The Florida Paralegal

Essential Rules, Documents, and Resources

The Florida Paralegal

Essential Rules, Documents, and Resources

INCLUDES

- A Comprehensive Legal Dictionary
- Florida Rules of Professional Conduct
- Paralegal Ethics
- Paralegal Registration
- Paralegal Certification
- Employment Resources
- Court Opinions on Paralegals
- CLE for Paralegals
- Employment Law Governing Paralegals
- Litigation Timelines
- Sample Documents
- State Research and Citation

William P. Statsky

Robert N. Diotalevi

Pamela McCoy Linquist

DELMAR
CENGAGE Learning

Australia • Canada • Mexico • Singapore • South Africa • Spain • United Kingdom • United States

DELMAR
CENGAGE Learning

The Florida Paralegal: Essential Rules, Documents, and Resources
William P. Statsky, Robert N. Diotalevi, and Pamela McCoy Linquist

Vice President, Career and Professional Editorial: Dave Garza

Director of Learning Solutions: Sandy Clark

Senior Acquisitions Editor: Shelley Esposito

Managing Editor: Larry Main

Senior Product Manager: Melissa Riveglia

Editorial Assistant: Lyss Zaza

Vice President, Career and Professional Marketing: Jennifer McAvey

Marketing Director: Deborah Yarnell

Marketing Manager: Erin Brennan

Marketing Coordinator: Jonathan Sheehan

Production Director: Wendy Troeger

Production Manager: Mark Bernard

Senior Content Project Manager: Betty Dickson

Senior Art Director: Joy Kocsis

Senior Director of Product Management for Career, Professional, and Languages: Tom Smith

Production Technology Analyst: Thomas Stover

Library of Congress Control Number: 2008933098

ISBN-13: 978-1-4180-1292-2

ISBN-10: 1-4180-1292-0

Delmar
5 Maxwell Drive
Clifton Park, NY 12065-2919
USA

Cengage Learning products are represented in Canada by Nelson Education, Ltd.

For your lifelong learning solutions, visit **delmar.cengage.com**

Visit our corporate website at **www.cengage.com**.

Printed in the United States of America
1 2 3 4 5 6 7 12 11 10 09

150

Dedication

To Pat Farrell Statsky. Ever the teacher and
spiritual guide. Namaste.

WPS

To my wife, Janet, for her devoted love and patience,
and my son Michael, the constant provider of youth and joy.
May God richly bless them.

BD

Thanks to my paralegal colleagues Karen, Steve, Chris, Carmen,
and Mary Lou for their professional expertise, Assistant Public Defender
Everett George, the Tampa United States Trustee staff for their encouragement,
and to my supportive and loving family: sons Michael, Eric, and Marc;
daughters-in-law Melody, Jacqueline, and Staci; and grandchildren Tiffany
and Michael Joseph. It has been a joy and a wonderful learning experience
working with Bill Statsky. Many thanks to Bill for his guidance, patience,
and understanding. A special *in memoriam* to my husband Major Allyn Linquist,
mother Alyce McCoy Thomas, and father Colonel Michael N. W. McCoy.

PML

Contents

Preface

What does it take to be an outstanding paralegal in Florida? Three key ingredients to your success are your paralegal education, native intelligence, and determination. This book seeks to complement all three by bringing together in one volume a vast amount of material that is either essential for all paralegals or useful for many.

Our focus is on the state of Florida—state resources, state laws, and state associations. Some federal laws and institutions will also be included when they are directly relevant to the state, e.g., federal government jobs for paralegals in federal agencies located in Florida.

The book has eight parts:

Part 1. The Paralegal Profession
Part 2. Paralegal Employment
Part 3. Ethics, Paralegals, and Attorneys
Part 4. Legal System
Part 5. Legal Research and Records Research
Part 6. Procedure: Some Basics
Part 7. Sample Documents
Part 8. Comprehensive Legal Dictionary

The last part contains a comprehensive legal dictionary with selected definitions specifically keyed to Florida law.

Within each of the first seven parts of the book, the sections will often include the following features:

Introduction: an overview of what is in the section and why it is included in the book.

Table of Contents: the main topics or areas covered in the section.

Abbreviations Used in the Section

Materials and Resources: the heart of the section.

More Information: leads to further materials, usually on the Internet.

Something to Check: questions that will help you expand and build on the material in the section.

In addition, there is an online page that will provide updates and related material. To use the page, go to *www.paralegal.delmar.cengage.com.*

The Florida Paralegal Reviewers:

Mary Conwell
Edison College
Ft. Myers, Florida

Susan Harrell
University of West Florida
Pensacola, Florida

Nekishia Lester
Keiser College
Ft. Lauderdale, Florida

The Paralegal Profession

A. Introduction

In the United States, a paralegal (sometimes called a legal assistant) is a person with substantive legal skills whose authority to use those skills is based on attorney supervision or special authorization from the government. By substantive skills, we mean skills that (1) are obtained through sophisticated training and (2) are significantly more advanced than those possessed by clerical personnel in most law offices.

Defining a Paralegal and Using the Paralegal Title

Florida has its own definition of a paralegal or legal assistant. These titles can be used *only* by persons who work under the supervision of an attorney. Unlike the vast majority of other states, Florida does not allow individuals who provide law-related services directly to the public without attorney supervision to call themselves paralegals or legal assistants. The Rules Regulating the Florida Bar provide as follows:

- A person who uses the title of paralegal, legal assistant, or other similar term when offering or providing services to the public must work for or under the direction or supervision of a lawyer or law firm. Rule 4-5.3
- A paralegal or legal assistant is a person qualified by education, training, or work experience, who works under the supervision of a member of the Florida Bar and who performs specifically delegated substantive legal work for which a member of The Florida Bar is responsible. Rule 10-2.1(b)
- For purposes of this chapter (establishing the Florida Registered Paralegal Program, examined later in this overview) . . . A paralegal is a person with education, training, or work experience, who works under the direction and supervision of a member of The Florida Bar and who performs specifically delegated substantive legal work for which a member of The Florida Bar is responsible. Rule 20-1.1(a)
- It shall constitute the unlicensed practice of law for a person who does not meet the definition of paralegal or legal assistant as set forth elsewhere in these rules to offer or provide legal services directly to the public or for a person who does not meet the definition of paralegal or legal assistant as set forth elsewhere in these rules to use the title paralegal, legal assistant, or other similar term in providing legal services or legal forms preparation services directly to the public. Rule 10-2.1(a)(2) (*www.floridabar.org*) (click "Lawyer Regulation" then "Rules Regulating The Florida Bar" then "10")

Fees and the Definition of a Paralegal

There is also an important Florida statute that defines legal assistant when attorney fees are awarded by the courts:

In any action in which attorneys' fees are to be determined or awarded by the court, the court shall consider, among other things, time and labor of any legal assistants who contributed nonclerical, meaningful legal support to the matter involved and who are working under the supervision of an attorney. For purposes of this section "legal assistant" means a person, who under the supervision and direction of a licensed attorney engages in legal research, and case development or planning in relation to modifications or initial proceedings, services, processes, or applications; or who prepares or interprets legal documents or selects, compiles, and uses technical information from references, such as digests, encyclopedias, or practice manuals and analyzes and follows procedural problems that involve independent decisions. F.S.A. § 57.104.

To find this statute, type "57.104" in the search box of a site containing Florida Statutes (for example, *www.leg.state.fl.us/statutes*).

Our Goals

This is a fascinating time to be a paralegal in Florida. Paralegals, working in a wide variety of settings, have made major contributions in the delivery of legal services. The state has a rich paralegal history. Our objective in this book is to give you the perspective of this history and to provide resources that will help you:

- Find paralegal employment
- Understand the unique features of our state government
- Find the laws that are the foundation of paralegal work
- Examine some of the major documents that paralegals prepare or help prepare for attorneys on behalf of clients
- Provide a comprehensive legal dictionary that defines all or most of the legal terms that give the legal system its unique character
- Abide by the ethics code
- Participate in organized efforts to continue the growth of the paralegal profession

Honoring Paralegals

See Exhibit 1.1A for the governor's proclamation recognizing the value of paralegals to the state.

EXHIBIT 1.1A	Paralegal Week in Florida

CHARLIE CRIST
GOVERNOR

PARALEGAL WEEK

WHEREAS, paralegals support attorneys in the provision of legal services to clients; and

WHEREAS, paralegals work to maintain integrity and a high degree of competence throughout the legal profession, while striving for professional enhancement through education; and

WHEREAS, the assistance of paralegals reduces the cost of providing legal service; and

WHEREAS, paralegals are highly educated, trained and experienced professionals with expertise in case research, correspondence writing, interviewing clients and witnesses, and other areas of law practice;

NOW, THEREFORE, I, Charlie Crist, Governor of the State of Florida, do hereby extend greetings and best wishes to all observing May 25–31, 2008 as *Paralegal Week*.

IN WITNESS WHEREOF, I have hereunto set my hand and caused the Great Seal of the State of Florida to be affixed at Tallahassee, the Capital, this 18ᵗʰ day of April, in the year two thousand eight.

Governer

THE CAPITOL
TALLAHASSEEE, FLORIDA 32399 • (850) 488-2272 • FAX (850) 922-4292

Source: *www.swfloridaparalegals.com/pdfiles/paralegal-week-2008.pdf*

B. Paralegals in the Twenty-First Century

Highlights

About 7 out of 10 paralegals in the country work for law firms; others work for corporate legal departments, government agencies, legal aid/service offices, and special interest organizations.

Employment is projected to grow much faster than average, as employers try to reduce costs by hiring paralegals to perform tasks that attorneys would otherwise have to perform.

Formally trained paralegals have the best employment opportunities as competition for jobs increases. (*www.bls.gov/oco/ocos114.htm*)

Work Settings

Most paralegals are employed by law firms, corporate legal departments, and government offices. In these organizations, they can work in many different areas of the law, including:

- litigation
- personal injury
- corporate law
- criminal law
- employee benefits
- intellectual property
- labor law
- bankruptcy
- immigration
- family law
- real estate

As the law has become more complex, paralegals have responded by becoming more specialized. Within specialties, functions often are broken down further so that paralegals may deal with a specific area. For example, paralegals specializing in labor law may concentrate exclusively on employee benefits. The U.S. Department of Labor has estimated that there are 238,000 paralegal jobs in the country. (See Exhibit 1.1B.) Bureau of Labor Statistics, U.S. Department of Labor. *Occupational Outlook Handbook*, 2008–09 Edition (*www.bls.gov/oco/ocos114.htm*).

A small number of paralegals own their own businesses and work as freelance paralegals, contracting their services to attorneys in law firms or corporate legal departments. Finally, some nonattorneys offer limited law-related services directly to the public without attorney supervision. As indicated, the absence of this supervision means they cannot call themselves paralegals or legal assistants. They are allowed to assist citizens in filling out certain court-approved legal forms without being charged with engaging in the unauthorized practice of law:

- It shall not constitute the unlicensed practice of law for a nonlawyer to engage in limited oral communications to assist a person in the completion of blanks on a legal form approved by the Supreme Court of Florida. Oral communications by nonlawyers are restricted to those communications reasonably necessary to elicit factual information to complete the blanks on the form and inform the person how to file the form. Rules Regulating the Florida Bar, Rule 10-2.1(a)(1) (*www.floridabar.org*) (click "Lawyer Regulation" then "Rules Regulating The Florida Bar" then "10")

For more on these restrictions, see sections 3.1 and 3.2.

Paralegal Work

Though attorneys assume ultimate responsibility for legal work, they often delegate tasks to paralegals.

In fact, paralegals continue to assume a growing range of tasks in the nation's legal offices and perform some of the same tasks as attorneys perform. Nevertheless, paralegals cannot give legal advice, set fees, represent clients in court, or engage in other categories of activities that constitute the unauthorized practice of law.

The variety and complexity of paralegal tasks depend on the kind of law practiced in the office, the competence and initiative of the paralegal, and the willingness of the attorney to delegate:

- Many paralegals provide litigation assistance by helping attorneys prepare for hearings and trials.
- Paralegals investigate the facts of cases and help ensure that all relevant information is considered.
- In the area of legal research, they perform cite checks, help determine the current validity of laws (through a process called shepardizing and keyciting), and perform other research tasks.
- When a lawsuit is filed, they help prepare pleadings and motions, summarize pretrial testimony, perform further factual research, and assist attorneys during the trial itself.
- A major duty of many litigation paralegals is file organization and tracking so that attorneys can easily access the numerous documents involved in client representation.
- Some paralegals coordinate and supervise the activities of other law office employees. Many of these paralegal supervisors have formed their own association, the International Paralegal Management Association (*www.paralegalmanagement.org*).

Transactional paralegals provide paralegal services for attorneys who represent clients in transactions such as entering contracts, incorporating a business, closing a real estate sale, or planning an estate. Paralegals who work for corporations assist attorneys with employee contracts, shareholder agreements, stock-option plans, employee benefit plans, and other transactional documents. They help prepare and file annual financial reports, corporate minutes, and corporate resolutions. They perform compliance work by monitoring and reviewing government regulations to ensure that the corporation is aware of new requirements and is operating within the law. Increasingly, experienced paralegals assume additional supervisory responsibilities, such as overseeing team projects and serving as a communications link between the legal team and the business staff of the corporation. When the corporation retains outside counsel, the corporate paralegal has additional liaison responsibilities.

Paralegals who work in government agencies analyze legal material for internal use, maintain office files, conduct factual and legal research for attorneys, and collect evidence for agency hearings. They may help prepare informative or explanatory material on laws, agency regulations, and agency policy for general use by the agency and the public. Paralegals employed in legal aid/legal service offices in the community help people who are poor, older people with limited means, and others who cannot afford private law firms. They file forms; conduct research; prepare documents; and, when authorized by law, represent clients at administrative hearings.

Paralegals in small and medium-size law firms often perform a variety of duties that require a general knowledge of the law. Those employed by large law firms, government agencies, and corporations, however, are more likely to specialize in one area of the law.

Familiarity with the use of computers in the law has become essential to paralegal work. Computer software packages and the Internet are used to search legal literature stored in computer databases and on CD-ROM. In litigation involving many supporting documents, paralegals often use computer databases to retrieve, organize, and index various materials. Imaging software allows paralegals to scan documents directly into a database, and billing programs help them track hours that will be billed to clients. Computer software packages are also used to perform tax computations and explore the consequences of various tax strategies for clients.

National Job Outlook According to the U.S. Department of Labor

Employment for paralegals and legal assistants is projected to grow much faster than average for all occupations through 2016. (Employment is expected to grow 22 percent between 2006 and 2016.) Employers are trying to reduce costs and increase the availability and efficiency of legal services by hiring paralegals to perform tasks formerly carried out by attorneys. Besides new jobs created by employment growth, additional job openings will arise as people retire and leave the field. Despite projections of rapid employment growth, competition for jobs should continue as many people seek to go into this profession. Experienced, formally trained paralegals often have the best employment opportunities.

Private law firms will continue to be the largest employers of paralegals, but a growing array of other organizations, such as corporate legal departments, insurance companies, real estate and title insurance firms, and banks hire paralegals. In particular, corporations are boosting their in-house legal departments to cut costs. Demand for paralegals is expected to grow as an expanding population increasingly requires legal services, especially in areas such as intellectual property, health care, elder law, criminal law, environmental law, and the global economy. Paralegals who specialize in areas such as real estate, bankruptcy, medical malpractice, and product liability are often in demand. The growth of prepaid legal plans should also contribute to the demand for legal services. (A prepaid plan is like health insurance in which a person pays an ongoing fee or premium for legal service needs that might arise in the future.) A growing number of experienced paralegals are expected to establish their own businesses as independent contractors.

Job opportunities for paralegals will expand in the public sector as well. Community legal aid/legal service programs (which provide assistance on the legal problems of poor people, older people with limited means, minority populations facing discrimination, and middle-income families just over the poverty line), will employ additional paralegals to minimize expenses and serve the most people. Federal, state, and local government agencies, consumer organizations, and the courts also should continue to hire paralegals in increasing numbers.

To a limited extent, paralegal jobs are affected by the business cycle. During recessions, demand declines for some discretionary legal services, such as estate planning, drafting wills, and real estate transactions. Corporations may be less inclined to initiate certain types of litigation when falling sales and profits lead to fiscal belt tightening. As a result, full-time paralegals employed in offices adversely affected by a recession may be laid off or have their work hours reduced. However, during recessions, corporations and individuals are more likely to face other problems that require legal assistance, such as bankruptcies, foreclosures, and divorces. Bureau of Labor Statistics, U.S. Department of Labor, *Occupational Outlook Handbook*, 2008–09 Edition (*www.bls.gov/oco/ocos114.htm*).

Career Video on Paralegals

To watch a short video that gives an overview of the paralegal career:

1. Go to *www.acinet.org/acinet*.
2. Look for video links on this page.
3. Also type "paralegal" in the search box.
4. Look for "Cluster and Career Videos."
5. Locate "Law and Public Safety" then "Paralegals."

C. Statistics on Paralegal Employment Nationally and in Florida

For employment trends in the state as well as nationally, see Exhibit 1.1B, which also provides comparable data on other legal occupations.

Earnings of paralegals vary greatly. Salaries depend on education, training, experience, the type and size of employer, and the geographic location of the job. In general, paralegals who work for large law firms or in large metropolitan areas earn more than those who work for smaller firms or in less populated regions. In addition to earning a salary, many paralegals receive bonuses. In May 2006, full-time wage and salary paralegals had median annual earnings, including bonuses, of $43,040. The middle 50 percent earned between $33,920 and $54,690. The top

EXHIBIT 1.1B	Employment Growth of Paralegals Compared with Other Legal Occupations in the Nation and in Florida				
United States	**Employment**		**Percentage Change**	**Job Openings***
	2006	**2016**		
Paralegals and legal assistants	237,700	290,600	+22%	8,410
Lawyers	760,700	844,200	+11%	22,780
Legal support workers, all other	47,900	50,300	+5%	1,040
Court reporters	19,100	23,800	+25%	790
Florida	**Employment**		**Percentage Change**	**Job Openings***
	2004	**2014**		
Paralegals and legal assistants	18,150	25,750	+42%	910
Lawyers	50,820	63,720	+25%	1,940
Legal support workers, all other	3,910	4,360	+12%	90
Court reporters	2,530	3,990	+58%	170

* Job Openings refers to the average annual job openings due to growth and net replacement.

Note: The data for the State Employment Trends and the National Employment Trends are not directly comparable. The projections period for state data is 2004–2014, while the projections period for national data is 2006–2016.

Source: Bureau of Labor Statistics, *Occupational Employment Survey*; Florida Agency for Workforce Innovation, *Labor Market Statistics*; America's Career InfoNet, a component of CareerOneStop (*www.acinet.org*).

EXHIBIT 1.1C Paralegal Wages Nationally and in Florida

Location	Pay Period	2007				
		10%	25%	Median	75%	90%
United States	Hourly	$13.64	$16.95	$21.63	$27.65	$34.37
	Yearly	$28,400	$35,300	$45,000	$57,500	$71,500
Florida	Hourly	$13.15	$15.90	$20.27	$25.15	$29.91
	Yearly	$27,400	$33,100	$42,200	$52,300	$62,200
Bradenton-Sarasota-Venice	Hourly	$13.70	$16.46	$19.52	$23.76	$30.38
	Yearly	$28,500	$34,200	$40,600	$49,400	$63,200
Deltona-Daytona Beach-Ormond Beach	Hourly	$13.64	$15.55	$17.28	$18.97	$22.48
	Yearly	$28,400	$32,300	$35,900	$39,500	$46,800
Fort Lauderdale-Pompano Beach-Deerfield Beach	Hourly	$14.59	$18.46	$22.33	$25.94	$29.17
	Yearly	$30,300	$38,400	$46,400	$54,000	$60,700
Gainesville	Hourly	$11.29	$14.16	$16.89	$19.08	$24.37
	Yearly	$23,500	$29,500	$35,100	$39,700	$50,700
Jacksonville	Hourly	$13.08	$15.03	$18.04	$22.55	$27.73
	Yearly	$27,200	$31,300	$37,500	$46,900	$57,700
Miami-Miami Beach-Kendall	Hourly	$12.42	$14.62	$21.31	$27.50	$33.45
	Yearly	$25,800	$30,400	$44,300	$57,200	$69,600
Orlando-Kissimmee	Hourly	$15.02	$17.99	$21.47	$25.25	$29.22
	Yearly	$31,200	$37,400	$44,700	$52,500	$60,800
Tallahassee	Hourly	$12.66	$13.96	$16.93	$22.17	$27.81
	Yearly	$26,300	$29,000	$35,200	$46,100	$57,800
Tampa-St. Petersburg-Clearwater	Hourly	$14.14	$17.32	$21.77	$26.75	$30.75
	Yearly	$29,400	$36,000	$45,300	$55,600	$64,000
West Palm Beach-Boca Raton-Boynton Beach	Hourly	$15.73	$18.39	$22.51	$26.72	$31.06
	Yearly	$32,700	$38,300	$46,800	$55,600	$64,600

Source: Bureau of Labor Statistics, *Occupational Employment Survey*; Florida Agency for Workforce Innovation, *Labor Market Statistics*; America's Career InfoNet, a component of CareerOneStop (*www.acinet.org*).

10 percent earned more than $67,540, and the bottom 10 percent earned just under $27,450. Median annual earnings in government and legal aid offices were as follows:

- Federal government: $56,080
- State government: $38,020
- Local government: $42,170
- Legal aid/service offices: $41,460
- Management of companies and enterprises: $52,220

Exhibit 1.1C provides an overview of national and Florida data on compensation.

Florida Economics and Law Office Management Survey

The following data from The Florida Bar's *Economics and Law Office Management Survey* covers 2006 unless otherwise indicated:

- Approximately two-thirds (66%) of law offices in Florida employ legal assistants/paralegals. See Exhibit 1.1D. This is a 10 percent increase since the year 2000.
- The mean salary of paralegals with 5–10 years of experience was $43,572. See Exhibit 1.1E. (In 2002, it was approximately $32,000.)

- The billing rate for legal assistants/paralegals was more than $100 an hour in 25 percent of offices. See Exhibit 1.1F.
- Legal assistants/paralegals in 43 percent of offices billed more than 1,000 hours a year. See Exhibit 1.1G.

Source: Florida Bar. *Results of the 2006 Economics and Law Office Management Survey* (December 2006). Available at: *www.floridabar.org* (click "Publications" and then "Research").

EXHIBIT 1.1D	Percentage of Florida Law Offices that Employ Legal Assistants/Paralegals

Does the Firm or Legal Office Employ Legal Assistants/Paralegals?

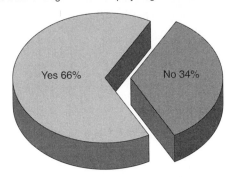

Yes 66%   No 34%

EXHIBIT 1.1E	Annual Salary for Legal Assistants/Paralegals in Florida Law Offices		
Paralegals	**Mean**	**Median**	**Mode**
New hires without experience	$31,371	$30,000	$25,000
Current employees with less than 5 years' experience	$36,672	$35,000	$30,000
Current employees with 5 to 10 years' experience	$43,572	$42,500	$40,000
Current employees with more than 10 years' experience	$49,007	$47,000	$45,000

EXHIBIT 1.1F	Average or Standard Hourly Rate that Florida Law Offices Bill for Legal Assistant/Paralegal Time
Hourly Rate	**Percentage**
$40 or less	9%
$41 to $60	11%
$61 to $80	31%
$81 to $100	24%
$101 to $120	11%
More than $120	14%

EXHIBIT 1.1G	Annual Average Number of Legal Assistant/Paralegal Billable Hours in Florida Law Offices (2005)
Billable Hours	**Percentage**
500 or fewer	40%
501 to 750	8%
751 to 1,000	9%
1,001 to 1,250	15%
1,251 to 1,500	13%
More than 1,500	15%

D. Paralegal Positions in Florida: Some Examples

As indicated, paralegals in Florida perform a rich variety of tasks in many different settings. No single job description encompasses them all. One way to understand this diversity is to look at selected paralegal profiles in Florida law offices. The paralegals we have selected are not representative of all or most paralegals in the state, but they do demonstrate the high level of confidence their employers place in them. In addition, we present comments by individual paralegals on how they define professional success.

Most attorneys specialize in one or more areas of practice. As you might imagine, the same is often true of the paralegals that they employ. The exception is the solo attorney in general practice. He or she provides a broad array of legal services in many areas of law. Similarly, paralegals who work for such attorneys often provide assistance in the variety of areas covered by their employers. In the main, most of the paralegals in the following profiles have specializations because they work in offices where their attorney supervisors specialize.

Paralegals Working in Law Firms: Examples

AnnaDanielle Carosiello

Becker & Poliakoff, P.A.
www.becker-poliakoff.com

AnnaDanielle Carosiello has been a paralegal at Becker & Poliakoff, P.A. for nine years, the last seven working as a community association paralegal. Her duties include drafting correspondence and legal documents including audit letters, demand letters, initial condominium prospectus filings, governing document revision projects, amendments, corporate merger documents, meeting notice packages, board resolutions, corporate reinstatements, Department of Business and Professional Regulation complaints, registered agent change forms,

Marketable Record Title Act filings, and construction lien documents. She also conducts legal research.

The attorneys she works with rely on paralegals to perform their jobs to the best of their ability every day. How paralegals carry out their work impacts client satisfaction, an attorney's reputation, their license to practice law, and their faith in a paralegal's ability to handle future assignments.

"To understand what it is like working at Becker & Poliakoff, one must understand the mission and reputation of the firm. It is one of the premier law firms in Florida. The firm's continuing effort to provide clients with quality legal services in the most cost-effective manner is demonstrated through the use of paralegals working under the direct supervision of attorneys. The talent and professionalism of attorneys and staff, and the commitment to excellence, is felt throughout the offices. Everyone works together as a team to meet the needs of our clients. We do what we can to get the job done."

According to Ms. Carosiello, the most important skills a paralegal must possess to succeed are the ability to:

- Understand legal terminology and complex legal concepts and theories
- Efficiently use computer programs to perform essential job functions
- Work in a team and respect the role of each team member, including clients, subordinates, and superiors
- Communicate clearly and concisely with clients and attorneys (using both written and oral communication)
- Multitask a demanding workload while prioritizing the most urgent matters and maintaining a high level of accuracy and efficiency in the work product

"If one is looking for an exciting, challenging, and rewarding career, this is the right career. It is the fast-paced, high volume, high-energy environment that keeps a paralegal on his/her toes."

H. Susan Coleman, CLA

Foley & Lardner LLP
apps.foley.com/staff

Susan Coleman has worked in the legal field for 28 years, and as a paralegal for the past 18 years. She earned her CLA (Certified Legal Assistant) credentials in 1992. As a general litigation paralegal at a large international firm, her duties include drafting pleadings and discovery; summarizing deposition transcripts and medical records; assisting in preparing position statements responsive to Equal Employment Opportunity Commission (EEOC) charges; preparing deposition notebooks, exhibits and outlines, trial notebooks, and exhibits; doing legal research using Westlaw and Lexis-Nexis; and locating/interviewing witnesses.

"This office has the most up-to-date technology of any place I have ever worked. The firm pays for paralegal association memberships and seminars. We have business cards. All of the paralegals have a window office and are assigned a secretary. It is a joy to work in an office like mine. I am challenged every day and treated like a professional. A few of the things that are different about this firm are as follows: our assignments are project-based (as opposed to attorney- or case-based); we work for all of the attorneys in the litigation department (we are not assigned to any particular attorney); and we get to work with great autonomy."

According to Ms. Coleman, the most important skills a paralegal must have are organization, flexibility, dependability, time management, technical/computer knowledge, the ability to perform legal research, the ability to comprehend and apply the *Federal Rules*, and the ability to multitask. She cites her most important references as the *Federal Rules of Civil Procedure*, the local rules for the applicable jurisdictions, *Florida Rules of Court*, the *Florida Bar Journal*, and a good legal dictionary.

Juana Cruz

Fowler White Burnett, P.A.
www.fowler-white.com/home.html

Juana Cruz is a paralegal with 17 years of experience. Currently employed as a commercial litigation legal assistant, her tasks include drafting pleadings and discovery documents, legal research, tracking deadlines, as well as maintaining client contact. The firm has three offices, employing a total of 26 paralegals, with a ratio of one paralegal and one legal secretary to one attorney. The environment is extremely fast-paced.

Ms. Cruz says that her opinion regarding the details and facts of a case is appreciated and taken into consideration. She is able to use her knowledge to the fullest, thereby freeing up the attorneys' time to work on more in-depth projects, where their expertise can be better utilized. This also is financially more beneficial to the clients, because paralegal billing time is at a lower rate. She believes that a paralegal must be able to multitask and remember the many different rules, regulations, and terminology that apply to cases. "Commercial litigation is so vast that you need to be up to date on many different procedures. You must know your legal terminology, because nothing is more important than understanding what you are expected to do. Don't be afraid to ask questions." Otherwise, you run the risk of having to redo tasks.

Cyndi Edwards

Buckingham, Doolittle & Burroughs, LLP
www.bdblaw.com

Cyndi Edwards works in litigation in the areas of corporate law, trusts and probate, and personal injury in state court (70% of the firm's cases) and federal court (30%). Her duties include drafting pleadings and discovery documents, performing legal research, and acting as client liaison.

"I work very closely with the attorneys in our firm. There is a strong team environment here. We work together in coming up with a game plan for the cases, and I feel that my opinions and ideas are greeted with respect. The department I work in has 11 attorneys, 4 paralegals, and 6 legal assistants. It is a small enough size to allow for easy flow of information, but is still large enough for a great deal of diversity of ideas. I have been a paralegal for 9 years, but have worked for only 1 other firm. I was previously with a very small firm, which consisted of only 1 attorney and myself. Both environments have their benefits. With only 1 attorney to report to, it was easier for me to know exactly how he wanted things done. Now I have to consider who I am doing work for and try to remember in what format he or she likes documents drafted. In contrast, when I worked for only 1 attorney there wasn't much diversity in the types of cases I handled, and now I work on several different types at a single time."

Ms. Edwards believes paralegals must be organized, detail-oriented, and have a strong grasp of the language arts. They also must know how the trial and appellate courts work together and the hierarchy of case law. Her advice is to ask questions, because attorneys are usually great teachers with a great deal of knowledge from years of schooling and practice.

Joanna Lubczanska

Santucci, Priore & Long
www.500law.com

Joanna Lubczanska is an intellectual property, corporate, and commercial litigation paralegal with seven years of experience. Her educational background consists of paralegal and legal studies, computer graphics, and fashion design.

Her duties include drafting all documents necessary to obtain and maintain federal and Florida trademark registrations as well as copyright registrations; drafting documents necessary to form various types of Florida entities; and drafting correspondence, pleadings, and discovery documents for civil commercial cases.

According to Ms. Lubczanska, the paralegal profession is fast-paced, challenging, and rewarding when working with attorneys who know how to use paralegal time correctly, as well as respect them and make them feel appreciated. You must be a team player, be efficient, and be energetic. Another crucial attribute is the ability to learn and adapt to the always changing needs and procedures of the legal profession.

The most important skills a paralegal must have are the ability to multitask, to perform legal research, and

to get the job done right with minimal instructions from attorneys, who are always busy. Paralegal work merges with the attorney's work product. Therefore, to get each project completed in a timely fashion, both paralegal and attorney must be able to communicate about any questions they may have.

"You must enjoy what you do. Whether you do so will depend on your dedication, effort, personality, the type of work you do, and the people you are surrounded by. There are many areas of law. Paralegals should try to gravitate toward areas that match their strengths and interests. I am an artist, so intellectual property cases, infringement, commercial litigation, and interacting with creative clients were perfect areas for me.

"You must be a self-motivated and driven individual to succeed in the legal field. Due to the amount of work involved, you must be able to prioritize, handle the work of two people, manage constant deadlines without feeling overwhelmed, be extremely organized and detail-oriented, and, most importantly, be patient. Each attorney has his or her own unique routine, style, and way of thinking. You will often have to go beyond your duties, especially in small firms, so that whatever needs to be done can be accomplished. It is very important to enjoy what you do and to feel accomplished and appreciated. You must have a positive relationship and develop open communication with the attorneys and staff you work with. There is nothing more frustrating than working where such an atmosphere does not exist."

Margaret Fahey McCoullough

Robert K. Kennett, Esq.
pview.findlaw.com/view/2060248_1

Margaret McCoullough has been a paralegal for 23 years. In addition to her paralegal and legal studies training, she has completed real estate, guardianship, and mediation courses. She currently works for a sole practitioner as the only paralegal in the office. She has been with this attorney for just over six years. Her last employment was also with a sole practitioner who practiced a different area of law.

Working in a sole practitioner environment affords many advantages, including flexibility of hours, periods of minimal distraction, and constant interaction with the attorney. This not only increases one's knowledge of law but also gives the paralegal freedom to use his or her own knowledge and skills.

The most important characteristic paralegals should have is possessing diverse communication skills. They must have the ability to speak to clients, attorneys, and court administrative staff (beginning with the clerks all the way up to the judge). Furthermore, paralegals must be profoundly empathetic with clients. Paralegals must constantly keep up to date with all periodicals, such as law journals, bar association publications, newspapers, and recent case law in relevant topic areas.

Anne M. Iacuzzo, CP

Freelance Paralegal

Anne Iacuzzo is currently working for four attorneys in Orlando and Naples in the areas of probate, estate planning, guardianship, and litigation. She says that "the working environment in any firm is totally controlled and fostered by the attorneys in the firm. Paralegals must remember that this is a business and that their function is to help this business become more profitable. The ideal office will foster an atmosphere of courtesy and cooperation so that all of its members work well together. You should be mindful of your place in the firm. Be courteous and kind. At the very least, always be civil. Develop interests of your own outside of the office to give your life balance and fun.

"You will encounter attorneys who do not realize the value of a paralegal and/or do not know how to utilize a paralegal's services. A law firm (or any business) is not going to be successful if attorneys sit behind their desks waiting for clients to materialize. They have to be out making contacts, promoting their firm and its services. Yet, the 'work' has to be done. Paralegals can and should 'hold down the fort' by drafting the documents and correspondence, and conducting the research as requested by the attorneys so that the attorneys can be the 'rainmakers' who bring in the business. It is important that you, as a paralegal, are able to listen carefully to your attorney, and to the client. And be discreet. You will meet people from all walks of life whose lifestyles and personal philosophy may be in direct conflict with yours.

"Other skills to be acquired are more obvious: good typing speed; the ability to edit and proofread; and keeping an even temperament in stressful situations. One of the most important skills is your ability to keep the attorney and yourself organized. You will be working on several different cases and must be able to track each case—court dockets, filing deadlines, etcetera. Your professional function is to assist your attorney, so whatever the attorney needs is your number one priority. The most important skill to develop is your sense of humor. You must still be able to see the joy in life, or you won't make it through the day. If you don't have patience and the ability to handle clients' anger without turning it inside yourself, this is not a profession for you."

Paralegals Working in Corporations, Legal Service Offices, and for the Government: Examples

Karen S. McLead, CP

Pinch a Penny, Inc.
www.pinchapenny.com

Karen S. McLead is one of the giants of the paralegal profession in Florida. In addition to her work in law firms and corporations, she has been active in helping give shape to the profession in the state. She is a former president of the Florida Association of Paralegals and chairperson of the Unlicensed Practice of Law Committee of The Florida Bar Association. Recently, she stood at the podium before the full bench of the Supreme Court of Florida to argue a position on paralegal regulation on behalf of the Florida Alliance of Paralegal Associations. The Florida Bar, recognizing her leadership, has appointed her to various committees and task forces involving issues of concern to the legal profession. Currently, Karen is a public member of the Florida Bar's Registered Paralegal Program Committee (*www.floridabar.org*; click "Inside the Bar" then "Committees").

Karen works for Pinch a Penny, Inc., a privately owned Florida corporation whose primary business is franchising pool and patio supply stores in Florida, Georgia, and Alabama. Prior to joining the company, she worked in law firms for more than 20 years.

Her duties at the company are varied. For example, the franchising arm of the company requires that she be familiar with Federal Trade Commission (FTC) guidelines that govern the sale of franchised businesses. She trains sales staff to ensure that they understand and adhere to the rules of the FTC relating to sales disclosures, profitability, and representations made to prospective buyers. In addition, she works to ensure that franchisees understand and comply with the laws and regulations of the Environmental Protection Agency (EPA).

She is also involved in the day-to-day operations of the franchisees, including the sale and purchase of the businesses. She works closely with the franchisee or buyer's attorneys, banks, and other business professionals. She makes presentations before city and county boards on issues relating to variances or special use exceptions of municipal codes and ordinances, which are required in connection with franchisee leases. She reviews in-house advertising copy to ensure that it complies with federal advertising laws. She also writes policies and procedures for the franchisee operating manual.

Her job includes work for one of the company's affiliates that markets inflatables and other toy products to its franchisees, requiring knowledge of laws governing imports and exports, patents, trademarks, and other intellectual property rights.

She serves as a corporate officer and registered agent for each of the companies and is responsible for maintaining the corporate record books. When litigation involving the company is brought, she works closely with outside law firms in all phases of the litigation. This has given her the unique opportunity to grow and be challenged in many arenas.

When asked about the traits a paralegal needs to perform such tasks, she said, "The traits I have found most useful are: (1) resourcefulness, (2) flexibility, (3) organization, (4) diversity, and (5) time management. Obviously, all areas that I oversee require more than general legal knowledge and expressly require certain abilities that are acquired over time. However, many of the matters I handle require nothing more than tenacity, good common sense, a willingness to do a good job, and the ability to impart that information in a manner that is understood by someone outside the legal arena.

"Florida is a unique state with many opportunities for paralegals to serve in non-traditional settings. We have many large corporations, both private and public, that employ paralegals, such as Publix Supermarkets, Disney World, Marriott Hotels, Fairfield Hotels, Raymond James Financial, and many others. As I've traveled around the state, I've had the opportunity to learn about the experiences of other paralegals, experiences that permit them to work outside the 'traditional' law firm setting and break through many barriers."

Steven Marciano

Amico Holdings, LLC

Steven is a paralegal at Amico Holdings, LLC, a multimillion dollar real estate acquisition and development company. "The following is a brief review of a few of my paralegal duties. Upon the purchase or sale of any property, I assist in the negotiation of the transaction. I meet and work closely with counsel to draft an acceptable contract, and I personally conduct all due diligence for each project. I am responsible for acquiring all financing for each project, as well as for the development and maintenance of new entities. I am administrator of the accounting and tax performance for each entity, together with our CPA (certified public accountant). I work closely with counsel on a daily basis regarding all legal matters for each company, for example, tenant matters, and both land use and zoning issues. In addition, I serve as corporate officer and registered agent for some of our entities.

"My experience working in the paralegal profession within Florida has been a wonderful learning experience. I began in the area of corporate and construction law and went on to bankruptcy and family law. I now work in the corporate and real estate areas of law. Involvement in local and state associations such as the Paralegal Association of Florida, Inc. (PAF) has been a wonderful experience. Involvement in local bar activities was also very rewarding. I was editor of a paralegal article for each issue of the Clearwater Bar Association's *Res Ipsa* newsletter for a few years, helping to educate attorneys and staff about our profession within the state of Florida."

Carmen Junquera

Bay Area Legal Services, Inc.
www.bals.org

Carmen Junquera is a public benefits paralegal at Bay Area Legal Services (BALS). She is a public benefits specialist in the Senior Advocacy Unit, which represents clients who are 60 years of age or older. "I do the initial interview with the client and obtain the facts of his or her problem. Depending on the legal problem, I may keep and work the case (always under the supervision of an attorney), or the case is transferred to the appropriate attorney or paralegal for representation. As the public benefits specialist for the unit, I assist clients who have been denied public benefits such as Medicaid and food stamps. I also represent clients who have been denied Supplemental Security Income (SSI) through the Social Security Administration. SSI is a means-based program for individuals who do not have enough hours of work to qualify for Social Security benefits, or whose income is below a certain level. I represent these clients in administrative hearings. I also work on landlord/tenant, guardianship, and home ownership/foreclosure cases. On most cases, I work on the case from beginning to the end, doing the pleadings and getting the case ready for the attorney to go to court."

To work in this area of the law, Ms. Junquera says you must be "compassionate, understanding, dedicated, and patient. The pay scale for attorneys, as well as paralegals, in a legal services office is not comparable to the pay scale in a private law firm. Therefore, dedication and love for what you do is a must."

Chris Griffiths

U.S. Attorney's Office
www.usdoj.gov/usao/flm

Chris Griffiths is a paralegal in the office of the U.S. Attorney's Office in Tampa, Florida. She is currently assigned to the Criminal Division, Drug Trafficking Section. "My main duties are organizing and disseminating discovery materials, preparing cases for trial, and utilizing legal research skills to draft responses to *pro se* habeas petitions. In addition, the government also has a catch-all phrase, 'other duties as assigned,' which ensures that I stay busy with a multitude of other assignments, including acting as Freedom of Information Act (FOIA) liaison, preparing and overseeing statistical reporting for narcotics cases, and drafting responses to clemency and pardon applications.

"My training and experience in researching legal issues has enriched my understanding of the criminal process from investigation to sentencing. Those skills enhance my professional abilities when litigation and technology intersect, which is now the norm in criminal litigation. Discovery and trial prep tend to go hand-in-hand. It is imperative to track what and when discovery materials are released to defense counsel to avoid trial delay or sanctions by the district court. This process also allows me to work closely with the trial attorney in assessing which documents and materials will be relevant as trial exhibits, will be responsive to various motions, or will facilitate trial strategy.

"The digital age is upon us. With automated litigation support, the role of the paralegal is changing to include a more significant emphasis on using the computer as a tool to present our case. Criminal case preparation is rapidly moving into a more automated format for providing discovery materials and presenting trial exhibits. Paper or analog discovery materials, such as documents, video and audio tapes, and photographs from the investigative agencies must be converted into a digital format. The task of providing automated litigation support for the trial attorney has, for the most part, fallen to paralegals.

"As part of the process of converting the materials to a digital or computerized format, paralegals must anticipate the next step of trial preparation. The type of file formats, as well as the indexing system, must be considered when copying relevant materials into a trial presentation program, such as Sanctions for use during trial. Just as Bates numbering helps account for the documents, the way you name and organize the electronic data makes trial preparation more manageable."

E. Certification

Florida paralegals have a number of options when seeking certification. Keep in mind, however, that none of these certification programs are mandatory. You can be a paralegal in Florida—or in any other state—without taking and passing a certification examination. Certification is voluntary. Yet, some paralegals feel that certification is an extra credential that can enhance their professionalism and commitment to the paralegal career.

Here is an overview of the major certification programs that are available:

National Certification

- CLA/CP certification of the National Association of Legal Assistants (NALA). Passing an exam and fulfilling the other requirements of NALA entitle you to be called a Certified Legal Assistant (CLA) or a Certified Paralegal (CP). (*www.nala.org*)
- PACE certification of the National Federation of Paralegal Associations (NFPA). Passing an exam and fulfilling the other requirements of NFPA entitle you to be called a Registered Paralegal (RP) or a PACE Registered Paralegal. (*www.paralegals.org*)
- PP certification of NALS, the Association for Legal Professionals. Passing an exam and fulfilling the other requirements of NALS entitle you to be called a Professional Paralegal (PP). (*www.nals.org*)
- AACP certification of the American Alliance of Paralegals, Inc. (AAPI). Fulfilling the requirements of AAPI (which does not include an examination) entitles you to be called an American Alliance Certified Paralegal (AACP). (*www.aapipara.org*)

Florida Certification

A Florida paralegal can become a Certified Florida Legal Assistant (CFLA) by passing an examination and meeting the other requirements set by the CFLA program administrator, the Paralegal Association of Florida (PAF) (*www.pafinc.org*). Established in 1980, the exam complements NALA's national certification program, meaning that CFLA certification has been designed for those who have already achieved the national certification from NALA as a CLA or CP.

Summary: How to Become a CFLA

There is a two-step process to become a CFLA:

1. Pass the CLA (Certified Legal Assistant/Certified Paralegal) test of National Association of Legal Assistants (NALA).
2. Pass the CFLA test of the Paralegal Association of Florida (PAF).

1. The CLA Exam

The first requirement is to meet the requirements of the Certified Legal Assistant/Certified Paralegal program of NALA.

National Association of Legal Assistants (NALA)
1516 South Boston, Suite 300
Tulsa, OK 74119
918-587-6828
www.nala.org

Once you do so, you can use the titles Certified Legal Assistant (CLA) or Certified Paralegal (CP). Here are examples of how John Smith could sign his name or have it printed on a business card once he fulfills the requirements of NALA:

John Smith, CLA
Paralegal

John Smith, CP
Legal Assistant

John Smith, Certified Legal
Assistant

John Smith, Certified
Paralegal

For ethical reasons, the designations CLA or CP should not be used alone. If they are not spelled out, the words *paralegal* or *legal assistant* should be used to make the person's nonlawyer status clear.

The CLA/CP program is popular in Florida. There are over 14,000 CLAs/CPs in the country. Approximately 25 percent of them are from Florida.

Eligibility to Take the CLA Exam

To be eligible for the CLA examination, a legal assistant must meet *one* of the following three requirements:

- Be a graduate of a legal assistant program that meets *one* of the following requirements:
  - Approved by the American Bar Association
  - An associate's degree program

- A post-baccalaureate certificate program in legal assistant studies
- A bachelor's degree program in legal assistant studies
- A legal assistant program that consists of a minimum of 60 semester hours (900 clock hours or 90 quarter hours) of which at least 15 semester hours (225 clock hours or 22.5 quarter hours) are substantive legal courses
- Have a bachelor's degree in any field plus one year's experience as a legal assistant. Successful completion of at least 15 semester hours (or 22.5 quarter hours or 225 clock hours) of substantive legal assistant courses will be considered equivalent to one year's experience as a legal assistant.
- Have a high school diploma or equivalent plus seven year's experience as a legal assistant under the supervision of a member of the Bar, plus evidence of a minimum of 20 hours of continuing legal education credit to have been completed within a two-year period prior to the CLA examination date.

Material Tested on the CLA Exam

The CLA examination is a two-day comprehensive examination based on federal law and procedure. It consists of five sections:

- **Communications.** Word usage and vocabulary, grammar/punctuation, writing skills, non-verbal communications, interviewing and client communications, and general communications related to interoffice/human relations situations.
- **Ethics.** Ethical responsibilities centering on performance of delegated work including confidentiality, unauthorized practice of law, legal advice, conflict of interest, billing and client communications; client/public contact including identification as a nonlawyer, advertising, and initial client contact; professional integrity/competence including knowledge of legal assistant codes of ethics; relationships with co-workers and support staff; and attorney codes/discipline.
- **Legal research.** Sources of law including primary authority and secondary authority, understanding how law is recorded, citing the law, updating decisions, identifying relevant facts and legal issues.
- **Judgment and analytical ability.** Comprehension of data—identifying and understanding a problem, ability to link facts or legal issues from other cases to the problem at hand, recognizing similarities and differences by analogy, evaluating and categorizing data, and organizing data and findings in a written document.
- **Substantive law.** This section is composed of five subsections. The first section is substantive law/general and covers the American legal system including court structure, legal concepts, and sources and classifications of law. All examinees must take this subsection, plus select any four other subsections from the following substantive areas of the law: administrative law, bankruptcy, business organizations, contracts, family law, criminal law and procedure, civil litigation, probate and estate planning, and real estate. These tests cover general knowledge and legal terminology of each practice area.

When and Where to Take the CLA Exam

The CLA exam is offered three times a year: March/April (depending on the holiday schedule), July, and December. Application forms and the requisite fees must be received by the published filing dates. Filing deadline dates are January 15 for the March/April examination, May 15 for the July examination, and October 1 for the December examination session.

The test can be taken at many schools, universities, and junior colleges throughout the country. A list is available from NALA (*www.nala.org*).

Cost of Taking the CLA Exam

You do not have to be a member of NALA to take the exam, but if you are a member, the fee for the exam is lower than for non-members. NALA members pay $250; non-members pay $275. Retakes of the exam are allowed. The retake fee is $60 per section. The CLA examination program has been approved by the Veterans Administration for qualified veterans (*gibill.va.gov*).

NALA also offers a separate specialty examination with different fees and requirements. This specialty exam is not, however, related to the CFLA exam in Florida.

2. The CFLA Exam

Once you have your CLA/CP certificate, you can go through a separate process of the Paralegal Association of Florida (PAF) to become a CFLA.

Paralegal Association of Florida
P.O. Box 7073
West Palm Beach, FL 33405
561-833-1408
www.pafinc.org

When you succeed, you can use the CFLA credential after your name. You can also use the CLA or CP title because, by definition, someone with CFLA certification also has CLA or CP certification. For example, a Florida paralegal who has passed the CFLA exam could be referred to as:

John Smith, CLA, CFLA
Paralegal

John Smith, CP, CFLA
Legal Assistant

John Smith, Certified Florida
Legal Assistant

John Smith, CFLA
Certified Paralegal

Eligibility to Take the CFLA Exam

To be eligible for the CFLA examination, you must meet *both* of the following requirements:

- You have taken and passed the CLA (Certified Legal Assistant) exam of the NALA. This means that you have met one of the three education requirements for the CLA exam. See the requirements above for the CLA exam.
- You are of good moral character and are aware of the ethical considerations of the profession. To this end, a Florida attorney signs an attestation on the CFLA application that states:

> I certify that this applicant for certification as a CERTIFIED LEGAL ASSISTANT by the Paralegal Association of Florida, Inc., has been employed by me for _____ years, _____ months, is aware of the ethical considerations of The Florida Bar and the Paralegal Association of Florida, Inc. I feel this applicant is of good moral character and is qualified to sit for the Florida Certification Examination.

Material Tested on the CFLA Exam

The CFLA exam is a three-hour exam that covers Florida law. The exam has two sections:

1. Ethics, civil procedure and Florida general law that includes Florida's court system, basic criminal law, basic property law, basic estate and probate law, basic family law, and basic business law
2. The choice of either real estate law, probate law, business law, family law, or criminal law

A passing grade for each section is 70 percent. Both sections must be passed to attain the CFLA designation.

Although ethics is not separately tested, each CFLA exam will include coverage of ethics rules as they pertain to attorneys, paralegals, and the practice of law. The applicant should be familiar with the Code of Ethics and Professional Responsibility of the National Association of Legal Assistants, the ethical rules of the American Bar Association, and the Florida State Bar Rules of Professional Conduct.

When and Where to Take the CFLA Exam

The CFLA exam is offered three times every year in conjunction with the CLA exam and at the Paralegal Association of Florida's mid-year meeting in the spring and annual meeting in September (*www.pafinc.org*). See also information on the test site and the CFLA workshop offered through the University of Central Florida (*www.ce.ucf.edu/pc_course.asp?prog=141*).

Cost of Taking the CFLA Exam

The cost of taking the CFLA (payable to PAF) is $100.00 for PAF members and $125.00 for non-members. A *CFLA Study Guide* ($85) is available from PAF.

Continuing Legal Education (CLE) Requirements

There are separate continuing legal education (CLE) requirements to maintain CLA/CP certification and CFLA certification:

- CLA/CP. You must complete 50 hours of CLE (or individual study programs) every five years. Credit can also be awarded for significant achievement in the area of continuing legal assistant education such as successful completion of a state certification test or teaching in a legal assistant program.
- CFLA. You must complete 30 hours of CLE over a five-year period. The CLE must be directly applicable to Florida law.

F. Florida Registered Paralegal (FRP)

"It is certainly an historic day for us," commented Karen McLead (former president of the Paralegal Association of Florida) when the Supreme Court of Florida announced its approval of the Florida Registered Paralegal Program in 2007.

In 2005, a proposal to institute a regulatory scheme for paralegals was introduced before the Florida legislature. The Florida Bar opposed the proposed legislation, in part because it believed that any regulation of paralegals should be in the judicial branch rather than the legislative branch. Eventually, the Bar submitted a proposal to the Supreme Court of Florida to establish the Florida Registered Paralegal Program. In November of 2007, the Court adopted the proposal. The program is now part of the Rules Regulating The Florida Bar in Chapter 20.

The Court did not answer the question of whether the judiciary or the legislature had jurisdiction to regulate paralegals. "The Court need not address whether it has jurisdiction to 'regulate' the paralegal profession because the rules proposed by the Bar that the Court adopts in this opinion do not establish 'regulation' of the paralegal profession. Rather, they create a registration program, participation in which is purely voluntary. The Bar urges the Court to approve this voluntary registration plan for members of a profession who perform work that is clearly related to the practice of law. We do so because we believe the program will inure to the benefit of the public in the same way the Florida Rules for Certified and Court-Appointed Mediators inured to the public's benefit and we are, therefore, comfortable with approving this program. It behooves us to tread with caution in implementing a registration program for professionals who have hitherto been largely self-regulated so that the efficacy of the program being adopted and its impact on both the legal and paralegal professions can be assessed before any mandatory plan is instituted." In *Re: Amendments to the Rules Regulating The Florida Bar: Florida Registered Paralegal Program,* 969 So. 2d 360 (Fla. 2007) (*www.floridasupremecourt.org/decisions/2007/sc06-1622.pdf*).

Because the registration program is voluntary, there are now, in effect, two tiers of paralegals in Florida:

- Those who meet the qualifications for registration and decide to pursue it
- Those who do not qualify for or who decide not to seek registration

Both kinds of paralegals are subject to the same ethical rules and restrictions on the use of the paralegal title. No individual can be called a paralegal unless he or she works under the supervision of a member of the Florida Bar. Furthermore, both kinds of paralegals can perform the same kinds of tasks. Registration does not broaden the scope of what a paralegal is authorized to do.

Eligibility

A Florida Registered Paralegal (FRP) must:

- Meet the definition of a paralegal
- Have designated education and work experience (see Rule 20-3.1 below) *or* have national certification from NALA or NFPA
- Complete an application and be registered by The Florida Bar
- Submit a sworn statement that you have read and will abide by the Code of Ethics and Responsibility
- Complete a minimum of 30 hours of continuing education every three years, five hours of which shall be in legal ethics or professionalism
- Pay a $150 application fee
- Register with The Florida Bar on an annual basis

Grandfathering provisions are available up to March of 2011 for those who do not meet the education or certification requirements (see Rule 20-3.1[c] below).

Definition of a Paralegal and Work Experience

A paralegal is defined as a person with education, training, or work experience, who works under the supervision of a member of the Florida Bar and who performs specifically delegated substantive legal work for which a member of the Florida Bar is responsible. To qualify as paralegal work or paralegal work experience for purposes of meeting the eligibility and renewal

requirements, the paralegal must primarily perform paralegal work and the work must be continuous and recent. Recent paralegal work means work performed during three of the previous five years, in connection with an initial registration. Time spent performing clerical work is specifically excluded.

Disclosure of Status

You must designate your status as a Florida registered paralegal at the outset of a relationship with a client, attorney, court personnel, agency personnel, or member of the general public. In written communication, you may either say Florida Registered Paralegal or FRP. If, however, you say FRP, you must also say paralegal to make your nonlawyer status clear. For example:

John Doe	John Doe, FRP
Florida Registered Paralegal	Paralegal
Smith & Smith	Smith & Smith

Here is the complete description of the registration program:

Rules Regulating the Florida Bar

Chapter 20 Florida Registered Paralegal Program
Subchapter 20-1 Preamble
Rule 20-1.1 Purpose

The purpose of this chapter is to set forth a definition that must be met in order to use the title paralegal, to establish the requirements to become a Florida Registered Paralegal, and to establish the requirements to maintain Florida Registered Paralegal status. This chapter is not intended to set forth the duties that a paralegal may perform because those restrictions are set forth in the Rules of Professional Conduct and various opinions of the Professional Ethics Committee. Nothing contained herein shall be deemed relevant in charging or awarding fees for legal services rendered by nonlawyers under the supervision of a member of The Florida Bar, such fees being based on the nature of the services rendered and not the title of the person rendering the services.

Subchapter 20-2 Definitions
Rule 20-2.1 Generally

For purposes of this chapter, the following terms shall have the following meaning:

(a) **Paralegal.** A paralegal is a person with education, training, or work experience, who works under the direction and supervision of a member of The Florida Bar and who performs specifically delegated substantive legal work for which a member of The Florida Bar is responsible.

(b) Florida Registered Paralegal. A Florida Registered Paralegal is someone who meets the definition of paralegal and the requirements for registration as set forth elsewhere in these rules.

(c) Paralegal Work and Paralegal Work Experience. Paralegal work and paralegal work experience are specifically delegated substantive legal work performed by a person with education, training, or work experience under the direction and supervision of a member of The Florida Bar for which a member of The Florida Bar is responsible. In order to qualify as paralegal work or paralegal work experience for purposes of meeting the eligibility and renewal requirements set forth herein, the paralegal must primarily perform paralegal work and the work must be continuous and recent. Recent paralegal work for the purposes of meeting the eligibility and renewal requirements set forth herein means work performed during 3 of the previous 5 years in connection with an initial registration, and during the preceding year in the case of a registration renewal. Time spent performing clerical work is specifically excluded.

(d) Approved Paralegal Program. An approved paralegal program is a program approved by the American Bar Association ("ABA") or a program that is in substantial compliance with the ABA guidelines and accredited by a nationally recognized accrediting agency approved by the United States Department of Education.

(e) Employing or Supervising Attorney. An employing or supervising attorney is the attorney having direct supervision over the work product of the paralegal or Florida Registered Paralegal.

(f) Board. The board is the Board of Governors of The Florida Bar.

(g) Respondent. A respondent is the individual whose conduct is under investigation.

(h) Designated Reviewer. The designated reviewer is a member of the board of governors appointed by the president of The Florida Bar from the district of the district paralegal committee and is responsible for review and other specific duties as assigned by the board of governors with respect to a particular district paralegal committee or matter. If a designated reviewer recuses or is unavailable, another board member from the district may be appointed by the president of The Florida Bar to serve as designated reviewer in that matter.

(i) Probable Cause. A finding of probable cause is a finding that there is cause to believe that a Florida Registered Paralegal is guilty of misconduct justifying disciplinary action.

(j) Bar Counsel. Bar counsel is a member of The Florida Bar representing The Florida Bar in any proceeding under these rules.

Subchapter 20-3 Eligibility Requirements
Rule 20-3.1 Requirements for Registration

In order to be a Florida Registered Paralegal under this chapter, an individual must meet 1 of the following requirements.

(a) Educational and Work Experience Requirements. A person may become a Florida Registered Paralegal by meeting 1 of the following education and paralegal work experience requirements:

(1) a bachelor's degree in paralegal studies from an approved paralegal program, plus a minimum of 1 year of paralegal work experience;

(2) a bachelor's degree from an institution accredited by a nationally recognized accrediting agency approved by the United States Department of Education or the Florida Department of Education, plus a minimum of 3 years of paralegal work experience;

(3) an associate's degree in paralegal studies from an approved paralegal program, plus a minimum of 2 years of paralegal work experience;

(4) an associate's degree from an institution accredited by a nationally recognized accrediting agency approved by the United States Department of Education or the Florida Department of Education, plus a minimum of 4 years of paralegal work experience; or

(5) a juris doctorate degree from an American Bar Association accredited institution, plus a minimum of 1 year of paralegal work experience.

(b) Certification. A person may become a Florida Registered Paralegal by obtaining 1 of the following certifications:

(1) successful completion of the Paralegal Advanced Competency Exam (PACE certification as offered by the National Federation of Paralegal Associations "NFPA") and good standing with NFPA; or

(2) successful completion of the Certified Legal Assistant/Certified Paralegal examination (CLA/CP certification as offered by the National Association of Legal Assistants "NALA") and good standing with NALA.

(c) Grandfathering. A person who does not meet the requirements of (a) or (b) may become a Florida Registered Paralegal by providing attestation from an employing or supervising attorney(s) that the person has paralegal work experience as defined elsewhere in these rules for 5 of the 8 years immediately preceding the date of such attestation. Any such attestation must be received by The Florida Bar not later than 3 years after the effective date of this chapter.

Subchapter 20-4 Registration
Rule 20-4.1 Generally

The following shall be filed with The Florida Bar by an individual seeking to be registered as a Florida Registered Paralegal:

(a) Educational, Certification, or Experience Requirement.
   (1) evidence that the individual has satisfied the requirements of rule 20-3.1(a) by supplying evidence of the degree and attestation from the employing or supervising attorney(s) showing that the individual has the appropriate paralegal work experience; or
   (2) a certificate showing that the individual has obtained 1 of the certifications set forth in rule 20-3.1(b); or
   (3) attestation from the employing or supervising attorney(s) that the individual has met the requirements of rule 20-3.1(c).

(b) **Statement of Compliance.** A sworn statement by the individual that the individual has read and will abide by the Code of Ethics and Responsibility set forth elsewhere in this chapter.

(c) **Registration Fee.** An appropriate registration fee set by the board.

(d) **Review by The Florida Bar.** Upon receipt of the items set forth in subdivision 20-4.1(a)–(c), The Florida Bar shall review the items for compliance with this chapter. Any incomplete submissions will be returned. If the individual meets all of the requirements of this chapter, the individual shall be added to the roll of Florida Registered Paralegals and a certificate evidencing such registration shall be issued.

(e) **Annual Renewal; Content and Registration Fee.** The registration pursuant to this subdivision shall be annual and consistent with that applicable to an attorney licensed to practice in the state of Florida. An annual registration fee shall be set by the board in an amount not more than the annual fees paid by inactive members of The Florida Bar. The renewal shall contain a statement that the individual is primarily performing paralegal work as defined elsewhere in this chapter and a statement that the individual is not ineligible for registration set forth elsewhere in this chapter. A Florida Registered Paralegal who is not primarily performing paralegal work shall not be eligible for renewal of the registration but may reapply for registration.

Subchapter 20-5 Ineligibility for Registration or Renewal
Rule 20-5.1 Generally

The following individuals are ineligible for registration as a Florida Registered Paralegal or for renewal of a registration that was previously granted:

(a) a person who is currently suspended or disbarred or who has resigned in lieu of discipline from the practice of law in any state or jurisdiction;

(b) a person who has been convicted of a felony in any state or jurisdiction and whose civil rights have not been restored;

(c) a person who has been found to have engaged in the unlicensed (unauthorized) practice of law in any state or jurisdiction;

(d) a person whose registration or license to practice has been terminated or revoked for disciplinary reasons by a professional organization, court, disciplinary board, or agency in any jurisdiction;

(e) a person who is no longer primarily performing paralegal work as defined elsewhere in these rules; or

(f) a person who fails to comply with prescribed continuing education requirements as set forth elsewhere in this chapter.

Rule 20-5.2 Duty to Update

An individual applying for registration as a Florida Registered Paralegal or who is registered as a Florida Registered Paralegal has a duty to inform The Florida Bar promptly of any fact or circumstance that would render the individual ineligible for registration or renewal.

Subchapter 20-6 Continuing Education
Rule 20-6.1 Generally

In order to maintain the status of Florida Registered Paralegal, a Florida Registered Paralegal must complete a minimum of 30 hours of continuing education every 3 years, 5 hours of which shall be in legal ethics or professionalism. Courses approved for credit by The Florida Bar, the National Association of Legal Assistants (NALA), or the National Federation of Paralegal Associations (NFPA) will be deemed acceptable for purposes of this rule.

Subchapter 20-7 Code of Ethics and Responsibility
Rule 20-7.1 Generally

A Florida Registered Paralegal shall adhere to the following Code of Ethics and Responsibility:

(a) Disclosure. A Florida Registered Paralegal shall disclose his or her status as a Florida Registered Paralegal at the outset of any professional relationship with a client, attorneys, a court or administrative agency or personnel thereof, and members of the general public.

(b) Confidentiality and Privilege. A Florida Registered Paralegal shall preserve the confidences and secrets of all clients. A Florida Registered Paralegal must protect the confidences of a client, and it shall be unethical for a Florida Registered Paralegal to violate any statute or rule now in effect or hereafter to be enacted controlling privileged communications.

(c) Appearance of Impropriety or Unethical Conduct. A Florida Registered Paralegal should understand the attorney's Rules of Professional Conduct and this code in order to avoid any action that would involve the attorney in a violation of the rules or give the appearance of professional impropriety. It is the obligation of the Florida Registered Paralegal to avoid conduct that would cause the lawyer to be unethical or even appear to be unethical, and loyalty to the lawyer is incumbent upon the Florida Registered Paralegal.

(d) Prohibited Conduct. A Florida Registered Paralegal should not:

(1) establish attorney-client relationships, accept cases, set legal fees, give legal opinions or advice, or represent a client before a court or other tribunal, unless authorized to do so by the court or tribunal;

(2) engage in, encourage, or contribute to any act that could constitute the unlicensed practice of law;

(3) engage in the practice of law;

(4) perform any of the duties that attorneys only may perform nor do things that attorneys themselves may not do; or

(5) act in matters involving professional legal judgment since the services of an attorney are essential in the public interest whenever the exercise of such judgment is required.

(e) Performance of Services. A Florida Registered Paralegal must act prudently in determining the extent to which a client may be assisted without the presence of an attorney. A Florida Registered Paralegal may perform services for an attorney in the representation of a client, provided:

(1) the services performed by the paralegal do not require the exercise of independent professional legal judgment;

(2) the attorney is responsible for the client, maintains a direct relationship with the client, and maintains control of all client matters;

(3) the attorney supervises the paralegal;

(4) the attorney remains professionally responsible for all work on behalf of the client and assumes full professional responsibility for the work product, including any actions taken or not taken by the paralegal in connection therewith; and

(5) the services performed supplement, merge with, and become the attorney's work product.

(f) Competence. A Florida Registered Paralegal shall work continually to maintain integrity and a high degree of competency throughout the legal profession.

(g) Conflict of Interest. A Florida Registered Paralegal who was employed by an opposing law firm has a duty not to disclose any information relating to the representation of the former firm's clients and must disclose the fact of the prior employment to the employing attorney.

(h) Reporting Known Misconduct. A Florida Registered Paralegal having knowledge that another Florida Registered Paralegal has committed a violation of this chapter or code shall inform The Florida Bar of the violation.

Subchapter 20-8 Revocation of Registration

The following rules and procedures shall apply to complaints against Florida Registered Paralegals:

Rule 20-8.1 Paralegal Committees

There shall be paralegal committees as are herein provided, each of which shall have the authority and jurisdiction required to perform the functions hereinafter assigned to the paralegal committee and which shall be constituted and appointed as follows:

(a) District Paralegal Committees. There shall be at least 1 paralegal committee for each appellate district of this state and as many more as shall be found desirable by the board. Such committees shall be continuing bodies notwithstanding changes in membership, and they shall have jurisdiction and the power to proceed in all matters properly before them.

(b) Membership, Appointment, and Eligibility. Each district paralegal committee shall consist of not fewer than 3 members, at least 1 of whom is a Florida Registered Paralegal and at least 1 of whom is a member of The Florida Bar. Members of district paralegal committees shall be nominated by the member of the board designated to review the actions of the committee and appointed by the board. All appointees shall be of legal age and shall be residents of the district or have their principal office in the district. For each district paralegal committee there shall be a chair designated by the designated reviewer of that committee. A vice-chair and secretary may be designated by the chair of each district committee.

(c) Terms. The terms of the members shall be for 3 years from the date of administration of the oath of service on the district paralegal committee or until such time as their successors are appointed and qualified. Continuous service of a member shall not exceed 6 years. A member shall not be reappointed for a period of 3 years after the end of the member's second term provided, however, the expiration of the term of any member shall not disqualify such member from concluding any investigation or participating in the disposition of cases that were pending before the committee when the member's term expired.

(d) Disqualification. No member of a district paralegal committee shall perform any district paralegal committee function when that member:

(1) is related by blood or marriage to the complainant or respondent;

(2) has a financial, business, property, or personal interest in the matter under consideration or with the complainant or respondent;

(3) has a personal interest that could be affected by the outcome of the proceedings or that could affect the outcome; or

(4) is prejudiced or biased toward either the complainant or the respondent.

Upon notice of the above prohibitions, the affected members should recuse themselves from further proceedings. The district paralegal committee chair shall have the power to disqualify any member from any proceeding in which any of the above prohibitions exists and is stated of record or in writing in the file by the chair.

(e) Removal. Any member may be removed from service by the designated reviewer of that committee or by the board.

(f) District Paralegal Committee Meetings. District paralegal committees should meet at regularly scheduled times, not less frequently than quarterly each year, and either the chair or vice-chair may call special meetings.

Rule 20-8.2 Duties and Authority

It is the duty of the district paralegal committees to receive and evaluate complaints against Florida Registered Paralegals. The district paralegal committees shall have the authority to remove or revoke an individual's registration as a Florida Registered Paralegal in accordance with the procedures set forth elsewhere in this chapter. A registration certificate issued pursuant to these rules may be suspended or revoked for any of the following reasons:

(a) conviction of a felony or of a misdemeanor involving moral turpitude, dishonesty, or false statement;

(b) fraud, dishonesty, or corruption that is related to the functions and duties of a Florida Registered Paralegal;

(c) gross incompetence or unprofessional or unethical conduct;

(d) willful, substantial, or repeated violation of any duty imposed by statute, rule, or order of court;

(e) fraud or misrepresentation in obtaining or renewing registration status;

(f) noncompliance with continuing education requirements;

(g) nonpayment of renewal fees; or

(h) violation of the Code of Ethics and Responsibility set forth elsewhere in these rules.

Rule 20-8.3 Complaint Processing

(a) Complaints. All complaints against a Florida Registered Paralegal may be initiated either by a sworn complaint asserting a violation of these rules or by The Florida Bar on its own motion.

(b) Review by Bar Counsel. Bar counsel shall review the complaint and determine whether the alleged conduct, if proven, would constitute a violation of these rules. Bar counsel may conduct a preliminary, informal investigation to aid in this determination and, if necessary, may employ a Florida Bar staff investigator to aid in the preliminary investigation. If bar counsel determines that the facts, if proven, would not constitute a violation, bar counsel may decline to pursue the complaint. The complainant shall be notified of a decision not to pursue a complaint and shall be given the reasons therefor.

(c) Closing by Bar Counsel and Committee Chair. Bar counsel may consult with the appropriate district paralegal committee chair to determine whether the alleged conduct of a complaint, if proven, would constitute a violation of these rules. If bar counsel and the district committee chair concur in a finding that the case should be closed, the complaint may be closed on such finding without referral to the district paralegal committee.

(d) Referral to District Paralegal Committee. Bar counsel may refer a file to the appropriate district paralegal committee for further investigation or action as authorized elsewhere in these rules.

(e) Notification of Violation. If a majority of the district paralegal committee finds probable cause to believe that a violation of these rules has occurred, bar counsel or the chair of the district paralegal committee will send written notice thereof to the Florida Registered Paralegal identifying the alleged violation. The notice shall be sent by certified U.S. mail directed to the last mailing address on file.

(f) Response to Notice of Violation. Within 30 days from the receipt of the notification, the Florida Registered Paralegal shall file a written response. If the Florida Registered Paralegal does not respond, the violations identified in the finding of probable cause shall be deemed admitted.

(g) Committee Review. After the filing of the written response to the finding of probable cause or following the expiration of the time within which to file a response if none is filed, the district paralegal committee shall review the complaint, the finding of probable cause, the response (if any), and any other pertinent materials, and decide whether to dismiss the proceeding or issue a proposed disposition. The committee shall promptly send written notice of its decision to the Florida Registered Paralegal by certified U.S. mail directed to the last mailing address on file.

Rule 20-8.4 Investigation

(a) Conduct of Proceedings. The proceedings of district paralegal committees when testimony is taken may be informal in nature and the committees shall not be bound by the rules of evidence.

(b) Taking Testimony. Bar counsel, each district paralegal committee, and members thereof conducting investigations are empowered to take and have transcribed the testimony and evidence of witnesses. If the testimony is recorded stenographically or otherwise, the witness shall be sworn by any person authorized by law to administer oaths.

(c) Rights and Responsibilities of Respondent. The respondent may be required to appear and to produce evidence as any other witness unless the respondent claims a privilege or right properly available to the respondent under applicable federal or state law. The respondent may be accompanied by counsel.

(d) Rights of Complaining Witness. The complaining witness is not a party to the investigation. The complainant may be granted the right to be present at any district paralegal committee proceeding when the respondent is present before the committee to give testimony. The complaining witness shall have no right to appeal the finding of the district paralegal committee.

Rule 20-8.5 Subpoenas

Subpoenas for the attendance of witnesses and the production of documentary evidence before a district paralegal committee shall be issued as follows:

(a) District Paralegal Committees. Subpoenas for the attendance of witnesses and the production of

documentary evidence shall be issued by the chair or vice-chair of a district paralegal committee in pursuance of an investigation authorized by the committee.

(b) Bar Counsel Investigations. Subpoenas for the attendance of witnesses and the production of documentary evidence before bar counsel when bar counsel is conducting an initial investigation shall be issued by the chair or vice-chair of a district paralegal committee to which the matter will be assigned.

(c) Service. Subpoenas may be served by an investigator employed by The Florida Bar or in the manner provided by law for the service of process.

Rule 20-8.6 Disposition of Complaints

Upon concluding its investigation, the district paralegal committee shall determine which of the following action(s) should be taken:

(a) close the matter on a finding of no violation;

(b) require that a specified continuing education course be taken;

(c) accept an affidavit from the Florida Registered Paralegal acknowledging that the conduct surrounding the complaint was a violation of these rules and that the Florida Registered Paralegal will refrain from conduct that would create a violation of these rules;

(d) suspension of the Florida Registered Paralegal's registration certificate for a period not to exceed 1 year;

(e) revocation of registration certificate; or

(f) denial of request for renewal.

Rule 20-8.7 Review of District Paralegal Committee Action

(a) Review by the Designated Reviewer. Notice of district paralegal committee action recommending either revocation or denial of renewal shall be given to the designated reviewer for review. Upon review of the district paralegal committee action, the designated reviewer may affirm the action of the district paralegal committee, request the district paralegal committee to reconsider its action, or refer the district paralegal committee action to the disciplinary review committee of the board of governors for its review. The request for a district paralegal committee reconsideration or referral to the disciplinary review committee shall be in writing and must be made within 30 days of notice of the district paralegal committee action. If the designated reviewer fails to make the request for reconsideration or referral within the time prescribed, the district paralegal committee action shall become final.

(b) Review by Disciplinary Review Committee. The disciplinary review committee shall review those district paralegal committee matters referred to it by a designated reviewer or the district paralegal committee and shall make a report to the board. The disciplinary review committee may confirm, reject, or amend the recommendation of the designated reviewer in whole or in part. The report of the disciplinary review committee shall be final unless overruled by the board.

(c) Board Action on Recommendations of the Disciplinary Review Committee. On review of a report and recommendation of the disciplinary review committee, the board of governors may confirm, reject, or amend the recommendation in whole or in part.

(d) Notice of Board Action. Bar counsel shall give notice of board action to the respondent, complainant, and district paralegal committee.

(e) Filing Service on Board of Governors. All matters to be filed with or served upon the board shall be addressed to the board of governors and filed with the executive director. The executive director shall be the custodian of the official records of the Florida Registered Paralegal Program.

Rule 20-8.8 Files

(a) Files Are Property of Bar. All matters, including files, preliminary investigation reports, interoffice memoranda, records of investigations, and the records of other proceedings under these rules are property of The Florida Bar.

(b) Investigatory Record. The investigatory record shall consist of the record before a district paralegal committee and any reports, correspondence, papers, and recordings and transcripts of hearings and transcribed testimony furnished to, served on, or received from the respondent or the complainant or a witness before the district paralegal committee. The record before the district paralegal committee shall consist of all reports, correspondence, papers, and recordings furnished to or received from the respondent and the transcript of district paralegal committee meetings or transcribed testimony, if the proceedings were attended by a court reporter; provided, however, that the committee may retire into private session to debate the issues involved and to reach a decision as to the action to be taken.

(c) Limitations on Disclosure. Any material provided to or promulgated by The Florida Bar that is confidential under applicable law shall remain confidential and shall not be disclosed except as authorized by the applicable law. If this type of material is made a part of the investigatory record, that portion of the investigatory record may be sealed by the district paralegal committee chair.

(d) Disclosure of Information. Unless otherwise ordered by a court, nothing in these rules shall prohibit the complainant, respondent, or any witness from disclosing the existence of proceedings under these rules or from disclosing any documents or correspondence served on or provided to those persons.

(e) Response to Inquiry. Representatives of The Florida Bar, authorized by the board, shall reply to inquiries regarding a pending or closed investigation. The Florida Bar may charge a reasonable fee for copying documents consistent with applicable law.

(f) Production of Investigatory Records Pursuant to Subpoena. The Florida Bar, pursuant to a valid subpoena issued by a regulatory agency, may provide any documents that are a portion of the investigatory record even if otherwise deemed confidential under these rules. The Florida Bar may charge a reasonable fee for copying the documents consistent with applicable law.

(g) Response to False or Misleading Statements. If public statements that are false and misleading are made about any investigation brought pursuant to this chapter, The Florida Bar may make any disclosure consistent with applicable law necessary to correct such false or misleading statements.

(h) Providing Material to Other Agencies. Nothing contained herein shall prohibit The Florida Bar from providing material to any state or federal law enforcement or regulatory agency, United States Attorney, state attorney, the National Association of Legal Assistants or the National Federation of Paralegal Associations and equivalent organizations, the Florida Board of Bar Examiners and equivalent entities in other jurisdictions, paralegal grievance committees and equivalent entities in other jurisdictions, and unlicensed practice of law committees and equivalent entities in other jurisdictions.

Subchapter 20-9 Immunity
Rule 20-9.1 Generally

The members of the district paralegal committees, the board, bar staff and counsel assisting the committees, shall have absolute immunity from civil liability for all acts in the course of their official duties.

Subchapter 20-10 Amendments
Rule 20-10.1 Generally

Rules governing the Florida Registered Paralegal Program may be amended in accordance with the procedures set forth elsewhere in these rules.

G. More Information

United States Department of Labor, Paralegals
www.bls.gov/oco/ocos114.htm

National and State Employment Data
www.labormarketinfo.com
www.uflib.ufl.edu/docs/guides/occupations.html

Paralegal Association of Florida (PAF)
www.pafinc.org (click "Certification")

National Federation of Paralegal Associations (NFPA)
www.paralegals.org

National Association of Legal Assistants (NALA)
www.nala.org

NALS, the Association for Legal Professionals
www.nals.org

American Bar Association Standing Committee on Paralegals (SCOP)
www.abanet.org/legalservices/paralegals

International Paralegal Management Association Survey
www.paralegalmanagement.org (click "Utilization Survey")

Law Firms in Florida
www.hg.org/northam-firms.html
www.lawresearchservices.com/firms/lawfirmUS.htm

NALP Directory of Legal Employers
www.nalpdirectory.com

America's Largest Law Firms
www.ilrg.com/nlj250

Law Firm Salaries
www.infirmation.com/shared/insider/payscale.tcl
swz.salary.com (type "paralegal" in the "Search by" box and your zip code in "Location")

The Florida Registered Paralegal Proposal
www.flabar.org (click "Search" then type "registered paralegal")

Legal Secretary's Handbook
www.flcourts18.org/PDF/legalsec.pdf (this handbook was developed to assist legal secretaries and other members of law office staffs in dealing with the Judge's Office)

American Freelance Paralegal Association
www.freelanceparalegal.org

Wikipedia on Paralegalism
en.wikipedia.org/wiki/Paralegal

H. Something to Check

1. Pick an area of practice that interests you. Find and compare three law firm descriptions of that area online. In what ways are the descriptions similar and different? To find law firms online, go to Google (*www.google.com*) or any general search engine and type "Florida law firm" and the area of law you are checking. For example:

   > "Florida law firm" "criminal law"
   > "Florida law firm" "adoption law"
   > "Florida law firm" "estate planning"

2. The definition of a paralegal from Rule 20-2.1(b) of Rules Regulating The Florida Bar is presented at the beginning of this section. Compare this definition to the definitions of a paralegal found on the web sites of NFPA, NALA, NALS, and SCOP. (See their Internet addresses immediately above.) List the similarities and differences among the definitions.

3. Go to the web sites of the paralegal associations in Florida (see section 1.2 for the addresses). Summarize what they say about the regulation of paralegals in Florida.

1.2 Paralegal Associations and Related Groups in Florida

A. Introduction

B. Paralegal Associations in Florida

C. National Paralegal Associations

D. Bar Association Affiliate/Associate Membership for Paralegals

E. Other Associations

F. Something to Check

A. Introduction

There are many vibrant paralegal associations in the state that have had a major impact on the development of the paralegal field. Associations can be helpful for finding employment and continuing your legal education while employed. One of the best networking opportunities available to you will be the various meetings regularly held by the associations. The essence of networking is locating other paralegals and exchanging ideas, resources, leads, and business cards with them. Such exchanges can be important even if the subject matter of a particular meeting does not interest you. Furthermore, your involvement in a paralegal association will help strengthen the association and the profession itself.

Paralegal certification is briefly mentioned below under Paralegal Association of Florida. For a more extensive treatment of certification and registration, see section 1.1.

This section presents an overview of the following Florida associations:

- Central Florida Paralegal Association
- Gainesville Association of Legal Assistants
- Gulf Coast Paralegal Association
- NALS of Central Florida
- Northeast Florida Paralegal Association
- Northwest Florida Paralegal Association
- Paralegal Associations of Florida
- South Florida Paralegal Association
- Southwest Florida Paralegal Association
- Tampa Bay Paralegal Association
- Volusia Association of Paralegals

Many of these associations are part of the Florida Alliance of Paralegal Associations (FAPA), formed in 1996 to promote the paralegal profession throughout the state. When you go to the web site of an association, find out what services it offers, if the association has a job bank that lists current paralegal openings, and whether there are special dues for different categories of members. Also, find out the date and location of the next meeting.

B. Paralegal Associations in Florida

CENTRAL FLORIDA PARALEGAL ASSOCIATION (CFPA)

P.O. Box 1107
Orlando, FL 32802
407-672-6372
www.cfpainc.com

Background: Founded in 1983, the Central Florida Paralegal Association (CFPA) is structured "to promote high standards of professionalism" for paralegals of central Florida. This is accomplished through a wide range of professional meetings, newsletters, continuing education offerings, employment referral services, and social activities. Members are thereby given a voice in issues affecting the paralegal profession at local, state, and national levels.

Membership: CFPA offers three classes of membership:

• Active ($45) • Student ($25) • Patron ($55)

Eligibility criteria are listed on the online application (*www.cfpainc.com*).

Attorney Attestation: Employed members of CFPA are required to have an attorney sign the following attestation: "I hereby attest that _____ is and has been employed by me as a paralegal/legal assistant since _____. I further attest that said applicant is aware of all governing bar and paralegal ethical rules, is of professional and honest character, and acts prudently in performing his/her duties."

School Attestation: Student members must have their schools sign the following attestation: "I hereby attest that _____ is currently enrolled in the legal assistant/paralegal program listed above. I further attest that said applicant is of professional and honest character."

National Affiliation: CFPA is an affiliate of the National Association of Legal Assistants (NALA) (*www.nala.org*).

Newsletter: CFPA's newsletter is the *CFPA FOCUS*. The current issue is available online (*www.cfainc.com*).

Services Offered: CFPA provides a job-referral service (via a job bank), continuing education, networking opportunities, scholarship awards, and a paralegal-of-the-year award.

GAINESVILLE ASSOCIATION OF LEGAL ASSISTANTS (GALA)

www.afn.org/~gala
(Note: The current status of this association is uncertain.)

GULF COAST PARALEGAL ASSOCIATION (GCPA)

Naples, Florida 34108
www.gcpa.info

Background: GCPA was founded in 2007 to promote continuing legal educational for local paralegals, to establish practice guidelines for the paralegal profession, and to provide a forum for networking among peers.

Membership: GCPA offers four classes of membership:

• Active ($50) • Student ($20)
• Associate ($30) • Sustaining ($50)

National Affiliation: GCPA is an affiliate of the National Association of Legal Assistants (NALA) (*www.nala.org*).

Newsletter: GCPA's newsletter is *Paralegal-Ease*. The current issue is available online (*www.gcpa.info*).

Services Offered: GCPA offers a job bank, paralegal student scholarships, legal education seminars, a newsletter, and bar liaison.

NALS OF CENTRAL FLORIDA

www.nals.org/membership/regions/Florida.html

National Affiliation: NALS of Central Florida is affiliate of NALS, the Association for Legal Professionals (*www.nals.org*).

NORTHEAST FLORIDA PARALEGAL ASSOCIATION (NEFPA)

221 North Hogan, P.O. Box 164
Jacksonville, FL 32202
www.nefpa.org

Background: Northeast Florida Paralegal Association (NEFPA) was established in 1984 under its former name, Jacksonville Legal Assistants, Inc. NEFPA promotes paralegal professionalism through its many programs.

Membership: NEFPA offers four categories of membership:

• Active ($55) • Student ($35)
• Associate ($35) • Sustaining ($100)

Eligibility criteria are listed on the online application (*www.nefpa.org/nefpa_membership_app.pdf*).

Attorney Attestation: Active members must have an attorney certify that the applicant "has been or was employed by me and/or by my firm or company as a paralegal/legal assistant during the period from _____." The attestation uses the definition of a paralegal as a person "qualified by education, training or work experience who is employed or retained by a lawyer, law office, corporation, governmental agency or other entity who performs specifically delegated substantive legal work for which a lawyer is responsible." One of the criteria for active membership includes "in-house training as a paralegal/legal assistant," which is defined as "attorney education of the employee solely as a paralegal/legal assistant, performing substantive legal work for which a lawyer would otherwise be responsible, including review and analysis of assignments and a reasonable amount of instruction related directly to the duties and obligations of the paralegal/legal assistant."

National Affiliation: NEFPA is an affiliate of the National Association of Legal Assistants (NALA) (*www. nala.org*).

Newsletter: NEFPA's newsletter is the *NEFPA Newsletter.* Current and prior issues are available online (*www. nefpa.org/newsletter.shtml*).

Services Offered: NEFPA encourages professional development by offering a job bank service, mentoring, networking opportunities, programs that promote certification, and volunteer opportunities at the office of Jacksonville Area Legal Aid and other community service outreach programs.

NORTHWEST FLORIDA PARALEGAL ASSOCIATION (NWFPA)
P.O. Box 1333
Pensacola, FL 32502
www.nwfpa.com

Background: The Northwest Florida Paralegal Association (NWFPA) was established in 1981 as Pensacola Legal Assistants to promote ethics, professionalism, and good fellowship within the legal community.

Membership: NWFPA offers five classes of membership:

- Active ($40)
- Student ($20)
- Associate ($35)
- Sustaining ($30)
- Institutional ($50)

Attorney Attestation: Some applicants for active membership must have an attorney/employer "hereby attest that _____ is employed by me and meets the qualifications for active membership in the Northwest Florida Paralegal Association."

National Affiliation: NWFPA is an affiliate of the National Association of Legal Assistants (NALA) (*www.nala.org*).

Services Offered: NWFPA offers seminars at its regularly scheduled meetings, networking opportunities, and job postings available on the association's web site (*www.nwfpa.com/jobs.htm*).

PARALEGAL ASSOCIATION OF FLORIDA (PAF)
P.O. Box 7073
West Palm Beach, FL 33405
800-433-4352,
561-833-1408
www.pafinc.org

Background: The Paralegal Association of Florida (PAF) was founded in 1976 as Florida Legal Assistants, Inc. With more than 1,000 members throughout the state,

PAF proudly proclaims that the "work we perform for our law firms, corporations, or governmental employers requires a high degree of professionalism, strong ethical standards, and initial and continuing legal education." The goal of PAF is to promote these goals.

Membership: PAF offers four classes of membership:

- Active ($65)
- Student ($35)
- Associate ($60)
- Sustaining ($150)

Membership requirements are listed on the online application (*www.pafinc.org/pdf/memberapp.pdf*).

Attorney Attestation: Some applicants for active membership must have an attorney/employer attest that the applicant "is employed by me and is recognized as a paralegal, and that she/he meets the criteria of the definition of a paralegal/legal assistant set forth by Fla. Stat. ch. 57.104 . . . [and] that the applicant's ethical and professional conduct are above reproach."

Chapters: PAF has the following chapters:

- Big Bend Chapter (Gadsden, Liberty, Leon, Wakulla, Jefferson, Franklin)
- Boca Raton Chapter
- Brevard Chapter
- Broward Chapter
- Hillsborough Chapter
- Palm Beach Chapter
- Pinellas Chapter
- Suncoast Chapter (Manatee, Hardee, Sarasota, De Soto)
- Southwest Chapter
- Treasure Coast Chapter (St. Lucie, Indian River, Okeechobee, Martin)

National Affiliation: PAF is an affiliate of the National Association of Legal Assistants (NALA) (*www.nala.org*).

Newsletter: PAF has two publications for its members, *IN BRIEF* and *IN BRIEF . . . Briefly* (*www.pafinc.org/ publications.php*).

Certification: In 1980, PAF established its state-specific certification program for paralegals who have already obtained national certification from NALA. Successful completion of PAF certification (including a three-hour examination on Florida law) allows one to be called a Certified Florida Legal Assistant (CFLA). The eligibility requirements and other details of the CFLA program are presented in section 1.1 of this book.

Other Services Offered: PAF offers continuing education, study groups to promote professional certification, networking opportunities, scholarship awards, and community service outreach opportunities.

SOUTH FLORIDA PARALEGAL ASSOCIATION (SFPA)
P.O. Box 31-0745
Miami, FL 33231-0745
305-944-0204
www.sfpa.info

Background: South Florida Paralegal Association (SFPA) was established in 1979 as the Dade Association of Legal

Assistants. Its goals are "to enhance the competence" and "to strive for the acceptance and effective use of professional paralegals in the South Florida area."

Membership: SFPA offers five classes of membership:

- Active ($70)
- Student ($60)
- Associate ($60)
- Sustaining ($125)
- Provisional ($70)

Membership requirements are listed on the online registration page (*www.sfpa.info/site/registration.aspx*).

National Affiliation: SFPA is an affiliate of the National Association of Legal Assistants (NALA) (*www.nala.org*).

Newsletter: SFPA's newsletter is the *SFPA Journal.* Current issues are available online (*www.sfpa.info*).

Services Offered: Continuing education, networking opportunities, mentoring, scholarships, and a job bank.

SOUTHWEST FLORIDA PARALEGAL ASSOCIATION (SWFPA)

P.O. Box 2094
Sarasota, FL 34230-2094
www.swfloridaparalegals.com

Background: Southwest Florida Paralegal Association (SWFPA) was established in 1997 to promote the professional interests of local paralegals.

Membership: SWFPA offers four classes of membership:

- Active ($45)
- Student ($15)
- Associate ($60)
- Sustaining ($60)

Attorney Attestation: Some applicants for active membership must obtain an attestation of an attorney/employer: "I hereby attest that _____ is employed by me and meets the qualifications for active membership."

National Affiliation: SWFPA is an affiliate of the National Association of Legal Assistants (NALA) (*www.nala.org*).

Newsletter: SWFPA's newsletter is the *Writ of Assistance.* Current issues are available to members online (*www.swfloridaparalegals.com*).

Services Offered: Continuing education, networking opportunities, and a job bank.

TAMPA BAY PARALEGAL ASSOCIATION (TBPA)

P.O. Box 2840
Tampa, FL 33601
813-229-3333
www.tbpa.org

Background: Tampa Bay Paralegal Association (TBPA) is a local Florida voice representing paralegals in the Tampa Bay area. The mayor recently praised its efforts and those of all Tampa paralegals by proclaiming September 23–30 as Paralegal Week. The Hillsborough County Commissioners have also issued a Paralegal Week Proclamation (*www.tbpa.org/archives.htm*).

Membership: TBPA has four classes of membership:

- Active ($50)
- Student ($20)
- Associate ($50)
- Sustaining ($100)

Active members must reside or work in Hernando, Hillsborough, Manatee, Pasco, Pinellas, or Polk counties.

National Affiliation: TBPA is an affiliate of the National Federation of Paralegal Associations (NFPA) (*www.paralegals.org*).

Services Offered: Continuing education, networking opportunities, and a job bank.

VOLUSIA COUNTY PARALEGAL ASSOCIATION (VCPA)

P.O. Box 15075
Daytona Beach, FL 32115-5075
www.volusiaparalegals.org

Background: The Volusia County Paralegal Association (VCPA) came into existence to promote the interests of local paralegals on the central east coast of Florida, particularly in Daytona Beach, Volusia County, and Flagler County.

Membership: VCPA offers three classes of membership:

- Associate ($100)
- Student ($25)
- General ($50)

Newsletter: VCPA's newsletter is the *Letter of the Law.* Current and past issues are available online (*www.volusiaparalegals.org*).

Services Offered: Continuing education, networking opportunities, mentoring, and a job bank.

C. National Paralegal Associations

There are a number of national paralegal associations that Florida paralegals have joined either directly or through one of their affiliates:

- National Association of Legal Assistants (NALA)
- National Federation of Paralegal Associations (NFPA)
- NALS, the Association of Legal Professionals (NALS)
- American Alliance of Paralegals (AAPI)

National Association of Legal Assistants (NALA)

Web Address: *www.nala.org*
E-mail: *nalanet@nala.org*
Certification Awarded: Certified Legal Assistant (CLA); Certified Paralegal (CP); Advanced Certified Paralegal (ACP)
Certification Requirements: *www.nala.org/cert.htm, www.nala.org/apcweb/index.html*
Ethics Code: *www.nala.org/benefits-code.htm, www.nala.org/98model.htm*
Newsletter: *FACTS & FINDINGS* (*www.nala.org/Facts_Findings.htm*)

Continuing Legal Education: *www.nalacampus.com*

Affiliated Associations: *www.nala.org/Affiliated_ Associations_Info.HTM*

National Federation of Paralegal Associations (NFPA)

Web Address: *www.paralegals.org*

E-mail: *info@paralegals.org*

Certification Awarded: PACE Registered Paralegal (RP)

Certification Requirements: *www.paralegals.org* (click "PACE/RP")

Ethics Code: *www.paralegals.org* (click " Positions & Issues")

Newsletter: *National Paralegal Reporter (www.paralegals. org)*

Continuing Legal Education: *www.paralegals.org* (click "CLE")

Career Center: *www.paralegals.org*

Affiliated Associations: *www.paralegals.org* (click "About NFPA" then "Local Member Associations")

NALS, The Association of Legal Professionals (NALS)

Web Address: *www.nals.org*

E-mail: *info@nals.org*

Certification Awarded: Professional Paralegal (PP)

Certification Requirements: *www.nals.org/certification*

Ethics Code: *www.nals.org/aboutnals/Code*

Newsletter: *@Law (www.nals.org/newsletters/index.html)*

Continuing Legal Education: *www.nals.org/ onlinelearning/index.html*

Career Center: *www.nals.org/careercenter/index.html*

Affiliated Associations: *www.nals.org/membership/ states/index.html*

American Alliance of Paralegals (AAPI)

Web Address: *www.aapipara.org*

E-mail: *info@aapipara.org*

Certification Awarded: American Alliance Certified Paralegal (AACP)

Certification Requirements: *www.aapipara.org/ Certification.htm*

Ethics Code: *www.aapipara.org/Ethicalstandards.htm*

Newsletter: *Alliance Echo (www.aapipara.org/Newsletter. htm)*

Continuing Legal Education: *www.aapipara.org/ Calendar.htm*

Job Bank: *www.aapipara.org/Jobbank.htm*

Continuing Legal Education: *www.aapipara.org*

D. Bar Association Affiliate/Associate Membership for Paralegals

Several bar associations in the state allow affiliate or associate membership for paralegals. For a list of these associations, see section 3.4.

E. Other Associations

The Florida Bar Association
www.flabar.org

Other Bar Associations in Florida
See section 3.4

American Bar Association Associate Membership for Paralegals
www.abanet.org/join

American Association of Legal Nurse Consultants, Jacksonville
www.aalnc.org/about/chapter_directory.cfm

American Association of Legal Nurse Consultants, Orlando
www.orlandoaalnc.org

American Association of Legal Nurse Consultants, Tampa Bay
www.tbaalnc.org

American Association of Legal Nurse Consultants, South Florida (Ft. Lauderdale)
www.sflaalnc.org

Association of Legal Administrators, Central Florida Chapter
www.cfcala.org

Association of Legal Administrators, Florida Capital Chapter
www.alatally.org

Association of Legal Administrators, Jacksonville Chapter
www.alajax.org

Association of Legal Administrators, Palm Beach County
www.pbcala.org

Association of Legal Administrators, Sarasota-Manatee Chapter
www.smcala.org

Association of Legal Administrators, Suncoast Chapter
www.alasuncoast.org

Association of Legal Administrators, South Florida Chapter
www.alasofla.org

Florida Association of Legal Support Specialists
www.falss.org

Broward County Association of Legal Support Specialists
www.falss.org/Home/CharteredChapters/Broward/Default.aspx

Collier Legal Support Professionals
www.falss.org/Home/CharteredChapters/Collier/Default.aspx

Florida Society of Enrolled Agents
www.fseaonline.org

Florida Association of Legal Support Specialists
www.falss.org/Home/Default.aspx
www.falss.org/Home/CharteredChapters/Default.aspx

Jacksonville Association of Legal Support Specialists
www.falss.org/Home/CharteredChapters/Jax/Default.aspx

Legal Support Specialists of North Pinellas
www.falss.org/Home/CharteredChapters/Northern%20Pinellas/Default.aspx

Marion County Legal Support Association
www.falss.org/Home/CharteredChapters/Marion/Default.aspx

Miami Dade Legal Support Association
www.falss.org/Home/CharteredChapters/Miami-Dade/Default.aspx

Okaloosa-Walton Legal Support Association
www.falss.org/Home/CharteredChapters/Okaloosa/Default.aspx

Orange County Association of Legal Support Specialists
www.falss.org/Home/CharteredChapters/Orange/Default.aspx

Pensacola Legal Support Specialists Association
www.falss.org/Home/CharteredChapters/Pensacola/Default.aspx

St. Augustine Legal Specialists Association
www.falss.org/Home/CharteredChapters/St.%20Augustine/Default.aspx

St. Petersburg Association of Legal Support Specialists
www.falss.org/Home/CharteredChapters/St.%20Petersburg/Default.aspx

Sarasota-Manatee Association of Legal Support Specialists
www.falss.org/Home/CharteredChapters/Sarasota/Default.aspx

Space Coast Association of Legal Support Specialists
www.falss.org/Home/CharteredChapters/SCALSS/Default.aspx

Tallahassee Association of Legal Support Specialists
www.falss.org/Home/CharteredChapters/Tallahassee/Default.aspx

West Pasco Legal Support Association
www.falss.org/Home/CharteredChapters/West%20Pasco/Default.aspx

Central Florida Association of Law Libraries
www.tblc.org/cfall

South Florida Association of Law Libraries
www.aallnet.org/chapter/sfall

South Florida Investigators Association
www.sfloridainvestigators.org

Florida Association of Licensed Investigators
www.fali.com

Florida Association of Computer Crime Investigators
www.facci.org

Florida Court Reporters Association
www.fcraonline.org

Association of Pretrial Professionals of Florida
www.appf.org

Florida Association of Court Clerks
www.floridabar.org (click "Links, Legal Groups, Statewide")

Independent Contractors ("Paralegals") in Florida (Examples)
www.tampaindependentparalegals.com
www.floridadivorcehelp.net
www.paraprofessionalservices.com

F. Something to Check

1. Examine any two online paralegal newsletters. Find an article or position statement in each that covers the same issue involving the regulation of Florida paralegals. Compare what each says about the issue.
2. For each of the following three topics, which paralegal association has the most comprehensive links: (a) Florida law, (b) paralegal employment, and (c) litigation services.

1.3 Sources of CLE for Paralegals
  A. Introduction
  B. CLE Options
  C. Something to Check

A. Introduction

CLE (continuing legal education) is training in the law (often short-term) that one receives after completing formal legal training. The training usually takes place at a rented hotel facility. Increasingly, however, you can take CLE offerings online from any location and at any time.

There are four reasons CLE is important for Florida paralegals:

- CLE allows paralegals to keep current on changing laws, new developments in law office management, and the dynamics of the practice of law.
- CLE programs can be an excellent way to network with paralegals and other professionals in the field of law; such networking can be valuable for future job leads as well as a resource for on-the-job needs.
- If you are a Florida Registered Paralegal (FRP) or a Certified Florida Legal Assistant (CFLA), you must complete designated hours of CLE to maintain your status. For more on Florida registration and certification, see section 1.1.
- If you have received national paralegal certification, you must submit proof of compliance with the CLE

requirements for maintaining your certification. For an explanation of these requirements, see:

- National Association of Legal Assistants (*www.nala.org*) for being a Certified Legal Assistant/Certified Paralegal
- National Federation of Paralegal Associations (*www.paralegals.org*) for being a PACE Registered Paralegal
- NALS, the Association for Legal Professionals (*www.nals.org*) for being a Professional Paralegal
- American Alliance of Paralegals (*www.aapipara.org*) for being an American Alliance Certified Paralegal

If you move to a state such as California that has mandatory/minimum continuing legal education (MCLE) requirements, you may be able to argue that the CLE you took in Florida will satisfy some of the CLE requirements of that state. (For more on California's requirements, see *www.caparalegal.org*.)

Keep careful records of your attendance at CLE courses and events even if you do not need to do so for certification. CLE helps demonstrate your expertise and can be a marketing tool when seeking a raise or other employment.

For more on the tax deductibility of CLE, see Appendix A of Part 2.

B. CLE Options

General Searches

- *www.google.com*
  (type "Florida CLE" in the search box)
- *www.yahoo.com*
  (type "Florida CLE" in the search box)
- *www.live.com*
  (type "Florida CLE" in the search box)

In the same search engines, type "CLE" and the name of your city. Examples: "Miami CLE" or "Tallahassee CLE."

Your Local Paralegal Association

Go to the web site of your paralegal association (see section 1.2). On the site, look for links that might be labeled Education, Continuing Legal Education, CLE, Professional Development, Career Center, Events, etc. Click these links to find out if the association sponsors or links to CLE programs. If there is a search box on the site, type in these terms. If there is an e-mail link to the association, send a message inquiring about CLE opportunities.

Examples of CLE through Paralegal Associations:

- *www.pafinc.org/events.php*
- *www.cfpainc.com/claeseminars.html*
- *www.sfpa.info/site/Events.aspx*

National Paralegal Associations
National Federation of Paralegal Associations
www.paralegals.org
(locate "CLE")

National Association of Legal Assistants
www.nala.org
(click "Continuing Education for Paralegals")

NALS, the Association for Legal Professionals
www.nals.org
(click "Online Learning Center")

Legal Administrator and Other Nonattorney Legal Organizations

Check the web sites of related associations in Florida such as chapters of the Association of Legal Administrators (see the links at the end of section 1.2). They may lead you to additional CLE options you should consider.

State and Local Bar Associations

Many paralegals attend the same CLE programs that attorneys attend. Go to the web site of state and local bar associations (see section 3.4 for their web addresses). Click "Education," "CLE," "Continuing Legal Education," or "Professional Development" to find out what is suggested or offered by the Bar.

Examples:

- *www.flabar.org* (click "CLE")
- *orangecountybar.org/cle*
- *www.dadecountybar.org/forms/cle.php*

Academy of Florida Trial Lawyers (AFTL)

"The Academy is the premier provider of continuing legal education for attorneys, paralegals and legal assistants in the state of Florida." AFTL offers monthly seminars on various topics that are vital to the practice of law. Paralegals can be members of AFTL (see section 3.4). As a benefit of membership, a paralegal has access to continuing education, audio tapes, and other continuing legal education resources.

Examples:

- *www.aftl.org*
- *www.aftl.org/CLE.asp*

Local Schools

Find out if local schools offer online or in-class courses in areas that you are interested in. The school might offer courses that qualify for CLE credits in compliance with paralegal certification. Example:

- *www.fau.edu/divdept/lifelong/smart/cla.htm*

American Bar Association CLE
www.abanet.org/cle/clenow
www.abanet.org/cle/ecle/home.html

Findlaw CLE
www.findlaw.com/07cle/list.html

Law.Com CLE Center–Florida
clecenter.com/default.aspx
(click "Florida" on the pull-down menu)

Law Library Association CLE Links
Go to the law library sites in your area (see section 5.8). Find out if they have any CLE links.
Example:

* *www.vclawlib.org/resources.htm*
(scroll down to the CLE tapes)

Taecan
www.taecan.com (locate "FL")

West Legal Education Center
westlegaledcenter.com (click "Paralegal Studies")

Institute for Paralegal Education
www.nbi-sems.com (type in your zip code)

Advanced Paralegal Education Group (APEG)
www.apeglegal.com (CLE for paralegals in corporate law)

International Paralegal Management Association
www.paralegalmanagement.org (click "Events" then "Webinar")

National Business Institute
www.nbi-sems.com
(click "Paralegal Knowledge")

Practising Law Institute
www.pli.edu

C. Something to Check

Pick an area of Florida law and practice. For that area, find five different CLE courses or offerings from different CLE providers. Describe and compare the five.

A. Introduction

One sign of the prominence of paralegals is the extent to which paralegal issues have been discussed in court opinions. This section demonstrates this prominence by presenting excerpts from a wide range of these opinions. Some of the opinions raise ethical issues, although most of the opinions cover broader themes such as the award of paralegal fees in fee-shifting cases, conflict of interest when a paralegal switches jobs, paralegal supervision, and paralegals on juries. Of course, even these themes often have ethical implications, but a more comprehensive treatment of ethics will come later in sections 3.2 and 3.3. Most of the cases involving the unauthorized practice of law (and defining the practice of law) are covered in section 3.1.

To compile the material for this section, we did a search on Westlaw (WL) that asked for every case that mentions paralegal, legal assistant, lay assistant, paraprofessional, nonlawyer, nonattorney, or rule 5.3.

Westlaw Query:

paralegal "legal assistant" "lay assistant" paraprofessional nonlawyer nonattorney "rule 5.3"

This query finds every case that mentions the word *paralegal* or any of the other words and phrases indicated. The databases in Westlaw selected to run this query were FL-CS (containing all state court cases), DCTFL (containing all cases from Florida's federal district courts), and CTA11 (containing all cases from the U.S. Court of Appeals for the Eleventh Circuit, which has jurisdiction over Florida). A database that combines both state and federal cases is FL-CS-ALL. The query produced more than a thousand hits from which excerpts have been selected. We have included excerpts of opinions that will be (or have been) published in traditional reporters such as the *Southern Reporter* (So. 2d). We have also included excerpts from those unpublished opinions (or opinions that have not been certified for publication) if they say something of interest to the paralegal community. If you wish further information about any of the cases, e.g., whether a case has been reversed or otherwise modified on appeal, check the cases in citators such as *Shepard's Citations* (on the shelf or online in Lexis-Nexis) and KeyCite (online in Westlaw).

B. Case Excerpts

Here are the major categories of issues covered by these courts when they mentioned paralegals, legal assistants, or other nonattorneys involved in the delivery of legal services:

Fees: Introduction
Fees: Tasks that Qualify for Paralegal Fees
Fees: Failure to Delegate
Fees: Overstaffing and Duplication of Services
Fees: Inadequate Documentation to Support an Award of Paralegal Fees
Fees: Improper Sharing of Fees with Nonlawyers
Fees: Other Fee Issues
Supervision of Paralegals

Disclosure of Nonlawyer status
Conflict of Interest: Switching Sides
Conflict of Interest: Personal Relationships
Attorney-Client Privilege and Work Product
Paralegal Mistakes
Crime and Fraud
Paralegal as Juror
Suspended Attorneys Acting as Paralegals
Miscellaneous

Fees: Introduction

Legal assistant time must be considered when awarding attorney fees (Fla. Stat. § 57.104)

- A trial court is required by § 57.104 to consider time expended by legal assistants when awarding attorney's fees. *Department of Transp. v. Robbins & Robbins, Inc.*, 700 So. 2d 782 (Fla. 5th DCA 1997) Section 57.104 provides as follows: "In any action in which attorneys' fees are to be determined or awarded by the court, the court shall consider, among other things, time and labor of any legal assistants who contributed nonclerical, meaningful legal support to the matter involved and who are working under the supervision of an attorney. For purposes of this section 'legal assistant' means a person, who under the supervision and direction of a licensed attorney engages in legal research, and case development or planning in relation to modifications or initial proceedings, services, processes, or applications; or who prepares or interprets legal documents or selects, compiles, and uses technical information from references such as digests, encyclopedias, or practice manuals and analyzes and follows procedural problems that involve independent decisions." (Fla. Stat. § 57.104)

Achieving efficiency and effectiveness through the use of skilled paralegals

- In awarding paralegal fees, the court said, "The efficient and effective presentation of evidence in a federal trial requires the assistance of skilled paralegals." *Minks v. Polaris Industries, Inc.*, 2007 WL 1725211 (M.D. Fla. 2007).

Delegation to paralegals reduces client fees

- This court finds that defendants' counsel diligently kept fees at a minimum by delegating the work down to be performed by an attorney or paralegal who was billed at a lower rate. *Jerelds v. City of Orlando*, 194 F. Supp. 2d 1305 (M.D. Fla. 2002).
- To deny reimbursement for clerk and paralegal time would be counterproductive because excluding reimbursement for such work might encourage attorneys to handle entire cases themselves, thereby achieving the same results at a higher overall cost. *Celeste v. Sullivan*, 988 F.2d 1069 (11th Cir. (Fla) 1992) (citing *Jean v. Nelson*, 863 F.2d 759 (11th Cir. 1988)).

Fees: Tasks that Qualify for Paralegal Fees

Paralegal fees are for tasks that require independent judgment under attorney supervision, not for clerical functions

- A paralegal should be engaged in matters, under the supervision of an attorney, that require some independent judgment or are matters that an attorney would be expected to perform but can, under an attorney's supervision, be performed by an individual with specialized training or experience. Clerical functions such as typing, office filing, photocopying, faxing, scanning, or filing documents either electronically or traditionally, are not such functions. Secretarial tasks are overhead expenses of the attorney and are not additionally compensable. *In re Carter*, 326 B.R. 892 (Bankr. S.D. Fla. 2005).

Attorneys performing clerical work; paralegal fees are given only to the extent that the paralegal performs work traditionally done by an attorney

- The efforts of a paralegal are recoverable only to the extent that the paralegal performs work traditionally done by an attorney. Where that is not the case, paralegal work is viewed as falling within the category of unrecoverable overhead expenses. See *Missouri v. Jenkins*, 491 U.S. 274, 288 n. 10 (1989). ("Of course, purely clerical or secretarial tasks should not be billed at a paralegal rate, regardless of who performs them.") Specifically, that portion of the block billing entry on October 10, 2005, spent researching corporate and PACER records is clerical work. Accordingly, that time should be

reduced by 1 hour for his performance of this task. *Hill v. Chequered Flag Auto Sales, Inc.*, 2007 WL 710139 (M.D. Fla. 2007).

- Counsel correctly points out that there is a substantial amount of claimed time that was spent doing clerical and secretarial work, such as gathering materials, copying them, mailing them, and refiling them. Such unrecoverable time amounts to 108 hours for Horan, and 72.2 hours for Knipp. These hours will be deducted from each individual's totals. *Scelta v. Delicatessen Support Services, Inc.*, 203 F. Supp. 2d 1328 (M.D. Fla. 2002).

Court rejects argument that paralegals performed merely clerical work

- Part of the losing party's argument against awarding fees is that the opposing party's paralegals performed merely clerical work, and that his attorneys ran up the fees due to their inexperience. The court disagreed, finding that the paralegals "contributed substantial non-clerical, meaningful legal support to the representation." *State, Dept. of Transp. v. Skidmore*, 720 So. 2d 1125 (Fla. 4th DCA 1998).
- The court has reviewed paralegal Thorn's billing statements and finds that the work for which the plaintiff seeks compensation—telephoning opposing counsel, conferencing with plaintiff's expert, attending the onsite inspection, drafting cover letters and e-mails—was the type of work traditionally performed by an attorney. Accordingly, the court will award plaintiff the full 4.7 hours claimed for paralegal Thorn. *Hansen v. Deercreek Plaza, LLC*, 420 F. Supp. 2d 1346 (S.D. Fla. 2006).
- The time spent by the paralegal was routine and bordered on the merely clerical. Although paralegals can (and do) perform many skilled tasks warranting fees of $90 or higher, the tasks performed by Ms. Ward (indexing pleadings and correspondence, telephoning counsel to schedule a meeting) involved no specialized skill or training and do not deserve to be compensated as such. *Brother International Beach Club Condominium Ass'n, Inc.*, 2005 WL 1027240 (M.D. Fla. 2005).

No paralegal fees for preparing civil cover sheet and summons; it was a clerical task

- Hamilton seeks an hourly rate of $95 for work performed by Nury Pacheco, apparently a paralegal. Yet no information has been provided regarding Pacheco's qualifications or experience. Additionally, the only work performed by Pacheco was 0.6 hours for "Preparation of Civil Cover Sheet and Summonses." (See time sheet.) These are non-reimbursable clerical tasks. *Hamilton v. Viking Protective Group, Inc.*, 2007 WL 2155575 (M.D. Fla., 2007).

Does electronic filing qualify for paralegal fees?

- Although electronic filing requires use of a login and password assigned to an attorney, electronically submitting a document is the equivalent of having a runner deliver the document to the court for filing. Although signing a document might reasonably be included in the work required by an attorney to prepare a document for filing, after the document has been delivered to staff for filing, counsel's work has been completed. Accordingly, a paralegal's work to electronically file a document is clerical work that is not compensable. *Reyes v. Falling Star Enterprises, Inc.*, 2006 WL 2927553 (M.D. Fla. 2006).

- A review of the billing sheets indicates numerous entries for "electronic filing" or "scanning and electronic filing" of documents. Indeed, the plaintiff submits more than two hours of paralegal time for filing and scanning, above and beyond time billed for research and drafting. The court finds that the task of e-filing is not a legal service, but is a ministerial matter, akin to mailing a letter or sending a facsimile. Though time spent on the substance of the matter filed is recoverable, time spent on the mere act of filing is not. The court deducts two hours of paralegal time from the total awarded. *Smith v. Richard's Restoration, Inc.*, 2006 WL 3898182 (M.D. Fla. 2006).

- Paralegal services for plaintiff's case involved electronic filing, work that is neither clerical nor secretarial in nature. Further, paralegal services are recoverable as fees under the EAJA [Equal Access to Justice Act] and are entitled to be billed at prevailing market rates. *McCullough v. Astrue*, 565 F. Supp. 2d 1327 (M.D. Fla., 2008).

Insufficient evidence the paralegal performed nonclerical duties

- Because the evidence is insufficient to justify a determination that the paralegals and law clerks performed any "nonclerical, meaningful legal support to the matter involved" as required by section 57.104, Florida Statutes (2003), we reduce the award by the $20,722 (276.3 hours at $75.00 per hour) allotted for their services. *Madden v. Madden*, 865 So. 2d 555 (Fla. App. 3d DCA 2003).

- Telephone charges, reasonable travel, postage, paralegal time, law clerk time, and computerized research expenses are all compensable under the Equal Access to Justice Act. 28 U.S.C.A. § 2412(d)(2)(A). Travel and living expenses of a legal assistant, who mainly performed secretarial services, were compensable under the Hyde Amendment, even though secretarial services otherwise would have been included in the attorney's overhead and would not have been separately compensable; the assistant made significant sacrifices by relocating for the entire trial and the assistant's services were invaluable to the preparation of the defense by assisting a number of attorneys

by helping them prepare documents, pleadings, and motions, often working long hours and weekends. Criminal Justice Act of 1964. *U.S. v. Adkinson*, 256 F. Supp. 2d 1297 (N.D. Fla. 2003).

- Manriquez seeks reimbursement for work that "legal assistant" Anthony Georges-Pierre performed. However, Mr. George-Pierre's time is not compensable because Manriquez has not demonstrated that he performed "work traditionally done by an attorney." Manriquez requests reimbursement for work that his attorneys performed, but which was clerical in nature. For example, he requests compensation for work that his lawyers performed with regards to deposition notices and subpoenas. Time for serving the amended deposition notices is purely clerical, and, therefore, any time billed for service is not compensable. Work related to deposition notices and subpoenas could be nonclerical in nature, depending on the circumstances. See, e.g., *Cuban Museum of Arts and Culture v. City of Miami*, 771 F. Supp. 1190, 1192 (S.D. Fla. 1991) (attorney's work in preparing subpoenas *duces tecum* compensable as non-clerical work because of the "speed, accuracy, and precision required in obtaining . . . documents" to which the subpoena related). However, Manriquez and his counsel have not met their burden of identifying any circumstances that rendered the work at issue nonclerical. Even if clerical work were compensable, it would not be compensable at a paralegal's rate, let alone the attorneys' rates that Manriquez seeks to recover for that work. Additionally, Manriquez has the burden to prove the prevailing market rate for the clerical work for which he seeks compensation. Manriquez has not even attempted to prove that prevailing market rate, and therefore he would not be entitled to compensation for the clerical work even if such work generally were compensable. *Manriquez v. Manuel Diaz Farms, Inc.*, 2002 WL 1050331 (S.D. Fla. 2002).

Fees: Failure to Delegate

- While recognizing that Mr. Lipman is a highly skilled attorney, the court believes his requested hourly fee for in-court work and for out-of-court work is excessive. This determination is based in part on the fact that a portion of the work performed by Mr. Lipman could have been performed by a nonlawyer at a lesser expense. *Dowdell v. City of Apopka*, 521 F. Supp. 297 (D.C. Fla. 1981).

- The district court abused no discretion in reducing the plaintiff's total hours claimed by 30 percent. The district court noted that the plaintiff's lawyers included time spent on "discrete unsuccessful claims," duplicated efforts, excessive meetings between attorneys, billing for administrative tasks, senior counsel's billing for legal research that could have been assigned to an associate or paralegal, and billing at full rates for non-legal tasks like travel and clerical functions. *St. Fleur v. City of Fort Lauderdale*, 149 Fed. Appx. 849 (11th Cir. (Fla). 2005).

Tasks performed by a partner that should have been delegated to an associate or paralegal

- Eighty-seven hours must be discounted to reflect that these hours were spent performing tasks that should have been delegated to an associate or paralegal at a lower rate. These entries consist of such tasks as reviewing documents, drafting documents, and researching case law. *U.S. E.E.O.C. v. Enterprise Leasing Co., Inc.* 2003 WL 21659097 (M.D. Fla. 2003).

- There was no testimony that paralegals were used to handle the routine matters of the class action litigation. Much of the necessary paper handling in a class action, particularly one involving a class of stockholders, should be handled by paralegals rather than attorneys; the fee should likewise reflect that judicious use was made of paralegal or clerical assistance. *Miller v. Mackey Intern., Inc.*, 70 F.R.D. 533 (S.D. Fla. 1976).

Fees: Overstaffing and Duplication of Services

Avoiding excessive billing due to duplication of services

- It is often important to analyze and exclude duplication of time spent on aspects of a case where several lawyers, paraprofessionals, and/or clerks are working simultaneously. *Brevard County v. Canaveral Properties, Inc.*, 696 So. 2d 1244 (Fla. 5th DCA 1997) (citing *Jane L. v. Bangerter*, 828 F. Supp. 1544).

How fast should paralegals be able to summarize deposition transcripts? And should they have been summarizing them at all?

- The plaintiff alleges the paralegal time claimed by the defendant for summarizing deposition transcripts was excessive. The plaintiff specifically complains of 9.1 hours for summarizing the 110 page deposition of plaintiff James R. Watson. The defendant's attorneys say their paralegals usually summarize 14 to 18 pages per hour. At that rate, a paralegal should have completed the plaintiff's 110 page deposition in 6.1 to 7.9 hours. The attorney records indicate that the first 30 pages of the deposition of "Mr. Watson" was summarized twice, the first time taking 1.8 hours; this is part of the 9.1 hours identified as devoted to his deposition. It is likely, however, that this was a typographical error, and that in fact this 1.8 hours was spent summarizing the deposition of Mr. Watson's *wife*, Mrs. Watson, who was also deposed. Even so, the defendant does not seriously contest disallowance of 1.8 hours as duplicative. This reduces the defendant's claim by $112.50. All remaining time devoted to summarizing depositions is properly compensable. With the possible exception of the 1.8 hours, the time devoted to summarizing depositions was a reasonable amount of time for completing this task. Some attorneys still have paralegals summarize depositions (a practice that developed when transcripts came without indexes and searchable text was unheard of), and the market still sometimes pays the charge. One might reasonably question why that is so. Searchable transcripts are now readily available, and laptop computers on counsel table are commonplace. Moreover, in a slip and fall case, one wonders how hard it could be to have a command of the depositions, perhaps with post-it® notes marking key passages, without the need for separate detailed summaries. Indeed, some might suggest that having summaries makes the attorney's job more difficult, not less; the summaries are one more source to keep track of or consult. It is perhaps no coincidence that some personal injury defense attorneys and commercial litigators (who typically charge by the hour, not only for their own time, but for paralegals) choose to have detailed summaries prepared, whereas most personal injury plaintiff's lawyers (who are paid based only on the result) do not. In the case at bar, however, the hourly rate paid to these attorneys was very low, and the overall fee was reasonable. Whatever might be said of a fee for summarizing depositions under other circumstances, in the case at bar this was just one component of an overall reasonable fee, and I choose to allow the claim. *Watson v. Wal-Mart Stores, Inc.*, 2005 WL 1266686 (N.D. Fla. 2005).

Twenty-nine paralegals working on one case was not excessive

- This construction defect litigation lasted five years. Although counsel alleges that "duplicative and excessive hours" were claimed, "he was unable to point to a single example of overstaffing." *Centex-Rooney Const. Co., Inc. v. Martin County*, 725 So. 2d 1255 (Fla. 4th DCA 1999).

"Astounding" number of attorney and paralegal hours claimed in a non-complex case

- It is "astounding" that three attorneys and a paralegal devoted 77-plus hours to preparing for and attending oral argument, given the relatively non-complex nature of this case. Many of the hours claimed reflect a certain amount of duplicative efforts, due no doubt to the fact that there were six professionals (three attorneys and three legal assistants) working on the file. Unfortunately, due to America Online's (AOL's) failure to claim only those services properly recoverable here, the court's estimation of the hours reasonably expended cannot be further identified by reference to a particular lawyer or legal assistant, at a particular hourly rate. *Action Sec. Service, Inc. v. America Online, Inc.*, 2007 WL 191308 (M.D. Fla. 2007).

Filling in the blanks on a one-page form should not take 48 minutes of paralegal time

- The preparation of a one-page form proof of claim, which is, essentially, a fill in the blanks form with numbers provided by the client, should not take 48 minutes of paralegal time and 18 minutes for attorney review. *In re Palmer*, 386 B.R. 875 (Bkrtcy. N.D. Fla. 2008).

- In the court's experience, the hourly rates billed for the work of paralegals in this matter, billed at varying hourly rates of $120 and up, are excessive, especially in light of the type of services often performed by these individuals. Certain matters were excessive and/or could have been performed by a paralegal or other assistant at a considerable savings. For example, the Receiver spent an extraordinary amount of time with automobile mechanics or detailers employed in preparation for the auction. Though such work was no doubt well-intended, it was unnecessary for the Receiver to "babysit" this work. Either the Receiver or his paralegal, but not both, were necessary at the auction previews, and the auctioneers or an assistant could have handled answering questions from prospective buyers. Multiple hours spent preparing a "to do" list or arranging a wire transfer are excessive in the exercise of good billing judgment. *F.T.C. v. Peoples Credit First, LLC*, 2006 WL 3747320 (M.D. Fla. 2006).

Fees: Inadequate Documentation to Support an Award of Paralegal Fees

- Although paralegal fees can be awarded in workers' compensation cases (Florida Statutes § 57.104), the burden is on the claimant to establish entitlement to such fees. There must be adequate documentation to support such an award of fees for paralegal services. In this case, the paralegal portion of the affidavit lists time for fax transmissions and for numerous telephone conferences with the judge's office and the attorney's office. Yet the affidavit did not establish that any of this time was nonclerical. *Dayco Products v. McLane*, 690 So. 2d 654 (Fla. 1st DCA 1997).

- Claimant in this workers' compensation case challenges the denial of costs associated with legal assistants. The claimant had the burden to establish that time spent by these legal assistants was nonclerical. She failed to do so. *Moore v. Hillsborough County School Bd.*, 987 So. 2d 1288 (Fla. App. 2008).

The importance of time sheet and accurate recordkeeping; questionable entries on associate and paralegal time

- Florida courts have emphasized the importance of keeping accurate and current records of work done and time spent on a case, particularly when someone other than the client may pay the fee. To accurately assess the labor involved, the attorney fee applicant should present records detailing the amount of work performed. Counsel is expected, of course, to claim only those hours that he could properly bill to his client. Inadequate documentation may result in a reduction in the number of hours claimed, as will a claim for hours that the court finds to be excessive or unnecessary. In the case before the court, there are questionable entries on the time sheets. *Haines v. Sophia*, 711 So. 2d 209 (Fla. 4th DCA 1998).

It is not enough to say that the paralegals are "highly skilled"; no fees can be awarded for clerical/administrative work

- With respect to the work of the paralegals, the defendants fail to fulfill their burden of presenting evidence to establish their background and experience. It is not enough simply to say that they are "highly skilled and well qualified." One paralegal spent 1.50 hours on "file organization," which would normally be purely clerical or administrative work not properly included within a request for attorneys' fees. Therefore, I recommend that this paralegal's time be reduced by 1.50 hours to account for this clerical/ administrative work. *Kolczynski v. United Space Alliance, LLC*, 2006 WL 3614919 (M.D. Fla. 2006).

Paralegal fees of $110 an hour (in a 1996 case) are too high

- The defendants challenge the rate of $110 per hour for Corry, a paralegal. There are no affidavits from local practitioners addressing the local market rates for paralegals. However, the court's experience in other matters led it to conclude that a rate of $110 per hour is way out of line. The rate of $65 per hour sought for the other paralegal from Hunton & Williams is within the range of prevailing market rates. Accordingly, Corry will be compensated at a rate of $65 per hour. *Wales v. Jack M. Berry, Inc.*, 192 F. Supp. 2d 1313 (M.D. Fla. 2001).

Paralegal fees are denied because of a failure to distinguish compensable from non-compensable paralegal task hours

- PODS, Inc. seeks payment for 314 hours at $165–$235 per hour ($62,020), for work done by Mark Scholl, a paralegal with PODS's New York counsel. The court found this request inappropriate. The vast majority of Mr. Scholl's work involved clerical and secretarial duties. Moreover, though a small portion of the hours may be compensable, PODS, Inc. has grouped these hours in the same entry with non-compensable hours; consequently, compensable and non-compensable hours are indistinguishable. The entire request for paralegal fees will be denied when non-compensable and compensable hours are grouped together. *PODS, Inc. v. Porta Stor, Inc.*, 2006 WL 2473627 (M.D. Fla. 2006).

- The attorney's affidavit states simply that $125 per hour is the reasonable rate for work performed by the firm. He does not distinguish or differentiate rates that would be charged for the work of a partner versus the rates for the work of an associate, law clerk, or paralegal. In this respect, the affidavit is insufficient and is of no help to the court in resolving this issue. *Resolution Trust Corp. v. Hallmark Builders, Inc.*, 143 F.R.D. 277 (M.D. Fla. 1992).

- The defendant asserts the paralegal time for "legal research" was unnecessary, and suggests that all 4.0 hours be deducted. The court was provided with no information about what the legal research concerned, and finds that the plaintiff has not satisfied his burden. The court will deduct 4.0 hours from the paralegal time. The defendant asserts that given the limited number of documents at trial (approximately two inches worth), the paralegal time spent in trial preparation and attendance at trial was excessive. The court concludes that the assistance and attendance of a paralegal during the trial was not necessary after the first day, and will deduct 22 hours from the paralegal time. The defendant asserts that 5.2 hours for paralegal Lexis research should be deducted. The court was provided with no information about research and finds that the plaintiff has not satisfied his burden. The court will deduct 5.2 hours from the paralegal time. *Drury v. Pena*, 1997 WL 718831 (M.D. Fla. 1997).

- Usually, secretarial work is included in an attorney's hourly fee although paralegal work may be charged separately. We are unable to make a proper determination of a reasonable attorney's fee on the basis of the record before us; consequently, we must remand for that purpose. *In re Estate of Platt*, 586 So. 2d 328 (Fla. 1991).

- The one document filed that includes an itemization of attorney fees and nonattorney fees by date and activity is insufficient because it fails to include the attorney and nonattorney billing rates and/or to differentiate the hours accrued as a result of the tasks associated with the case. *Crescent Shores Properties, Inc. v. Landmark American Ins. Co.*, 2006 WL 3762056 (N.D. Fla. 2006).

- Counsel claims the work of two legal assistants, at $45 per hour and $95 per hour, although the declaration does not explain the discrepancy in rates between the two assistants in the same office. Redacted billing records are presented for the court's review, and the only evidence of the reasonableness of the fees sought is Ms. Tanner's opinion that the fees charged are "reasonable for the market place." *Microsoft Corp. v. Raven Technology, Inc.*, 2007 WL 438803 (M.D. Fla. 2007).

Fees: Improper Sharing of Fees with Nonlawyers

7% bonus to paralegal

- The attorney engaged in misconduct by instituting a bonus system where he agreed to pay a nonlawyer a seven percent fee. His paralegal was to receive seven percent of the fees generated in excess of his overhead. The attorney admitted that he improperly shared fees with nonlawyers as a result of his bonus plan. *The Florida Bar v. Shankman*, 908 So. 2d 379 (Fla. 2005).

Paralegal can enforce a bonus agreement even though it violates the fee-sharing prohibition of the ethics code

- An agreement between an attorney and a paralegal pursuant to which the paralegal would receive a bonus of ten percent of the attorney fees in cases she worked on was enforceable by the paralegal, even though the agreement violated the professional conduct rule barring sharing of fees with nonlawyers. The paralegal was not bound by the professional conduct rules and did not know that the agreement was against the rules when she entered into it. Preventing enforcement of the agreement would reward the attorney's noncompliance with the rules and penalize the innocent party. The public interest is not advanced if an attorney is permitted to promise a bonus arrangement that violates the fee-sharing rule, and then invoke the Rules as a shield from liability under that arrangement. We specifically limit our holding to the factual circumstances of this case involving an employment relationship between an attorney and a paralegal. This opinion is not to be construed to apply to a proscribed referral fee arrangement, which is distinguishable because it raises a separate set of policy considerations. *Patterson v. Law Office of Lauri J. Goldstein, P.A.*, 980 So. 2d 1234 (Fla. App. 2008).

Paralegal is told, to "do whatever you need to do to bring in some business"

- An attorney was disciplined for engaging in improper solicitation through a paralegal and for fee splitting. Barrett hired Cooper, an ordained minister, as a "paralegal." Although Cooper had previously worked for a law firm, Cooper's primary duty at Barrett's law firm was to bring in new clients. As Cooper testified, Barrett told him to "do whatever you need to do to bring in some business" and "go out and . . . get some clients." Cooper was paid a salary averaging $20,000 per year and, in addition to his salary, yearly "bonuses" that generally exceeded his yearly salary. In fact, Cooper testified that Barrett offered him $100,000 if he brought in a large case. *The Florida Bar v. Barrett*, 897 So. 2d 1269 (Fla. 2005).

- The case involved allegations that an attorney shared fees with nonlawyers by paying a percentage of the fees to his investigators and legal assistants. *The Florida Bar v. Rue*, 643 So. 2d 1080 (Fla. 1994).

Fees: Other Fee Issues

A nonattorney representative at an administrative agency hearing is not entitled to an award of attorney fees

- At a Department of Insurance hearing, a bank was represented by a nonattorney employee of the bank who was qualified by the agency to provide this representation. There is a section of the Administrative Procedure Act that authorizes an award of attorney fees for representation in agency proceedings (§ 120.595). This section does not, however, authorize such fees when the representation is provided by a nonattorney rather than by an attorney. *State, Dept. of Ins. v. Florida Bankers Ass'n*, 764 So. 2d 660 (Fla. 1st DCA 2000).

It is illogical to lower client costs by using paralegals and then seek to recoup the paralegal's time at an attorney rate

- Paralegal hours cannot be blended with attorney hours in calculating the lodestar amount. Section 57.104 requires consideration of legal assistant time in the award of attorneys' fees. This court, however, has never held that paralegal time can be "blended" with attorney time to set a reasonable attorney rate. Further, it is not logical to use a paralegal to help on a client's case because it is cheaper for the client, then seek to recoup the paralegal time at an attorney rate. Coupling that with the admission that the paralegal would not reap the benefit of this windfall shows that this "blending" is simply another method to increase the attorneys' fees in the case. Upon remand, the trial court will separate out the paralegal time of 122.7 hours and, if appropriate for compensation, multiply the number of paralegal hours by the hourly rate of $75. *Department of Transp. v. Robbins & Robbins, Inc.*, 700 So. 2d 782 (Fla. 5th DCA 1997).

Paralegals are not required to testify

- When a hearing is held (under § 57.105) on the award of attorney fees, including paralegal fees, it is not required that the paralegal testify at the hear-

ing. *Banks v. Maxwell Bldg. Corp.*, 925 So. 2d 473 (Fla. 4th DCA 2006).

No fees for a quasi paralegal versus an actual paralegal

- Defendants urge the court to reject the plaintiffs' claim to payment for fees related to Mr. Johnson. Defendants contend that Mr. Johnson acted as a quasi-paralegal prior to and during trial but note he is not an actual paralegal. This court agrees that Mr. Johnson's fees are not recoverable; he is not an attorney, law clerk, or paralegal and thus cannot be paid under the attorneys' fees provision. *U.S. ex rel. Southeast Enterprise Group, Inc. v. Skanska USA Bldg., Inc.*, 2005 WL 2179774 (M.D. Fla. 2005).

Legal assistants are able to perform many legal tasks with greater efficiency than lawyers

- *Sirgany Intern. of Orlando, Inc. v. Greater Orlando Aviation Authority*, 1988 WL 493668 (M.D. Fla. 1988).

Supervision of Paralegals

Paralegals as agents of the attorney

- The court emphasized that an attorney's nonlawyer personnel are agents of the attorney and that the attorney is responsible for seeing that the agents' actions do not violate the Code of Professional Responsibility. *The Florida Bar v. Rogowski*, 399 So. 2d 1390 (Fla. 1981).

Undue reliance on a paralegal

- The attorney failed to supervise a paralegal who had formed a corporation to assist immigrants. The attorney assumed the title of managing attorney of the corporation but did not provide competent client representation. The paralegal acted substantially alone in assisting clients, e.g., the attorney relied exclusively on the paralegal's analysis of the cases. *The Florida Bar v. Abrams*, 919 So. 2d 425 (Fla. 2006).

Failure to review answers to interrogatories given to a paralegal by the client

- An attorney has a duty to review a client's sworn answers to interrogatories for correctness, even when the answers have been prepared by the client and a paralegal. *The Florida Bar v. Burkich-Burrell*, 659 So. 2d 1082 (Fla. 1995).

Failure to manage a paralegal who was assigned trust account duties

- An attorney was charged with dishonesty and misrepresentation in connection with the misuse of funds held in a trust account. Blaming his paralegal, the attorney argued that he had not acted intentionally. The court held that when an attorney knowingly assigns his trust account responsibilities to his paralegal and then fails to manage the paralegal's activities, the attorney has the requisite intent needed to establish a violation of the rule against engaging in conduct involving dishonesty or misrepresentation. *The Florida Bar v. Riggs*, 944 So. 2d 167 (Fla. 2006).

Failure to give instructions to nonattorney employee on regulations governing trust accounts

- The attorney employed an office manager, who was given substantial authority and control over the attorney's trust and office operating accounts. The attorney failed to instruct the office manager concerning the regulations governing trust account operations. The office manager allegedly mishandled the trust funds. This violates the former Florida Bar Code of Professional Responsibility, Disciplinary Rule 3-104(C), which provides as follows: "A lawyer or law firm that employs nonlawyer personnel shall exercise a high standard of care to assure compliance by the nonlawyer personnel with the applicable provisions of the Code of Professional Responsibility." *The Florida Bar v. Armas*, 518 So. 2d 919 (Fla. 1988).

- The attorney failed to supervise nonlawyer personnel properly in the recordkeeping of estates, failed to ensure nonlawyer compliance with the Code of Professional Responsibility, and failed to examine and be responsible for all work delegated to nonlawyer personnel. *The Florida Bar v. Carter*, 502 So. 2d 904 (Fla. 1987).

- The attorney allowed his nonlawyer employee to manage and control his trust and general accounts without adequate supervision or control. *The Florida Bar v. Whitlock*, 426 So. 2d 955 (Fla. 1982).

- The attorney failed to adequately supervise his staff. He also assisted in the unauthorized practice of law because the letters authored by his nonlawyer employees contained legal advice that only a lawyer can give. *The Florida Bar v. Spann*, 682 So. 2d 1070 (Fla. 1996).

- The failure of an attorney to adequately supervise a paralegal in an immigration matter warrants a 90-day suspension. *The Florida Bar v. Lawless*, 640 So. 2d 1098 (Fla. 1994).

- An attorney is disciplined for failure to properly supervise nonlawyer personnel and failure to examine and be responsible for work delegated to nonlawyer personnel. In view of the complications involved in this case, the attorney was not entitled to rely solely on the assurances of his nonlawyer personnel that the title was clear. *The Florida Bar v. Greene*, 515 So. 2d 1280 (Fla. 1987).

Disclosure of Nonlawyer Status

- The attorney is disciplined for permitting a nonlawyer member of his staff to discuss a legal matter with a client without first advising the client that the nonlawyer staff member was not a lawyer. *The Florida Bar v. Bowles*, 480 So. 2d 636 (Fla. 1985).

- All correspondence from the Florida office that is on the stationery of the firm shall be signed by an individual who is either a member or associate of the firm admitted to the Florida Bar or, when otherwise proper, by an individual whose status is otherwise clearly indicated (e.g., legal assistant, law clerk, or the like). *The Florida Bar v. Savitt*, 363 So. 2d 559 (Fla. 1978).

- The attorney allowed several of his nonlawyer employees to sign letters "for the firm," which failed to disclose their nonlawyer status, and advertisements for legal services were placed in the phone book for one of his employees, even though the employee was not admitted to practice law in Florida. *The Florida Bar v. Spann*, 682 So. 2d 1070 (Fla. 1996).

- An attorney was disciplined for permitting a nonlawyer to sign correspondence that did not disclose the signer's nonlawyer status. *The Florida Bar v. Sheppard*, 529 So. 2d 1101 (Fla. 1988).

Conflict of Interest: Switching Sides

- The court adopted the following standard in determining whether a law firm that hires a nonlawyer employee of an opposing firm must be disqualified from the litigation. The burden of proving that disqualification is required rests at all times upon the movant (the client of the former firm), which also has the initial burden of presenting credible evidence that the nonlawyer employee was exposed to confidential information that is material to the representation of the former firm's client in the matter at issue before the lower tribunal. When presented, this evidence raises two rebuttable presumptions:
  - That the nonlawyer employee actually obtained confidential information material to the case
  - That the nonlawyer employee disclosed or will disclose such confidential information to the hiring firm

  The burden of going forward then shifts to the client of the hiring firm, who must attempt to rebut at least one of these presumptions by proving to the trier of fact either:
  - That the nonlawyer employee did not acquire any confidential information material to the matter at issue while employed by the former firm
  - That the nonlawyer employee has not disclosed any material confidential information and that the hiring firm has taken adequate measures to ensure that no such disclosure will occur

If the client of the hiring firm convinces the trier of fact by the greater weight of the evidence that the nonlawyer employee did not acquire any material confidential information while employed by the former firm, the motion for disqualification of the hiring firm will be denied. However, if the trier of fact is not so convinced, it must then determine whether the evidence rebuts the second presumption, that the nonlawyer employee disclosed material confidential information to the hiring firm. At this point, the burden of going forward shifts to the client of the former firm, who must present evidence of either of the following:

- That the nonlawyer employee has actually disclosed material confidential information to the hiring firm
- That the nonlawyer employee has worked on the case or will necessarily be required to work on the case, or that the measures taken by the hiring firm to ensure that the nonlawyer employee does not disclose material confidential information are, or will be, ineffective

If the trier of fact is persuaded that confidential information has not been disclosed to the hiring firm and that the hiring firm has implemented adequate measures to reasonably ensure that no such disclosure will occur, the motion will be denied. If the trier of fact is persuaded that confidential information has actually been disclosed to the hiring firm, or that the nonlawyer employee has worked or will necessarily work on the case, or that adequate screening measures have not been implemented, or that screening measures would be ineffective, the motion will be granted. Florida Bar Ethics Opinion 86-5, states:

> A law firm that hires a nonlawyer who was employed by an opposing law firm has a duty not to seek or permit disclosure by the employee of the confidences or secrets of the opposing firm's clients. The firm from which the employee departs has a corresponding duty to admonish the employee that he or she is obligated to preserve the confidences and secrets of the clients.

Obviously the canons, ethical considerations, and disciplinary rules cannot apply to nonlawyers; however, they do define the type of ethical conduct that the public has a right to expect not only of lawyers but also of their non-professional employees and associates in all matters pertaining to professional employment. *Stewart v. Bee-Dee Neon & Signs, Inc.*, 751 So. 2d 196 (Fla. 1st DCA 2000).

- Doctor Koulisis, who was a defendant in a medical malpractice case, filed a motion to disqualify the plaintiffs' law firm after the law firm hired a legal secretary from the law firm that was defending the doctor in the case. Once it is established that this nonlawyer had actual knowledge of confidential information material to the case while at the prior firm, the disqualification of the firm that hired her will be ordered even if the latter firm screens the nonlawyer from the case. *Koulisis v. Rivers*, 730 So. 2d 289 (Fla. 4th DCA 1999).

- The fact that an individual who had formerly worked as a legal secretary for plaintiff's counsel was briefly used by defendant's counsel as an independent contractor in a non-legal capacity did not require disqualification of defendant's counsel in this premises liability action. The individual worked for the defendant's firm for only 10 hours, over two days, entering billing data into a computer, and the billing records did not concern the underlying case. *Eastrich No. 157 Corp. v. Gatto*, 868 So. 2d 1266 (Fla. 4th DCA 2004).

- This court is faced with considering the standard for disqualification where:
  - A nonlawyer employee has been exposed to confidential information on an underlying case while working for the former firm;
  - The nonlawyer employee leaves the former firm to work for opposing counsel; and
  - The hiring firm screens the nonlawyer employee from working on the case in which he or she had been exposed to confidential information

This court adopts the burden shifting test from the *Koulisis* opinion as the standard in this District for determining when the hiring of a nonlawyer employee of an opposing firm requires the imputed disqualification of the hiring firm. Under this standard, actual knowledge of confidential information is required to obtain disqualification. *First Miami Securities, Inc. v. Sylvia*, 780 So. 2d 250 (Fla. 3d DCA 2001).

- The affidavits submitted by counsel establish that Ms. Rechner had done the primary secretarial work in the case while employed with the Kreeger & Kreeger firm and, thus, was privy to confidences of Lackow. Nothing more was required to be shown to support the disqualification of the Heller firm where the secretary now works. If information provided by a client in confidence to an attorney for the purpose of obtaining legal advice could be used against the client because a member of the attorney's nonlawyer support staff left the attorney's employment, it would have a devastating effect both on the free flow of information between client and attorney and on the cost and quality of the legal services rendered by an attorney. Every departing secretary, investigator, or paralegal would be free to impart confidential information to the opposition without effective restraint. The only practical way to ensure that this will not happen and to preserve public trust in the scrupulous administration of justice is to subject these "agents" of lawyers to the same disability lawyers have when they leave legal employment with confidential information. *Lackow v. Walter E. Heller & Co. Southeast, Inc.*, 466 So. 2d 1120 (Fla. 3th DCA 1985).

- Where a legal secretary or other support person moves from the law firm representing one party to the law firm representing the opposing party, disqualification of the support person's new law firm is required only when there is evidence that the law firm obtained confidential information from its new employee, thereby gaining unfair advantage over the opposing party. In this case, the new employer had effectively screened the secretary from involvement in the lawsuit and had taken those steps that a responsible firm should take to ensure there was no impropriety. The defendant had not obtained confidential information or unfair advantage over the plaintiff. *City of Apopka v. All Corners, Inc.*, 701 So. 2d 641 (Fla. 5th DCA 1997).

- The fact that the secretary for the defendant's attorney became employed by the attorney for the plaintiffs while the litigation was ongoing did not require that plaintiffs' law firm be disqualified absent a showing that the plaintiffs had obtained an unfair advantage over the defendants that could be alleviated only by removal of the attorney. It is not enough simply to show that the secretary had access to confidential information at the former firm. *Esquire Care, Inc. v. Maguire*, 532 So. 2d 740 (Fla. 2d DCA 1988).

- Disqualification denied. In this case, the trial court concluded that no confidential, privileged information was involved and the former employees were not employed by the opposition at the time the current lawsuit was filed. The facts are distinguishable from cases in which an attorney hires a secretary or paralegal who previously worked for the opposing party's attorney. See, e.g., *In re Complex Asbestos Litigation*, 283 Cal. Rptr. 732 (1991) (law firm employing a paralegal previously employed by an opposing law firm is disqualified, absent the former employer's consent or an effective screening procedure, where the employee had possession of privileged information). The common elements in these cases are that they all involve employees with confidential, privileged information, and they all relate to employees hired by opposing parties during a single lawsuit. *Carnival Corp. v. Romero*, 710 So. 2d 690 (Fla. 5th DCA 1998).

- A husband files a motion to disqualify his wife's attorney in this dissolution of marriage proceeding based on the fact that a secretary for the husband's former counsel is now employed by the wife's attorney. If the trier of fact is persuaded that confidential information has not been disclosed to the hiring law firm by the nonlawyer employee and that the law firm has implemented adequate measures to reasonably ensure that no such disclosure will occur, the motion to disqualify the hiring firm will be denied; if the trier of fact is persuaded that confidential information has actually been disclosed to the hiring firm, or that the nonlawyer employee has worked or will necessarily work on the case, or that adequate screening measures have not been implemented, or that screening measures would be ineffective, the motion will be granted. *Lansing v. Lansing*, 784 So. 2d 1254 (Fla. 5th DCA 2001).

- Plaintiffs (the Walkers) filed suit against Universal Baptist Church of Coral Gables (UBC) and Miami-Dade County for injuries sustained when swimming in a county park while enrolled in a summer camp at UBC. The plaintiffs' counsel hired a paralegal who had previously worked for UBC's counsel. While employed by UBC's counsel, this paralegal worked on the plaintiffs' lawsuit. Upon learning of this situation, UBC moved to disqualify plaintiffs' counsel. The trial court granted UBC's motion to disqualify. *Miami-Dade County v. Walker*, 948 So. 2d 68 (Fla. App. 3d DCA, 2007).

Conflict of Interest: Personal Relationships

Defense counsel's legal assistant has an affair with the detective working with the prosecution

- The defendant in this criminal case argued that his defense counsel's legal assistant and the lead detective were having an affair. This was argued to support his claim that "trial counsel labored under an actual conflict of interest . . . and that, but for this conflict, created by the personal relationship between counsel's assistant and the lead detective, there is a reasonable probability that the outcome" of his criminal trial would have been different. The legal assistant testified that she first met the detective during this trial and that the extent of their conversation was small talk. She said that, after the trial, it developed into "a friendship that did have a physical aspect to it" but that it "did not last long and [that] it went back to a friendship." The detective testified that the relationship occurred after the trial and sentencing and that he did not discuss the case with her at any time during the trial. The trial court determined that though there might have been a relationship between the detective and the defense counsel's legal assistant, that relationship occurred after the trial ended. Hence, there was no ineffective assistance of counsel due to this relationship. *Brown v. State*, 894 So. 2d 137 (Fla. 2004).

Attorney-Client Privilege and Work Product

Paralegal bound by the attorney-client privilege

- When a client reveals confidential information to his attorney, the attorney is generally not considered to be disclosing that information in violation of attorney-client privilege or the duty of confidentiality by revealing factual details to firm partners, his secretary, his paralegal, or firm associates involved in the case. All of those people would be bound by the attorney-client privilege and the duty of confidentiality from disclosing the confidential information to anyone outside that circle. *Estate of Stephens ex rel. Clark v. Galen Health Care, Inc.*, 911 So. 2d 277 (Fla. 2d DCA 2005).

- A letter received by a nonattorney advocate is protected by the attorney-client privilege. *Sanchez v. State*, 641 So. 2d 433 (Fla. 3d DCA 1994).

- Work product includes as protected material those materials that are prepared by nonattorneys so long as the preparation is in anticipation of litigation or preparation for trial. *Procter & Gamble Co. v. Swilley*, 462 So. 2d 1188 (Fla. 1st DCA 1985) (citing a Maryland case with approval).

Paralegal Mistakes

Paralegal's responses to requests for admissions concede the entire case!

- At the beginning of the trial, defense counsel moved to amend the responses to the plaintiff's request for admissions. He established that the wrong responses were filed due to clerical error. His paralegal had filed responses that admitted causation, permanency, and negligence. In short, the responses admitted all relevant issues to be tried. His paralegal testified regarding the mistake. The appellate court held that the trial court erred in not granting the motion to amend the responses. *Istache v. Pierre*, 876 So. 2d 1217 (Fla. 4th DCA 2004).

Paralegal mistakenly bids $15,500 rather than $115,500

- Wells Fargo was represented at a judicial sale by a paralegal employed by its attorney. There is no dispute that the paralegal was experienced with public foreclosure sales and had attended more than one thousand similar sales. She arrived before the sale began and had ample time to prepare for this sale. She brought a form document that had been prepared either by Wells Fargo or its attorneys, containing specific information and instructions for this sale. The instructions informed her to make one bid of $115,500. This was the tax-appraised value of the property after deducting the homestead exemption. Unfortunately, the form was filled in by hand, and the handwriting was not very clear. The first "1" in the number was close to the "$" and slightly separated from the "15,500.00." The paralegal misread the bid instruction as $15,500.00. This sale was the fourteenth sale on the docket, and the paralegal opened the bidding at $15,500. Wells Fargo filed a motion to set aside the judicial sale. A hearing was held in which the paralegal explained her actions. The trial court refused to set the sale aside. We accept the trial court's conclusion that the amount of the sale was grossly inadequate. This inadequacy, however, occurred due to an avoidable, unilateral mistake by an agent of Wells Fargo. As between Wells Fargo and a good faith purchaser at the judicial sale, the trial court had the discretion to place the risk of this mistake upon Wells Fargo. Thus, we affirm the trial court's orders denying relief to Wells Fargo. *Wells Fargo Credit Corp. v. Martin*, 605 So. 2d 531 (Fla. 2d DCA 1992).

Paralegal mislays the suit papers

- The Department of Insurance forwarded the complaint to Lloyd's registered agent at the New York law firm of Mendes & Mount. A paralegal with the firm mislaid the suit papers until June 26, when the firm sent the summons and complaint to London. The law firm's transmittal letter did not tell Lloyd's that it faced an impending deadline for a responsive pleading. The court held that the foreign insurer's failure to respond in a timely manner to the lawsuit amounted to excusable neglect. *Lloyd's Underwriter's at London v. Ruby, Inc.* 801 So. 2d 138 (Fla. 4th DCA 2001).

Inadvertent disclosure of privileged documents

- A lawyer and paralegal were given the task of reviewing documents that were to be produced before deposition and production. Twenty-three privileged documents were inadvertently disclosed. They were within 21 boxes that were copied. The scope of the discovery in this case was rather voluminous, and the disclosure was very small by comparison. "Mistakes of this type are likely to occur in cases with voluminous discovery." Petitioners demonstrated that they took reasonable precautions to prevent inadvertent disclosures. *Abamar Housing and Development, Inc. v. Lisa Daly Lady Decor, Inc.* 698 So. 2d 276 (Fla. 3d DCA 1997).

A $6,700 mistake

- Five apartments in a building had been converted into a condominium by its then owner and sold to a foreign corporation called Transiera Corporation. At the closing of this transaction, a paralegal of Cohen,

Angel & Rogovin, the law firm representing the seller, made a $6,700 mistake in Transiera's favor. When the mistake was discovered, requests for reimbursement were made on Transiera's attorney, and when reimbursement was not forthcoming, BBA sued Transiera to recover the money. *First American Title Ins. Co. v. Kessler*, 452 So. 2d 35 (Fla. 3d DCA 1984).

Miscalendaring

* The party filed an amended response in early November, attributing the untimely response to a paralegal's scheduling error. Bowytz said that his paralegal had miscalendared the date when the documents should have been produced. Discovery sanctions were approved. *Precision Tune Auto Care, Inc. v. Radcliffe*, 804 So. 2d 1287 (Fla. 4th DCA 2002).

Attorney "dropped the ball" in failing to respond, blaming his staff for the failure

* In failing to respond to a request for discovery documents, the attorney completely "dropped the ball." The attorney claims that his staff was responsible for the failure to respond to the request. Because, however, the staff members in question are nonattorneys, the burden of responding falls squarely on the attorney's shoulders. We agree with the trial court's conclusion that the attorney's actions constituted gross negligence. *Woodall v. Hillsborough County Hosp. Authority*, 778 So. 2d 320 (Fla. 2d DCA 2000).

Confusion of cases

* The affidavit of the attorney's legal assistant states that the attorney directed the assistant to prepare a notice of appeal for signature and filing with the court. The legal assistant believed that the notice of appeal was filed on October 27, 2006. The affidavit further asserts that the legal assistant confused this defendant's notice of appeal with the notice of appeal filed in another case that same day. The request to file a late notice of appeal was denied. *U.S. v. Brinson*, 2007 WL 446439 (S.D. Fla. 2007).

Crime and Fraud

* An attorney and sole practitioner brought an action against his former paralegal for embezzlement of funds from his trust account. In a two-count complaint, he accused the paralegal of fraud and civil theft, later amending the complaint to include additional counts of racketeering, civil conspiracy, and libel. The trial court, however, concluded that the attorney, not the paralegal, "stole his client's money." *Ramos v. Mast*, 789 So. 2d 1226 (Fla. 4th DCA 2001).

* An attorney was charged with dishonesty and misrepresentation in connection with the misuse of funds held in a trust account. He asserted that his former paralegal stole from the account. *The Florida Bar v. Riggs*, 944 So. 2d 167 (Fla. 2006).

Paralegal charged by attorney with forgery

* *Kerben v. Intercontinental Bank*, 573 So. 2d 976 (Fla. 5th DCA 1991).

Paralegal as Juror

Fear that a juror (who was a paralegal) might dominate the other jurors; paralegals are generally presumed to have analytical and forensic abilities that a layperson does not possess

* An error was committed in seating a juror against whom the defense had interposed a peremptory challenge. The prospective juror, Ms. Stone, had informed the court during *voir dire* that she worked for a law firm as a certified paralegal. Defense counsel exercised a peremptory challenge but the state asserted that the defense was simply attempting to exclude women from the jury. Defense counsel countered that she did not want someone on the jury with a strong legal background who could dominate the other jurors. The court, however, rejected the challenge and ordered that Stone be seated as a juror. The reason offered by the defense for the peremptory challenge was a legitimate, non-discriminatory one, and it was an error for the trial court to overrule the challenge. A person with formal legal training is generally presumed to have analytical and forensic abilities that a layperson does not possess and thus could have a disproportionate influence on the deliberations. This status constituted a legitimate, gender-neutral reason for the peremptory challenge. *Santiago v. State*, 652 So. 2d 485 (Fla. 5th DCA, 1995).

Juror Number 6 (a paralegal student) is dismissed

* When the judge asked Juror Number 6 about her reasons for sending notes to the court that asked questions about search warrants, she replied that, because of her knowledge of the law, she wanted to see if the search warrant was directed specifically to other evidence in the case. She said she did not have contact with anyone not connected to the case but that she had been reading her paralegal materials and attending classes. She denied having discussed the case with her husband, although she admitted that he had attempted to talk with her about it. At the conclusion of this inquiry, the court decided to dismiss Juror Number 6. This juror had earlier sent another note asking whether she could bring a tape recorder to court so that she could study her lessons

during recesses. The court did not allow her to do so. *U.S. v. Register*, 182 F.3d 820 (11th Cir. (Fla.) 1999).

Suspended Attorneys Acting as Paralegals

- Though a suspended attorney may work as a law clerk, investigator, or paralegal, employment in such a capacity contemplates supervision of the suspended attorney by a member of the Bar in good standing. This supervision did not take place in this case. *The Florida Bar v. Forrester*, 916 So. 2d 647 (Fla. 2005).

- Under Rule 3-6.1 of the Rules Regulating The Florida Bar, a suspended or disbarred attorney can be an employee of a law firm with the following restriction: "No employee shall have direct contact with any client. Direct client contact does not include the participation of the employee as an observer in any meeting, hearing, or interaction between a supervising attorney and a client." *The Florida Bar v. Neiman*, 816 So. 2d 587 (Fla. 2002).

- After an attorney was suspended for two years, he was employed by two attorneys as their paralegal. Suspended attorneys who are employed to perform legal services that laypeople may ethically perform are on notice that direct contact with clients is strictly forbidden. In this case, however, "it cannot be said that all client contact was strictly and specifically forbidden by this Court's order." The attorney did not hold himself out to be an attorney in his contact with clients. The contact was largely for the purpose of relaying information to attorneys out of the office and did not include the rendering of legal advice. The client contact was casual and minimal. Nothing in this opinion, however, is to be taken as an indication that this court, in the future, will tolerate direct client contact by a suspended attorney performing lay legal services. *The Florida Bar v. Thomson*, 354 So. 2d 872 (Fla. 1978).

Miscellaneous

Paralegals sue for overtime compensation

- The plaintiff has filed suit under the Fair Labor Standards Act, alleging that she and others similarly situated were not compensated for overtime hours during their employment as paralegals with the defendants. Though the parties agree it is appropriate to give notice of this suit to paralegals formerly employed with defendant, as well as their right to opt into the suit, there is some disagreement as to what length of time should be used in determining which paralegals should be included, i.e., those who worked within two years from the date of the filing of the suit, or those who worked within three years from the date of filing. The court held that the two-

year period would apply. *Nunnery v. Groelle & Salmon*, 2007 WL 781369 (M.D. Fla., 2007).

Paralegal who is sexually harassed at the law firm is ineligible for unemployment compensation

- Fran Brown appealed the denial of her claim for unemployment benefits. She was a legal assistant at an Orlando law firm, where she was sexually harassed by a male coworker over a period of some five months. She did not report this to her employers. When they learned of it through another employee, they met with Brown and then placed her on paid administrative leave. Several days thereafter, they advised Brown that they wanted her to return to work and would change her work location to the firm's main building. The administrator of the law firm, the harasser's wife, worked in the main building. Brown refused to return to work based on the presence of the harasser's wife, and on the advice of her attorney and her psychologist. Brown said she would have refused to return to work even if the harasser were not permitted to be near her. She also felt she could not work around the harasser's wife, even though the latter was without fault. Brown was asked to cooperate in the investigation conducted by the employer and refused to do so—again, on advice of counsel. She quit her job after her leave of absence expired. The court held that Brown failed to establish "good cause" for voluntarily leaving her employment after the employer had corrected the alleged sexual harassment situation. Hence, she was ineligible for unemployment compensation. *Brown v. Unemployment Appeals Com'n*, 633 So. 2d 36 (Fla. 5th DCA 1994).

Defendant is not entitled to a copy of a paralegal's summary of psychological reports prepared for the prosecution

- A death-row inmate is not entitled to a copy of the sheets summarizing psychological reports prepared by the attorney general's paralegal for use by the assistant attorney general. The paralegal's summary is not a public record. *Bryan v. Butterworth*, 692 So. 2d 878 (Fla. 1997).

A swearing contest between secretaries and a paralegal

- The court had to weigh conflicting testimony of secretaries and a paralegal on whether counsel was in compliance with rules and court orders. In exasperation, the court said, "This has created a swearing contest between secretaries and a paralegal to determine their veracity. None of these persons is a lawyer, and our power to discipline them for lack of candor is limited. It simply cannot be that the rules permit such an evasion of the responsibility placed on lawyers, as officers of the court. We rely on the representations made to us by lawyers, not their support staff." *Merritt v. Promo Graphics, Inc.*, 679 So. 2d 1277 (Fla. App. 5th DCA, 1996).

Misleading work-at-home paralegal opportunities

- The defendants continued to market, sell, and distribute work-at-home paralegal opportunities by promising financial rewards that were misleading and contain gross misrepresentations of actual financial rewards and opportunities available and actually obtained by similarly situated individuals. *F.T.C. v. Para-Link Intern., Inc.*, 2001 WL 1701537 (M.D. Fla. 2001).

Improper use of a paralegal in an adoption proceeding

- An attorney "impermissibly and intentionally allowed" her paralegal "to fulfill adoption-related duties without having obtained the requisite qualifications." *The Florida Bar v. Dove*, 985 So. 2d 1001 (Fla. 2008).

Allegation that a runner/messenger falsely called himself a paralegal

- *Florida Bd. of Bar Examiners ex rel. O.C.M.*, 850 So. 2d 497 (Fla. 2003).

C. Something to Check

- Go to the online sources that provide free access to state court opinions in Florida. (See the chart in section 5.1.) Do a search for the terms "paralegal" or "legal assistant." Select one of the opinions found by these search terms. Summarize (brief) the opinion.

Becoming an Attorney in Florida

A. Introduction

B. Requirements to Become a Florida Attorney

C. Law Schools in Florida

D. Sample Bar Exam Question

E. More Information

F. Something to Check

A. Introduction

A question that arises in the minds of some paralegals during their career is: Should I become an attorney? Most paralegals answer no, particularly in light of the stress that they see in the lives of many practicing attorneys and the massive law school debt that they carry well into the early years of their career. Yet some paralegals wish to pursue the law school option. If you look at the résumés of Florida attorneys posted on their law firm web sites, you will occasionally see that they were employed as paralegals before attending law school. Some attorneys worked part-time as paralegals while going to law school. In this section, we explore what is involved in becoming an attorney in this state.

For a statistical overview of attorneys in Florida (including salaries and bar passage rates), see section 3.4. For a timeline of the disciplinary process in Florida, see Part 3, Appendix A.

B. Requirements to Become a Florida Attorney

Admission to the practice of law in Florida is controlled by the Florida Supreme Court. Under the Florida Constitution, "the supreme court shall have exclusive jurisdiction to regulate the admission of persons to the practice of law and the discipline of persons admitted." (Article V, § 15.) The Court regulates admission to the bar through its administrative arm, the Florida Board of Bar Examiners, a 15 member board of lawyers and nonlawyer public members. The board conducts background investigations of attorney applicants, develops and administers the bar examination, and submits names of qualified attorney applicants to the Supreme Court of Florida for approval.

Florida Board of Bar Examiners	Supreme Court of Florida	The Florida Bar
1891 Eider Ct.	500 South Duval St.	651 East Jefferson St.
Tallahassee,	Tallahassee,	Tallahassee,
FL 32399-1750	FL 32399-1925	FL 32399-2300
850-487-1292	850-488-0125	850-561-5600
www.floridabarexam.org	*www.floridasupremecourt.org*	*www.floridabar.org*

Summary of Admission Requirements

To become a member of the Florida Bar, an applicant shall:

- Be at least 18 years of age or older
- Have a Bachelor of Laws or Doctor of Jurisprudence (JD) from an ABA-accredited law school (most law schools require an undergraduate degree for admission to their JD program)
- Have demonstrated (prior to taking the Florida bar examination) the requisite character, fitness, and moral qualifications for admission to the practice of law as approved by the Florida Board of Bar Examiners (law students are encouraged to file for admission to the bar upon entering their senior year in law school; the board's investigation can take up to eight months)
- Have submitted (prior to taking The Florida Bar examination) an affidavit attesting that the applicant has read Chapter 4, "Rules of Professional Conduct," and Chapter 5, "Rules Regulating Trust Accounts," of the Rules Regulating The Florida Bar
- Have passed:
  - the Florida Bar examination
  - the Multistate Bar Examination (MBE)
  - the Multistate Professional Responsibility Examination (MPRE)
- Have taken the oath of office.

Restrictions

- Florida is *not* one of the few states in the country where law office apprenticeship or correspondence schools can take the place of obtaining an ABA-approved law school degree.
- Persons who have been disbarred from the practice of law or who have resigned pending disciplinary proceedings shall not be eligible to apply for a period of five years from the date of disbarment or three years from the date of resignation or such longer period as is set for readmission by the jurisdictional authority.

Fees to Take the Examination and Apply for Admission

- $375: For law students who filed an early registration and are now converting to a regular applicant and plan to take the Bar Examination
- $875 For law students who did not file an early registration

Fee to Take the Multistate Professional Responsibility Exam (MPRE)

- $60 (*www.ncbex.org/multistate-tests*)

Bar Exam Structure

Summary: the Florida Bar Examination consists of a General Bar Examination and the Multistate Professional Responsibility Examination (MPRE). The General Bar Examination has two parts:

- Part A: Florida-prepared Examination
- Part B: Multistate Bar Examination (MBE)

The General Bar Examination is taken after completing law school; the MPRE can be taken prior to graduation from law school.

General Bar Examination

The General Bar Examination is a two-day exam consisting of essays and multiple choice questions. (See a sample question later in this appendix.) It tests the applicant's ability to reason logically, to accurately analyze the problem presented, and to demonstrate a thorough knowledge of the fundamental principles of law and their application.

Part A: Florida Law

Part A consists of six one-hour segments. One segment will be on the subject of Florida Rules of Civil and Criminal Procedure and the Florida Rules of Judicial Administration. The other five segments can be selected from the following subjects: Florida constitutional law, federal constitutional law, business entities including corporations and partnerships, wills and the administration of estates, trusts, real property, evidence, torts, criminal law, contracts, family law, Chapter 4 of the *Rules of Professional Conduct,* and Chapter 5 of the rules regulating trust accounts in the Rules Regulating The Florida Bar.

Part B: Multistate Bar Exam (MBE)

Part B is the MBE, offered through the National Conference of Bar Examiners (*www.ncbex.or*g). It is a six-hour, 200 question multiple-choice examination covering the following six areas: contracts, constitutional law, criminal law, evidence, real property, and torts (*www.ncbex.org/multistate-tests/mbe*).

Multistate Professional Responsibility Examination (MPRE)

The MPRE is a 125-minute, 60 question multiple-choice examination on ethics, based primarily on the ABA Model Rules of Professional Conduct (*www.ncbex.org/multistate-tests/mpre*).

C. Law Schools in Florida

To practice law in Florida, one does not need to attend a Florida law school. Most Florida attorneys, however, do attend one of the following schools in the state:

Ave Maria Law School
www.avemarialaw.com

Barry University School of Law (Andreas)
www.barry.edu/law

Florida A&M University College of Law
www.famu.edu/index.cfm?a=law&p=CollegeofLawHome

Florida Coastal School of Law
www.fcsl.edu

Florida International University College of Law
law.fiu.edu

Florida State University College of Law
www.law.fsu.edu

Nova Southeastern University (Broad)
www.nsulaw.nova.edu

Stetson University College of Law
www.law.stetson.edu

St. Thomas University School of Law
www.stu.edu/stu-law-school-section-134.html

University of Florida Levin College of Law
www.law.ufl.edu

University of Miami School of Law
www.law.miami.edu

D. Sample Bar Exam Question

Exhibit B.1 contains an example of a bar exam essay question, one that was actually administered by the Board of Bar Examiners on a recent bar exam. It will give you some idea of what the essay portion of the exam is like. For more sample questions (and answers):

- Go to the site of the Board of Bar Examiners (*www.floridabarexam.org*)
- Click "Site Map"
- Click "Study Guide"

E. More Information

So You Want to Be a Lawyer
www.floridabar.org
(click "Public Information" then "Consumer Information")

EXHIBIT B.1   **Example of an Essay Question on the Florida Bar Examination**

BAR EXAMINATION–FAMILY LAW ESSAY QUESTION

Wilma, a successful architect, married her bookkeeper, Hudson. Hudson worked full-time until the birth of their son, Chad. Thereafter, Hudson worked part-time at Wilma's firm so that he could care for Chad. After nine years, Wilma and Hudson began having marital difficulties. Without consulting an attorney, in contemplation of separating, Wilma and Hudson agreed in writing to the following:

• To equally divide all marital assets and debts;
• To waive any claim for alimony and child support; and,
• To have rotating custody of Chad.

The parties remained together for another six months. Hudson then moved to a modest two-bedroom apartment nearby. Wilma became upset, fired Hudson, and did not allow him visitation or communication with Chad. Wilma, through her attorney, filed for divorce seeking custody, child support, and supervised visitation.

Hudson, through his attorney, counter-petitioned to vacate the parties' agreement because he was under emotional stress when entering into the agreement, and sought alimony, custody, child support, and attorney's fees. Hudson is currently unemployed.

As the Judge's staff attorney, prepare a memorandum regarding:

(1) Should the agreement be set aside?

(2) What should the outcome of the case be regarding alimony, child support, custody, and visitation, given the parties' agreement?

(3) Does Hudson have a claim for attorney's fees?

Source: Florida Board of Bar Examiners, Study Guide *(www.floridabarexam.org/public/main.nsf/SG0306.PDF/$file/SG0306.PDF)*

The Florida Board of Bar Examiners Study Guide is copyrighted and is reproduced under the express written permission of the Florida Board of Bar Examiners.

Florida Board of Bar Examiners
www.floridabarexam.org

Florida Law Schools
www.alllaw.com/state_resources/florida/law_schools
stu.findlaw.com/schools/usaschools/florida.html

The Cost of Law School: Some Examples
www.barry.edu/law/financialAid/cost.htm
www.law.ufl.edu/admissions
(click "Fees & Expenses")

Financial Aid For Law School
www.lsac.org/Financing/financial-aid-introduction.asp
studentaid.ed.gov
www.fafsa.ed.gov

Multistate Bar Exam Study Aids
www.ncbex.org/multistate-tests/mbe
www.ncbex.org/multistate-tests/mpre

Bar Exam Preparation
www.law.miami.edu/library/barexamguide.php
www.law.ufl.edu/students/flabarapp.shtml

Florida Bar Review Courses
www.celebration-bar-exam-review.com
www.thestudygroup.com/floridabarreview.htm
www.micromash.net
www.floridabarreview.com

Six-Hour Video on the Florida Bar Examination
www.law.fsu.edu/current_students/student_affairs/
Florida_Bar_Exam_video.html

"Inside" the Florida Bar Exam
www.chesslaw.com/insidetheflabar.htm

Ten Top Mistakes to Avoid in Applying to Law School
www.chss.montclair.edu/leclair/LS/lsprep.html
www.accepted.com/Law/vault_article.aspx

Why Law School Is So Stressful
www.law.fsu.edu/academic_programs/humanizing_lawschool/
images/EP.pdf

Bar Admission in All States
www.abanet.org/legaled/baradmissions/basicoverview.html
www.ncbex.org/fileadmin/mediafiles/downloads/
Comp_Guide/2007CompGuide.pdf

More Resources
www.asl.edu/current/barexam.php
academic.udayton.edu/legaled/barpass
www.washlaw.edu/postlaw/barprep.html

Online Advice
www.google.com
(type "Should I Go to Law School" in the search box)

F.   **Something to Check**

Law school library web sites often have excellent legal research guides. Select any three law schools listed in section C above. At the web sites of these law schools, locate their law library link. At these law library sites, compare the information provided (including further links) on Florida legal research. Describe what you are led to. Which law library leads you to the most comprehensive links?

Paralegal Employment

2.1 Resources for Finding Employment in Florida

A. Introduction

B. General Strategies for Finding Employment

C. Specific Resources

D. More Information

E. Something to Check

A. Introduction

How do new paralegals find their first jobs? How do experienced paralegals interested in a job change find opportunities that build on their experience? In this section, we present ideas and resources that can be helpful in answering these questions for full-time and part-time work. In addition to general strategies, you will find specific Internet sites that should be checked. Some of the sites cover the entire state; others focus on specific areas of the state.

Most of the leads will be to traditional employment agencies that match employers with applicants. In addition, staffing agencies are included. A staffing agency is an employment agency that places temporary workers, often directly paying the workers and handling all of the financial aspects of the placement. A law office will pay the staffing agency, which in turn pays the paralegal's salary for work at the law office. Many employment and staffing agencies do not charge job applicants for their services. Of course, you should confirm that this is true before deciding to work with any agency.

B. General Strategies for Finding Employment

The starting point in your job search should be the school where you received your paralegal education. The program director will be your best guide on what is available. Here are some additional strategies:

▶ *Local paralegal associations.* Section 1.2 lists every paralegal association in the state. It also gives you related groups such as legal administrator associations. Go to the web site of every association near the cities or towns where you want to work. Find out if any job leads are available on these web sites. Some associations give current openings that non-members can access. If the newsletter of an association is online, look through recent issues. They may list job openings that are not found elsewhere on the association's web site. Send an e-mail to the association, asking for leads to employment and staffing agencies in the area. If there is a search box on the site, type in search words such as "employment," "job bank," "paralegal work," and "legal assistant employment."

▶ *National paralegal associations.* Check the career resources of the national paralegal associations:

National Federation of Paralegal Associations
www.paralegals.org (click "NFPA Career Center")

NALS, the Association for Legal Professionals
www.nals.org (click "Career Center")

American Alliance of Paralegals
www.aapipara.org (click "Job Bank")

▶ *Attorney job search resources.* There are many resources in the state that focus on the search for attorney employment. (Some are listed below.) Don't be reluctant to check out web sites for attorney employment. Many have pages about or links to paralegal employment. If not, call them or send them an e-mail message, asking for leads on paralegal employment in the area. In the search box on the site, type in search words such as "paralegal" and "legal assistant."

▶ *Bar associations.* Bar associations sometimes have employment services or career centers that can be helpful for paralegals. For example, at the Hillsborough County Bar Association site (*www.hillsbar.com*), click "Legal Placement" for leads to paralegal positions in the Tampa area. (For a list of all the bar associations in the state, see section 3.4.) Go to the web sites of the associations to find out if any leads are available on paralegal employment. In the search box on the site, type in search words such as "employment," "paralegal," and "legal assistant."

▶ *General circulation and legal newspapers.* General circulation newspapers often have want ads for paralegals. These newspapers are worth checking, particularly their online editions. Also find out what the legal newspaper is for your area, hard copy and online. It may have want ads for paralegals.

Florida newspapers online
www.abyznewslinks.com/unitefl.htm
newslink.org/flnews.html
www.usnpl.com/flnews.php
www.50states.com/news/florida.htm

▶ *General search engines.* Go to general search engines (e.g., *www.google.com*, *www.live.com*, *www.yahoo.com*, *www.ask.com*). In these engines, try the following searches that include the name of the state or the city where you want to work:

paralegal job Florida
paralegal job Miami
paralegal job Tallahassee

▶ *Legal search engines.*

Findlaw
www.findlaw.com (click "Jobs")
careers.findlaw.com

Rominger Legal

www.romingerlegal.com (click "Legal Job Center")

Hieros Gamos

www.hg.org (see the entries under "Legal Employment Center"; under "Job Listings" select "Paralegal")

LawGuru

www.lawguru.com/pro.php (click "Legal Career Center" then under "Job Search" select "Paralegal")

▶ *Networking.* Many paralegals find employment through the networking contacts they make with attorneys, paralegals, legal secretaries, etc. whom they meet at school, at paralegal associations, at social clubs, at church or synagogue, etc. At these settings, always be ready to ask, "Who do you know who might be looking for paralegals?" There are few more powerful networking questions that you could ask of anyone with any connection to the practice of law.

▶ *Legal Assistant Today job bank*
www.legalassistanttoday.com/jobbank

▶ *Paralegal jobs in the public sector.* If you are seeking employment in the public sector:

- See section 2.2 for employment in state government
- See section 2.3 for employment in federal agencies located in Florida
- See section 4.2 for links to employment in Florida state courts and section 4.3 for links to employment in federal courts in Florida
- See section 2.4 for the links to legal aid/legal services offices and other public sector offices in Florida

For directories of public defender offices and associations, check:
www.flpda.org/pages/public_defenders.htm#
www.llrx.com/features/publicdefense.htm

▶ *Paralegal jobs in corporations.* Check the web site of the Association of Corporate Counsel (*www.acc.com*):

1. Click "Careers" and "Find A Job"
2. Click "Florida"
3. Look through the attorney jobs to see if any paralegal (or related) jobs are listed
4. For attorney jobs, contact some of the agencies listed to determine if they place paralegals in corporations or can direct you to agencies that do
5. In the search box, type "paralegal" or "legal assistant"

▶ *Law firm web sites.* Most law firms have a web site and the largest ones invariably have a job section, often under the caption "careers" or "employment." Look for links to "legal support," "staff & support,"

"careers," "professional legal staff," "legal assistants," "paralegals," and the like. These sections usually include a description of the firm, specific jobs available, and instructions on how to apply for a job. For lists of some Florida law offices, check:

lawyers.findlaw.com/lawyer/state/Florida
www.lawresearchservices.com/firms/florida.htm
www.washlaw.edu/lfirms/index.php?c=13
washlaw.edu/lfirms/index.php?c=8
www.nalpdirectory.com
www.hg.org/northam-firms.html

● *Paralegal manager positions.*

International Paralegal Management Association
www.paralegalmanagement.org (click "Job Bank")

Association of Legal Administrators
www.alanet.org (under Job Bank, select "Job Seekers"; type "paralegal" as a keyword and as a location, select "Florida")

C. Specific Resources
Statewide
Association of Legal Administrators
www.alanet.org/jobs/current.asp (for Florida, type "paralegal")

Career Builder
jobs.careerbuilder.com/al.ic/Florida_Legal.htm
www.careerbuilder.com (type "paralegal" and a Florida city)

Craigslist
www.craigslist.org (click "Florida and a city"; under Jobs, click "Legal/Paralegal")

Detod.com
detod.legalstaff.com

FindLaw Careers, Florida
careers.findlaw.com

Florida Association for Women Lawyers
fawl.legalstaff.com

Flipdog
www.flipdog.com
(type "Paralegal" and your zip code)

Hire Counsel
www.hirecounsel.com (under Title, click "Paralegal" or "Legal Assistant," and then select a Florida job city)

Indeed
www.indeed.com/q-Paralegal-l-Florida-jobs.html (type "Paralegal" and your zip code)

IntJobs
intjobs.org/law/paralegal.html

Job Search
legal.jobsearch.com

JobsNet Florida
legal.jobs.net/Florida.htm

Law Crossing
www.lawcrossing.com/lclegalstaff.php (select "Legal Staff"; under Browse Jobs by Location, select "Florida")

LawGuru
lawguru.legalstaff.com

LawJobs
www.lawjobs.com

Legal Resource Center
www.thelccn.com/JobSeekers.aspx

Legal Staff
www.legalstaff.com

Monster, Florida
www.monster.com
jobsearch.monster.com

National Legal Aid & Defender Association
www.nlada.org/Jobs (select "Florida")

Nation Job Network
www.nationjob.com/legal

Paralegal Gateway
paralegalgateway.com (click "Career Center")

Robert Half Legal
800-870-8367
roberthalflegal.com

SimplyHired
www.simplyhired.com/job-search/l-Florida/o-232000/t-Paralegal (click "Paralegal" and type your zip code)

Smart Hunt
smarthunt.com (type "paralegal" and a Florida city)

Vault
www.vault.com (click "Jobs" then "Florida" and type "paralegal" as a keyword)

Yahoo Hotjobs, Legaljobs, Florida
hotjobs.yahoo.com/jobs/FL/legal-jobs
hotjobs.yahoo.com/jobs/FL/All/Legal-jobs

Resources for Selected Counties and Cities

Clearwater Bar Association
clearbar.legalstaff.com
www.clwbar.org/classified.html

Fort Lauderdale
legal.jobs.net/Florida-FortLauderdale.htm
fortlauderdale.craigslist.org/lgl

Gainesville Association of Legal Assistants, Inc.
www.afn.org/~gala/jobs.html

Jacksonville
legal.jobs.net/Florida-Jacksonville.htm
hotjobs.yahoo.com/jobs/FL/Jacksonville/Legal-jobs
jacksonville.craigslist.org/lgl

Miami
legal.jobs.net/Florida-Miami.htm
hotjobs.yahoo.com/jobs/FL/Miami/Legal-jobs
miami.employmentguide.com/Legal_jobs/apply.html

Northwest Florida Paralegal Association
www.nwfpa.com/jobs.htm
www.nwfpa.com/career.htm

Northeast Florida Paralegal Association, Inc.
www.nefpa.org/job.shtml

Orlando
legal.jobs.net/Florida-Orlando.htm
www.orlandorecruiter.com
orlando.craigslist.org/lgl

Palm Beach County Bar Association
www.palmbeachbar.org/job.php

Southwest Florida Paralegal Association, Inc.
www.swfloridaparalegals.com/employment/opps.html

St. Petersburg
legal.jobs.net/Florida-StPetersburg.htm
legal.careers.com/Florida-StPetersburg.htm

Tallahassee
legal.jobs.net/Florida-Tallahassee.htm
tallahassee.craigslist.org/lgl

Tampa
legal.jobs.net/Florida-Tampa.htm
jobs.careerbuilder.com/al.ic/Florida_Tampa_Legal.htm?
IPath=OCP

Volusia Association of Paralegals
www.volusiaparalegals.org/careers.htm

D. More Information

U.S. Department of Labor
Paralegals and Legal Assistants
www.bls.gov/oco/ocos114.htm

Paralegal Salaries
See section 1.1.

Job Strategy Toolbox for Paralegals (Gailynne Ferguson)
www.law.com/jsp/law/careercenter/lawArticleCareerCenter.jsp?
id=1176973460690&rss=careercenter

25 Things You Should Never Put on a Résumé
www.hrworld.com/features/25-things-not-to-put-on-resume-121807

E. **Something to Check**

1. List and compare the services of two paralegal employment sites that allow you to submit your résumé online.
2. What direct or indirect paralegal employment services are available to you at two paralegal associations and two bar associations closest to your area?
3. What useful information can you obtain at any of the legal administrator or legal secretary association sites in Florida? (See the end of section 1.2 for a list of these sites.)

2.2 Sample Paralegal Job Descriptions in State Government
A. Introduction
B. Paralegals and Legal Assistants
C. Other State Positions to Consider
D. More Information
E. Something to Check

A. Introduction

There are four major categories of state government jobs that have been filled by persons with paralegal skills:

- Paralegals and legal assistants (sometimes still called paralegal specialists)
- Law clerks
- Judicial assistants
- Legislative aides

A fifth category we will consider are workers in office and administrative support (executive secretaries and administrative assistants). Although many of these positions are clerical, they sometimes require legal skills and can lead to paralegal positions.

Summary of Steps to Take When Seeking Employment in State Government

1. Go to the People First site (*peoplefirst.myflorida.com*), which is designed for people seeking a position in Florida state government.
2. Select a region: west, north, central, or south.
3. Select a county.
4a. Scroll down to the Keywords search box. Type "paralegal" in the box. Also try "legal."
4b. Or, select "Paralegals and Legal Assistants" under "Select Occupation."
5. If you find a vacancy you wish to pursue, select it.
6. Read the qualifications.
7. If qualified, and if the position accepts online applications, submit an application. Otherwise, download the application, fill it out, and submit it as instructed.
8. For positions within the state court system, go to the main site on state courts (*www.flcourts.org*). Click "Court Employment."
9. For positions within the state legislature, go to the main site on the state legislature (*www.leg.state.fl.us*). Click "Legislative Employment" Also contact the office of your state representative (*www.myfloridahouse.gov*) and state senator (*flsenate.gov*) to inquire about positions in the legislature for persons with legal training.

B. Paralegals and Legal Assistants

Occupation: Paralegals and Legal Assistants (23-2011) (sometimes referred to as Paralegal Specialists prior to the current broadbanding classification system)

Web Information:
www.myflorida.com (type "paralegal" or "23-2011" in "Finding Jobs in Florida")
sun6.dms.state.fl.us/owa_broadband/owa/broadband_www.BROADBAND_MENU.BB_MENU (click "Legal" then "Legal Support" then "Paralegals")

Job Family: Legal
Occupational Group: Legal Support
Broadband Levels: Level 1 – Pay Band 005
Pay Band Information: *dms.myflorida.com/dms/content/view/full/1872*
Description: This is work assisting lawyers by researching legal precedent, investigating facts, or preparing legal documents. Incumbents conduct research to support a legal proceeding, to formulate a defense, or to initiate legal action. They may also be responsible for coordinating work and supervising employees.

Work Examples:
- Supervises employees by assigning work, reviewing progress, and assessing performance
- Gathers and analyzes research data
- Reviews documents to determine type and manner of service of process
- Prepares legal documents
- Conducts research and fact finding to assist in case preparation
- Maintains case and other administrative files, court calendars, and litigation timetables
- Files pleadings and other legal documents with the court clerk
- Assists victims and witnesses with court proceedings
- Answers routine questions regarding legal issues
- Directs and coordinates law office activity

- Keeps and monitors legal volumes and/or software to ensure that the law library is up-to-date
- Attends depositions, hearings, and/or trials in order to assist lawyers

Examples of Job Characteristics:

- **O**bserving, receiving, and otherwise obtaining information from all relevant sources.
- Identifying information received by making estimates or categorizations, recognizing differences or similarities, or sensing changes in circumstances or events.
- Identifying underlying principles, reasons, or facts by breaking down information or data into separate parts.
- Providing information to supervisors, fellow workers, and subordinates. This information can be exchanged face-to-face, in writing, or via telephone/ electronic transfer.
- Evaluating information against a set of standards and verifying that it is correct.
- Entering, transcribing, recording, storing, and maintaining information in either written form or by electronic/magnetic recording.
- Communicating with persons outside the organization, representing the organization to customers, the public, government, and other external sources. This information can be exchanged face-to-face, in writing, or via telephone/electronic transfer.
- Combining, evaluating, and reasoning with information and data to make decisions and solve problems. These processes involve making decisions about the relative importance of information and choosing the best solution.
- Monitoring and reviewing information from materials, events, or the environment, often to detect problems or to find out when things are finished.

Examples of Knowledge, Skills, and Abilities:

- *Information Gathering* Knowing how to find information and identifying essential information
- *Reading Comprehension* Understanding written sentences and paragraphs in work-related documents
- *Writing* Communicating effectively with others in writing as indicated by the needs of the audience
- *Critical Thinking* Using logic and analysis to identify the strengths and weaknesses of different approaches
- *Speaking* Talking to others to effectively convey information
- *Information Organization* Finding ways to structure or classify multiple pieces of information
- *Negotiation* Bringing others together and trying to reconcile differences
- *Active Listening* Listening to what other people are saying and asking questions as appropriate

- *Coordination* Adjusting actions in relation to others' actions
- *Management of Personnel Resources* Motivating, developing, and directing people as they work, identifying the best people for the job
- *Synthesis/Reorganization* Reorganizing information to get a better approach to problems or tasks
- *Law, Government, and Jurisprudence* Knowledge of laws, legal codes, court procedures, precedents, government regulations, executive orders, agency rules, and the democratic political process
- *Clerical* Knowledge of administrative and clerical procedures and systems
- *English Language* Knowledge of the structure and content of the English language including the meaning and spelling of words, rules of composition, and grammar
- *Computer* Knowledge of computer software including applications

Qualifications:

Under the broadbanding classification system, the individual agency or the supervisor determines the level of qualifications preferred for a particular position. The following are *examples* of possible preferences:

- Completion of a training program to become a legal assistant or a paralegal
- A degree or certificate in legal studies or allied legal services
- Graduation from a school of law
- A bachelor's degree from an accredited college
- Four years of experience involving paralegal work
- Four years of experience in legal secretarial work

C. Other State Positions to Consider

Persons with paralegal skills have also held positions as law clerks, executive secretaries, administrative assistants, judicial assistants, and legislative aides.

- Law Clerks

Description: This position assists hearing officers, attorneys, and/or judges with various legal responsibilities such as legal document preparation, research, maintaining records, and coordinating responsibilities. Some positions will be supervisory.

Web Information: *www.state.fl.us/dms/hrm/BROADBAND/ profiles/23-2092.doc*

Qualifications: The individual agency or the supervisor determines the level of qualifications preferred for a particular position. (Note that law clerks who work in state courts must be attorneys.)

- Executive Secretaries and Administrative Assistants

Description: This is work providing high-level administrative support by conducting research, preparing reports, handling information requests, assisting with program management, assisting constituents, and performing administrative and clerical functions such as preparing correspondence, receiving visitors, arranging conference calls, and scheduling meetings. Incumbents may also train and supervise lower-level clerical staff, maintain various databases, and coordinate legislative work.

Web Information: *www.state.fl.us/dms/hrm/BROADBAND/ profiles/43-6011.doc*

Qualifications: The individual agency or the supervisor determines the level of qualifications preferred for a particular position. For example, an agency might require a bachelor's degree with three years of administrative experience.

- Judicial Assistants (Circuit and County Courts)

Description: These are highly demanding, responsible positions entailing a variety of duties for a circuit or county court judge. The judicial assistant manages the judge's calendars and schedules pretrial hearings and other meetings. The person in this position also reviews files for formatting and accuracy and acts as the judge's liaison to other personnel and attorneys. Much of the work is confidential and requires the judicial assistant to have high standards of conduct.

Web Information:
www.flcourts.org (click "Court Employment")
www.flcourts.org/gen_public/employment/bin/jacircuit.pdf
www.flcourts.org/gen_public/employment/bin/jacountycrt.pdf

Qualifications: High school diploma and four years of experience in the legal profession as a legal secretary or a paralegal/legal assistant.

- Legislative Aides

When looking for employment within the state legislature or within the offices of individual legislators, contact the office of your state representative (*www.myfloridahouse.gov*) and state senator (*flsenate.gov*) to inquire about positions in the legislature for persons with legal training. Also check the legislature's employment sites:

Legislative Employment
www.leg.state.fl.us
(click "Legislative Employment")

Legislative Job Application
www.leg.state.fl.us
(click "Legislative Employment" then check "Applications")

D. More Information

General Search Engine
In a general search engine (e.g., *www.google.com*, *www.yahoo.com*, *www.live.com*, *www.ask.com*), run the following search: state government jobs Florida

Human Resource Management
4050 Esplanade Way, Suite 235
Tallahassee, FL 32399-0950
850-922-5449
dms.myflorida.com/dms/workforce/human_resource_ management

Department of Management Services
dms.myflorida.com/dms

Broadband Classifications
Job Families
sun6.dms.state.fl.us/owa_broadband/owa/ broadband_www.BROADBAND_MENU.BB_MENU
(click "Legal" then "Legal Support")

Legal Assistants and Paralegals
www.myflorida.com (type "paralegal" or "23-2011" in "Finding Jobs in Florida")

Salary Information, State Agencies
www.dep.state.fl.us/admin/broadband/default.htm
(click "Pay Bands")

Salary Information, Courts
www.flcourts.org/gen_public/employment/salary_schedule1. shtml

County Government
www.stateofflorida.com/Portal/DesktopDefault.aspx?tabid=35
(click employment links within your county government)

City Government
www.flcities.com/city_links.asp
(click employment links within your city government)

Florida Public Defender Association
www.flpda.org
(click "Employment")

General Information
www.myflorida.com/agency/50
(click "Job Search – State")

E. Something to Check

1. Use the links above to find an example of a current job opening for a paralegal in a state government agency.
2. Give an example of the salary range for (a) a paralegal in a state government agency and (b) a judicial assistant in a state county or circuit court.

2.3 Sample Paralegal Job Description in a Federal Agency Located in Florida

A. Introduction

B. Sample Job Description

C. More Information

D. Something to Check

A. Introduction

The federal government is the largest employer of paralegals in the United States. Its paralegal position is the Paralegal Specialist. (There is also a Legal Assistant position that has substantial clerical responsibility.) The role of the Paralegal Specialist can be somewhat different from paralegals in the private sector. A Paralegal Specialist can be a document examiner, an investigator, or a law clerk, among other descriptions. He or she may work independently in the federal government and does not always work directly for or under the supervision of an attorney.

To make listings of federal job vacancies accessible, an official, centralized web site called USAJobs has been created. It is managed by the Office of Personnel Management (OPM), the agency responsible for federal personnel matters. Vacancies from all federal agencies can be posted at USAJobs.

How to Use USAJobs
www.usajobs.opm.gov

1. Type "paralegal" in the "Search Jobs" box and your zip code.
2. After you complete the search, check the link that will e-mail you future paralegal job openings.

The government identification code for the Paralegal Specialist is GS-950. The positions range from GS-5 to GS-11 on the federal General Schedule (GS) pay scale. (See the salary link below.) The pay levels include yearly cost-of-living increases passed by Congress, as well as locality pay.

In addition to the USAJobs web site, an agency might advertise its employment openings in local newspapers and on the agency's online site. Check standard telephone directories for a list of U.S. government offices in your area.

For additional leads to finding federal employment, see "More Information" below.

Elsewhere in this book, you will find additional information on employment:

- In state government agencies (section 2.2)
- In private law firms (section 2.1)
- In corporations (section 2.1)
- In legal service offices (sections 2.1 and 2.4)

B. Sample Job Description

The following job description is for a paralegal position in a federal government agency located in Florida. It is an example only. The position may no longer be open. We present it here solely to give you an idea of the kinds of positions available in the federal government for Florida paralegals. Note that the listing also includes sample questions used in evaluating applicants. The questions are the equivalent of interview questions. You should consider preparing answers to such questions when applying for *any* paralegal job.

Overview

Title: Paralegal Specialist
Series, Grade: GS-950-7/9/11
Salary Range: $35,116 to $67,567 per annum
Promotion Potential: To GS-11
Vacancy Announcement Number: ORL 06-2122-88
Duty Location: U.S. Trustee Program, Orlando, FL
Number of Vacancies: 1 vacancy
Appointment: Full-time, permanent, excepted service appointment. Applicants must serve a two-year trial period.
Who May Apply: Open to all qualified persons. Eligible displaced/surplus Department of Justice and federal employees in the local commuting area may apply. Veterans who are preference eligible or who have been separated from the armed forces under honorable conditions after three (3) years or more of continuous active service may apply. This position offers career mobility opportunities.

Duties

The incumbent is responsible for performing a variety of duties that require the application of legal knowledge and financial analysis skills to the examination and processing of cases initiated under the U.S. Bankruptcy Code and are directly in support of the United States Trustee.

Representative duties:

1. Review Chapter 7 or 11 bankruptcy petitions and schedules for legal and procedural compliance with the Bankruptcy Code and related state statutes.
2. In cases of debtor noncompliance with legal requirements, make recommendations regarding U.S. Trustee action and draft motions commensurate with recommendations.
3. Review applications for retention of professionals, ensuring qualifications; where necessary, draft motions regarding applications for payment of professionals' fees and expenses.
4. Conduct analysis of disclosure statements for legal sufficiency; determine financial condition of debtor and advise attorney or analyst.
5. Analyze facts and technical questions on case administration received by phone or correspondence, answering those that have been settled by interpretations of applicable legal provisions and researching those that present legal issues.
6. Perform thorough audits of trustee final reports to assure that all assets have been properly liquidated and accounted for; participate in monitoring and reviewing the performance of trustees.
7. As necessary, perform research to assist attorneys and draft pleadings.

Qualifications

Applicants must possess one year of specialized experience equivalent to the next lower grade level in the Federal service. Specialized experience is experience which demonstrates knowledge of law, rules, regulations, policies, and precedents, and skill in interpreting and applying them to varying situations. Skill in analyzing case issues, summarizing pertinent data on the issues involved, developing and/or evaluating evidence, resolving conflicting data, clarifying factual and legal issues, and recommending appropriate actions.

Substitution of Education for Experience for Applicants at the GS-7 Level

The experience requirement may be met by successful completion of one full academic year of graduate-level education or law school OR successfully meeting the requirements of the Superior Academic Achievement provisions.

Substitution of Education for Experience for Applicants at the GS-9 Level

The experience requirement may be met by two (2) full academic years of graduate-level education or completion of all requirements for a master's or equivalent graduate degree, or completion of all requirements for an LL.B. or J.D. degree.

Substitution of Education for Experience for Applicants at the GS-11 Level

The experience requirements may be met by three (3) full academic years of graduate-level education or the successful completion of a Ph.D. or equivalent doctoral degree or completion of all requirements for LL.M.

Combination of Education and Experience

Equivalent combinations of successfully completed education and experience may be used to meet the experience requirements.

Selective Placement Factors

Selective Placement Factors are knowledge, skills, abilities, or special qualifications that are in addition to the minimum requirements but determined to be essential to perform the duties of the position to be filled. The Selective Placement Factor for this position is as follows: At least six months bankruptcy experience that exhibits knowledge of bankruptcy regulations and procedures. Education cannot be substituted for the six months' bankruptcy experience requirement.

Quality Ranking Factors

Quality Ranking Factors are knowledge, skills, and abilities which could be expected to enhance significantly the performance of the position. The Quality Ranking Factors for this position are as follows:

1. Knowledge and skill in fact finding, analysis, and communication including ability to correspond and elicit information from debtors, creditors, and their counsel.
2. Skill in the use and application of established instructions, procedures, policies, or precedents of the Bankruptcy Code and rules of procedures, local rules of practice, applicable case law, and other reference material.
3. Skill in business arithmetic and familiarity with basic accounting principles.
4. Knowledge of automated office systems.
5. Ability to communicate orally and in writing.

Applicants are encouraged to submit a *separate narrative* addressing the selective placement factors and quality ranking factors to ensure that full credit is received for the appropriate work experience as it relates to the position.

Evaluation Methods

Applicants will be evaluated based on experience as it relates to the quality ranking factors. Information provided in the separate narrative is heavily relied upon in the rating process. Basically qualified applicants may be further evaluated to determine those who are best qualified.

Special Notes

- Applicants must meet all eligibility requirements, including time-in-grade restrictions, as of the closing date.
- Selectee not currently employed by the offices, boards, or divisions of the Department of Justice will be required to submit to urinalysis screening for illegal drug use prior to appointment.
- A security investigation will be conducted to determine the suitability for this position. Employment is contingent upon completion of a satisfactory background investigation as adjudicated by the Department of Justice.
- Position subject to restrictions of PL 103-94, Section 8, Political Recommendations.
- Relocation expenses not authorized.
- Selectee will be eligible for health and life insurance, annual and sick leave and will be covered under the Federal Employees Retirement System (FERS).
- This is a multiple grade level recruitment. If you do not specify a grade level, you will only be considered at the highest level for which you are qualified.
- Applicants must serve a two-year trial period.

- All Federal employees are required by PL 104-134 to have federal payments made by Direct Deposit/ Electronic Funds Transfer.
- If selected, a male applicant born after December 31, 1959, and at least 18 years of age must be registered with the Selective Service System unless covered by an exemption under the Selective Service Law, in accordance with 5 U.S.C. § 3328.
- Applicants must be U.S. citizens.

How to Apply

Applicants must submit one of the following: a résumé; an OF-612, Optional Application for Federal Employment; or an SF-171, Application for Federal Employment. Résumés must include information outlined in the U.S. Office of Personnel Management's flyer (OF-510, Applying for a Federal Job), full name, mailing address, phone number, Social Security number, country of citizenship, and veterans' preference. Forms OF-510 and OF-612 may be obtained on the Office of Personnel Management's web site (*www.opm.gov/forms*). In addition, current/former Federal employees must submit a performance appraisal issued within the last 12 months and the latest SF-50, Notification of Personnel Action.

Sample Questions Used in Evaluating Applicants

(Note: Your responses are subject to verification through background checks, job interviews, or any other information obtained during the application process.)

- In the past three years how many different paying jobs have you held for more than two weeks?
- On your present or most recent job, how did your supervisor rate you: outstanding; above average; average; below average; not employed or received no rating?
- How many civic or social organizations (which have regular meetings and a defined membership) have you belonged to?
- Have you successfully done work where your primary responsibility was to help others work out their problems?
- Have you successfully done work that constantly required you to work under difficult time constraints?
- Have you successfully planned an event such as a conference, fund-raiser, etc.?
- Have you successfully learned a hobby or leisure activity requiring extensive study or use of complex directions?
- Have you effectively served on a problem-solving, planning, or goal-setting committee or team?
- Have you successfully completed a long-term project outside of work where you were solely responsible for doing the work?
- Have you successfully done work that required extensive on-the-job training?

- Have you worked on several major assignments or projects at the same time with minimal supervision and completed the work on time or ahead of schedule?
- Have you often been asked to proofread or edit the writing of others for content, punctuation, spelling, and grammar?
- Have you suggested or made changes to products or procedures that resulted in better meeting customer needs?
- Have you successfully done work that required you to interact with people at many levels in an organization?
- Have you successfully done work that regularly involved composing letters or writing reports containing several short paragraphs, such as investigation reports, accident reports, performance evaluations, etc.?
- Have you successfully done work that regularly involved answering questions, gathering nonsensitive information, or providing assistance to others, either in person or by telephone?
- Have you successfully done work where you had to coordinate vacation schedules, lunch breaks, etc., with other workers?
- Have you designed or developed something, on your own initiative, to help you or other employees better complete assignments?
- Have you successfully done work that regularly involved being on duty by yourself, or completing nonroutine assignments with minimal or no close supervision?
- Have you taught yourself skills that improved your performance in school or at work (e.g., taught yourself typing, computer skills, a foreign language, etc.)?
- Have you successfully completed a complex research project that included collecting and analyzing information, and reporting conclusions or recommendations?
- Have you successfully done work where your supervisor regularly relied on you to make decisions while he or she was in meetings or out of the office?
- Have you taken the initiative to learn new skills or acquire additional knowledge that improved your performance at work or school, or in leisure activities?
- Have you participated in training classes, workshops, or seminars outside of school that helped you improve your teamwork skills?
- Have you been given additional responsibilities because of your ability to organize and complete your regular work more quickly than expected?

C. More Information

General Search Engines

In a general search engine (e.g., *www.google.com, www.yahoo.com, www.live.com, www.ask.com*), run the following search: federal government jobs Florida

Finding a Federal Job
USAJobs
www.usajobs.opm.gov
jobsearch.usajobs.opm.gov/a9opm.asp

Federal Job Search
www.federaljobsearch.com
(In Career Field, click "Legal"; in Location, click "Florida")

Applying for a Federal Job
www.gpo.gov/careers/pdfs/of0510.pdf

Official/Standard Forms Used in Federal Hiring
www.opm.gov/forms

FedWorld
usajobs.opm.gov

Federal Jobs Digest
www.jobsfed.com
(click "Florida" on the map)

Yahoo HotJobs/Government
hotjobs.yahoo.com/governmentjobs

Lists of U.S. Government Departments and Agencies
www.usa.gov
(click "A–Z Agency Index")
www.congress.org
(click "Federal Agencies")

Federal Salaries
www.opm.gov/oca/06tables/index.asp

Qualification Standards for General Schedule (GS) Positions
www.opm.gov/qualifications/SEC-IV/A/gs-admin.asp

D. Something to Check

1. Use the links above to find three examples of federal job openings for paralegals in agencies located in Florida.
2. Go to a list of the web sites of U.S. senators (*www.senate.gov*) and U.S. representatives (*www.house.gov*) in Congress for Florida. Give examples of information on these sites that might be helpful for someone looking for work as a paralegal in the federal government.

2.4 Pro Bono Opportunities for Paralegals

A. Introduction
B. Finding Pro Bono Opportunities
C. More Information
D. Something to Check

A. Introduction

In this section, you will learn a great deal about working in the public sector as we explore pro bono opportunities for paralegals. Pro bono (or pro bono publico) means for the public good. (See the dictionary definition at the end of the book.) It refers to work performed without fee or compensation, for the benefit of society. Certain kinds of law offices often welcome volunteer or pro bono help. Here are the main categories of such offices:

- A legal aid office, also called a legal service office, that provides free legal services to the poor; an example is Legal Services of Greater Miami (*www.lsgmi.org*)
- A public interest law office that brings test cases that raise broad issues of social justice; an example is ACLU of Florida (*www.aclufl.org*)
- A government office; an example is the Office of the State Attorney in the Fifteenth Judicial Circuit (Palm Beach County), which "augments regular staff with volunteers" (*www.sa15.state.fl.us/Divisions/Volunteer%20Services.htm*)

Organizations and agencies such as these sometimes use volunteer paralegal services because the demand for services by individuals who cannot afford to hire an attorney far exceeds available resources. Paralegals with full-time jobs might devote an evening a month or every other Saturday to pro bono work. Some employers give their paralegals time off during the work week to do such work.

Paralegals perform a great range of tasks in these settings. For example, they might:

- Interview prospective clients to help screen applicants for the services that the office provides
- Perform factual research
- Draft pleadings, particularly in high-volume categories of cases such as divorce or eviction

In addition to substantive tasks such as these, pro bono paralegals might be asked to perform administrative and clerical tasks such as photocopying documents or entering data in a computer database.

Why Paralegals Engage in Pro Bono Work

Why do paralegals engage in pro bono work? Here are some of the major reasons:

- *Personal satisfaction.* The primary reason is the personal satisfaction derived from working for organizations or agencies engaged in socially worthy ventures. Many paralegals feel a professional responsibility to help ensure that disadvantaged individuals have greater access to our justice system.
- *Ethical obligation.* Professional legal associations often say that pro bono work is an ethical obligation

that is either required or strongly encouraged. See, for example:

- Guideline 4 of the model standards and guidelines of the National Association of Legal Assistants (*www.nala.org/98model.htm*)
- Guideline 10 of the model guidelines of the American Bar Association Standing Committee on Paralegals (*www.abanet.org/legalservices/paralegals/downloads/modelguidelines.pdf*)

- *New experience.* Through pro bono work, paralegals often gain practical experience in areas of the law outside their primary expertise.
- *Networking.* Even if pro bono work in some offices is more administrative or clerical than legal, paralegals can obtain valuable insights and networking contacts by interacting with the staffs of these offices.
- *Résumé building.* Unemployed paralegals, particularly those just out of school, have an added incentive to do pro bono work. Anything you can say on your résumé about real-world law office experience might help distinguish your résumé from that of someone without such experience.
- *Possible job leads.* All or most of the offices that accept volunteers have regular salaried employees. It is not uncommon for a paralegal to be hired by a law office where he or she once did work as a pro bono volunteer.

Ethical Concerns

Before outlining some of the major ways to explore pro bono opportunities, two ethical cautions should be covered: confidentiality and conflict of interest.

- *Confidentiality.* Everything you learn about a client when working pro bono should be kept confidential. The fact that some of these clients do not pay for their services is irrelevant. A poor person seeking a divorce in a legal aid office has the same right of confidentiality as a Fortune 500 company involved in complex litigation.
- *Conflict of interest.* As you know from your course in ethics (and as will be examined later in sections 3.2 and 3.3), you need to be aware of the danger that prior client work by an attorney or paralegal could create a conflict of interest for another client in another office. One of the ways this can occur is when the prior work was on behalf of a client who now has an adverse interest with a current client in a different office.

Example: Jim works on behalf of a client named Smith in the case of *Smith v. Jones* while Jim is volunteering at the ABC law office. Later, Jim applies for work at the XYZ law office. One of the clients of this firm is Jones, who is now suing Smith in a case that is different from (but yet related to) the case Smith had at the ABC office.

If XYZ hires Jim, there may be a conflict of interest because of Jim's prior work on behalf of Smith. Hiring Jim might eventually disqualify XYZ from continuing to represent Jones, particularly if Jim gives an XYZ attorney confidential information about Smith that Jim learned while at the ABC office. If this occurs, the prior work of the paralegal at the ABC office has "contaminated" the XYZ office.

It is unlikely that pro bono work will create such conflicts of interest, but the cautious paralegal needs to be alert to the possibility. Keep a personal journal in which you note the names of all the parties involved in cases on which you work in *any* law office. The journal should be private because it contains confidential information. (Client names, for example, are confidential.) Yet, when applying for a job, one of the ways an office can determine whether you pose conflict-of-interest risks is to find out what cases you have worked on in the past. It is ethically permissible for you to reveal this information when you are in serious discussions about a new position.

B. Finding Pro Bono Opportunities

To learn about pro bono opportunities for paralegals in your area, start by asking paralegals you know (from school, at the office, at a paralegal association meeting, etc.) if they have done any pro bono work, and, if not, whether they know of others who have. Networking with other paralegals in this way can be productive. Also ask attorneys you know where they or other attorneys do pro bono work. As pointed out later, paralegals often do pro bono work in the same offices where attorneys do such work.

1. Paralegal Associations

Check with the local paralegal associations near you (see the address of all state associations in section 1.2). Follow these steps:

(a) Find out if the association's web site lists pro bono opportunities or a pro bono coordinator for the association.

(b) Check the titles of board members and officers for the association to see if anyone on the list covers pro bono matters.

(c) If the newsletter of the association is online, find out if recent issues of the newsletter mention offices that use pro bono help.

(d) E-mail the president of the association or the association's general-information e-mail address to inquire about leads to pro bono work in the area.

(e) If there is a search box on the site, type in "pro bono."

(f) Click the e-mail address name of any paralegal on the site, introduce yourself, state that you are trying to learn about pro bono opportunities in the area, and ask if this person has any leads. Often all you need to get started is the name of one paralegal doing pro bono work. Such a person will tell you where he or she does such work and who would know if additional volunteers are needed.

2. CASA: Court Appointed Special Advocate Florida Guardian ad Litem (GAL) Program

800-628-3233 (national headquarters: inquire about Florida GAL)

www.gal.alachua.fl.us/info.htm

When a court must intervene to help an abused or neglected child, CASA/GAL volunteers (who do not have to be attorneys) are there to tell the child's story and to help protect the child's future. Volunteers do not work under attorney supervision but are given training to serve as informed, independent, and objective voices in court for abused and neglected children. Volunteers work as fact finders, interviewers, and investigators. They gather pertinent information relative to the child's case and report on these findings in court. Their goal is to gather as much information as possible to help the court make the best decision regarding the child's future. They also monitor the case to ensure the child's needs are being met.

3. Attorney Pro Bono as a Lead to Paralegal Pro Bono

Very often, a law office that accepts pro bono volunteer work by attorneys also accepts (or would be willing to consider) pro bono volunteer work by paralegals. For the ethical obligation of Florida attorneys to perform pro bono work, see Rule 4–6.1, covered in section 3.2 of this book. ("Each member of The Florida Bar in good standing, as part of that member's professional responsibility, should (1) render pro bono legal services to the poor and (2) participate, to the extent possible, in other pro bono service activities that directly relate to the legal needs of the poor.") Call or e-mail offices that use attorney pro bono help to ask if they accept pro bono work by paralegals. If not, ask if they could suggest any offices in the area that do. Here are some sites that will help you find out where attorneys do pro bono work:

(a) Florida Bar Resource Center/Opportunities Guide
www.floridaprobono.org/oppsguide.cfm

(b) Legal Aid/Pro Bono Directory
Go to *www.floridabar.org*, click "Public Information," and click "Legal Aid/Pro Bono."

(c) Bar associations
Go to the web sites of all bar associations in your area (see the addresses in section 3.4). Look for committees, sections, or special programs on pro bono. Type "pro bono" in the association's search box. Send an e-mail to the information office at the association in which you say: "I'm looking for leads to offices that accept pro bono work by paralegals and would appreciate any help you can provide."

(d) ABA pro bono site
Go to *www.abanet.org/legalservices/probono/volunteer. html*, click "National Pro Bono Volunteer Opportunities Guide," and click "Florida" on the map.
These steps should lead you to a site that lists pro bono programs throughout the state. See also:
www.probono.net/aba_oppsguide.cfm
www.abanet.org/legalservices/probono

(e) General search engines
In Google, run a search that contains the name of your city or county, the phrase *pro bono*, and the word *~attorney*. The tilde (~) before the word *attorney* means you want to include synonyms of attorney such as lawyer and counsel. Here are examples of such queries (add the word Florida if you obtain many non-Florida hits):

> Orlando "pro bono" ~attorney
> Miami "pro bono" ~attorney
> "Lee County" Florida "pro bono" ~attorney

Try the same searches on other general search engines (*www.yahoo.com, www.live.com, www.ask.com*, etc.).

(f) Volunteer lawyers
Do the following search in Google or in any search engine:

> "volunteer lawyers" Florida

(g) Law firms' web sites
Law firms often boast about the pro bono contributions of their attorneys. If you have the web site of any Florida law firm, particularly large ones, type "pro bono" in the search box of the site. You will often be given the names of specific offices or organizations in the state where attorneys at that firm have volunteered.

(h) FLAdvocate.org
www.fladvocate.org
This site is run by an organization of "Florida lawyers serving the public good." Click any of the leads on the site to pro bono opportunities in the state.

(i) Florida Pro Bono Coordinator's Association
www. floridalegal.org/ProBono/fpbca.htm

(j) Florida Bar Foundation
www.flabarfndn.org

(k) Local legal aid web sites
www.flcourts.org/gen_public/family/self_help/legal_aid.shtml

(l) Legal Services Corporation
www.lsc.gov
This is the federal government agency that funds legal service programs. Click "Florida" on the map or type "Florida" in the search box. You will be led to a list of all

of the legal service programs in the state, many of which welcome pro bono assistance.

(m) Florida Law Help
www.lawhelp.org/fl
floridalawhelp.org
This site lists numerous programs in the state that provide legal services to low-income persons. Almost all of these programs accept pro bono assistance.

(n) Aardvarc
www.aardvarc.org/dv/states/fldv.shtml
This site contains resources for victims of domestic violence. It has an extensive list of legal aid/legal services offices in the counties of the state. These offices can be contacted not only about the need for pro bono help in domestic violence cases but also in other areas of the law in which they practice.

(o) Volunteer Match
www.volunteermatch.org
Type in your zip code and "law" as a keyword. You will be led to organizations seeking people who can provide direct or indirect legal help.

(p) Florida Bar Directory
www.floridabar.org/tfb/flabarwe.nsf
Click "Contact Us" on this site. Scroll down the directory until you see the contact information for Pro Bono. Click on the e-mail link to send a message inquiring about pro bono leads for paralegals.

(q) State Attorney
sa18.state.fl.us/general/saolist.htm
stateattorney14.com/state-attorneys.html
Check the Office of the State Attorney in your judicial circuit to see if there are pro bono opportunities.

(r) Public defenders: state
www.flpda.org/pages/public_defenders.htm
Find out if the state public defender in your judicial circuit has pro bono opportunities.

(s) Public defenders: federal
www.fd.org/pdf_lib/defenderdir.pdf
Find out if the federal public defender in your judicial circuit has pro bono opportunities.

C. More Information

How to Use Legal Assistants in Pro Bono Publico Programs
www.abanet.org/legalservices/paralegals/
  probonobrochure.html

Corporate Pro Bono
www.corporateprobono.org

Pro Bono Institute
www.probonoinst.org

National Association of Pro Bono Professionals
www.abanet.org/legalservices/probono/napbpro/
  home.html

Miscellaneous Pro Bono Links
www.ptla.org/ptlasite/probono.htm

Lawyer Referral Services
www.abanet.org/legalservices/lris/directory
www.legal-aid.com/lawyer_referral_services.html

D. Something to Check

1. Find an office in Florida that accepts pro bono help for adopted children who are seeking information and possible contact with their birth parents.
2. Pick any other area of the law. Find three offices in Florida that accept pro bono help for those areas of the law.

2.5 Becoming a Notary Public in Florida
  A. Introduction
  B. Duties, Liabilities, and Prohibited Acts of a Notary
  C. More Information
  D. Something to Check

A. Introduction

Very often, law offices work with documents that must be notarized. This is particularly true in offices that do a fair amount of transactional work. Transactional paralegals provide paralegal services for attorneys who represent clients in transactions such as entering contracts, incorporating a business, closing a real estate sale, or planning an estate. If someone is not available in the office to notarize documents involved in such transactions, outside notary services must be used (and paid for). Paralegals should consider becoming notaries. It can be valuable even if this credential is used only occasionally as a backup when others are not readily available to notarize documents.

Caution, however, is needed when performing notary services. Attorney supervisors have been known to pressure their employees to notarize documents improperly, such as by asking them to notarize a signature that the employee did not personally observe being placed on a document. In fact, when paralegals are named as defendants in a suit, the most common reason is false notarization of a signature.

Qualifications and Steps to Apply

To become a notary public and to provide notary services, you must:

1. Be at least 18 years of age
2. Be a legal resident of Florida (proof of residence may be required)
3. Be able to read and write English

4. Complete a three-hour course of study (which includes quizzes)
5. Be a U.S. citizen or submit a recorded Declaration of Domicile (available at the county clerk's office)
6. Swear or affirm that you have read the notary laws and will obey them
7. Take a constitutional oath of office (see exhibit 2.5A)
8. Obtain a surety bond in the amount of $7,500
9. Submit an application through the bonding agency
10. Submit an Affidavit of Character signed by a person unrelated to you and who has known you at least one year (note that special steps are required if the applicant has had a felony conviction)

EXHIBIT 2.5A | **Oath of Office of a Notary Public**

I do solemnly (swear) (affirm) that I will support, protect, and defend the Constitution and Government of the United States and of the State of Florida; that I am duly qualified to hold office under the Constitution of the State of Florida; that I have read Chapter 117, Florida Statutes, and any amendments thereto, and know the duties, responsibilities, limitations, and powers of a notary public, and that I will honestly, diligently, and faithfully discharge the duties of Notary Public, State of Florida, on which I am now about to enter (, so help me God). . . . I accept the office of Notary Public, State of Florida.

Source: Notary Public Commission Application
(notaries.dos.state.fl.us/pdf/applpkg.pdf)

The state fee for becoming a Florida notary is $39. This does not include the cost of the three-hour course (a requirement added in 2002), but the course can be taken online at no charge through the state web site. Obtaining the surety bond is an additional cost (see below).

A notary must also purchase a stamp or seal that meets state requirements. The stamp must contain the notary's exact commissioned name, the commission number, the words *Notary Public of the State of Florida*, and the notary's commission expiration date. The notary must keep the seal in a safe location where it cannot be stolen or used improperly.

A notary's commission as a notary public is valid for four years, unless revoked for misconduct, incapacity, or moving out of state.

Role of Notary Commissions and Certifications Section

The Notary Commissions and Certifications Section of the Department of State processes notary applications and issues commissions, once approved for appointment. The Department also maintains records on notaries by keeping applications on file. Its computer database is accessible to the public. The Notary Commissions and Certifications Section does not assist notaries with questions about their duties.

Department of State
Division of Corporations
Notary Commissions and Certifications Section
P.O. Box 6327
Tallahassee, FL 32314
850-245-6975
notaries.dos.state.fl.us/index.html

Role of Notary Section of the Executive Office of the Governor

The Notary Section of the Executive Office of the Governor educates and assists notaries by:

- Publishing educational materials (e.g., the *Governor's Reference Manual for Notaries*)
- Answering telephone inquiries from notaries
- Conducting notary seminars
- Maintaining the online Notary Education Course
- Reviewing problems related to a person's eligibility for appointment as a notary
- Investigating complaints against notaries
- Recommending disciplinary action when appropriate

Executive Office of the Governor
Notary Section
209, The Capitol
Tallahassee, FL 32399
850-922-6400
www.flgov.com/notary
www.flgov.com/notary_contact

Role of Bonding Companies

Bonding companies in the state can:

- Provide you with an application to become a notary
- Submit the application for you (electronically) to the Notary Commissions and Certifications Section of the Department of State) along with your $39 application fee
- Sell you the required $7,500 bond that you must have
- Sell you an optional errors and omissions policy
- Sell you a notary seal

The bond is not an insurance policy for the notary. It protects the public by providing a limited fund for paying claims against the notary. The notary remains personally liable to the full extent of any harm he or she causes and may be required to reimburse the bonding company for sums paid by the company because of misconduct or negligence of the notary. The errors and omissions policy, on the other hand, is a liability policy that protects the notary for covered incidents up to the limits of the policy.

List of Approved Bonding Companies
notaries.dos.state.fl.us/notagn97.html

Role of Approved Schools

Applicants for a notary commission must submit proof that they have, within one year prior to their application, completed at least three hours of interactive or classroom instruction, including electronic notarization, and covering the duties of the notary public. Courses satisfying this section may be offered by any public or private sector person or entity registered with the Executive Office of the Governor. (*notaries.dos.state. fl.us/education/index.html*)

Online Notary Course Offered by the Governor's Office
notaries.dos.state.fl.us/education
notaries.dos.state.fl.us/education/instructions.html

Approved Notary Education Providers
www.flgov.com/notary_education

B. Duties, Liabilities, and Prohibited Acts of a Notary

Six Basic Duties of Notaries Public:

- Administer oaths or affirmations (§ 117.05, Florida Statutes)
- Take acknowledgments (§ 117.05, Florida Statutes)
- Attest to photocopies of certain documents (§ 117.05(12), Florida Statutes)
- Solemnize marriage (§ 741.08, Florida Statutes)
- Verify vehicle identification numbers (VINs)
- Certify the contents of a safe-deposit box (§ 655. 94(1), Florida Statutes)

Notaries must keep a sequential journal of all notarial acts they perform.

Fees

- Performing notarial acts: $10 is the maximum fee notaries can charge for each notarial act of administering an oath, taking an acknowledgment, attesting to a photocopy, verifying a VIN, or certifying the contents of a safe-deposit box.
- Performing a marriage ceremony: $20 is the maximum fee they can charge to solemnize marriage.

Note, however, that notaries can charge less than the maximum fee or no fee.

Law Office Employers of Notaries

Private employers such as law firms can enter into agreements with their employees for the payment of costs such as bond premiums. The agreements can also specify who will receive fees collected by the notary. The employer may limit the employee to providing notarial services during the workday solely to transactions directly associated with the business purposes of the employer.

Liability

Although notaries are bonded, they may be held personally liable for any misconduct or negligence in the performance of their official duties. For example, they could be sued if an improper notarization causes loss to another individual or company. Furthermore, the notary's employer may also be held liable if the notarization in question was performed within the scope of the notary's employment (§ 117.05(6), Florida Statutes). As indicated earlier, if notaries and their employers have purchased a liability policy (an errors and omissions policy), they may be able to recover some or all of what they have been obligated to pay.

Prohibited Acts

- A notary may not notarize a signature on a document if:
    - The person whose signature is being notarized is not in the presence of the notary at the time the signature is notarized.
    - The notary does not personally know the signer or have satisfactory evidence of identification.
    - The document is incomplete.
    - The notary public actually knows that the person signing the document has been adjudicated mentally incapacitated.
    - The person whose signature is to be notarized is the spouse, son, daughter, mother, or father of the notary.
    - The notary has a financial interest in or is a party to the underlying transaction.
- A notary may not:
    - Give legal advice, unless the notary is a licensed attorney.
    - Prepare legal documents if doing so would constitute UPL (unauthorized practice of law) in the state. (On the UPL in Florida, see sections 3.1, 3.2, and 3.3.)
- A notary may not:
    - Change anything in a written instrument after it has been signed by anyone.
    - Notarize his or her own signature.
    - Translate the phrase *Notary Public* into a language other than English in an advertisement for notarial services.
    - Take the acknowledgment of a person who does not speak or understand the English language, unless the nature and effect of the instrument to be notarized is translated into a language that the person does understand.

Wills

The Florida State Bar advises that when a notary is asked to notarize a document that purports to be a will, he or she should decline and advise the person requesting the notarization to consult a member of the Florida State Bar. If an attorney recommends that the document be notarized, a notary may do so.

C. More Information

Overview of Florida Notaries
www.flgov.com/notary
notaries.dos.state.fl.us

Notary Reference Manual
www.flgov.com/notary_ref_manual
notaries.dos.state.fl.us/education/index.html (click "Notary Reference Manual")

Laws Relating to Florida Notaries Public
www.flgov.com/notary_laws
www.floridanotaryservice.com/laws.aspx

Educational Resources for Florida Notaries
notaries.dos.state.fl.us/education/index.html
www.flgov.com/notary_education

Notary Forms and Sample Documents
notaries.dos.state.fl.us/appdwnld.html
notaries.dos.state.fl.us

The Unlawful Notary
www.lastwordedits.com/unlawfulnotary.pdf

Prohibitions Applicable to Notaries
www.flnotary.com/ImportantInfo.asp (click "Dos" and "Don'ts")

Searching for a Specific Florida Notary
notaries.dos.state.fl.us/not001.html

The Notary View (newsletter on Florida notaries)
www.flgov.com/notary_view

Electronic Notarization
notaries.dos.state.fl.us/education/elecnot.html

American Society of Notaries
800-522-3392
www.asnnotary.org
www.flgov.com/notary_natl_orgs

Florida Notary Association
800-432-4254
www.flnotary.com

National Notary Association, Florida Office
800-833-1211
www.nationalnotary.org
www.flgov.com/notary_natl_orgs

American Notary Exchange
www.americannotaryexchange.com (click "Florida")

American Society of Notaries
www.asnnotary.org/?form=stateinfo (click "Florida")

D. Something to Check

1. Go to the Florida Statutes (*www.leg.state.fl.us/statutes*). Click "Title X" and then "Chapter 117" to find the statutes on notaries. When can a notary's commission be revoked or suspended?

2. What is the function of a Florida civil law appointment for attorneys? (*notaries.dos.state.fl.us/civil.html*)

3. On Google (*www.google.com*) or another general search engine, run the following search: "Florida notary public." Summarize the categories of information found with this search.

2.6 An Employee or an Independent Contractor?
A. Introduction
B. Standards Under Florida and Federal Law
C. More Information
D. Something to Check

A. Introduction

Most paralegals are employees of law firms, corporations, or other groups where they work in full-time or part-time positions. (The technical terms sometimes used for employer and employee in labor and employment law are *master* and *servant*.) There are, however, a fair number of paralegals who have left the security of a regular paycheck to open their own businesses. They have become independent paralegals (sometimes called freelance paralegals) who offer services to more than one law office, usually charging the firm an hourly rate or a per-project flat fee. We are *not* referring to individuals who offer their services directly to the public without attorney supervision. In Florida, such individuals cannot be called paralegals or legal assistants because they are not supervised by attorneys. Our focus in this section is the independent who can still use the titles of paralegal or legal assistant because they do work under the supervision of an attorney. Yet, they are not on the traditional payroll of a single law office. They provide a variety of services to different firms. For example, they might:

- Digest the transcripts of depositions or other litigation documents
- Encode or enter documents into a computer database
- Collect and help interpret medical records
- Prepare a 706 federal estate tax return
- Prepare all the documents needed to probate an estate
- Prepare trial exhibits
- Conduct asset searches
- Compile chain-of-title reports on real property

Such work is performed in the paralegal's office (often in his or her own home) or at the law firms that have retained the paralegal.

The problem is that Florida and the federal government (particularly the Internal Revenue Service) may conclude that these independent paralegals are not independent enough. They might be considered *employees* regardless of their title or where they do their work.

For its *employees*, a law office is required to withhold federal and state income taxes, withhold and pay Social Security and Medicare taxes, pay unemployment tax on wages, pay overtime compensation, provide workers' compensation coverage, etc. In general, however, none of this is required for *independent contractors* that the office hires. In light of this disparity of treatment, offices are occasionally charged with improperly classifying workers as independent contractors to avoid their tax withholding and other employee-related (i.e., human resource) obligations.

This raises the basic question: What is an employee? The answer to this question is not always clear.

- The sole test is *not* whether you are on the payroll.
- The sole test is *not* your title.
- The sole test is *not* whether you work full-time or part-time.
- The sole test is *not* whether the law office considers you an independent contractor nor whether you consider yourself to be one.
- The sole test is *not* whether you have signed an agreement with the law office specifying that you are an independent contractor rather than an employee.

It is quite possible for everyone to consider a worker to be an independent contractor—*except the government!* The Florida state government and/or the federal government may take the position that a particular "independent contractor" is in fact an employee in disguise. When such a conclusion is reached, back employment taxes must be paid and civil penalties are possible. The law office may not be trying to avoid its tax and other responsibilities. It may simply have been mistaken in its definition of an employee. This is not uncommon. Many businesses have been told that workers being paid as independent contractors should have been classified as employees.

Sometimes the issue arises through tort law. For example:

> The ABC law firm hires Mary as an "independent contractor." One of Mary's tasks for the firm is to file pleadings in court. While driving to court one day in her own car, Mary has an accident. The other driver now wants to sue Mary *and* the ABC law firm as her employer.

Whether the driver can also recover against ABC depends, in part, on whether Mary is an employee of ABC.

B. Standards Under Florida and Federal Law

Under both Florida and federal law, the key to determining whether someone is an independent contractor is the amount of control that exists over what he or she does and how he or she does it. Related factors are also considered, but control is key. Figure 2.6A summarizes the test.

FIGURE 2.6A | **Independent Contractor or Employee?**

General Guidelines for Determining Who Is an Independent Contractor and Who Is an Employee

- An individual is an independent contractor if the person for whom the services are performed:
  - Has the right to control or direct only the result of the work
  - Does not have the right to control or direct the means and methods of accomplishing the result
- Anyone who performs services for an office is an employee if the office can control what will be done *and* how it will be done through instructions, training, or other means. This is so even when the office gives the worker freedom of action. What matters is that the office has the *right* to control the details of how the services are performed.
- Here is how one Florida court explained the test: "Control has always been the critical test for determining whether one is an employee or an independent contractor . . . , the decisive question being who has the right to direct what shall be done, and when, where, and how it shall be done . . . . In other words, an 'independent contractor' is one who represents his employer as to the *results* of his work, but not as to the *means* by which the results are achieved." *Edwards v. Caulfield*, 560 So. 2d 364, 370 (Fla. 1st DCA 1990).

No two independent paralegals operate exactly alike. Different paralegals have different relationships with their attorney clients. Some are given much more independence than others. Hence, there is no one answer to the question of whether independent paralegals are employees or independent contractors. Each case must be examined separately.

There is Florida law and federal law on when a worker is an employee as opposed to an independent contractor. Florida applies its own law on state issues such as whether a worker must be covered by workers' compensation. The federal government applies its law when the issue is whether federal income and Social Security taxes must be withheld. Yet, there is substantial similarity between Florida and federal law on the question. The right of control is central under both laws.

Factors Considered Under Florida Law

Whether a worker is an employee or independent contractor under Florida law depends on a number of factors, all of which must be considered, and none of which is controlling by itself. These factors are laid out by the Florida Supreme Court in *Cantor v. Cochran*, 184 So.[2d 173 (Fla. 1966). The *Cantor* case adopts the approach taken by section 220 of the *Restatement (Second) of Agency.*

Under § 220, a worker is an employee (referred to as a "servant"), if his or her services are subject to the hirer's "control or right to control." In determining whether a worker is a servant (employee) or an independent contractor, the following matters of fact, among others, are considered:

- The extent of control that, by agreement, the hirer may exercise over the details of the work
- Whether the worker is engaged in a distinct occupation or business
- The kind of occupation, with reference to whether, in the locality, the work is usually done under the direction of the hirer or whether it is usually done by a specialist without supervision
- The skill required in the particular occupation
- Whether the hirer or the worker supplies the instrumentalities, tools, and the place of work for the worker to do the work
- The length of time for which the worker does the work
- The method of payment, whether by time or by the job
- Whether the work is a part of the regular business of the hirer
- Whether the parties believe they are creating the relation of master and servant (employer and employee)
- Whether the hirer is or is not in business

The workers' compensation statute in Florida also has provisions for determining when someone is an independent contractor:

Florida Statutes Annotated § 440.02(d) (Workers' Compensation Definitions)

"Employee" does not include:

1. An independent contractor who is not engaged in the construction industry.

a. In order to meet the definition of independent contractor, at least four of the following criteria must be met:

(I) The independent contractor maintains a separate business with his or her own work facility, truck, equipment, materials, or similar accommodations;

(II) The independent contractor holds or has applied for a federal employer identification number, unless the independent contractor is a sole proprietor who is not required to obtain a federal employer identification number under state or federal regulations;

(III) The independent contractor receives compensation for services rendered or work performed and such compensation is paid to a business rather than to an individual;

(IV) The independent contractor holds one or more bank accounts in the name of the business entity for purposes of paying business expenses or other expenses related to services rendered or work performed for compensation;

(V) The independent contractor performs work or is able to perform work for any entity in addition to or besides the employer at his or her own election without the necessity of completing an employment application or process; or

(VI) The independent contractor receives compensation for work or services rendered on a competitive-bid basis or completion of a task or a set of tasks as defined by a contractual agreement, unless such contractual agreement expressly states that an employment relationship exists.

b. If four of the criteria listed in sub-subparagraph a do not exist, an individual may still be presumed to be an independent contractor and not an employee based on full consideration of the nature of the individual situation with regard to satisfying any of the following conditions:

(I) The independent contractor performs or agrees to perform specific services or work for a specific amount of money and controls the means of performing the services or work.

(II) The independent contractor incurs the principal expenses related to the service or work that he or she performs or agrees to perform.

(III) The independent contractor is responsible for the satisfactory completion of the work or services that he or she performs or agrees to perform.

(IV) The independent contractor receives compensation for work or services performed for a commission or on a per-job basis and not on any other basis.

(V) The independent contractor may realize a profit or suffer a loss in connection with performing work or services.

(VI) The independent contractor has continuing or recurring business liabilities or obligations.

(VII) The success or failure of the independent contractor's business depends on the relationship of business receipts to expenditures.

Also, under Florida Statutes Annotated § 121.021(50) covering the Florida's retirement system:

"Independent contractor" means an individual who is not subject to the control and direction of the employer for whom work is being performed, with respect not only to what shall be done but to how it shall be done. If the employer has the right to exert such control, an employee-employer relationship exists, and, for purposes of this chapter, the person is an employee and not an independent contractor. The division shall adopt rules providing criteria for determining whether an individual is an employee or an independent contractor.

See also Florida Statutes Annotated § 112.3187, which defines employee and independent contractor under the Whistle-blower's Act.

Factors Considered Under Federal Law

Federal law reaches substantially the same conclusion, but uses different terminology in describing the factors involved. Under federal law, three categories of evidence on control and independence are considered: (1) behavioral control, (2) financial control, and (3) type of relationship. Evidence in these categories provides factors to be weighed; they are not absolute guidelines or definitions.

(1) Behavioral Control

Does the office have the right to direct and control *how* the worker does the task for which he or she is hired? Two behavioral facts that help answer this question are the type and degree of instructions received, and the training provided.

- Instructions the office gives the worker. In general, employees are subject to instructions about when, where, and how to work. Here are examples of the kinds of instructions an office could give on how work should be done:
    - When and where to do the work
    - What tools or equipment to use
    - What other workers to use to assist with the work
    - Where to purchase supplies and services
    - What work must be performed by a specified individual
    - What order or sequence to follow

The amount of instruction needed varies among different jobs. Even if no instructions are given, sufficient behavioral control may exist if the office has the *right* to control how the work results are achieved. An office may lack the knowledge to instruct some highly specialized professionals; in other cases, the task may require little or no instruction. The key consideration is whether the office has retained the right to control the details of a worker's performance or has given up this right.

- Training the office gives the worker. An employee may be given training on performing the services in a particular manner. Independent contractors, on the other hand, ordinarily use their own methods.

(2) Financial Control

Factors that show whether the office has a right to control the business aspects of the worker's job include:

- The extent to which the worker has unreimbursed business expenses. Independent contractors are more likely to have unreimbursed expenses than are employees. Fixed ongoing costs that are incurred regardless of whether work is currently being performed are especially important. Note, however, that it is possible for employees to incur unreimbursed expenses in connection with the services they perform for their office.
- The extent of the worker's investment. An independent contractor (unlike an employee) often has a significant investment in the facilities he or she uses in performing services for someone else. This is not to say, however, that a significant investment is required for independent contractor status.
- The extent to which the worker makes services available to the relevant market. An independent contractor is generally free to seek out business opportunities. Independent contractors often advertise, maintain a visible business location, and are available to work in the relevant market.
- How the office pays the worker. Assume that a worker is guaranteed a regular wage amount for an hourly, weekly, or other period of time. This usually indicates that he or she is an employee, even when the wage or salary is supplemented by a commission. An independent contractor is usually paid a flat fee for the job. In some professions, however, such as law, independent contractors are often paid hourly.
- The extent to which the worker can realize a profit or loss. An independent contractor can make a profit or suffer a loss.

(3) Type of Relationship

Facts that show the parties' type of relationship include:

- Written contracts describing the relationship the parties intended to create. Employees often do not have such contracts.
- Whether the office provides the worker with employee-type benefits, such as insurance, a pension plan, vacation pay, or sick pay. Independent contractors are seldom given such benefits.
- The permanency of the relationship. If the office engages a worker with the expectation that the relationship will continue indefinitely, rather than for a specific project or period, this is generally considered evidence that the intent of the office was to create an employer-employee relationship.
- The extent to which services performed by the worker are a key aspect of the regular business of the office. If a worker provides services that are a key aspect of the office's regular business activity, it is more likely that it will have the right to direct and control his or her activities and, therefore, this factor indicates an employer-employee relationship.

Conclusion

When the status of a paralegal is challenged, the various factors under Florida or federal law will be weighed one by one. The evidence may conflict. Some aspects of what a paralegal does may clearly indicate an independent contractor status, and others may point to an employee-employer relationship. A court will examine the factors to determine where, on balance, a particular worker fits.

C. More Information

Search Engine
In Google or a other general search engine, run the following search:
employee "independent contractor" Florida

IRS Guidance
Who Are Employees?
www.irs.gov/pub/irs-pdf/p15a.pdf

Distinguishing Between Self-Employed Individuals and Independent Contractors
tlc-mag.com/TLC_self_employed.html

Who is Self-Employed?
www.irs.gov/businesses/small/article/0,,id=115045,00.html

Independent Contractors vs. Employees
www.irs.gov/businesses/small/article/0,,id=99921,00.html

IRS Telephone Help for Employment Questions
800-829-4933

Office of the General Counsel (Florida Gulf Coast University): Employee or Independent Contractor
www.fgcu.edu/generalcounsel/contracts-employee-vs-independent.asp

Office of the Controller (Florida International University): Employee or Independent Contractor?
finance.fiu.edu/controller/contractor.html

Employee vs. Independent Contractor Classification
www.peakconsultinginc.com/evsc.htm

StaffMarket (Bradenton, Florida): The Employee vs. Independent Contractor Issue
www.staffmarket.com/employee-leasing/contractor-employee.asp

D. Something to Check

1. Using any general search engine (e.g., *www.google.com*) or legal search engine (e.g., *www.findlaw.com*), find and summarize a court opinion (other than the *Cantor* case discussed above) from any Florida state court (or any federal court sitting in Florida) in which the issue was whether a worker was an employee or independent contractor.
2. Interview an independent or freelance paralegal who has his or her own office in Florida. Find out how this paralegal typically provides services to law firms. Then apply the Florida guidelines and the federal guidelines to identify evidence of both independent contractor status and employee status.

2.7 Overtime Pay under Federal Law
A. Introduction
B. Federal Overtime Law: Fair Labor Standards Act (FLSA)
C. Filing a Complaint
D. More Information
E. Something to Check

A. Introduction

Overtime law relevant to paralegals is governed by the FLSA, the Fair Labor Standards Act. (A separate set of overtime rules can apply to manual laborers in Florida.) Under the FLSA, eligibility for overtime compensation depends on job duties, not on job titles. Regardless of what an employee is called, his or her right to overtime compensation will depend on a close analysis of the nature of the actual work performed by individual employees. If an employee is eligible for overtime, he or she cannot be asked to waive this entitlement as a condition of obtaining or maintaining employment.

Disputes over entitlement to overtime compensation can involve substantial sums of money, particularly when a law firm is charged with violating overtime laws over a number of years. Such a dispute recently led to litigation in a Florida federal court in which a paralegal alleged "that she and others similarly situated were not compensated for overtime hours during their employment as paralegals" with the Florida law firm of Groelle & Salmon. The litigation is in its early stages. An early issue before the court is whether the case can be brought as a class action that includes current and former paralegal employees of the firm. *Nunnery v. Groelle & Salmon, P.A.*, 2007 WL 781369 (U.S. District Court, Middle District, Florida, 2007).

Some paralegals would prefer *not* to receive overtime compensation even if they are entitled to it. They would rather have their extra work hours rewarded by bonuses and other perks, similar to the way attorneys are rewarded. Yet, even these paralegals should know what they are entitled to under the law in the event that they need to use it at some point in the future, particularly when leaving a position.

In general, as you will see in the following discussion, many paralegal *supervisors* are not eligible for overtime compensation; they are exempt. Most paralegals who do not have managerial or supervisory responsibility, however, are entitled to overtime compensation; they are not exempt. This discussion assumes that a paralegal at a particular job site is *not* covered by a union contract, which can provide greater wage benefits than those guaranteed by federal law.

B. Federal Overtime Law: Fair Labor Standards Act (FLSA)

Federal overtime law is enforced by the Wage and Hour Division (WHD) of the United States Department of Labor (DOL):

U.S. Department of Labor
Employment Standards Administration
Wage and Hour Division
200 Constitution, NW
Washington, DC 20210
866-4-USWAGE
www.dol.gov/esa/whd

Workers are entitled to overtime compensation if they are paid either hourly or on a salary basis and earn under $455 a week ($23,660 a year). Most paralegals earn more than this amount. Are they also entitled to overtime compensation? In general, the answer is yes, *unless they are exempt.*

There are three main categories of exempt employees under federal law: executive, professional, and administrative (referred to as the white collar exemptions). Do paralegals fit within any of them? The answer depends on their primary duties, meaning the main or most important tasks they perform. It does not depend on title, which can vary from employer to employer. Furthermore, because paralegals perform a variety of tasks in many different settings, the question of whether they are exempt must be determined on a person-by-person basis—one paralegal at a time. It is possible for a paralegal in a particular office to be exempt while another paralegal in the same office is non-exempt.

Here is an overview of the three exemptions and how they might apply to paralegals.

• *Executive Exemption under Federal Law.* The employee (1) manages an enterprise such as a department or subdivision that has a permanent status or function in the office; (2) customarily and regularly directs the work of two or more employees; and (3) either has the authority to hire, promote, or fire other employees or can recommend such action and the recommendation is given particular weight.

Many paralegal supervisors meet all three tests of the executive exemption. They often manage the paralegal unit of the firm; supervise more than two employees; and have great influence on who is hired, promoted, or fired in their department. This is not so, however, for non-supervisory paralegals. Hence, the latter are not exempt under the executive exemption, but many paralegal supervisors would be.

• *Professional Exemption under Federal Law.* The employee performs work that requires advanced knowledge that is customarily acquired by a prolonged course of

specialized intellectual instruction. (Advanced knowledge involves work that is predominantly intellectual in character and includes work requiring the consistent exercise of discretion and judgment.) There are two categories of exempt professional employees: learned professionals (whose specialized academic training is a standard prerequisite for entrance into the profession) and creative professionals (who work mainly in the creative arts).

Paralegals normally do not fit within the professional exemption. They are not "creative professionals" because law is not in the same category as music, theater, or one of the other creative arts. Nor are they "learned professionals" because prolonged specialized instruction is not a standard prerequisite to entering the field. A bachelor's degree, for example, is not a prerequisite to becoming a paralegal. An example of a support occupation that *would* qualify as a learned profession is the registered nurse because having a specialized advanced degree is a standard prerequisite for becoming a registered nurse.

A paralegal who applies professional knowledge from *another* field to his or her paralegal work could be considered exempt. A recent opinion from the Wage and Hour Division (U.S. Department of Labor Employment Standards Administration) discussed this type of exemption: "For example, if a law firm hires an engineer as a paralegal to provide expert advice on product liability cases or to assist on patent matters, that engineer could qualify for exemption." Similarly, a paralegal "who possesses an MBA and an accounting degree and passed the uniform CPA exam, might . . . qualify for exemption if she performed primarily expert work in her advanced fields of study." (*www.dol.gov/esa/whd/opinion/FLSA/2005/2005_12_16_54_FLSA.htm*)

• *Administrative Exemption under Federal Law.* The employee (1) performs office work that is directly related to the management or general business operations of the employer or of the employer's customers and (2) exercises discretion and independent judgment with respect to matters of significance.

The question of whether the administrative exemption applies to paralegals is less clear. The first test under the administrative exemption is that the employees perform office work that is "directly related to the management or general business operations of the employer or of the employer's customers." This means "assisting with the running or servicing of the business" such as working on budgets, purchasing equipment, or administering the office's computer database (*www.dol.gov/esa/regs/compliance/whd/fairpay*). Such tasks, however, are not the primary duties of most paralegals, although they may help out in these areas. In the main, paralegals spend most of their time working on individual cases and hence do not meet the first test.

The second test (which also must be met for the administrative exemption to apply) is that the employees exercise "discretion and independent judgment with respect to matters of significance." The phrase *discretion and independent judgment* involves (1) comparing and evaluating possible courses of conduct and (2) acting or making a decision after the various possibilities have been considered. The phrase implies that the employee has authority to make an independent choice, "free from immediate direction or supervision." An employee does *not* exercise discretion and independent judgment if he or she merely uses skills in applying well-established techniques, procedures, or standards described in manuals or other sources.

Do paralegals meet the second test of exercising "discretion and independent judgment with respect to matters of significance"? They certainly work on "matters of significance." Yet, it is not clear whether they exercise "discretion and independent judgment." Paralegals are often given some leeway in the performance of their work. Yet, if they operate "within closely prescribed limits," they are not exercising discretion and independent judgment. Federal officials argue that paralegals could not have the kind of independence this exemption requires in light of the ethical obligation of attorneys to supervise and approve the work of paralegals. If paralegals make independent choices on client matters, they run the risk of being charged with engaging in the unauthorized practice of law, and their attorneys could be charged with violating their ethical duty of supervision.

To summarize federal overtime law:

- Most paralegals are not exempt under the executive exemption (not exempt means overtime pay is required)
- Many paralegal supervisors are exempt under the executive exemption (hence, no overtime pay for them)
- Most paralegals are not exempt under the professional exemption
- Most paralegals are probably not exempt under the administrative exemption

C. Filing a Complaint

To file a federal complaint for failing to receive overtime compensation, contact:

Florida District Offices
Wage and Hour Division
www.dol.gov/esa/contacts/whd/america2.htm
Fort Lauderdale Area Office (954-356-6896; 866-4-USWAGE)
Jacksonville District Office (904-359-9292; 866-4-USWAGE)
Miami District Office (305-598-6607; 866-4-USWAGE)

Orlando District Office (407-648-6471; 866-4-USWAGE)
Tampa District Office (813-288-1242; 866-4-USWAGE)

There is a two-year statute of limitations (three years for willful violations). Failure to file a federal claim within this period may mean that the claim is lost.

D. More Information

Opinion of Wage and Hour Division of the U.S. Department of Labor on Paralegal Entitlement to Overtime Compensation
www.dol.gov/esa/whd/opinion/FLSA/2005/2005_12_16_54_FLSA.htm

Federal Overtime
www.dol.gov
www.dol.gov/esa/regs/compliance/whd/fairpay/complaint.htm

Fair Labor Standards Act
www.opm.gov/flsa/overview.asp
www.law.cornell.edu/uscode/29/usc_sup_01_29_10_8.html
en.wikipedia.org/wiki/Fair_Labor_Standards_Act

State Wage Law
www.jacksonlewis.com/legalupdates/article.cfm?aid=699
hr.blr.com/BLR_Shared/topic/Florida_Overtime_Law.cfm

Florida Labor Law
www.megalaw.com/fl/top/fllabor.php
www.stateofflorida.com/Portal/DesktopDefault.aspx?tabid=10
www.floridajobs.org/minimumwage/index.htm
www.floridawagelaw.com

E. Something to Check

1. Find section 448.01 in Florida Statutes (*www.leg.state.fl.us/Statutes/index.cfm*; click "Title XXXI, Labor"). What overtime rights do manual laborers have?
2. Go to the Fair Labor Standards Act (FLSA) in the United States Code (see site above under More Information). Quote any sentence in the FSLA that mentions any of the exemptions from overtime laws.

A. Introduction

It can happen. You're working as a paralegal and suddenly find yourself out of work with no immediate prospects for new employment. One resource to consider while continuing to look for work is unemployment compensation (UC), which provides temporary income payments to make up part of the wages lost by workers who lose their jobs through no fault of their own, but who are able to work and are available for work. Even if you are still able to work part time, you may be able to receive UC benefits. Eligibility for benefits is not based on need. UC is not a public assistance program.

To be eligible for benefits, you must, for each week benefits are claimed:

- Be totally or partially unemployed
- File an initial claim for benefits and report as directed to file for subsequent weeks
- Have the necessary wage credits for work in covered employment during the base period
- Have worked and earned three times the current weekly benefit amount since the filing date of the prior claim, providing you received benefits on the prior claim
- Be able to work, be available for work, be registered for work, and be seeking work
- Participate in reemployment services (e.g., job search assistance services), whenever you have been determined to be likely to exhaust regular benefits and be in need of reemployment services
- Serve a waiting week, for which no benefits are payable, after filing an initial claim

UC is part of a federal program administered in Florida by the Agency for Workforce Innovation (AWI). UC is financed by employers who pay unemployment taxes on up to $7,000 in wages paid to each worker. (There are no deductions from the wages of workers themselves.) The actual tax rate varies for each employer, depending in part on the amount of UC benefits paid to former employees. Employers, therefore, can earn a lower tax rate when fewer claims are made on the employer's account by former employees.

The maximum weekly benefit is $275; the minimum is $32. The maximum total benefits that can be received are $7,500 or 26 full weeks. Benefits are based on a claimant's earnings in a 12-month "base period" consisting of four quarters of three months each. In periods of high unemployment in the economy, extended benefits may be available.

For federal tax purposes, UC benefits are fully taxable if you are required to file a tax return. You have a choice on whether to have the tax withheld from your benefit checks. If you choose withholding, 10 percent of your weekly benefit amount will be withheld.

Monetary Qualifications

To qualify for UC benefits in Florida, you must have worked in covered employment and earned a minimum amount of wages in the base period.

- The claimant's base period is the first four of the last five completed calendar quarters.
- There must be wages in two or more quarters in the base period.
- The total base period wages must equal at least $3,400 and must be at least the amount of 1.5 times the quarter containing the highest wages.

B. Filing a UC Claim

- File online: At *www.fluidnow.com*, click "Internet Unemployment Compensation Claim Application"
- File by phone: 850-921-7400 (Leon County); 407-228-1501 (Orange County); 954-625-3000 (Miami-Dade/Broward County); 800-204-2418 (everywhere else)

Information and Documents You Will Need to Provide

- Your Social Security number
- The names, addresses, and phone numbers of all your employers during the past 18 months
- The dates you worked and gross earnings from each employer
- Gross earnings for this week since 12:01 A.M. Sunday
- Driver's license or state identification card number, voter registration number, or other type of ID that will verify your identity
- The name and local number of your labor union hall, if applicable
- If not a U.S. citizen, your Alien Registration Number and work permit expiration date
- Your DD-214 form (if you were in the military within the past two years)
- If you were a federal employee within the past two years, your SF-50 form or SF-8 form and check stubs or W-2 proof of earnings
- If you would like for your benefits to be deposited directly to your bank account, have one of your checks or deposit slips available

Reasons Benefit Payments Are Denied

Benefits can be denied for reasons such as the following:

- Quitting your job for personal reasons. If you quit for personal reasons, benefit payments can be paid only if you quit for good cause attributable to your employer or for a personal illness or disability that made it necessary for you to leave the job.

- Being discharged for misconduct connected with work. Misconduct is an intentional or controllable act or failure to take action, which shows a deliberate disregard of the employer's interests. Misconduct may include breaking a known company policy.
- Not being able to work or not being available for work. You must be able, ready, and willing to accept a suitable job immediately. You must also be able to get to work and have adequate child care in order to be able to work.
- Refusing an offer of suitable work.
- Being on a leave of absence that you requested.
- Knowingly making false statements to obtain benefit payments.

C. Appeals

Different levels of appeal exist if you are denied UC benefits.

Unemployment Compensation Office of Appeals (UCOA)

A claimant can appeal a determination that denies benefits; the former employer can appeal a determination that grants benefits. The appeal must be filed within 20 calendar days of the date the notice of determination was mailed or, if not mailed, from the date of delivery. If the appeal is not filed in a timely manner, it will be dismissed.

There are two ways to file the appeal:

1. On the Internet: *www.fluidnow.com/appeals*
2. In writing to any of the unemployment claim adjudication offices operated by the Agency for Workforce Innovation or to the central Unemployment Compensation Office of Appeals (UCOA):

Office of Appeals
MSC 347, Caldwell Building
107 East Madison
Tallahassee, FL 32399-4143

At least 10 days prior to the hearing date, the appeals referee will mail notice of the hearing to all parties. The appeal is heard by an appeals referee of the Unemployment Compensation Office of Appeals. The referee considers testimony taken under oath. "Parties may obtain discovery through the means and in the manner provided in Rules 1.280 through 1.400, Florida Rules of Civil Procedure." (60BB-5.018) (*www.floridajobs.org/unemployment/apprefrules.html*) Upon conclusion of the hearing, the appeals referee issues a written decision.

Representation

Any person compelled to appear, or who appears voluntarily, at any proceeding before an appeals referee may, at his or her own expense, be accompanied, represented, or advised by an attorney or authorized representative. Florida Administrative Code, 60BB-5.008 (Appearances).

Fees

1. Any attorney or authorized representative who represents a claimant in any proceeding governed by these rules shall disclose orally on the record, or by post-hearing motion, the amount, if any, the claimant has agreed to pay for his or her services. The attorney or representative shall also disclose the hourly rate charged or other method used to compute the proposed fee and the nature and extent of the services rendered.
2. The appeals referee shall approve, reduce, or deny the proposed fee by written order, which may be included in the decision upon the merits of the appeal. Florida Administrative Code, 60BB-5.009 (Fees). (*www.floridajobs.org/unemployment/apprefrules.html*)

Unemployment Appeals Commission (UAC)

Either a claimant or an employer has the right to file a written appeal of the decision of the Unemployment Compensation Office of Appeals. The appeal is to the Unemployment Appeals Commission (UAC), a quasi-judicial administrative appellate body that is the highest level of administrative review of contested unemployment cases decided by appeals referees. At the administrative level, its decision is final.

Unemployment Appeals Commission
300 Webster Building
2671 Executive Center Circle West
Tallahassee, FL 32399-0681
850-488-2123
www.floridajobs.org/unemployment/apploff.html

The appeal must be filed within 20 calendar days after the mailing of the decision of the appeals referee or, if not mailed, within 20 calendar days after the date of delivery. The appeal can be submitted either by U.S. Postal Service or by facsimile. Appeals filed after the 20 calendar day deadline are generally dismissed, although the UAC will consider valid requests that explain why this deadline was not met.

The UAC will review the record of the hearing. Based on this review, the UAC may affirm, reverse, or modify the decision of the hearing officer. If a significant error or deficiency occurred, the UAC may remand the case to the Office of Appeals for further action. The UAC will not hold a hearing or consider evidence being presented for the first time that could have been brought to the attention of the hearing officer by an exercise of due diligence. Additionally, the UAC will not reweigh the evidence, substitute its factual findings for those of the referee, nor overturn a decision supported by competent substantial evidence that complies with the law.

Steps for filing an appeal to the UAC are available online:

www.fluidnow.com/appeals

www.floridajobs.org/unemployment/uc_app_comm_overview.html

Court

After exhausting avenues of appeal within the agency, dissatisfied parties can file a court appeal in the District Court of Appeal covering the county from which the referee rendered its decision or the county where the appellant (the party filing the appeal) resides.

D. Contacts

Telephone Assistance
Unemployment Insurance
866-778-7356

Employment Development Office
Agency for Workforce Development
107 East Madison
Caldwell Building
Tallahassee, FL 32399-4120
850-245-7105

Unemployment Compensation
Claims and Benefits
Post Office Drawer 5350
Tallahassee, FL 32314-5350
866-778-7356

Central Office Appeals
107 East Madison
Caldwell Building, MSC 347
Tallahassee, FL 32399-4143
850-921-3511

Alien Labor Certification
107 East Madison
Caldwell Building, MSC G-300
Tallahassee, FL 32399-4140
850-921-3299

Labor Market Statistics
107 East Madison
Caldwell Building, MSC G-020
Tallahassee, FL 32399-4111
850-245-7205
866-537-3615

Office for Civil Rights
107 East Madison
Caldwell Building, MSC 150
Tallahassee, FL 32399-4129
850-921-3201

Florida Unemployment Appeals Commission
2671 Executive Center Circle West
Suite 300, Webster Building
Tallahassee, FL 32399-0681
850-487-2685

E. More Information

Overview of Unemployment Compensation
www.myflorida.com/dor/uc
taxlaw.state.fl.us/ut/eh/uct48ehb.pdf
www.fluidnow.com
www.floridajobs.org/unemployment/uc_emp_claims.html
www.floridajobs.org/unemployment/uc_claimbooklet.html
www.floridajobs.org/unemployment/index.html
www.myflorida.com/dor/uc/GT-800058.html
www.hr.ufl.edu/class_comp/compensation/unemployment.asp

Unemployment Compensation Employer Handbook
taxlaw.state.fl.us/uct_ehb.aspx?file=uct_ehb
taxlaw.state.fl.us/ut/eh/uct48ehb.pdf

Filing a Claim
www.fluidnow.com (click "File a Claim" or "Internet Unemployment Compensation Claim Application")

Filing an Appeal
www.fluidnow.com (click "File an Appeal")

"Important Notice in Unemployment Compensation Cases"
District Court of Appeal, Third District
www.3dca.flcourts.org/Clerk/UnemplCompNotice.pdf

Unemployment Compensation Statutes
www.leg.state.fl.us/Statutes (click "Title XXXI, Labor" then "Chapter 443" (Unemployment Compensation))

Unemployment Compensation Regulations
www.flrules.org/gateway/ChapterHome.asp?Chapter=60BB-3
www.flrules.org (type "60BB-3" and then "60BB-5" in the Chapter Number search box)

Unemployment Compensation Forms
www.floridajobs.org/unemployment (click "Claim Forms" or "Unemployment Compensation Forms")
taxlaw.state.fl.us/ut/eh/sect7.pdf

F. Something to Check

Assume that a worker applies for UC benefits after being terminated from a job for misconduct.

1. Use the online UC statutes to find and summarize any two statutes covering such workers.
2. Use the online UC regulations to find and summarize any two regulations covering such workers.

A. Introduction

There are two main reasons Florida paralegals should know about workers' compensation law: (1) understanding your rights when injured on the job and (2) being better able to assist attorneys who practice workers' compensation law. A recent litigation report pointed out that in some Florida law firms that practice workers' compensation law, "paralegals do almost all of the work on cases" *(www.jcc.state.fl.us/jcc/files/reports/2005AnnualReport.pdf)*. Note, however, that in Florida, unlike some other states, paralegals are not allowed to represent clients in workers' compensation cases on their own.

Florida's system of workers' compensation is compulsory. This means that employers are required to provide workers' compensation insurance for their employees either through private insurance carriers or through self-insurance. (Occasionally, waivers are permitted.) Employers with fewer than four employees are exempt from the state's workers' compensation act.

What happens if you are injured on your paralegal job? Although paralegal work certainly does not qualify as inherently dangerous, accidents can occur.

Examples:

- You have an accident while driving to a court clerk's office to file a pleading
- You slip in the hallway on the way back from your supervisor's office
- You drop a laptop on your toe

The primary system covering such mishaps is workers' compensation. Florida Statutes provide that an employer must pay compensation or furnish benefits if an employee suffers an accidental compensable injury or death arising out of work performed in the course and scope of employment. The injury, its occupational cause, and any resulting manifestations or disability must be established to a reasonable degree of medical certainty, and the accidental compensable injury must be the major contributing cause of any resulting injuries.

In this section, we will provide an overview of this program. Workers' compensation is a no-fault system, meaning that injured employees need not prove the injury was someone else's fault to receive workers' compensation benefits. In exchange for an assurance of compensation for every job-related injury regardless of fault, workers give up the right to sue their employers for negligence. The primary requirement for receiving benefits is to sustain an injury arising out of and in the course of employment.

Workers' compensation claims are not filed in the state circuit court or county court systems, nor in the federal court system. All workers' compensation petitions and initial pleadings are filed with the OJCC (Office of the Judges of Compensation Claims). The OJCC is within the Department of Management Services, Division of Administrative Hearings. As we will see, however, appeals can be made to the Florida courts after a case has proceeded through the OJCC.

Regarding representation of clients, according to Rule 60Q-6.104 of the Florida Rules of Procedure for Workers' Compensation:

> (1) Appearance of Counsel. An attorney who files a petition or claim on behalf of a party has entered an appearance and shall be deemed the party's attorney of record . . . . The notice of appearance shall include the style of the proceeding; the case number; the name of the party on whose behalf the attorney is appearing; and the name, mailing address, telephone number, and Florida Bar number of the attorney. *(www.jcc.state.fl.us/JCC/rules.asp)*

Paralegals can assist the attorney by preparing pleadings, handling discovery, calculating deadlines, etc., but, as indicated, they cannot represent clients on their own.

Attorney fees in workers' compensation claims are set by statute at 20 percent of the first $5,000; 15 percent of the second $5,000; 10 percent on the remaining amount received over the first 10 years; and 5 percent of the benefits secured after 10 years. In certain cases, the attorney fee may be added to the award. *(www.flsenate.gov/Statutes; Title XXXI, Chapter 440, Section 440.34)*

B. Overview of the Benefit Delivery Process

Thousands of claims for work-related injuries, diseases, and deaths are filed in Florida every year. The workers' compensation system is run by the Division of Workers' Compensation (DWC). See the addresses below under Contacts. Unless self-insured, employers purchase workers' compensation coverage for their employees, generally from an insurance carrier. All medical care is provided through a managed care arrangement controlled by the employer or the workers' compensation carrier.

There are six basic types of workers' compensation benefits, depending on the nature, date, and severity of the employee's injury:

1. *Medical Benefits.* The employer must provide any medically necessary remedial treatment, care, and attendance for as long as the nature of the injury or the process of recovery requires.
2. *Temporary Total Disability Benefits (TTD).* These benefits are provided as a result of an injury that temporarily prevents the employee from returning to work and the employee has not reached MMI (maximum medical improvement).
3. *Temporary Partial Disability Benefits (TPD).* These benefits are provided when the doctor releases the employee to return to work, but the employee has not reached MMI (maximum medical improvement) and earns less than 80 percent of the pre-injury wage. The benefit is equal to 80 percent of the difference between 80 percent of the pre-injury wage and the post-injury wage. (The maximum length of time the injured employee can receive temporary benefits is 104 weeks or until the date MMI is determined, whichever is earlier.)
4. *Permanent Total Disability Benefits (PTD).* These benefits are provided when the injury causes the employee to be permanently and totally disabled according to the conditions stated in law.
5. *Permanent Impairment Benefits.* These benefits are provided when the injury causes any physical, psychological, or functional loss and the impairment exists after the date of MMI (maximum medical improvement). A doctor will assign a permanent impairment rating, expressed as a percentage, to the injury.
6. *Death Benefits.* The maximum benefit is $150,000 for a death resulting from a workplace accident.

Steps Involved

1. Worker informs employer of injury as soon as possible
2. Worker chooses a doctor from a list of physicians provided by the employer's medical care arrangement or insurance carrier (note that going to medical providers not authorized by the employer may result in the worker paying for his or her own medical care)
3. Employer notifies its insurance carrier (filing a First Report of Illness or Injury); employer must report deaths resulting from workplace accidents to the DWC (Division of Workers' Compensation)

For an overview of the benefits delivery process, see Exhibit 2.9A.

EXHIBIT 2.9A   Overview of the Workers' Compensation Benefit Delivery Process

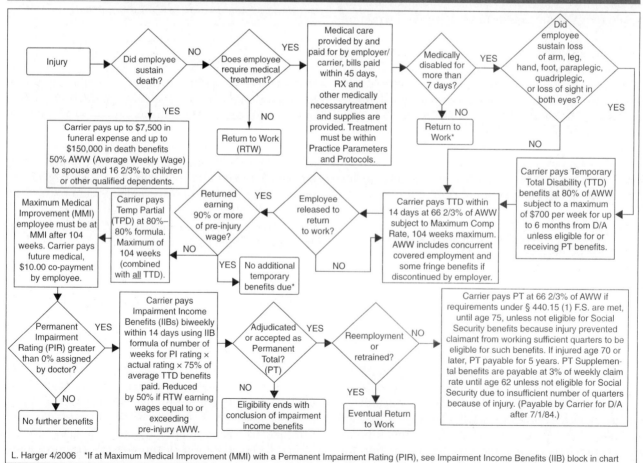

L. Harger 4/2006   *If at Maximum Medical Improvement (MMI) with a Permanent Impairment Rating (PIR), see Impairment Income Benefits (IIB) block in chart

Source: *www.fldfs.com/WC/pdf/flowchart.pdf*

Abbreviations used in Exhibit 2.9A

AWW average weekly wage
D/A date of accident
IIB impairment income benefit
MMI maximum medical improvement
PIR permanent impairment rating
PT permanent total
RTW return to work
TPD temporary partial disability
TTD temporary total disability

C. Statute of Limitations and Fraud

Statute of Limitations

Once employees are injured at work or become aware of a workers' compensation injury, they have 30 days in which to report their injury to their employer. Generally, they have two years from the date of injury to file a claim. Failure to report the injury within 30 days may be used as a defense against the claim regardless of the two-year statute of limitations for filing a claim.

Fraud

Workers' compensation fraud occurs when any person knowingly and with intent to injure, defraud, or deceive any employer or employee, insurance carrier, or self-insured program files false or misleading information. Workers' compensation fraud is a third-degree felony. Rewards of up to $25,000 may be paid to individuals who provide information that leads to arrest and conviction of persons committing insurance fraud. The state has established a toll-free number to report suspected workers' compensation fraud: 800-378-0445.

D. Denial of Benefits: Procedures for Mediation and Hearing

When a worker and a carrier disagree over a benefit, the worker can file a Petition for Benefits with the Division of Administrative Hearings (DOAH), invoking the jurisdiction of the Office of Judges of Compensation Claims (OJCC). The employer (usually via its insurer) must file a response to the petition within 14 days. The OJCC holds a mediation within 130 days. (Private mediation is necessary if no state mediator is available within that time.)

The mediators gather the parties and their representatives in a conference room to discuss settlement, then separate the parties into different rooms, shuttling offers and counteroffers back and forth. If some issues remain in dispute after mediation, the case is set for trial and discovery begins. (Difficulty in scheduling depositions of doctors often leads to a request for a delay of trial.) The trial is conducted by a Judge of Compensation Claims. At the trial, most of the witnesses testify by deposition rather than live. The witnesses who do appear are questioned and cross-examined. Attorneys may make brief closing arguments. The proceedings are recorded on tape. At the conclusion, the judge reviews the depositions and notes from the testimony and is required to make a decision within 30 days. A party who thinks there is a legal basis for overturning the judge's decision can appeal to the First District Court of Appeal (1st DCA) and then possibly to the Supreme Court of Florida.

For an overview of the procedures for mediation and hearing, see Exhibit 2.9B.

E. Contacts

Division of Workers' Compensation (DWC)
Employee Assistance Office
200 East Gaines
Tallahassee, FL 32399-4228
800-342-1741, 850-413-1601
www.fldfs.com/WC/contacts.html
www.fldfs.com/WC/directory.html
www.fldfs.com/WC/dist_offices.html

Office of the Judges of Compensation Claims (OJCC)
850-487-1911
www.jcc.state.fl.us/jcc
www.jcc.state.fl.us/JCC/n-o-r.asp

Employee Assistance District Offices (EADO)
Compliance District Offices (CDO)
www.fldfs.com/wc/organization/eao_offices.html
www.fldfs.com/wc/organization/boc_offices.html

Daytona
EADO: 386-323-0907

Daytona Beach
EADO: 386-323-0907
CDO: 386-323-0906

Fort Myers
EADO: 239-938-1841
CDO: 239-938-1840

Fort Walton Beach
CDO: 850-833-9019

Jacksonville
EADO: 904-798-5807
CDO: 904-798-5806

Miami
EADO: 305-536-0307
CDO: 305-536-0306

Ocala
EADO: 352-401-5339
CDO: 352-401–5350

Orlando
EADO: 407-853-4407
CDO: 407-835-4406

Panama City
CDO: 850-747-5425

Pensacola
EADO: 850-453-7805
CDO: 850-453-7804

Plantation
EADO: 954-321-2907
CDO: 954-321-2906

Port Richey
CDO: 727-816-1967

Sarasota
CDO: 941-329-1120

St. Augustine
CDO: 904-461-2469

Tallahassee
EADO: 850-413-1610
CDO: 850-413-1609

EXHIBIT 2.9B | **Procedures for Mediation and Hearings**

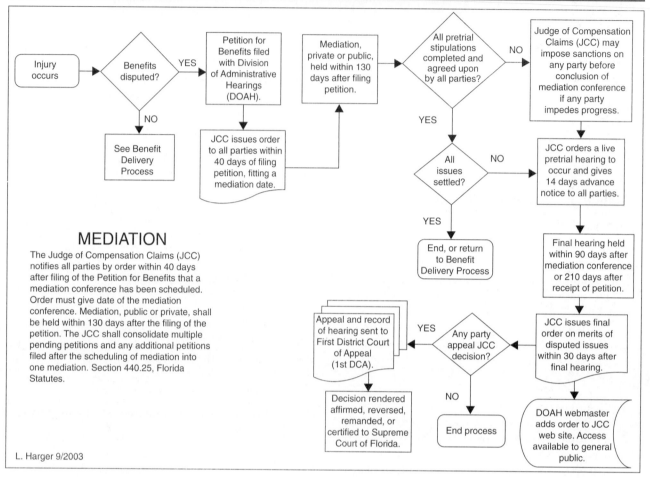

Source: *www.fldfs.com/WC/pdf/mediation.pdf*

Tampa
EADO: 813-221-6507
CDO: 813-221-6506

Tavares
CDO: 352-343-9653 x5577

Titusville
CDO: 321-264-4050

West Palm Beach
EADO: 561-837-5293
CDO: 561-837-5716

F. | **More Information**

Overview of Florida Workers' Compensation
www.fldfs.com/WC/faq/faqwrkrs.html
www.fldfs.com/WC/pdf/DFS-F2-DWC-60.pdf
www.fldfs.com/WC/pdf/DFS-F2-DWC-65.pdf

Workers' Compensation Databases
www.fldfs.com/WC/databases.html

Overview of Administrative Hearing Process
(Representing Yourself)
www.doah.state.fl.us/internet/RepYourself.cfm

Workers' Compensation Procedures and Forms
www.fldfs.com/wc/forms.html

Work-Related Injuries and Illnesses in Florida
www.fldfs.com/WC/statistics.html

Workers' Compensation Managed Care
www.fdhc.state.fl.us/MCHQ/Managed_Health_Care/WCMC

Workers' Compensation Section of The Florida Bar
www.flworkerscomp.org

Board Certified Workers' Compensation Attorneys
www.floridabar.org
(click "Professional Practice," "Certification," "Board Certified Lawyer Directory," then "Workers' Compensation")

National Employment Lawyers Association: Florida Chapter
www.floridanela.org

Florida Workers' Compensation Newsletter (*News & 440 Report*)
www.flworkerscomp.org/News440.aspx

Pro Se Workers' Compensation Mediation
www.flworkerscomp.org/News440.aspx
(click "2006 Volume XXVIII, No.1" then go to page 20)

Workers' Compensation Statutes
www.fldfs.com/WC/claimflow.html
(Click "FL Workers' Comp Statutes")

www.flsenate.gov/statutes
(click "Title XXXI, Labor")
(click "Chapter 440, Workers' Compensation")

Florida Workers' Compensation Institute
www.fwciweb.org

Florida Workers' Compensation Joint Underwriting Association
www.fwcjua.com

MegaLaw: Florida Workers' Compensation
www.megalaw.com/fl/top/fllabor.php

Workers' Compensation Oversight Board
www.fldfs.com/WC/pdf/2kAR_OversightBoard.PDF

Occupational Safety & Health Administration (OSHA)
(Florida office)
www.osha.gov/oshdir/florida.html

U.S. Occupational Safety & Health Administration (OSHA)
www.osha.gov

Florida Medical Association
www.fmaonline.org

Workers Injury Law & Advocacy Group
www.wilg.org

WorkersCompensation.com
www.workerscompensation.com
(click "Florida")

Workers Comp Rx
www.workerscomprx.com

G. Something to Check

1. Find three Florida law firms online that represent clients in workers' compensation cases. Compare their descriptions of the services they offer.
2. Go to Rule 60Q-6.104 of the Florida Rules of Procedure for Workers' Compensation regarding representation in workers' compensation cases (*www.jcc.state.fl.us/JCC/rules.asp*). What must the notice of appearance include?

Deductibility of Paralegal Education or Training

A. Introduction

B. Qualifying Work-Related Education (QWRE) that Is Deductible

C. More Information

D. Something to Check

A. Introduction

Paralegals can incur education and training expenses:

- Before they obtain their first job
- While employed
- While looking for a new position after leaving an old one

Are any of these expenses deductible on federal income tax returns as business expenses? In this section, we examine the tax law governing this question.

The cost of obtaining a paralegal education by way of a bachelor's degree, associate's degree, or certificate can be significant. In addition, there are the fees involved when applying for and maintaining one's status as a Florida Registered Paralegal (FRP) or Certified Florida Legal Assistant (CFLA), as discussed in section 1.1. The costs of attending continuing legal education (CLE) sessions to keep current in the law can be considerable. When paralegals spend their own money for any of these purposes, are they deductible?

B. Qualifying Work-Related Education (QWRE) that Is Deductible

You can deduct education costs as a business expense if the education can be classified as *qualifying work-related education* (QWRE). What is QWRE? The following three principles apply:

1. The education must fit within *either* (a) or (b):
   (a) The education is required by your employer or by the law to keep your present salary, status, or job, and this required education serves a bona fide business purpose of the employer OR
   (b) The education is used to maintain or improve skills that are needed in your present work.
2. Education that meets the minimum educational requirements of your present trade or business is *not* QWRE.
3. Education that is part of a program of study to qualify you for a new trade or business is *not* QWRE.

Figure A.1 summarizes these principles.

CLE Expenses

Florida paralegals often pay for continuing legal education (CLE) courses offered by associations, schools, or institutes. (See section 1.3 on CLE for paralegals.) Although CLE is not required to be a paralegal in Florida, it certainly helps you maintain or improve your paralegal skills. Indeed, skill maintenance or skill improvement is a major purpose of CLE. Consequently, when you pay for such CLE yourself, the cost constitutes deductible QWRE.

Certification Expenses

The same is true of courses you take to maintain your voluntary certification/registration status, as long as they maintain or improve skills needed in your present work. (For an overview of the certification/registration requirements of state and national programs, see section 1.1.)

Initial Education Expenses

Of course, your largest education expense will probably be for your *initial* paralegal training. Can this be QWRE? For most students, the answer is *no* because it is a program of study to qualify you for a "new trade or business."

Suppose, however, that you are a legal secretary paying your own way to go to paralegal school part-time or during an extended break from work. Can the cost of this education be QWRE? This is a more difficult question to answer. If as a secretary you were performing some paralegal tasks (even though you were not called a paralegal), an argument can be made that you are not trying to enter a "new trade or business." You are simply expanding (improving) what you already do. It's not clear whether the Internal Revenue Service (IRS) would accept this argument. If it does, the cost of the paralegal education would be QWRE.

Suppose that you are an experienced paralegal who wants to become an attorney. Can your law school education be QWRE? Because the requirements for being an attorney are substantially different from what is required to be a paralegal, the IRS would probably take the position that going from paralegal to attorney is entering a new trade or business. In an example provided

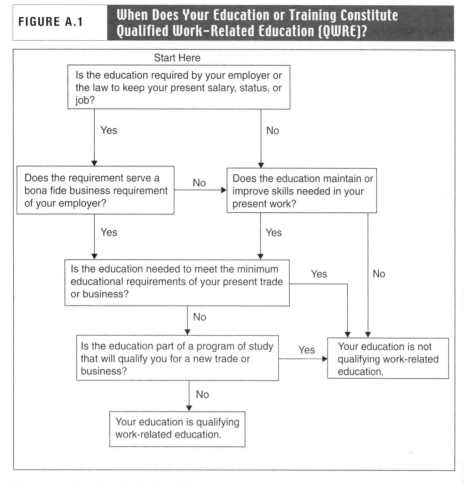

FIGURE A.1 | **When Does Your Education or Training Constitute Qualified Work–Related Education (QWRE)?**

Source: *www.irs.gov/pub/irs-pdf/p970.pdf*

by the IRS, if an accountant decides to become an attorney, his or her law school education would not be QWRE even if the employer requires the accountant to obtain a law degree. According to the IRS, going from accountant to attorney qualifies the accountant for a new trade or business.

C. More Information

Federal Tax Benefits for Education
www.irs.gov/pub/irs-pdf/p970.pdf
www.irs.gov/publications/p970/ch12.html
taxguide.completetax.com/text/Q04_5120.asp
*www.unclefed.com/TaxHelpArchives/2002/HTML/
  p508toc.html*

Hope Education Tax Credit
Form 8863
www.irs.gov/pub/irs-pdf/f8863.pdf

Lifetime Learning Credit
www.irs.gov/individuals/article/0,,id=96273,00.html

Paralegals as State Employees
Section 1009.265(1), Florida Statutes, provides: "As a benefit to the employer and employees of the state, subject to approval by an employee's agency head or the equivalent, each state university and community college shall waive tuition and fees for state employees to enroll for up to 6 credit hours of courses per term on a space-available basis."
www.fldfs.com/Treasurer/Educ/EducAssistanceProgram.htm

D. Something to Check

Go to the Internal Revenue Service site (*www.irs.gov*). Use its search boxes to try to find material relevant to the following case. Mary is a legal investigator who works for a Florida law firm. She wants to take an evidence course at a local paralegal school. If she pays for the course herself, under what circumstances, if any, can she deduct the cost as QWRE?

Ethics, Paralegals, and Attorneys

A. Introduction

No statute in Florida defines the practice of law. Therefore, there is no clear statutory definition of what constitutes the unauthorized practice of law (UPL). There are statutes saying who is allowed to practice law and what the legal consequences are for engaging in the unauthorized practice of law. Most of the definitions of the practice of law have come from court opinions, which are our major focus here. For related sections, see:

- Section 3.2, containing the text of the Rules of Professional Conduct, some of which pertain to UPL
- Section 3.3, which discusses ethical opinions, some of which pertain to UPL
- Appendix A of Part 1, covering paralegals in court opinions, some of which involve UPL
- Appendix A of Part 3, which discusses attorney discipline for offenses such as aiding nonattorneys in engaging in UPL

B. Themes Covered

Why the practice of law is regulated	Using the paralegal title
Who can practice law?	Preparing pleadings and briefs
Who decides who can practice law?	Agency representation: state
Federal supremacy over Florida law	Agency representation: federal
Role of The Florida Bar	Representing corporations
Penalty for engaging in UPL	Control of law offices
Defining the practice of law	Bankruptcy and immigration
Providing assistance on forms	Inmate legal assistance
	Miscellaneous UPL issues

C. Applicable Laws

Why the Practice of Law Is Regulated

▶ A primary responsibility of the Florida Supreme Court is to define and regulate the practice of law to protect the public from incompetent, unethical, or irresponsible representation. *Florida Bar v. Schramek*, 616 So. 2d 979 (Fla. 1993).

▶ The reason for prohibiting the practice of law by those who have not been examined and found qualified to practice is frequently misunderstood. It is not done to aid or protect the members of the legal profession either in creating or maintaining a monopoly or closed shop. It is done to protect the public from being advised and represented in legal matters by unqualified persons over whom the judicial department can exercise little, if any, control in the matter of infractions of the code of conduct which, in the public interest, lawyers are bound to observe. *State ex rel. Florida Bar v. Sperry*, 140 So. 2d 587 (Fla. 1962), vacated on other grounds, 373 U.S. 379 (1963).

▶ Because the regulation of the unlicensed practice of law serves the critical role of protecting the public from unqualified individuals who attempt to perform legal services, nonlawyers do not have a constitutional equal protection right to practice law by participating in settlement negotiations or giving legal advice. There is simply no constitutional right to engage in the unlicensed practice of law. *The Florida Bar v. Neiman*, 816 So. 2d 587 (Fla. 2002).

Who Can Practice Law?

▶ "All persons in good standing as members of The Florida Bar shall be permitted to practice in Florida." (Florida Rules of Judicial Administration, Rule 2.505(a).)

Who Decides Who Can Practice Law?

▶ "The Supreme Court of Florida has the exclusive jurisdiction to regulate the admission of persons to the practice of law and the discipline of persons admitted." (Art. V, § 15, Florida Constitution.)

▶ Pursuant to the provisions of article V, section 15, of the Florida Constitution, the Supreme Court of Florida has inherent jurisdiction to prohibit the unlicensed practice of law. (Rule 10-1.1, Rules Regulating The Florida Bar.)

▶ The Florida Supreme Court acts well within its constitutional authority to limit the practice of law by nonlawyers, given significant state interest in protecting the public, and does not thereby deprive nonlawyers of a constitutionally protected right to engage in trade, in violation of federal and state RICO (Racketeer Influenced and Corrupt Organizations Act) and antitrust laws. *Florida Bar v. Schramek*, 616 So. 2d 979 (Fla. 1993).

Federal Supremacy over Florida Law

▸ The U.S. Supreme Court has determined that Florida cannot enjoin a nonlawyer registered to practice before the United States Patent Office from preparing and prosecuting patent applications in Florida, even though those activities constitute the practice of law. The Court's ruling was based on the Supremacy Clause of the U.S. Constitution. Federal statute and patent regulations specifically authorize practice before the patent office by nonlawyer agents. "Florida has a substantial interest in regulating the practice of law within the State and . . . , *in the absence of federal legislation,* it could validly prohibit nonlawyers from engaging in this circumscribed form of patent practice" (emphasis added). The Court further noted that because "patent practitioners are authorized to practice only before the Patent Office, the State maintains control over the practice of law within its borders except to the limited extent necessary for the accomplishment of the federal objectives." *Sperry v. Florida ex rel. Florida Bar,* 373 U.S. 379 (1963).

▸ **Preparation of Pension Plans**
Currently, the preparation of pension plans is substantially regulated by federal law, the Employee Retirement Income Security Act of 1974 (ERISA). Nonlawyers, such as certified public accountants (CPAs), are authorized by federal statutes and regulations to prepare and present such plans for Internal Revenue Service (IRS) approval. Also, federal statutes and regulations provide that a number of major functions in the operation of pension plans be carried out by nonlawyer professionals. A Florida court cannot prohibit authorized professionals from preparing and presenting the necessary documents to federal agencies before which they are admitted to practice. *The Florida Bar Re Advisory Opinion: Nonlawyer Preparation of Pension Plans,* 571 So. 2d 430 (Fla. 1990).

Role of The Florida Bar

▸ The Florida Bar, as an official arm of the court, is charged with the duty of considering, investigating, and seeking the prohibition of matters pertaining to the unlicensed practice of law and the prosecution of alleged offenders. The court shall establish a standing committee on the unlicensed practice of law and at least one circuit committee on unlicensed practice of law in each judicial circuit. (Rule 10-1.2, Rules Regulating The Florida Bar.)

▸ The Unlicensed Practice of Law (UPL) program of The Florida Bar was established by the Supreme Court of Florida to protect the public against harm caused by unlicensed individuals practicing law. (*www.floridabar.org;* click "Unlicensed Practice.")

▸ Rules Governing the Investigation and Prosecution of the Unauthorized Practice of Law. (*www.floridabar.org;* click "Lawyer Regulation," then "Rules Regulating The Florida Bar," then "10.")

Penalty for Engaging in Unauthorized Practice of Law

▸ Any person not licensed or otherwise authorized to practice law in this state who practices law in this state or holds himself or herself out to the public as qualified to practice law in this state, or who willfully pretends to be, or willfully takes or uses any name, title, addition, or description implying that he or she is qualified, or recognized by law as qualified, to practice law in this state, commits a felony of the third degree. (Florida Statutes § 454.23.)

▸ A court has the authority to issue a preliminary or temporary injunction when public harm or the possibility thereof is made apparent to the court in order that such harm may be summarily prevented or speedily enjoined. (Rules Regulating The Florida Bar, Rule 10-7.1(f).)

Defining the Practice of Law

▸ **An all-encompassing attempt to define the practice of law is not possible**
It is somewhat difficult to define exactly what constitutes the practice of law in all instances. Indeed, any attempt to formulate a lasting, all-encompassing definition of the practice of law is doomed to failure for the reason that under our system of jurisprudence, such practice must necessarily change with the ever-changing business and social order. *Florida Bar v. Brumbaugh,* 355 So. 2d 1186 (Fla. 1978).

▸ **The difficulty of defining the practice of law does not mean that an ordinary person exercising ordinary common sense would not know what it is**
An inflexible, permanent definition of the practice of law is simply impracticable. This does not mean, however, that the practice of law cannot be defined or that an attempt to interpret section 454.23 (which makes it a felony to practice law without a license or other authorization) must involve guesswork and chance. The law regulating the practice of law (in § 454.23 and the cases and rules interpreting it) is set out in terms that an ordinary person exercising ordinary common sense can sufficiently understand and comply with, without sacrifice to the public interest. *State v. Foster,* 674 So. 2d 747 (Fla. 1st DCA 1996).

▸ **Scope of the practice of law; services affecting important rights requiring legal skill and knowledge greater than that possessed by an average citizen**
It is generally understood that the performance of services in representing another before the courts is the practice of law. But the practice of law also includes the giving of legal advice and counsel to others as to their rights and obligations under the law

and the preparation of legal instruments, including contracts, by which legal rights are either obtained, secured, or given away, although such matters may not then or ever be the subject of proceedings in a court. . . . In determining whether the giving of advice and counsel and the performance of services in legal matters for compensation constitute the practice of law, it is safe to follow the rule that if the giving of such advice and performance of such services affect important rights of a person under the law, and if the reasonable protection of the rights and property of those advised and served requires that the persons giving such advice possess legal skill and a knowledge of the law greater than that possessed by the average citizen, then the giving of such advice and the performance of such services by one for another as a course of conduct constitute the practice of law. *State ex rel. Florida Bar v. Sperry,* 140 So. 2d 587 (Fla. 1962), vacated on other grounds, 373 U.S. 379 (1963); see also *The Florida Bar v. Neiman,* 816 So. 2d 587 (Fla. 2002).

▶ **The practice of law can exist even if compensation is not provided**
Compensation is not a necessary element of proving that an individual has engaged in the unlicensed practice of law. The court permanently enjoined two nonattorneys in this case from appearing in court on behalf of others other than as a witness; drafting, signing, or filing pleadings or memoranda of law for others; giving legal advice; and engaging in the practice of law in Florida in any other matter. They may not give legal advice, regardless of whether they charge compensation. *The Florida Bar v. Smania,* 701 So. 2d 835 (Fla. 1997).

▶ **Sources of the definition of the practice of law**
The definition of the practice of law in Florida is not confined to the language in section 454.23 (which makes it a felony to practice law without a license or other authorization), but, rather, is shaped by the decisional law and court rules as well as common understanding and practices. *State v. Foster,* 674 So. 2d 747 (Fla. 1st DCA 1996).

Providing Assistance on Forms

▶ **Limited oral communications to assist in completing blanks on approved forms: Rule 10-2.1, Rules Regulating The Florida Bar**

(a) Unlicensed Practice of Law. The unlicensed practice of law shall mean the practice of law, as prohibited by statute, court rule, and case law of the state of Florida. For purposes of this chapter:

(1) It shall not constitute the unlicensed practice of law for a nonlawyer to engage in limited oral communications to assist a person in the completion of blanks on a legal form approved by the Supreme Court of Florida. Oral communi-

cations by nonlawyers are restricted to those communications reasonably necessary to elicit factual information to complete the blanks on the form and inform the person how to file the form. Legal forms approved by the Supreme Court of Florida which may be completed as set forth herein shall only include and are limited to forms approved by the Supreme Court of Florida pursuant to rule 10-2.1(a) [formerly rule 10-1.1(b)] of the Rules Regulating The Florida Bar, the Family Law Forms contained in the Florida Family Law Rules of Procedure, and the Florida Supreme Court Approved Family Law Forms contained in the Florida Family Law Rules of Procedure.

(A) Except for forms filed by the petitioner in an action for an injunction for protection against domestic or repeat violence, the [language in exhibit 3.1A] shall appear on any form completed by a nonlawyer and any individuals assisting in the completion of the form shall provide their name, business name, address, and telephone number on the form.

EXHIBIT 3.1A	Language That Must Appear on Documents Prepared with the Assistance of Nonlawyers

This form was completed with the assistance of:
Name of Individual
Name of Business
Address
Telephone Number

(B) Before a nonlawyer assists a person in the completion of a form, the nonlawyer shall provide the person with a copy of a disclosure which contains the [provisions stated in Exhibit 3.1B].

(C) A copy of the disclosure, signed by both the nonlawyer and the person, shall be given to the person to retain and the nonlawyer shall keep a copy in the person's file. The nonlawyer shall also keep copies for at least 6 years of all forms given to the person being assisted. The disclosure does not act as or constitute a waiver, disclaimer, or limitation of liability.

(2) It shall constitute the unlicensed practice of law for a person who does not meet the definition of paralegal or legal assistant as set forth elsewhere in these rules to offer or provide legal services directly to the public or for a person

EXHIBIT 3.1B	Disclosures by a Nonlawyer Who Provides Assistance on Approved Legal Forms; Who can be Called a Paralegal

- (Name) told me that he/she is a nonlawyer and may not give legal advice, cannot tell me what my rights or remedies are, cannot tell me how to testify in court, and cannot represent me in court.
- Rule 10-2.1(b) of the Rules Regulating The Florida Bar defines a paralegal as a person who works under the supervision of a member of The Florida Bar and who performs specifically delegated substantive legal work for which a member of The Florida Bar is responsible. Only persons who meet the definition may call themselves paralegals. (Name) informed me that he/she is not a paralegal as defined by the rule and cannot call himself/herself a paralegal.
- (Name) told me that he/she may only type the factual information provided by me in writing into the blanks on the form. (Name) may not help me fill in the form and may not complete the form for me. If using a form approved by the Supreme Court of Florida, (Name) may ask me factual questions to fill in the blanks on the form and may also tell me how to file the form.

———— I can read English

———— I cannot read English but this notice was read to me by (Name) in (Language) which I understand.

who does not meet the definition of paralegal or legal assistant as set forth elsewhere in these rules to use the title paralegal, legal assistant, or other similar term in providing legal services or legal forms preparation services directly to the public.

(3) It shall constitute the unlicensed practice of law for a lawyer admitted in a state other than Florida to advertise to provide legal services in Florida which the lawyer is not authorized to provide.

(b) Paralegal or Legal Assistant. A paralegal or legal assistant is a person qualified by education, training, or work experience, who works under the supervision of a member of The Florida Bar and who performs specifically delegated substantive legal work for which a member of The Florida Bar is responsible. A nonlawyer or a group of nonlawyers may not offer legal services directly to the public by employing a lawyer to provide the lawyer supervision required under this rule.

(c) Nonlawyer or Nonattorney. For purposes of this chapter, a nonlawyer or nonattorney is an individual who is not a member of The Florida Bar. This includes, but is not limited to, lawyers admitted in other jurisdictions, law students, law graduates, applicants to The Florida Bar, disbarred lawyers, and lawyers who have resigned from The Florida Bar.

A suspended lawyer, while a member of The Florida Bar during the period of suspension as provided elsewhere in these rules, does not have the privilege of practicing law in Florida during the period of suspension.

See also In re Amendments to the Florida Family Law Rules of Procedure, 940 So. 2d 409 (Fla. 2006) and The Florida Bar re Amendment to Rules Regulating The Florida Bar (Chapter 10), 510 So. 2d 596 (Fla. 1987).

Caution on Using the Forms

▶ **A Court's caution on the use of self-help forms**
We take this opportunity to comment upon the use of these "self-help" forms. While we applaud the desire and efforts of our supreme court to make our courts more accessible to our citizens, we nevertheless caution those who would proceed without professional assistance to do so with great care. That very accessibility and reliance upon self-help may work to the great disadvantage of a pro se litigant. Professionals in all walks of life are by their training uniquely able and qualified to help those people who do not have the training or expertise to help themselves. Particularly, this is true in regard to the legal profession where those individuals involved in litigation have financial and property rights at issue. Trial judges should not be required or expected to give advice in order to protect pro se litigants. Even lawyers who are tempted to represent themselves are warned by the old adage that "a lawyer who represents himself has a fool as a client." A book full of suggested forms and legal definitions will likely not provide a sufficient guide to navigate the treacherous waters of what may appear to be an amicable divorce. Even our supreme court approved "Notice to Parties Who Are Not Represented by an Attorney Who Is a Member in Good Standing of The Florida Bar" [which]concludes with the following attempted absolvement: "[i]n no event will the Florida Supreme Court, The Florida Bar, or anyone contributing to the production of these forms, or instructions, be liable for any direct, indirect, or consequential damages resulting from their use." *Buscemi v. Intachai*, 730 So. 2d 329 (Fla. App. 2d DCA, 1999).

Cases on Forms Assistance

▶ The approval of these forms in no way authorizes a nonlawyer to modify the forms. *Approval of Forms-Family Law Rules*, 663 So. 2d 1314 (Fla. 1995).

▶ Approved simplified forms are not intended to be used by nonlawyers as a means to practice law or to give legal advice. *Rules Regulating The Fla. Bar-Approval of Forms*, 581 So. 2d 902 (Fla. 1991).

▶ Conducting interviews with "clients" and choosing particular forms based on their responses; drafting entries on forms; directly contacting persons for consultations, explanations, recommendations, advice, and assistance in completion of forms; directing and participating in the accumulation of evidence; and offering advice and making decisions that require legal skill and knowledge of law constituted practice of law. *The Florida Bar v. King*, 468 So. 2d 982 (Fla. 1985).

▶ Marilyn Brumbaugh may sell printed material purporting to explain legal practice and procedure to the public in general and she may sell sample legal forms on the dissolution of marriage. Our holding also applies to the preparation of wills or real estate transaction documents. While Ms. Brumbaugh may legally sell forms in these areas, and type up instruments that have been completed by clients, she must not engage in personal legal assistance in conjunction with her business activities, including the correction of errors and omissions. *Florida Bar v. Brumbaugh*, 355 So. 2d 1186 (Fla. 1978).

▶ In the case before us, Schramek modified forms approved by this Court, used forms not approved by this court for use by nonlawyers, and provided legal advice regarding a number of areas, including, but not limited to, living trusts, the transfer of real property, bankruptcy, the formation of corporations, and the appellate process. This court has specifically determined that each of those activities constitutes the unauthorized practice of law because they require a knowledge of the law greater than that possessed by the average citizen. *Florida Bar v. Schramek*, 616 So. 2d 979 (Fla. 1993).

▶ An operator of a legal form preparation service engaged in the unauthorized practice of law by engaging in oral communication, taking information from written documents, and conducting legal research for the purpose of preparing legal documents not approved by Supreme Court, and by using the word legal in its business name and in advertisements, which listed legal fields in which they offered assistance. *The Florida Bar v. Miravalle*, 761 So. 2d 1049 (Fla. 2000).

▶ Providers of legal form preparation services engaged in the UPL, where they provided customers with legal assistance in the selection, preparation, and completion of legal forms; corrected customers' errors or omissions; prepared or assisted in the preparation of pleadings and other legal documents for customers; corresponded with opposing parties or attorneys for opposing parties as representative of a customer in a legal matter; hired an attorney to provide legal advice to customers; held this attorney out to their customers as the providers' supervising attorney; and advertised their services in such a way as to lead the public to believe that the providers were capable of providing legal services. *The Florida Bar v. We The People Forms and Service Center of Sarasota*, 883 So. 2d 1280 (Fla. 2004).

▶ A nonlawyer does not engage in the unauthorized practice of law by selling printed material purporting to explain legal practice and procedure to the public in general, or standardized legal forms, including general directions on how to fill out such forms. What is prohibited is personal legal assistance by nonlawyers on an individual's specific legal problems. *The Florida Bar v. Peake*, 364 So. 2d 431 (Fla. 1978).

Titles

▶ Paralegal or Legal Assistant. A paralegal or legal assistant is a person qualified by education, training, or work experience, who works under the supervision of a member of The Florida Bar and who performs specifically delegated substantive legal work for which a member of The Florida Bar is responsible. A nonlawyer or a group of nonlawyers may not offer legal services directly to the public by employing a lawyer to provide the lawyer supervision required under this rule. Rules Regulating The Florida Bar, Rule 10-2.1(b).

▶ It shall constitute the unlicensed practice of law for a person who does not meet the definition of paralegal or legal assistant . . . to use the title paralegal, legal assistant, or other similar term in providing legal services or legal forms preparation services directly to the public. Rules Regulating The Florida Bar, Rule 10-2.1(a)(2).

▶ The forms center is enjoined from using the titles paralegal or legal assistant unless he or she is working for and under the supervision of a member of The Florida Bar and performs specifically delegated substantive legal work for which a member of The Florida Bar is responsible. *The Florida Bar v. We The People Forms and Service Center of Sarasota, Inc.*, 883 So. 2d 1280 (Fla. 2004).

Pleadings and Briefs

▶ **Nonlawyers cannot sign pleadings**
Pursuant to Rule 2.515(c)(2) of the Florida Rules of Judicial Administration, "An attorney, party, or other person who files a pleading or paper by electronic transmission that does not contain the original signature of that attorney, party, or other person shall file that identical pleading or paper in paper form containing an original signature of that attorney, party, or other person . . . immediately thereafter." The use of the words *other person* in this rule is not meant to allow a nonlawyer to sign and file pleadings or other papers on behalf of another. Such conduct would constitute the unauthorized practice of law. *In re Amendments to the Florida Rules of Judicial Admin.* 939 So. 2d 966 (Fla. 2006).

▶ **Pleadings and briefs filed by a nonattorney for another are a nullity**
Pleadings filed by a nonlawyer on behalf of another are a nullity. The same rule applies to briefs filed in

this court. Ms. Leftow's power of attorney to act on her mother's behalf authorizes her to act as her mother's agent, not as her mother's attorney at law. *Forman v. State Dept. of Children & Families*, 956 So. 2d 476 (Fla. 4th DCA 2007). The rule is the product of the policy against the unauthorized practice of law. *Torrey v. Leesburg Regional Medical Center*, 769 So. 2d 1040 (Fla. 2000).

Agency Representation: State

▸ **State agency authorization of nonattorney practice**
We have recognized that state administrative agencies have the authority to permit nonlawyers to practice before them. *The Florida Bar v. Moses*, 380 So. 2d 412 (Fla. 1980).

▸ **Attorneys do not have the exclusive right to appear at agencies**
Lawyers have no exclusive right to appear before non-adjudicative bodies, as they do before a court. Florida Rules of Professional Conduct, Rule 4-3.9 (Official Comment).

▸ **Nonattorney representation at Florida administrative agency hearings: overview**
When a state agency proposes to take some action that is adverse to a person, the affected person is normally entitled to request an administrative hearing to determine the matter. Requests for hearings are initially made to the appropriate state agency. If the case does not involve disputed facts, the agency itself will conduct a proceeding and subsequently render a decision. If the request for hearing indicates that the affected person disputes facts upon which the proposed action is based, the agency ordinarily refers the case to the Division of Administrative Hearings (DOAH) for a hearing (*www.doah.state.fl.us*). DOAH provides a hearing conducted by an independent and neutral administrative law judge (ALJ), who thereafter writes a decision, either a Recommended or Final Order, which is provided to the state agency and the parties in the case. At a DOAH hearing, you may be represented at the hearing by a nonlawyer who is determined by the ALJ to be qualified to protect your rights. This generally requires a prehearing conference or affidavit filed by the individual representing you showing that he or she is conversant with the law and procedures involved in your case and can protect your right to appeal. (*www.doah.state.fl.us/internet/RepYourself.cfm*)

▸ **Administrative Procedure Act: agency representation by "other qualified representatives"**
Any person compelled to appear, or who appears voluntarily, before any presiding officer or agency in an investigation or in any agency proceeding has the right, at his or her own expense, to be accompanied, represented, and advised by counsel or by other qualified representatives. Florida Statutes § 120.62.

▸ **Qualifications of nonattorney representatives at Florida administrative hearings: Florida Administrative Code, Rule 28-106.106**
Who May Appear; Criteria for Qualified Representatives.

(1) Any party who appears in any agency proceeding has the right, at his or her own expense, to be represented by counsel or by a qualified representative. Counsel means a member of the Florida Bar or a law student certified pursuant to Chapter 11 of the Rules Regulating the Florida Bar. An attorney disbarred in any state shall not be authorized to serve as a qualified representative.

(2) **(a)** A party seeking representation by a qualified representative shall file a written request with the presiding officer as soon as practicable. The request shall identify the name, address, and telephone number of the representative and shall state that the party is aware of the services which the representative can provide, and is aware that the party can be represented by counsel at the party's own expense and has chosen otherwise.

(b) The presiding officer shall consider whether the representative is qualified to appear in the administrative proceeding and capable of representing the rights and interests of the party. The presiding officer may consider a representative's sworn affidavit setting forth the representative's qualifications . . . .

(3) The presiding officer shall authorize the representative to appear if the presiding officer is satisfied that the representative has the necessary qualifications to responsibly represent the party's interests in a manner which will not impair the fairness of the proceeding or the correctness of the action to be taken.

(4) The presiding officer shall make a determination of the qualifications of the representative in light of the nature of the proceedings and the applicable law. The presiding officer shall consider:

(a) The representative's knowledge of jurisdiction;

(b) The representative's knowledge of the Florida Rules of Civil Procedure relating to discovery in an administrative proceeding;

(c) The representative's knowledge regarding the rules of evidence, including the concept of hearsay in an administrative proceeding;

(d) The representative's knowledge regarding the factual and legal issues involved in the proceedings; and

(e) The representative's knowledge of and compliance with the Standards of Conduct for Qualified Representatives (*www.flrules.org/gateway/ruleNo.asp?ID=28-106.106*) (*www.flrules.org/Gateway/View_notice.asp?id=3399285*)

▶ **Nonattorney representation before the Public Employees Relations Commission; the unauthorized practice of law and the practice of law by nonlawyers are not synonymous**

The issue is whether a nonlawyer's appearance in a representative capacity before a hearing officer in an unfair labor practice proceeding constituted the unauthorized practice of law. The Supreme Court held that (1) the nonlawyer's conduct constituted the practice of law; (2) the legislature may oust the Supreme Court's responsibility to define the practice of law in proceedings before agencies and can convert the practice of law by a nonlawyer into authorized representation (the unauthorized practice of law and the practice of law by nonlawyers are not synonymous); (3) the legislature, through delegation in the Administrative Procedure Act extending authority for party representation by nonlawyers to qualified lay representatives, ousted the Supreme Court's responsibility in proceedings before the Public Employees Relations Commission which could convert practice of law by lay representative into authorized representation; (4) however, the rule of the Public Employees Relations Commission authorizing lay representation in its proceedings without setting standards for nonlawyer representation constituted an invalid exercise of delegated authority because the Administrative Procedure Act authorized agencies to permit only "qualified" lay representatives to appear in agency proceedings. *The Florida Bar v. Moses,* 380 So. 2d 412 (Fla. 1980).

● Any full-time employee or officer of any public employer or employee organization may represent his employer or any member of a bargaining unit in any proceeding authorized in this part, excluding the representation of any person or public employer in a court of law by a person who is not a licensed attorney. Florida Statutes § 447.609.

Agency Representation: Federal

● Under the federal Administrative Procedure Act, a person compelled to appear in person before an agency or representative thereof is entitled to be accompanied, represented, and advised by counsel or, if permitted by the agency, by other qualified representative. 5 U.S.C. § 555(b).

▶ **The right of a nonattorney parent to present evidence and cross-examine witnesses in an agency proceeding does not confer the right to represent the child in court**

Parents of an autistic minor brought an action against the school board under the federal Individuals with Disabilities Education Act (IDEA). Although it is true that parents have the right to present evidence and examine witnesses in due process hearings held pursuant to IDEA (see 20 U.S.C. § 1415(d)(2); 34 C.F.R. § 303.422(b)(2)), there is no indication that Congress intended to carry this requirement over to federal court proceedings. In the absence of such intent, we are compelled to follow the usual rule—that parents who are not attorneys may not bring a pro se action on their child's behalf—because it helps to ensure that children rightfully entitled to legal relief are not deprived of their day in court by unskilled, if caring, parents. *Devine v. Indian River County School Bd.,* 121 F.3d 576 (11th Cir. (Fla.) (1997)).

Nonattorney Representatives of Corporations

General rule

▶ A nonlawyer employee of a corporation cannot sign pleadings seeking eviction of a tenant. A corporation is not a person and, therefore, a corporation cannot designate a nonattorney employee to represent it. Instead, a corporation must be represented by an attorney. *Quinn v. Housing Authority of City of Orlando,* 385 So. 2d 1167 (Fla. 5th DCA 1980).

▶ A corporation may not represent itself through nonlawyer employees, officers, or shareholders. This rule applies even where the nonlawyer purporting to represent the corporation is its sole shareholder. *Richter v. Higdon Homes, Inc.,* 544 So. 2d 300 (Fla. 1st DCA 1989).

▶ Defendants argue that an individual nonlawyer plaintiff cannot represent a corporate co-plaintiff. Defendants are correct. It is a well-settled principle of law that a corporation cannot appear pro se and must be represented by counsel. *Native Assur. Co., Inc. v. Florida Dept. of Financial Services,* 2003 WL 22135976 (S.D. Fla. 2003).

▶ **Exception in small claims cases**

A corporation may be represented at any stage of the trial court proceedings by an officer of the corporation or any employee authorized in writing by an officer of the corporation. Florida Small Claims Rules, Rule 7.050.

▶ **Collection cases**

A corporation can employ nonlawyer employees to make non-legal collection efforts, but only a lawyer can represent a corporation in taking legal collection steps. Actions brought in small claims court (Fla.R.Summ.P. 7.050(a)(2)) are an exception to this rule. *Golden Cleaver Packing, Inc. v. G & M Hughes Corp.,* 490 So. 2d 1381 (Fla. 5th DCA 1986).

▶ **Articles of incorporation**

Drafting articles of incorporation is the practice of law. *The Fla. Bar v. Mills,* 398 So. 2d 1368 (Fla. 1981).

Nonattorney Control of Law Offices

▶ A corporation engaged in the unlicensed practice of law where its officers and stockholders were nonlawyers with no legal training who supervised and maintained a degree of control over the legal services it furnished through its lawyer employees. *Florida Bar v. Consol. Bus. & Legal Forms, Inc.,* 386 So. 2d 797 (Fla. 1980).

Bankruptcy and Immigration

▸ A nonlawyer engages in the unauthorized practice of law by having direct contact with individuals on their bankruptcy cases, and by giving explanations, recommendations, advice, and assistance in the provision, selection, and completion of legal forms. The Bar's regulation of the defendant's conduct was not preempted by 11 U.S.C. § 110 (1994), which also regulates the conduct of a "bankruptcy petition preparer." *Florida Bar v. Catarcio,* 709 So. 2d 96 (Fla. 1998).

▸ Robert Palmer is a nonattorney (a disbarred attorney) who operates a business called Legal Clinic. As part of that business, he provides services to bankruptcy debtors. He distributes business cards that reflect the name Legal Clinic and uses that name in advertising and on signs at his place of business. Under federal law, a bankruptcy petition preparer shall not use the word legal or any similar term in any advertisements, or advertise under any category that includes the word legal or any similar term. (11 U.S.C. § 110(f)(1).) A preparer shall be fined for a violation of this provision in an amount not to exceed $500 for each such violation. *In re Brummitt,* 323 B.R. 522 (Bankr. M.D. Fla. 2005).

▸ An individual or entity in the United States may choose to be represented by an attorney *or accredited representative* when filing applications or petitions with U.S. Citizenship and Immigration Services (USCIS). Accredited representatives must work for a Recognized Organization in order to be eligible to represent you before USCIS and file a Form G-28. They may be authorized to practice before the Immigration Courts, the Board of Immigration Appeals (BIA), and/or USCIS. Recognized organizations may only charge nominal fees, if any, for providing services in immigration matters. While other individuals (notary publics and immigration consultants) may assist you by filling in the blanks on pre-printed USCIS forms with information provided by you, these individuals may NOT represent you before USCIS. In addition, notary publics and immigration consultants may only charge nominal fees as regulated by state law. Individuals helping you in this way are required by law to disclose to USCIS their assistance by completing the section at the bottom of a petition or application concerning the "Preparer" of the form. (Type "immigration consultants" in the search box at *www.uscis.gov/portal/site/uscis.*)

▸ The preparation of forms to effect a change in immigration status requires legal training and familiarity with immigration laws. The failure to properly prepare the forms could result in great harm, including deportation. The respondent held himself out as legally qualified to perform immigration services, which constitutes the unauthorized practice of law in Florida. We therefore permanently enjoin and restrain respondent from engaging in the acts complained of and from otherwise engaging in the practice of law in this state. *The Florida Bar v. Matus,* 528 So. 2d 895 (Fla. 1988).

Inmate Legal Assistance

▸ It would be virtually impossible to provide each prisoner who wished to file a petition with individual counsel. Without the assistance of a "jailhouse lawyer," a great many of these prisoners would never be capable of articulating a petition or letter requesting relief. *Coonts v. Wainwright,* 282 F. Supp. 893 (M.D. Fla. 1968).

▸ We hold that the fundamental constitutional right of access to the courts requires prison authorities to assist inmates in the preparation and filing of meaningful legal papers by providing prisoners with adequate law libraries or adequate assistance from persons trained in the law. *Demps v. State,* 696 So. 2d 1296 (Fla. 3d DCA 1997).

▸ A nonattorney jailhouse lawyer may help fellow prisoners file initial papers in habeas corpus actions when the state has failed to provide alternative aid to such prisoners in seeking post-conviction relief. This exception does not include the right to represent another in court. *Bauer v. State,* 610 So. 2d 1326 (Fla. 2d DCA 1992).

▸ Criminal defendants do not have the right to nonattorney representation in court. There is no constitutional guarantee that nonattorneys may represent other people in litigation. There is a narrow exception to this conclusion: a jailhouse lawyer may help fellow prisoners file initial papers in habeas corpus actions when the state has failed to provide alternative aid to such prisoners in seeking post-conviction relief. *Bauer v. State,* 610 So. 2d 1326 (Fla. 2d DCA 1992).

Miscellaneous UPL Issues

▸ **Rosemary Furman's Secretarial Service**
This is a case that received national attention. The Florida Bar filed a petition with the court alleging that the activities of the Northside Secretarial Service of Rosemary Furman, a nonattorney, constituted the unauthorized practice of law by giving legal advice and by rendering legal services in connection with do-it-yourself divorce kits and adoptions. More specifically, the Bar alleged that Furman performed legal services by soliciting information from customers and by preparing legal pleadings for them in

violation of Florida law and that, through advertising, the respondent held herself out to the public as having legal expertise in Florida family law. She was found guilty, enjoined from continuing to engage in such activities, and sentenced to 120 days in jail. The widespread publicity generated by the case helped convince the governor to grant her clemency so that she did not have to serve any time in jail. *The Florida Bar v. Furman*, 451 So. 2d 808 (Fla. 1984).

▶ **County Court small claims mediation**
A nonlawyer representative may appear on behalf of a party to a small claims mediation if the representative has the party's signed written authority to appear and has full authority to settle without further consultation. Rule 1.750(e) Florida Rules of Civil Procedure; *In re Amendments to Florida Rules of Civil Procedure*, 682 So. 2d 105 (Fla. 1996); Rule 7.090(f) Small Claims Rules; *In re Amendments to Florida Small Claims Rule 7.090*, 985 So. 2d 1033 (Fla. 2008).

▶ **Nonattorney sued for giving negligent legal advice**
A nonlawyer is sued for giving negligent legal advice concerning a divorce. He now argues that as a nonlawyer, he cannot be held liable for a failure to give proper legal advice and counsel. This argument overlooks the fact that whether a lawyer or not, if he undertakes to give legal advice, he is subject to a standard of due care. When anyone undertakes to do a particular act for another, the act undertaken must be done with reasonable care so as not to injure the other person by reason of the act performed. *Buscemi v. Intachai*, 730 So. 2d 329 (Fla. 2d DCA 1999).

▶ **Dependency cases**
A nonattorney counselor's preparation of documents and presentation of non-contested dependency cases, including the filing of documents, request for relief, and testimony of counselors, constituted the unauthorized practice of law. *The Florida Bar re Advisory Opinion HRS Nonlawyer Counselor*, 518 So. 2d 1270 (Fla. 1988). The Florida Department of Health and Rehabilitative Services (HRS or Department) lay counselors are engaged in the practice of law in drafting legal documents and representing HRS in court in uncontested juvenile dependency proceedings. *The Florida Bar In re Advisory Opinion HRS Nonlawyer Counselor*, 547 So. 2d 909 (Fla. 1989).

▶ **Real estate deeds**
Preparation of deeds for individuals other than one's self constitutes the unauthorized practice of law. *The Fla. Bar v. Valdes*, 464 So. 2d 1183 (Fla. 1985).

▶ **Real estate closing**
A paralegal who represented a party at the closing of a restaurant purchase without attorney supervision, who gave legal advice to the purchaser of the restaurant, and who corresponded with another attorney,

and signed *For the Firm* without a disclaimer of nonattorney status, engaged in the unauthorized practice of law and would be permanently enjoined from doing so. *The Florida Bar v. Pascual*, 424 So. 2d 757 (Fla. 1982).

▶ **Evictions**
The respondent is restrained from conducting the following activities: (a) filing the initial complaints for residential landlords, (b) counseling landlords about legal matters regarding tenant eviction actions, (c) typing or printing information on the tenant eviction forms set forth in the petition where the landlord orally communicates such information to the respondent, and (d) appearing in court or in any judicial proceeding that is part of the tenant eviction process. *The Florida Bar v. Mickens*, 505 So. 2d 1319 (Fla. 1987).

▶ **Representation of landlords by nonlawyer property managers**
Designated nonlawyer property managers may handle uncontested residential evictions on behalf of both individual and corporate landlords. It is not the unlicensed practice of law for a property manager to draft and serve a three-day notice. It is the unlicensed practice of law for a nonlawyer to draft and file a complaint for eviction and motion for default and to obtain a final judgment and writ of possession for a landlord in an uncontested residential eviction. *The Florida Bar re Advisory Opinion—Nonlawyer Preparation of and Representation of Landlord in Uncontested Residential Evictions*, 627 So. 2d 485 (Fla. 1993); see also 605 So. 2d 868.

▶ **Mechanic lien notices**
It is not the unlicensed practice of law for nonlawyers to engage in communications with their customers for the purpose of completing the notice-to-owner (NTO) forms and preliminary notice-to-contractor forms with respect to mechanics' liens. But nonlawyers may give no legal advice in connection with the preparation and service of the notices. The construction industry, which is served by those who fill out the forms, is aware of their significance and generally knowledgeable of the requirements pertaining to the perfection of mechanics' lien rights. The two forms in question are statutory forms requiring only a minimum of information, which may be easily obtained from the customer or the public records. There has been no showing that the public is being harmed by the preparation of these forms by nonlawyers. *The Florida Bar In re Advisory Opinion-Nonlawyer Preparation of Notice to Owner and Notice to Contractor*, 544 So. 2d 1013 (Fla. 1989).

▶ **Living trusts**
The assembly, drafting, execution, and funding of a living trust document constitute the practice of law. A lawyer must make the determination as to the client's need for a living trust and identify the

type of living trust most appropriate for the client. Legal advice on the application, preparation, advisability or quality of any legal instrument or document or forms in connection with the disposition of property inter vivos or upon death constitutes the practice of law and may not be carried on by nonlawyers. A living trust document involves the disposition of property at death, and consequently requires legal expertise. However, gathering the necessary information for the living trust does not constitute the practice of law, and nonlawyers may properly perform this activity. *The Florida Bar re Advisory Opinion-Nonlawyer Preparation of Living Trusts,* 613 So. 2d 426 (Fla. 1992).

▶ A corporation in the business of creating and selling complex estate planning documents engaged in unauthorized practice of law when its nonlawyer employees answered specific legal questions; determined appropriateness of living trusts based on a customer's particular needs and circumstances; assembled, drafted, and executed documents; and funded living trusts. *The Florida Bar v. American Senior Citizens Alliance, Inc.,* 689 So. 2d 255 (Fla. 1997).

▶ **Bidding at judicial sales**
An attorney may employ a nonattorney to bid at a judicial sale in a mortgage foreclosure. A judicial sale is part of the judicial process, but it is not a judicial proceeding. *Heilman v. Suburban Coastal Corp.,* 506 So. 2d 1088 (Fla. 4th DCA 1987).

▶ **Securities arbitration**
A nonlawyer who is retained to represent an investor, for compensation, in securities arbitration against a broker is engaged in the unauthorized practice of law. Such representatives give specific legal advice and perform the traditional tasks of the lawyer at every stage of the arbitration proceeding in an effort to protect the investor's important legal and financial interests. When performed by nonlawyers, such activities, wholly unregulated and unsanctionable, must be enjoined. *The Florida Bar re Advisory Opinion on Nonlawyer Representation in Securities Arbitration,* 696 So. 2d 1178 (Fla. 1997).

▶ **Advice on pursuing an appeal**
Giving advice regarding procedures to follow for an appeal constitutes the unauthorized practice of law. *The Fla. Bar v. Mills,* 410 So. 2d 498 (Fla. 1982).

▶ **Questioning witnesses at depositions**
The taking of a deposition constitutes the practice of law. Absent express authorization from the Supreme Court, there is no provision in Florida law or in the rules of The Florida Bar permitting a nonlawyer, representing another person, to participate actively in the questioning of witnesses in depositions even under the immediate guidance and supervision of a licensed attorney. Lacking adequate legal training, a nonattorney participating in the examination of a witness poses the dangers of incompetent or irresponsible representation. *State v. Foster,* 674 So. 2d 747 (Fla. 1st DCA 1996).

▶ **The limits of powers of attorney**
The trial court was correct in not allowing the appellant's wife, who was armed with his power of attorney, to represent him in this case. *Pryor v. King,* 485 So. 2d 28 (Fla. 1st DCA 1986).

▶ **Community association managers**
A licensed community association manager (CAM) petitioned for an advisory opinion on whether several aspects of community association management would constitute the unlicensed practice of law. The Supreme Court held that (1) ministerial actions taken by CAMs that do not require significant legal expertise and interpretation do not constitute unauthorized practice of law, such as completing various forms and drafting notices, but (2) CAMs would engage in unauthorized practice of law by drafting documents requiring the legal description of property or establishing rights of the community association, by making determinations and drafting documents requiring interpretations of statutes and various rules, or by giving advice as to the legal consequences of taking certain courses of action. *The Florida Bar re Advisory Opinion Activities of Community Ass'n Managers,* 681 So. 2d 1119 (Fla. 1996).

▶ **Advertising**
The court enjoined a nonlawyer from advertising in any fashion that may lead a reasonable layperson to believe that the nonlawyer may offer to the public legal services, legal advice, or personal legal assistance. *Florida Bar v. Becerra,* 661 So. 2d 299 (Fla. 1995).

D. More Information

The Florida Bar
www.flabar.org
(click "Unlicensed Practice")

Rules Regulating The Florida Bar
www.flabar.org
(click "Lawyer Regulation" then "Rules Regulating The Florida Bar")

Rules of Professional Conduct
www.flabar.org
(click "Lawyer Regulation," then "Rules Regulating The Florida Bar," then "Rules Of Professional Conduct")

Ethics Opinions of The Florida Bar on UPL
www.flabar.org
(click on "Member Services," then "Ethics Opinions," then "Subject Index of Ethics Opinions," then "Unlicensed Practice of Law")

Formal Advisory Opinions of The Florida Bar on UPL
www.flabar.org
(click "Unlicensed Practice" then "Formal Advisory Opinions")

Filing a UPL Complaint
www.flabar.org
(click "Public Information," then "Consumer Information," then "Filing an Unlicensed Practice of Law Complaint")

Self-Representation at Florida Administrative Agencies
www.doah.state.fl.us (click "Rep. Yourself")

American Legal Ethics Library
www.law.cornell.edu/ethics
(click "Listing by jurisdiction" then "Florida")

Florida Ethics Resources
www.law.cornell.edu/ethics/fl/narr
www.ll.georgetown.edu/states/florida.cfm

E. Something to Check

1. Run the following search ("unauthorized practice of law" Florida) in any three general search engines (e.g., *www.google.com, www.yahoo.com, www.live.com, Ask.com*). Prepare a report on the categories of sites to which each search engine leads you. Cluster the same kinds of sites you find into categories, e.g., sites giving you cases on UPL in Florida, sites giving you bar associations in Florida that have UPL resources, and sites that lead you to attorneys who represent clients suing other attorneys for UPL. Give a brief description of each category with a minimum of five examples of web sites under each category. After you finish the report for the three general search engines, comment on which engine was the most productive and why.

2. Pick any three legal search engines or portals (e.g., *www.findLaw.com, www.washlaw.edu, www.lawguru.com, RomingerLegal.com*). How effective is each in leading you to material about the unauthorized practice of law in Florida? Describe what you are able to find.

3.2 Florida Rules of Professional Conduct (FRPC) and Trust Account Rules

A. Introduction

The Florida Supreme Court promulgated the Rules Regulating The Florida Bar. Chapter 4 of these rules contains the Florida Rules of Professional Conduct (FRPC), the ethics code that governs the legal profession in the state. The FRPC is based on the American Bar Association's Model Rules of Professional Conduct, as modified by the Florida Supreme Court. Numbered brackets have been added to the official comments to facilitate cross-referencing.

For other material on or related to ethics, see also:

- Section 1.1, "Florida Registered Paralegal Rules"
- Part 1, Appendix A, "Paralegals in Court Opinions" (some of the court opinions summarized in Appendix A cover ethical issues)
- Section 3.1, "Defining the Practice of Law (Authorized and Unauthorized) in Florida"
- Section 3.3, "Ethical Opinions of the Bar Association Involving Paralegals and Other Nonlawyers"
- Part 3, Appendix A, "Disciplinary Proceedings Against an Attorney"

B. Rules and Official Comments of Particular Relevance to Paralegals and Other Nonlawyers

While all of the rules and official comments in the FRPC are important, some are of particular relevance to paralegals and other nonlawyers. In the following list of such rules and comments, the bracketed numbers refer to specific paragraphs in the official comments. These bracketed numbers have been added for clarity of reference. The comment paragraphs in the FRPC itself are unnumbered. For example, 4-1.10[7] in the following list refers to the seventh paragraph in the official comments to rule 4-1.10.

Preamble (see the definition of *screened* in the "Terminology" section of the Preamble found at the beginning of the FRPC; screening is important in conflict of interest cases; see also the discussion of screening in paragraphs [8] and [9] of the official comments on the Preamble)

> **4-1.4[4]** (a member of the lawyer's staff should acknowledge receipt of a client request and advise the client when a response may be expected)
>
> **4-1.5[3]** (general overhead should be accounted for in a lawyer's fee)
>
> **4-1.5[4]** (informing the client about the costs of paralegal services)
>
> **4-1.10[7]** (the screening of paralegals to avoid disqualification due to a conflict of interest)
>
> **4-3.9[2]** ("Lawyers have no exclusive right to appear before nonadjudicative bodies, as they do before a court.")
>
> **4-5.3** (responsibilities regarding nonlawyer assistants)

Summary of Rules and Comments of Particular Relevance to Paralegals and Other Nonlawyers

4-5.3(b)(1)&(2) (managers must take reasonable efforts to ensure that measures are in place that give reasonable assurance that paralegals and other nonlawyer assistants will comply with ethical rules)

4-5.3(c) (paralegals may perform the duties delegated to them by the lawyer without the presence or active involvement of the lawyer; the lawyer shall review and be responsible for the work product of the paralegals)

4-5.3[1] (lawyers must give paralegals and other nonlawyer assistants appropriate instruction and supervision concerning the ethical aspects of their employment, particularly regarding the obligation not to disclose information relating to representation of the client, and should be responsible for their work product)

4-5.3[3] (ownership or partnership interest by non-lawyers)

4-5.4(a) (sharing fees with a nonlawyer))

4-5.4(a)(4) (limitations on paying bonuses to a nonlawyer)

4-5.4(b) (nonlawyers can participate in a pension, profit-sharing, or retirement plan)

4-5.4(c) (lawyers cannot form a partnership with a nonlawyer)

4-5.4(e)(1) (nonlawyers cannot own an interest in a law practice)

4-5.4(e)(2) (nonlawyers cannot be directors or officers of a law practice)

4-5.4(e)(3) (nonlawyers cannot have the right to direct or control the professional judgment of a lawyer)

4-5.4[3] (nonlawyer compensation may not be based on legal fees)

4-5.5[2] (a lawyer can employ the services of para-professionals and delegate functions to them, so long as the lawyer supervises the delegated work and retains responsibility for their work)

4-5.5[2] (a lawyer can provide professional advice and instruction to nonlawyers whose employment requires knowledge of law, e.g., claims adjusters, employees of financial or commercial institutions, social workers, accountants, and persons employed in government agencies)

4-5.5[2] (a lawyer may counsel nonlawyers who wish to proceed pro se)

4-7.2(c)(14) (lawyers shall not give anything of value to someone for recommending the lawyer's services)

4-7.2[8] (payment to a secretary to prepare advertising communications)

4-7.4 (employees or agents of a lawyer are prohibited from soliciting on the lawyer's behalf)

4-8.4[1] (lawyers must not request or instruct their agents to violate an ethical rule)

20 (Florida Registered Paralegal Program)

C. Table of Contents of FRPC and Trust Account Rules

4. Rules of Professional Conduct

Preamble: A Lawyer's Responsibilities

Scope

Terminology

Table of Contents of Ethics Rules

4-1 Client-Lawyer Relationship

4-2 Counselor

4-3 Advocate

D. Index to the FRPC and Trust Account Rules

Bracketed numbers refer to paragraph numbers that have been added to the official comments to the rules; letters and numbers in parentheses refer to the rules themselves.

> Index to the FRPC and Trust Account Rules

a client's legal affairs and reporting about them to the client or to others.

In addition to these representational functions, a lawyer may serve as a third-party neutral, a nonrepresentational role helping the parties to resolve a dispute or other matter. Some of these rules apply directly to lawyers who are or have served as third-party neutrals. See, e.g., rules 4-1.12 and 4-2.4. In addition, there are rules that apply to lawyers who are not active in the practice of law or to practicing lawyers even when they are acting in a nonprofessional capacity. For example, a lawyer who commits fraud in the conduct of a business is subject to discipline for engaging in conduct involving dishonesty, fraud, deceit, or misrepresentation. See rule 4-8.4.

In all professional functions a lawyer should be competent, prompt, and diligent. A lawyer should maintain communication with a client concerning the representation. A lawyer should keep in confidence information relating to representation of a client except so far as disclosure is required or permitted by the Rules of Professional Conduct or by law.

> **Summary of Many Ethical Duties**

A lawyer's conduct should conform to the requirements of the law, both in professional service to clients and in the lawyer's business and personal affairs. A lawyer should use the law's procedures only for legitimate purposes and not to harass or intimidate others.

A lawyer should demonstrate respect for the legal system and for those who serve it, including judges, other lawyers, and public officials. While it is a lawyer's duty, when necessary, to challenge the rectitude of official action, it is also a lawyer's duty to uphold legal process.

> **Respect for the Legal System**

As a public citizen, a lawyer should seek improvement of the law, access to the legal system, the administration of justice, and the quality of service rendered by the legal profession. As a member of a learned profession, a lawyer should cultivate knowledge of the law beyond its use for clients, employ that knowledge in reform of the law, and work to strengthen legal education. In addition, a lawyer should further the public's understanding of and confidence in the rule of law and the justice system, because legal institutions in a constitutional democracy depend on popular participation and support to maintain their authority.

A lawyer should be mindful of deficiencies in the administration of justice and of the fact that the poor, and sometimes persons who are not poor, cannot afford adequate legal assistance. Therefore, all lawyers should devote professional time and resources and use civic influence to ensure equal access to our system of justice for all those who because of economic or social barriers cannot

> **Helping Those Who Cannot Afford Legal Services**

E. Text of the FRPC and Trust Account Rules with Official Comments

4. Rules of Professional Conduct

Preamble: A Lawyer's Responsibilities

> **Text of the Rules and Official Comments**

A lawyer, as a member of the legal profession, is a representative of clients, an officer of the legal system, and a public citizen having special responsibility for the quality of justice.

> **Lawyer as Advisor, Advocate, Negotiator, Evaluator, and Third-Party Neutral**

As a representative of clients, a lawyer performs various functions. As an adviser, a lawyer provides a client with an informed understanding of the client's legal rights and obligations and explains their practical implications. As an advocate, a lawyer zealously asserts the client's position under the rules of the adversary system. As a negotiator, a lawyer seeks a result advantageous to the client but consistent with requirements of honest dealing with others. As an evaluator, a lawyer acts by examining afford or secure adequate legal counsel. A lawyer should aid the legal profession in pursuing these objectives and should help the Bar regulate itself in the public interest.

Many of the lawyer's professional responsibilities are prescribed in the Rules of Professional Conduct and in substantive and procedural law. A lawyer is also

The Conscience of a Lawyer

guided by personal conscience and the approbation of professional peers. A lawyer should strive to attain the highest level of skill, to improve the law and the legal profession, and to exemplify the legal profession's ideals of public service.

A lawyer's responsibilities as a representative of clients, an officer of the legal system, and a public citizen are usually harmonious. Zealous advocacy is not inconsistent with justice. Moreover, unless violations of law or injury to another or another's property is involved, preserving client confidences ordinarily serves the public interest because people are more likely to seek legal advice, and thereby heed their legal obligations, when they know their communications will be private.

In the practice of law conflicting responsibilities are often encountered. Difficult ethical problems may arise from a conflict between a lawyer's responsibility to a client and the lawyer's own sense of personal honor, including obligations to society and the legal profession. The Rules of Professional Conduct often prescribe terms for resolving such conflicts. Within the framework of these rules, however, many difficult issues of professional discretion can arise. Such issues must be resolved through the exercise of sensitive professional and moral judgment guided by the basic principles underlying the rules. These principles include the lawyer's obligation to protect and pursue a client's legitimate interests, within the bounds of the law, while maintaining a professional, courteous, and civil attitude toward all persons involved in the legal system.

Self-Regulation in the Legal Profession

Lawyers are officers of the court and they are responsible to the judiciary for the propriety of their professional activities. Within that context, the legal profession has been granted powers of self-government. Self-regulation helps maintain the legal profession's independence from undue government domination. An independent legal profession is an important force in preserving government under law, for abuse of legal authority is more readily challenged by a profession whose members are not dependent on the executive and legislative branches of government for the right to practice. Supervision by an independent judiciary, and conformity with the rules the judiciary adopts for the profession, assures both independence and responsibility.

Thus, every lawyer is responsible for observance of the Rules of Professional Conduct. A lawyer should also aid in securing their observance by other lawyers. Neglect of these responsibilities compromises the independence of the profession and the public interest that it serves.

Scope:

The Rules of Professional Conduct are rules of reason. They should be interpreted with reference to the

Ethics Rules That Are Imperatives vs Those That Are Permissive

purposes of legal representation and of the law itself. Some of the rules are imperatives, cast in the terms of "shall" or "shall not." These define proper conduct for purposes of professional discipline. Others, generally cast in the term "may," are permissive and define areas under the rules in which the lawyer has discretion to exercise professional judgment. No disciplinary action should be taken when the lawyer chooses not to act or acts within the bounds of such discretion. Other rules define the nature of relationships between the lawyer and others. The rules are thus partly obligatory and disciplinary and partly constitutive and descriptive in that they define a lawyer's professional role.

The comment accompanying each rule explains and illustrates the meaning and purpose of the rule.

Rules vs Comments in the Code

The comments are intended only as guides to interpretation, whereas the text of each rule is authoritative. Thus, comments, even when they use the term "should," do not add obligations to the rules but merely provide guidance for practicing in compliance with the rules.

The rules presuppose a larger legal context shaping the lawyer's role. That context includes court rules and statutes relating to matters of licensure, laws defining specific obligations of lawyers, and substantive and procedural law in general. Compliance with the rules, as with all law in an open society, depends primarily upon understanding and voluntary compliance, secondarily upon reinforcement by peer and public opinion, and finally, when necessary, upon enforcement through disciplinary proceedings. The rules do not, however, exhaust the moral and ethical considerations that should inform a lawyer, for no worthwhile human activity can be completely defined by legal rules. The rules simply provide a framework for the ethical practice of law. The comments are sometimes used to alert lawyers to their responsibilities under other law.

Furthermore, for purposes of determining the lawyer's authority and responsibility, principles of substantive law external to these rules determine whether a client-lawyer relationship exists. Most of the duties flowing from the client-lawyer relationship attach only after the client has requested the lawyer to

Determining the Existence of an Attorney-Client Relationship; Confidentiality Prior to this Time

render legal services and the lawyer has agreed to do so. But there are some duties, such as that of confidentiality under rule 4-1.6, which attach when the lawyer agrees to consider whether a client-lawyer relationship shall be established. See rule 4-1.18. Whether a client-lawyer relationship exists for any specific purpose can depend on the circumstances and may be a question of fact.

Failure to comply with an obligation or prohibition imposed by a rule is a basis for invoking the disciplinary process. The rules presuppose that disciplinary assessment of a lawyer's conduct will be made on the basis of the facts and circumstances as they existed at the time of the conduct in question in recognition of the fact that a lawyer often has to act upon uncertain or incomplete evidence of the situation. Moreover, the rules presuppose that whether discipline should be imposed for a violation, and the severity of a sanction, depend on all the circumstances, such as the willfulness and seriousness of the violation, extenuating factors, and whether there have been previous violations.

| Ethics Violations vs Civil Liability |

Violation of a rule should not itself give rise to a cause of action against a lawyer nor should it create any presumption in such a case that a legal duty has been breached. In addition, violation of a rule does not necessarily warrant any other nondisciplinary remedy, such as disqualification of a lawyer in pending litigation. The rules are designed to provide guidance to lawyers and to provide a structure for regulating conduct through disciplinary agencies. They are not designed to be a basis for civil liability.

| Using Ethics as a Procedural Weapon |

Furthermore, the purpose of the rules can be subverted when they are invoked by opposing parties as procedural weapons. The fact that a rule is a just basis for a lawyer's self-assessment, or for sanctioning a lawyer under the administration of a disciplinary authority, does not imply that an antagonist in a collateral proceeding or transaction has standing to seek enforcement of the rule. Accordingly, nothing in the rules should be deemed to augment any substantive legal duty of lawyers or the extra-disciplinary consequences of violating such duty. Nevertheless, since the rules do establish standards of conduct by lawyers, a lawyer's violation of a rule may be evidence of a breach of the applicable standard of conduct.

Terminology:

"*Belief*" or "*believes*" denotes that the person involved actually supposed the fact in question to be true. A person's belief may be inferred from circumstances.

"*Consult*" or "*consultation*" denotes communication of information reasonably sufficient to permit the client to appreciate the significance of the matter in question.

| Definitions of Key Terms in the FRPC |

"*Confirmed in writing*," when used in reference to the informed consent of a person, denotes informed consent that is given in writing by the person or a writing that a lawyer promptly transmits to the person confirming an oral informed consent. See "informed consent" below. If it is not feasible to obtain or transmit the writing at the time the person gives informed consent, then the lawyer must obtain or transmit it within a reasonable time thereafter.

"*Firm*" or "*law firm*" denotes a lawyer or lawyers in a law partnership, professional corporation, sole proprietorship, or other association authorized to practice law; or lawyers employed in the legal department of a corporation or other organization.

"*Fraud*" or "*fraudulent*" denotes conduct having a purpose to deceive and not merely negligent misrepresentation or failure to apprise another of relevant information.

| Defining *Fraud* |

"*Informed consent*" denotes the agreement by a person to a proposed course of conduct after the lawyer has communicated adequate information and explanation about the material risks of and reasonably available alternatives to the proposed course of conduct.

"*Knowingly*," "*known*," or "*knows*" denotes actual knowledge of the fact in question. A person's knowledge may be inferred from circumstances.

"*Lawyer*" denotes a person who is a member of The Florida Bar or otherwise authorized to practice in any court of the State of Florida.

"*Partner*" denotes a member of a partnership and a shareholder in a law firm organized as a professional corporation, or a member of an association authorized to practice law.

"*Reasonable*" or "*reasonably*" when used in relation to conduct by a lawyer denotes the conduct of a reasonably prudent and competent lawyer.

"*Reasonable belief*" or "*reasonably believes*" when used in reference to a lawyer denotes that the lawyer believes the matter in question and that the circumstances are such that the belief is reasonable.

"*Reasonably should know*" when used in reference to a lawyer denotes that a lawyer of reasonable prudence and competence would ascertain the matter in question.

"*Screened*" denotes the isolation of a lawyer from any participation in a matter through the timely imposition of procedures within a firm that are reasonably adequate under the circumstances to protect information that the isolated lawyer is obligated to protect under these rules or other law.

| Defining *Screened* in Conflict of Interest Cases |

"*Substantial*" when used in reference to degree or extent denotes a material matter of clear and weighty importance.

"Tribunal" denotes a court, an arbitrator in a binding arbitration proceeding, or a legislative body, administrative agency, or other body acting in an adjudicative capacity. A legislative body, administrative agency, or other body acts in an adjudicative capacity when a neutral official, after the presentation of evidence or legal argument by a party or parties, will render a binding legal judgment directly affecting a party's interests in a particular matter.

"Writing" or *"written"* denotes a tangible or electronic record of a communication or representation, including handwriting, typewriting, printing, photostating, photography, audio or video recording, and e-mail. A *"signed"* writing includes an electronic sound, symbol or process attached to or logically associated with a writing and executed or adopted by a person with the intent to sign the writing.

Official Comments on Preamble

Confirmed in writing

[1] If it is not feasible to obtain or transmit a written confirmation at the time the client gives informed consent, then the lawyer must obtain or transmit it within a reasonable time thereafter. If a lawyer has obtained a client's informed consent, the lawyer may act in reliance on that consent so long as it is confirmed in writing within a reasonable time thereafter.

Firm

[2] Whether two or more lawyers constitute a firm above can depend on the specific facts. For example, two

> **Office Sharing**

practitioners who share office space and occasionally consult or assist each other ordinarily would not be regarded as constituting a firm. However, if they present themselves to the public in a way that suggests that they are a firm or conduct themselves as a firm, they should be regarded as a firm for purposes of the rules. The terms of any formal agreement between associated lawyers are relevant in determining whether they are a firm, as is the fact that they have mutual access to information concerning the clients they serve. Furthermore, it is relevant in doubtful cases to consider the underlying purpose of the rule that is involved. A group of lawyers could be regarded as a firm for purposes of the rule that the same lawyer should not represent opposing parties in litigation, while it might not be so regarded for purposes of the rule that information acquired by one lawyer is attributed to another. With respect to the law department of an organization, including the government, there is ordinarily no question that the members of the department constitute a firm within the meaning of the Rules of Professional Conduct.

[3] There can be uncertainty, however, as to the identity of the client. For example, it may not

> **Identity of the Client**

be clear whether the law department of a corporation represents a subsidiary or an affiliated corporation, as well as the corporation by which the members of the department are directly employed. A similar question can arise concerning an unincorporated association and its local affiliates. Similar questions can also arise with respect to lawyers in legal aid and legal services organizations. Depending upon the structure of the organization, the entire organization or different components of it may constitute a firm or firms for purposes of these rules.

Fraud

[4] When used in these rules, the terms "fraud" or "fraudulent" re-

> **Fraud vs Negligence**

fer to conduct that has a purpose to deceive. This does not include merely negligent misrepresentation or negligent failure to apprise another of relevant information. For purposes of these rules, it is not necessary that anyone has suffered damages or relied on the misrepresentation or failure to inform.

Informed consent

[5] Many of the Rules of Professional Conduct require the lawyer to obtain the informed

> **Informed Consent**

consent of a client or other person (e.g., a former client or, under certain circumstances, a prospective client) before accepting or continuing representation or pursuing a course of conduct. See, e.g., rules 4-1.2(c), 4-1.6(a), 4-1.7(b), and 4-1.18. The communication necessary to obtain such consent will vary according to the rule involved and the circumstances giving rise to the need to obtain informed consent. The lawyer must make reasonable efforts to ensure that the client or other person possesses information reasonably adequate to make an informed decision. Ordinarily, this will require communication that includes a disclosure of the facts and circumstances giving rise to the situation, any explanation reasonably necessary to inform the client or other person of the material advantages and disadvantages of the proposed course of conduct, and a discussion of the client's or other person's options and alternatives.

[6] In some circumstances it may be appropriate for a lawyer to advise a client or other person to seek the advice of other counsel. A lawyer need not inform a client or other person of facts or implications already known to the client or other person; nevertheless, a lawyer who does not personally inform the client or other person assumes the risk that the

client or other person is inadequately informed and the consent is invalid. In determining whether the information and explanation provided are reasonably adequate, relevant factors include whether the client or other person is experienced in legal matters generally and in making decisions of the type involved, and whether the client or other person is independently represented by other counsel in giving the consent. Normally, such persons need less information and explanation than others, and generally a client or other person who is independently represented by other counsel in giving the consent should be assumed to have given informed consent.

[7] Obtaining informed consent will usually require an affirmative response by the client or other person. In general, a lawyer may not assume consent from a client's or other person's silence. Consent may be inferred, however, from the conduct of a client or other person who has reasonably adequate information about the matter. A number of rules state that a person's consent be confirmed in writing. See, e.g., rule 4-1.7(b). For a definition of "writing" and "confirmed in writing," see terminology above. Other rules require that a client's consent be obtained in a writing signed by the client. See, e.g., rule 4-1.8(a). For a definition of "signed," see terminology above.

Screened

[8] This definition applies to situations where screening of a personally disqualified lawyer is permitted to remove imputation of a conflict of interest under rules 4-1.11, 4-1.12, or 4-1.18. The purpose of screening is to assure the affected parties that confidential information known by the personally disqualified lawyer remains protected. The personally disqualified lawyer should acknowledge the obligation not to communicate with any of the other lawyers in the firm with respect to the matter. Similarly, other lawyers in the firm who are working on the matter should be informed that the screening is in place and that they may not communicate with the personally disqualified lawyer with respect to the matter. Additional screening measures that are appropriate for the particular matter will depend on the circumstances.

[9] To implement, reinforce, and remind all affected lawyers of the presence of the screening, it may be appropriate for the firm to undertake such procedures as a written undertaking by the screened lawyer to avoid any communication with other firm personnel and any contact with any firm files or other materials relating to the matter, written notice and instructions to all other firm personnel forbidding any communication

Components of Screening in Conflict of Interest Cases

with the screened lawyer relating to the matter, denial of access by the screened lawyer to firm files or other materials relating to the matter, and periodic reminders of the screen to the screened lawyer and all other firm personnel. In order to be effective, screening measures must be implemented as soon as practicable after a lawyer or law firm knows or reasonably should know that there is a need for screening.

4-1. Client-Lawyer Relationship

Rule 4-1.1. Competence

A lawyer shall provide competent representation to a client. Competent representation requires the legal knowledge, skill, thoroughness, and preparation reasonably necessary for the representation.

Defining Competence

Official Comments on Rule 4-1.1 (Competence)

Legal knowledge and skill (Comment on Rule 4-1.1)

[1] In determining whether a lawyer employs the requisite knowledge and skill in a particular matter, relevant factors include the relative complexity and specialized nature of the matter, the lawyer's general experience, the lawyer's training and experience in the field in question, the preparation and study the lawyer is able to give the matter, and whether it is feasible to refer the matter to, or associate or consult with, a lawyer of established competence in the field in question. In many instances the required proficiency is that of a general practitioner. Expertise in a particular field of law may be required in some circumstances.

Factors Determining Competence

[2] A lawyer need not necessarily have special training or prior experience to handle legal problems of a type with which the lawyer is unfamiliar. A newly admitted lawyer can be as competent as a practitioner with long experience. Some important legal skills, such as the analysis of precedent, the evaluation of evidence and legal drafting, are required in all legal problems. Perhaps the most fundamental legal skill consists of determining what kind of legal problems a situation may involve, a skill that necessarily transcends any particular specialized knowledge. A lawyer can provide adequate representation in a wholly novel field through necessary study. Competent representation can also be provided through the association of a lawyer of established competence in the field in question.

The Skills a Lawyer Should Have

[3] In an emergency a lawyer may give advice or assistance in a matter in which the lawyer does not

Giving Legal Advice in an Emergency

have the skill ordinarily required where referral to or consultation or association with another lawyer would be impractical. Even in an emergency, however, assistance should be limited to that reasonably necessary in the circumstances, for ill-considered action under emergency conditions can jeopardize the client's interest.

[4] A lawyer may accept representation where the requisite level of competence can be achieved by reasonable preparation. This applies as well to a lawyer who is appointed as counsel for an unrepresented person. See also rule 4-6.2.

Thoroughness and preparation (Comment on Rule 4-1.1)

[5] Competent handling of a particular matter includes inquiry into and analysis of the factual and legal elements of the problem, and use of methods and procedures meeting the standards of competent practitioners. It also includes adequate preparation. The required attention and preparation are determined in part by what is at stake; major litigation and complex transactions ordinarily require more extensive treatment than matters of lesser complexity and consequence. The lawyer should consult with the client about the degree of thoroughness and the level of preparation required as well as the estimated costs involved under the circumstances.

| A Lawyer's Requirement to Prepare Adequately |

Maintaining competence (Comment on Rule 4-1.1)

[6] To maintain the requisite knowledge and skill, a lawyer should keep abreast of changes in the law and its practice, engage in continuing study and education, and comply with all continuing legal education requirements to which the lawyer is subject.

| CLE: Continuing Legal Education |

Rule 4-1.2. Objectives and Scope of Representation

(a) Lawyer to Abide by Client's Decisions. Subject to subdivisions (c) and (d), a lawyer shall abide by a client's decisions concerning the objectives of representation, and, as required by rule 4-1.4, shall reasonably consult with the client as to the means by which they are to be pursued. A lawyer may take such action on behalf of the client as is impliedly authorized to carry out the representation. A lawyer shall abide by a client's decision whether to settle a matter. In a criminal case, the lawyer shall abide by the client's decision, after consultation with the lawyer, as to a plea to be entered, whether to waive jury trial, and whether the client will testify.

| Determining a Client's Wishes |

(b) No Endorsement of Client's Views or Activities. A lawyer's representation of a client, including representation by appointment, does not constitute an endorsement of the client's political, economic, social, or moral views or activities.

| The Political and Moral Views of a Client |

(c) Limitation of Objectives and Scope of Representation. If not prohibited by law or rule, a lawyer and client may agree to limit the objectives or scope of the representation if the limitation is reasonable under the circumstances and the client gives informed consent in writing. If the attorney and client agree to limit the scope of the representation, the lawyer shall advise the client regarding applicability of the rule prohibiting communication with a represented person.

(d) Criminal or Fraudulent Conduct. A lawyer shall not counsel a client to engage, or assist a client, in conduct that the lawyer knows or reasonably should know is criminal or fraudulent. However, a lawyer may discuss the legal consequences of any proposed course of conduct with a client and may counsel or assist a client to make a good faith effort to determine the validity, scope, meaning, or application of the law.

| Criminal or Fraudulent Conduct |

Official Comments on Rule 4-1.2 (Objectives and Scope of Representation)

Allocation of authority between client and lawyer (Comment on Rule 4-1.2)

[1] Subdivision (a) confers upon the client the ultimate authority to determine the purposes to be served by legal representation, within the limits imposed by law and the lawyer's professional obligations. Within those limits, a client also has a right to consult with the lawyer about the means to be used in pursuing those objectives. At the same time, a lawyer is not required to pursue objectives or employ means simply because a client may wish that the lawyer do so.

[2] A clear distinction between objectives and means sometimes cannot be drawn, and in many cases the client-lawyer relationship partakes of a joint undertaking. In questions of means, the lawyer should assume responsibility for technical and legal tactical issues but should defer to the client regarding such questions as the expense to be incurred and concern for third persons who might be adversely affected. Law defining the lawyer's scope of authority in litigation varies among jurisdictions. The decisions specified

| The Objectives of Representation vs the Means to Accomplish Them |

in subdivision (a), such as whether to settle a civil matter, must also be made by the client. See rule 4-1.4(a)(1) for the lawyer's duty to communicate with the client about such decisions. With respect to the means by which the client's objectives are to be pursued, the lawyer shall consult with the client as required by rule 4-1.4(a)(2) and may take such action as is impliedly authorized to carry out the representation.

[3] On occasion, however, a lawyer and a client may disagree about the means to be used to accomplish the client's objectives. The lawyer should consult with the client and seek a mutually acceptable resolution of the disagreement. If such efforts are unavailing and the lawyer has a fundamental disagreement with the client, the lawyer may withdraw from the representation. See rule 4-1.16(b)(4). Conversely, the client may resolve the disagreement by discharging the lawyer. See rule 4-1.16(a)(3).

[4] At the outset of a representation, the client may authorize the lawyer to take specific action on the client's behalf without further consultation. Absent a material change in circumstances and subject to rule 4-1.4, a lawyer may rely on such an advance authorization. The client may, however, revoke such authority at any time.

[5] In a case in which the client appears to be suffering mental disability, the lawyer's duty to abide by the client's decisions is to be guided by reference to rule 4-1.14.

Independence from client's views or activities (Comment on Rule 4-1.2)

[6] Legal representation should not be denied to people who are unable to afford legal services or whose cause is controversial or the subject of popular disapproval. By the same token representing a client does not constitute approval of the client's views or activities.

> **The Independence of a Lawyer**

Agreements limiting scope of representation (Comment on Rule 4-1.2)

[7] The scope of services to be provided by a lawyer may be limited by agreement with the client or by the terms under which the lawyer's services are made available to the client. When a lawyer has been retained by an insurer to represent an insured, for example, the representation may be limited to matters related to the insurance coverage. A limited representation may be appropriate because the client has limited objectives for the representation. In addition, the terms upon which representation is undertaken may exclude specific means that might otherwise be used to accomplish the client's objectives.

> **Limiting the Scope of Representation**

[8] Such limitations may exclude actions that the client thinks are too costly or that the lawyer regards as repugnant or imprudent, or which the client regards as financially impractical.

> **Repugnant, Imprudent, or Impractical Actions**

[9] Although this rule affords the lawyer and client substantial latitude to limit the representation if not prohibited by law or rule, the limitation must be reasonable under the circumstances. If, for example, a client's objective is limited to securing general information about the law the client needs in order to handle a common and typically uncomplicated legal problem, the lawyer and client may agree that the lawyer's services will be limited to a brief consultation. Such a limitation, however, would not be reasonable if the time allotted was not sufficient to yield advice upon which the client could rely. In addition, a lawyer and client may agree that the representation will be limited to providing assistance out of court, including providing advice on the operation of the court system and drafting pleadings and responses.

[10] If the lawyer assists a pro se litigant by drafting any document to be submitted to a court, the lawyer is not obligated to sign the document. However, the lawyer must indicate "Prepared with the assistance of counsel" on the document to avoid misleading the court, which otherwise might be under the impression that the person, who appears to be proceeding pro se, has received no assistance from a lawyer.

> **Assisting a Pro Se Litigant**

[11] If not prohibited by law or rule, a lawyer and client may agree that any in-court representation in a family law proceeding be limited as provided for in Family Law Rule of Procedure 12.040. For example, a lawyer and client may agree that the lawyer will represent the client at a hearing regarding child support and not at the final hearing or in any other hearings. For limited in-court representation in family law proceedings, the attorney shall communicate to the client the specific boundaries and limitations of the representation so that the client is able to give informed consent to the representation.

> **Family Law Representation**

[12] Regardless of the circumstances, a lawyer providing limited representation forms an attorney-client relationship with the litigant, and owes the client all attendant ethical obligations and duties imposed by the Rules Regulating The Florida Bar, including, but not limited to, duties of competence, communication, confidentiality, and avoidance of conflicts of interest. Although an agreement for limited representation does not exempt a lawyer from the duty to provide competent representation, the limitation is a factor to be considered when determining the legal knowledge, skill,

thoroughness, and preparation reasonably necessary for the representation. See rule 4-1.1.

[13] An agreement concerning the scope of representation must accord with the Rules of Professional Conduct and law. For example, the client may not be asked to agree to representation so limited in scope as to violate rule 4-1.1 or to surrender the right to terminate the lawyer's services or the right to settle litigation that the lawyer might wish to continue.

Criminal, fraudulent, and prohibited transactions (Comment on Rule 4-1.2)

[14] A lawyer is required to give an honest opinion about the actual consequences that

> **Assisting Client in Criminal or Fraudulent Conduct**

appear likely to result from a client's conduct. The fact that a client uses advice in a course of action that is criminal or fraudulent does not, of itself, make a lawyer a party to the course of action. However, a lawyer may not assist a client in conduct that the lawyer knows or reasonably should know to be criminal or fraudulent. There is a critical distinction between presenting an analysis of legal aspects of questionable conduct and recommending the means by which a crime or fraud might be committed with impunity.

[15] When the client's course of action has already begun and is continuing, the lawyer's

> **Improperly Assisting the Concealment of Wrongdoing**

responsibility is especially delicate. The lawyer is required to avoid assisting the client, for example, by drafting or delivering documents that the lawyer knows are fraudulent or by suggesting how the wrongdoing might be concealed. A lawyer may not continue assisting a client in conduct that the lawyer originally supposed was legally proper but then discovers is criminal or fraudulent. The lawyer must, therefore, withdraw from the representation of the client in the matter. See rule 4-1.16(a). In some cases, withdrawal alone might be insufficient. It may be necessary for the lawyer to give notice of the fact of withdrawal and to disaffirm any opinion, document, affirmation, or the like. See rule 4-4.1.

[16] Where the client is a fiduciary, the lawyer may be charged with special obligations in dealings with a beneficiary.

[17] Subdivision (d) applies whether or not the defrauded party is a party to the trans-

> **Advice on Criminal or Fraudulent Avoidance of Tax Liability**

action. For example, a lawyer must not participate in a transaction to effectuate criminal or fraudulent avoidance of tax liability. Subdivision (d) does not preclude undertaking a criminal defense incident to a general retainer for legal services to a lawful enterprise. The last sentence of subdivision (d) recognizes that determining the validity or interpretation of a statute or regulation may require a course of action involving disobedience of the statute or regulation or of the interpretation placed upon it by governmental authorities.

[18] If a lawyer comes to know or reasonably should know that a client expects assistance not permitted by the Rules of Professional Conduct or other law or if the lawyer intends to act contrary to the client's instructions, the lawyer must consult with the client regarding the limitations on the lawyer's conduct. See rule 4-1.4(a)(5).

Rule 4-1.3. Diligence

A lawyer shall act with reasonable diligence and promptness in representing a client.

> **Diligence in Representing a Client**

Official Comments on Rule 4-1.3 (Diligence)

[1] A lawyer should pursue a matter on behalf of a client despite opposition, obstruction, or personal inconvenience to the lawyer and take whatever lawful and ethical measures are required to vindicate a client's cause or endeavor. A lawyer must also act with commitment and dedication to the interests of the client and with zeal in advocacy upon the client's behalf. A lawyer is not bound, however, to press for every advantage that might be realized for a client. For example, a lawyer may have authority to exercise professional discretion in determining the means by which a matter should be pursued. See rule 4-1.2. The lawyer's duty to act with reasonable diligence does not require the use of offensive tactics or preclude the treating of all persons involved in the legal process with courtesy and respect.

[2] A lawyer's workload must be controlled so that each matter can be handled competently.

> **Controlling the Law Firm's Workload**

[3] Perhaps no professional shortcoming is more widely resented than procrastination. A client's interests often can be adversely affected by the passage of time

> **Procrastination; Missing the Statute of Limitations**

or the change of conditions; in extreme instances, as when a lawyer overlooks a statute of limitations, the client's legal position may be destroyed. Even when the client's interests are not affected in substance, however, unreasonable delay can cause a client needless anxiety and undermine confidence in the lawyer. A lawyer's duty to act with reasonable promptness, however, does not preclude the lawyer from agreeing to a reasonable request for a postponement that will not prejudice the lawyer's client.

[4] Unless the relationship is terminated as provided in

rule 4-1.16, a lawyer should carry through to conclusion all matters undertaken for a client. If a lawyer's employment is limited to a specific matter, the relationship terminates when the matter has been resolved. If a lawyer has served a client over a substantial period in a variety of matters, the client sometimes may assume that the lawyer will continue to serve on a continuing basis unless the lawyer gives notice of withdrawal. Doubt about whether a client-lawyer relationship still exists should be clarified by the lawyer, preferably in writing, so that the client will not mistakenly suppose the lawyer is looking after the client's affairs when the lawyer has ceased to do so. For example, if a lawyer has handled a judicial or administrative proceeding that produced a result adverse to the client and the lawyer and the client have not agreed that the lawyer will handle the matter on appeal, the lawyer must consult with the client about the possibility of appeal before relinquishing responsibility for the matter. See rule 4-1.4(a)(2). Whether the lawyer is obligated to prosecute the appeal for the client depends on the scope of the representation the lawyer has agreed to provide to the client. See rule 4-1.2.

Rule 4-1.4. Communication

(a) Informing Client of Status of Representation. A lawyer shall:

(1) promptly inform the client of any decision or circumstance with respect to which

Keeping the Client Informed

the client's informed consent, as defined in terminology, is required by these rules;

(2) reasonably consult with the client about the means by which the client's objectives are to be accomplished;

(3) keep the client reasonably informed about the status of the matter;

(4) promptly comply with reasonable requests for information; and

(5) consult with the client about any relevant limitation on the lawyer's conduct when the lawyer knows or reasonably should know that the client expects assistance not permitted by the Rules of Professional Conduct or other law.

(b) Duty to Explain Matters to Client. A lawyer shall explain a matter to the extent reasonably necessary to permit the client to make informed decisions regarding the representation.

Official Comments on Rule 4-1.4 (Communication)

[1] Reasonable communication between the lawyer and the client is necessary for the client to effectively participate in the representation.

Communicating with client (Comment on Rule 4-1.4)

[2] If these rules require that a particular decision about the representation be made by the client, subdivision (a)(1) requires that the lawyer promptly consult with and secure the client's consent prior to taking action unless prior discussions with the client have resolved what action the client wants the lawyer to take. For example, a lawyer who receives from opposing counsel an offer of settlement in a civil controversy or a proffered plea bargain in a criminal case must promptly inform the client of its substance unless the client has previously indicated that the proposal will be acceptable or unacceptable or has authorized the lawyer to accept or to reject the offer. See rule 4-1.2(a).

[3] Subdivision (a)(2) requires the lawyer to reasonably consult with the client about the means to be used to accomplish the client's objectives. In some situations—depending on both the importance of the action under consideration and the feasibility of consulting with the client—this duty will require consultation prior to taking action. In other circumstances, such as during a trial when an immediate decision must be made, the exigency of the situation may require the lawyer to act without prior consultation. In such cases the lawyer must nonetheless act reasonably to inform the client of actions the lawyer has taken on the client's behalf. Additionally, subdivision (a)(3) requires that the lawyer keep the client reasonably informed about the status of the matter, such as significant developments affecting the timing or the substance of the representation.

[4] A lawyer's regular communication with clients will minimize the occasions on which a client will need to request information concerning the represen-

Promptly Answering a Client's Questions; Duty of Lawyer's Staff

tation. When a client makes a reasonable request for information, however, subdivision (a)(4) requires prompt compliance with the request, or if a prompt response is not feasible, that the lawyer, or *a member of the lawyer's staff, acknowledge receipt of the request and advise the client when a response may be expected.* (Emphasis added.)

Explaining Matters (Comment on Rule 4-1.4)

[5] The client should have sufficient information to participate intelligently in decisions concerning the objectives of the representation and the means by which they are to be pursued, to the extent the client is willing and able to do so.

[6] Adequacy of communication depends in part on the kind of advice or assistance that is involved. For example, when there is time to explain a proposal made in a

Explaining Strategy and the Prospect of Success to a Client

negotiation, the lawyer should review all important provisions with the client before proceeding to an agreement. In litigation a lawyer should explain the general strategy and prospects of success and ordinarily should consult the client on tactics that are likely to result in significant expense or to injure or coerce others. On the other hand, a lawyer ordinarily will not be expected to describe trial or negotiation strategy in detail. The guiding principle is that the lawyer should fulfill reasonable client expectations for information consistent with the duty to act in the client's best interests and the client's overall requirements as to the character of representation. In certain circumstances, such as when a lawyer asks a client to consent to a representation affected by a conflict of interest, the client must give informed consent, as defined in terminology.

[7] Ordinarily, the information to be provided is that

Representing an Organization

appropriate for a client who is a comprehending and responsible adult. However, fully informing the client according to this standard may be impracticable, for example, where the client is a child or suffers from mental disability. See rule 4-1.14. When the client is an organization or group, it is often impossible or inappropriate to inform every one of its members about its legal affairs; ordinarily, the lawyer should address communications to the appropriate officials of the organization. See rule 4-1.13. Where many routine matters are involved, a system of limited or occasional reporting may be arranged with the client.

Withholding Information (Comment on Rule 4-1.4)

[8] In some circumstances, a lawyer may be justified in delaying transmission of information when the client

Withholding Information from a Client

would be likely to react imprudently to an immediate communication. Thus, a lawyer might withhold a psychiatric diagnosis of a client when the examining psychiatrist indicates that disclosure would harm the client. A lawyer may not withhold information to serve the lawyer's own interest or convenience or the interests or convenience of another person. Rules or court orders governing litigation may provide that information supplied to a lawyer may not be disclosed to the client. Rule 4-3.4(c) directs compliance with such rules or orders.

Rule 4-1.5. Fees and Costs for Legal Services

(a) Illegal, Prohibited, or Clearly Excessive Fees and Costs. An attorney shall not enter into an agree-

Improper Legal Fees

ment for, charge, or collect an illegal, prohibited, or clearly excessive fee or cost, or a fee generated by

employment that was obtained through advertising or solicitation not in compliance with the Rules Regulating The Florida Bar. A fee or cost is clearly excessive when:

(1) after a review of the facts, a lawyer of ordinary prudence would be left with a definite and firm conviction that the fee or the cost exceeds a reasonable fee or cost for services provided to such a degree as to constitute clear over-reaching or an unconscionable demand by the attorney; or

(2) the fee or cost is sought or secured by the attorney by means of intentional misrepresentation or fraud upon the client, a nonclient party, or any court, as to either entitlement to, or amount of, the fee.

(b) Factors to Be Considered in Determining Reasonable Fees and Costs.

(1) Factors to be considered as guides in determining a reasonable fee include:

Factors That Determine the Reasonableness of Fees

(A) the time and labor required, the novelty, complexity, and difficulty of the questions involved, and the skill requisite to perform the legal service properly;

(B) the likelihood that the acceptance of the particular employment will preclude other employment by the lawyer;

(C) the fee, or rate of fee, customarily charged in the locality for legal services of a comparable or similar nature;

(D) the significance of, or amount involved in, the subject matter of the representation, the responsibility involved in the representation, and the results obtained;

(E) the time limitations imposed by the client or by the circumstances and, as between attorney and client, any additional or special time demands or requests of the attorney by the client;

(F) the nature and length of the professional relationship with the client;

(G) the experience, reputation, diligence, and ability of the lawyer or lawyers performing the service and the skill, expertise, or efficiency of effort reflected in the actual providing of such services; and

(H) whether the fee is fixed or contingent, and, if fixed as to amount or rate, then whether the client's ability to pay rested to any significant degree on the outcome of the representation.

(2) Factors to be considered as guides in determining reasonable costs include:

(A) the nature and extent of the disclosure made to the client about the costs;

(B) whether a specific agreement exists between the lawyer and client as to the costs a client is expected to pay and how a cost is calculated that is charged to a client;

Factors That Determine the Reasonableness of Costs

(C) the actual amount charged by third party providers of services to the attorney;

(D) whether specific costs can be identified and allocated to an individual client or a reasonable basis exists to estimate the costs charged;

(E) the reasonable charges for providing in-house service to a client if the cost is an in-house charge for services; and

(F) the relationship and past course of conduct between the lawyer and the client.

All costs are subject to the test of reasonableness set forth in subdivision (a) above. When the parties have a written contract in which the method is established for charging costs, the costs charged thereunder shall be presumed reasonable.

(c) Consideration of All Factors. In determining a reasonable fee, the time devoted to the representation and customary rate of fee need not be the sole or controlling factors. All factors set forth in this rule should be considered, and may be applied, in justification of a fee higher or lower than that which would result from application of only the time and rate factors.

(d) Enforceability of Fee Contracts. Contracts or agreements for attorney's fees between attorney and client will ordinarily be enforceable according to the terms of such contracts or agreements, unless found to be illegal, obtained through advertising or solicitation not in compliance with the Rules Regulating The Florida Bar, prohibited by this rule, or clearly excessive as defined by this rule.

Fee Agreements

(e) Duty to Communicate Basis or Rate of Fee or Costs to Client. When the lawyer has not regularly represented the client, the basis or rate of the fee and costs shall be communicated to the client, preferably in writing, before or within a reasonable time after commencing the representation.

The fact that a contract may not be in accord with these rules is an issue between the attorney and client and a matter of professional ethics, but is not the proper basis for an action or defense by an opposing party when fee-shifting litigation is involved.

Fee-Shifting Litigation

(f) Contingent Fees. As to contingent fees:

(1) A fee may be contingent on the outcome of the matter for which the service is rendered, except in a matter in which a contingent fee is prohibited

Contingent Fees

by subdivision (f)(3) or by law. A contingent fee agreement shall be in writing and shall state the method by which the fee is to be determined, including the percentage or percentages that shall accrue to the lawyer in the event of settlement, trial, or appeal, litigation and other expenses to be deducted from the recovery, and whether such expenses are to be deducted before or after the contingent fee is calculated. Upon conclusion of a contingent fee matter, the lawyer shall provide the client with a written statement stating the outcome of the matter and, if there is a recovery, showing the remittance to the client and the method of its determination.

(2) Every lawyer who accepts a retainer or enters into an agreement, express or implied, for compensation for services rendered or to be rendered in any action, claim, or proceeding whereby the lawyer's compensation is to be dependent or contingent in whole or in part upon the successful prosecution or settlement thereof shall do so only where such fee arrangement is reduced to a written contract, signed by the client, and by a lawyer for the lawyer or for the law firm representing the client. No lawyer or firm may participate in the fee without the consent of the client in writing. Each participating lawyer or law firm shall sign the contract with the client and shall agree to assume joint legal responsibility to the client for the performance of the services in question as if each were partners of the other lawyer or law firm involved. The client shall be furnished with a copy of the signed contract and any subsequent notices or consents. All provisions of this rule shall apply to such fee contracts.

Contingent Fee Agreements Must Be in Writing

(3) A lawyer shall not enter into an arrangement for, charge, or collect:

(A) any fee in a domestic relations matter, the payment or amount of which is contingent upon the securing of a divorce or upon the amount of alimony or support, or property settlement in lieu thereof; or

(B) a contingent fee for representing a defendant in a criminal case.

Contingent Fees in Domestic Relations and Criminal Cases

(4) A lawyer who enters into an arrangement for, charges, or collects any fee in an action or claim for personal injury or for property damages or for death or loss of services resulting from personal injuries based upon tortious

Contingent Fees in Tort and Property Damage Cases

conduct of another, including products liability claims, whereby the compensation is to be dependent or contingent in whole or in part upon the successful prosecution or settlement thereof shall do so only under the following requirements:

(A) The contract shall contain the . . . provisions in Exhibit 3.2A.

EXHIBIT 3.2A	Required Client Disclosures When a Contingent Fee is Sought in Tort and Property Cases Under Rule 4-1.5(f)(4)(A)

(i) "The undersigned client has, before signing this contract, received and read the statement of client's rights and understands each of the rights set forth therein. The undersigned client has signed the statement and received a signed copy to refer to while being represented by the undersigned attorney(s)."

(ii) "This contract may be cancelled by written notification to the attorney at any time within 3 business days of the date the contract was signed, as shown below, and if cancelled the client shall not be obligated to pay any fees to the attorney for the work performed during that time. If the attorney has advanced funds to others in representation of the client, the attorney is entitled to be reimbursed for such amounts as the attorney has reasonably advanced on behalf of the client."

(B) The contract for representation of a client in a matter set forth in subdivision (f)(4) may provide for a contingent fee arrangement as agreed upon by the client and the lawyer, except as limited by the following provisions:

Contingent Fees That Are Presumed to Be Excessive

(i) Without prior court approval as specified below, any contingent fee that exceeds the following standards shall be presumed, unless rebutted, to be clearly excessive:

a. Before the filing of an answer or the demand for appointment of arbitrators or, if no answer is filed or no demand for appointment of arbitrators is made, the expiration of the time period provided for such action:
1. 33 1/3% of any recovery up to $1 million; plus
2. 30% of any portion of the recovery between $1 million and $2 million; plus
3. 20% of any portion of the recovery exceeding $2 million.

b. After the filing of an answer or the demand for appointment of arbi-

trators or, if no answer is filed or no demand for appointment of arbitrators is made, the expiration of the time period provided for such action, through the entry of judgment:
1. 40% of any recovery up to $1 million; plus
2. 30% of any portion of the recovery between $1 million and $2 million; plus
3. 20% of any portion of the recovery exceeding $2 million.

c. If all defendants admit liability at the time of filing their answers and request a trial only on damages:
1. 33 1/3% of any recovery up to $1 million; plus
2. 20% of any portion of the recovery between $1 million and $2 million; plus
3. 15% of any portion of the recovery exceeding $2 million.

d. An additional 5% of any recovery after institution of any appellate proceeding is filed or post-judgment relief or action is required for recovery on the judgment.

(ii) If any client is unable to obtain an attorney of the client's choice because of the limitations set forth in subdivision (f)(4)(B)(i), the client may petition the court in which the matter would be filed, if litigation is necessary, or if such court will not accept jurisdiction for the fee division, the circuit court wherein the cause of action arose, for approval of any fee contract between the client and an attorney of the client's choosing. Such authorization shall be given if the court determines the client has a complete understanding of the client's rights and the terms of the proposed contract. The application for authorization of such a contract can be filed as a separate proceeding before suit or simultaneously with the filing of a complaint. Proceedings thereon may occur before service on the defendant and this aspect of the file may be sealed. A petition under this subdivision shall contain a certificate showing service on the client and, if the petition is denied, a copy of the petition and order denying the petition shall be served on The Florida Bar in Tallahassee by the member of the bar who filed the petition. Authorization of such a contract shall not bar subsequent inquiry as to whether the fee actually claimed or charged is clearly excessive under subdivisions (a) and (b).

(iii) Subject to the provisions of 4-1.5(f)(4)(B)(i) and (ii) a lawyer who enters into an arrangement for, charges, or collects any fee in an action or claim for medical liability whereby the compensation is dependent or contingent in whole or in part upon the successful prosecution or settlement thereof shall provide the language of *article I, section 26 of the Florida Constitution* to the client in writing and shall orally inform the client that:

| Contingent Fees in Medical Liability Cases |

a. [See Exhibit 3.2B]

| EXHIBIT 3.2B | **Required Client Disclosure When a Contingent Fee Is Sought in a Medical Liability Case under Rule 4-1.5(f)(4)(B)(iii)(a)** |

Unless waived, in any medical liability claim involving a contingency fee,

- The claimant is entitled to receive no less than 70% of the first $250,000.00 of all damages received by the claimant, exclusive of reasonable and customary costs, whether received by judgment, settlement, or otherwise, and regardless of the number of defendants.
- The claimant is entitled to 90% of all damages in excess of $250,000.00, exclusive of reasonable and customary costs and regardless of the number of defendants.

---

b. If a lawyer chooses not to accept the representation of a client under the terms of *article I, section 26 of the Florida Constitution*, the lawyer shall advise the client, both orally and in writing of alternative terms, if any, under which the lawyer would accept the representation of the client, as well as the client's right to seek representation by another lawyer willing to accept the representation under the terms of *article I, section 26 of the Florida Constitution*, or a lawyer willing to accept the representation on a fee basis that is not contingent.

c. If any client desires to waive any rights under *article I, section 26 of the Florida Constitution* in order to obtain a lawyer of the client's choice, a client may do so by waiving such rights in writing, under oath, and in the form provided in this rule. The lawyer shall provide each client a copy of the written waiver and shall afford each client a full and complete opportunity to understand the rights being waived as set forth in the waiver. A copy of the waiver, signed by each client and lawyer, shall be given to each client to retain, and the lawyer shall keep a copy in the lawyer's file pertaining to the client. The waiver shall be retained by the lawyer with the written fee contract and closing statement under the same conditions and requirements provided in 4-1.5(f)(5). [See Exhibit 3.2C]

| Waiver of Client Rights in Medical Liability Contingent Cases |

(C) Before a lawyer enters into a contingent fee contract for representation of a client in a matter set forth in this rule, the lawyer shall provide the client with a copy of the statement of client's rights and shall afford the client a full and complete opportunity to understand each of the rights as set forth therein. A copy of the statement, signed by both the client and the lawyer, shall be given to the client to retain and the lawyer shall keep a copy in the client's file. The statement shall be retained by the lawyer with the written fee contract and closing statement under the same conditions and requirements as subdivision (f)(5).

(D) As to lawyers not in the same firm, a division of any fee within subdivision (f)(4) shall be on the following basis:

| Division of Fees in a Contingent Fee Medical Liability Case |

(i) To the lawyer assuming primary responsibility for the legal services on behalf of the client, a minimum of 75% of the total fee.

(ii) To the lawyer assuming secondary responsibility for the legal services on behalf of the client, a maximum of 25% of the total fee. Any fee in excess of 25% shall be presumed to be clearly excessive.

(iii) The 25% limitation shall not apply to those cases in which 2 or more lawyers

EXHIBIT 3.2C	Waiver When a Contingent Fee Is Sought in a Medical Liability Case Under Rule 4–1.5(f)(4)(B)(iii)(c)

WAIVER OF THE CONSTITUTIONAL RIGHT PROVIDED IN *ARTICLE I, SECTION 26 OF THE FLORIDA CONSTITUTION*

On November 2, 2004, voters in the State of Florida approved The Medical Liability Claimant's Compensation Amendment that was identified as Amendment 3 on the ballot. The amendment is set forth below:

The Florida Constitution

Article I, Section 26 is created to read "Claimant's right to fair compensation." In any medical liability claim involving a contingency fee, the claimant is entitled to receive no less than 70% of the first $250,000 in all damages received by the claimant, exclusive of reasonable and customary costs, whether received by judgment, settlement or otherwise, and regardless of the number of defendants. The claimant is entitled to 90% of all damages in excess of $250,000, exclusive of reasonable and customary costs and regardless of the number of defendants. This provision is self-executing and does not require implementing legislation.

The undersigned client understands and acknowledges that (initial each provision):
_____ I have been advised that signing this waiver releases an important constitutional right; and
_____ I have been advised that I may consult with separate counsel before signing this waiver; and that I may request a hearing before a judge to further explain this waiver; and
_____ By signing this waiver I agree to an **increase in the attorney fee** that might otherwise be owed if the constitutional provision listed above is not waived. Without prior court approval, the increased fee that I agree to may be up to the maximum contingency fee percentages set forth in Rule Regulating The Florida Bar 4-1.5(f)(4)(B)(i). Depending on the circumstances of my case, the maximum agreed upon fee may range from 33 1/3% to 40% of any recovery up to $1 million; plus 20% to 30% of any portion of the recovery between $1 million and $2 million; plus 15% to 20% of any recovery exceeding $2 million; and
_____ I have three (3) business days following execution of this waiver in which to cancel this waiver; and
_____ I wish to engage the legal services of the lawyers or law firms listed below in an action or claim for medical liability the fee for which is contingent in whole or in part upon the successful prosecution or settlement thereof, but I am unable to do so because of the provisions of the constitutional limitation set forth above. In consideration of the lawyers' or law firms' agreements to represent me and my desire to employ the lawyers or law firms listed below, I hereby knowingly, willingly, and voluntarily waive any and all rights and privileges that I may have under the constitutional provision set forth above, as apply to the contingency fee agreement only. Specifically, I waive the percentage restrictions that are the subject of the constitutional provision and confirm the fee percentages set forth in the contingency fee agreement; and
_____ I have selected the lawyers or law firms listed below as my counsel of choice in this matter and would not be able to engage their services without this waiver; and I expressly state that this waiver is made freely and voluntarily, with full knowledge of its terms, and that all questions have been answered to my satisfaction.

ACKNOWLEDGMENT BY CLIENT FOR PRESENTATION TO THE COURT

The undersigned client hereby acknowledges, under oath, the following:

- I have read and understand this entire waiver of my rights under the constitutional provision set forth above.
- I am not under the influence of any substance, drug, or condition (physical, mental, or emotional) that interferes with my understanding of this entire waiver in which I am entering and all the consequences thereof.
- I have entered into and signed this waiver freely and voluntarily.
- I authorize my lawyers or law firms listed below to present this waiver to the appropriate court, if required for purposes of approval of the contingency fee agreement. Unless the court requires my attendance at a hearing for that purpose, my lawyers or law firms are authorized to provide this waiver to the court for its consideration without my presence.

DATED this _____ day of _____, _____.

By: _____

CLIENT

Sworn to and subscribed before me this _____ day of _____, _____ by _____, who is personally known to me, or has produced the following identification: _____.

Notary Public

My Commission Expires:

Dated this _____ day of _____, _____.

By: _____

ATTORNEY

or firms accept substantially equal active participation in the providing of legal services. In such circumstances counsel shall apply to the court in which the matter would be filed, if litigation is necessary, or if such court will not accept jurisdiction for the fee division, the circuit court wherein the cause of action arose, for authorization of the fee division in excess of 25%, based upon a sworn petition signed by all counsel that shall disclose in detail those services to be performed. The application for authorization of such a contract may be filed as a separate proceeding before suit or simultaneously with the filing of a complaint, or within 10 days of execution of a contract for division of fees when new counsel is engaged. Proceedings thereon may occur before service of process on any party and this aspect of the file may be sealed. Authorization of such contract shall not bar subsequent inquiry as to whether the fee actually claimed or charged is clearly excessive. An application under this subdivision shall contain a certificate showing service on the client and, if the application is denied, a copy of the petition and order denying the petition shall be served on The Florida Bar in Tallahassee by the member of the bar who filed the petition. Counsel may proceed with representation of the client pending court approval.

(iv) The percentages required by this subdivision shall be applicable after deduction of any fee payable to separate counsel retained especially for appellate purposes.

(5) In the event there is a recovery, upon the conclusion of the representation, the lawyer shall prepare a closing statement reflecting an itemization of all costs and expenses, together with the amount of fee received by each participating lawyer or law firm. A copy of the closing statement shall be executed by all participating lawyers, as well as the client, and each shall receive a copy. Each participating lawyer shall retain a copy of the written fee contract and closing statement for 6 years after execution of the closing statement. Any contingent fee contract and closing statement shall be available for inspection at reasonable times by the client, by any other person upon judicial order, or by the appropriate disciplinary agency.

| Closing Statement Itemizing Costs, Expenses, and Fees |

(6) In cases in which the client is to receive a recovery that will be paid to the client on a future

| Structured Verdict or Settlement |

structured or periodic basis, the contingent fee percentage shall be calculated only on the cost of the structured verdict or settlement or, if the cost is unknown, on the present money value of the structured verdict or settlement, whichever is less. If the damages and the fee are to be paid out over the long term future schedule, this limitation does not apply. No attorney may negotiate separately with the defendant for that attorney's fee in a structured verdict or settlement when such separate negotiations would place the attorney in a position of conflict.

(g) Division of Fees Between Lawyers in Different Firms. Subject to the provisions of subdivision (f)(4)(D), a division of fee between lawyers who are not in the same firm may be made only if the total fee is reasonable and:

| Fee Division Between Lawyers in Different Law Firms |

(1) the division is in proportion to the services performed by each lawyer; or

(2) by written agreement with the client:

    (A) each lawyer assumes joint legal responsibility for the representation and agrees to be available for consultation with the client; and

    (B) the agreement fully discloses that a division of fees will be made and the basis upon which the division of fees will be made.

(h) Credit Plans. A lawyer or law firm may accept payment under a credit plan. No higher fee shall be charged and no additional charge shall be imposed by reason of a lawyer's or law firm's participation in a credit plan.

| Payment of Fees by Credit |

[See Exhibit 3.2D for a summary statement of client rights in contingency cases.]

Official Comments on Rule 4-1.5 (Fees and Costs of Legal Services)

Bases or rate of fees and costs (Comment on Rule 4-1.5)

[1] When the lawyer has regularly represented a client, they ordinarily will have evolved an understanding concerning the basis or rate of the fee. The conduct of the lawyer and client in prior relationships is relevant when analyzing the requirements of this rule. In a new client-lawyer relationship, however, an understanding as to the fee should be promptly established. It is not necessary to recite all the factors that underlie the basis of the fee

| Communication with Clients about Fees |

EXHIBIT 3.2D	**Statement Of Client's Rights for Contingency Fees**

Before you, the prospective client, arrange a contingent fee agreement with a lawyer, you should understand this statement of your rights as a client. This statement is not a part of the actual contract between you and your lawyer, but, as a prospective client, you should be aware of these rights:

1　There is no legal requirement that a lawyer charge a client a set fee or a percentage of money recovered in a case. You, the client, have the right to talk with your lawyer about the proposed fee and to bargain about the rate or percentage as in any other contract. If you do not reach an agreement with 1 lawyer you may talk with other lawyers.

2.　Any contingent fee contract must be in writing and you have 3 business days to reconsider the contract. You may cancel the contract without any reason if you notify your lawyer in writing within 3 business days of signing the contract. If you withdraw from the contract within the first 3 business days, you do not owe the lawyer a fee although you may be responsible for the lawyer's actual costs during that time. If your lawyer begins to represent you, your lawyer may not withdraw from the case without giving you notice, delivering necessary papers to you, and allowing you time to employ another lawyer. Often, your lawyer must obtain court approval before withdrawing from a case. If you discharge your lawyer without good cause after the 3-day period, you may have to pay a fee for work the lawyer has done.

3.　Before hiring a lawyer, you, the client, have the right to know about the lawyer's education, training, and experience. If you ask, the lawyer should tell you specifically about the lawyer's actual experience dealing with cases similar to yours. If you ask, the lawyer should provide information about special training or knowledge and give you this information in writing if you request it.

4.　Before signing a contingent fee contract with you, a lawyer must advise you whether the lawyer intends to handle your case alone or whether other lawyers will be helping with the case. If your lawyer intends to refer the case to other lawyers, the lawyer should tell you what kind of fee sharing arrangement will be made with the other lawyers. If lawyers from different law firms will represent you, at least 1 lawyer from each law firm must sign the contingent fee contract.

5.　If your lawyer intends to refer your case to another lawyer or counsel with other lawyers, your lawyer should tell you about that at the beginning. If your lawyer takes the case and later decides to refer it to another lawyer or to associate with other lawyers, you should sign a new contract that includes the new lawyers. You, the client, also have the right to consult with each lawyer working on your case and each lawyer is legally responsible to represent your interests and is legally responsible for the acts of the other lawyers involved in the case.

6.　You, the client, have the right to know in advance how you will need to pay the expenses and the legal fees at the end of the case. If you pay a deposit in advance for costs, you may ask reasonable questions about how the money will be or has been spent and how much of it remains unspent. Your lawyer should give a reasonable estimate about future necessary costs. If your lawyer agrees to lend or advance you money to prepare or research the case, you have the right to know periodically how much money your lawyer has spent on your behalf. You also have the right to decide, after consulting with your lawyer, how much money is to be spent to prepare a case. If you pay the expenses, you have the right to decide how much to spend. Your lawyer should also inform you whether the fee will be based on the gross amount recovered or on the amount recovered minus the costs.

7　You, the client, have the right to be told by your lawyer about possible adverse consequences if you lose the case. Those adverse consequences might include money that you might have to pay to your lawyer for costs and liability you might have for attorney's fees, costs, and expenses to the other side.

8.　You, the client, have the right to receive and approve a closing statement at the end of the case before you pay any money. The statement must list all of the financial details of the entire case, including the amount recovered, all expenses, and a precise statement of your lawyer's fee. Until you approve the closing statement your lawyer cannot pay any money to anyone, including you, without an appropriate order of the court. You also have the right to have every lawyer or law firm working on your case sign this closing statement.

9.　You, the client, have the right to ask your lawyer at reasonable intervals how the case is progressing and to have these questions answered to the best of your lawyer's ability.

10.　You, the client, have the right to make the final decision regarding settlement of a case. Your lawyer must notify you of all offers of settlement before and after the trial. Offers during the trial must be immediately communicated and you should consult with your lawyer regarding whether to accept a settlement. However, you must make the final decision to accept or reject a settlement.

11.　If at any time you, the client, believe that your lawyer has charged an excessive or illegal fee, you have the right to report the matter to The Florida Bar, the agency that oversees the practice and behavior of all lawyers in Florida. For information on how to reach The Florida Bar, call 850/561- 5600, or contact the local bar association. Any disagreement between you and your lawyer about a fee can be taken to court and you may wish to hire another lawyer to help you resolve this disagreement. Usually fee disputes must be handled in a separate lawsuit, unless your fee contract provides for arbitration. You can request, but may not require, that a provision for arbitration (under chapter 682, Florida Statutes, or under the fee arbitration rule of the Rules Regulating The Florida Bar) be included in your fee contract.

_____　　_____

Client Signature　　　　　　　Attorney Signature

_____　　_____

Date　　　　　　　　　　　　　Date

but only those that are directly involved in its computation. It is sufficient, for example, to state the basic rate is an hourly charge or a fixed amount or an estimated amount, or to identify the factors that may be taken into account in finally fixing the fee. Although hourly billing or a fixed fee may be the most common bases for computing fees in an area of practice, these may not be the only bases for computing fees.

[2] A lawyer should, where appropriate, discuss alternative billing methods with the

| Alternative Billing Methods |

client. When developments occur during the representation that render an earlier estimate substantially inaccurate, a revised estimate should be provided to the client. A written statement concerning the fee reduces the possibility of misunderstanding. Furnishing the client with a simple memorandum or a copy of the lawyer's customary fee schedule is sufficient if the basis or rate of the fee is set forth.

[3] General overhead should be accounted for in a lawyer's fee, whether the lawyer

| Overhead |

charges hourly, flat, or contingent fees. Filing fees, transcription, and the like should be charged to the client at the actual amount paid by the lawyer.

[4] A lawyer may agree with the client to charge a reasonable amount for in-house costs

| Charging for In-House Costs and Services, Including Paralegal Services |

or services. In-house costs include items such as copying, faxing, long distance telephone, and computerized research. *In-house services include paralegal services*, investigative services, accounting services, and courier services. (Emphasis added.)

[5] The lawyer should sufficiently communicate with the client regarding the costs charged to the client so that the client understands the amount of costs being charged or the method for calculation of those costs. Costs appearing in sufficient detail on closing statements and approved by the parties to the transaction should meet the requirements of this rule. Rule 4-1.8(e) should be consulted regarding a lawyer's providing financial assistance to a client in connection with litigation.

Terms of payment (Comment on Rule 4-1.5)

[6] A lawyer may require advance payment of a fee but

| Nonrefundable Retainers |

is obliged to return any unearned portion. See rule 4-1.16(d). A lawyer is not, however, required to return retainers that, pursuant to an agreement with a client, are not refundable.

[7] A lawyer may accept property in payment for services, such as an ownership interest

| Fees Paid in Property Other Than Money |

in an enterprise, providing this does not involve acquisition of a proprietary interest in the cause of action

or subject matter of the litigation contrary to rule 4-1.8(i). However, a fee paid in property instead of money may be subject to special scrutiny because it involves questions concerning both the value of the services and the lawyer's special knowledge of the value of the property.

[8] An agreement may not be made whose terms might induce the lawyer improperly to curtail services for the client or perform them in a way contrary to the client's interest. For example, a lawyer should not enter into an agreement whereby services are to be provided only up to a stated amount when it is foreseeable that more extensive services probably will be required, unless the situation is adequately explained to the client. Otherwise, the client might have to bargain for further assistance in the midst of a proceeding or transaction. However, it is proper to define the extent of services in light of the client's ability to pay.

[9] A lawyer should not exploit a fee arrangement based primarily on hourly charges by using wasteful procedures. When there is doubt whether a contingent fee is con-

| Hourly Charges for Wasteful Services (Padding) |

sistent with the client's best interest, the lawyer should offer the client alternative bases for the fee and explain their implications. Applicable law may impose limitations on contingent fees, such as a ceiling on the percentage.

Prohibited contingent fees (Comment on Rule 4-1.5)

[10] Subdivision (f)(3)(A) prohibits a lawyer from charging a contingent fee in a domestic rela-

| Improper Contingent Fees |

tions matter when payment is contingent upon the securing of a divorce or upon the amount of alimony or support or property settlement to be obtained. This provision does not preclude a contract for a contingent fee for legal representation in connection with the recovery of post-judgment balances due under support, alimony, or other financial orders because such contracts do not implicate the same policy concerns.

Contingent fee regulation

[11] Subdivision (e) is intended to clarify that whether the lawyer's fee contract complies with these rules is a matter between the lawyer and client and an issue for professional disciplinary enforcement. The rules and subdivision (e) are not intended to be used as procedural weapons or defenses by others. Allowing opposing parties to assert noncompliance with these rules as a defense, including whether the fee is fixed or contingent, allows for potential inequity if the opposing party is allowed to escape responsibility for their actions solely through application of these rules.

[12] Rule 4-1.5(f)(4) should not be construed to apply to actions or claims seeking property or other damages arising in the commercial litigation context.

[13] Rule 4-1.5(f)(4)(B) is intended to apply only to contingent aspects of fee agreements. In the situation where a lawyer and client enter a contract for part noncontingent and part contingent attorney's fees, rule 4-1.5(f)(4)(B) should not be construed to apply to and prohibit or limit the noncontingent portion of the fee agreement. An attorney could properly charge and retain the noncontingent portion of the fee even if the matter was not successfully prosecuted or if the noncontingent portion of the fee exceeded the schedule set forth in rule 4-1.5(f)(4)(B). Rule 4-1.5(f)(4)(B) should, however, be construed to apply to any additional contingent portion of such a contract when considered together with earned noncontingent fees. Thus, under such a contract a lawyer may demand or collect only such additional contingent fees as would not cause the total fees to exceed the schedule set forth in rule 4-1.5(f)(4)(B).

[14] The limitations in rule 4-1.5(f)(4)(B)(i)(c) are only to be applied in the case where all the defendants admit liability at the time they file their initial answer and the trial is only on the issue of the amount or extent of the loss or the extent of injury suffered by the client. If the trial involves not only the issue of damages but also such questions as proximate cause, affirmative defenses, seat belt defense, or other similar matters, the limitations are not to be applied because of the contingent nature of the case being left for resolution by the trier of fact.

[15] Rule 4-1.5(f)(4)(B)(ii) provides the limitations set forth in subdivision (f)(4)(B)(i) | **Client Waiver in Contingency Fee Cases** | may be waived by the client upon approval by the appropriate judge. This waiver provision may not be used to authorize a lawyer to charge a client a fee that would exceed rule 4-1.5(a) or (b). It is contemplated that this waiver provision will not be necessary except where the client wants to retain a particular lawyer to represent the client or the case involves complex, difficult, or novel questions of law or fact that would justify a contingent fee greater than the schedule but not a contingent fee that would exceed rule 4-1.5(b).

[16] Upon a petition by a client, the trial court reviewing the waiver request must grant that request if the trial court finds the client: (a) understands the right to have the limitations in rule 4-1.5(f)(4)(B) applied in the specific matter; and (b) understands and approves the terms of the proposed contract. The consideration by the trial court of the waiver petition is not to be used as an opportunity for the court to inquire into the merits or details of the particular action or claim that is the subject of the contract.

[17] The proceedings before the trial court and the trial court's decision on a waiver request are to be confidential and not subject to discovery by any of the parties to the action or by any other individual or entity except The Florida Bar. However, terms of the contract approved by the trial court may be subject to discovery if the contract (without court approval) was subject to discovery under applicable case law or rules of evidence.

[18] Rule 4-1.5(f)(4)(B)(iii) is added to acknowledge the provisions of article 1, section 26 of the Florida Constitution, and to create an affirmative obligation on the part of an attorney contemplating a contingency | **Contingent Fees in Medical Liability Cases** | fee contract to notify a potential client with a medical liability claim of the limitations provided in that constitutional provision. This addition to the rule is adopted prior to any judicial interpretation of the meaning or scope of the constitutional provision and this rule is not intended to make any substantive interpretation of the meaning or scope of that provision. The rule also provides that a client who wishes to waive the rights of the constitutional provision, as those rights may relate to attorney's fees, must do so in the form contained in the rule.

[19] Rule 4-1.5(f)(6) prohibits a lawyer from charging the contingent fee percentage on the total, future value of a recovery being paid on a structured or periodic basis. This prohibition does not apply if the lawyer's fee is being paid over the same length of time as the schedule of payments to the client.

[20] Contingent fees are prohibited in criminal and certain domestic relations matters. In domestic | **Bonus or Additional Fees** | tic relations cases, fees that include a bonus provision or additional fee to be determined at a later time and based on results obtained have been held to be impermissible contingency fees and therefore subject to restitution and disciplinary sanction as elsewhere stated in these Rules Regulating The Florida Bar. Fees that provide for a bonus or additional fees and that otherwise are not prohibited under the Rules Regulating The Florida Bar can be effective tools for structuring fees. For example, a fee contract calling for a flat fee and the payment of a bonus based on the amount of property retained or recovered in a general civil action is not prohibited by these rules. However, the bonus or additional fee must be stated clearly in amount or formula for calculation of the fee (basis or rate). Courts have held that unilateral bonus fees are unenforceable. The test of reasonableness and other requirements of this rule apply to permissible bonus fees.

Division of fee (Comment on Rule 4-1.5)

[21] A division of fee is a single billing to a client cover-

Fee Division

ing the fee of 2 or more lawyers who are not in the same firm. A division of fee facilitates association of more than 1 lawyer in a matter in which neither alone could serve the client as well, and most often is used when the fee is contingent and the division is between a referring lawyer and a trial specialist. Subject to the provisions of subdivision (f)(4)(D), subdivision (g) permits the lawyers to divide a fee on either the basis of the proportion of services they render or by agreement between the participating lawyers if all assume responsibility for the representation as a whole and the client is advised and does not object. It does require disclosure to the client of the share that each lawyer is to receive. Joint responsibility for the representation entails the obligations stated in rule 4-5.1 for purposes of the matter involved.

Disputes over fees (Comment on Rule 4-1.5)

[22] Since the fee arbitration rule (chapter 14) has

Fee Disputes

been established by the bar to provide a procedure for resolution of fee disputes, the lawyer should conscientiously consider submitting to it. Where law prescribes a procedure for determining a lawyer's fee, for example, in representation of an executor or administrator, a class, or a person entitled to a reasonable fee as part of the measure of damages, the lawyer entitled to such a fee and a lawyer representing another party concerned with the fee should comply with the prescribed procedure.

Referral fees and practices (Comment on Rule 4-1.5)

[23] A secondary lawyer shall not be entitled to a fee

Referral Fees

greater than the limitation set forth in rule 4-1.5(f)(4)(D)(ii) merely because the lawyer agrees to do some or all of the following: (a) consults with the client; (b) answers interrogatories; (c) attends depositions; (d) reviews pleadings; (e) attends the trial; or (f) assumes joint legal responsibility to the client. However, the provisions do not contemplate that a secondary lawyer who does more than the above is necessarily entitled to a larger percentage of the fee than that allowed by the limitation.

[24] The provisions of rule 4-1.5(f)(4)(D)(iii) only apply

Co-Counsel Relationships

where the participating lawyers have for purposes of the specific case established a co-counsel relationship. The need for court approval of a referral fee arrangement under rule 4-1.5(f)(4)(D)(iii) should only occur in a small percentage of cases arising under rule 4-1.5(f)(4) and usually occurs prior to the commencement of litigation or at the onset of the representation. However, in those cases in which litigation has been commenced or the representation has already begun, approval of the fee division should be sought within a reasonable period of time after the need for court approval of the fee division arises.

[25] In determining if a co-counsel relationship exists, the court should look to see if the lawyers have established a special partnership agreement for the purpose of the specific case or matter. If such an agreement does exist, it must provide for a sharing of services or responsibility and the fee division is based upon a division of the services to be rendered or the responsibility assumed.

[26] It is contemplated that a co-counsel situation would exist where a division of responsibility is based upon, but not limited to, the following: (a) based upon geographic considerations, the lawyers agree to divide the legal work, responsibility, and representation in a convenient fashion. Such a situation would occur when different aspects of a case must be handled in different locations; (b) where the lawyers agree to divide the legal work and representation based upon their particular expertise in the substantive areas of law involved in the litigation; or (c) where the lawyers agree to divide the legal work and representation along established lines of division, such as liability and damages, causation and damages, or other similar factors.

[27] The trial court's responsibility when reviewing an application for authorization of a fee division under rule 4-1.5(f)(4)(D)(iii) is to determine if a co-counsel relationship exists in that particular case. If the court determines a co-counsel relationship exists and authorizes the fee division requested, the court does not have any responsibility to review or approve the specific amount of the fee division agreed upon by the lawyers and the client.

[28] Rule 4-1.5(f)(4)(D)(iv) applies to the situation where appellate counsel is retained during the trial of the case to assist with the appeal of the case. The percentages set forth in subdivision (f)(4)(D) are to be applicable after appellate counsel's fee is established. However, the effect should not be to impose an unreasonable fee on the client.

Credit Plans (Comment on Rule 4-1.5)

[29] Credit plans include credit cards. If a lawyer accepts payment from

Payment of Fees by Credit Card

a credit plan for an advance of fees and costs, the amount must be held in trust in accordance with chapter 5, Rules Regulating The Florida Bar, and the lawyer must add the lawyer's own money to the trust account in an amount equal to the amount charged by the credit plan for doing business with the credit plan.

Rule 4-1.6. Confidentiality of Information

(a) Consent Required to Reveal Information. A lawyer shall not reveal information relating to representation of a client except as stated in subdivisions (b), (c), and (d), unless the client gives informed consent.

| Duty of Confidentiality |

(b) When Lawyer Must Reveal Information. A lawyer shall reveal such information to the extent the lawyer reasonably believes necessary:

| When the Confidentiality Rule Does Not Apply; Death or Substantial Bodily Harm |

(1) to prevent a client from committing a crime; or

(2) to prevent a death or substantial bodily harm to another.

(c) When Lawyer May Reveal Information. A lawyer may reveal such information to the extent the lawyer reasonably believes necessary:

(1) to serve the client's interest unless it is information the client specifically requires not to be disclosed;

(2) to establish a claim or defense on behalf of the lawyer in a controversy between the lawyer and client;

(3) to establish a defense to a criminal charge or civil claim against the lawyer based upon conduct in which the client was involved;

(4) to respond to allegations in any proceeding concerning the lawyer's representation of the client; or

(5) to comply with the Rules of Professional Conduct.

(d) Exhaustion of Appellate Remedies. When required by a tribunal to reveal such information, a lawyer may first exhaust all appellate remedies.

(e) Limitation on Amount of Disclosure. When disclosure is mandated or permitted, the lawyer shall disclose no more information than is required to meet the requirements or accomplish the purposes of this rule.

Official Comments on Rule 4-1.6 (Confidentiality of Information)

[1] The lawyer is part of a judicial system charged with upholding the law. One of the lawyer's functions is to advise clients so that they avoid any violation of the law in the proper exercise of their rights.

This rule governs the disclosure by a lawyer of information relating to the representation of a client during the lawyer's representation of the client. See rule 4-1.18 for the lawyer's duties with respect to information provided to the lawyer by a prospective client, rule 4-1.9(b) for the lawyer's duty not to reveal information relating to the lawyer's prior representation of a former client, and rules 4-1.8(b) and 4-1.9(b) for the lawyer's duties with respect to the use of such information to the disadvantage of clients and former clients.

[2] A fundamental principle in the client-lawyer relationship is that, in the absence of the client's informed consent, the lawyer must

| Why the Confidentiality Rule Exists |

not reveal information relating to the representation. See terminology for the definition of informed consent. This contributes to the trust that is the hallmark of the client-lawyer relationship. The client is thereby encouraged to seek legal assistance and to communicate fully and frankly with the lawyer even as to embarrassing or legally damaging subject matter. The lawyer needs this information to represent the client effectively and, if necessary, to advise the client to refrain from wrongful conduct. Almost without exception, clients come to lawyers in order to determine their rights and what is, in the complex of laws and regulations, deemed to be legal and correct. Based upon experience, lawyers know that almost all clients follow the advice given, and the law is upheld.

[3] The principle of confidentiality is given effect in 2 related bodies of law, the attorney-client privilege (which includes the work product doctrine) in the

| Attorney-Client Privilege, Work-Product Rule, and Confidentiality |

law of evidence and the rule of confidentiality established in professional ethics. The attorney-client privilege applies in judicial and other proceedings in which a lawyer may be called as a witness or otherwise required to produce evidence concerning a client. The rule of client-lawyer confidentiality applies in situations other than those where evidence is sought from the lawyer through compulsion of law. The confidentiality rule applies not merely to matters communicated in confidence by the client but also to all information relating to the representation, whatever its source. A lawyer may not disclose such information except as authorized or required by the Rules of Professional Conduct or by law. However, none of the foregoing limits the requirement of disclosure in subdivision (b). This disclosure is required to prevent a lawyer from becoming an unwitting accomplice in the fraudulent acts of a client. See also Scope.

[4] The requirement of maintaining confidentiality of information relating to representation applies to government lawyers who may disagree with the policy goals that their representation is designed to advance.

Authorized disclosure (Comment on Rule 4-1.6)

[5] A lawyer is impliedly authorized to make disclosures about a client when appropriate in carrying out the representation, except to the extent that the client's instructions or special circumstances limit that authority. In litigation, for

| Revealing Confidential Information |

example, a lawyer may disclose information by admitting a fact that cannot properly be disputed or in negotiation by making a disclosure that facilitates a satisfactory conclusion.

[6] Lawyers in a firm may, in the course of the firm's practice, disclose to each other information relating to a client of the firm, unless the client has instructed that particular information be confined to specified lawyers.

Disclosure Adverse to Client (Comment on Rule 4-1.6)

[7] The confidentiality rule is subject to limited exceptions. In becoming privy to information

| A Client Who Intends to Commit Serious Harm |

about a client, a lawyer may foresee that the client intends serious harm to another person. However, to the extent a lawyer is required or permitted to disclose a client's purposes, the client will be inhibited from revealing facts that would enable the lawyer to counsel against a wrongful course of action. While the public may be protected if full and open communication by the client is encouraged, several situations must be distinguished.

[8] First, the lawyer may not counsel or assist a client in conduct that is criminal or fraudulent. See rule

| Using False Evidence |

4-1.2(d). Similarly, a lawyer has a duty under rule 4-3.3(a)(4) not to use false evidence. This duty is essentially a special instance of the duty prescribed in rule 4-1.2(d) to avoid assisting a client in criminal or fraudulent conduct.

[9] Second, the lawyer may have been innocently involved in past conduct by the client that was criminal or fraudulent. In such a situation the lawyer has not violated rule 4-1.2(d), because to "counsel or assist" criminal or fraudulent conduct requires knowing that the conduct is of that character.

[10] Third, the lawyer may learn that a client intends prospective conduct that is criminal. As stated in subdivision (b)(1), the lawyer shall reveal information in order to prevent such consequences. It is admittedly difficult for a lawyer to "know" when the criminal intent will actually be carried out, for the client may have a change of mind.

[11] Subdivision (b)(2) contemplates past acts on the part of a client that may result in present or future

| Death or Substantial Bodily Harm |

consequences that may be avoided by disclosure of otherwise confidential communications. Rule 4-1.6(b)(2) would now require the attorney to disclose information reasonably necessary to prevent the future death or substantial bodily harm to another, even though the act of the client has been completed.

[12] The lawyer's exercise of discretion requires consideration of such factors as the nature of the

lawyer's relationship with the client and with those who might be injured by the client, the lawyer's own involvement in the transaction, and factors that may extenuate the conduct in question. Where practical the lawyer should seek to persuade the client to take suitable action. In any case, a disclosure adverse to the client's interest should be no greater than the lawyer reasonably believes necessary to the purpose.

Withdrawal (Comment on Rule 4-1.6)

[13] If the lawyer's services will be used by the client in materially furthering a course of criminal

| Mandatory Withdrawal |

or fraudulent conduct, the lawyer must withdraw, as stated in rule 4-1.16(a)(1). After withdrawal the lawyer is required to refrain from making disclosure of the client's confidences, except as otherwise provided in rule 4-1.6. Neither this rule nor rule 4-1.8(b) nor rule 4-1.16(d) prevents the lawyer from giving notice of the fact of withdrawal, and the lawyer may also withdraw or disaffirm any opinion, document, affirmation, or the like.

[14] Where the client is an organization, the lawyer may be in doubt whether contemplated conduct will actually be carried out by the organization. Where necessary to guide conduct in connection with the rule, the lawyer may make inquiry within the organization as indicated in rule 4-1.13(b).

Dispute Concerning Lawyer's Conduct (Comment on Rule 4-1.6)

[15] A lawyer's confidentiality obligations do not preclude a lawyer from securing confidential legal advice about the lawyer's personal responsibility to comply with these rules. In most situations, disclosing information to secure such advice will be impliedly authorized for the lawyer to carry out the representation. Even when the disclosure is not impliedly authorized, subdivision (c)(5) permits such disclosure because of the importance of a lawyer's compliance with the Rules of Professional Conduct.

[16] Where a legal claim or disciplinary charge alleges complicity of the lawyer in a client's conduct or other misconduct of the

| Authorized Disclosure of Confidential Information |

lawyer involving representation of the client, the lawyer may respond to the extent the lawyer reasonably believes necessary to establish a defense. The same is true with respect to a claim involving the conduct or representation of a former client. The lawyer's right to respond arises when an assertion of such complicity has been made. Subdivision (c) does not require the lawyer to await the commencement of an action or proceeding that charges such complicity, so that the defense may be established by responding directly to a third party who has made such an assertion. The right to defend, of course, applies where a proceeding has been commenced. Where practicable and not prejudicial to the lawyer's ability to establish the defense, the lawyer should advise the client of the third party's assertion and request that the client respond appropriately. In any event, disclosure should be no greater than the lawyer reasonably believes is necessary to vindicate innocence, the disclosure should be made in a manner that limits access to the information to the tribunal or other persons having a need to know it, and appropriate protective orders or other arrangements should be sought by the lawyer to the fullest extent practicable.

[17] If the lawyer is charged with wrongdoing in which

Alleged Wrongdoing by a Lawyer

the client's conduct is implicated, the rule of confidentiality should not prevent the lawyer from defending against the charge. Such a charge can arise in a civil, criminal, or professional disciplinary proceeding and can be based on a wrong allegedly committed by the lawyer against the client or on a wrong alleged by a third person; for example, a person claiming to have been defrauded by the lawyer and client acting together. A lawyer entitled to a fee is permitted by subdivision (c) to prove the services rendered in an action to collect it. This aspect of the rule expresses the principle that the beneficiary of a fiduciary relationship may not exploit it to the detriment of the fiduciary. As stated above, the lawyer must make every effort practicable to avoid unnecessary disclosure of information relating to a representation, to limit disclosure to those having the need to know it, and to obtain protective orders or make other arrangements minimizing the risk of disclosure.

Disclosures otherwise required or authorized (Comment on Rule 4-1.6)

[18] The attorney-client privilege is differently defined in various jurisdictions. If a lawyer is called as a

Attorney-Client Privilege

witness to give testimony concerning a client, absent waiver by the client, rule 4-1.6(a) requires the lawyer to invoke the privilege when it is applicable. The lawyer must comply with the final orders of a court or other tribunal of competent jurisdiction requiring the lawyer to give information about the client.

[19] The Rules of Professional Conduct in various circumstances permit or require a lawyer to disclose information relating to the representation. See rules 4-2.3, 4-3.3, and 4-4.1. In addition to these provisions, a lawyer may be obligated or permitted by other provisions of law to give information about a client. Whether another provision of law

supersedes rule 4-1.6 is a matter of interpretation beyond the scope of these rules, but a presumption should exist against such a supersession.

Former client (Comment on Rule 4-1.6)

[20] The duty of confidentiality continues after the client-lawyer relationship has terminated. See rule 4-1.9 for the prohibition against using such information to the disadvantage of the former client.

Rule 4-1.7. Conflict of Interest; Current Clients

(a) **Representing Adverse Interests.** Except as provided in subdivision (b), a lawyer shall not represent a client if:
(1) the representation of 1 client will be directly adverse to another client; or

Conflict of Interest; Current Clients; Adverse Interests

(2) there is a substantial risk that the representation of 1 or more clients will be materially limited by the lawyer's responsibilities to another client, a former client or a third person or by a personal interest of the lawyer.

(b) Notwithstanding the existence of a conflict of interest under subdivision (a), a lawyer may represent a client if:
(1) the lawyer reasonably believes that the lawyer will be able to provide competent and diligent representation to each affected client;
(2) the representation is not prohibited by law;
(3) the representation does not involve the assertion of a position adverse to another client when the lawyer represents both clients in the same proceeding before a tribunal; and
(4) each affected client gives informed consent, confirmed in writing or clearly stated on the record at a hearing.

(c) **Explanation to Clients.** When representation of multiple clients in a single matter is undertaken, the consultation shall include explanation of the implications of the common representation and the advantages and risks involved.

Multiple Clients: Common Representation

(d) **Lawyers Related by Blood or Marriage.** A lawyer related to another lawyer as parent, child, sibling, or spouse shall not represent a client in a representation directly adverse to a person who the lawyer knows is represented by the other lawyer except upon consent by the client after consultation regarding the relationship.

(e) **Representation of Insureds.** Upon undertaking the representation of an insured client at the expense of the insurer, a lawyer has a duty to ascertain whether the lawyer will be representing both the insurer

Insurance Companies; Scope of Representation

and the insured as clients, or only the insured, and to inform both the insured and the insurer regarding the scope of the representation. All other Rules Regulating The Florida Bar related to conflicts of interest apply to the representation as they would in any other situation.

Official Comments on Rule 4-1.7 (Conflict of Interest; Current Clients)

Loyalty to a Client (Comment on Rule 4-1.7)

[1] Loyalty and independent judgment are essential elements in the lawyer's relationship to a client. Conflicts

Three Categories of Conflict

of interest can arise from the lawyer's responsibilities to another client, a former client or a third person, or from the lawyer's own interests. For specific rules regarding certain conflicts of interest, see rule 4-1.8. For former client conflicts of interest, see rule 4-1.9. For conflicts of interest involving prospective clients, see rule 4-1.18. For definitions of "informed consent" and "confirmed in writing," see terminology.

[2] An impermissible conflict of interest may exist before representation is undertaken, in which event the representation should be declined. If such a conflict arises after representation has been undertaken, the lawyer should withdraw from the representation. See rule 4-1.16. Where more than 1 client is involved and the lawyer withdraws because a conflict arises after representation, whether the lawyer may continue to represent any of the clients is determined by rule 4-1.9. As to whether a client-lawyer relationship exists or, having once been established, is continuing, see comment to rule 4-1.3 and scope.

[3] As a general proposition, loyalty to a client pro-

Loyalty to a Client

hibits undertaking representation directly adverse to that client's or another client's interests without the affected client's consent. Subdivision (a)(1) expresses that general rule. Thus, a lawyer ordinarily may not act as advocate against a person the lawyer represents in some other matter, even if it is wholly unrelated. On the other hand, simultaneous representation in unrelated matters of clients whose interests are only generally adverse, such as competing economic enterprises, does not require consent of the respective clients. Subdivision (a)(1) applies only when the representation of 1 client would be directly adverse to the other and where the lawyer's responsibilities of loyalty and confidentiality of the other client might be compromised.

[4] Loyalty to a client is also impaired when a lawyer cannot consider, recommend, or carry out an appropriate course of action for the client because of the

Independent Professional Judgment

lawyer's other responsibilities or interests. The conflict in effect forecloses alternatives that would otherwise be available to the client. Subdivision

(a)(2) addresses such situations. A possible conflict does not itself preclude the representation. The critical questions are the likelihood that a conflict will eventuate and, if it does, whether it will materially interfere with the lawyer's independent professional judgment in considering alternatives or foreclose courses of action that reasonably should be pursued on behalf of the client. Consideration should be given to whether the client wishes to accommodate the other interest involved.

Consultation and Consent (Comment on Rule 4-1.7)

[5] A client may consent to representation notwithstanding a conflict. However, as indicated in subdivision (a)(1) with respect

When Consent Will Not Cure a Conflict

to representation directly adverse to a client and subdivision (a)(2) with respect to material limitations on representation of a client, when a disinterested lawyer would conclude that the client should not agree to the representation under the circumstances, the lawyer involved cannot properly ask for such agreement or provide representation on the basis of the client's consent. When more than 1 client is involved, the question of conflict must be resolved as to each client. Moreover, there may be circumstances where it is impossible to make the disclosure necessary to obtain consent. For example, when the lawyer represents different clients in related matters and 1 of the clients refuses to consent to the disclosure necessary to permit the other client to make an informed decision, the lawyer cannot properly ask the latter to consent.

Lawyer's interests (Comment on Rule 4-1.7)

[6] The lawyer's own interests should not be permitted to have adverse effect on representation of a client. For example, a lawyer's need for income should not lead

Conflicts Caused by Personal Interests of a Lawyer

the lawyer to undertake matters that cannot be handled competently and at a reasonable fee. See rules 4-1.1 and 4-1.5. If the probity of a lawyer's own conduct in a transaction is in serious question, it may be difficult or impossible for the lawyer to give a client detached advice. A lawyer may not allow related business interests to affect representation, for example, by referring clients to an enterprise in which the lawyer has an undisclosed interest.

Conflicts in Litigation

[7] Subdivision (a)(1) prohibits representation of opposing parties in litigation. Simultaneous representation of parties whose interests in litigation may conflict, such as co-plaintiffs or co-defendants, is governed by subdivisions (a), (b),

Simultaneous Representation of Opposing Parties

and (c). An impermissible conflict may exist by reason of substantial discrepancy in the parties' testimony, incompatibility in positions in relation to an opposing party, or the fact that there are substantially different possibilities of settlement of the claims or liabilities in question. Such conflicts can arise in criminal cases as well as civil. The potential for conflict of interest in representing multiple defendants in a criminal case is so grave that ordinarily a lawyer should decline to represent more than 1 co-defendant. On the other hand, common representation of persons having similar interests is proper if the risk of adverse effect is minimal and the requirements of subdivision (c) are met.

[8] Ordinarily, a lawyer may not act as advocate against

An Advocate Against One's Own Client

a client the lawyer represents in some other matter, even if the other matter is wholly unrelated. However, there are circumstances in which a lawyer may act as advocate against a client. For example, a lawyer representing an enterprise with diverse operations may accept employment as an advocate against the enterprise in an unrelated matter if doing so will not adversely affect the lawyer's relationship with the enterprise or conduct of the suit and if both clients consent upon consultation. By the same token, government lawyers in some circumstances may represent government employees in proceedings in which a government agency is the opposing party. The propriety of concurrent representation can depend on the nature of the litigation. For example, a suit charging fraud entails conflict to a degree not involved in a suit for a declaratory judgment concerning statutory interpretation.

[9] A lawyer may represent parties having antagonistic

Antagonistic Positions on Legal Issues

positions on a legal question that has arisen in different cases, unless representation of either client would be adversely affected. Thus, it is ordinarily not improper to assert such positions in cases pending in different trial courts, but it may be improper to do so in cases pending at the same time in an appellate court.

Interest of person paying for a lawyer's service (Comment on Rule 4-1.7)

[10] A lawyer may be paid from a source other than

Conflicts When Someone Other Than the Client is Paying the Lawyer

the client, if the client is informed of that fact and consents and the arrangement does not compromise the lawyer's duty of loyalty to the client. See rule 4-1.8(f). For example, when an insurer and its insured have conflicting interests in a matter arising from a liability insurance agreement and the insurer is required to

provide special counsel for the insured, the arrangement should assure the special counsel's professional independence. So also, when a corporation and its directors or employees are involved in a controversy in which they have conflicting interests, the corporation may provide funds for separate legal representation of the directors or employees, if the clients consent after consultation and the arrangement ensures the lawyer's professional independence.

Other conflict situations (Comment on Rule 4-1.7)

[11] Conflicts of interest in contexts other than litigation sometimes may be difficult to assess. Relevant factors in determining whether there is potential for adverse effect include the duration and intimacy of the lawyer's relationship with the client or clients involved, the functions being performed by the lawyer, the likelihood that actual conflict will arise, and the likely prejudice to the client from the conflict if it does arise. The question is often one of proximity and degree.

[12] For example, a lawyer may not represent multiple parties to a

Common Representation

negotiation whose interests are fundamentally antagonistic to each other, but common representation is permissible where the clients are generally aligned in interest even though there is some difference of interest among them.

[13] Conflict questions may also arise in estate planning and

Estate Cases

estate administration. A lawyer may be called upon to prepare wills for several family members, such as husband and wife, and, depending upon the circumstances, a conflict of interest may arise. In estate administration the identity of the client may be unclear under the law of some jurisdictions. In Florida, the personal representative is the client rather than the estate or the beneficiaries. The lawyer should make clear the relationship to the parties involved.

[14] A lawyer for a corporation or other organization who is also a member of its board of direc-

Corporate Lawyers

tors should determine whether the responsibilities of the 2 roles may conflict. The lawyer may be called on to advise the corporation in matters involving actions of the directors. Consideration should be given to the frequency with which such situations may arise, the potential intensity of the conflict, the effect of the lawyer's resignation from the board, and the possibility of the corporation's obtaining legal advice from another lawyer in such situations. If there is material risk that the dual role will compromise the lawyer's independence of professional judgment, the lawyer should not serve as a director.

Conflict Charged by an Opposing Party (Comment on Rule 4-1.7)

[15] Resolving questions of conflict of interest is primarily the responsibility of the lawyer undertaking the representation. In litigation, a court may raise the question when there is reason to infer that the lawyer has neglected the responsibility. In a criminal case, inquiry by the court is generally required when a lawyer represents multiple defendants. Where the conflict is such as clearly to call in question the fair or efficient administration of justice, opposing counsel may properly raise the question. Such an objection should be viewed with caution, however, for it can be misused as a technique of harassment. See scope.

Family relationships between lawyers (Comment on Rule 4-1.7)

[16] Rule 4-1.7(d) applies to related lawyers who are in different firms. Related lawyers in the same firm are also governed by rules 4-1.9 and 4-1.10. The disqualification stated in rule 4-1.7(d) is personal and is not imputed to members of firms with whom the lawyers are associated.

Representation of Insureds (Comment on Rule 4-1.7)

[17] The unique tripartite relationship of insured, insurer, and lawyer can lead to ambiguity as to whom a lawyer represents. In a particular case, the lawyer may represent only the insured, with the insurer having the status of a non-client third party payor of the lawyer's fees. Alternatively, the lawyer may represent both as dual clients, in the absence of a disqualifying conflict of interest, upon compliance with applicable rules. Establishing clarity as to the role of the lawyer at the inception of the representation avoids misunderstanding that may ethically compromise the lawyer. This is a general duty of every lawyer undertaking representation of a client, which is made specific in this context due to the desire to minimize confusion and inconsistent expectations that may arise.

> Insurance Companies

[18] **Consent Confirmed in Writing or Stated on the Record at a Hearing**

Subdivision (b) requires the lawyer to obtain the informed consent of the client, confirmed in writing or clearly stated on the record at a hearing. With regard to being confirmed in writing, such a writing may consist of a document executed by the client or one that the lawyer promptly records and transmits to the client following an oral consent. See terminology. If it is not feasible to obtain or transmit the writing at the time the client gives informed consent, then the lawyer must obtain or

> Informed Consent

transmit it within a reasonable time thereafter. See terminology. The requirement of a writing does not supplant the need in most cases for the lawyer to talk with the client, to explain the risks and advantages, if any, of representation burdened with a conflict of interest, as well as reasonably available alternatives, and to afford the client a reasonable opportunity to consider the risks and alternatives and to raise questions and concerns. Rather, the writing is required in order to impress upon clients the seriousness of the decision the client is being asked to make and to avoid disputes or ambiguities that might later occur in the absence of a writing.

Rule 4-1.8. Conflict of Interest; Prohibited and Other Transactions

(a) **Business Transactions with or Acquiring Interest Adverse to Client.** A lawyer shall not enter into a business transaction with a client or knowingly acquire an ownership, possessory, security, or other pecuniary interest adverse to a client, except a lien granted by law to secure a lawyer's fee or expenses, unless:

> Informed Consent from a Client Regarding Business Transactions with a Lawyer

   (1) the transaction and terms on which the lawyer acquires the interest are fair and reasonable to the client and are fully disclosed and transmitted in writing to the client in a manner that can be reasonably understood by the client;

   (2) the client is advised in writing of the desirability of seeking and is given a reasonable opportunity to seek the advice of independent legal counsel on the transaction; and

   (3) the client gives informed consent, in a writing signed by the client, to the essential terms of the transaction and the lawyer's role in the transaction, including whether the lawyer is representing the client in the transaction.

(b) **Using Information to Disadvantage of Client.** A lawyer shall not use information relating to representation of a client to the disadvantage of the client unless the client gives informed consent, except as permitted or required by these rules.

(c) **Gifts to Lawyer or Lawyer's Family.** A lawyer shall not solicit any substantial gift from a client, including a testamentary gift, or prepare on behalf of a client an instrument giving the lawyer or a person related to the lawyer any substantial gift unless the lawyer or other recipient of the gift is related to the client. For purposes of this subdivision, related persons include a spouse, child, grandchild, parent, grandparent, or other relative with whom the lawyer or the client maintains a close, familial relationship.

> Substantial Gifts to a Lawyer

(d) Acquiring Literary or Media Rights. Prior to the conclusion of representation of a client, a lawyer shall not make or negotiate an agreement giving the lawyer literary or media rights to a portrayal or account based in substantial part on information relating to the representation.

(e) Financial Assistance to Client. A lawyer shall not provide financial assistance to a client in connection with pending or contemplated litigation, except that:

| A Lawyer's Payment of the Client's Litigation Expenses |

(1) a lawyer may advance court costs and expenses of litigation, the repayment of which may be contingent on the outcome of the matter; and

(2) a lawyer representing an indigent client may pay court costs and expenses of litigation on behalf of the client.

(f) Compensation by Third Party. A lawyer shall not accept compensation for representing a client from one other than the client unless:

(1) the client gives informed consent;

| Third-Party Payment of Legal Fees |

(2) there is no interference with the lawyer's independence of professional judgment or with the client-lawyer relationship; and

(3) information relating to representation of a client is protected as required by rule 4-1.6.

(g) Settlement of Claims for Multiple Clients. A lawyer who represents 2 or more clients

| Settlement |

shall not participate in making an aggregate settlement of the claims of or against the clients, or in a criminal case an aggregated agreement as to guilty or nolo contendere pleas, unless each client gives informed consent, in a writing signed by the client. The lawyer's disclosure shall include the existence and nature of all the claims or pleas involved and of the participation of each person in the settlement.

(h) Limiting Liability for Malpractice. A lawyer shall not make an agreement prospectively limiting the

| Legal Malpractice Liability |

lawyer's liability to a client for malpractice unless permitted by law and the client is independently represented in making the agreement. A lawyer shall not settle a claim for such liability with an unrepresented client or former client without first advising that person in writing that independent representation is appropriate in connection therewith.

(i) Acquiring Proprietary Interest in Cause of Action.

| Lien to Secure a Fee |

A lawyer shall not acquire a proprietary interest in the cause of action or subject matter of litigation the lawyer is conducting for a client, except that the lawyer may:

(1) acquire a lien granted by law to secure the lawyer's fee or expenses; and

(2) contract with a client for a reasonable contingent fee.

(j) Representation of Insureds. When a lawyer undertakes the defense of an insured other than a governmental entity, at the expense of an insurance company, in regard to an action or claim for personal injury or for property damages, or for death or loss of services resulting from personal injuries based upon tortious conduct, including product liability claims, the Statement of Insured Client's Rights shall be provided to the insured at the commencement of the representation. The lawyer shall sign the statement certifying the date on which the statement was provided to the insured. The lawyer shall keep a copy of the signed statement in the client's file and shall retain a copy of the signed statement for 6 years after the representation is completed. The statement shall be available for inspection at reasonable times by the insured, or by the appropriate disciplinary agency. Nothing in the Statement of Insured Client's Rights shall be deemed to augment or detract from any substantive or ethical duty of a lawyer or affect the extradisciplinary consequences of violating an existing substantive legal or ethical duty; nor shall any matter set forth in the Statement of Insured Client's Rights give rise to an independent cause of action or create any presumption that an existing legal or ethical duty has been breached. [See Exhibit 3.2E.]

| Insurance Company; Insured Client Rights |

(k) While lawyers are associated in a firm, a prohibition in the foregoing subdivisions (a) through (i) that applies to any one of them shall apply to all of them.

Official Comments on Rule 4-1.8 (Conflict of Interest: Prohibited and Other Transactions)

Business transactions between client and lawyer (Comment on Rule 4-1.8)

[1] A lawyer's legal skill and training, together with the relationship of trust and confidence between lawyer and client, create the possibility of overreaching when the lawyer participates in a business, property, or financial transaction with a client. The requirements of subdivision (a) must be met even when the transaction is not closely related to the subject matter of the representation. The rule applies to lawyers engaged in the sale of goods or services related to the practice of law. See rule 4-5.7. It does not apply to ordinary fee arrangements between client and lawyer, which are governed by rule 4-1.5, although its requirements must be met when the lawyer accepts an interest in the client's business or other nonmonetary property as payment for all or part of a fee. In addition, the

| Overreaching by a Lawyer |

EXHIBIT 3.2E   Statement of Insured Client's Rights

An insurance company has selected a lawyer to defend a lawsuit or claim against you. This Statement of Insured Client's Rights is being given to you to assure that you are aware of your rights regarding your legal representation. This disclosure statement highlights many, but not all, of your rights when your legal representation is being provided by the insurance company.

1. **Your Lawyer.** If you have questions concerning the selection of the lawyer by the insurance company, you should discuss the matter with the insurance company and the lawyer. As a client, you have the right to know about the lawyer's education, training, and experience. If you ask, the lawyer should tell you specifically about the lawyer's actual experience dealing with cases similar to yours and give you this information in writing, if you request it. Your lawyer is responsible for keeping you reasonably informed regarding the case and promptly complying with your reasonable requests for information. You are entitled to be informed of the final disposition of your case within a reasonable time.

2. **Fees and Costs.** Usually the insurance company pays all of the fees and costs of defending the claim. If you are responsible for directly paying the lawyer for any fees or costs, your lawyer must promptly inform you of that.

3. **Directing the Lawyer.** If your policy, like most insurance policies, provides for the insurance company to control the defense of the lawsuit, the lawyer will be taking instructions from the insurance company. Under such policies, the lawyer cannot act solely on your instructions, and at the same time, cannot act contrary to your interests. Your preferences should be communicated to the lawyer.

4. **Litigation Guidelines.** Many insurance companies establish guidelines governing how lawyers are to proceed in defending a claim. Sometimes those guidelines affect the range of actions the lawyer can take and may require authorization of the insurance company before certain actions are undertaken. You are entitled to know the guidelines affecting the extent and level of legal services being provided to you. Upon request, the lawyer or the insurance company should either explain the guidelines to you or provide you with a copy. If the lawyer is denied authorization to provide a service or undertake an action the lawyer believes necessary to your defense, you are entitled to be informed that the insurance company has declined authorization for the service or action.

5. **Confidentiality.** Lawyers have a general duty to keep secret the confidential information a client provides, subject to limited exceptions. However, the lawyer chosen to represent you also may have a duty to share with the insurance company information relating to the defense or settlement of the claim. If the lawyer learns of information indicating that the insurance company is not obligated under the policy to cover the claim or provide a defense, the lawyer's duty is to maintain that information in confidence. If the lawyer cannot do so, the lawyer may be required to withdraw from the representation without disclosing to the insurance company the nature of the conflict of interest which has arisen. Whenever a waiver of the lawyer-client confidentiality privilege is needed, your lawyer has a duty to consult with you and obtain your informed consent. Some insurance companies retain auditing companies to review the billings and files of the lawyers they hire to represent policyholders. If the lawyer believes a bill review or other action releases information in a manner that is contrary to your interests, the lawyer should advise you regarding the matter.

6. **Conflicts of Interest.** Most insurance policies state that the insurance company will provide a lawyer to represent your interests as well as those of the insurance company. The lawyer is responsible for identifying conflicts of interest and advising you of them. If at any time you believe the lawyer provided by the insurance company cannot fairly represent you because of conflicts of interest between you and the company (such as whether there is insurance coverage for the claim against you), you should discuss this with the lawyer and explain why you believe there is a conflict. If an actual conflict of interest arises that cannot be resolved, the insurance company may be required to provide you with another lawyer.

7. **Settlement.** Many policies state that the insurance company alone may make a final decision regarding settlement of a claim, but under some policies your agreement is required. If you want to object to or encourage a settlement within policy limits, you should discuss your concerns with your lawyer to learn your rights and possible consequences. No settlement of the case requiring you to pay money in excess of your policy limits can be reached without your agreement, following full disclosure.

8. **Your Risk.** If you lose the case, there might be a judgment entered against you for more than the amount of your insurance, and you might have to pay it. Your lawyer has a duty to advise you about this risk and other reasonably foreseeable adverse results.

9. **Hiring Your Own Lawyer.** The lawyer provided by the insurance company is representing you only to defend the lawsuit. If you desire to pursue a claim against the other side, or desire legal services not directly related to the defense of the lawsuit against you, you will need to make your own arrangements with this or another lawyer. You also may hire another lawyer, at your own expense, to monitor the defense being provided by the insurance company. If there is a reasonable risk that the claim made against you exceeds the amount of coverage under your policy, you should consider consulting another lawyer.

10. **Reporting Violations.** If at any time you believe that your lawyer has acted in violation of your rights, you have the right to report the matter to The Florida Bar, the agency that oversees the practice and behavior of all lawyers in Florida. For information on how to reach The Florida Bar call (850) 561-5839 or you may access the Bar at *www.FlaBar.org.*

IF YOU HAVE ANY QUESTIONS ABOUT YOUR RIGHTS, PLEASE ASK FOR AN EXPLANATION.

CERTIFICATE

The undersigned hereby certifies that this Statement of Insured Client's Rights has been provided to . . . . . (name of insured/client(s)) . . . . . by . . . . . (mail/hand delivery) . . . . . at . . . . . (address of insured/client(s) to which mailed or delivered, on . . . . . (date) . . . . .
[Signature of Attorney]

[Print/Type Name]
Florida Bar No.:

rule does not apply to standard commercial transactions between the lawyer and the client for products or services that the client generally markets to others, for example, banking or brokerage services, medical services, products manufactured or distributed by the client, and utilities services. In such transactions the lawyer has no advantage in dealing with the client, and the restrictions in subdivision (a) are unnecessary and impracticable. Likewise, subdivision (a) does not prohibit a lawyer from acquiring or asserting a lien granted by law to secure the lawyer's fee or expenses.

[2] Subdivision (a)(1) requires that the transaction itself

Fairness to the Client

be fair to the client and that its essential terms be communicated to the client, in writing, in a manner that can be reasonably understood. Subdivision (a)(2) requires that the client also be advised, in writing, of the desirability of seeking the advice of independent legal counsel. It also requires that the client be given a reasonable opportunity to obtain such advice. Subdivision (a)(3) requires that the lawyer obtain the client's informed consent, in a writing signed by the client, both to the essential terms of the transaction and to the lawyer's role.

[3] When necessary, the lawyer should discuss both the material risks of the proposed transaction, including any risk presented by the lawyer's involvement, and the existence of reasonably available alternatives and should explain why the advice of independent legal counsel is desirable. See terminology (definition of informed consent).

[4] The risk to a client is greatest when the client expects the lawyer to represent the client in the transaction itself or when the lawyer's financial interest otherwise poses a significant risk that the lawyer's representation of the client will be materially limited by the lawyer's financial interest in the transaction. Here the lawyer's role requires that the lawyer must comply, not only with the requirements of subdivision (a), but also with the requirements of rule 4-1.7. Under that rule, the lawyer must disclose the risks associated with the lawyer's dual role as both legal adviser and participant in the transaction, such as the risk that the lawyer will structure the transaction or give legal advice in a way that favors the lawyer's interests at the expense of the client. Moreover, the lawyer must obtain the client's informed consent. In some cases, the lawyer's interest may be such that rule 4-1.7 will preclude the lawyer from seeking the client's consent to the transaction.

[5] If the client is independently represented in the transaction, subdivision (a)(2) of this rule is inapplicable, and the subdivision (a)(1) requirement for full disclosure is satisfied either by a written disclosure by the lawyer involved in the transaction or by the client's independent counsel. The fact that the client was independently represented in the transaction is relevant in determining whether the agreement was fair and reasonable to the client as subdivision (a)(1) further requires.

Gifts to lawyers (Comment on Rule 4-1.8)

[6] A lawyer may accept a gift from a client, if the transaction meets general standards of fairness and if the lawyer does not prepare the instrument bestowing the gift.

Gifts to Lawyers; Undue Influence

For example, a simple gift such as a present given at a holiday or as a token of appreciation is permitted. If a client offers the lawyer a more substantial gift, subdivision (c) does not prohibit the lawyer from accepting it, although such a gift may be voidable by the client under the doctrine of undue influence, which treats client gifts as presumptively fraudulent. In any event, due to concerns about overreaching and imposition on clients, a lawyer may not suggest that a substantial gift be made to the lawyer or for the lawyer's benefit, except where the lawyer is related to the client as set forth in subdivision (c). If effectuation of a substantial gift requires preparing a legal instrument such as a will or conveyance, however, the client should have the detached advice that another lawyer can provide and the lawyer should advise the client to seek advice of independent counsel. Subdivision (c) recognizes an exception where the client is a relative of the donee or the gift is not substantial.

[7] This rule does not prohibit a lawyer from seeking to have the lawyer or a partner or associate of the lawyer named as personal representative of the client's estate or to another potentially lucrative fiduciary position.

Conflicts of Interest in Potentially Lucrative Fiduciary Services

Nevertheless, such appointments will be subject to the general conflict of interest provision in rule 4-1.7 when there is a significant risk that the lawyer's interest in obtaining the appointment will materially limit the lawyer's independent professional judgment in advising the client concerning the choice of a personal representative or other fiduciary. In obtaining the client's informed consent to the conflict, the lawyer should advise the client concerning the nature and extent of the lawyer's financial interest in the appointment, as well as the availability of alternative candidates for the position.

Literary rights (Comment on Rule 4-1.8)

[8] An agreement by which a lawyer acquires literary or media rights concerning the conduct of the representation creates a conflict between the interests of the client and

Literary Rights

the personal interests of the lawyer. Measures suitable in the representation of the client may detract from the publication value of an account of the representation. Subdivision (d) does not prohibit a lawyer representing a client in a transaction concerning literary property from agreeing that the lawyer's fee shall consist of a share in ownership in the property if the arrangement conforms to rule 4-1.5 and subdivisions (a) and (i).

Financial Assistance (Comment on Rule 4-1.8)

[9] Lawyers may not subsidize lawsuits or administrative proceedings brought on behalf of

> **Financial Assistance by a Lawyer to a Client; Stirring Up Litigation**

their clients, including making or guaranteeing loans to their clients for living expenses, because to do so would encourage clients to pursue lawsuits that might not otherwise be brought and because such assistance gives lawyers too great a financial stake in the litigation. These dangers do not warrant a prohibition on a lawyer advancing a client court costs and litigation expenses, including the expenses of medical examination and the reasonable costs of obtaining and presenting evidence, because these advances are virtually indistinguishable from contingent fees and help ensure access to the courts. Similarly, an exception allowing lawyers representing indigent clients to pay court costs and litigation expenses regardless of whether these funds will be repaid is warranted.

Person Paying for lawyer's Services (Comment on Rule 4-1.8)

[10] Lawyers are frequently asked to represent a client under circumstances in which a third person will compensate the lawyer, in whole or in part. The

> **Third-Party Payment of a Lawyer's Fees; Independent Professional Judgment**

third person might be a relative or friend, an indemnitor (such as a liability insurance company), or a co-client (such as a corporation sued along with one or more of its employees). Because third-party payers frequently have interests that differ from those of the client, including interests in minimizing the amount spent on the representation and in learning how the representation is progressing, lawyers are prohibited from accepting or continuing such representations unless the lawyer determines that there will be no interference with the lawyer's independent professional judgment and there is informed consent from the client. See also rule 4-5.4(d) (prohibiting interference with a lawyer's professional judgment by one who recommends, employs, or pays the lawyer to render legal services for another).

[11] Sometimes, it will be sufficient for the lawyer to obtain the client's informed consent regarding the fact of the payment and the identity of the third-party payer. If, however, the fee arrangement creates a conflict of interest for the lawyer, then the lawyer must comply with rule 4-1.7. The lawyer must also conform to the requirements of rule 4-1.6

concerning confidentiality. Under rule 4-1.7(a), a conflict of interest exists if there is significant risk that the lawyer's representation of the client will be materially limited by the lawyer's own interest in the fee arrangement or by the lawyer's responsibilities to the third-party payer (for example, when the third-party payer is a co-client). Under rule 4-1.7(b), the lawyer may accept or continue the representation with the informed consent of each affected client, unless the conflict is nonconsentable under that subdivision. Under rule 4-1.7(b), the informed consent must be confirmed in writing or clearly stated on the record at a hearing.

Aggregate Settlements (Comment on Rule 4-1.8)

[12] Differences in willingness to make or accept an offer of settlement are among the risks of common representation of multiple clients by a single lawyer. Under rule 4-1.7, this is one of the risks that should be discussed before undertaking the representation, as part of

> **Settlement in Common Representation Cases**

the process of obtaining the clients' informed consent. In addition, rule 4-1.2(a) protects each client's right to have the final say in deciding whether to accept or reject an offer of settlement and in deciding whether to enter a guilty or nolo contendere plea in a criminal case. The rule stated in this subdivision is a corollary of both these rules and provides that, before any settlement offer or plea bargain is made or accepted on behalf of multiple clients, the lawyer must inform each of them about all the material terms of the settlement, including what the other clients will receive or pay if the settlement or plea offer is accepted. See also terminology (definition of informed consent). Lawyers representing a class of plaintiffs or defendants, or those proceeding derivatively, must comply with applicable rules regulating notification of class members and other procedural requirements designed to ensure adequate protection of the entire class.

Acquisition of Interest in Litigation (Comment on Rule 4-1.8)

[13] Subdivision (i) states the traditional general rule that lawyers are prohibited from acquiring a proprietary interest in litigation. This general rule, which has its basis in common law champerty and maintenance, is subject to specific exceptions developed in decisional law and continued in these rules, such as the exception for reasonable contingent fees set forth in rule 4-1.5 and the exception for certain advances of the costs of litigation set forth in subdivision (e).

> **Improper Proprietary Interest in Litigation; Champerty**

This rule is not intended to apply to customary qualification and limitations in legal opinions and memoranda.

Representation of Insureds (Comment on Rule 4-1.8)

[14] As with any representation of a client when another person or client is paying for the representation, the representation of an insured client at the request of the insurer creates a special need for the lawyer to be cognizant of the potential for ethical risks. The nature of the relationship between a lawyer and a client can lead to the insured or the insurer having expectations inconsistent with the duty of the lawyer to maintain confidences, avoid conflicts of interest, and otherwise comply with professional standards. When a lawyer undertakes the representation of an insured client at the expense of the insurer, the lawyer should ascertain whether the lawyer will be representing both the insured and the insurer, or only the insured. Communication with both the insured and the insurer promotes their mutual understanding of the role of the lawyer in the particular representation.

> *Representing an Insured Client*

[15] The Statement of Insured Client's Rights has been developed to facilitate the lawyer's performance of ethical responsibilities. The highly variable nature of insurance and the responsiveness of the insurance industry in developing new types of coverages for risks arising in the dynamic American economy render it impractical to establish a statement of rights applicable to all forms of insurance. The Statement of Insured Client's Rights is intended to apply to personal injury and property damage tort cases. It is not intended to apply to workers' compensation cases. Even in that relatively narrow area of insurance coverage, there is variability among policies. For that reason, the statement is necessarily broad. It is the responsibility of the lawyer to explain the statement to the insured. In particular cases, the lawyer may need to provide additional information to the insured.

> *Statement of Insured Client's Rights (Exhibit 3.2E)*

[16] Because the purpose of the statement is to assist laypersons in understanding their basic rights as clients, it is necessarily abbreviated. Although brevity promotes the purpose for which the statement was developed, it also necessitates incompleteness. For these reasons, it is specifically provided that the statement shall not serve to establish any legal rights or duties, nor create any presumption that an existing legal or ethical duty has been breached. As a result, the statement and its contents should not be invoked by opposing parties as grounds for disqualification of a lawyer or for procedural purposes. The purpose of the statement would be subverted if it could be used in such a manner.

[17] The statement is to be signed by the lawyer to establish that it was timely provided to the insured, but the insured client is not required to sign it. It is in the best interests of the lawyer to have the insured client sign the statement to avoid future questions, but it is considered impractical to require the lawyer to obtain the insured client's signature in all instances.

[18] Establishment of the statement and the duty to provide it to an insured in tort cases involving personal injury or property damage should not be construed as lessening the duty of the lawyer to inform clients of their rights in other circumstances. When other types of insurance are involved, when there are other third-party payors of fees, or when multiple clients are represented, similar needs for fully informing clients exist, as recognized in rules 4-1.7(c) and 4-1.8(f).

Imputation of Prohibitions (Comment on Rule 4-1.8)

[19] Under subdivision (k), a prohibition on conduct by an individual lawyer in subdivisions (a) through (i) also applies to all lawyers associated in a firm with the personally prohibited lawyer. For example, 1 lawyer in a firm may not enter into a business transaction with a client of another member of the firm without complying with subdivision (a), even if the first lawyer is not personally involved in the representation of the client.

> *Prohibitions Imputed to All Lawyers in the Firm*

Rule 4-1.9. Conflict of Interest; Former Client

A lawyer who has formerly represented a client in a matter shall not thereafter:

> *Material Adverse Interest; Conflicts with Former Clients*

(a) represent another person in the same or a substantially related matter in which that person's interests are materially adverse to the interests of the former client unless the former client gives informed consent; or

(b) use information relating to the representation to the disadvantage of the former client except as rule 4-1.6 would permit with respect to a client or when the information has become generally known.

Official Comments on Rule 4-1.9 (Conflict of Interest; Former Client)

[1] After termination of a client-lawyer relationship, a lawyer may not represent another client except in conformity with this rule. The principles in rule 4-1.7 determine whether the interests of the present and former client are adverse. Thus, a lawyer could not properly seek to rescind on behalf of a new client a contract drafted on behalf of the former client. So also a lawyer who has prosecuted an accused person

could not properly represent the accused in a subsequent civil action against the government concerning the same transaction.

[2] The scope of a "matter" for purposes of rule 4-1.9(a) may depend on the facts of a particular situation or transaction. The lawyer's involvement in a matter can also be a question of degree. When a lawyer has been directly involved in a specific transaction, subsequent representation of other clients with materially adverse interests clearly is prohibited. On the other hand, a lawyer who recurrently handled a type of problem for a former client is not precluded from later representing another client in a wholly distinct problem of that type even though the subsequent representation involves a position adverse to the prior client.

[3] Similar considerations can apply to the reassignment of military lawyers between defense and prosecution functions within the same military jurisdiction. The underlying question is whether the lawyer was so involved in the matter that the subsequent representation can be justly regarded as a changing of sides in the matter in question.

Changing Sides; Substantial Relationship

Matters are "substantially related" for purposes of this rule if they involve the same transaction or legal dispute, or if the current matter would involve the lawyer attacking work that the lawyer performed for the former client. For example, a lawyer who has previously represented a client in securing environmental permits to build a shopping center would be precluded from representing neighbors seeking to oppose rezoning of the property on the basis of environmental considerations; however, the lawyer would not be precluded, on the grounds of substantial relationship, from defending a tenant of the completed shopping center in resisting eviction for nonpayment of rent.

[4] Lawyers owe confidentiality obligations to former clients, and thus information acquired by the lawyer in the course of representing a client may not subsequently be used by the lawyer to the disadvantage of the client without the former client's consent. For example, a lawyer who has represented a businessperson and learned extensive private financial information about that person may not then represent that person's spouse in seeking a divorce. However, the fact that a lawyer has once served a client does not preclude the lawyer from using generally known information about that client when later representing another client. Information that has been widely disseminated by the media to the public, or that typically would be obtained by any reasonably prudent lawyer who had never represented the former client, should be considered generally known and ordinarily will not be disqualifying. The essential question is whether, but for having represented the

Misuse of Private Financial Information by a Lawyer

former client, the lawyer would know or discover the information.

[5] Information acquired in a prior representation may have been rendered obsolete by the passage of time. In the case of an organizational client, general knowledge of the client's policies and practices ordinarily will not preclude a subsequent representation; on the other hand, knowledge of specific facts gained in a prior representation that are relevant to the matter in question ordinarily will preclude such a representation. A former client is not required to reveal the confidential information learned by the lawyer in order to establish a substantial risk that the lawyer has confidential information to use in the subsequent matter. A conclusion about the possession of such information may be based on the nature of the services the lawyer provided the former client and information that would in ordinary practice be learned by a lawyer providing such services.

[6] The provisions of this rule are for the protection of clients and can be waived if the former client gives informed consent. See terminology. With regard to an opposing party's raising a question of conflict of interest, see comment to rule 4-1.7. With regard to disqualification of a firm with which a lawyer is associated, see rule 4-1.10.

Rule 4-1.10. Imputation of Conflicts of Interest; General Rule

(a) Imputed Disqualification of All Lawyers in Firm. While lawyers are associated in a firm, none of them shall knowingly represent a client when any 1 of them practicing alone would be prohibited from doing so by rule 4-1.7 or 4-1.9 except as provided elsewhere in this rule, or unless the prohibition is based on a personal interest of the prohibited lawyer and does not present a significant risk of materially limiting the representation of the client by the remaining lawyers in the firm.

Imputed Disqualification

(b) Former Clients of Newly Associated Lawyer. When a lawyer becomes associated with a firm, the firm may not knowingly represent a person in the same or a substantially related matter in which that lawyer, or a firm with which the lawyer was associated, had previously represented a client whose interests are materially adverse to that person and about whom the lawyer had acquired information protected by rules 4-1.6 and 4-1.9(b) that is material to the matter.

Imputed Conflict of Interest When Switching Jobs

(c) Representing Interests Adverse to Clients of Formerly Associated Lawyer. When a lawyer has terminated an association with a firm, the firm is not prohibited from thereafter representing a person with interests materially adverse to those of a client represented by the formerly associated lawyer unless:

(1) the matter is the same or substantially related to that in which the formerly associated lawyer represented the client; and

(2) any lawyer remaining in the firm has information protected by rules 4-1.6 and 4-1.9(b) that is material to the matter.

(d) Waiver of Conflict. A disqualification prescribed by this rule may be waived by the affected client under the conditions stated in rule 4-1.7.

(e) Government Lawyers. The disqualification of lawyers associated in a firm with former or current government lawyers is governed by rule 4-1.11.

Official Comments on Rule 4-1.10 (Imputation of Conflicts of Interest; General Rule)

Definition of "firm" (Comment on Rule 4-1.10)

[1] With respect to the law department of an organization, there is ordinarily no question that the members of the department constitute a firm within the meaning

> **Identity of the Client**

of the Rules of Professional Conduct. However, there can be uncertainty as to the identity of the client. For example, it may not be clear whether the law department of a corporation represents a subsidiary or an affiliated corporation, as well as the corporation by which the members of the department are directly employed. A similar question can arise concerning an unincorporated association and its local affiliates.

[2] Similar questions can also arise with respect to lawyers in legal aid. Lawyers employed in the same unit of a legal

> **Legal Aid Office**

service organization constitute a firm, but not necessarily those employed in separate units. As in the case of independent practitioners, whether the lawyers should be treated as associated with each other can depend on the particular rule that is involved and on the specific facts of the situation.

[3] Where a lawyer has joined a private firm after having represented the government, the situation is governed by rule 4-1.11(a) and (b); where a lawyer represents the government after having served private clients, the situation is governed by rule 4-1.11(c)(1). The individual lawyer involved is bound by the rules generally, including rules 4-1.6, 4-1.7, and 4-1.9.

[4] Different provisions are thus made for movement of a lawyer from 1 private firm to another and for movement of a lawyer between a private firm and the government. The government is entitled to protection of its client confidences and, therefore, to the protections provided in rules 4-1.6, 4-1.9, and 4-1.11. However, if the more extensive disqualification in rule 4-1.10 were applied to former government lawyers, the potential effect on the government would be unduly burdensome. The government deals with all private

citizens and organizations and thus has a much wider circle of adverse legal interests than does any private law firm. In these circumstances, the government's recruitment of lawyers would be seriously impaired if rule 4-1.10 were applied to the government. On balance, therefore, the government is better served in the long run by the protections stated in rule 4-1.11.

Principles of Imputed Disqualification (Comment on Rule 4-1.10)

[5] The rule of imputed disqualification stated in subdivision (a)

> **Loyalty to the Client**

gives effect to the principle of loyalty to the client as it applies to lawyers who practice in a law firm. Such situations can be considered from the premise that a firm of lawyers is essentially 1 lawyer for purposes of the rules governing loyalty to the client or from the premise that each lawyer is vicariously bound by the obligation of loyalty owed by each lawyer with whom the lawyer is associated. Subdivision (a) operates only among the lawyers currently associated in a firm. When a lawyer moves from 1 firm to another the situation is governed by subdivisions (b) and (c).

[6] The rule in subdivision (a) does not prohibit representation where neither questions of client loyalty nor protection of confidential information are presented. Where 1 lawyer in

> **A Lawyer's Strong Political Beliefs**

a firm could not effectively represent a given client because of strong political beliefs, for example, but that lawyer will do no work on the case and the personal beliefs of the lawyer will not materially limit the representation by others in the firm, the firm should not be disqualified. On the other hand, if an opposing party in a case were owned by a lawyer in the law firm, and others in the firm would be materially limited in pursuing the matter because of loyalty to that lawyer, the personal disqualification of the lawyer would be imputed to all others in the firm.

[7] *The rule in subdivision (a) also does not prohibit representation by others in the law firm where the person prohibited from involvement in a matter is a nonlawyer, such*

> **The Screening of Paralegals**

as a paralegal or legal secretary. Such persons, however, ordinarily must be screened from any personal participation in the matter to avoid communication to others in the firm of confidential information that both the nonlawyers and the firm have a legal duty to protect. See terminology and rule 4-5.3. (Emphasis added.)

Lawyers Moving between Firms (Comment on Rule 4-1.10)

[8] When lawyers have been associated in a firm but then end their association, however, the problem is more complicated. The fiction that the law firm is the same as a

> **Switching Jobs**

single lawyer is no longer wholly realistic. There are several competing considerations. First, the client previously represented must be reasonably assured that the principle of loyalty to the client is not compromised. Second, the rule of disqualification should not be so broadly cast as to preclude other persons from having reasonable choice of legal counsel. Third, the rule of disqualification should not unreasonably hamper lawyers from forming new associations and taking on new clients after having left a previous association. In this connection, it should be recognized that today many lawyers practice in firms, that many to some degree limit their practice to 1 field or another, and that many move from 1 association to another several times in their careers. If the concept of imputed disqualification were defined with unqualified rigor, the result would be radical curtailment of the opportunity of lawyers to move from 1 practice setting to another and of the opportunity of clients to change counsel.

[9] Reconciliation of these competing principles in the past has been attempted under 2 rubrics. One approach has been to seek per se rules of disqualification. For example, it has been held that a partner in a law firm is conclusively presumed to have access to all confidences concerning all clients of the firm. Under this analysis, if a lawyer has been a partner in one law firm and then becomes a partner in another law firm, there is a presumption that all confidences known by a partner in the first firm are known to all partners in the second firm. This presumption might properly be applied in some circumstances, especially where the client has been extensively represented, but may be unrealistic where the client was represented only for limited purposes. Furthermore, such a rigid rule exaggerates the difference between a partner and an associate in modern law firms.

[10] The other rubric formerly used for dealing with vicarious disqualification is the appearance of impropriety and was proscribed in former Canon 9 of the Code of Professional Responsibility. This rubric has a two-fold problem. First, the appearance of impropriety can be taken to include any new client-lawyer relationship that might make a former client feel anxious. If that meaning were adopted, disqualification would become little more than a question of subjective judgment by the former client. Second, since "impropriety" is undefined, the term "appearance of impropriety" is question-begging. It therefore has to be recognized that the problem of imputed disqualification cannot be properly resolved either by simple analogy to a lawyer practicing alone or by the very general concept of appearance of impropriety.

[11] A rule based on a functional analysis is more appropriate for determining the question of vicarious disqualification. Two functions are involved: preserving confidentiality and avoiding positions adverse to a client.

Confidentiality (Comment on Rule 4-1.10)

[12] Preserving confidentiality is a question of access to information. Access to information, in turn, is essentially a question of fact in particular circumstances, aided by inferences, deductions, or working presumptions that reasonably may be made about the way in which lawyers work together. A lawyer may have general access to files of all clients of a law firm and may regularly participate in discussions of their affairs; it should be inferred that such a lawyer in fact is privy to all information about all the firm's clients. In contrast, another lawyer may have access to the files of only a limited number of clients and participate in discussion of the affairs of no other clients; in the absence of information to the contrary, it should be inferred that such a lawyer in fact is privy to information about the clients actually served but not information about other clients.

> Access to Information and Confidentiality

[13] Application of subdivisions (b) and (c) depends on a situation's particular facts. In any such inquiry, the burden of proof should rest upon the firm whose disqualification is sought.

[14] Subdivisions (b) and (c) operate to disqualify the firm only when the lawyer involved has actual knowledge of information protected by rules 4-1.6 and 4-1.9(b). Thus, if a lawyer while with 1 firm acquired no knowledge or information relating to a particular client of the firm and that lawyer later joined another firm, neither the lawyer individually nor the second firm is disqualified from representing another client in the same or a related matter even though the interests of the 2 clients conflict.

> Actual Knowledge of Protected Information

[15] Independent of the question of disqualification of a firm, a lawyer changing professional association has a continuing duty to preserve confidentiality of information about a client formerly represented. See rules 4-1.6 and 4-1.9.

Adverse Positions (Comment on Rule 4-1.10)

[16] The second aspect of loyalty to client is the lawyer's obligation to decline subsequent representations involving positions adverse to a former client arising in substantially related matters. This obligation requires abstention from adverse representation by the individual lawyer involved, but does not properly entail abstention of

> Adverse Positions in Substantially Related Matters

other lawyers through imputed disqualification. Hence, this aspect of the problem is governed by rule 4-1. 9(a). Thus, if a lawyer left 1 firm for another, the new affiliation would not preclude the firms involved from continuing to represent clients with adverse interests in the same or related matters so long as the conditions of rule 4-1.10(b) and (c) concerning confidentiality have been met.

[17] Rule 4-1.10(d) removes imputation with the informed consent of the affected client or former client under the conditions stated in rule 4-1.7. The conditions stated in rule 4-1.7 require the lawyer to determine that the representation is not prohibited by rule 4-1.7(b) and that each affected client or former client has given informed consent to the representation, confirmed in writing or clearly stated on the record. In some cases, the risk may be so severe that the conflict may not be cured by client consent. For a definition of informed consent, see terminology.

[18] Where a lawyer is prohibited from engaging in certain transactions under rule 4-1.8, subdivision (k) of that rule, and not this rule, determines whether that prohibition also applies to other lawyers associated in a firm with the personally prohibited lawyer.

Rule 4-1.13. Organization as Client

| Corporations and Other Organizations as Clients |

(a) Representation of Organization. A lawyer employed or retained by an organization represents the organization acting through its duly authorized constituents.

(b) Violations by Officers or Employees of Organization. If a lawyer for an organization knows that an officer, employee, or other person associated with the organization is engaged in action, intends to act, or refuses to act in a matter related to the representation that is a violation of a legal obligation to the organization or a violation of law that reasonably might be imputed to the organization and is likely to result in substantial injury to the organization, the lawyer shall proceed as is reasonably necessary in the best interest of the organization. In determining how to proceed, the lawyer shall give due consideration to the seriousness of the violation and its consequences, the scope and nature of the lawyer's representation, the responsibility in the organization and the apparent motivation of the person involved, the policies of the organization concerning such matters, and any other relevant considerations. Any measures taken shall be designed to minimize disruption of the organization and the risk of revealing information relating to the representation to persons outside the organization. Such measures may include among others:

(1) asking reconsideration of the matter;

(2) advising that a separate legal opinion on the matter be sought for presentation to appropriate authority in the organization; and

(3) referring the matter to higher authority in the organization, including, if warranted by the seriousness of the matter, referral to the highest authority that can act in behalf of the organization as determined by applicable law.

| Reporting Matters up the Chain of Command within the Organization |

(c) Resignation as Counsel for Organization. If, despite the lawyer's efforts in accordance with subdivision (b), the highest authority that can act on behalf of the organization insists upon action, or a refusal to act, that is clearly a violation of law and is likely to result in substantial injury to the organization, the lawyer may resign in accordance with rule 4-1.16.

(d) Identification of Client. In dealing with an organization's directors, officers, employees, members, shareholders, or other constituents, a lawyer shall explain the identity of the client when the lawyer knows or reasonably should know that the organization's interests are adverse to those of the constituents with whom the lawyer is dealing.

(e) Representing Directors, Officers, Employees, Members, Shareholders, or Other Constituents of Organization. A lawyer representing an organization may also represent any of its directors, officers, employees, members, shareholders, or other constituents, subject to the provisions of rule 4-1.7. If the organization's consent to the dual representation is required by rule 4-1.7, the consent shall be given by an appropriate official of the organization other than the individual who is to be represented, or by the shareholders.

| Dual Representation |

Official Comments on Rule 4-1.13 (Organization as Client)

The Entity as the Client (Comment on Rule 4-1.13)

[1] An organizational client is a legal entity, but it cannot act except through its officers, directors, employees, shareholders, and other constituents. Officers, directors, employees, and shareholders are the constituents of the corporate organizational client. The duties defined in this comment apply equally to unincorporated associations. "Other constituents" as used in this comment means the positions equivalent to officers, directors, employees, and shareholders held by persons acting for organizational clients that are not corporations.

[2] When 1 of the constituents of an organizational client communicates with the organization's lawyer in that person's organizational capacity, the communication is protected by rule 4-1.6. Thus, by way of

example, if an organizational client requests its lawyer to investigate allegations of wrongdoing, interviews made in the course of that investigation between the lawyer and the client's employees or other constituents are covered by rule 4-1.6. This does not mean, however, that constituents of an organizational client are the clients of the lawyer. The lawyer may not disclose to such constituents information relating to the representation except for disclosures explicitly or impliedly authorized by the organizational client in order to carry out the representation or as otherwise permitted by rule 4-1.6.

[3] When constituents of the organization make decisions for it, the decisions ordinarily must be accepted by the lawyer even if their utility or prudence is doubtful. Decisions concerning policy and operations, including ones entailing serious risk, are not as such in the lawyer's province. However, different considerations arise when the lawyer knows that the organization may be substantially injured by action of a constituent that is in violation of law. In such a circumstance, it may be reasonably necessary for the lawyer to ask the constituent to reconsider the matter.

> **Violations of Law within the Organization**

[4] If that fails, or if the matter is of sufficient seriousness and importance to the organization, it may be reasonably necessary for the lawyer to take steps to have the matter reviewed by a higher authority in the organization. Clear justification should exist for seeking review over the head of the constituent normally responsible for it. The stated policy of the organization may define circumstances and prescribe channels for such review, and a lawyer should encourage the formulation of such a policy. Even in the absence of organization policy, however, the lawyer may have an obligation to refer a matter to higher authority, depending on the seriousness of the matter and whether the constituent in question has apparent motives to act at variance with the organization's interest. Review by the chief executive officer or by the board of directors may be required when the matter is of importance commensurate with their authority. At some point it may be useful or essential to obtain an independent legal opinion.

> **Review by a Higher Authority within the Organization**

[5] The organization's highest authority to whom a matter may be referred ordinarily will be the board of directors or similar governing body. However, applicable law may prescribe that under certain conditions highest authority reposes elsewhere; for example, in the independent directors of a corporation.

Relation to other Rules (Comment on 4-1.13)

[6] The authority and responsibility provided in this rule are concurrent with the authority and responsibility provided in other rules. In particular, this rule does not limit or expand the lawyer's responsibility under rule 4-1.6, 4-1.8, 4-1.16, 4-3.3, or 4-4.1. If the lawyer's services are being used by an organization to further a crime or fraud by the organization, rule 4-1.2(d) can be applicable.

Government Agency (Comment on Rule 4-1.13)

[7] The duty defined in this rule applies to governmental organizations. However, when the client is a governmental organization, a different balance may be appropriate between maintaining confidentiality and assuring that the wrongful official act is prevented or rectified, for public business is involved. In addition, duties of lawyers employed by the government or lawyers in military service may be defined by statutes and regulation. Defining precisely the identity of the client and prescribing the resulting obligations of such lawyers may be more difficult in the government context and is a matter beyond the scope of these rules. Although in some circumstances the client may be a specific agency, it may also be a branch of the government, such as the executive branch, or the government as a whole. For example, if the action or failure to act involves the head of a bureau, either the department of which the bureau is a part or the relevant branch of government may be the client for purposes of this rule. Moreover, in a matter involving the conduct of government officials, a government lawyer may have authority under applicable law to question such conduct more extensively than that of a lawyer for a private organization in similar circumstances. This rule does not limit that authority.

Clarifying the Lawyer's Role (Comment on Rule 4-1.13)

[8] There are times when the organization's interest may be or becomes adverse to those of 1 or more of its constituents. In such circumstances the lawyer should advise any constituent whose interest the lawyer finds adverse to

> **When a Lawyer for an Organization Cannot Represent One of Its Constituents**

that of the organization of the conflict or potential conflict of interest that the lawyer cannot represent such constituent and that such person may wish to obtain independent representation. Care must be taken to assure that the constituent understands that, when there is such adversity of interest, the lawyer for the organization cannot provide legal representation for that constituent and that discussions between the lawyer for the organization and the constituent may not be privileged. Whether such a warning should be given by the lawyer for the organization to any constituent may turn on the facts of each case.

Dual Representation (Comment on Rule 4-1.13)

[9] Subdivision (e) recognizes that a lawyer for an organization may also represent a principal officer or major shareholder.

Derivative Actions (Comment on Rule 4-1.13)

[10] Under generally prevailing law, the shareholders or members of a corporation may bring suit to compel the directors to perform their legal obligations in the supervision of the organization. Members of unincorporated associations have essentially the same right. Such an action may be brought nominally by the organization, but usually is, in fact, a legal controversy over management of the organization. The question can arise whether counsel for the organization may defend such an action. The proposition that the organization is the lawyer's client does not alone resolve the issue. Most derivative actions are a normal incident of an organization's affairs, to be defended by the organization's lawyer like any other suit. However, if the claim involves serious charges of wrongdoing by those in control of the organization, a conflict may arise between the lawyer's duty to the organization and the lawyer's relationship with the board. In those circumstances, rule 4-1.7 governs who should represent the directors and the organization.

| Shareholder's Derivative Actions |

Representing Related Organizations (Comment on Rule 4-1.13)

[11] Consistent with the principle expressed in subdivision (a) of this rule, a lawyer or law firm who represents or has represented a corporation (or other organization) ordinarily is not presumed to also represent, solely by virtue of representing or having represented the client, an organization (such as a corporate parent or subsidiary) that is affiliated with the client. There are exceptions to this general proposition, such as, for example, when an affiliate actually is the alter ego of the organizational client or when the client has revealed confidential information to an attorney with the reasonable expectation that the information would not be used adversely to the client's affiliate(s). Absent such an exception, an attorney or law firm is not ethically precluded from undertaking representations adverse to affiliates of an existing or former client.

Rule 4-1.14. Client under a Disability

(a) Maintenance of Normal Relationship. When a client's ability to make adequately considered decisions in connection with the representation is impaired, whether because of minority, mental disability, or for some other

| Impaired Clients |

reason, the lawyer shall, as far as reasonably possible, maintain a normal client-lawyer relationship with the client.

(b) Appointment of Guardian. A lawyer may seek the appointment of a guardian or take other protective action with respect to a client only when the lawyer reasonably believes that the client cannot adequately act in the client's own interest.

Official Comments on Rule 4-1.14 (Client under a Disability)

[1] The normal client-lawyer relationship is based on the assumption that the client, when properly advised and assisted, is capable of making decisions about important matters. When the client is a minor or suffers from a mental disorder or disability, however, maintaining the ordinary client-lawyer relationship may not be possible in all respects. In particular, an incapacitated person may have no power to make legally binding decisions. Nevertheless, a client lacking legal competence often has the ability to understand, deliberate upon, and reach conclusions about matters affecting the client's own well-being. Furthermore, to an increasing extent the law recognizes intermediate degrees of competence. For example, children as young as 5 or 6 years of age, and certainly those of 10 or 12, are regarded as having opinions that are entitled to weight in legal proceedings concerning their custody. So also, it is recognized that some persons of advanced age can be quite capable of handling routine financial matters while needing special legal protection concerning major transactions.

| Client Who Lacks Legal Competence |

[2] The fact that a client suffers a disability does not diminish the lawyer's obligation to treat the client with attention and respect. If the person has no guardian or legal representative, the lawyer often must act as de facto guardian. Even if the person does have a legal representative, the lawyer should as far as possible accord the represented person the status of client, particularly in maintaining communication.

| Lawyer as De Facto Guardian |

[3] If a legal representative has already been appointed for the client, the lawyer should ordinarily look to the representative for decisions on behalf of the client. If a legal representative has not been appointed, the lawyer should see to such an appointment where it would serve the client's best interests. Thus, if a disabled client has substantial property that should be sold for the client's benefit, effective completion of the transaction ordinarily requires appointment of a legal representative. In many circumstances, however, appointment of a legal representative may be expensive or traumatic for the

client. Evaluation of these considerations is a matter of professional judgment on the lawyer's part.

[4] If the lawyer represents the guardian as distinct from the ward and is aware that the guardian is acting adversely to the ward's interest, the lawyer may have an obligation to prevent or rectify the guardian's misconduct. See rule 4-1.2(d).

Disclosure of Client's Condition (Comment on Rule 4-1.14)

[5] Rules of procedure in litigation generally provide that minors or persons suffering mental disability shall be represented by a guardian or next friend if they do not have a general guardian. However, disclosure of the client's disability can adversely affect the client's interests. The lawyer may seek guidance from an appropriate diagnostician.

Rule 4-1.15. Safekeeping Property

Compliance with Trust Accounting Rules. A lawyer shall comply with The Florida Bar Rules Regulating Trust Accounts. [See Rule 5-1.1 and 5-1.2 below.]

Rule 4-1.16. Declining or Terminating Representation

(a) When Lawyer Must Decline or Terminate Representation. Except as stated in subdivision (c), a lawyer shall not represent a client or, where representation has commenced, shall withdraw from the representation of a client if:

| Accepting Clients; Withdrawal |

(1) the representation will result in violation of the Rules of Professional Conduct or law;

| A Lawyer's Physical or Mental Impairment |

(2) the lawyer's physical or mental condition materially impairs the lawyer's ability to represent the client;

(3) the lawyer is discharged;

(4) the client persists in a course of action involving the lawyer's services that the lawyer reasonably believes is criminal or fraudulent, unless the client agrees to disclose and rectify the crime or fraud; or

(5) the client has used the lawyer's services to perpetrate a crime or fraud, unless the client agrees to disclose and rectify the crime or fraud.

(b) When Withdrawal Is Allowed. Except as stated in subdivision (c), a lawyer may withdraw from representing a client if:

| Withdrawing from Representation |

(1) withdrawal can be accomplished without material adverse effect on the interests of the client;

(2) the client insists upon taking action that the lawyer considers repugnant, imprudent, or with which the lawyer has a fundamental disagreement;

(3) the client fails substantially to fulfill an obligation to the lawyer regarding the lawyer's services and has been given reasonable warning that the lawyer will withdraw unless the obligation is fulfilled;

(4) the representation will result in an unreasonable financial burden on the lawyer or has been rendered unreasonably difficult by the client; or

(5) other good cause for withdrawal exists.

(c) Compliance with Order of Tribunal. A lawyer must comply with applicable law requiring notice or permission of a tribunal when terminating a representation. When ordered to do so by a tribunal, a lawyer shall continue representation notwithstanding good cause for terminating the representation.

(d) Protection of Client's Interest. Upon termination of representation, a lawyer shall take steps to the extent reasonably practicable to protect a client's interest, such as giving reasonable notice to the client, allowing time for employment of other counsel, surrendering papers and property to which the client is entitled, and refunding any advance payment of fee or expense that has not been earned or incurred. The lawyer may retain papers and other property relating to or belonging to the client to the extent permitted by law.

| Returning Client Papers and Property; Refunding Unearned Fees |

Official Comments on Rule 4-1.16 (Declining or Terminating Representation)

[1] A lawyer should not accept representation in a matter unless it can be performed competently, promptly, without improper conflict of interest, and to completion. Ordinarily, a representation in a matter is completed when the agreed-upon assistance has been concluded. See rule 4-1.2, and the comment to rule 4-1.3.

Mandatory Withdrawal (Comment on Rule 4-1.16)

[2] A lawyer ordinarily must decline or withdraw from representation if the client demands that the lawyer engage in conduct that is illegal or violates the Rules of Professional Conduct or law. The lawyer is not obliged to decline or withdraw simply because the client suggests such a course of conduct; a client may make such a suggestion in the hope that a lawyer will not be constrained by a professional obligation. Withdrawal is also mandatory if the client persists in a course of action that the lawyer reasonably believes is criminal or fraudulent, unless the client agrees to disclose and rectify the crime or fraud. Withdrawal is also required if the lawyer's services were misused in the past even if that would materially prejudice the client.

| Mandatory Withdrawal |

Court Permission to Withdraw

[3] When a lawyer has been appointed to represent a client, withdrawal ordinarily requires approval of the appointing authority. See also rule 4-6.2. Similarly, court approval or notice to the court is often required by applicable law before a lawyer withdraws from pending litigation. Difficulty may be encountered if withdrawal is based on the client's demand that the lawyer engage in unprofessional conduct. The court may request an explanation for the withdrawal, while the lawyer may be bound to keep confidential the facts that would constitute such an explanation. The lawyer's statement that professional considerations require termination of the representation ordinarily should be accepted as sufficient. Lawyers should be mindful of their obligations to both clients and the court under rules 4-1.6 and 4-3.3.

Discharge (Comment on Rule 4-1.16)

[4] A client has a right to discharge a lawyer at any time, with or without cause, subject to liability for payment for the lawyer's services. Where future dispute about the withdrawal may be anticipated, it may be advisable to prepare a written statement reciting the circumstances.

Discharging a Lawyer

[5] Whether a client can discharge appointed counsel may depend on applicable law. A client seeking to do so should be given a full explanation of the consequences. These consequences may include a decision by the appointing authority that appointment of successor counsel is unjustified, thus requiring the client to be self-represented.

[6] If the client is mentally incompetent, the client may lack the legal capacity to discharge the lawyer, and in any event the discharge may be seriously adverse to the client's interests. The lawyer should make special effort to help the client consider the consequences and may take reasonably necessary protective action as provided in rule 4-1.14.

Optional Withdrawal (Comment on Rule 4-1.16)

[7] A lawyer may withdraw from representation in some circumstances. The lawyer has the option to withdraw if it can be accomplished without material adverse effect on the client's interests. The lawyer also may withdraw where the client insists on taking action that the lawyer considers repugnant, imprudent, or with which the lawyer has a fundamental disagreement.

Optional Withdrawal

[8] A lawyer may withdraw if the client refuses to abide by the terms of an agreement relating to the representation, such as an agreement concerning fees or court costs or an agreement limiting the objectives of the representation.

Assisting the Client upon Withdrawal (Comment on Rule 4-1.16)

[9] Even if the lawyer has been unfairly discharged by the client, a lawyer must take all reasonable steps to mitigate the consequences to the client. The lawyer may retain papers and other property as security for a fee only to the extent permitted by law.

Minimizing the Adverse Effects of Withdrawal

Refunding Advance Payment of Unearned Fee

[10] Upon termination of representation, a lawyer should refund to the client any advance payment of a fee that has not been earned. This does not preclude a lawyer from retaining any reasonable nonrefundable fee that the client agreed would be deemed earned when the lawyer commenced the client's representation. See also rule 4-1.5.

Rule 4-1.18. Duties to Prospective Client

(a) **Prospective Client.** A person who discusses with a lawyer the possibility of forming a client-lawyer relationship with respect to a matter is a prospective client.

(b) **Confidentiality of Information.** Even when no client-lawyer relationship ensues, a lawyer who has had discussions with a prospective client shall not use or reveal information learned in the consultation, except as rule 4-1.9 would permit with respect to information of a former client.

The Duty of Confidentiality to Someone Who Is Not a Client

(c) **Subsequent Representation.** A lawyer subject to subdivision (b) shall not represent a client with interests materially adverse to those of a prospective client in the same or a substantially related matter if the lawyer received information from the prospective client that could be used to the disadvantage of that person in the matter, except as provided in subdivision (d). If a lawyer is disqualified from representation under this rule, no lawyer in a firm with which that lawyer is associated may knowingly undertake or continue representation in such a matter, except as provided in subdivision (d).

(d) **Permissible Representation.** When the lawyer has received disqualifying information as defined in subdivision (c), representation is permissible if:

(1) both the affected client and the prospective client have given informed consent, confirmed in writing; or

(2) the lawyer who received the information took reasonable measures to avoid exposure to more disqualifying information than was reasonably necessary to determine whether to represent the prospective client; and

Screening to Avoid Disqualification

(i) the disqualified lawyer is timely screened from any participation in the matter and is apportioned no part of the fee therefrom; and

(ii) written notice is promptly given to the prospective client.

Official Comments on Rule 4-1.18 (Duties to Prospective Client)

[1] Prospective clients, like clients, may disclose information to a lawyer, place documents or other property in the lawyer's custody, or rely on the lawyer's advice.

Partial Protection for Prospective Clients

A lawyer's discussions with a prospective client usually are limited in time and depth and leave both the prospective client and the lawyer free (and the lawyer sometimes required) to proceed no further. Hence, prospective clients should receive some but not all of the protection afforded clients.

[2] Not all persons who communicate information to a lawyer are entitled to protection under this rule. A person who communicates information unilaterally to a lawyer, without any reasonable expectation that the lawyer is willing to discuss the possibility of forming a client-lawyer relationship, is not a "prospective client" within the meaning of subdivision (a).

[3] It is often necessary for a prospective client to reveal information to the lawyer during an initial consultation prior to the decision about formation of a client-lawyer relationship. The lawyer

Dynamics of the Initial Interview

often must learn such information to determine whether there is a conflict of interest with an existing client and whether the matter is one that the lawyer is willing to undertake. Subdivision (b) prohibits the lawyer from using or revealing that information, except as permitted by rule 4-1.9, even if the client or lawyer decides not to proceed with the representation. The duty exists regardless of how brief the initial conference may be.

[4] In order to avoid acquiring disqualifying information from a prospective client, a lawyer considering whether to undertake a new matter should limit the initial interview to only such information as reasonably appears necessary for that purpose. Where the information indicates that a conflict of interest or other reason for non-representation exists, the lawyer should so inform the prospective client or decline the representation. If the prospective client wishes to retain the lawyer, and if consent is possible under rule 4-1.7, then consent from all affected present or former clients must be obtained before accepting the representation.

[5] A lawyer may condition conversations with a prospective client on the person's informed consent that no information disclosed during the consultation will prohibit the lawyer from representing a different client in the matter. See terminology for the definition of informed consent. If the agreement expressly so provides, the prospective client may also consent to the lawyer's subsequent use of information received from the prospective client.

[6] Even in the absence of an agreement, under subdivision (c), the lawyer is not prohibited from representing a client with interests adverse to those of the prospective client in the same or a substantially related matter unless the lawyer has received from the prospective client information that could be used to the disadvantage of the prospective client in the matter.

[7] Under subdivision (c), the prohibition in this rule is imputed to other lawyers as provided in rule 4-1.10, but, under subdivision

Screening to Avoid Disqualification

(d)(1), the prohibition and its imputation may be avoided if the lawyer obtains the informed consent, confirmed in writing, of both the prospective and affected clients. In the alternative, the prohibition and its imputation may be avoided if the conditions of subdivision (d)(2) are met and all disqualified lawyers are timely screened and written notice is promptly given to the prospective client. See Rule terminology (requirements for screening procedures). Paragraph (d)(2)(i) does not prohibit the screened lawyer from receiving a salary or partnership share established by prior independent agreement, but that lawyer may not receive compensation directly related to the matter in which the lawyer is disqualified.

[8] Notice, including a general description of the subject matter about which the lawyer was consulted, and of the screening procedures employed, generally should be given as soon as practicable after the need for screening becomes apparent.

[9] The duties under this rule presume that the prospective client consults the lawyer in good faith.

Sham Consultation

A person who consults a lawyer simply with the intent of disqualifying the lawyer from the matter, with no intent of possibly hiring the lawyer, has engaged in a sham and should not be able to invoke this rule to create a disqualification.

[10] For the duty of competence of a lawyer who gives assistance on the merits of a matter to a prospective client, see rule 4-1.1. For a lawyer's duties when a prospective client entrusts valuables or papers to the lawyer's care, see chapter 5, Rules Regulating The Florida Bar.

4-2. Counselor

Rule 4-2.1. Adviser

In representing a client, a lawyer shall exercise independent professional judgment and render candid

Independent Professional Judgment and Legal Advice

advice. In rendering advice, a lawyer may refer not only to law but to other considerations such as moral, economic, social, and political factors that may be relevant to the client's situation.

Official Comments on Rule 4-2.1 (Adviser)

Scope of advice (Comment on Rule 4-2.1)

[1] A client is entitled to straightforward advice express-

| Giving Candid Legal Advice |

ing the lawyer's honest assessment. Legal advice often involves unpleasant facts and alternatives that a client may be disinclined to confront. In presenting advice, a lawyer endeavors to sustain the client's morale and may put advice in as acceptable a form as honesty permits. However, a lawyer should not be deterred from giving candid advice by the prospect that the advice will be unpalatable to the client.

[2] Advice couched in narrowly legal terms may be of lit-

| Moral Considerations in Giving Legal Advice |

tle value to a client, especially where practical considerations, such as cost or effects on other people, are predominant. Purely technical legal advice, therefore, can sometimes be inadequate. It is proper for a lawyer to refer to relevant moral and ethical considerations in giving advice. Although a lawyer is not a moral adviser as such, moral and ethical considerations impinge upon most legal questions and may decisively influence how the law will be applied.

[3] A client may expressly or impliedly ask the lawyer for purely technical advice. When such a request is made by a client experienced in legal matters, the lawyer may accept it at face value. When such a request is made by a client inexperienced in legal matters, however, the lawyer's responsibility as adviser may include indicating that more may be involved than strictly legal considerations.

[4] Matters that go beyond strictly legal questions may also be in the domain of another profession. Family

| Recommending Other Professional Help |

matters can involve problems within the professional competence of psychiatry, clinical psychology, or social work; business matters can involve problems within the competence of the accounting profession or of financial specialists. Where consultation with a professional in another field is itself something a competent lawyer would recommend, the lawyer should make such a recommendation. At the same time, a lawyer's advice at its best often consists of recommending a course of action in the face of conflicting recommendations of experts.

Offering advice (Comment on Rule 4-2.1)

| Giving Legal Advice When It Is Not Sought |

[5] In general, a lawyer is not expected to give advice until asked by the client. However, when a lawyer knows that a client proposes

a course of action that is likely to result in substantial adverse legal consequences to the client, the lawyer's duty to the client under rule 4-1.4 may require that the lawyer offer advice if the client's course of action is related to the representation. Similarly, when a matter is likely to involve litigation, it may be necessary under rule 4-1.4 to inform the client of forms of dispute resolution that might constitute reasonable alternatives to litigation. A lawyer ordinarily has no duty to initiate investigation of a client's affairs or to give advice that the client has indicated is unwanted, but a lawyer may initiate advice to a client when doing so appears to be in the client's interest.

Rule 4-2.2. [left vacant by the Court]

Rule 4-2.3. Evaluation for Use by Third Persons

(a) **When Lawyer May Provide Evaluation.** A lawyer may provide an evaluation of a matter affecting a client for the use of someone other than the client if:

| Legal Evaluations on a Matter Affecting the Client That Others Will Use |

  (1) the lawyer reasonably believes that making the evaluation is compatible with other aspects of the lawyer's relationship with the client; and

  (2) the client gives informed consent.

(b) **Limitation on Scope of Evaluation.** In reporting the evaluation, the lawyer shall indicate any material limitations that were imposed on the scope of the inquiry or on the disclosure of information.

(c) **Maintaining Client Confidences.** Except as disclosure is required in connection with a report of an evaluation, information relating to the evaluation is otherwise protected by rule 4-1.6.

Official Comments on Rule 4-2.3 (Evaluation for Use by Third Parties)

Definition (Comment on Rule 4-2.3)

[1] An evaluation may be performed at the client's direction but for the primary purpose of establishing information for the benefit of third parties; for example, an opinion concerning the title of property rendered at the behest of a vendor for the information of a prospective purchaser or at the behest of a borrower for the information of a prospective lender. In some situations, the evaluation may be required by a government agency; for example, an opinion concerning the legality of the securities registered for sale under the securities laws. In other instances, the evaluation may be required by a third person, such as a purchaser of a business.

[2] A legal evaluation should be distinguished from an investigation of a person with whom the lawyer does not have a client-lawyer relationship. For example, a lawyer retained by a purchaser to analyze a vendor's title to property does not have a client-lawyer relationship with the vendor. So also, an

investigation into a person's affairs by a government lawyer, or by special counsel employed by the government, is not an evaluation as that term is used in this rule. The question is whether the lawyer is retained by the person whose affairs are being examined. When the lawyer is retained by that person, the general rules concerning loyalty to client and preservation of confidences apply, which is not the case if the lawyer is retained by someone else. For this reason, it is essential to identify the person by whom the lawyer is retained. This should be made clear not only to the person under examination, but also to others to whom the results are to be made available.

Duty to Third Person (Comment on Rule 4-2.3)

[3] When the evaluation is intended for the information or use of a third person, a legal duty to that person may or may not arise. That legal question is beyond the scope of this rule. However, since such an evaluation involves a departure from the normal client-lawyer relationship, careful analysis of the situation is required. The lawyer must be satisfied as a matter of professional judgment that making the evaluation is compatible with other functions undertaken in behalf of the client. For example, if the lawyer is acting as an advocate in defending the client against charges of fraud, it would normally be incompatible with that responsibility for the lawyer to perform an evaluation for others concerning the same or a related transaction. Assuming no such impediment is apparent, however, the lawyer should advise the client of the implications of the evaluation, particularly the lawyer's responsibilities to third persons and the duty to disseminate the findings.

Access to and Disclosure of Information (Comment on Rule 4-2.3)

[4] The quality of an evaluation depends on the freedom and extent of the investigation upon which it is based. Ordinarily, a lawyer should have whatever latitude of investigation seems necessary as a matter of professional judgment. Under some circumstances, however, the terms of the evaluation may be limited. For example, certain issues or sources may be categorically excluded or the scope of search may be limited by time constraints or the noncooperation of persons having relevant information. Any such limitations that are material to the evaluation should be described in the report. If, after a lawyer has commenced an evaluation, the client refuses to comply with the terms upon which it was understood the evaluation was to have been made, the lawyer's obligations are determined by law, having reference to the terms of the client's agreement and the surrounding circumstances. In no circumstances is the lawyer permitted to knowingly make a false statement of material fact or law in providing an evaluation under this rule. See rule 4-4.1.

Financial Auditors' Requests for Information (Comment on Rule 4-2.3)

[5] When a question concerning the legal situation of a client arises at the instance of the client's financial auditor and the question is referred to the lawyer, the lawyer's response may be made in accordance with procedures recognized in the legal profession. Such a procedure is set forth in the American Bar Association Statement of Policy Regarding Lawyers' Responses to Auditors' Requests for Information, adopted in 1975.

Rule 4-2.4. Lawyer Serving as Third-Party Neutral

(a) A lawyer serves as a third-party neutral when the lawyer assists 2 or more persons who are not clients of the lawyer to reach a resolution of a dispute or other matter that has arisen between them. Service as a third-party neutral may include service as an arbitrator, a mediator, or in such other capacity as will enable the lawyer to assist the parties to resolve the matter.

> **Lawyers Assisting People without Representing Them**

(b) A lawyer serving as a third-party neutral shall inform unrepresented parties that the lawyer is not representing them. When the lawyer knows or reasonably should know that a party does not understand the lawyer's role in the matter, the lawyer shall explain the difference between the lawyer's role as a third-party neutral and a lawyer's role as one who represents a client.

Official Comments on Rule 4-2.4 (Lawyer Serving as Third-Party Neutral)

> **ADR: Alternative Dispute Resolution**

[1] Alternative dispute resolution has become a substantial part of the civil justice system. Aside from representing clients in dispute-resolution processes, lawyers often serve as third-party neutrals. A third-party neutral is a person, such as a mediator, arbitrator, conciliator, or evaluator, who assists the parties, represented or unrepresented, in the resolution of a dispute or in the arrangement of a transaction. Whether a third-party neutral serves primarily as a facilitator, evaluator, or decisionmaker depends on the particular process that is either selected by the parties or mandated by a court.

[2] The role of a third-party neutral is not unique to lawyers, although, in some court-connected contexts, only lawyers are allowed to serve in this role or to handle certain types of cases. In performing this role, the lawyer may be subject to court rules or other law

that apply either to third-party neutrals generally or to lawyers serving as third-party neutrals. Lawyer-neutrals may also be subject to various codes of ethics, such as the Code of Ethics for Arbitration in Commercial Disputes prepared by a joint committee of the American Bar Association and the American Arbitration Association, or the Model Standards of Conduct for Mediators jointly prepared by the American Bar Association, the American Arbitration Association, and the Society of Professionals in Dispute Resolution. A Florida Bar member who is a certified mediator is governed by the applicable law and rules relating to certified mediators.

[3] Unlike nonlawyers who serve as third-party neutrals, lawyers serving in this role may experience unique problems as a result of differences between the role of a third-party neutral and a lawyer's service as a client representative. The potential for confusion is significant when the parties are unrepresented in the process. Thus, subdivision (b) requires a lawyer-neutral to inform unrepresented parties that the lawyer is not representing them. For some parties, particularly parties who frequently use dispute-resolution processes, this information will be sufficient. For others, particularly those who are using the process for the first time, more information will be required. Where appropriate, the lawyer should inform unrepresented parties of the important differences between the lawyer's role as third-party neutral and a lawyer's role as a client representative, including the inapplicability of the attorney-client evidentiary privilege. The extent of disclosure required under this subdivision will depend on the particular parties involved and the subject matter of the proceeding, as well as the particular features of the dispute-resolution process selected.

[4] A lawyer who serves as a third-party neutral subsequently may be asked to serve as a lawyer representing a client in the same matter. The conflicts of interest that arise for both the individual lawyer and the lawyer's law firm are addressed in rule 4-1.12.

[5] Lawyers who represent clients in alternative dispute-resolution processes are governed by the Rules of Professional Conduct. When the dispute-resolution process takes place before a tribunal, as in binding arbitration (see terminology), the lawyer's duty of candor is governed by rule 4-3.3. Otherwise, the lawyer's duty of candor toward both the third-party neutral and other parties is governed by rule 4-4.1.

4-3. Advocate

Rule 4-3.1. Meritorious Claims and Contentions

| Avoiding Frivolous Claims |

A lawyer shall not bring or defend a proceeding, or assert or controvert an issue therein, unless there is a basis in law and fact for doing so that is not frivolous, which includes a good faith argument for an extension, modification, or reversal of existing law. A lawyer for the defendant in a criminal proceeding, or the respondent in a proceeding that could result in incarceration, may nevertheless so defend the proceeding as to require that every element of the case be established.

Official Comments on Rule 4-3.1 (Meritorious Claims and Contentions)

[1] The advocate has a duty to use legal procedure for the fullest benefit of the client's cause, but also a duty not to abuse legal procedure. The law, both procedural and substantive, establishes the limits within which an advocate may proceed. However, the law is not always clear and never is static. Accordingly, in determining the proper scope of advocacy, account must be taken of the law's ambiguities and potential for change.

[2] The filing of an action or defense or similar action taken for a client is not frivolous merely because the facts have not first been fully substantiated or because the lawyer expects to develop | Good Faith Arguments | vital evidence only by discovery. What is required of lawyers, however, is that they inform themselves about the facts of their clients' cases and the applicable law and determine that they can make good faith arguments in support of their clients' positions. Such action is not frivolous even though the lawyer believes that the client's position ultimately will not prevail. The action is frivolous, however, if the lawyer is unable either to make a good faith argument on the merits of the action taken or to support the action taken by a good faith argument for an extension, modification, or reversal of existing law.

[3] The lawyer's obligations under this rule are subordinate to federal or state constitutional law that entitles a defendant in a criminal matter to the assistance of counsel in presenting a claim or contention that otherwise would be prohibited by this rule.

Rule 4-3.2. Expediting Litigation

A lawyer shall make reasonable efforts to expedite litigation consistent with the interests of the client. | Avoiding Dilatory Tactics |

Official Comments on Rule 4-3.2 (Expediting Litigation)

[1] Dilatory practices bring the administration of justice into disrepute. Although there will be occasions when a lawyer may properly seek a postponement for personal reasons, it is not proper for a lawyer to routinely fail to expedite litigation solely for the convenience of the advocates. Nor will a

failure to expedite be reasonable if done for the purpose of frustrating an opposing party's attempt to obtain rightful redress or repose. It is not a justification that similar conduct is often tolerated by the bench and bar. The question is whether a competent lawyer acting in good faith would regard the course of action as having some substantial purpose other than delay. Realizing financial or other benefit from otherwise improper delay in litigation is not a legitimate interest of the client.

Rule 4-3.3. Candor Toward the Tribunal

(a) **False Evidence; Duty to Disclose.** A lawyer shall not knowingly:

> **Making False Statements; Failure to Disclose**

(1) make a false statement of material fact or law to a tribunal;

(2) fail to disclose a material fact to a tribunal when disclosure is necessary to avoid assisting a criminal or fraudulent act by the client;

(3) fail to disclose to the tribunal legal authority in the controlling jurisdiction known to the lawyer to be directly adverse to the position of the client and not disclosed by opposing counsel; or

(4) permit any witness, including a criminal defendant, to offer testimony or other evidence that the lawyer knows to be false. A lawyer may not offer testimony that the lawyer knows to be false in the form of a narrative unless so ordered by the tribunal. If a lawyer has offered material evidence and thereafter comes to know of its falsity, the lawyer shall take reasonable remedial measures.

(b) **Extent of Lawyer's Duties.** The duties stated in subdivision (a) continue beyond the conclusion of the proceeding and apply even if compliance requires disclosure of information otherwise protected by rule 4-1.6.

(c) **Evidence Believed to Be False.** A lawyer may refuse to offer evidence that the lawyer reasonably believes is false.

(d) **Ex Parte Proceedings.** In an ex parte proceeding a lawyer shall inform the tribunal of all material facts known to the lawyer that will enable the tribunal to make an informed decision, whether or not the facts are adverse.

Official Comments on Rule 4-3.3 (Candor Toward the Tribunal)

[1] The advocate's task is to present the client's case with persuasive force. Performance of that duty while maintaining confidences of the client is qualified by the advocate's duty of candor to the tribunal. However, an advocate does not vouch for the evidence submitted in a cause; the tribunal is responsible for assessing its probative value.

Representations by a Lawyer (Comment on Rule 4-3.3)

[2] An advocate is responsible for pleadings and other documents prepared for litigation, but is usually not required to have personal knowledge of matters asserted therein, for litigation documents ordinarily present assertions by the client, or by someone on the client's behalf, and not assertions by the lawyer. Compare rule 4-3.1. However, an assertion purporting to be on the lawyer's own knowledge, as in an affidavit by the lawyer or in a statement in open court, may properly be made only when the lawyer knows the assertion is true or believes it to be true on the basis of a reasonably diligent inquiry. There are circumstances where failure to make a disclosure is the equivalent of an affirmative misrepresentation. The obligation prescribed in rule 4-1.2(d) not to counsel a client to commit or assist the client in committing a fraud applies in litigation. Regarding compliance with rule 4-1.2(d), see the comment to that rule. See also the comment to rule 4-8.4(b).

Misleading Legal Argument (Comment on Rule 4-3.3)

[3] Legal argument based on a knowingly false representation of law constitutes dishonesty toward the tribunal. A lawyer is

> **Duty to Disclose Adverse Legal Authority**

not required to make a disinterested exposition of the law, but must recognize the existence of pertinent legal authorities. Furthermore, as stated in subdivision (a)(3), an advocate has a duty to disclose directly adverse authority in the controlling jurisdiction that has not been disclosed by the opposing party. The underlying concept is that legal argument is a discussion seeking to determine the legal premises properly applicable to the case.

False Evidence (Comment on Rule 4-3.3)

[4] When evidence that a lawyer knows to be false is provided by a person who is not the client, the lawyer must refuse to offer it regardless of the client's wishes.

[5] When false evidence is offered by the client, however, a conflict may arise between the lawyer's duty to keep the client's revelations confidential and the duty of candor to the court. Upon ascertaining that material evidence is false, the lawyer should seek to persuade the client that the evidence should not be offered or, if it has been offered, that its false character should immediately be disclosed. If the persuasion is ineffective, the lawyer must take reasonable remedial measures.

[6] Except in the defense of a criminally accused, the rule generally recognized is that, if necessary to rectify the situation, an advocate must disclose the existence of the client's deception to the court. Such a disclosure can result in grave consequences to

> **Disclosing a Client's Deception; Perjury**

the client, including not only a sense of betrayal but also loss of the case and perhaps a prosecution for perjury. But the alternative is that the lawyer co-operate in deceiving the court, thereby subverting the truth-finding process that the adversary system is designed to implement. See rule 4-1.2(d). Furthermore, unless it is clearly understood that the lawyer will act upon the duty to disclose the existence of false evidence, the client can simply reject the lawyer's advice to reveal the false evidence and insist that the lawyer keep silent. Thus, the client could in effect coerce the lawyer into being a party to fraud on the court.

Perjury by a Criminal Defendant (Comment on Rule 4-3.3)

[7] Whether an advocate for a criminally accused has the same duty of disclosure has been intensely debated. While it is agreed that the lawyer should seek to persuade the client to refrain from perjurious testimony, there has been dispute concerning the lawyer's duty when that persuasion fails. If the confrontation with the client occurs before trial, the lawyer ordinarily can withdraw. Withdrawal before trial may not be possible if trial is imminent, if the confrontation with the client does not take place until the trial itself, or if no other counsel is available.

[8] The most difficult situation, therefore, arises in a criminal case where the accused insists on testifying when the lawyer knows that the testimony is perjurious. The lawyer's effort to rectify the situation can increase the likelihood of the client's being convicted as well as opening the possibility of a prosecution for perjury. On the other hand, if the lawyer does not exercise control over the proof, the lawyer participates, although in a merely passive way, in deception of the court.

[9] Although the offering of perjured testimony or false evidence is considered a fraud on the tribunal, these situations are distinguishable from that of a client who, upon being arrested, provides false identification to a law enforcement officer. The client's past act of lying to a law enforcement officer does not constitute a fraud on the tribunal, and thus does not trigger the disclosure obligation under this rule, because a false statement to an arresting officer is unsworn and occurs prior to the institution of a court proceeding. If the client testifies, the lawyer must attempt to have the client respond to any questions truthfully or by asserting an applicable privilege. Any false statements by the client in the course of the court proceeding will trigger the duties under this rule.

Remedial Measures (Comment on Rule 4-3.3)

[10] If perjured testimony or false evidence has been offered, the advocate's proper course ordinarily is to remonstrate with the client confidentially. If that fails, the advocate should seek to withdraw if that will remedy the situation. Subject to the caveat

> **Withdrawal and/or Disclosure by Lawyer to Court of Client's Perjury**

expressed in the next section of this comment, if withdrawal will not remedy the situation or is impossible and the advocate determines that disclosure is the only measure that will avert a fraud on the court, the advocate should make disclosure to the court. It is for the court then to determine what should be done—making a statement about the matter to the trier of fact, ordering a mistrial, or perhaps nothing. If the false testimony was that of the client, the client may controvert the lawyer's version of their communication when the lawyer discloses the situation to the court. If there is an issue whether the client has committed perjury, the lawyer cannot represent the client in resolution of the issue and a mistrial may be unavoidable. An unscrupulous client might in this way attempt to produce a series of mistrials and thus escape prosecution. However, a second such encounter could be construed as a deliberate abuse of the right to counsel and as such a waiver of the right to further representation.

Constitutional Requirements (Comment on Rule 4-3.3)

[11] The general rule—that an advocate must disclose the existence of perjury with respect to a material fact, even that of a client—applies to defense counsel in criminal cases, as well as in other instances. However, the definition of the lawyer's ethical duty in such a situation may be qualified by constitutional provisions for due process and the right to counsel in criminal cases.

Refusing to Offer Proof Believed to be False (Comment on Rule 4-3.3)

[12] Generally speaking, a lawyer has authority to refuse to offer testimony or other proof that

> **Untrustworthy Evidence**

the lawyer believes is untrustworthy. Offering such proof may reflect adversely on the lawyer's ability to discriminate in the quality of evidence and thus impair the lawyer's effectiveness as an advocate. In criminal cases, however, a lawyer may, in some jurisdictions, be denied this authority by constitutional requirements governing the right to counsel.

[13] A lawyer may not assist the client or any witness in offering false testimony or other false evidence, nor may the lawyer permit the client or any other witness to testify falsely in the narrative form unless ordered to do so by the tribunal. If a lawyer knows that the client intends to commit perjury, the lawyer's first duty is to attempt to persuade

> **Threat of Disclosure**

the client to testify truthfully. If the client still insists on committing perjury, the lawyer must threaten to disclose the client's intent to commit perjury to the judge. If the threat of disclosure does not successfully persuade the client to testify truthfully, the lawyer must disclose the fact that the client intends to lie to the tribunal and, per 4-1.6, information sufficient to prevent the commission of the crime of perjury.

[14] The lawyer's duty not to assist witnesses, including the lawyer's own client, in offering false evidence stems from the Rules of Professional Conduct, Florida statutes, and caselaw.

[15] Rule 4-1.2(d) prohibits the lawyer from assisting a client in conduct that the lawyer knows or reasonably should know is criminal or fraudulent.

[16] Rule 4-3.4(b) prohibits a lawyer from fabricating evidence or assisting a witness to testify falsely.

[17] Rule 4-8.4(a) prohibits the lawyer from violating the Rules of Professional Conduct or knowingly assisting another to do so.

[18] Rule 4-8.4(b) prohibits a lawyer from committing a criminal act that reflects adversely on the lawyer's honesty, trustworthiness, or fitness as a lawyer.

[19] Rule 4-8.4(c) prohibits a lawyer from engaging in conduct involving dishonesty, fraud, deceit, or misrepresentation.

[20] Rule 4-8.4(d) prohibits a lawyer from engaging in conduct that is prejudicial to the administration of justice.

[21] Rule 4-1.6(b) requires a lawyer to reveal information to the extent the lawyer reasonably believes necessary to prevent a client from committing a crime.

[22] This rule, 4-3.3(a)(2), requires a lawyer to reveal a material fact to the tribunal when disclosure is necessary to avoid assisting a criminal or fraudulent act by the client, and 4-3.3(a)(4) prohibits a lawyer from offering false evidence and requires the lawyer to take reasonable remedial measures when false material evidence has been offered.

[23] Rule 4-1.16 prohibits a lawyer from representing a client if the representation will result in a violation of the Rules of Professional Conduct or law and permits the lawyer to withdraw from representation if the client persists in a course of action that the lawyer reasonably believes is criminal or fraudulent or repugnant or imprudent. Rule 4-1.16(c) recognizes that notwithstanding good cause for terminating representation of a client, a lawyer is obliged to continue representation if so ordered by a tribunal.

[24] To permit or assist a client or other witness to testify falsely is prohibited by section 837.02, Florida Statutes (1991), which makes perjury in an official proceeding a felony, and by section 777.011, Florida Statutes (1991), which proscribes aiding, abetting, or counseling commission of a felony.

[25] Florida caselaw prohibits lawyers from presenting false testimony or evidence. *Kneale v. Williams*, 30 So. 2d 284 (Fla. 1947), states that perpetration of a fraud is outside the scope of the professional duty of an attorney and no privilege attaches to communication between an attorney and a client with respect to transactions constituting the making of a false claim or the perpetration of a fraud. *Dodd v. The Florida Bar*, 118 So. 2d 17 (Fla. 1960), reminds us that "the courts are . . . dependent on members of the bar to . . . present the true facts of each cause . . . to enable the judge or the jury to [decide the facts] to which the law may be applied. When an attorney . . . allows false testimony . . . [the attorney] . . . makes it impossible for the scales [of justice] to balance." See *The Fla. Bar v. Agar*, 394 So. 2d 405 (Fla. 1981), and *The Fla. Bar v. Simons*, 391 So. 2d 684 (Fla. 1980).

[26] The United States Supreme Court in *Nix v. Whiteside*, 475 U.S. 157 (1986), answered in the negative the constitutional issue of whether it is ineffective assistance of counsel for an attorney to threaten disclosure of a client's (a criminal defendant's) intention to testify falsely.

Ex parte Proceedings (Comment on Rule 4-3.3)

[27] Ordinarily, an advocate has the limited responsibility of presenting 1 side of the matters that a tribunal should consider in reaching a decision; the conflicting position is expected to be presented by the opposing party. However, in an ex parte proceeding, such as an application for a temporary injunction, there is no balance of presentation by opposing advocates. The object of an ex parte proceeding is nevertheless to yield a substantially just result. The judge has an affirmative responsibility to accord the absent party just consideration. The lawyer for the represented party has the correlative duty to make disclosures of material facts known to the lawyer and that the lawyer reasonably believes are necessary to an informed decision.

> Disclosures During Ex Parte Proceedings

Rule 4-3.4. Fairness to Opposing Party and Counsel

A lawyer shall not:

(a) unlawfully obstruct another party's access to evidence or otherwise unlawfully alter, destroy, or conceal a document or other material that the lawyer knows or reasonably should know is relevant to a pending or a reasonably foreseeable proceeding; nor counsel or assist another person to do any such act;

> Unethical Interference with an Opponent

(b) fabricate evidence, counsel or assist a witness to testify falsely, or offer an inducement to a witness, except a lawyer may pay a witness reasonable expenses incurred by the witness in attending or testifying at proceedings; a reasonable, noncontingent fee for professional services of an expert witness; and reasonable compensation to reimburse a witness for the loss of compensation incurred by reason of preparing for, attending, or testifying at proceedings;

(c) knowingly disobey an obligation under the rules of a tribunal except for an open refusal based on an assertion that no valid obligation exists;

(d) in pretrial procedure, make a frivolous discovery request or intentionally fail to comply with a legally proper discovery request by an opposing party;

| Frivolous Discovery Requests |

(e) in trial, state a personal opinion about the credibility of a witness unless the statement is authorized by current rule or case law, allude to any matter that the lawyer does not reasonably believe is relevant or that will not be supported by admissible evidence, assert personal knowledge of facts in issue except when testifying as a witness, or state a personal opinion as to the justness of a cause, the culpability of a civil litigant, or the guilt or innocence of an accused;

(f) request a person other than a client to refrain from voluntarily giving relevant information to another party unless the person is a relative or an employee or other agent of a client, and it is reasonable to believe that the person's interests will not be adversely affected by refraining from giving such information;

| Threatening Criminal Charges |

(g) present, participate in presenting, or threaten to present criminal charges solely to obtain an advantage in a civil matter; or

(h) present, participate in presenting, or threaten to present disciplinary charges under these rules solely to obtain an advantage in a civil matter.

Official Comments on Rule 4-3.4 (Fairness to Opposing Party and Counsel)

[1] The procedure of the adversary system contemplates that the evidence in a case is to be marshalled competitively by the contending parties. Fair competition in the adversary system is secured by prohibitions against destruction or concealment of evidence, improperly influencing witnesses, obstructive tactics in discovery procedure, and the like.

| Destruction or Concealment of Evidence |

[2] Documents and other items of evidence are often essential to establish a claim or defense. Subject to evidentiary privileges, the right of an opposing party, including the government, to obtain evidence through discovery or subpoena is an important procedural right. The exercise of that right can be frustrated if relevant material is altered, concealed, or destroyed. Applicable law in many ju-risdictions makes it an offense to destroy material for the purpose of impairing its availability in a pending proceeding or one whose commencement can be foreseen. Falsifying evidence is also generally a criminal offense. Subdivision (a) applies to evidentiary material generally, including computerized information.

[3] With regard to subdivision (b), it is not improper to pay a witness's expenses or to compensate an expert witness on terms permitted by law. The common law rule in most jurisdictions is that it is improper to pay an occurrence witness any fee for testifying and that it is improper to pay an expert witness a contingent fee.

| Improper Contingent Fee to a Witness |

[4] Previously, subdivision (e) also proscribed statements about the credibility of witnesses. However, in 2000, the Supreme Court of Florida entered an opinion in *Murphy v. International Robotic Systems, Inc.*, 766 So. 2d 1010 (Fla. 2000), wherein the court allowed counsel in closing argument to call a witness a "liar" or to state that the witness "lied." There the court stated: "First, it is not improper for counsel to state during closing argument that a witness 'lied' or is a 'liar,' provided such characterizations are supported by the record." *Murphy*, id., at 1028. Members of the bar are advised to check the status of the law in this area.

| Calling a Witness a "Liar" |

[5] Subdivision (f) permits a lawyer to advise employees of a client to refrain from giving information to another party, for the employees may identify their interests with those of the client. See also rule 4-4.2.

Rule 4-3.5. Impartiality and Decorum of the Tribunal

(a) Influencing Decision Maker. A lawyer shall not seek to influence a judge, juror, prospective juror, or other decision maker except as permitted by law or the rules of court.

| Improper Communications with Judge or Jury |

(b) Communication with Judge or Official. In an adversary proceeding a lawyer shall not communicate or cause another to communicate as to the merits of the cause with a judge or an official before whom the proceeding is pending except:

(1) in the course of the official proceeding in the cause;

(2) in writing if the lawyer promptly delivers a copy of the writing to the opposing counsel or to the adverse party if not represented by a lawyer;

(3) orally upon notice to opposing counsel or to the adverse party if not represented by a lawyer; or

(4) as otherwise authorized by law.

(c) Disruption of Tribunal. A lawyer shall not engage in conduct intended to disrupt a tribunal.

(d) Communication With Jurors. A lawyer shall not:

(1) before the trial of a case with which the lawyer is connected, communicate or cause another to communicate with anyone the lawyer knows to be a member of the venire from which the jury will be selected;

(2) during the trial of a case with which the lawyer is connected, communicate or cause another to communicate with any member of the jury;

(3) during the trial of a case with which the lawyer is not connected, communicate or cause another to communicate with a juror concerning the case;

(4) after dismissal of the jury in a case with which the lawyer is connected, initiate communication with or cause another to initiate communication with any juror regarding the trial except to determine whether the verdict may be subject to legal challenge; provided, a lawyer may not interview jurors for this purpose unless the lawyer has reason to believe that grounds for such challenge may exist; and provided further, before conducting any such interview the lawyer must file in the cause a notice of intention to interview setting forth the name of the juror or jurors to be interviewed. A copy of the notice must be delivered to the trial judge and opposing counsel a reasonable time before such interview. The provisions of this rule do not prohibit a lawyer from communicating with members of the venire or jurors in the course of official proceedings or as authorized by court rule or written order of the court.

| Post-Trial Interview of Jurors |

Official Comments on Rule 4-3.5 (Impartiality and Decorum of the Tribunal)

[1] Many forms of improper influence upon a tribunal are proscribed by criminal law. Others are specified in Florida's Code of Judicial Conduct, with which an advocate should be familiar. A lawyer is required to avoid contributing to a violation of such provisions.

[2] The advocate's function is to present evidence and argument so that the cause may be decided according to law. Refraining from abusive or obstreperous conduct is a corollary of the advocate's right to speak on behalf of litigants. A lawyer may stand firm against abuse by a judge but should avoid reciprocation; the judge's default is no justification for similar dereliction by an advocate. An advocate can present the cause, protect the record for subsequent review, and preserve professional integrity by patient firmness no less effectively than by belligerence or theatrics.

| Abusive, Obstreperous, Belligerent, Theatrical Conduct |

Rule 4-3.6. Trial Publicity

| Prejudicial Statements Made Out of Court |

(a) Prejudicial Extrajudicial Statements Prohibited. A lawyer shall not make an extrajudicial statement that a reasonable person would expect to be disseminated by means of public communication if the lawyer knows or reasonably should know that it will have a substantial likelihood of materially prejudicing an adjudicative proceeding due to its creation of an imminent and substantial detrimental effect on that proceeding.

(b) Statements of Third Parties. A lawyer shall not counsel or assist another person to make such a statement. Counsel shall exercise reasonable care to prevent investigators, employees, or other persons assisting in or associated with a case from making extrajudicial statements that are prohibited under this rule.

Official Comments on Rule 4-3.6 (Trial Publicity)

[1] It is difficult to strike a balance between protecting the right to a fair trial and safeguarding the right of free expression. Preserving the right to a fair trial necessarily entails some curtailment of the information that may be disseminated about a party prior to trial, particularly where trial by jury is involved. If there were no such limits, the result would be the practical nullification of the protective effect of the rules of forensic decorum and the exclusionary rules of evidence. On the other hand, there are vital social interests served by the free dissemination of information about events having legal consequences and about legal proceedings themselves. The public has a right to know about threats to its safety and measures aimed at assuring its security. It also has a legitimate interest in the conduct of judicial proceedings, particularly in matters of general public concern. Furthermore, the subject matter of legal proceedings is often of direct significance in debate and deliberation over questions of public policy.

| The Public's Right to Know vs. a Fair Trial |

Rule 4-3.7. Lawyer as Witness

(a) When Lawyer May Testify. A lawyer shall not act as advocate at a trial in which the lawyer is likely to be a necessary witness on behalf of the client unless:

| Inconsistency in a Lawyer's Role as Advocate and Witness |

(1) the testimony relates to an uncontested issue;

(2) the testimony will relate solely to a matter of formality and there is no reason to believe that substantial evidence will be offered in opposition to the testimony;

(3) the testimony relates to the nature and value of legal services rendered in the case; or

(4) disqualification of the lawyer would work substantial hardship on the client.

(b) Other Members of Law Firm as Witnesses. A lawyer may act as advocate in a trial in which another lawyer in the lawyer's firm is likely to be called as a witness unless precluded from doing so by rule 4-1.7 or 4-1.9.

Official Comments on Rule 4-3.7 (Lawyer as Witness)

[1] Combining the roles of advocate and witness can prejudice the tribunal and the opposing party and can also involve a conflict of interest between the lawyer and client.

[2] The trier of fact may be confused or misled by a lawyer serving as both advocate and witness. The combination of roles may prejudice another party's rights in the litigation. A witness is required to testify on the basis of personal knowledge, while an advocate is expected to explain and comment on evidence given by others. It may not be clear whether a statement by an advocate-witness should be taken as proof or as an analysis of the proof.

> **Analysis or Proof?**

[3] To protect the tribunal, subdivision (a) prohibits a lawyer from simultaneously serving as advocate and necessary witness except in those circumstances specified. Subdivision (a)(1) recognizes that if the testimony will be uncontested, the ambiguities in the dual role are purely theoretical. Subdivisions (a)(2) and (3) recognize that, where the testimony concerns the extent and value of legal services rendered in the action in which the testimony is offered, permitting the lawyers to testify avoids the need for a second trial with new counsel to resolve that issue. Moreover, in such a situation the judge has first-hand knowledge of the matter in issue; hence, there is less dependence on the adversary process to test the credibility of the testimony.

[4] Apart from these 2 exceptions, subdivision (a)(4) recognizes that a balancing is required between the interests of the client and those of the tribunal and the opposing party. Whether the tribunal is likely to be misled or the opposing party is likely to suffer prejudice depends on the nature of the case, the importance and probable tenor of the lawyer's testimony, and the probability that the lawyer's testimony will conflict with that of other witnesses. Even if there is risk of such prejudice, in determining whether the lawyer should be disqualified, due regard must be given to the effect of disqualification on the lawyer's client. It is relevant that one or both parties could reasonably foresee that the lawyer would probably be a witness. The conflict of interest principles stated in rules 4-1.7, 4-1.9, and 4-1.10 have no application to this aspect of the problem.

[5] Because the tribunal is not likely to be misled when a lawyer acts as advocate in a trial in which another lawyer in the lawyer's firm will testify as a necessary witness, subdivision (b) permits the lawyer to do so except in situations involving a conflict of interest.

[6] In determining if it is permissible to act as advocate in a trial in which the lawyer will be a necessary witness, the lawyer must also consider that the dual role may give rise to a conflict of interest that will require compliance with rules 4-1.7 or 4-1.9. For example, if there is likely to be substantial conflict between the testimony of the client and that of the lawyer, the representation involves a conflict of interest that requires compliance with rule 4-1.7. This would be true even though the lawyer might not be prohibited by subdivision (a) from simultaneously serving as advocate and witness because the lawyer's disqualification would work a substantial hardship on the client. Similarly, a lawyer who might be permitted to simultaneously serve as an advocate and a witness by subdivision (a)(3) might be precluded from doing so by rule 4-1.9. The problem can arise whether the lawyer is called as a witness on behalf of the client or is called by the opposing party. Determining whether such a conflict exists is primarily the responsibility of the lawyer involved. If there is a conflict of interest, the lawyer must secure the client's informed consent. In some cases, the lawyer will be precluded from seeking the client's consent. See rule 4-1.7. If a lawyer who is a member of a firm may not act as both advocate and witness by reason of conflict of interest, rule 4-1.10 disqualifies the firm also. See terminology for the definition of "confirmed in writing" and "informed consent."

[7] Subdivision (b) provides that a lawyer is not disqualified from serving as an advocate because a lawyer with whom the lawyer is associated in a firm is precluded from doing so by subdivision (a). If, however, the testifying lawyer would also be disqualified by rule 4-1.7 or 4-1.9 from representing the client in the matter, other lawyers in the firm will be precluded from representing the client by rule 4-1.10 unless the client gives informed consent under the conditions stated in rule 4-1.7.

Rule 4-3.8. Special Responsibilities of a Prosecutor

The prosecutor in a criminal case shall:

(a) refrain from prosecuting a charge that the prosecutor knows is not supported by probable cause;

(b) not seek to obtain from an unrepresented accused a waiver of important pre-trial rights such as a right to a preliminary hearing;

(c) make timely disclosure to the defense of all evidence or information known to the prosecutor that tends to negate the guilt of the accused or mitigates the offense, and, in

> **Disclosing Exculpatory Evidence**

connection with sentencing, disclose to the defense and to the tribunal all unprivileged mitigating information known to the prosecutor, except when the prosecutor is relieved of this responsibility by a protective order of the tribunal.

Official Comments on Rule 4-3.8 (Special Responsibilities of a Prosecutor)

[1] A prosecutor has the responsibility of a minister of justice and not simply that of an advocate. This responsibility carries with it specific obligations such as making a reasonable effort to assure that the accused has been advised of the right to and the procedure for obtaining counsel and has been given a reasonable opportunity to obtain counsel so that guilt is decided upon the basis of sufficient evidence. Precisely how far the prosecutor is required to go in this direction is a matter of debate. Florida has adopted the American Bar Association Standards of Criminal Justice Relating to Prosecution Function. This is the product of prolonged and careful deliberation by lawyers experienced in criminal prosecution and defense and should be consulted for further guidance. See also rule 4-3.3(d) governing ex parte proceedings, among which grand jury proceedings are included. Applicable law may require other measures by the prosecutor and knowing disregard of these obligations or systematic abuse of prosecutorial discretion could constitute a violation of rule 4-8.4.

[2] Subdivision (b) does not apply to an accused appearing pro se with the approval of the tribunal, nor does it forbid the lawful questioning of a suspect who has knowingly waived the rights to counsel and silence.

[3] The exception in subdivision (c) recognizes that a prosecutor may seek an appropriate protective order from the tribunal if disclosure of information to the defense could result in substantial harm to an individual or to the public interest.

Rule 4-3.9. Advocate in Nonadjudicative Proceedings

A lawyer representing a client before a legislative body or administrative agency in a nonadjudicative proceeding shall disclose that the appearance is in a representative capacity and shall conform to the provisions of rules 4-3.3(a) through (d), and 4-3.4(a) through (c).

> **Appearances before Legislatures or Agencies**

Official Comments on Rule 4-3.9 (Advocate in Nonadjudicative Proceedings)

[1] In representation before bodies such as legislatures, municipal councils, and executive and administrative agencies acting in a rule-making or policy-making capacity, lawyers present facts, formulate issues, and advance argument in the matters under consideration. The decision-making

body, like a court, should be able to rely on the integrity of the submissions made to it. A lawyer appearing before such a body must deal with the tribunal honestly and in conformity with applicable rules of procedure. See rules 4-3.3(a) through (d), and 4-3.4(a) through (c).

[2] *Lawyers have no exclusive right to appear before nonadjudicative bodies, as they do before a court*. The requirements of this rule therefore may subject lawyers to regulations inapplicable to advocates who are not lawyers. However, legislatures and administrative agencies have a right to expect lawyers to deal with them as they deal with courts. (Emphasis added.)

> "Lawyers have no exclusive right to appear before nonadjudicative bodies, as they do before a court"

[3] This rule only applies when a lawyer represents a client in connection with an official hearing or meeting of a governmental agency or a legislative body to which the lawyer or the lawyer's client is presenting evidence or argument. It does not apply to representation of a client in a negotiation or other bilateral transaction with a governmental agency or in connection with an application for a license or other privilege or the client's compliance with generally applicable reporting requirements, such as the filing of income-tax returns. Nor does it apply to the representation of a client in connection with an investigation or examination of the client's affairs conducted by government investigators or examiners. Representation in such matters is governed by rules 4-4.1 through 4-4.4.

4-4. Transactions with Persons Other Than Clients

Rule 4-4.1. Truthfulness in Statements to Others

In the course of representing a client a lawyer shall not knowingly:

> **False Statement/ Failure to Disclose Material Facts**

(a) make a false statement of material fact or law to a third person; or

(b) fail to disclose a material fact to a third person when disclosure is necessary to avoid assisting a criminal or fraudulent act by a client, unless disclosure is prohibited by rule 4-1.6.

Official Comments on Rule 4-4.1 (Truthfulness in Statements to Others)

Misrepresentation (Comment on Rule 4-4.1)

[1] A lawyer is required to be truthful when dealing with others on a client's behalf, but generally has no affirmative duty to inform an opposing party of relevant facts. A misrepresentation can occur if the lawyer incorporates or affirms a statement of another person that the lawyer knows is false. Misrepresentations can also occur by partially true but misleading statements or

> "No affirmative duty to inform an opposing party of relevant facts"

omissions that are the equivalent of affirmative false statements. For dishonest conduct that does not amount to a false statement or for misrepresentations by a lawyer other than in the course of representing a client, see rule 4-8.4.

Statements of Fact (Comment on Rule 4-4.1)

[2] This rule refers to statements of fact. Whether a particular statement should be regarded as one of fact can depend on the circumstances. Under generally accepted conventions in negotiation, certain types of statements ordinarily are not taken as statements of material fact. Estimates of price or value placed on the subject of a transaction and a party's intentions as to an acceptable settlement of a claim are ordinarily in this category, and so is the existence of an undisclosed principal except where nondisclosure of the principal would constitute fraud. Lawyers should be mindful of their obligations under applicable law to avoid criminal and tortious misrepresentation.

Crime or Fraud by Client (Comment on Rule 4-4.1)

[3] Under rule 4-1.2(d), a lawyer is prohibited from counseling or assisting a client in

> **Assisting a Client Commit Fraud or a Crime**

conduct that the lawyer knows is criminal or fraudulent. Subdivision (b) states a specific application of the principle set forth in rule 4-1.2(d) and addresses the situation where a client's crime or fraud takes the form of a lie or misrepresentation. Ordinarily, a lawyer can avoid assisting a client's crime or fraud by withdrawing from the representation. Sometimes it may be necessary for the lawyer to give notice of the fact of withdrawal and to disaffirm an opinion, document, affirmation, or the like. In extreme cases, substantive law may require a lawyer to disclose information relating to the representation to avoid being deemed to have assisted the client's crime or fraud. If the lawyer can avoid assisting a client's crime or fraud only by disclosing this information, then under subdivision (b) the lawyer is required to do so, unless the disclosure is prohibited by rule 4-1.6.

Rule 4-4.2. Communication with Person Represented by Counsel

(a) In representing a client, a lawyer shall not communi-

> **Noncontact Rule: Represented Persons**

cate about the subject of the representation with a person the lawyer knows to be represented by another lawyer in the matter, unless the lawyer has the consent of the other lawyer. Notwithstanding the foregoing, an attorney may, without such prior consent, communicate with another's client in order to meet the requirements of any court rule, statute, or contract requiring notice or service of process directly on an adverse party, in which event the communication shall be strictly restricted to that required by the court rule, statute, or contract, and a copy shall be provided to the adverse party's attorney.

(b) An otherwise unrepresented person to whom limited representation is being provided or has been provided in accordance with Rule Regulating The Florida Bar 4-1.2 is considered to be unrepresented for purposes of this rule unless the opposing lawyer knows of, or has been provided with, a written notice of appearance under which, or a written notice of time period during which, the opposing lawyer is to communicate with the limited representation lawyer as to the subject matter within the limited scope of the representation.

Official Comments on Rule 4-4.2 (Communication with Person Represented by Counsel)

[1] This rule contributes to the proper functioning of the legal system by protecting a person who has chosen to be represented by a lawyer in a matter against possible overreaching by other lawyers who are participating in the matter, interference by those lawyers with the client-lawyer relationship, and the uncounseled disclosure of information relating to the representation.

[2] This rule applies to communications with any person who is represented by counsel concerning the matter to which the communication relates.

[3] The rule applies even though the represented person initiates or consents to the communication. A lawyer must immediately terminate communication with a person if, after commencing communication, the lawyer learns that the person is one with whom communication is not permitted by this rule.

[4] This rule does not prohibit communication with a represented person, or an employee or agent of such a person, concerning mat-

> **Permissible Contacts with Represented Parties**

ters outside the representation. For example, the existence of a controversy between a government agency and a private party, or between 2 organizations, does not prohibit a lawyer for either from communicating with nonlawyer representatives of the other regarding a separate matter. Nor does this rule preclude communication with a represented person who is seeking advice from a lawyer who is not otherwise representing a client in the matter. A lawyer may not make a communication prohibited by this rule through the acts of another. See rule 4-8.4(a).

[5] Parties to a matter may communicate directly with each other, and a lawyer is not prohibited from advising a client concerning a communication that the client is legally entitled to make, provided that the client is not used to indirectly violate the Rules of Professional Conduct. Also, a lawyer having independent justification for communicating with the

other party is permitted to do so. Permitted communications include, for example, the right of a party to a controversy with a government agency to speak with government officials about the matter.

[6] In the case of a represented organization, this rule prohibits communications with a constituent of the organization who supervises, directs, or regularly consults with the organization's lawyer concerning the matter or has authority to obligate the organization with respect to the matter or whose act or omission in connection with the matter may be imputed to the organization for purposes of civil or criminal liability. Consent of the organization's lawyer is not required for communication with a former constituent. If a constituent of the organization is represented in the matter by the agent's or employee's own counsel, the consent by that counsel to a communication will be sufficient for purposes of this rule. Compare rule 4-3.4(f). In communication with a current or former constituent of an organization, a lawyer must not use methods of obtaining evidence that violate the legal rights of the organization. See rule 4-4.4.

[7] The prohibition on communications with a represented person only applies in circumstances where the lawyer knows that the person is in fact represented in the matter to be discussed. This means that the lawyer has actual knowledge of the fact of the representation; but such actual knowledge may be inferred from the circumstances. See terminology. Thus, the lawyer cannot evade the requirement of obtaining the consent of counsel by closing eyes to the obvious.

[8] In the event the person with whom the lawyer communicates is not known to be represented by counsel in the matter, the lawyer's communications are subject to rule 4-4.3.

Rule 4-4.3. Dealing with Unrepresented Persons

(a) In dealing on behalf of a client with a person who is not represented by counsel, a lawyer shall not state or

Unrepresented Persons: Clarifying the Lawyer's Role

imply that the lawyer is disinterested. When the lawyer knows or reasonably should know that the unrepresented person misunderstands the lawyer's role in the matter, the lawyer shall make reasonable efforts to correct the misunderstanding. The lawyer shall not give legal advice to an unrepresented person, other than the advice to secure counsel.

(b) An otherwise unrepresented person to whom limited representation is being provided or has been provided in accordance with Rule Regulating The Florida Bar 4-1.2 is considered to be unrepresented for purposes of this rule unless the opposing lawyer knows of, or has been provided with, a written notice

of appearance under which, or a written notice of time period during which, the opposing lawyer is to communicate with the limited representation lawyer as to the subject matter within the limited scope of the representation.

Official Comments on Rule 4-4.3 (Dealing with Unrepresented Persons)

[1] An unrepresented person, particularly one not experienced in dealing with legal matters, might assume that a lawyer is disinterested in loyalties or is a disinterested authority on the law even when the lawyer represents a client. In order to avoid a misunderstanding, a lawyer will typically need to identify the lawyer's client and, where necessary, explain that the client has interests opposed to those of the unrepresented person. For misunderstandings that sometimes arise when a lawyer for an organization deals with an unrepresented constituent, see rule 4-1.13(d).

[2] This rule does not prohibit a lawyer from negotiating the terms of a transaction or settling a dispute with an unrepresented person. So long as the lawyer has explained that the lawyer represents an adverse party and is not representing the person, the lawyer may inform the person of the terms on which the lawyer's client will enter into an agreement or settle a matter, prepare documents that require the person's signature, and explain the lawyer's own view of the meaning of the document or the lawyer's view of the underlying legal obligations.

Settlement

Rule 4-4.4. Respect for Rights of Third Persons

(a) In representing a client, a lawyer shall not use means that have no substantial purpose other than to embarrass, delay, or burden a third person or knowingly use methods of obtaining evidence that violate the legal rights of such a person.

Harassment

(b) A lawyer who receives a document relating to the representation of the lawyer's client and knows or reasonably should know that the document was inadvertently sent shall promptly notify the sender.

Misdelivery of E-Mail and Other Documents

Official Comments on Rule 4-4.4 (Respect for Rights of Third Persons)

[1] Responsibility to a client requires a lawyer to subordinate the interests of others to those of the client, but that responsibility does not imply that a lawyer may disregard the rights of third persons. It is impractical to catalogue all such rights, but they include legal restrictions on methods of obtaining evidence from third persons and unwarranted intrusions into privileged relationships, such as the client-lawyer relationship.

[2] Subdivision (b) recognizes that lawyers sometimes receive documents that were mistakenly sent or produced by opposing parties or their lawyers. If a lawyer knows or reasonably should know that such a document was sent inadvertently, then this rule requires the lawyer to promptly notify the sender in order to permit that person to take protective measures. Whether the lawyer is required to take additional steps, such as returning the original document, is a matter of law beyond the scope of these rules, as is the question of whether the privileged status of a document has been waived. Similarly, this rule does not address the legal duties of a lawyer who receives a document that the lawyer knows or reasonably should know may have been wrongfully obtained by the sending person. For purposes of this rule, "document" includes e-mail or other electronic modes of transmission subject to being read or put into readable form.

[3] Some lawyers may choose to return a document unread, for example, when the lawyer learns before receiving the document that it was inadvertently sent to the wrong address. Where a lawyer is not required by applicable law to do so, the decision to voluntarily return such a document is a matter of professional judgment ordinarily reserved to the lawyer. See rules 4-1.2 and 4-1.4.

4-5. Law Firms and Associations

Rule 4-5.1. Responsibilities of Partners, Managers, and Supervisory Lawyers

(a) Duties Concerning Adherence to Rules of Professional Conduct. A partner in a law firm, and a lawyer who individually or together with other lawyers possesses comparable managerial authority

Lawyer Supervision of Other Lawyers in the Firm

in a law firm, shall make reasonable efforts to ensure that the firm has in effect measures giving reasonable assurance that all lawyers therein conform to the Rules of Professional Conduct.

(b) Supervisory Lawyer's Duties. Any lawyer having direct supervisory authority over another lawyer shall make reasonable efforts to ensure that the other lawyer conforms to the Rules of Professional Conduct.

(c) Responsibility for Rules Violations. A lawyer shall be responsible for another lawyer's violation of the Rules of Professional Conduct if:

(1) the lawyer orders the specific conduct or, with knowledge thereof, ratifies the conduct involved; or

(2) the lawyer is a partner or has comparable managerial authority in the law firm in which the other lawyer practices or has direct supervisory authority over the other lawyer, and knows of the conduct at a time when its consequences can be avoided or mitigated but fails to take reasonable remedial action.

Official Comments on Rule 4-5.1 (Responsibilities of Partners, Managers, and Supervisory Lawyers)

[1] Subdivision (a) applies to lawyers who have managerial authority over the professional work of a firm. See terminology. This includes members of a partnership, the shareholders in a law firm organized as a professional corporation, and members of other associations authorized to practice law; lawyers having comparable managerial authority in a legal services organization or a law department of an enterprise or government agency, and lawyers who have intermediate managerial responsibilities in a firm. Subdivision (b) applies to lawyers who have supervisory authority over the work of other lawyers in a firm.

[2] Subdivision (a) requires lawyers with managerial authority within a firm to make reasonable efforts to establish internal policies and procedures designed to provide reasonable assurance that all lawyers in the firm will conform to the Rules of Professional Conduct. Such policies and procedures include those designed to detect and resolve conflicts of interest, identify dates by which actions must be taken in pending matters, account for client funds and property, and ensure that inexperienced lawyers are properly supervised.

[3] Other measures that may be required to fulfill the responsibility prescribed in subdivision (a) can

Duties in Small vs Large Firm

depend on the firm's structure and the nature of its practice. In a small firm of experienced lawyers, informal supervision and periodic review of compliance with the required systems ordinarily will suffice. In a large firm, or in practice situations in which difficult ethical problems frequently arise, more elaborate measures may be necessary. Some firms, for example, have a procedure whereby junior lawyers can make confidential referral of ethical problems directly to a designated supervising lawyer or special committee. See rule 4-5.2. Firms, whether large or small, may also rely on continuing legal education in professional ethics. In any event the ethical atmosphere of a firm can influence the conduct of all its members and the partners may not assume that all lawyers associated with the firm will inevitably conform to the rules.

[4] Subdivision (c) expresses a general principle of personal responsibility for acts of another. See also rule 4-8.4(a).

[5] Subdivision (c)(2) defines the duty of a partner or other lawyer having comparable managerial

Supervisory Duty: Preventing Misconduct

authority in a law firm, as well as a lawyer having supervisory authority over performance of specific legal work by another lawyer. Whether a lawyer has such supervisory authority in particular circumstances is a question of fact. Partners and lawyers with comparable authority have at least indirect responsibility for all work being done by the firm, while a partner or manager in charge of a particular matter ordinarily also has supervisory responsibility for the work of other firm lawyers engaged in the matter. Appropriate remedial action by a partner or managing lawyer would depend on the immediacy of that lawyer's involvement and the seriousness of the misconduct. A supervisor is required to intervene to prevent avoidable consequences of misconduct if the supervisor knows that the misconduct occurred. Thus, if a supervising lawyer knows that a subordinate misrepresented a matter to an opposing party in negotiation, the supervisor as well as the subordinate has a duty to correct the resulting misapprehension.

[6] Professional misconduct by a lawyer under supervision could reveal a violation of subdivision (b) on the part of the supervisory lawyer even though it does not entail a violation of subdivision (c) because there was no direction, ratification, or knowledge of the violation.

[7] Apart from this rule and rule 4-8.4(a), a lawyer does not have disciplinary liability for the conduct of a partner, shareholder, member of a limited liability company, officer, director, manager, associate, or subordinate. Whether a lawyer may be liable civilly or criminally for another lawyer's conduct is a question of law beyond the scope of these rules.

[8] The duties imposed by this rule on managing and supervising lawyers do not alter the personal duty of each lawyer in a firm to abide by the Rules of Professional Conduct. See rule 4-5.2(a).

Rule 4-5.2. Responsibilities of a Subordinate Lawyer

(a) Rules of Professional Conduct Apply. A lawyer is

Following Orders Is No Defense to Ethics Violations Charge

bound by the Rules of Professional Conduct notwithstanding that the lawyer acted at the direction of another person.

(b) Reliance on Supervisor's Opinion. A subordinate lawyer does not violate the Rules of Professional Conduct if that lawyer acts in accordance with a supervisory lawyer's reasonable resolution of an arguable question of professional duty.

Official Comments on Rule 4-5.2 (Responsibilities of a Subordinate Lawyer)

[1] Although a lawyer is not relieved of responsibility for a violation by the fact that the lawyer acted at the direction of a supervisor, that fact may be

relevant in determining whether a lawyer had the knowledge required to render conduct a violation of the rules. For example, if a subordinate filed a frivolous

The Relevance of What the Subordinate Knew

pleading at the direction of a supervisor, the subordinate would not be guilty of a professional violation unless the subordinate knew of the document's frivolous character.

[2] When lawyers in a supervisor-subordinate relationship encounter a matter involving professional judgment as to ethical duty, the supervisor may assume responsibility for making the judgment. Otherwise a consistent course of action or position could not be taken. If the question can reasonably be answered only 1 way, the duty of both lawyers is clear and they are equally responsible for fulfilling it. However, if the question is reasonably arguable, someone has to decide upon the course of action. That authority ordinarily reposes in the supervisor, and a subordinate may be guided accordingly. For example, if a question arises whether the interests of 2 clients conflict under rule 4-1.7, the supervisor's reasonable resolution of the question should protect the subordinate professionally if the resolution is subsequently challenged.

Rule 4-5.3. Responsibilities Regarding Nonlawyer Assistants

(a) Use of Titles by Nonlawyer Assistants. A person who uses the title of paralegal, legal assistant,

Paralegals and Legal Assistants

or other similar term when offering or providing services to the public must work for or under the direction or supervision of a lawyer or law firm.

(b) Supervisory Responsibility. With respect to a nonlawyer employed or retained by or associated with a lawyer or an authorized business entity as defined elsewhere in these Rules Regulating The Florida Bar:

(1) a partner, and a lawyer who individually or together with other lawyers possesses comparable managerial authority in a law firm, shall make reasonable efforts to ensure that the firm has in effect measures giving reasonable assurance that the person's conduct is compatible with the professional obligations of the lawyer;

(2) a lawyer having direct supervisory authority over the nonlawyer shall make reasonable efforts to ensure that the person's conduct is compatible with the professional obligations of the lawyer; and

(3) a lawyer shall be responsible for conduct of such a person that would be a violation of

Lawyer Responsibility for Paralegal Misconduct

the Rules of Professional Conduct if engaged in by a lawyer if:

(A) the lawyer orders or, with the knowledge of the specific conduct, ratifies the conduct involved; or

(B) the lawyer is a partner or has comparable managerial authority in the law firm in which the person is employed, or has direct supervisory authority over the person, and knows of the conduct at a time when its consequences can be avoided or mitigated but fails to take reasonable remedial action.

(c) Ultimate Responsibility of Lawyer. Although para-

Paralegals acting "without the presence or active involvement of the lawyer"; ultimate responsibility

legals or legal assistants may perform the duties delegated to them by the lawyer without the presence or active involvement of the lawyer, the lawyer shall review and be responsible for the work product of the paralegals or legal assistants.

Official Comments on Rule 4-5.3 (Responsibilities Regarding Nonlawyer Assistants)

[1] Lawyers generally employ assistants in their practice, including secretaries, investigators, law student interns, and paraprofessionals such as paralegals and legal assistants. Such assistants,

Appropriate Instruction to and Supervision of Paralegals on Ethics

whether employees or independent contractors, act for the lawyer in rendition of the lawyer's professional services. A lawyer must give such assistants appropriate instruction and supervision concerning the ethical aspects of their employment, particularly regarding the obligation not to disclose information relating to representation of the client. The measures employed in supervising nonlawyers should take account of the level of their legal training and the fact that they are not subject to professional discipline. If an activity requires the independent judgment and participation of the lawyer, it cannot be properly delegated to a nonlawyer employee.

[2] Subdivision (b)(1) requires lawyers with managerial authority within a law firm to make reasonable efforts to establish internal policies and procedures designed to provide reasonable assurance that nonlawyers in the firm will act in a way compatible with the Rules of Professional Conduct. See comment to rule 4-5.1. Subdivision (b)(2) applies to lawyers who have supervisory authority over the work of a nonlawyer. Subdivision (b)(3) specifies the circumstances in which a lawyer is responsible for conduct of a nonlawyer that would be a violation of the Rules of Professional Conduct if engaged in by a lawyer.

[3] Nothing provided in this rule should be interpreted to mean that a nonlawyer may have any

ownership or partnership interest in a law firm, which is prohibited by rule 4-5.4. Additionally, this rule would not permit a

Ownership or Partnership Interest

lawyer to accept employment by a nonlawyer or group of nonlawyers, the purpose of which is to provide the supervision required under this rule. Such conduct is prohibited by rules 4-5.4 and 4-5.5.

Rule 4-5.4. Professional Independence of a Lawyer

(a) Sharing Fees with Nonlawyers. A lawyer or law firm shall not share legal fees with a nonlawyer, except that:

(1) an agreement by a lawyer with the lawyer's firm, partner, or associate may provide

Sharing Fees with a Nonlawyer

for the payment of money, over a reasonable period of time after the lawyer's death, to the lawyer's estate or to 1 or more specified persons;

(2) a lawyer who undertakes to complete unfinished legal business of a deceased lawyer may pay to the estate of the deceased lawyer that proportion of the total compensation that fairly represents the services rendered by the deceased lawyer;

(3) a lawyer who purchases the practice of a deceased, disabled, or disappeared lawyer may, in accordance with the provisions of rule 4-1.17, pay to the estate or other legally authorized representative of that lawyer the agreed upon purchase price;

(4) bonuses may be paid to non-lawyer employees for work

Paying Bonuses to Nonlawyers

performed, and may be based on their extraordinary efforts on a particular case or over a specified time period. Bonus payments shall not be based on cases or clients brought to the lawyer or law firm by the actions of the nonlawyer. A lawyer shall not provide a bonus payment that is calculated as a percentage of legal fees received by the lawyer or law firm; and

(5) a lawyer may share court-awarded fees with a nonprofit, pro bono legal services organization that employed, retained, or recommended employment of the lawyer in the matter.

(b) Qualified Pension Plans. A lawyer or law firm may include non-lawyer employees in a qualified pension, profit-sharing, or retirement plan, even though the

Nonlawyers in a Pension, Profit-Sharing, or Retirement Plan

lawyer's or law firm's contribution to the plan is based in whole or in part on a profit-sharing arrangement.

(c) Partnership with Nonlawyer. A lawyer shall not form a partnership with a nonlawyer if any of the activities of the partnership consist of the practice of law.

(d) Exercise of Independent Professional Judgment. A lawyer shall not permit a person who recommends,

Independent Professional Judgment

employs, or pays the lawyer to render legal services for another to direct or regulate the lawyer's professional judgment in rendering such legal services.

(e) Nonlawyer Ownership of Authorized Business Entity. A lawyer shall not practice with or in the form of a business entity authorized to practice law for a profit if:

(1) a nonlawyer owns any interest therein, except that a fiduciary representative of the estate of a lawyer may hold the stock or interest of the lawyer for a reasonable time during administration; or

(2) a nonlawyer is a corporate director or officer thereof or occupies the position of similar responsibility in any form of association other than a corporation; or

(3) a nonlawyer has the right to direct or control the professional judgment of a lawyer.

Official Comments on Rule 4-5.4 (Professional Independence of a Lawyer)

[1] The provisions of this rule express traditional limitations on sharing fees. These limitations are to protect the lawyer's professional independence of judgment. Where someone other than the client pays the lawyer's fee or salary, or recommends employment of the lawyer, that arrangement does not modify the lawyer's obligation to the client. As stated in subdivision (d), such arrangements should not interfere with the lawyer's professional judgment.

[2] This rule also expresses traditional limitations on permitting a third party to direct or regulate the lawyer's professional judgment in rendering legal services to another. See also rule 4-1.8(f) (lawyer may accept compensation from a third party as long as there is no interference with the lawyer's independent professional judgment and the client gives informed consent).

[3] The prohibition against sharing legal fees with nonlawyer employees is not intended to prohibit profit-

Nonlawyer Compensation Plans May Not Be Based on Legal Fees

sharing arrangements that are part of a qualified pension, profit-sharing, or retirement plan. Compensation plans, as opposed to retirement plans, may not be based on legal fees.

Rule 4-5.5. Unlicensed Practice of Law; Multijurisdictional Practice of Law

(a) Practice of Law. A lawyer shall not practice law in a jurisdiction other than the lawyer's home state, in violation of the regulation of the legal profession in

Authorization to Practice Law in Florida

that jurisdiction, or in violation of the regulation of the legal profession in the lawyer's home state, or assist another in doing so.

(b) Prohibited Conduct. A lawyer who is not admitted to practice in Florida shall not:

(1) except as authorized by other law, establish an office or other regular presence in Florida for the practice of law;

(2) hold out to the public or otherwise represent that the lawyer is admitted to practice law in Florida; or

(3) appear in court, before an administrative agency, or before any other tribunal unless authorized to do so by the court, administrative agency, or tribunal pursuant to the applicable rules of the court, administrative agency, or tribunal . . . .

Official Comments on Rule 4-5.5 (Unlicensed Practice of Law; Multijurisdictional Practice of Law)

[1] Subdivision (a) applies to unlicensed practice of law by a lawyer, whether through the lawyer's direct action or by the lawyer assisting another person. A lawyer may practice law only in a jurisdiction in which the lawyer is authorized to practice. A lawyer may be admitted to practice law in a jurisdiction on a regular basis or may be authorized by court rule or order or by law to practice for a limited purpose or on a restricted basis. Regardless of whether the lawyer is admitted to practice law on a regular basis or is practicing as the result of an authorization granted by court rule or order or by the law, the lawyer must comply with the standards of ethical and professional conduct set forth in these Rules Regulating The Florida Bar.

[2] The definition of the practice of law is established by law and varies from one jurisdiction to another. Whatever the definition, limiting the practice of law to members of the bar protects the public against rendition of legal services by unqualified

A Lawyer May Employ Paraprofessionals, Give Advice to Nonlawyers Such as Claims Adjusters, and Counsel Pro Se Nonlawyers

persons. *This rule does not prohibit a lawyer from employing the services of paraprofessionals and delegating functions to them, so long as the lawyer supervises the delegated work and retains responsibility for their work. See rule 4-5.3. Likewise, it does not prohibit lawyers from providing professional advice and instruction to nonlawyers whose employment requires knowledge of law; for example, claims adjusters, employees of financial or commercial institutions, social workers, accountants, and persons employed in government agencies. In addition, a lawyer may counsel nonlawyers who wish to proceed pro se.* (Emphasis added.)

[3] Other than as authorized by law, a lawyer who is not admitted to practice in Florida violates subdivision (b) if the lawyer establishes an office or other regular presence in Florida for the practice of law. Presence may be regular even if the lawyer is not physically present here. Such a lawyer must not hold out to the

public or otherwise represent that the lawyer is admitted to practice law in Florida . . . .

Rule 4-5.6. Restrictions on Right to Practice

A lawyer shall not participate in offering or making:

(a) a partnership, shareholders, operating, employment,

> Restrictions on Practice after Leaving a Law Firm

or other similar type of agreement that restricts the rights of a lawyer to practice after termination of the relationship, except an agreement concerning benefits upon retirement; or

(b) an agreement in which a restriction on the lawyer's right to practice is part of the settlement of a client controversy.

Official Comments on Rule 4-5.6 (Restrictions on Right to Practice)

[1] An agreement restricting the right of lawyers to practice after leaving a firm not only limits their professional autonomy, but also limits the freedom of clients to choose a lawyer. Subdivision (a) prohibits such agreements except for restrictions incident to provisions concerning retirement benefits for service with the firm.

[2] Subdivision (b) prohibits a lawyer from agreeing not to represent other persons in connection with settling a claim on behalf of a client.

[3] This rule does not apply to prohibit restrictions that may be included in the terms of the sale of a law practice in accordance with the provisions of rule 4-1.17.

[4] This rule is not a per se prohibition against severance agreements between lawyers

> Severance Agreements

and law firms. Severance agreements containing reasonable and fair compensation provisions designed to avoid disputes requiring time-consuming quantum meruit analysis are not prohibited by this rule. Severance agreements, on the other hand, that contain punitive clauses, the effect of which are to restrict competition or encroach upon a client's inherent right to select counsel, are prohibited. The percentage limitations found in rule 4-1.5(f)(4)(D) do not apply to fees divided pursuant to a severance agreement. No severance agreement shall contain a fee-splitting arrangement that results in a fee prohibited by the Rules Regulating The Florida Bar.

Rule 4-5.7. Responsibilities Regarding Nonlegal Services

(a) Services Not Distinct From Legal Services. A lawyer

> Ancillary Services

who provides nonlegal services to a recipient that are not distinct from legal services provided to that recipient is subject to the Rules Regulating The Florida Bar with respect to the provision of both legal and nonlegal services.

(b) Services Distinct From Legal Services. A lawyer who provides nonlegal services to a recipient that are distinct from any legal services provided to the recipient is subject to the Rules Regulating The Florida Bar with respect to the nonlegal services if the lawyer knows or reasonably should know that the recipient might believe that the recipient is receiving the protection of a client-lawyer relationship . . . .

Official Comments on Rule 4-5.7 (Responsibilities Regarding Nonlegal Services)

[1] For many years, lawyers have provided to their clients nonlegal services that are ancillary to the practice of law. A broad range of economic and other interests of clients may be served by lawyers participating in the delivery of these services. In recent years, however, there has been significant debate about the role the rules of professional conduct should play in regulating the degree and manner in which a lawyer participates in the delivery of nonlegal services. The ABA, for example, adopted, repealed, and then adopted a different version of ABA Model Rule 5.7. In the course of this debate, several ABA sections offered competing versions of ABA Model Rule 5.7.

[2] One approach to the issue of nonlegal services is to try to substantively limit the type of nonlegal services a lawyer may provide to a recipient or the manner in which the services are provided. A competing approach does not try to substantively limit the lawyer's provision of nonlegal services, but instead attempts to clarify the conduct to which the Rules Regulating The Florida Bar apply and to avoid misunderstanding on the part of the recipient of the nonlegal services. This rule adopts the latter approach.

The Potential for Misunderstanding (Comment on Rule 4-5.7)

[3] Whenever a lawyer directly provides nonlegal services, there exists the potential for ethical problems. Principal among these is the possibility that the person for whom the nonlegal services are performed may fail to understand that the services may not carry with them the protection normally afforded by the client-lawyer relationship. The recipient of the nonlegal services may expect, for example, that the protection of client confidences, prohibitions against representation of persons with conflicting interests, and obligations of a lawyer to maintain professional independence apply to the provision of nonlegal services when that may not be the case. The risk of confusion is acute especially when the lawyer renders both types of services with respect to the same matter . . . .

Rule 4-5.8. Procedures for Lawyers Leaving Law Firms and Dissolution of Law Firms

(a) **Contractual Relationship Between Law Firm and Clients.** The contract for legal services creates the legal relationships between the client and law firm and between the client and individual members of the law firm, including the ownership of the files maintained by the lawyer or law firm. Nothing in these rules creates or defines those relationships.

(b) **Client's Right to Counsel of Choice.** Clients have the right to expect that they may choose counsel when legal services are required and, with few exceptions, nothing that lawyers and law firms do shall have any effect on the exercise of that right.

(c) **Contact With Clients.**

(1) *Lawyers Leaving Law Firms.* Absent a specific agreement otherwise, a lawyer who is leaving a law firm shall not unilaterally contact those clients of the law firm for purposes of notifying them about the anticipated departure or to solicit representation of the clients unless the lawyer has approached an authorized representative of the law firm and attempted to negotiate a joint communication to the clients concerning the lawyer leaving the law firm and bona fide negotiations have been unsuccessful.

| Contacting Clients When Leaving a Law Firm |

(2) *Dissolution of Law Firm.* Absent a specific agreement otherwise, a lawyer involved in the dissolution of a law firm shall not unilaterally contact clients of the law firm unless, after bona fide negotiations, authorized members of the law firm have been unable to agree on a method to provide notice to clients . . . .

Official Comments on Rule 4-5.8 (Procedures for Lawyers Leaving Law Firms and Dissolution of Law Firms)

[1] The current rule of law regarding ownership of client files is discussed in *Donahue v. Vaughn*, 721 So. 2d 356 (Fla. 5th DCA 1998), and *Dowda & Fields, P.A. v. Cobb*, 452 So. 2d 1140 (Fla. 5th DCA 1984). A lawyer leaving a law firm, when the law firm remains available to continue legal representation, has no right nor expectation to take client files without an agreement with the law firm to do so.

| Ownership of Client Files |

[2] While clients have the right to choose counsel, such choice may implicate obligations. Those obligations may include a requirement to pay for legal services previously rendered and costs expended in connection with the representation as well as a reasonable fee for copying the client's file . . . .

4-6. Public Service

Rule 4-6.1. Pro Bono Public Service

(a) **Professional Responsibility.** Each member of The Florida Bar in good standing, as part of that member's professional responsibility, should (1) render pro bono legal services to the poor and (2) participate, to the extent possible, in other pro bono service activities that directly relate to the legal needs of the poor. This professional responsibility does not apply to members of the judiciary or their staffs or to government lawyers who are prohibited from performing legal services by constitutional, statutory, rule, or regulatory prohibitions. Neither does this professional responsibility apply to those members of the bar who are retired, inactive, or suspended, or who have been placed on the inactive list for incapacity not related to discipline.

| Ethical Duty to Provide Legal Services to the Poor |

(b) **Discharge of the Professional Responsibility to Provide Pro Bono Legal Service to the Poor.** The professional responsibility to provide pro bono legal services as established under this rule is aspirational rather than mandatory in nature. The failure to fulfill one's professional responsibility under this rule will not subject a lawyer to discipline. The professional responsibility to provide pro bono legal service to the poor may be discharged by:

| 20 Hours or $350 |

(1) annually providing at least 20 hours of pro bono legal service to the poor; or

(2) making an annual contribution of at least $350 to a legal aid organization.

(c) **Collective Discharge of the Professional Responsibility to Provide Pro Bono Legal Service to the Poor.** Each member of the bar should strive to individually satisfy the member's professional responsibility to provide pro bono legal service to the poor. Collective satisfaction of this professional responsibility is permitted by law firms only under a collective satisfaction plan that has been filed previously with the circuit pro bono committee and only when providing pro bono legal service to the poor:

(1) in a major case or matter involving a substantial expenditure of time and resources; or

(2) through a full-time community or public service staff; or

(3) in any other manner that has been approved by the circuit pro bono committee in the circuit in which the firm practices.

(d) **Reporting Requirement.** Each member of the bar shall annually report whether the member has satisfied the member's professional responsibility to provide pro bono legal services

| Reporting Pro Bono Activity |

to the poor. Each member shall report this information through a simplified reporting form that is made a part of the member's annual membership fees statement. The form will contain the . . . categories [in Exhibit 3.2F] from which each member will be allowed to choose in reporting whether the member has provided pro bono legal services to the poor. The failure to report this information shall constitute a disciplinary offense under these rules.

EXHIBIT 3.2F Reporting Pro Bono Activity

(1) I have personally provided _____ hours of pro bono legal services;

(2) I have provided pro bono legal services collectively by: (indicate type of case and manner in which service was provided);

(3) I have contributed $_____ to: (indicate organization to which funds were provided);

(4) I have provided legal services to the poor in the following special manner: (indicate manner in which services were provided); or

(5) I have been unable to provide pro bono legal services to the poor this year; or

(6) I am deferred from the provision of pro bono legal services to the poor because I am: (indicate whether lawyer is: a member of the judiciary or judicial staff; a government lawyer prohibited by statute, rule, or regulation from providing services; retired; or inactive).

(e) Credit Toward Professional Responsibility in Future Years. In the event that more than 20 hours of pro bono legal service to the poor are provided and reported in any 1 year, the hours in excess of 20 hours may be carried forward and reported as such for up to 2 succeeding years for the purpose of determining whether a lawyer has fulfilled the professional responsibility to provide pro bono legal service to the poor in those succeeding years . . . .

Official Comments on Rule 4-6.1 (Pro Bono Public Service)

[1] Pro bono legal service to the poor is an integral and particular part of a lawyer's pro bono public service responsibility. As our society has become one in which rights and responsibilities are increasingly defined in legal terms, access to legal services has become of critical importance. This is true for all people, be they rich, poor, or of moderate means. However, because the legal problems of the poor often involve areas of basic need, their inability to obtain legal services can have dire consequences. The vast unmet legal needs of the poor in Florida have been recognized by the Supreme Court of Florida and by several studies undertaken in Florida over the past two decades.

"The vast unmet legal needs of the poor"

[2] The Supreme Court of Florida has further recognized the necessity of finding a solution to the problem of providing the poor greater access to legal service and the unique role of lawyers in our adversarial system of representing and defending persons against the actions and conduct of governmental entities, individuals, and nongovernmental entities. As an officer of the court, each member of The Florida Bar in good standing has a professional responsibility to provide pro bono legal service to the poor. Certain lawyers, however, are prohibited from performing legal services by constitutional, statutory, rule, or other regulatory prohibitions. Consequently, members of the judiciary and their staffs, government lawyers who are prohibited from performing legal services by constitutional, statutory, rule, or regulatory prohibitions, members of the bar who are retired, inactive, or suspended, or who have been placed on the inactive list for incapacity not related to discipline are deferred from participation in this program.

[3] In discharging the professional responsibility to provide pro bono legal service to the poor, each lawyer should furnish a minimum of twenty hours of pro bono legal service to the poor annually or contribute $350 to a legal aid organization. "Pro bono legal service" means legal service rendered without charge or expectation of a fee for the lawyer at the time the service commences. Legal services written off as bad debts do not qualify as pro bono service. Most pro bono service should involve civil proceedings given that government must provide indigent representation in most criminal matters.

[4] Pro bono legal service to the poor is to be provided not only to those persons whose household incomes are below the federal poverty standard but also to those persons frequently referred to as the "working poor." Lawyers providing pro bono legal service on their own need not undertake an investigation to determine client eligibility. Rather, a good faith determination by the lawyer of client eligibility is sufficient. Pro bono legal service to the poor need not be provided only through legal services to individuals; it can also be provided through legal services to charitable, religious, or educational organizations whose overall mission and activities are designed predominately to address the needs of the poor. For example, legal service to organizations such as a church, civic, or community service organizations relating to a project seeking to address the problems of the poor would qualify.

Legal Help for the Working Poor

[5] While the personal involvement of each lawyer in the provision of pro bono legal service to the poor is generally preferable, such personal involvement may not always be possible or produce the ultimate desired result, that is, a significant maximum

increase in the quantity and quality of legal service provided to the poor. The annual contribution alternative recognizes a lawyer's professional responsibility to provide financial assistance to increase and improve the delivery of legal service to the poor when a lawyer cannot or decides not to provide legal service to the poor through the contribution of time. Also, there is no prohibition against a lawyer contributing a combination of hours and financial support. The limited provision allowing for collective satisfaction of the 20-hour standard recognizes the importance of encouraging law firms to undertake the pro bono legal representation of the poor in substantial, complex matters requiring significant expenditures of law firm resources and time and costs, such as class actions and post-conviction death penalty appeal cases, and through the establishment of full-time community or public service staffs. When a law firm uses collective satisfaction, the total hours of legal services provided in such substantial, complex matters or through a full-time community or public service staff should be credited among the firm's lawyers in a fair and reasonable manner as determined by the firm.

[6] The reporting requirement is designed to provide a sound basis for evaluating the results achieved by this rule, reveal the strengths and weaknesses of the pro bono plan, and to remind lawyers of their professional responsibility under this rule. The fourth alternative of the reporting requirements allows members to indicate that they have fulfilled their service in some manner not specifically envisioned by the plan.

[7] The 20-hour standard for the provision of pro bono legal service to the poor is a minimum. Additional hours of service are to be encouraged. Many lawyers will, as they have before the adoption of this rule, contribute many more hours than the minimum. To ensure that a lawyer receives credit for the time required to handle a particularly involved matter, this rule provides that the lawyer may carry forward, over the next 2 successive years, any time expended in excess of 20 hours in any 1 year.

Rule 4-6.2. Accepting Appointments

Lawyer as Appointed Counsel

A lawyer shall not seek to avoid appointment by a tribunal to represent a person except for good cause, such as when:

(a) representing the client is likely to result in violation of the Rules of Professional Conduct or of the law;

(b) representing the client is likely to result in an unreasonable financial burden on the lawyer; or

(c) the client or the cause is so repugnant to the lawyer as to be likely to impair the client-lawyer relationship or the lawyer's ability to represent the client.

Official Comments on Rule 4-6.2 (Accepting Appointments)

[1] A lawyer ordinarily is not obliged to accept a client whose character or cause the lawyer regards as repugnant. The lawyer's freedom to select clients is, however,

Clients or Causes That Are "Repugnant" or Unpopular

qualified. All lawyers have a responsibility to assist in providing pro bono public service as provided in these rules. See rule 4-6.1. In the course of fulfilling a lawyer's obligation to provide legal services to the poor, a lawyer should not avoid or decline representation of a client simply because a client is unpopular or involved in unpopular matters. Although these rules do not contemplate court appointment as a primary means of achieving pro bono service, a lawyer may be subject to appointment by a court to serve unpopular clients or persons unable to afford legal services.

[2] For good cause a lawyer may seek to decline an appointment to represent a person who cannot afford to retain counsel or whose cause is unpopular. Good cause exists if the lawyer could not handle the matter competently, see rule 4-1.1, or if undertaking the representation would result in an improper conflict of interest, for example, when the client or the cause is so repugnant to the lawyer as to be likely to impair the client-lawyer relationship or the lawyer's ability to represent the client. A lawyer may also seek to decline an appointment if acceptance would be unreasonably burdensome, for example, when it would impose a financial sacrifice so great as to be unjust.

[3] An appointed lawyer has the same obligations to the client as retained counsel, including the obligations of loyalty and confidentiality, and is subject to the same limitations on the client-lawyer relationship, such as the obligation to refrain from assisting the client in violation of the rules.

Rule 4-6.3. Membership in Legal Services Organization

A lawyer may serve as a director, officer, or member of a legal services organization, apart from the law firm in which the lawyer practices, notwithstanding that the organization serves persons having interests adverse to the client of the lawyer. The lawyer shall not knowingly participate in a decision or action of the organization: (a) if participating in the decision would be incompatible with the lawyer's obligations to a client under rule 4-1.7; or (b) where the decision could have a material adverse effect on the representation of a client of the organization whose interests are adverse to a client of the lawyer.

Official Comments on Rule 4-6.3 (Membership in Legal Service Organization)

[1] Lawyers should be encouraged to support and participate in legal service organizations. A lawyer who is an officer or a member of such an organization does not thereby have a client-lawyer relationship with persons served by the organization. However, there is potential conflict between the interests of such persons and the interests of the lawyer's clients. If the possibility of such conflict disqualified a lawyer from serving on the board of a legal services organization, the profession's involvement in such organizations would be severely curtailed.

[2] It may be necessary in appropriate cases to reassure a client of the organization that the representation will not be affected by conflicting loyalties of a member of the board. Established, written policies in this respect can enhance the credibility of such assurances.

Rule 4-6.4. Law Reform Activities Affecting Client Interests

A lawyer may serve as a director, officer, or member of an organization involved in reform of the law or its administration notwithstanding that the reform may affect the interests of a client of the lawyer. When the lawyer knows that the interests of a client may be materially affected by a decision in which the lawyer participates, the lawyer shall disclose that fact but need not identify the client.

Official Comments on Rule 4-6.4 (Legal Reform Activities Affecting Client Interests)

[1] Lawyers involved in organizations seeking law reform generally do not have a client-lawyer relationship with the organization. Otherwise, it might follow that a lawyer could not be involved in a bar association law reform program that might indirectly affect a client. See also rule 4-1.2(b). For example, a lawyer specializing in antitrust litigation might be regarded as disqualified from participating in drafting revisions of rules governing that subject. In determining the nature and scope of participation in such activities, a lawyer should be mindful of obligations to clients under other rules, particularly rule 4-1.7. A lawyer is professionally obligated to protect the integrity of the program by making an appropriate disclosure within the organization when the lawyer knows a private client might be materially affected.

Rule 4-6.5. Voluntary Pro Bono Plan

(a) **Purpose.** The purpose of the voluntary pro bono attorney plan is to increase the availability of legal service to the poor. . . .

(d) **Suggested Pro Bono Service Opportunities.** The following are suggested pro bono service opportunities that should be included in each circuit plan:
1. representation of clients through case referral;
2. interviewing of prospective clients;
3. participation in pro se clinics and other clinics in which lawyers provide advice and counsel;
4. acting as co-counsel on cases or matters with legal assistance providers and other pro bono lawyers;
5. providing consultation services to legal assistance providers for case reviews and evaluations;
6. participation in policy advocacy;
7. providing training to the staff of legal assistance providers and other volunteer pro bono attorneys;
8. making presentations to groups of poor persons regarding their rights and obligations under the law;
9. providing legal research;
10. providing guardian ad litem services;
11. providing assistance in the formation and operation of legal entities for groups of poor persons; and
12. serving as a mediator or arbitrator at no fee to the client-eligible party.

4-7. Information About Legal Services

Rule 4-7.1. General

(a) **Permissible Forms of Advertising.** Subject to all the requirements set forth in this subchapter 4-7, including the filing requirements of rule 4-7.7, a lawyer may advertise services through public media, including but not limited to: print media, such as a telephone directory, legal directory, newspaper, or other periodical; outdoor advertising, such as billboards and other signs; radio, television, and computer-accessed communications; recorded messages the public may access by dialing a telephone number; and written communication in accordance with rule 4-7.4. | Lawyer Advertising |

(b) **Advertisements Disseminated in Florida.** Subchapter 4-7 shall apply to lawyers admitted to practice law in Florida who solicit or advertise for legal employment in Florida or who target solicitations or advertisements for legal employment at Florida residents.

(c) **Advertisements by Out-of-State Lawyers.** Subchapter 4-7 shall apply to lawyers admitted to practice law in jurisdictions other than Florida:
(1) who have established a regular and/or permanent presence in Florida for the practice of law as authorized by other law; and
(2) who solicit or advertise for legal employment in Florida or who target solicitations or advertisements for legal employment at Florida residents.

(d) Advertisements Not Disseminated in Florida. Subchapter 4-7 shall not apply to any advertisement broadcast or disseminated in another jurisdiction in which the advertising lawyer is admitted if such advertisement complies with the rules governing lawyer advertising in that jurisdiction and is not intended for broadcast or dissemination within the state of Florida.

(e) Communications with Family Members. Subchapter 4-7 shall not apply to communications between a lawyer and that lawyer's own family members.

(f) Communications at a Prospective Client's Request. Subchapter 4-7 shall not apply to communications between a lawyer and a prospective client if made at the request of that prospective client.

(g) Application of General Misconduct Rule. The general rule prohibiting a lawyer from engaging in conduct involving dishonesty, deceit, or misrepresentation applies to all communications by a lawyer, whether or not subchapter 4-7 applies to that communication.

Official Comments on Rule 4-7.1 (General)

[1] To assist the public in obtaining legal services, lawyers should be allowed to make known their services not only through reputation but also through organized information campaigns in the form of advertising. The public's need to know about legal services can be fulfilled in part through advertising that provides the public with useful, factual information about legal rights and needs and the availability and terms of legal services from a particular lawyer or law firm. This need is particularly acute in the case of persons of moderate means who have not made extensive use of legal services. Nevertheless, certain types of advertising by lawyers create the risk of practices that are misleading or overreaching and can create unwarranted expectations by persons untrained in the law. Such advertising can also adversely affect the public's confidence and trust in our judicial system.

[2] In order to balance the public's need for useful information, the state's need to ensure a system by which justice will be administered fairly and properly, as well as the state's need to regulate and monitor the advertising practices of lawyers, and a lawyer's right to advertise the availability of the lawyer's services to the public, these rules permit public dissemination of information concerning a lawyer's name or firm name, address, and telephone number; the kinds of services the lawyer will undertake; the basis on which the lawyer's fees are determined, including prices for specific services and payment and credit arrangements; a lawyer's foreign language ability; names of references and, with

| Categories of Lawyer Information That Can Be Advertised |

their consent, names of clients regularly represented; and other factual information that might invite the attention of those seeking legal assistance.

[3] Regardless of medium, a lawyer's advertisement should provide only useful, factual information presented in a nonsensational manner. Advertisements utilizing slogans or jingles, oversized electrical and neon signs, or sound trucks fail to meet these standards and diminish public confidence in the legal system.

| Nonsensational Advertising |

[4] These rules do not prohibit communications authorized by law, such as notice to members of a class in class action litigation.

[5] These rules apply to advertisements and written communications directed at prospective clients and concerning a lawyer's or law firm's availability to provide legal services. These rules do not apply to communications between lawyers and their own family members, or communications with a prospective client at that prospective client's request.

Rule 4-7.2. Communications Concerning a Lawyer's Services

The following shall apply to any communication conveying information about a lawyer's or a law firm's services except as provided in subdivision (e) of rule 4-7.1:

(a) Required Content of Advertisements and Unsolicited Written Communications.

(1) *Name of Lawyer or Lawyer Referral Service.* All advertisements and written communications pursuant to these rules shall include the name of at least 1 lawyer or the lawyer referral service responsible for their content.

| Required Content |

(2) *Location of Practice.* All advertisements and written communications provided for under these rules shall disclose, by city or town, 1 or more bona fide office locations of the lawyer or lawyers who will actually perform the services advertised. If the office location is outside a city or town, the county in which the office is located must be disclosed. A lawyer referral service shall disclose the geographic area in which the lawyer practices when a referral is made. For the purposes of this rule, a bona fide office is defined as a physical location maintained by the lawyer or law firm where the lawyer or law firm reasonably expects to furnish legal services in a substantial way on a regular and continuing basis.

(b) Permissible Content of Advertisements and Unsolicited Written Communications. If the content of an advertisement in any public media or unsolicited written communication is limited to the

| Permissible Content |

following information, the advertisement or unsolicited written communication is exempt from the filing and review requirement and, if true, shall be presumed not to be misleading or deceptive.

(1) *Lawyers and Law Firms.* A lawyer or law firm may include the following information in advertisements and unsolicited written communications:

(A) the name of the lawyer or law firm subject to the requirements of this rule and rule 4-7.9, a listing of lawyers associated with the firm, office locations and parking arrangements, disability accommodations, telephone numbers, web site addresses, and electronic mail addresses, office and telephone service hours, and a designation such as "attorney" or "law firm";

(B) date of admission to The Florida Bar and any other bars, current membership or positions held in The Florida Bar or its sections or committees, former membership or positions held in The Florida Bar or its sections or committees with dates of membership, former positions of employment held in the legal profession with dates the positions were held, years of experience practicing law, number of lawyers in the advertising law firm, and a listing of federal courts and jurisdictions other than Florida where the lawyer is licensed to practice;

(C) technical and professional licenses granted by the state or other recognized licensing authorities and educational degrees received, including dates and institutions;

(D) military service, including branch and dates of service;

(E) foreign language ability;

(F) fields of law in which the lawyer practices, including official certification logos, subject to the requirements of subdivision (c)(6) of this rule regarding use of terms such as certified, specialist, and expert;

(G) prepaid or group legal service plans in which the lawyer participates;

(H) acceptance of credit cards;

(I) fee for initial consultation and fee schedule, subject to the requirements of subdivisions (c)(7) and (c)(8) of this rule regarding cost disclosures and honoring advertised fees;

(J) common salutary language such as "best wishes," "good luck," "happy holidays," or "pleased to announce";

(K) punctuation marks and common typographical marks;

(L) an illustration of the scales of justice not deceptively similar to official certification logos

or The Florida Bar logo, a gavel, traditional renditions of Lady Justice, the Statue of Liberty, the American flag, the American eagle, the State of Florida flag, an unadorned set of law books, the inside or outside of a courthouse, column(s), diploma(s), or a photograph of the lawyer or lawyers who are members of or employed by the firm against a plain background consisting of a single solid color or a plain unadorned set of law books.

(2) *Lawyer Referral Services.* A lawyer referral service may advertise its name, location, telephone number, the referral fee charged, its hours of operation, the process by which referrals are made, the areas of law in which referrals are offered, the geographic area in which the lawyers practice to whom those responding to the advertisement will be referred, and, if applicable, its nonprofit status, its status as a lawyer referral service approved by The Florida Bar, and the logo of its sponsoring bar association.

(3) *Public Service Announcements.* A lawyer or law firm may be listed as a sponsor of a public service announcement or charitable, civic, or community program or event as long as the information about the lawyer or law firm is limited to the permissible content set forth in subdivision (b)(1) of this rule.

(c) **Prohibitions and General Regulations Governing Content of Advertisements and Unsolicited Written Communications.**

(1) *Statements about Legal Services.* A lawyer shall not make or permit to be made a false, misleading, or deceptive communication about the lawyer or the lawyer's services. A communication violates this rule if it:

> Prohibited Content

(A) contains a material misrepresentation of fact or law;

(B) is false or misleading;

(C) fails to disclose material information necessary to prevent the information supplied from being false or misleading;

(D) is unsubstantiated in fact;

(E) is deceptive;

(F) contains any reference to past successes or results obtained;

(G) promises results;

(H) states or implies that the lawyer can achieve results by means that violate the Rules of Professional Conduct or other law;

(I) compares the lawyer's services with other lawyers' services, unless the comparison can be factually substantiated; or

(J) contains a testimonial.

(2) *Descriptive Statements.* A lawyer shall not make statements describing or characterizing the quality of the lawyer's services in advertisements and unsolicited written communications.

(3) *Prohibited Visual and Verbal Portrayals and Illustrations.* A lawyer shall not include in any advertisement or unsolicited written communication any visual or verbal descriptions, depictions, illustrations, or portrayals of persons, things, or events that are deceptive, misleading, manipulative, or likely to confuse the viewer.

(4) *Advertising Areas of Practice.* A lawyer or law firm shall not advertise for legal employment in an area of practice in which the advertising lawyer or law firm does not currently practice law.

(5) *Stating or Implying Florida Bar Approval.* A lawyer or law firm shall not make any statement that directly or impliedly indicates that the communication has received any kind of approval from The Florida Bar.

(6) *Communication of Fields of Practice.* A lawyer may

| Statement of Certification |

communicate the fact that the lawyer does or does not practice in particular fields of law. A lawyer shall not state or imply that the lawyer is "certified," "board certified," a "specialist," or an "expert" except as follows:

(A) Florida Bar Certified Lawyers. A lawyer who complies with the Florida certification plan as set forth in chapter 6, Rules Regulating The Florida Bar, may inform the public and other lawyers of the lawyer's certified areas of legal practice. Such communications should identify The Florida Bar as the certifying organization and may state that the lawyer is "certified," "board certified," a "specialist in (area of certification)," or an expert in (area of certification)."

(B) Lawyers Certified by Organizations Other Than The Florida Bar or Another State Bar. A lawyer certified by an organization other than The Florida Bar or another state bar may inform the public and other lawyers of the lawyer's certified area(s) of legal practice by stating that the lawyer is "certified," "board certified," a "specialist in (area of certification)," or an "expert in (area of certification)" if:

   (i) the organization's program has been accredited by The Florida Bar as provided elsewhere in these Rules Regulating The Florida Bar; and,

   (ii) the member includes the full name of the organization in all communications pertaining to such certification.

(C) Certification by Other State Bars. A lawyer certified by another state bar may inform

the public and other lawyers of the lawyer's certified area(s) of legal practice and may state in communications to the public that the lawyer is "certified," "board certified," a "specialist in (area of certification)," or an "expert in (area of certification)" if:

   (i) the state bar program grants certification on the basis of standards reasonably comparable to the standards of the Florida certification plan as set forth in chapter 6, Rules Regulating The Florida Bar, as determined by The Florida Bar; and,

   (ii) the member includes the name of the state bar in all communications pertaining to such certification.

(7) *Disclosure of Liability for Expenses Other Than Fees.* Every advertisement and unsolicited written communication that contains information about the lawyer's fee, including those that indicate no fee will be

| Disclosure of Expenses in Addition to Fees |

charged in the absence of a recovery, shall disclose whether the client will be liable for any expenses in addition to the fee.

(8) *Period for Which Advertised Fee Must Be Honored.* A lawyer who advertises a specific fee or range of fees for a particular service shall honor the advertised fee or range of fees for at least 90 days unless the advertisement specifies a shorter period; provided that, for advertisements in the yellow pages of telephone directories or other media not published more frequently than annually, the advertised fee or range of fees shall be honored for no less than 1 year following publication.

(9) *Firm Name.* A lawyer shall not advertise services under a name that violates the provisions of rule 4-7.9.

(10) *Language of Required Statements.* Any words or statements required by this subchapter to appear in an advertisement or direct mail communication must appear in the same language in which the advertisement appears. If more than 1 language is used in an advertisement or direct mail communication, any words or statements required by this subchapter must appear in each language used in the advertisement or direct mail communication.

(11) *Appearance of Required Statements.* Any words or statements required by this subchapter to appear in an advertisement or direct mail communication must be clearly legible if written or intelligible if spoken aloud.

(12) *Payment by Nonadvertising Lawyer.* No lawyer shall, directly or indirectly, pay all or a part of the cost of an advertisement by a lawyer not in

the same firm. Rule 4-1.5(f)(4)(D) (regarding the division of contingency fees) is not affected by this provision even though the lawyer covered by rule 4-1.5(f)(4)(D)(ii) advertises.

(13) *Referrals to Another Lawyer.* If the case or matter will be referred to another lawyer or law firm, the communication shall include a statement so advising the prospective client.

(14) *Payment for Recommendations; Lawyer Referral Service Fees.* A lawyer shall not give anything of value to a person for recommending the lawyer's services, except that a lawyer may pay the reasonable cost of advertising or written or recorded communication permitted by these rules, may pay the usual charges of a lawyer referral service or other legal service organization, and may purchase a law practice in accordance with rule 4-1.17.

> **Paying Someone for Recommending a Lawyer's Services**

Official Comments on Rule 4-7.2 (Communications Concerning a Lawyer's Services)

[1] This rule governs all communications about a lawyer's services, including advertising permitted by this subchapter. Whatever means are used to make known a lawyer's services, statements about them must be truthful. This precludes any material misrepresentation or misleading omission, such as where a lawyer states or implies certification or recognition as a specialist other than in accordance with this rule, where a lawyer implies that any court, tribunal, or other public body or official can be improperly influenced, or where a lawyer advertises a particular fee or a contingency fee without disclosing whether the client will also be liable for costs.

[2] Another example of a misleading omission is an advertisement for a law firm that states that all the firm's lawyers are juris doctors but does not disclose that a juris doctorate is a law degree rather than a medical degree of some sort and that virtually any law firm in the United States can make the same claim. Although this rule permits lawyers to list the jurisdictions and courts to which they are admitted, it also would be misleading for a lawyer who does not list other jurisdictions or courts to state that the lawyer is a member of The Florida Bar. Standing by itself, that otherwise truthful statement implies falsely that the lawyer possesses a qualification not common to virtually all lawyers practicing in Florida.

> **Juris Doctor Is Not a Medical Degree**

Prohibited Information (Comment on Rule 4-7.2)

[3] The prohibition in subdivision (c)(1)(F) precludes advertisements about results obtained on behalf of a client, such as the amount of a damage award or the lawyer's record in obtaining favorable

> **Advertisements That Refer to Results**

verdicts. Such information may create the unjustified expectation that similar results can be obtained for others without reference to the specific factual and legal circumstances.

[4] The prohibition in subdivision (c)(1)(I) of comparisons that cannot be factually substantiated would preclude a lawyer from representing that the lawyer or the lawyer's law firm is "the best," "one of the best," or "one of the most experienced" in a field of law.

[5] The prohibition in subdivision (c)(1)(J) precludes endorsements or testimonials, whether from clients or anyone else, because they are inherently misleading to a person untrained in the law. Potential clients are likely to infer from the testimonial that the lawyer will reach similar results in future cases. Because the lawyer cannot directly make this assertion, the lawyer is not permitted to indirectly make that assertion through the use of testimonials.

> **Endorsements and Testimonials**

[6] Subdivision (c)(3) prohibits visual or verbal descriptions, depictions, portrayals, or illustrations in any advertisement which create suspense, or contain exaggerations or appeals to the emotions, call for legal services, or create consumer problems through characterization and dialogue ending with the lawyer solving the problem. Illustrations permitted under *Zauderer v. Office of Disciplinary Counsel of the Supreme Court of Ohio*, 471 U.S. 626 (1985), are informational and not misleading, and are therefore permissible. As an example, a drawing of a fist, to suggest the lawyer's ability to achieve results, would be barred. Examples of permissible illustrations would include a graphic rendering of the scales of justice to indicate that the advertising attorney practices law, a picture of the lawyer, or a map of the office location.

> **Prohibited Illustration: A Drawing of a Fist**

Communication of Fields of Practice (Comment on Rule 4-7.2)

[7] This rule permits a lawyer or law firm to indicate areas of practice in communications about the lawyer's or law firm's services, such as in a telephone directory or other advertising, provided the advertising lawyer or law firm actually practices in those areas of law at the time the advertisement is disseminated. If a lawyer practices only in certain fields, or will not accept matters except in such fields, the lawyer is permitted so to indicate. However, no lawyer who is not certified by The Florida Bar, by another state bar with comparable standards, or an organization accredited by The Florida Bar may be described to the public as a "specialist" or as "specializing," "certified," "board certified," being an "expert" or having "expertise

in," or any variation of similar import. A lawyer may indicate that the lawyer concentrates in, focuses on, or limits the lawyer's practice to particular areas of practice as long as the statements are true.

Paying Others to Recommend a Lawyer (Comment on Rule 4-7.2)

[8] A lawyer is allowed to pay for advertising permitted by this rule and for the purchase of a law practice in accordance with the provisions of

> Paying to Procure Professional Work

rule 4-1.17, but otherwise is not permitted to pay or provide other tangible benefits to another person for procuring professional work. However, a legal aid agency or prepaid legal services plan may pay to advertise legal services provided under its auspices. Likewise, a lawyer may participate in lawyer referral programs and pay the usual fees charged by such programs, subject, however, to the limitations imposed by rule 4-7.10. *This rule does not prohibit paying regular compensation to an assistant, such as a secretary or advertising consultant, to prepare communications permitted by this rule.* (Emphasis added.)

Required Disclosures (Comment on Rule 4-7.2)

Required disclosures would be ineffective if they appeared in an advertisement so briefly or minutely as to be overlooked or ignored. Thus, required information must be legible if written or intelligible if spoken aloud to ensure that the recipient receives the information.

Rule 4-7.3. Advertisements in the Public Print Media

Advertisements disseminated in the public print media are subject to the requirements of rule 4-7.2.

Rule 4-7.4. Direct Contact With Prospective Clients

(a) Solicitation. Except as provided in subdivision (b) of this rule, a lawyer shall not solicit professional employment from a prospective client

> Employee Who Solicit Clients for a Lawyer: Ambulance Chasing

with whom the lawyer has no family or prior professional relationship, in person or otherwise, when a significant motive for the lawyer's doing so is the lawyer's pecuniary gain. *A lawyer shall not permit employees or agents of the lawyer to solicit in the lawyer's behalf.* A lawyer shall not enter into an agreement for, charge, or collect a fee for professional employment obtained in violation of this rule. The term "solicit" includes contact in person, by telephone, telegraph, or facsimile, or by other communication directed to a specific recipient and includes (i) any written form of communication directed to a specific recipient and not meeting the requirements of subdivision (b) of this rule,

and (ii) any electronic mail communication directed to a specific recipient and not meeting the requirements of subdivision (c) of rule 4-7.6. (Emphasis added.)

(b) Written Communication Sent on an Unsolicited Basis.

(1) A lawyer shall not send, or knowingly permit to be sent, on the lawyer's behalf or on behalf of the lawyer's firm

> Unsolicited Written Communication

or partner, an associate, or any other lawyer affiliated with the lawyer or the lawyer's firm, an unsolicited written communication directly or indirectly to a prospective client for the purpose of obtaining professional employment if:

(A) the written communication concerns an action for personal injury or wrongful death or otherwise relates to an accident or disaster involving the person to whom the communication is addressed or a relative of that person, unless the accident or disaster occurred more than 30 days prior to the mailing of the communication;

(B) the written communication concerns a specific matter and the lawyer knows or reasonably should know that the person to whom the communication is directed is represented by a lawyer in the matter;

(C) it has been made known to the lawyer that the person does not want to receive such communications from the lawyer;

(D) the communication involves coercion, duress, fraud, overreaching, harassment, intimidation, or undue influence;

(E) the communication contains a false, fraudulent, misleading, or deceptive statement or claim or is improper under subdivision (c)(1) of rule 4-7.2; or

(F) the lawyer knows or reasonably should know that the physical, emotional, or mental state of the person makes it unlikely that the person would exercise reasonable judgment in employing a lawyer.

(2) Written communications to prospective clients for the purpose of obtaining professional employment are subject to the following requirements:

(A) Written communications to a prospective client are subject to the requirements of rule 4-7.2.

(B) The first page of such written communications shall be plainly marked

> The Word "Advertisement" in Red Ink

"advertisement" in red ink, and the lower left corner of the face of the envelope containing a written communication likewise shall carry a prominent, red "advertisement" mark. If the written communication is in the form of a self-mailing brochure or pamphlet, the "advertisement" mark in red ink shall appear on the address panel of the brochure or pamphlet and on the inside of the brochure or pamphlet. Brochures solicited by clients or prospective clients need not contain the "advertisement" mark.

(C) Written communications mailed to prospective clients shall be sent only by regular U.S. mail, not by registered mail or other forms of restricted delivery.

(D) Every written communication shall be accompanied by a written statement detailing the background, training, and experience of the lawyer or law firm. This statement must include information about the specific experience of the advertising lawyer or law firm in the area or areas of law for which professional employment is sought. Every written communication disseminated by a lawyer referral service shall be accompanied by a written statement detailing the background, training, and experience of each lawyer to whom the recipient may be referred.

(E) If a contract for representation is mailed with the written communication, the top of

"DO NOT SIGN"

each page of the contract shall be marked "SAMPLE" in red ink in a type size 1 size larger than the largest type used in the contract and the words "DO NOT SIGN" shall appear on the client signature line.

(F) The first sentence of any written communication prompted by a specific occurrence involving or affecting the intended recipient of the communication or a family member shall be: "If you have already retained a lawyer for this matter, please disregard this letter."

(G) Written communications shall not be made to resemble legal pleadings or other legal documents. This provision does not preclude the mailing of brochures and pamphlets.

(H) If a lawyer other than the lawyer whose name or signature appears on the communication will actually handle the case or matter, any written communication concerning a specific matter shall include a statement so advising the client.

(I) Any written communication prompted by a specific occurrence involving or affecting the intended recipient of the communication or a family member shall disclose how the lawyer obtained the information prompting the communication. The disclosure re-

quired by this rule shall be specific enough to help the recipient understand the extent of the lawyer's knowledge regarding the recipient's particular situation.

(J) A written communication seeking employment by a specific prospective client in a specific matter shall not reveal on the envelope, or on the outside of a self-mailing brochure or pamphlet, the nature of the client's legal problem.

Official Comments on Rule 4-7.4 (Direct Contact with Prospective Clients)

[1] There is a potential for abuse inherent in direct solicitation by a lawyer of prospective clients known to need legal services. It subjects the person to the private importuning of a trained advocate, in a direct interpersonal encounter. A prospective client often feels overwhelmed by the situation giving rise to the need for legal services and may have an impaired capacity for reason, judgment, and protective self-interest. Furthermore, the lawyer seeking the retainer is faced with a conflict stemming from the lawyer's own interest, which may color the advice and representation offered the vulnerable prospect.

[2] The situation is therefore fraught with the possibility of undue influence, intimidation, and overreaching. This potential for abuse inherent in direct solicitation of prospective clients justifies the 30-day restriction, particularly since lawyer advertising permitted under these rules offers an alternative means of communicating necessary information to those who may be in need of legal services.

[3] Advertising makes it possible for a prospective client to be informed about the need for legal services, and about the qualifications of available lawyers and law firms, without subjecting the prospective client to direct personal persuasion that may overwhelm the client's judgment.

[4] The use of general advertising to transmit information from lawyer to prospective client, rather than direct private contact, will help to assure that the information flows cleanly as well as freely. Advertising is out in public view, thus subject to scrutiny by those who know the lawyer. This informal review is itself likely to help guard against statements and claims that might constitute false or misleading communications. Direct private communications from a lawyer to a prospective client are not subject to such third-party scrutiny and consequently are much more likely to approach (and perhaps cross) the dividing line between accurate representations and those that are false and misleading.

[5] Direct written communications seeking employment by specific prospective clients generally present less potential for abuse or overreaching than

In-Person Solicitation

in-person solicitation and are therefore not prohibited for most types of legal matters, but are subject to reasonable restrictions, as set forth in this rule, designed to minimize or preclude abuse and over-reaching and to ensure lawyer accountability if such should occur.

[6] This rule allows targeted mail solicitation of potential plaintiffs or claimants in personal injury and

| Target Mail Solicitation |

wrongful death causes of action or other causes of action that relate to an accident, disaster, death, or injury, but only if mailed at least 30 days after the incident. This restriction is reasonably required by the sensitized state of the potential clients, who may be either injured or grieving over the loss of a family member, and the abuses that experience has shown exist in this type of solicitation.

[7] Letters of solicitation and their envelopes must be clearly marked "advertisement." This will avoid the recipient's perceiving that there is a need to open the envelope because it is from a lawyer or law firm, only to find the recipient is being solicited for legal services. With the envelope and letter marked "advertisement," the recipient can choose to read the solicitation, or not to read it, without fear of legal repercussions.

[8] In addition, the lawyer or law firm should reveal the source of information used to determine that the recipient has a potential legal problem. Disclosure of the information source will help the recipient to understand the extent of knowledge the lawyer or law firm has regarding the recipient's particular situation and will avoid misleading the recipient into believing that the lawyer has particularized knowledge about the recipient's matter if the lawyer does not. The lawyer or law firm must disclose sufficient information or explanation to allow the recipient to locate for himself or herself the information that prompted the communication from the lawyer.

[9] This rule would not prohibit a lawyer from contacting representatives of organizations or groups that may be interested in establishing a group or prepaid legal plan for its members, insureds, beneficiaries, or other third parties for the purpose of informing such entities of the availability of and details concerning the plan or arrangement that the lawyer or the lawyer's law firm is willing to offer. This form of communication is not directed to a specific prospective client known to need legal services related to a particular matter. Rather, it is usually addressed to an individual acting in a fiduciary capacity seeking a supplier of legal services for others who may, if they choose, become prospective clients of the lawyer. Under these circumstances, the activity that the lawyer undertakes in communicating with such representatives and the type of information transmitted to the individual

are functionally similar to and serve the same purpose as advertising permitted under other rules in this subchapter.

Rule 4-7.5. Advertisements in the Electronic Media Other Than Computer-Accessed Communications

(a) **Generally.** With the exception of computer-based advertisements (which are subject to the special requirements set forth in rule 4-7.6), all advertisements in the electronic media, in-

| TV and Radio Advertising |

cluding but not limited to television and radio, are subject to the requirements of rule 4-7.2.

(b) **Appearance on Television or Radio.** Advertisements on the electronic media such as television and radio shall conform to the requirements of this rule.

(1) *Prohibited Content.* Television and radio advertisement shall not contain:

(A) any feature that is deceptive, misleading, manipulative, or that is likely to confuse the viewer;

(B) any spokesperson's voice or image that is recognizable to the public; or

(C) any background sound other than instrumental music.

(2) *Permissible Content.* Television and radio advertisements may contain:

(A) images that otherwise conform to the requirements of these rules; or

(B) a nonattorney spokesperson speaking on behalf of the lawyer or law firm, as long as the spokesperson is not a celebrity recognizable to the public. If a spokesperson is used, the spokesperson shall provide a spoken disclosure identifying the spokesperson as a spokesperson and disclosing that the spokesperson is not a lawyer.

Official Comments on Rule 4-7.5 (Advertisements in the Electronic Media Other Than Computer-Accessed Communications)

[1] Television is now one of the most powerful media for conveying information to the public; a blanket prohibition against television advertising, therefore, would impede the flow of information about legal services to many sectors of the public. However, the unique characteristics of electronic media, including the pervasiveness of television and radio, the ease with which these media are abused, and the passiveness of the viewer or listener, make the electronic media especially subject to regulation in the public interest. Therefore, greater restrictions on the manner of television and radio advertising are justified than might be appropriate for advertisements in the other media.

[2] To prevent abuses, including potential interferences with the fair and proper administration

| Public Confidence in the Legal Profession |

of justice and the creation of incorrect public perceptions or assumptions about the manner in which our legal system works, and to promote the public's confidence in the legal profession and this country's system of justice while not interfering with the free flow of useful information to prospective users of legal services, it is necessary also to restrict the techniques used in television and radio advertising.

[3] This rule is designed to ensure that the advertising is not misleading and does not create unreasonable or unrealistic expectations about the results the lawyer may be able to obtain in any particular case, and to encourage the provision of useful information to the public about the availability and terms of legal services. Thus, the rule allows lawyer advertisements in which a lawyer who is a member of the advertising firm personally appears to speak regarding the legal services the lawyer or law firm is available to perform, the fees to be charged for such services, and the background and experience of the lawyer or law firm.

[4] The prohibition against false, misleading, or manipulative advertising is intended to pre-

| Inappropriate Dramatization; No Sounds of Car Crashes |

clude, among other things, the use of scenes creating suspense, scenes containing exaggerations, or situations calling for legal services, scenes creating consumer problems through characterization and dialogue ending with the lawyer solving the problem, and the audio or video portrayal of an event or situation. Although dialogue is not necessarily prohibited under this rule, advertisements using dialogue are more likely to be misleading or manipulative than those advertisements using a single lawyer to articulate factual information about the lawyer or law firm's services.

[5] The prohibition against any background sound other than instrumental music precludes, for example, the sound of sirens or car crashes and the use of jingles.

Rule 4-7.6. Computer-Accessed Communications

(a) Definition. For purposes of this subchapter, "com-

| Internet Advertising |

puter-accessed communications" are defined as information regarding a lawyer's or law firm's services that is read, viewed, or heard directly through the use of a computer. Computer-accessed communications include, but are not limited to, Internet presences such as home pages or World Wide Web sites, unsolicited electronic mail communications, and information concerning a lawyer's or law firm's services that appears on World Wide Web search engine screens and elsewhere.

(b) Internet Presence. All World Wide Web sites and home pages accessed via the Internet that are controlled or sponsored by a lawyer or law firm and that contain information concerning the lawyer's or law firm's services:

(1) shall disclose all jurisdictions in which the lawyer or members of the law firm are licensed to practice law;

(2) shall disclose 1 or more bona fide office locations of the lawyer or law firm, in accordance with subdivision (a)(2) of rule 4-7.2; and

(3) are considered to be information provided upon request and, therefore, are otherwise governed by the requirements of rule 4-7.9.

(c) Electronic Mail Communications. A lawyer shall not send, or knowingly permit to be sent, on the lawyer's behalf or on behalf of the lawyer's

| E-Mail Communication |

firm or partner, an associate, or any other lawyer affiliated with the lawyer or the lawyer's firm, an unsolicited electronic mail communication directly or indirectly to a prospective client for the purpose of obtaining professional employment unless:

(1) the requirements of subdivisions (b)(1), (b)(2)(A), (b)(2)(E), (b)(2)(F), (b)(2)(G), (b)(2)(I), and (b)(2)(J) of rule 4-7.4 are met;

(2) the communication discloses 1 or more bona fide office locations of the lawyer or lawyers who will actually perform the services advertised, in accordance with subdivision (a)(2) of rule 4-7.2; and

(3) the subject line of the communication states "legal advertisement."

(d) Advertisements. All computer-accessed communications concerning a lawyer's or law firm's services, other than those subject to subdivisions (b) and (c) of this rule, are subject to the requirements of rule 4-7.2.

Official Comments on Rule 4-7.6 (Computer-Accessed Communications)

[1] Advances in telecommunications and computer technology allow lawyers to communicate with other lawyers, clients, prospective clients, and others in increasingly quicker and more efficient ways. Regardless of the particular technology used, however, a lawyer's communications with prospective clients for the purpose of obtaining professional employment must meet standards designed to protect the public from false, deceptive, misleading, or confusing messages about lawyers or the legal system and to encourage the free flow of useful legal-related information to the public.

[2] The specific regulations that govern computer-accessed communications differ according to the

| A Lawyer's Web Site |

particular variety of communication employed. For example, a lawyer's Internet web site is accessed by the viewer upon the viewer's initiative and, accordingly, the standards governing such communications correspond to the rules applicable to information provided to a prospective client at the prospective client's request.

[3] In contrast, unsolicited electronic mail messages from lawyers to prospective clients are functionally comparable to direct mail communications and thus are governed by similar rules. Additionally, communications advertising or promoting a lawyer's services that are posted on search engine screens or elsewhere by the lawyer, or at the lawyer's behest, with the hope that they will be seen by prospective clients are simply a form of lawyer advertising and are treated as such by the rules.

[4] This rule is not triggered merely because someone other than the lawyer gratuitously links to, or comments on, a lawyer's Internet web site.

Rule 4-7.7. Evaluation of Advertisements

(a) Filing and Advisory Opinion. Subject to the exemptions stated in rule 4-7.8, any lawyer who advertises services through any public media or through written communications sent on an unsolicited basis to prospective clients shall file a copy of each such advertisement with The Florida Bar at its headquarters address in Tallahassee for evaluation of compliance with these rules. . . .

Official Comments on Rule 4-7.7 (Evaluation of Advertisements)

[1] This rule has a dual purpose: to enhance the court's and the bar's ability to monitor advertising practices for the protection of the public and to assist members of the bar to conform their advertisements to the requirements of these rules.

[2] . . . The Florida Bar will advise the filing lawyer in writing whether the advertisement appears to comply with the rules.

Rule 4-7.8. Exemptions from the Filing and Review Requirement

The following are exempt from the filing requirements of rule 4-7.7:

(a) any advertisement in any of the public media, including the yellow pages of telephone directories, that contains neither illustrations nor information other than permissible content of advertisements listed in rule 4-7.2(b).

(b) a brief announcement in any of the public media that identifies a lawyer or law firm as a contributor to a specified charity or as a sponsor of a public service announcement or a specified charitable, community,

or public interest program, activity, or event, provided that the announcement contains no information about the lawyer or law firm other than permissible content of advertisements listed in rule 4-7.2(b) and the fact of the sponsorship or contribution. In determining whether an announcement is a public service announcement for purposes of this rule and the rule setting forth permissible content of advertisements, the following are criteria that may be considered:

(1) whether the content of the announcement appears to serve the particular interests of the lawyer or law firm as much as or more than the interests of the public;

(2) whether the announcement contains information concerning the lawyer's or law firm's area of practice, legal background, or experience;

(3) whether the announcement contains the address or telephone number of the lawyer or law firm;

(4) whether the announcement concerns a legal subject;

(5) whether the announcement contains legal advice; and

(6) whether the lawyer or law firm paid to have the announcement published.

(c) A listing or entry in a law list or bar publication.

(d) Professional announcement cards stating new or changed associations, new offices, and similar changes relating to a lawyer or law firm, and that are mailed only to other lawyers, relatives, close personal friends, and existing or former clients.

(e) Computer-accessed communications as described in subdivision (b) of rule 4-7.6.

Official Comments on Rule 4-7.8 (Exemptions from the Filing and Review Requirement)

In *The Florida Bar v. Doe*, 634 So. 2d 160 (Fla. 1994), the court recognized the need for specific guidelines to aid lawyers and the bar in determining whether a particular announcement in the public media is a public service announcement as contemplated in this rule and rule 4-7.2. Subdivisions (b)(1)–(6) of this rule respond to the court's concern by setting forth criteria that, while not intended to be exclusive, provide the needed guidance. With the exception of subdivision (b)(3), these criteria are based on factors considered by the court in *Doe*.

Rule 4-7.9 Firm Names and Letterhead

(a) False, Misleading, or Deceptive. A lawyer shall not use a firm name, letterhead, or other professional designation that is false, misleading, or deceptive as set forth in subdivision (c)(1) of rule 4-7.2.

(b) Trade Names. A lawyer may practice under a trade name if the name is not deceptive and does not imply a connection with a government agency or with a public or charitable legal services organization, does not imply that the firm is something other

Misleading Law Firm Names; Using the Phrases "Legal Clinic" or "Legal Services"

than a private law firm, and is not misleading, or deceptive as set forth in subdivision (c)(1) of rule 4-7.2. A lawyer in private practice may use the term "legal clinic" or "legal services" in conjunction with the lawyer's own name if the lawyer's practice is devoted to providing routine legal services for fees that are lower than the prevailing rate in the community for those services.

(c) Advertising Under Trade Name. A lawyer shall not advertise under a trade or fictitious name, except that a lawyer who actually practices under a trade name as authorized by subdivision (b) may use that name in advertisements. A lawyer who advertises under a trade or fictitious name shall be in violation of this rule unless the same name is the law firm name that appears on the lawyer's letterhead, business cards, office sign, and fee contracts, and appears with the lawyer's signature on pleadings and other legal documents.

(d) Law Firm with Offices in More Than 1 Jurisdiction. A law firm with offices in more than 1 jurisdiction may use the same name in each jurisdiction, but identification of the lawyers in an office of the firm shall indicate the jurisdictional limitations on those not licensed to practice in the jurisdiction where the office is located.

(e) Name of Public Officer in Firm Name. The name of a lawyer holding a public office shall not be used in the name of a law firm, or in communications on its behalf, during any substantial period in which the lawyer is not actively and regularly practicing with the firm.

(f) Partnerships and Authorized Business Entities. Lawyers may state or imply that they practice in a partnership or authorized business entity only when that is the fact.

(g) Insurance Staff Attorneys. Where otherwise consistent with these rules, lawyers who practice law as employees within a separate unit of a liability insurer representing others pursuant to policies of liability insurance may practice under a name that does not constitute a material misrepresentation. In order for the use of a name other than the name of the insurer not to constitute a material misrepresentation, all lawyers in the unit must comply with all of the following:

(1) the firm name must include the name of a lawyer who has supervisory responsibility for all lawyers in the unit;

(2) the office entry signs, letterhead, business cards, web sites, announcements, advertising, and listings or entries in a law list or bar publication bearing the name must disclose that the lawyers in the unit are employees of the insurer;

(3) the name of the insurer and the employment relationship must be disclosed to all insured clients and prospective clients of the lawyers, and must be disclosed in the official file at the lawyers' first appearance in the tribunal in which the lawyers appear under such name;

(4) the offices, personnel, and records of the unit must be functionally and physically separate from other operations of the insurer to the extent that would be required by these rules if the lawyers were private practitioners sharing space with the insurer; and

(5) additional disclosure should occur whenever the lawyer knows or reasonably should know that the lawyer's role is misunderstood by the insured client or prospective clients.

Official Comments on Rule 4-7.9 (Firm Names and Letterhead)

[1] A firm may be designated by the names of all or some of its members, by the names of deceased members where there has been a continuing succession in the firm's identity, or by a trade name such as "Family Legal Clinic." Although the United States Supreme Court has held that legislation may prohibit the use of trade names in professional practice, use of such names in law practice is acceptable so long as it is not misleading. If a private firm uses a trade name that includes a geographical name such as "Springfield Legal Clinic," an express disclaimer that it is not a public legal aid agency may be required to avoid a misleading implication. It may be observed that any firm name including the name of a deceased partner is, strictly speaking, a trade name. The use of such names to designate law firms has proven a useful means of identification. However, it is misleading to use the name of a lawyer not associated with the firm or a predecessor of the firm.

[2] Subdivision (a) precludes use in a law firm name of terms that imply that the firm is something other than a private law firm. Two examples of such terms are "academy" and "institute." Subdivision (b) precludes use of a trade or fictitious name suggesting that the firm is named for a person when in fact such a person does not exist or is not associated with the firm. An example of such an improper name is "A. Aaron Able." Although not prohibited per se, the terms "legal clinic" and "legal services" would be misleading if used by a law firm that did not devote its practice to providing routine legal services at prices below those prevailing in the community for like services.

[3] Subdivision (c) of this rule precludes a lawyer from advertising under a nonsense name designed to obtain an advantageous position for the lawyer in alphabetical directory listings unless the lawyer actually practices under that nonsense name. Advertising under a law firm name that differs from the firm name under which the lawyer actually practices violates both this rule and the prohibition against false, misleading, or deceptive communications as set forth in subdivision (c)(1) of rule 4-7.2.

> **Nonsense Names**

[4] With regard to subdivision (f), lawyers sharing office facilities, but who are not in fact partners, may not denominate themselves as, for example, "Smith and Jones," for that title suggests partnership in the practice of law.

> **Office Sharing**

[5] All lawyers who practice under trade or firm names are required to observe and comply with the requirements of the Rules Regulating The Florida Bar, including but not limited to rules regarding conflicts of interest, imputation of conflicts, firm names and letterhead, and candor toward tribunals and third parties.

[6] Some liability insurers employ lawyers on a full-time basis to represent their insured clients in defense of claims covered by the contract of insurance. Use of a name to identify these attorneys is permissible if there is such physical and functional separation as to constitute a separate law firm. In the absence of such separation, it would be a misrepresentation to use a name implying that a firm exists. Practicing under the name of an attorney inherently represents that the identified person has supervisory responsibility. Practicing under a name prohibited by subsection (f) is not permitted. Candor requires disclosure of the employment relationship on letterhead, business cards, and in certain other communications that are not presented to a jury. The legislature of the State of Florida has enacted, as public policy, laws prohibiting the joinder of a liability insurer in most such litigation, and Florida courts have recognized the public policy of not disclosing the existence of insurance coverage to juries. Requiring lawyers who are so employed to disclose to juries the employment relationship would negate Florida public policy. For this reason, the rule does not require the disclosure of the employment relationship on all pleadings and papers filed in court proceedings. The general duty of candor of all lawyers may be implicated in other circumstances, but does not require disclosure on all pleadings.

Rule 4-7.10 Lawyer Referral Services

(a) When Lawyers May Accept Referrals. A lawyer shall not accept referrals from a lawyer referral service unless the service:

(1) engages in no communication with the public and in no direct contact with prospective clients in a manner that would violate the Rules of Professional Conduct if the communication or contact were made by the lawyer;

(2) receives no fee or charge that constitutes a division or sharing of fees, unless the service is a not-for-profit service approved by The Florida Bar pursuant to chapter 8 of these rules;

(3) refers clients only to persons lawfully permitted to practice law in Florida when the services to be rendered constitute the practice of law in Florida;

(4) carries or requires each lawyer participating in the service to carry professional liability insurance in an amount not less than $100,000 per claim or occurrence;

> **Minimum Malpractice Insurance**

(5) furnishes The Florida Bar, on a quarterly basis, with the names and Florida bar membership numbers of all lawyers participating in the service;

(6) furnishes The Florida Bar, on a quarterly basis, the names of all persons authorized to act on behalf of the service;

(7) responds in writing, within 15 days, to any official inquiry by bar counsel when bar counsel is seeking information described in this subdivision or conducting an investigation into the conduct of the service or an attorney who accepts referrals from the service;

(8) neither represents nor implies to the public that the service is endorsed or approved by The Florida Bar, unless the service is subject to chapter 8 of these rules;

(9) uses its actual legal name or a registered fictitious name in all communications with the public; and

(10) affirmatively states in all advertisements that it is a lawyer referral service.

(b) Responsibility of Lawyer. A lawyer who accepts referrals from a lawyer referral service is responsible for ensuring that any advertisements or written communications used by the service comply with the requirements of the Rules Regulating The Florida Bar, and that the service is in compliance with the provisions of this subchapter.

(c) Definition of Lawyer Referral Service. A "lawyer referral service" is:

(1) any person, group of persons, association, organization, or entity that receives a fee or charge for referring or causing the direct or indirect referral of a potential client to a lawyer drawn from a specific group or panel of lawyers; or

(2) any group or pooled advertising program operated by any person, group of persons, association,

organization, or entity wherein the legal services advertisements utilize a common telephone number and potential clients are then referred only to lawyers or law firms participating in the group or pooled advertising program.

A pro bono referral program, in which the participating lawyers do not pay a fee or charge of any kind to receive referrals or to belong to the referral panel, and are undertaking the referred matters without expectation of remuneration, is not a lawyer referral service within the definition of this rule.

Official Comments on Rule 4-7.10 (Lawyer Referral Services)

[1] Every citizen of the state should have ready access to the legal system. A person's access to the legal system is enhanced by the assistance of a lawyer qualified to handle that person's legal needs. Many of the citizens of the state who are potential consumers of legal services encounter difficulty in identifying and locating lawyers who are willing and qualified to consult with them about their legal needs. Lawyer referral services can facilitate the identification and intelligent selection of lawyers qualified to render assistance. However, because a potential for abuse exists, the participation of lawyers in referral services must be regulated to ensure protection of the public.

[2] It is in the public interest that a person seeking the assistance of counsel receive accurate information to select or be matched with counsel qualified to render the needed services. Therefore, a lawyer should not participate in a lawyer referral service that communicates misleading information to the public or that directly contacts prospective clients about available legal services in a manner that constitutes impermissible solicitation.

> **Unethical Lawyer Referral Services**

[3] One who avails oneself of legal services is well served only if those services are rendered by a lawyer who exercises independent legal judgment. The division or sharing of a fee risks the creation of an obligation that impairs a lawyer's ability to exercise independent legal judgment. Therefore, the public interest usually compels the ethical prohibition against the division or sharing of fees and that ethical prohibition should likewise apply to the division or sharing of fees with a lawyer referral service.

[4] The prohibition does not extend to the lawyer's paying a pre-arranged, fixed-sum participation fee. Furthermore, the prohibition does not apply when the referring agency is a not-for-profit service operated by a bona fide state or local bar association under the supervision of and approved by The Florida Bar in order to ensure that such service fulfills the public-interest purposes of a lawyer referral service

and to ensure that the risk of impairment of the lawyer's ability to exercise independent legal judgment is in that circumstance minimal.

[5] It is in the public interest that a person receive legal services only from someone who is qualified to render them. Lawyers should strive to prevent harm resulting from the rendering of legal services by persons not legally qualified to do so. Therefore, a lawyer should not participate in a lawyer referral service that refers clients to persons not lawfully permitted to practice law in Florida when the services to be rendered constitute the practice of law in Florida. The quasi-institutionalization of legal services by a lawyer referral service implies that the service has screened the qualifications and financial responsibility of its participating lawyers. That implication may be misleading and does not exist when a prospective client directly selects a lawyer at arm's length. Therefore, it is in the public interest that only lawyers who have established a certain amount of financial responsibility for professional liability participate in a lawyer referral service. Accordingly, a lawyer should participate in a lawyer referral service only if the service requires proof of that financial responsibility.

[6] To enable The Florida Bar to fulfill its obligation to protect the public from unethical or other improper conduct by those who practice law in Florida, The Florida Bar must have available to it the identity of all lawyers participating in a lawyer referral service. Therefore, a lawyer should participate in a lawyer referral service only if the service furnishes The Florida Bar with the names of its participating lawyers.

4-8. Maintaing the Integrity of the Profession

Rule 4-8.1. Bar Admission and Disciplinary Matters

An applicant for admission to the bar, or a lawyer in connection with a bar admission application or in connection with a disciplinary matter, shall not:

(a) knowingly make a false statement of material fact;

(b) fail to disclose a fact necessary to correct a misapprehension known by the person to have arisen in the matter or knowingly fail to respond to a lawful demand for information from an admissions or disciplinary authority, except that this rule does not require disclosure of information otherwise protected by rule 4-1.6; or

(c) commit an act that adversely reflects on the applicant's fitness to practice law. An applicant who commits such an act before admission, but which is discovered after admission, shall be subject to discipline under these rules.

> **Fitness to Practice Law**

Official Comments on Rule 4-8.1 (Bar Admission and Disciplinary Matters)

[1] The duty imposed by this rule extends to persons seeking admission to the bar as well as to lawyers. Hence, if a person makes a material false statement in connection with an application for admission, it may be the basis for subsequent disciplinary action if the person is admitted and in any event may be relevant in a subsequent admission application. The duty imposed by this rule applies to a lawyer's own admission or discipline as well as that of others. Thus, it is a separate professional offense for a lawyer to knowingly make a misrepresentation or omission in connection with a disciplinary investigation of the lawyer's own conduct. Subdivision (b) of this rule also requires correction of any prior misstatement in the matter that the applicant or lawyer may have made and affirmative clarification of any misunderstanding on the part of the admissions or disciplinary authority of which the person involved becomes aware.

[2] This rule is subject to the provisions of the fifth amendment of the United States Constitution and the corresponding provisions of the Florida Constitution. A person relying on such a provision in response to a question, however, should do so openly and not use the right of nondisclosure as a justification for failure to comply with this rule.

[3] A lawyer representing an applicant for admission to the bar, or representing a lawyer who is the subject of a disciplinary inquiry or proceeding, is governed by the rules applicable to the client-lawyer relationship, including rule 4-1.6 and, in some cases, rule 4-3.3.

[4] An applicant for admission may commit acts that adversely reflect on the applicant's fitness to practice law and which are discovered only after the applicant becomes a member of the bar. This rule provides a means to address such misconduct in the absence of such a provision in the Rules of the Supreme Court Relating to Admissions to the Bar.

Rule 4-8.2. Judicial and Legal Officials

(a) **Impugning Qualifications and Integrity of Judges or Other Officers.** A lawyer shall not make a statement that the lawyer knows to be false or with reckless disregard as to its truth or falsity concerning the qualifications or integrity of a judge, mediator, arbitrator, adjudicatory officer, public legal officer, juror or member of the venire, or candidate for election or appointment to judicial or legal office.

| Attacking the Integrity of Judges and Others |

(b) **Candidates for Judicial Office; Code of Judicial Conduct Applies.** A lawyer who is a candidate for judicial office shall comply with the applicable provisions of Florida's Code of Judicial Conduct.

Official Comments on Rule 4-8.2 (Judicial and Legal Officials)

[1] Assessments by lawyers are relied on in evaluating the professional or personal fitness of persons being considered for election or appointment to judicial office and to public legal offices, such as attorney general, prosecuting attorney, and public defender. Expressing honest and candid opinions on such matters contributes to improving the administration of justice. Conversely, false statements by a lawyer can unfairly undermine public confidence in the administration of justice.

| Honest and Candid Opinions |

[2] False statements or statements made with reckless disregard for truth or falsity concerning potential jurors, jurors serving in pending cases, or jurors who served in concluded cases undermine the impartiality of future jurors who may fear to execute their duty if their decisions are ridiculed. Lawyers may not make false statements or any statement made with the intent to ridicule or harass jurors.

[3] When a lawyer seeks judicial office, the lawyer should be bound by applicable limitations on political activity.

[4] To maintain the fair and independent administration of justice, lawyers are encouraged to continue traditional efforts to defend judges and courts unjustly criticized.

Rule 4-8.3. Reporting Professional Misconduct

(a) **Reporting Misconduct of Other Lawyers.** A lawyer who knows that another lawyer has committed a violation of the Rules of Professional Conduct that raises a substantial question as to that lawyer's honesty, trustworthiness, or fitness as a lawyer in other respects shall inform the appropriate professional authority.

| One Lawyer Reporting Misconduct of Another Lawyer |

(b) **Reporting Misconduct of Judges.** A lawyer who knows that a judge has committed a violation of applicable rules of judicial conduct that raises a substantial question as to the judge's fitness for office shall inform the appropriate authority.

(c) **Confidences Preserved.** This rule does not require disclosure of information otherwise protected by rule 4-1.6 or information gained by a lawyer or judge while participating in an approved lawyers assistance program. Provided further, however, that if a lawyer's participation in an approved lawyers assistance program is part of a disciplinary sanction this limitation shall not be applicable and a report about the lawyer who is participating as part of a disciplinary sanction shall be made to the appropriate disciplinary agency.

(d) **Limited Exception for LOMAS Counsel.** A lawyer employed by or acting on behalf of the Law Office

Management Assistance Service (LOMAS) shall not have an obligation to disclose knowledge of the conduct of another member of The Florida Bar that raises a substantial question as to the other lawyer's fitness to practice, if the lawyer employed by or acting on behalf of LOMAS acquired the knowledge while engaged in a LOMAS review of the other lawyer's practice. Provided further, however, that if the LOMAS review is conducted as a part of a disciplinary sanction this limitation shall not be applicable and a report shall be made to the appropriate disciplinary agency.

Official Comments on Rule 4-8.3 (Reporting Professional Misconduct)

[1] Self-regulation of the legal profession requires that members of the profession initiate disciplinary investigation when they know of a violation of the Rules of Professional Conduct. Lawyers have a similar obligation with respect to judicial misconduct. An apparently isolated violation may indicate a pattern of misconduct that only a disciplinary investigation can uncover. Reporting a violation is especially important where the victim is unlikely to discover the offense.

[2] A report about misconduct is not required where it would involve violation of rule 4-1.6. However, a lawyer should encourage a client to consent to disclosure where prosecution would not substantially prejudice the client's interests.

[3] If a lawyer were obliged to report every violation of the rules, the failure to report any violation would itself be a professional offense. Such a requirement existed in many jurisdictions, but proved to be unenforceable. This rule limits the reporting obligation to those offenses that a self-regulating profession must vigorously endeavor to prevent. A measure of judgment is, therefore, required in complying with the provisions of this rule. The term "substantial" refers to the seriousness of the possible offense and not the quantum of evidence of which the lawyer is aware.

[4] The duty to report professional misconduct does not apply to a lawyer retained to represent a lawyer whose professional conduct is in question. Such a situation is governed by the rules applicable to the client-lawyer relationship.

[5] Information about a lawyer's or judge's misconduct or fitness may be received by a lawyer in the course of that lawyer's participation in an approved lawyers or judges assistance program. In that circumstance, providing for an exception to the reporting requirements of subdivisions (a) and (b) of this rule encourages lawyers and judges to seek treatment through such a program. Conversely, without such an exception, lawyers and judges may hesitate to seek assistance from these programs, which may then result in additional harm to their professional careers and additional injury to the welfare of clients and the public. These rules do not otherwise address the confidentiality of information received by a lawyer or judge participating in an approved lawyers assistance program; such an obligation, however, may be imposed by the rules of the program or other law.

Rule 4-8.4. Misconduct

A lawyer shall not:

(a) violate or attempt to violate the Rules of Professional Conduct, knowingly assist or induce another to do so, or do so through the acts of another;

(b) commit a criminal act that reflects adversely on the lawyer's honesty, trustworthiness, or fitness as a lawyer in other respects;

(c) engage in conduct involving dishonesty, fraud, deceit, or misrepresentation, except that it shall not be professional misconduct for a lawyer for a criminal law enforcement agency or regulatory agency to advise others about or to supervise another in an undercover investigation, unless prohibited by law or rule, and it shall not be professional misconduct for a lawyer employed in a capacity other than as a lawyer by a criminal law enforcement agency or regulatory agency to participate in an undercover investigation, unless prohibited by law or rule;

(d) engage in conduct in connection with the practice of law that is prejudicial to the administration of justice, including to knowingly, or through callous indifference, disparage, humiliate, or discriminate against litigants, jurors, witnesses, court personnel, or other

> Conduct That Humiliates Judges, Litigants, Other Lawyers, etc.

lawyers on any basis, including, but not limited to, on account of race, ethnicity, gender, religion, national origin, disability, marital status, sexual orientation, age, socioeconomic status, employment, or physical characteristic;

(e) state or imply an ability to influence improperly a government agency or official or to achieve results by means that violate the Rules of Professional Conduct or other law;

(f) knowingly assist a judge or judicial officer in conduct that is a violation of applicable rules of judicial conduct or other law;

(g) fail to respond, in writing, to any official inquiry by bar counsel or a disciplinary agency, as defined elsewhere in these rules, when bar counsel or the agency is conducting an investigation into the

> Responding to an Investigation

lawyer's conduct. A written response shall be made:

(1) within 15 days of the date of the initial written investigative inquiry by bar counsel, grievance committee, or board of governors;

(2) within 10 days of the date of any follow-up written investigative inquiries by bar counsel, grievance committee, or board of governors;

(3) within the time stated in any subpoena issued under these Rules Regulating The Florida Bar (without additional time allowed for mailing);

(4) as provided in the Florida Rules of Civil Procedure or order of the referee in matters assigned to a referee; and

(5) as provided in the Florida Rules of Appellate Procedure or order of the Supreme Court of Florida for matters pending action by that court.

Except as stated otherwise herein or in the applicable rules, all times for response shall be calculated as provided elsewhere in these Rules Regulating The Florida Bar and may be extended or shortened by the inquirer upon good cause shown;

| Failure to Pay Child Support |

(h) willfully refuse, as determined by a court of competent jurisdiction, to timely pay a child support obligation; or

| Sexual Exploitation of a Client or Client's Representative |

(i) engage in sexual conduct with a client or a representative of a client that exploits or adversely affects the interests of the client or the lawyer-client relationship including, but not limited to:

(1) requiring or demanding sexual relations with a client or a representative of a client incident to or as a condition of a legal representation;

(2) employing coercion, intimidation, or undue influence in entering into sexual relations with a client or a representative of a client; or

(3) continuing to represent a client if the lawyer's sexual relations with the client or a representative of the client cause the lawyer to render incompetent representation.

Official Comments on Rule 4-8.4 (Misconduct)

[1] Lawyers are subject to discipline when they violate or attempt to violate the Rules of Professional Conduct, knowingly assist or induce another to do so, or do so through the acts of another, as when they request or instruct an agent to do so on the lawyer's behalf. Subdivision (a), however, does not prohibit a lawyer from advising a client concerning action the client is legally entitled to take, provided that the client is not used to indirectly violate the Rules of Professional Conduct.

[2] Many kinds of illegal conduct reflect adversely on

| Moral Turpitude |

fitness to practice law, such as offenses involving fraud and the offense of willful failure to file an income tax return. However, some kinds of offense carry no such implication. Traditionally, the distinction was drawn in terms of offenses involving "moral turpitude." That concept can be construed to include offenses concerning some matters of personal morality, such as adultery and comparable offenses, that have no specific connection to fitness for the practice of law. Although a lawyer is personally answerable to the entire criminal law, a lawyer should be professionally answerable only for offenses that indicate lack of those characteristics relevant to law practice. Offenses involving violence, dishonesty, or breach of trust or serious interference with the administration of justice are in that category. A pattern of repeated offenses, even ones of minor significance when considered separately, can indicate indifference to legal obligation.

[3] A lawyer may refuse to comply with an obligation imposed by law upon a good faith belief that no valid obligation exists. The provisions of rule 4-1.2(d) concerning a good faith challenge to the validity, scope, meaning, or application of the law apply to challenges of legal regulation of the practice of law.

[4] Subdivision (c) recognizes instances where lawyers in criminal law enforcement agencies or regulatory agencies advise others about or supervise others in undercover investigations, and provides an exception to allow the activity without the lawyer engaging in professional misconduct. The exception acknowledges current, acceptable practice of these agencies. Although the exception appears in this rule, it is also applicable to rules 4-4.1 and 4-4.3. However, nothing in the rule allows the lawyer to engage in such conduct if otherwise prohibited by law or rule.

[5] Subdivision (d) of this rule proscribes conduct that is prejudicial to the administration of justice. Such proscription includes the prohibition against discriminatory conduct committed by a lawyer while performing duties in connection with the practice of law. The proscription extends to any characteristic or status that is not relevant to the proof of any legal or factual issue in dispute. Such conduct, when directed towards litigants, jurors, witnesses, court personnel, or other lawyers, whether based on race, ethnicity, gender, religion, national origin, disability, marital status, sexual orientation, age, socioeconomic status, employment, physical characteristic, or any other basis, subverts the administration of justice and undermines the public's confidence in our system of justice, as well as notions of equality. This subdivision does not prohibit a lawyer from representing a client as may

be permitted by applicable law, such as, by way of example, representing a client accused of committing discriminatory conduct.

[6] Lawyers holding public office assume legal responsibilities going beyond those of other citizens. A lawyer's abuse of public office can suggest an inability to fulfill the professional role of attorney. The same is true of abuse of positions of private trust such as trustee, executor, administrator, guardian, or agent and officer, director, or manager of a corporation or other organization.

[7] A lawyer's obligation to respond to an inquiry by a disciplinary agency is stated in subdivision (g) and rule 3-7.6(h)(2). While response is mandatory, the lawyer may deny the charges or assert any available privilege or immunity or interpose any disability that prevents disclosure of certain matter. A response containing a proper invocation thereof is sufficient under the Rules Regulating The Florida Bar. This obligation is necessary to ensure the proper and efficient operation of the disciplinary system.

[8] Subdivision (h) of this rule was added to make consistent the treatment of attorneys who fail to pay child support with the treatment of other professionals who fail to pay child support, in accordance with the provisions of section 61.13015, Florida Statutes. That section provides for the suspension or denial of a professional license due to delinquent child support payments after all other available remedies for the collection of child support have been exhausted. Likewise, subdivision (h) of this rule should not be used as the primary means for collecting child support, but should be used only after all other available remedies for the collection of child support have been exhausted. Before a grievance may be filed or a grievance procedure initiated under this subdivision, the court that entered the child support order must first make a finding of willful refusal to pay. The child support obligation at issue under this rule includes both domestic (Florida) and out-of-state (URESA) child support obligations, as well as arrearages.

[9] Subdivision (i) proscribes exploitation of the client and the lawyer-client relationship by means of commencement of sexual conduct. The lawyer-client relationship is grounded on mutual trust. A sexual relationship that exploits that trust compromises the lawyer-client relationship. For purposes of this subdivision, client means an individual, or a representative of the client, including but not limited to a duly authorized constituent of a corporate or other non-personal entity, and lawyer refers only to the lawyer(s) engaged in the legal representation and not other members of the law firm.

Rule 4-8.5. Jurisdiction

A lawyer admitted to practice in this jurisdiction is subject to the disciplinary authority of this jurisdiction although engaged in practice elsewhere.

Official Comments on Rule 4-8.5 (Jurisdiction)

[1] In modern practice lawyers frequently act outside the territorial limits of the jurisdiction in which they are licensed to practice, either in another state or outside the United States. In doing so, they remain subject to the governing authority of the jurisdiction in which they are licensed to practice. If their activity in another jurisdiction is substantial and continuous, it may constitute the practice of law in that jurisdiction. See rule 4-5.5.

[2] If the Rules of Professional Conduct in the 2 jurisdictions differ, principles of conflict of laws may apply. Similar problems can arise when a lawyer is licensed to practice in more than 1 jurisdiction.

[3] Where the lawyer is licensed to practice law in 2 jurisdictions that impose conflicting obligations, applicable rules of choice of law may govern the situation. A related problem arises with respect to practice before a federal tribunal where the general authority of the states to regulate the practice of law must be reconciled with such authority as federal tribunals may have to regulate practice before them.

Rule 4-8.6. Authorized Business Entities

(a) Authorized Business Entities. Lawyers may practice law in the form of professional service corporations, professional limited liability companies, sole proprietorships, general partnerships, or limited liability partnerships organized or qualified under applicable law. Such forms of practice are authorized business entities under these rules.

> Professional Corporations, Partnerships, Limited Liability Companies, Sole Proprietorships

(b) Practice of Law Limited to Members of The Florida Bar. No authorized business entity may engage in the practice of law in the state of Florida or render advice under or interpretations of Florida law except through officers, directors, partners, managers, agents, or employees who are qualified to render legal services in this state. . . .

(f) Cessation of Legal Services. Whenever all shareholders of a professional service corporation, or all members of a professional limited liability company, the proprietor of a solo practice, or all partners in a limited liability partnership become legally disqualified to render legal services in this state, the authorized business entity shall cease the rendition of legal services in Florida. . . .

5. Rules Regulating Trust Accounts

5-1 Generally

Rule 5-1.1 Trust Accounts

(a) Nature of Money or Property Entrusted to Attorney.

(1) *Trust Account Required; Commingling Prohibited.* A lawyer shall hold in trust, separate from the lawyer's own property, funds and property of clients or third persons that are in a lawyer's possession in connection with a representation. All funds, including advances for fees, costs, and expenses, shall be kept in a separate bank or savings and loan association account maintained in the state where the lawyer's office is situated or elsewhere with the consent of the client or third person and clearly labeled and designated as a trust account. A lawyer may maintain funds belonging to the lawyer in the trust account in an amount no more than is reasonably sufficient to pay bank charges relating to the trust account.

Commingling Funds

(2) *Compliance with Client Directives.* Trust funds may be separately held and maintained other than in a bank or savings and loan association account if the lawyer receives written permission from the client to do so and provided that written permission is received before maintaining the funds other than in a separate account.

(3) *Safe Deposit Boxes.* If a member of the bar uses a safe deposit box to store trust funds or property, the member shall advise the institution in which the deposit box is located that it may include property of clients or third persons.

(b) Application of Trust Funds or Property to Specific Purpose. Money or other property entrusted to an attorney for a specific purpose, including advances for fees, costs, and expenses, is held in trust and must be applied only to that purpose. Money and other property of clients coming into the hands of an attorney are not subject to counterclaim or setoff for attorney's fees, and a refusal to account for and deliver over such property upon demand shall be deemed a conversion.

(c) Liens Permitted. This subchapter does not preclude the retention of money or other property upon which the lawyer has a valid lien for services nor does it preclude the payment of agreed fees from the proceeds of transactions or collection.

Lawyer's Lien

(d) Controversies as to Amount of Fees. Controversies as to the amount of fees are not grounds for disciplinary proceedings unless the amount demanded is clearly excessive, extortionate, or fraudulent. In a controversy alleging a clearly excessive, extortion- ate, or fraudulent fee, announced willingness of an attorney to sub- mit a dispute as to the amount of a fee to a competent tribunal for determination may be considered in any determi- nation as to intent or in mitigation of discipline; provided, such willingness shall not preclude ad- mission of any other relevant admissible evidence re- lating to such controversy, including evidence as to the withholding of funds or property of the client, or to other injury to the client occasioned by such con- troversy.

Fees That Are Excessive, Extortionate, or Fraudulent

(e) Notice of Receipt of Trust Funds; Delivery; Account- ing. Upon receiving funds or other property in which a client or third person has an interest, a lawyer shall promptly notify the client or third per- son. Except as stated in this rule or otherwise per- mitted by law or by agreement with the client, a lawyer shall promptly deliver to the client or third person any funds or other property that the client or third person is entitled to receive and, upon re- quest by the client or third person, shall promptly render a full accounting regarding such property.

(f) Disputed Ownership of Trust Funds. When in the course of representation a lawyer is in possession of property in which 2 or more persons (1 of whom may be the lawyer) claim interests, the property shall be treated by the lawyer as trust property, but the portion belonging to the lawyer or law firm shall be withdrawn within a reasonable time after it becomes due unless the right of the lawyer or law firm to re- ceive it is disputed, in which event the portion in dis- pute shall be kept separate by the lawyer until the dispute is resolved. The lawyer shall promptly dis- tribute all portions of the property as to which the interests are not in dispute.

(g) Interest on Trust Accounts (IOTA) Program.

(1) *Definitions.* As used herein, the term:

  (A) "nominal or short term" describes funds of a client or third person that, pursuant to subdivision (3), below, the lawyer has deter- mined cannot practicably be invested for the benefit of the client or third person;

  (B) "Foundation" means The Florida Bar Foun- dation, Inc.;

  (C) "IOTA account" means an interest or dividend-bearing trust account benefitting The Florida Bar Foundation established in an eligible institution for the deposit of nominal or short-term funds of clients or third persons;

  (D) "eligible institution" means any bank or sav- ings and loan association authorized by fed- eral or state laws to do business in Florida and insured by the Federal Savings and

Loan Insurance Corporation, or any successor insurance corporation(s) established by federal or state laws, or any open-end investment company registered with the Securities and Exchange Commission and authorized by federal or state laws to do business in Florida, all of which must meet the requirements set out in subdivision (5), below.

(E) "interest or dividend-bearing trust account" means a federally insured checking account or investment product, including a daily financial institution repurchase agreement or a money market fund. A daily financial institution repurchase agreement must be fully collateralized by, and an open-end money market fund must consist solely of, United States Government Securities. A daily financial institution repurchase agreement may be established only with an eligible institution that is deemed to be "well capitalized" or "adequately capitalized" as defined by applicable federal statutes and regulations. An openend money market fund must hold itself out as a money market fund as defined by applicable federal statutes and regulations under the Investment Company Act of 1940, and have total assets of at least $250,000,000. The funds covered by this rule shall be subject to withdrawal upon request and without delay.

(2) *Required Participation.* All nominal or short-term funds belonging to clients or third persons that are placed in trust with any member of The Florida Bar practicing law from an office or other business location within the state of Florida shall be deposited into one or more IOTA accounts, except as provided elsewhere in this chapter. Only trust funds that are nominal or short term shall be deposited into an IOTA account. The member shall certify annually, in writing, that the member is in compliance with, or is exempt from, the provisions of this rule.

(3) *Determination of Nominal or Short-Term Funds.* The lawyer shall exercise good faith judgment in determining upon receipt whether the funds of a client or third person are nominal or short term. In the exercise of this good faith judgment, the lawyer shall consider such factors as:

(A) the amount of a client's or third person's funds to be held by the lawyer or law firm;

(B) the period of time such funds are expected to be held;

(C) the likelihood of delay in the relevant transaction(s) or proceeding(s);

(D) the cost to the lawyer or law firm of establishing and maintaining an interest-bearing account or other appropriate investment for the benefit of the client or third person; and

(E) minimum balance requirements and/or service charges or fees imposed by the eligible institution.

The determination of whether a client's or third person's funds are nominal or short term shall rest in the sound judgment of the lawyer or law firm. No lawyer shall be charged with ethical impropriety or other breach of professional conduct based on the exercise of such good faith judgment.

(4) *Notice to Foundation.* Lawyers or law firms shall advise the Foundation, at Post Office Box 1553, Orlando, Florida 32802-1553, of the establishment of an IOTA account for funds covered by this rule. Such notice shall include: the IOTA account number as assigned by the eligible institution; the name of the lawyer or law firm on the IOTA account; the eligible institution name; the eligible institution address; and the name and Florida Bar attorney number of the lawyer, or of each member of The Florida Bar in a law firm, practicing from an office or other business location within the state of Florida that has established the IOTA account.

> Notice of IOTA Account

(5) *Eligible Institution Participation in IOTA.* Participation in the IOTA program is voluntary for banks, savings and loan associations, and investment companies. . . .

(6) *Small Fund Amounts.* The Foundation may establish procedures for a lawyer or law firm to maintain an interest-free trust account for client and third-person funds that are nominal or short term when their nominal or short-term trust funds cannot reasonably be expected to produce or have not produced interest income net of reasonable eligible institution service charges or fees.

(7) *Confidentiality.* The Foundation shall protect the confidentiality of information regarding a lawyer's or law firm's trust account obtained by virtue of this rule.

(h) **Interest on Funds That Are Not Nominal or Short Term.** A lawyer who holds funds for a client or third person and who determines that the funds are not nominal or short term as defined elsewhere in this subchapter shall not receive benefit from interest on funds held in trust.

(i) **Unidentifiable Trust Fund Accumulations and Trust Funds Held for Missing Owners.** When an attorney's trust account contains an unidentifiable accumulation of trust funds or property, or trust funds or property held for missing owners, such funds or property shall be so designated. Diligent search and inquiry shall then be made by the attorney to determine the beneficial owner of any unidentifiable accumulation or the address of any missing owner. If the beneficial owner of an unidentified accumulation is determined, the funds shall be properly identified as the lawyer's trust property. If a missing beneficial owner is located, the trust funds or property shall be paid over or delivered to the beneficial owner if the owner is then entitled to receive the same. Trust funds and property that remain unidentifiable and funds or property that are held for missing owners after being designated as such shall, after diligent search and inquiry fail to identify the beneficial owner or owner's address, be disposed of as provided in applicable Florida law.

(j) **Disbursement Against Uncollected Funds.** A lawyer generally may not use, endanger, or encumber money held in trust for a client for purposes of carrying out the business of another client without the permission of the owner given after full disclosure of the circumstances. However, certain categories of trust account deposits are considered to carry a limited and acceptable risk of failure so that disbursements of trust account funds may be made in reliance on such deposits without disclosure to and permission of clients owning trust account funds subject to possibly being affected. Except for disbursements based upon any of the 6 categories of limited-risk uncollected deposits enumerated below, a lawyer may not disburse funds held for a client or on behalf of that client unless the funds held for that client are collected funds. For purposes of this provision, "collected funds" means funds deposited, finally settled, and credited to the lawyer's trust account. Notwithstanding that a deposit made to the lawyer's trust account has not been finally settled and credited to the account, the lawyer may disburse funds from the trust account in reliance on such deposit:

(1) when the deposit is made by certified check or cashier's check;

(2) when the deposit is made by a check or draft representing loan proceeds issued by a federally or state-chartered bank, savings bank, savings and loan association, credit union, or other duly licensed or chartered institutional lender;

(3) when the deposit is made by a bank check, official check, treasurer's check, money order, or other such instrument issued by a bank, savings and loan association, or credit union when the lawyer has reasonable and prudent grounds to believe the instrument will clear and constitute collected funds in the lawyer's trust account within a reasonable period of time;

(4) when the deposit is made by a check drawn on the trust account of a lawyer licensed to practice in the state of Florida or on the escrow or trust account of a real estate broker licensed under applicable Florida law when the lawyer has a reasonable and prudent belief that the deposit will clear and constitute collected funds in the lawyer's trust account within a reasonable period of time;

(5) when the deposit is made by a check issued by the United States, the State of Florida, or any agency or political subdivision of the State of Florida;

(6) when the deposit is made by a check or draft issued by an insurance company, title insurance company, or a licensed title insurance agency authorized to do business in the state of Florida and the lawyer has a reasonable and prudent belief that the instrument will clear and constitute collected funds in the trust account within a reasonable period of time.

A lawyer's disbursement of funds from a trust account in reliance on deposits that are not yet collected funds in any circumstances other than those set forth above, when it results in funds of other clients being used, endangered, or encumbered without authorization, may be grounds for a finding of professional misconduct. In any event, such a disbursement is at the risk of the lawyer making the disbursement. If any of the deposits fail, the lawyer, upon obtaining knowledge of the failure, must immediately act to protect the property of the lawyer's other clients. However, if the lawyer accepting any such check personally pays the amount of any failed deposit or secures or arranges payment from sources available to the lawyer other than trust account funds of other clients, the lawyer shall not be considered guilty of professional misconduct.

Official Comments on Rule 5-1.1 (Trust Accounts)

[1] A lawyer must hold property of others with the care required of a professional fiduciary. This chapter requires maintenance of a bank or savings and

> **Lawyer as Fiduciary**

loan association account, clearly labeled as a trust account and in which only client or third party trust funds are held.

[2] Securities should be kept in a safe deposit box, except when some other form of safekeeping is warranted by special circumstances.

[3] All property that is the property of clients or third persons should be kept separate from the lawyer's business and personal property and, if money, in 1 or more trust accounts, unless requested otherwise in writing by the client. Separate trust accounts may be warranted when administering estate money or acting in similar fiduciary capacities.

[4] A lawyer who holds funds for a client or third person and who determines that the funds are not nominal or short term as defined elsewhere in this subchapter should hold the funds in a separate interest-bearing account with the interest accruing to the benefit of the client or third person unless directed otherwise in writing by the client or third person.

[5] Lawyers often receive funds from which the lawyer's fee will be paid. The lawyer is not required

Holding Funds to Coerce a Client

to remit to the client funds that the lawyer reasonably believes represent fees owed. However, a lawyer may not hold funds to coerce a client into accepting the lawyer's contention. The disputed portion of the funds must be kept in a trust account and the lawyer should suggest means for prompt resolution of the dispute, such as arbitration. The undisputed portion of the funds shall be promptly distributed.

[6] Third parties, such as a client's creditors, may have lawful claims against funds or other property in a lawyer's custody. A lawyer may have a duty under applicable law to protect such third party claims against wrongful interference by the client. When the lawyer has a duty under applicable law to protect the third-party claim and the third-party claim is not frivolous under applicable law, the lawyer must refuse to surrender the property to the client until the claims are resolved. However, a lawyer should not unilaterally assume to arbitrate a dispute between the client and the third party, and, where appropriate, the lawyer should consider the possibility of depositing the property or funds in dispute into the registry of the applicable court so that the matter may be adjudicated.

[7] The obligations of a lawyer under this chapter are independent of those arising from activity other than rendering legal services. For example, a lawyer who serves only as an escrow agent is governed by the applicable law relating to fiduciaries even though the lawyer does not render legal services in the transaction and is not governed by this rule.

[8] Each lawyer is required to be familiar with and comply with the Rules Regulating Trust Accounts as adopted by the Supreme Court of Florida.

[9] Money or other property entrusted to a lawyer for a specific purpose, including advances for fees, costs, and expenses, is held in trust and must be applied only to that purpose. Money and other property of clients coming into the hands of a lawyer are not subject to counterclaim or setoff for attorney's fees, and a refusal to account for and deliver over such property upon demand shall be a conversion. This does not preclude the retention of money or other property upon which a lawyer has a valid lien for services or to preclude the payment of agreed fees from the proceeds of transactions or collections.

[10] Advances for fees and costs (funds against which costs and fees are billed) are the property of the

Retainers

client or third party paying same on a client's behalf and are required to be maintained in trust, separate from the lawyer's property. Retainers are not funds against which future services are billed. Retainers are funds paid to guarantee the future availability of the lawyer's legal services and are earned by the lawyer upon receipt. Retainers, being funds of the lawyer, may not be placed in the client's trust account.

[11] The test of excessiveness found elsewhere in the Rules Regulating The Florida Bar applies to all fees for legal services including retainers, nonrefundable retainers, and minimum or flat fees.

Rule 5-1.2 Trust Accounting Records And Procedures

(a) **Applicability.** The provisions of these rules apply to all trust funds received or disbursed by members of The Florida Bar in the course of their professional practice of law as members of The Florida Bar

Trust Account Recordkeeping

except special trust funds received or disbursed by an attorney as guardian, personal representative, receiver, or in a similar capacity such as trustee under a specific trust document where the trust funds are maintained in a segregated special trust account and not the general trust account and wherein this special trust position has been created, approved, or sanctioned by law or an order of a court that has authority or duty to issue orders pertaining to maintenance of such special trust account. These rules shall apply to matters wherein a choice of laws analysis indicates that such matters are governed by the laws of Florida.

(b) **Minimum Trust Accounting Records.** The following are the minimum trust accounting records that shall be maintained:

(1) A separate bank or savings and loan association account or accounts in the name of the lawyer or law firm and clearly labeled and designated as a "trust account."

(2) Original or duplicate deposit slips and, in the case of currency or coin, an additional cash receipts book, clearly identifying:

   (A) the date and source of all trust funds received; and

   (B) the client or matter for which the funds were received.

(3) Original canceled checks, all of which must be numbered consecutively, or, if the financial institution wherein the trust account is maintained does not return the original checks, copies that include all endorsements, as provided by the financial institution.

(4) Other documentary support for all disbursements and transfers from the trust account.

(5) A separate cash receipts and disbursements journal, including columns for receipts, disbursements, transfers, and the account balance, and containing at least:

   (A) the identification of the client or matter for which the funds were received, disbursed, or transferred;

(B) the date on which all trust funds were received, disbursed, or transferred;

(C) the check number for all disbursements; and

(D) the reason for which all trust funds were received, disbursed, or transferred.

(6) A separate file or ledger with an individual card or page for each client or matter, showing all individual receipts, disbursements, or transfers and any unexpended balance, and containing:

(A) the identification of the client or matter for which trust funds were received, disbursed, or transferred;

(B) the date on which all trust funds were received, disbursed, or transferred;

(C) the check number for all disbursements; and

(D) the reason for which all trust funds were received, disbursed, or transferred.

(7) All bank or savings and loan association statements for all trust accounts.

(c) **Minimum Trust Accounting Procedures**. The minimum trust accounting procedures that shall be followed by all members of The Florida Bar (when a choice of laws analysis indicates that the laws of Florida apply) who receive or disburse trust money or property are as follows:

> **Trust Account Accounting Procedures**

(1) The lawyer shall cause to be made monthly:

(A) reconciliations of all trust bank or savings and loan association accounts, disclosing the balance per bank, deposits in transit, outstanding checks identified by date and check number, and any other items necessary to reconcile the balance per bank with the balance per the checkbook and the cash receipts and disbursements journal; and

(B) a comparison between the total of the reconciled balances of all trust accounts and the total of the trust ledger cards or pages, together with specific descriptions of any differences between the 2 totals and reasons therefor.

(2) At least annually, the lawyer shall prepare a detailed listing identifying the balance of the unexpended trust money held for each client or matter.

(3) The above reconciliations, comparisons, and listing shall be retained for at least 6 years.

(4) The lawyer or law firm shall authorize and request any bank or savings and loan association where the lawyer is a signatory on a trust account to notify Staff Counsel, The Florida Bar, 651 East Jefferson Street, Tallahassee, Florida 32399-2300, in the event any trust check is returned due to insufficient funds or uncollected funds, absent bank error.

(5) The lawyer shall file with The Florida Bar between June 1 and August 15 of each year a trust accounting certificate showing compliance with these rules on a form approved by the board of governors.

(d) **Record Retention.** A lawyer or law firm that receives and disburses client or third party funds or property shall maintain the records required by this chapter for 6 years subsequent to the final conclusion of each representation in which the trust funds or property were received.

(e) **Audits.** Any of the following shall be cause for The Florida Bar to order an audit of a trust account:

> **Trust Account Audits**

(1) failure to file the trust account certificate required by rule 5-1.2(c)(5);

(2) return of a trust account check for insufficient funds or for uncollected funds, absent bank error;

(3) filing of a petition for creditor relief on behalf of an attorney;

(4) filing of felony charges against an attorney;

(5) adjudication of insanity or incompetence or hospitalization of the attorney under the Florida Mental Health Act;

(6) filing of a claim against the attorney with the Clients' Security Fund;

(7) when requested by a grievance committee or the board of governors; or

(8) upon court order.

(f) **Cost of Audit.** Audits conducted in any of the circumstances enumerated in this rule shall be at the cost of the attorney audited only when the audit reveals that the attorney was not in substantial compliance with the trust accounting requirements. It shall be the obligation of any attorney who is being audited to produce all records and papers concerning property and funds held in trust and to provide such explanations as may be required for the audit. Records of general accounts are not required to be produced except to verify that trust money has not been deposited thereto. If it has been determined that trust money has been deposited into a general account, all of the transactions pertaining to any firm account will be subject to audit.

(g) **Failure to Comply With Subpoena.**

(1) Members of the bar are under an obligation to maintain trust accounting records as required by these rules and, as a condition of the privilege of practicing law in Florida, may not assert any privilege personal to the lawyer that may be applicable to production of same in these disciplinary proceedings.

(2) Notice of noncompliance with a subpoena may be filed with the Supreme Court of Florida only if a grievance committee or a referee shall

first find that no good cause exists for failure to comply. A grievance committee or referee shall hear the issue of noncompliance and issue findings thereon within 30 days of the request for issuance of the notice of noncompliance.

(3) After notice is filed with the Supreme Court of Florida by The Florida Bar that a member of the bar has failed to fully comply with a properly issued subpoena directing the production of any trust accounting records that are required by these rules, unless good cause for the failure to comply is shown, the member may be suspended from the practice of law in Florida, by order of the Supreme Court of Florida, until such time as the member fully complies with the subpoena and/or until further order of the court.

(4) Any member subject to suspension under this rule may petition the court, within 10 days of the filing of the notice, to withhold entry of the order of suspension or at any time after entry of an order of suspension may petition the court to terminate or modify the order of suspension. If the court determines it necessary to refer the petition to terminate or modify the suspension to a referee for receipt of evidence, the referee proceedings shall be conducted in the same manner as proceedings before a referee on a petition to withhold, terminate, or modify an order of emergency suspension, as elsewhere provided in these rules.

20. Florida Registered Paralegal Program

[For the text of the rules in chapter 20, see section 1.1 of this book. In chapter 20 the Court promulgates the rules governing the establishment of the voluntary Florida Registered Paralegal Program.]

F.   More Information

The Florida Bar
www.flabar.org
(click "Unlicensed Practice")

Rules of Professional Conduct
www.flabar.org
(click "Lawyer Regulation," then "Rules Regulating The Florida Bar," then "Rules of Professional Conduct")
www.law.cornell.edu/ethics/fl/code
www.sunethics.com/rpc_index.htm

Rules Regulating The Florida Bar
www.flabar.org
(click "Lawyer Regulation" then "Rules Regulating The Florida Bar")

Florida Legal Ethics
www.law.cornell.edu/ethics/fl/narr
www.ethics.state.fl.us

Florida Commission on Ethics
www.ethics.state.fl.us

Researching Ethics Questions in Florida
www.flabar.org
(click "Lawyer Regulation" then "Ethics Opinions")

Ethics Opinions of The Florida Bar on UPL
www.flabar.org
(click "Member Services," then "Ethics Opinions," then "Subject Index of Ethics Opinions," then "Unlicensed Practice of Law")

Formal Advisory Opinions of The Florida Bar on UPL
www.flabar.org
(click "Unlicensed Practice" then "Formal Advisory Opinions")

Filing a UPL Complaint
www.flabar.org
(click "Public Information," then "Consumer Information," then "Filing an Unlicensed Practice of Law Complaint")

Self-Representation at Florida Administrative Agencies
www.doah.state.fl.us/internet/RepYourself.cfm

Self-Representation—General
www.floridalawhelp.org
www.floridabar.org
(click "Public Information" then "Legal Aid/Pro Bono")

American Legal Ethics Library
www.law.cornell.edu/ethics
(click "Listing by jurisdiction" then "Florida")

G.   Something to Check

1. Use the online sites for Florida court opinions (see section 5.1). Find and summarize (brief) one opinion from any Florida state court on solicitation under the Florida Rules of Professional Conduct.

2. Run the following search (Florida "rules of professional conduct") in any three general search engines (e.g., *www.google.com, www.yahoo.com, www.live.com, www.ask.com*). Prepare a report on the categories of sites to which each search engine leads you. Cluster the same kinds of sites you find into categories (sites giving you the text of the rules, opinions interpreting the rules, law firms that represent attorneys charged with violating the rules, etc.). Give a brief description of each category with a minimum of five examples of web sites under each category. After you finish the report for the three general search engines, comment on which engine was the most productive and why.

A. Introduction

The text of the ethical rules governing attorneys are found in section 3.2. Here we will cover some of the major interpretations of these rules involving paralegals and other nonattorneys. The interpretations are in opinions written by courts and by The Florida Bar's Committee on Professional Ethics. The Committee on Professional Ethics answers ethics inquiries from members of the Bar concerning the inquirer's own proposed conduct. The committee also publishes formal advisory opinions that interpret ethics rules.

The ethical opinions interpret both the Florida Rules of Professional Conduct (FRPC) and the Florida Code of Professional Responsibility (FCPR). Although the FRPC replaced the FCPR, opinions interpreting the FCPR are often relied on as persuasive authority.

This section covers some aspects of the unauthorized practice of law (UPL). See section 3.1, however, for a more complete coverage of the practice of law and the unauthorized practice of law involving paralegals and other nonattorneys.

B. Ethical Opinions Involving Paralegals and Other Nonlawyers

Issues Covered

ABA 65-4; 68-58; 76-33; 88-6; 95-1

Accountant 76-33

Adjusting Insurance Claims 74-35; 76-33; 92-3

Administrator See Office Manager

Advertising 71-39; 88-15; 89-4

Advice See Legal Advice

Agency Representation 65-4; 95-1

Aiding the Unauthorized Practice of Law See UPL

American Bar Association See ABA

Appearance of Impropriety 76-33

Arbitrator 66-57

Associate Defined 86-1

Attorney (Disbarred) as Paralegal 62-26

Attorney Signature 87-11

Authorized Practice of Law 95-1

Billing 75-29; 76-33; 07-2

Bonus 02-1

Business Card 71-39; 86-4; 89-4

Card See Business Card

Certified Paralegals 86-4

Clerk 76-33

Client Billing 76-33

Client Consent 76-33

Client Files 70-62; 88-15

Client Funds 64-40

Client Interviewing 88-6

Clients, Direct Relationship with 74-35; 88-6; 95-2

Closings 70-62; 89-5. See also Real Estate

Collection Agency 62-18; 81-3

Commissions See Referral Fees; Sharing Fees

Computer files 07-2

Confidentiality 76-33; 86-5; 88-15; 07-2

Conflict of Interest 86-5; 07-2

Consent 76-33; 07-2

Contingent Fee 76-33; 07-2

Contract Paralegal 07-2

Corporations 65-4

Defining the Practice of Law 74-35

Delegation 70-62; 74-35; 76-33; 87-11; 88-6

Depositions 70-62; 73-41; 76-33

Disbarred Attorney 62-26

Disclosure of Status 86-4; 88-6; 89-5

Disqualification 86-5

Dividing Fees See Referral Fees; Sharing Fees

Double Billing 76-33

Drafting 76-33

Evaluation 88-6

Extraordinary Efforts 75-29; 02-1

Factual Information 88-6

Family Law 02-1

Federal Law 65-4; 95-1

Fees 75-29; 76-33; 07-2. See also Forwarding Fee; Referral Fees; Securities; Sharing Fees

Fiduciary 76-33

Files See Client Files

Forwarding Fee 62-18

Fringe Benefits 68-58

Generating Clients See Referral Fees

Hearings, Representation at 65-4; 95-1

Heir Hunting 97-3

Independent Contractor 76-33

Insurance Claims 74-35; 76-33; 92-3

Interference with Client Relationship 95-2

Intern 70-1

Interrogatories 70-62

Interviewing 70-1; 70-62; 88-6

Investigation and Investigators 71-39; 76-33; 86-4

Judgment 70-62; 74-35; 88-6

Law Clerk 76-33; 70-1

Law Firm Letterhead See Letterhead

Law Student 70-1

Lay Assistant 70-62

Legal Advice 88-6; 89-5

Legal Intern 70-1

Legal Research 62-26; 76-33; 07-2

Legal Secretary See Secretary

Letterhead 65-4; 86-4; 94-6

Letters, Signing 86-4

Living Trusts 95-2

Loyalty 95-2

Marketing 89-4

Mediation 94-6

Merged Work Product 76-33; 88-6

Ministerial Acts 89-5

Misleading Conduct See Advertising; Status Identification; Titles

Negotiating Claims 74-35. See also Insurance Claims

Nonlawyer Status Identification 86-4; 88-6; 89-4; 94-6

Non-legal Problem Solving 70-1

Office Managers and Administrators 64-40; 76-33; 87-11

Office Space See Sharing Office Space

Outsourcing 07-2

Ownership Interest in Law Practice 65-4; 94-6

Overhead 75-29; 76-33;
07-2
Overtime 76-33
**Partnership with Non-
lawyers** 65-4; 94-6
Pecuniary Gain 97-3. See
also Solicitation
Personal Injury Claims
See Insurance Claims
Pleadings 87-11
Practice of Law 73-41;
74-35
Probate 70-62
Professional Judgment
70-62; 74-35
Profit Sharing 68-58. See
also Sharing Fees
Public Adjuster See
Adjusting Insurance
Claims
**Quasi-Legal Representa-
tion** 95-1
Real Estate 70-62; 73-43;
76-33; 89-5
Recommending Clients
See Referral Fees
Referral Fees 88-15; 97-3;
02-1; 02-8. See also
Forwarding Fee
Retirement Plan 68-58
Scheduling 70-62
Secretary 70-62; 75-29;
76-33; 86-5
Securities 95-2; 02-8
Sharing Fees 66-57; 68-
58; 88-15; 92-3; 94-6;
95-1; 97-3; 02-1; 02-8

Sharing Office Space
66-57; 88-15
Signature 64-40; 86-4;
87-11
**Social Security Represen-
tation** 95-1
Solicitation 65-4; 71-39;
88-15; 89-4; 97-3
Sperry v. State of Florida
95-1
Splitting Fees See Refer-
ral Fees; Sharing Fees
Students 70-1
Status Identification 86-
4; 88-6; 89-4; 94-6
Supervision 64-40; 70-1;
76-33; 87-11; 88-6;
89-5; 07-2
**Suspended Attorney as
Paralegal** 62-26
Switching Sides 86-5
Title Companies 89-5
Title, Paralegal 86-4
**Transcribing dictation
tapes** 07-2
Trust Accounts 64-40
Trusts 95-2
**Unauthorized Practice of
Law** See UPL; See also
section 3.1
Undignified 75-29
Unprofessional 75-29
UPL 65-4; 73-41; 74-35;
87-11; 89-5; 92-3; 94-6;
97-3
Witness Assistance
70-62

Florida Ethics Opinions Excerpted

Abbreviations

Canon A Canon of the CPR
CPR Code of Professional Responsibility (in effect be-
fore the RPC was adopted)
DR Disciplinary Rule (part of the CPR)
EC Ethical Consideration (part of the CPR)
FEO Florida Ethics Opinion of the Committee on Pro-
fessional Ethics
RPC Rules of Professional Conduct
Rule A rule within the RPC
WL Westlaw

Florida Ethics Opinions

Florida Ethics Opinion 62-18 (1962)

Committee on Professional Ethics, Florida Bar Association
www.floridabar.org (Click "Lawyer Regulation" then
"Ethics Opinions," then type "62-18")
1962 WL 8225
Summary: A collection agency referred a claim to an attorney, who collected the claim after suit, paid the
client, sent a check to the collection agency as for-
warder, and then stopped payment on the grounds that
he could not ethically pay a layman a fee. The question
is whether under these circumstances he can be disciplined. An attorney cannot be subject to disciplinary
proceedings for refusing to pay a forwarding fee to a
collection agency inasmuch as the applicable Canons
prohibit payment of a forwarding fee to a layman.

Florida Ethics Opinion 62-26 (1986)

Committee on Professional Ethics, Florida Bar Association
www.floridabar.org (Click "Lawyer Regulation" then
"Ethics Opinions," then type "62-26")
1986 WL 84404
Summary: It is permissible for a suspended attorney to
be employed by a law firm to perform the type of duties
permitted of nonlawyer personnel, provided that the
required notice and periodic reports are submitted to
The Florida Bar and the suspended attorney is not allowed to have any direct contact with clients or to handle client funds or property.

In *Opinion 62-26*, the Committee declined to respond to a suspended attorney's inquiry concerning the
permissibility of his accepting employment with a law
firm to do legal research during the period of his suspension. At the time of the inquiry, there was no counterpart
to the current Integration Rule 11.10(8), which permits
law firms to employ suspended and disbarred attorneys
to perform only such work as is permitted nonlawyer
staff. See Rule 3-6.1 of the Rules Regulating The Florida
Bar (effective January 1, 1987). Integration Rule 11.10(8)
compels the conclusion that it is permissible for a suspended attorney to be employed by a law firm, provided

that the attorney and the employing firm comply with the restrictions and requirements of the rule.

Florida Ethics Opinion 64-40 (1987)

Committee on Professional Ethics, Florida Bar Association
www.floridabar.org (Click "Lawyer Regulation" then
"Ethics Opinions," then type "64-40")
1987 WL 125112

Summary: While it is permissible for properly authorized and supervised nonlawyer employees to be signatories on lawyers' trust accounts, it is the lawyers who are ultimately responsible for compliance with rules relating to trust accounts and client funds.

In *Opinion 64-40*, the Committee found no ethical impropriety in a law firm office manager who is not a lawyer drawing checks for the firm on its trust account upon proper authorization from the attorney responsible for the case. The Committee continues to be of the view that it is permissible for a trusted nonlawyer employee to draw checks on the trust account upon proper authorization and under appropriate supervision. Attorneys are cautioned, however, that they remain ultimately responsible for compliance with all rules relating to trust accounts and client funds, and that they are subject to discipline for an employee's misconduct involving client funds.

Florida Ethics Opinion 65-4 (1965)

Committee on Professional Ethics, Florida Bar Association
www.floridabar.org (Click "Lawyer Regulation" then
"Ethics Opinions," then type "65-4")
1965 WL 6947

Summary: It would be improper for a lawyer to form a partnership with a nonlawyer for the purpose of representing clients before certain state and federal agencies, notwithstanding that the other person is authorized to practice before those agencies, unless the lawyer completely withdraws from the practice of law and limits his activities to those that can be performed by nonlawyers.

A member of The Florida Bar inquires whether it would be ethically proper for him to form a partnership with a person who is not a lawyer and is not admitted to The Florida Bar for the purpose of practicing before the Interstate Commerce Commission and the Florida Public Utilities Commission. The proposed partner is a Class B practitioner, admitted to practice before both of the agencies mentioned. He proposes to establish a partnership that would be limited strictly to performing services as transportation consultants and to practice before the regulatory bodies mentioned. The proposed partnership would in no way engage in the general practice of law, but the lawyer would continue to practice law in a separate office located several miles from the office of the proposed partnership.

He also inquires whether it would be proper for him and his proposed partner to form a corporation and act as the principals of that corporation for the purpose of preparing transportation tariffs, preparing transportation reports, and doing research regarding transportation matters for attorneys who practice before both federal and state agencies that regulate transportation. The staff would be neither attorneys nor persons otherwise permitted to practice before the agencies concerned. Also, whether it would be proper under such circumstances for the corporation to solicit business from attorneys engaged in the general practice of law and from attorneys who are admitted to practice before the regulatory agencies. The letterhead of the corporation would carry only the corporate name and there would be no reference to the fact that either of the principals are attorneys or are persons admitted to practice before transportation agencies.

It is the unanimous view of this Committee that it would be improper to form the partnership mentioned above, and the Committee therefore answers the first inquiry in the negative. Opinions 57, 225, 233, 234, 257, 269, 272, 297, and 305 of the Professional Ethics Committee of the American Bar Association are pertinent to the inquiry. Especially pertinent are ABA Opinions 257 and 269 where, in each instance, that Committee disapproved a partnership between a lawyer and a layman admitted to practice before a federal regulatory agency. It was the view of the American Bar Committee, and it is our view, that such partnerships are improper unless the lawyer ceases entirely to offer his services as a lawyer and confines his activities strictly to those opened to persons who are not admitted to practice law. Canons 33 and 34 are involved.

Regarding the second inquiry, the Committee expresses some doubt as to whether it has sufficient information to formulate a final judgment. The plan set forth in the second inquiry supposedly might involve unauthorized practice of law, but this Committee has no jurisdiction over such matters. Assuming unauthorized practice is not involved, and assuming further that the lawyer member of the organization ceased the practice of law, there would be no ethical objection to the plan. If, however, the lawyer member did not cease the practice of law, the arrangement could well offend the provisions of Canon 27, particularly if the corporation's activities resulted in legal work being forwarded to the lawyer member of the corporation. Further, if the data accumulated and sold by the corporation is of such nature that the lawyer's association with the corporation would add to the reliance that purchasers place upon the data, or if the data in any way involved the interpretation or construction of laws or regulatory rules, then the lawyer's association with such corporation would, in our opinion, be improper.

Florida Ethics Opinion 66-57 (1967)
Committee on Professional Ethics, Florida Bar Association
www.floridabar.org (Click "Lawyer Regulation" then
"Ethics Opinions," then type "66-57")
1967 WL 7210
Summary: Although the sharing of office space by a lawyer with a nonlawyer is not to be encouraged, members of The Florida Bar who rent space in their office for occasional use by an arbitrator may place on their door a legend bearing the name of the arbitrator. The listing must be clearly separate from the listing of the law firm.

———————————

AB, a professional arbitrator with a principal office in another state, desires to rent space in an office of members of The Florida Bar. The arbitrator is a member of the bar of the state in which he has his principal office but is not engaged in the practice of law, devoting his time exclusively to his work as an arbitrator and impartial chairman. He is not admitted to The Florida Bar. The members of The Florida Bar to whom the request for rental is addressed have inquired of this Committee whether it would be appropriate to place on the office door below and distinguished from their own names a legend reading "AB, Arbitrator and Impartial Chairman—Not a Member of The Florida Bar." It would be contemplated that the office space to be rented would be used only when the occasion arises for the arbitrator to act in his capacity as arbitrator in Florida. No reference to his presence in the suite of offices would be made in answering the telephone, nor would such reference appear on the firm stationery.

Although in our judgment the sharing of office space by a lawyer with a nonlawyer is not to be encouraged, we do not think the proposed arrangement is proscribed by the canons so long as the listing on the door is physically arranged to avoid any misleading connotation that the arbitrator is connected with the firm. In our judgment if the listing is clearly separate from that of the law firm, it is not necessary to add the words "Not a Member of The Florida Bar" because this legend might suggest a lawyer relationship. Most importantly the inquiring members of the Bar must be careful that the sharing of offices does not result in a "feeder" to their practice, indirect advertising of their professional services, sharing of professional fees or professional responsibilities with the arbitrator, or any implication to visitors that their practice is related to the work of the arbitrator.

Florida Ethics Opinion 68-58 (1969)
Committee on Professional Ethics, Florida Bar Association
www.floridabar.org (Click "Lawyer Regulation" then
"Ethics Opinions," then type "68-58")
1969 WL 8673

Summary: It is permissible that a retirement plan for nonlawyer employees is based in part on firm profits.

———————————

We are . . . asked whether it is possible for members or stockholders in the professional service corporation to make contributions to retirement or pension plans for their employees [who] find a basis in the profits of the corporation. In its *Opinion 303*, the American Bar Association Committee observed:

"However, if the salary of a nonlawyer employee is based on the percentage of the net profits, a division of fees for legal services would be involved and Canon 34 would prohibit it. Thus, if a professional association or professional corporation is organized to practice law and it is approved as a corporation for federal income tax purposes, it would not be ethically proper for it to have a profit-sharing plan if nonlawyers were included as the beneficiaries of the plan."

It seems to us that a subsequent opinion of the American Bar Association Committee, *Opinion 311* (rendered April 8, 1964), may be inconsistent with the quoted portion of *Opinion 303*. There the American Bar Association Committee held that a retirement plan by attorneys for themselves and their lay employees under federal income tax provisions governing self-employed persons was not unethical even though the benefits were measured by the employee's salary and were payable only if profits existed from which to pay them, commenting that "profits are not a measure of the additional compensation but only a contingent limitation . . . ."

In any event, and without at all endeavoring to launch into a technical discussion of the niceties of tax law, it seems to us that so long as a law firm adopts a conventional deferred compensation or retirement plan for lay and legal personnel, funded by contributions from the firm profits, and if such plan is a reasonable and ordinary method of giving fringe benefit additional compensation to bona fide employees, it is irrelevant whether or not the firm is organized as a professional association, and that the basic concern of Canon 34, to preclude fee splitting, is not offended. As a practical matter, it is our understanding that lay employees would ordinarily find the contribution of the firm for their benefit would be based on their salary even though presumably arising from firm profits just as the original salary did, and thus, the reasoning set forth in *Opinion 311* would apply. However, even if the particular plan utilized caused contributions to be made on a basis other than salary, we would be unable to share the concern expressed in *Opinion 303*, if the plan in fact was a bona fide retirement or deferred compensation plan as contrasted with a subterfuge to avoid Canon 34.

Florida Ethics Opinion 70-1 (1970)
Committee on Professional Ethics, Florida Bar Association
www.floridabar.org (Click "Lawyer Regulation" then
"Ethics Opinions," then type "70-1")
1970 WL 10141

Summary: Nonlawyers may be employed as clerks to interview prospective clients for the purpose of determining their eligibility to participate in the program and to ascertain the general nature of a prospective client's problem.

[Part and full-time law students] would interview prospective clients of Law, Inc. for the purpose of determining the interviewee's eligibility to participate in the program and to ascertain the general nature of his problem. In the event that the problem were legal, he would be referred to a member of the Bar employed by Law, Inc. In some instances, the interviewer would endeavor to solve non-legal problems and in others he would refer the person to an appropriate source of assistance. It would be understood that the law clerk or intern would at all times be under the supervision of a member of The Florida Bar who ultimately will be professionally responsible for his actions.

We see no ethical objection to members of The Florida Bar permitting such action on behalf of the employees of Law, Inc.

Florida Ethics Opinion 70-62 (1971)

Committee on Professional Ethics, Florida Bar Association
www.floridabar.org (Click "Lawyer Regulation" then "Ethics Opinions," then type "70-62")
1971 WL 16810

Summary: Lay personnel may be used in a law office only to the extent that they are delegated mechanical, clerical, or administrative duties. The attorney may not ethically delegate to a lay employee any activity that requires the attorney's personal judgment and participation.

Inquiry is made pertaining to the use of lay personnel within a law office. The opinion will be divided into two parts.

The first portion is quoted from the inquiry as follows:
We anticipate using the lay person in the real estate field to handle the following matters:

[1] After the contract between the parties has been executed and a file set up by the attorney's secretary, the file will be delivered to the lay specialist who will obtain all preliminary data. This would include location and ordering of abstracts and survey where appropriate, checking our internal files to determine if a prior opinion or title policy has been issued by our firm on said property, obtaining pay-off or assumption figures on existing mortgages and liens and, in general, gathering all necessary data involving said transaction.

[2] We envision that after the contract stage the next time the file would come back to the attorney would be after the abstract continuation, surveys, and all necessary data have been compiled. The lay assistant would then forward the file back to the responsible attorney with all such data included. The responsible attorney would then examine the abstract and dictate either an Opinion of Title or title binder based on his examination. The file would then go back to the lay assistant who would, following the directives of the attorney, prepare closing statements, and notify all parties of the scheduled closing.

[3] All work and documents prepared by the lay assistant would be forwarded back to the responsible attorney at some predetermined time prior to the closing for the attorney's review and approval.

[4] The attorney closes the real estate transaction.

[5] After the closing the attorney forwards a file back to the lay assistant with appropriate directives as to the recording of documents, pay-off of any liens, and disbursements of expenses not disbursed during the closing.

The Committee basically approves the proposal as outlined in the inquiry, finding that there is no ethical problem. The sole reservation to be expressed by the Committee is that the attorney should at no time leave to the lay employee those matters calling for the expertise of an attorney. For example, if lay personnel prepare all closing documents, such lay personnel should not be allowed to draw complicated escrow agreements or other collateral contracts. See Canon 3 and ethical considerations thereunder (EC 3-5 and 3-6).

The second part of the inquiry is not quite as easy to answer. It asks of the propriety of: In the probate field we propose the utilization of lay personnel to prepare estate forms, accountings, and tax returns; obtain necessary facts from outside sources for preparation of such estate pleadings; and perform other duties of this nature. In the litigation field we propose utilization of lay personnel to index depositions, prepare interrogatories, prepare schedules of witnesses to be deposed, schedules of witnesses necessary for trial, summarize facts, interview witnesses, and other such related matters. We propose that all work done by a layperson in our office shall be reviewed and approved by a responsible attorney before any item either goes to the files or outside of the office as a completed item of work.

These plans are similar to the proposal as to real estate transactions but not as detailed. Again, the Committee does recognize and approve the use of lay personnel in probate and litigation under the appropriate considerations of Canon 3. Delegation to lay employees of the mechanical, clerical, and administrative duties is encouraged. However, the attorney may not ethically delegate an activity in which he personally should give his judgment and participation.

While generally approving the concept stated in this second part of the inquiry, the Committee gives it but a qualified approval as the Committee would prefer to determine such matters on specific factual cases. This is true because the Committee does have reservations as to authorizing lay personnel to prepare interrogatories and to interview all witnesses in every case. What may be permissible in a "run-of-the-mill" case may not be so in complicated, unusual matters.

Florida Ethics Opinion 71-39 (1971)
Committee on Professional Ethics, Florida Bar Association
www.floridabar.org (Click "Lawyer Regulation" then "Ethics Opinions," then type "71-39")
1971 WL 16838
Summary: An investigator employed full time by a law firm may use the law firm's name on his business card.

A member of The Florida Bar employs an investigator. He desires to have a card imprinted as follows:

NAME
INVESTIGATOR
Street and Number
City, State, Zip

There will be no indication that the address is one of a law office. The Committee finds there is no impropriety in the proposed action, assuming the investigator is a full-time employee working for no one else. The Committee further assumes the activity of the investigator is that duly and ethically allowed to be handled by a law assistant.

As a matter of interest, the ABA has considered similar questions in informal opinions 881 (1965), 909 (1966) and 1185 (1971). The ABA opinions determine a law firm does not necessarily violate ethical principles by permitting an investigator, also an employee, to use a business card bearing his name and position and additionally the law firm's name, address and telephone number. The ABA committee determined the firm would be accountable for the lay assistant's actions and conduct and would have to ensure the investigator's activities did not result in advertising or solicitation on behalf of the law firm, or even appear to do so. A majority of this Committee would adopt the view expressed by the ABA. A minority finds the use of the law firm's name on the card to be improper, but do agree to the use of the card with address and telephone number thereon.

Florida Ethics Opinion 73-41 (1974)
Committee on Professional Ethics, Florida Bar Association
www.floridabar.org (Click "Lawyer Regulation" then "Ethics Opinions," then type "73-41")
1974 WL 20334
Summary: Law firm employees who are not admitted to practice in Florida may not take depositions for the firm, nor may they do any work that constitutes the practice of law, even though the employees are law school graduates and are admitted in other jurisdictions.

Florida Ethics Opinion 73-43 (1974)
Committee on Professional Ethics, Florida Bar Association
www.floridabar.org (Click "Lawyer Regulation" then "Ethics Opinions," then type "73-43")
1974 WL 20335
Summary: A graduate of a paralegal institute who is employed by a law firm may, under the supervision and direction of an attorney, prepare real estate documents for which the attorney takes complete professional responsibility.

Florida Ethics Opinion 74-35 (1974)
Committee on Professional Ethics, Florida Bar Association
www.floridabar.org (Click "Lawyer Regulation" then "Ethics Opinions," then type "74-35")
1974 WL 20350
Summary: Lawyers are not permitted to delegate to laypersons the handling of negotiations with insurance company adjustors regarding claims of the lawyer's clients.

The Board of Governors of The Florida Bar has requested the Committee on Professional Ethics to review and reconsider Florida *Ethics Opinion 70-7*, issued June 2, 1970, in light of the provisions of the Code of Professional Responsibility that became effective October 1, 1970, and related opinions issued since that date concerning the use of "paralegals" or "lay assistants." (See Florida *Opinions 70-62, 73-41*, and *73-43*.) *Opinion 70-7* gave qualified approval to a lawyer's use of lay personnel in handling contacts and negotiations with insurance company adjusters in respect to personal injury claims of the lawyer's clients. The opinion cautioned lawyers against permitting such lay employees to assume duties and responsibilities in such negotiations that would amount to unauthorized practice of law, but it did not undertake to define what would constitute the practice of law in respect to such negotiations.

The Board of Governors has been confronted with widely differing interpretations of this opinion in respect to activities that the lawyer may ethically delegate to such laypersons. Such negotiations always involve the exercise of the lawyer's professional judgment, so that, as a practical matter, it is doubtful that a lawyer may delegate any responsibility for negotiation to lay employees and avoid the proscription on aiding the unauthorized practice of law.

Canon 3 of the Code of Professional Responsibility and DR 3-101(A) implementing that canon specifically require that "A lawyer shall not aid a nonlawyer in the unauthorized practice of law." The ethical considerations underlying this disciplinary rule emphasize "the need of the public for integrity and competence of those who undertake to render legal services" (EC 3-1), and further state that "[t]he sensitive variations in the considerations that bear on legal determinations often make it difficult even for a lawyer to exercise appropriate professional judgment, and it is therefore essential that the personal nature of the relationship of client and lawyer be preserved. Competent professional judgment is the product of a trained familiarity with law and legal processes; a disciplined, analytical approach to legal problems; and a firm ethical commitment" (EC 3-2).

Accordingly, EC 3-4 states that "[p]roper protection of members of the public demands that no person be permitted to act in the confidential and demanding capacity of a lawyer unless he is subject to the regulations of the legal profession."

Neither the disciplinary rules nor the ethical considerations under Canon 3 of the CPR state whether the negotiation of claims by laypersons amounts to unauthorized practice of law. EC 3-5 provides only some broad guidelines: It is neither necessary nor desirable to attempt the formulation of a single, specific definition of what constitutes the practice of law. Functionally, the practice of law relates to the rendition of services for others that call for the professional judgment of a lawyer. The essence of the professional judgment of the lawyer is his educated ability to relate the general body and philosophy of law to a specific legal problem of a client; and thus, the public interest will be better served if only lawyers are permitted to act in matters involving professional judgment. Where this professional judgment is not involved, nonlawyers, such as court clerks, police officers, abstracters, and many governmental employees, may engage in occupations that require a special knowledge of law in certain areas. But the services of a lawyer are essential in the public interest whenever the exercise of professional legal judgment is required.

Although EC 3-6 recognizes that lawyers may often delegate tasks to lay employees in order to render legal services more economically and efficiently, the functions that may be ethically delegated are quite limited (see *Florida Opinions 70-62, 73-41,* and *73-43*). *Opinion 70-62* specifically states that EC 3-6 does not permit a lawyer to delegate any activity in which the lawyer personally should give his judgment and participation. It seems to us that, even in the simplest of personal injury cases, negotiation of a settlement most favorable to the client necessarily requires the exercise of the lawyer's professional judgment and participation to some extent.

Moreover, there is a valid distinction between the status of a licensed adjuster and that of the attorney's lay employee handling negotiations. The adjuster is hired directly by the insurance company to adjust claims within the limitations permitted by the relevant provisions of Chapter 626, Florida Statutes. The lay employee of an attorney is not a "public adjuster" as defined in that chapter. The client employs the attorney, not a "public adjuster," to prosecute his claim against the wrongdoer and the insurer, and is entitled to the lawyer's participation and judgment in the conduct of negotiations.

For the foregoing reasons, it is the Committee's opinion that DR 3-101(A) and the ethical considerations quoted above do not permit lawyers to delegate to laypersons the handling of negotiations with adjusters in respect to claims being handled on behalf of the attorney's clients. To this extent, the Committee recedes from its prior *Opinion 70-7.*

Florida Ethics Opinions 75-29 (1975)

Committee on Professional Ethics, Florida Bar Association
www.floridabar.org (Click "Lawyer Regulation" then "Ethics Opinions," then type "75-29")
1975 WL 21306

Summary: It is unprofessional and undignified for an attorney to separately charge a client for costs of secretarial work unless such work is extraordinary or unusual.

A member of The Florida Bar asks about the propriety of charging clients as a cost item for the secretarial time the firm spends for the client on a particular matter. The charge would be listed separately on the statement sent to the client and would pass on to the client the cost of the secretary's salary determined on an hourly rate. The Committee is of the opinion that, while the proposal is not specifically prohibited by the Code of Professional Responsibility (see particularly DR 2-206, EC 2-17, 2-18, 2-19, DR 5-103, and EC 5-8), the proposal is unprofessional and undignified and should be discouraged. Regular and usual secretarial services have traditionally been considered part of a lawyer's overhead expense that the lawyer includes in the fee he charges the client. We are not suggesting that a lawyer may not charge a client for extra and unusual secretarial services, for example, overtime work for which a secretary is paid in addition to her regular salary or for secretarial work incident to the matter the lawyer is handling but that is not ordinarily done by a legal secretary. But we believe that office overhead, expenses the lawyer would routinely incur without reference to a particular matter for a particular client, should be included as an element of the fee charged and not billed as separate cost items.

Florida Ethics Opinions 76-33 & 76-38 (1977)

Committee on Professional Ethics, Florida Bar Association
www.floridabar.org (Click "Lawyer Regulation" then "Ethics Opinions," then type "76-33" and "76-38")
1977 WL 23158

Summary: In billing a client a lawyer may separately itemize for legal research and other similar services performed by salaried nonlawyer personnel, but care should be taken to avoid the double-billing that could result if such charges are already accounted for in overhead.

Members of The Florida Bar ask about the propriety of separately itemizing on a bill to a client time devoted to a legal matter for that client by a lawyer's nonlawyer employees for work involving legal research, investigation, or drafting of pleadings done under the supervision of the lawyer.

The Code of Professional Conduct [sic] does not specifically answer the present inquiries. However, the Code does specifically authorize the delegation by a lawyer of functions of the lawyer to "nonlawyers such as secretaries, law clerks, investigators, researchers, legal assistants, accountants, draftsmen, office administrators, and other lay personnel to assist the lawyer in the delivery of legal services," subject to certain qualifications. EC 3-6. DR 3-104, as to "nonlawyer personnel," specifically sets out circumstances and conditions under which such personnel may and may not be utilized. Both EC 3-6 and DR 3-104 stress, among other things, that the work should be done under the direct supervision of the lawyer, who shall be responsible for such work, which will be merged into the lawyer's own completed product.

This Committee's *Opinion 75-29* states that a lawyer may not charge a client as a cost item for the secretarial time the firm spends for the client if such time is a part of the lawyer's regular and usual overhead. However, that opinion does not proscribe such charges for extra and unusual secretarial services, e.g., overtime or other work for the client not ordinarily done by the legal secretary. The Committee believes that the Code does not contemplate that such work of nonlawyer personnel described in EC 3-6 and DR 3-104 will be free of charge and believes that the Code does not prohibit a lawyer from separately itemizing on his bill to the client the time of nonlawyer personnel of the type referred to in the inquiries.

We believe that the foregoing conclusion of this Committee is not inconsistent with *Opinion 75-29* and that the types of work described in the present inquiries and in EC 3-6 and DR 3-104 are work that might otherwise have been done by the lawyer himself and that is delegated by the lawyer and is not that referred to in *Opinion 75-29* as ordinarily done by a legal secretary, the salary for which is part of the normal office overhead that a lawyer would routinely incur without reference to a particular matter for a particular client.

The work described in the present inquiries is such that the lawyer, in our opinion, could charge therefore as separate itemization on his bill if done by outside independent contractors, e.g., legal research services, research computer systems, private investigators, and the like, and there should not be a difference in that respect if those same types of services are performed by salaried personnel employed by the lawyer. See ABA *Informal Opinion 343* (1970 Supplement to *The Digest of Bar Association Ethics Opinions, No. 5050*), stating that

where a lawyer employs an accountant with the client's consent, he can bill the accountant's fee as a separate item of expense.

Also, see especially ABA *Informal Opinion 1333*, which does not prohibit such separate itemization for time devoted to a legal matter by a non-admitted law clerk, with or without degree, subject to the caveat, to which this Committee also subscribes, that care is taken to avoid the appearance of the unauthorized practice of law. We add the further, more specific caveats that all conditions of DR 3-104 be fully complied with, that care is taken to avoid the slightest appearance otherwise, that the charges for such nonlawyer work reflect only the time spent on the particular matter that is being billed and are not based on the nonlawyer's salary as a whole, and that such charges not be excessive or disproportionate to charges for like services, if reasonably available, performed by independent contractors.

The use of nonlawyer personnel should never be permitted to detract or appear to detract from the "fiduciary and personal character of the lawyer-client relationship" (EC 3-1). See our *Opinion 74-35* that a lawyer may not delegate to nonlawyer personnel the handling of negotiations with adjusters, and stressing EC 3-4, which says that "[p]roper protection of members of the public demands that no person be permitted to act in the confidential and demanding capacity of a lawyer unless he is subject to the regulations of the legal profession."

See also our *Opinions 73-41* and *73-43*, proscribing the use of nonlawyer personnel in the taking of depositions and attending closings without the presence of the lawyer-employer.

The Committee also believes that, consistent with ABA *Informal Opinion 1333*, the lawyer is not required to so separately itemize such work of nonlawyer personnel described in EC 3-6 and DR 3-104 but that time for such work may, in the alternative, be included as an element considered in arriving at the lawyer's fee in the same manner as the lawyer's normal and usual overhead expenses are treated. See also our *Opinion 75-29*. However, the lawyer should not in fact or effect duplicate charges for services of nonlawyer personnel, and if those charges are separately itemized, the salaries of such personnel employed by the lawyer should in some reasonable fashion be excluded from consideration as an overhead element in fixing the lawyer's own fee. If that exclusion cannot, as a practical matter, be accomplished in some rational and reasonably accurate fashion, then the charges for nonlawyer time should be credited against the lawyer's own fee.

As to whether knowledge and specific advance consent of the client as to such uses of nonlawyer personnel, and charges therefor, are necessary, the Committee majority feels that it is in some instances and is not in others. For example, it would not seem appropriate for a lawyer to always have to seek the consent of the client as to use of a law clerk in conducting legal research. And under EC 3-6 and DR 3-104, the work delegated to nonlawyer personnel should be so much under the lawyer's supervision and ultimately merged into the lawyer's own product that the work will be, in effect, that of the lawyer himself, who presumably has entered into a "clear agreement with his client as to the basis of the fee charges to be made" (EC 2-19). However, we feel that such "clear agreement" could not exist in many situations where the lawyer intends to make substantial use of nonlawyer personnel, and to bill directly or indirectly therefor, unless the client is informed of that intention at the time the fee agreement is entered into.

Therefore, if there is a potentiality of dispute with, or of lack of clear agreement with and understanding by, the client as to the basis of the lawyer's charges, including the foregoing elements of nonlawyer time, whether or not the nonlawyer personnel time is to be separately itemized, the lawyer's intention to so use nonlawyer personnel and charge directly or indirectly therefor should be discussed in advance with, and approved by, the client. This would seem especially the case where substantial use is to be made of any kind of such nonlawyer services. See also EC 2-19 as to explaining to clients the reasons for particular fee arrangements proposed.

The Committee suggests that the potentiality of such dispute or lack of clear agreement and understanding referred to in the foregoing paragraph may exist in the case of work to be done by nonlawyer personnel who are employed by the lawyer and who perform services of a type known by the lay public to be regularly available through independent contractors, e.g., investigators. The Committee feels that such potentiality especially may exist where the lawyer enters into a contingent fee arrangement with the client and then separately itemizes charges to the client for the time of nonlawyer personnel who are full-time employees of the lawyer; the arrangement may be susceptible of interpretation as involving charging the client for such nonlawyer services and at the same time, in fact or effect, duplicating the charges by including the salaries of such personnel as overhead and an element of the lawyer's own fee, as proscribed hereinabove.

Again, as stated above, care should be taken to avoid the appearance of any unauthorized practice of law or of the use of such nonlawyer personnel in any way other than as set forth in Canon 3. Accordingly, even where the advance specific consent of the client as to the use of nonlawyer personnel may not seem necessary, as referred to above, the lawyer, when intending to separately itemize on his bill for the services of nonlawyer personnel, should, when arriving at the fee agreement with the client, acquaint the client with the legal limitations on any such personnel whose services might be used and with the conditions applicable to the use of such personnel as provided in Canon 3.

Florida Ethics Opinion 81-3 (1981)

Committee on Professional Ethics, Florida Bar Association
www.floridabar.org (Click "Lawyer Regulation" then "Ethics Opinions," then type "81-3")
1981 WL 125112

Summary: When a law firm uses a collection agency to collect delinquent fees, the "collection agency so employed by the attorney should be viewed as 'nonlawyer personnel' within the purview of DR 3-104. The employing lawyer therefore has a continuing duty of exercising a high standard of care to assure that the delegated collection efforts of the agency are not conducted in a manner contrary to the Florida Code of Professional Responsibility."

Florida Ethics Opinion 86-1 (1986)

Committee on Professional Ethics, Florida Bar Association
www.floridabar.org (Click "Lawyer Regulation" then "Ethics Opinions," then type "86-1")
1986 WL 84405

Summary: The Court has defined "associate" narrowly to mean "a salaried lawyer-employee who is not a partner of the firm" and to exclude nonlawyer employees of the firm. *The Florida Bar v. Fetterman*, 439 So. 2d 835 (Fla. 1983).

Florida Ethics Opinion 86-4 (1986)

Committee on Professional Ethics, Florida Bar Association
www.floridabar.org (Click "Lawyer Regulation" then "Ethics Opinions," then type "86-4")
1986 WL 84408

Summary: It is permissible for nonlawyer employees to be listed on a law firm's letterhead along with their titles signifying their nonlawyer status. It also is permissible to issue nonlawyer employees business cards bearing their name and title along with the firm name, address, and telephone number.

One of the most frequently asked ethics questions in the last year or two has been whether it is permissible to list nonlawyer employees—paralegals and legal assistants in particular—with their titles on law firm letterhead. A related question of similar frequency is whether it is permissible to issue nonlawyer employees business cards bearing their name and title along with the firm's name, address, and telephone number. Both are permissible.

The Committee's prior opinions on the permissibility of letterhead listings and business cards for nonlawyer employees are somewhat inconsistent and dated. In *Opinion 71-39*, the Committee found it to be permissible for a law firm's investigator to carry business cards imprinted with the investigator's name and the law firm's name, address, and telephone number. In *Opinion 73-43*, the Committee found it impermissible, because of the possibility of solicitation, for a law firm's name to be imprinted on a lay employee's business card. The Committee also found it impermissible for a law firm's trained paralegal to write letters on firm stationary with the title "Legal Assistant" appearing below the paralegal's signature and name. The Committee reasoned that the terms "Legal Assistant" and "Paralegal" had "no official meaning and no precise definition that [was] generally applied or accepted" and could mislead clients into believing that nonlawyer assistants were lawyers.

Opinion 77-14 found it impermissible for a law firm to signify and name a legal assistant on the firm letterhead. The Committee found the practice not to be authorized by DR 2-102(A) as it existed in 1977. In its 1977 form, the rule imposed detailed restrictions on letterhead, business cards, and signs. In its current form, DR 2-102 simply requires that letterhead and business cards not include any statement that is false, fraudulent, misleading, or deceptive. Proposed Rule of Professional Conduct 4-7.5 is essentially the same as the current DR 2-102.

At the same time that the Committee in *Opinion 77-14* disapproved the listing of legal assistants on firm letterhead, the Committee permitted a legal assistant to sign letters as "Legal Assistant." This time the Committee noted that EC 3-6 provides for an indication of the letter-writer's nonlawyer status. DR 3-104(E) requires that a nonlawyer disclose his or her nonlawyer status in communications with clients, lawyers outside the firm, and members of the public.

In light of the growing presence of formally trained and/or experienced legal assistants and paralegals in the practice of law, the popular recognition of their status and role, and the current DR 2-102 and DR 3-104(E), the Committee now concludes that it is permissible for paralegals and legal assistants to be named and their titles signified on firm letterhead. The Committee considers it unlikely that anyone will be misled by titles such as Paralegal and Legal Assistant to believe that the person named is a lawyer.

The Committee further concludes that it is permissible for nonlawyer employees to carry business cards imprinted with the nonlawyer employee's name and title and the firm's name, address, and telephone number. Finally, the Committee reaffirms the conclusion of *Opinion 77-14* that a nonlawyer's title indicating nonlawyer status should appear beneath the employee's name on correspondence signed by the employee. Lawyers should take care not to hold a paralegal or legal assistant out as "certified" if the employee is not in fact certified. (DR 2-102.)

Florida Ethics Opinion 86-5 (1986)

Committee on Professional Ethics, Florida Bar Association
www.floridabar.org (Click "Lawyer Regulation" then "Ethics Opinions," then type "86-5")
1986 WL 84409

Summary: A law firm that hires a nonlawyer who was employed by an opposing law firm has a duty not to seek or permit disclosure by the employee of the confidences or secrets of the opposing firm's clients. The firm from which the employee departs has a corresponding duty to admonish the employee that he or she is obligated to preserve the confidences and secrets of the clients.

The Committee has been asked to consider how the conflict-of-interest and confidentiality rules apply when nonlawyer employees move from one law firm to another. The issue usually arises when a paralegal, legal assistant, or legal secretary "switches sides," that is, moves from one firm to a second firm that is opposing counsel in some matter after having worked on the matter for the first firm or having otherwise been exposed to confidences and secrets of the first firm's client.

DR 4-101(E) requires a lawyer to "exercise reasonable care to prevent his employees . . . from disclosing or using confidences or secrets of a client." DR 3-104(C) requires a lawyer or law firm to "exercise a high standard of care to assure compliance by the nonlawyer personnel with the applicable provisions of the Code of Professional Responsibility." See Proposed Rule of Professional Conduct 4-5.3 ("Responsibilities Regarding Nonlawyer Assistants"). The Preamble to the Code of Professional Responsibility recognizes: "Obviously the canons, ethical considerations, and disciplinary rules cannot apply to nonlawyers; however, they do define the type of ethical conduct that the public has a right to expect not only of lawyers but also of their nonprofessional employees and associates in all matters pertaining to professional employment. A lawyer should ultimately be responsible for the conduct of his employees and associates in the course of the professional representation of the client. The Code does not directly regulate the conduct of nonlawyer employees of a law firm. The Code recognizes, however, that nonlawyer employees necessarily share in confidential and secret information and therefore necessarily share the attorney's ethical obligation not to disclose or use such information without the client's consent. For that reason, lawyers are required to use care to ensure that their nonlawyer employees appreciate and conduct themselves in accordance with the shared duty of confidentiality."

Thus, while the new employer of an attorney who switched sides would be disqualified automatically from representation in the matter, the new employer of a nonlawyer employee who switched sides would not be disqualified. However, both the hiring firm and the former firm still must meet their obligations under DR 4-101(E) and DR 3-104(C). That is, the former firm has a duty to admonish the departing employee that the employee has an ethical or moral obligation not to reveal confidences or secrets of any client to the hiring firm. The hiring firm has a corresponding duty not to seek or permit a disclosure of confidences or secrets by the employee and not to use such information.

The former firm has a second duty when a paralegal or legal assistant switches sides. If the employee had a close relationship with the client, the former firm must advise the client of the employee's departure and new employment. The client is entitled to be kept informed of significant developments in the representation. Proposed Rule of Professional Conduct 4-1.4 ("Communication").

Florida Ethics Opinion 87-11 (1988)

Committee on Professional Ethics, Florida Bar Association
www.floridabar.org (Click "Lawyer Regulation" then "Ethics Opinions," then type "87-11")
1988 WL 281582

Summary: Under no circumstances should an attorney permit a nonlawyer employee to sign the attorney's name, together with the nonlawyer's initials, to notices of hearing and other pleadings.

———————————

The inquiring attorney requests an opinion regarding the ethical permissibility of the following conduct:

[1] An attorney who is on vacation authorizes his secretary, via a telephone call, to sign the attorney's name, together with the secretary's initials, to discovery and notices of hearing.
[2] An attorney with a large case load authorizes his secretary or paralegal office manager to sign notices of hearings as a convenience.

Under the Rules of Professional Conduct (Chapter 4, Rules Regulating The Florida Bar), an attorney may delegate functions to a nonlawyer employee so long as the attorney supervises and retains responsibility for the work (Rule 4-5.5, Comment). The delegating attorney has a duty to make reasonable efforts to ensure that the nonlawyer employee's conduct is compatible with the professional obligations of the attorney (Rule 4-5.3(b)). One of the attorney's professional obligations is to refrain from knowingly disobeying the rules of a tribunal (Rule 4-3.4(c)).

Thus, an attorney practicing in Florida courts is obligated to comply personally with the Rules of Judicial Administration and to ensure that the conduct of his nonlawyer employees is compatible with this obligation.

In this respect, Rule 2.060(d) of the Rules of Judicial Administration provides in pertinent part: "Every pleading and other paper of a party represented by an attorney shall be signed by at least one attorney of record in his individual name whose address and telephone number, including area code, shall be stated, and who shall be duly licensed to practice law in Florida or who shall have received permission to appear in the particular case as provided in subsection(b). . . ."

In view of the rules referred to above, the Committee concludes that an attorney should not under any circumstances permit nonlawyer employees to sign notices of hearing.

The Committee is aware of *Hankin v. Blissett*, 475 So. 2d 1303 (Fla. 3d DCA 1985), which held that a notice of appeal on which an attorney's secretary signed the attorney's name met the requirements of Rule 2.060(d) because "a pleading signed in the name of the attorney by the attorney's authorized agent is, in effect, a pleading signed by the attorney." *Hankin* addressed only the legal sufficiency of pleadings signed by nonlawyer for lawyers. The ruling does not relieve attorneys of their ethical obligation to comply with the letter of Rule 2.060(d). Failure to comply with the letter of the rule carries danger of aiding the unlicensed practice of law in violation of Rule 4-5.5(b).

Florida Ethics Opinion 88-6 (1988)

Committee on Professional Ethics, Florida Bar Association
www.floridabar.org (Click "Lawyer Regulation" then "Ethics Opinions," then type "88-6")
1988 WL 281586

Summary: It is not impermissible per se for a lawyer to have a nonlawyer employee conduct the initial interview with a new client, although the practice is discouraged and must adhere to certain guidelines.

———————————

The Committee has been asked to consider what a legal assistant or other nonlawyer employee may and may not do in an initial interview with prospective clients. Rule 4-5.3 of the Rules Regulating The Florida Bar provides in pertinent part: With respect to a nonlawyer employed or retained by or associated with a lawyer: (a) A partner in a law firm shall make reasonable efforts to ensure that the firm has in effect measures giving reasonable assurance that the person's conduct is compatible with the professional obligations of the lawyer; (b) A lawyer having direct supervisory authority over the nonlawyer shall make reasonable efforts to ensure that the person's conduct is compatible with the professional obligations of the lawyer.

Although this rule does not specifically address the question posed to the Committee, the former rule that governed this area (DR 3-104, Code of Professional Responsibility) provided some insights that remain valid under the current rules. DR 3-104 states that while nonlawyer employees may perform delegated functions under the direct supervision of a lawyer, they may not counsel clients about legal matters or otherwise engage in the unauthorized practice of law. The disciplinary rule further states that the initial and continuing relationship with the client is the responsibility of the lawyer, with the work of the nonlawyer employee being merged into the attorney's completed product. Of course, the lawyer must examine and be responsible for all work delegated to the nonlawyer employee. In addition, DR 3-104 points out that nonlawyer employees must first disclose their nonlawyer status before communicating with clients or the public.

Further insight in this area may be gained from two Florida ethics opinions. *Opinion 70-62* provides that an attorney may not delegate to a legal assistant any activity requiring the attorney's personal judgment and participation. *Opinion 73-41* states that an attorney may use a legal assistant only for work that does not constitute the practice of law. This is consistent with Rule 4-5.5(b).

Although the Florida opinions do not address the specific issue presented to the Committee, an ABA opinion does. ABA *Informal Opinion 998* concludes: While we think it is appropriate for a lawyer to provide himself with such assistance as he deems necessary in order efficiently and economically to perform his work and that of his office, any layman hired by him should not give legal advice or act as a lawyer. We think that the system of conducting initial interviews with clients by nonlawyers could be a violation of the Canons of Ethics, if any advice were given or if the client did not subsequently actually see the lawyer and confer with him. Accordingly, although we do not condemn the practice which you suggest in all instances, we do think it has great dangers and should be carefully supervised so that in practice it complies with the Canons. It would be better if the prospective client were first interviewed by the lawyer and then by the lay assistant. However, as above stated, we do not categorically state that this is essential.

After a review of the above-stated information, the Committee concludes that while it is preferred that an attorney conduct the initial interview with prospective clients, the use of nonlawyer employees for this purpose is not prohibited per se. However, the lawyer is responsible for careful, direct supervision of nonlawyer employees and must make certain that (1) they clearly identify their nonlawyer status to prospective clients, (2) they are used for the purpose of obtaining only factual information from prospective clients, and (3) they give no legal advice concerning the case itself or the representation agreement. Any questions concerning an assessment of the case, the applicable law, or the representation agreement would have to be answered by the lawyer. Furthermore, it is imperative that the lawyer evaluate all information obtained by a nonlawyer employee during the client interview and that the lawyer subsequently confer with the client and establish a personal and continuing relationship.

Florida Ethics Opinion 88-15 (1988)
Committee on Professional Ethics, Florida Bar Association
www.floridabar.org (Click "Lawyer Regulation" then "Ethics Opinions," then type "88-15")
1988 WL 281593
Summary: Lawyers may share office space with nonlawyers, but certain ethical limitations apply.

An attorney asks whether . . . an attorney ethically may share office space with a nonlawyer. [This is permitted if certain ethical guidelines are observed.] Generally speaking, the attorney must preserve client confidences, avoid misleading appearances, refrain from prohibited solicitation practices, and not participate in improper division of legal fees.

Rule 4-1.6, Rules Regulating The Florida Bar, provides that an attorney must preserve in confidence all information relating to representation of his or her clients. An attorney sharing space with a nonlawyer must ensure that the nonlawyer and his or her employees do not have access to the attorney's client files. This can be done, for example, by keeping client files in a room to which the nonlawyers do not have access or by keeping the files in locking file cabinets. Additionally, the nonlawyers should not be able to overhear confidential attorney-client conversations.

Any advertising or other statements concerning an attorney or his or her law practice must be truthful and not misleading (Rules 4-7.1 and 4-7.2). Consequently, an attorney must take steps to avoid misleading the public as to the nature of the business activities being conducted within his or her offices. This means there should be a separate sign at the office entrance and on the building directory (if there is one) for each business or profession operated within the attorney's offices. For example, . . . if John Smith operated a law practice and Jane Jones operated a real estate brokerage in the same office suite, there should be a sign for each business. Furthermore, it is recommended that two businesses or professions that share space have separate telephone lines even if those lines will be answered by a common receptionist. If there is only a central incoming line, the receptionist must answer in a neutral manner (such as "professional offices") in order to avoid misleading callers.

An attorney is prohibited from engaging in in-person solicitation of legal employment, except from relatives, clients, and former clients (Rule 4-7.4(a)). This prohibition may not be evaded through the use of nonlawyer agents (Rule 4-8.4(a)). In addition, Rule 4-7.2(c) provides that an attorney may not give "anything of value" in exchange for a recommendation. Of course, an attorney may not divide legal fees with a nonlawyer. (Rule 4-5.4(a)). These rules therefore prohibit an attorney from using a nonlawyer with whom he or she shares space as an agent for solicitation of legal employment or from paying the nonlawyer for referrals. . . .

Florida Ethics Opinion 89-4 (1989)
Committee on Professional Ethics, Florida Bar Association
www.floridabar.org (Click "Lawyer Regulation" then "Ethics Opinions," then type "89-4")
1989 WL 380142

Summary: A law firm may not allow its nonlawyer marketing director to solicit business for the firm in any manner forbidden to lawyers themselves. A nonlawyer marketing director may not be paid commissions representing a percentage of fees generated from business brought to the firm by him.

The inquiring attorney's law firm wishes to hire a nonlawyer to solicit legal business for the firm. The lawyer expresses his view that while advertising is unprofessional and should not be allowed, straightforward solicitation should be permitted. In this regard, the attorney presents several questions:

[1] Can the firm hire a nonlawyer to solicit business?

[2] Can the firm pay the nonlawyer either a straight salary, a salary plus commission, or a straight commission?

[3] Are there any new rules, regulations, or guidelines that govern?

[4] May the firm provide the nonlawyer with a business card indicating that the nonlawyer is a solicitor, a salesperson, a production manager, or is involved in marketing?

[1] An attorney may hire a nonlawyer to do only such solicitation as the attorney himself is permitted to do by the Rules of Professional Conduct. The rules do not permit in-person solicitation or telephone solicitation by a lawyer or by any agent of the lawyer. The prohibition against in-person and telephone solicitation is set forth in Rule 4-7.4(a). If a lawyer orders a nonlawyer employee to engage in conduct that would be a violation of the rules if engaged in by the lawyer, or if the lawyer ratifies such misconduct, under Rule 4-5.3(c) the lawyer is held responsible for the misconduct. All that the rules would allow a nonlawyer "solicitor" to do on behalf of the inquiring attorney's firm is manage whatever marketing activities the firm may wish to undertake in conformance with Rules 4-7.1 through 4-7.7 of the Rules of Professional Conduct. These include advertising in public media and through direct mail campaigns.

[2] A nonlawyer hired to engage in permissible marketing activities on behalf of a lawyer may be paid a straight salary. If commissions would be tied to legal fees derived from business brought to the firm by the nonlawyer's efforts, payment of those commissions would constitute a violation of Rule 4-5.4(a)(3), which forbids a lawyer to divide a legal fee with a nonlawyer.

[3] The rules that govern are those identified above: Rules 4-7.1 through 4-7.7 (advertising and solicitation), Rule 4-5.3 (conduct of nonlawyer employees), and Rule 4-5.4(a)(3) (dividing a legal fee with a nonlawyer).

[4] It is permissible for nonlawyer employees to be issued business cards that clearly indicate their nonlawyer status. This Committee so ruled in *Opinion 86-4*. Thus the nonlawyer "solicitor's" business cards must carry a disclaimer such as "not a member of the Bar" or "not a lawyer." Neither of the titles suggested by the attorney—solicitor, salesperson, production manager—is permissible for the nonlawyer's business card. The first two refer to activities that the attorney cannot ethically permit the nonlawyer to do, and thus are misleading in violation of Rule 4-7.1 and 4-7.6(a). Neither permissible advertising nor impermissible solicitation is synonymous with production management, so the third term also is misleading. "Marketing director" would be an appropriate title for a nonlawyer employee responsible for permitted marketing functions.

Florida Ethics Opinion 89-5 (1989)

Committee on Professional Ethics, Florida Bar Association
www.floridabar.org (Click "Lawyer Regulation" then "Ethics Opinions," then type "89-5")
1989 WL 380143

Summary: A law firm may permit a paralegal or other trained employee to handle a real estate closing at which no lawyer in the firm is present if certain conditions are met. (RPC: 4-5.5(b).)

In *Opinion 73-43*, this Committee concluded that it was permissible for a lawyer to have a legal assistant prepare real estate documents under the lawyer's supervision, but that it would be improper for the legal assistant to attend closings at which no attorney in the firm was present. The committee reasoned that there was no purpose for the legal assistant to attend closings except to give legal advice and that the legal assistant's presence could be construed by the clients as answering unasked questions about the propriety or legality of the closing documents.

The Unlicensed Practice of Law Committee has requested that we reconsider the issue of whether a legal assistant or other nonlawyer employee with real estate expertise may be permitted to conduct or otherwise participate in a closing in place of a lawyer in the firm. That committee does not agree with the premise of *Opinion 73-43*: that conducting a closing necessarily involves the giving of legal advice, in fact or by implication. That committee notes that title companies are permitted by the supreme court to conduct closings. (*Cooperman v. West Coast Title Company*, 75 So. 2d 818 (Fla. 1954).) The committee also points out that the typical residential real estate transaction is nonadversarial and that allowing a trained paralegal to handle the closing will enable a law firm to assist in real estate transactions at a lower cost to clients.

The majority of this Committee (seven members dissent) now concludes that law firms should be permitted to have trained nonlawyer employees conduct closings at which no lawyer in the firm is present if certain conditions are met. Accordingly, this Committee recedes from *Opinion 73-43*.

Rule 4-5.5(b), Rules Regulating The Florida Bar, forbids a lawyer to assist a person who is not a member of the Bar in the performance of activity that constitutes the unlicensed practice of law. But, as the comment states, this rule "does not prohibit a lawyer from employing the services of paraprofessionals and delegating functions to them, so long as the lawyer supervises the delegated work and retains responsibility for their work."

The majority of this Committee concluded that under Rule 4-5.5(b), a law firm may permit a nonlawyer employee to conduct or attend a closing if the following conditions are met:

[1] A lawyer supervises and reviews all work done up to the closing.

[2] The supervising lawyer determines that handling or attending the closing will be no more than a ministerial act. Handling the closing will constitute a ministerial act only if the supervising lawyer determines that the client understands the closing documents in advance of the closing.

[3] The clients consent to the closing being handled by a nonlawyer employee of the firm. This requires that written disclosure be made to the clients that the person who will handle or attend the closing is a nonlawyer and will not be able to give legal advice at the closing.

[4] The supervising lawyer is readily available, in person or by telephone, to provide legal advice or answer legal questions should the need arise.

[5] The nonlawyer employee will not give legal advice at the closing or make impromptu decisions that should be made by the supervising lawyer.

When a law firm's involvement in a real estate transaction is limited to issuing title insurance as an agent for a title insurance company, and does not involve representation of either party to the transaction, condition number 3 does not apply. However, the law firm should take care that the parties understand that the firm does not represent their interests.

Florida Ethics Opinion 92-3 (1992)

Committee on Professional Ethics, Florida Bar Association
www.floridabar.org (Click "Lawyer Regulation" then "Ethics Opinions," then type "92-3")
1992 WL 602494
Summary: An attorney cannot share fees with a lay company (a public adjusting firm) engaged in the business of settling personal injury claims with insurance companies. The company would refer clients to the attorney. This would violate Rule 4-5.3(a) which prohibits attorneys from sharing legal fees with nonlawyers. "The Company's

fee would be paid out of the attorney's portion of the recovery, which clearly would constitute improper fee splitting." "Furthermore, the Bar's Unlicensed Practice of Law Counsel has taken the position that a public adjuster engages in the unlicensed practice of law if the adjuster acts on behalf of a claimant against a tortfeasor's insurance company; the authorized activities of a public adjuster are limited to adjusting claims with the claimant's insurer."

Florida Ethics Opinion 94-6 (1995)

Committee on Professional Ethics, Florida Bar Association
www.floridabar.org (Click "Lawyer Regulation" then "Ethics Opinions," then type "94-6")
1995 WL 815247
Summary: Nonlawyer mediators employed by the inquirer's law firm may not have an ownership interest in either the law firm or the mediation department. To do so would implicate rules prohibiting sharing fees with nonlawyers, partnership with nonlawyers, and assisting in the unauthorized practice of law. See Rules 4-5.4(a), 4-5.4(b), and 4-5.5(b).... Regarding letterhead, nonlawyer mediators employed by the firm may be listed on the letterhead only if their nonlawyer status is clearly indicated. [See also *Advisory Opinion 2000-009*, Mediator Ethics Committee (*www.tfapm.org/Drc/opinionlist/2000-09.shtml*).]

Florida Ethics Opinion 95-1 (1995)

Committee on Professional Ethics, Florida Bar Association
www.floridabar.org (Click "Lawyer Regulation" then "Ethics Opinions," then type "95-1")
1995 WL 815245
Summary: A [lawyer] may not ethically enter into a business arrangement with a nonlawyer to represent claimants in social security disability matters. Fees claimed by or paid to the bar member for such representation are considered legal fees, and thus the proposed arrangement would violate Rule 4-5.4, which prohibits a lawyer from sharing legal fees with a nonlawyer. (RPC: 4-5.4)

A member of The Florida Bar has requested an advisory ethics opinion regarding the following: I have recently been approached by a nonattorney who wishes to start a business representing claimants in social security disability matters. The Code of Federal [R]egulations §§ 404.1705 and 416.1505 allow for nonattorneys to represent claimants in these matters. The nonattorney has asked me to work for his company and act as a claimant representative employed by his company. I would act not only as the representative but also as the management of the company. The nonattorney would be the sole shareholder in the company, but all management and decisions concerning the representation of clients would be made by me. The company would incur all costs associated with the representation and collect all fees resulting from it, as allowed by CFR §§ 404.1720 and 416.1520. I as an employee would receive a salary and bonuses based upon the profitability of the company. All work performed for the company would fit within the social security disability area, thus could be performed by nonattorneys. The company would engage in some advertising but would not advertise the services of an attorney.

[1] My question is, would this association of quasi-legal representation with the company violate Rule 4-5.4 of the Professional Rules of Conduct, or any other rule of conduct?

[2] If the above-discussed association does not violate a rule of conduct would I still be able to practice law independently of the company in areas other than social security? I the attorney would incur all expenses involved in the representation of clients and receive all fees resulting from that representation. The legal representation performed by me would be conducted from my office with the company but would have no other connection to the company.

[3] Lastly, would I as an independent attorney be able to represent the company's clients in Federal District Court proceedings resulting from their social security claim? I the attorney would bear the court costs and expenses associated with the district court case and would receive any Equal Access to Justice Act fees that may result from this action.

As noted by the inquirer, federal legislation permits nonlawyers to practice in certain specified subject areas. States are preempted from enjoining conduct that Congress has expressly sanctioned by such legislation (*Sperry v. State of Florida ex rel. the Florida Bar*, 373 U.S. 379 (1963)). Nevertheless, states "maintain control over the practice of law within [their] borders except to the limited extent necessary for the accomplishment of the federal objectives" (Id. at 402). It therefore appears that a state may properly proscribe, by application of its ethics rules, activities by lawyers with nonlawyers as long as the proscription does not infringe on the authorization granted the latter by Congress (*ABA Informal Opinion 1241*). This conclusion is consistent with our *Florida Ethics Opinion 65-4*. Moreover, ethics authorities from other jurisdictions have generally disapproved the type of arrangement proposed above. See *Kansas Opinion 93-11*. See also, for example, *Indiana Opinion 6 of 1994*, *Maryland Opinion 84-92*, *Wisconsin Opinion E-84-4*.

Additionally, it is important to note that a particular activity constituting the practice of law does not cease to be the practice of law simply because nonlawyers may legally perform it (*ABA Informal Opinion 1241*). When engaged in by laypersons, such activity is simply the authorized practice of law. Thus, it is our opinion that members of The Florida Bar who, while maintaining a law practice or otherwise holding themselves out as

attorneys, represent claimants in social security disability matters are providing legal services for which they are receiving a "legal" fee even though the matters may properly be handled by nonlawyers. See *ABA Informal Opinion 1241*. Under those circumstances, the Florida lawyer may not join with a nonlawyer to provide such services without running afoul of Rule 4-5.4.

Florida Ethics Opinion 95-2 (1995)
Committee on Professional Ethics, Florida Bar Association
www.floridabar.org (Click "Lawyer Regulation" then "Ethics Opinions," then type "95-2")
1995 WL 815244

Summary: It would be unethical for an attorney to enter an arrangement with a lay company to provide representation in securities disputes for clients obtained by the company. Nonattorney company employees could interfere with the direct relationship the attorney must have with the client. "In a similar arrangement regarding living trust preparation, the Florida Supreme Court stated: 'If the lawyer is employed by the corporation selling the living trust rather than by the client, then the lawyer's duty of loyalty to the client could be compromised'" (*The Florida Bar re: Advisory Opinion: Nonlawyer Preparation of Living Trusts*, 613 So. 2d 426 (Fla. 1992)). The Court went on to say, "In light of this duty of loyalty to the client, a lawyer who assembles, reviews, executes, and funds a living trust document should be an independent counsel paid by the client and representing the client's interests alone."

Florida Ethics Opinion 97-3 (1997)
Committee on Professional Ethics, Florida Bar Association
www.floridabar.org (Click "Lawyer Regulation" then "Ethics Opinions," then type "97-3")
1997 WL 912330

Summary: An attorney may not accept referrals from an heir hunting service if this service improperly solicits the heirs.

An attorney's agent is subject to the same ethical restrictions on solicitation as the attorney. See Florida *Ethics Opinions 77-8, 74-15,* and *92-3.* Rule 4-7.4(a) provides the following: A lawyer shall not solicit professional employment from a prospective client with whom the lawyer has no family or prior professional relationship, in person or otherwise, when a significant motive for the lawyer's doing so is the lawyer's pecuniary gain. A lawyer shall not permit employees or agents of the lawyer to solicit in the lawyer's behalf. A lawyer shall not enter into an agreement for, charge, or collect a fee for professional employment obtained in violation of this rule. The term *solicit* includes contact in person, by telephone, telegraph, or facsimile, or by other communication directed to a specific recipient and includes any written form of communication directed to a specific recipient and not meeting the requirements of subdivision (b) of this rule. . . .

If the methods employed by heir hunting services to contact prospective heirs do not comply with the rules regulating attorney solicitation and advertising, an attorney would be prohibited from accepting referrals from such a source. Such a referral scheme also implicates the rules prohibiting fee splitting with nonlawyers and assisting in the unauthorized practice of law. See Rules 4-5.4(a) & (d) and 4-5.5(b), Rules Regulating The Florida Bar.

Florida Ethics Opinion 02-1 (2002)
Committee on Professional Ethics, Florida Bar Association
www.floridabar.org (Click "Lawyer Regulation" then "Ethics Opinions," then type "02-1")
2002 WL 405113
Summary: An attorney may not give a bonus to a nonlawyer employee solely based on the number of hours worked by the employee (RPC: 4-5.4).

———

A member of The Florida Bar has requested an advisory ethics opinion. [The] attorney inquires: May I bonus a nonlawyer employee based on the number of hours the nonlawyer employee has worked on a case for a particular client?

As a family law attorney, I do virtually nothing at a flat rate and certainly no work is done by percentage. I bill my time and the time of my legal assistant at separate hourly rates, which are itemized on the client's bill and described in the written fee agreement with the client. I would like to bonus my employees based on their own productivity. I would not be utilizing any portion of the fees received by me for that purpose.

Although the attorney did not specifically state it in the written request, during the hotline call, the attorney proposed the following: If the legal assistant works ten hours on a case and the attorney bills the client ten hours of legal assistant time, may the attorney pay a bonus to the legal assistant based on a certain rate times ten hours?

Rule 4-5.4(a), Florida Rules of Professional Conduct, provides that a lawyer or law firm "shall not share legal fees with a nonlawyer." Rule 4-5.4(a)(4) specifically deals with the issue of "bonus" payments to nonlawyer personnel in a law firm. The rule provides as follows:

(a) Sharing Fees with Nonlawyers. A lawyer or law firm shall not share legal fees with a nonlawyer, except that: . . . (4) bonuses may be paid to nonlawyer employees based on their extraordinary efforts on a particular case or over a specified time period, provided that the payment is not based on the generation of clients or business and is not calculated as a percentage of legal fees received by the lawyer or law firm.

Pursuant to Rule 4-5.4(a)(4), the inquirer may pay the firm's legal assistant a bonus, but that bonus cannot be based in any way upon a percentage of fees generated by the legal assistant or the firm and cannot be based upon generating clients for the firm. Bonuses to nonlawyer employees cannot be calculated as a percentage

of the firm's fees or of the gross recovery in cases on which the nonlawyer worked. See *Florida Ethics Opinion 89-4* (a law firm cannot pay to a firm marketing manager a bonus based on a percentage of business he or she generates for the firm). Rule 4-7.2(c)(8) . . . further prohibits attorneys from giving "anything of value to a person for recommending the lawyer's services. . . ."

Based on the rules and opinion, the inquiring attorney may pay the legal assistant a bonus based on the legal assistant's extraordinary efforts on a particular case or over a specific period of time. While the number of hours the legal assistant works on a particular case or over a specific period of time is one of several factors that can be considered in determining a bonus for the legal assistant, it is not the sole factor to be considered. It must be remembered that the rule allows a bonus to be paid to a nonlawyer based on "extraordinary efforts" either in a particular case or over a specific time period. A bonus that is solely calculated on the number of hours incurred by the legal assistant on the matter is tantamount to a finding that every single hour incurred was an extraordinary effort, and such a finding is very unlikely to be true. Therefore, unless every single hour incurred by the legal assistant was a truly extraordinary effort, it would be impermissible for the inquiring attorney to pay a bonus to his legal assistant calculated in the manner the inquiring attorney has proposed. However, the number of hours incurred by the legal assistant on the particular matter or over a specified time period may be considered by the lawyer as one of the factors in determining the legal assistant's bonus.

Florida Ethics Opinion 02-8 (2004)
Committee on Professional Ethics, Florida Bar Association
www.floridabar.org (Click "Lawyer Regulation" then "Ethics Opinions," then type "02-8")
2004 WL 4953224
Summary: A lawyer may not enter into a referral arrangement with a nonlawyer who is a securities dealer to refer the lawyer's clients to the securities dealer, who would then pay the lawyer a portion of the advisory fee for the clients referred.

Proposed Advisory Opinion 07-2 (September 7, 2007)
Committee on Professional Ethics, Florida Bar Association
www.floridabar.org (Click "Lawyer Regulation," then "Ethics Opinions," then "Proposed Advisory Opinions")
Summary: Law firms can outsource paralegal functions to nonattorneys in India if adequate supervision is maintained, conflicts of interest are avoided, confidentiality is preserved, client consent is obtained, and billing arrangements are proper.

———

A member of The Florida Bar has inquired whether a law firm may ethically outsource legal work to overseas attorneys or paralegals. The overseas attorneys, who are not admitted to The Florida Bar, would do work, including document preparation, for the creation of business entities, business closings, and immigration forms and letters. Paralegals, who are not foreign attorneys, would transcribe dictation tapes. The foreign attorneys and paralegals would have remote access to the firm's computer files and may contact the clients to obtain information needed to complete a form. In addition to the facts presented in the written inquiry, the Committee was advised that the outsourcing company employs lawyers admitted to practice in India who are capable of providing much broader assistance to law firms in the United States besides outsourcing merely paralegal work, including contract drafting, litigation support, legal research, and forms preparation. . . .

Law firms frequently hire contract paralegals to perform services such as legal research and document preparation. It is the Committee's opinion that there is no ethical distinction when hiring an overseas provider of such services versus a local provider, and that contracting for such services does not constitute aiding the unlicensed practice of law, provided that there is adequate supervision by the law firm. [(The work delegated to nonlawyer personnel should be so much under the lawyer's supervision and ultimately merged into the lawyer's own product that the work will be, in effect, that of the lawyer himself . . . . Under Rule 4-5.3, A lawyer must give nonlawyer assistants appropriate instruction and supervision concerning the ethical aspects of their employment, particularly regarding the obligation not to disclose information relating to representation of the client.)]

Attorneys who use overseas legal outsourcing companies should recognize that providing adequate supervision may be difficult when dealing with employees who are in a different country. . . . An attorney may need to take extra steps to ensure that the foreign employees are familiar with Florida's ethics rules governing conflicts of interest and confidentiality. [(The attorney must also recognize that he or she could be held responsible for any conflict of interest that may be created by the hiring of [a foreign company] and which could arise from relationships that company develops with others during the attorney's relationship with company.)]

Of particular concern is the ethical obligation of confidentiality. The inquirer states that the foreign attorneys will have remote access to the firm's computer files. The committee believes that the law firm should instead limit the overseas provider's access to only the information necessary to complete the work for the particular client. The law firm should provide no access to information about other clients of the firm. The committee believes that the law firm should obtain prior client consent to disclose information that the firm reasonably believes is necessary to serve the client's interests.

Additionally, . . . regarding billing for nonlawyer personnel . . . , the lawyer should not in fact or effect duplicate charges for services of nonlawyer personnel, and if those charges are separately itemized, the salaries of such personnel employed by the lawyer should in some reasonable fashion be excluded from consideration as an overhead element in fixing the lawyer's own fee. If that exclusion cannot, as a practical matter, be accomplished in some rational and reasonably accurate fashion, then the charges for nonlawyer time should be credited against the lawyer's own fee. . . . The law firm may charge a client the actual cost of the overseas provider, unless the charge would normally be covered as overhead. However, in a contingent fee case, it would be improper to charge separately for work that is usually otherwise accomplished by a client's own attorney and incorporated into the standard fee paid to the attorney, even if that cost is paid to a third-party provider.

C. More Information

Florida Ethics Opinions
www.floridabar.org
(Click "Lawyer Regulation" then "Ethics Opinions")

Lexis
www.lexis.com
(ETHICS library FLBPE file)

Westlaw
www.westlaw.com
(FLETH-EO database)

Florida Ethics
www.law.cornell.edu/ethics/florida.html
www.ll.georgetown.edu/states/ethics/florida.cfm
www.sunethics.com
www.sunethics.com/newsarchive.htm

Researching Ethics Opinions
www.floridabar.org
(Click "Lawyer Regulation," then "Ethics Opinions," then "Researching Ethics Questions")

Florida Bar Ethics Hotline
800-235-8619
www.floridabar.org
(Click "Lawyer Regulation," then "Ethics Opinions," then "The Florida Bar Ethics Hotline")

Ethics Opinion Request Form
www.floridabar.org
(Click "Lawyer Regulation," then "Ethics Opinions," then "Ethics Inquiry Form")

Ethics in General
www.abanet.org/cpr/links.html
www.legalethics.com

D. Something to Check

1. Go to the web site containing ethical opinions of The Florida Bar (*www.floridabar.org*; click "Lawyer Regulation" then "Ethics Opinions"). Find and summarize (brief) one opinion (not mentioned in this section) on each of the following topics:
   a. Attorney advertising
   b. In-person solicitation

2. A paralegal works in a solo-attorney's law office, whose practice is confined to workers' compensation law. The attorney is out of the office a substantial amount of time. The paralegal, who has been fully trained in this area of the law, meets and greets the prospective clients, conducts the initial client interviews, fills out the worksheets, and prepares the documents needed to file with the workers' compensation agency. The attorney does not see clients until there are court appearances or administrative hearings. On occasion, the attorney has allowed the paralegal to sign the attorney's name on court pleadings. The paralegal's name is on the law firm letterhead without a title. Identify each ethical violation and the applicable ethical opinion(s) and/or rule(s).

3.4 Florida Bar Associations, Related Attorney Organizations, and Paralegal Membership Opportunities

A. Introduction
B. Attorneys in Florida: A Snapshot
C. State Bar Association
D. Other Statewide and Regional Associations
E. Local Bar Associations
F. More Information
G. Something to Check

A. Introduction

This section seeks to identify every major attorney organization in the state, particularly the bar associations. Many of the web sites for these groups have search boxes. To find out what the group may have said about paralegals, type "paralegal" or "legal assistant" in the search box. You could be led to news, committee or section activities, or ethical material pertaining to paralegals and related nonattorneys.

Before examining these associations, here is an overview—a snapshot—of the world of Florida attorneys.

B. Attorneys in Florida: A Snapshot

Number of attorneys in Florida	81,534
Percentage of attorneys who are male	69.1%
Percentage of attorneys who are female	30.9%
Percentage in private practice	78%
Percentage of sole practitioners	29%
Percentage in the public sector	15%
Percentage in corporations/other	8%
Median income before taxes (all attorneys)	$100,000
Percentage whose median net exceeds $100,000	50%
Percentage whose median net is under $50,000	17%
Median net income for male attorneys	$78,000
Median net income for female attorneys	$54,500
Total number taking bar exam	4,566
Number passing	3,024
Percentage passing	66%
Number taking bar exam for the first time	3,505
Number of first-time takers who passed	2,718
Percentage of first-time takers who passed	80%
Number of repeat takers	476
Number of repeat takers who passed	130
Percentage of repeat takers who passed	27%
Number admitted as foreign legal consultants	13

Sources:
www.ncbex.org
www.floridabar.org

C. State Bar Association

The Florida Bar
651 E. Jefferson Street
Tallahassee, FL 32399-2300
850-561-5600
www.floridabar.org

The Florida Bar is an *integrated* bar association, meaning that membership is a requirement to be able to practice law in the state. It is one of the largest mandatory state bar associations in the country. Headquartered in Tallahassee, the bar has branch offices in Tallahassee, Orlando, Tampa, Fort Lauderdale, and Miami. The Florida Bar itself does not license attorneys. The Florida Board of Bar Examiners, an arm of the Florida Supreme Court, is the licensing body for the state.

State Bar Committees or Sections of Interest to Paralegals

- Florida Registered Paralegal Program Committee
- Special Committee on Paralegals in the Legal Profession
- Special Committee to Study Paralegal Regulation
- Standing Committee on Professional Ethics
- Board Disciplinary Review Committee
- Standing Committee on Unlicensed Practice of Law

Paralegals as Members of State Bar Sections and Committees

Some of the sections of The Florida Bar allow affiliate memberships for nonlawyers and non-members. Examples:

Florida Registered Paralegal Program Committee
www.floridabar.org
(click "Inside the Bar" then "Committees")
Three of the seven members of the committee are paralegals, at least two of whom are Florida Registered Paralegals (FRP). One member is a paralegal educator who may be a lawyer or a nonlawyer.

Administrative Law Section Affiliate Membership

www.flaadminlaw.org

www.flaadminlaw.org/documents/affapp.pdf

"Affiliate membership in the Administrative Law Section is open to . . . law students, legal assistants, members of the legislature and legislative staff, and other administrative personnel. . . . The dues for affiliate membership are $25 per individual."

Entertainment, Arts and Sports Law Section Affiliate Membership

www.easl.info

easl.info/index.php?module=Static_Docs&func=view&f= affiliate.pdf

"Membership . . . will provide you with interesting and informative ideas. It will help keep you informed on new developments in this field. You will receive . . . discounts on continuing legal education opportunities offered by the section. As an affiliate member of the section, you will meet with lawyers sharing similar interests and problems and work with them in forwarding the public and professional needs of the Bar." Dues: $35 a year.

Environmental and Land Use Law Section Affiliate Membership

www.eluls.org

www.eluls.org/membership.html

Dues: $50 a year.

Health Law Section Affiliate Membership

www.flabarhls.org

www.flabarhls.org/about/index.asp

Affiliate membership is open to "paralegals, legal administrators or other persons who hold positions directly related to health law." Dues: $50 a year.

Equal Opportunities Section Affiliate Membership

www.floridabar.org (click "Inside The Bar" then "Sections & Divisions")

"Law school students and graduates, legal assistants and members of agencies, firms or companies dealing with or affecting minorities, women, and persons with disabilities are encouraged to join as affiliate members." Dues: $25 a year.

Public Interest Law Section Affiliate Membership

www.floridabar.org (click "Inside The Bar" then "Sections & Divisions")

Dues: $25 a year.

D. Other Statewide and Regional Associations

Academy of Florida Management Attorneys

theafma.com

Academy of Florida Trial Lawyers

See Florida Justice Association below

ACLU of Florida

786-363-2700

www.aclufl.org

American Academy of Matrimonial Lawyers, Florida Chapter

813-995-0970

www.aamlflorida.org

American Board of Trial Advocates, Florida Chapters

www.abota.org (click "Chapters")

American Immigration Lawyers Association, Florida Chapters

www.aila.org/content/default.aspx?bc=20618

Asian Pacific American Bar Association of South Florida

305-441-8900

apabasfla.org

Association of Corporate Counsel, Florida Chapters

www.acc.com/php/cms/index.php?id=23

Bankruptcy Bar Association—Southern District of Florida

www.bbasdfl.org

Black Lawyers Association (Miami-Dade County)

See Wilkie D. Ferguson Jr. Bar Association below

Caribbean Bar Association, South Florida Chapter

www.caribbeanbar.org

Caribbean Bar Association, South Florida Chapter, Associate Membership for Nonlawyers

www.caribbeanbar.org/members/register

Associate membership for nonlawyers: $30

Central Florida Association for Women Lawyers

www.cfawl.org

Central Florida Association of Criminal Defense Attorneys

www.floridabar.org

(click "Links" then "Voluntary Bar" then "County" then "Orange")

Central Florida Bankruptcy Law Association

www.cfbla.org

Central Florida Bankruptcy Law Association, Paralegal Associate Membership

www.cfbla.org

Associate membership for nonattorneys: $40. "By profession or occupation I . . . am a paralegal employed by or associated with a regular member."

Central Florida Gay & Lesbian Law Association

www.cfglla.org

Colombian-American Bar Association (Coral Gables)

305-448-0511

www.colbar.org

Cuban American Bar Association (Miami)
www.cabaonline.com

D.W. Perkins Bar Association (African-American; Jacksonville)
904-355-6002
www.dwperkinsbar.org

Eighth Judicial Circuit Bar Association
(Alachua, Baker, Bradford, Gilchrist, Levy, and Union Counties)
www.8jcba.org

Escambia-Santa Rosa Bar Association
www.esrba.com

Federal Bar Association, Florida Chapters
(Broward County, Gainesville, Jacksonville, Northwest Florida, Orlando, Palm Beach County, South Florida, Southwest Florida, Tallahassee, Tampa Bay)
www.fedbar.org/chapters.html

Florida Academy of Professional Mediators
www.tfapm.org

Florida Association for Women Lawyers
www.fawl.org

Florida Association of Attorney-CPAs
www.floridabar.org
(click "Links" then "Voluntary Bar" then "Statewide")
www.attorney-cpa.com
(click "National, Chapter & State")

Florida Association of County Attorneys
www.fl-counties.com/legal/faca.shtml

Florida Association of Police Attorneys
www.fapa-inc.org

Florida Association of Criminal Defense Lawyers
800-369-9503
www.facdl.org

Florida Association of Criminal Defense Lawyers Affiliate Membership
www.facdl.org/MemberCenter/Member_Center.html

Florida Bar Foundation
800-541-2195
www.flabarfndn.org

Florida Defense Lawyers Association
813-885-9888
www.fdla.org

Florida Government Bar Association
www.floridabar.org
(click "Links" then "Voluntary Bar" then "County" then "Leon")

Florida Justice Association
850-224-9403
www.floridajusticeassociation.org
www.aftl.org

Florida Justice Association, Paralegal Membership
850-224-9403
www.aftl.org/join.asp
"Your membership as a paralegal or legal assistant affords you the opportunity to gain from the experience of others in many ways: through intense legal seminars, through one-on-one discussions, and through access to a network of fellow paralegal and legal assistants across the state."

Florida Justice Association, Women's Caucus
850-224-9403
www.aftl.org/womensCaucus.asp

Florida Prosecuting Attorneys Association
850-488-3070
www.myfpaa.org

Florida Public Defender Association, Inc.
850-488-6850
www.flpda.org

Florida Trial Court Staff Attorneys Association
ftcsaa.org

F. Malcolm Cunningham Sr. Bar Association (African-American; West Palm Beach)
www.cunninghambar.org

Gay and Lesbian Lawyers Association of South Florida
www.google.com (type the name of the association as a search term)

George Edgecomb Bar Association (African-American; Tampa)
www.gebaonline.com

Haitian Lawyers Association
www.floridabar.org
(click "Links" then "Voluntary Bar" then "Regional")

Hispanic Bar Association, Central and Northeast Florida
www.floridabar.org
(click "Links" then "Voluntary Bar" then "Regional")

Intellectual Property Law Association of South Florida
www.floridabar.org
(click "Links" then "Voluntary Bar" then "Regional")
www.intellectualpropertyassociation.com/contact-us

Juvenile Justice Attorneys Association
www.floridabar.org
(click "Links" then "Voluntary Bar" then "Regional")

Josiah T. Walls Bar Association (African-American; Gainesville)
352-372-0519
www.floridabar.org/DIVCOM/PI/PIMasDir.nsf/ABARS? OpenView

National Employment Lawyers Association, Florida Chapter
800-631-7870
www.floridanela.org

National Employment Lawyers Association, Florida Chapter, Paraprofessional Membership
800-631-7870
www.floridanela.org/pdf/application.pdf
(Student/Paraprofessional Membership: $50)

Paul C. Perkins Bar Association (African-American; Orlando)
www.pcpbar.com

Puerto Rican Bar Association of Florida
www.floridabar.org
(click "Links" then "Voluntary Bar" then "Regional")

Southwest Florida Bankruptcy Professionals Association
www.floridabar.org
(click "Links" then "Voluntary Bar" then "Regional")

Third Judicial Circuit Bar Association, Lake City
www.floridabar.org
(click "Links" then "Voluntary Bar" then "Regional")

Trial Lawyer Section of the Florida Bar
www.flatls.org

Virgil Hawkins Florida Chapter National Bar Association (African-American)
www.vhfcnba.org

Wilkie D. Ferguson Jr. Bar Association
www.blacklawyerassociation-miami.com

Young Lawyers Division of the Florida Bar
www.flayld.org

E. Local Bar Associations

BRANDON
Brandon Bar Association
www.brandonbar.org

BREVARD COUNTY
Brevard County Bar Association
321-254-8801
www.brevardbar.org

BROWARD COUNTY
Broward County Bar Association
954-764-8040
www.browardbar.org

Broward County Hispanic Bar Association
www.browardcountyhispanicbar.com

Broward County Trial Lawyers Association
www.bctla.org/br

Broward County Women Lawyers' Association
www.bcwla.com

Broward Association of Criminal Defense Lawyers
www.floridabar.org
(click "Links" then "Voluntary Bar" then "County" then "Broward")

Broward Christian Legal Society
www.floridabar.org
(click "Links" then "Voluntary Bar" then "County" then "Broward")

Federal Bar Association, Broward Chapter
www.fedbar.org/browardcounty.html

CLEARWATER
Clearwater Bar Association
www.clwbar.org
www.clearwaterbar.org

COLLIER COUNTY
Collier County Bar Association
239-774-8711
www.colliercountybar.org

COLLIER COUNTY
Collier County Bar Association Associate Membership for Certified Legal Assistants
www.colliercountybar.org

Collier County Women's Bar Association
www.ccwba.org

CORAL GABLES
Coral Gables Bar Association
www.coralgablesbar.org

DADE COUNTY
Dade County Bar Association
305-371-2220
www.dadecountybar.org

Association of Corporate Counsel, Miami Chapter
www.acc.com
(type "Florida" in the search box)

Colombian-American Bar Association (Coral Gables)
305-448-0511
www.colbar.org

Dade County Defense Bar Association
www.floridabar.org
(click "Links" then "Voluntary Bar" then "County"
then "Dade")

Miami Beach Bar Association
www.miamibeachbar.org

Miami-Dade Justice Association
305-458-1298
www.miamidadejustice.org

Wilkie D. Ferguson Jr. Bar Association
www.blacklawyerassociation-miami.com

HILLSBOROUGH COUNTY
Hillsborough County Bar Association
813-226-6431
www.hillsbar.com

Brandon Bar Association
www.brandonbar.org

Carrollwood Community Bar Association
www.carrollwoodbar.com

Federal Bar Association, Tampa Bay Chapter
www.fedbar.org/tampabay.html

Hillsborough Association for Women Attorneys
www.hawl.org

INDIAN RIVER COUNTY
Indian River County Bar Association
www.irclaw.org

JACKSONVILLE
Jacksonville Bar Association
904-399-4486
www.jaxbar.org

D.W. Perkins Bar Association (African-American)
904-355-6002
www.dwperkinsbar.org

Federal Bar Association, Jacksonville Chapter
www.fedbar.org/jacksonville.html

Jackson Bankruptcy Bar Association
jaxbkybar.com

Jacksonville Trial Lawyers Association
www.floridabar.org
(click "Links" then "Voluntary Bar" then "Regional")

Jacksonville Women Lawyers Association
www.jwla.org

LEE COUNTY
Lee County Bar Association
239-334-0047

www.leebar.org

ORANGE COUNTY
Orange County Bar Association
407-422-4551
www.orangecountybar.org

Orange County Bar Association Paralegal Affiliate Membership
www.orangecountybar.org
www.orangecountybar.org/Prospective/join.asp

Central Florida Association for Women Lawyers
www.cfawl.org

Central Florida Bankruptcy Law Association
www.cfbla.org

Federal Bar Association, Orlando Chapter
www.fedbar.org/orlando.html

PALM BEACH COUNTY
Palm Beach County Bar Association
561-687-2800
www.palmbeachbar.org

Palm Beach County Justice Association
561-999-9490
www.pbctla.org

F. Malcolm Cunningham Sr. Bar Association
www.cunninghambar.org

Federal Bar Association—Palm Beach County Chapter
www.fedbar.org/palmbeachcounty.html

SARASOTA COUNTY
Sarasota County Bar Association
941-366-6703
www.sarasotabar.com

SAINT LUCIE COUNTY
St. Lucie County Bar Association
www.slcba.org

SAINT PETERSBURG
St. Petersburg Bar Association
727-823-7474
www.stpetebar.com

SOUTH PALM BEACH COUNTY
South Palm Beach County Bar Association
561-482-3838
www.southpalmbeachbar.org

South Palm Beach County Bar Association-Associates
561-482-3838
www.southpalmbeachbar.org
(Now accepting nonattorney/associate membership applications: $100)

TALLAHASSEE
Tallahassee Bar Association
www.tallahasseebar.org

Federal Bar Association, Tallahassee Chapter
www.fedbar.org/tallahassee.html

VOLUSIA COUNTY
Volusia County Bar Association
386-253-9471
www.volusiabar.org

WEST PASCO
West Pasco Bar Association
www.wpba.net

Other Bar Associations

For contact information on the following bar associations, go to *www.floridabar.org*

(click "Links" then "Voluntary Bar" then "County")

Bay County Bar Association

B'nai B'rith Justice Unit 5360

Cape Coral Bar Association

Capital City Hispanic Bar Association

Charlotte County Bar Association

Citrus County Bar Association

Clay County Bar Association

Flagler County Bar Association

Florida Government Bar Association

Gadsten County Bar Association

Hardee County Bar Association

Hernando County Bar Association

Hialeah-Miami Lakes Bar Association

Highlands County Bar Association

Hispanic Bar of Palm Beach County

Homestead Bar Association

Jacksonville Beaches Bar Association

Jefferson County Bar Association

Lake County Bar Association

Lakeland Bar Association

Manatee County Bar Association

Marion County Bar Association

Martin County Bar Association

Monroe County Bar Association

Nassau County Bar Association

North Dade Bar Association

Okeechobee Bar Association

Osceola County Bar Association

Pasco County Bar Association

Pinellas County Mid-County Bar Association

Pinellas County Trial Lawyers Bar Association

Plant City Bar Association

Polk County Trial Lawyers Bar Association

Port St. Lucie Bar Association

Putnam County Bar Association

Saint Johns County Bar Association

Seminole County Bar Association

Sumter County Bar Association

Upper Keys Bar Association

F. More Information

Florida Bar Associations
www.floridabar.org/DIVCOM/PI/PIMasDir.nsf/
 WBARS?OpenView
www.legaltrek.com/HELPSITE/States/State_Contents/
 Florida.htm

Lawyer Referral Services
www3.flabar.org/DIVPGM/lronline.nsf/wReferral6?OpenForm
www.abanet.org/legalservices/lris/directory
www.legal-aid.com/lawyer_referral_services.html#Florida

Directory of Florida Attorneys
www.attorneylocate.com/city.asp?city_statecode=FL
www.floridabar.org
(click "Find A Lawyer")
www.lawyers.findlaw.com/lawyer/state/Florida
www.lawyers.com/Florida/browse-by-city.html

Statistics on Florida Attorneys
www.abanet.org/marketresearch
www.abanet.org/marketresearch/resource.html

G. Something to Check

1. Find three bar sites that have the most comprehensive links to Florida law.
2. Find two bar sites that have useful information on the area of the law in which you work or hope to work.

APPENDIX A

Timeline: Disciplinary Proceedings against an Attorney

A. Introduction

In this section, we will outline the steps involved in bringing a complaint against a Florida attorney for violating one or more of the standards of conduct set forth in the Rules Regulating The Florida Bar. Before we begin, here is an overview of the punishments that can be imposed and the statistics on their imposition in the state.

The types of discipline, as specifically set out in Rule 3-5 of the Rules of Discipline in the Rules Regulating The Florida Bar, include:

- *Admonishment.* Admonishments or reprimands are issued for minor misconduct such as not communicating with clients or failing to diligently pursue a case. Rule 3-5.1(b) specifically states that the following are *not* considered minor in nature:
  - Misappropriation of client's funds or property
  - Loss of a person's money, legal rights, or valuable property rights
  - Prior public discipline of the attorney (in the past three years)
  - Prior discipline of the attorney (in the past five years) for misconduct of the "same nature"
  - Dishonesty, misrepresentation, deceit, or fraud
  - A felony

If, however, one of the above conditions exists but "unusual circumstances" are involved, the attorney may be admonished or diverted to a practice and professionalism enhancement program.

- *Probation.* The attorney is allowed to continue practicing law under certain conditions. The probation period may be for a definite period of time (not less than six months nor more than three years) or for an indefinite period of time.
- *Public reprimand.* The attorney is required to personally appear before the Supreme Court of Florida, the board of governors, a designated judge, or the referee for public reprimand. All public reprimands are reported in the *Southern Reporter* (the regional case reporter that contains Florida court opinions; see section 5.1 on Florida research).

- *Suspension.* The attorney remains a member of The Florida Bar but without the privilege of practicing law. Suspension can be for a definite period of time (not to exceed three years) or for an indefinite period of time. If an attorney is suspended for more than 90 days, proof of rehabilitation is required and passage of all or a portion of the Florida bar examination may be required.
- *Emergency suspension.* The attorney remains a member of The Florida Bar but without the privilege of practicing law, pending the outcome of final discipline.
- *Disbarment.* The attorney's status as a member of The Florida Bar is terminated. The attorney can apply for readmission five years from the date of disbarment unless the attorney has been permanently disbarred.

In addition to the above types of discipline, the Rules provide that an attorney may be required to notify the client, opposing counsel, and the court in which the attorney practices of the discipline imposed; forfeit fees; and pay restitution. In some cases, the Supreme Court may allow an attorney to resign from The Florida Bar rather than face discipline. If an attorney selects voluntary resignation, the same rules apply as for disbarment.

The Florida Bar, Rule 3-5.1, Rules Regulating The Florida Bar (2005). (*www.floridabar.org*; click "Lawyer Regulation," then "Rules Regulating The Florida Bar," then "Rules Of Discipline")

For statistics on discipline in Florida, see Exhibit A.1.

B. Timeline

The main participants in the disciplinary process are bar counsel (an employee of The Florida Bar), grievance committee (volunteers), referee (an appointed circuit or county court judge), and the Florida Supreme Court.

1. Prior to Filing a Complaint

Prior to filing a complaint, The Florida Bar recommends that a dissatisfied client consider taking the following actions:

EXHIBIT A.1	Discipline in Florida	
	2006–2007	1996–1997
Bar Population	81,534	56,379
Complaints Received	9,063	9,436
Disbarments	48	36
Suspensions	22	27
Public Reprimands	39	66
Disciplinary Resignations	0	36
Admonishments	74	88
Probations	22	71
Injunctions	1	4
Total Final Orders	391	428
Administration Cost of Discipline System	$9,462,926	$5,993,790
Number of Staff Attorneys	33	
Number of Staff Legal Assistants/Paralegals	10	

Source: www.floridabar.org (click "Lawyer Regulation" then "Lawyer Conduct" then "The Florida Bar Disciplinary Statistics")
www.abanet.org/cpr/discipline/sold/home.html

- Write a "non-threatening letter" to the attorney and explain the issue prompting the complaint. The purpose of this letter is twofold: It may result in the resolution of the issue or, if the issue remains unresolved, it will serve to "document" the client's good faith effort to resolve the issue prior to filing a "formal complaint."
- Contact the Bar's Attorney Consumer Assistance Program (ACAP) for assistance in resolving the issue at 866-352-0707 or
  www.floridabar.org (click "Public Information" then "Attorney Consumer Assistance Program")

A dissatisfied client may also consider using alternative ways of resolving disputes with attorneys such as the Bar's programs for grievance mediation (866-352-0707) and fee arbitration (850-561-5719).

2. Filing a Complaint

If the issue remains unresolved after taking the above steps, a formal complaint can be filed with the Florida Bar within six years from the time the issue constituting the complaint was discovered or should have been discovered. (It can be filed after six years if the complaint alleges theft or a felony.) The complaint must be in writing and made under oath. The complaint should be sent to the Attorney Consumer Assistance Program (ACAP).

www.floridabar.org
(click "Public Information" then "Consumer Information" then "Inquiry Concerning A Florida Lawyer")

Downloading the complaint form:
www.flabar.org

(click "Public Information" then "Attorney Consumer Assistance Program" then "Attorney Complaint Form")

3. Inquiry Becomes a Complaint; Investigation

The first step is the creation of an *inquiry file* to be reviewed by bar counsel. After reviewing the inquiry file, bar counsel may take one of the following actions:

- If it is determined that The Florida Bar does not have jurisdiction to investigate the alleged misconduct, the file is closed.
- If it is determined that The Florida Bar does have jurisdiction to investigate the alleged misconduct, a disciplinary file is created.

If a *disciplinary file* is created, the matter is no longer referred to as an *inquiry* but is referred to as a *complaint*. The person complaining is the complaining witness, not a party. Bar counsel does not represent the complaining witness.

Following further investigation, such as the review of a required written response by the attorney, the complaint may then be dismissed, classified as minor misconduct, or referred to a "grievance committee" for even further investigation.

4. Grievance Committee

Each circuit in Florida has at least one grievance committee comprised of at least three volunteer members, with one member of the three being a non-lawyer. The main purpose of the grievance committee is to decide "whether there is probable cause to believe a lawyer violated the professional conduct rules imposed by the Supreme Court of Florida and whether discipline against the lawyer appears to be warranted." Probable cause, as defined by The Florida Bar, is "a finding by an authorized agency that there is cause to believe that a member of The Florida Bar is guilty of misconduct justifying disciplinary action." (Rule 3-7.4.)

The grievance committee may require the attorney "to testify and to produce evidence." The attorney will be provided copies of "all materials" that the committee takes into consideration in making its determination. After the grievance committee's full investigation of the matter, it may take one of the following actions:

- Determine that probable cause does not exist and terminate the investigation (in some cases, a letter of advice may be provided to the attorney)
- Determine that minor misconduct does exist and recommend admonishment or diversion to a remedial program
- Determine that probable cause does exist

If the grievance committee finds probable cause, the most likely next step would be filing the complaint with the Supreme Court of Florida.

5. Referee

If a complaint is filed with the Supreme Court of Florida and if the attorney contests the complaint, a referee may be assigned to try the case. In accordance with Rule 3-7.6, the referee's findings of fact are filed with the Supreme Court in the form of a report and recommendation.

6. Supreme Court of Florida

Unless it is appealed, a referee's report that does not recommend probation, public reprimand, suspension, disbarment, or resignation pending disciplinary proceedings is considered final. If any of the foregoing is recommended in the referee's report, the Supreme Court must commence its review within 60 days of service of the report on the respondent and The Florida Bar (Rule 3-7.7). The Florida Constitution (Article V, § 15) provides that the Supreme Court has "exclusive jurisdiction" and is the final authority in making the determination regarding the discipline of Florida attorneys.

C. Clients' Security Fund

Aggrieved clients have a number of options:

- File an ethics complaint against the attorney (see above)
- Sue the attorney for civil malpractice (e.g., negligence)
- File claim under the Clients' Security Fund

The Clients' Security Fund was established by the Board of Governors of The Florida Bar for the purpose of providing compensation (up to $50,000) to clients who have suffered financial or property losses due to the misappropriation, embezzlement, or other wrongful taking or conversion by a licensed Florida attorney acting in a fiduciary or legal capacity. (A designated portion of annual dues to The Florida Bar support this fund.) Since its inception in 1967, the Fund has awarded $6,858,856 to 2,550 claimants. (Bruce M. Smith, *Clients' Security Fund, Annual Report*, 79-Jun FLBJ 44.)

To be considered for reimbursement by the Fund, application must be made to:

Public Service Programs
The Florida Bar
651 E. Jefferson Street
Tallahassee, FL 32399-2300
850-561-5812

www.floridabar.org
(click "Public Information" then "Clients' Security Fund")

D. Grading the Florida Disciplinary System

HALT: An Organization of Americans for Legal Reform (*www.halt.org*) grades the disciplinary system of every state by issuing its Lawyer Discipline Report Card. The 2006 grade it gave Florida was C+. See Exhibit A.2. Its 2002 grade was also C+.

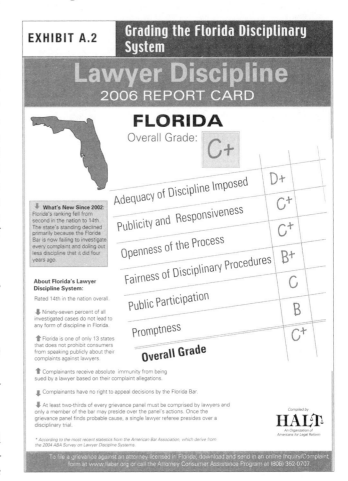

EXHIBIT A.2 | Grading the Florida Disciplinary System

Source: HALT (*www.halt.org/reform_projects/lawyer_accountability/report_card_2006/pdf/FL_LDRC_06.pdf*)

E.   More Information

Overview
www.floridabar.org (click "Lawyer Regulation")

Consumer Information
www.floridabar.org (click "Public Information")

Disciplinary Statistics
www.abanet.org/cpr/discipline/sold/home.html
www.floridabar.org (click "Lawyer Regulation" then "Lawyer Conduct" then "The Florida Bar Disciplinary Statistics")

Report Card on Effectiveness of Florida's System of Disciplining Attorneys (2006)

www.halt.org/reform_projects/lawyer_accountability/ report_card_2006

Report Card on Effectiveness of Florida's System of Disciplining Attorneys (2002)

www.halt.org/reform_projects/lawyer_accountability/ report_card

F. Something to Check

1. What are the factors used by HALT (see site above) to determine the B+ grade it gave Florida for the fairness of its disciplinary procedures?

2. Find and summarize (brief) an opinion of the Supreme Court of Florida in which an attorney was disciplined. (On finding opinions, see sections 4.2 and 5.1.)

Legal System

A. Introduction

In this section, we present an overview of Florida state government. More detailed information about the major components of our state government is available in:

- Section 4.2 on our state courts
- Section 4.4 on the state legislature
- Section 4.5 on administrative agencies in the executive branch
- Section 4.6 on county and city government

B. Overview

The Florida Constitution divides the powers of government into three branches: executive, legislative, and judicial (*www.myflorida.com*). There is, however, some overlap in this allocation of powers such as the state senate's power to sit as a court to try some elected officers who have been impeached for misconduct in office. Exhibit 4.1A presents an overview of the major units of our state government.

C. Executive, Legislative, and Judicial Branches

Executive Branch

Governor

The supreme executive power of the state is vested in the governor, whose constitutional mandate is to see "that the laws be faithfully executed" (Art. IV, § 1(a),

Fla. Const.). He or she is the chief administrative officer of the state responsible for planning and budgeting. In matters of clemency, the governor can "with the approval of two members of the cabinet, grant full or conditional pardons, restore civil rights, commute punishment, and remit fines and forfeitures for offenses." (Art. IV, § 8.)

In addition to strictly executive functions, the governor has an important role in the state's legislative process. He or she submits to the legislature the annual budget and sets forth statements of the state government's anticipated revenues and expenses. All bills enacted by the legislature are subject to the governor's approval before becoming law. The governor has the power to veto bills; a veto can be set aside only by a two-thirds vote of both the state house of representatives and the state senate. The governor may exercise selective veto powers over general appropriation bills to eliminate any appropriation while approving others covered in the same bill. The common name for this practice is the *line-item veto*.

Governor
The Capitol
400 South Monroe Street
Tallahassee, FL 32399
850-488-7146; 850-488-4441
www.flgov.com

Governor's Staff
www.flgov.com/ governors_staff
Office of Cabinet Affairs
850-488-5152
www.flgov.com/cabinet_affairs

Other Statewide Elected Offices

The governor's cabinet is comprised of an attorney general, a chief financial officer, and a commissioner of agriculture, all elected statewide (Fla. Const. Art. IV, § 4).

Lieutenant Governor
850-488-7146
ltgov.flgov.com/meet_lt_gov

The only constitutional duty of the lieutenant governor is to become the governor should that office become vacant due to death, impeachment trial, or incapacity. The lieutenant governor serves as a policy adviser to (and carries out duties delegated by) the governor. He or she assists with gubernatorial appointments, negotiations with the state legislature, and coordination among state agencies.

EXHIBIT 4.1A	Florida State Government	
EXECUTIVE BRANCH	**LEGISLATIVE BRANCH**	**JUDICIARY BRANCH**
• Governor • Lieutenant Governor • Attorney General • Chief Financial Officer • Commissioner of Agriculture • Numerous other departments, agencies, and boards	• State Senate • State House of Representatives • Legislative Committees • Office of Program Policy Analysis and Government Accountability (OPPAGA)	• Florida Supreme Court • Florida District Courts of Appeals • Florida Circuit Courts • Florida County Courts

Attorney General
850-414-3300
myfloridalegal.com

The attorney general is the chief state legal officer. His or her responsibilities include:

- Enforcing state consumer protection and antitrust laws
- Civilly prosecuting criminal racketeering
- Representing the state when convicted defendants appeal their convictions, including capital murder cases
- Issuing formal legal opinions at the request of various public officials on questions relating to the application of state law
- Defending the constitutionality of statutes duly enacted by the legislature
- Exercising (through a statewide prosecutor) concurrent jurisdiction with the state attorneys to prosecute crimes occurring in two or more judicial circuits

Chief Financial Officer
850-413-3100
www.fldfs.com

The chief financial officer oversees the Department of Financial Services, which is responsible for assisting consumers in matters of financial services, including banking, securities, and insurance. Responsibilities that fall directly under the chief financial officer include:

- Overseeing the state's accounting and auditing functions
- Monitoring the investment of state funds
- Investigating fraud, including identity theft and insurance fraud
- Overseeing cemeteries and funeral homes that sell preneed contracts
- Licensing and providing oversight of insurance agents and agencies
- Operating the Division of Workers' Compensation
- Investigating fires and suppressing arson (as state fire marshal)

Commissioner of Agriculture
850-488-3022
www.doacs.state.fl.us

The commissioner of agriculture runs the Department of Agriculture and Consumer Services. Responsibilities of the department include:

- Ensuring the safety and wholesomeness of food and other consumer products through inspection and testing programs
- Protecting consumers from unfair and deceptive business practices and providing consumer information
- Assisting Florida's farmers and agricultural industries with the production and promotion of agricultural products
- Conserving and protecting the state's agricultural and natural resources by reducing wildfires, promoting environmentally safe agricultural practices, and managing public lands

State Agencies, Departments, and Commissions

For a list of the major state agencies, departments, and commissions, see section 4.5 and the following sites:

www.myflorida.com/directory
www.myflorida.com/taxonomy/government
dlis.dos.state.fl.us/fgils/government.html

Legislative Branch

Under the Florida Constitution, the legislative power of the state is vested in the Florida Legislature, which consists of the Senate and House of Representatives. Legislators are elected by district: one senator in each senatorial district and one member of the house from each representative district.

For an overview of the legislative process (how a bill becomes a law), see section 4.4.

Florida House of Representatives
850-488-1157
www.myfloridahouse.gov

Committees of the Florida House of Representatives
www.myfloridahouse.gov
(click "Councils & Committees")

Florida Senate
850-488-4371; 800-342-1827
www.flsenate.gov

Committees of the Florida Senate
www.flsenate.gov/Committees

Office of Program Policy Analysis and Government Accountability (OPPAGA)
850-488-0021
www.oppaga.state.fl.us

The Office of Program Policy Analysis and Government Accountability (OPPAGA) provides objective research and analysis to the Florida legislature. The research concentrates on state government programs, agencies, and school district performance. In addition, the OPPAGA provides assistance to legislators, produces a weekly newsletter for policymakers, and produces an electronic encyclopedia of evaluations of all major state programs.

Judicial Branch

The judicial power of the State of Florida is vested in the Supreme Court, district courts of appeals, circuit courts, and county courts. For details on the jurisdiction and the lines of appeal in the Florida state court system, see section 4.2.

Florida Supreme Court
850-488-0125
www.floridasupremecourt.org

District Courts of Appeal
www.flcourts.org/courts/dca/dca.shtml

Circuit Courts
www.flcourts.org/courts/circuit/circuit.shtml

County Courts
www.flcourts.org/courts/county/county.shtml

Office of the State Courts Administrator
850-922-5081
www.flcourts.org/courts/crtadmin/crtadmin.shtml

Exhibit 4.1B presents a detailed listing of state and local government offices.

D. More Information

State Government Home Page
www.myflorida.com

State Government Overview
www.myflorida.com/directory
www.legaltrek.com/HELPSITE/States/Florida.htm

Functions of the Executive Office
www.flgov.com/summary_functions

Online State Government Phone Directory
411.myflorida.com

State Constitution
www.leg.state.fl.us
(click "Statutes, Constitution, & Laws of Florida")

E. Something to Check

1. Use the online resources in this section to determine last year's state government deficit (or surplus) in Florida.

2. Identify any one problem that you think exists in your community. Use the online sites in this section to identify government entities (e.g., bureaus, departments, committees) or persons in the executive and legislative branches that would probably have authority to solve or address this problem.

EXHIBIT 4.1B State and Local Government Branches, Agencies, and Offices

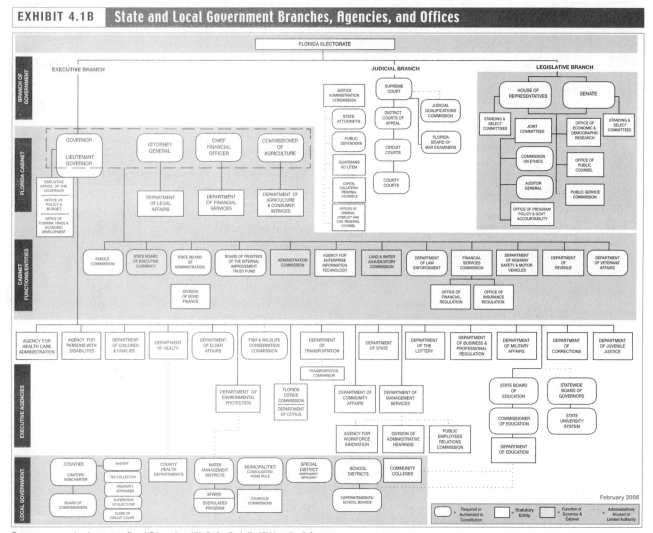

Source: *www.ebudget.state.fl.us/(S(wpzims45io3pfee5c1zjie45))/motherinfo.aspx*
www.ebudget.state.fl.us/(S(wpzims45io3pfee5c1zjie45))/ExecBranchOrgChartJan2008.pdf

A. Introduction

The major Florida state courts are as follows:

- Supreme Court of Florida
- District Courts of Appeal
- Circuit Courts
- County Courts

See also the following related sections in the book:

- Florida state legal research (section 5.1)
- Citation of legal materials (section 5.2)
- Timeline of civil litigation (section 6.1)
- Timeline of criminal litigation (section 6.4)
- Selected rules of procedure (section 6.2)
- Civil complaints (section 7.4)
- Appellate briefs (section 7.4)

Exhibit 4.2A summarizes the jurisdiction and lines of appeal among the Florida state courts.

B. Florida State Courts

Supreme Court of Florida

There are seven justices on the Florida Supreme Court, one chief justice and six justices. They reach the court (and remain there) through a *merit retention system*. Under this system, the governor appoints new justices from a list of three to six names submitted by the Judicial Nominating Commission. The governor must select from the list. Once appointed, justices eventually must face the voters in a "yes" or "no" vote as to whether they should remain in office. New justices face their first merit retention vote in the next general statewide election that occurs more than one year after their appointment. If retained, the justice serves a six-year term. Justices then will again face an up-or-down vote in the general election occurring just before the six-year term expires. The Florida Constitution establishes a mandatory retirement age for justices that occurs on or after their 70th birthdays.

Supreme Court of Florida
500 South Duval St.
Tallahassee, FL 32399
850-488-0125
www.floridasupremecourt.org

Supreme Court: Jurisdiction and Functions

Mandatory Jurisdiction. The Supreme Court must review:

- Final orders imposing death sentences
- District court decisions declaring a state statute or provision of the state constitution invalid
- Bond validations
- Certain orders of the Public Service Commission on utility rates and services

Discretionary Jurisdiction. The Supreme Court can review:

- Any decision of a district court of appeal that expressly declares valid a state statute, construes a provision of the state or federal constitution, affects a class of constitutional or state officers, or directly conflicts with a decision of another district court or of the Supreme Court on the same question of law
- Certain categories of judgments, decisions, and questions of law certified to it by the district courts of appeal and federal appellate courts

Writs. It can issue the extraordinary writs of prohibition, mandamus, quo warranto, and habeas corpus, and all other writs necessary to the complete exercise of its jurisdiction.

Advisory Opinions. It renders advisory opinions to the governor, upon request, on questions relating to the governor's constitutional duties and powers.

Regulation of Florida Courts. It promulgates rules governing practice and procedure in all Florida courts, subject to the power of the legislature to repeal any rule by a two-thirds vote of its membership.

Regulation of Attorneys. It has exclusive authority to regulate the admission and discipline of attorneys in Florida. In the exercise of this authority, it has adopted the Rules of Professional Conduct, established the Board of Bar Examiners to administer the admissions process, and created The Florida Bar to superintend bar governance.

Regulation of Judicial Officers. It has authority to discipline and remove judicial officers through its Code of Judicial Conduct and the Judicial Qualifications Commission.

Supreme Court: Internal Operating Procedures
www.floridasupremecourt.org/pub_info/documents/IOPs.pdf
www.floridasupremecourt.org/pub_info/documents/juris.pdf

Supreme Court: Florida Rules of Appellate Procedure
www.4dca.org/applellate%20rules.pdf
www.floridasupremecourt.org/decisions/barrules.shtml

Supreme Court: Biographies of Justices
www.floridasupremecourt.org/justices/index.shtml

Supreme Court: Schedule
www.floridasupremecourt.org/pub_info/calendar.pdf

EXHIBIT 4.2A **Florida State Court System**

Legend

= Appellate level

= Trial level

COLR = Court of Last Resort
IAC = Intermediate Appellate Court
GJC = General Jurisdiction Court
LJC = Limited Jurisdiction Court
A = Appeal from Admin. Agency
↑ = Route of appeal

Supreme Court   COLR
7 justices sit en banc   A

Case Types:
- Mandatory jurisdiction in civil, capital criminal, criminal administrative agency, juvenile, disciplinary, advisory opinion cases
- Discretionary jurisdiction in civil, non-capital criminal, administrative agency, juvenile, advisory opinion, original proceeding, interlocutory decision cases

District Courts of Appeal (5 courts)   IAC
62 judges sit in 3-judge panels   A

Case Types:
- Mandatory jurisdiction in civil, non-capital criminal, administrative agency, juvenile, original proceeding, interlocutory decision cases
- Discretionary jurisdiction in civil, non-capital criminal, juvenile, original proceeding, interlocutory decision cases

Circuit Court (20 circuits)   GJC
527 judges
Jury trials except in appeals

Case Types:
- Tort, contract, real property ($15,001–no maximum), miscellaneous civil.
- Exclusive mental health, probate/estate, civil appeals
- Exclusive domestic relations
- Exclusive felony, criminal appeals
- Juvenile

County Court (67 counties)   LJC
280 judges

Case Types:
- Tort contract, real property ($5,001–$15,000), miscellaneous civil.
- Exclusive small claims (up to $5,000)
- Exclusive misdemeanor, preliminary hearings
- Exclusive traffic/other violation jurisdiction, except parking (which is handled administratively)

Source: Court Statistics Project, State Court Caseload Statistics, 2004 (National Center for State Courts 2005)
(*www.ncsconline.org/D_Research/Ct_Struct/state_inc.asp?STATE=FL*)

Supreme Court: Opinions
www.floridasupremecourt.org/decisions/index.shtml
www.findlaw.com/11stategov/fl/flca.html
www.law.ufl.edu/opinions/supreme
www.law.fsu.edu/library/flsupct

Supreme Court: Webcasts of Oral Arguments
wfsu.org/gavel2gavel
www.floridasupremecourt.org/pub_info/press.shtml

Supreme Court: Appellate Briefs (Since 1987)
www.law.fsu.edu/library/flsupct

Supreme Court: Appellate Briefs (Font and Point Size)

All briefs that are computer-generated are to be submitted in either Times New Roman 14-point font or Courier New 12-point font. These are the only font types that are acceptable. Also, all briefs that are computer-generated shall contain a certificate of compliance signed by the counsel, or the party if unrepresented, certifying that the brief complies with the font requirements of this rule. This certification shall be included right after the certificate of service. Florida Rule of Appellate Procedure 9.210(a) (*www.floridasupremecourt.org/clerk/faq.shtml*).

Supreme Court: Employment
www.floridasupremecourt.org/employment/index.shtml

Florida District Courts of Appeal

The District Courts of Appeal (DCA) are headquartered in Tallahassee, Lakeland, Miami, West Palm Beach, and Daytona Beach. Cases are reviewed by three-judge panels. District court judges serve terms of six years and are eligible for successive terms under a merit retention vote of the electors in their districts.

District Courts: Jurisdiction

The district courts of appeal can:

- Hear appeals from final judgments
- Review certain non-final orders
- Review final actions taken by state agencies in carrying out the duties of the executive branch of government
- Issue the extraordinary writs of certiorari, prohibition, mandamus, quo warranto, habeas corpus, and other writs necessary to the complete exercise of their jurisdiction

First District Court of Appeal, Tallahassee

First District Court of Appeal
301 S. Martin Luther King Blvd.
Tallahassee, FL 32399
850-487-1000; 850-488-6151
www.1dca.org

First District Court of Appeals: Biographies of Judges
www.1dca.org/judges.html

First District Court of Appeals: Calendar and Docket
calendar.1dca.org
199.242.69.70/pls/ds/ds_docket_search?pscourt=1

First District Court of Appeals: Opinions
opinions.1dca.org
opinions.1dca.org/written
opinions.1dca.org/written/archiveframe.htm
www.findlaw.com/11stategov/fl/flca.html

First District Court of Appeals: Florida Rules of Appellate Procedure
www.floridasupremecourt.org/decisions/barrules.shtml
www.4dca.org/applellate%20rules.pdf

First District Court of Appeals: Filing Procedures
www.1dca.org/filings.html
www.1dca.org/notice.pdf

First District Court of Appeals: E-Access
www.1dca.org/eaccess.shtml

First District Court of Appeals: Employment
www.1dca.org/jobs.html

Second District Court of Appeal, Lakeland and Tampa

Second District Court of Appeal
1005 East Memorial Blvd.
Lakeland, FL 33801
863-499-2290
www.2dca.org

Second District Court of Appeal
1700 North Tampa St., Ste 300
Tampa, FL 33602
813-272-3430

Second District Court of Appeal: Biographies of Judges
www.2dca.org/Judges/judges.shtml

Second District Court of Appeal: Calendar and Docket
www.2dca.org/Clerk/clerks_office.shtml
199.242.69.70/pls/ds/ds_docket_search

Second District Court of Appeal: Opinions
www.2dca.org/opinions/opinions.shtml
www.findlaw.com/11stategov/fl/flca.html

Second District Court of Appeal: Procedures
www.2dca.org/Clerk/clerks_office.shtml

Second District Court of Appeals: Florida Rules of Appellate Procedure
www.floridasupremecourt.org/decisions/barrules.shtml

Second District Court of Appeal: E-Mail Filing
www.2dca.org/Clerk/clerks_office.shtml

Pro Se Appellate Handbook: Representing Yourself on Appeal
www.flabarappellate.org/asp/pro_sehandbook.asp

Second District Court of Appeal: Employment
www.2dca.org/Employment/employment.shtml

Third District Court of Appeal, Miami

Third District Court of Appeal
2001 SW 117 Ave.
Miami, FL 33175-1716
305-229-3200
www.3dca.flcourts.org

Third District Court of Appeal: Biographies of Judges
www.3dca.flcourts.org
(click "Judges")

Third District Court of Appeal: Calendar and Docket
www.3dca.flcourts.org
(click "Clerk's Office")

Third District Court of Appeal: Procedures
www.3dca.flcourts.org
(click "Clerk's Office" then "General Information")

Third District Court of Appeal: Opinions
www.3dca.flcourts.org
(click "Opinions")
www.findlaw.com/11stategov/fl/flca.html

Third District Court of Appeals: Florida Rules of Appellate Procedure
www.floridasupremecourt.org/decisions/barrules.shtml
www.4dca.org/appllellate%20rules.pdf

Third District Court of Appeal: Employment
www.3dca.flcourts.org
(click "Clerk's Office")

Fourth District Court of Appeal, West Palm Beach

Fourth District Court of Appeal
1525 Palm Beach Lakes Blvd.
West Palm Beach, FL 33401
561-242-2000
www.4dca.org

Fourth District Court of Appeal: Biographies of Judges
www.4dca.org/judgesfrm.html

Fourth District Court of Appeal: Calendar
www.4dca.org/calendarfrm.html

Fourth District Court of Appeal: Procedures
www.4dca.org/geniformfrm.html

Fourth District Court of Appeal: Court Forms
www.4dca.org/policiesfrm.html

Fourth District Court of Appeal: Opinions
www.4dca.org/recentopfrm.html
www.findlaw.com/11stategov/fl/flca.html
199.242.69.27/SCRIPTS/texis.exe/webinator/search?pr=4DCA

Fourth District Court of Appeals: Florida Rules of Appellate Procedure
www.4dca.org/appllellate%20rules.pdf
www.floridasupremecourt.org/decisions/barrules.shtml

Fourth District Court of Appeal: Understanding the Appellate Process
www.4dca.org/geniformfrm.html

Fourth District Court of Appeal: Unemployment Compensation Appeals
www.4dca.org/geniformfrm.html

Fourth District Court of Appeal: Employment
www.4dca.org/employment.html

Fifth District Court of Appeal, Daytona Beach

Fifth District Court of Appeal
300 South Beach St.
Daytona Beach, FL 32114
386-947-1500; 386-255-8600
www.5dca.org

Fifth District Court of Appeal: Biographies of Judges
www.5dca.org/JudgesFrame.htm

Fifth District Court of Appeal: Calendar and Docket
www.5dca.org
(click "Oral Argument Calendar")
199.242.69.70/pls/ds/ds_docket_search?pscourt=5

Fifth District Court of Appeal: Procedures
www.5dca.org/Clerk/ClerkFrameset.htm
(click "Notice to Attorneys and Parties")

Fifth District Court of Appeal: Opinions
www.5dca.org/Opinions/OpinionFrameset.htm
www.findlaw.com/11stategov/fl/flca.html

Fifth District Court of Appeals: Florida Rules of Appellate Procedure
www.floridasupremecourt.org/decisions/barrules.shtml
www.4dca.org/appllellate%20rules.pdf

Fifth District Court of Appeal: Employment
www.5dca.org
(click "Employment")

Florida Circuit Courts

The 20 circuit courts in Florida have both trial and appellate jurisdiction. Circuit court judges are elected by the voters of the circuits in non-partisan, contested elections. They serve for six-year terms and are subject to the same disciplinary standards and procedures as Supreme Court justices and district court judges.

Circuit Courts: Jurisdiction

Trial Jurisdiction of Circuit Courts

Circuit courts have general trial jurisdiction over matters not assigned by statute to the county courts. Specifically:

- Original jurisdiction over civil disputes involving more than $15,000
- Controversies involving the estates of decedents, minors, and persons adjudicated as incapacitated
- Cases relating to juveniles
- Criminal prosecutions for all felonies
- Tax disputes
- Actions to determine the title and boundaries of real property
- Suits for declaratory judgments (to determine the legal rights or responsibilities of parties under the terms of written instruments, laws, or regulations before a dispute arises and leads to litigation)

- Requests for injunctions to prevent persons or entities from acting in a manner that is asserted to be unlawful

Appellate Jurisdiction of Circuit Courts

Circuit courts hear appeals from county court cases and have the power to issue the extraordinary writs of certiorari, prohibition, mandamus, quo warranto, habeas corpus, and all other writs necessary to the complete exercise of their jurisdiction.

Circuit Courts: Web Sites

www.flcourts.org/courts/circuit/circuit.shtml
www.17th.flcourts.org/html/florida_judicial_sites.html

The locations of the circuit courts are presented in Exhibit 4.2B.

| EXHIBIT 4.2B | Florida Circuit Courts |

1st	Escambia, Okaloosa, Santa Rose, Walton
2nd	Franklin, Gadsden, Jefferson, Leon, Liberty, Wakulla
3rd	Columbia, Dixie, Hamilton, Lafayette, Madison, Suwanee, Taylor
4th	Clay, Duval, Nassau
5th	Citrus, Hernando, Lake, Mairon, Sumter
6th	Pasco, Pinellas
7th	Flagler, Putnam, St. Johns, Volusia
8th	Alachua, Baker, Bradford, Gilchrist, Levy, Union
9th	Orange, Osceola
10th	Hardee, Highlands, Polk
11th	Dade
12th	Desoto, Manatee, Sarasota
13th	Hillsborough
14th	Bay, Calhoun, Gulf, Holmes, Jackson, Washington
15th	Palm Beach
16th	Monroe
17th	Broward
18th	Brevard, Seminole
19th	Indian River, Martin, Okeechobee, St. Lucie
20th	Charlotte, Collier, Glades, Hendry, Lee

Source: *www.jud10.org/circuits.htm*
www.flcourts.org/gen_public/family/self_help/map.shtml

Florida County Courts

Florida has 67 county courts, one for each county. County judges serve six-year terms. They are subject to the same disciplinary standards, and to the jurisdiction of the Judicial Qualifications Commission, as all other judicial officers.

County Courts: Jurisdiction

The trial jurisdiction of county courts consists of:

- Civil disputes involving $15,000 or less
- Small claims (up to $5,000)

- Traffic offenses
- Less serious criminal matters (misdemeanors)

County Courts: Web Sites

www.countyjudges.com/judicial.htm
www.flcourts.org/courts/county/county.shtml
www.countyjudges.com/Judges/index.htm

Small Claims

www.jud10.org/CountyCourt/SmallClaims/claims.htm
www.circuit8.org/sc
www.fllawonweb.com/SmallClaims.htm
www.consumeraffairs.com/consumerism/small_fl.html

| C. | **More Information** |

Overview

www.flcourts.org
www.floridasupremecourt.org/pub_info/system2.shtml
www.floridasupremecourt.org/pub_info/documents/juris.pdf
www.legalengine.com/state_trial_appellate_district_supreme_courts/florida.html

Court Statistics

www.flcourts.org/gen_public/stats/index.shtml
www.flcourts.org/gen_public/stats/bin/Factsheet1.pdf
www.ncsconline.org/D_Research/csp/CSP_Main_Page.html
(select "Florida")

Court Forms

www.flcourts.org/gen_public/family/forms_rules

Drug Court

www.ninja9.org/courts/Drug/DrugCourt.htm
www.flcourts.org/gen_public/family/drug_court/index.shtml

Teen Court

www.flteencourt.net

Court Employment

www.flcourts.org/gen_public/employment/index.shtml

Wikipedia on Florida State Courts

en.wikipedia.org/wiki/Florida_Supreme_Court
en.wikipedia.org/wiki/Category:Florida_state_courts
en.wikipedia.org/wiki/Category:Florida_appellate_courts

| D. | **Something to Check** |

1. Go to the sites that give you online access to court opinions of the Florida Supreme Court. (See sites above and those in section 5.1.) Use the search features of the sites to find an opinion on any broad legal topic, e.g., capital punishment or adoption. Summarize (brief) what the opinion says about your topic.
2. Go to the web sites of any three trial courts mentioned in this section. For the same general kind of litigant filing (e.g., a complaint, an amendment to a prior filing) state the filing fee in each of the three courts.

3. For one of the five District Courts of Appeal, go to the biographies of the judges. Pick one judge. Identify a prior job of this judge that might indicate a possible conservative or liberal philosophy of deciding cases. Explain your answer.

4.3 Federal Courts in Florida

- A. Introduction
- B. Federal Courts
- C. PACER
- D. More Information
- E. Something to Check

A. Introduction

There are four types of federal courts either sitting in Florida or with jurisdiction over the state (not including the U.S. Supreme Court):

- U.S. Court of Appeals for the Eleventh Circuit
- U.S. District Courts (Southern District, Middle District, and Northern District)
- U.S. Bankruptcy Courts (Southern District, Middle
- District, and Northern District)
- U.S. Immigration Courts

In this section we present an overview of these courts, how they operate, and some of the major resources that are available when working with them.

Links to Most Courts Covered in This Section
www.ca11.uscourts.gov/links/index.php

For related sections in this book, see also:

- Section 6.3 (comparison of state and federal court procedures)
- Section 7.2 (federal court complaint)

B. Federal Courts

U.S. Court of Appeals for the Eleventh Circuit

The United States is divided geographically into 11 numbered federal judicial circuits (also called regional circuits). Each circuit has a court of appeals (the U.S. Court of Appeals for the First Circuit, the U.S. Court of Appeals for the Second Circuit, etc.). These federal courts of appeals are intermediate appellate courts just below the U.S. Supreme Court. In addition to the 11 numbered circuits, there are two other circuits: the District of Columbia Circuit and the Federal Circuit, both located in Washington, DC. (The Federal Circuit is a separate and unique court of appeals that has nationwide jurisdiction in specialized cases.)

Each of the 50 states (plus the territories of Guam, Puerto Rico, and the U.S. Virgin Islands) is assigned to one of the 11 numbered circuits. The states of Florida, Alabama, and Georgia are in the Eleventh Circuit. The court of appeals for our circuit is the U.S. Court of Appeals for the Eleventh Circuit, sometimes abbreviated as CA11 or 11th Cir.

The U.S. Court of Appeals for the Eleventh Circuit hears appeals (1) from the U.S. district courts in Florida, Alabama, and Georgia, and (2) from the U.S. Tax Court and from certain federal administrative agencies where the non-governmental parties are from one of the three states that make up the Eleventh Circuit. The other regional circuits do the same for their circuits. Decisions of the U.S. courts of appeals are final except as they are subject to review on writ of certiorari by the U.S. Supreme Court. Judges on the court of appeals have lifetime tenure; they are nominated by the president and confirmed by the U.S. Senate.

11th Circuit: Address
United States Court of Appeals, Eleventh Circuit
Elbert P. Tuttle Court of Appeals Building
56 Forsyth St. N.W.
Atlanta, GA 30303
404-335-6100
www.ca11.uscourts.gov

11th Circuit: Judges
www.ca11.uscourts.gov/about/judges.php

11th Circuit: Opinions
www.ca11.uscourts.gov/opinions
www.findlaw.com/casecode/courts/11th.html
www.law.cornell.edu/federal/opinions.html
www.law.emory.edu/11circuit

11th Circuit: PACER login
800-676-6856
pacer.login.uscourts.gov/cgi-bin/login.pl?court_id=11ca

11th Circuit: Rules
Federal Rules of Appellate Procedure (FRAP)
www.ca11.uscourts.gov
(click "Rules/Addenda" then "FRCP")
www.uscourts.gov/rules/appel2007.pdf
www.law.cornell.edu/rules/frap

Eleventh Circuit Rules; Eleventh Circuit Internal Operating Procedures (IOP)
www.ca11.uscourts.gov/rules

11th Circuit: Forms
www.ca11.uscourts.gov/documents
www.ca11.uscourts.gov/documents/cja.php

11th Circuit: Briefing and Filing Instructions
www.ca11.uscourts.gov/offices/filing2.php

Checklist for Appellate Briefs
(covers colors, length restrictions, etc.)
www.ca11.uscourts.gov/documents/pdfs/BriefsChecklist.pdf

11th Circuit: Common Fees

For docketing an appeal: $450
Search (and certification) of court records: $26
Reproducing records: $0.50 per page
Opinions: $4.00 each copy
Attorney admission to 11th Circuit Bar: $170
www.ca11.uscourts.gov/about/fees.php

11th Circuit: Law Library

404-335-6500
www.ca11.uscourts.gov/library

11th Circuit: Lower Courts

www.ca11.uscourts.gov/links/index.php

U.S. District Courts

U.S. district courts exist within the judicial districts that are part of the regional circuits. In the 50 states, there are 89 district courts. Each state has at least one district court. Florida has three: Southern District, Middle District, and Northern District. In addition to a district court for the District of Columbia, the Commonwealth of Puerto Rico has a district court with jurisdiction corresponding to that of district courts in the various states. Finally, district courts also exist in the territories of the Virgin Islands, Guam, and the Northern Mariana Islands for a total of 94 district courts in the federal judicial system.

U.S. district courts are trial courts of general federal jurisdiction. Within limits set by Congress and the Constitution, they can hear nearly all categories of federal cases, including both civil and criminal matters. Typically, federal courts hear civil cases in which the United States is a party or those involving the U.S. Constitution, laws enacted by Congress, treaties, and laws relating to navigable waters. Examples include bankruptcy and violations of federal environmental laws. Another large source of civil cases in district courts are those involving disputes between citizens of different states (diversity of citizenship) if the amount in dispute exceeds $75,000. Federal criminal cases in district courts are filed by the U.S. attorney who represents the United States. Examples of federal crimes prosecuted in district court include illegal importation of drugs and certain categories of bank fraud.

At present, each district court has from 2 to 28 federal district judgeships, depending on the amount of judicial work within its boundaries. Only one judge is usually required to hear and decide a case in a district court, but in limited cases, three judges are called together to comprise the court. Judges of district courts have lifetime tenure; they are nominated by the president and confirmed by the U.S. Senate.

Each district court has one or more magistrate and bankruptcy judges, a clerk, a U.S. attorney, a U.S. marshal, probation officers, and court reporters. A United States magistrate judge is a federal trial judge appointed for a term of eight years by the life-tenured judges of a district court. Magistrates do not have all the powers of a district judge. The latter can assign some trials to magistrates upon consent of the parties.

Cases from a district court are reviewable on appeal by the U.S. court of appeals in the circuit where the district court sits.

As indicated, there are three United States district courts sitting in Florida:

- U.S. District Court, Southern District of Florida
- U.S. District Court, Middle District of Florida
- U.S. District Court, Northern District of Florida

United States District Court, Southern District of Florida

United States District Court
Southern District of Florida
Clerks Office, Rm 150
301 North Miami Ave.
Miami, FL 33128
305-523-5100

Southern District: Divisional Offices

Fort Lauderdale (954-769-5400)
Fort Pierce (772-467-2300)
Key West (305-295-8100)
West Palm Beach (561-803-3400)

Southern District: Web Site

www.flsd.uscourts.gov
www.law.cornell.edu/federal/districts.html

Southern District: Judges

www.flsd.uscourts.gov
(click entries under "Judge Information")
*www.floridabar.org/DIVPGM/PU/FCPCSurvey.nsf/
    WFCPCArea?Openview&Start=1&Expand=3#3*

Southern District: Opinions

www.flsd.uscourts.gov
(under "Case Information," click "Orders & Opinions")

Southern District: Filings and Verdicts

www.flsd.uscourts.gov
(under "Case Information," click "Filings & Verdicts")

Southern District: Local Rules and Court Orders

www.flsd.uscourts.gov
(under "Rules," click "Local Rules")
www.flsd.uscourts.gov/localrules/localrules.pdf

Southern District: Administrative Orders

www.flsd.uscourts.gov
(under "Rules," click "Administrative Orders")

Southern District: Federal Rules of Civil Procedure

www.law.cornell.edu/rules/frcp
www.uscourts.gov/rules/civil2007.pdf
www.federalrulesofcivilprocedure.info/frcp

Southern District: Federal Rules of Criminal Procedure
www.law.cornell.edu/rules/frcrmp
www.uscourts.gov/rules/crim2007.pdf

Southern District: Case Management/Electronic Case Files (CM/ECF)
www.flsd.uscourts.gov/default.asp?file=/CMECF/index2.html
www.flsd.uscourts.gov/default.asp?file=/eFile/index.html

Southern District: ECF/Pacer Login
pacer.login.uscourts.gov/cgi-bin/login.pl?court_id=flsdc

Southern District: Forms
www.flsd.uscourts.gov
(under "General Information," click "Forms")

Southern District: Fees
www.flsd.uscourts.gov
(under "General Information," click "Fee Schedule")

Southern District: Juror Handbook
www.txnd.uscourts.gov/pdf/jurybook.pdf
www.dcd.uscourts.gov/Handbook-for-Trial-Jurors.pdf

Southern District: Employment Opportunities
www.flsd.uscourts.gov
(under "Employment," click "Vacancies")
www.uscourts.gov/employment.html

U.S. District Court, Middle District of Florida

United States District
 Court
Middle District of
 Florida
Jacksonville Division
300 North Hogan St.
Jacksonville, FL 32202
904-549-1900

Ft. Myers Division
2110 First St.
Ft. Myers, FL 33901
239-461-2000

Ocala Division
207 NW Second St.
Ocala, FL 34475
352-369-4860

Orlando Division
80 North Hughey Ave.
Orlando, Florida 32801
407-835-4200

Tampa Division
801 North Florida Ave.
Tampa, FL 33602
813-301-5400

Middle District: Web Site
www.flmd.uscourts.gov
www.law.cornell.edu/federal/districts.html#circuit

Middle District: Judges
www.flmd.uscourts.gov
(click "Judicial Info")

Middle District: Calendar
www.flmd.uscourts.gov
(click "Calendars")

Middle District: Opinions
www.flmd.uscourts.gov
(click "Notable Cases")

Middle District: Local Rules
www.flmd.uscourts.gov
(click "Local Rules")

Middle District: Federal Rules of Civil Procedure
www.law.cornell.edu/rules/frcp
www.uscourts.gov/rules/civil2007.pdf
www.federalrulesofcivilprocedure.info/frcp

Middle District: Federal Rules of Criminal Procedure
www.law.cornell.edu/rules/frcrmp
www.uscourts.gov/rules/crim2007.pdf

Middle District: Case Management/Electronic Case Files (CM/ECF)
www.flmd.uscourts.gov
(click "CM/ECF")

Middle District: Forms
www.flmd.uscourts.gov
(click "Forms & Publications")

Middle District: Fees
www.flmd.uscourts.gov
(click "FAQs" then "Fees")

Middle District: Juror Handbook
www.txnd.uscourts.gov/pdf/jurybook.pdf
www.dcd.uscourts.gov/Handbook-for-Trial-Jurors.pdf

Middle District: Employment Opportunities
www.flmd.uscourts.gov
(click "Career Opportunities")
www.uscourts.gov/employment.html

United States District Court, Northern District of Florida

United States District
 Court
Northern District of
 Florida
Gainesville Division
401 SE First, Ave. Rm 243
Gainesville, FL 32601
352-380-2400

Panama City Division
30 W. Government St.
Panama City, FL 32401
850-769-4556

Pensacola Division
1 North Palafox St.
Pensacola, FL 32502
850-435-8440

Tallahassee Division
111 N. Adams St.
Tallahassee, FL 32301
850-521-3501

Northern District: Web Site
www.flnd.uscourts.gov
www.law.cornell.edu/federal/districts.html#circuit

Northern District: Judges
www.flnd.uscourts.gov
(click "Contact Us")

Northern District: Local Rules
www.flnd.uscourts.gov/forms/Court%20Rules/local_rules.pdf
www.flnd.uscourts.gov/forms/index.cfm#rules

Northern District: Federal Rules of Civil Procedure
www.law.cornell.edu/rules/frcp
www.uscourts.gov/rules/civil2007.pdf
www.federalrulesofcivilprocedure.info/frcp

Northern District: Federal Rules of Criminal Procedure
www.law.cornell.edu/rules/frcrmp

Northern District: Case Management/Electronic Case Filing (CM/ECF)
www.flnd.uscourts.gov/attorneys/cmecf

Northern District: Forms
www.flnd.uscourts.gov/forms

Northern District: Fees
www.flnd.uscourts.gov/attorneys/filingFees.cfm

Northern District: Juror Handbook
www.txnd.uscourts.gov/pdf/jurybook.pdf
www.dcd.uscourts.gov/Handbook-for-Trial-Jurors.pdf

U.S. Bankruptcy Courts

Federal courts have exclusive jurisdiction over bankruptcy cases. Such cases cannot be filed in state court. Although U.S. district courts have jurisdiction over all bankruptcy matters (28 U.S.C. § 1334), they have the authority (28 U.S.C. § 157) to delegate or refer bankruptcy cases to the U.S. bankruptcy courts. There is a bankruptcy court in each of the 94 federal judicial districts. Bankruptcy courts are usually in the same physical location as the U.S. district courts. However, in some areas, based on local space availability, the bankruptcy court may be located in space other than the U.S. courthouse where the district court is situated. A U.S. bankruptcy judge is a judicial officer of the U.S. district court and is appointed for a 14-year term by the majority of judges of the U.S. court of appeals in the circuit.

The primary purposes of bankruptcy law are (1) to give an honest debtor a fresh start in life by relieving the debtor of most debts and (2) to repay creditors in an orderly manner to the extent that the debtor has property available for payment.

Kinds of Bankruptcy
www.uscourts.gov/bankruptcycourts/bankruptcybasics.html

Bankruptcy Basics
www.uscourts.gov/bankruptcycourts/bankruptcybasics/process.html
www.uscourts.gov/bankruptcycourts/BB101705final2column.pdf

United States Code: Title 11 (Bankruptcy)
uscode.house.gov/download/title_11.shtml
www.law.cornell.edu/uscode/html/uscode11/usc_sup_01_11.html

Federal Rules of Bankruptcy Procedure
www.law.cornell.edu/rules/frbp
www.uscourts.gov/rules/newrules4.html

U.S. Bankruptcy Court, Southern District of Florida

United States Bankruptcy Court
Southern District of Florida
51 S.W. 1st Ave., Rm 1517
Miami, FL 33130
305-714-1800

299 E. Broward Blvd., Rm 112
Fort Lauderdale, FL 33301
954-769-5700

1675 Palm Beach Lakes
West Palm Beach, FL 33401
561-514-4100

Southern District: Web Site
www.flsb.uscourts.gov

Southern District: Judges
www.flsb.uscourts.gov
(click "Judges Information")

Southern District: Opinions
www.flsb.uscourts.gov
(click "Court Opinions")

Southern District: Case Management/Electronic Case Filing (CM/ECF)
ecf.flsb.uscourts.gov
www.flsb.uscourts.gov/cm_ecf/cmecf_frame.html

Southern District: Calendar
www.flsb.uscourts.gov
(click "Court Calendars")

Southern District: Rules
www.flsb.uscourts.gov
(click "Rules, Forms, & Guidelines")

Southern District: Forms
www.flsb.uscourts.gov
(click "Rules, Forms, & Guidelines")
www.uscourts.gov/bkforms

Southern District: Fees
www.flsb.uscourts.gov
(click "Filing & Fee Information")

Southern District: Employment
www.flsb.uscourts.gov
(click "Employment")
www.uscourts.gov/employment.html

U.S. Bankruptcy Court, Middle District of Florida

United States Bankruptcy Court
Middle District of Florida
801 N. Florida Ave.
Tampa, FL 33602
813-301-5065

Orlando Courthouse
135 West Central Blvd.
Orlando, FL 32801
407-648-6365

Jacksonville Courthouse
300 North Hogan St.
Jacksonville, FL 32202
904-301-6490

Ft. Myers Courthouse
2110 First St.
Ft. Myers, FL 33901
(Ft. Myers cases are filed and maintained in the Tampa Division)

Middle District: Web Site
www.flmb.uscourts.gov

Middle District: Opinions
www.flmb.uscourts.gov
(click entries under "Opinions")

Middle District: Judges
www.flmb.uscourts.gov
(click entries under "Judges' Corner")

Middle District: Case Management/Electronic Case Filing (CM/ECF)
ecf.flmb.uscourts.gov

Middle District: Calendar
pacer.flmb.uscourts.gov/jcal/index.htm

Middle District: Rules
www.flmb.uscourts.gov/localrules/default.htm

Middle District: Forms
www.flmb.uscourts.gov/forms
www.uscourts.gov/bkforms/index.html

Middle District: Fees
www.flmb.uscourts.gov/filingfees

Middle District: Procedures
www.flmb.uscourts.gov/procedures

Middle District: Employment
www.flmb.uscourts.gov/employment
www.uscourts.gov/employment.html

United States Bankruptcy Court, Northern District of Florida

United States Bankruptcy
  Court
Northern District of Florida
110 East Park Ave., Ste 100
Tallahassee, FL 32301
850-521-5001

Pensacola Office
220 West Garden St.,
  Ste 700
Pensacola, FL 32502
850-435-8475

Northern District: Web Site
www.flnb.uscourts.gov

Northern District: Judges
www.flnb.uscourts.gov
(click entries under "Contact Us")

Northern District: Opinions
www.flnb.uscourts.gov/webapps/opinions

Northern District: Case Management/Electronic Case Files (CM/ECF)
ecf.flnb.uscourts.gov/cgi-bin/login.pl

Northern District: Calendar
www.flnb.uscourts.gov
(click "Public Calendar")

Northern District: Rules
www.flnb.uscourts.gov
(click "Local Rules")

Northern District: Forms
www.flnb.uscourts.gov
(click the links under "Forms")
www.uscourts.gov/bkforms

Northern District: Bankruptcy Forms Manual
www.flnb.uscourts.gov
(click "National Bankruptcy Forms")

Northern District: Fees
www.flnb.uscourts.gov
(click "Filing Fees")

Northern District: Pro Se Bankruptcy
(filing without an attorney)
www.flnb.uscourts.gov/pro_se/Default.aspx

Northern District: Employment Opportunities
www.flnb.uscourts.gov
(under "Contact Us" click "Employment")
www.uscourts.gov/employment.html

U.S. Immigration Courts

The Executive Office for Immigration Review (EOIR) (*www.usdoj.gov/eoir*) adjudicates matters brought under various immigration statutes to its three administrative tribunals: the Board of Immigration Appeals, the Office of the Chief Immigration Judge, and the Office of the Chief Administrative Hearing Officer.

The Board of Immigration Appeals has nationwide jurisdiction to hear appeals from certain decisions made by immigration judges and by district directors of the Department of Homeland Security (DHS). The Office of the Chief Immigration Judge provides overall direction for more than 200 immigration judges located in 53 immigration courts throughout the nation. Immigration judges are responsible for conducting formal administrative proceedings and act independently in their decision-making capacity. Their decisions are administratively final, unless appealed or certified to the Board.

Florida has two court locations: Miami and Orlando. (The Bradenton location was recently closed.) The Miami court is presently composed of 20 judges and has a pending caseload of approximately 16,000. The Orlando court has 3 judges.

Immigration Court Locations in Florida

U.S. Immigration Court
333 S. Miami Ave., Ste 700
Miami, FL 33130
305-789-4221; 800-898-7180
www.usdoj.gov/eoir/sibpages/mia/geninfo2.htm

U.S. Immigration Court
5449 Semoran Blvd., Ste 200
Orlando, FL 32822
407-648-6565
www.usdoj.gov/eoir/sibpages/orl/orlmain.htm

Local Operating Rules and Procedures
www.usdoj.gov/eoir/efoia/ocij/locopproc.htm

C. PACER

Public Access to Court Electronic Records (PACER) is an electronic public access service that allows users to obtain case and docket information from federal appellate, district, and bankruptcy courts, and from the U.S. Party/Case Index. PACER is a service of the U.S. Judiciary. The PACER Service Center is operated by the Administrative Office of the U.S. Courts (*pacer.psc.uscourts.gov*).

Currently most courts are available on the Internet. Links to these courts are provided at the PACER site (*pacer.psc.uscourts.gov/cgi-bin/links.pl*). However, a few systems are not available on the Internet and must be dialed directly using communication software (such as Procomm Plus, pcAnywhere, or HyperTerminal) and a modem. Electronic access is available for most courts by registering with the PACER Service Center, the judiciary's centralized registration, billing, and technical support center. You can register online or by phone at 800-676-6856; 210-301-6440.

Each court maintains its own databases with case information. Because PACER database systems are maintained within each court, each jurisdiction will have a different URL or modem number. Accessing and querying information from each service is comparable. The format and content of information provided, however, may differ slightly.

D. More Information

Federal Judiciary Overview
www.uscourts.gov
www.firstgov.gov/Agencies/Federal/Judicial.shtml

Guide to the Federal Courts
www.uscourts.gov/journalistguide/welcome.html
www.uscourts.gov/understand02

Federal Court Links
www.uscourts.gov/links.html

Federal Judicial Center
www.fjc.gov

U.S. Immigration Courts
www.usdoj.gov/eoir/sibpages/ICadr.htm#Immigration

Federal Public Defender
flm.fd.org
www.fpd-fln.org
www.fd.org/pdf_lib/defenderdir.pdf

Filing for Bankruptcy Without an Attorney
www.uscourts.gov/bankruptcycourts/prose.html

Employment Opportunities in the Federal Courts
www.uscourts.gov/employment/vacancies.html#

Florida Federal Court Judges Practice Guide
www.floridabar.org/DIVPGM/PU/FCPCSurvey.nsf/
  WFCPCArea?Openview&Start=1&Expand=3#3

Wikipedia on Federal Courts in Florida
en.wikipedia.org/wiki/11th_Circuit_Court_of_Appeals

E. Something to Check

1. Go to the sites that give you online access to court opinions of the U.S. Court of Appeals for the Eleventh Circuit. Use the search features of the sites to find an opinion on any broad legal topic, e.g., capital punishment or adoption. Summarize (brief) what the opinion says about your topic.
2. For one of the three district courts in Florida, find the calendar of any judge on the court you select. Name one case on the calendar of that judge.
3. You have a case that you want to file in U.S. Bankruptcy Court. The client resides in Sarasota, Florida. In what court should you file this case? How do you find out?

4.4 State Legislation: How a Bill Becomes a Florida Statute
  A. Introduction
  B. How a Bill Becomes a Florida Statute
  C. More Information
  D. Something to Check

A. Introduction

In this section, we provide an overview of the legislative process in Florida, specifically, how a bill becomes a law. For related information, see:

- Section 4.1 (introduction to the state government of Florida, including the major units of the state legislature)
- Section 5.1 (doing legal research in Florida law, including finding state statutes online and on the shelves)

B. How a Bill Becomes a Florida Statute

Introduction

The Florida state legislature is a two-chamber (bicameral) legislature consisting of the Florida Senate and the Florida House of Representatives.

Senate	House
850-488-4371;	850-488-1157;
800-342-1827	800-342-1827
www.flsenate.gov	*www.myfloridahouse.gov*
www.leg.state.fl.us	*www.leg.state.fl.us*

There are 40 senators and 120 representatives in the state legislature. The leader of the Senate is the President of the Senate. The leader of the House is the Speaker of the House. The legislative process occurs annually with each regular session beginning on the first Tuesday after the first Monday in March, not to exceed 60 days. The committees of each chamber meet during the months preceding the regular session on a schedule set by the presiding officers. By proclamation, special sessions may be called by the governor or by the leaders of both chambers acting jointly. Special sessions deal with specific issues that cannot wait for the next regular session.

Idea for a Bill

A *bill* is a proposal to add to or change current law filed in either chamber of the legislature. Through the bill, a legislator seeks to enact a new law or to amend or repeal an existing law. After passing both chambers, the bill becomes an *act* and must be presented to the governor for acceptance or rejection. If accepted, it becomes a *law.*

Ideas for bills can come from many sources: individual legislators, the governor, administrative agencies, lobbyists, businesses, community groups, and private citizens. The first step is to have a legislator (a senator or representative) sponsor or author the bill. Either chamber may originate any type of legislation.

Drafting

The legislator will send the idea for the bill to the House Bill Drafting Service (BDS) or to the Office of Senate Legal Research and Drafting Services, where it will be drafted into bill form. Once a bill is drafted for the House, it is forwarded to the Office of the Clerk for review to make sure the requirements set forth in the Florida Constitution are met. Here the bill receives an official number and is then considered prefiled. In the Senate, a bill is filed with the Secretary and numbered. When the draft of the bill is completed and approved by the legislator who is sponsoring it, the bill is ready for the next step: formal introduction in the Senate or in the House.

First Consideration: Introducing the Bill

The Florida Constitution requires a bill to receive three readings in each chamber on three separate days before enactment. (A two-thirds vote can suspend this requirement.) The first consideration of a bill consists of its introduction by publication in the *Journal* for the Senate or the House.

The *Journal* is the official legal record of the proceedings of the Senate or the House of Representatives. Each chamber publishes a *Journal* for each day of session. The *Journal* records only the formal action that occurs in the legislature and committees. Its contents include titles of bills introduced and considered, a record of members' votes on issues, as well as motions and other business before the legislature. Debates are usually not included in the *Journal.*

Second Consideration: Assignment to Standing Committee

After introduction, a House bill is referred by the Speaker of the House to House committees for review. A Senate bill is referred by the Senate President to Senate committees for review. Bills are assigned to policy committees according to subject area. Committee chairs may refer the bill to their subcommittees for review.

Committee Action

There are several different actions a committee may take on a bill. The committee may hold a hearing during which testimony can be heard in support of or in opposition to the bill. It may report a bill favorably with no changes; adopt amendments and report the bill favorably with amendments; redraft the bill or adopt numerous or lengthy amendments and report it as a committee substitute bill; combine two or more bills into one amended or substitute bill; indefinitely postpone the bill, thereby defeating it; report it unfavorably; or take no action at all.

If the chairperson of a committee decides that a bill should be considered by a subcommittee, he or she will designate several members of the committee to serve on a subcommittee to consider the bill while the full committee goes ahead with other business. A subcommittee proceeds in much the same manner as the full committee. It may hold subcommittee hearings on the bill and decide to report it back to the full committee without changes, amend it, prepare a substitute bill, or recommend its defeat.

For bills accepted by the full committee, the next step is consideration of possible floor action by the Senate Rules Committee or by the House Rules and Calendar Council by being placed on the Special Order Calendar for chamber consideration.

Second Reading

When a bill is read from the House or Senate Special Order Calendar in that chamber, it is the second reading. In both the Senate and the House, the bill may still be amended. If there are any amendments to the bill, it is sent to the engrossing section, where the amendments are incorporated into the bill. (Engrossing is the process of incorporating amendments adopted by a chamber into a new version of the bill. See the comprehensive dictionary in Part 8 of this book.)

Bill Analysis

Each committee that considers a bill prepares a *bill analysis*, sometimes referred to as a staff analysis. The bill analysis is updated as the bill moves through the legislative process. The analysis (1) summarizes the bill, (2) explains how current law is affected by the bill, (3) spells out the likely impact of the bill, (4) raises any constitutional issues presented by the bill, and (5) summarizes committee amendments, if any, brought forward with the bill. An analysis is prepared for the use of committee members. After meetings of a committee, the analysis is updated to include changes recommended by the committee. The post-meeting analysis prepared by staff of the last committee reporting the bill is made available to members during floor sessions.

Additionally, a specific administrative agency of the Florida government may be required to prepare an analysis if a particular bill affects that agency.

Third Consideration: Floor Action

The point in the legislative process at which the full membership of the House or Senate votes on a bill is the third reading, also known as floor action. During a formal session of the Senate or the House, the bill is read for the third time and is discussed or debated. The bill is then considered for a final vote.

Repeat Process in Other Chamber

When a bill is passed by the first chamber after debate on the floor, it is forwarded to the second chamber, where it undergoes essentially the same process of introduction, referral to committee, committee hearings, and floor action. The second chamber may pass the measure without change, amend it, prepare a substitute bill, indefinitely postpone it, or defeat it.

Resolution of Differences

If a bill is amended in the second chamber, it must go back to the chamber of origin for concurrence, meaning agreement on those amendments. If the chamber of origin does not concur in those amendments, the bill is referred to a two-chamber or two-house *conference committee* to resolve the differences. (A conference committee is actually two committees, one appointed by the House Speaker and the other by the Senate President to resolve differences.) A majority of the members of the committee from each chamber must agree before a conference committee report may be returned to both chambers for a vote.

Governor

If both chambers approve a bill, it goes to enrollment and then to the governor. (An enrolled bill is a measure approved by both chambers, signed by the legislative officers, and sent to the governor for action.) The governor has three choices:

- Sign the bill into law
- Allow it to become law without his or her signature by not acting on it within 10 days of receiving it
- Veto it

A governor's veto can be overridden by a two-thirds vote in each chamber.

Revised Code and Laws of Florida

Once enacted into law, the act is filed with the secretary of state, who assigns it a chapter number. These chaptered acts are statutes and ordinarily become part of the *Florida Statutes*. The *Florida Statutes* is a comprehensive collection of statutes organized by subject matter. In addition, at the end of each annual legislative session, the secretary of state publishes *Laws of Florida* in paper and electronic format. It is a compilation of all acts passed by that Florida legislature. The acts appear in the order they were numbered. *Florida Statutes* is the official state code and is published annually. To research effective dates of legislation affecting statutory provisions, consult the laws listed in the History provision that follows each statutes section.

Exhibits 4.4A and 4.4B outline the legislative process depending on whether a bill ordinates in the Senate or House.

c. | **More Information**

Overview of Legislative Process
www.leg.state.fl.us/Info_Center/index.cfm

EXHIBIT 4.4A   Life Cycle of a Bill That Originates in the Florida Senate

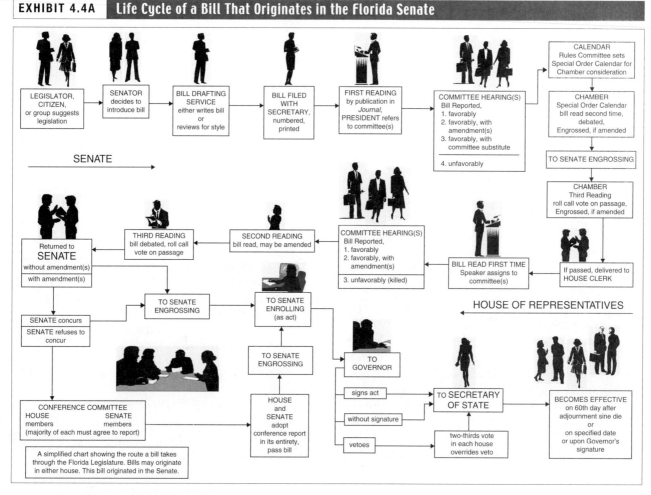

Source: www.leg.state.fl.us/data/civics/senate_idealaw.pdf
(www.flsenate.gov/data/civics/idea_to_law_chart.pdf) (www.leg.state.fl.us/Info_Center/index.cfm)

Current Bills of the Florida Legislature
Senate: *www.flsenate.gov/Session/index.cfm*
House: *www.myfloridahouse.gov/Sections/Bills/bills.aspx*

Florida Constitution
www.leg.state.fl.us/Welcome/index.cfm?CFID=6136514&
  CFTOKEN=70487514 (click "Florida Constitution")

Florida Statutes
www.leg.state.fl.us/Statutes/index.cfm

Broadcasting Legislative Sessions
www.myfloridahouse.gov/Sections/HouseCalendar/
  broadcast.aspx

Legislative News
www.lobbytools.com (subscriber service)

Florida Legislative History Research
www.leg.state.fl.us
(click "Senate" or "House")
law.miami.edu/library/flhistguide.php
www.law.ufl.edu/lic/guides/florida/fllegislative_history.shtml
dlis.dos.state.fl.us/index_Researchers.cfm
www.law.ufl.edu/lic/guides/florida/LEG_HIST06.pdf

www.myfloridahouse.gov/Sections/HouseCalendar/
  broadcast.aspx
library.flcourts.org/screens/Legislative_History.pdf

Senate Handbook; Senate Rules
www.flsenate.gov/publications/2004/Senate/Administrative/
  handbook.pdf
www.flsenate.gov/publications/2004/Senate/Administrative/
  rulebook.pdf

Employment Opportunities in the Legislature
www.leg.state.fl.us
(click "Employment")

Glossary of Legislative Terms
www.myfloridahouse.gov/Sections/Glossary/
  glossary.aspx?Filter=L
www.flsenate.gov/Info_Center/index.cfm?Mode=Glossary&
  Submenu=3&Tab=info_center

Governor
www.flgov.com

Secretary of State
www.dos.state.fl.us

| EXHIBIT 4.4B | **Life Cycle of a Bill That Originates in the Florida House of Representatives** |

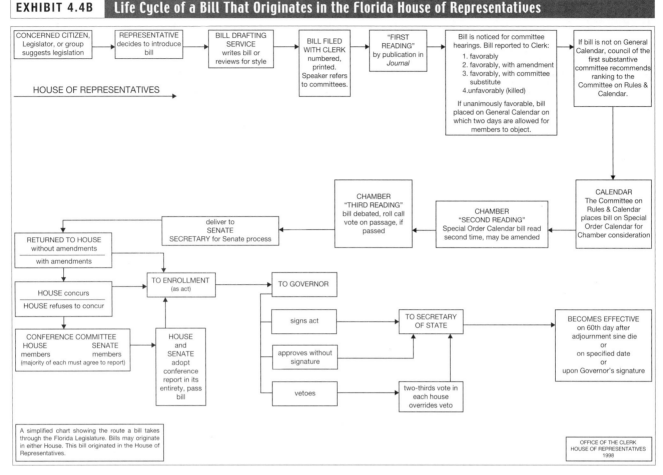

Source: *www.leg.state.fl.us/data/civics/house_idealaw.pdf*
(*www.leg.state.fl.us/Info_Center/index.cfm*)

Federal Legislative Process

www.thomas.gov

thomas.loc.gov/home/lawsmade.toc.html

| D. | **Something to Check** |

1. Find a bill currently before the legislature on any:
   a. Family law topic
   b. Criminal law topic
2. Cite one bill or statute that was introduced, authored, or sponsored:
   a. By your state senator
   b. By your state representative
3. Locate any pending bill regarding health care.

4.5 State Agencies, Offices, and Boards
A. Introduction
B. Contacts
C. More Information
D. Something to Check

A. Introduction

This section covers the major state agencies, offices, and boards in Florida. See also:

- Section 4.1 (overview of state government)
- Section 4.2 (state courts)
- Section 4.4 (state legislature)
- Section 4.6 (county and city governments)
- Section 5.9 (hotline resources and complaint directories)

For legal research leads to issues that pertain to many of these state governmental entities, see the starter cites in section 5.5.

Main Information Number on Florida Government

850-488-1234; 850-488-7146

Florida Government Information

dlis.dos.state.fl.us/fgils

www.stateofflorida.com

B. Contacts

Accountants
Addiction
Administration
Adoption
Aerospace Support
African Americans
Aging
Agriculture
AIDS
Air
Alcohol and Drugs
Antitrust
Architects
Archives
Arts and Humanities
Athletics
Attorney General
Audits
Banks
Bar, State
Birth Records
Boating
Budget
Building
Business
Cemetery
Child Support Services
Chiropractors
Cities
Civil Rights
Claims against State
Commerce
Complaints Directory
Computer Crimes
Conservation
Construction
Consumer Services
Corporations
Corrections
Cosmetology
Counties
Courts
Death Records
Dentistry
Disabilities
Dissolution Records
Domestic Violence
Drugs

Economic Development
Education
Elections
Emergency
Employment
Energy
Environment
Estate Tax
Ethics
Families
Finance
Fire Marshal
Fish
Food and Beverage
Forensic Sciences
Forestry
Funeral Services
Gambling
Game and Hunting
Governor
Health
Highway Patrol
Hospitals
House of Representatives
Housing
Hurricanes
Identity Theft
Information on
   Florida Government
Information Technology
Inspector General
Insurance
Investigation
Jobs
Justice
Labor
Law Enforcement
Law Library
Legislature
Library
Licensing
Lieutenant Governor
Lobbying
Local Government
Lottery
Marriage Records
Mediation
Medicine

Mental Health
Military
Missing Persons
Motor Vehicles
National Guard
Natural Resources
Nursing
Occupational Safety
Parks
Permits
Personnel
Pharmacy
Prison
Privacy
Probate
Public Assistance
Public Defender
Public Utilities
Real Estate
Recreation
Recycling
Retirement
Secretary of State
Senate
Sex Offenders
Social Services
Sports
Tax
Teachers
Tourism
Traffic Safety
Transportation
Treasury
Unclaimed Property
Unemployment Insurance
Universities, Public
Veterans
Veterinary Medicine
Victim Services
Vital Records
Voting
Water
Welfare
Whistle Blower
Women
Workers' Compensation

Accountants

(See also Audits, Finance, Tax)

Board of Accountancy
850-487-1395
www.myflorida.com/dbpr/divisions.html
(click "Certified Public Accounting")

Addiction

(See also Alcohol and Drugs, Drugs, Health)

Florida Certification Board
850-222-6314
www.flcertificationboard.org

Administration

(See also Courts, Legislature)

Governor
850-488-4441
www.flgov.com
www.flgov.com/executive_office

State Government
850-488-1234
www.myflorida.com
www.flgov.com

Office of Policy and Budget
850-488-7810
www.flgov.com/opb_office

State Board of Administration
850-488-4406
www.sbafla.com

Office of the Chief Inspector General
850-922-4637
www.flgov.com/inspector_general_office

Adoption

(See also Social Services)

Department of Children and Families
904-353-0679; 800-96-ADOPT
www.dcf.state.fl.us/adoption

Aerospace Support

Space Florida
321-730-5301
www.spaceflorida.gov

African Americans

Florida Black Business Investment Board
850-878-0826
www.fbbib.com

Aging

Department of Elder Affairs
800-963-5337; 850-414-2000
elderaffairs.state.fl.us

Council on Aging
850-222-8877
www.fcoa.org

Independent Living Council
877-822-1993; 850-488-5624
flailc.org

Ombudsman Program
888-831-0404; 850-414-2323
ltcop.myflorida.com

Agriculture

(See also Food and Beverage)

Department of Agriculture and Consumer Services
850-488-3022
doacs.state.fl.us

AIDS

(See also Health)

Bureau of HIV/AIDS
850-245-4334
www.doh.state.fl.us/disease_ctrl/aids

Air

(See also Environment)

Clean Air Florida
850-488-0114
www.dep.state.fl.us/air/cleanair.htm

Alcohol and Drugs

(See also Addiction, Drugs, Food and Beverage, Health, Law Enforcement, Pharmacy)

Office of Drug Control
850-921-0485
www.flgov.com/drug_control

Division of Alcoholic Beverages and Tobacco
850-488-3227
www.myflorida.com/dbpr/divisions.html
(click "Alcoholic Beverages and Tobacco")

Alcohol and Drug Abuse Association
850-878-2196
www.fadaa.org

Antitrust

(See Attorney General)

Architects

Board of Architecture
850-487-1395
www.myflorida.com/dbpr/divisions.html

Archives

(See also Library)

State Library and Archives
850-245-6700
dlis.dos.state.fl.us/index_researchers.cfm

Arts and Humanities

(See also Tourism)

Division of Cultural Affairs
850-245-6470
www.florida-arts.org

Bureau of Archaeological Research
850-245-6444
dhr.dos.state.fl.us/archaeology

Bureau of Historic Preservation
850-245-6333
www.flheritage.com/preservation

Museum of Florida History
850-245-6400
dhr.dos.state.fl.us/museum

Office of Cultural and Historical Preservation
850-245-6300; 850-245-6333
www.flheritage.com

Office of Film and Entertainment
850-410-4765; 877-FLA-FILM
www.filminflorida.com

Athletics

(See also Arts, Gambling, Tourism)

Board of Athlete Agents
850-487-1395
www.myflorida.com/dbpr/divisions.html

Florida Sports Foundation
850-488-8347
www.flasports.com

Attorney General

(See also Law Enforcement)

Office of the Attorney General
850-414-3300
www.myfloridalegal.com

Audits

(See also Finance)

Auditor General
850-488-5534
www.state.fl.us/audgen

Banks

(See also Finance)

Office of Financial Regulation
800-342-2762; 800-848-3792
www.flofr.com/banking

Bar Association, State

(See also section 3.4)

The Florida Bar
850-561-5600
www.floridabar.org

Birth Records

(See Vital Records; see also section 5.7)

Boating

(See also Natural Resources, Tourism)

Boat Registrations and Titles
850-922-9000
www.hsmv.state.fl.us/dmv/faqboat.html

Boating and Waterways
www.myfwc.com/boating

Budget

(See also Administration)

Office of Policy and Budget
850-488-7810
www.flgov.com/opb_office

Legislative Budget Commission
www.leg.state.fl.us
(click "Joint Legislative Committees" then "Legislative Budget Commission")

Building

(See Construction)

Business

Department of Business and Professional Regulation
850-413-7046
www.myflorida.com/dbpr

Division of Corporations
800-755-5111
www.sunbiz.org
www.dos.state.fl.us
(click "Corporations")

Department of State
850-245-6500
www.dos.state.fl.us

Cemetery

(See Funeral Services)

Child Support Services

(See also Social Services)

Child Support Enforcement
800-622-5437; 800-622-KIDS
dor.myflorida.com/dor/childsupport
sun6.dms.state.fl.us/dor/childsupport

Online Child Support Services
www.myfloridacounty.com/services/child_support

Children's Medical Services
850-245-4200
www.doh.state.fl.us/cms

Chiropractors

Board of Chiropractic Medicine
www.doh.state.fl.us/mqa/chiro

Cities

(See Local Government)

Civil Rights

(See also Attorney General, Law Enforcement, Privacy)

Commission on Human Relations
800-342-8170; 850-488-7082
fchr.state.fl.us

Office for Civil Rights
850-921-3201
www.floridajobs.org/civilrights/index.html

Claims Against State

Bureau of State Liability Claims
850-413-3122
www.fldfs.com/Risk/SLC/index.htm

Commerce

(See Business)

Complaints Directory

Consumer Complaints
www.800helpfla.com/ccform.html
www.stateofflorida.com
(click "Consumer Complaints")

Computer Crimes

(See also Law Enforcement)

Computer Crime Center
850-410-7052
www.fdle.state.fl.us/Fc3

Conservation

(See also Emergency, Environment, Natural Resources)

Division of Waste Management
850-245-8705
www.dep.state.fl.us/waste

Energy Office
850-245-8002
www.dep.state.fl.us/energy/default.htm

Construction

(See also Consumer Services)

Board of Architecture
850-487-1395
www.myflorida.com/dbpr/divisions.html

Building Code
850-487-1824
www.floridabuilding.org/c

Construction Industry Licensing Board
850-487-1395
www.myflorida.com/dbpr/divisions.html

Housing and Community Development
850-488-7956
www.floridacommunitydevelopment.org

Consumer Services

(See also Law Enforcement)

Consumer Protection
850-414-3300
myfloridalegal.com/consumer

Department of Agriculture and Consumer Services
850-488-3022
doacs.state.fl.us

Division of Consumer Services
800-435-7352
www.800helpfla.com

Lemon Law
800-321-5366; 850-410-3807
www.800helpfla.com/lemonlaw.html

Corporations

(See also Business)

Division of Corporations
800-755-5111
www.sunbiz.org
www.dos.state.fl.us
(click "Corporations")

Corrections

(See also Law Enforcement)

Department of Corrections
850-488-2533
www.dc.state.fl.us

Department of Juvenile Justice
850-488-1850
www.djj.state.fl.us

Parole Commission
850-922-0000
fpc.state.fl.us

Board of Executive Clemency
850-488-2952
fpc.state.fl.us/Clemency.htm

Corrections Commission
850-413-9330
www.flaccreditation.org

Cosmetology

Board of Cosmetology
850-487-1395
www.myflorida.com/dbpr/divisions.html

Counties

(See Local Government)

Courts

(See also section 4.2)

State Courts
www.flcourts.org

Death Records

(See Vital Records; see also section 5.7)

Dentistry

(See also Health)

Bureau of Dental Health
850-245-4333
www.doh.state.fl.us/family/fdhdescription.html

Disabilities

(See also Health, Workers' Compensation)

Agency for Persons with Disabilities
850-488-4257
apd.myflorida.com

Developmental Disabilities Council
800-580-7801; 850-488-4180
www.fddc.org

Division of Disability Determinations
850-488-4222
www.doh.state.fl.us/DD/DDDdescription.html

Division of Vocational Rehabilitation
800-451-4327; 850-245-3399
www.rehabworks.org

Division of Blind Services
800-672-7038; 850-245-0370
dbs.myflorida.com

Statewide Advocacy Council
800-342-0825; 850-488-6173
www.floridasac.org

Commission for the Transportation Disadvantaged
850-410-5700
www.dot.state.fl.us/ctd

Mental Health Services
www.dcf.state.fl.us/mentalhealth

Florida State Hospital
850-663-7536
www.dcf.state.fl.us/INSTITUTIONS/FSH

Northeast Florida State Hospital
904-259-6211
www.dcf.state.fl.us/INSTITUTIONS/neFSH

Dissolution Records

(See Vital Records; see also section 5.7)

Domestic Violence

(See also Law Enforcement)

Domestic Violence
800-500-1119
www.dcf.state.fl.us/domesticviolence

Drugs

(See also Addiction, Alcohol, Health, Law Enforcement, Pharmacy)

Alcohol and Drug Abuse Association
850-878-2196
www.fadaa.org

Florida Highway Patrol
850-617-2399
www.fhp.state.fl.us
(click "Contraband Interdiction Program")

Office of Drug Control
850-921-0485
www.flgov.com/drug_control

Economic Development

(See also Business)

Economic Development Council
850-201-3332
www.fedc.net

Office of Tourism, Trade and Economic Development
850-487-2568
www.flgov.com/otted_office

Growth Management Study Commission
877-429-1296
1000friendsofflorida.org
www.1000fof.reform/GMSC_Report.asp

Education

Department of Education
850-245-0505
www.fldoe.org

State Board of Education
850-245-0505
www.fldoe.org/board

Assessment and School Performance
850-245-0513
www.fldoe.org/asp

Division of Educator Quality
850-245-0441
www.fldoe.org/dpe

Association of Community Colleges
850-222-3222
www.facc.org

Community Colleges
www.fldoe.org/cc/colleges.asp

State University System
850-245-0466
www.fldcu.org

Florida State University
850-644-2525
www.fsu.edu

University of Florida
352-392-3261
www.ufl.edu

Sunshine Connections
850-245-9840
www.sunshineconnections.org

Division of Blind Services
800-672-7038; 850-245-0370
dbs.myflorida.com

Elections

(See also Secretary of State)

Division of Elections
800-955-8771; 850-245-6200
election.dos.state.fl.us

Elections Commission
850-922-4539
www.fec.state.fl.us

County Election Supervisors
election.dos.state.fl.us/SOE/supervisor_elections.shtml

Emergency

(See also Environment, Health)

Department of Law Enforcement
850-410-7000
www.fdle.state.fl.us

Emergency Management
850-413-9900
www.myflorida.com/agency/23

Emergency Operations Center
www.floridadisaster.org

Division of Emergency Medical Operations
850-245-4440
doh.state.fl.us/demo

Department of Community Affairs
850-488-8466
www.dca.state.fl.us

Florida Highway Patrol
www.fhp.state.fl.us
www.hsmv.state.fl.us/offices

Department of Highway Safety and Motor Vehicles
850-922-9000
www.hsmv.state.fl.us

Travel Information
www.fl511.com

Employment

(See also Labor, Occupational Safety, Unemployment Insurance, Workers' Compensation)

Agency for Workforce Innovation
850-245-7105
www.floridajobs.org

Employment and Labor
www.stateofflorida.com
(click "Employment and Jobs")

Workforce Florida
850-921-1119
www.workforceflorida.com

Energy

(See also Conservation, Environment, Natural Resources)

Energy Office
850-245-8002
www.dep.state.fl.us/energy

Environment

(See also Agriculture, Emergency, Natural Resources, Recycling, Water)

Department of Environmental Protection
850-245-2118
www.dep.state.fl.us

Clean Air Florida
850-488-0114
www.dep.state.fl.us/air/cleanair.htm

Estate Tax

(See also Tax)

Department of Revenue, Estate Tax
800-352-3671; 850-488-6800;
dor.myflorida.com/dor/taxes/estate_tax.html

Probate Guide
850-487-1345
www.stateofflorida.com
(click "Probate Guide")

Ethics

(See also sections 3.2 and 3.3)

Commission on Ethics
850-488-7864
www.ethics.state.fl.us

Families

(See also Child Support Services, Health, Social Services)

Department of Children and Families
850-487-1111
www.myflorida.com/cf_web

Finance

(See also Banks, Housing)

Department of Financial Services
800-342-2762; 850-413-3100
www.fldfs.com

Division of Treasury
850-413-3165
www.fltreasury.org

Fire Marshal

Division of State Fire Marshal
850-413-3170
www.fldfs.com/sfm

Fish

(See also Game and Hunting, Natural Resources)

Fish and Wildlife Conservation Commission
850-488-4676
www.floridaconservation.org
www.myfwc.com/fishingareas.html

Licenses and Permits
888-347-4356
www.myfwc.com/license_permit

Food and Beverage

Department of Agriculture and Consumer Services
850-488-3022
www.doacs.state.fl.us

Department of Citrus
863-499-2500
www.floridajuice.com

Division of Alcoholic Beverages and Tobacco
850-488-3227
www.myflorida.com/dbpr/divisions.html

Division of Dairy Industry
850-487-1450
www.doacs.state.fl.us/dairy

Division of Food Safety
850-245-5520
www.doacs.state.fl.us/fs

Forensic Sciences

(See also Law Enforcement)

Division of the International Association for Identification
305-460-5435
www.fdiai.org

Forestry

(See also Environment, Natural Resources)

Division of Forestry
850-488-4274
www.fl-dof.com

Funeral Services

Division of Funeral, Cemetery, and Consumer Services
850-413-3039
www.fldfs.com/FuneralCemetery

Gambling

(See also Athletics, Law Enforcement, Sports)

Department of Lottery
850-487-7777
www.oppaga.state.fl.us/profiles/2090

Florida Lottery
850-487-7725
www.flalottery.com

Division of Pari-Mutuel Wagering
850-488-9130
www.myflorida.com/dbpr/divisions.html

Game Promotions/Sweepstakes
800-HELP-FLA; 850-922-2966
www.800helpfla.com/sweepstakes.html

Game and Hunting

(See also Natural Resources)

Division of Hunting and Game Management
myfwc.com/hunting

Hunting Licenses and Permits
888-486-8356; 850-488-4676
myfwc.com/license_permit

Fish and Wildlife Conservation Commission
850-488-4676
myfwc.com/sitemap.htm

Governor

Office of the Governor
850-488-7146
www.flgov.com

Health

(See also AIDS, Disabilities, Emergency, Hospitals, Insurance, Occupational Safety)

Department of Health
850-245-4147
www.doh.state.fl.us

Agency for Health Care Administration
888-419-3456
www.fdhc.state.fl.us

Children's Medical Services
850-245-4200
www.doh.state.fl.us/cms

Maternal and Child Health
850-245-4465
www.doh.state.fl.us/family/mch

Division of Family Health Services
850-245-4100
www.doh.state.fl.us/family/fhdescription.html

Division of Environmental Health
850-245-4250
www.doh.state.fl.us/environment

Public Health Services
850-245-4229
www.doh.state.fl.us/planning_eval/phealth/services.htm

Division of Emergency Medical Operations
850-245-4440
doh.state.fl.us/demo

HealthStat
www.floridahealthfinder.gov

Department of Health, Vital Records
904-359-6900
www.doh.state.fl.us/planning_eval/vital_statistics

Medical Quality Assurance
850-488-0595
www.doh.state.fl.us/mqa

Board of Medicine
850-245-4131
www.stateofflorida.com
(click "Medicine, Florida Board of")

Disease Control
850-245-4300
www.doh.state.fl.us/Disease_ctrl/dcdescription.html

Division of Health Access and Tobacco
850-245-4144
www.doh.state.fl.us/Tobacco

Healthcare Licensing Services
850-444-9814
www.healthcarelicensing.com

Highway Patrol

(See also Law Enforcement, Motor Vehicles)

Florida Highway Patrol
850-617-2301
www.fhp.state.fl.us

Department of Highway Safety and Motor Vehicles
850-922-9000
www.hsmv.state.fl.us

Hospitals

(See Disabilities, Health)

House of Representatives

(See also Senate and section 4.4)

House of Representatives
850-488-1157
www.myfloridahouse.gov

Housing

(See also Real Estate)

Division of Housing and Community Development
850-488-7956
www.dca.state.fl.us/fhcd

Housing
dlis.dos.state.fl.us/fgils/housing.html

Department of Community Affairs
850-488-8466
www.dca.state.fl.us

Housing Coalition
850-878-4219
www.flhousing.org

Housing Finance Corporation
850-488-4197
www.floridahousing.org

State Housing Initiatives Partnership
850-488-4197
*www.floridahousing.org/Home/HousingPartners/
    LocalGovernments*

Hurricanes

(See also Emergency)

Disaster Recovery Fund
800-825-3786
www.flahurricanefund.org

Division of Emergency Management
800-342-3557
www.floridadisaster.org

Hurricane Safety
850-222-1996
www.hurricanesafety.org

Identity Theft

(See also Law Enforcement, Privacy)

Consumer Protection; Attorney General
866-966-7226; 850-414-3300;
myfloridalegal.com/consumer
www.myfloridalegal.com/identitytheft

Department of Law Enforcement
850-410-7898
www.fdle.state.fl.us/CompID

Information on Florida Government

850-488-1234; 850-488-7146
dlis.dos.state.fl.us/fgils

Information Technology

IT Florida
800-748-1120
www.itflorida.com

Inspector General

Office of the Chief Inspector General
850-922-4637
www.flgov.com/inspector_general_office

Insurance

(See also Unemployment Insurance)

Office of Insurance Regulation
850-413-3140
www.floir.com

Division of Insurance Fraud
850-488-5768
www.fldfs.com/fraud

Division of Rehabilitation and Liquidation
850-413-3179
www.fldfs.com/Receiver

Investigation

(See also Forensic Sciences, Law Enforcement)

Florida Highway Patrol
Bureau of Investigations
850-617-2301
www.fhp.state.fl.us/BuOfIn

Jobs

(See Employment, Labor)

Justice

(See Attorney General, Courts, Law Enforcement)

Labor

(See also Employment, Occupational Safety, Unemployment Insurance, Workers' Compensation)

Employment and Labor
www.stateofflorida.com
(click "Employment and Jobs")

Agency for Workforce Innovation
850-245-7105
www.floridajobs.org

Alien Labor Certification
850-921-3299
www.floridajobs.org/alc

Bureau of Child Labor
800-226-2536; 850-488-3131
www.myflorida.com/dbpr/reg/childlabor/index.html

Bureau of Farm Labor
850-488-3131
www.myflorida.com/dbpr/reg/farmLabor.html

Labor Market Statistics
866-537-3615; 850-245-7205
www.labormarketinfo.com

Workforce Florida
850-921-1119
www.workforceflorida.com

Law Enforcement

(See also Corrections, Fire Marshal, Military, Missing Persons, Public Defender, Sex Offenders)

Department of Law Enforcement
850-410-7000
www.fdle.state.fl.us

Domestic Security
850-410-8690
www.fdle.state.fl.us/Domestic_Security
www.fdle.state.fl.us/osi/DomesticSecurity

Office of the Attorney General
850-414-3300
www.myfloridalegal.com

Department of Highway Safety and Motor Vehicles
850-922-9000
www.hsmv.state.fl.us

Florida Highway Patrol
850-617-2399
www.fhp.state.fl.us

Statistical Analysis Center
850-410-7140
www.fdle.state.fl.us/FSAC

Domestic Violence
800-500-1119
www.dcf.state.fl.us/domesticviolence

T.H.U.G.S. (Taking Hoodlums Using Guns Seriously)
800-704-0231
www.fdle.state.fl.us/OSI/THUGS

Division of State Fire Marshal
850-413-3170
www.fldfs.com/sfm

FBI, Florida Offices
jacksonville.fbi.gov
miami.fbi.gov
tampa.fbi.gov

Law Library

(See also Archives, Library; see also section 5.8)

Supreme Court Law Library
850-488-8919
library.flcourts.org

Tax Law Library
taxlaw.state.fl.us

Legislature

(See also section 4.4)

House of Representatives
850-488-1157
www.myfloridahouse.gov

Senate
www.flsenate.gov

Legislative Information Service
800-342-1827; 850-488-4371

Library

(See also Archives, Law Library; see also section 5.8)

State Library and Archives
850-245-6700
dlis.dos.state.fl.us/index_researchers.cfm

State Library
850-245-6600
dlis.dos.state.fl.us/library

Electronic Library
850-245-6626
www.flelibrary.org

Licensing

(See also Business, Consumer Services)

**Department of Agriculture and Consumer Services
Division of Licensing**
850-245-5691
licgweb.doacs.state.fl.us

**Department of Business and Professional Regulation
Licensing Portal**
850-487-1395
www.myfloridalicense.com/dbpr

Healthcare Licensing Services
850-444-9814
www.healthcarelicensing.com

Permits and Licenses
www.stateofflorida.com
(click "Permits and Licenses (All Types)")

Lieutenant Governor

Lieutenant Governor
850-488-7146
ltgov.flgov.com

Lobbying

Lobbyist Registration Office
850-922-4990
www.leg.state.fl.us/lobbyist

Local Government

(See also section 4.6)

League of Cities
800-342-8112; 850-222-9684
www.flcities.com

Florida Association of Counties
850-922-4300
www.fl-counties.com
www.myfloridacounty.com

Lottery

(See also Gambling)

Florida Lottery
850-487-7725
www.flalottery.com

Department of Lottery
850-487-7777
www.oppaga.state.fl.us/profiles/2090

Marriage Records

(See Vital Records; see also section 5.7)

Mediation

(See also Labor)

**Florida Supreme Court
Dispute Resolution Center**
850-921-2910
www.tfapm.org/supreme.shtml

Medicine

(See Health)

Mental Health

(See Disabilities, Health)

Military

(See also National Guard)

Department of Military Affairs
904-823-0364
www.dma.state.fl.us

National Guard
904-823-0364
www.floridaguard.army.mil

Florida Department of Veterans' Affairs
850-487-1533
www.floridavets.org

Missing Persons

(See also Law Enforcement)

Department of Law Enforcement
888-356-4774
www.fdle.state.fl.us/a-z_index.html
(click "Missing Persons")

Missing Endangered Persons Information Clearinghouse
888-356-4774; 850-410-8585
www3.fdle.state.fl.us/MCICSearch

Motor Vehicles

(See also Highway Patrol, Transportation)

Department Highway Safety and Motor Vehicles
850-922-9000
www.hsmv.state.fl.us

Division of Driver Licenses
850-922-9000
www.hsmv.state.fl.us
(click "Driver License")

Alcohol Testing Program
850-410-7810
www.fdle.state.fl.us/atp

Safety Programs
850-414-4590
www.dot.state.fl.us/safety

National Guard

(See Military)

Natural Resources

(See also Environment, Water)

Division of State Lands
850-245-2555
www.dep.state.fl.us/lands

Division of Forestry
850-488-4274
www.fl-dof.com

Division of Recreation and Parks
850-245-2157
www.dep.state.fl.us/parks
www.floridastateparks.org

Fish and Wildlife Conservation Commission
850-488-4676
www.floridaconservation.org
www.myfwc.com/fishingareas.html

Fish and Wildlife Research Institute
727-896-8626
www.floridamarine.org

Coastal Management Program
850-245-2161
www.dep.state.fl.us/cmp

Department of Environmental Protection
850-245-2118
www.dep.state.fl.us

Clean Air Florida
850-488-0114
www.dep.state.fl.us/air/cleanair.htm

Air Resource Management
850-488-0114
www.dep.state.fl.us/air

Boating and Waterways
www.myfwc.com/boating

Division of Hunting and Game Management
myfwc.com/hunting

Energy Office
850-245-8002
www.dep.state.fl.us/energy

Geological Survey
850-488-4191
www.dep.state.fl.us/geology

Public Service Commission
800-342-3552; 850-413-6100
www.psc.state.fl.us

Nursing

(See also Health)

Board of Nursing
850-245-4746
www.doh.state.fl.us/mqa/nursing

Occupational Safety

(See also Employment, Health, Labor, Workers' Compensation)

Occupational Safety and Health Administration
904-232-2895; 954-424-0242; 813-626-1177
www.osha.gov/oshdir/florida.html

Parks

(See also Environment, Natural Resources)

Division of Recreation and Parks
850-245-2157
www.dep.state.fl.us/parks
www.floridastateparks.org

Permits

(See also Business)

Permits and Licenses
www.stateofflorida.com
(click "Permits and Licenses (All Types)")

Personnel

(See Employment, Labor)

Pharmacy

(See also Health)

Board of Pharmacy
850-245-4292
www.doh.state.fl.us/mqa/pharmacy

Prison

(See Corrections)

Privacy

(See also Civil Rights, Identity Theft, Law Enforcement)

Attorney General, Consumer Protection
866-966-7226; 850-414-3300
myfloridalegal.com/consumer
(type "privacy" in the search box)

Driver Privacy Protection Act
www.hsmv.state.fl.us/ddl/DPPAInfo.html

Probate

(See also Courts, Estate Tax)

Probate Guide
850-487-1345
www.stateofflorida.com
(click "Probate Guide")

Public Assistance

(See Child Support Services, Social Services)

Public Defender

Public Defenders
www.flpda.org
www.justiceadmin.org/pd
publicdefender.cjis20.org/public_defenders.htm
(click "Public Defender Sites")

Public Utilities

(See also Natural Resources)

Public Service Commission
800-342-3552; 850-413-6100
www.psc.state.fl.us

Real Estate

(See also Housing)

Division of Real Estate
850-487-1395
www.myflorida.com/dbpr/divisions.html

Real Estate Commission
850-487-1395
www.myflorida.com/dbpr/re/frec.html

Real Estate Development and Management
850-488-1817
dms.myflorida.com/dms2/business_operations
(click "Real Estate Development & Management")

Recreation

(See Environment, Natural Resources, Parks)

Recycling

(See also Conservation)

Recycle Florida Today
877-867-4RFT; 800-CLEANUP
www.recyclefloridatoday.org

Waste Management Recycling
800-CLEANUP; 850-245-8705
www.dep.state.fl.us/waste/categories/recycling

Waste Management
850-245-8707
www.dep.state.fl.us/waste

Retirement

(See also Employment)

Division of Retirement
850-488-2786
dms.myflorida.com
(click "Florida Retirement System")

Secretary of State

Office of Secretary
850-245-6500
oss.dos.state.fl.us

Senate

(See also Legislature; see also section 4.4)

The Florida Senate
850-487-5072
www.flsenate.gov

Sex Offenders

(See also Computer Crimes, Law Enforcement)

Sexual Offenders and Predators
888-357-7332
offender.fdle.state.fl.us/offender

Sexual Offender Database
www.fdle.state.fl.us

Social Services

(See also Adoption, Child Support Services, Health)

Department of Children and Families
850-487-1111
www.myflorida.com/cf_web

Women, Infants and Children (WIC)
850-245-4202
www.doh.state.fl.us/family/wic

Sports

(See Athletics, Game and Hunting)

Tax

(See also Estate Tax)

Department of Revenue, Taxes
800-352-3671; 850-488-6800
sun6.dms.state.fl.us/dor
(click "Taxes")

Tax Registration
www.sunbiz.org/taxes.html
dor.myflorida.com/dor/eservices/apps/register

Teachers

(See also Education, Employment)

Educator Certification
800-445-6739; 850-245-5049
www.fldoe.org/edcert

Tourism

(See also Arts)

Tourism and Recreation
dlis.dos.state.fl.us/fgils/tourism.html

Office of Tourism, Trade, and Economic Development
850-487-2568
www.flgov.com/otted_office

Traffic Safety

(See Law Enforcement, Motor Vehicles, Transportation)

Transportation

(See also Motor Vehicles)

Department of Transportation
866-374-3368; 850-414-4100
www.dot.state.fl.us

Department of Highway Safety and Motor Vehicles
850-922-9000
www.hsmv.state.fl.us

Transportation Commission
850-414-4105
www.ftc.state.fl.us

Commission for the Transportation Disadvantaged
850-410-5700
www.dot.state.fl.us/ctd

Treasury

Division of Treasury
850-413-3165
www.fltreasury.org

Department of Financial Services
800-342-2762; 850-413-3100
www.fldfs.com

Unclaimed Property

Bureau of Unclaimed Property
888-258-2253; 850-413-5555
www.fltreasurehunt.org

Unemployment Insurance

(See also Employment, Insurance, Labor, Workers' Compensation; see also section 2.8)

Unemployment Compensation
866-778-7356
www.floridajobs.org/unemployment

Universities, Public

(See Education)

Veterans

(See Military)

Veterinary Medicine

Board of Veterinary Medicine
850-487-1395
www.myflorida.com/dbpr/divisions.html

Victim Services

(See also Computer Crimes, Law Enforcement, Privacy)

Attorney General, Crime Victims' Services
850-414-3300
myfloridalegal.com/victims

Victims Assistance
877-884-2846
www.dc.state.fl.us
(click "Victims Assistance")

Victim's Rights
800-435-8286
fpc.state.fl.us/Victims.htm

Vital Records

(See also section 5.7)

Department of Health, Vital Records
904-359-6900
www.doh.state.fl.us/planning_eval/vital_statistics

Voting

(See Elections)

Water

(See also Environment, Natural Resources)

Water Resource Management
850-245-8335
www.dep.state.fl.us/water

Office of Agricultural Water Policy
850-617-1700
www.floridaagwaterpolicy.com

Water Management Districts
www.dep.state.fl.us/secretary/watman

Department of Boating and Waterways
www.myfwc.com/boating

Welfare

(See Child Support Services, Social Services)

Whistle Blower

Office of Inspector General
800-543-5353; 850-922-1060
www.flgov.com/ig_home
*www.dcf.state.fl.us/admin/ig/publications/
    wbhotlinebrochure.pdf*
www.browardbar.org/articles/166.htm

Women

(See also Civil Rights, Social Services)

Commission on the Status of Women
850-414-3300
www.fcsw.net

Women, Infants and Children (WIC)
850-245-4202
www.doh.state.fl.us/family/wic

Workers' Compensation

(See also Employment, Labor, Occupational Safety,
Unemployment Insurance; see also section 2.9)

Division of Workers' Compensation
850-413-1601
www.fldfs.com/wc

C. More Information

Florida State Agencies
www.myflorida.com/contactus
www.seflin.org/govdoct/flcore.html
www.statelocalgov.net/state-fl.cfm
www.findlaw.com/11stategov/fl/state.html
www.legaltrek.com/HELPSITE/States/Florida.htm
www.firstgov.gov/Agencies/State_and_Territories.shtml
dir.yahoo.com/Regional/U_S__States/Florida/government

Other States
www.statelocalgov.net

D. Something to Check

1. Find the web sites for three Florida agencies, offices, or boards that refer to paralegals employed within them.
2. Identify what Florida agencies, offices, or boards would have relevant information on (1) abortion, (2) the plight of an insolvent business, and (3) police misconduct.

> **4.6 Counties and Cities: Some Useful Law-Related Sites**
> A. Information
> B. Sites
> C. More Information
> D. Something to Check

A. Information

Florida has 67 counties, each with a county seat where the county courthouse is located. This section presents contact information on the following major county and city law-related sites:

- Main government site
- Administrative agency list
- Child support enforcement agency
- County/city attorney
- Local courts/clerks
- County ordinances
- Public defender
- Public records
- Sheriff/police
- State attorney

For related information:

- About state government, see section 4.1
- About state courts, see section 4.2
- About public records, see section 5.7
- About law libraries, see section 5.8
- About federal courts in Florida, see section 4.3
- About bar associations, see section 3.4
- About paralegal associations, see section 1.2

B. Sites

Alachua County	Hardee County	Okeechobee County
Baker County	Hendry County	Orange County
Bay County	Hernando County	Orlando, City of
Bradford County	Hialeah, City of	Osceola County
Brevard County	Highlands County	Palm Beach County
Broward County	Hillsborough County	Pasco County
Calhoun County	Hollywood, City of	Pembroke Pines, City of
Cape Coral, City of	Holmes County	Pinellas County
Charlotte County	Indian River County	Polk County
Citrus County	Jackson County	Putnam County
Clay County	Jacksonville, City of	Santa Rosa County
Clearwater, City of	Jefferson County	Sarasota County
Collier County	Lafayette County	Seminole County
Columbia County	Lake County	St. Johns County
Coral Springs, City of	Lee County	St. Lucie County
DeSoto County	Leon County	St. Petersburg, City of
Dixie County	Levy County	Sumter County
Duval County	Liberty County	Suwannee County
Escambia County	Madison County	Tallahassee, City of
Flagler County	Manatee County	Tampa, City of
Fort Lauderdale	Marion County	Taylor County
Franklin County	Martin County	Union County
Gadsden County	Miami, City of	Volusia County
Gilchrist County	Miami-Dade County	Wakulla County
Glades County	Monroe County	Walton County
Gulf County	Nassau County	Washington County
Hamilton County	Okaloosa County	

Alachua County

Alachua: County Government
352-374-5210
www.co.alachua.fl.us/government
www.co.alachua.fl.us/government/bocc

Alachua: Administrative Agencies
www.co.alachua.fl.us/government/depts.

Alachua: Charter and Ordinances
www.co.alachua.fl.us/government/attorney
(click "Home Rule Charter/Ordinances")

Alachua: Child Support Enforcement
circuit8.org/family/support.html

Alachua: Clerk of the Court
352-374-3636
www.alachuaclerk.org/Clerk/index.cfm

Alachua: County Attorney
352-374-5218
www.co.alachua.fl.us/government/attorney

Alachua: Courts
352-374-3636
www.circuit8.org
www.alachuaclerk.org/Clerk/index.cfm

Alachua: Laws and Ordinances
www.municode.com
(click "ONLINE LIBRARY" then "Florida" then "Alachua County")

Alachua: Public Defender
352-338-7370

Alachua: Public Records Search
www.alachuacounty.us/government/clerk/records
www.doh.state.fl.us/planning_eval/vital_statistics
www.myfloridacounty.com/services/officialrecords_intro.shtml

Alachua: Sheriff
352-367-4040
www.alachuasheriff.org

Alachua: State Attorney
352-374-3670
www.sao8.org
sawww.co.alachua.fl.us

Baker County

Baker: County Government
904-259-3613
www.bakercountyfl.org
bakercountyfl.org/board

Baker: Administrative Agencies
www.bakercountyfl.org
bakercountyfl.org/clerk/local.htm

Baker: Child Support Enforcement
circuit8.org/family/support.html

Baker: Courts
www.circuit8.org
bakercountyfl.org/clerk

Baker: Public Defender
352-338-7370

Baker: Public Records Search
bakercountyfl.org/clerk
(click "Order Official Records")
www.doh.state.fl.us/planning_eval/vital_statistics
www.myfloridacounty.com/services/officialrecords_intro.shtml

Baker: Sheriff
904-239-2231
www.bakercountyfl.org/bcso
www.doh.state.fl.us/planning_eval/vital_statistics

Baker: State Attorney
352-374-3670
sawww.co.alachua.fl.us

Bay County

Bay: County Government
850-784-4013
www.bay.fl.us
www.co.bay.fl.us/area/contact.php

Bay: Administrative Agencies
www.co.bay.fl.us/area/contact.php

Bay: Child Support Enforcement
www.myfloridacounty.com/services/child_support

Bay: Courts
850-747-5102
www.baycoclerk.com
www.jud14.flcourts.org

Bay: Laws and Ordinances
www.municode.com
(click "ONLINE LIBRARY" then "Florida" then "Bay County")
www.municode.com/Resources/gateway.asp?pid=14281&
sid=9

Bay: Public Defender
850-784-6155
www.jud14.flcourts.org/CircuitLinks/PublicDefender.htm

Bay: Public Records Search
www.baycoclerk.com
www.doh.state.fl.us/planning_eval/vital_statistics
www.myfloridacounty.com/services/officialrecords_intro.shtml

Bay: Sheriff
850-747-4700
www.bayso.org

Bay: State Attorney
800-842-0103; 850-872-4473
stateattorney14.com

Bradford County

Bradford: County Government
www.bradford-co-fla.org

Bradford: Administrative Agencies
www.bradford-co-fla.org

Bradford: Child Support Enforcement
www.myfloridacounty.com/services/child_support
www.bradford-co-fla.org/clerkCourts.html

Bradford: Courts
904-966-6280
www.bradford-co-fla.org/clerkIndex.html
www.bradford-co-fla.org/clerkCourts.html
www.circuit8.org

Bradford: Laws and Ordinances
www.municode.com
(click "ONLINE LIBRARY" then "Florida" then "Bradford County")

Bradford: Public Defender
352-338-7370

Bradford: Public Records Search
www.bradford-co-fla.org/clerkCourts.html
(click "Order Official Records")
www.doh.state.fl.us/planning_eval/vital_statistics
www.myfloridacounty.com/services/officialrecords_intro.shtml

Bradford: Sheriff
904-966-6380
www.bradfordsheriff.org

Bradford: State Attorney
904-966-6208
sawww.co.alachua.fl.us

Brevard County

Brevard: County Government
www.brevardcounty.us/commission
www.brevardcounty.us/county_manager

Brevard: Administrative Agencies
www.brevardcounty.us/bcc/bccdeptindex.cfm

Brevard: Charter and Ordinances
www.brevardcounty.us/commission
(click "County Charter" and "Ordinances")
www.municode.com
(click "ONLINE LIBRARY" then "Florida" then "Brevard County")

Brevard: Child Support Enforcement
800-622-5437
199.241.8.125/index.cfm?FuseAction=ChildSupport.Home

Brevard: Consumer Protection
321-617-7510
www.sa18.state.fl.us/consume/consumer.htm

Brevard: Courts
321-637-7373
www.flcourts18.org

Brevard: Public Defender
321-617-7373
www.brevardcounty.us/publicdefender

Brevard: Public Records Search
webinfo5.brevardclerk.us/webapps_ssl/rcrc/default.cfm
www.doh.state.fl.us/planning_eval/vital_statistics
www.myfloridacounty.com/services/officialrecords_intro.shtml

Brevard: Sheriff
321-264-5201
www.brevardsheriff.com

Brevard: State Attorney
321-617-7510
www.sa18.state.fl.us

Broward County

Broward: County Government
954-357-7000
www.broward.org/countygov.htm

Broward: Administrative Agencies
www.broward.org/findanagency.htm

Broward: Charter
www.broward.org/charter/welcome.htm

Broward: Child Support Enforcement
dor.myflorida.com/dor/childsupport/phone.html
www.myfloridacounty.com/services/child_support/index.shtml

Broward: Consumer Protection
954-357-5350
www.broward.org/consumer/coi00600.htm

Broward: County Attorney
954-357-7600
www.broward.org/legal/welcome.htm

Broward: Courts
954-831-7019
www.17th.flcourts.org
www.clerk-17th-flcourts.org

Broward: Laws and Ordinances
www.municode.com
(click "ONLINE LIBRARY" then "Florida" then "Broward County")

Broward: Public Defender
954-831-8650
www.browarddefender.org

Broward: Public Records Search
www.co.broward.fl.us/records/welcome.htm
www.doh.state.fl.us/planning_eval/vital_statistics
www.myfloridacounty.com/services/officialrecords_intro.shtml

Broward: Sheriff
954-831-8900
www.flsheriffs.org/sheriffs/broward.htm

Broward: State Attorney
954-831-6955
www.sao17.state.fl.us

Calhoun County

Calhoun: County Government
mycalhouncounty.com

Calhoun: Administrative Agencies
mycalhouncounty.com

Calhoun: Child Support Enforcement
dor.myflorida.com/dor/childsupport/phone.html
www.myfloridacounty.com/services/child_support/
index.shtml

Calhoun: Courts
850-674-4545
www2.myfloridacounty.com/wps/wcm/connect/calhounclerk
www2.myfloridacounty.com/wps/wcm/connect/
calhounclerk/Home/Courts

Calhoun: Public Defender
850-674-9301
www.jud14.flcourts.org/CircuitLinks/PublicDefender.htm

Calhoun: Public Records Search
mycalhouncounty.com
(click "Official Records Search")
www.doh.state.fl.us/planning_eval/vital_statistics
www.myfloridacounty.com/services/officialrecords_intro.shtml

Calhoun: Sheriff
850-674-5049
www.calhounsheriff.com

Calhoun: State Attorney
800-248-9270; 850-674-4589
stateattorney14.com

Cape Coral, City of

Cape Coral: City Government
239-574-0437
www.capecoral.net

Cape Coral: Administrative Agencies
www.capecoral.net
(click "City Government")

Cape Coral: City Attorney
239-574-0408
www.capecoral.net
(under "City Government" click "City Departments")

Cape Coral: City Police
239-574-0676
www.capecoral.net
(under "City Government" click "City Departments")

Cape Coral: Codes and Ordinances
www.capecoral.net
(under "Laws and Codes" click code entries)

Cape Coral: Public Records Search
239-574-0411
www.capecoral.net
(under "Request Help with" click "Public Records Request")
www.doh.state.fl.us/planning_eval/vital_statistics
www.myfloridacounty.com/services/officialrecords_intro.shtml

Charlotte County

Charlotte: County Government
941-743-1200
www.charlottecountyfl.com/government.asp

Charlotte: Administrative Agencies
www.charlottecountyfl.com/depts.htm

Charlotte: Child Support Enforcement
dor.myflorida.com/dor/childsupport

Charlotte: Consumer Protection
sao.cjis20.org/Economic_Crimes.htm

Charlotte: Courts
941-637-2199
www.co.charlotte.fl.us/clrkinfo/clerk_default.htm
www.ca.cjis20.org/web/main/index.asp

Charlotte: Laws and Ordinances
www.municode.com
(click "ONLINE LIBRARY" then "Florida" then "Charlotte County")
www.municode.com/resources/gateway.asp?pid=10526&sid=9

Charlotte: Public Defender
941-637-2181
pd.cjis20.org

Charlotte: Public Records Search
www.ccappraiser.com/record.asp?
www.doh.state.fl.us/planning_eval/vital_statistics
www.myfloridacounty.com/services/officialrecords_intro.shtml

Charlotte: Sheriff
941-639-2101
www.ccso.org

Charlotte: State Attorney
941-637-2104
sao.cjis20.org

Citrus County

Citrus: County Government
www.bocc.citrus.fl.us

Citrus: Administrative Agencies
www.citruscountyfl.org/commserv/community_services.htm

Citrus: Child Support Enforcement
dor.myflorida.com/dor/childsupport/phone.html
www.myfloridacounty.com/services/child_support/index.shtml

Citrus: Code Of Ordinances
www.municode.com/resources/gateway.asp?sid=9&pid=12785

Citrus: Courts
352-341-6400
www.clerk.citrus.fl.us/home.jsp

Citrus: Laws and Ordinances
www.municode.com
(click "ONLINE LIBRARY" then "Florida" then "Citrus County")

Citrus: Public Defender
352-742-4270
www.co.hernando.fl.us/judicial/pubdef.htm

Citrus: Public Records Search
www.clerk.citrus.fl.us/nws/home.jsp
www.doh.state.fl.us/planning_eval/vital_statistics
www.myfloridacounty.com/services/officialrecords_intro.shtml

Citrus: Sheriff
352-726-1121
www.sheriffcitrus.org

Citrus: State Attorney
352-341-6670
jud5.flcourts.org/sao/index.htm

Clay County

Clay: County Government
904-269-6347
www.claycountygov.com

Clay: Administrative Agencies
www.claycountygov.com/Departments/dptlist.html

Clay: Child Support Enforcement
clerk.co.clay.fl.us/child_support_DL.htm
www.myfloridacounty.com/services/child_support

Clay: Courts
904-284-6317
clerk.co.clay.fl.us
www.coj.net/Departments/Fourth+Judicial+Circuit+Court/default.htm

Clay: Laws and Ordinances
www.municode.com
(click "ONLINE LIBRARY" then "Florida" then "Clay County")

Clay: Public Defender
904-284-6318
www.coj.net/Departments/Public+Defender

Clay: Public Records Search
www.doh.state.fl.us/planning_eval/vital_statistics
www.myfloridacounty.com/services/officialrecords_intro.shtml

Clay: Sheriff
904-264-6512
claysheriff.com

Clay: State Attorney
904-630-2400
*www.coj.net/Departments/State+Attorneys+Office+/
   default.htm*

Clearwater, City of

Clearwatwer: City Government
www.clearwater-fl.com

Clearwatwer: Administrative Agencies
www.clearwater-fl.com/gov/index.asp
www.clearwater-fl.com/gov/depts/index.asp

Clearwatwer: City Attorney
727-562-4010
www.clearwater-fl.com/gov/depts/city_attorney/index.asp

Clearwatwer: City Police
727-562-4080
www.clearwaterpolice.org

Clearwatwer: Code Of Ordinances
www.clearwater-fl.com/gov/codes/index.asp

Clearwatwer: Public Records Search
www.clearwater-fl.com/gov/depts/official_records/index.asp
www.doh.state.fl.us/planning_eval/vital_statistics
www.myfloridacounty.com/services/officialrecords_intro.shtml

Collier County

Collier: County Government
239-774-8999
www.co.collier.fl.us

Collier: Administrative Agencies
www.co.collier.fl.us/Index.aspx?page=818
www.colliergov.net/Index.aspx?page=8

Collier: Child Support Enforcement
www.collierclerk.com
(click "Child Support")

Collier: County Attorney
239-774-8400
www.co.collier.fl.us/Index.aspx?page=97

Collier: Courts
www.collierclerk.com
www.ca.cjis20.org/web/main/index.asp

Collier: Laws and Ordinances
www.municode.com
(click "ONLINE LIBRARY" then "Florida" then
"Collier County")

Collier: Public Defender
239-252-8397
pd.cjis20.org

Collier: Public Records Search
www.collierappraiser.com
www.collierclerk.com
(click entries under "Records Search")
www.doh.state.fl.us/planning_eval/vital_statistics
www.myfloridacounty.com/services/officialrecords_intro.shtml

Collier: Sheriff
239-774-4434
www.colliersheriff.org

Collier: State Attorney
239-252-8470
sao.cjis20.org

Columbia County

Columbia: County Government
www.mycolumbiacounty.com

Columbia: Administrative Agencies
www.columbiacountyfla.com/Financial_Managment.asp

Columbia: Child Support Enforcement
www.myfloridacounty.com/services/child_support

Columbia: County Attorney
386-752-7191
www.columbiacountyfla.com/Attorney.asp

Columbia: Courts
386-758-1342
www.jud3.flcourts.org
www.columbiacountyfla.com/CO_Clerk_of_Courts.asp
www2.myfloridacounty.com/wps/wcm/connect/columbiaclerk

Columbia: Public Defender
386-758-0540
www.columbiacountyfla.com/CO_Public_Defender.asp

Columbia Public Records Search
www2.myfloridacounty.com/wps/wcm/connect/columbiaclerk
(click "Public County Search")
www.doh.state.fl.us/planning_eval/vital_statistics
www.myfloridacounty.com/services/officialrecords_intro.shtml

Columbia: Sheriff
386-752-9212
www.columbiasheriff.com

Columbia: State Attorney
386-362-2320
www.columbiacountyfla.com/CO_State_Attorney.asp

Coral Springs, City of

Coral Springs: City Government
954-344-1000
www.coralsprings.org

Coral Springs: Administrative Agencies
www.coralsprings.org/departments/index.cfm

Coral Springs: City Police
www.coralsprings.org/police

Coral Springs: Codes and Ordinances
www.municode.com
(click "ONLINE LIBRARY" then "Florida" then "Coral Springs")
www.municode.com/resources/gateway.asp?pid=10537&sid=9%20

De Soto County

DeSoto: County Government
www.co.desoto.fl.us

DeSoto: Administrative Agencies
www.co.desoto.fl.us
(click entries under "Administration")

DeSoto: Child Support Enforcement
desotoclerk.com/ChildSup.htm

DeSoto: Courts
863-993-4876
12circuit.state.fl.us
desotoclerk.com/Info.htm

DeSoto: Laws and Ordinances
www.municode.com
(click "ONLINE LIBRARY" then "Florida" then "DeSoto County")

DeSoto: Public Defender
941-861-5500

DeSoto: Public Records Search
desotoclerk.com/dpa/cvweb.asp
www.doh.state.fl.us/planning_eval/vital_statistics
www.myfloridacounty.com/services/officialrecords_intro.shtml

DeSoto: Sheriff
863-993-4700
www.desotosheriff.com

DeSoto: State Attorney
863-993-4881
sao.co.sarasota.fl.us

Dixie County

Dixie: County Government
352-498-1206
www.mydixiecounty.com
dixie.fl.gov

Dixie: Administrative Agencies
dixie.fl.gov/directory.html
dixie.fl.gov/directory.html#personnel

Dixie: Child Support Enforcement
dor.myflorida.com/dor/childsupport/phone.html
www.myfloridacounty.com/services/child_support/index.shtml

Dixie: County Attorney
dixie.fl.gov/directory.html#personnel

Dixie: Courts
352-498-1200
www.jud3.flcourts.org
www2.myfloridacounty.com/wps/wcm/connect/dixieclerk

Dixie: Public Defender
386-758-0540
www.columbiacountyfla.com/CO_Public_Defender.asp

Dixie: Public Records Search
www.doh.state.fl.us/planning_eval/vital_statistics
www.myfloridacounty.com/services/officialrecords_intro.shtml

Dixie: Sheriff
352-498-1220
www.flsheriffs.org/sheriffs/dixie.htm

Dixie: State Attorney
386-362-2320
www.columbiacountyfla.com/CO_State_Attorney.asp

Duval County

Duval: County Government
www.coj.net/Departments/default.htm
www.floridacountiesmap.com/duval_county.shtml

Duval: Administrative Agencies
www.coj.net/Departments/default.htm

Duval: Child Support Enforcement
dor.myflorida.com/dor/childsupport/phone.html
www.myfloridacounty.com/services/child_support/index.shtml

Duval: Courts
904-630-2031
www.duvalclerk.com/ccWebsite

Duval: Public Defender
904-630-1501
www.coj.net/Departments/Public+Defender/default.htm

Duval: Public Records Search
www.doh.state.fl.us/planning_eval/vital_statistics
www.myfloridacounty.com/services/officialrecords_intro.shtml

Duval: Sheriff
904-630-0500
www.coj.net/Departments/Sheriffs+Office/default.htm

Duval: State Attorney
904-630-2400
www.coj.net/Departments/State+Attorneys+Office+/default.htm

Escambia County

Escambia: County Government
850-595-4946
www.co.escambia.fl.us

Escambia: Administrative Agencies
www.co.escambia.fl.us/departments.php

Escambia: Child Support Enforcement
dor.myflorida.com/dor/childsupport/phone.html
www.myfloridacounty.com/services/child_support/index.shtml

Escambia: County Attorney
*www.co.escambia.fl.us/departments/county_attorney/
   default.php*

Escambia: Courts
850-595-4310
www.clerk.co.escambia.fl.us
www.firstjudicialcircuit.org

Escambria: Laws and Ordinances
www.municode.com
(click "ONLINE LIBRARY" then "Florida" then
"Escambria County")

Escambia: Laws and Ordinances
www.municode.com/resources/gateway.asp?pid=10700&sid=9

Escambia: Public Defender
850-595-4100
www.pdo1.org/index.htm

Escambia: Public Records Search
www.clerk.co.escambia.fl.us
(click "Public Records")
www.doh.state.fl.us/planning_eval/vital_statistics
www.myfloridacounty.com/services/officialrecords_intro.shtml

Escambia: Sheriff
850-436-9630
www.escambiaso.com

Escambia: State Attorney
850-595-4200
sao1.co.escambia.fl.us

Flagler County

Flagler: County Government
www.flaglercounty.org

Flagler: Administrative Agencies
www.flaglercounty.org

Flagler: Child Support Enforcement
dor.myflorida.com/dor/childsupport/phone.html
www.myfloridacounty.com/services/child_support/index.shtml

Flagler: Courts
www.flaglerclerk.com
(click "Courts")

Flagler: County Attorney
386-313-4005
www.flaglercounty.org/pages.php?PB=187

Flagler: Courts
386-313-4400
www.flaglerclerk.com
www.circuit7.org

Flagler: Laws and Ordinances
www.municode.com
(click "ONLINE LIBRARY" then "Florida" then "Flagler County")
www.municode.com/resources/gateway.asp?pid=12218&sid=9

Flagler: Public Defender
386-313-4545
www.volusia.org/publicdefender

Flagler: Public Records Search
www.flaglerclerk.com
(click "Official Records")
www.doh.state.fl.us/planning_eval/vital_statistics
www.myfloridacounty.com/services/officialrecords_intro.shtml

Flagler: Sheriff
386-437-4116
www.myfcso.us

Flagler: State Attorney
386-313-4300
www.sao7.com

Fort Lauderdale, City of

Fort Lauderdale: City Government
954-828-5000
ci.ftlaud.fl.us/cityhall.htm

Fort Lauderdale: Administrative Agencies
ci.ftlaud.fl.us/cityhall.htm

Fort Lauderdale: City Police
954-828-5700
ci.ftlaud.fl.us/police

Fort Lauderdale: Codes and Ordinances
www.municode.com
(click "ONLINE LIBRARY" then "Florida" then "Fort Lauderdale County")
www.municode.com/resources/gateway.asp?pid=10787&sid=9

Fort Lauderdale: Public Records Search
ci.ftlaud.fl.us/pio
www.doh.state.fl.us/planning_eval/vital_statistics
www.myfloridacounty.com/services/officialrecords_intro.shtml

Franklin County

Franklin: County Government
www.franklincountyflorida.com

Franklin: Administrative Agencies
www.franklincountyflorida.com

Franklin: Child Support Enforcement
www.myfloridacounty.com/services/child_support

Franklin: Courts
850-653-8861
www.2ndcircuit.leon.fl.us
www2.myfloridacounty.com/wps/wcm/connect/franklinclerk

Franklin: Laws and Ordinances
www.municode.com
(click "ONLINE LIBRARY" then "Florida" then "Franklin County")

Franklin: Public Defender
850-653-9506
www.co.leon.fl.us/PD/index.asp
www.co.leon.fl.us/pd/location.asp

Franklin: Public Records Search
www.doh.state.fl.us/planning_eval/vital_statistics
www.myfloridacounty.com/services/officialrecords_intro.shtml

Franklin: Sheriff
(850) 670-8500
www.franklinsheriff.com

Franklin: State Attorney
850-653-8181
www.sao2fl.org

Gadsden County

Gadsden: County Government
850-875-8650
www.gadsdengov.net

Gadsden: Administrative Agencies
www.gadsdengov.net/departments.html
www.gadsdengov.net/contactus.html

Gadsden: Child Support Enforcement
myfloridacounty.com/services/child_support

Gadsden: Courts
850-875-8601
www.clerk.co.gadsden.fl.us
www.2ndcircuit.leon.fl.us

Gadsden: Laws and Ordinances
www.municode.com
(click "ONLINE LIBRARY" then "Florida" then "Gadsden County")
www.municode.com/Resources/gateway.asp?pid=13425&sid=9

Gadsden: Public Defender
850-627-9241
www.co.leon.fl.us/pd

Gadsden: Public Records Search
www.doh.state.fl.us/planning_eval/vital_statistics
www.myfloridacounty.com/services/officialrecords_intro.shtml

Gadsden: Sheriff
850-627-9233
gadsdensheriff.org

Gadsden: State Attorney
850-627-9647; 850-488-6701
www.sao2fl.org

Gilchrist County

Gilchrist: County Government
gilchrist.fl.us

Gilchrist: Administrative Agencies
gilchrist.fl.us/Directory/Directory.htm

Gilchrist: Child Support Enforcement
dor.myflorida.com/dor/childsupport/phone.html
www.myfloridacounty.com/services/child_support/index.shtml

Gilchrist: County Attorney
352-378-5827

Gilchrist: Courts
800-267-3182; 352-463-3170
www2.myfloridacounty.com/wps/wcm/connect/gilchristclerk
www.circuit8.org

Gilchrist: Laws and Ordinances
gilchrist.fl.us
(click "Code of Ordinances")

Gilchrist: Public Defender
352-338-7370

Gilchrist: Public Records Search
records.gilchrist.fl.us/oncoreweb/Search.aspx
www.doh.state.fl.us/planning_eval/vital_statistics
www.myfloridacounty.com/services/officialrecords_intro.shtml

Gilchrist: Sheriff
352-463-3410
www.gilcso.org

Gilchrist: State Attorney
352-463-3406
sawww.co.alachua.fl.us

Glades County

Glades: County Government
863-946-6000
www.gladescofl.us
mygladescounty.com

Glades: Administrative Agencies
www.gladescofl.us
(click "Departments")

Glades: Child Support Enforcement
dor.myflorida.com/dor/childsupport/phone.html
www.myfloridacounty.com/services/child_support/index.shtml

Glades: Courts
863-946-6010
www2.myfloridacounty.com/wps/wcm/connect/gladesclerk
www.ca.cjis20.org

Glades: Public Defender
863-675-5263
pd.cjis20.org

Glades: Public Records Search
www.doh.state.fl.us/planning_eval/vital_statistics
www.myfloridacounty.com/services/officialrecords_intro.shtml

Glades: Sheriff
863-946-1600
www.gladessheriff.org

Glades: State Attorney
863-946-0077
sao.cjis20.org/Glades.htm

Gulf County

Gulf: County Government
850-229-6111
www.gulfcountygovernment.com

Gulf: Administrative Agencies
www.gulfcountygovernment.com/departments.cfm

Gulf: Child Support Enforcement
dor.myflorida.com/dor/childsupport/phone.html
www.myfloridacounty.com/services/child_support/index.shtml

Gulf: Courts
850-229-6112
www2.myfloridacounty.com/wps/wcm/connect/gulfclerk
www.jud14.flcourts.org

Gulf: Public Defender
850-229-9600
www.jud14.flcourts.org/CircuitLinks/PublicDefender.htm

Gulf: Public Records Search
www.doh.state.fl.us/planning_eval/vital_statistics
www.myfloridacounty.com/services/officialrecords_intro.shtml

Gulf: Sheriff
850-227-1115
www.gulfsheriff.com

Gulf: State Attorney
850-800-545-8272; 850-229-6131
stateattorney14.com/office-locations.html
www.jud14.flcourts.org/CircuitLinks/StateAttorney.htm

Hamilton County

Hamilton: County Government
www.hamiltoncountyflorida.com

Hamilton: Administrative Agencies
www.hamiltoncountyflorida.com

Hamilton: Child Support Enforcement
dor.myflorida.com/dor/childsupport/phone.html
www.myfloridacounty.com/services/child_support/index.shtml

Hamilton: County Attorney
386-792-2395
www.hamiltoncountyflorida.com/cd_attorney.aspx

Hamilton: Courts
386-792-1288
www.hamiltoncountyflorida.com/cd_clerk.aspx

Hamilton: Public Defender
386-758-0540
www.columbiacountyfla.com/CO_Public_Defender.asp

Hamilton: Public Records Search
www.doh.state.fl.us/planning_eval/vital_statistics
www.myfloridacounty.com/services/officialrecords_intro.shtml

Hamilton: Sheriff
850-877-2165
www.hamiltoncountyflorida.com/cd_sherrif.aspx

Hamilton: State Attorney
386-362-2320
www.columbiacountyfla.com/CO_State_Attorney.asp

Hardee County

Hardee: County Government
863-773-6952
www.hardeecounty.net

Hardee: Administrative Agencies
www.hardeecounty.net
(click "Departments")

Hardee: Child Support Enforcement
dor.myflorida.com/dor/childsupport/phone.html
www.myfloridacounty.com/services/child_support/index.shtml

Hardee: Courts
863-773-4174
www2.myfloridacounty.com/wps/wcm/connect/hardeeclerk
www.jud10.org

Hardee: Public Defender
863-534-4200
www.jud10.org/pd.htm
www.public-defender10-fl.org

Hardee: Public Records Search
www.doh.state.fl.us/planning_eval/vital_statistics
www.myfloridacounty.com/services/officialrecords_intro.shtml

Hardee: Sheriff
863-773-0304
www.hardeeso.com

Hardee: State Attorney
863-773-6613
www.sao10.com

Hendry County

Hendry: County Government
863-675-5220
www.hendryfla.net

Hendry: Administrative Agencies
www.hendryfla.net/agencies.htm

Hendry: Child Support Enforcement
800-622-5437
www.hendryclerk.org/cse.htm

Hendry: Courts
863-675-5217
www.hendryclerk.org
www.hendryclerk.org/courts.htm
www.ca.cjis20.org/web/main/index.asp

Hendry: Laws and Ordinances
www.hendryclerk.org/records.htm
(click "Code of Ordinances")

Hendry: Public Defender
863-675-5263
pd.cjis20.org

Hendry: Public Records Search
www.doh.state.fl.us/planning_eval/vital_statistics
www.myfloridacounty.com/services/officialrecords_intro.shtml

Hendry: Sheriff
863-674-4060
www.hendrysheriff.org

Hendry: State Attorney
863-674-4033
sao.cjis20.org

Hernando County

Hernando: County Government
352-754-4000
www.co.hernando.fl.us

Hernando: Child Support Enforcement
352-540-6336
www.clerk.co.hernando.fl.us/Other/ChildSupport.html

Hernando: Courts
352-540-6216
www.clerk.co.hernando.fl.us
www.circuit5.org

Hernando: Laws and Ordinances
www.co.hernando.fl.us
(click "County Ordinances")

Hernando: Public Defender
352-742-4270
www.hernandocounty.us/judicial/pubdef.htm

Hernando: Public Records Search
www.doh.state.fl.us/planning_eval/vital_statistics
www.myfloridacounty.com/services/officialrecords_intro.shtml

Hernando: Sheriff
352-754-6830
www.hcso.hernando.fl.us

Hernando: State Attorney
352-620-3800; 352-754-4255
jud5.flcourts.org/sao/index.htm
www.hernandocounty.us/judicial/stateatty.htm

Hialeah, City of

Hialeah: City Government
305-883-5800
www.hialeahfl.gov

Hialeah: Administrative Agencies
www.hialeahfl.gov/dept

Hialeah: Laws and Ordinances
www.municode.com
(click "ONLINE LIBRARY" then "Florida" then "Hialeah")

Hialeah: City Attorney
305-883-5853
www.hialeahfl.gov/dept/law/default.asp

Hialeah: City Police
305-687-2525
www.hialeahfl.gov/dept/police/default.asp

Hialeah: Public Records Search
www.doh.state.fl.us/planning_eval/vital_statistics
www.myfloridacounty.com/services/officialrecords_intro.shtml

Highlands County

Highlands: County Government
www.hcbcc.net/#

Highlands: Administrative Agencies
www.hcbcc.net/BoardsCommiti.html

Highlands: Child Support Enforcement
dor.myflorida.com/dor/childsupport/phone.html
www.myfloridacounty.com/services/child_support/index.shtml

Highlands: Courts
863-402-6564
www.clerk.co.highlands.fl.us
www.hcclerk.org
www.jud10.org

Highlands: Laws and Ordinances
www.hcbcc.net/#
(under "For Citizens" click "Read County Ordinances")

Highlands: Public Defender
863-402-6724
www.public-defender10-fl.org
www.jud10.org/pd.htm

Highlands: Public Records Search
www.appraiser.co.highlands.fl.us/index.shtml
www.hcclerk.org/SearchOfficialRecords.aspx
www.doh.state.fl.us/planning_eval/vital_statistics
www.myfloridacounty.com/services/officialrecords_intro.shtml

Highlands: Sheriff
863-402-7200
www.highlandssheriff.org

Highlands: State Attorney
863-534-4800
www.sao10.com

Hillsborough County

Hillsborough: County Government
813-272-5750
www.hillsboroughcounty.org

Hillsborough: Administrative Agencies
www.hillsboroughcounty.org/departments

Hillsborough: Child Support Enforcement
www.myfloridacounty.com/services/child_support/index.shtml

Hillsborough: County Attorney
813-272-5670
www.hillsboroughcounty.org/countyattorney

Hillsborough: Courts
813-276-8100
www.hillsclerk.com
www.fljud13.org

Hillsborough: Laws and Ordinances
www.hillsboroughcounty.org/sitemap.cfm
(click "Codes (Hillsborough County)")

Hillsborough: Public Defender
813-272-5980
pd13.state.fl.us

Hillsborough: Public Records Search
www.hillsboroughcounty.org/sitemap.cfm
(click "Public Records")
propmap2.hcpafl.org
www.doh.state.fl.us/planning_eval/vital_statistics
www.myfloridacounty.com/services/officialrecords_intro.shtml

Hillsborough: Sheriff
813-247-8000
www.hcso.tampa.fl.us

Hillsborough: State Attorney
813-272-5400
www.sao13th.com

Hollywood, City of

Hollywood: City Government
954-921-3321
www.hollywoodfl.org

Hollywood: Administrative Agencies
www.hollywoodfl.org/city_directory/hlwd_tel.htm

Hollywood: City Police
954-967-4636
www.hollywoodpolice.org

Hollywood: Codes and Ordinances
www.hollywoodfl.org/city_clerks/directory.htm
(click "Code of Ordinances")

www.amlegal.com/library/fl/hollywood.shtml

Hollywood: Public Records Search
www.doh.state.fl.us/planning_eval/vital_statistics
www.myfloridacounty.com/services/officialrecords_intro.shtml

Holmes County

Holmes: County Government
www.myholmescounty.com

Holmes: Child Support Enforcement
dor.myflorida.com/dor/childsupport/phone.html
www.myfloridacounty.com/services/child_support/index.shtml

Holmes: Courts
850-547-1100
www2.myfloridacounty.com/wps/wcm/connect/holmesclerk
www.jud14.flcourts.org

Holmes: Public Defender
850-638-6000
www.jud14.flcourts.org/CircuitLinks/PublicDefender.htm

Holmes: Public Records Search
www.doh.state.fl.us/planning_eval/vital_statistics
www.myfloridacounty.com/services/officialrecords_intro.shtml

Holmes: Sheriff
850-547-4421
www.holmescosheriff.org

Holmes: State Attorney
850-547-2262
stateattorney14.com/office-locations.html

Indian River County

Indian River: County Government
772-567-8000
www.ircgov.com
indian-river.fl.us/government

Indian River: Administrative Agencies
www.ircgov.com/Departments/Index.htm

Indian River: Child Support Enforcement
dor.myflorida.com/dor/childsupport/phone.html
www.myfloridacounty.com/services/child_support/index.shtml

Indian River: Courts
772-770-5185
www.clerk.indian-river.org
www.circuit19.org

Indian River: Laws and Ordinances
www.municode.com
(click "ONLINE LIBRARY" then "Florida" then "Indian River County")

Indian River: County Attorney
772-567-8000
www.ircgov.com/Departments/Attorney/Index.htm

Indian River: Public Defender
772-770-5080
www.pd19.org

Indian River: Public Records Search
www.ircpa.org
www.doh.state.fl.us/planning_eval/vital_statistics
www.myfloridacounty.com/services/officialrecords_intro.shtml

Indian River: Sheriff
772-569-6700
ircsheriff.org

Indian River: State Attorney
772-465-3000; 772-288-5646
sa18.state.fl.us/general/saolist.htm

Jackson County

Jackson: County Government
850-482-9633
www.jacksoncountyfl.com

Jackson: Administrative Agencies
www.jacksoncountyfl.com/#Departments

Jackson: Child Support Enforcement
dor.myflorida.com/dor/childsupport/phone.html
www.myfloridacounty.com/services/child_support/
   index.shtml

Jackson: Courts
850-482-9552
www.myfloridaclerks.com/countytemplate.cfm?countyid=
   Jackson
www2.myfloridacounty.com/wps/wcm/connect/jacksonclerk
www.jud14.flcourts.org

Jackson: Laws and Ordinances
www.jacksoncountyfl.com
(click "Community Development" then "County Regulations")
www.municode.com
(click "ONLINE LIBRARY" then "Florida" then "Jackson County")

Jackson: Public Defender
850-482-9366
www.jud14.flcourts.org/CircuitLinks/PublicDefender.htm

Jackson: Public Records Search
www.doh.state.fl.us/planning_eval/vital_statistics
www.myfloridacounty.com/services/officialrecords_intro.shtml

Jackson: Sheriff
850-482-9624
www.jcsheriff.com

Jackson: State Attorney
800-344-7532; 850-482-9555
stateattorney14.com/office-locations.html

Jacksonville, City of

Jacksonville: City Government
904-630-2489
www.coj.net

Jacksonville: Administrative Agencies
www.coj.net/Departments/default.htm

Jacksonville: Laws and Ordinances
www.municode.com
(click "ONLINE LIBRARY" then "Florida" then "Jacksonville")

Jacksonville: City Police
www.jacksonvillepd.com

Jacksonville: Public Records Search
www.doh.state.fl.us/planning_eval/vital_statistics
www.myfloridacounty.com/services/officialrecords_intro.shtml

Jefferson County

Jefferson: County Government
850-342-0187
www.co.jefferson.fl.us
myjeffersoncounty.com

Jefferson: Administrative Agencies
www.co.jefferson.fl.us
(click "Departments")

Jefferson: Child Support Enforcement
www.myfloridacounty.com/services/child_support/
   index.shtml

Jefferson: Courts
850-342-0218; 850-342-0218
www.myfloridaclerks.com/countytemplate.cfm?countyid=
   Jefferson
www.2ndcircuit.leon.fl.us

Jefferson: Public Defender
850-342-0202
www.co.leon.fl.us/pd/location.asp

Jefferson: Public Records Search
www.doh.state.fl.us/planning_eval/vital_statistics
www.myfloridacounty.com/services/officialrecords_intro.shtml

Jefferson: Sheriff
850-997-2523
www.flsheriffs.org/sheriffs/jefferso.htm

Jefferson: State Attorney
850-653-8181; 850-488-6701
www.sao2fl.org

Lafayette County

Lafayette: County Government
www.uflib.ufl.edu/fefdl/counties/lafayette.html
en.wikipedia.org/wiki/Lafayette_County,_Florida

Lafayette: Child Support Enforcement
dor.myflorida.com/dor/childsupport/phone.html
*www.myfloridacounty.com/services/child_support/
    index.shtml*

Lafayette: Courts
386-294-1600
*www.myfloridaclerks.com/countytemplate.cfm?countyid=
    Lafayette*
www2.myfloridacounty.com/wps/wcm/connect/lafayetteclerk
www.jud3.flcourts.org

Lafayette: Property Appraiser
386-294-1991
www.lafayettepa.com

Lafayette: Public Defender
386-758-0540
www.columbiacountyfla.com/CO_Public_Defender.asp

Lafayette: Public Records Search
www.doh.state.fl.us/planning_eval/vital_statistics
www.myfloridacounty.com/services/officialrecords_intro.shtml

Lafayette: Sheriff
flsheriffs.org/sheriffs/lafayette.htm

Lafayette: State Attorney
386-362-2320
www.columbiacountyfla.com/CO_State_Attorney.asp

Lake County

Lake: County Government
www.lakecountyfl.gov

Lake: Administrative Agencies
www.co.lake.fl.us/departments

Lake: Child Support Enforcement
*www.lakecountyclerk.org/departments.asp?subject=
    Child_Support*

Lake: County Attorney
352-343-9787
www.lakecountyfl.gov/departments/county_attorney

Lake: Courts
352-742-4100
www.lakecountyclerk.org
www.myfloridaclerks.com/countytemplate.cfm?countyid=Lake
www.circuit5.org

Lake: Laws and Ordinances
www.lakecountyfl.gov/departments/county_attorney
(click "Ordinances")

Lake: Public Defender
352-742-4270
www.hernandocounty.us/judicial/pubdef.htm

Lake: Public Records Search
www.doh.state.fl.us/planning_eval/vital_statistics
www.myfloridacounty.com/services/officialrecords_intro.shtml

Lake: Sheriff
352-343-2101
www.lcso.org

Lake: State Attorney
352-742-4255
www.hernandocounty.us/judicial/stateatty.htm

Lee County

Lee: County Government
239-533-2737
www.lee-county.com

Lee: Administrative Agencies
www.lee-county.com
(under "Government" click "Departments")

Lee: Child Support Enforcement
dor.myflorida.com/dor/childsupport/phone.html
*www.myfloridacounty.com/services/child_support/
    index.shtml*

Lee: County Attorney
239-335-2236
www.lee-county.com/countyattorney

Lee: Courts
239-533-5000
www.myfloridaclerks.com/countytemplate.cfm?countyid=Lee
www.ca.cjis20.org/web/main/index.asp

Lee: Laws and Ordinances
www.municode.com
(click "ONLINE LIBRARY" then "Florida" then "Lee
County")
www.lee-county.com
(under "Government" click "Online Resources" then
"Administrative Codes")

Lee: Public Defender
239-335-2921
pd.cjis20.org

Lee: Public Records Search
www.doh.state.fl.us/planning_eval/vital_statistics
www.myfloridacounty.com/services/officialrecords_intro.shtml

Lee: Sheriff
239-477-1200
www.sheriffleefl.org

Lee: State Attorney
239-335-2700
sao.cjis20.org/Lee.htm

Leon County

Leon: County Government
850-606-5300
www.leoncountyfl.gov

Leon: Administrative Agencies
www.leoncountyfl.gov/departments.asp

Leon: Child Support Enforcement
dor.myflorida.com/dor/childsupport/phone.html
www.myfloridacounty.com/services/child_support/index.shtml

Leon: County Attorney
850-606-2500
www.leoncountyfl.gov/LCAO

Leon: Courts
850-577-4000
www.clerk.leon.fl.us
www.2ndcircuit.leon.fl.us

Leon: Laws and Ordinances
www.leoncountyfl.gov/documents.asp

Leon: Public Defender
850-606-1000
www.co.leon.fl.us/pd/index.asp

Leon: Public Records Search
dta.co.leon.fl.us/prop/Search2.cfm
www.doh.state.fl.us/planning_eval/vital_statistics
www.myfloridacounty.com/services/officialrecords_intro.shtml

Leon: Sheriff
850-922-3346
lcso.leonfl.org

Leon: State Attorney
850-606-6000
www.sao2fl.org

Levy County

Levy: County Government
352-486-5218
www.levycounty.org

Levy: Administrative Agencies
www.levycounty.org
(click "County Departments")

Levy: Child Support Enforcement
dor.myflorida.com/dor/childsupport/phone.html
www.myfloridacounty.com/services/child_support/index.shtml

Levy: County Attorney
352-486-3389
www.levycounty.org
(click "County Departments" then "County Attorney")

Levy: Courts
352-486-5266
levyclerk.com
www.myfloridaclerks.com/countytemplate.cfm?countyid=Levy
www.circuit8.org

Levy: Laws and Ordinances
www.municode.com
(click "ONLINE LIBRARY" then "Florida" then "Levy County")

Levy: Public Defender
352-338-7370

Levy: Public Records Search
oncore.levyclerk.com/oncoreweb
www.doh.state.fl.us/planning_eval/vital_statistics
www.myfloridacounty.com/services/officialrecords_intro.shtml

Levy: Sheriff
352-486-5111
www.levyso.com

Levy: State Attorney
352-486-5140
sawww.co.alachua.fl.us

Liberty County

Liberty: County Government
www.uflib.ufl.edu/fefdl/counties/liberty.html
www.freenet.tlh.fl.us/Liberty_County/government.html
en.wikipedia.org/wiki/Liberty_County,_Florida

Liberty: Child Support Enforcement
dor.myflorida.com/dor/childsupport/phone.html
www.myfloridacounty.com/services/child_support/index.shtml

Liberty: Courts
850-643-2215
www.myfloridaclerks.com/countytemplate.cfm?countyid=Liberty
www.myfloridacounty.com/mfcTemplate/view.jsp?countyid=LIBERTY
www.2ndcircuit.leon.fl.us

Liberty: Public Defender
850-627-9241
www.co.leon.fl.us/pd/index.asp

Liberty: Public Records Search
www.doh.state.fl.us/planning_eval/vital_statistics
www.myfloridacounty.com/services/officialrecords_intro.shtml

Liberty: Sheriff
850-643-2235

Liberty: State Attorney
850-606-6000
www.sao2fl.org

Madison County

Madison: County Government
850-973-3179
www.madisoncountyfl.com

Madison: Administrative Agencies
www.madisoncountyfl.com/departments.aspx

Madison: Child Support Enforcement
dor.myflorida.com/dor/childsupport/phone.html
www.myfloridacounty.com/services/child_support/index.shtml

Madison: Courts
850-973-1500
www.madisonclerk.com
(click "Courts")
www.myfloridaclerks.com/countytemplate.cfm?countyid=Madison
www.jud3.flcourts.org

Madison: Public Defender
386-758-0540
www.columbiacountyfla.com/CO_Public_Defender.asp

Madison: Public Records Search
www.doh.state.fl.us/planning_eval/vital_statistics
www.myfloridacounty.com/services/officialrecords_intro.shtml

Madison: Sheriff
850-973-4151
www.flsheriffs.org/sheriffs/madison.htm

Madison: State Attorney
386-362-2320
www.columbiacountyfla.com/CO_State_Attorney.asp

Manatee County

Manatee: County Government
941-748-4501
www.co.manatee.fl.us

Manatee: Administrative Agencies
www.co.manatee.fl.us
(click "Departments")

Manatee: Child Support Enforcement
www.clerkofcourts.com/cvpcaseapp/csform.asp

Manatee: County Attorney
941-745-3750
www.co.manatee.fl.us
(click "Departments" then "County Attorney")

Manatee: Courts
941-749-1800
www.myfloridaclerks.com/countytemplate.cfm?countyid=
Manatee
www.clerkofcourts.com
12circuit.state.fl.us

Manatee: Laws and Ordinances
www.municode.com
(click "ONLINE LIBRARY" then "Florida" then "Manatee County")

Manatee: Public Defender
941-861-5500

Manatee: Public Records Search
www.doh.state.fl.us/planning_eval/vital_statistics
www.myfloridacounty.com/services/officialrecords_intro.shtml

Manatee: Sheriff
941-747-3011
www.manateesheriff.com

Manatee: State Attorney
941-747-3077
sao.co.sarasota.fl.us

Marion County

Marion: County Government
352-438-2300
www.marioncountyfl.org

Marion: Administrative Agencies
www.marioncountyfl.org
(click "Departments")

Marion: Child Support Enforcement
dor.myflorida.com/dor/childsupport/phone.html
www.myfloridacounty.com/services/child_support/
index.shtml

Marion: County Attorney
352-438-2330
www.marioncountyfl.org/Attorney/attorney.aspx

Marion: Courts
352-671-5604
www.myfloridaclerks.com/countytemplate.cfm?countyid=
Marion
www.marioncountyclerk.org
www.co.hernando.fl.us/judicial/#Fifth

Marion: Laws and Ordinances
www.marioncountyfl.org
(under "I Want To" click "Find County Code of Ordinances")

Marion: Public Defender
352-742-4270
www.hernandocounty.us/judicial/pubdef.htm

Marion: Public Records Search
www.propappr.marion.fl.us/agree.html
www.marioncountyclerk.org
(click "Official Records Search")
www.doh.state.fl.us/planning_eval/vital_statistics
*www.myfloridacounty.com/services/officialrecords_*
intro.shtml

Marion: Sheriff
352-732-8181
www.marionso.com

Marion: State Attorney
352-620-3800
jud5.flcourts.org/sao/index.htm
www.co.hernando.fl.us/judicial/stateatty.htm

Martin County

Martin: County Government
772-281-2360
www.martin.fl.us

Martin: Administrative Agencies
www.martin.fl.us
(click "Departments")

Martin: Child Support Enforcement
www.myfloridacounty.com/services/child_support

Martin: County Attorney
772-228-5440
www.martin.fl.us
(click "Departments" then "County Attorney")

Martin: Courts
772-288-5576; 772-288-5736
clerk-web.martin.fl.us/ClerkWeb
www.myfloridaclerks.com/countytemplate.cfm?countyid=Martin

Martin: Laws and Ordinances
www.martin.fl.us
(click "Martin County Code")

Martin: Public Defender
772-288-5581
www.pd19.org

Martin: Public Records Search
clerk-web.martin.fl.us/ClerkWeb/courts/criminal.htm
(click "Public Records")
www.doh.state.fl.us/planning_eval/vital_statistics
www.myfloridacounty.com/services/officialrecords_intro.shtml

Martin: Sheriff
772-220-7000
www.sheriff.martin.fl.us

Martin: State Attorney
772-288-5646

Miami, City of

Miami: City Government
305-250-5300
www.miamigov.com/cms

Miami: Administrative Agencies
egov.ci.miami.fl.us/directory/citydirectory.aspx

Miami: City Attorney
305-416-1800
www.miamigov.com/cityattorney/pages

Miami: City Police
www.miami-police.org

Miami: Codes and Ordinances
www.municode.com/resources/gateway.asp?pid=10933&sid=9

Miami: Public Records Search
www.doh.state.fl.us/planning_eval/vital_statistics
www.myfloridacounty.com/services/officialrecords_intro.shtml

Miami-Dade County

Miami-Dade: County Government
311; 305-468-5900
www.miamidade.gov

Miami-Dade: Administrative Agencies
www.miamidade.gov
(click "County Agencies")

Miami-Dade: Child Support Enforcement
dor.myflorida.com/dor/childsupport/phone.html
www.myfloridacounty.com/services/child_support/index.shtml

Miami-Dade: County Attorney
305-375-5151
attorney.miamidade.gov

Miami-Dade: Courts
305-349-7333; 305-275-1155
www.myfloridaclerks.com/countytemplate.cfm?countyid=Miami-Dade
www.miami-dadeclerk.com/dadecoc/Contact_Us.asp
www.jud11.flcourts.org

Miami-Dade: Laws and Ordinances
www.municode.com
(click "ONLINE LIBRARY" then "Florida" then "Miami-Dade County")
www.municode.com/resources/gateway.asp?pid=10620&sid=9

Miami-Dade: Public Defender
305-545-1600
www.pdmiami.com

Miami-Dade: Public Records Search
www.miami-dadeclerk.com/public-records
www.doh.state.fl.us/planning_eval/vital_statistics
www.myfloridacounty.com/services/officialrecords_intro.shtml

Miami-Dade: Police
305-4-POLICE
www.mdpd.com

Miami-Dade: State Attorney
305-547-0100
miamisao.com

Monroe County

Monroe: County Government
305-292-4441
www.uflib.ufl.edu/ElectedOfficials/County2.asp?County=Monroe
monroecofl.virtualtownhall.net/Pages/MonroeCoFL_WebDocs/divisions

Monroe: Child Support Enforcement
800-622-5437
www.clerk-of-the-court.com/Other/ChildSupport.html

Monroe: Courts
305-294-4641
www.clerk-of-the-court.com
www.myfloridaclerks.com/countytemplate.cfm?countyid=Monroe
www.keyscourts.net

Monroe: Laws and Ordinances
www.municode.com
(click "ONLINE LIBRARY" then "Florida" then "Monroe County")

Monroe: Public Defender
305-294-2501

Monroe: Public Records Search
www.doh.state.fl.us/planning_eval/vital_statistics
www.myfloridacounty.com/services/officialrecords_intro.shtml

Monroe: Sheriff
305-296-2424
www.keysso.net

Monroe: State Attorney
305-292-3400
www.keyssao.org

Nassau County

Nassau: County Government
800-958-3496; 904-548-4600
www.nassaucountyfl.com
www.nassauclerk.com

Nassau: Administrative Agencies
www.nassauclerk.com
(click "Contact Information")

Nassau: Child Support Enforcement
800-622-5437
www.nassauclerk.com
(click "Child Support")

Nassau: Courts
904-548-4600
www.myfloridaclerks.com/countytemplate.cfm?countyid=Nassau

Nassau: Laws and Ordinances
www.nassaucountyfl.com
(click "County Ordinances")

Nassau: Public Defender
904-630-1501
www.coj.net/Departments/Public+Defender/default.htm

Nassau: Public Records Search
www.nassauclerk.com
(click "Official Records Search")
www.doh.state.fl.us/planning_eval/vital_statistics
www.myfloridacounty.com/services/officialrecords_intro.shtml

Nassau: Sheriff
904-225-9189
www.nassaucountysheriff.com

Nassau: State Attorney
904-630-2400
www.coj.net/Departments/State+Attorneys+Office+/default.htm

Okaloosa County

Okaloosa: County Government
850-651-7515
www.co.okaloosa.fl.us

Okaloosa: Administrative Agencies
www.co.okaloosa.fl.us
(click "Departments")

Okaloosa: Child Support Enforcement
dor.myflorida.com/dor/childsupport/phone.html
www.myfloridacounty.com/services/child_support/index.shtml

Okaloosa: Courts
850-689-5821; 850-689-5000
www.clerkofcourts.cc
www.myfloridaclerks.com/countytemplate.cfm?countyid=Okaloosa
www.firstjudicialcircuit.org

Okaloosa: Laws and Ordinances
www.municode.com
(click "ONLINE LIBRARY" then "Florida" then "Okaloosa County")
www.municode.com/resources/gateway.asp?pid=11900&sid=9

Okaloosa: Public Defender
850-651-7350; 850-689-5580
www.pdo1.org/okaloosa.htm

Okaloosa: Public Records Search
www.clerkofcourts.cc/orsearch/choice.htm
www.doh.state.fl.us/planning_eval/vital_statistics
www.myfloridacounty.com/services/officialrecords_intro.shtml

Okaloosa: Sheriff
850-651-7410
www.sheriff-okaloosa.org

Okaloosa: State Attorney
850-595-4200
sao1.co.escambia.fl.us

Okeechobee County

Okeechobee: County Government
863-763-6441
www.co.okeechobee.fl.us
www.floridatc.com/government.html

Okeechobee: Administrative Agencies
www.co.okeechobee.fl.us/listings.htm

Okeechobee: Child Support Enforcement
dor.myflorida.com/dor/childsupport/phone.html
www.myfloridacounty.com/services/child_support/index.shtml

Okeechobee: Courts
863-763-2131
www.clerk.co.okeechobee.fl.us
www.clerk.co.okeechobee.fl.us/Local_Websites.htm
www.circuit19.org

Okeechobee: Laws and Ordinances
www.co.okeechobee.fl.us
(click "Code of Ordinances")

Okeechobee: Public Defender
863-763-7977
www.pd19.org

Okeechobee: Public Records Search
www.doh.state.fl.us/planning_eval/vital_statistics
www.myfloridacounty.com/services/officialrecords_intro.shtml

Okeechobee: Sheriff
863-763-3117
www.sheriff.co.okeechobee.fl.us

Okeechobee: State Attorney
772-288-5646

Orange County

Orange: County Government
407-836-3111
www.orangecountyfl.net

Orange: Administrative Agencies
www.occompt.com/sitemap.html

Orange: Child Support Enforcement
dor.myflorida.com/dor/childsupport/phone.html
www.myfloridacounty.com/services/child_support/index.shtml

Orange: Courts
407-836-2200
www.myorangeclerk.com
www.ninja9.org

Orange: Laws and Ordinances
www.orangecountyfl.net/cms/DEPT/CEsrvcs/code
(click "Municipal Code Corporation")

Orange: Public Defender
407-836-4800
pd.circuit9.org

Orange: Public Records Search
www.occompt.com/records.html
www.doh.state.fl.us/planning_eval/vital_statistics
www.myfloridacounty.com/services/officialrecords_intro.shtml

Orange: Sheriff
407-254-7000
www.ocso.com

Orange: State Attorney
407-836-2400

Orlando, City of

Orlando: City Government
407-246-4990
www.cityoforlando.net

Orlando: Administrative Agencies
www.cityoforlando.net/contact.htm

Orlando: City Attorney
407-246-2221
www.cityoforlando.net/elected/mayor/cityattorney.htm

Orlando: City Police
321-246-2470
www.cityoforlando.net/police

Orlando: Codes and Ordinances
www.municode.com/resources/gateway.asp?pid=13349&sid=9

Orlando: Public Records Search
www.doh.state.fl.us/planning_eval/vital_statistics
www.myfloridacounty.com/services/officialrecords_intro.shtml

Osceola County

Osceola: County Government
407-343-2275
www.osceola.org

Osceola: Administrative Agencies
www.osceola.org
(click "Department Directory")

Osceola: Charter
www.osceola.org/index.cfm?lsFuses=department/
AboutOsceola/Charter

Osceola: Child Support Enforcement
dor.myflorida.com/dor/childsupport/phone.html
www.myfloridacounty.com/services/child_support/index.shtml

Osceola: County Attorney
407-343-2330
www.osceola.org/index.cfm?lsFuses=department/
CountyAttorney

Osceola: Courts
407-343-3500
www.osceolaclerk.com
www.ninja9.org

Osceola: Laws and Ordinances
www.municode.com
(click "ONLINE LIBRARY" then "Florida" then "Osceola County")

Osceola: Public Defender
407-343-7100
pd.circuit9.org

Osceola: Public Records Search
www.doh.state.fl.us/planning_eval/vital_statistics
www.myfloridacounty.com/services/officialrecords_intro.shtml

Osceola: Sheriff
407-348-2222
www.osceolasheriff.org

Osceola: State Attorney
407- 836-2400

Palm Beach County

Palm Beach: County Government
561-355-2754
www.co.palm-beach.fl.us

Palm Beach: Administrative Agencies
www.co.palm-beach.fl.us/departments.htm

Palm Beach: Child Support Enforcement
www.pbcountyclerk.com
(click "Child Support")

Palm Beach: County Attorney
561-355-2225
www.co.palm-beach.fl.us/countyattorney

Palm Beach: Courts
561-355-2996
www.myfloridaclerks.com/countytemplate.cfm?countyid=
Palm+Beach
www.pbcountyclerk.com
www.co.palm-beach.fl.us/cadmin

Palm Beach: Laws and Ordinances
www.co.palm-beach.fl.us/government.htm
(click "County Code")

Palm Beach: Public Defender
561-355-7500
www.pd15.state.fl.us

Palm Beach: Public Records Search
www.co.palm-beach.fl.us/papa/index.htm
www.pbcountyclerk.com/oris/records_home.html
www.doh.state.fl.us/planning_eval/vital_statistics
www.myfloridacounty.com/services/officialrecords_intro.shtml

Palm Beach: Sheriff
561-688-3000
www.pbso.org

Palm Beach: State Attorney
561-355-7100
www.sa15.state.fl.us

Pasco County

Pasco: County Government
727-847-2411; 352-521-4274
www.pascocountyfl.net

Pasco: Administrative Agencies
www.pascocountyfl.net
(click "County Agencies")

Pasco: Child Support Enforcement
dor.myflorida.com/dor/childsupport/phone.html
www.myfloridacounty.com/services/child_support/
index.shtml

Pasco: Courts
727-847-2411
www.myfloridaclerks.com/countytemplate.cfm?countyid=
Pasco
www.jud6.org

Pasco: Laws and Ordinances
www.municode.com
(click "ONLINE LIBRARY" then "Florida" then "Pasco County")

Pasco: Public Defender
352-521-4388
www.wearethehope.org

Pasco: Public Records Search
www.pascoclerk.com/public-sup-svcs-record-search.asp
appraiser.pascogov.com
www.doh.state.fl.us/planning_eval/vital_statistics
*www.myfloridacounty.com/services/officialrecords_*
intro.shtml

Pasco: Sheriff
727-847-5878
pascosheriff.com/webapps/index.pgm

Pasco: State Attorney
727-464-6221
statty.co.pinellas.fl.us

Pembroke Pines, City of

Pembroke Pines: City Government
954-435-6500
www.ppines.com

Pembroke Pines: City Police
www.ppines.com/police/index.html

Pembroke Pines: Codes and Ordinances
www.ppines.com/cityclerk/ordinances.html

Pembroke Pines: Public Records Search
www.doh.state.fl.us/planning_eval/vital_statistics
*www.myfloridacounty.com/services/officialrecords_*
intro.shtml

Pinellas County

Pinellas: County Government
727-464-3000
www.pinellascounty.org

Pinellas: Administrative Agencies
www.pinellascounty.org/phone.htm

Pinellas: Child Support Enforcement
dor.myflorida.com/dor/childsupport/phone.html
www.myfloridacounty.com/services/child_support/
index.shtml

Pinellas: Laws and Ordinances
www.pinellascounty.org/attorney/Code.htm

Pinellas: Courts
727-464-3341
www.myfloridaclerks.com/countytemplate.cfm?countyid=
Pinellas
www.jud6.org

Pinellas: Public Defender
727-464-6516
www.wearethehope.org

Pinellas: Public Records Search
www.pcpao.org
pubtitlet.co.pinellas.fl.us/mainmenux.jsp
www.doh.state.fl.us/planning_eval/vital_statistics
www.myfloridacounty.com/services/officialrecords_intro.shtml

Pinellas: Sheriff
727-582-6200
www.pcsoweb.com/index.aspx

Pinellas: State Attorney
727-464-6221
statty.co.pinellas.fl.us

Polk County

Polk: County Government
863-534-6000
www.polk-county.net

Polk: Administrative Agencies
www.polk-county.net
(click "Government" then "Department and Agency Listing")

Polk: Child Support Enforcement
dor.myflorida.com/dor/childsupport/phone.html
www.myfloridacounty.com/services/child_support/index.shtml

Polk: County Attorney
863-534-6730
www.polk-county.net
(click "Government" then "Department and Agency Listing")

Polk: Courts
863-534-4540
www.myfloridaclerks.com/countytemplate.cfm?countyid=Polk
www.polkcountyclerk.net/?pg=co
www.jud10.org

Polk: Laws and Ordinances
www.municode.com
(click "ONLINE LIBRARY" then "Florida" then "Polk County")

Polk: Public Defender
863-534-4200
www.jud10.org/pd.htm

Polk: Public Records Search
www.polkcountyclerk.net
www.doh.state.fl.us/planning_eval/vital_statistics
www.myfloridacounty.com/services/officialrecords_intro.shtml

Polk: Sheriff
800-226-0344; 863-533-0344
www.polksheriff.org

Polk: State Attorney
863-534-4800
www.sao10.com

Putnam County

Putnam: County Government
www1.putnam-fl.com

Putnam: Administrative Agencies
www1.putnam-fl.com/live/default.asp

Putnam: Child Support Enforcement
www.myfloridacounty.com/services/child_support/index.shtml

Putnam: Courts
386-329-0361
www.myfloridaclerks.com/countytemplate.cfm?countyid=Putnam
www1.putnam-fl.com/live/clkmain.asp
www.circuit7.org

Putnam: Public Defender
386-329-7730
www.volusia.org/publicdefender

Putnam: Public Records Search
www.doh.state.fl.us/planning_eval/vital_statistics
www.myfloridacounty.com/services/officialrecords_intro.shtml

Putnam: Sheriff
386-329-0800
www.putnamsheriff.org

Putnam: State Attorney
386-329-0259
www.sao7.com

Santa Rosa County

Santa Rosa: County Government
850-983-1877
www.santarosa.fl.gov
www.co.santa-rosa.fl.us

Santa Rosa: Administrative Agencies
www.santarosa.fl.gov/phone/index.html
www.santarosa.fl.gov/departments/index.html

Santa Rosa: Child Support Enforcement
dor.myflorida.com/dor/childsupport/phone.html
www.myfloridacounty.com/services/child_support/index.shtml

Santa Rosa: Courts
850-983-1987
www.myfloridaclerks.com/countytemplate.cfm?countyid=Santa+Rosa
www2.myfloridacounty.com/wps/wcm/connect/santarosaclerk

Santa Rosa: Laws and Ordinances
www.co.santa-rosa.fl.us
(click "County Code")

Santa Rosa: Public Defender
850-981-5600
www.pdo1.org/santarosa.htm

Santa Rosa: Public Records Search
www.doh.state.fl.us/planning_eval/vital_statistics
www.myfloridacounty.com/services/officialrecords_intro.shtml

Santa Rosa: Sheriff
850-983-1100
www.srso.net
www.santarosasheriff.org

Santa Rosa: State Attorney
850-981-5500
sao1.co.escambia.fl.us

Sarasota County

Sarasota: County Government
941-861-5000
www.co.sarasota.fl.us

Sarasota: Administrative Agencies
www.co.sarasota.fl.us/departmentsaz.asp

Sarasota: Child Support Enforcement
dor.myflorida.com/dor/childsupport/phone.html
www.myfloridacounty.com/services/child_support/index.shtml

Sarasota: County Attorney
941-861-7272
oca.co.sarasota.fl.us

Sarasota: Courts
941-861-7400
www.sarasotaclerk.com
12circuit.state.fl.us

Sarasota: Laws and Ordinances
www.municode.com
(click "ONLINE LIBRARY" then "Florida" then "Sarasota County")

Sarasota: Public Defender
941-861-5500

Sarasota: Public Records Search
www.sarasotaproperty.net/scpa_record_search.asp
www.doh.state.fl.us/planning_eval/vital_statistics
www.myfloridacounty.com/services/officialrecords_intro.shtml

Sarasota: Sheriff
941-861-5800
www.sarasotasheriff.org

Sarasota: State Attorney
941-861-4400
sao.co.sarasota.fl.us

Seminole County

Seminole: County Government
407-665-7211
www.seminolecountyfl.gov/cm

Seminole: Administrative Agencies
www.seminolecountyfl.gov/guide/deptlist.asp

Seminole: Child Support Enforcement
dor.myflorida.com/dor/childsupport/phone.html
www.myfloridacounty.com/services/child_support/index.shtml

Seminole: County Attorney
407-665-7254
www.seminolecountyfl.gov/ca

Seminole: Courts
407-665-4330
www.myfloridaclerks.com/countytemplate.cfm?countyid=Seminole
www.seminoleclerk.org
www.flcourts18.org

Seminole: Laws and Ordinances
www.seminolecountyfl.gov/guide/codes.asp

Seminole: Public Defender
321-617-7373
www.brevardcounty.us/publicdefender

Seminole: Public Records Search
www.doh.state.fl.us/planning_eval/vital_statistics
www.myfloridacounty.com/services/officialrecords_intro.shtml

Seminole: Sheriff
407-665-6600
seminolesheriff.org

Seminole: State Attorney
407-665-6000
www.sa18.state.fl.us

St. Johns County

St. Johns: County Government
904-209-0655
www.co.st-johns.fl.us

St. Johns: Administrative Agencies
www.co.st-johns.fl.us/BCC/index.aspx

St. Johns: Child Support Enforcement
dor.myflorida.com/dor/childsupport/phone.html
www.myfloridacounty.com/services/child_support/index.shtml

St. Johns: Courts
904-819-3600
www.clk.co.st-johns.fl.us
www.circuit7.org

St. Johns: Laws and Ordinances
www.co.st-johns.fl.us
(under "SJC Services" click "Code Enforcement")

St. Johns: Public Defender
904-824-8623
www.volusia.org/publicdefender

St. Johns: Public Records Search
www.doh.state.fl.us/planning_eval/vital_statistics
www.myfloridacounty.com/services/officialrecords_intro.shtml

St. Johns: Sheriff
800-346-7596; 904-824-8304
www.sjso.org

St. Johns: State Attorney
904-823-2300
www.sao7.com

St. Lucie County

St. Lucie: County Government
772-462-1100
www.stlucieco.gov

St. Lucie: Administrative Agencies
www.stlucieco.gov
(under "Government" click "Departments")

St. Lucie: Child Support Enforcement
www.myfloridacounty.com/services/child_support

St. Lucie: County Attorney
772-462-1441
www.stlucieco.gov/attorney

St. Lucie: Courts
772-462-6900
www.slcclerkofcourt.com
www.circuit19.org

St. Lucie: Public Defender
772-462-2048
www.pd19.org

St. Lucie: Public Records Search
www.paslc.org
oncore.slcclerkofcourt.com/oncorewebpublic
www.doh.state.fl.us/planning_eval/vital_statistics
www.myfloridacounty.com/services/officialrecords_intro.shtml

St. Lucie: Sheriff
772-462-7300
www.stluciesheriff.com

St. Petersburg, City of

St. Petersburg: City Government
727-893-7111
www.stpete.org

St. Petersburg: Administrative Agencies
www.stpete.org/citydep.asp

St. Petersburg: City Police
727-893-7780
www.stpete.org/police

St. Petersburg: Codes and Ordinances
www.stpete.org
(click "city government" then "City Code")

St. Petersburg: Legal Counsel
727-893-7401
www.stpete.org/legal

St. Petersburg: Public Records Search
www.doh.state.fl.us/planning_eval/vital_statistics
www.myfloridacounty.com/services/officialrecords_intro.shtml

Sumter County

Sumter: County Government
352-793-0200
sumtercountyfl.gov

Sumter: Administrative Agencies
sumtercountyfl.gov/links.htm

Sumter: Child Support Enforcement
dor.myflorida.com/dor/childsupport/phone.html
www.myfloridacounty.com/services/child_support/index.shtml

Sumter: Courts
352-793-0211
www.sumterclerk.com/public
www.myfloridaclerks.com/countytemplate.cfm?countyid=Sumter

Sumter: Laws and Ordinances
sumtercountyfl.gov
(click "Search County Codes")

Sumter: Public Defender
352-742-4270
www.hernandocounty.us/judicial/pubdef.htm

Sumter: Public Records Search
www.sumterclerk.com/public
(click "Public Records")
www.doh.state.fl.us/planning_eval/vital_statistics
www.myfloridacounty.com/services/officialrecords_intro.shtml

Sumter: Sheriff
352-793-0222
www.sumtercountysheriff.org

Sumter: State Attorney
352-620-3800
jud5.flcourts.org/sao/index.htm

Suwannee County

Suwannee: County Government
386-364-3410
www.suwcounty.org

Suwannee: Administrative Agencies
www.suwcounty.org
(click "Departments")

Suwannee: Child Support Enforcement
dor.myflorida.com/dor/childsupport/phone.html
www.myfloridacounty.com/services/child_support/index.shtml

Suwannee: Courts
386-362-0500
www.suwclerk.org
www.suwclerk.org/mambo
www.jud3.flcourts.org

Suwannee: Laws and Ordinances
www.suwcounty.org
(click "Code Compliance")

Suwannee: Public Defender
386-758-0540
www.columbiacountyfla.com/CO_Public_Defender.asp

Suwanee: Public Records Search
www.suwclerk.org/mambo
(click "Official Records")
www.doh.state.fl.us/planning_eval/vital_statistics
www.myfloridacounty.com/services/officialrecords_intro.shtml

Suwannee: Sheriff
386-364-3443
www.suwanneesheriff.com

Suwannee: State Attorney
386-362-2320
www.columbiacountyfla.com/CO_State_Attorney.asp

Tallahassee, City of

Tallahassee: City Government
850-891-0000
www.talgov.com

Tallahassee: Administrative Agencies
www.talgov.com
(click "Departments")

Tallahassee: City Attorney
850-891-8554
www.talgov.com/legal

Tallahassee: City Police
850-891-4200
www.talgov.com/tpd/chief.cfm

Tallahassee: Codes and Ordinances
www.talgov.com/dncs/code.cfm

Tallahassee: Public Records Search
www.doh.state.fl.us/planning_eval/vital_statistics
www.myfloridacounty.com/services/officialrecords_intro.shtml

Tampa, City of

Tampa: City Government
813-274-8211
www.tampagov.net

Tampa: Administrative Agencies
www.tampagov.net/contact_us/index.asp

Tampa: City Attorney
813-274-8996
www.tampagov.net/dept_city_attorney

Tampa: City Police
813-276-3200
www.tampagov.net/dept_police

Tampa: Codes and Ordinances
www.tampagov.net/dept_code_enforcement

Tampa: Public Records Search
www.tampagov.net/programs_and_services/_online_tools/search.asp
www.doh.state.fl.us/planning_eval/vital_statistics
www.myfloridacounty.com/services/officialrecords_intro.shtml

Taylor County

Taylor: County Government
www.taylorcountygov.com

Taylor: Administrative Agencies
www.taylorcountygov.com/directory.html

Taylor: Child Support Enforcement
dor.myflorida.com/dor/childsupport/phone.html
www.myfloridacounty.com/services/child_support/index.shtml

Taylor: Courts
850-838-3506
www.jud3.flcourts.org
www.myfloridaclerks.com/countytemplate.cfm?countyid=Taylor
www2.myfloridacounty.com/wps/wcm/connect/taylorclerk

Taylor: Laws and Ordinances
www.municode.com
(click "ONLINE LIBRARY" then "Florida" then "Taylor County")
www.municode.com/resources/gateway.asp?pid=13410&sid=9

Taylor: Public Defender
386-758-0540
www.columbiacountyfla.com/CO_Public_Defender.asp

Taylor: Public Records Search
www.myfloridacounty.com/services/officialrecords_intro.shtml
www.doh.state.fl.us/planning_eval/vital_statistics

Taylor: Sheriff
850-584-4225
www.taylorcountysherifffl.org

Taylor: State Attorney
386-362-2320
www.columbiacountyfla.com/CO_State_Attorney.asp

Taylor County: Tax Collector
850-838-3517

Union County

Union: County Government
www.myfloridacounty.com/mfcTemplate/view.jsp?countyid=UNION
www.floridanetlink.com/union.php

Union: Child Support Enforcement
dor.myflorida.com/dor/childsupport/phone.html
www.myfloridacounty.com/services/child_support/index.shtml

Union: Courts
386-496-3711
www.circuit8.org
www.myfloridaclerks.com/countytemplate.cfm?countyid=Union

Union: Public Defender
352-338-7370

Union: Public Records Search
www.doh.state.fl.us/planning_eval/vital_statistics
www.myfloridacounty.com/services/officialrecords_intro.shtml

Union: Sheriff
386-496-2501
www.flsheriffs.org
(type "Union" in the search box)

Union: State Attorney
386-496-6280
sawww.co.alachua.fl.us

Volusia County

Volusia: County Government
866-345-0345
www.volusia.org

Volusia: Administrative Agencies
www.volusia.org/county

Volusia: Child Support Enforcement
dor.myflorida.com/dor/childsupport/phone.html
*www.myfloridacounty.com/services/child_support/
index.shtml*

Volusia: Courts
386-822-5710; 386-736-5915
*www.myfloridaclerks.com/countytemplate.cfm?countyid=
Volusia*
www.volusia.org/courts/default.htm

Volusia: Laws and Ordinances
www.municode.com
(click "ONLINE LIBRARY" then "Florida" then "Volusia County")

Volusia: Public Defender
386-239-7730
www.volusia.org/publicdefender

Volusia: Public Records Search
webserver.vcgov.org/vc_search.html
www.doh.state.fl.us/planning_eval/vital_statistics
www.myfloridacounty.com/services/officialrecords_intro.shtml

Volusia: Sheriff
386-736-5961
volusia.org/sheriff

Volusia: State Attorney
386-329-7710
www.sao7.com

Wakulla County

Wakulla: County Government
850-926-0919
www.mywakulla.com

Wakulla: Administrative Agencies
www.mywakulla.com
(click "Departments")

Wakulla: Child Support Enforcement
dor.myflorida.com/dor/childsupport/phone.html
www.myfloridacounty.com/services/child_support/index.shtml

Wakulla: County Attorney
850-926-7666

Wakulla: Courts
850-926-0905
*www.myfloridaclerks.com/countytemplate.cfm?countyid=
Wakulla*
www.wakullaclerk.com

Wakulla: Laws and Ordinances
www.municode.com
(click "ONLINE LIBRARY" then "Florida" then
"Wakulla County")

Wakulla: Public Defender
850-926-0912
www.co.leon.fl.us/pd/location.asp

Wakulla: Public Records Search
www.wakullaclerk.com/oncoreweb/Search.aspx
www.doh.state.fl.us/planning_eval/vital_statistics
*www.myfloridacounty.com/services/officialrecords_
intro.shtml*

Wakulla: Sheriff
850-926-0800
www.wcso.org

Wakulla: State Attorney
850-926-0914; 850-606-6000
www.sao2fl.org

Walton County

Walton: County Government
850-892-8155
www.co.walton.fl.us

Walton: Administrative Agencies
www.co.walton.fl.us/citizen_services/Website%20Directory.pdf

Walton: Child Support Enforcement
dor.myflorida.com/dor/childsupport/phone.html
www.myfloridacounty.com/services/child_support/index.shtml

Walton: County Attorney
850-892-8110
www.co.walton.fl.us/citizen_services/Website%20Directory.pdf

Walton: Courts
850-595-4400; 850-892-8115
www.firstjudicialcircuit.org
clerkofcourts.co.walton.fl.us
*www.myfloridaclerks.com/countytemplate.cfm?countyid=
Walton*

Walton: Laws and Ordinances
www.municode.com
(click "ONLINE LIBRARY" then "Florida" then "Walton County")

Walton: Public Defender
850-892-8090
www.pdo1.org/walton.htm

Walton: Public Records Search
www.doh.state.fl.us/planning_eval/vital_statistics
www.myfloridacounty.com/services/officialrecords_intro.shtml

Walton: Resolutions and Ordinances
gisftp.co.walton.fl.us/search

Walton: Sheriff
850-892-8186
waltonso.org/home.html

Walton: State Attorney
850-892-8080
sao1.co.escambia.fl.us

Washington County

Washington: County Government
850-638-6200
www.washingtonfl.com

Washington: Administrative Agencies
www.washingtonfl.com

Washington: Child Support Enforcement
dor.myflorida.com/dor/childsupport/phone.html
www.myfloridacounty.com/services/child_support/index.shtml

Washington: Courts
850-638-6289
www.washingtonfl.com
(click "County Judge")
www2.myfloridacounty.com/wps/wcm/connect/washingtonclerk

Washington: Laws and Ordinances
www.municode.com
(click "ONLINE LIBRARY" then "Florida" then "Washington County")
www.municode.com/resources/gateway.asp?pid=10982&sid=9

Washington: Public Defender
850-784-6155
www.jud14.flcourts.org/CircuitLinks/PublicDefender.htm

Washington: Public Records Search
www.doh.state.fl.us/planning_eval/vital_statistics
www.myfloridacounty.com/services/officialrecords_intro.shtml

Washington: Sheriff
850-638-6111
www.wcso.us

Washington: State Attorney
850-638-6150
stateattorney14.com/office-locations.html

C. More Information

Child Support Services
www.myfloridacounty.com/services/child_support/index.shtml

Clerks
www.stateofflorida.com/Portal/DesktopDefault.aspx?tabid=51
www.myfloridaclerks.com
dlis.dos.state.fl.us/fgils/coclerks.html

Consumer Protection
myfloridalegal.com/consumer

County/City Governments
www.stateofflorida.com/Portal/DesktopDefault.aspx?tabid=35
www.fl-counties.com/
www.myfloridacounty.com
www.flcities.com/city_links.asp
www.chesslaw.com/floridalaw.htm
www.fccma.org

County Ordinances and Codes
www.municode.com
(click "ONLINE LIBRARY" then "Florida")
www.findlaw.com/11stategov/fl/laws.html

County Statistics/Profiles
www.fl-counties.com/aboutflco/flmap.shtml
www.myflorida.com
(type "county profiles" in the search box)

Courts
www.flcourts.org

Department of State
www.dos.state.fl.us

Domestic Violence Resources
www.dcf.state.fl.us/domesticviolence
www.aardvarc.org/dv/states/fldv.shtml
www.fcadv.org

Florida Electronic Federal Depository Library
www.uflib.ufl.edu/fefdl
(click your county on the map)

Florida Prosecuting Attorneys
850-488-3070
www.myfpaa.org/?form=contactus

Health Officers, Registrars, and Recorders
www.doh.state.fl.us/planning_eval/vital_statistics/index.html
www.doh.state.fl.us/chdsitelist.htm

Highway Safety (all county offices)
www.hsmv.state.fl.us/offices

Jail Inmate Search
www.ancestorhunt.com/county-jail-inmates-search.htm

Legal Aid/Legal Service Offices
www.floridalawhelp.org
www.floridalegal.org

Property Appraisers
dor.myflorida.com/dor/property/appraisers.html

Public Defenders
850-488-6850
www.flpda.org

Public Records
www.legaltrek.com/HELPSITE/States/Florida.htm
(click "Public Records")
www.doh.state.fl.us/planning_eval/vital_statistics
www.myfloridacounty.com/services/officialrecords_intro.shtml
www.vitalrec.com/fl.html#County

Sheriffs
www.flsheriffs.org

Florida Counties and Cities on Wikepedia
en.wikipedia.org/wiki/List_of_counties_in_Florida
en.wikipedia.org/wiki/List_of_cities_in_Florida

D. Something to Check

1. Pick one kind of information pertaining to law and government (e.g., enforcement of the dog leash law). Find the address of where this information would be found in any 10 Florida counties or cities.

2. For any county you select, identify the kind of information available online about any aspect of real property in that county.

P A R T
5

Legal Research and Records Research

A. Introduction

In this section we answer the following question: Where can you find Florida primary authority (e.g., cases, statutes) and secondary authority (e.g., legal encyclopedias and treatises) if you need to research an issue of Florida law?

We will cover both traditional book sources as well as what is available online. For related material, see:

- State courts in Florida, including links to their opinions (section 4.2)
- Federal courts in Florida, including links to their opinions (section 4.3)
- Citing Florida legal materials (section 5.2)
- Research starters for 78 major Florida topics (section 5.5)
- Finding Florida public records (section 5.7)
- Finding law libraries in your area that often have materials on Florida law (section 5.8)
- Finding continuing legal education (CLE) resources in Florida (section 1.3)

B. Finding Florida State Law

Exhibit 5.1A presents an overview of Florida law found in traditional and online sources.

C. Publishers of Materials on Florida Law

Aspen Publishers
www.aspenpublishers.com
(type "Florida" in the search box)

CaseClerk
www.caseclerk.com

Fastcase
www.fastcase.com

Florida Law Weekly
www.floridalawweekly.com

James Publishing
www.jamespublishing.com
(type "Florida" in the search box)

LexisNexis/Matthew Bender
www.lexisone.com
bender.lexisnexis.com
(type "Florida" in the search box)

Loislaw
www.loislaw.com

The Florida Bar
www.floridabar.org
(click "Publications")

TheLaw.net
thelaw.net

VersusLaw
www.versuslaw.com

West/Thomson
west.thomson.com/store/default.asp
(type "Florida" in the search box)

D. More Information

Online Portals to Florida Law
www.floridalawonline.net
www.loc.gov/law/guide/us-fl.html
www.chesslaw.com/floridalaw.htm
www.washlaw.edu/uslaw/states/Florida/index.html
www.legaltrek.com/HELPSITE/States/State_Contents/Florida.htm
www.megalaw.com/fl/fl.php
www.ll.georgetown.edu/states/florida.cfm
www.lawsource.com/also/usa.cgi?fl
www.law.miami.edu/library/guides.php#florida
www.law.ufl.edu/lic/links/florida
www.law.fsu.edu/library/databases/index.html
library.ucf.edu/Reference/Guides/legal/florida.asp
www.romingerlegal.com/state/florida.html
www.law.cornell.edu/states/florida.html
www.alllaw.com/state_resources/florida
www.findlaw.com/11stategov/fl/index.html
dlis.dos.state.fl.us/fgils/government.html
www.lexisone.com/legalresearch/legalguide/states/florida.htm
www.hg.org/usstates.html (click "Florida")
www.aallnet.org/sis/lisp/florida.pdf

E. Something to Check

1. Pick any legal issue (e.g., capital punishment, abortion, divorce). Using the free online materials referred to in this section, find and summarize one case and one statute on your topic.
2. Use any of the sites to locate a Florida legal form that can be used on a family law case.

EXHIBIT 5.1A	Florida Law on the Shelf and Online		
CATEGORY	WHERE TO FIND IT ON THE SHELF	WHERE TO FIND IT ONLINE FOR A FEE	WHERE TO FIND IT ONLINE FREE (complete, partial, or links)
Florida Constitution	• *Florida Statutes* • *Florida Statutes Annotated* (West) • *LexisNexis Florida Statutes Annotated* (LexisNexis)	• Lexis: *www.lexis.com* FLA library FLCNST file; CODES library FLCNST file; CONLAW library FLCNST file • Westlaw: *www.westlaw.com* FL-ST-ANN database • Others: see addresses on p. 266 for Fastcase, Loislaw, TheLaw.net, VersusLaw	• *www.flsenate.gov* (click "Statutes & Constitution") • *www.floridalawonline.net* (click "Florida Constitution") • *www.leg.state.fl.us* (click "Florida Constitution") • *www.megalaw.com/fl/flconstitution.php* • *www.law.fsu.edu/crc/conhist/contents.html* • *www.law.fsu.edu/crc* (Florida Constitution Revision Commission)
State Statutes (Florida Codes)	• *Florida Statutes* • *Florida Statutes Annotated* (FSA)(West) • *Florida Annotated Statutes* (LexisNexis)	• Lexis: *www.lexis.com* FLA library CODE file • Westlaw: *www.westlaw.com* FL-ST-ANN database; FL-ST database • Others: see addresses on p. 266 for Fastcase, Loislaw, TheLaw.net, VersusLaw	• *www.flsenate.gov* (click "Statutes & Constitution") • *www.floridalawonline.net* (click "Florida Statutes") • *www.leg.state.fl.us* (click "Florida Statutes") • *www.megalaw.com/fl/flcode.php*
State Statutes (session laws & advance services)	• *Laws of Florida* • *Florida Session Law Service* (West) • *Florida Session Law Reporter* (Florida Legal Periodicals)	• Lexis: *www.lexis.com* FLA library FLALS file • Westlaw: *www.westlaw.com* FL-LEGIS database • *www.floridalegalperiodicals.com/session*	• *www.floridalawonline.net* (click "Session Laws") • *www.leg.state.fl.us* (click "Laws of Florida")
Pending Bills/ Bill Tracking		• Lexis: *www.lexis.com* LEGIS library FLTRCK file FLA library FLALS file • Westlaw: *www.westlaw.com* FL-BILLTRK database; FL-BILLTXT database	• *www.leg.state.fl.us* (click "Senate" or "House")
Legislative Journals	• *Journal of the House of Representatives* • *Journal of the Senate*	• Westlaw: *www.westlaw.com* FL-LH-JRNLS database	• *www.myfloridahouse.gov* (click "General Information" then "House Journal") • *www.flsenate.gov* (click "Journals")

CATEGORY	WHERE TO FIND IT ON THE SHELF	WHERE TO FIND IT ONLINE FOR A FEE	WHERE TO FIND IT ONLINE FREE (complete, partial, or links)
Legislative History		• Lexis: www.lexis.com FLA library FLTEXT file • Westlaw: www.westlaw.com FL-LH database; FL-LH-JRNLS database	• www.leg.state.fl.us (click "Senate" or "House") • www.law.miami.edu/library/flhistguide.php • www.law.ufl.edu/lic/guides/florida/fllegislative_history.shtml • dlis.dos.state.fl.us/index_Researchers.cfm • www.law.ufl.edu/lic/guides/florida/LEG_HIST06.pdf • library.ucf.edu/GovDocs/training/flaleghist.asp • library.flcourts.org/screens/Legislative_History.pdf
Online Legislative Sessions			• www.myfloridahouse.gov (click "Session Live!") • www.leg.state.fl.us (click "Senate" then "Video Broadcasts")
State Ballot Propositions			• election.dos.state.fl.us/initiatives/initiativelist.asp
State Administrative Regulations (Code and Register)	• Florida Administrative Code Annotated (FAC) (LexisNexis) • Florida Administrative Weekly (FAW)	• Lexis: www.lexis.com FLA library FLADMN file; FLA library FLRGST file • Westlaw: www.westlaw.com FL-ADC database • Others: see addresses on p. 266 for Fastcase, Loislaw, TheLaw.net, VersusLaw	• www.doah.state.fl.us/internet • www.flrules.org • www.floridalawonline.net (click "Administrative Code") • www.floridalawonline.net (click "Administrative Weekly") • faw.dos.state.fl.us • faw.dos.state.fl.us/pdf/Rmhb.pdf (Rulemaking Handbook) • dlis.dos.state.fl.us/fgils/agencies.html • www.law.miami.edu/library/fladminguide.php • www.leg.state.fl.us/Statutes/index.cfm?App_mode=Display_Statute&URL=Ch0120/ch0120.htm (Florida Administrative Procedure Act)

CATEGORY	WHERE TO FIND IT ON THE SHELF	WHERE TO FIND IT ONLINE FOR A FEE	WHERE TO FIND IT ONLINE FREE (complete, partial, or links)
Executive Orders of the Governor			• *www.floridalawonline.net* (click "Executive Orders") • *www.flgov.com/orders_search* • *www.flgov.com* (click "Media Center" then "Executive Orders")
State Administrative Decisions	• *Florida Administrative Law Reports* (FALR, Inc.) Examples: • *Florida Public Service Commission Reporter* (FALR, Inc.) • *Florida Career Service Reporter* (FALR, Inc.)	• Lexis: *www.lexis.com* FLA library, FLPUC file; FLA library, FLPER file; FLA file, FLSEC file; FLA file, FLTAX file; CCHTAX library FLCOMP file • Westlaw: *www.westlaw.com* FL-PUR database; FLTAX database; FL-PER database; FLSEC-ADMIN database	• *www.floridalawonline.net* (click "Div. Admin. Hearings Orders") • *www.doah.state.fl.us* (click "Case Search") • *www.law.miami.edu/library/fladminguide.php* • *dlis.dos.state.fl.us/fgils/agencies.html*
State Court Opinions of: • Florida Supreme Court • Florida Court of Appeals	• *Florida Reports* • *Florida Supplement* • *Florida Supplement 2d* • *Southern Reporter* • *Southern Reporter 2d* • *Southern Reporter 2d, Florida Cases* • *Florida Law Weekly* • *Florida Law Weekly Supplement* • *Official Slip Opinions*	• Lexis: *www.lexis.com* FLA library FLMEGA file; FLA library FLCTS file • Westlaw: *www.westlaw.com* FL-CS database • Others: see addresses on p. 266 for Fastcase, Loislaw, TheLaw.net, VersusLaw	• *www.floridalawonline.net* (click entries under "Florida Courts") • *www.floridasupremecourt.org* (click "Court Decisions & Rules") • *www.floridasupremecourt.org/decisions/index.shtml* (click "DCA" entries under "Opinions") • *www.floridalawonline.net* (click "Dist. Ct. Appeals Opinions" under "Florida Courts") • *www.lexisone.com/caselaw/freecaselaw* • *www.law.miami.edu/library/guides.php#florida*
State Court Rules (Rules of Court)	• *Florida Rules of Court* (West) • *Florida Rules of Court Service* (LexisNexis)	• Lexis: *www.lexis.com* FLA library FLRULE file • Westlaw: *www.westlaw.com* FL-RULES database; FL-TRIALRULES database • Others: see addresses on p. 266 for Fastcase, Loislaw, TheLaw.net, VersusLaw	• *www.floridalawonline.net* (click "Rules of Court") • *www.floridalawonline.net/courts.html# courtrules* • *www.floridasupremecourt.org* (Click "Court Decisions & Rules") • *www.megalaw.com/fl/flrules.php* • *www.llrx.com/courtrules-gen/state-Florida.html* • *phonl.com/fl_law/rules/frcp* (Florida Rules of Civil Procedure)

CATEGORY	WHERE TO FIND IT ON THE SHELF	WHERE TO FIND IT ONLINE FOR A FEE	WHERE TO FIND IT ONLINE FREE (complete, partial, or links)
Ethics/Disciplinary Opinions	• Advisory Opinions of the Board of Commissioners on Ethics (State of Florida) • Opinions of the Judicial Ethics Advisory Committee	• Lexis: www.lexis.com FLA library FLETOP file; ETHICS library FLETH file • Westlaw: www.westlaw.com FLETH-EO database; FLETH-CS database; FL-ETH database	• www.floridalawonline.net/courts.html#ethics • www.floridabar.org (click "Member Services" then "Ethics Opinions") • www.floridabar.org/tfb/TFBETOpin.nsf/EthicsIndex?OpenForm • www.floridasupremecourt.org/decisions/opinions.shtml (click "Search" and type in "Ethics") • www.sunethics.com • www.ll.georgetown.edu/states/ethics/florida.cfm
Ethics Code/Rules	• Rules of Professional Conduct	• Lexis: www.lexis.com CLE library FLBPE file; ETHICS library FLBPE file; FLA library FLBPE file • Westlaw: www.westlaw.com FL-ST database Search: ci(cpr), ci(bar)	• www.floridabar.org (click "Lawyer Regulation" then "Rules Regulating The Florida Bar") • www.sunethics.com • www.ll.georgetown.edu/states/ethics/florida.cfm
Citators	• Shepard's Florida Citations • Shepard's Southern Reporter Citations	• Lexis: www.lexis.com FLA Library • KeyCite: www.westlaw.com • Globalcite: Loislaw (see address on p. 266)	
Digests of Florida State Court Opinions	• West's Florida Digest 2d	• Westlaw: www.westlaw.com Example of a digest search in the FL-CS database containing all Florida state cases: di(murder)	
Florida Attorney General Opinions	• Annual Report of the Attorney General	• Lexis: www.lexis.com FLA library FLAG file • Westlaw: www.westlaw.com FL-AG database	• myfloridalegal.com/opinions • www.floridalawonline.net (click "Attorney General Opinions")

CATEGORY	WHERE TO FIND IT ON THE SHELF	WHERE TO FIND IT ONLINE FOR A FEE	WHERE TO FIND IT ONLINE FREE (complete, partial, or links)
Local Government Laws (charters, codes, ordinances)	Available through local county law libraries. Examples: • *Code of Ordinances – Marion County* • *Municipal Code of Jacksonville*	• Lexis: *www.lexis.com* FLA library FLMCDE file • Westlaw: *www.westlaw.com* FL-MUNCLE database; FLJUR-MUN database • *www.municode.com*	• *www.municode.com/resources/code_list. asp?stateID=9* • *bpcnet.com* (click "Florida") • *www.amlegal.com/library* (click Florida on the map) • *www.floridalawonline.net* (click "Codes & Ordinances" under "Local Government") • *www.fl-counties.com* • *www.flcities.com*
State Archives of Florida Government Documents			• *dlis.dos.state.fl.us/index_researchers.cfm*
State Legal Encyclopedia	*Florida Jurisprudence, 2d* (West)	• Lexis: *www.lexis.com* FLA library FLJUR file • Westlaw: *www.westlaw.com* FLJUR database	
Legal Treatises on State Law	Examples: • *Basic Estate Planning in Florida* (LexisNexis) • *Florida Mortgages* (West)	• Lexis: *www.lexis.com* FLA library FLBEP file • Westlaw: *www.westlaw.com* FL-MORTGAGES database	
Jury Instructions	• *Florida Standard Jury Instructions in Civil Cases* (Florida Bar) • *Florida Standard Jury Instructions in Criminal Cases* (Florida Bar) • *Florida Forms of Jury Instruction* (Matthew Bender)	• Lexis: *www.lexis.com* FLA library FFJURY file; FLA library FLJINS file; CLE file FLSJIC file • Westlaw: *www.westlaw.com* FL-JICIV database; FL-JICRIM database	• *www.floridasupremecourt.org* (click "Criminal Jury Instructions")
Jury Verdicts	• *Florida Jury Verdict Reporter* (Florida Legal Periodicals)	• *www.floridalegalperiodicals.com*	
Legal Research Manuals/Guides on Florida Law	• *Guide to Florida Legal Research 6th Ed.* (The Florida Bar/LexisNexis) • *Florida Legal Research 3d Ed.* (Carolina Press)		See "Online Portals to Florida Law" in More Information on p. 266

CATEGORY	WHERE TO FIND IT ON THE SHELF	WHERE TO FIND IT ONLINE FOR A FEE	WHERE TO FIND IT ONLINE FREE (complete, partial, or links)
Legal Newspapers & Business Newspapers with Features of Interest to the Practice of Law	• *Miami Daily Business Review* • *Palm Beach Daily Business Review* • *The Financial News and Daily Record* • *The Florida Bar News* • *Gulf Coast Business Review*	• Westlaw: *www.westlaw.com* LEGNEWSL database	• *www.dailybusinessreview.com* • *www.jaxdailyrecord.com* • *www.review.net* • *www.floridabar.org* (click "Publications")
Blogs on Florida Law			• *www.justia.com/us-states/florida* (click "Florida Law Blogs") • *blawgsearch.justia.com* (click "US States" then "Florida") • *abstractappeal.com* • *floridalegalblog.blogspot.com* • *injurylaw.labovick.com* • *www.fladivorcelawblog.com* • *criminaldefenseblog.blogspot.com* • *www.sdfla.blogspot.com* • *www.floridaipblog.com* • *floridaerisa.blogspot.com* • *fsulawlibraryblog.typepad.com* • *www.flprobatelitigation.com* • *www.bankruptcyorlando.com* • *floridamediator.blogspot.com* • *floridaassetprotection.blogs.com/alperlaw*
Discussion Groups (List-servs)			• *Florida Lawyers list* FL-LAW@pd.net (Send the following message to law@pd.net: subscribe fl-law Your Name) • *www.bulletinboards.com/chkpswd.cfm?comcode=1233321*
Appellate Briefs (Florida Supreme Court)		• Lexis: *www.lexis.com* FLA library FLBRFS library • Westlaw: *www.westlaw.com* FL-SCT-BRIEF database	• *www.floridalawonline.net* (click "Supreme Court Briefs" under "Florida Courts") • *www.law.fsu.edu/library/flsupct/index.html* • *www.floridasupremecourt.org/pub_info/summaries/archives.shtml*

CATEGORY	WHERE TO FIND IT ON THE SHELF	WHERE TO FIND IT ONLINE FOR A FEE	WHERE TO FIND IT ONLINE FREE (complete, partial, or links)
Oral Arguments before the Florida Supreme Court			• wfsu.org/gavel2gavel
Native American Government in Florida			• www.seminoletribe.com (Seminole Tribe of Florida) • en.wikipedia.org/wiki/Seminole • www.epa.gov/region4indian/tribal.htm
Locating Florida Attorneys	• Martindale-Hubbell Law Directory • Florida Bar Journal (annual directory issue)	• Lexis: www.lexis.com MARHUB library FLDIR file • Westlaw: www.westlaw.com WLD-FL database	• www.floridalawonline.net (click "Florida Bar Directory" under "Florida Legal Directories") • www.floridabar.org (click "Inside the Bar" then "Find A Lawyer") • www.martindale.com • lawyers.findlaw.com
Florida Law Library Online Catalogs			• library.flcourts.org • www.law.ufl.edu/lic • www.mdcll.org • library.uwf.edu/eli/general/Florida Documents.shtml • famu.catalog.fcla.edu/am.jsp
Ask a Florida Librarian (submit a legal research question on Florida law)			• www.askalibrarian.org/aal.asp • www.askalibrarian.org/vrl_intro.asp?library=FLCC2400 • pbclibrary.org/email.htm • library.fiu.edu/Home/AskaLibrarian.aspx • www.ipl.org/div/askus

> **5.2. Citation Examples: Some Comparisons**
> A. Introduction: Sources of Citation Rules
> B. Citation Comparisons
> C. More Information
> D. Something to Check

A. Introduction: Sources of Citation Rules

In this section we will examine examples from different citation guidelines:

Source of Citation Rules	Referred to Here As:
Florida Rules of Appellate Procedure (Rule 9.800) (the state's "Uniform Citation System")	Rule 9.800
The Bluebook: A Uniform System of Citation (Columbia Law Review Ass'n, et al., eds., 18th ed., 2005)	Bluebook
Florida Style Manual (Florida State University Law Review, 6th ed., 2003)	FSM

The priority among these rules is as follows:

- First, follow Rule 9.800
- If Rule 9.800 does not have a rule that covers what you want to cite, follow the rules in the Bluebook
- If neither Rule 9.800 nor the Bluebook cover what you want to cite, follow the rules in the FSM

A fourth source that is becoming increasingly popular in the United States is the *ALWD Citation Manual:*

ALWD Citation Manual: A Professional System of Citation (2d ed., Aspen Publishers, 2003) (Assn. of Legal Writing Directors and Darby Dickerson)	ALWD

There is considerable similarity in how these sources cite laws and other categories of legal materials. Yet, there are some important differences you should know about. In this section, we provide examples of the formats required by the sources. When you compare the examples, make careful note of large differences (e.g., how words are abbreviated) as well as seemingly small ones (e.g., the use of spaces and commas).

B. Citation Comparisons

Within the sources of citation rules listed above there are lists of abbreviations that each recommends or requires. For more on abbreviations in citations, see

section 5.3 in this book. The following list strives to present the most commonly cited legal authority. The examples assume that the citation is being used in a document that will be submitted to a Florida court.

- **Florida Constitution**

Rule 9.800:	Art. V, § 3(b)(3), Fla. Const.
Bluebook:	Fla. Const. art. V, § 3(b)(3)
ALWD:	Fla. Const. art. V, § 3(b)(3)

- **Florida Statutes (official)**

Rule 9.800:	§ 350.34, Fla. Stat. (1973)
Bluebook:	Fla. Stat. § 350.34 (1973)
ALWD:	Fla. Stat. § 350.34 (1973)

- **Florida Statutes (unofficial)**

Rule 9.800:	32 Fla. Stat. Ann. 116 (1975)
Bluebook:	Fla. Stat. Ann. § 32.116 (West 1975)
ALWD:	Fla. Stat. Ann. § 32.116 (West 1975)

- **Florida Administrative Code**

Rule 9.800	Fla. Admin. Code R. 28-5.604
Bluebook:	Fla. Admin. Code Ann. r. 28-5.604 (1990)
ALWD:	Fla. Admin. Code Ann. r. 28-5.604 (1990)

- **Florida State Court Opinions**
  - Florida Supreme Court

Rule 9.800:	*Fenelon v. State*, 594 So. 2d 292 (Fla. 1992)
Bluebook:	*Fenelon v. State*, 594 So. 2d 292 (Fla. 1992)
ALWD:	*Fenelon v. State*, 594 So. 2d 292 (Fla. 1992)

  - Florida District Courts of Appeal

Rule 9.800:	*Sotolongo v. State*, 530 So. 2d 514 (Fla. 2d DCA 1988)
Bluebook:	*Sotolongo v. State*, 530 So. 2d 514 (Fla. Dist. Ct. App. 1988)
ALWD:	*Sotolongo v. State*, 530 So. 2d 514 (Fla. 2d Dist. App. 1988)

  - Florida Circuit Courts

Rule 9.800:	*Whidden v. Francis*, 27 Fla. Supp. 80 (Fla. 11th Cir. Ct. 1966)
Bluebook:	*Whidden v. Francis*, 27 Fla. Supp. 80 (Fla. Cir. Ct. 1966)
ALWD:	*Whidden v. Francis*, 27 Fla. Supp. 80 (Fla. Cir. 1966)

  - Florida County Courts

Rule 9.800:	*State v. Alvarez*, 42 Fla. Supp. 83 (Fla. Dade Cty. Ct. 1975)
Bluebook:	*State v. Alvarez*, 42 Fla. Supp. 83 (Fla. Dade County Ct. 1975)
ALWD:	*State v. Alvarez*, 42 Fla. Supp. 83 (Fla. Dade County Ct. 1975)

- **Federal Court Opinions Applicable in Florida**
  - United States Supreme Court

  Rule 9.800: *Sansone v. United States,* 380 U.S. 343 (1965)

  Bluebook: *Sansone v. United States,* 380 U.S. 343 (1965)

  ALWD: *Sansone v. U.S.,* 380 U.S. 343 (1965)

  - United States Court of Appeals for the Eleventh Circuit

  Rule 9.800: *Scott v. Taylor,* 405 F.3d 1251 (11th Cir. 2005)

  Bluebook: *Scott v. Taylor,* 405 F.3d 1251 (11th Cir. 2005)

  ALWD: *Scott v. Taylor,* 405 F.3d 1251 (11th Cir. 2005)

  - United States District Court in Florida

  Rule 9.800: *Valdes v. Crosby,* 390 F. Supp. 2d 1084 (M.D. Fla. 2005)

  Bluebook: *Valdes v. Crosby,* 390 F. Supp. 2d 1084 (M.D. Fla. 2005)

  ALWD: *Valdes v. Crosby,* 390 F. Supp. 2d 1084 (M.D. Fla. 2005)

- **Florida Attorney General Opinions**

  Rule 9.800: Op. Att'y Gen. Fla. 73-178 (1973)
  Bluebook: 73 Fla. Att'y Gen. Op. No. 178 (1973)
  ALWD: Fla. Atty. Gen. Op. 73-178 (1973)

- **Florida Rules of Court**

  Rule 9.800: Fla. R. Civ. P. 1.180
  Bluebook: Fla. R. Civ. P. 1.180
  ALWD: Fla. R. Civ. P. 1.180

- **Law Reviews**

  Bluebook: Kristen Osenga, *Entrance Ramps, Tolls, and Express Lanes: Proposals for Decreasing Traffic Congestion in the Patent Office,* 33 Fla. St. U. L. Rev. 119 (2005)

  ALWD: Kristen Osenga, *Entrance Ramps, Tolls, and Express Lanes: Proposals for Decreasing Traffic Congestion in the Patent Office,* 33 Fla. St. U. L. Rev. 119 (2005)

- **Legal Encyclopedias**

  Bluebook: 4 Fla. Jur. 2d *Appellate Review* § 208 (1996)

  ALWD: 4 Fla. Jur. 2d *Appellate Review* § 208 (1996)

- **Treatises**

  Bluebook: Jerome Ira Solkoff, *Florida Elder Law* (2005)

  ALWD: Jerome Ira Solkoff, *Florida Elder Law* (West 2005)

- **Dictionaries**

  Bluebook: *Black's Law Dictionary* 101 (8th ed., 2004)

  ALWD: *Black's Law Dictionary* 101 (Bryan A. Garner, ed. 8th ed., West 2004)

C. More Information

Florida Rules of Appellate Procedure Rule 9.800
www.4dca.org/applellate%20rules.pdf
www.floridasupremecourt.org/decisions/barrules.shtml

The Florida Style Manual (5th ed. 2001)
www.law.fsu.edu/journals/lawreview/downloads/293/FlaStyle.pdf

The Florida Style Manual (4th edition 1997)
www.law.fsu.edu/Journals/lawreview/downloads/242/fsm.pdf
24 Fla. St. U. L. Rev. 507 (1997)

"Citation Form [in Florida]: Keeping Up with the Times"
(81 Florida Bar Journal 23, January 2007)
www.floridabar.org
(click "Publications" then "The Florida Bar Journal" and type "citation" in the search box)

Florida Bar Legal Citations
www.floridabar.org
(click "Publications" then "The Florida Bar Journal" and type "citation" in the search box)

Bluebook Citation
www.law.cornell.edu/citation
www.law.cornell.edu/citation/state_samples/sample_florida.htm
www.legalbluebook.com

ALWD Citation
www.alwd.org
www.alwd.org/publications/citation_manual.html

Wikipedia on Citation
en.wikipedia.org/wiki/Case_citation

Citation in General
www.freedomlaw.com/LegCitations.html

Cite-Checking
lib.law.washington.edu/ref/citecheck.html

Universal Citation Guide (Florida)
www.aallnet.org/committee/citation/ucg/appe-index.html

Other Citation Systems
www.bedfordstmartins.com/online/citex.html

D. Something to Check

Assume you are given the following information about a legal authority that you wish to cite for inclusion in a document to be submitted to a Florida state court. Write the citation in proper form. (If you need a date, you can make one up.)

1. Sec. 14, Art. 1, Constitution of the State of Florida
2. Section 113:4-01 of the Administrative Code of Florida
3. Florida Rules of Civil Procedure, Rule 36
4. Florida Statutes section 775.080
5. The 1987 opinion of the Florida Supreme Court called Rogers versus the state found on page 526 of volume 511 of the Southern Reporter second series

5.3 Abbreviations in Citations: Some Comparisons

A. Introduction
B. Abbreviation Comparisons
C. Abbreviation Guidelines
D. Abbreviations for Major Florida Newspapers
E. More Information
F. Something to Check

A. Introduction

As we saw in section 5.2, citation rules can be found in several sources: The *Florida Rules of Appellate Procedure* (Rule 9.800), *The Bluebook: A Uniform System of Citation* (Bluebook), and the *Florida Style Manual* (Florida State University Law Review, 6th ed., 2003). Also mentioned as an alternative source is the *ALWD Citation Manual: A Professional System of Citation* (ALWD).

An important citation concern is the abbreviation of words and phrases in legal writing. Citation systems do not always agree on how something should be abbreviated or whether something should be abbreviated at all. In this section, we will compare how three systems abbreviate important words and phrases. Our focus will be on those abbreviations that *differ* among any one of the three major systems, although for major entries we will show the abbreviations even if all three systems agree. Often the only difference is whether a space is used between specific letters of the abbreviation.

Rule 9.800 of the *Rules of Appellate Procedure* applies to all legal documents, including court opinions, and *takes precedence* over all other citation rules. It is the primary authority in determining how to cite a source. The scope of the *Rules of Appellate Procedure*, however, is limited and Rule 9.800 does not encompass many of the sources that one may wish to cite. As we saw in section 5.2, when Rule 9.800 does not address a particular citation, the Bluebook controls. If the Bluebook does not address a particular citation, the *Florida Style Manual* controls.

B. Abbreviation Comparisons

	Rule 9.800	Florida Style Manual	Bluebook	ALWD
Administrative	Admin.	Admin.	Admin.	Admin.
Association	Ass'n		Ass'n	Assn.
Attorney	Att'y	Att'y	Att'y	Atty.
Attorney General	Att'y Gen.	Att'y Gen.	Att'y Gen.	Atty. Gen.
Bankruptcy		Bankr.	Bankr.	Bankr.
Chapter	ch.		ch.	ch.
Commission	Comm'n	Comm'n	Comm'n	Commn.
Committee		Comm.	Comm.	Comm.
Constitution	Const.	Const.	Const.	Const.
Division		Div.	Div.	Div.
Federal Rules of Appellate Procedure			Fed. R. App. P.	Fed. R. App. P.
Federal Rules of Civil Procedure			Fed. R. Civ. P.	Fed. R. Civ. P.
Federal Rules of Criminal Procedure			Fed. R. Crim. P.	Fed. R. Crim. P.
Federal Rules of Evidence			Fed. R. Evid.	Fed. R. Evid.
Federal Supplement	F. Supp.		F. Supp.	F. Supp.
Federal Supplement Second			F. Supp. 2d	F. Supp. 2d
Florida	Fla.	Fla.	Fla.	Fla.

Florida Administrative Code	Fla. Admin. Code R.	Fla. Admin. Code R.	Fla. Admin. Code Ann. r.	Fla. Admin. Code Ann. r.
Florida Administrative Weekly		Fla. Admin. W.	Fla. Admin. Weekly	Fla. Admin. Wkly.
Florida Attorney General Opinions	Op. Att'y Gen. Fla.	Op. Att'y Gen. Fla.	Fla. Att'y Gen. Op.	Fla. Atty. Gen. Op.
Florida Bar Admissions Rules	Fla. Bar Admiss. R.	Fla. Bar Admiss. R.		
Florida Bar Foundation By-Laws	Fla. Bar Found. By-Laws	Fla. Bar Found. By-Laws		
Florida Bar Foundation Charter	Fla. Bar Found. Charter	Fla. Bar Found. Charter		
Florida Bar Integration Rule	Fla. Bar. Integr. R.			
Florida Bar Journal		Fla. B.J.		Fla. B.J.
Florida Circuit Court	Fla. [number of circuit] Cir. Ct.	Fla. [number of circuit] Cir. Ct.	Fla. Cir. Ct.	Fla. [number of circuit] Cir.
Florida County Court	Fla. [name of county] Cty. Ct.	Fla. [name of county] Cty. Ct.	Fla. [name of county] County Ct.	Fla. [name of County] Co. Ct.
Florida District Court of Appeal	Fla. [number of district] DCA (year).	Fla. [number of district] DCA (year)	Fla. Dist. Ct. App.	Fla. [number of district] Dist. App.
Florida Family Law Rules of Procedure	Fla. Fam. L. R. P.	Fla. Fam. L. R. P.		
Florida Judicial Qualifications Commission	Fla. Jud. Qual. Comm'n	Fla. Jud. Quals. Comm'n		
Florida Law Weekly	Fla. L. Weekly	Fla. L. Weekly	Fla. L. Weekly	Fla. L. Wkly.
Florida Law Weekly Federal	Fla. L. Weekly Fed.			
Florida Law Weekly Supplement	Fla. L. Weekly Supp.	Fla. L. Weekly Supp.	Fla. L. Weekly Supp.	Fla. L. Wkly. Supp.
Florida Probate Rules	Fla. Prob. R.	Fla. Prob. R.		
Florida Public Service Commission	Fla. Public Serv. Comm'n	Fla. Public Serv. Comm'n		
Florida Rules for Mediators	Fla. R. Med.	Fla. R. Cert. & Ct.- Apptd. Mediators		
Florida Rules of Appellate Procedure	Fla. R. App. P.	Fla. R. App. P.	Fla. R. App. P.	Fla. R. App. P.
Florida Rules of Arbitration	Fla. R. Arb.			
Florida Rules of Civil Procedure	Fla. R. Civ. P.	Fla. R. Civ. P.	Fla. R. Civ. P.	Fla. R. Civ. P.
Florida Rules of Criminal Procedure	Fla. R. Crim. P.	Fla. R. Crim. P.	Fla. R. Crim. P.	Fla. R. Crim. P.
Florida Rules of Judicial Administration	Fla. R. Jud. Admin.	Fla. R. Jud. Admin.	Fla. R. Jud. Admin.	Fla. R. Jud. Admin.
Florida Rules of Juvenile Procedure	Fla. R. Juv. P.	Fla. R. Juv. P.	Fla. R. Juv. P.	Fla. R. Juv. P.
Florida Rules of Traffic Court	Fla. R. Traf. Ct.	Fla. R. Traf. Ct.	Fla. R. Traffic Ct.	
Florida Rules of Workers' Compensation	Fla. R. Work. Comp. P.	Fla. R. Work. Comp. P.		
Florida Small Claims Rules	Fla. Sm. Cl. R.	Fla. Sm. Cl. R.		
Florida Standard Jury Instructions (Civil)	Fla. Std. Jury Instr. (Civ.)	Fla. Std. Jury Instr. (Civ.)		
Florida Standard Jury Instructions (Criminal)	Fla. Std. Jury Instr. (Crim.)	Fla. Std. Jury Instr. (Crim.)		

Florida Standards for Imposing Lawyer Sanctions	Fla. Stds. Imposing Law. Sancs.	Fla. Stds. Imposing Law. Sancs.		
Florida Statutes	Fla. Stat.	Fla. Stat.	Fla. Stat.	Fla. Stat.
Florida Statutes Annotated	Fla. Stat. Ann.	Fla. Stat. Ann.	Fla. Stat. Ann.	Fla. Stat. Ann.
Florida Supplement	Fla. Supp.	Fla. Supp.	Fla. Supp.	Fla. Supp.
Florida Supplement Second	Fla. Supp. 2d	Fla. Supp. 2d	Fla. Supp. 2d	Fla. Supp. 2ed
Footnote	n.	n.	n.	n.
Government	Gov't	Gov't	Gov't	Govt.
Government Code	Gov't Code	Gov't Code	Gov't Code	Govt. Code
International		Int'l	Int'l	Intl.
Juvenile Court	Juv. Ct.		Juv. Ct.	Juv. Ct.
Management		Mgmt.	Mgmt.	Mgt.
National		Nat'l	Nat'l	Natl.
Opinion	Op.	Op.	Op.	Op.
Paragraph		¶	para. (¶ if used in source)	¶
Probate Court	Prob. Ct.	Prob. Ct.	Prob. Ct.	Prob. Ct.
Regulation	Reg.	Reg.	Reg.	Reg.
Rules Regulating The Florida Bar	R. Regulating Fla. Bar	R. Regulating Fla. Bar	R. Regulating Fla. Bar	
Secretary		Sec'y	Sec'y	Sec.
Senate Bill Number		SB	S.	Sen.
Senate Committee			S. Comm.	Sen. Comm.
Southern Reporter Second	So. 2d	So. 2d	So. 2d	So. 2d
Statutes	Stat.	Stat.	Stat.	Stat.
University		U.	Univ.	U.
U.S. Bankruptcy Court Middle District			Bankr. M.D. Fla.	Bankr. M.D. Fla.
U.S. Bankruptcy Court Northern District			Bankr. N.D. Fla.	Bankr. N.D. Fla.
U.S. Bankruptcy Court Southern District	Bankr. S.D. Fla.		Bankr. S.D. Fla.	Bankr. S.D. Fla.
U.S. District Court Middle District	M.D. Fla.		M.D. Fla.	M.D. Fla.
U.S. District Court Northern District	N.D. Fla.		N.D. Fla.	N.D. Fla.
U.S. District Court Southern District	S.D. Fla.		S.D. Fla.	S.D. Fla.

C. Abbreviation Guidelines

Rule 9.800, Uniform Citation System. This rule applies to all legal documents, including court opinions. Except for citations to case reporters, all citation forms should be spelled out in full if used as an integral part of a sentence either in the text or in footnotes. Abbreviated forms as shown in this rule should be used if the citation is intended to stand alone either in the text or in footnotes.

The Bluebook recommends using "(Fla. Dist. Ct. App.)" as the parenthetical identifier when citing to a district court of appeal decision. This form, however, does not indicate to which of Florida's five district courts of appeal the citation refers. Thus, accepted practice in Florida is to indicate the number of the district court, followed by the abbreviation "DCA."

Rule 2.2 of the Florida Style Manual states that if a month is used in a citation, then the month should be abbreviated. When abbreviating a state, do not use the two-letter postal abbreviations.

Rule 5.51 of the Florida Style Manual states that you should abbreviate section references in a footnote citation sentence by using the section symbol (§). Use a single section symbol with a space between the section symbol and the section's number for a single section reference. Use two section symbols with no space between them for citing consecutive sections.

D. Abbreviations for Major Florida Newspapers

EXHIBIT 5.3B	Abbreviations of Florida Newspapers (Florida Style Manual)

The following is a list of abbreviations for major Florida newspapers as set forth in the *Florida Style Manual*

NEWSPAPER	ABBREVIATION
Florida Times-Union	Fla. Times-Union
Fort Lauderdale Sun Sentinel	Ft. Laud. Sun Sent.
The Miami Herald	Miami Herald
The Orlando Sentinel	Orlando Sent.
The Palm Beach Post	Palm Bch. Post
St. Petersburg Times	St. Pete. Times
Tallahassee Democrat	Tall. Dem.
The Tampa Tribune	Tampa Trib.

E. More Information

Florida Bar Legal Citations
www.floridabar.org
(click "Publications" then "The Florida Bar Journal" and type "citation" in the search box)

Florida Rules of Appellate Procedure (including Rule 9.800)
www.4dca.org/applellate%20rules.pdf

Florida Style Manual
www.law.fsu.edu/Journals/lawreview/downloads/242/fsm.pdf

Basic Legal Citation
www.law.cornell.edu/citation/3-400.htm

University of Central Florida, Legal Citations Information
library.ucf.edu/GovDocs/legal/Default.asp

Miscellaneous
www.llrx.com/columns/reference37.htm
www.aallnet.org/sis/lisp/cite.htm
www.ulib.iupui.edu/subjectareas/gov/docs_abbrev.html
www.legalabbrevs.cardiff.ac.uk

F. Something to Check

1. Open any law book, e.g., a school textbook, a case reporter, a statutory code. Find any two abbreviations used in this book that do *not* conform with the Rule 9.800. Describe the discrepancies.

2. Use the examples and other material in sections 5.2 and 5.3 to determine if there are any improper abbreviations in the following citations according to Rule 9.800:

   Fenelon v. State, 594 So.2d (Fla. 1992)

   Sotolongo v. State, 530 So.2d 514 (Fla. DCA 1988)

   Section 350.34, Fla. Stat. (1973)

   Fla. Admin. Code R.62D-2.014

5.4 Abbreviations for Notetaking
   A. Introduction
   B. Notetaking Abbreviations
   C. More Information

A. Introduction

There are many settings in which paralegals must be able to write quickly. Examples include notetaking:

- In class
- While studying school textbooks
- While conducting legal research
- While receiving instructions from a supervisor
- While interviewing a client or witness
- When listening to a deposition witness give testimony
- When listening to a trial witness give testimony

Using abbreviations in such settings can be helpful. This section presents some commonly used notetaking abbreviations in the law. Some entries have more than one abbreviation, e.g., c/a and coa for cause of action. When a choice is available, pick an abbreviation with which you are comfortable.

These abbreviations are for use in notetaking, *not for use in citations or formal writing*. (For some abbreviations used in citations, see section 5.3.) The primary purpose of the following abbreviations is to help you take notes that only you will read. Hence feel free to try out, adapt, and add to the following list.

B. Notetaking Abbreviations

a action
A Atlantic Reporter (or answer)
A2d Atlantic Reporter Second
aa administrative agency
a/b appellate brief
ABA American Bar Association
a/c appellate court
acct account
acctg accounting
ad administrative decision
admr administrator

ADR alternate dispute resolution

aff affirmed

a/g attorney general

agt agent

aka also known as

a/l administrative law

alj administrative law judge

AmJur American Jurisprudence

amt amount

ans answer

aple appellee

aplt appellant

app appeal

appee appellee

appnt appellant

apt apartment

ar administrative regulation

a/r assumption of the risk

asap as soon as possible

assn association

atty attorney

b business (or bill)

b. born

b/4 before

ba bar association

bankr bankruptcy

b/c because

bd board

betw/ between

bfp bona fide purchaser

b/k breach of contract

bldg building

b/p burden of proof

bus business

b/w breach of warranty

c. circa [about]

© consideration

¢ complaint

ca court of appeals

CA11 Eleventh Circuit

c/a cause of action

cc child custody

CC Civil Code (or Circuit Court)

c/c counterclaim

c-dr creditor

c/e cross examination

cert certiorari

cf compare

ch chapter (or charter)

CiCt Circuit Court

c/l common law

cle continuing legal education

co company (or county)

coa cause of action

comm committee

commn commission

commnr commissioner

compl. complaint (or compliance)

conf conference

con law constitutional law

consv conservative

cont continued

corp corporation

cp community property

CP Common Pleas

cr criminal (or creditor)

cr-c criminal court

cs child support

ct court

cty county

cv civil

cy calendar year

CyCt County Court

cz cause

△ defendant

d danger (or dangerous)

d. died (or death)

DA district attorney

DC Drug Court

DCA District Court of Appeals

d/e direct examination

decrg decreasing

depo deposition

dept department

df defendant

dist district

div division

dkt docket

dmg damages

dob date of birth

dod date of death

dom dissolution of marriage

d-r debtor

dv domestic violence

= equals

e evidence

e/d eminent domain

ee employee

eg example

egs examples

emp employment

eng engineer (or engineering)

ent enterprise

eo executive order

eq equity

eqbl equitable

er employer

est estimate (or established)

ev evidence

ex exhibit

exr executor

f fact

F Federal Reporter (or Florida)

F2 Federal Reporter Second

F3 Federal Reporter Third

FAC Florida Administrative Code

FALR Florida Administrative Law Reports

faq frequently asked questions

FAW Florida Administrative Weekly

FB Florida Bar

FBJ Florida Bar Journal

FBN Florida Bar News

FC Florida Circuit Court (or Family Court)

4cb foreseeable

fed federal

FJ Florida Jurisprudence

FL Laws of Florida

Fla Florida Reports (or Supreme Court of Florida)

FlaBar Florida Bar Association

FlaBJ Florida Bar Journal

FlaCir Florida Circuit Court

FlaDistApp Florida District Court of Appeal

FlaJur Florida Jurisprudence

FlaLaws Laws of Florida

FlaStat Florida Statute

FlaStatAnn Florida Statutes Annotated

fn footnote

FRAP Federal Rules of Appellate Procedure

FRCP Federal Rules of Civil Procedure

FRCRP Federal Rules of Criminal Procedure

FRE Federal Rules of Evidence

FS Federal Supplement

fs facts

FSA Florida Statutes Annotated

FSC Florida Supreme Court

f-st federal statute

FSt Florida Statute

fy fiscal year

g govern

GA General Assembly

g/r general rule

gt government

gvt government

h husband

hb House Bill

hdc holder in due course

HR House of Representatives

hrg hearing

i interest

ij injury

immig immigration

in interest

inc incorporated

incrg increasing

indl individual

indp independent

info information

inj injunction

ins insurance

intl international

i-p in personam

i-r in rem

IRC Internal Revenue Code

IRS Internal Revenue Service

J judge (justice or judgment)

JC Juvenile Court

j/d judgment for defendant

JJ judges (or justices)

jp justice of the peace

j/p judgment for plaintiff

jt judgment
jud judicial (or judgment)
jur jurisdiction
juv juvenile
jxn jurisdiction
K contract
l liable (or liability)
< less than (or smaller than)
LF Laws of Florida
l/h legislative history
liab liability (or liable)
lit litigation
l/l limited liability
ll landlord
l/lc limited liability company
l/lp limited liability partnership
ll/s looseleaf service
LN Lexis-Nexis
LOF Laws of Florida
lr legal research
ltd limited
Lx Lexis
max maximum
MC Municipal Court
mem memorial (or member)
mfg manufacturing
mfr manufacturer
mgmt management
min minimum
misc miscellaneous
mj major
mkt market
mo majority opinion
> more than (or greater than)
mtg mortgage (or meeting)
mtge mortgagee
mtgr mortgagor
mtn motion
mun municipal
n/a irrelevant (or not applicable)
natl national
neg negligence (or negligent)
negl negligence
noh notice of hearing
nt nothing (or note or not)
ntry notary

number
O owner
o degree
oa opposing attorney
obj object (or objective)
oc opposing counsel
occ occupation
oee offeree
oer offeror
ol online
op opinion
ord ordinance
π plaintiff
p plaintiff
p. page
PC Penal Code
p/c proximate cause
pee promisee
petr petitioner
p/f prima facie
pg page
pgs pages
pj personal judgment
PL public law
pl plaintiff
+ plus
pol practice of law
por promisor
pp public policy
p/r personal representative
priv private
pub public
pub-op public opinion
pvg privilege
pvt private
Q equity (or equitable)
? question
?d questioned
r regulation
® reasonable
re real estate (or regarding)
rec record
rec'd received
reg regulation
rel related to
rep representative (or representation)
rev reverse
revd reversed
r/o restraining order
roc rules of court
rogs interrogatories
RPC Rules of Professional Conduct

rr railroad
rsb reasonable
s sum
S statute
$ suppose
sb Senate Bill
s/b should be
sc supreme court
SCF Supreme Court of Florida
secy secretary
s/f statute of frauds
s-h self-help
Sh Shepard's Citations (or shepardize)
Sh-z shepardize
s/j summary judgment
sl strict liability
s/l statute of limitations
s-mj subject-matter jurisdiction
sn/b should not be
So Southern Reporter
So2 Southern Reporter Second
SOL statute of limitations
sop service of process
SOS secretary of state
ss sections
s-st state statute
st something (or sometimes)
stat statute
Stat United States Statutes at Large
stats statistics
std standard
st-st state statute
sub substantial
subj subject (or subjective)
t testimony
T tort
t/c trial court

tee trustee
test testimony
**** therefore
tp third party
tpr trespasser
tro temporary restraining order
u understanding
U university
uc unemployment compensation
ucc Uniform Commercial Code
ui unemployment insurance
usc United States Code
ussc United States Supreme Court
v versus (or against)
vs against (or versus)
w wife
w/ with
wc workers' compensation
w/i within
WL Westlaw
w/o without
x cross
xe cross examination
© consideration
¢ complaint
Δ defendant
= equals
< less than (or smaller than)
> more than (or greater than)
number
π plaintiff
+ plus
? question
?d questioned
® reasonable
$ suppose
**** therefore

C. More Information

Taking Notes
www.nyls.edu/pages/3083.asp

Abbreviations
lib.law.washington.edu/pubs/acron.html
www.llrx.com/columns/reference37.htm?
www.aboutlawschools.org/law/resources/legalabbreviations
www.abbreviations.com

5.5 Research Starters for 78 Major Florida Topics
A. Introduction
B. Abbreviations
C. Topics Covered
D. Research Starter Cites and Sites
E. More Information on Florida Law
F. Something to Check

A. Introduction

Often in legal research, the first hurdle is finding your first lead. You need a *starting point* that will guide you into the various categories of case law, statutory law, administrative law, etc. You may also need a lead to secondary authority such as a legal treatise or legal encyclopedia that will provide an overview of an area of the law that may be new to you. In this section, we provide you with such leads to 78 major topics of Florida law. They are *starter cites* in the sense that they may lead you—directly or indirectly—to what you need.

See also the following related areas of the book:

- Section 5.1 on legal research in Florida law
- Section 5.6 on self-help resources on Florida law
- Section 5.7 on public records research
- Section 4.5 on state agencies, offices, and boards

B. Abbreviations

The starter sites use the following abbreviations to legal materials covered, many of which are online as well as on the shelves of moderate-sized law libraries:

FAC: Florida Administrative Code

FD: Florida Digest, 2d
(the FD will lead you to key numbers within the West Group digest system)

FJ: Florida Jurisprudence 2d
(Florida is one of the few states that has its own legal encyclopedia)

FSA: Florida Statutes Annotated

C. Topics Covered

Abortion	Affidavits
Administrative	Agency
Law	Alimony
Adoption	Annulment

Appeal and Error
Arbitration
Attorney-Client
  Privilege
Attorneys
Banking
Child Custody
Child Support
Civil Procedure
Commercial Code
Constitutional
  Law
Consumer Protection
Contracts
Corporations
Courts in
  Florida
Criminal Law
Damages
Deeds
Discovery
Divorce/Dissolution of
  Marriage
Domestic
  Violence
Employment
  Discrimination
Enforcement of
  Judgment
Environment
Equity
Estates
Evidence
Family Law
Fraud
Garnishment
Government
Guardianship
Illegitimacy
Injunctions
Insurance
Intellectual
  Property
Labor Relations
Landlord and
  Tenant

Legal Separation
Limited Liability
  Companies
Marriage
Mediation
Medical
  Malpractice
Mineral, Water,
  and Fishing
  Rights
Minors
Mortgages
Motor Vehicles
Negligence
Notary Public
Paralegals
Partnerships
Pleading
Power of
  Attorney
Privacy
Privileged
  Communications
Products Liability
Property Division in
  Dissolution of Marriage
Real Property
Service of
  Process
Statute of
  Frauds
Statute of
  Limitations
Summary Judgment
Summons
Taxation
Torts
Traffic Laws
Trusts
Unemployment
  Insurance
Venue
Water Rights
Wills
Workers'
  Compensation

D. Research Starter Cites and Sites
Abortion

Statutes: FSA §§ 390.011 et seq.
Regulations: FAC Chapter 59-A9
Cases: FD: check the key numbers (☞) under Abortion and Birth Control
Encyclopedia: FJ: check Criminal Law §§ 3208 et seq.; Family Law §§ 3, 236; Physicians § 3214

Internet:

megalaw.com/fl/top/flfamily.php

www.guttmacher.org/pubs/sfaa/florida.html

Administrative Law

Statutes: FSA Chapter 120
Regulations: FAC Titles 1-69
Cases: FD: check the key numbers (☞) under Administrative Law and Procedure
Encyclopedia: FJ: check Administrative Law §§ 1 et seq.
Internet:
www.falr.com
www.law.ufl.edu/lic/guides
(click "Florida Administrative Code")

Adoption

Statutes: FSA § 39.812; Chapter 63
Regulations: FAC Chapter 10M-8 (Adoptions)
Cases: FD: check the key numbers (☞) under Adoption
Encyclopedia: FJ: check Family Law §§ 152 et seq.
Internet:
www.Florida.adoption.com
www.adoption.org/adopt/state-of-Florida-adoption-laws.php
www.state.fl.us/cf_web
megalaw.com/fl/top/flfamily.php

Affidavits

Statutes: FSA §§ 92.50 et seq.
Cases: FD: check the key numbers (☞) under Affidavits
Encyclopedia: FJ: check Acknowledgments §§ 31 et seq.
Internet:
www.ilrg.com/forms/affidavit-gen/us/fl
www.hsmv.state.fl.us/forms/insurance.html

Agency

Statutes: FSA Chapter 475
Cases: FD: check the key numbers (☞) under Principal and Agent
Encyclopedia: FJ: Agency and Employment §§ 1 et seq.

Alimony

Statutes: FSA §§ 61.08, 61.043
Cases: FD: check the key numbers (☞) under Divorce 199 et seq.
Encyclopedia: FJ: check Family Law §§ 593 et seq.
Internet:
megalaw.com/fl/top/flfamily.php
www.divorcenet.com/states/florida

Annulment

Statutes: FSA Chapter 61
Regulations: FAC Rule 64V-1.021
Cases: FD: check the key numbers (☞) under Marriage 56 et seq.

Encyclopedia: FJ: check Family Law §§ 482 et seq.
Internet:
megalaw.com/fl/top/flfamily.php
www.divorcenet.com/states/florida/divorce_and_annulment

Appeal and Error

Statutes: FSA: see Florida Rules of Appellate Procedure
Cases: FD: check the key numbers (☞) under Appeal and Error
Encyclopedia: FJ: check Appellate Review §§ 1 et seq.
Internet:
megalaw.com/fl/top/flcivpro.php
www.flcourts.org

Arbitration

Statutes: FSA Chapters 44, 682
Regulations: FAC Rules 22I-7.001 et seq. (medical malpractice arbitration)
Cases: FD: check the key numbers (☞) under Alternative Dispute Resolution 110 et seq.
Encyclopedia: FJ: check Arbitration and Award §§ 1 et seq.
Internet:
www.flcourts.org/gen_public/adr/index.shtml
floridaarbitrationlaw.com

Attorney-Client Privilege

Statutes: FSA § 90.502
Cases: FD: check the key numbers (☞) under Witnesses 67
Encyclopedia: FJ: check Evidence and Witnesses §§ 695 et seq.
Internet:
www.law.cornell.edu/ethics/fl/code/CRule_4-1.6.htm
www.fgcu.edu/generalcounsel/privilege.asp

Attorneys

Statutes: FSA Chapter 454
Regulations: FAC Rule 2-37.010
Cases: FD: check the key numbers (☞) under Attorney and Client
Encyclopedia: FJ: check Attorneys at Law §§ 1 et seq.
Internet:
www.flabar.org

Banking

Statutes: FSA Chapters 652 et seq.
Regulations: FAC Title 3 (Department of Banking and Finance)
Cases: FD: check the key numbers (☞) under Banks and Banking
Encyclopedia: FJ: check Banks and Lending Institutions §§ 1 et seq.

Internet*:*
www.fldfs.com
www.leg.state.fl.us/statutes
   (click "Title XXXVIII")

Child Custody

Statutes: FSA Chapter 61
Regulations: FAC Rule 64B19-18.077
Cases: FD: check the key numbers (⟐) under Child Custody
Encyclopedia: FJ: check Family Law §§ 91 et seq., 772 et seq.
Internet*:*
megalaw.com/fl/top/flfamily.php
www.divorcenet.com/states/florida

Child Support

Statutes: FSA Chapters 61, 88, 409, 742
Regulations: FAC Title 10, Chapter 10C-25 (Child Support Enforcement Program)
Cases: FD: check the key numbers (⟐) under Child Support
Encyclopedia: FJ: check Family Law §§ 506, 841 et seq.
Internet:
dor.myflorida.com/dor/childsupport
megalaw.com/fl/top/flfamily.php
www.divorcenet.com/states/florida

Civil Procedure

Statutes: FSA: see Florida Rules of Civil Procedure
Cases: FD: check the key numbers (⟐) under Appeal and Error; Evidence; Pretrial Procedure; Trial; Witnesses
Encyclopedia: FJ: check Actions §§ 1 et seq.; Appellate Review §§ 1 et seq.; Discovery and Depositions §§ 1 et seq.; Judgments and Decrees §§ 1 et seq.; Parties §§ 1 et seq.; Pleadings §§ 1 et seq.; Trial §§ 1 et seq.; Venue §§ 1 et seq.
Internet:
megalaw.com/fl/top/flcivpro.php
www.floridasupremecourt.org/decisions/index.shtml
   (click "Florida Rules of Civil procedure")

Commercial Code

Statutes: FSA Chapters 670 et seq.
Cases: FD: check the key numbers (⟐) under Bills and Notes; Sales
Encyclopedia: FJ: check Assignments §§ 1 et seq., Banks and Lending Institutions §§ 1 et seq.; Bills, Notes §§ 1 et seq.; Contracts § 42; Investment Securities and Securities Act §§ 1 et seq.; Sales §§ 1 et seq., Secured Transactions §§ 1 et seq.
Internet:
www.leg.state.fl.us/statutes
   (click "Title XXXIX")
www.floridaucc.com

Constitutional Law

Statutes: See index to Florida Constitution within FSA
Cases: FD: check the key numbers (⟐) under Constitutional Law
Encyclopedia: FJ: check Constitutional Law §§ 1 et seq.
Internet:
megalaw.com/fl/flconstitution.php
www.law.fsu.edu/crc

Consumer Protection

Statutes: FSA Chapter 501
Cases: FD: check the key numbers (⟐) under Consumer Credit; Debtor and Creditor; Fraud
Encyclopedia: FJ: Consumer and Borrower Protection §§ 1 et seq.
Internet:
www.myfloridalegal.com/consumer
www.stateofflorida.com/Portal/DesktopDefault.aspx?tabid=57

Contracts

Statutes: FSA Chapters 670, 725
Cases: FD: check the key numbers (⟐) under Contracts; Sales
Encyclopedia: FJ: check Contracts §§ 1 et seq.; Sales §§ 1 et seq.
Internet:
www.weblocator.com/attorney/fl/law/contcon.html

Corporations

Statutes: FSA Chapter 607
Regulations: FAC Title 1, Chapter 1C-6 (Division of Corporations)
Cases: FD: check the key numbers (⟐) under Corporations; Securities Regulation
Encyclopedia: FJ: check Business Relationships §§ 1 et seq.
Internet:
sunbiz.org
www.dos.state.fl.us
www.flabuslaw.org

Courts in Florida

Statutes: FSA: Florida Constitution Article V
Cases: FD: check the key numbers (⟐) under Courts
Encyclopedia: FJ: check Courts and Judges §§ 1 et seq.
Internet:
www.flcourts.org
megalaw.com/fl/flconstitution.php#A05

Criminal Law

Statutes: FSA Chapters 775 et seq., 900 et seq.. See also Florida Rules of Criminal Procedure

Cases: FD: check the key numbers (☞) under Criminal Law; Sentencing and Punishment
Encyclopedia: FJ: check Criminal Law §§ 1 et seq.
Internet:
myfloridalegal.com
megalaw.com/fl/top/flcriminal.php

Damages

Statutes: FSA §§ 768.71 et seq.
Cases: FD: check the key numbers (☞) under Damages
Encyclopedia: FJ: check Damages §§ 1 et seq.
Internet:
www.megalaw.com/fl/top/fltorts.php

Deeds

Statutes: FSA Chapters 689, 695
Cases: FD: check the key numbers (☞) under Deeds; Property
Encyclopedia: FJ: check Deeds §§ 1 et seq.; Mortgages and Deeds of Trust §§ 1 et seq.
Internet:
dor.myflorida.com/dor/taxes/doc_stamp.html
www.lectlaw.com/inll/106.htm
www.weblocator.com/attorney/fl/law/resreal.html

Discovery

Statutes: FSA Florida Rules of Civil Procedure Rules 1.280 et seq.
Cases: FD: check the key numbers (☞) under Pretrial Procedure 11 et seq.
Encyclopedia: FJ: check Discovery and Depositions §§ 1 et seq.
Internet:
megalaw.com/fl/top/flcivpro.php

Divorce/Dissolution of Marriage

Statutes: FSA Chapter 61
Cases: FD: check the key numbers (☞) under Divorce; Husband and Wife
Encyclopedia: FJ: check Family Law §§ 876 et seq.
Internet:
www.flcourts.org/gen_public/family/forms_rules/index.shtml
www.hodgsonruss.com/article_564.html
www.divorcenet.com/states/florida
www.stateofflorida.com/Portal/DesktopDefault.aspx?tabid=64
megalaw.com/fl/top/flfamily.php

Domestic Violence

Statutes: FSA §§ 39.901 et seq.; 414.157, 741.01
Regulations: FAC Chapters 10A-8, 10M-48; 65C-6 (Domestic Violence)

Cases: FD: check the key numbers (☞) under Breach of the Peace 15
Encyclopedia: FJ: check Family Law §§ 75 et seq.
Internet:
www.fcadv.org
www.aardvarc.org/dv/states/fldv.shtml
www.dcf.state.fl.us/domesticviolence

Employment Discrimination

Statutes: FSA Chapter 760; Florida Constitution, Article 1 §§ 2 et seq.
Regulations: FAC §§ Rules 60BB-1.013, 60L-36.005
Cases: FD: check the key numbers (☞) under Civil Rights 1101
Encyclopedia: FJ: check Civil Rights §§ 13 et seq.; Labor Law §§ 192, 194
Internet:
megalaw.com/fl/top/fllabor.php
www.stateofflorida.com/Portal/DesktopDefault.aspx?tabid=10

Enforcement of Judgment

Statutes: FSA Chapter 55; Florida Rules of Civil Procedure Rule 1.570
Cases: FD: check the key numbers (☞) under the Judgment
Encyclopedia: FJ: check Creditors' Rights §§ 57 et seq.; Judgments and Decrees §§ 367 et seq.
Internet:
megalaw.com/fl/top/flcivpro.php

Environment

Statutes: FSA Chapters 369 et seq., 403
Regulations: FAC Title 17 (Department of Environmental Regulation); Title 62 (Department of Environmental Protection)
Cases: FD: check the key numbers (☞) under Environmental Law
Encyclopedia: FJ: check Environmental Rights and Remedies §§ 1 et seq.
Internet:
www.dep.state.fl.us
megalaw.com/fl/top/flenvironmental.php

Equity

Statutes: FSA §§ 68.01 et seq., 625.75, 702.01
Cases: FD: check the key numbers (☞) under Equity
Encyclopedia: FJ: check Equity and Equitable Matters §§ 1 et seq.
Internet:
megalaw.com/fl/top/flcivpro.php
megalaw.com/fl/top/flfamily.php

Estates

Statutes: FSA: Chapters 689, 731 et seq.
Cases: FD: check the key numbers (☞) under the Estates in Property; Trusts; Wills
Encyclopedia: FJ: check Estates, Powers §§ 1 et seq.
Internet:
megalaw.com/fl/top/flprobate.php
dor.myflorida.com/dor/taxes/estate_tax.html

Evidence

Statutes: FSA Chapters 90 et seq.
Regulations: FAC Rules 28-106.213; 60Q-6.121; 65-2.060
Cases: FD: check the key numbers (☞) under Evidence; Witnesses
Encyclopedia: FJ: check Evidence and Witnesses §§ 1 et seq.
Internet:
megalaw.com/fl/top/flcivpro.php

Family Law

Statutes: FSA §§ 20.19 et seq.; Chapters 39, 61
Regulations: FAC Title 65 (Department of Children and Family Services)
Cases: FD: check the key numbers (☞) under the vols. for Child Custody; Child Support; Divorce; Husband and Wife; Marriage
Encyclopedia: FJ: check Family Law §§ 1 et seq.
Internet:
megalaw.com/fl/top/flfamily.php
www.dcf.state.fl.us/ess
www.dcf.state.fl.us/childcare

Fraud

Statutes: FSA § 222.30; Chapters 726, 817
Regulations: FAC Rules 1S-2.025; 10C-24.020; 59G-7.073
Cases: FD: check the key numbers (☞) under Fraud
Encyclopedia: FJ: check Fraud and Deceit §§ 1 et seq.
Internet*:*
www.800helpfla.com
myfloridalegal.com
www.fldfs.com/fraud

Garnishment

Statutes: FSA Chapter 77
Regulations: FAC Rules 3A-31.801 et seq.; 12-21.201 et seq.
Cases: FD: check the key numbers (☞) under Garnishment; Judgment
Encyclopedia: FJ: check Creditors' Rights §§ 133 et seq.
Internet*:*
library.findlaw.com/1998/Dec/1/126478.html
www.fair-debt-collection.com/state-wage-garnishments.html

Government

Statutes: FSA Chapters 6, 10, 12, 25
Cases: FD: check the key numbers (☞) under the vols. for Counties; Municipal Corporations; Officers and Public Employees; States; Towns
Encyclopedia: FJ: check State of Florida §§ 1 et seq.
Internet:
www.myflorida.com
www.myflorida.com/taxonomy/government

Guardianship

Statutes: FSA Chapter 744
Regulations: FAC Rules 58M-2.001 et seq. (Public Guardianship Office)
Cases: FD: check the key numbers (☞) under Child Custody; Guardian and Ward
Encyclopedia: FJ: check Decedents' Estates; Family Law §§ 1 et seq.; Guardian and Ward §§ 1 et seq.
Internet:
megalaw.com/fl/top/flfamily.php
www.flcourts.org/gen_public/family/self_help/guardianship

Illegitimacy

Statutes: FSA Chapter 742
Regulations: FAC Rules 12E-1.003(3); 59G-7.0601(10); 65C-23.002
Cases: FD: check the key numbers (☞) under Children Out-of-Wedlock
Encyclopedia: FJ: check Declaratory Judgments § 23; Family Law § 111 (Children under Descent)
Internet:
megalaw.com/fl/top/flfamily.php

Injunctions

Statutes: FSA Chapter 60
Regulations: FAC Rule 25-22.030
Cases: FD: check the key numbers (☞) under Injunction
Encyclopedia: FJ: check Injunctions §§ 1 et seq.
Internet:
megalaw.com/fl/top/flcivpro.php

Insurance

Statutes: FSA Chapters 624 et seq.
Regulations: FAC Title 4 (Department of Insurance)
Cases: FD: check the key numbers (☞) under Insurance
Encyclopedia: FJ: check Insurance §§ 1 et seq.
Internet:
www.floir.com
www.hsmv.state.fl.us/ddl/insurancemenu.html

Intellectual Property

Statutes: FSA §§ 540.11 et seq.
Regulations: FAC Rules 6C3-10.142; 20-42.003; 20-107.002 et seq.
Cases: FD: check the key numbers (☞) under Copyrights and Intellectual Property
Encyclopedia: FJ: check Literary Property and Copyright §§ 1 et seq.; Trademarks §§ 1 et seq.
Internet:
grove.ufl.edu/~techlaw/links/
library.findlaw.com/1999/Jul/1/126833.html
en.wikipedia.org/wiki/Intellectual_property

Labor Relations

Statutes: FSA Chapters 447 et seq.
Regulations: FAC Title 38 (Department of Labor and Employment Security)
Cases: FD: check the key numbers (☞) under Labor and Employment
Encyclopedia: FJ: check Labor and Labor relations §§ 1 et seq.
Internet:
dlis.dos.state.fl.us/fgils/laborlaw.html
megalaw.com/fl/top/fllabor.php
www.stateofflorida.com
(click entries under "Employment" and "Labor")

Landlord and Tenant

Statutes: FSA Chapter 83
Cases: FD: check the key numbers (☞) under Landlord and Tenant
Encyclopedia: FJ: check Landlord and Tenant §§ 1 et seq.
Internet:
megalaw.com/fl/top/fllandlord.php
www.800helpfla.com/landlord_text.html

Legal Separation

Statutes: FSA Chapter 61
Cases: FD: check the key numbers (☞) under Divorce 155
Encyclopedia: FJ: check Family Law § 880
Internet:
www.hodgsonruss.com/article_564.html
www.divorcenet.com/states/florida
www.megalaw.com/fl/top/flfamily.php

Limited Liability Companies

Statutes: FSA Chapters 608, 621
Regulations: FAC Rules 61H1-26.002; 12C-2.006
Cases: FD: check the key numbers (☞) under Limited Liability Companies
Encyclopedia: FJ: check Business Relationships §§ 437 et seq.

Internet:
form.sunbiz.org/cor_llc.html
www.llrx.com/features/llc.htm

Marriage

Statutes: FSA Chapter 741
Regulations: FAC Rules 21CC-1.001 et seq.; 64V-1.021
Cases: FD: check the key numbers (☞) under Husband and Wife; Marriage
Encyclopedia: FJ: check Family Law §§ 11 et seq.
Internet:
megalaw.com/fl/top/flfamily.php

Mediation

Statutes: Chapter 44
Regulations: FAC Rules 2-41.001; 4-166.031; 7D-25.001
Cases: FD: check the key numbers (☞) under Alternative Dispute Resolution
Encyclopedia: FJ: check Arbitration and Award §§ 140 et seq.
Internet:
www.flcourts.org/gen_public/adr/index.shtml
www.tfapm.org/supreme.shtml

Medical Malpractice

Statutes: FSA Chapter 766
Regulations: FAC Rules 4-31.069; 4-39.001; 4-187.001; 22I-7.001 et seq. (medical malpractice arbitration)
Cases: FD: check the key numbers (☞) under Health 600 et seq.
Encyclopedia: FJ: check Medical Malpractice §§ 1 et seq.
Internet:
www.mcandl.com/florida.html
www.floridamalpractice.com

Mineral, Water, and Fishing Rights

Statutes: FSA Chapters 369 et seq.
Regulations: FAC Titles 16 (Natural Resources); 39 (Fish Commission); 40 (Water Management)
Cases: FD: check the key numbers (☞) under Environmental Law; Fish; Game; Mines and Minerals; Water and Water Courses
Encyclopedia: FJ: check Fish and Game §§ 1 et seq.; Mines and Minerals §§ 1 et seq.; Water §§ 1 et seq.
Internet:
www.dep.state.fl.us/geology/geologictopics/minerals.htm
www.dep.state.fl.us/water
www.floridaagwaterpolicy.com
megalaw.com/fl/top/flenvironmental.php

Minors

Statutes: FSA Chapters 61, 743
Regulations: FAC Rule 38C-3.031 (child labor); Title 65 (Department of Children and Family Services)

Cases: FD: check the key numbers (☞) under Infants; Child Custody
Encyclopedia: FJ: check Family Law §§ 229 et seq.
Internet:
megalaw.com/fl/top/flfamily.php

Mortgages

Statutes: FSA Chapters 697 et seq.
Regulations: FAC Rule 4-2.005 (mortgage guarantee insurance)
Cases: FD: check the key numbers (☞) under Mortgages
Encyclopedia: FJ: check Mortgages and Deeds of Trust §§ 1 et seq.
Internet:
www.famb.org/consumers/index.html

Motor Vehicles

Statutes: FSA Chapters 316 et seq.
Regulations: FAC Title 15 (Department of Highway Safety and Motor Vehicles)
Cases: FD: check the key numbers (☞) under Automobiles
Encyclopedia: FJ: check Automobiles and Other Vehicles §§ 1 et seq.
Internet:
www.hsmv.state.fl.us

Negligence

Statutes: Chapter 768; § 784.05
Cases: FD: check the key numbers (☞) under Negligence; Torts
Encyclopedia: FJ: check Medical Malpractice §§ 1 et seq.; Negligence §§ 1 et seq.; Premises Liability §§ 1 et seq.; Product Liability §§ 1 et seq.; Torts §§ 1 et seq.
Internet:
megalaw.com/fl/top/fltorts.php

Notary Public

Statutes: Chapter 117
Regulations: FAC Rule 1C-13.001 (fees)
Cases: FD: check the key numbers (☞) under Notaries
Encyclopedia: FJ: check Acknowledgements §§ 41 et seq.
Internet:
notaries.dos.state.fl.us

Paralegals

Statutes: FSA §§ 57.104, 744.108(i)
Regulations: FAC Rules 2-37.030 (paralegal billing); 58A-1.001 (legal assistance)
Cases: FD: check the key numbers (☞) under the Attorney and Client 11; Costs 194.50; Prisons 4(13)
Encyclopedia: FJ: check Attorneys at Law §§ 62, 73, 94, 311; Costs § 115

Internet:
www.pafinc.org
floridalegalblog.blogspot.com/2006/06/paralegal-regulation.html

Partnerships

Statutes: Chapter 620
Cases: FD: check the key numbers (☞) under Partnership
Encyclopedia: FJ: check Business Relationships §§ 487 et seq.
Internet:
form.sunbiz.org/cor_gp.html
www.law.fsu.edu/Journals/lawreview/issues/232/larson.html

Pleading

Statutes: Florida Rules of Civil Procedure Rules 1.100 et seq.
Cases: FD: check the key numbers (☞) under Pleading
Encyclopedia: FJ: check Actions §§ 1 et seq.; Parties §§ 1 et seq.; Pleadings §§ 1 et seq.
Internet:
megalaw.com/fl/top/flcivpro.php

Power of Attorney

Statutes: FSA Chapter 709
Regulations: FAC Rule 9H-2.005
Cases: FD: check the key numbers (☞) under Principal and Agent 10
Encyclopedia: FJ: check Agency and Employment §§ 23 et seq.
Internet:
library.findlaw.com/1999/Apr/1/130594.html
www.ilrg.com/forms/powerofattorney-gd-disab/us/fl

Privacy

Statutes: FSA §§ 381.026 et seq.; Chapters 760 et seq.; Florida Constitution Article I, §§ 23 et seq.
Regulations: FAC Rules 4-128.001 et seq. (financial and health information); 65C-15.013 (right to privacy); 69B-128.001 (financial and health information)
Cases: FD: check the key numbers (☞) under Health 257; Insurance 2300; Records 61; Search and Seizure 26; Torts 329
Encyclopedia: FJ: check Constitutional Law §§ 370 et seq.; Criminal Law §§ 631 et seq.; Defamation and Privacy §§ 1 et seq.
Internet:
myfloridalegal.com/consumer
(type "privacy" in the search box)

Privileged Communications

Statutes: FSA §§ 90.501 et seq.
Cases: FD: check the key numbers (☞) under Witnesses 51 et seq.

Encyclopedia: FJ: check Evidence and Witnesses §§ 674 et seq.
Internet:
megalaw.com/fl/top/flcivpro.php

Products Liability

Statutes: FSA §§ 46.051, 686.41; Chapter 768
Cases: FD: check the key numbers (☞) under Products Liability; Torts
Encyclopedia: FJ: check Products Liability §§ 1 et seq.
Internet:
megalaw.com/fl/top/fltorts.php
www.ferrarolaw.com/PracticeAreas/Product-Liability.asp

Property Division in Dissolution of Marriage

Statutes: FSA § 61.075
Cases: FD: check the key numbers (☞) under Divorce 248 et seq.
Encyclopedia: FJ: check Family Law §§ 706 et seq.
Internet:
megalaw.com/fl/top/flfamily.php

Real Property

Statutes: FSA Chapter 475, 689, 731
Regulations: FAC Title 61, subtitle 61J1 (Division of Real Estate), subtitle 61J2 (Real Estate Commission)
Cases: FD: check the key numbers (☞) under Deeds; Estates in Property; Property
Encyclopedia: FJ: check Deeds §§ 1 et seq.; Property §§ 1 et seq.
Internet:
www.myflorida.com/dbpr/divisions.html
(click "Real Estate")
www.myfloridalicense.com/dbpr/re/frec.html
www.weblocator.com/attorney/fl/law/resreal.html

Service of Process

Statutes: FSA Chapter 48; Florida Rules of Civil Procedure Rule 1.070
Cases: FD: check the key numbers (☞) under Process
Encyclopedia: FJ: check Process §§ 1 et seq.
Internet:
megalaw.com/fl/top/flcivpro.php

Statute of Frauds

Statutes: FSA Chapter 725
Cases: FD: check the key numbers (☞) under Frauds, Statute of
Encyclopedia: FJ: check Frauds, Stataute of §§ 1 et seq.
Internet:
megalaw.com/fl/top/flcivpro.php
www.weblocator.com/attorney/fl/law/contcon.html

Statute of Limitations

Statutes: FSA Chapter 95
Cases: FD: check the key numbers (☞) under Limitation of Actions
Encyclopedia: FJ: check Limitations and Laches §§ 1 et seq.
Internet:
megalaw.com/fl/top/flcivpro.php

Summary Judgment

Statutes: FSA Florida Rules of Civil Procedure Rule 1.510
Cases: FD: check the key numbers (☞) under Judgment 178 et seq.
Encyclopedia: FJ: check Summary Judgment §§ 1 et seq.
Internet:
megalaw.com/fl/top/flcivpro.php

Summons

Statutes: FSA Florida Rules of Civil Procedure Rule 1.070
Cases: FD: check the key numbers (☞) under Process 10 et seq.
Encyclopedia: FJ: check Criminal Law §§ 81 et seq.; Process §§ 1 et seq.
Internet:
megalaw.com/fl/top/flcivpro.php

Taxation

Statutes: FSA Title 12 (Department of Revenue)
Regulations: FAC §§ 12 et seq.
Cases: FD: check the key numbers (☞) under Taxation
Encyclopedia: FJ: check Taxation §§ 1 et seq.; Taxpayers' Actions §§ 1 et seq.
Internet:
dor.myflorida.com/dor/taxes
sun6.dms.state.fl.us/dor
(click "Taxes")

Torts

Statutes: FSA Chapters 766 et seq.
Regulations: FAC Rules 22I-7.001 et seq. (medical malpractice arbitration)
Cases: FD: check the key numbers (☞) under Negligence; Products Liability; Torts
Encyclopedia: FJ: check Medical Malpractice §§ 1 et seq.; Negligence §§ 1 et seq.; Premises Liability §§ 1 et seq.; Product Liability §§ 1 et seq.; Torts §§ 1 et seq.
Internet:
megalaw.com/fl/top/fltorts.php

Traffic Laws

Statutes: Chapter 316 et seq.
Regulations: FAC Title 15 (Department of Highway Safety and Motor Vehicles) Subtitle 15B (highway patrol)

Cases: FD: check the key numbers (⬡) under Automobiles 335
Encyclopedia: FJ: check Automobiles §§ 237 et seq.
Internet:
www.findlaw.com/11stategov/fl/laws.html

Trusts

Statutes: FSA Chapter 737
Cases: FD: check the key numbers (⬡) under Trusts
Encyclopedia: FJ: check Estates §§ 1 et seq.; Trusts §§ 1 et seq.
Internet:
megalaw.com/fl/top/flprobate.php

Unemployment Insurance

Statutes: FSA Chapter 443 et seq.
Regulations: FAC Title 38, Subtitle 38B (Division of Unemployment Compensation)
Cases: FD: check the key numbers (⬡) under Unemployment Compensation
Encyclopedia: FJ: check Unemployment Compensation §§ 1 et seq.
Internet:
www.floridajobs.org/unemployment
megalaw.com/fl/top/fllabor.php

Venue

Statutes: FSA § 47.011
Cases: FD: check the key numbers (⬡) under Venue
Encyclopedia: FJ: check Venue §§ 1 et seq.
Internet:
megalaw.com/fl/top/flcivpro.php

Water Rights

Statutes: FSA Chapter 373
Regulations: FAC Title 16 (Department of Natural Resources)
Cases: FD: check the key numbers (⬡) under Waters and Water Courses
Encyclopedia: FJ: check Water §§ 1 et seq.
Internet:
www.dep.state.fl.us/water
www.myflorida.com/agency/27
www.myflorida.com/agency/24

Wills

Statutes: FSA §§ 732.501 et seq.
Cases: FD: check the key numbers (⬡) under Wills
Encyclopedia: FJ: check Decedents' Property §§ 214 et seq.
Internet:
megalaw.com/fl/top/flprobate.php

Workers' Compensation

Statutes: FSA Chapter 440 et seq.
Regulations: FAC Title 38, Subtitle 38F (Division of Workers' Compensation)
Cases: FD: check the key numbers (⬡) under Workers' Compensation
Encyclopedia: FJ: check Workers' Compensation §§ 1 et seq.
Internet:
www.fldfs.com/WC
megalaw.com/fl/top/fllabor.php

E. More Information on Florida Law

(See also section 5.1 on Florida legal research)
www.findlaw.com/11stategov/fl/laws.html
www.leg.state.fl.us/Welcome/index.cfm
www.megalaw.com/fl/fl.php
www.romingerlegal.com/state/florida.html
www.floridasupremecourt.org
www.flcourts.org
www.floridabar.org
www.floridalawweekly.com

F. Something to Check

One of the ways that law firms try to attract clients is to provide law summaries and overviews on their web sites. Pick any two topics covered in this section (e.g., adoption, limited liability companies). For each topic, find three Florida law firm web sites that provide summaries or overviews of Florida law on the topic. Compare the quality and quantity of what you learn about the law at each site. To locate the law firms, go to any search engine (e.g., *www.google.com*) and type in "Florida," "law" or "lawyer," and your topic.
Examples:

Florida law adoption
Florida lawyer adoption

5.6 Self-Help Resources in Florida
   A. Introduction
   B. Resources
   C. More Information
   D. Something to Check

A. Introduction

When citizens act on their own behalf on legal matters, they are acting pro se, engaging in what is called self-help. Florida has a wide variety of self-help resources and materials for those who wish to represent themselves or to learn more about the law in order to communicate with their attorney more effectively.

Self-help resources play a number of roles in our legal system:

- A law office may provide partial (i.e., unbundled) legal services to clients who are representing themselves.
- A law office will sometimes refer citizens to self-help materials when the office cannot provide representation.
- Self-help resources can provide excellent overviews of the law that everyone should know about. The overviews provide links to additional research sources that can be of help when conducting traditional research.
- Even if persons have attorney representation, they may sometimes consult self-help materials in order to be able to communicate with their attorneys more intelligently.

An American Bar Association study of self-represented litigants showed:

- Persons with incomes less than $50,000 are more likely to represent themselves.
- About 20 percent of self-represented litigants report they can afford an attorney but do not want one.
- Self-represented persons are more likely to be satisfied with the judicial process than those who are represented by attorneys.
- Almost 75 percent of those who represented themselves in court said they would do it again (*www. pro-selaw.org/pro-selaw/index.asp*).

Many of the self-help resources in this section involve family law and small claims matters. The links in the sites, however, often lead to resources for other kinds of cases as well.

For related sections in this book, see also:

- Section 2.4 on pro bono opportunities
- Section 4.2 on state courts in Florida
- Section 5.1 on Florida state legal research
- Section 5.5 on research starters
- Section 5.7 on public records research
- Section 6.1 on civil case timelines
- Section 6.4 on criminal case timelines

B. Resources

1. General
2. Self-Help in Specific Counties
3. Self-Help in Specific Legal Subjects

1. General

Florida State Courts Self-Help
www.flcourts.org/gen_public/family/self_help/index.shtml

This excellent resource provides access to information for local self-help centers; lawyer referral services; free and low-cost legal aid; and family law forms for use in dissolution, paternity, child support, name change, and grandparent visitation cases. The forms are free, up-to-date, and in engrossed (ready to use) format with all amendments incorporated.

Consumers' Guide to Self-Help: Florida
www.abanet.org/legalservices/findlegalhelp/home.cfm
www.abanet.org/legalservices/findlegalhelp/selfhelp.cfm? id=FL
www.law.ufl.edu/lic/guides
(click entries under "Florida Research Guides")

Florida Small Claims Court
www.law.ufl.edu/lic/guides/florida/small_claims.pdf

Pro Se Appellate Handbook: Representing Yourself on Appeal
www.flabarappellate.org/asp/pro_sehandbook.asp

Florida Self-Help Books
www.law.ufl.edu/lic/guides/florida/SELFHELP06.pdf
www.vclawlib.org/resources.htm#books
www.galtpress.com/SHLBF.html

Florida Law Help
www.floridalawhelp.org
888-895-7873
A helpline for senior citizens with materials relevant to a wide variety of legal issues that all citizens can find helpful.

Lawton Chiles Legal Information Center: Florida Self-Help Law
www.law.ufl.edu/lic/guides
(click "Florida Self-Help Law")

Peoples Law Guide
www.browardbar.org
(click "Public Resources" and "Peoples Law Guide")

LawInfo.org
www.abalawinfo.org

Pro Se Law Center
www.pro-selaw.org
(click "Court Pro Se Sites" then the link to Florida)

Self-Help Law ExPress (SHLEP)
blogs.law.harvard.edu/shlep/about

Resources for Self-Represented Litigants
www.selfhelpsupport.org

Legal Hotlines Technical Assistance Guide
www.legalhotlines.org/library/index.cfm

Protecting Your Rights
www.justice.org

Pre Se Forum
www.ajs.org/prose/home.asp

How to Research a Legal Problem: A Guide for Non-Lawyers
www.aallnet.org/sis/lisp/research.htm

Ask a Librarian (National)
www.loc.gov/rr/askalib/ask-law.html
www.lawlib.state.ma.us/ask.htm
www.mncourts.gov/selfhelp/?page=268

Ask a Librarian (Florida)
www.askalibrarian.org/aal.asp
info.askalibrarian.org
www.uflib.ufl.edu/ask

A Layman's Guide to Legal Terms
courts.co.calhoun.mi.us/book008.htm

2. Self-Help in Specific Counties

www.flcourts.org/gen_public/family/self_help/map.shtml
(Click the map for your area of the state to locate local self-help programs.)

3. Self-Help in Specific Legal Subjects

Legal Guide to Doing Business in Florida
www.lexmundi.com/images/lexmundi/PDF/guide-florida.pdf

- Corporate law
- Limited liability companies
- State taxation
- Immigration
- Banking in Florida
- Securities law
- Real estate law
- Intellectual property

Representing Yourself in Family Court
www.jud6.org/GeneralPublic/RepresentingYourselfInCourt.html

Family Law Forms
www.flcourts.org/gen_public/family/forms_rules/index.shtml

Florida Auto Repair
www.law.ufl.edu/lic/guides/florida/Auto%20Repair.pdf

Florida Business Law (Legal Guide)
www.citmedialaw.org/legal-guide

Florida Family Law Handbook
www.alachuacounty.us/government/clerk/famlaw/handbook.aspx

Florida Identity Theft
myfloridalegal.com/idkitprintable.pdf

Florida Landlord-Tenant Law
www.law.ufl.edu/lic/guides/florida/Landlord.pdf

Landlord and Tenant Handbook
www.ca.cjis20.org/landlord%20tenant%20handbook.pdf

Bankruptcy in Florida
www.floridabankruptcylaws.com

Filing for Bankruptcy Without an Attorney
www.uscourts.gov/bankruptcycourts/prose.html

Florida Lemon Law
www.law.ufl.edu/lic/guides/florida/lemon-law.pdf

WomensLaw Domestic Violence Assistance
www.womenslaw.org/natl_links.htm

Liability for Online Conduct
www.citmedialaw.org
www.citmedialaw.org/legal-guide

Consumer Pamphlets on the Law
www.floridabar.org
(click "Public Information" and "Consumer Pamphlets")

Topics Covered:

- Adoption in Florida
- Applying for Credit or Loans
- Attorney Consumer Assistance Program
- Attorney's Fees
- Automobile Insurance
- Bankruptcy
- Buying a Home
- Clients' Security Fund
- Consumer Guide to the Legal Fee Arbitration
- A Consumer Guide to Clients' Rights
- Divorce in Florida
- Do You Have a Will?
- Filing an Unlicensed Practice of Law Complaint
- Florida Powers of Attorney
- Grievance Mediation
- Handbook for Jurors
- How to Find a Lawyer in Florida
- Immigration Update
- Inquiry Concerning a Florida Lawyer
- Legal Aid in Florida
- Legal Guide for New Adults
- Mass Disaster
- Mortgage Fraud
- Notaries, Immigration, and the Law
- Shared Parenting After Divorce
- The Revocable Trust in Florida
- U.S. Lawful Permanent Residents
- What Is Guardianship?

Miscellaneous Subjects
www.browardbar.org/articles.php

- Appeals
- Bankruptcy
- Criminal Law
- Employment Law
- Family Law
- Health Law
- Immigration
- Insurance
- Mediation
- Personal Injury
- Probate
- Wills
- Trusts

C. More Information

Florida Statutes
www.leg.state.fl.us/Statutes

Legal Information Institute
www.law.cornell.edu/index.html
www.law.cornell.edu/topics/state_statutes.html

Rominger Legal: Florida Law
www.romingerlegal.com/state/florida.html

Florida Forms
www.findforms.com
(type "Florida" in the search box)

Nolo Press (Self-Help Legal Materials)
www.nolo.com

Yahoo Self-Help Resources
dir.yahoo.com/Government/Law/Self_Help

Legal Web Sites: Separating the Good from the Bad and the Ugly
www.peoples-law.org/finding/legal-sites/select%20websites.htm

D. Something to Check

1. Find online self-help information on collecting child support in Florida.
2. Find online self-help information on suing your neighbor in Florida for damage done to a common fence.

5.7 Public Records Research

A. Introduction
B. A Right of Access: Florida's Public Records Law
C. Search Resources
D. More Information
E. Something to Check

A. Introduction

There are a large variety of public records that a law firm may seek to obtain. For example:

Business Records

- Corporations
- Limited liability companies
- Partnerships
- Fictitious names
- Real estate
- Sales tax registrations
- Tax liens
- Trademarks and service marks
- UCC filings

Individual Records

- Accident reports
- Bankruptcies
- Birth
- Court judgments
- Criminal records
- Death
- Divorce
- Marriage
- Occupational licenses
- Vehicle ownership
- Workers' compensation claims

Access to these records varies. Some are available to the general public, while others are subject to substantial restrictions.

This section will provide some starting points in finding out what is available. Some of the Internet sites and phone numbers in this section will lead you to complete access to the records involved. Others will simply be locations where you can begin making inquiries about what might be available - free or for a fee.

County Clerks of Court

Many public records are available at the county level, particularly through the offices of the county clerks of court. See section 4.6 for leads to county clerks of court, often through court links. For some counties, section 4.6 will also provide direct links to the county's record search system.

County Public Records Search
www.myfloridacounty.com/services/officialrecords_intro.shtml

B. A Right of Access: Florida's Public Records Law

Florida law provides a constitutional and statutory right of access to public records, subject to specified exemptions.

Florida Constitution

Article 1, Section 24. Access to public records and meetings.—

(a) Every person has the right to inspect or copy any public record made or received in connection with the official business of any public body, officer, or employee of the state, or persons acting on their behalf, except with respect to records exempted pursuant to this section or specifically made confidential by this Constitution. This section specifically includes the legislative, executive, and judicial branches of government and each agency or department created thereunder; counties, municipalities, and districts; and each constitutional officer, board, and commission, or entity created pursuant to law or this Constitution. . . .

(c) The legislature . . . may provide by general law passed by a two-thirds vote of each house for the exemption of records from the requirements of subsection (a). . . , provided that such law shall state with specificity the public necessity justifying the exemption and shall be no broader than necessary to accomplish the stated purpose of the law. (*www.leg.state.fl.us*) (click "Florida Constitution" then "Article I" and "Section 24")

Florida Statutes

Section 119.01(1) General state policy on public records. It is the policy of this state that all state, county, and municipal records are open for personal inspection and copying by any person. Providing access to public records is a duty of each agency.
Section 119.011(11). Definitions. "Public records" means all documents, papers, letters, maps, books, tapes, photographs, films, sound recordings, data processing software, or other material, regardless of the physical form, characteristics, or means of transmission, made or received pursuant to law or ordinance or in connection with the transaction of official business by any agency. (*www.leg.state.fl.us*) (click "Florida Statutes" then "Title X" and "Chapter 119")

Exemptions

There are numerous exemptions from inspection or copying of public records. Here are some examples:

- Abuse records received by the Department of Children and Families
- Active criminal investigative and intelligence information (except time, date, location, and nature of a reported crime)
- Attorney work product
- Autopsy photographs, video, or audio records
- Bank account numbers; debit, charge, and credit card numbers
- Bids

Summary of Exemptions
myfloridalegal.com/sun.nsf/manual
(Click sections on "exemptions")

Public Records Guides in Florida

- Florida Government-in-the-Sunshine Manual
  myfloridalegal.com/sunshine
  www.floridafaf.org
  myfloridalegal.com/sun.nsf/manual

- Pocket Guide to Florida Government-in-the-Sunshine Laws
  www.floridafaf.org/pktguide.htm

- Florida Public Records Handbook
  www.idiganswers.com/pages/handbook.html
  www.floridafaf.org

- Florida Public Records Guide
  www.stateofflorida.com/Portal/DesktopDefault.
  aspx?tabid=13

Public Meetings Requirement
www.leg.state.fl.us
(click "Florida Statutes" then "Title XIX" and "Chapter 286")

C. Search Resources

Accident Reports
Highway Patrol
850-617-3416 (crash reports)
850-617-2306 (traffic homicide report)
www.fhp.state.fl.us/html/fhpfaqsa.html

Highway Patrol Local Offices
www.hsmv.state.fl.us/offices
Sheriff's Local Offices
www.flsheriffs.org
(click "Meet the Sheriffs")

Accountants (license records)
Board of Accountancy
850-487-1395
www.ficpa.org/ficpa/ResourceCenter/FLBOA
www.myflorida.com/dbpr/cpa/index.html

Acupuncturists (license records)
Florida Department of Health
Board of Acupuncture
850-245-4161
www.doh.state.fl.us/mqa/acupunct

Acupuncture: Health Care Provider License Search
ww2.doh.state.fl.us/IRM00PRAES/PRASLIST.ASP

Alcohol Beverage Control (license records)
Department of Business and Professional Regulation
Division of Alcoholic Beverages and Tobacco
850-488-3227
www.myflorida.com/dbpr/abt/index.html
www.myflorida.com/dbpr/divisions.html
(click "Alcoholic Beverages and Tobacco")

Appraiser Records (property ownership and valuation)
Department of Revenue
Property Appraisers
dor.myflorida.com/dor/property/appraisers.html
(click your county)

Architects (license records)
(See also Construction Industry)
Board of Architecture and Interior Design
850-487-1395
www.myflorida.com/licensee/cat
(Select "Architect" links)
www.myfloridalicense.com/dbpr/pro/arch

Attorneys (license records)
The Florida Bar
850-561-5832; 850-561-5600
www.floridabar.org/names.nsf/MESearch?OpenForm

Automobile Driving Records
www.stateofflorida.com/Portal/DesktopDefault.aspx?tabid=23

Automobile VIN Records Check
www.dmv.org/vehicle-history.php#tz_FL

Background Checks
www.fdle.state.fl.us/CriminalHistory
www2.fdle.state.fl.us/cchinet

Banks
(See Financial Institutions)

Barbers (license records)
Barbers' Board
850-487-13956
www.myflorida.com/dbpr/pro/barb/barb_index.shtml

Birth Records
Department of Health, Office of Vital Records
904-359-6900 x9000
www.doh.state.fl.us/planning_eval/vital_statistics
www.familybirthrecords.com
www.50states.com/vitalrecords/florida.htm

County Vital Records Offices
www.vitalrec.com/fl.html#County

Boat Records (stolen property)
pas.fdle.state.fl.us/pas/item/displayLicenseDecalSearch.a

Brokers
(See Financial Services, Real Estate)

Business Filings
(See also Companies, Corporations Records, UCC Filings)
850-488-1234
www.stateofflorida.com/portal/desktopdefault.aspx?tabid=8
www.secstates.com

Regulated Industries
www.stateofflorida.com/Portal/DesktopDefault.aspx?tabid=25
www.myflorida.com/licensee/cat

Cable Franchise
Department of State, Division of Corporations
800-755-5111
www.sunbiz.org/index.html
(click "Document Searches")

Campaigns
(See Elections)

Cemeteries (license records)
Department of Financial Services
Board of Funeral, Cemetery, and Consumer Services
800-342-2762; 800-323-2627
www.fldfs.com/FuneralCemetery
www.fldfs.com/FuneralCemetery/fc_app_info.htm

Charities Look-up Database
app1.800helpfla.com/giftgiversguide
www.doacs.state.fl.us/onestop/cs/solicit.html/giftgiversguide

Check Cashers
Office of Financial Regulation, Division of Securities and Finance
800-848-3792; 850-410-9898
www.flofr.com/Licensing
www.flofr.com/Finance/licensing-i.htm

Chiropractic
Chiropractic Physician: Health Care Provider License Search
ww2.doh.state.fl.us/IRM00PRAES/PRASLIST.ASP

Cities
www.searchsystems.net/list.php?nid=21

Listing of Cities
www.stateofflorida.com/Portal/DesktopDefault.aspx?tabid=34
(links to city governments and records kept by them)

Clerk of Court Records
www.stateofflorida.com/Portal/DesktopDefault.aspx?tabid=51

Collection Agencies (license records)
Office of Financial Regulation, Division of Securities and Finance
800-848-3792; 850-410-9898
www.flofr.com/Licensing

Companies
(See also Corporations Records)
www.sunbiz.org/index.html
(click "Document Searches")

Regulated Industries
www.stateofflorida.com/Portal/DesktopDefault.aspx?tabid=25

Construction Industry (license records)
(See also Architects)
850-487-1395
www.myflorida.com/dbpr/pro/cilb/cilb_index.shtml

Consumer Finance Companies (license records)
Office of Financial Regulation, Division of Securities and Finance
800-848-3792; 850-410-9898
www.flofr.com/Licensing

Contractors
(See Architects, Construction Industry)

Contribution (campaign records)
(See also Elections)
election.dos.state.fl.us/campaign-finance/contrib.asp

Corporations Records
Department of State, Division of Corporations
800-755-5111
www.sunbiz.org
www.secstates.com

Regulated Industries
*www.stateofflorida.com/Portal/DesktopDefault.
  aspx?tabid=25*

Cosmetologists (license records)
Board of Cosmetology
850-487-1395
www.myflorida.com/dbpr/pro/cosmo/cos_index.shtml

County Records
(See also section 4.6)
www.myfloridacounty.com/howdoi
www.myfloridacounty.com/services/officialrecords_intro.shtml
www.publicrecordfinder.com/states/florida.html
www.searchsystems.net/list.php?nid=21

Listing of Counties
*www.stateofflorida.com/Portal/DesktopDefault.
  aspx?tabid=35*
(links to county governments and records kept by
them)

Clerk of Court Records
*www.stateofflorida.com/Portal/DesktopDefault.
  aspx?tabid=51*
www.myfloridacounty.com/howdoi

County Vital Records Offices
www.vitalrec.com/fl.html#County

Court Opinions
(See also section 5.1)
Opinions of the Florida Supreme Court and Courts of
Appeal
www.floridasupremecourt.org/decisions/index.shtml
www.findlaw.com/11stategov/fl/flca.html

Credit Unions
(See Financial Institutions)

Criminal Records
Florida Department of Law Enforcement
Criminal History Repository
850-410-8109
www.fdle.state.fl.us/CriminalHistory
www2.fdle.state.fl.us/cchinet

Florida Department of Corrections
Corrections Offender Network
www.dc.state.fl.us/AppCommon

Sexual Offenders and Predators
offender.fdle.state.fl.us/offender/homepage.do

Wanted List
pas.fdle.state.fl.us/pas/pashome.a

Death Records
Department of Health, Office of Vital Records
904-359-6900 x9000
www.doh.state.fl.us/planning_eval/vital_statistics

www.doh.state.fl.us/planning_eval/vital_statistics/deaths.htm
ssdi.rootsweb.com

County Vital Records Offices
www.vitalrec.com/fl.html#County

Deeds
dor.myflorida.com/dor/taxes/doc_stamp.html

Dental Hygienists/Assistants (license records)
Dental Hygienist: Health Care Provider License Search
ww2.doh.state.fl.us/IRM00PRAES/PRASLIST.ASP

Dentists (license records)
Florida Department of Health
Board of Dentistry
www.doh.state.fl.us/mqa/dentistry
ww2.doh.state.fl.us/IRM00PRAES/PRASLIST.ASP

Dieticians
Dietitian: Health Care Provider License Search
ww2.doh.state.fl.us/IRM00PRAES/PRASLIST.ASP

Divorce/Dissolution of Marriage Records
Department of Health, Office of Vital Records
904-359-6900 x9000
www.doh.state.fl.us/planning_eval/vital_statistics
*www.doh.state.fl.us/planning_eval/vital_statistics/
  marriage.htm*
www.50states.com/vitalrecords/florida.htm
www.vitalrec.com/fl.html

Doctors
(See Dentists, Physicians)

Driving Records
(See also Vehicle Records)
www.stateofflorida.com/Portal/DesktopDefault.aspx?tabid=23

Elections
Department of State, Division of Elections
850-245-6200
election.dos.state.fl.us

Campaign Contribution Records
*election.dos.state.fl.us/campaign-finance/
  cam-finance-index.shtml*

Engineers (license records)
Board of Professional Engineers
850-521-0500
www.fbpe.org
www.myflorida.com/licensee/cat
(Click "Engineering")

Environmental Permit Records
tlhora6.dep.state.fl.us/www_pa/pa_statewide_count.asp
tlhora6.dep.state.fl.us/www_pa/pa_county_count.asp

Federal Lien Registrations
Department of State, Division of Corporations
800-755-5111
www.sunbiz.org/index.html
(click "Document Searches")

Fictitious Name Records
Department of State, Division of Corporations
800-755-5111
www.sunbiz.org/index.html
(click "Document Searches")
www.sunbiz.org/ficinam.html

Financial Institutions
(banks, credit unions, savings & loan associations, trust companies)
Office of Financial Regulation
800-848-3792; 850-410-9898
www.flofr.com/banking
www.flofr.com/banking/dogi.htm
(click "Institution Search" and "Licensing Search")

Financial Services (license records)
(financial planners, insurance brokers, investment advisers, securities brokers)
Florida Department of Financial Services
800-342-2762
www.fldfs.com
www.fldfs.com/data/aar_alis1

Firearms Records
licgweb.doacs.state.fl.us/access/records.html
licgweb.doacs.state.fl.us/weapons
www.fdle.state.fl.us
(click "FAQ" then "Firearms Checks")

Funeral Trade (license records)
(See Cemeteries)

Guns
(See Firearms)

Health Statistics
Florida Center for Health Information and Policy Analysis
850-922-7036
www.fdhc.state.fl.us/SCHS
www.floridahealthfinder.gov

Hearing Aids
Hearing Aid Specialists: Health Care Provider License Search
ww2.doh.state.fl.us/IRM00PRAES/PRASLIST.ASP

Hotels
850-922-8981
www.myflorida.com/dbpr/divisions.html
(click "Hotels and Restaurants")

Insurance Brokers and Companies (license records)
Florida Office of Insurance Regulation
850-413-3140
www.floir.com

Department of Financial Services
800-342-2762
www.fldfs.com
www.fldfs.com/data/aar_alis1

Inmate Records and Locator
Department of Corrections
www.dc.state.fl.us/ActiveInmates/search.asp
www.dc.state.fl.us/oth/inmates/index.html
www.ancestorhunt.com/county-jail-inmates-search.htm

Interior Design (license records)
(See also Architects, Construction Industry)
Board of Architecture and Interior Design
850-487-1395
www.myflorida.com/dbpr/divisions.html

Investment Advisors
(See Financial Services)

Judgment Liens
Department of State, Division of Corporations
800-755-5111
www.sunbiz.org/index.html
(click "Document Searches")

Jury Verdicts
www.flajury.com

Licenses
(See Occupational Licenses)

Liens
(See Federal Lien Registrations, Judgment Liens)

Limited Liability Companies Records
Department of State, Division of Corporations
800-755-5111
www.sunbiz.org/index.html
(click "Document Searches")
*www.stateofflorida.com/Portal/DesktopDefault.
    aspx?tabid=155*
www.secstates.com

Limited Partnership Records
Department of State, Division of Corporations
800-755-5111
www.secstates.com
www.sunbiz.org/index.html
(click "Document Searches")

Lobbying Records
(See also Elections)
www.leg.state.fl.us/lobbyist/index.cfm

Marriage Records
Department of Health, Office of Vital Records
904-359-6900 x9000
www.doh.state.fl.us/planning_eval/vital_statistics
*www.doh.state.fl.us/planning_eval/vital_statistics/
    marriage.htm*
www.50states.com/vitalrecords/florida.htm
www.vitalrec.com/fl.html

Massage Therapy
Massage Therapist: Health Care Provider License Search
ww2.doh.state.fl.us/IRM00PRAES/PRASLIST.ASP

Midwifery
Midwives: Health Care Provider License Search
ww2.doh.state.fl.us/IRM00PRAES/PRASLIST.ASP

Military Discharge/Separation Records
freepages.military.rootsweb.com/~xander/florida-records.htm
dlis.dos.state.fl.us/archives/militarypension

Missing Persons Database
pas.fdle.state.fl.us/pas/person/
 displayMissingPersonsSearch.a

Mortgage Brokers (license records)
Office of Financial Regulation, Division of Securities
and Finance
800-848-3792; 850-410-9898
www.flofr.com/Licensing

Motor Vehicles
(See Automobile, Vehicle Records)

Notary Public Database
(See also section 2.5)
notaries.dos.state.fl.us/not001.html

Nurses (license records)
Florida Board of Nursing
850-245-4125
www.doh.state.fl.us/mqa/nursing
www.doh.state.fl.us/mqa/proflist.htm
ww2.doh.state.fl.us/IRM00PRAES/PRASLIST.ASP

Occupational License Records
(See specific occupations in this section)
www.myflorida.com/licensee/cat
www.stateofflorida.com/Portal/DesktopDefault.aspx?tabid=25

County Licensing (links to county governments)
www.stateofflorida.com/Portal/DesktopDefault.aspx?tabid=35

City Licensing (links to city governments)
www.stateofflorida.com/Portal/DesktopDefault.aspx?tabid=34

Occupational Therapy (license records)
Occupational Therapist: Health Care Provider License
Search
ww2.doh.state.fl.us/IRM00PRAES/PRASLIST.ASP

Opticians (license records)
850-245-4474
www.doh.state.fl.us/mqa/opticianry

Optician: Health Care Provider License Search
ww2.doh.state.fl.us/IRM00PRAES/PRASLIST.ASP

Optometrists (license records)
Board of Optometry
850-245-4355
www.doh.state.fl.us/mqa/optometry
ww2.doh.state.fl.us/IRM00PRAES/PRASLIST.ASP

Paramedics
Paramedic: Health Care Provider License Search
ww2.doh.state.fl.us/IRM00PRAES/PRASLIST.ASP

Partnership Records
Department of State, Division of Corporations
800-755-5111
www.sunbiz.org/index.html
(click "Document Searches")

Pharmacists (license records)
Board of Pharmacy
850-245-4292
www.doh.state.fl.us/mqa/pharmacy

Pharmacist: Health Care Provider License Search
ww2.doh.state.fl.us/IRM00PRAES/PRASLIST.ASP

Physical Therapists (license records)
Board of Physical Therapy
850-488-0595
www.doh.state.fl.us/mqa/physical
ww2.doh.state.fl.us/IRM00PRAES/PRASLIST.ASP

Physician Assistants (license records)
Department of Health
ww2.doh.state.fl.us/IRM00PRAES/PRASLIST.ASP
www.doh.state.fl.us/mqa/PhysAsst/pa_applicant.html

Physicians (license records)
Florida Board of Medicine
888-275-3287
Medical Quality Assurance (850-245-4224)
www.fsmb.org
(click "FCVS")
www.stateofflorida.com/Portal/DesktopDefault.
 aspx?tabid=115

Medical Doctor: Health Care Provider
License Search
ww2.doh.state.fl.us/IRM00PRAES/PRASLIST.ASP

Disciplinary Data
www.fsmb.org
(click "Physician Data Center")
www.fsmb.org/fpdc_basummary.html

Probate Records
(See Death Records)

Psychology
Psychologist: Health Care Provider License Search
ww2.doh.state.fl.us/IRM00PRAES/PRASLIST.ASP

Real Estate (license records)
(See also Deeds)
Department of Business and Professional Regulation
Division of Real Estate
850-487-1395
www.myflorida.com/dbpr/re/index.html
www.stateofflorida.com/Portal/DesktopDefault.aspx?tabid=9

Restaurant Disciplinary Records
850-922-8981
www.myflorida.com/dbpr/divisions.html
(click "Hotels and Restaurants")

Sales and Use Tax Registrations
Department of Revenue, Sales and Use Tax
800-352-3671; 850-488-6800
dor.myflorida.com/dor/taxes/sales_tax.html
www.stateofflorida.com/Portal/DesktopDefault.aspx?tabid=29

Savings & Loan Associations
(See Financial Institutions)

School Districts
(See also Teacher)
www.floridasmart.com/education/districts.htm
www.fldoe.org
(click "Public Schools/Districts")

Securities
(See also Financial Services)
Office of Financial Regulation, Division of Securities
and Finance
800-848-3792; 850-410-9898
www.flofr.com/Licensing

Sex Offender Registration Records
(See also Criminal Records)
Florida Sexual Offenders and Predators
888-357-7332
www.fdle.state.fl.us/a-z_index.html
www.fdle.state.fl.us/CriminalHistory
www.sexcriminals.com/regs/1016.html

Social Worker
Social Worker: Health Care Provider License Search
ww2.doh.state.fl.us/IRM00PRAES/PRASLIST.ASP

Board of Clinical Social Work, Marriage and Family
www.doh.state.fl.us/mqa/491

Statistics on the State of Florida
www.fedstats.gov/qf/states/12000.html
www.doh.state.fl.us

Stolen Property Database
pas.fdle.state.fl.us/pas/pashome.a

Taxation
www.stateofflorida.com/Portal/DesktopDefault.aspx?tabid=29

Teacher, Public School (credential records)
Department of Education, Bureau of Educator
Certification
800-445-6739
www.fldoe.org/edcert

Therapists (license records)
(See also Social Worker)
Department of Health
850-488-0595
ww2.doh.state.fl.us/IRM00PRAES/PRASLIST.ASP
www.doh.state.fl.us/mqa/PRAES

Title Loan Companies
Office of Financial Regulation, Division of Securities
and Finance

800-848-3792; 850-410-9898
www.flofr.com/Licensing

Tobacco Industries (license records)
Department of Business and Professional Regulation
Division of Alcoholic Beverages and Tobacco
850-488-3227
www.myflorida.com/dbpr/divisions.html
(click "Alcoholic Beverages and Tobacco")

Trademarks and Service Mark Registration Records
Department of State, Division of Corporations
800-755-5111
www.sunbiz.org/index.html
(click "Document Searches")
www.secstates.com
www.stateofflorida.com/portal/desktopdefault.aspx?tabid=8

Trust Companies
(See Financial Institutions)

UCC (Uniform Commercial Code) Filings
Department of State, Division of Corporations
800-755-5111
www.sunbiz.org/index.html
(click "Document Searches")

Unclaimed Property Records
Bureau of Unclaimed Property
888-258-2253; 850-413-5555
www.fltreasurehunt.org

Uniform Commercial Code Filings
(See UCC)

Unions
unionreports.gov

Vehicle Records
Department of Highway Safety and Motor Vehicles
850-922-9000
www.hsmv.state.fl.us
www.stateofflorida.com/Portal/DesktopDefault.aspx?tabid=23

Department of Motor Vehicles
www.dmv.org/fl-florida/department-motor-vehicles.php

Veterinarians (license records)
Board of Veterinary Medicine
850-487-1395
www.myflorida.com/dbpr/pro/vetm/vet_index.shtml
www.myflorida.com/licensee/cat
(click "Veterinarians")

VIN Motor Vehicle Records Check
(See also Vehicle Records)
www.dmv.org/vehicle-history.php#tz_FL

Workers' Compensation
Department of Financial Services, Division of Workers'
Compensation

800-742-2214; 850-413-1601
www.fldfs.com/WC
www.fldfs.com/WC/databases.html

Compliance Records
www.fldfs.com/WCAPPS/Compliance_POC/wPages/query.asp

D. More Information

State Archives
Department of State, Bureau of Archives & Records
Management 850-245-6700
www.fdle.state.fl.us
(click "Open Government" then entries under "Public
Records")
dlis.dos.state.fl.us/index_researchers.cfm

General Information and Links (free and fee-based)
www.legaltrek.com/HELPSITE/States/Florida.htm
(click "Public Records")
www.zabasearch.com
www.publicrecordfinder.com/states/florida.html
www.myfloridacounty.com/services/officialrecords_intro.shtml
www.stateofflorida.com/Portal/DesktopDefault.
  aspx?tabid=13
www.searchsystems.net/list.php?nid=21
florida.iaf.net/states/florida.html
www.business.com/directory/law/state_law/florida/
  public_records
www.oatis.com/publicrecords.htm
www.50states.com/publicrecords/florida.htm
www.virtualchase.com/topics/introduction_public_records.
  shtml
www.casebreakers.com
www.brbpub.com/freeresources/pubrecsites.aspx
www.skipease.com/free_public_record_searches.html
wikis.ala.org/godort/index.php/State_Agency_Databases

Westlaw
www.westlaw.com
www.westlaw.com/empower/publicrecords.wl
Examples of public records databases: People Finder-
Person Tracker, Name Tracker, Telephone Tracker, Ad-
dress Alert, Skip Tracer, Social Security Number Alert,
Death Records, Professional Licenses; People Finder
Plus Assets Library-Combined Asset Locator, Aircraft
Registration Records, Watercraft Registration Records,
Stock Locater Records, Motor Vehicle Registration
Records, Real Property Assessor Records, Real Prop-
erty Transactions; People Finder, Assets Plus Adverse
Filings Library – Combined Adverse Filings, Bank-
ruptcy Records, UCC, Liens/Civil Judgment Filings,
Uniform Commercial Code Filings, Liens/Civil Judg-
ment Filings; Public Records Library – U.S. Business
Finder Records, Corporate and Limited Partnership
Records, "Doing Business As" Records, Litigation
Preparation Records, Executive Affiliation Records,
Name Availability Records

Lexis
www.lexis.com; www.lexisnexis.com
Examples of public records databases: Bankruptcy Filings, Business Locators, Corporate Filings (Business and
Corporate Information, Limited Partnership Information, Fictitious Business Name Information, Franchise
Index), Civil and Criminal Court Filings, Judgments and
Liens (including UCC and State Tax Liens), Jury Verdicts and Settlements, Professional Licenses Information, Person Locators (Military Locator, Voter Registration Record Information from 26 states, Social Security
Death Records from 1962, Inmate Records from six
states, Criminal History Records from 37 states), Personal Property Records (including Aircraft Registrations, Boat Registrations, Motor Vehicle Registrations
from 20 states), Real Property Records (Deed Transfers,
Tax Assessor Records, Mortgage Records).

E. Something to Check

1. In the yellow pages, select three persons or businesses in three different categories of services that
   probably require a license in Florida (e.g., contractor, funeral homes). Go to the web site for each
   service.

   a. What kinds of information are available
      about that service?
   b. What information can you find about the
      three persons or businesses you selected,
      e.g., were you able to verify that the person
      or business has a current valid license?

2. Go to one of the search sites that allows you to find
   public records on individuals. Type in someone's
   name (e.g., your own) to find out what public
   records are available online.

5.8 Finding Law Libraries in Your Area
   A.   Introduction
   B.   Law Library Listings by City and County
   C.   Ask a Librarian
   D.   Your Neighborhood Public Library
   E.   More Information
   F.   Something to Check

A. Introduction

Elsewhere we cover the extensive availability of
Florida law that you can read online. (See sections 5.1
and 5.5.) Suppose, however, that you want to go to a
bricks and mortar law library to use its resources. You
want to go to a facility where you can take books off the
shelf. What options are available to you?

There are three major kinds of law libraries in Florida to which you have full or partial access:

- County Law Libraries (CLL)
- Federal Depository Libraries (FDL)
- State Document Depository Libraries (SDDL)

The list below will tell you which libraries fall into these three categories. Some libraries fall into more than one category. After each entry you will find the designations CLL, FDL, or SDDL to indicate the kind of library it is or the kind of legal materials in it to which you are entitled to have free access.

Before you visit any of the libraries on this list, you should phone the library and check its web site to determine its location, hours, and any restrictions on using its materials.

- County Law Libraries (CLL)

There are many county law libraries (CLLs) in the state. Some are large facilities to which the general public has access, either without charge or by paying a fee. The use of others is limited to judges and attorneys of the county. Many are relatively small and are stored in the offices of private attorneys.

- Federal Depository Libraries (FDL)

www.gpoaccess.gov/libraries.html

A federal depository library is a public or private library that receives free federal government publications to which it must allow access by the general public without charge. The publications include federal statutes, federal regulations, and federal court opinions. If the library is private, e.g., a private university library, the public right of free access may be limited to those publications the library receives from the federal government under the federal depository program. The private library has the right to prevent the public from using the rest of its collection.

- State Document Depository Libraries (SDDL)

dlis.dos.state.fl.us/library/deplist.cfm

A state document depository is a public or private library that receives free state government publications to which it must allow access by the general public without charge. The state documents include state agency reports, legislative proceedings and hearings, directories, etc. If the library is private, it can restrict the public from the rest of its collection.

B. Law Library Listings by City and County

Alachua County	Brooksville
Bartow	Broward County
Bay County	Bunnell
Boca Raton	Chiefland
Bradenton	Clearwater
Brevard County	Cocoa

Collier County	New Port Richey
Coral Gables	Okaloosa County
Dade City	Orange County
Daytona Beach	Orlando
DeLand	Osceola County
Duval County	Palm Beach County
Escambia County	Panama City
Flagler County	Pasco County
Fort Myers	Pensacola
Fort Pierce	Pinellas County
Gainesville	Polk County
Gulfport	Saint Lucie County
Hernando County	Saint Petersburg
Highlands County	Sanford
Hillsborough County	Santa Rosa County
Indian River County	Sarasota
Jacksonville	Sarasota County
Kissimmee	Sebring
Lake County	Seminole County
Lakeland	Shalimar
Lee County	Stuart
Leesburg	Sumter County
Leon County	Tallahassee
Levy County	Tampa
Manatee County	Tavares
Marion County	Vero Beach
Melbourne	Viera
Miami	Volusia County
Miami-Dade County	West Palm Beach
Milton	Winter Park
Naples	

AAA

Alachua County
See Gainesville

BBB

Bartow
Polk County Law Library (CLL)
863-534-4013
www.pclc.lib.fl.us/location/polk_law/info/
www.pclc.lib.fl.us/location

Bay County
See Panama City

Boca Raton
Florida Atlantic Univ. Wimberly Library (FDL) (SDDL)
561-297-3788
www.library.fau.edu/depts/govdocs/govdocs.htm
www.library.fau.edu/depts/govdocs/govdoc.htm

Bradenton
Manatee County Law Library (CLL)
941-741-4090
clerkofcourts.com/CourtServices/LawLib/library.htm

Manatee County Public Library System (FDL)(SDDL)
941-748-5555
www.co.manatee.fl.us/library/master.html

Brevard County
See Cocoa, Melbourne, Viera

Brooksville
Hernando County Law Library (CLL)
www.clerk.co.hernando.fl.us/Other/LawLibrary.html

Broward County
See Fort Lauderdale

Bunnell
Bunnell Branch Library of Flagler County (CLL)
386-437-7390
www.flaglerlibrary.org/bunnell/libraryinfo.htm

CCC

Chiefland
Luther Calloway Public Library (SDDL)
352-493-2758
dlis.dos.state.fl.us/library/deplist.cfm

Clearwater
Clearwater Public Library (FDL)
727-562-4970
www.clearwater-fl.com/cpl/ref/govdocs.asp

Pinellas County Law Library (CLL)
727-464-3411
www.jud6.org/LegalCommunity/LawLibraries.html

Cocoa
Brevard County Library (FDL) (SDDL)
321-633-1794
www.brev.org/websites/government.htm
www.brev.org/about_bcl/federal_repository/index.htm

Collier County
See Naples

Coral Gables
Univ. of Miami Law Library (FDL) (SDDL)
305-284-4722
www.library.miami.edu/research/guides/
   governmentinformation.html
www.library.miami.edu/index.html

DDD

Dade City
Pasco County Law Library, East (CLL)
352-521-4274; 352-521-4399

Daytona Beach`
Volusia County Public Library (FDL)(SDDL)
386-257-6036
www.vcpl.lib.fl.us/services.html

DeLand
Stetson Univ. duPont-Ball Library (FDL) (SDDL)
386-822-7185
www.stetson.edu/library/departments_govdocs.php
www.stetson.edu/library/databases_government.php

Duval County
See Jacksonville

EEE

Escambia County
See Pensacola

FFF

Flagler County
See Bunnell

Broward County Library (FDL)(SDDL)
954-357-7439
www.broward.org/library
www.browardlibrary.org

Nova Southeastern Univ. Law Library (FDL)
954-262-6202; 954-262-6213
www.nsulaw.nova.edu/library_tech/library/index.cfm

Lee County Library System (SDDL)
239-479-4636
www.lee-county.com/library

Fort Pierce
Indian River Community College Miley Library (FDL)
772-462-7600
www.ircc.edu
(click "Libraries" then "Government Documents")

Saint Lucie County Law Library (CLL)
772-462-2370
www.rjslawlibrary.org/locations.htm

GGG

Gainesville
John A. H. Murphree Law Library (CLL)
352-374-3659
www.circuit8.org/library

Univ. of Florida College of Law (FDL)
352-273-0367; 352-273-0369
www.law.ufl.edu/lic

Univ. of Florida Smathers Libraries Documents Dept
(FDL)(SDDL)
352-273-0367
web.uflib.ufl.edu/docs

Univ. of Florida Lawton Chiles Legal Information
Center (FDL)
352-273-0724
www.law.ufl.edu/lic

Gulfport
Stetson Univ. College of Law Library (FDL)
727-562-7821; 727-562-7826
www.law.stetson.edu
(click "Law Library")

HHH

Hernando County
See Brooksville

Highlands County
See Sebring

Hillsborough County
See Tampa

III

Indian River County
See Fort Pierce, Vero Beach

JJJ

Jacksonville
Duval County Law Library (CLL)
904-630-2560
*www.coj.net/Departments/Fourth+Judicial+Circuit+Court/
    Duval+County/Law+Library.htm*

Jacksonville Public Library (FDL) (SDDL)
904-630-2665; 904-630-1994
jpl.coj.net

Jacksonville Univ. Swisher Library (FDL) (SDDL)
904-256-7263; 904-256-7267
www.ju.edu/library/government.aspx

Univ. of North Florida Carpenter Library
(FDL) (SDDL)
904-620-2616
www.unf.edu/library/doc

KKK

Kissimmee
Ray Shanks Law Library (CLL)
Osceola Library System
407-935-0777
www.osceolalibrary.org

LLL

Lake County
See Leesburg, Tavares

Lakeland
Lakeland Public Library (FDL)
863-834-4280; 863-284-4265
www.lakelandgov.net/library/docsearch.html

Lee County
See Fort Myers

Leesburg
Lake-Sumter Community College Library (FDL)
352-365-3563
www.lscc.edu/library
catalog.gpo.gov/fdlpdir/FDLPdir.jsp?mode=1&pid=8

Leon County
See Tallahassee

Levy County
See Chiefland

MMM

Manatee County
See Bradenton

Marion County
See Stuart

Melbourne
Florida Institute of Technology Evans Library (FDL)
321-674-8086; 321-674-7531
www.lib.fit.edu/links
(click "Government Resources")

Miami
Florida International Univ. Green Library
(FDL) (SDDL)
305-348-2481; 305-919-5721
library.fiu.edu/files/govdocs/index.html

Miami-Dade County Law Library (CLL)
305-349-7548
www.mdcll.org

Miami-Dade Public Library System (FDL)
305-375-5575
www.mdpls.org

St. Thomas Univ. Library (FDL)
305-628-6667; 305-628-6668
catalog.gpo.gov/fdlpdir/FDLPdir.jsp?mode=1&pid=16
www.stu.edu/lawlib

Miami-Dade County
See Coral Gables, Miami

Milton
Santa Rosa County Law Library (CLL)
850-981-5597
www.firstjudicialcircuit.org/PageView.asp?edit_id=310

NNN

Naples
Hodges Univ. Lib. (FDL)
239-513-1122
catalog.gpo.gov/fdlpdir/FDLPdir.jsp?mode=1&pid=6

New Port Richey
Pasco County Law Library - West (CLL)
727-847-8107

OOO

Okaloosa County
See Shalimar

Orange County
See Orlando, Winter Park

Orlando
Orange County Library System (SDDL)
407-835-7323
www.ocls.info/flashDefault.asp?bhcp=1

Univ. of Central Florida Library (FDL)(SDDL)
407-823-5880; 407-823-2562
library.ucf.edu/govdocs

Osceola County
See Kissimmee

PPP

Palm Beach County
See Boca Raton, West Palm Beach

Panama City
Bay County Law Library (CLL)
850-747-5323
www.jud14.flcourts.org/CircuitLinks/BCLL.htm

Pasco County
See Dade City, New Port Richey

Pensacola
Escambia County Law Library (CLL)
850-595-4469
www.firstjudicialcircuit.org/PageView.asp?edit_id=310

Univ. of West Florida Libraries (FDL)(SDDL)
850-474-2424; 850-474-2410
library.uwf.edu/index.htm
catalog.gpo.gov/fdlpdir/FDLPdir.jsp?mode=1&pid=5

Pinellas County
See Clearwater, Saint Petersburg

Polk County
See Bartow

SSS

Saint Lucie County
See Fort Pierce

Saint Petersburg
Pinellas County Law Library (CLL)
727-582-7875
www.jud6.org/LegalCommunity/LawLibraries.html

Saint Petersburg Public Library (FDL)(SDDL)
727-893-7928
www.splibraries.org/weblinks/government.htm

Sanford
Seminole County Wilson Memorial Law Library (CLL)

407-665-4576
*en.wikipedia.org/wiki/Fred_R._Wilson_Memorial_Law_
Library*
www.seminoleclerk.org

Santa Rosa County
See Milton

Sarasota
Univ. of South Florida/New College of
Florida(FDL)(SDDL)
941-487-4301
lib.sar.usf.edu/collections.htm

Selby Public Library (FDL)
941-861-1100; 941-861-1164
*suncat.co.sarasota.fl.us/Collections/GovernmentDocuments.
aspx*

Sarasota County
See Sarasota

Sebring
Highlands County Law Library (CLL)
863-402-6621
nthomas@bcc.co.highlands.fl.us

Seminole County
See Sanford

Shalimar
Okaloosa County Law Library (CLL)
850-651-7497; 850-651-7256
www.firstjudicialcircuit.org/PageView.asp?edit_id=310

Stuart
Marion County Law Library (CLL)
772-221-1427

Sumter County
See Leesburg

TTT

Tallahassee
Florida A & M Univ. Coleman Library (FDL)(SDDL)
850-599-3714; 850-599-3714
*www.famu.edu/index.cfm?a=library&
p=GovernmentDocuments*
catalog.gpo.gov/fdlpdir/FDLPdir.jsp?mode=1&pid=7

Florida State Univ. Law Library (FDL)
850-644-7479; 850-644-4095
www.law.fsu.edu/library
catalog.gpo.gov/fdlpdir/FDLPdir.jsp?mode=1&pid=34

Florida State Univ. Strozier Library (FDL)(SDDL)
850-644-1486
www.lib.fsu.edu/find/documents

Florida Supreme Court Library (FDL)
850-488-8919
library.flcourts.org

State Library and Archives of Florida (FDL) (SDDL)
850-245-6600
dlis.dos.state.fl.us

Tampa
Hillsborough County Law Library (CLL)
813-272-5818
www.hillsboroughcounty.org/directoryofservices/legalassist.cfm

Tampa-Hillsborough County Public Library
(FDL)(SDDL)
813-273-3652; 813-301-7187
thpl.org
www.hcplc.org
www.hcplc.org/hcplc/ig/government.html

Univ. of South Florida Library (FDL)(SDDL)
813-974-2729
www.lib.usf.edu/public/index.cfm?Pg=GovernmentDocuments

Univ. of Tampa Kelce Library (FDL)
813-253-6231
utopia.ut.edu
utopia.ut.edu/govdocs.htm

Tavares
Lake County Law Library (CLL)
352-742-4161
www.lakecountyclerk.org/services.asp?subject=Law_Library
*www.lakeline.lib.fl.us/programs_and_services/
   legal_services.aspx*

VVV

Vero Beach
Indian River County Law Library (CLL)
772-770-5157
www.irclibrary.org/lawlib
catalog.irclibrary.org/polaris/default.aspx?ctx=6.1033.0.0.1

Viera
Brevard County Law Library (CLL)
321-617-7295
www.brev.org/locations/brevard_law/index.htm

Volusia County
See Daytona Beach, DeLand

WWW

West Palm Beach
Palm Beach County Law Library (CLL)
561-355-2928
www.pbcgov.com/cadminlawlibrary

Winter Park
Rollins College Olin Library (FDL)
407-646-2507; 407-646-2693
www.rollins.edu/olin/index.html
www.rollins.edu/olin/documents/index.html

C. Ask a Librarian

When thinking about library resources, you should consider the free "Ask a Librarian" programs in Florida and around the country. Most are available by e-mail to help answer specific questions, particularly about research materials and factual information. Of course, you can't send them a set of facts and ask them to tell you what law applies to those facts. This would be the equivalent of giving legal advice, which they are not allowed to provide. But they can often be helpful in giving you leads for answering narrow questions such as, "Where can I find the administrative decisions of the XYZ agency?" or "Where can I check to find out the percentage of Florida judges who are women?" Good "Googling" skills may allow you to find answers to such questions on your own, but when you are having difficulty, the Ask programs might be able to provide what you need.

Some Ask programs are limited to designated populations such as the students of a particular university. The web site of the program will list any restrictions that exist. Don't be reluctant to contact Ask programs located outside Florida. Many are eager to help no matter where the inquirer is located.

Finding Ask a Librarian Programs
* Run the following search in Google or any search engine:
  "ask a librarian"
  "ask a librarian" law
  "ask a librarian" Florida
  "ask a librarian" law Florida
* Some Possibilities:
www.loc.gov/rr/askalib
www.askalibrarian.org/aal.asp
www.askalibrarian.org/vrl_intro.asp?library=FLCC2400
pbclibrary.org/email.htm
www.lib.usf.edu/public/#ResearchHelp
library.fiu.edu/Home/AskaLibrarian.aspx
www.ipl.org/div/askus

D. Your Neighborhood Public Library

Surprisingly, many local public libraries have legal materials on their shelves. For example, here is what the catalog of one neighborhood library lists as available:

Official Florida Statutes
The Law of Florida Homeowners' Associations
Florida Criminal and Traffic Law Manual
Florida Real Estate Principles, Practices & Law

Florida Divorce Handbook

Florida Law: A Layman's Guide

Some of these materials may not be kept up to date. The next time you are in your library, you should find out what is available.

E. More Information

Federal Depository Libraries
www.uflib.ufl.edu/fedl
(click "Directory")
catalog.gpo.gov/fdlpdir/FDLPdir.jsp

State Document Depository Libraries
dlis.dos.state.fl.us/library/deplist.cfm

Florida Electronic Federal Depository Library
www.uflib.ufl.edu/fedl

Southeastern Chapter of the American Association of Law Libraries
www.aallnet.org/chapter/seaall/states/fl.htm
www.aallnet.org/chapter/seaall/index.html

South Florida Association of Law Libraries
www.aallnet.org/chapter/sfall/members.htm

State, Court, and County Law Libraries
www.aallnet.org/sis/sccll/membership/libraries.htm#f
www.aallnet.org/sis/sccll

Florida Library Index
www.libdex.com/country/USA-Florida.html

F. Something to Check

1. Call the federal depository library (FDL) nearest to you that is not fully public. An example would be one at a private university. Assume that you want to go to this library to use the Code of Federal Regulations (CFR) volumes on the shelves of this library. (You want to look at a "hard copy" of the CFR rather than examine it online.) Ask the library how you would do this. Do you need a special pass? Are there any restrictions on your use of the rest of the library? In short, how do you gain admission to use the materials (like the CFR) that this private library receives under the federal depository program? Repeat this assignment for any other federal depository library in the state and compare your answers for the two libraries.

2. Contact the nearest state document depository library (SDDL) by phone or online. Find out what state legal materials it receives from the State Library of Florida or from any state agency. What restrictions, if any, are there on your access to these materials?

5.9 Hotline Resources and Complaint Directories
A. Introduction
B. Help and Complaint Hotline Resources
C. Something to Check

A. Introduction

On the job you sometimes need quick access to a phone number or web site of commonly used resources. This section provides many of them. See also section 4.5 for similar leads.

B. Help and Complaint Hotline Resources

Topics Covered

AARP	Business Fraud
Abandoned Property	Cancer
Abortion	CEB
Abuse	Cellular Phone
Accountants	Cemetery
ACLU Florida	Charities Fraud
Acupuncture	Check Cashers
ADA	Child Abuse
Adoption	Child Labor
Adult Abuse	Children: Missing
Agriculture	Children
AIDS	Children's Health
Airline Complaints	Insurance
Air Pollution	Children's Defense Fund
Alcohol and Drug Abuse	Child Support
Alien Labor Certification	Chiropractic
Alternative Dispute	Citizenship
Resolution	City Governments
Alzheimer's	Civil Rights
Architects	Clean Air
Assisted Living Facility	Clemency
Attorney	Coast Guard
Attorney General	Collection Agency
Attorney Referral	Communicable Diseases
Automobiles	Continuing Education
Bank Regulation	of the Bar
Bankruptcy	Congress
Bar Associations	Conservation
Battered Women	Construction Industry
Better Business Bureau	Consumer Complaint
Betting	Consumer Product Safety
Birth Records	Commission
Board of Medicine	Consumer Resource Guide
Boating Accidents	Corporations
Brain Injury	County Governments
Brokers Regulation	Courts
Building Contractor	Credit Bureaus
Business	Credit Union

Crime Statistics
Crime Victim Assistance
Day Care
Death Records
Debt Collection
Dental Professions
Disability
Disasters
Discrimination
Divorce/Dissolution
Doctors
Domestic Security
Domestic Violence
Do Not Call Registry
Drug and Alcohol Abuse
Drug Court
Education
Elder Abuse
Elder Affairs
Elections
Electricity
Emergency Management
Employment
Energy
Environmental Health
Environmental Protection
Equal Employment
    Opportunity
Estate Taxes
Ethics
Fair Housing
Family Advocate
Farmworker
Federal Communications
    Commission
Federal Government
Federal Trade Commission
FEMA
Financial Regulation and
    Services
Fire Departments
Fish and Wildlife
FLAIRS
Food and Drug
    Administration
Food Safety
Food Stamps
Foster Care
Fraud
Funeral Home
    Regulation
Gambling Regulation
Game Promotion
Gas
Gay and Lesbian Rights
Get Lean
Government
Government Employment

Government Waste
    Hotline
Governor
Health and Human
    Services
Healthcare Facility
Healthcare Practitioner
Health Studios
Helpline Services
Highway Patrol
Highway Safety
Home Health Care
Homeland Security
Homelessness
House of Representatives
Housing Coalition
Housing Discrimination
Housing Finance
Hospital
Human Relations
Hurricane
Identity Theft
Immigration Services
Incest
Information and Referral
    Services
Injured Worker
Insurance
Internet Crime
Investment
IRS
Job Safety
KidCare
Lawyer Referral Services
Legal Aid/Legal Services
Legislature
Lemon Law
LexisNexis
Licenses
Lifeline
Liquor Enforcement
Local Government
Long-term Care
Lottery
Marriage/Family Therapist
Marriage Records
Mediation
Medical Board
Medicare
Medicaid
Mental Health
Mental Retardation
Missing Children
Mortgage Regulation
Motor Vehicles
Movers
Natural Gas
No-Scam

Nurses
Nursing Home
Occupational Safety
Occupational Therapist
Ombudsman
Parent
Parole
Passport Services
Pensions
Pesticide
Pharmacist
Physicians
Poison
Police
Postal Fraud
Psychologists
Public Defenders
Public Utility
Putative Fathers
Rape
Rates
Red Cross
Runaway
Savings and Loans
Secretary of State
Securities
Secured Transaction
Senate
Seniors
Sex Offender
Sexually Transmitted
    Disease

Sheriff
Small Business
Social Security
STD
Substance Abuse
Suicide
Sweepstakes
Tax
Telecommunications
Telemarketers
Telephone
Tourism
Travel Agents
Unclaimed Property
Unemployment
    Compensation
Utilities
Vehicle Repair
Venereal Disease
Veterans
Victim Resources
Vital Records
Voting
Water
Weather
West Group
Whistle Blower
White House
Wildlife
Workers' Compensation
Youth Crisis

AARP Hotline (American Association of Retired Persons)
888-687-2277
www.aarp.org

Abandoned Property
888-258-2253; 850-413-5555
www.fltreasurehunt.org

Abortion
800-230-PLAN
www.plannedparenthood.org
(enter "Florida" in drop-down state box)

Abuse
(See also Substance Abuse)
Reporting Abuse/Neglect/Exploitation
(See also Child Abuse, Elder Abuse, Elder Affairs, Seniors)
800-422-4453
www.helpguide.org
(click "Abuse & Addictions")

Accountants, Complaints Against
www.myfloridalicense.com/dbpr/cpa/complaint.html

ACLU Florida
786-363-2700
www.aclufl.org

Acupuncture: Reporting Unlicensed Activity
www.doh.state.fl.us/mqa/acupunct/acu_consumer.html
www.doh.state.fl.us/mqa/updates.html

ADA (Americans with Disabilities Act)
(See Disability)

Adoption
800-96-ADOPT
www.dcf.state.fl.us/adoption

Adoption Reunion Registry
Florida Adoption Reunion Registry (FARR)
850-488-8000
www.adoptflorida.com/Reunion-Registry.htm

Adult Abuse
(See Elder Abuse, Elder Affairs, Seniors)

Agriculture, Florida Department of
850-488-3022
www.doacs.state.fl.us

AIDS Hotline
800-332-2437; 800-FLA-AIDS
www.211bigbend.com/hotlines/hiv

Airline Complaints
866-TELL-FAA
www.dep.state.fl.us/Air/contacts.htm
airconsumer.ost.dot.gov
866-289-9673
contact.tsa.dhs.gov/default.aspx

Air Pollution
(See Environmental Health)

Alcohol and Drug Abuse
(See also Substance Abuse)
800-729-6686
ncadi.samhsa.gov

Alcohol Regulation
www.myflorida.com/dbpr/abt/index.shtml
www.atf.treas.gov (federal)

Liquor Enforcement Hotline
866-540-SUDS
www.myflorida.com/dbpr/abt/index.html

Alien Labor Certification
850-921-3299
www.floridajobs.org/alc/index.html

Alternative Dispute Resolution
www.flcourts.org/gen_public/adr/brochure.shtml

Alzheimer's Helpline
800-272-3900 (national); 407-228-4299 (Florida)
www.alzflorida.org
www.alz.org

Architects, Complaints Against
850-402-1570
www.stslaw.com/adboard.asp
www.myflorida.com/dbpr/pro/arch/index.html

Assisted Living Facility Complaint Hotline
888-419-3456; 850-487-2515
www.fdhc.state.fl.us/Contact/call_center.shtml

Attorney (Bar Associations)
(See also Part 3, appendix A on attorney discipline)
850-561-5600
www.floridabar.org

Attorney: Continuing Education of the Bar (CEB)
(See also section 1.3)
850-561-5600 x5842
www.floridabar.org
(click on "Member Services," then "CLER/BSCR")

Attorney Discipline Records
(See also Part 3, appendix A on attorney discipline)
800-342-8060 x5839
www.floridabar.org

Attorney General (Florida)
850-414-3300; 866-966-7226 (fraud hotline)
myfloridalegal.com

Attorney, Grievances Against
866-352-0707
www.floridabar.org
(click "Public Information" then "Attorney Consumer
Assistance")

Attorney Referral Services
800-342-8011
www.floridabar.org/divpgm/lronline.nsf/wreferral6?openform

Automobiles
(See also Motor Vehicles)
Department of Highway Safety and Motor Vehicles
850-922-9000
www.hsmv.state.fl.us

Bank Regulation/Consumer Complaints
800-848-3792; 800-342-2762 (state)
800-613-6743; 800-842-6929 (federal)
www.flofr.com/banking
www.flofr.com/Director/ofrcontacts.htm
www.occ.treas.gov/index.htm

Bankruptcy
(See Bankruptcy courts in Florida in section 4.3)

Bar Associations
(See Attorney and section 3.4)

Battered Women
(See Domestic Violence)

Better Business Bureau
www.bbb.org
(type in your zip code)

Betting
(See also Lottery)
www.myflorida.com/dbpr/pmw/index.shtml

Birth Records
904-359-6900; 877-550-7330
www.doh.state.fl.us/planning_eval/vital_statistics
www.cdc.gov/nchs/howto/w2w/florida.htm
www.vitalrec.com

Board of Medicine
(See Doctors, Health, Medical Board)

Boating Accidents/Theft of Boats
myfwc.com/law/boating
pas.fdle.state.fl.us/pas/item/displayLicenseDecalSearch.a

Brain Injury
800-992-3442
www.biaf.org

Brokers Regulation, Securities
800-848-3792; 800-342-2762 (complaints)
www.flofr.com/licensing

Building Contractor
(See Construction Industry)

Business (formation, assistance, taxation)
800-755-5111
www.sunbiz.org
www.stateofflorida.com
(click entries under "Business")
www.sba.gov
(type "Florida" in the search box)
www.stateofflorida.com/Portal/DesktopDefault.aspx?
   tabid=8

Small Business Development Center
850-473-7800
www.floridasbdc.com

Business Fraud
Federal Trade Commission
877-FTC-HELP
www.ftc.gov

Business Fraud (New Business Opportunities)
Complaint Hotline
800-HELP-FLA
www.800helpfla.com/complnt.html

Cancer Hotline
800-4-CANCER
www.cancer.gov/newscenter

CEB
(See Attorney)

Cellular Phone Complaints
888-CALL-FCC
www.fcc.gov/cgb/complaints.html

Cemetery Consumer Hotline
800-323-2627
www.fldfs.com/funeralcemetery

Charities Fraud Complaint Hotline
800-HELP-FLA
www.800helpfla.com/complnt.html

Check Cashers Regulation
800-848-3792
www.flofr.com/licensing

Child Abuse Hotline
800-96-ABUSE; 800-4-A-CHILD; 888-PREVENT;
800-FLA-LOVE
www.childhelpusa.org
www.childwelfare.gov/pubs/reslist/tollfree.cfm

Child Labor
800-226-2536
www.myflorida.com/dbpr/reg/childlabor/index.html

Children: Missing Children Hotline
800-THE-LOST; 800-I-AM-LOST (national)
888-356-4774 (Florida)
www.fdle.state.fl.us/mcicsearch/
www.missingkids.com
www.childwelfare.gov/pubs/reslist/tollfree.cfm

Children's Health Insurance
Florida KidCare
888-540-5437
www.floridakidcare.org

Healthy Kids
800-821-KIDS
www.healthykids.org

Children's Defense Fund
800-233-1200
www.childrensdefense.org

Child Support
800-622-KIDS
dor.myflorida.com/dor/childsupport
dor.myflorida.com/dor/childsupport/phone.html

Chiropractic Board (Department of Health)
850-245-4355
www.doh.state.fl.us/mqa/chiro

Chiropractic Physician Complaint Hotline
888-419-3456
www.doh.state.fl.us/mqa/enforcement/enforce_howto.htm

Citizenship
800-375-5283
www.uscis.gov

City Governments
(See Government; see also section 4.6)

Civil Rights
Disability Rights
800-514-0301
www.ada.gov

Equal Employment Opportunity Commission
800-669-4000
www.eeoc.gov

Fair Housing
800-669-9777
www.hud.gov/offices/fheo

Florida Commission on Human Relations
850-488-7082; 800-342-8170
fchr.state.fl.us

U.S. Commission on Civil Rights
800-552-6843
www.usccr.gov

Clean Air
(See Environmental Health)

Clemency
850-488-2952
fpc.state.fl.us/Clemency.htm

Coast Guard
800-368-5647
www.uscg.mil/default.asp

Collection Agency Regulation
800-848-3792
www.flofr.com/licensing

Communicable Diseases (Department of Health)
(See also Sexually Transmitted Disease)
850-245-4300
www.doh.state.fl.us/Disease_ctrl/epi/diseases.htm

Continuing Education of the Bar
(See Attorney)

Congress
www.house.gov
202-225-3121
www.senate.gov
202-224-3121

Conservation
(See Energy, Fish and Wildlife)

Construction Industry Regulation
850-487-1395
www.myflorida.com/dbpr/pro/cilb/index.html

Consumer Complaint Hotline
800-HELP-FLA
myfloridalegal.com/consumer
www.800helpfla.com/complnt.html
www.stateofflorida.com/Portal/DesktopDefault.
   aspx?tabid=57

Consumer Product Safety Commission Hotline
800-638-2772
www.cpsc.gov

Consumer Protection
myfloridalegal.com/consumer
www.fraud.org

Consumer Resource Guide
www.800helpfla.com/azguide.html

Corporations
(See also Business)
800-755-5111
www.sunbiz.org/index.html

County Governments
(see Government)

Courts (federal courts in Florida)
(See also section 4.3)
www.uscourts.gov/courtlinks
(click Florida on the map)

Courts (state)
(See also section 4.2)
www.flcourts.org

Credit Bureaus
Equifax
800-685-1111
www.equifax.com

Experian
888-397-3742
www.experian.com

TransUnion
800-916-8800; 800-888-4213
www.transunion.com

Credit Union Regulation
800-848-3792
www.flofr.com/banking

Crime Statistics in Florida
850-410-7000
www.fdle.state.fl.us/Crime_Statistics

Crime Victim Assistance
(See Victim Resources)

Day Care Regulation
www.dcf.state.fl.us/childcare
www.dcf.state.fl.us/childcare/links.shtml

Death Records
877-550-7330; 904-359-6900; 866-441-NCHS
www.doh.state.fl.us/planning_eval/vital_statistics
www.cdc.gov/nchs/howto/w2w/florida.htm
www.vitalrec.com

Debt Collection
(See Collection Agency)

Dental Professions Complaint Hotline
888-419-3456
www.doh.state.fl.us/mqa/enforcement/enforce_howto.htm
www.doh.state.fl.us/mqa/updates.html

Disability Rights and Services
(See also Civil Rights)
800-514-0301; 202-457-0046; 850-488-9071; 800-840-8844
www.ada.gov
www.aapd-dc.org
www.advocacycenter.org

Disasters
(See Emergency Management)

Discrimination
(See Civil Rights)

Divorce/Dissolution Records
904-359-6900; 866-441-NCHS
www.doh.state.fl.us/planning_eval/vital_statistics
www.cdc.gov/nchs/howto/w2w/florida.htm
www.vitalrec.com

Divorce Resources
www.fldivorceonline.com
www.divorcenet.com/states/florida/index_html

Doctors
(See also Medical Board)
888-419-3456
www.floridahealthfinder.gov
www.fdhc.state.fl.us/Contact/call_center.shtml
www.stateofflorida.com/Portal/DesktopDefault.aspx?tabid=
    115#practitioners

Domestic Security in Florida
850-410-7233; 202-282-8000
www.fdle.state.fl.us/a-z_index.html
(click "Domestic Security")
www.dhs.gov/index.shtm

Domestic Violence Hotlines
800-500-1119 (Florida hotline)
863-534-4989 (Florida Attorney Office Domestic Violence)
800-799-SAFE
www.fcadv.org
www.aardvarc.org/dv/states/fldv.shtml
www.ndvh.org

Do Not Call Registry
800-HELP-FLA (state); 888-382-1222 (federal)
www.800helpfla.com/complnt.html
www.donotcall.gov/default.aspx

Drug and Alcohol Abuse
(See also Substance Abuse)
800-729-6686; 800-DRUGHELP
ncadi.samhsa.gov

Drug Court
www.flcourts.org
(click "Drug Court Program")

Education, Department of
850-245-0505
www.fldoe.org

Elder Abuse Hotline
800-96-ABUSE
www.elderabusecenter.org

Special Needs Adult Hotline
800-962-2873
www.dcf.state.fl.us/abuse/report

Elder Affairs
850-414-2000
elderaffairs.state.fl.us

Long-term Care Ombudsman
888-831-0404
ombudsman.myflorida.com

Senior Legal Helpline
888-895-7873
www.legalhotlines.org/hotlines.cfm
elder.law.stetson.edu
www.legalhotlines.org/directory2003/index.cfm
(select "Florida" in the search box)

Elections: Voter Assistance Hotline
866-308-6739
election.dos.state.fl.us

Florida Elections Commission
850-922-4539
www.fec.state.fl.us

Reporting Voter Fraud
877-868-3737
election.dos.state.fl.us/fraud.shtml

Electricity Regulation
(See Public Utility)

Emergency Management (state)
800-342-3557
www.floridadisaster.org

Disaster Recovery Fund
800-825-3786
www.flahurricanefund.org

Emergency Management (federal)
800-621-FEMA
www.fema.gov

Employment Discrimination
(See Civil Rights)

Employment in State Government
(See also section 2.2)
866-ONE-HRFL
peoplefirst.myflorida.com

Employment: Job Safety
(See also Child Labor)
800-321-OSHA (national)
800-321-6742; 954-424-0242 (Florida)
www.osha.gov
www.osha.gov/oshdir/fl.html

Injured Worker Hotline
800-342-1741
www.fldfs.com/wc/faq/faqwrkrs.html

Employment Rights
(See Civil Rights)

Energy Conservation
850-245-8002
www.dep.state.fl.us/energy/default.htm

Energy, Low-Income Energy Assistance
850-488-7541
www.floridacommunitydevelopment.org/liheap

Environmental Health
850-245-4250
www.doh.state.fl.us/environment/index.html

Air Pollution
850-488-0114
www.dep.state.fl.us/Air/contacts.htm

Clean Indoor Air
800-337-3742
www.broward.org/air/air_faq.htm

Environmental Protection (federal)
800-621-8431; 800-424-8802
www.epa.gov

Environmental Protection (state)
(See also Fish and Wildlife)
850-245-2118
www.dep.state.fl.us

Equal Employment Opportunity
(See Civil Rights)

Estate Taxes, Florida
(See also Tax)
800-352-3671; 850-488-6800
www.myflorida.com/dor/taxes/estate_tax.html
sun6.dms.state.fl.us/dor/taxes/estate_tax.html

Ethics
(See also Attorney)
Florida Commission on Ethics
850-488-7864
www.ethics.state.fl.us

Fair Housing
(See Civil Rights)

Family Advocate
(See Disability, Mental Retardation)

Farmworker Hotline
800-633-3572
www.floridajobs.org/alc

Federal Communications Commission
888-CALL-FCC
www.fcc.gov

Federal Government
(See Government)

Federal Trade Commission
877-FTC-HELP; 202-326-2222
www.ftc.gov

FEMA (Federal Emergency Management Agency)
(See Emergency)

Financial Regulation and Services
Department of Financial Services Hotline
800-342-2762
www.fldfs.com

Office of Financial Regulation
800-848-3792
www.flofr.com/licensing

Securities and Exchange Commission
800-SEC-0330
www.sec.gov

Florida Alliance for Information and Referral Services
flairs.org

Florida Bankers Association
850-224-2265
www.floridabankers.com

Fire Departments
www.fldfs.com/sfm/Links/LinksDepartments.htm

Fire Marshal
800-342-2762; 850-413-3100
www.fldfs.com/sfm

Fish and Wildlife Conservation
(See also Conservation)
850-488-4676
wildflorida.org

FLAIRS (Florida Alliance for Information and Referral Services)
flairs.org

Food and Drug Administration
888-INFO-FDA
www.fda.gov

Food Safety (federal regulation)
United States Department of Agriculture
800-535-4555
www.fsis.usda.gov/oa/topics/foodsec_cons.htm

Food Safety (state regulation)
850-245-5520
www.doacs.state.fl.us/fs/contact.html

Food Stamps
www.dcf.state.fl.us/ess/foodstamps.shtml
www.dcf.state.fl.us/ess/fsfactsheet.pdf

Foster Care
www.dcf.state.fl.us/fostercare

Fraud Complaints
(See also Identity Theft, Insurance, Medicaid, Postal Fraud)
myfloridalegal.com/consumer
www.fraud.org
elder.law.stetson.edu

Funeral Home Regulation
800-323-2627; 850-413-3039
myfloridacfo.com/FuneralCemetery/fc_special.htm

Gambling Regulation
(See also Lottery)
www.myflorida.com/dbpr/pmw/index.shtml

Game Promotion Complaint Hotline
(See also Sweepstakes)
800-HELP-FLA
www.800helpfla.com/complnt.html

Gas
(See Public Utility)

Gay and Lesbian Rights
(See also Civil Rights)
ACLU of Florida
786-363-2700
www.aclufl.org/issues

Get Lean
(See Government Waste)

Government: Federal
800-FED-INFO; 800-333-4636
www.firstgov.gov
www.consumeraction.gov/selected.shtml

Government: Florida
(See also sections 4.1, 4.2, 4.4, 4.5, and 4.6)
850-488-1234 (state government information)
www.myflorida.com
www.myflorida.com/directory

Government: City and County
www.govengine.com/localgov/florida.html
www.megalaw.com/fl/flcities.php

Government Employment
866-663-4735
peoplefirst.myflorida.com

Government Waste Hotline
Get Lean
800-438-5326
www.fldfs.com/aadir/contact.htm
oacr.ufl.edu/Investigations.htm

Governor
850-488-7146
www.flgov.com

Health and Human Services Information Helpline
866-762-2237
www.dcf.state.fl.us/ess/dist14.shtml

Healthcare Facility Complaint Hotline
888-419-3456
www.fdhc.state.fl.us/Contact/call_center.shtml

Long-term Care Ombudsman
888-831-0404
ombudsman.myflorida.com

Healthcare Practitioner Complaint Hotline
888-419-3456
www.doh.state.fl.us/mqa/enforcement/enforce_howto.htm

Health Studios Complaint Hotline
800-HELP-FLA
www.800helpfla.com/complnt.html

Helpline (Human Services)
flairs.org/index.htm

Highway Patrol
850-922-9000
www.fhp.state.fl.us

Patrol Stations
www.fhp.state.fl.us/misc/fhpstations.htm

Highway Safety (all county offices)
www.hsmv.state.fl.us/offices

Home Health Care Complaint Hotline
888-419-3456
www.fdhc.state.fl.us/Contact/call_center.shtml

Homeland (Domestic) Security–Florida
850-410-7000
www.fdle.state.fl.us

Homelessness
850-922-4691
www.dcf.state.fl.us/homelessness

House of Representatives
(See Congress, Legislature)

Housing Coalition
800-677-4548
www.flhousing.org

Housing Discrimination
(See Civil Rights)

Housing Finance Corporation
850-488-4197
www.floridahousing.org/home

Hospital Complaint Hotline
888-419-3456
www.fdhc.state.fl.us/Contact/call_center.shtml

Human Relations
(See Civil Rights)

Hurricane Relief Fund
(See Emergency Management)

Identity Theft
(See also Fraud)
877-ID-THEFT; 850-414-3300
www.myfloridalegal.com/identitytheft
101-identitytheft.com/identity-theft-florida.htm
www.consumer.gov/idtheft
www.idtheftcenter.org
www.ftc.gov/bcp/index.shtml
(click "File a Complaint")

Immigration Services
800-375-5283
www.uscis.gov

Incest Counseling Hotline
Parent Helpline
800-352-5683; 800-FLA-LOVE
www.floridanetwork.org/parent_tip_sheet.htm

Information and Referral Services (FLAIRS)
flairs.org

Injured Worker Hotline
(See Employment: Job Safety; Workers'
Compensation)

Insurance for Children
(See Children's Health Insurance)

Insurance: Consumer Hotline
800-342-2762
www.fldfs.com

Insurance Fraud
800-378-0445; 800-342-2762
www.fldfs.com/fraud

Insurance Regulation
850-413-3140
www.floir.com

Internet Crime
(See also Fraud)
www.ic3.gov

Investment Regulation
(See Financial Regulation and Services)

IRS
800-829-1040
(See also Tax)
www.irs.gov

Job Safety
(See Employment)

KidCare
(See Children's Health Insurance)

Lawyer Referral Services
(See Attorney)

Legal Aid/Legal Services of Florida
(See also section 2.4)
850-385-7900; 888-895-7873

www.floridalegal.org
www.lawhelp.org/FL

Legislature (state Senate and House)
(See also Congress)
800-342-1827
www.flsenate.gov
www.myfloridahouse.gov
850-488-1157
www.leg.state.fl.us

Legislature (bill information)
850-488-4371
www.myfloridahouse.gov

Lemon Law Hotline
800-321-5366
www.800helpfla.com/lemonlaw.html

LexisNexis
800-223-1940; 800-356-6548
www.lexisnexis.com
www.lexisone.com

Licenses, Business and Professional
850-487-1395
www.myfloridalicense.com

Lifeline (telephone)
800-342-3552
www.floridapsc.com/utilities/telecomm/lifeline

Liquor Enforcement Hotline
(See Alcohol)

Local Government
(See Government)

Long-term Care Ombudsman
888-831-0404
ombudsman.myflorida.com

Lottery
850-487-7777
www.flalottery.com

Marriage/Family Therapist Complaint Hotline
888-419-3456
www.doh.state.fl.us/mqa/enforcement/enforce_howto.htm

Marriage Records
904-359-6900
www.cdc.gov/nchs/howto/w2w/florida.htm

Mediation Resources
850-921-2910
www.flcourts.org/gen_public/adr/brochure.shtml

Medical Board (Florida Board of Medicine)
(See also Doctors, Health)
850-245-4131
www.doh.state.fl.us/mqa/medical
www.stateofflorida.com/Portal/DesktopDefault.aspx?tabid=115
www.doh.state.fl.us/mqa/updates.html

Complaints Against Doctors
888-419-3456
www.doh.state.fl.us/mqa/enforcement/enforce_csu.html
www.fdhc.state.fl.us/Contact/call_center.shtml

Medicare and Medicaid Services
ahca.myflorida.com/Medicaid/index.shtml
www.cms.hhs.gov/MedicaidGenInfo
www.cms.hhs.gov/PrescriptionDrugCovGenIn

Medicare: Florida
800-MEDICARE
www.floridamedicare.com

Medicare Hotline
800-633-4227
www.medicare.gov/CallCenter.asp

Medicaid: Florida
850-488-3560
www.floridamedicaid.com

Medicaid Fraud Hotline
866-966-7226
myfloridalegal.com
(under "Crime and Fraud" click "Medicaid Fraud")
www.ssa.gov/oig/hotline

Mental Health Services
www.dcf.state.fl.us/mentalhealth

Mental Health Information Hotline
800-950-6264; 877-626-4352
www.nami.org
mentalhealth.samhsa.gov/resources/faqs.aspx

Community Mental Health
850-224-6048
www.fccmh.org

Mental Retardation
(See also Disability)
Family Advocate
954-975-5159
www.floridasvoice.org
fccflorida.org/resources/state.htm

Missing Children Hotline
(See Children)

Mortgage Regulation/Consumer Complaints
800-848-3792; 800-342-2762
www.flofr.com/banking
www.flofr.com/Director/ofrcontacts.htm

Motor Vehicles (Highway Safety & Motor Vehicles)
850-922-9000
www.hsmv.state.fl.us

Motor Vehicle Complaint Hotline
(See also Lemon Law)
800-HELP-FLA
www.800helpfla.com/complnt.html

Movers Complaint Hotline
800-HELP-FLA
www.800helpfla.com/complnt.html

Natural Gas Regulation
(See Public Utility)

No-Scam Hotline
866-9-NO-SCAM

Nurses (Complaints Against)
www.doh.state.fl.us/mqa/nursing/nur_consumer.html

Nursing Home Complaint Hotline
888-419-3456
www.fdhc.state.fl.us/Contact/call_center.shtml

Nursing Home Ratings
www.memberofthefamily.net/registry/fl.htm

Occupational Safety and Health
(See Employment: Job Safety)

Occupational Therapist Complaint Hotline
www.doh.state.fl.us/mqa/occupational/ot_consumer.html

Ombudsman: Long-term Care
888-831-0404
ombudsman.myflorida.com

Parent Helpline
800-352-5683; 800-FLA-LOVE

Parole
(See also Clemency)
850-922-0000.
fpc.state.fl.us

Passport Services
877-487-2778
travel.state.gov/passport/passport_1738.html

Pensions
866-275-7922
www.floridappta.org
www.dol.gov/dol/topic/retirement/retirementsavings.htm

Pesticide Hotline
800-858-7378
npic.orst.edu

Pharmacist Complaint Hotline
888-419-3456
www.doh.state.fl.us/mqa/pharmacy/ph_consumer.html

Physicians
(See Doctors)

Poison Control Hotline
800-222-1222
www.poison.org
www.fasthealth.com/poison/fl.php

Police Departments
(See also Highway Patrol)
www.policeemployment.com/city/fl

www.usacops.com/fl
www.the911site.com/911pd/florida.shtml

Postal Fraud
800-372-8347
postalinspectors.uspis.gov

Psychologists, Complaints against
888-419-3456
www.doh.state.fl.us/mqa/psychology/psy_consumer.html

Public Defenders
www.flpda.org
publicdefender.cjis20.org/public_defenders.htm

Public Utility/Public Service Commission
800-342-3552
www.flpsc.com

Public Utilities Complaints
800-342-3552
www.psc.state.fl.us
www.psc.state.fl.us/consumers/complaints

Putative Fathers Registry
904-359-6900
www.doh.state.fl.us/planning_eval/vital_statistics/
    Putative.htm

Rape Hotline/Rape Crisis Centers
(See also Domestic Violence)
800-656-HOPE
www.rainn.org

Florida Council Against Sexual Violence
888-956-RAPE
www.fcasv.org

Rates
(See Public Utility)

Red Cross
800-435-7669
www.redcross.org

Runaway Hotline
(See Youth Crisis)
800-RUNAWAY; 800-621-4000
www.nrscrisisline.org
www.djj.state.fl.us/Prevention/index.html

Savings and Loans Regulation
800-848-3792; 202-906-6000
www.flofr.com/banking
www.ots.treas.gov/default.cfm

Secretary of State, Florida
850-245-6500
oss.dos.state.fl.us

Securities Regulation/Consumer Complaints
800-848-3792; 800-342-2762
www.flofr.com/banking
www.flofr.com/Director/ofrcontacts.htm

Secured Transaction Registry
850-222-8526
www.floridaucc.com

Senate
(See Congress, Legislature)

Seniors
(See also Elder)

Senior Health Insurance Information
800-963-5337
www.floridahealthfinder.gov

Senior Legal Helpline
888-895-7873; 813-232-1222
elderaffairs.state.fl.us

Sex Offender Information
(See also Rape)
888-357-7332
offender.fdle.state.fl.us/offender/homepage.do
www.fbi.gov/hq/cid/cac/registry.htm

Sexually Transmitted Disease Hotline
(See also Communicable Diseases)
800-227-8922; 850-245-4303; 800-FLA-AIDS
www.doh.state.fl.us/Disease_ctrl/std/index.html
www.211bigbend.com/hotlines/hiv/stds.htm

Venereal Disease Hotline
800-232-4636
www.cdc.gov/std

Sheriff Offices
www.flsheriffs.org

Small Business
(See Business)

Social Security Information Hotline
800-772-1213; 800-269-0271 (fraud hotline)
www.ssa.gov
www.ssa.gov/atlanta/southeast/fl/florida.htm

STD Hotline
(See Sexually Transmitted Diseases)

Substance Abuse Information Hotline
(See also Drug and Alcohol Abuse)
800-662-HELP; 800-66-AYUDA
850-878-2196; 850-487-2920
www.fadaa.org
www.dcf.state.fl.us/mentalhealth/sa

Suicide Prevention Hotline
800-273-TALK; 800-SUICIDE
www.suicidepreventionlifeline.org
www.floridasuicideprevention.org
www.sprc.org/stateinformation/statepages/florida.asp

Sweepstakes Complaint Hotline
(See also Game Promotion)
800-HELP-FLA
www.800helpfla.com/complnt.html

Tax (federal income)
800-829-1040 (individuals)
800-829-4933 (businesses)
www.irs.gov
www.irs.gov/localcontacts
(click "Florida")

Tax (state income)
(See also Estate Taxes)
800-352-3671
dor.myflorida.com/dor/taxes/new.html

Taxpayer Assistance
www.tax-coalition.org/programs.cfm
dor.myflorida.com/dor

Telecommunications Research and Action Center
800-344-8722
www.trac.org

Telemarketers Complaint Hotline
800-HELP-FLA
www.800helpfla.com/complnt.html

Telephone Regulation
(See Cellular Phone, Federal Communications Commission, Public Utility)

Lifeline (telephone)
800-342-3552
www.floridapsc.com/utilities/telecomm/lifeline

Tourism in Florida
888-735-2872; 850-488-5607
www.visitflorida.com

Travel Agents Complaint Hotline
800-HELP-FLA
www.800helpfla.com/complnt.html

Unclaimed Property
888-258-2253; 850-413-5555
www.fltreasurehunt.org

Unemployment Compensation
866-778-7356
www.floridajobs.org/unemployment

Utilities
(See Public Utility)

Vehicle Repair Complaint Hotline
(See Motor Vehicles)

Venereal Disease Hotline
(See Sexually Transmitted Disease)

Veterans Services
850-487-1533
www.floridavets.org

Victim Resources (crime)
877-8-VICTIM; 800-226-6667
www.dc.state.fl.us/oth/victasst
myfloridalegal.com/victims

Vital Records
904-359-6900; 866-441-NCHS
www.doh.state.fl.us/planning_eval/vital_statistics
www.cdc.gov/nchs/howto/w2w/florida.htm
www.vitalrec.com

Voting
(See Elections)

Water Regulation
(See Public Utility)

Weather
www.nws.noaa.gov
www.weathercentral.com/weather/us/states/FL

West Group/Westlaw
800-328-4880; 800-WESTLAW
www.west.thomson.com

Whistle Blower Hotline
800-543-5353
www.dcf.state.fl.us/admin/ig/publications/
wbhotlinebrochure.pdf

White House
202-456-1414
www.whitehouse.gov

Wildlife Conservation
850-488-4676
wildflorida.org

Workers' Compensation
800-742-2214; 800-303-3649; 850-413-1601
www.fldfs.com/WC

Injured Worker Hotline
800-342-1741
www.fldfs.com/wc/faq/faqwrkrs.html

Youth Crisis Hotline
800-442-HOPE; 800-HIT-HOME
www.nrscrisisline.org
www.athealth.com/Consumer/issues/hotlines.html
www.ycc.org

Runaway
800-RUNAWAY; 800-621-4000
www.djj.state.fl.us/Prevention/index.html

C. Something to Check

What hotline or complaint resources might help a client concerned about the following circumstances:

1. Stalking
2. Insolvency
3. Credit discrimination

PART

6

Procedure: Some Basics

6.1 Timeline: Civil Case in the Florida State Courts
A. Introduction
B. Overview
C. More Information
D. Something to Check

A. Introduction

Our main focus in this section will be the litigation procedures followed in cases where one private party asserts a tort or contract cause of action against another private party. We will not cover criminal cases or civil claims against the state. Probate and domestic relations or family law cases are also civil matters, but they have their own special procedures.

The timeline in this section describes many of the major events in contested civil cases commonly filed in the state courts of Florida. Keep in mind, however, that civil cases can vary a great deal in complexity, depending on the nature of the case, the magnitude of the issues, the amount of potential damages, the extent of contention between the parties, and the caliber of the attorneys. Also adding diversity and complexity are the local rules that apply only to the court in which a case is being litigated. Our timeline primarily covers rules of statewide applicability.

See also the following related sections:

- Venue, process, pleadings, and discovery (section 6.2)
- Overview of Florida state courts (section 4.2)
- Example of a civil complaint (section 7.1)
- Rules for, and example of, an appellate brief filed in state court (section 7.4)
- Self-help resources in Florida (section 5.6)
- Overview of federal courts sitting in Florida (section 4.3)
- Some comparisons between state and federal civil procedure (section 6.3)
- Timeline of a criminal case in state court (section 6.4)

B. Overview

Exhibit 6.1A presents an overview of many of the major events involved in the litigation of a relatively large contract or tort civil case in Florida state courts.

Preliminary Considerations

Statute of limitations. The statute of limitations places time limits on filing a lawsuit. For example, an action for wrongful death must be filed within two years of the date of death. (Florida Statutes, § 95.11(4).) If you do not bring suit within this time period, the suit is barred, meaning that you can no longer sue on that cause of action.

Subject-matter jurisdiction. To hear a case, a court must have power over that kind of case. This power is its subject-matter jurisdiction. For example, claims between private parties in which the amount in dispute is more than $15,000 are brought in Circuit Court (commonly referred to as a court of general jurisdiction). Claims between private parties in which the amount in dispute is between $5,001 and $15,000 are brought in a County Court. This court also has procedures for hearing small claims under $5,000. For an overview of the subject-matter jurisdiction of Florida courts, see exhibit 4.2A in section 4.2.

Personal jurisdiction. Personal jurisdiction (also called in personam jurisdiction) is the court's power over a particular party to adjudicate his or her personal rights. The main way in which this power is acquired is by serving the defendant with process in the state. The long-arm statute allows the state to acquire personal jurisdiction over an out-of-state defendant based upon certain contacts that the defendant has had within Florida. (Florida Statutes, § 48.193.) An example of such contact would be marketing of a product in Florida by an out-of-state manufacturer.

Venue. There may be more than one court that has subject-matter jurisdiction over a case as well as personal jurisdiction over the defendant. If so, the place of the trial is referred to as its venue. (Selecting the venue is called choice of venue.) Florida's general venue statute provides that "Actions shall be brought only in the county where the defendant resides, where the cause of action accrued, or where the property in litigation is located." (Florida Statutes, § 47.011.)

Arbitration and mediation. Throughout the case, efforts to resolve the dispute without litigation are often made. This can include arbitration, mediation, and other methods of alternative dispute resolution (ADR). (See the discussion of alternative dispute resolution below.)

Commencement of the Case; Pleadings and Motions

Complaint. A civil action commences with the filing of a complaint or petition with the clerk of the court. ("Every action of a civil nature shall be deemed commenced when the complaint or petition is filed. . . ." Florida Rules of Civil Procedure, Rule 1.050.) This pleading "must state a cause of action and shall contain (1) a short and plain statement of the grounds upon which the court's jurisdiction depends . . . , (2) a short and plain statement of the ultimate facts showing that

EXHIBIT 6.1A   Bringing and Defending a Civil Case in Florida State Courts

(The following overview covers many of the major events in a relatively large contract or tort case filed in a Florida state court; variations will depend on factors such the complexity of the case and the applicability of local rules.)

PRELIMINARY CONSIDERATIONS	COMMENCEMENT OF THE CASE; PLEADINGS & MOTIONS	DISCOVERY	ALTERNATIVE DISPUTE RESOLUTION (ADR)	PRETRIAL	TRIAL	POST-TRIAL	APPEALS
• Statute of limitations • Subject-matter jurisdiction • Personal jurisdiction • Venue • Arbitration and mediation	• Complaint • Civil cover sheet • Summons • Service of process • Proof of service • Answer • Responsive motions • Counterclaim • Crossclaim • Third-party complaint • Sham pleadings • Amendments to pleadings • Supplemental pleadings	• Methods and scope of discovery • Deposition upon oral examination • Deposition upon written questions • Interrogatories • Request for production of documents and things and entry upon land or other property for inspection and other purposes • Request for admissions • Physical or mental examination • Motion for order compelling discovery • Motion for protective order	• General rules • Mediation • Arbitration • Proposal for settlement	• Case management conference • Motion for summary judgment • Pretrial conference	• Jury demand • Notice for trial; setting for trial • Jury selection (voir dire) • Opening statements • Invoke the rule • Examination of witnesses • Exhibits • Motion for a directed verdict/ motion for involuntary dismissal • Closing statements • Instructions to jury • Verdict	• Remittitur and additur • Motion for a new trial • Final judgment/ enforcement	• Florida Court of Appeals • Supreme Court of Florida

the pleader is entitled to relief, and (3) a demand for judgment for the relief to which the pleader deems himself or herself entitled." Florida Rules of Civil Procedure, Rule 1.110(b). Special pleading rules exist for certain kinds of cases. For example, in a medical malpractice case, the attorney must make a "reasonable investigation" of the grounds for such an action and the complaint "shall contain a certificate of counsel that such reasonable investigation gave rise to a good faith belief that grounds exist for an action against each named defendant." (Florida Statutes, § 766.104(1).) Upon filing with the appropriate court, the court will assign a case number to the action.

Civil case cover sheet. Florida Rules of Civil Procedure requires that a civil cover sheet (Form 1.997) must be completed and filed with the clerk of the court at the same time the initial complaint is filed. The clerk of the court will complete the civil cover sheet for a *pro se* litigant. On the cover sheet, specific information must be provided such as the case style, type of case, and whether a jury trial is demanded. (Florida Rules of Civil Procedure, Rule 1.100(c)(2).)

Summons. The plaintiff must complete the summons and present it to the court clerk for issuance. The summons contains the clerk's or judge's signature as well as the seal of the court. The summons notifies the defendant(s) of the action and the time within which the defendant(s) must file a written response (20 days after service of process) to the complaint in order to avoid a default judgment. (Florida Rules of Civil Procedure, Rule 1.070(a).)

Service of process. Bringing a suit requires you to provide formal notice that you have commenced legal process. This is called service of process. When serving the other side, you provide copies of the papers you filed in court to commence the action. For a civil case, the summons and complaint must be served on each defendant named in the complaint. For personal service, the server personally delivers the summons and complaint to the defendant or someone qualified to accept service for the defendant. Service of process may be made by (1) an officer authorized by law to serve process, or (2) a competent person not interested in the action and appointed by the court. In special circumstances, service of process by publication is allowed. There is also a provision in the Florida Rules of Civil Procedure for notifying a defendant of the commencement of a lawsuit via certified mail, return receipt requested. The defendant is asked to waive service of process. Generally, if a defendant has not been properly served within 120 days after the filing of the initial complaint or petition, the court will direct that service must be effected within a specific time or the court will dismiss the action without prejudice or drop the defendant not

served as a party. (Florida Rules of Civil Procedure, Rule 1.070.)

Proof of service. The person serving the summons and complaint must complete and sign a proof of service, which states the date and time the defendant was served. After a defendant is served, the proof of service, together with the original summons, is filed with the court. (Florida Statutes, § 48.21.)

Answer. To avoid a default judgment, the defendant must file an answer to the complaint within 20 days after service of process. "In the answer a pleader shall state in short and plain terms the pleader's defenses to each claim asserted and shall admit or deny the averments on which the adverse party relies. If the defendant is without knowledge, the defendant shall so state and such statement shall operate as a denial." (Florida Rules of Civil Procedure, Rule 1.110(c).) An example of a defense is the expiration of the statute of limitations. If the defendant's answer contains a counterclaim or crossclaim (see below), the plaintiff must file an answer within 20 days. (Florida Rules of Civil Procedure, Rule 1.140(a)(1).)

Responsive motions. In addition to or in place of filing an answer, the defendant can respond by motion (which is not a pleading). "[T]he following defenses may be made by motion at the option of the pleader: (1) lack of jurisdiction over the subject matter, (2) lack of jurisdiction over the person, (3) improper venue, (4) insufficiency of process, (5) insufficiency of service of process, (6) failure to state a cause of action, and (7) failure to join indispensable parties. A motion making any of these defenses shall be made before pleading if a further pleading is permitted." (Florida Rules of Civil Procedure, Rule 1.040(b).)

Counterclaim. If the defendant has a claim against the plaintiff, the defendant can state the claim (called a counterclaim) in his or her answer. The claim may arise out of the transaction or occurrence that is the subject matter of the plaintiff's claim (compulsory counterclaim) or it may not so arise (permissive counterclaim). (Florida Rules of Civil Procedure, Rule 1.070(a).) An example of a counterclaim that does arise out of the same transaction or occurrence is the defendant's claim that the plaintiff wrongfully injured the defendant in the car collision that the plaintiff's complaint initially asserted was caused by the defendant.

Crossclaim. In addition to filing an answer, the defendant can file a crossclaim against another defendant (co-defendant) in the action arising out of the transaction or occurrence that is the subject matter of the original action or a counterclaim, or that relates to any property that is the subject matter of the original action. (Florida Rules of Civil Procedure, Rule 1.070(g).)

Third-party complaint. A third-party complaint is a defendant's complaint against someone who is not currently a party. A "defendant may have a summons and complaint served on a person not a party to the action who is or may be liable to the defendant for all or part of the plaintiff's claim against the defendant, and may also assert any other claim that arises out of the transaction or occurrence that is the subject matter of the plaintiff's claim." (Florida Rules of Civil Procedure, Rule 1.180(a).) If, for example, Smith sues Jones for damaging Smith's fence, Jones may be able to assert a third-party complaint against the gardening company that Jones hired on the basis that the company caused the damage to the fence. The gardening company is called the third-party defendant. If a third-party complaint is filed more than 20 days after the defendant serves the original answer, the defendant must obtain leave of court for permission to file the third-party complaint. If the defendant has filed a counterclaim, the plaintiff may also bring a third-party into the original action. (Florida Rules of Civil Procedure, Rule 1.180(b).)

Sham pleadings. If a party believes a pleading or any part of a pleading to be a sham, that party may file a motion to strike. Once filed, the court will hear the motion, take evidence, and if the motion is sustained, the pleading to which the motion is directed will be stricken or a summary judgment may be entered. The motion to strike must be verified by the party filing the motion. (Florida Rules of Civil Procedure, Rule 1.150.)

Amendments to pleadings. Once a party has filed a complaint or other pleading, he or she may wish to alter or amend it. "A party may amend a pleading once as a matter of course at any time before a responsive pleading is served or, if the pleading is one to which no responsive pleading is permitted and the action has not been placed on the trial calendar, may so amend it at any time within 20 days after it is served. Otherwise a party may amend a pleading only by leave of court or by written consent of the adverse party." (Florida Rules of Civil Procedure, Rule 1.190(a).)

Supplemental pleadings. "Upon motion of a party the court may permit that party, upon reasonable notice and upon such terms as are just, to serve a supplemental pleading setting forth transactions or occurrences or events which have happened since the date of the pleading sought to be supplemented. If the court deems it advisable that the adverse party plead thereto, it shall so order, specifying the time therefor." (Florida Rules of Civil Procedure, Rule 1.190(d).)

Discovery

Methods and scope of discovery. Before trial, parties can use discovery methods to obtain facts from an opponent in order to prepare for trial. These methods are:

- Depositions upon oral examination or written questions
- Written interrogatories
- Production of documents or things or permission to enter upon land or other property for inspection and other purposes
- Physical and mental examinations
- Requests for admission (Florida Rules of Civil Procedure, Rule 1.280(a))

What is discoverable by these methods? "Parties may obtain discovery regarding any matter, not privileged, that is relevant to the subject matter of the pending action. . . . It is not ground for objection that the information sought will be inadmissible at the trial if the information sought appears reasonably calculated to lead to the discovery of admissible evidence." (Florida Rules of Civil Procedure, Rule 1.280(b)(1).)

Deposition upon oral examination. A deposition upon oral examination is the oral questioning of a witness under oath in the presence of a court reporter, who writes down or records the testimony of the deposition witness (called the deponent). "After commencement of the action any party may take the testimony of any person, including a party, by deposition upon oral examination. Leave of court, granted with or without notice, must be obtained only if the plaintiff seeks to take a deposition within 30 days after service of the process and initial pleading upon any defendant, except that leave is not required (1) if a defendant has served a notice of taking deposition or otherwise sought discovery, or (2) if special notice is given" as provided in the rules. (Florida Rules of Civil Procedure, Rule 1.310(a).)

Deposition upon written questions. A deposition upon written questions is the submission of written questions to a witness who answers them orally under oath in the presence of a court reporter, who writes down or records the testimony of the deponent. "After commencement of the action any party may take the testimony of any person, including a party, by deposition upon written questions. The attendance of witnesses may be compelled by the use of subpoena. . . . Within 30 days after the notice and written questions are served, a party may serve cross questions upon all other parties. Within 10 days after being served with cross questions, a party may serve redirect questions upon all other parties. Within 10 days after being served with redirect questions, a party may serve recross questions upon all other parties." (Florida Rules of Civil Procedure, Rule 1.320(a).)

Interrogatories. Interrogatories are written questions posed to a party, requiring a written response. The number of interrogatories allowed is limited to 30 questions, including subparts, unless the court permits a larger number. The Supreme Court has approved a form of interrogatories for some types of actions. A party must use an approved form but is allowed to add additional questions as long as the number of questions does not exceed 30. "Each interrogatory shall be answered separately and fully in writing under oath unless it is objected to, in which event the grounds for objection shall be stated and signed by the attorney making it. The party to whom the interrogatories are directed shall serve the answers and any objections within 30 days after the service of the interrogatories, except that a defendant may serve answers or objections within 45 days after service of the process and initial pleading upon that defendant." Answers are not filed with the court unless the court orders that a copy be submitted. (Florida Rules of Civil Procedure, Rule 1.340(a).)

Request for production of documents or things and entry upon land or other property for inspection and other purposes. "Any party may request any other party (1) to produce and permit the party making the request. . . to inspect and copy any designated documents, including writings, drawings, graphs, charts, photographs, phono-records, and other data compilations. . . in the possession, custody, or control of the party to whom the request is directed; (2) to inspect and copy, test, or sample any tangible things. . . in the possession, custody, or control of the party to whom the request is directed; or (3) to permit entry upon designated land or other property in the possession or control of the party upon whom the request is served for the purpose of inspection and measuring, surveying, photographing, testing, or sampling the property or any designated object or operation on it. . . ." (Florida Rules of Civil Procedure, Rule 1.350(a).) The request may be served on the plaintiff "after commencement of the action and on any other party with or after service of the process and initial pleading on that party." The party to whom the request is directed shall serve a written response within 30 days after service of the request, "except that a defendant may serve a response within 45 days after service of the process and initial pleading on that defendant." (Rule 1.350(b).)

Request for admissions. Requests for admissions (RFA) are written requests from a party that any other party to the action admit the truth of matters that relate to statements or opinions of fact or of the application of law to fact, including the genuineness of any documents described in the request. The requests (not to exceed 30, including subparts) can be served on the plaintiff after the action is commenced and on any other party after service or process and initial pleading upon that party. "The matter is admitted unless the party to whom the request is directed serves upon the party requesting the admission a written answer . . .

within 30 days after service of the request. . . but. . . a defendant shall not be required to serve answers or objections before the expiration of 45 days after service of the process and initial pleading upon the defendant." (Florida Rules of Civil Procedure, Rule 1.370(a).)

Physical or mental examination. Discovery can also include a request by one party that another party (or someone under the control of the other party) submit to a physical or mental examination by a qualified expert when the condition of the person to be examined is in controversy. The party requesting the exam must have "good cause" to seek it. The request may be served on the plaintiff after commencement of the action and on any other person with or after service of the process and initial pleading on that party. "The party to whom the request is directed shall serve a response within 30 days after service of the request, except that a defendant need not serve a response until 45 days after service of the process and initial pleading on that defendant." (Florida Rules of Civil Procedure, Rule 1.360(a).)

Motion for order compelling discovery. Upon failure to comply with valid discovery requests (e.g., refusing to answer a deposition question or providing an evasive or incomplete answer), a party can request the court to force compliance by filing a motion for an order compelling discovery. The prevailing party may be required to reimburse the other party for reasonable expenses, including attorneys' fees, associated with obtaining or defending the motion. (Florida Rules of Civil Procedure, Rule 1.380.)

Motion for a protective order. If a party is abusing the discovery process to harass the other side or is demanding information that is privileged or otherwise protected from disclosure by law, the responding party may bring a motion for a protective order. The motion must be brought for good cause. The prevailing party may be required to reimburse the other party for reasonable expenses, including attorneys' fees, associated with obtaining or defending the motion. (Florida Rules of Civil Procedure, Rule 1.280(c).)

Alternative Dispute Resolution (ADR)

General rules. Alternative dispute resolution (ADR) is a method of resolving a legal dispute without litigation. ADR can occur before or after a lawsuit is filed. The presiding judge has the authority to enter an order referring all or any part of a contested civil matter to mediation or arbitration. Also, the parties may file a written stipulation to mediate or arbitrate any issue between them at any time. This stipulation will be incorporated into the order of referral. The first mediation conference or arbitration hearing shall be held within

60 days of the order of referral. (Florida Rules of Civil Procedure, Rule 1.700.)

Mediation. Mediation is a process in which a neutral third party encourages and facilitates the resolution of a dispute between two or more parties. Mediation is informal and nonadversarial, its purpose being a mutually acceptable and voluntary agreement between the parties. In mediation, the parties have the sole authority to decide whether to resolve their differences. The mediator assists the parties in identifying the issues, fosters joint problem solving, and explores settlement alternatives. (Florida Statutes, § 44.1011(2).) "Mediation shall be completed within 45 days of the first mediation conference unless extended by order of the court or by stipulation of the parties." (Florida Rules of Civil Procedure, Rule 1.710.)

Arbitration. Arbitration as a process whereby a neutral third party or panel (called an arbitrator or arbitration panel) considers the facts and arguments presented by the parties and renders a decision. The process may be binding or nonbinding. (Florida Statutes, § 44.1011(1).)

Proposal for settlement. A proposal for settlement, also referred to as an offer or demand, may be served on a defendant no earlier than 90 days after service of process. A proposal for settlement may be served on a plaintiff no earlier than 90 days after the action has been commenced. No proposal may be served later than 45 days before the date set for trial or the first day of the docket on which the case is set for trial, whichever occurs first. A proposal may be withdrawn (in writing) prior to written acceptance. A proposal shall be deemed rejected unless accepted by delivery of a written notice of acceptance within 30 days after service of the proposal. (Florida Rules of Civil Procedure, Rule 1.442.)

Pretrial

Case management conference. At any time after responsive pleadings are due, a court may order (or a party may convene after notice) a case management conference to:

- Schedule service of motions, pleadings, and other papers
- Set or reset the date and time of trials
- Coordinate progress of the action in complex litigation
- Limit, schedule, order, or expedite discovery
- Schedule disclosure of expert witnesses and their opinions
- Schedule or hear motions in limine
- Explore settlement possibilities
- Require filing of preliminary stipulations

- Refer issues to a magistrate for findings of fact
- Schedule conferences or discuss matters that may aid in the disposition of the case (Florida Rules of Civil Procedure, Rule 1.200(a))

Motion for summary judgment. A motion for summary judgment is a resolution of a claim or defense without a trial when it can be shown by the admissible evidence on file that there is no genuine issue as to any material fact and that the moving party is entitled to a judgment on the claim or defense as a matter of law. The motion can be made at any time after the expiration of 20 days from the commencement of the action or after service of a motion for summary judgment by the adverse party. The movant shall serve the motion at least 20 days before the time fixed for the hearing, and shall also serve at that time copies of any summary judgment evidence on which the movant relies that has not already been filed with the court. The adverse party shall identify, by notice mailed to the movant's attorney at least five days prior to the day of the hearing, or delivered no later than 5:00 p.m. two business days prior to the day of the hearing, any summary judgment evidence on which the adverse party relies. (Florida Rules of Civil Procedure, Rule 1.510.)

Pretrial conference. Once the action is at issue, a party may request or a court on its own may schedule, with 20 days' notice, a pretrial conference to:

- Simplify the issues
- Determine the necessity of amending the pleadings
- Obtain admissions pertaining to facts and documents
- Determine the number of expert witnesses allowed
- Resolve case management matters (see above) (Florida Rules of Civil Procedure, Rule 1.200(b))

Trial

Jury demand. Any party may demand a trial by jury of any issue triable by a jury by serving upon the other party a demand in writing for a jury trial at any time after commencement of the action and not later than 10 days after the service of the last pleading directed to such issue. If a party does not make such a written demand, then the demand for a jury trial is waived. (Florida Rules of Civil Procedure, Rule 1.430.)

Notice for trial; setting for trial. Twenty days after service of the last pleading, or after disposition of any motions directed to the last pleading served, a party may file a notice for trial. This notice must include an estimate of the time required for trial, whether the trial is to be by a jury, and whether the trial is on the original action or on a subsequent proceeding. If the court determines that the matter is ready to be set for trial, the court will enter an order fixing a date for trial. The trial shall be set not less than 30 days from the service of the notice for trial. (Florida Rules of Civil Procedure, Rule 1.440.)

Jury selection (voir dire). In a civil trial, the jury usually consists of six jurors. During jury selection (voir dire), prospective jurors are asked questions by the judge and attorneys (and also sometimes by questionnaire) to determine their fitness to sit on the jury. Prospective jurors can be challenged for cause (e.g., they may not be impartial because they are related to one of the parties). A prospective juror can also be dismissed by a peremptory challenge, which is a right to challenge and remove a prospective juror without giving any reasons. Each party has three peremptory challenges. When a challenge is made, it is addressed outside the hearing of the jury so that the jury is not aware "of the nature of the challenge, the party making the challenge, or the basis of the court's ruling on the challenge." (Florida Rules of Civil Procedure, Rule 1.431.)

Opening statements. Once the jury has been sworn in, the court will give each side an opportunity to make an opening statement. In a civil trial, the plaintiff presents its opening statement first. In most cases, the defendant makes its opening statement immediately after the plaintiff's opening statement. An opening statement tells the jury what the party expects the evidence to show.

Invoke the rule. At the request of a party (or on its own motion), the court may order witnesses excluded from a proceeding so that they cannot hear the testimony of other witnesses. This exclusion is known as invoking the rule (Florida Statutes, § 90.616) on excluding witnesses. A party who is a natural person, however, cannot be excluded.

Examination of witnesses. The plaintiff presents its case first, since the plaintiff has the burden of proof. After each witness has testified under direct examination, the other side may cross-examine the witness regarding the testimony already given. After cross-examination, the party who called the witness may conduct a redirect examination, followed by a possible recross-examination by the other side. After all plaintiff's witnesses have testified, the plaintiff will "rest." Then it is the defendant's turn to present its version of the case. (24 Florida Jurisprudence 2d, Evidence and Witnesses § 811 et seq.)

Exhibits. Exhibits to be introduced into evidence are usually pre-marked before the start of the trial. The courtroom clerk labels each exhibit with a number or letter. When introducing evidence, it is generally necessary to establish a legal basis for considering the evidence through the witness who will be testifying about the exhibit. Establishing a legal basis for considering evidence is called "laying an evidentiary foundation." Before accepting an item into evidence, the judge will ask the opposing side if there is any objection to admitting the exhibit into evidence.

Motion for a directed verdict/motion for involuntary dismissal. Either side can request a directed verdict. "A motion for a directed verdict shall state the specific grounds therefor." If granted, the court essentially instructs the jury that there is no issue of fact for them to resolve, and as a matter of law, the result of the case must be decided a certain way. If the motion is granted, the jury does not deliberate. "When a motion for a directed verdict made at the close of all of the evidence is denied or for any reason is not granted, the court is deemed to have submitted the action to the jury subject to a later determination of the legal questions raised by the motion." (Florida Rules of Civil Procedure, Rule 1.480.) If the case is being tried without a jury, the motion that seeks the same result is a motion for involuntary dismissal. (Rule 1.420(b).)

Closing statements. Assuming that directed verdicts have not been granted, the attorneys then make their closing arguments to the jury, summarizing their case and argument for a favorable verdict.

Instructions to jury. Jury instructions are the trial judge's explanation to the jury of the law and the manner in which the jury should go about reaching a verdict. Each party is allowed to make a written request of any instructions it would like the court to give the jury. "Not later than at the close of the evidence, the parties shall file written requests that the court charge the jury on the law set forth in such requests. The court shall then require counsel to appear before it to settle the charges to be given." (Florida Rules of Civil Procedure, Rule 1.470.) "The forms of Florida Standard Jury Instructions published by The Florida Bar pursuant to authority of the supreme court may be used by the trial judges of this state in charging the jury in civil actions to the extent that the forms are applicable." (Florida Rules of Civil Procedure, Form 1.985.) The jury must follow the judge's instruction in arriving at its verdict.

Verdict. After receiving instructions, the jury goes to the jury room to deliberate and reach a verdict. The moderator of the discussions is a foreperson whom the jurors select from among themselves. In civil cases, the jury must decide if the party with the burden of proof has proven its case by a preponderance of the evidence. Under this standard, the greater weight of the evidence must support every element of the party's claim. This means that the evidence on one side of the scale outweighs that on the other. Most verdicts are general verdicts, which simply state which side wins and the amount awarded, if the verdict includes an award of damages. When punitive damages are sought, the amount of these damages must be stated separately from amounts of the other damages awarded. (Florida Rules of Civil Procedure, Rule 1.481.) In certain kinds of cases, e.g., medical malpractice, the jury must itemize categories of damages such as past and future economic losses. (Florida Statutes, § 768.77.)

Post-Trial

Remittitur and additur. The court has the responsibility, upon proper motion by a party, to review the amount of the damages awarded to determine whether the amount is excessive or inadequate based on certain criteria and the facts and circumstances presented at trial. The court may order a remittitur if it finds the amount excessive or may order an additur if it finds the amount inadequate. "If the party adversely affected by such remittitur or additur does not agree, the court shall order a new trial in the cause on the issue of damages only." (Florida Statutes, § 768.74(4).)

Motion for a new trial. A motion for a new trial asks the trial court to order a new trial on all or part of the issues. The motion "shall be served not later than 10 days after the return of the verdict in a jury action or the date of filing of the judgment in a non-jury action." (Florida Rules of Civil Procedure, Rule 1.530.)

Final judgment/enforcement. The trial court's final disposition of the case is the final judgment. When a sum of money has been awarded as damages, the final judgment reflects the amount, after taking into account setoffs and other considerations. The final judgment is, in effect, the plaintiff's legal right to damages. It is the responsibility of the prevailing party to take the necessary steps for acquiring satisfaction of the damages awarded in the judgment. "Final process to enforce a judgment solely for the payment of money shall be by execution, writ of garnishment, or other appropriate process or proceedings. . . . Final process to enforce a judgment for the recovery of property shall be by a writ of possession for real property and by a writ of replevin, distress writ, writ of garnishment, or other appropriate process or proceedings for other property." (Florida Rules of Civil Procedure, Rule 1.570.)

Appeals

Florida Court of Appeals. The first level of appeal from judgments is the district court of appeal. (See section 4.2 for an overview of appellate courts.) The first step in the appeal process is the filing of two copies of a Notice of Appeal (accompanied by filing fees prescribed by law) with the clerk of the court that rendered the judgment to be reviewed within 30 days from entry of the judg-ment. The clerk at the lower court will prepare the record and index and transmit the appellate packet to the appeals court within 110 days of filing the notice. (Florida Rule of Appellate Procedure 9.110.) The court of appeals (consisting of a three-judge panel) decides (on the basis of oral arguments and appellate briefs) whether any errors of law were made by the trial court. The court of appeals may affirm, reverse, or modify the judgment, or it can send the case back to the trial court (remand it) for further proceedings.

Supreme Court of Florida. A party dissatisfied with the decision of the court of appeals can request the Supreme Court of Florida to review the decision of the court of appeals. If the request is granted, the court decides (on the basis of oral arguments and appellate briefs) whether any errors of law were made. (See section 4.2 for an overview of the Supreme Court.) The Supreme Court has the discretion to accept or deny a review; it often denies requests to review a decision of the court of appeals, but it must hear appeals if the decision involves the unconstitutionality of a state statute or provision of the Florida Constitution.

C. **More Information**

Overview of Civil Litigation in Florida
*www.floridabar.org/DIVCOM/PI/RHandbook01.nsf/
    Form+List?OpenForm*
(click "Reporter's Guide to a Civil Lawsuit")
www.clerk.leon.fl.us
(click "Frequently Asked Questions")
www.weblocator.com/attorney/fl/law/processcon.html
*www.delmarlearning.com/companions/content/140184829X/
    state/FL/kerley_FL_v5.pdf*

Florida Civil Procedure and Practice
www.megalaw.com/fl/top/flcivpro.php

Handbook on Florida Discovery Practice
www.flatls.org/Handbook/Handbook.pdf

Florida State Trial and Appellate Courts
www.flcourts.org

Florida Civil Standard Jury Instructions
www.flcourts18.org/PDF/civil.pdf
www.lexisnexis.com/flabar/jury_instructions.asp

ADR (alternative dispute resolution)
www.flcourts.org
(click "Alternative Dispute Resolution/Mediation")
www.tfapm.org

Summary Jury Trial
www.2ndcircuit.leon.fl.us/Resources/summary_trial.pdf

Florida Statutes
www.leg.state.fl.us/Statutes/index.cfm

Florida Rules of Civil Procedure
www.floridabar.org
(click "Professional Practice" then "Rules of Procedure")

Jury Information
www.flcourts.org/gen_public/jury/index.shtml

Understanding the Appellate Process
www.4dca.org/geniformfrm.html

Pro Se Appellate Handbook: Representing Yourself on Appeal
www.4dca.org/geniformfrm.html

D. Something to Check

1. Go to the web site of the circuit court in your county and to the court of appeal to which decisions of that circuit court are appealed (see section 4.2). What information is available on these sites for trials and appeals of civil cases in those courts?

2. Go to the online Florida Rules of Civil Procedure. Assuming that a circuit civil case was filed and served on a defendant on August 4, 2009, compute when the answer would have been due.

6.2 Venue, Process, Pleadings, and Discovery: 40 Rules Even Non-Litigation Paralegals Should Know

A. Introduction
B. The Rules
C. More Information
D. Something to Check

A. Introduction

Even if you do not work in litigation now, at some time in your career there is a good chance that you will. A majority of the paralegals you will meet at paralegal association gatherings work in some phase of litigation, either on the front lines or in indirect capacities. Even attorneys and paralegals who work in transaction practices often have litigation on their mind—from the perspective of how to avoid it! In short, litigation dominates a large portion of the legal world. Knowing some of the essential rules of civil litigation in the Florida courts will help you communicate intelligently with (and perhaps be better prepared one day to join) attorneys and paralegals in the world of litigation.

In this section, we introduce excerpts from 40 of the most important litigation rules in Florida, primarily in two areas where paralegals have their most prominent roles: pleadings and discovery. Because the rules are excerpted rather than presented in full, you, of course, will need to go to the codes or rules themselves to obtain the full text whenever working on a client's case.

Consider this recommendation: read through the excerpts at least once or twice a year. Each time you do, you will increase your "litigation literacy," and gain a richer context for many of the non-litigation tasks you perform.

For related material in this book, see:

- Section 4.2, state courts in Florida
- Section 4.3, federal courts in Florida
- Section 6.1, timeline: a civil case in the Florida state courts
- Section 6.3, state vs. federal civil litigation in Florida
- Section 7.1, example of a civil complaint
- Section 7.4, example of an appellate brief

B. The Rules
Table of Contents

State Courts
Venue
Summons
Service of Process
Time Computation
Pleadings
Pretrial Procedure
Class Action
Discovery: Overview
Discovery: Depositions
Discovery: Interrogatories
Discovery: Production of Documents and Things; Entry upon Land
Discovery: Physical or Other Kind of Examination
Discovery: Requests for Admission
Discovery: Sanctions
Lawyer-Client Privilege

STATE COURTS

State courts in Florida (Constitution of the State of Florida, Art. V, § 1)

The judicial power shall be vested in a supreme court, district courts of appeal, circuit courts, and county courts. No other courts may be established by the state, any political subdivision, or any municipality. The legislature shall, by general law, divide the state into appellate court districts and judicial circuits following county lines. Commissions established by law, or administrative officers or bodies may be granted quasi-judicial power in matters connected with the functions of their offices. The legislature may establish by general law a civil traffic hearing officer system for the purpose of hearing civil traffic infractions. The legislature may, by general law, authorize

| Levels of Florida Courts |

a military court-martial to be conducted by military judges of the Florida National Guard, with direct appeal of a decision to the District Court of Appeal, First District.

VENUE

Where actions may be begun (Florida Statutes § 47.11)

Actions shall be brought only in the county where the defendant resides, where the cause of action accrued,

> **Where Venue Can Lie**

or where the property in litigation is located. This section shall not apply to actions against nonresidents.

Actions against defendants residing in different counties (Florida Statutes § 47.021)

Actions against two or more defendants residing in different counties may be brought in any county in which any defendant resides.

Actions on several causes of action (Florida Statutes § 47.041)

Actions on several causes of action may be brought in any county where any of the causes of action arose. When two or more causes of action joined arose in different counties, venue may be laid in any of such counties, but the court may order separate trials if expedient.

Actions against corporations (Florida Statutes § 47.051)

Actions against domestic corporations shall be brought only in the county where such corporation has, or usually keeps, an office for transaction of its customary business, where the cause of action accrued, or where the property in litigation is located. Actions against foreign corporations doing business in this state shall be brought in a county where such corporation has an agent or other representative, where the cause of action accrued, or where the property in litigation is located.

SUMMONS

Summons; issuance (Florida Rules of Civil Procedure, Rule 1.070(a))

Upon the commencement of the action, summons or other process authorized by law shall be issued forth-

> **Summons: Issuance and Form**

with by the clerk or judge under the clerk's or the judge's signature and the seal of the court and delivered for service without praecipe.

Summons: general form (Florida Rules of Civil Procedure, Form 1.902)

THE STATE OF FLORIDA:
To Each Sheriff of the State:

YOU ARE COMMANDED to serve this summons and a copy of the complaint or petition in this action on defendant _____.

Each defendant is required to serve written defenses to the complaint or petition on _____, plaintiff's attorney, whose address is _____, within 20 days after service of this summons on that defendant, exclusive of the day of service, and to file the original of the defenses with the clerk of this court either before service on plaintiff's attorney or immediately thereafter. If a defendant fails to do so, a default will be entered against that defendant for the relief demanded in the complaint or petition.

SERVICE OF PROCESS

Who may serve process (Florida Rules of Civil Procedure, Rule 1.070(b))

Service of process may be made by an officer authorized by law to serve process, but the court may appoint

> **Service of Process Rules**

any competent person not interested in the action to serve the process. When so appointed, the person serving process shall make proof of service by affidavit promptly and in any event within the time during which the person served must respond to the process. Failure to make proof of service shall not affect the validity of the service. When any process is returned not executed or returned improperly executed for any defendant, the party causing its issuance shall be entitled to such additional process against the unserved party as is required to effect service.

Copies of initial pleading (Florida Rules of Civil Procedure, Rule 1.070(e))

At the time of personal service of process a copy of the initial pleading shall be delivered to the party upon whom service is made. The date and hour of service shall be endorsed on the original process and all copies of it by the person making the service. The party seeking to effect personal service shall furnish the person making service with the necessary copies. . . .

How to serve an attorney or a party (Florida Rules of Civil Procedure, Rule 1.080(b))

When service is required or permitted to be made upon a party represented by an attorney, service shall be made upon the attorney unless

> **Service of Process on an Attorney or Party**

service upon the party is ordered by the court. Service on the attorney or party shall be made by delivering a copy or mailing it to the attorney or the party at the last known address or, if no address is known, by leaving it with the clerk of the court. Service by mail shall be complete upon mailing. Delivery of a copy within this rule shall be complete upon: (1) handing it to the attorney or to the party, (2) leaving it at the attorney's or party's office with a clerk or other person in charge thereof, (3) if there is no one in charge, leaving it in a conspicuous place therein, (4) if the office is closed or the person to be served has no office, leaving it at the person's usual place of abode with some person of his or her family above 15 years of age and informing such person of the contents, or (5) transmitting it by facsimile to the attorney's or party's office with a cover sheet containing the sender's name, firm, address, telephone number, and facsimile number, and the number of pages transmitted. When service is made by facsimile, a copy shall also be served by any other method permitted by this rule. Facsimile service occurs when transmission is complete. Service by delivery after 5:00 p.m. shall be deemed to have been made on the next day that is not a Saturday, Sunday, or legal holiday.

Original Documents (Florida Rules of Civil Procedure, Rule 1.080(d))

All original papers shall be filed with the court either before service or immediately thereafter. If the original of any bond or other paper is not placed in the court file, a certified copy shall be so placed by the clerk.

TIME COMPUTATION

Determination of time periods (Florida Rules of Civil Procedure, Rule 1.090(a))

In computing any period of time prescribed or allowed by these rules, by order of court, or by any applicable

| Time Computations |

statute, the day of the act, event, or default from which the designated period of time begins to run shall not be included. The last day of the period so computed shall be included unless it is a Saturday, Sunday, or legal holiday, in which event the period shall run until the end of the next day which is neither a Saturday, Sunday, or legal holiday. When the period of time prescribed or allowed is less than 7 days, intermediate Saturdays, Sundays, and legal holidays shall be excluded in the computation.

PLEADINGS

Pleadings (Florida Rules of Civil Procedure, Rule 1.100(a))

There shall be a complaint or, when so designated by a statute or rule, a petition, and an answer to it; an answer

| Kinds of Pleadings Allowed |

to a counterclaim denominated as such; an answer to a crossclaim if the answer contains a crossclaim; a third-party complaint if a person who was not an original party is summoned as a third-party defendant; and a third-party answer if a third-party complaint is served. If an answer or

third-party answer contains an affirmative defense and the opposing party seeks to avoid it, the opposing party shall file a reply containing the avoidance. No other pleadings shall be allowed.

Captions of pleadings (Florida Rules of Civil Procedure, Rule 1.100(c))

Every pleading, motion, order, judgment, or other paper shall have a caption containing the name of the

| Required Content of Captions |

court, the file number, the name of the first party on each side with an appropriate indication of other parties, and a designation identifying the party filing it and its nature or the nature of the order, as the case may be. All papers filed in the action shall be styled in such a manner as to indicate clearly the subject matter of the paper and the party requesting or obtaining relief.

Claims for relief (Florida Rules of Civil Procedure, Rule 1.110(b))

A pleading which sets forth a claim for relief, whether an original claim, counterclaim, crossclaim, or third-party claim, must state a cause of ac-

| Pleading a Cause of Action: Ultimate Facts |

tion and shall contain (1) a short and plain statement of the grounds upon which the court's jurisdiction depends, unless the court already has jurisdiction and the claim needs no new grounds of jurisdiction to support it, (2) a short and plain statement of the ultimate facts showing that the pleader is entitled to relief, and (3) a demand for judgment for the relief to which the pleader deems himself or herself entitled. Relief in the alternative or of several different types may be demanded. Every complaint shall be considered to demand general relief.

The answer (Florida Rules of Civil Procedure, Rule 1.110(c))

In the answer a pleader shall state in short and plain terms the pleader's defenses to each claim asserted and

| Pleading an Answer: How to Deny Something |

shall admit or deny the averments on which the adverse party relies. If the defendant is without knowledge, the defendant shall so state and such statement shall operate as a denial. Denial shall fairly meet the substance of the averments denied. When a pleader intends in good faith to deny only a part of an averment, the pleader shall specify so much of it as is true and shall deny the remainder. Unless the pleader intends in good faith to controvert all of the averments of the preceding pleading, the pleader may make denials as specific denials of designated averments or may generally deny all of the averments except such designated averments as the pleader expressly admits, but when the pleader does so intend to controvert all of its averments, including averments of the grounds upon which the court's jurisdiction depends, the pleader may do so by general denial.

Affirmative defenses (Florida Rules of Civil Procedure, Rule 1.110(d))

In pleading to a preceding pleading a party shall set forth affirmatively accord and satisfaction,

> Nineteen
> Affirmative Defense

arbitration and award, assumption of risk, contributory negligence, discharge in bankruptcy, duress, estoppel, failure of consideration, fraud, illegality, injury by fellow servant, laches, license, payment, release, res judicata, statute of frauds, statute of limitations, waiver, and any other matter constituting an avoidance or affirmative defense. When a party has mistakenly designated a defense as a counterclaim or a counterclaim as a defense, the court, on terms if justice so requires, shall treat the pleading as if there had been a proper designation. . . .

Fraud, mistake, condition of the mind (Florida Rules of Civil Procedure, Rule 1.120(b))

In all averments of fraud or mistake, the circumstances constituting fraud or mistake shall be stated with such particularity as the circumstances

> When You Must
> Plead with
> Particularity

may permit. Malice, intent, knowledge, mental attitude, and other condition of mind of a person may be averred generally.

PRETRIAL PROCEDURE

Case management conference (Florida Rules of Civil Procedure, Rule 1.200(a))

At any time after responsive pleadings or motions are due, the court may order, or a party, by serving a notice, may convene, a case management conference. The matter to be considered shall be specified in the order or notice setting the conference. At such a conference the court may:

> Goals of the Case
> Management
> Conference

(1) schedule or reschedule the service of motions, pleadings, and other papers;
(2) set or reset the time of trials, subject to rule 1.440(c);
(3) coordinate the progress of the action if complex litigation factors are present;
(4) limit, schedule, order, or expedite discovery;
(5) schedule disclosure of expert witnesses and the discovery of facts known and opinions held by such experts;
(6) schedule or hear motions in limine;
(7) pursue the possibilities of settlement;
(8) require filing of preliminary stipulations if issues can be narrowed;
(9) consider referring issues to a magistrate for findings of fact; and
(10) schedule other conferences or determine other matters that may aid in the disposition of the action.

Pretrial conference (Florida Rules of Civil Procedure, Rule 1.200(b))

After the action is at issue the court itself may or shall on the timely motion of any party require the parties to appear for a conference to consider and determine:

> Goals of the
> Pretrial
> Conference

(1) the simplification of the issues;
(2) the necessity or desirability of amendments to the pleadings;
(3) the possibility of obtaining admissions of fact and of documents that will avoid unnecessary proof;
(4) the limitation of the number of expert witnesses; and
(5) any matters permitted under subdivision (a) of this rule.

CLASS ACTIONS

Prerequisites to class representation (Florida Rules of Civil Procedure, Rule 1.220(a))

Before any claim or defense may be maintained on behalf of a class by one party or more suing or being sued as the representative of all the members of a class, the court shall first conclude that:

> Requirements for
> a Class Action

(1) the members of the class are so numerous that separate joinder of each member is impracticable,
(2) the claim or defense of the representative party raises questions of law or fact common to the questions of law or fact raised by the claim or defense of each member of the class,
(3) the claim or defense of the representative party is typical of the claim or defense of each member of the class, and
(4) the representative party can fairly and adequately protect and represent the interests of each member of the class.

Claims and defenses maintainable (Florida Rules of Civil Procedure, Rule 1.220(b))

A claim or defense may be maintained on behalf of a class if the court concludes that the prerequisites of subdivision (a) are satisfied, and that:

> Additional
> Requirements to
> Bring a Class
> Action

(1) the prosecution of separate claims or defenses by or against individual members of the class would create a risk of either:
 (A) inconsistent or varying adjudications concerning individual members of the class which

would establish incompatible standards of conduct for the party opposing the class; or

(B) adjudications concerning individual members of the class which would, as a practical matter, be dispositive of the interests of other members of the class who are not parties to the adjudications, or substantially impair or impede the ability of other members of the class who are not parties to the adjudications to protect their interests; or

(2) the party opposing the class has acted or refused to act on grounds generally applicable to all the members of the class, thereby making final injunctive relief or declaratory relief concerning the class as a whole appropriate; or

(3) the claim or defense is not maintainable under either subdivision (b)(1) or (b)(2), but the questions of law or fact common to the claim or defense of the representative party and the claim or defense of each member of the class predominate over any question of law or fact affecting only individual members of the class, and class representation is superior to other available methods for the fair and efficient adjudication of the controversy. . . .

DISCOVERY: OVERVIEW

Discovery methods (Florida Rules of Civil Procedure, Rule 1.280(a))

Parties may obtain discovery by one or more of the following methods:

Five Kinds of Discovery

- depositions upon oral examination or written questions;

- written interrogatories;

- production of documents or things or permission to enter upon land or other property for inspection and other purposes;

- physical or other kind of examination; and

- requests for admission.

Unless the court orders otherwise and under subdivision (c) of this rule, the frequency of use of these methods is not limited, except as provided in rule 1.200 and rule 1.340.

Scope of discovery (Florida Rules of Civil Procedure, Rule 1.280(b))

What Can Be Obtained through Discovery

Unless otherwise limited by order of the court in accordance with these rules, the scope of discovery is as follows:

(1) In General. Parties may obtain discovery regarding any matter, not privileged, that is relevant to the subject matter of the pending action, whether it relates to the claim or defense of the party seeking discovery or the claim or defense of any other party, including the existence, description, nature, custody, condition, and location of any books, documents, or other tangible things and the identity and location of persons having knowledge of any discoverable matter. It is not ground for objection that the information sought will be inadmissible at the trial if the information sought appears reasonably calculated to lead to the discovery of admissible evidence.

(2) Indemnity Agreements. A party may obtain discovery of the existence and contents of any agreement under which any person may be liable to satisfy part or all of a judgment that may be entered in the action or to indemnify or to reimburse a party for payments made to satisfy the judgment. Information concerning the agreement is not admissible in evidence at trial by reason of disclosure.

Trial preparation: materials (Florida Rules of Civil Procedure, Rule 1.280(b)(3))

The Attorney Work-Product Rule

Subject to the provisions of subdivision (b)(4) of this rule [covering discovery of expert witnesses], a party may obtain discovery of documents and tangible things otherwise discoverable under subdivision (b)(1) of this rule and prepared in anticipation of litigation or for trial by or for another party or by or for that party's representative, including that party's attorney, consultant, surety, indemnitor, insurer, or agent, only upon a showing that the party seeking discovery has need of the materials in the preparation of the case and is unable without undue hardship to obtain the substantial equivalent of the materials by other means. In ordering discovery of the materials when the required showing has been made, the court shall protect against disclosure of the mental impressions, conclusions, opinions, or legal theories of an attorney or other representative of a party concerning the litigation. Without the required showing a party may obtain a copy of a statement concerning the action or its subject matter previously made by that party. . . . For purposes of this paragraph, a statement previously made is a written statement signed or otherwise adopted or approved by the person making it, or a stenographic, mechanical, electrical, or other recording or transcription of it that is a substantially verbatim recital of an oral statement by the person making it and contemporaneously recorded.

Claims of privilege or protection of trial preparation materials (Florida Rules of Civil Procedure, Rule 1.280(b)(5))

How to Protect Privileged Material from Discovery

When a party withholds information otherwise discoverable under these rules by claiming that it is privileged or subject to protection as trial preparation material, the party shall make the claim expressly and shall describe the nature of the documents, communications, or things not produced or disclosed in a manner that, without revealing information itself privileged or protected, will enable other parties to assess the applicability of the privilege or protection.

Protective orders (Florida Rules of Civil Procedure, Rule 1.280(c))

Protection against Annoyance, Embarrassment, Oppression, or Undue Burden or Expense

Upon motion by a party or by the person from whom discovery is sought, and for good cause shown, the court in which the action is pending may make any order to protect a party or person from annoyance, embarrassment, oppression, or undue burden or expense that justice requires, including one or more of the following:

(1) that the discovery not be had;
(2) that the discovery may be had only on specified terms and conditions, including a designation of the time or place;
(3) that the discovery may be had only by a method of discovery other than that selected by the party seeking discovery;
(4) that certain matters not be inquired into, or that the scope of the discovery be limited to certain matters;
(5) that discovery be conducted with no one present except persons designated by the court;
(6) that a deposition after being sealed be opened only by order of the court;
(7) that a trade secret or other confidential research, development, or commercial information not be disclosed or be disclosed only in a designated way; and
(8) that the parties simultaneously file specified documents or information enclosed in sealed envelopes to be opened as directed by the court. . . .

DISCOVERY: DEPOSITIONS

Who can be deposed (Florida Rules of Civil Procedure, Rule 1.310(a))

After commencement of the action any party may take

Deposition upon Oral Examination

the testimony of any person, including a party, by deposition upon oral examination.

Production of materials at the deposition (Florida Rules of Civil Procedure, Rule 1.310(b))

If a subpoena duces tecum is to be served on the person to be examined, the designation of the materials to be produced under the subpoena shall be attached to or included in the notice.

Examination and cross-examination; record of examination; oath; objections (Florida Rules of Civil Procedure, Rule 1.310(c))

Examination and cross-examination of witnesses may proceed as permitted at the trial. The officer before

What Occurs at a Deposition

whom the deposition is to be taken shall put the witness on oath and shall personally, or by someone acting under the officer's direction and in the officer's presence, record the testimony of the witness, except that when a deposition is being taken by telephone, the witness shall be sworn by a person present with the witness who is qualified to administer an oath in that location. The testimony shall be taken stenographically or recorded by any other means ordered. . . . If requested by one of the parties, the testimony shall be transcribed at the initial cost of the requesting party and prompt notice of the request shall be given to all other parties. All objections made at time of the examination to the qualifications of the officer taking the deposition, the manner of taking it, the evidence presented, or the conduct of any party, and any other objection to the proceedings shall be noted by the officer upon the deposition. Any objection during a deposition shall be stated concisely and in a nonargumentative and nonsuggestive manner. A party may instruct a deponent not to answer only when necessary to preserve a privilege, to enforce a limitation on evidence directed by the court, or to present a motion. . . . Otherwise, evidence objected to shall be taken subject to the objections. Instead of participating in the oral examination, parties may serve written questions in a sealed envelope on the party taking the deposition and that party shall transmit them to the officer, who shall propound them to the witness and record the answers verbatim.

DISCOVERY: INTERROGATORIES

Procedure for using interrogatories (Florida Rules of Civil Procedure, Rule 1.340(a))

Without leave of court, any party may serve upon any other party written interrogatories to be answered

Written Interrogatories to Parties

(1) by the party to whom the interrogatories are directed, or
(2) if that party is a public or private corporation or partnership or association or governmental agency, by any officer or agent, who shall furnish the information available to that party.

Interrogatories may be served on the plaintiff after commencement of the action and on any other party with or after service of the process and initial pleading upon that party. The interrogatories shall not exceed 30, including all subparts, unless the court permits a larger number on motion and notice and for good cause. If the supreme court has approved a form of interrogatories for the type of action, the initial interrogatories shall be in the form approved by the court. . . .

Each interrogatory shall be answered separately and fully in writing under oath unless it is objected to, in which event the grounds for objection shall be stated and signed by the attorney making it. The party to whom the interrogatories are directed shall serve the answers and any objections within 30 days after the service of the interrogatories, except that a defendant may serve answers or objections within 45 days after service of the process and initial pleading upon that defendant. The court may allow a shorter or longer time. . . .

Arranging the interrogatories (Florida Rules of Civil Procedure, Rule 1.340(e))

Interrogatories shall be arranged so that a blank space is provided after each separately num-

> Space for Answering Interrogatories

bered interrogatory. The space shall be reasonably sufficient to enable the answering party to insert the answer within the space. If sufficient space is not provided, the answering party may attach additional papers with answers and refer to them in the space provided in the interrogatories.

DISCOVERY: PRODUCTION OF DOCUMENTS AND THINGS; ENTRY UPON LAND

Request; scope (Florida Rules of Civil Procedure, Rule 1.350(a))

Any party may request any other party (1) to produce and permit the party making the request, or some-

> Scope of Production

one acting in the requesting party's behalf, to inspect and copy any designated documents, including writings, drawings, graphs, charts, photographs, phono-records, and other data compilations from which information can be obtained, translated, if necessary, by the party to whom the request is directed through detection devices into reasonably usable form, that constitute or contain matters within the scope of rule 1.280(b) and that are in the possession, custody, or control of the party to whom the request is directed; (2) to inspect and copy, test, or sample any tangible things that constitute or contain matters within the scope of rule 1.280(b) and that are in the possession, custody, or control of the party to whom the request is directed; or (3) to permit entry upon designated land or other property in the possession or control of the party upon whom the request is served for the purpose of inspection and measuring, surveying, photographing, testing, or sampling the property or any designated object or operation on it within the scope of rule 1.280(b).

Request; scope (Florida Rules of Civil Procedure, Rule 1.350(b))

The request [for production] shall set forth the items to be inspected,

> Procedures for Obtaining Production

either by individual item or category, and describe each item and category with reasonable particularity. The request shall specify a reasonable time, place, and manner of making the inspection or performing the related acts. The party to whom the request is directed shall serve a written response. . . . For each item or category the response shall state that inspection and related activities will be permitted as requested unless the request is objected to, in which event the reasons for the objection shall be stated. If an objection is made to part of an item or category, the part shall be specified. When producing documents, the producing party shall either produce them as they are kept in the usual course of business or shall identify them to correspond with the categories in the request. . . .

DISCOVERY: PHYSICAL OR OTHER KIND OF EXAMINATION

Request; scope (Florida Rules of Civil Procedure, Rule 1.360(a))

(1) A party may request any other party to submit to, or to produce a person in that other party's custody or legal control for, ex-

> Good Cause to Obtain a Physical or Other Kind of Examination of a Party

amination by a qualified expert when the condition that is the subject of the requested examination is in controversy.

    (A) . . . The request shall specify a reasonable time, place, manner, conditions, and scope of the examination and the person or persons by whom the examination is to be made. . . . The response shall state that the examination will be permitted as requested unless the request is objected to, in which event the reasons for the objection shall be stated.

    (B) In cases where the condition in controversy is not physical, a party may move for an examination by a qualified expert as in subdivision (a)(1). The order for examination shall be made only after notice to the person to be examined and to all parties, and shall specify the time, place, manner, conditions, and scope of the examination and the person or persons by whom it is to be made.

(2) An examination under this rule is authorized only when the party submitting the request has good cause for the examination. At any hearing the party submitting the request shall have the burden of showing good cause.

DISCOVERY: REQUESTS FOR ADMISSIONS

Request for admission (Florida Rules of Civil Procedure, Rule 1.370(a))

A party may serve upon any other party a written request for the admission of the truth of any matters

| What a Party Can Be Requested to Admit |

within the scope of rule 1.280(b) set forth in the request that relate to statements or opinions of fact or of the application of law to fact, including the genuineness of any documents described in the request. Copies of documents shall be served with the request unless they have been or are otherwise furnished or made available for inspection and copying. . . . The request for admission shall not exceed 30 requests, including all subparts, unless the court permits a larger number on motion and notice and for good cause, or the parties propounding and responding to the requests stipulate to a larger number. Each matter of which an admission is requested shall be separately set forth.

Response (Florida Rules of Civil Procedure, Rule 1.370(a))

| Responding to a Request for Admission |

The matter is admitted unless the party to whom the request is directed serves upon the party requesting the admission a written answer or objection addressed to the matter. . . . If objection is made, the reasons shall be stated. The answer shall specifically deny the matter or set forth in detail the reasons why the answering party cannot truthfully admit or deny the matter. A denial shall fairly meet the substance of the requested admission, and when good faith requires that a party qualify an answer or deny only a part of the matter of which an admission is requested, the party shall specify so much of it as is true and qualify or deny the remainder. An answering party may not give lack of information or knowledge as a reason for failure to admit or deny unless that party states that that party has made reasonable inquiry and that the information known or readily obtainable by that party is insufficient to enable that party to admit or deny. A party who considers that a matter of which an admission has been requested presents a genuine issue for trial may not object to the request on that ground alone; the party may deny the matter or set forth reasons why the party cannot admit or deny it, . . .

DISCOVERY: SANCTIONS

Motion (Florida Rules of Civil Procedure, Rule 1.380(a)(2))

If a deponent fails to answer a question propounded or submitted under rule 1.310 or 1.320, or a corporation or other entity fails to make a designation under rule 1.310(b)(6) or 1.320(a), or

| Seeking an Order Compelling Discovery |

a party fails to answer an interrogatory submitted under rule 1.340, or if a party in response to a request for inspection submitted under rule 1.350 fails to respond that inspection will be permitted as requested or fails to permit inspection as requested, or if a party in response to a request for examination of a person submitted under rule 1.360(a) objects to the examination, fails to respond that the examination will be permitted as requested, or fails to submit to or to produce a person in that party's custody or legal control for examination, the discovering party may move for an order compelling an answer, or a designation or an order compelling inspection, or an order compelling an examination in accordance with the request. The motion must include a certification that the movant, in good faith, has conferred or attempted to confer with the person or party failing to make the discovery in an effort to secure the information or material without court action. . . . [For purposes of this subdivision an evasive or incomplete answer shall be treated as a failure to answer. 1.380(a)(3)]

Award of expenses and fees (Florida Rules of Civil Procedure, Rule 1.380(a)(4))

If the motion is granted and after opportunity for hearing, the court shall require the party or deponent whose conduct necessitated the motion or the party or counsel advising

| Expenses and Attorney Fees for the Motion to Compel Discovery |

the conduct to pay to the moving party the reasonable expenses incurred in obtaining the order that may include attorneys' fees, unless the court finds that the movant failed to certify in the motion that a good faith effort was made to obtain the discovery without court action, that the opposition to the motion was justified, or that other circumstances make an award of expenses unjust. If the motion is denied and after opportunity for hearing, the court shall require the moving party to pay to the party or deponent who opposed the motion the reasonable expenses incurred in opposing the motion that may include attorneys' fees, unless the court finds that the making of the motion was substantially justified or that other circumstances make an award of expenses unjust.

LAWYER-CLIENT PRIVILEGE

Lawyer-Client Privilege (Florida Statutes, § 90.502)

(1) For purposes of this section:
  (a) A "lawyer" is a person authorized, or reasonably believed by the client to be authorized, to practice law in any state or nation.
  (b) A "client" is any person, public officer, corporation, association, or other organization or

| Confidential Communications between Lawyer and Client |

entity, either public or private, who consults a lawyer with the purpose of obtaining legal services or who is rendered legal services by a lawyer.

(c) A communication between lawyer and client is "confidential" if it is not intended to be disclosed to third persons other than:

1. Those to whom disclosure is in furtherance of the rendition of legal services to the client.
2. Those reasonably necessary for the transmission of the communication.

(2) A client has a privilege to refuse to disclose, and to prevent any other person from disclosing, the contents of confidential communications when such other person learned of the communications because they were made in the rendition of legal services to the client.

(3) The privilege may be claimed by:
(a) The client.
(b) A guardian or conservator of the client.
(c) The personal representative of a deceased client.
(d) A successor, assignee, trustee in dissolution, or any similar representative of an organization, corporation, or association or other entity, either public or private, whether or not in existence.
(e) The lawyer, but only on behalf of the client. The lawyer's authority to claim the privilege is presumed in the absence of contrary evidence.

(4) There is no lawyer-client privilege under this section when:
(a) The services of the lawyer were sought or obtained to enable or aid anyone to commit or plan to commit what the client knew was a crime or fraud.
(b) A communication is relevant to an issue between parties who claim through the same deceased client.
(c) A communication is relevant to an issue of breach of duty by the lawyer to the client or by the client to the lawyer, arising from the lawyer-client relationship.
(d) A communication is relevant to an issue concerning the intention or competence of a client executing an attested document to which the lawyer is an attesting witness, or concerning the execution or attestation of the document.
(e) A communication is relevant to a matter of common interest between two or more clients, or their successors in interest, if the communication was made by any of them to a lawyer retained or consulted in common when offered in a civil action between the clients or their successors in interest.

(5) Communications made by a person who seeks or receives services from the Department of Revenue under the child support enforcement program to the attorney representing the department shall be confidential and privileged as provided for in this section. Such communications shall not be disclosed to anyone other than the agency except as provided for in this section. Such disclosures shall be protected as if there were an attorney-client relationship between the attorney for the agency and the person who seeks services from the department. . . .

C. More Information

Florida Civil Procedure and Practice
www.megalaw.com/fl/top/flcivpro.php

Florida Rules of Civil Procedure
www.floridabar.org
(click "Professional Practice" then "Rules of Procedure")
www.phonl.com/fl_law/rules/frcp

Florida Statutes
www.leg.state.fl.us/Statutes/index.cfm

Constitution of the State of Florida
www.leg.state.fl.us
(click "Florida Constitution")

Florida State Trial and Appellate Courts
www.flcourts.org

Handbook on Florida Discovery Practice
www.flatls.org/Handbook/Handbook.pdf

Overview of Civil Litigation in Florida
www.floridabar.org/DIVCOM/PI/RHandbook01.nsf/Form+List?OpenForm
(click "Reporter's Guide to a Civil Lawsuit")
www.clerk.leon.fl.us
(click "Frequently Asked Questions")
www.weblocator.com/attorney/fl/law/processcon.html
www.delmarlearning.com/companions/content/140184829X/state/FL/kerley_FL_v5.pdf

Serving Process
www.serve-now.com/resources/process-serving-laws/Florida

D. Something to Check

1. Go to a web site that contains the Florida Rules of Civil Procedure (see More Information above). Do a search for any three topics covered in the rules excerpted here in section 6.2. Look for additional statutes on these topics. Summarize what you find.

2. Go to a web site that contains Florida Statutes (see More Information above). Go to title VII, chapter 90 on evidence. What is the statutory definition of hearsay? Summarize any two exceptions to the hearsay rule.

6.3 State and Federal Civil Litigation in Florida: Some Comparisons

A. Introduction

B. Comparisons

C. More Information

D. Something to Check

A. Introduction

In this section, we will briefly outline some comparisons between litigating civil cases in Florida courts and in the federal courts. See also the following related sections:

- Section 4.2, state court subject-matter jurisdiction
- Section 4.3, federal court subject-matter jurisdiction
- Section 6.1, timeline: a civil case in Florida state courts
- Section 6.2, selected litigation rules in Florida state courts
- Section 7.1, example of a civil complaint filed in state court
- Section 7.2, example of a civil complaint filed in federal court
- Section 7.4, example of an appellate brief filed in state court
- Section 6.4, timeline: a criminal case in Florida state courts

Abbreviations

Fla.R.Civ.P.: Florida Rules of Civil Procedure

F.R.Civ.P.: Federal Rules of Civil Procedure

F.S.: Florida Statutes

USC: United States Code

B. COMPARISONS

Comparisons between state and federal civil litigation are presented in Exhibit 6.3A.

EXHIBIT 6.3A	State and Federal Civil Litigation: Some Points of Comparison

State Litigation	Federal Litigation
Major Courts • Florida Supreme Court • Florida District Courts of Appeal • Circuit Courts • County Courts	Major Courts • Supreme Court of the United States • United States Courts of Appeals • United States District Courts • United States Immigration Courts • United States Court of International Trade • United States Court of Federal Claims • United States Court of Appeals for the Armed Services
	• United States Tax Court • United States Court of Appeals for Veterans Claims • Judicial Panel on Multidistrict Litigation
Subject-Matter Jurisdiction of Main Trial Court • Circuit Courts (a court of general jurisdiction) • civil disputes involving more than $15,000; • disputes involving the estates of decedents, minors, and persons adjudicated as incapacitated • cases relating to juveniles • all felony cases • tax disputes • property boundary and title disputes • suits for declaratory judgments • requests for injunctions (F.S. § 26.012) • County Court (a court of limited jurisdiction) • civil disputes involving $15,000 or less • small claims (up to $5,000) • traffic offenses • less serious criminal matters (misdemeanors) (F.S. § 34.01)	*Subject-Matter Jurisdiction of Main Trial Court* • United States District Court (a court of general jurisdiction) • federal questions • diversity cases (over $75,000) (28 USC §§ 1331; 1332; 1345; 1346)
Venue Examples: • county where defendant resides • county where the cause of action accrued • county where the property in litigation is located • county where domestic corporation keeps office to conduct customary business (F.S. §§ 47.011, 47.051)	*Venue* Examples: • district where a substantial part of the events or omissions giving rise to the claim occurred or where the property in dispute is located • any district if the defendant is an alien (28 USC § 1391)
Forum non conveniens For the convenience of the parties or in the interest of justice, any court of record may transfer any civil action to any other court of record in which it might have been brought. (F.S. § 47.122)	*Forum non conveniens* For the convenience of parties and witnesses, in the interest of justice, a district court may transfer any civil action to any other district or division where it might have been brought. (28 USC § 1404(a))
Joinder of Parties • Permissive (Fla.R.Civ.P. 1.210) • Compulsory (An indispensable party is one whose interest in the controversy makes it impossible to completely adjudicate the matter without affecting either that party's interest or the interests of another party in the action. *Florida Dept. of Revenue v. Cummings,* 930 So. 2d 604 (Fla. 2006)	*Joinder of Parties* • Permissive (F.R.Civ.P. 20) • Compulsory (F.R.Civ.P. 19)
Pleadings Allowed There shall be • a complaint or, when so designated by a statute or rule, a petition, and an answer to it; • an answer to a counterclaim denominated as such; • an answer to a crossclaim if the answer contains a crossclaim; • a third-party complaint if a person who was not an original party is summoned as a third-party defendant; and • a third party answer if a third-party complaint is served. • If an answer or third-party answer contains an affirmative defense and the opposing party seeks to avoid it, the opposing party shall file a reply containing the avoidance. No other pleadings shall be allowed. (Fla.R.Civ.P. 1.100(a))	*Pleadings Allowed* Only these pleadings are allowed: (1) a complaint; (2) an answer to a complaint; (3) an answer to a counterclaim designated as a counterclaim; (4) an answer to a crossclaim; (5) a third-party complaint; (6) an answer to a third-party complaint; and (7) if the court orders one, a reply to an answer. (F.R.Civ.P. 7(a))

State Litigation	Federal Litigation
Complaint A pleading which sets forth a claim for relief must state a cause of action and shall contain: (1) a short and plain statement of the grounds upon which the court's jurisdiction depends, (2) a short and plain statement of the ultimate facts showing that the pleader is entitled to relief, and (3) a demand for judgment for relief to which the pleader deems himself or herself entitled. Relief in the alternative or of several different types may be demanded. (Fla.R.Civ.P. 1.110(b).) Forms of action and technical forms for seeking relief of pleas, pleadings, or motions are abolished. (Fla.R.Civ.P. 1.110(a).)	*Complaint* Notice Pleading. Claim for Relief. A pleading that states a claim for relief must contain: (1) a short and plain statement of the grounds for the court's jurisdiction, unless the court already has jurisdiction and the claim needs no new jurisdictional support; (2) a short and plain statement of the claim showing that the pleader is entitled to relief; and (3) a demand for the relief sought, which may include relief in the alternative or different types of relief. (F.R.Civ.P. (8)(a).)
Special Damages When items of special damages are claimed, they shall be specifically stated. (Fla.R.Civ.P. 1.120(g).)	*Special Damages* If an item of special damage is claimed, it must be specifically stated. (F.R.Civ.P. 9(g).)
Caption Every pleading, motion, order, judgment, or other paper shall have a caption containing the name of the court, the file number, the name of the first party on each side with an appropriate indication of other parties, and a designation identifying the party filing it and its nature or the nature of the order, as the case may be. All papers filed in the action shall be styled in such a manner as to indicate clearly the subject matter of the paper and the party requesting or obtaining relief. (Fla.R.Civ.P. 1.100(c)(1).)	*Caption* Every pleading must have a caption with the court's name, a title, a file number, and a Rule 7(a) designation. The title of the complaint must name all the parties; the title of other pleadings, after naming the first party on each side, may refer generally to other parties. (F.R.Civ.P. 10(a).)
Time Limit for Service If service of the initial process and initial pleading is not made upon a defendant within 120 days after filing of the initial pleading directed to that defendant the court, on its own initiative after notice or on motion, shall direct that service be effected within a specified time or shall dismiss the action without prejudice or drop that defendant as a party; provided that if the plaintiff shows good cause or excusable neglect for the failure, the courts shall extend the time for service for an appropriate period. (Fla.R.Civ.P. 1.070(j).)	*Time Limit for Service* If a defendant is not served within 120 days after the complaint is filed, the court—on motion or on its own after notice to the plaintiff—must dismiss the action without prejudice against that defendant or order that service be made within a specified time. But if the plaintiff shows good cause for the failure, the court must extend the time for service for an appropriate period. (F.R.Civ.P. 4(m).)
Motion for More Definite Statement If a pleading to which a responsive pleading is permitted is so vague or ambiguous that a party cannot reasonably be required to frame a responsive pleading, that party may move for a more definite statement before interposing a responsive pleading. The motion shall point out the defects complained of and of the details desired. If the motion is granted and the order of the court is not obeyed within 10 days after notice of the order or such other time as the court may fix, the court may strike the pleading to which the motion was directed or make such order as it deems just. (Fla.R.Civ.P. 1.140(e).)	*Motion for More Definite Statement* A party may move for a more definite statement of a pleading to which a responsive pleading is allowed but which is so vague or ambiguous that the party cannot reasonably prepare a response. The motion must be made before filing a responsive pleading and must point out the defects complained of and the details desired. If the court orders a more definite statement and the order is not obeyed within 10 days after notice of the order or within the time the court sets, the court may strike the pleading or issue any other appropriate order. (F.R.Civ.P. 12(e).)
Answer In the answer a pleader shall state in short and plain terms the pleader's defenses to each claim asserted and shall admit or deny the averments on which the adverse party relies. If the defendant is	*Answer* • In General. In responding to a pleading, a party must: (A) state in short and plain terms its defenses to each claim asserted against it; and

State Litigation	Federal Litigation
without knowledge, the defendant shall so state and such statement shall operate as a denial. (Fla.R.Civ.P. 1.110(c).) Forms of action and technical forms for seeking relief of pleas, pleadings, or motions are abolished. (Fla.R.Civ.P. 1.110(a).)	(B) admit or deny the allegations asserted against it by an opposing party. (F.R.Civ.P. (8)(b)(1).) • Denials—Responding to the Substance. A denial must fairly respond to the substance of the allegation. • General and Specific Denials. A party that intends in good faith to deny all the allegations of a pleading—including the jurisdictional grounds—may do so by a general denial. A party that does not intend to deny all the allegations must either specifically deny designated allegations or generally deny all except those specifically admitted. (F.R.Civ.P. (8)(b)(2).)
Time Limit for Answer A defendant shall serve an answer within 20 days after service of original process and the initial pleading on the defendant, or not later than the date fixed in a notice by publication. (Fla.R.Civ.P. 1.140(a)(1).)	*Time Limit For Answer* Unless another time is specified by this rule or a federal statute, the time for serving a responsive pleading is as follows: (A) A defendant must serve an answer: (i) within 20 days after being served with the summons and complaint. (F.R.Civ.P. 12(a)(1).)
Amendments to Pleadings A party may amend a pleading once as a matter of course at any time before a responsive pleading is served, or if the pleading is one to which no responsive pleading is permitted and the action has not been placed on the trial calendar, may so amend it at any time within 20 days after it is served. Otherwise a party may amend a pleading only by leave of court or by written consent of the adverse party. If a party files a motion to amend a pleading, the party shall attach the proposed amended pleading to the motion. Leave of court shall be given freely when justice so requires. A party shall plead in response to an amended pleading within 10 days after service of the amended pleading unless the court otherwise orders. (Fla.R.Civ.P. 1.190(a).)	*Amendments to Pleadings* (1) Amending as a Matter of Course. A party may amend its pleading once as a matter of course: (A) before being served with a responsive pleading; or (B) within 20 days after serving the pleading if a responsive pleading is not allowed and the action is not yet on the trial calendar. (2) Other Amendments. In all other cases, a party may amend its pleading only with the opposing party's written consent or the court's leave. The court should freely give leave when justice so requires. (F.R.Civ.P. 15(a).)
What is Discoverable: Scope of Discovery Parties may obtain discovery regarding any matter, not privileged, that is relevant to the subject matter of the pending action, whether it relates to the claim or defense of the party seeking discovery or the claim or defense of any other party, including the existence, description, nature, custody, condition, and location of any books, documents, or other tangible things and the identity and location of persons having knowledge of any discoverable matter. It is not ground for objection that the information sought will be inadmissible at the trial if the information sought appears reasonably calculated to lead to the discovery of admissible evidence. (Fla.R.Civ.P. 1.280(b)(1).)	*What is Discoverable: Scope of Discovery* Parties may obtain discovery regarding any nonprivileged matter that is relevant to any party's claim or defense—including the existence, description, nature, custody, condition, and location of any documents or other tangible things and the identity and location of persons who know of any discoverable matter. For good cause, the court may order discovery of any matter relevant to the subject matter involved in the action. Relevant information need not be admissible at the trial if the discovery appears reasonably calculated to lead to the discovery of admissible evidence. (F.R.Civ.P. Rule 26(b)(1).)
Attorney Work-Product Rule A party may obtain discovery of documents and tangible things otherwise discoverable under Rule 1.280(b)(1) of the Florida Rules of Civil Procedure and prepared in anticipation of litigation or for trial by or for another party or by or for that party's representative, including that party's attorney, consultant, surety, indemnitor, insurer, or agent, only upon a showing that the party seeking discovery has need of the materials in the preparation of the case and is unable	*Attorney Work-Product Rule* • Documents and Tangible Things. Ordinarily, a party may not discover documents and tangible things that are prepared in anticipation of litigation or for trial by or for another party or its representative (including the other party's attorney, consultant, surety, indemnitor, insurer, or agent). But, subject to Rule 26(b)(4), those materials may be discovered if: (i) they are otherwise discoverable under Rule 26(b)(1); and

State Litigation	Federal Litigation
without undue hardship to obtain the substantial equivalent of the materials by other means. In ordering discovery of the materials when the required showing has been made, the court shall protect against disclosure of the mental impressions, conclusions, opinions, or legal theories of an attorney or other representative of a party concerning the litigation. (Fla.R.Civ.P. 1.280(b)(3).)	(ii) the party shows that it has substantial need for the materials to prepare its case and cannot, without undue hardship, obtain their substantial equivalent by other means. (F.R.Civ.P. 26(b)(3)(A).) • Protection Against Disclosure. If the court orders discovery of those materials, it must protect against disclosure of the mental impressions, conclusions, opinions, or legal theories of a party's attorney or other representative concerning the litigation. (F.R.Civ.P. 26(b)(3)(B).)
Lawyer-Client Privilege A communication between lawyer and client is "confidential" if it is not intended to be disclosed to third persons other than: 1. Those to whom disclosure is in furtherance of the rendition of legal services to the client. and 2. Those reasonably necessary for the transmission of the communication. (F.S. § 90.502(1)(c).) Exceptions to the attorney-client privilege (e.g., the services of the lawyer were sought to enable or aid anyone to commit what the client knew was a crime or fraud) can be found at F.S. § 90.502(4).	*Lawyer-Client Privilege* The attorney-client privilege, "the oldest of the privileges for confidential communications known to the common law," protects the disclosures that a client makes to his attorney, in confidence, for the purpose of securing legal advice or assistance. Based on the theory that "sound legal advice or advocacy . . . depends upon the lawyer's being fully informed by the client," the privilege is designed "to encourage full and frank communication between attorneys and their clients and thereby promote broader public interests in the observance of law and administration of justice." *Cox v. Administrator U.S. Steel & Carnegie*, 17 F.3d 1386, 1414 (11th Cir. 1994).
Methods of Discovery • Interrogatories (Fla.R.Civ.P. 1.340) • Depositions upon oral examination or written questions (Fla.R.Civ.P. 1.310 and 1.320) • Requests for admission (Fla.R.Civ.P. 1.370) • Production of documents or things or permission to enter upon land or other property for inspection and other purposes (Fla.R.Civ.P. 1.350) • Examination of persons (physical or other kind of examination) (Fla.R.Civ.P. 1.360)	*Methods of Discovery* • Interrogatories (F.R.Civ.P. 33) • Deposition by oral examination (F.R.Civ.P. 30) • Deposition by written questions (F.R.Civ.P. 31) • Requests for admissions (F.R.Civ. P. 36) • Production of documents, electronically stored information, and tangible things, or entry on land for inspection and other purposes (F.R.Civ.P. 34) • Physical or mental examination (F.R.Civ.P. 35)
Default Judgment When a party against whom affirmative relief is sought has failed to file or serve any paper in the action, the party seeking the relief may request the clerk to enter a default against that party. Final judgments after default may be entered by the court at any time after the default. If it is necessary to take an account or to determine the amount of damages or to establish the truth of any averment by evidence or to make an investigation of any other matter to enable the court to enter judgment or to effectuate it, the court may receive affidavits, make references, or conduct hearings as it deems necessary and shall accord a right of trial by jury to the parties when required by the Constitution or any statute. (Fla.R.Civ.P. 1.500.)	*Default Judgment* (a) Entering a Default. When a party against whom a judgment for affirmative relief is sought has failed to plead or otherwise defend, and that failure is shown by affidavit or otherwise, the clerk must enter the party's default. (F.R.Civ. P. 55(a).) • Entering a Default Judgment. (1) By the Clerk. If the plaintiff's claim is for a sum certain or a sum that can be made certain by computation, the clerk—on the plaintiff's request, with an affidavit showing the amount due—must enter judgment for that amount and costs against a defendant who has been defaulted for not appearing and who is neither a minor nor an incompetent person. (2) By the Court. In all other cases, the party must apply to the court for a default judgment. . . . The court may conduct hearings or make referrals—preserving any federal statutory right to a jury

State Litigation	Federal Litigation
	trial—when, to enter or effectuate judgment, it needs to: (A) conduct an accounting; (B) determine the amount of damages; (C) establish the truth of any allegation by evidence; or (D) investigate any other matter. (F.R.Civ.P. 55(b))
Summary Judgment A party seeking to recover upon a claim, counterclaim, crossclaim, or third-party claim or to obtain a declaratory judgment may move for a summary judgment in that party's favor upon all or any part thereof with or without supporting affidavits at any time after the expiration of 20 days from the commencement of the action or after service of a motion for summary judgment by the adverse party. (Fla.R.Civ.P. 1.510(a).) A party against whom a claim, counterclaim, crossclaim, or third-party claim is asserted or a declaratory judgment is sought may move for a summary judgment in that party's favor as to all or any part thereof at any time with or without supporting affidavits. (Fla.R.Civ.P. 1.510(b).) The motion shall state with particularity the grounds upon which it is based and the substantial matters of law to be argued and shall specifically identify any affidavits, answers to interrogatories, admissions, depositions, and other materials as would be admissible in evidence ("summary judgment evidence") on which the movant relies. (Fla.R.Civ.P. 1.510(c).) The judgment sought shall be rendered forthwith if the pleadings, depositions, answers to interrogatories, admissions, affidavits, and other materials as would be admissible in evidence on file show that there is no genuine issue as to any material fact and that the moving party is entitled to a judgment as a matter of law. A summary judgment, interlocutory in character, may be rendered on the issue of liability alone although there is a genuine issue as to the amount of damages. (Fla.R.Civ.P. 1.510(c).)	*Summary Judgment* • A party claiming relief may move, with or without supporting affidavits, for summary judgment on all or part of the claim. The motion may be filed at any time after: (1) 20 days have passed from commencement of the action; or (2) the opposing party serves a motion for summary judgment. (F.R.Civ.P. 56(a).) • A party against whom relief is sought may move at any time, with or without supporting affidavits, for summary judgment on all or part of the claim. (F.R.Civ.P. 56(b).) • The motion must be served at least 10 days before the day set for the hearing. An opposing party may serve opposing affidavits before the hearing day. The judgment sought should be rendered if the pleadings, the discovery and disclosure materials on file, and any affidavits show that there is no genuine issue as to any material fact and that the movant is entitled to judgment as a matter of law. (F.R.Civ.P. 56(c).)
Pretrial Planning Procedures • Case management conference (Fla.R.Civ.P. 1.200(a)) • Pretrial conference (Fla.R.Civ.P. 1.200(b))	*Pretrial Planning Procedures* • Pretrial conferences (F.R.Civ.P. 16(a-c)) • Final pretrial conferences (F.R.Civ.P. 16(d))
Alternate Dispute Resolution • The presiding judge may enter an order referring all or any part of a contested civil matter to mediation or arbitration. The parties to any contested civil matter may file a written stipulation to mediate or arbitrate any issue between them at any time. Such stipulation shall be incorporated into the order of referral. (Fla.R.Civ.P. 1.700(a).) • For definitions of arbitration and mediation, see F.S. §§ 44.1011(1) and (2).	*Alternate Dispute Resolution* An alternative dispute resolution process includes any process or procedure, other than an adjudication by a presiding judge, in which a neutral third party participates to assist in the resolution of issues in controversy, through processes such as early neutral evaluation, mediation, minitrial, and arbitration. Each United States district court shall authorize, by local rule, the use of alternative dispute resolution processes in all civil actions. Each United States district court shall devise and implement its own alternative dispute resolution program to encourage and promote the use of alternative dispute resolution in its district. (28 USC § 651.)

C. More Information

Florida Rules of Civil Procedure

www.floridalawonline.net/courts.html#courtrules

www.floridabar.org

(click "Professional Practice" then "Rules of Procedure")

Florida Rules (more)

www.floridasupremecourt.org

(click "Court Decisions & Rules)

www.floridalawonline.net/courts.html#courtrules

www.llrx.com/courtrules-gen/state-Florida.html

Federal Rules of Civil Procedure

www.law.cornell.edu/rules/frcp/?

Federal Courts Overview

www.uscourts.gov/journalistguide/welcome.html

Understanding the Federal Courts

www.uscourts.gov/understand03

Inside the Federal Courts

www.fjc.gov/federal/courts.nsf

Juror Handbook in Federal Court

www.txnd.uscourts.gov/pdf/jurybook.pdf

www.dcd.uscourts.gov/Handbook-for-Trial-Jurors.pdf

Alternative Dispute Resolution (ADR)

www.flcourts.org/gen_public/adr/index.shtml

Handbook on Discovery Practice (state)

www.flatls.org/Handbook/Handbook.pdf

Handbook on Civil Discovery Practice (federal)

*www.flmd.uscourts.gov/Forms/Civil/Discovery_Practice_*
   Manual.pdf

D. Something to Check

Using the online sites that give the text of state and federal statutes (see More Information above), compare the state and federal rules on:

1. Interrogatories
2. Sanctions for failure to comply with discovery requests

6.4 Timeline: Criminal Case in the Florida State Courts

A. Introduction

B. Overview of a Criminal Case

C. More Information

D. Something to Check

A. Introduction

In this section, we will focus on the major procedural steps involved in prosecuting serious criminal cases in Florida state courts. In a recent 12-month period, over 200,000 defendants were charged with crimes in the circuit courts of Florida (*trialstats.flcourts.org/TrialCourtStats. aspx*). Such cases can vary a great deal in complexity depending on the nature of the charge, the extent of contention between the state and the accused, and the caliber of attorneys representing both sides. With this qualification in mind, the overview presented here will apply to many serious criminal cases brought in Florida state courts. See also the following related sections:

- Overview of Florida state courts (section 4.2)
- Example of a criminal complaint (section 7.5)
- Rules for, and example of, an appellate brief (section 7.4)
- Legal research in state law (section 5.1)
- Overview of federal courts sitting in Florida (section 4.3)

B. Overview of a Criminal Case

Exhibit 6.4A presents an overview of a typical criminal case in the Florida state courts.

Offense Alleged

Section 775.08 of Florida Statutes provides three major classes of offenses that can be committed in Florida, although only two of the classes constitute a crime: felonies and misdemeanors. The third class of offenses, which does not constitute a crime, is called a noncriminal violation.

Felony. A crime punishable by death or imprisonment in a state penitentiary for a term exceeding one year. Examples include capital murder, robbery, burglary, and most drug offenses. For sentencing purposes, felonies are classified as: (1) capital felony, (2) life felony, (3) first degree felony, (4) second degree felony, and (5) third degree felony. (Florida Statutes § 775.081(1).)

Misdemeanor. A crime punishable by imprisonment in a county correctional facility for a term not exceeding one year. For sentencing purposes, misdemeanors are classified as: (1) first degree misdemeanor and (2) second degree misdemeanor. (Florida Statutes § 775.081(2).)

Noncriminal violation. An offense punishable by a fine, forfeiture, or other civil penalty. (Florida Statutes § 775.081(3).)

Commencement of Case

"If you have been the victim of a crime or believe that a crime has been committed, you should first contact a law enforcement agency that has jurisdiction in the city or county where the physical acts of the crime occurred." (*www.co.leon.fl.us/statty/Initiating_a_Case.htm*)

EXHIBIT 6.4A	The Prosecution of a Criminal Case in Florida State Courts						
OFFENSE ALLEGED	COMMENCEMENT OF CASE	PRELIMINARY PROCEEDINGS	ARRAIGNMENT AND PLEAS	MOTIONS AND DISCOVERY	TRIAL	POST-TRIAL MOTIONS; SENTENCING	POST-CONVICTION RELIEF AND APPEAL
• Felony • Misdemeanor • Noncriminal violation	• Complaint filed with law enforcement official or with the state attorney • Investigation • Arrest with warrant • Arrest without warrant • Notice to appear	• First appearance • Pretrial release • Bond hearing • Decision to charge • Information filed • Grand jury indictment filed	• Arraignment • Entering a plea • Plea bargaining • Right to a speedy trial	• Pretrial motions • Notice of discovery • Prosecutor's discovery obligation • Disclosure to prosecution • Defendant's discovery obligation • Pretrial conferences	• Bench trial • Jury selection • Opening statements • State's case • Defense's case • Closing arguments • Motion for judgment of acquittal • Jury instructions • Jury deliberations • Verdict	• Motion for new trial • Motion for arrest of judgment • Rendition of judgment • Presentence report • Allocution • Sentencing	• Post-conviction motions • Appeal

Complaint. In many cases, the case commences when a victim of an alleged crime or a person believing that a crime has been committed files a written complaint with law enforcement officials or with the state attorney's office.

Investigation. Once a complaint has been filed, law enforcement officials and/or the state attorney's office may investigate reported crimes by interviewing the victim, witnesses, and suspects in order to determine whether "probable cause" exists that a crime has been committed. An investigation does not always lead to an arrest. "If the perpetrator cannot be readily located within their jurisdiction [the police department or sheriff's office] may apply to a judge to have an arrest warrant issued and sent to the area where the offender is located or entered into law enforcement computer databases nationwide." (*www.co.leon.fl.us/statty/Initiating_a_Case.htm*)

Arrest with a warrant. A judge or other designated court official can issue a warrant that directs a police officer to arrest a person if satisfied that the latter violated the criminal laws of Florida. Once arrested, the person will be transported to a jail facility for the booking process.

Arrest without a warrant. A police officer can arrest a person without a warrant: (1) if the officer has probable cause to believe that the person has committed a felony, (2) if the person has committed a misdemeanor in the presence of the officer, or (3) if the officer has reasonable cause to believe that the person has committed certain misdemeanors such as shoplifting or domestic violence. Once arrested, the arrested person will be transported to a jail facility for the booking process.

Notice to appear. Instead of arresting an accused person, a law enforcement official may issue a written order (Notice to Appear) that requires the accused person to appear before a judicial officer at a specific date and time. If the police (or other law enforcement) officer

arrests the accused as opposed to issuing a Notice to Appear and the booking officer subsequently determines that the accused will appear as directed, the booking officer has the authority to release the person and issue a Notice to Appear.

Preliminary Proceedings

First appearance. Persons arrested in Florida must be taken before a judicial officer within 24 hours of arrest. At this first appearance, the judicial officer determines if there was probable cause to make the arrest, informs the defendants of the charge, and provides them with a copy of the complaint. This officer also advises them that: (1) they are not required to say anything, (2) anything they say may be used against them, (3) they have a right to legal representation and that counsel will be appointed (usually a public defender) if they cannot afford private counsel, and (4) they have the right to communicate with counsel, family, or friends. (Florida Rules of Criminal Procedure, Rule 3.130.)

Pretrial release. Persons charged with a crime are entitled to pretrial release on reasonable conditions unless the charge is a capital offense or an offense punishable by life imprisonment and "the proof of guilt is evident or the presumption is great." (Florida Rules of Criminal Procedure, Rule 3.131.) If eligible for pretrial release, the judge will review a defendant's background, criminal history, and other factors. The judge has the discretion to release defendants on their own recognizance (promise to appear), on a cash or surety bond, on monitored release, or to the custody of another. The terms *bail* or *bond* include "any or all forms of pretrial release." (Florida Statutes § 903.011.)

Bond hearing. When a judge decides that defendants can be released with a cash or surety bond condition, the amount of the bond/bail must be set. In some misdemeanor cases, however, a preset amount of bail can be paid by the accused at the police station without a court hearing. The forms of bail are (1) secured bail bond in which nonappearance results in forfeiture of a surety bond, which the accused often buys from a bail bondsman; (2) unsecured bail bond in which nonappearance results in forfeiture of property not covered by security; and (3) 10 percent bond in which nonappearance results in forfeiture of the minimum amount the accused was allowed to deposit in court, which is 10 percent of the full bond. At any later time, defendants may request a hearing to consider reducing the amount of bail.

Decision to charge. It is the responsibility of the state attorney's office to make the decision on whether to bring formal charges. In making this determination, the state attorney will review police reports and statements made by witnesses and victims. Formal charges must be filed on defendants in custody within 30 days from the date of arrest or from the date of the service of capias upon them. (Capias is a writ commanding that someone be taken into custody.) If formal charges are not brought within this time period, the court shall order that the defendants automatically be released on their own recognizance on the 33rd day unless the state files formal charges by that date, or, if the state shows good cause, order that the defendants automatically be released on their own recognizance on the 40th day unless the state files formal charges by that date. (Florida Rules of Criminal Procedure, Rule 3.134.) Formal charges are filed by either an information or an indictment. Indictments are returned by a grand jury in cases involving capital crime punishable by death or life imprisonment. Other crimes can be charged through the filing of an information by the state attorney. (Florida Rules of Criminal Procedure, Rule 3.140(a).) If defendants are not charged via information or indictment, within 21 days from the date of arrest or service of capias on them, they have a right to an adversary preliminary hearing on any felony charge then pending against them. (Florida Rules of Criminal Procedure, Rule 3.133(b).)

Information filed. Once the state attorney has reviewed the particulars of a case, the state attorney may file an information. This is a formal charging document alleging crimes based on the facts supplied to the state attorney. It is signed by the state attorney and has the effect of an indictment. (*www.coj.net/Departments/State+Attorneys+Office+/Legal+Terms.htm*)

The information must be a "plain, concise, and definite written statement of the essential facts constituting the offense charged." (Florida Rules of Criminal Procedure, Rule 3.140(b).)

Grand jury indictment filed. Another way a person can be formally charged with a violation of law is by indictment, a document issued by a grand jury, usually charging a felony punishable by the death penalty or life imprisonment.

It is based upon the facts and circumstances of a case as presented to the grand jury by the prosecution. Like an information, an indictment must be a "plain, concise, and definite written statement of the essential facts constituting the offense charged." (Florida Rules of Criminal Procedure, Rule 3.140(b).)

Arraignment and Pleas

Arraignment. At any time following the filing of formal charges, arraignment can take place. At the arraignment, the defendant is brought before a judge in open court (or in some instances, by an audiovisual device). He or she is informed of the charges and is required to enter a plea or formal response to those charges.

Entering a plea. The following pleas can be entered by the accused at any time, such as during the arraignment: (1) guilty, (2) not guilty, or (3) nolo contendere (with the consent of the court). In a nolo contendere or no-contest plea, the defendant neither admits nor denies the charges, but the plea is the equivalent of a guilty plea insofar as it gives court power to punish the defendant. At any time during the process, a defendant may change a plea to guilty or nolo contendere. If a defendant stands mute, or pleads evasively, a plea of not guilty shall be entered. If the defendant is a corporation and fails to appear, a plea of not guilty shall be entered of record. If a defendant pleads guilty or nolo contendere, the next step in the process will be the sentencing proceedings. (Florida Rules of Criminal Procedure, Rule 3.170.)

Plea bargaining. The accused may be allowed to plead guilty to a less serious offense than the one charged. When the prosecution makes a plea offer, defense counsel must present it to the defendant for his or her acceptance or rejection. The "prosecuting attorney and the defense attorney, or the defendant when representing himself or herself, are encouraged to discuss and to agree on pleas that may be entered by a defendant," although ultimate authority for sentencing rests with the trial judge. (Florida Rules of Criminal Procedure, Rule 3.171.)

Right to a speedy trial. A major incentive for the prosecution to make decisions in the early stages of a case is the defendant's right to a speedy trial. Generally, every person charged with a crime by indictment or information shall be brought to trial within 90 days if the crime charged is a misdemeanor or within 175 days if the crime is a felony. The time period commences when the person is taken into custody, *i.e.*, the person is arrested or receives a Notice to Appear in lieu of arrest. A person shall be considered to have been brought to trial if the trial commences within the time period provided and when the trial jury panel is sworn for voir dire examination, or on waiver of a jury trial, when the trial proceedings begin.

Motions and Discovery

Pretrial motions. All motions, as well as pleadings in response to a motion, must be in writing and signed by the moving party or the moving party's legal counsel. (Upon good cause, a court can waive this requirement.) The motion or pleading must state the ground(s) on which it is based and a copy must be served on the opposing party with an accompanying certificate of service. Pretrial motions include motion to dismiss, motion to suppress evidence in an unlawful search, motion to suppress evidence of a confession or admission illegally obtained, motion for continuance, motion to take deposition to perpetuate testimony, and motion to expedite. (Florida Rules of Criminal Procedure, Rule 3.190.)

Notice of discovery. After the filing of the information or indictment, the defendant may elect to participate in the discovery process by filing and serving on the prosecuting attorney a Notice of Discovery.

Prosecutor's discovery obligation. Within 15 days of the receipt of the defendant's Notice of Discovery, certain discovery obligations attach to the prosecutor such as giving the defendant a Discovery Exhibit that lists the names and addresses of all persons identified by the state as having relevant information related to the charges against the defendant. The defendant must also be given any statement made by those named persons. The prosecutor has a continuing duty to disclose to the defendant any "material information within the state's possession or control that tends to negate the guilt of the defendant as to any offense charged, regardless of whether the defendant has incurred reciprocal discovery obligations." (Florida Rules of Criminal Procedure, Rule 3.220(b)(4).)

Disclosure to prosecution. After the filing of the charging document, the court may require the defendant to submit to procedures such as appearing in a lineup; speaking for identification purposes; being fingerprinted; posing for photographs not involving re-enactment of the alleged offense; trying on articles of clothing; permitting the taking of certain specimens such as the defendant's blood; and providing samples of the defendant's handwriting. (Florida Rules of Criminal Procedure, Rule 3.220(c).)

Defendant's discovery obligation. By filing a Notice of Discovery or participating in any discovery process, which includes the taking of a discovery deposition, the defendant must give the prosecutor a Discovery Exhibit within 15 days of the receipt of the state's Discovery Exhibit. The defendant must provide the prosecutor certain information such as the names and addresses of witnesses that may be called to testify at trial, as well as copies of their written statement, if any. (Florida Rules of Criminal Procedure, Rule 3.220(d).)

Pretrial conferences. Pretrial conferences can be held with the prosecutor, defense attorney, and defendant (unless the defendant has waived his or her appearance in writing) for any purpose related to promoting a fair and expeditious trial. An example would be the discussion of a discovery schedule. (Florida Rules of Criminal Procedure, Rule 3.220(p).)

Trial

Criminal trials are relatively rare. Most criminal cases are disposed of by pleas of guilty in plea bargaining. When a trial is held, the steps are often as follows.

Bench trial. All accused persons have the right to a trial by jury. Defendants can elect to waive their right to a jury trial by submitting the waiver in writing. In a bench trial, the judge is the trier of fact.

Jury selection. The jury consists of twelve jurors in all capital cases and six jurors in all other criminal cases. (Florida Rules of Criminal Procedure, Rule 3.270.) Additionally, the court may direct that alternate jurors be selected in the same manner as the jurors. Alternate jurors, except in capital cases, are usually excused when the jury enters into the stage of considering the verdict. After the judge calls the case, the first step in a jury case is *voir dire*, the selection of the jury. After taking an oath to answer all questions truthfully, prospective jurors are questioned by the judge and the attorneys for each side. (Florida Rules of Criminal Procedure, Rule 3.300.) All prospective jurors can be challenged for cause (e.g., they may not be impartial because they are related to one of the parties). A prospective juror can also be dismissed by a peremptory challenge from either side. (No reason need be given for a peremptory challenge.) Each side has ten peremptory challenges in the case of a felony punishable by death or imprisonment for life; six in the case of all other felonies; and three in the case of misdemeanors. (Florida Rules of Criminal Procedure, Rule 3.350.) Each juror takes an oath that he or she "will well and truly try the issues between the State of Florida and the defendant and render a true verdict according to the law and the evidence." (Florida Rules of Criminal Procedure, Rule 3.360.)

Opening statements. Once the jury has been sworn in, the attorneys give their opening statements to the jury, beginning with the prosecution. The statement outlines what the party expects to prove during the trial.

State's case. The prosecutor presents its case by conducting a direct examination of the witnesses it calls and by offering physical evidence. The defendant can cross-examine the state's witnesses. The prosecution then rests.

Defense's case. At the conclusion of the state's case, the defendant presents its case by conducting a direct examination of the witnesses it calls and by offering physical evidence. The prosecutor can cross-examine the defendant's witnesses. The defendant then rests.

Closing arguments. The attorney for each side then presents to the jury its closing argument that summarizes and interprets the evidence presented during the trial. "In all criminal trials, excluding the sentencing phase of a capital case, at the close of all the evidence, the prosecuting attorney shall be entitled to an initial closing argument and a rebuttal closing argument before the jury or the court sitting without a jury." (Florida Rules of Criminal Procedure, Rule 3.381.)

Motion for judgment of acquittal. If, at the close of the evidence for the state or at the close of all the evidence in the cause, the court is of the opinion that the evidence is insufficient to warrant a conviction, it may, and on the motion of the prosecuting attorney or the defendant shall, enter a judgment of acquittal. (Florida Rules of Criminal Procedure, Rule 3.380.)

Jury instructions. If no judgment of acquittal has been entered, the judge will give the jury detailed legal instructions about the crimes and explains the deliberation process it should follow in reaching a verdict. This is called instructing or charging the jury. Before delivering the charge, the judge will decide whether to include any of the instructions the attorneys may have submitted as requests for instructions. When applicable, standard jury instructions published by The Florida Bar may be utilized by the trial judges. (Florida Rules of Criminal Procedure, Rule 3.390.)

Jury deliberations. Rule 3.400, Florida Rules of Criminal Procedure, provides that the court has the discretion of allowing the jury to take to the jury room a copy of the charges against the defendant, verdict forms, the instructions given, and all evidence except depositions. In any capital case, it is mandatory that the jury be given a copy of all instructions to review in the jury room. (Florida Rules of Criminal Procedure, Rule 3.400.) The jury then goes to the jury room to deliberate a verdict.

Verdict. Once in the jury room, the moderator of their discussion is a foreperson whom the jurors select from among themselves. The jury must decide that the defendant is guilty beyond a reasonable doubt by a unanimous verdict. When the verdict is announced, the attorneys can ask that the jurors be polled individually on whether each agreed with (voted for) the verdict. A verdict may be rendered on any day, including Sundays and legal holidays. (Florida Rules of Criminal Procedure, Rules 3.440 and 3.540.)

Post-Trial Motions and Sentencing

Motion for new trial. In most cases, a motion for new trial must be made within 10 days after the verdict or finding of the court. The motion will be granted if the jurors reached the verdict by lot, the verdict is contrary to law or the weight of the evidence, or if the defendant provides newly discovered evidence that was unavailable at the trial and the result would have more than likely been different had such evidence been presented. (Florida Rules of Criminal Procedure, Rules 3.590 and 3.600.)

Motion for arrest of judgment. A motion to arrest judgment is a request that the court stay or refrain from rendering or enforcing the judgment. In most cases, this motion must be made within 10 days after the verdict or finding of the court. The motion will be granted if: (1) the indictment or information on which the defendant was tried is so defective that it will not support a judgment of conviction, (2) the court is without jurisdiction of the cause, (3) the verdict is so uncertain that it does not appear therefrom that the jurors intended to convict the defendant of an offense of which the defendant could be convicted under the indictment or information under which the defendant was tried, or (4) the defendant was convicted of an offense for which the defendant could not be convicted under the indictment or information under which the defendant was tried. (Florida Rules of Criminal Procedure, Rules 3.590 and 3.610.)

Rendition of judgment. A judgment is the adjudication by the court that the defendant is guilty or not guilty. If the defendant is found guilty, a judgment of guilty and, if the defendant has been acquitted, a judgment of not guilty shall be rendered in open court and in writing, signed by the judge, filed, and recorded. However, where allowed by law, the judge may withhold an adjudication of guilt if the judge places the defendant on probation. (Florida Rules of Criminal Procedure, Rules 3.650 and 3.670.)

Presentence report. In all cases in which the court has discretion as to what sentence may be imposed, the court may refer the case to the Department of Corrections for investigation and recommendation. No sentence or sentences other than probation shall be imposed on any defendant found guilty of a first felony offense or found guilty of a felony while under the age of 18 years, until after such investigation has first been made and the recommendations of the Department of Corrections received and considered by the sentencing judge. The report provides extensive biographical information about the defendant and other pertinent facts about the case in order to help the court impose an appropriate sentence under the guidelines established by the legislature and the courts. (Florida Rules of Criminal Procedure, Rule 3.710.)

Allocution. The court shall inform the defendant of the finding of guilt against the defendant and of the judgment and ask the defendant whether there is any legal cause to show why sentence should not be pronounced. (Florida Rules of Criminal Procedure, Rule 3.720.)

Sentencing. Sentencing is the pronouncement by the court of the penalty imposed on a defendant for the offense of which the defendant has been adjudged guilty. The sentencing must take place in open court. In minor cases, sentencing can occur immediately after a guilty verdict is announced. (Florida Rules of Criminal Procedure, Rule 3.700.)

Post-Conviction Relief and Appeal

Post-conviction motions. The defendant may file a motion for post-conviction relief (motion to vacate, set aside, or correct the sentence) in the court in which he or she was convicted on the following grounds: the judgment or sentence violated the federal or state Constitution or laws; the court lacked jurisdiction to enter the judgment or impose the sentence; the sentence exceeded the maximum authorized by law; the plea was involuntary; or the judgment or sentence is otherwise subject to collateral attack. (Florida Rules of Criminal Procedure, Rule 3.850.)

Appeal. After a guilty verdict or judgment, a defendant may appeal the trial court's decision to the appropriate district appeals court at any time between the entry of the judgment and the sentence or 30 days after the date of sentencing. The notice of appeal is filed with the clerk of the trial court. (Florida Rules of Appellate Procedure, Rule 9.140(b)(3).) A further appeal may be possible to the Supreme Court of Florida. If the death penalty is imposed, a defendant may appeal directly to the Supreme Court of Florida from the trial court. Under limited situations, a defendant may appeal a plea entered. Under limited situations, the *state* may be allowed to appeal. Appeals are governed by Florida Rules of Appellate Procedure. The party filing an appeal is referred to as the appellant. The party against whom an appeal is filed is referred to as the appellee. (Florida Rules of Appellate Procedure, Rules 9.020(g) and 9.140 et seq.)

C. More Information

Florida Rules of Criminal Procedure
www.floridasupremecourt.org/decisions/barrules.shtml
(click "Documents" then "Criminal Procedure")

Florida Statutes on Crimes
www.leg.state.fl.us/Statutes
(click "Title XLVI")

Florida Rules of Appellate Procedure
www.floridasupremecourt.org/decisions/barrules.shtml
(click "Documents" then "Appellate Procedure")

Initiating a Criminal Case
www.co.leon.fl.us/statty/Initiating_a_Case.htm
www.co.leon.fl.us/statty/Understanding_the_Criminal_Justice_System.htm

Prosecuting Crimes
www.sa18.state.fl.us/prosecute/division.htm
www.coj.net/Departments/State+Attorneys+Office+/Prosecuting+Criminals.htm

Felony, Misdemeanor & Criminal Traffic Case Process
www.pdmiami.com/adult_case_process.htm

Felony and Misdemeanor Procedures
www.public-defender10-fl.org/felonyandmis.html

How a Case Proceeds
www.wearethehope.org/faq.htm#arraign

Criminal Justice Process
sao.co.sarasota.fl.us/legal.htm

Criminal Process in Florida
research.lawyers.com/Florida/Criminal-Process-in-Florida.html

Florida Criminal Law Guide
www.richardhornsby.com/criminal/guide/index.html

Overview of a Criminal Case
www.brevardcounty.us/publicdefender/client.htm#FApd13.state.fl.us/forms.htm
pd13.state.fl.us/pdf/About-your-day-in-county-court.pdf
sao1.co.escambia.fl.us/faq.htm
www.keyssao.org/CJS%20Overview.htm

Defining Criminal Law Terms
www.sa18.state.fl.us/legterm/terms.htm
sao.co.sarasota.fl.us/glossary.htm
www.coj.net/Departments/State+Attorneys+Office+/Legal+Terms.htm
www.pdo1.org/legalglossary.htm

Florida Attorney General
myfloridalegal.com

Florida State Attorneys
www.stateofflorida.com/Portal/DesktopDefault.aspx?tabid=140

Florida Prosecuting Attorneys Association
www.myfpaa.org

Florida Public Defenders
www.flpda.org/pages/public_defenders.htm
publicdefender.cjis20.org/public_defenders.htm
www.flpda.org/pages/public_defenders.htm

Crime Victim Services

myfloridalegal.com/victims

Jury Instructions in Criminal Cases

www.floridasupremecourt.org
(click "Criminal Jury Instructions")

Crime Statistics in Florida

www.flcourts.org
(click "press & media" then "Statistics")
www.fdle.state.fl.us/Crime_Statistics
www.dc.state.fl.us/pub/index.html

Florida Courts

www.flcourts.org

Florida Criminal Defense Law Blog

blog.justiceflorida.com

Criminal Law Links

www.crimelynx.com/research.html
talkjustice.com/browse.asp
www.findlaw.com/01topics/09criminal/sites.html

D. Something to Check

1. Go to the web site for the state courts in your county (see sections 4.2 and 4.6). What information or assistance does it provide for defendants, witnesses, or jurors in criminal cases?

2. Select any three general search engines (e.g., *www.google.com*) and any three legal search engines or portals (e.g., *www.findlaw.com*). At these sites run this search: "Florida criminal cases." What are the different categories of results you find? Compare the six sites you used for this search.

Sample Documents

A. Introduction

This section presents an example of a civil complaint filed in a Florida state court. The complaint is being brought against the following person:

> Robert E. Moneyhan a/k/a Demon Moon, an individual; d/b/a (doing business as) Katrinahelp.com; Katrinadonations.com; Katrinarelieffund.com; and Katrinarelief.com

The complaint is for an injunction, damages, civil penalties, and other statutory relief regarding alleged deceptive and unfair trade practices after Hurricane Katrina.

Compare this complaint to the sample *federal* civil complaint printed in section 7.2. See also:

- Section 4.2, overview of Florida state courts
- Section 6.3, some distinctions between state and federal civil procedure
- Section 6.2, some of the major statutes covering pretrial procedures, including the drafting of complaints and other pleadings
- Section 7.5, a state criminal complaint

B. A State Civil Complaint

Exhibit 7.1A contains a sample complaint filed in a Florida state court.

C. ▌ More Information

Overview of Civil Litigation in Florida
www.floridabar.org/DIVCOM/PI/RHandbook01.nsf/Form+ List?OpenForm
(click "Reporter's Guide to a Civil Lawsuit")
www.clerk.leon.fl.us
(click "Frequently Asked Questions")

www.weblocator.com/attorney/fl/law/processcon.html
www.delmarlearning.com/companions/content/140184829X/ state/FL/kerley_FL_v5.pdf

Florida State Courts System
www.flcourts.org

Florida Statutes
www.leg.state.fl.us/Statutes

Florida Civil Procedure and Practice
www.megalaw.com/fl/top/flcivpro.php

Florida Rules of Civil Procedure
www.floridabar.org
(click "Professional Practice" then "Rules of Procedure")
www.phonl.com/fl_law/rules/frcp

Selected Forms
partners.uslegalforms.com/enter5.cgi?legallawhelp^/Florida/ samplesearch.htm

Lawton Chiles Legal Information Center: Florida Self-Help Law
www.law.ufl.edu/lic/guides
(click "Florida Self-Help Law")

Resources for Self-Represented Litigants
www.flcourts.org/gen_public/family/forms_rules/index.shtml
www.selfhelpsupport.org
(click "Self Help Programs")

Library of Congress: Florida Law
www.loc.gov/law/guide/us-fl.html

Florida Tort Law Information
www.megalaw.com/fl/top/fltorts.php

D. ▌ Something to Check

1. What different kinds of complaint forms are made available both online and in hard copy by the Florida state courts system?

2. Go to the Internet and perform searches on the individuals who took part in the proceedings involving the Moneyhan complaint. Use Google or any search engine to find information about the litigation initiated by the Moneyhan complaint. Give a brief legal synopsis as well as an overall perspective of what happened in the case.

3. The beginning of the Moneyhan complaint tells you about the office of the attorney general. Find and visit the web site of this office. Briefly describe other kinds of civil actions filed by the attorney general's office.

EXHIBIT 7.1A — Sample Civil Complaint Filed in a Florida State Court

**IN THE CIRCUIT COURT OF THE FOURTH JUDICIAL CIRCUIT
IN AND FOR NASSAU COUNTY, FLORIDA**

CIVIL ACTION

STATE OF FLORIDA,
DEPARTMENT OF LEGAL AFFAIRS,
OFFICE OF THE ATTORNEY GENERAL,

    Plaintiff,   CASE NO. _____

vs.   DIVISION: _____

ROBERT E. MONEYHAN a/k/a DEMON MOON, an individual,
d/b/a KATRINAHELP.COM, KATRINADONATIONS.COM,
KATRINARELIEFFUND.COM, and KATRINARELIEF.COM,

    Defendant.
_____

**COMPLAINT FOR INJUNCTION, DAMAGES,
CIVIL PENALTIES AND OTHER STATUTORY RELIEF**

Plaintiff, STATE OF FLORIDA, DEPARTMENT OF LEGAL AFFAIRS, OFFICE OF THE ATTORNEY GENERAL (the "Attorney General"), sues Defendant, ROBERT E. MONEYHAN, an individual, also known as Demon Moon, an individual, doing business as katrinahelp.com, katrinadonations.com, katrinarelief.com, katrinarelieffund.com, and other assumed names and web sites unknown at this time, and alleges:

JURISDICTION AND VENUE

1. This is an action for damages, declaratory relief, injunctive relief, and other statutory relief pursuant to the Florida Deceptive and Unfair Trade Practices Act, Chapter 501, Part II, Florida Statutes (2004).

2. This Court has jurisdiction pursuant to the provisions of the Florida Deceptive and Unfair Trade Practices Act, Chapter 501, Part II, Florida Statutes.

3. The acts or practices complained of herein occurred in the conduct of a trade or

---

EXHIBIT 7.1A

commerce within Florida as defined in Section 501.203(8). Florida Statutes, including Hillsborough and Nassau counties and affecting multiple judicial circuits.

THE PARTIES

4. The Department of Legal Affairs is an enforcing authority pursuant to Section 501.203(2), Florida Statutes, and is authorized to seek damages and injunctive and other statutory relief.

5. The Office of the Attorney General conducted an investigation and Attorney General, Charles J. Crist, Jr., reviewed this matter and determined that this enforcement action is in the public interest.

6. At all times material hereto, Defendant, a/k/a Demon Moon, d/b/a katrinahelp.com, katrinadonations.com, katrinarelief.com, katrinarelieffund.com, and other web sites and assumed names unknown at this time, conducted business in and resided in Florida. Defendant is currently residing at 32668 St. Jarvis Road, Yulee, Florida 32097.

OVERVIEW

7. On August 26, 2005, Hurricane Katrina at category 1 strength hit southeast Florida's densely populated coast. Upon exiting Florida, Katrina strengthened in the warm gulf waters before packing category 4 winds on August 29th of 145 mph into the gulf coast of Louisiana, Mississippi, Alabama and the western portion of the Florida panhandle. The devastation from Hurricane Katrina and the after effects has been absolutely horrific. With hundreds declared dead and thousands without homes and in dire need of the essentials of life at the most basic levels, the need for human compassion and charitable giving to assist those affected is great.

2

EXHIBIT 7.1A | **Sample Civil Complaint Filed in a Florida State Court**

DEFENDANT'S COURSE OF CONDUCT

8. On August 28, 2005, Defendant Robert Moneyhan, utilizing the alias of Demon Moon at a post office box in Yulee, Florida, registered at least four domain names for use with maintaining web sites on the Internet. Defendant registered the following domain names for one year.

> katrinahelp.com
> katrinadonations.com
> katrinarelief.com
> katrinarelieffund.com.

9. From at least August 31, 2005, Defendant has participated in or controlled the operation of and continues to operate web sites that have solicited or may in the future solicit charitable donations. On August 31, 2005, the web site katrinahelp.com proclaimed above a large picture of Hurricane Katrina headed for the gulf coast:

> "Welcome to Katrina HELP.com"
> (Made necessary by Hurrican(sic) Katrina's devastation)
> Click this 'DONATE' button to share YOUR good fortune with Hurricane Katrina's victims.
> (100% of donations used for relief purposes!)

An icon which says "DONATE" permits donations by mastercard or visa and is visible on the web page. A copy of the web site is attached as Exhibit "A" hereto.

10. On August 31, 2005, the web site katrinadonations.com contained virtually identical content and solicited donations. It is believed that the other two web sites known to be registered to Defendant, katrinarelief.com and katrinarelieffund.com, contained similar content and solicited donations.

11. Pursuant to Florida law, before soliciting charitable donations, a person must file

3

EXHIBIT 7.1A

registration documents with the Department of Agriculture and Consumer Services, Division of Consumer Services. On information and belief, Defendant has not applied for or obtained appropriate registration to permit solicitation of donations by Defendant or any of the websites that Defendant registered. On information and belief, this is not a legitimate charity and any money raised would not go to the victims.

12. Defendant has procured and maintained a Paypal account to collect payments from each of the web sites soliciting donations. Pursuant to Paypal policies and procedures, Paypal collects a fee for receiving payments of 2.9%. Defendant misrepresents "100% of donations used for relief." By way of example, for a $100 donation through Defendant's web site, only $97 could possibly be used for relief as Defendant is assessed the Paypal fee.

13. Defendant further fails to specify how the victims of Hurricane Katrina are identified and the particulars of what Defendant deems as relief.

14. As of September 1, 2005, Defendant appears to have changed the content of the web sites to attempt to sell the web site domain names to the highest bidder. It is unknown whether Defendant will change the sites at any given time to again deceptively and unfairly solicit funds to Defendant's paypal accounts or otherwise to his benefit.

COUNT I
DECEPTIVE AND UNFAIR TRADE PRACTICES
CHAPTER 501, PART II, FLORIDA STATUTES

15. Paragraphs 1 to 14 are hereby realleged and incorporated herein by reference, as if fully set forth below.

16. Section 501.204(1), Florida Statutes, provides that "Unfair methods of competition, unconscionable acts or practices, and unfair or deceptive acts or practices in the

4

EXHIBIT 7.1A Sample Civil Complaint Filed in a Florida State Court

conduct of any trade or commerce are hereby declared unlawful."

17. As set forth herein, Defendant, acting individually or in concert with others, has engaged in representations, acts, practices or omissions in trade or commerce which are material, and which are likely to mislead consumers acting reasonably under the circumstances; or Defendant has engaged in acts or practices in trade or commerce which offend established public policy and are unethical, oppressive, unscrupulous or substantially injurious to consumers.

18. By engaging in the foregoing, Defendant has engaged in deceptive and unfair trade practices in violation of Section 501.204, Florida Statutes.

19. Defendant knew or should have known that the methods, acts or practices alleged herein were deceptive or unfair.

20. Unless Defendant is permanently enjoined from engaging further in the acts and practices alleged herein, the continued activities of Defendant will result in irreparable injury to the public, for which there is no adequate remedy at law.

COUNT II
DECEPTIVE AND UNFAIR TRADE PRACTICES
CONDUCT VIOLATING CHAPTER 496, FLORIDA STATUTES
VIOLATES CHAPTER 501, PART II, FLORIDA STATUTES

21. Paragraphs 1 to 14 are hereby realleged and incorporated herein by reference, as if fully set forth below.

22. As alleged in paragraphs 8-14, Defendant, acting individually or in concert with others, has solicited or attempted to solicit and obtain donations from Defendant registered and controlled web sites under the guise of relief for Hurricane Katrina victims, without applying for or obtaining registration pursuant to Section 496.405, Florida Statutes. On

EXHIBIT 7.1A

information and belief, Defendant failed to file a registration statement required by Section 496.405(1).

23. Section 496.405(1)(a), Florida Statutes, requires registration and provides:

A charitable organization or sponsor, unless exempted pursuant to s. 496.406, which intends to solicit contributions in this state by any means or have funds solicited on its behalf by any person, charitable organization, sponsor, commercial co-venturer, or professional solicitor, or that participates in a charitable sales promotion or sponsor sales promotion, must, prior to engaging in any of these activities, file an annual registration statement, and a renewal statement annually thereafter, with the department.

24. Pursuant to Section 496.416, Florida Statutes, "any person who commits an act or practice that violates any provision of ss. 496.401-496.424 commits an unfair or deceptive practice in violation of chapter 501, part II, and is subject to the penalties and remedies provided for such violation."

25. Section 501.203(3)(c), Florida Statutes, states that a violation of Chapter 501, Part II, may be based on a violation of any law which proscribes a deceptive act or practice.

26. Defendant, acting individually or in concert with others, has engaged in representations, acts, practices or omissions in trade or commerce which are material, and which are likely to mislead consumers acting reasonably under the circumstances; or Defendant has engaged in acts or practices in trade or commerce which offend established public policy and are unethical, oppressive, unscrupulous or substantially injurious to consumers.

27. By engaging in the foregoing activities in violation of Section 496.405, Florida Statutes, Defendant has engaged in deceptive and unfair trade practices in violation of Section 501.204, Florida Statutes.

EXHIBIT 7.1A   Sample Civil Complaint Filed in a Florida State Court

28. Defendant knew or should have known that the methods, acts or practices alleged herein were deceptive or unfair.

29. Unless Defendant is permanently enjoined from engaging further in the acts and practices alleged herein, the continued activities of Defendant will result in irreparable injury to the public, for which there is no adequate remedy at law.

COUNT III
DECEPTIVE AND UNFAIR TRADE PRACTICES
CONDUCT VIOLATING CHAPTER 817, FLORIDA STATUTES
VIOLATES CHAPTER 501, PART II, FLORIDA STATUTES

30. Paragraphs 1 to 14 are hereby realleged and incorporated herein by reference, as if fully set forth below.

31. As alleged in paragraphs 8-12, Defendant, acting individually or in concert with others, has solicited or attempted to solicit and obtain donations from Defendant registered and controlled web sites under the guise of relief for Hurricane Katrina victims, by assuring "100% of ALL donations used for relief." In fact, 100% of the donations cannot be used as represented as a Paypal fee is deducted from the donation and less than 100% of any such donation would be remitted to Defendant for disbursement under his control.

32. Section 817.41(1), Florida Statutes, provides:

It shall be unlawful for any person to make or disseminate or cause to be disseminated before the general public of the state, or any portion thereof, any misleading advertisement. Such making or dissemination of misleading advertisement shall constitute and is hereby declared to be fraudulent and unlawful, designed and intended for obtaining money or property under false pretenses.

33. By undertaking the activities and practices set forth herein, Defendant made or

EXHIBIT 7.1A

disseminated, or caused to be disseminated, before the general public of Florida, or any portion thereof, misleading advertising, in violation of Section 817.41(1), Florida Statutes. Such making or dissemination of misleading advertisements is fraudulent and unlawful, and designed and intended for obtaining money or property under false pretenses.

34. Section 501.203(3)(c), Florida Statutes, states that a violation of Chapter 501, Part II, may be based on a violation of any law which proscribes a deceptive act or practice.

35. Defendant, acting individually or in concert with others, has engaged in representations, acts, practices or omissions in trade or commerce which are material, and which are likely to mislead consumers acting reasonably under the circumstances; or Defendant has engaged in acts or practices in trade or commerce which offend established public policy and are unethical, oppressive, unscrupulous or substantially injurious to consumers.

36. By engaging in the foregoing activities in violation of Section 817.41, Florida Statutes, Defendant has engaged in deceptive and unfair trade practices in violation of Section 501.204, Florida Statutes.

37. Defendant knew or should have known that the methods, acts or practices alleged herein were deceptive or unfair.

38. Unless Defendant is permanently enjoined from engaging further in the acts and practices alleged herein, the continued activities of Defendant will result in irreparable injury to the public, for which there is no adequate remedy at law.

PRAYER FOR RELIEF

WHEREFORE, Plaintiff, State of Florida, Department of Legal Affairs,

Office of the Attorney General, asks for judgment:

EXHIBIT 7.1A — Sample Civil Complaint Filed in a Florida State Court

A. Temporarily and permanently enjoining Defendant, his agents and those persons in active concert or participation with him who receive actual notice of the injunction, from engaging in the acts and practices in violation of provisions of Chapter 501, Part II, Florida Statutes (2004), as specifically alleged above, and any similar acts and practices;

B. Awarding the Attorney General attorney's fees and costs pursuant Section 501.2105, Florida Statutes;

C. Assessing against Defendant, civil penalties in the amount of Ten Thousand Dollars ($10,000) for each violation of Chapter 501, Part II, Florida Statutes, in accordance with Section 501.2075, Florida Statutes; and Fifteen Thousand Dollars ($15,000) for each such violation that victimizes, or attempts to victimize, a senior citizen or handicapped person, in accordance with Section 501.2077, Florida Statutes. (2004).

D. Awarding restitution for consumers injured by Defendant.

E. Requiring that Defendant disgorge all revenues, and all interest or proceeds derived therefrom, generated as a result of the unconscionable, unfair and deceptive practices set forth in this complaint;

F. In Granting Injunctive Relief, enjoining Defendant from forming a business or organizational identity as a method of avoiding the terms and conditions of the Injunction; requiring Defendant to disclose the terms and conditions of the Injunction to all officers, employees, representatives, agents, successors, assigns, or any other person who acts under or who will act under, by, through, or on behalf of Defendant engaged in any activity involving solicitation of donations through commercial e-mail, instant messaging, or any internet

9

EXHIBIT 7.1A

promotion for a period of 2 years; and:

(1) Appointing a Receiver over Defendant's assets and property, and providing for the liquidation of assets (a) procured through monies obtained through unlawful activities, or (b) procured through financing obtained in reliance on assets, revenues, draws, or income derived through unlawful means.

(2) Freezing Defendant's assets, except as provided by the Court; and

(3) Temporarily enjoining Defendant from transferring an interest in or title to real estate located in Florida, unless Defendant provides 60 days notice to the Court and the parties of intent to transfer such an interest or title and 10 days notice of closing on the sale or transfer of any such interest in property.

G. Declaring the practices described in this complaint unlawful; and

H. Granting such other relief as this court deems just and proper.

Respectfully submitted,

CHARLES J. CRIST, JR.
ATTORNEY GENERAL

JULIA A. HARRIS
SENIOR ASSISTANT ATTORNEY GENERAL
Florida Bar No. 884235
Department of Legal Affairs
Concourse Center 4
3507 East Frontage Road, Suite 325
Tampa, Florida 33607
(813)287-7950
(813)281-5515 (facsimile)

10

7.2 Sample Civil Complaint Filed in a Federal District Court in Florida

A. Introduction

B. A Federal Civil Complaint

C. More Information

D. Something to Check

A. Introduction

In this section, we look at a civil complaint filed in a U.S. District Court sitting in Florida. The complaint alleges a violation of civil rights under § 1983 and the Fourteenth Amendment due to alleged excessive force by a police officer and common law torts (negligence and battery) growing out of the incident.

Compare this complaint to the sample state court civil complaint in section 7.1. See also section 6.3 covering some of the distinctions between state and federal civil procedure.

For more on federal courts in Florida, see section 4.3.

B. A Federal Civil Complaint

Exhibit 7.2A contains a sample civil complaint and civil cover sheet filed in a federal district court sitting in Florida.

C. More Information

Federal Judiciary Overview
www.uscourts.gov
www.firstgov.gov/Agencies/Federal/Judicial.shtml

Guide to the Federal Courts
www.uscourts.gov/journalistguide/welcome.html
www.uscourts.gov/understand02

Florida Southern District
www.flsd.uscourts.gov
(click "Forms")

Florida Northern District
www.flnd.uscourts.gov
(click "Forms & Publications" then "Attorney")

Florida Middle District
www.flmd.uscourts.gov
(type "complaint" in the search box)

Florida Federal Court Judges' Practice Guide
www.floridabar.org/DIVPGM/PU/FCPCSurvey.nsf/ WFCPCArea?Openview&Start=1&Expand=3#3

D. Something to Check

1. What information can you find online about (a) the attorney who represented the plaintiff in this case, (b) the plaintiff, and (c) the defendant police officer? (Caution: The attorney may have misspelled the officer's last name in the complaint.)

2. This was a § 1983 complaint. List the kinds of information you can find online about § 1983 litigation.

EXHIBIT 7.2A | **Sample Civil Complaint (with Civil Cover Sheet) Filed in a United States District Court**

IN THE UNITED STATES DISTRICT COURT
FOR THE SOUTHERN DISTRICT OF FLORIDA

FORT LAUDERDALE DIVISION

CASE NO: **06-61469**
CIV- COOKE
MAGISTRATE JUDGE BROWN

ANDREA SWICHKOW,

Plaintiff,

vs.

CITY OF PLANTATION and
GRAIG BOEMEESTER,

Defendants.

COMPLAINT FOR DAMAGES AND DEMAND FOR JURY TRIAL

Plaintiff, ANDREA SWICHKOW ("SWICHKOW"), by and through her undersigned counsel, hereby sues Defendants, CITY OF PLANTATION and GRAIG BOEMEESTER ("BOEMEESTER"), and alleges as follows:

INTRODUCTION

1. This action arises under Title 42 of the United States Code, Section 1983 and the Fourteenth Amendments to the United States Constitution. In addition to civil rights claims, pendent claims pursuant to state law are raised in this Complaint.

JURISDICTION AND VENUE

2. This Court has jurisdiction under Title 28 of the United States Code, Section 1331.

3. Venue is proper in this district based on Title 28 United States Code, Section 1391 (b). Some or all of the Defendants reside in, and all claims arose within, this District.

EXHIBIT 7.2A

PARTIES

4. At all times material to this Complaint, SWICHKOW was and is sui juris and a resident of Broward County, Florida.

5. The Defendant, THE CITY OF PLANTATION, is a municipal corporation and governmental subdivision of the State of Florida, existing and organized under the laws of the State of Florida with its principal place of business located at 451 NW 70TH Terrace, Plantation, Florida, 33317.

6. The Defendant, BOEMEESTER, was and is sui juris and, on information and belief, is a resident of Broward County, Florida.

GENERAL ALLEGATIONS

7. On or about June 14, 2005, SWICHKOW was alone in her vehicle when she was stopped at a stop sign at the entrance of a parking lot in Broward County, Florida.

8. At said time and place, SWICHKOW was approached by an unidentified male with his arms above his head.

9. As he approached, the man identified himself as a police officer and ordered SWICHKOW to step out of her vehicle.

10. Because he was not wearing a uniform, SWICHKOW requested that he provide her with identification verifying that he was indeed a police officer. Simultaneously and while still remaining in the relative safety of her vehicle, SWICHKOW placed a call to her husband on her cell phone.

11. While still communicating with her husband on the cell phone an Officer from THE CITY OF PLANTATION POLICE DEPARTMENT arrived on the scene and identified himself as BOEMEESTER.

EXHIBIT 7.2A — Sample Civil Complaint [with Civil Cover Sheet] Filed in a United States District Court

12. As Mr. Boemeester approached Ms. Swichkow's vehicle she requested that he speak to her husband with whom she was still in communication with on her cell phone. Mr. Boemeester flatly refused to speak to Ms. Swichkow's husband.

13. Without any warning or provocation, Mr. Boemeester grabbed Ms. Swichkow's cell phone out of her hand, threw it on the ground and proceeded to forcibly remove Ms. Swichkow from her vehicle.

14. Once he dragged Ms. Swichkow out of her vehicle, Mr. Boemeester threw her onto the hood of her vehicle causing her to sustain severe and permanent personal injuries to her person.

15. In accordance with Florida Statutes § 68.28, written notice of this claim was presented to the Defendant and the State Department of Insurance. See Letter of Notification of Claim attached hereto as Exhibit "A". The Claim has been denied or is deemed denied by operation of law.

16. All conditions precedent to the filing of the instant action have occurred or have been waived.

COUNT ONE
(Violation of 42 U.S.C. §983)

17. Plaintiff, Ms. Swichkow realleges and incorporates herein by reference the allegations in paragraphs 1-16 above.

18. This cause of action is brought pursuant to 42 U.S.C. § 983 and the Constitution of the United States, in particular, but not limited to, the Fourteenth Amendment thereto.

EXHIBIT 7.2A

19. Acting under color of law, Defendant, Mr. Boemeester used excessive force upon Plaintiff, Ms. Swichkow, unreasonably and unnecessarily and for no proper or lawful purpose.

20. Plaintiff, Ms. Swichkow had the right, under the Fourteenth Amendment to the United States Constitution, to be free from the unreasonable seizure of her person, which right protects against the use of excessive force under color of law.

21. Defendant, the City and its agent and/or employee, Defendant, Mr. Boemeester violated Plaintiff, Ms. Swichkow's right to be free from the unreasonable seizure of her person when Defendant, Mr. Boemeester used unreasonable, unnecessary and excessive force in the course of arresting Plaintiff, Ms. Swichkow.

22. As a direct and proximate result of the Defendants' intentional and deliberate violation of Plaintiff, Ms. Swichkow's Constitutionally protected right, Plaintiff, Ms. Swichkow suffered great bodily harm and injury.

WHEREFORE, Plaintiff, Ms. Swichkow demands judgment against Defendants for damages, costs, disbursements, expert fees and attorney's fees pursuant to 42 U.S.C. § 988, prejudgment interest pursuant to 42 U.S.C. § 1988, and such further and additional relief as the Court deems just and proper.

COUNT TWO
(Negligent Hiring, Retention and Supervision)

23. Plaintiff, Ms. Swichkow realleges and incorporates herein by reference the allegations in paragraphs 1-16 above.

24. At all times material hereto, Defendant, the City, had a duty to hire, supervise and retain competent staff which would not engage in unwarranted

EXHIBIT 7.2A | **Sample Civil Complaint (with Civil Cover Sheet) Filed in a United States District Court**

and unlawful physical abuse of, and wrongful assault and battery on residents of Broward County, Florida including Plaintiff, Ms. Swichkow.

25. On information and belief, Defendant, Mr. Boemeester's history prior to being employed by, and conduct while an employee of, Defendant, the City, was such that Defendant, the City knew or should have known of Defendant, Mr. Boemeester's propensity for violence and hence was on notice of his violent propensities.

26. Defendant, the City, breached its duty to hire, supervise and retain competent staff which would not engage in unwarranted and unlawful physical abuse of, and wrongful assault and battery on, residents of Broward County, Florida, including Plaintiff, Ms. Swichkow.

27. Defendant, the City's, breach of that duty was the proximate cause of Plaintiff, Ms. Swichkow's injuries.

WHEREFORE, Plaintiff, Ms. Swichkow demands judgment against Defendant, the City for damages and for such further and additional relief as the Court deems just and proper.

COUNT THREE
(Negligence)

28. Plaintiff, Ms. Swichkow realleges and incorporates herein by reference the allegations in paragraphs 1-16 above.

29. At all times material hereto, Defendant, Mr. Boemeester committed a tortuous act against Plaintiff, Ms. Swichkow during the course of his employment with and to further a purpose or interest of Defendant, the City.

30. At all times material hereto, Defendant, Mr. Boemeester was under the control of Defendant, the City.

EXHIBIT 7.2A

31. At all times material hereto, Defendant, the City, owed Plaintiff, Ms. Swichkow a duty to ensure that Defendant, Mr. Boemeester does not act in a tortuous manner towards her.

32. Defendant, the City's breach of that duty was the proximate cause of Plaintiff, Ms. Swichkow's injury.

WHEREFORE, Plaintiff, Ms. Swichkow demands judgment against Defendant, the City for the damages and such further and additional relief as the Court deems just and proper.

COUNT FOUR
(Battery)

33. Plaintiff, Ms. Swichkow realleges and incorporates herein by reference the allegations in paragraphs 1-16 above.

34. Defendant, Mr. Boemeester, purposefully, intentionally, and without consent, justification, or authority of law, touched Ms. Swichkow's person.

35. At no time was Defendant, Mr. Boemeester, authorized to touch Plaintiff, Ms. Swichkow, in the manner in which he did.

36. Defendant, Mr. Boemeester did, in fact, cause an intentional and offensive contact with Plaintiff, Ms. Swichkow's person.

37. As a direct and proximate consequence of Defendant, Mr. Boemeester's purposeful, intentional, and unlawful actions, Plaintiff, Ms. Swichkow suffered bodily harm and injury to her person.

WHEREFORE, Plaintiff, Ms. Swichkow demands judgment against the Defendant, Mr. Boemeester for damages and for such further and additional relief as the Court deems just and proper.

EXHIBIT 7.2A — Sample Civil Complaint (with Civil Cover Sheet) Filed in a United States District Court

DEMAND FOR JURY TRIAL

Plaintiff, Ms. Swichkow, hereby demands a trial by jury of all issues so triable herein.

Dated: September 26, 2006.

Respectfully Submitted,

DAVID A. HOWARD, P.A.
Attorneys for Plaintiff
44 West Flagler Street
Suite 675
Miami, Florida 33130-6801
Telephone: 305.357.0295
Facsimile: 305.374.9572

_____
DAVID A. HOWARD, ESQUIRE
Florida Bar No. 956589

Exhibit 7.2A

Case: 0:06-cv-61469-MGC   Document 1   Filed 09/27/2006   Page 8 of 8

JS 44   **CIVIL COVER SHEET**   **06 - 61469**

The JS 44 civil cover sheet and the information contained herein neither replace nor supplement the filing and service of pleadings or other papers as required by law, except as provided by local rules of court. This form, approved by the Judicial Conference of the United States in September 1974, is required for the use of the Clerk of Court for the purpose of initiating the civil docket sheet.   (SEE INSTRUCTIONS ON THE REVERSE OF THE FORM.)

I. (a) PLAINTIFFS
ANDREA SWICHKOW

DEFENDANTS
CITY OF PLANTATION & CRAIG BOEMBESTER

(b) County of Residence of First Listed Plaintiff BROWARD
(EXCEPT IN U.S. PLAINTIFF CASES)

County of Residence of First Listed Defendant _____
(IN U.S. PLAINTIFF CASES ONLY)
NOTE: IN LAND CONDEMNATION CASES, USE THE LOCATION OF THE LAND INVOLVED.

(c) Attorney's (Firm Name, Address, and Telephone Number)
DAVID A. HOWARD
44 W FLAGLER ST, MIAMI, FL 33130 - (305)357-0295

Attorneys (If Known)

(d)
Broward/ 06-61469-CIV-Cooke/Brown

II. BASIS OF JURISDICTION (Place an "X" in One Box Only)
- ☐ 1 U.S. Government Plaintiff
- ☐ 2 U.S. Government Defendant
- ☒ 3 Federal Question (U.S. Government Not a Party)
- ☐ 4 Diversity (Indicate Citizenship of Parties in Item III)

III. CITIZENSHIP OF PRINCIPAL PARTIES (Place an "X" in One Box for Plaintiff and One Box for Defendant)
(For Diversity Cases Only)

	PTF	DEF		PTF	DEF
Citizen of This State	☐ 1	☐ 1	Incorporated or Principal Place of Business In This State	☐ 4	☐ 4
Citizen of Another State	☐ 2	☐ 2	Incorporated and Principal Place of Business In Another State	☐ 5	☐ 5
Citizen or Subject of a Foreign Country	☐ 3	☐ 3	Foreign Nation	☐ 6	☐ 6

IV. NATURE OF SUIT (Place an "X" in One Box Only)

CONTRACT
- ☐ 110 Insurance
- ☐ 120 Marine
- ☐ 130 Miller Act
- ☐ 140 Negotiable Instrument
- ☐ 150 Recovery of Overpayment & Enforcement of Judgment
- ☐ 151 Medicare Act
- ☐ 152 Recovery of Defaulted Student Loans (Excl. Veterans)
- ☐ 153 Recovery of Overpayment of Veteran's Benefits
- ☐ 160 Stockholders' Suits
- ☐ 190 Other Contract
- ☐ 195 Contract Product Liability
- ☐ 196 Franchise

REAL PROPERTY
- ☐ 210 Land Condemnation
- ☐ 220 Foreclosure
- ☐ 230 Rent Lease & Ejectment
- ☐ 240 Torts to Land
- ☐ 245 Tort Product Liability
- ☐ 290 All Other Real Property

TORTS

PERSONAL INJURY
- ☐ 310 Airplane
- ☐ 315 Airplane Product Liability
- ☐ 320 Assault, Libel & Slander
- ☐ 330 Federal Employers' Liability
- ☐ 340 Marine
- ☐ 345 Marine Product Liability
- ☐ 350 Motor Vehicle
- ☐ 355 Motor Vehicle Product Liability
- ☐ 360 Other Personal Injury

PERSONAL INJURY
- ☐ 362 Personal Injury - Med. Malpractice
- ☐ 365 Personal Injury - Product Liability
- ☐ 368 Asbestos Personal Injury Product Liability

PERSONAL PROPERTY
- ☐ 370 Other Fraud
- ☐ 371 Truth in Lending
- ☐ 380 Other Personal Property Damage
- ☐ 385 Property Damage Product Liability

CIVIL RIGHTS
- ☐ 441 Voting
- ☐ 442 Employment
- ☐ 443 Housing/ Accommodations
- ☐ 444 Welfare
- ☐ 445 Amer. w/Disabilities - Employment
- ☐ 446 Amer. w/Disabilities - Other
- ☐ 440 Other Civil Rights

PRISONER PETITIONS
- ☐ 510 Motions to Vacate Sentence
- *Habeas Corpus:*
- ☐ 530 General
- ☐ 535 Death Penalty
- ☐ 540 Mandamus & Other
- ☐ 550 Civil Rights
- ☐ 555 Prison Condition

FORFEITURE/PENALTY
- ☐ 610 Agriculture
- ☐ 620 Other Food & Drug
- ☐ 625 Drug Related Seizure of Property 21 USC 881
- ☐ 630 Liquor Laws
- ☐ 640 R.R. & Truck
- ☐ 650 Airline Regs.
- ☐ 660 Occupational Safety/Health
- ☐ 690 Other

LABOR
- ☐ 710 Fair Labor Standards Act
- ☐ 720 Labor/Mgmt. Relations
- ☐ 730 Labor/Mgmt. Reporting & Disclosure Act
- ☐ 740 Railway Labor Act
- ☐ 790 Other Labor Litigation
- ☐ 791 Empl. Ret. Inc. Security Act

IMMIGRATION
- ☐ 462 Naturalization Application
- ☐ 463 Habeas Corpus - Alien Detainee
- ☐ 465 Other Immigration Actions

BANKRUPTCY
- ☐ 422 Appeal 28 USC 158
- ☐ 423 Withdrawal 28 USC 157

PROPERTY RIGHTS
- ☐ 820 Copyrights
- ☐ 830 Patent
- ☐ 840 Trademark

SOCIAL SECURITY
- ☐ 861 HIA (1395ff)
- ☐ 862 Black Lung (923)
- ☐ 863 DIWC/DIWW (405(g))
- ☐ 864 SSID Title XVI
- ☐ 865 RSI (405(g))

FEDERAL TAX SUITS
- ☐ 870 Taxes (U.S. Plaintiff or Defendant)
- ☐ 871 IRS—Third Party 26 USC 7609

OTHER STATUTES
- ☐ 400 State Reapportionment
- ☐ 410 Antitrust
- ☐ 430 Banks and Banking
- ☐ 450 Commerce
- ☐ 460 Deportation
- ☐ 470 Racketeer Influenced and Corrupt Organizations
- ☐ 480 Consumer Credit
- ☐ 490 Cable/Sat TV
- ☐ 810 Selective Service
- ☐ 850 Securities/Commodities/ Exchange
- ☐ 875 Customer Challenge 12 USC 3410
- ☐ 890 Other Statutory Actions
- ☐ 891 Agricultural Acts
- ☐ 892 Economic Stabilization Act
- ☐ 893 Environmental Matters
- ☐ 894 Energy Allocation Act
- ☐ 895 Freedom of Information Act
- ☐ 900 Appeal of Fee Determination Under Equal Access to Justice
- ☐ 950 Constitutionality of State Statutes

V. ORIGIN (Place an "X" in One Box Only)
- ☒ 1 Original Proceeding
- ☐ 2 Removed from State Court
- ☐ 3 Remanded from Appellate Court
- ☐ 4 Reinstated or Reopened
- ☐ 5 Transferred from another district (specify)
- ☐ 6 Multidistrict Litigation
- ☐ 7 Appeal to District Judge from Magistrate Judgment

VI. RELATED/RE-FILED CASE(S) (See instructions):
a) Re-filed cases: ☐ Yes ☒ No   b) Related cases: ☐ Yes ☒ No
JUDGE _____   DOCKET NUMBER _____

VII. CAUSE OF ACTION
Cite the U.S. Civil Statute under which you are filing (Do not cite jurisdictional statutes unless diversity):
42 U.S.C. SECTION 1983
42 U.S.C. § 1983 - Police officer assaulted plaintiff
LENGHT OF TRIAL

VIII. REQUESTED IN COMPLAINT:
☐ CHECK IF THIS IS A CLASS ACTION UNDER F.R.C.P. 23
DEMAND $ _____
CHECK YES only if demanded in complaint:
JURY DEMAND: ☒ Yes ☐ No

ABOVE INFORMATION TRUE & CORRECT TO THE BEST OF MY KNOWLEDGE

SIGNATURE OF ATTORNEY OF RECORD
_____

DATE: 9/26/06

FOR OFFICE USE ONLY
AMOUNT $350.00   RECEIPT 9473560   DT 09/27/06

Source: Swichkow v. City of Plantation and Boemester; 2006 WL 3033310 (S.D.Fla. September 27, 2006) (No. 06-61469 Civ-Cooke).

A. Introduction

This section presents a sample legal memorandum that applies Florida law. It is an office memo in the sense that it will not be filed with the court nor shown to anyone outside the office. It is designed for discussion and analysis solely for members of the firm working on the case of a client. The memo is not an advocacy document; it is not designed to convince a court or an opponent to take a particular position. Consequently, the memo does not hide or downplay any weaknesses in the client's position. It presents the strengths and weaknesses of the client's case.

All law firms do not use the same format for an office memorandum. Most firms, however, have the same basic five components: facts, issues or questions, brief answer, analysis or discussion, and conclusion. Firms may package these components in different ways (and may add others), but all of the five basic components are often present.

The format selected for our sample memorandum of law in Exhibit 7.3A has five parts presented in the following order:

I. Statement of Facts
II. Questions Presented
III. Brief Answers
IV. Discussion
V. Conclusion

B. Sample Memorandum of Law

Exhibit 7.3A   Sample Memorandum of Law

MEMORANDUM OF LAW

TO: Ms. Robin Kane, Esquire

FROM: Mr. Aaron Gunther, Paralegal

DATE: November 4, 2009

RE: Negligence stemming from a Spider Bite

              Paul Simpson v. Middle Medical Center

              Case No. 09-1234

I. STATEMENT OF FACTS

An ambulance brought Paul Simpson to the emergency room of the Middle Medical Center in Tampa (MMC) after he sustained minor injuries in an automobile accident. Dr. Charles Casten, the emergency room physician at MMC, ordered x-rays. Simpson was given a hospital gown and placed on the x-ray table. He then felt what seemed like flea bites. When he told the technician that he had been bitten by fleas, the technician laughed, as if Simpson were joking.

When Simpson returned to the emergency room, he showed Dr. Casten a mark near his left rib cage, but did not say he believed he had been bitten. Casten speculated that the mark might indicate seat belt trauma and ordered a CT scan. While the CT scan was taking place, Simpson again felt something biting him. When he emerged from the scanner, he reached inside his gown, pulled out a black widow spider, and threw it on the floor. He immediately returned to the emergency room, where Casten began treatment for the bite.

Simpson has retained our law firm to pursue his remedies against MMC for the physical or emotional distress arising from the spider bite.

II. QUESTIONS PRESENTED

1. Does a hospital have a duty to guard an invitee against attack by a poisonous spider bite within the hospital?

2. Was the hospital negligent in failing to prevent the spider bite?

EXHIBIT 7.3A

III. BRIEF ANSWERS

1. Yes. Although no Florida case has ruled on the issue, a good argument can be made that landowners have a duty to prevent attacks by animals that are not in their natural habitat.

2. The evidence collected to date, however, fails to establish that the hospital was unreasonable in failing to prevent the spider bite of Simpson, one of its patients.

IV. DISCUSSION

Simpson's negligence claim would be a premises liability action against the landowner-hospital by a business invitee, a hospital patient.

In Florida, a landowner owes two duties to a business invitee: (1) to use reasonable care in maintaining the premises in a reasonably safe condition; and (2) to give the invitee warning of concealed perils which are or should be known to the landowner, and which are unknown to the invitee and cannot be discovered by him through the exercise of due care. Knight v. Waltman, 774 So. 2d 731, 733 (Fla. 2d DCA 2000).

See also Emmons v. Baptist Hosp., 478 So. 2d 440, 442 (Fla. 1st DCA 1985). Simpson can try to assert that MMC breached both duties.

Issue 1

The first issue is whether a hospital has a duty to guard an invitee against attack by a poisonous spider within the hospital.

The hospital does have a the duty to maintain its facility in a reasonably safe condition. This duty requires the hospital to exercise ordinary care. Emmons, 478 So. 2d at 442. A landowner, however, is not an insurer of the safety of its business invitees. An inference of negligence is not warranted by the mere happening of an accident. "It is . . . fundamental, of course, that the mere occurrence of an accident does not give rise to an inference of negligence, and is not sufficient for a finding of negligence on the part of anyone." Cassel v. Price, 396 So. 2d 258, 264 (Fla. 1st DCA 1981).

No Florida cases specifically address a premises liability action based on a spider or insect bite. Generally, Florida law holds that landowners do not have a duty to guard an invitee against harm from a wild animal, which is broadly defined to include insects. See Wamser v. City of St. Petersburg, 339 So. 2d 244 (Fla. 2d DCA 1976) (addressing a shark attack in the waters off one of the city's beaches); Palumbo v. State Game & Fresh Water Fish Comm'n, 487 So. 2d 352 (Fla. 1st DCA 1986) (concerning an alligator attack at a lake). Note, however,

Exhibit 7.3A Sample Memorandum of Law

that the Wamser and Palumbo cases involved injuries from an animal attack that took place in the animal's natural habitat.

Cases in other jurisdictions have come to different conclusions. A Texas court, for example, held that a landowner could owe a duty with regard to wild animals found inside an artificial structure:

We do not say a landowner can never be negligent with regard to the indigenous wild animals found on its property. A premises owner could be negligent with regard to wild animals found in artificial structures or places where they are not normally found; that is, stores, hotels, apartment houses, or billboards, if the landowner knows or should know of the unreasonable risk of harm posed by an animal on its premises, and cannot expect patrons to realize the danger or guard against it. Nicholson v. Smith, 986 S.W. 2d 54, 63-64 (Tex.Ct.App.1999).

A California court, however, held, as a matter of law, that a homeowner owed no duty to an invitee to prevent injury from a spider bite. Brunelle v. Signore, 215 Cal. App. 3d 122, 263 Cal. Rptr. 415, 416 (1989). In this case, a guest had suffered serious injuries after he was bitten by a brown recluse spider at a vacation home owned by the defendant.

Issue 2

Assuming a duty can exist because of the nonnatural environment in which the spider bit Simpson, a more serious problem is whether the hospital breached that duty. As indicated, the hospital is not an insurer. It is not required to prevent injuries; its obligation is limited to exercising reasonable care in preventing injury. Cassel, 396 So. 2d at 264.

The following evidence collected thus far in the case would suggest that MMC has not breached this duty:

• MMC had contracted with a pest control company (Code Safe Control, Inc.) to provide preventive maintenance and to respond to reports of pests in the hospital. A technician from the company is expected to testify that he has serviced the hospital for four years and has never seen a black widow spider or spider infestation of any kind at the hospital.

• John Anderson, the expert entomologist we have hired, has told us (1) that black widow spiders are native to Florida and can be found inside buildings; (2) that spiders could be excluded from a structure only by completely isolating it from the outside world, and (3) that such measures would make it impossible for a hospital to remain open to the public.

EXHIBIT 7.3A

• On the day Simpson was bit, no evidence has been uncovered to date that Dr. Casten or anyone else treating Simpson saw a spider before he was bitten.

We need to conduct further investigation and discovery to try to determine what policies are in place at MMC to prevent insect attacks, whether spiders and similar insects have been seen on the premises in the past, and if so, how the hospital responded.

V. CONCLUSION

A good argument can be made that a duty of reasonable care exists to prevent spider bites to patients in a hospital because the hospital is not the natural environment of spiders, although authority exists outside Florida that such a duty does not exist. The evidence collected, to date, however, casts doubt on whether MMC breached this duty, assuming a Florida court finds that it exists. Further investigation and discovery are needed to find out MMC's prior experience with such insects, whether it has adequate preventive procedures in place to prevent bites, and whether such procedures have been consistently followed.

Memo Format

www.ualr.edu/cmbarger
(click "Format Guidelines")
www.alwd.org/publications/pdf/CM2_Appendix6.pdf
www.alwd.org/publications/pdf/CM1_Appendix6.pdf
users.ipfw.edu/vetterw/a339-research-sample-memo.htm

Sample Memorandum of Law

users.ipfw.edu/vetterw/a339-research-sample-memo.htm
www.chessconsulting.org/financialaid/sample02.htm

Find a memorandum of law online on any legal issue in any state. Run the search, "memorandum of law" in Google or another search engine. Try to find an internal memo rather than one that was filed in court. Compare its format or structure to the sample memorandum presented here in the spider case.

7.4 Sample Appellate Brief Filed in the Florida Supreme Court

A. Introduction

B. Florida Rules of Appellate Procedure on the Content and Form of Appellate Briefs

C. Sample Appellate Brief Filed in the Florida Supreme Court

D. More Information

E. Something to Check

A. Introduction

An appellate brief is a document submitted by a party to an appellate court and served on the opposing party in which arguments are presented on why the appellate court should affirm (approve), reverse, or otherwise modify what a lower court has done. There are a number of roles that paralegals perform in this area of appellate practice. They might be asked to go through the transcript of the trial record to find references that the attorney wants to use in the brief. They might be asked to cite check the brief by making sure that:

- All quotations are accurate
- All citations are in the format required by court rules
- The brief itself is in the format required by court rules
- All laws cited are still valid

The last role is performed by using citators such as Shepard's Citations, KeyCite, or GlobalCite. A citator allows you to check each case, statute, or other law to make sure that it has not been overruled or changed since the time the appellate brief was drafted. Occasionally, an experienced paralegal will be asked to draft a portion of an appellate brief.

The main courts in which appellate briefs are filed are the District Courts of Appeal and the Florida Supreme Court. In this section, we present an example of an appellate brief filed in the Florida Supreme Court. See also the following related sections in the book:

- Florida state legal research (section 5.1)
- Citation of legal materials (section 5.2)
- Timeline of civil litigation (section 6.1)
- Timeline of criminal litigation (section 6.4)
- Selected rules of procedure (section 6.2)
- Comparison of state and federal civil procedure (section 6.3)
- Civil complaints (section 7.4)

An appeal is initiated by filing two copies of a Notice of Appeal with the court that rendered the judgment to be reviewed. This must be done (with appropriate filing fees) within 30 days from entry of the judgment. As indicated in section 6.1, the clerk of the lower court will prepare the record and index and transmit the appellate packet to the appeals court within 110 days of filing the notice. Once the case is docketed in the appeals court, the briefing process described here commences. (Florida Rule of Appellate Procedure 9.110.) A Notice of Appeal and related forms can be found in Florida Rules of Appellate Procedure, Rule 9.900(a)-(h).

B. Florida Rules of Appellate Procedure on the Content and Form of Appellate Briefs

Before examining a sample brief in Exhibit 7.4A, review the following rules from the Florida Rules of Appellate Procedure on the content and form of appellate briefs in Florida state courts.

Florida Rules of Appellate Procedure

www.floridasupremecourt.org/decisions/barrules.shtml
(click "Documents" then "Appellate Procedure")

RULE 9.210. BRIEFS

(a) **Generally.** In addition to briefs on jurisdiction under rule 9.120(d), the only briefs permitted to be filed by the parties in any one proceeding are the initial brief, the answer brief, a reply brief, and a cross-reply brief. All briefs required by these rules shall be prepared as follows:

(1) Briefs shall be printed, typewritten, or duplicated on opaque, white, unglossed 8 1/2-by-11 inch paper. | Required Format for an Appellate Brief

(2) The lettering in briefs shall be black and in distinct type, double-spaced, with margins no less

than 1 inch. Lettering in script or type made in imitation of handwriting shall not be permitted. Footnotes and quotations may be single spaced and shall be in the same size type, with the same spacing between characters, as the text. Computer-generated briefs shall be submitted in either Times New Roman 14-point font or Courier New 12-point font. All computer-generated briefs shall contain a certificate of compliance signed by counsel, or the party if unrepresented, certifying that the brief complies with the font requirements of this rule. The certificate of compliance shall be contained in the brief immediately following the certificate of service.

(3) Briefs shall be securely bound in book form and fastened along the left side in a manner that will allow them to lie flat when opened or be securely stapled in the upper left corner. Headings and subheadings shall be at least as large as the brief text and may be single spaced.

(4) The cover sheet of each brief shall state the name of the court, the style of the cause, including the case number if assigned, the lower tribunal, the party on whose behalf the brief is filed, the type of brief, and the name and address of the attorney filing the brief.

<u>Cover Sheet</u>

(5) The initial and answer briefs shall not exceed 50 pages in length, provided that if a cross-appeal has been filed, the answer brief/initial brief on cross-appeal shall not exceed 85 pages. Reply briefs shall not exceed 15 pages in length; provided that if a cross-appeal has been filed, the reply brief shall not exceed 50 pages, not more than 15 of which shall be devoted to argument replying to the answer portion of the appellee/cross-appellant's brief. Crossreply briefs shall not exceed 15 pages. Briefs on jurisdiction shall not exceed 10 pages. The table of contents and the citation of authorities shall be excluded from the computation. Longer briefs may be permitted by the court.

<u>Restrictions on Length</u>

(b) Contents of Initial Brief. The initial brief shall contain the following, in order:

(1) A table of contents listing the issues presented for review, with references to pages.

(2) A table of citations with cases listed alphabetically, statutes and other authorities, and the pages of the brief on which each citation appears. See rule 9.800 for a uniform citation system.

<u>Table of Citations</u>

(3) A statement of the case and of the facts, which shall include the nature of the case, the course of the proceedings, and the disposition in the lower tribunal. References to the appropriate volume and pages of the record or transcript shall be made.

(4) A summary of argument, suitably paragraphed, condensing succinctly, accurately, and clearly the argument actually made in the body of the brief. It should not be a mere repetition of the headings under which the argument is arranged. It should seldom exceed 2 and never 5 pages.

(5) Argument with regard to each issue including the applicable appellate standard of review.

(6) A conclusion, of not more than 1 page, setting forth the precise relief sought.

(c) Contents of Answer Brief. The answer brief shall be prepared in the same manner as the initial brief; provided that the statement of the case and of the facts may be omitted. If a cross-appeal has been filed, the answer brief shall include the issues in the cross-appeal that are presented for review, and argument in support of those issues.

<u>Other Appellate Briefs</u>

(d) Contents of Reply Brief. The reply brief shall contain argument in response and rebuttal to argument presented in the answer brief.

(e) Contents of Cross-Reply Brief. The cross-reply brief is limited to rebuttal of argument of the cross-appellee.

(f) Times for Service of Briefs. The times for serving jurisdiction and initial briefs are prescribed by rules 9.110, 9.120, 9.130, and 9.140. Unless otherwise required, the answer brief shall be served within 20 days after service of the initial brief; the reply brief, if any, shall be served within 20 days after service of the answer brief; and the cross-reply brief, if any, shall be served within 20 days thereafter.

(g) Filing with Courts. The filing requirements of the courts are as follows:

<u>Filing Requirements</u>

(1) Circuit Courts. Original and 1 copy.

(2) District Courts of Appeal. Original and 3 copies.

(3) Supreme Court. Original and 7 copies; except that 5 copies only shall accompany the original jurisdictional briefs prescribed in rule 9.120(d).

RULE 9.220. APPENDIX

(a) Purpose. The purpose of an appendix is to permit the parties to prepare and transmit copies of those portions of the record deemed necessary to an understanding of the issues presented. It may be served with any petition, brief, motion, response, or reply but shall be served as otherwise required by these rules. In any proceeding in which an appendix is required, if the court finds that the appendix is incomplete, it shall direct a party to supply the omitted parts of the appendix. No proceeding shall be determined until an opportunity to supplement the appendix has been given.

(b) **Contents.** The appendix shall contain an index and a conformed copy of the opinion or order to be reviewed and may contain any other portions of the record and other authorities. It shall be separately bound or separated from the petition, brief, motion, response, or reply by a divider and appropriate tab. Asterisks should be used to indicate omissions in documents or testimony of witnesses. If the appendix includes documents filed before January 1991 on paper measuring $8\frac{1}{2}$ by 14 inches, the documents should be reduced in copying to $8\frac{1}{2}$ by 11 inches, if practicable. If impracticable, the appen-

> The Appendix to
> an Appellate brief

dix may measure $8\frac{1}{2}$ by 14 inches, but it should be bound separately from the document that it accompanies.

RULE 9.225. NOTICE OF SUPPLEMENTAL AUTHORITY

Notices of supplemental authority may be filed with the court before a decision has been rendered to call attention to decisions, rules, statutes, or other authorities that are significant to the issues raised and that have been discovered after the last brief served in the cause. The notice may identify briefly the points argued on appeal to which the supplemental authorities are pertinent, but shall not contain argument. Copies of the supplemental authorities shall be attached to the notice.

C. Sample Appellate Brief Filed in the Florida Supreme Court

EXHIBIT 7.4A   Appellate Brief

IN THE SUPREME COURT OF FLORIDA

THE FLORIDA BAR,

    Complainant

v.

ALAN S. GLUECK,

    Respondent.

Supreme Court Case
No. SC06-1101, SC07-1

The Florida Bar File
Nos. 2005-51,065(17J)
2005-51,354(17J)
2005-51,440(17J)
2005-51,469(17J)
2006-50,254(17J)
2006-50,780(17J)
2006-51,397(17J)
2006-51,490(17J)

THE FLORIDA BAR'S INITIAL BRIEF

JUAN CARLOS ARIAS, #0076414
Bar Counsel
The Florida Bar
5900 North Andrews Ave., Suite 900
Fort Lauderdale, FL 33309
(954) 772-2245

KENNETH L. MARVIN, #200999
Staff Counsel
The Florida Bar
651 E. Jefferson Street
Tallahassee, FL 32399-2300
(850)-561-5600

JOHN F. HARKNESS, JR., #123390
Executive Director
The Florida Bar
651 E. Jefferson Street
Tallahassee, FL 32399-2300
(850) 561-5600

EXHIBIT 7.4A

TABLE OF CONTENTS

ii

EXHIBIT 7.4A Appellate Brief

TABLE OF AUTHORITIES

Cases

R. Regulating Fla. Bar

Standards

iii

EXHIBIT 7.4A

PRELIMINARY STATEMENT

Throughout this Initial Brief, The Florida Bar will refer to specific parts of the record as follows: The Report of Referee dated March 29, 2007, will be designated as RR _____ (indicating the referenced page number). The Florida Bar will be referred to as "the Bar." Alan S. Glueck will be referred to as "respondent."

1

EXHIBIT 7.4A Appellate Brief

STATEMENT OF THE CASE AND FACTS

This case arises from respondent's participation in a business venture with a non-lawyer that included the practice of law, assisting the non-lawyer in the violation of an injunction from the Supreme Court of Florida, neglecting clients, and lying to the Bar during an official investigation. The 2 consolidated Supreme Court cases involve 8 different clients whose immigration cases were neglected by the respondent.

The referee found clear and convincing evidence that respondent violated the 28 counts of misconduct contained in the complaint. The referee concluded that the respondent: 1) entered into an improper "partnership" or "business relationship" with a non-lawyer that included the practice of law [RR 18]; 2) that the respondent "intentionally violated the UPL injunction" ordered by the Supreme Court of Florida [RR 3]; and 3) that the respondent "intentionally mislead The Florid[sic] Bar and knowingly concealed his relationship" with the non-lawyer. [RR12]

The final hearing focused on respondent's knowledge of an injunction that prohibited a non-lawyer from advising persons on legal and immigration matters. The evidence showed that respondent represented the non-lawyer in the 1997 Unlicensed Practice of Law action that concluded with an injunction from the Supreme Court prohibiting the non-lawyer from advising persons on immigration

2

Exhibit 7.4A

matters. The referee found that the respondent "knowingly assisted" and "intentionally violated the UPL injunction." [RR 3]

The final hearing also focused on the respondent's business relationship with the non-lawyer and the quality of the legal service provided by the partnership. The uncontroverted evidence showed that respondent entered into an inappropriate partnership with the non-lawyer's translation and accounting business that "blended together into one operation sharing the same office manager, location, employees, and sharing control over bank accounts." [RR 48]. The referee concluded that this partnership included the practice of law. [RR 48]

As to the quality of legal service provided by the respondent and the non-lawyer partner, the evidence showed that respondent never personally met with most of the complainants, did not properly communicate or explain legal matters to them, and failed to diligently represent the clients. The referee found that the respondent visited the legal operation "every two to three weeks" [RR 5] and that the non-lawyer was responsible for the day to day operation, serving as the "conduit for factual and legal information." [RR 9]

In her report the referee concluded that during the Bar's investigation, the respondent misrepresented and failed to reveal his inappropriate partnership with the non-lawyer. The referee found that respondent "intentionally mislead The

3

EXHIBIT 7.4A   Appellate Brief

Florid[a] Bar and knowingly concealed his relationship" with the non-lawyer. [RR12]

The Bar recommended disbarment but the referee, even though she found respondent guilty of all the alleged violations, recommended only a 3 year suspension. The Florida Bar does not challenge the referee findings but instead asserts that the referee recommended a sanction too lenient considering the severity of the cumulative misconduct.

4

Exhibit 7.4A

SUMMARY OF THE ARGUMENT

The referee correctly found respondent guilty of the 11 rule violations contained within the Bar's complaint but erred in failing to recommend an appropriate sanction against respondent. In her 87 page-long report, the referee found that the Bar presented clear and convincing evidence of respondent's 28 counts of ethical rule violations affecting 8 different complainants, but only recommended a 3 year suspension instead of disbarment.

Beyond the specific facts of the 8 individual cases, the referee described in her report the inappropriateness of respondent's general conduct. The referee found that: 1) the respondent entered into an improper "partnership" or "business relationship" with a non-lawyer that included the practice of law [RR 18]; 2) that the respondent "intentionally violated UPL injunction" ordered by the Supreme Court of Florida [RR 3]; 3) and that the respondent "intentionally mislead The Florid[sic] Bar and knowingly concealed his relationship" with the non-lawyer. [RR12]

The referee found that the following ethical violations were proven through clear and convincing evidence: R. Regulating Fla. Bar 3-4.2 [Violation of the Rules of Professional Conduct as adopted by the rules governing The Florida Bar is a cause for discipline.]; 3-4.3 [The commission by a lawyer of an act that is unlawful or contrary to honesty and justice, whether the act is committed in the

5

EXHIBIT 7.4A | Appellate Brief

course of the attorney's relations as an attorney or otherwise, whether committed within or outside the state of Florida and whether or not the act is a felony or misdemeanor, may constitute a cause for discipline.]; **4-1.1** [A lawyer shall provide competent representation to a client. Competent representation requires the legal knowledge, skill, thoroughness, and preparation reasonably necessary for the representation.]; **4-1.3** [A lawyer shall act with reasonable diligence and promptness in representing a client.]; **4-1.4(a)** [A lawyer shall keep a client reasonably informed about the status of a matter and promptly comply with reasonable requests for information.]; **4-1.4(b)** [A lawyer shall explain a matter to the extent reasonably necessary to permit the client to make informed decisions regarding the representation.]; **4-5.4(c)** [A lawyer shall not form a partnership with a non-lawyer if any of the activities of the partnership consist of the practice of law.]; **4-8.1(a)** [An applicant for admission to the bar, or a lawyer in connection with a bar admission application or on connection with a disciplinary matter shall not knowingly make a false statement of material fact.]; **4-8.1(b)** [An applicant for admission to the bar, or a lawyer in connection with a bar admission application or on connection with a disciplinary matter shall not knowingly fail to disclose a fact necessary to correct a misapprehension known by the person to have arisen in the matter.]; **4-8.4(a)** [A lawyer shall not violate or attempt to violate the Rules of Professional Conduct, knowingly assist or induce another to do so, or do so

6

Exhibit 7.4A

through the acts of another.]; **4-8.4(c)** [A lawyer shall not engage in conduct involving dishonesty, fraud, deceit or misrepresentation.].

The Bar also provided the referee with case law and the appropriate Florida Standards for Imposing Lawyer Sanctions warranting disbarment based on respondent's serious pattern of ethical misconduct. The Bar requests that this Court order respondent's disbarment based on the severity of the overwhelming evidence found in the record, the Florida Standards for Imposing Lawyer Sanctions, and relevant case law.

7

EXHIBIT 7.4A Appellate Brief

ARGUMENT

THE REFEREE ERRED BY RECOMMENDING A 3 YEAR SUSPENSION INSTEAD OF DISBARMENT BASED ON FLORIDA STANDARDS FOR IMPOSING LAWYER SANCTIONS AND FLORIDA CASE LAW.

While a referee's findings of fact should be upheld unless clearly erroneous, this Court is not bound by the referee's recommendations in determining the appropriate level of discipline. *The Florida Bar v. Vannier*, 498 So.2d 896 (Fla. 1986); *The Florida Bar v. Rue*, 643 So.2d 1080 (Fla. 1994). Furthermore, this Court has stated the review of the discipline recommendation does not receive the same deference as the guilt recommendation because this Court has the ultimate authority to determine the appropriate sanction. *The Florida Bar v. Grief*, 701 So.2d 555 (Fla. 1997); *The Florida Bar. v. Wilson*, 643 So.2d 1063 (Ha. 1994). In *The Florida Bar v. Pahules*, 233 So.2d 130 (Fla. 1970), this Court held three purposes must be held in mind when deciding the appropriate sanction for an attorney's misconduct: 1) the judgment must be fair to society; 2) the judgment must be fair to the attorney; and 3) the judgment must be severe enough to deter others attorneys from similar conduct. This Court has further stated a referee's recommended discipline must have a reasonable basis in existing case law or the Standards for Imposing Lawyer Sanctions. *The Florida Bar v. Sweeney*, 730 So.2d 1269 (Fla. 1998); *The Florida Bar v. Leznar*, 690 So.2d 1284 (Fla. 1997). The

8

Exhibit 7.4A

Court will not second guess a referee's recommended discipline "as long as that discipline has a reasonable basis in existing case law." *The Florida Bar v. Laing*, 695 So.2d 299, 304 (Fla. 1997).

In the instant case, while the referee found respondent guilty of all the allegations raised by the bar and found various aggravating factors present, the referee did not disbar respondent. This is contrary to existing case law. This Court has ruled that it "deals more harshly with cumulative misconduct than it does with isolated misconduct." *The Florida Bar v. Williams*, 604 So.2d 447 (Fla. 1992). The *Williams* decision follows the line of cases such as *The Florida Bar v. Mitchell*, 385 So.2d 96 (Fla. 1980), where this court upheld the referee's recommendation for disbarment and his finding that "the totality and frequency of the different complaints evidence to me a reckless and wanton disregard by the Respondent for the rights and needs of his clients."

The case before the Court also involves cumulative misconduct, as described in the 28 counts of the complaint, which demonstrates respondent's disregard for the profession and his unfitness to practice law. The referee recognized the principle of "cumulative misconduct" outlined in *Mitchell* and *Williams* when she explained in her report that:

The Supreme Court held in *The Florida Bar v. Abrams*, 919 So.2d 425 (Fla. 2006) that an attorney who allowed his name and title to be used by a non-lawyer in a corporation doing immigration work violated the prohibition against conduct involving dishonesty, fraud,

9

EXHIBIT 7.4A Appellate Brief

deceit or misrepresentation, warranting a one-year suspension. The Court in *Abrams* found that the paralegal was the person in control of the corporation's day-to-day operations, met with the clients, conducted the client interviews, and made the decisions as to the appropriate course of action for the clients, and that the lawyer himself visited the office several times a month. The present case involves similar facts as in *Abrams*, but is more egregious in that Respondent participated in creating a "store front" for the Law Office of Alan S. Glueck and received the benefits of a free location, utilities, employees, secretarial and bookkeeping services. Furthermore, the current case involves eight cases of misconduct and not just one as in the *Abrams* case. [RR 84]

The referee's recommendation of a 3 year suspension is not appropriate given the severity of the respondent's misconduct.

This case bears some similarities to the case of *The Florida Bar v. Elster*, 770 So.2d 1184 (Fla. 2000), where an attorney received a 3 year suspension for failing to accomplish any meaningful work on behalf of immigration clients, misrepresentation to clients, and issuance of misleading business cards. This Court upheld the referee's findings and explained that:

"[F]irst, '[c]onfidence in, and proper utilization of, the legal system is adversely affected when a lawyer fails to diligently pursue a legal matter entrusted to that lawyer's care. A failure to do so is a direct violation of the oath a lawyer takes upon his admission to the bar.' Second, the gravity of Elster's misconduct is heightened by one very important aggravating factor not present in any other case involving a pattern of conduct as serious as that in which Elster has engaged; vulnerability of the victims. The facts of these four cases, considered together, clearly show a pattern of egregious exploitation by Elster of a very vulnerable class of individuals."

10

Exhibit 7.4A

The case before this court is more egregious than *Elster* and requires the imposition of a more severe sanction. While both cases involve complainants who were immigrants seeking the legalization of their status in the United States, in the instant case, as a direct result of respondent's misconduct, several complainants had to return to their country of origin and 1 was detained for several months after missing an immigration hearing because of respondent's failure to inform her of the hearing date. In this particular case, the referee found that:

Respondent did not transfer Nakad's case to Attorney Kimmel until 2004 but still attempts to blame Attorney Kimmel for the deportation order being enforced. The referee finds this the most egregious case out of all that has been pleaded and heard. Nakad was arrested and detained for seven months with the threat of the loss of custody of her daughter. She expended thousands of dollars to get her Immigration status clarified and to retain her rights to raise her daughter in the United States. The emotional distress caused by the process was abundantly clear by her testimony and demeanor at the final hearing. Respondent's blame of the subsequent counsel is unfounded and unacceptable." [RR 70]

Put simply, the referee's recommendation of a 3 year suspension, in light of these circumstances, is not consistent with the prior rulings of this court.

Not only did this respondent exploit a very vulnerable class of individuals and failed to perform meaningful work on behalf of his clients, but he also intentionally assisted a non-lawyer in violating an injunction ordered by the Supreme Court of Florida [RR 11], entered into an inappropriate business relationship or partnership with the non-lawyer [RR 16], and intentionally misled the Bar in an official

11

EXHIBIT 7.4A Appellate Brief

investigation. [RR 12]. This additional aggravating misconduct demonstrates "a reckless and wanton disregard by the Respondent for the rights and needs of his clients." *The Florida Bar v. Mitchell*, 385 So.2d 96 (Fla. 1980).

Not only is Mr. Glueck's disbarment supported by existing case law coupled with the aggravating factors, but The Florida Standards for Imposing Lawyer Sanctions provide a reasonable basis for this Court to impose disbarment. Standard 4.41(a) states that disbarment is appropriate when a lawyer abandons the practice and causes serious or potentially serious injury to a client. The referee in this case found that respondent in essence abandoned some of his clients by not notifying them of the closure of his office in Aventura and by failing to transfer the mail service from the closed location to his other office. [RR 14, 27, 28, 29, 36, 37, 45, 46, 61, 63, 64, 73, and 76]

Standard 4.61 is also applicable and warrants disbarment. This standard states that disbarment is appropriate when a lawyer knowingly or intentionally deceives a client with the intent to benefit the lawyer or another regardless of injury or potential injury to the client. After respondent closed his office in Aventura, he told one of the complainants that he was not retained by him to handle the client's legal matter when in fact the opposite was true. The referee found, however, that respondent "told Ramos that he contracted with Millennia and that he paid Millennia. Respondent blamed Millennia for the problems with the application and

12

Exhibit 7.4A

refused to return money to Ramos" [RR 15]. It is uncontroverted that respondent misled his client by blaming Millennia, his business venture with the non-lawyer, in order to protect himself financially.

Disbarment is also warranted here pursuant to Standard 6.11 which states that disbarment is appropriate when a lawyer (a) with the intent to deceive the court, knowingly makes a false statement or submits a false document; or (b) improperly withholds material information, and causes serious or potentially serious injury to a party, or causes a significant or potentially significant adverse effect on the legal proceeding. The referee found that respondent violated 8 counts of Rule of Professional conduct 4-8.1(a), a lawyer shall not knowingly make a false statement of material fact in connection with a disciplinary matter; 7 counts of Rule of Professional conduct 4-8.1(b), a lawyer shall not knowingly fail to disclose a fact necessary to correct a misapprehension known by the person to have arisen in a disciplinary matter; and 7 counts of Rule of Professional conduct 4-8.4(c), a lawyer shall not engage in conduct involving dishonesty, fraud, deceit, or misrepresentation. The referee concluded that "the Bar has proven by clear and convincing evidence that Respondent intentionally mislead The Florid[sic] Bar and knowingly concealed his relationship with Betchinger and Millennia." [RR 12]

Finally, under Standard 7.1 disbarment is also appropriate. Standard 7.1 states that disbarment is appropriate when a lawyer intentionally engages in

13

Exhibit 7.4A

CONCLUSION

The referee erred in failing to recommend disbarment. The Bar proved by clear and convincing evidence 28 counts of misconduct. Respondent's conduct in forming a partnership or business relationship with a non-lawyer; assisting the non-lawyer in violating an injunction from the Supreme Court of Florida; his failure to communicate and diligently represent clients; intentionally misleading the Bar in an official investigation; and engaging in conduct involving dishonesty, fraud, deceit or misrepresentation, warrant disbarment.

The Bar respectfully requests that this Court disbar respondent from the practice of law based on the Florida Standards for Imposing Lawyer Sanctions and relevant case law.

15

Exhibit 7.4A   Appellate Brief

conduct that is a violation of a duty owed as a professional with the intent to obtain a benefit for the lawyer or another, and causes serious or potentially serious injury to a client, the public, or the legal system. It is uncontroverted that respondent, for his personal financial gain, entered into a partnership with a non-lawyer and assisted him in violating an injunction ultimately injuring several clients in the process. [RR 3]

Based on the foregoing, the Bar respectfully requests that this Honorable Court reject the referee's recommendation of a 3 year suspension and disbar the respondent based on his egregious cumulative misconduct. Disbarment is warranted given the ethical misconduct involved in this case, is supported by The Standards for Imposing Lawyer Sanctions, and has a reasonable basis in similar cases brought before the Court.

14

Exhibit 7.4A   Appellate Brief

Respectfully submitted,

_____

JUAN CARLOS ARIAS
Bar Counsel
The Florida Bar
Cypress Financial Center
5900 North Andrews Ave., Suite 900
Fort Lauderdale, FL 33309
(954) 772-2245

CERTIFICATE OF SERVICE

I **HEREBY CERTIFY** the original and 7 copies of The Florida Bar's Initial Brief has been furnished via regular U.S. mail to The Honorable Thomas D. Hall, Clerk, Supreme Court of Florida, Supreme Court Building, 500 South Duval Street, Tallahassee, FL 32399-1927 and has been electronically filed; a true and correct copies have been furnished by regular U.S. mail to Kevin P. Tynan, attorney for respondent, 8142 N. University Drive, Tamarac, FL 33321, and to Staff Counsel, The Florida Bar, 651 East Jefferson Street, Tallahassee, Florida 32399-2300, on this _____ day of _____, 2007.

_____

JUAN CARLOS ARIAS

CERTIFICATE OF TYPE, SIZE STYLE AND ANTI-VIRUS SCAN

Undersigned counsel hereby certifies The Florida Bar's Initial Brief is submitted in 14 point, proportionately spaced, Times New Roman font, and the computer file has been scanned and found to be free of viruses by Norton Anti-Virus for Windows.

_____

JUAN CARLOS ARIAS

16

For Florida cases, see also section 5.1.

1. Check the accuracy of the location information in the citations by determining whether the three cases are found in the volumes and on the pages indicated in their citations.

2. Check the accuracy of what the brief says about the three cases. For example, the brief cites *The Florida Bar v. Vannier* in support of the position that while a referee's findings of fact should be upheld unless clearly erroneous, the Court is not bound by the referee's recommendations in determining the appropriate level of discipline. Go to the *Vannier* case to determine if it takes this position.

D. More Information

Florida Rules
www.floridasupremecourt.org
(click "Court Decisions & Rules")
www.floridalawonline.net/courts.html#courtrules
www.llrx.com/courtrules-gen/state-Florida.html

Florida Civil Procedure and Practice
www.megalaw.com/fl/top/flcivpro.php

Florida Statutes
www.leg.state.fl.us/Statutes/index.cfm

Florida State Trial and Appellate Courts
www.flcourts.org

Understanding the Appellate Process
www.4dca.org/geniformfrm.html

Pro Se Appellate Handbook: Representing Yourself on Appeal
www.4dca.org/geniformfrm.html

Guide to Appellate Briefs Online
www.llrx.com/features/briefsonline.htm#free%20by%20jurisdiction
www.llrx.com/columns/reference43.htm
www.legaline.com/freebriefslinks.html
www.lawsource.com/also/usa.cgi?usb

E. Something to Check

Assume that you have been asked to cite check the appellate brief in this section in the case of *The Florida Bar v. Glueck*. Pick any three cases cited in the brief. Try to find them in a large law library or online. On finding cases online, check:
www.law.cornell.edu/states/florida.html
www.findlaw.com/11stategov/fl/laws.html

7.5 Sample Criminal Indictment Filed in a Florida State Court
A. Introduction
B. A State Criminal Indictment
C. More Information
D. Something to Check

A. Introduction

This section presents an example of an indictment filed in a Florida circuit court. The case involves the kidnapping and murder of a 9-year-old Citrus County girl by a registered sex offender. The case gained national notoriety and prompted Florida legislators to propose legislation that would require registered sex offenders to wear electronic tracking devices at all times. The indictment sets out four counts: murder in the first degree, burglary of a dwelling with battery, kidnapping, and sexual battery upon a person under 12 years of age.

B. A State Criminal Indictment

Exhibit 7.5A contains the original indictment and probable cause affidavit.

Exhibit 7.5A	**Indictment and Probable Cause Affidavit**

IN THE CIRCUIT COURT OF THE FIFTH JUDICIAL CIRCUIT OF THE STATE OF
FLORIDA, IN AND FOR CITRUS COUNTY, IN THE SPRING TERM THEREOF, IN THE YEAR OF OUR
LORD, TWO THOUSAND-FIVE.

THE STATE OF FLORIDA   CASE NO. 2005-CF-000298-A

vs   **INDICTMENT**

JOHN EVANDER COUEY

IN THE NAME AND BY THE AUTHORITY OF THE STATE OF FLORIDA:

THE GRAND JURORS OF THE STATE OF FLORIDA, impaneled and sworn to inquire and true
presentment make, in and for the body of the County of Citrus, upon their oaths do present, that: JOHN
EVANDER COUEY (R/G: W/M, DOB: 08/19/1958, SSN: ▌▌▌▌▌▌) in the County of Citrus, and the State
of Florida, between the 23rd day of February and the 7th day of March, inclusive, in the year of Our Lord, two
thousand-five:

COUNT I
MURDER IN THE FIRST DEGREE (FC)

did unlawfully and from a premeditated design to effect the death of ▌▌▌▌▌▌▌▌▌▌▌▌▌▌▌▌ , a human
being, kill and murder the said ▌▌▌▌▌▌▌▌▌▌▌▌▌▌ by causing her to asphyxiate, in violation of
Florida Statute 782.04(1)(a)1;

COUNT II
BURGLARY OF A DWELLING WITH BATTERY (F1L)

and said Grand Jurors aforesaid, under oath, further present that JOHN EVANDER COUEY (R/G: W/M, DOB:
08/19/1958, SSN: ▌▌▌▌▌▌), in the County of Citrus and the State of Florida, between the 23rd and 24th day
of February, inclusive, in the year of Our Lord, two thousand-five, did unlawfully enter or remain in a certain
dwelling or curtilage thereof, located at ▌▌▌▌▌▌▌▌▌▌▌▌▌▌▌▌▌▌▌▌ , in the County and State
aforesaid, the property of ▌▌▌▌▌▌▌▌▌▌▌▌▌▌▌▌ , as owners or custodians thereof, without said
persons' consent with the intent to commit an offense therein, and, in the course thereof, did commit a battery
upon ▌▌▌▌▌▌▌▌▌▌▌▌▌▌▌▌ , by actually and intentionally touching or striking ▌▌▌▌▌▌▌▌▌
against her will, in violation of Florida Statutes 810.02(1), 810.02(2)(a) and 784.03;

COUNT III
KIDNAPPING (FL)

and said Grand Jurors aforesaid, under oath, further present that JOHN EVANDER COUEY (R/G: W/M, DOB:
08/19/1958, SSN: ▌▌▌▌▌▌), in the County of Citrus and the State of Florida, between the 23rd day of
February and the 7th day of March, inclusive, in the year of Our Lord, two thousand-five, did forcibly, secretly,
or by threat, confine, abduct, or imprison ▌▌▌▌▌▌▌▌▌▌▌▌▌▌ , a child under the age of thirteen (13) years
of age, against her will, without lawful authority, with the intent to commit or facilitate the commission of a
felony, and in the course of said kidnapping, did commit a sexual battery upon the said ▌▌▌▌▌▌▌▌▌▌
▌▌▌▌▌▌▌▌ , in violation of Florida Statute 787.01(1) and 787.01(3);

C-2005-15300

Exhibit 7.5A **Indictment and Probable Cause Affidavit**

PAGE 2
STATE OF FLORIDA
VS
JOHN EVANDER COUEY
2005-CF-000298-A

<u>COUNT IV</u>
SEXUAL BATTERY UPON PERSON UNDER TWELVE YOA (FL)

and said Grand Jurors aforesaid, under oath, further present that JOHN EVANDER COUEY (R/G: W/M, DOB: 08/19/1958, SSN: ▮▮▮▮▮▮▮▮), in the County of Citrus and the State of Florida, between the 23rd day of February and the 7th day of March, inclusive, in the year of Our Lord, two thousand-five, did, being a person eighteen (18) years of age or older, unlawfully commit sexual battery upon ▮▮▮▮▮▮▮▮▮▮▮▮▮▮▮▮▮▮▮▮▮▮▮▮▮▮▮▮▮ , date of birth: ▮▮▮▮▮▮▮▮▮▮▮▮▮ a person less than twelve (12) years of age, by causing his ▮▮▮▮▮▮▮▮▮▮▮▮▮▮▮▮▮ of ▮▮▮▮▮▮▮▮▮▮▮▮▮▮▮▮▮ in violation of Florida Statute 794.011(2);

contrary to the form of the statute in such cases made and provided and against the peace and dignity of the State of Florida.

A TRUE BILL

(signature)
FOREPERSON OF THE GRAND JURY

I HEREBY CERTIFY that as authorized and required by law, I have advised the GRAND JURY returning this indictment.

(signature)
Richard D. Ridgway, Assistant State Attorney
Fifth Judicial Circuit of Florida
Florida Bar No. 261114

Presented and filed in the CIRCUIT Court this ___1___ day of _April_, 2005.

BETTY STRIFLER
CLERK OF CIRCUIT COURT

BY _(signature)_ D.C.

C-2005-15300

Exhibit 7.5A **Indictment and Probable Cause Affidavit**

Complaint/Arrest Affidavit Continuation	Court Case No. 05CF298	Agency Case No. 05020760

Defendant's Name: COUEY, JOHN EVANDER   Date of Birth: 08191958

JAIL LOG: (To be completed by booking officer)   Jail Inmate No. 05-1254

Date booked 3-21-05	Time Booked am pm 1450	Booking Officer	Fingerprinted By	Photographed By	Bin Number 03W

Advised of Rights By	Check for Warrant HCIC[ ] FCIC[ ] LOCAL[ ]	Holds Yes[ ] No[ ]	Agency of Held

Attorney (If known)	Religion J[ ] Pr[ ] C[ ] Other[ ]	Marital Status S[ ] M[ ] D[ ] Sep[ ]	Telephone Call Logged Time am pm # ( )

Next of Kin/PARENTS OF JUVENILE (for emergency)	Relation Address	Phone: (352) - Phone:

Bond Date	Returnable Court Date	Returnable Court Time	Release Date	Release Time am pm	Releasing Officer

Bond Charge A	Bond Charge B	Bond Charge C	Bond Charge D	

NAME AND ADDRESS OF BONDSMAN:_____   Bond Type: ROR[ ] SURETY[ ] Cash [ ]

Bail Bond[ ] Cert[ ] Other[ ]

APPROVING OFFICER SIGNATURE:_____

PROBABLE CAUSE AFFIDAVIT:
(specify probable cause for each charge)
     Before Me, the undersigned authority, personally appeared GRACE, SCOTT DETECTIVE who being duly sworn, alleges, on information and belief, that on the 24 day of February, 2005 in Citrus County, Florida the defendant did:

SUBMITTED BY: GRACE, SCOTT 2095/ATCHISON, GARY 1414 (AR05001532)
DID COMMIT THE OFFENSE OF BURGLARY WITH BATTERY, IN VIOLATION OF FLORIDA STATE STATUTE 810.02 (2)A, AND

DID COMMIT THE OFFENSE OF KIDNAPPING A CHILD UNDER THE AGE OF THIRTEEN, BY PLACING SAID CHILD IN CONFINEMENT AGAINST HIS OR HER WILL, IN VIOLATION OF FLORIDA STATE STATUTE 787.01(1) (B), AND

DID COMMIT THE OFFENSE OF SEXUAL BATTERY OF A PERSON UNDER THE AGE OF TWELVE, WHICH IS IN VIOLATION OF FLORIDA STATE STATUTE 794.011(2)A, AND

DID COMMIT THE OFFENSE OF HOMICIDE WHEN HE PERPETRATED FROM A PREMEDITATED DESIGN TO AFFECT THE DEATH OF THE PERSON KILLED OR ANY HUMAN BEING, WHICH IS IN VIOLATION OF FLORIDA STATE STATUTE 782.04 (1) (A)1, TO WIT:

ON 022405, THE VICTIM, A WHITE FEMALE JUVENILE WITH THE DATE OF BIRTH ███████████, WAS REPORTED MISSING FROM HER RESIDENCE LOCATED AT ████████████████ CITRUS COUNTY, FLORIDA. THE VICTIM WAS LAST SEEN WEARING A PINK NIGHTGOWN AND WHITE SILK SHORTS AND A BLUE STUFFED DOLPHIN WAS MISSING WITH HER. SINCE 022405 MEMBERS OF THE CITRUS COUNTY SHERIFF'S OFFICE AND OTHERS WALKED AND SEARCHED THE HOMOSASSA AREA IN ATTEMPTS TO LOCATE THE VICTIM. AS OF 031805, THERE WAS NO CONFIRMED CONTACT WITH THE VICTIM.

Source: Citrus County Clerk of Court, Criminal Division (*www.clerk.citrus.fl.us/home.jsp*)

C. More Information

Florida Criminal Law Resources

www.megalaw.com/fl/top/flcriminal.php

Obtaining Criminal History Information

www.fdle.state.fl.us/CriminalHistory

Florida Department of Law Enforcement

www.fdle.state.fl.us

Florida Crime Statistics

www.fdle.state.fl.us/fsac

Florida Sexual Offender Database

www.fdle.state.fl.us

Florida Criminal Defense Law Blog

blog.justiceflorida.com

Criminal Law and Procedure

www.law.cornell.edu/wex/index.php/Criminal_law
www.law.cornell.edu/wex/index.php/Criminal_procedure

Florida State Courts

www.flcourts.org

Florida Statutes

www.leg.state.fl.us/statutes

Criminal Law Links

www.crimelynx.com/research.html
talkjustice.com/browse.asp
www.findlaw.com/01topics/09criminal/sites.html

D. Something to Check

1. Describe the respective roles of the grand jury and the state attorney in the indictment found in Exhibit 7.5A. To find out, use the sites in More Information in this section and in section 6.4.

2. Go to Florida Statutes online (see More Information above). Quote from any one of the statutes cited in the indictment shown in Exhibit 6.4A.

3. Find online information about paralegals who work in criminal law offices in Florida.

Comprehensive Legal Dictionary

A

AAA American Arbitration Association (*www.adr.org*).

AAfPE See American Association for Paralegal Education (*www.aafpe.org*).

AALS Association of American Law Schools (*www.aals.org*).

a aver et tener To have and to hold. See habendem clause.

ABA American Bar Association (*www.abanet.org*).

abaction Stealing animals, often by driving them off.

abandonee The person to whom something is abandoned or relinquished.

abandonment A total surrender of property, persons, or rights.

> An abandoned child, for purposes of dependency proceeding, is one whose parent or caregiver, while being able, makes no provision for the child's support and makes no effort to communicate with the child. West's F.S.A. § 39.01(2). *J.B.M.*, 870 So.2d 946 (Fla. App. 1 Dist., 2004)

abatable nuisance A nuisance that can be diminished or eliminated.

abatement 1. Termination or nullification. 2. A suspension of proceedings. 3. A reduction of testamentary legacies because estate assets are insufficient to pay debts and other legacies.

abatement of action A complete ending or quashing of a suit.

abator Someone who abates a nuisance.

abdication A voluntary renunciation of a privilege or office.

abduction The unlawful taking away of someone (e.g., child, wife, ward, servant) by force or trickery.

abet To encourage or assist another, often in criminal activity.

> To aid and abet means to help the person who actually committed the crime by doing or saying something that caused, encouraged, incited, or assisted the criminal. F.S.A. § 777.011. *Gale*, 726 So.2d 328 (Fla.App. 2 Dist.,1999)

abettor A person who encourages another to commit a crime.

abeyance Suspension; not finally settled or vested.

ability The power or capacity to perform.

ab initio From the beginning.

abjuration Renunciation under oath, formally giving up rights.

abnormally dangerous Extrahazardous (ultrahazardous) even if reasonable care is used.

abode Dwelling place; residence.

abogado An advocate or lawyer (Spanish).

abolish To eliminate or cancel.

aboriginal Pertaining to inhabitants from earliest times.

abortifacient Causing abortion.

abortion 1. An induced termination of a pregnancy. 2. A miscarriage.

> Abortion means the termination of human pregnancy with an intention other than to produce a live birth or to remove a dead fetus. F.S.A. § 390.011(1).

above 1. With a superior status. 2. Earlier or before.

abridge 1. To diminish. 2. To condense or shorten.

abrogate To annul, cancel, or destroy.

abscond To flee in order to avoid arrest or legal process.

absentee landlord A lessor who does not live on the leased premises.

absolute Unconditional; final.

absolute deed A deed that transfers land without encumbrances.

absolute law An immutable law of nature.

absolute liability See strict liability.

absolute nuisance A nuisance for which one is liable without regard to whether it occurred through negligence or other fault.

absolution Release from an obligation or penalty.

absolutism A political system in which one person has total power.

absorption The assimilation of one entity or right into another.

abstain To refrain from; to refuse to use the jurisdiction that a court has.

abstention doctrine If a matter can be tried in federal or state court, a federal court can decline its jurisdiction to avoid unnecessary interference with the state.

abstract A summary or abridgment.

abstraction Taking something, often wrongfully, with intent to defraud.

abstract of record Abbreviated history of court proceedings to date.

abstract of title A condensed history or summary of conveyances, interests, and encumbrances that affect title to land.

abuse 1. Improper use. 2. Physical or mental mistreatment.

abuse of discretion A decision that is manifestly unreasonable, depriving someone of a substantive right.

abuse of process A tort consisting of the following elements: (a) the use of a civil or criminal process, (b) for a purpose for which the process is not designed, (c) resulting in actual damage.

> Under Florida law, abuse of process involves the use of criminal or civil legal process against another primarily to accomplish a purpose for which it was not designed. *Whitney Information Network*, 353 F.Supp.2d 1208 (M.D.Fla.,2005)

abut To be next to or touch; to share a common border.

abutters Owners of property joined at a common border.

accede 1. To agree. 2. To attain an office.

accelerated depreciation Taking more depreciation deductions during the early years of the life of an asset.

acceleration Causing something to occur sooner, e.g., to pay an obligation, to enjoy a benefit.

acceleration clause A clause in a contract or instrument stating what will trigger an earlier payment schedule.

acceptance 1. Agreement (express or implied) with the terms of an offer. 2. The act of receiving a thing with the intention of retaining it. 3. The commitment to honor a draft or bill of exchange.

> The term "acceptance" means the drawee's signed agreement to pay a draft as presented. Acceptance must be written on the draft and may consist of the drawee's signature alone. F.S.A. § 673.4091(1)

access Opportunity to enter, visit with, or be intimate with.

access easement See easement of access.

accession 1. An increase through addition. 2. A country's acceptance of a treaty. 3. The right to own what is added to land by improvements or natural growth.

accessory 1. One who, without being present, helps another commit or conceal a crime. 2. A subordinate part.

accessory after the fact One who knows a crime has been committed (although not present at the time) and who helps the offender escape.

accessory before the fact One who assists or encourages another to commit a crime, although not present at the time it is committed.

accident An unexpected misfortune whether or not caused by negligence or other fault.

> "Accident" means an occurrence resulting in injury or death to one or more persons which is not the result of willful action by a party. F.S.A. § 90.4026(a)

accommodated party See accommodation party.

accommodation 1. A favor, e.g., making a loan, acting as a cosigner. 2. An adjustment or settlement. 3. Lodging.

accommodation indorser See accommodation party.

accommodation paper A promissory note or bill of exchange that is cosigned by a person (who does not receive payment or other consideration) in order to help someone else secure credit or a loan. The person signing is the accommodation party.

accommodation party Someone who signs a promissory note or other negotiable instrument in any capacity, e.g., as indorser, without receiving payment or other consideration, in order to act as surety for another party (called the accommodated party).

accomplice A person who participates with another in an offense before, during, or after its commission.

> An "accomplice" is one who knowingly, voluntarily, and with common intent unites with others in commission of a crime. *Newton*, 178 So.2d 341 (Fla.App.1965)

accord 1. An agreement or contract to settle a dispute. 2. An agreement for the future discharge of an existing debt by a substituted performance. Also called executory accord. Once the debt is discharged, the arrangement is called an accord and satisfaction.

accord and satisfaction See accord (2).

account 1. A financial record of debts, credits, transactions, etc. 2. An action or suit to force the defendant to explain his or her handling of a fund in which the plaintiff has an interest. Also called accounting.

> An "account" means a demand deposit account, checking or negotiable withdrawal order account, savings account, time deposit account, or money-market mutual fund account. F.S.A. § 409.25657(b)

accountable Responsible; liable.

accountant A person skilled in keeping financial records and accounts.

account debtor The person who has obligations on an account.

accounting 1. A bookkeeping system for recording financial transactions. 2. A settling of an account with a determination of what is owed. 3. See account (2).

accounting period The period of time, e.g., a year, used by a taxpayer for the determination of tax liability.

account payable A regular business debt not yet paid.

account receivable A regular business debt not yet collected.

account stated An agreement on the accuracy of an account, stating the balance due.

accredit 1. To acknowledge or recognize officially. 2. To accept the credentials of a foreign envoy.

accredited investor An investor who is financially sophisticated.

accretion Growth in size by gradual accumulation. An increase of land by natural forces, e.g., soil added to a shore.

> Accretion is the extension of land area due to a gradual, natural, and imperceptible build up of additional land by the accumulation of alluvium material. Reliction is a similar increase of land area due to the lowering of the water level by natural causes. *State, Dept. of Natural Resources v. Contemporary Land Sales*, 400 So.2d 488 (Fla.App., 1981)

accrual basis A method of accounting in which revenues are recorded when earned or due, even though not collected, and expenditures are recorded when liabilities are incurred, whether paid or not.

accrue To come into existence as a right; to vest.

accrued dividend A declared dividend yet to be paid.

accumulated earnings tax A penalty tax on a corporation that retains its earnings beyond the reasonable needs of the business.

accumulation trust A trust in which the trustee must invest trust income rather than pay it out to beneficiaries.

accumulative sentence See consecutive sentences.

accusation A charge that one has committed a crime or other wrong.

accusatory instrument A document charging someone with a crime, e.g., an indictment.

> Accusatory pleading, as used in defining permissive lesser included offense, does not refer to all counts pleaded in the information, but just the count for which the request for a lesser included instruction is made. *Wilson*, 749 So.2d 516 (Fla.App. 5 Dist.,1999)

accused The person accused or formally charged with a crime.

acknowledgment 1. An affirmation that something is genuine. 2. A formal statement of a person executing an instrument that he or she is doing so as a free act. 3. An acceptance of responsibility.

acknowledgment of paternity A formal admission by a father that a child is his.

ACLU American Civil Liberties Union (*www.aclu.com*).

acquaintance rape Rape by someone the victim knows.

acquest Property acquired by a means other than inheritance.

acquiesce To consent passively; to comply without protest.

acquire To obtain; to gain ownership of.

acquit 1. To release someone from an obligation. 2. To declare that the accused is innocent of the crime.

acquittal 1. A discharge or release from an obligation. 2. A formal declaration of innocence of a crime.

acquittance A written discharge from an obligation.

ACRS Accelerated cost-recovery system.

act 1. Something done voluntarily; an external manifestation of the will. 2. A law passed by the legislature.

acting Temporarily functioning as or substituting for.

actio A right or claim.

action 1. A civil or criminal court proceeding. 2. Conduct.

actionable Pertaining to that which can become the basis of a lawsuit.

actionable per se Pertaining to words that on their face and without the aid of extrinsic proof are defamatory. They are called actionable words.

actionable words See actionable per se.

action at law An action in a court of law, not in a court of equity.

action on the case An action to recover for damages caused indirectly rather than directly or immediately. Also called trespass on the case.

active trust See special trust.

act of bankruptcy Debtor's conduct that could trigger involuntary bankruptcy.

act of God A force of nature; an unusual force of nature.

act of state doctrine Courts of one country should not judge the validity of an act of another country that occurs within the latter.

> The "act of state doctrine" prohibits the United States courts from reaching the merits of an issue in order to avoid embarrassment of foreign governments in politically sensitive matters and interference with foreign policy. *Glen,* 365 F.Supp.2d 1263 (S.D.Fla.,2005)

actual Real; existing in fact.

actual authority The authority a principal intentionally confers on an agent or permits the agent to believe has been conferred.

actual cash value 1. Fair market value. 2. Replacement cost less depreciation.

actual damages Damages that compensate for an actual or proven loss.

actual fraud See positive fraud.

actual loss Amounts paid or payable as a result of a substantial loss.

actual malice 1. Conscious wrongdoing; intent to injure. Also called malice in fact. 2. Knowledge of the falsity of a defamatory statement or a reckless disregard as to truth or falsity.

actual notice Notice given to a person directly and personally. Also called express notice.

actual value Fair market value.

actuary One skilled in statistics for risk and premium calculations.

actus reus The physical deed or act that is wrongful.

> Intent is a purpose or objective fixed in the mind. Knowledge is the perception of the mind as to facts. Intent and knowledge constitute the mens rea (evil intent or guilty mind) of a crime while the physical act or conduct constitutes the actus reus (act of the person). *People v. Tracey A.,* 413 N.Y.S.2d 92 (N.Y.Co.Ct., 1979)

ADA Americans with Disabilities Act (*www.eeoc.gov/ada*).

ad damnum clause A clause stating the damages claimed.

addict A habitual user of something, e.g., a drug.

additur A practice by which a judge offers a defendant the choice between a new trial and accepting a damage award higher than what the jury awarded.

adduce To present or introduce; to offer as evidence or authority.

ADEA Age Discrimination in Employment Act (*www.eeoc.gov/policy/adea.html*).

adeem To take away; to revoke a bequest.

ademption The extinction of a specific bequest or devise because of the disappearance of or disposition of the subject matter from the estate of the testator in his or her lifetime.

> Ademption occurs when a specific devise made in the will is no longer in the estate at the time of the testator's death. *In re Estate of Walters,* 700 So.2d 434 (Fla.App. 4 Dist.,1997)

adequate consideration Fair and reasonable consideration under the circumstances of the agreement. See also consideration.

adequate remedy at law A legal remedy, e.g., damages, that is complete, practical, and efficient.

adhesion contract A standard contract offered on a take-it-or-leave-it basis to a consumer who has no meaningful choice as to its terms.

ad hoc For this special purpose only.

ad hominem Appealing to emotions or personal matters, not to reason.

ad idem On the same matter.

ad interim Temporarily.

adjacent Lying near or close by; next to.

adjective law Procedural law; rules of practice.

adjoining Touching; contiguous.

adjourn To postpone or suspend until another time.

adjournment Postponing of a session until another time.

adjudge To decide judicially.

adjudicate To judge; to resolve a dispute judicially.

adjudication A determination or judgment by a court of law.

> The adjudication of any controversy contemplates that the claims of all the parties thereto have been considered and set at rest. *Miller,* 11 So.2d 892 (Fla.1943)

adjudicative facts Facts concerning the who, what, when, where, and how pertaining to a particular case.

adjunction Adding or attaching one thing to another.

adjure To request solemnly.

adjust 1. To assess and determine what will be paid under an insurance policy. 2. To set a new payment plan for debts.

adjustable-rate mortgage (ARM) A mortgage with a fluctuating interest rate tied to a market index. Also called variable-rate mortgage (VRM).

adjusted basis The cost or other original basis of an asset reduced by deductions for depreciation and increased by capital improvements.

adjusted gross income (AGI) Gross income less allowable deductions.

adjuster One who determines (or settles) the amount of a claim.

ad litem For the suit; for purposes of this litigation.

administration 1. The persons or entities managing an estate, a government agency, or other organization. 2. The management and settlement of the estate of a decedent. 3. The management and settlement of a bankruptcy estate.

administrative agency See agency (2).

administrative discretion An administrative agency's power to use judgment in choosing among available alternatives.

administrative law The laws governing and created by administrative agencies.

Administrative Law Judge (ALJ) A hearing officer within an administrative agency. Also called hearing examiner.

Administrative Procedure Act (APA) A federal or state statute on rulemaking and hearing procedures before administrative agencies.

administrative remedy Relief granted by an administrative agency.

administrator 1. A manager. 2. A person appointed by the court to manage the estate of someone who dies without a will (i.e., intestate) or who dies with a will that does not name a functioning executor.

administrator ad litem An administrator appointed by the court to represent an estate of a decedent in a court proceeding.

> When an estate must be represented and the personal representative is unable to do so, the court shall appoint an administrator ad litem without bond to represent the estate in that proceeding. F.S.A. § 733.308

administrator cum testamento annexo (cta) See cum testamento annexo.

administrator de bonis non (dbn) See de bonis non.

administratrix A woman who administers the estate of the deceased.

admiralty The law that applies to maritime disputes or offenses involving ships and navigation. Also called maritime law.

admissible Allowed into court to determine its truth or believability.

admission 1. An assertion of the truth of a fact. 2. An official acknowledgment of someone's right to practice law.

admission against interest A statement by a party that is harmful to a position he or she is taking in the litigation.

> An admission is made by a person against whose interest the admission operates or someone speaking in his or her behalf. *In re Kleiner's Estate*, 176 A.2d 410 (Pa.1962)

admit To accept as true or valid.

admonition 1. A reprimand. 2. A warning from a judge to a jury.

adopt To go through a formal process of establishing a relationship of parent and child between persons.

adoptee The person adopted.

ADR See alternative dispute resolution.

ad testificandum To or for testifying.

adult A person who has reached the age of majority (e.g., 21, 18).

adulterate To contaminate by adding something inferior.

adultery Sexual relations between a married person and someone other than his or her spouse.

ad valorem tax A tax based on a percentage of the value of property.

advance 1. To lend. 2. To pay or supply something before it is due.

advance directive A statement of one's wishes regarding medical treatment upon becoming incompetent. Also called living will or healthcare proxy.

advancement A gift in advance, usually by a parent to a child. The amount or value of the gift is deducted from what the recipient eventually receives when the giver dies intestate (i.e., without a valid will).

> An inter vivos gift made by a parent to a child with the intent that such gift represents a part or the whole of the donor's estate that the donee would inherit on the death of the donor. *West*, 427 So.2d 813 (Fla.App. 5 Dist.,1983)

advance sheet A pamphlet containing laws (e.g., court opinions) that comes out before a later volume of the same set.

adventure A risky business venture, e.g., a shipment of goods at sea.

adversary An opponent.

adversary proceeding 1. A hearing involving opposing parties. 2. Litigation brought within a bankruptcy proceeding based on conflicting claims between a debtor, a creditor, or other interested party.

adversary system A method of resolving a legal dispute whereby the parties argue their conflicting claims before a neutral decision-maker.

adverse Having opposite interests; against.

adverse interest A goal or claim of one person that is different from or opposed to the goal or claim of another.

adverse parties Parties in a suit with conflicting interests.

adverse possession A method of obtaining title to the land of another by using the land under a claim of right in a way that is open, exclusive, hostile to the current owner, and continuous.

> There is a distinction between acquiring of title by adverse possession and the acquiring of a prescriptive right. In the former, title must be through possession. In the latter, a prescriptive right is through the use of the privilege without actual possession. In acquisition of the title by adverse possession, the possession must be exclusive, while in acquisition of a prescriptive right, the use may be in common with the owner or the public. *Hunt*, 121 So.2d 697 (Fla.App.1960)

adverse witness See hostile witness.

advice 1. An opinion offered as guidance. 2. Notice that a draft has been drawn.

advice and consent The U.S. Senate's approval power on treaties and major presidential appointments. U.S. Const. Art. II, § 2.

advisement Careful consideration.

advisory jury A jury whose verdict is not binding on the court.

> An advisory jury is a procedural tool that a trial court may utilize in cases in which the trial court determines that an advisory jury is likely to be helpful to the court in discharging its function; even with an advisory jury, the trial court is the trier of both law and fact and it is the trial court's ultimate finding and judgment alone which are subject to review. *Vista Centre Venture*, 603 So.2d 576 (Fla.App. 5 Dist.,1992)

advisory opinion An opinion of a court that is not binding.

advocacy Arguing for or against something; pleading.

advocate One who argues or pleads for another.

AFDC See Aid to Families with Dependent Children.

aff'd Affirmed.

affect To act on (upon); to influence.

affected class 1. Persons who suffered job discrimination. 2. Persons who constitute a class for bringing a class action.

affecting commerce Involving commerce or trade.

aff'g Affirming.

affiant Someone who makes an affidavit.

affidavit A written or printed statement of facts made under oath before a person with authority to administer the oath.

affidavit of service A sworn statement that a document (e.g., summons) has been delivered (served) to a designated person.

affiliate A subsidiary; one corporation controlled by another.

affiliation order An order determining paternity.

affinity Relationship by marriage, not by blood.

affirm 1. To declare that a judgment is valid. 2. To assert formally, but not under oath. The noun is *affirmance*.

affirmance See affirm.

affirmation A solemn declaration, often a substitute for an oath.

affirmative action Steps designed to eliminate existing and continuing discrimination, to remedy the effects of past discrimination, and to create systems to prevent future discrimination.

affirmative charge An instruction that removes an issue from the jury.

affirmative defense A defense raising new facts that will defeat the plaintiff's claim even if the plaintiff's fact allegations are proven.

> An affirmative defense is a defense which admits the cause of action, but avoids liability, in whole or in part, by alleging an excuse, justification, or other matter negating or limiting liability. *St. Paul Mercury Ins.*, 837 So.2d 483 (Fla.App. 5 Dist.,2002)

affirmative easement An easement that forces the landowner to allow the easement holder to do specific acts on the land.

affirmative relief Relief (e.g., damages) a defendant could have sought in his or her own suit, but instead is sought in a counterclaim or cross-claim.

affirmative warranty An insurance warranty that asserts the existence of a fact at the time the policy is entered into.

affix To attach; to add to permanently.

affray Fighting in a public place so as to cause terror to the public.

affreightment A contract to transport goods by ship.

aforementioned See aforesaid.

aforesaid Mentioned earlier in the document.

aforethought Thought of beforehand; premeditated.

a fortiori With greater force; all the more so.

after-acquired property Property acquired after a particular event, e.g., after making a will, after giving a security interest.

after-acquired title rule When a seller does not obtain title to an asset until after attempting to sell it, title automatically vests in the buyer the moment the seller obtained it.

after-born child A child born after the execution of a will.

age discrimination Discrimination on the basis of one's age.

agency 1. A relationship in which one person acts for and can bind another. 2. A governmental body, other than a court or legislature, that carries out the law.

> Agency means any state, county, district, authority, or municipal officer, department, division, board, bureau, commission, or other separate unit of government created or established by law including, for the purposes of this chapter, the Commission on Ethics, the Public Service Commission, and the Office of Public Counsel, and any other public or private agency, person, partnership, corporation, or business entity acting on behalf of any public agency. West's F.S.A. § 119.011(2)

agency shop A business or other entity that collects union dues from all employees, even those who decided not to join the union.

agent 1. A person authorized to act for another. 2. A power or force that produces an effect.

age of consent The age at which one can marry without parental consent or have sexual intercourse without the partner committing statutory rape.

age of majority The age at which a person has the right to vote, enter a contract that cannot be disaffirmed, make a will, etc. Also called full age.

age of reason The age at which a child is deemed capable of making reasoned judgments and, therefore, can commit a crime or tort.

aggravated assault The crime of assault committed with the intent to cause serious bodily harm or other circumstances that make the crime more severe than simple assault.

> An assault either with deadly weapon without intent to kill or assault with intent to commit felony. *Grinage*, 641 So.2d 1362 (Fla.App. 5 Dist.,1994)

aggravation Circumstances that increase the enormity of a crime or tort, e.g., using a weapon.

aggregate Combined into a whole.

aggregation The unpatentability of an invention because its parts lack a composite integrated mechanism.

aggregation doctrine To reach the jurisdictional amount in a federal diversity case, the total of all the claims cannot be added.

aggrieved party One whose legal rights have been invaded.

AGI See adjusted gross income.

agio Money paid to convert one kind of money into another.

agreed case Facts agreed upon by the parties, allowing a court to limit itself to deciding the questions of law on those facts. Also called case agreed, case stated.

agreement Mutual assent by the parties; a meeting of the minds.

aid and abet Assist or encourage someone to commit a crime.

> To help a person who actually committed a crime by doing or saying something that caused, encouraged, incited, or assisted the criminal. F.S.A. § 777.011. *Gale*, 726 So.2d 328 (Fla.App. 2 Dist.,1999)

aider by verdict A jury verdict cures technical pleading defects.

Aid to Families with Dependent Children (AFDC) Federal public assistance replaced by TANF (Temporary Assistance for Needy Families).

airbill A bill of lading used in a shipment of goods by air.

air rights The right of a landowner to use all or part of the airspace above his or her land.

air piracy Using force or threats to seize or hijack an aircraft.

aka Also known as.

alderman A member of the local legislative body.

aleatory Depending on uncertain circumstances or contingencies.

aleatory contract A contract in which performance depends on uncertain events, e.g., an insurance contract.

> A contract is aleatory or hazardous when the performance of that which is one of its objects depends on an uncertain event. It is certain when the thing to be done is supposed to depend on the will of the party, or when in the usual course of events it must happen in the manner stipulated. *Miller*, 573 So.2d 24 (Fla.App. 3 Dist.,1990)

ALI See American Law Institute (*www.ali.org*).

Alford **plea** A defendant's plea-bargained guilty plea that does not actually admit guilt. *North Carolina v. Alford*, 91 S. Ct. 160 (1970).

alias Otherwise known as; an assumed name.

alias summons; alias writ A new summons or writ given when the original one was issued without effect.

alibi A defense alleging absence from the scene of the crime.

alien One who is not a citizen of the country where he or she resides.

alienable Legally transferable to the ownership of another.

alienage The condition or status of an alien.

alienate To transfer; to transfer title.

alienation clause A clause in an insurance policy that voids the policy if the property being insured is sold or transferred.

alienation of affections The tort of causing a diminishment of the marital relationship between the plaintiff and his or her spouse.

> We also disagree that the statutory abolition of an action for alienation of affections precludes a cause of action for intentional interference with the parent-child relationship. They are separate torts. *Stone*, 734 So.2d 1038 (Fla.,1999)

alienee A person to whom property is conveyed or transferred.

alieni juris Under another's power.

alienor A person who transfers or conveys property.

alimony A court-ordered payment of money or other property by one spouse to another for support after divorce or separation. Also called spousal support.

alimony in gross Alimony in the form of a single definite sum that cannot be modified. Also called lump-sum alimony.

alimony pendente lite See temporary alimony.

aliquot An exact division or fractional part.

aliunde rule Jury deliberations may not be scrutinized, unless there is evidence from a source other than a juror to impeach the jury verdict.

ALJ See Administrative Law Judge.

allegation A statement of fact that one expects to prove.

alleged Asserted as true, but not yet proven.

allegiance Loyalty owed to a government, a cause, or a person.

Allen **charge** A supplementary instruction given to a deadlocked jury to encourage it to reach a verdict. Also called dynamite charge. *Allen v. U.S.*, 17 S. Ct. 154 (1896)

all faults A sale of goods "as is," in their present condition.

all fours See on all fours.

allocation A setting aside or designation for a purpose.

allocatur It is allowed. In Pennsylvania, the permission to appeal.

allocution 1. The judge asks a convicted defendant if he or she has anything to say before sentence is imposed. 2. The defendant's right to make such a statement.

> Allocution is the right of the defendant to make a final plea on his own behalf to the sentencer before the imposition of sentence. It is a right of ancient origin. *U.S. v. Prouty*, 303 F.3d 1249 (11th Cir. 2002).

allodial Owned absolutely, free and clear.

allograph A writing or signature made by one person for another.

allonge A slip of paper attached to a negotiable instrument to provide space for more indorsements.

allotment A share, e.g., the land awarded to an individual American Indian; a portion of one's pay deducted to meet an obligation such as child support.

allotment certificate A document stating the number of shares of a security to be purchased, payment terms, etc.

allowance 1. Portion assigned or bestowed. 2. Deduction or discount.

alluvion The washing up of sand or soil so as to form firm ground.

alteration Making something different, e.g., modifying real property, changing the language or meaning of a document.

alter ego rule Personal liability can be imposed on shareholders who use the corporation for personal business.

> Under the basic alter ego theory (confusion of identities), the personal affairs of the shareholder become confused with the business affairs of the corporation. Individual liability under this theory rests in part on the fact that a shareholder has taken it upon himself to disregard the corporate entity. *Solomon*, 550 So.2d 1182 (Fla.App. 5 Dist.,1989)

alternate valuation The value of assets six months after death.

alternative contract A contract that gives options for performance.

alternative dispute resolution (ADR) Arbitration, mediation, and similar methods of resolving a dispute without litigation.

alternative minimum tax (AMT) A tax imposed to ensure that enough income tax is paid by persons with large deductions, credits, or exclusions.

alternative pleading Alleging facts or claims in a complaint or other pleading that are not necessarily consistent.

alternative relief Inconsistent relief sought on the same claim.

alternative writ A writ requiring a person to do a specified thing or to show cause why he or she should not be compelled to do it.

amalgamation Consolidation, e.g., two corporations into a new one.

ambassador An officer of high diplomatic rank representing a country.

ambit Boundary; the limits of a power.

ambulance chasing Soliciting injury victims by or for an attorney.

ambulatory 1. Revocable. 2. Able to walk.

ameliorating waste Waste by a tenant that in fact improves the land.

amenable 1. Legally accountable or answerable; subject to answer to the law. 2. Submissive.

amendment A formal change (e.g., addition, subtraction, correction) made in the text of a document (e.g., statute, legislative bill, pleading, contract).

> An amendment of a constitution repeals or changes some provision in, or adds something to the instrument amended. *Wilson*, 34 So.2d 114 (Fla.1948)

amercement A fine or punishment imposed (e.g., on a public official) at the court's discretion.

American Law Institute (ALI) An organization of scholars that writes model acts and restatements of the law (*www.ali.org*).

American Association for Paralegal Education (AAfPE) A national association of paralegal schools (*www.aafpe.org*).

American Bar Association (ABA) A national voluntary association of attorneys (*www.abanet.org*).

American rule Each side in litigation pays its own attorney fees and court costs unless a statute provides otherwise. Under the English rule, also called loser-pays, the losing party may be required to pay the attorney fees and court costs incurred by the winning side.

Americans with Disabilities Act (ADA) A federal statute that prohibits discrimination against persons with disabilities in employment and other public services. 42 USC § 12101

> See Florida Americans with Disabilities Accessibility Implementation Act. Florida Statutes, § 553.501

amicable action An action brought by mutual consent of the parties to seek a ruling on facts they do not dispute.

amicus curiae Friend of the court. A nonparty who obtains court permission to file a brief with its views on the case.

> Briefs from amicus curiae, which means "friend of the court," are generally for the purpose of assisting the court in cases which are of general public interest, or aiding in the presentation of difficult issues. F.S.A. R.App.P.Rule 9.370. *Ciba-Geigy Ltd.*,683 So.2d 522 (Fla.App. 4 Dist.,1996)

amnesty A pardon for crimes, often granted to a group.

amortization 1. The gradual elimination of a debt, often by making regular payments toward principal along with interest payments. 2. Writing off the cost of an intangible asset over its useful life.

amotion Removing or turning someone out.

amount in controversy The amount sued for. The amount needed (over $75,000) to establish diversity jurisdiction in federal court. Also called jurisdictional amount (28 U.S.C. 1332(a)).

analogous 1. Sufficiently similar to lend support. 2. Involving facts and rules that are similar to those now under consideration.

anarchist One who believes government should not exist.

anarchy The absence of political authority or order.

ancestor A person from whom one is descended; a forebear.

ancient documents Deeds and other writings 20 or more years old that are presumed to be genuine if kept in proper custody.

> Introduction of a map into evidence as an ancient document was not error where map appeared to be regular on its face, bore date resembling rest of document, appeared from date to have been over 30 years of age, and came from proper custody. *Drake*, 227 So.2d 709 (Fla.App. 1969)

ancient lights rule Windows with outside light for a period of time (e.g., 20 years) cannot be blocked off by an adjoining landowner.

ancillary Supplementary; subsidiary.

ancillary administration An administrator appointed by the court for property or the decedent located in a different jurisdiction.

ancillary jurisdiction Authority of a court to hear claims that otherwise would not be within its jurisdiction if these claims are sufficiently related to the case properly before the court.

and his heirs Words that give a transferee a fee simple absolute.

animo With the intention.

animus 1. Intention, e.g., animus furandi (intent to steal), animus testandi (intent to make a will). 2. Animosity; ill will.

annexation 1. Merging or attaching one thing to another. 2. The formal takeover or appropriation of something (e.g., territory).

annotated statutes A collection of statutes that include research references such as case summaries interpreting the statutes.

annotation A remark or note on a law, e.g., a summary of a case.

annual exclusion The amount one can give away each year gift-tax free.

annual percentage rate (APR) The true cost of borrowing money expressed as an annual interest rate.

annual report A corporation's annual financial report to stockholders.

annuitant A beneficiary of an annuity.

annuity A fixed sum payable periodically to a person for life or a specific period of time.

> Annual payments for life derived as provided in this chapter from the accumulated contributions of a member. All annuities shall be paid in equal monthly installments. F.S.A. § 238.01(15)

annuity certain An annuity that continues paying for a set period even if the annuitant dies within the period.

annuity due An annuity payable at the start of each pay period.

annul To obliterate or nullify.

annulment 1. A nullification or voiding. 2. A declaration that a valid marriage never existed or that an attempted marriage is invalid.

answer 1. The first pleading of the defendant that responds to the plaintiff's claims. 2. To assume someone else's liability.

ante Before; prior to.

ante litem motam Before the suit began or arose.

antecedent Preexisting.

antecedent debt A debt that preexists an event, e.g., filing for bankruptcy. A prior debt may be consideration for a new promise to pay.

antedate 1. To backdate; to place a date on a document that is earlier than the date the document was written. 2. To precede.

antenuptial Occurring before marriage. See premarital agreement.

antichresis An agreement giving the creditor the income from and possession of the property pledged, instead of interest.

anticipation 1. Doing something before its scheduled time. 2. Prior disclosure or use of an invention, jeopardizing its patentability.

anticipatory breach A repudiation of a contract duty before the time fixed in the contract for the performance of that duty.

> An anticipatory breach is deemed to "accrue," if at all, in the county from which the "breachor" transmits the repudiation, rather than where the "breachee" receives it. *Kumar*, 696 So.2d 393 (Fla.App. 3 Dist.,1997)

anticipatory search warrant A search warrant usable only on a future date, not upon issuance.

antidumping law A law against selling imported goods at less than their fair price if the imports hurt comparable domestic products.

antilapse A gift in a will goes to the heirs of the beneficiary to prevent the gift from failing because the beneficiary predeceases the testator.

antinomy A contradiction between two laws or propositions.

anti-racketeering See RICO.

antitrust law Laws against price fixing, monopolies, and other anticompetitive practices and restraints of trade.

APA See Administrative Procedure Act.

apostille A certificate authenticating foreign documents.

apparent 1. Capable of being seen; visible. 2. Seeming.

apparent authority An agent's authority that the principal reasonably leads another to believe the agent has. Also called ostensible authority.

> Apparent authority, for purposes of determining whether a principal is liable for the acts of an agent, is authority which a principal knowingly tolerates or permits, or which the principal by its actions or words holds the agent out as possessing. *Roessler*, 858 So.2d 1158 (Fla.App. 2 Dist., 2003)

apparent defects Defects observable upon reasonable inspection. Also called patent defects.

apparent heir An heir who will inherit unless he or she predeceases the ancestor or is disinherited by will. Also called heir apparent.

app. Appellate; appeal.

appeal Asking a higher tribunal to review or reconsider the decision of an inferior tribunal.

appealable Sufficiently final so that it can be appealed.

> A partial summary judgment granted to a counterdefendant on a counterclaim was not an "appealable final judgment" despite contention that it disposed of a different cause of action containing a different element than the claim, where the disposed of and remaining causes of action were interrelated. *Taddie Underground Utility Co.*, 497 So.2d 701 (Fla.App. 2 Dist.,1986)

appeal bond A bond of a party filing an appeal to cover the opponent's costs if the appeal is later deemed to have been not genuine.

appearance Formally coming before a tribunal as a party or as a representative of a party.

appellant The person or party who brings the appeal.

appellate Concerning appeals or an appellate court.

appellate brief See brief (1).

appellate jurisdiction The power of an appellate court to review and correct the decisions of a lower tribunal.

appellee The person against whom an appeal is brought. Respondent.

append To attach.

appoint To give someone a power or authority.

appointee The person selected.

apportionment 1. A proportional division. 2. The process of allocating legislators among several political subdivisions.

> In the case of apportionment, as opposed to allocation, the taxpayer's normal or business income is mathematically divided among various jurisdictions in which it does business, to determine the measure of local tax. F.S.A. § 220.01. *Roger Dean Enterprises*, 387 So.2d 358 (Fla.,1980)

appraisal Estimation of value or worth.

appraisal remedy A shareholder's right to have its shares bought back by the corporation due to dissent with an extraordinary corporate decision.

appraiser Someone who impartially evaluates (appraises) property.

appreciation Increase in property value, often due to inflation.

apprehension 1. Knowledge. 2. Fear. 3. Seizure or arrest.

appropriation 1. Taking control or possession. 2. An invasion-of-privacy tort committed by the use of a person's name, likeness, or personality for commercial gain without authorization. 3. The legislature's setting aside of money for a specific purpose.

approval sale See sale on approval.

appurtenance A thing or right belonging or attached to something else.

appurtenant Belonging to; incident to the principal property.

appurtenant easement See easement appurtenant.

APR See annual percentage rate.

a priori Deductively; derived from logic or self-evident propositions, without reference to observed experience.

arbiter A referee or judge, someone who can resolve a dispute.

arbitrage Simultaneous matched purchase and sale of identical or equivalent securities in order to profit from price discrepancies.

arbitrament 1. The decision of an arbitrator. 2. The act of deciding.

arbitrary Capricious, subjective. Biased on individual preferences.

> An arbitrary decision is one not supported by facts or logic. *Board of Clinical Laboratory Personnel*, 721 So.2d 317 (Fla.App. 1 Dist.,1998)

arbitration A method of alternative dispute resolution (ADR) in which the parties submit their dispute to an impartial third person (the arbitrator) who renders a decision that can resolve the dispute without litigation. The decision is either nonbinding or, usually upon prior agreement of the parties, binding.

> [A] process whereby a neutral third person or panel, called an arbitrator or arbitration panel, considers the facts and arguments presented by the parties and renders a decision which may be binding or nonbinding as provided in this chapter. F.S.A. § 44.1011(1)

arbitration clause A contract clause providing for compulsory arbitration of disputes under the contract.

arbitrator The person rendering the decision in arbitration.

arguendo In arguing; for the sake of argument.

argument A presentation of reasons for a legal position.

argumentative Containing conclusions as well as facts; contentious.

arise 1. To stem from or originate. 2. To come into notice.

aristocracy A government ruled by a superior or privileged class.

ARM See adjustable-rate mortgage.

armed robbery Robbery committed while armed with a dangerous weapon.

arm's length As between two strangers who are looking out for their own self-interests.

arraignment A court proceeding in which the accused is formally charged with a crime and enters a plea of guilty, not guilty, etc. The verb is *arraign*.

arrangement with creditors A plan whereby the debtor settles with his or her creditors or obtains more time to repay debts.

array A group of persons summoned to be considered for jury duty.

arrearages, arrears Unpaid debts; overdue debts.

> Child support arrearage occurs when a court orders support, but a party does not pay it. *Penalver v. Columbo*, 810 So.2d 563 (Fla.App. 2 Dist.,2002)

arrest Taking someone into custody to answer a criminal charge.

arrest of judgment A court's staying of a judgment because of errors.

arrest record 1. A form filled out when the police arrest someone. 2. A list of a person's prior arrests.

arrest warrant A written order of a judge or magistrate that a person be arrested and brought before the court.

arrogation Claiming or seizing something without authority or right.

arson The willful and malicious burning of property.

> Any person who willfully and unlawfully, or while in the commission of any felony, by fire or explosion, damages or causes to be damaged: (a) Any dwelling, whether occupied or not, or its contents; . . . is guilty of arson in the first degree, . . . F.S.A. § 806.01(1)

art 1. Applying knowledge and skill to produce a desired result. 2. A process or method to produce a useful result. 3. See term of art.

art Article.

artful pleading An attempt to phrase a federal claim as a state claim.

article A part or subdivision of a law or document.

Article I court A federal court created by legislation. Also called legislative courts.

Article III court A federal court created by the U.S. Constitution in article III. Also called constitutional court.

articled clerk In England, one apprenticed to a solicitor.

Articles of Confederation The governing document for the 13 original states.

articles of dissolution A document filed with the secretary of state or other state official that pertains to the dissolving of a corporation or other business entity. It must state that the debts of the entity have been settled.

> Requirements for the content of articles of dissolution of a limited liability company are set forth in F.S.A. § 608.445.

articles of impeachment Formal accusations against a public official asserted as grounds for removing him or her from office.

articles of incorporation The document that establishes (incorporates) a corporation and identifies its basic functions and rules.

artifice Contrivance, trick, or fraud.

artificial person A legal person. An entity, such as a corporation, created under the laws of the state and treated in some respects as a human being. Also called fictitious person, juristic person.

artisan's lien See mechanic's lien.

ascendant An ancestor, e.g., grandparent.

as is In its present condition; no warranty given.

asportation Carrying away for purposes of larceny.

> Asportation required for crime of larceny may be completed by the slightest removal of article from its original position or place where the owner placed it or wanted it to be. *Johnson*, 432 So.2d 758 (Fla.App. 1 Dist.,1983)

assailant One who attacks or assaults another.

assault 1. As a tort, assault is an act intended to cause harmful or offensive contact with another or an imminent apprehension of such contact and the other is thereby placed in such imminent apprehension. 2. As a crime, assault may require an intent to cause physical harm and actual contact with the victim.

> An assault is an intentional, unlawful threat by word or act to do violence to the person of another, coupled with an apparent ability to do so, and doing some act which creates a well-founded fear in such other person that such violence is imminent. F.S.A. § 784.011(1)

assault and battery The crime of battery. See battery.

assay An examination to test the quality and quantity of metals.

assembly 1. A gathering of people for a common goal. 2. One of the houses of the legislature in many states.

assent Agreement, approval.

assert To declare; to state as true.

assessable stock Stock that subjects the holder to an additional assessment or contribution.

assessment 1. A determination of the value of something, often for purposes of taxation. 2. A determination of the share that is due from someone; an amount assessed. 3. The requirement of an additional payment to a business.

> Assessment means a share of the funds which are required for the payment of common expenses, which from time to time is assessed against the unit owner. F.S.A. § 718.103(1)

assessed ratio The ratio of assessed value to fair market value.

assessment work Labor on a mining claim each year to maintain the claim.

assessor A technical expert or adviser, e.g., on making assessments.

asset Anything of value; tangible or intangible property.

asset depreciation range IRS's range of depreciable lives of assets.

asseveration A solemn declaration.

assign 1. To transfer or convey property or rights. 2. To point out or specify, e.g., errors. 3. See assigns.

assigned counsel A court-appointed attorney for a poor person.

assigned risk A person an insurance company is required to insure.

assignee The person to whom property or rights are transferred.

assignment The transfer of ownership or rights.

assignment for benefit of creditors A transfer of the debtor's property to a trustee, with authority to liquidate the debtor's affairs and distribute the proceeds equitably to creditors.

assignment of errors A party's list of errors claimed to have been made by a trial court submitted to an appellate court on appeal.

assignor The person who transfers property or rights.

assigns Assignees; persons to whom property or rights are transferred.

assise; assize An old English court, law, or writ.

assistance of counsel See effective assistance of counsel.

assisted living facility Any building or buildings, section or distinct part of a building, private home, boarding home, home for the aged, or other residential facility, whether operated for profit or not, which undertakes through its ownership or management to provide housing, meals, and one or more personal services for a period exceeding 24 hours to one or more adults who are not relatives of the owner or administrator. F.S.A. § 429.02

associate An attorney employee who hopes one day to be promoted to partner.

associate justice An appellate court judge who is not the chief justice.

association 1. An organization of people joined for a common purpose. 2. An unincorporated company or other organization.

assume 1. To take upon oneself. 2. To suppose without proof.

assumpsit 1. A promise. 2. An action for breach of contract.

assumption 1. The act of taking something upon oneself. 2. Something taken for granted without proof.

assumption of mortgage A property buyer's agreement to be personally liable for payment of an already existing mortgage.

assumption of the risk The knowing and voluntary acceptance of the risk of being harmed by someone's negligence or other conduct.

> Preliminary to any finding of express assumption of risk is a showing that the particular risk was known or should have been known and appreciated by the person injured. *Donaldson*, 675 So.2d 228 (Fla.App. 1 Dist.,1996)

assurance 1. A statement tending to inspire confidence. 2. Insurance. 3. A pledge or guarantee. 4. The act (and the document) that conveys real property.

assured A person who has been insured.

asylum 1. A sanctuary or hiding place. 2. A government's protection given to a political refugee from another country. Also called political asylum.

at bar Currently before the court.

at issue In dispute.

at large 1. Free. 2. An entire area rather than one of its districts.

at law Pertaining to a court of law as opposed to a court of equity.

at risk Pertaining to an investment that could lead to actual loss.

attaché A person in a diplomatic office with a specific specialty.

attachment The act or process of taking, apprehending, or seizing persons or property, by virtue of writ, summons, or other judicial order, and bringing same into custody of the law.

> The writ of attachment shall command the sheriff to attach and take into custody so much of the lands, tenements, goods, and chattels of the party against whose property the writ is issued as is sufficient to satisfy the debt demanded with costs. F.S.A. § 76.13(1)

attachment bond A bond given by one whose property has been attached in order to reclaim it and provide protection to the party who attached it.

attainder The loss of civil rights upon receiving a death sentence or being designated as an outlaw.

attaint 1. To disgrace or condemn to attainder. 2. To accuse a jury of giving a false verdict.

attempt An overt act or conduct (beyond mere preparation) performed with the intent to commit a crime that was not completed.

attendant circumstances Relevant facts surrounding an event.

attenuation Illegally obtained evidence might be admissible if the link between the illegal conduct and the evidence is so attenuated as to dissipate the taint.

attest To affirm to be true or genuine; to bear witness.

attestation clause A clause stating that you saw (witnessed) someone sign a document or perform other tasks related to the validity of the document.

attorn 1. To transfer something to another. 2. To acknowledge being the tenant of a new landlord.

attorney 1. One licensed to practice law. A lawyer. Also called attorney at law. 2. One authorized to act in place of or for another. Also called attorney-in-fact.

attorney at law See attorney (1).

attorney-client privilege A client and an attorney can refuse to disclose communications between them if their purpose was to facilitate the provision of legal services to the client.

> A client has a privilege to refuse to disclose, and to prevent any other person from disclosing, the contents of confidential communications when such other person learned of the communications because they were made in the rendition of legal services to the client. F.S.A. § 90.502(2)

attorney general The chief attorney for the government.

Attorney-in-fact See attorney (2).

attorney of record The attorney noted in the court files as the attorney representing a particular party.

attorney's lien The right of an attorney to retain possession of money or property of a client until his or her proper fees have been paid.

attorney work product See work product rule.

attornment See attorn.

attractive nuisance doctrine A duty of reasonable care is owed to prevent injury to a trespassing child unable to appreciate the danger from an artificial condition or activity on land to which the child can be expected to be attracted. Also called turntable doctrine.

> The possessor of land is liable for injury to trespassing young children caused by a structure or other artificial condition, if the possessor knows or should know that children are likely to trespass thereon and that such condition involves unreasonable risk of death or serious injury to children and children do not realize the risk involved and the utility to the possessor of maintaining condition is slight as compared to such risk. *Banks*, 132 So.2d 219 (Fla.App.1961)

attribution Assigning one taxpayer's ownership interest to another.

at-will employee An employee with no contract protection. An employee who can quit or be terminated at any time and for any reason.

auction A public sale of assets to the highest bidder.

audit An examination of records to verify financial or other data.

auditor Someone who performs audits, often an accountant.

augmented estate A decedent's estate with adjustments keyed to the length of marriage and gifts decedent made shortly before death.

authentication Evidence that a writing or other physical item is genuine and is what it purports to be.

author An originator of a work in various media (e.g., print, film) plus other participants with copyright protection, e.g., translators.

authority 1. The power or right to act. 2. A source relied upon.

authorize To give power or permission; to approve.

authorized stock See capital stock (1).

automobile guest statute See guest statute.

autopsy An examination of a cadaver to identify the cause of death. Also called postmortem.

autoptic evidence See demonstrative evidence.

autrefois acquit A plea that one has already been acquitted of the offense.

autre vie Another's life.

aver To assert or allege.

average 1. Usual, ordinary, norm. 2. Mean, median. 3. Partial loss or damage.

averment A positive allegation or assertion of fact.

avoid 1. To annul or cancel. 2. To escape.

avoidable consequences See mitigation-of-damages rule.

avoidance Escaping; invalidating. See also confession and avoidance.

> An avoidance is an allegation of additional facts intended to overcome an affirmative defense. *Buss Aluminum Products*, 651 So.2d 694 (Fla.App. 2 Dist.,1995)

avowal 1. An offer to prove. 2. An acknowledgment.

avulsion The sudden loss or addition to land caused by flood or by a shift in the bed or course of a stream.

award What a court or other tribunal gives or grants via its decision.

axiom An established or self-evident principle.

AWOL Absent without leave or permission. See also desertion.

B

baby act A minor's defense of infancy in a breach of contract action.

BAC See blood alcohol concentration.

bachelor of laws See LL.B.

back To assume financial responsibility for; to indorse.

bad 1. Defective. 2. Void or invalid.

bad check A check dishonored for insufficient funds.

bad debt An uncollectible debt.

bad faith 1. Dishonest purpose. Also called mala fides. 2. The absence of a reasonable basis to delay or deny an insurance claim.

> Bad faith in connection with insured's settlement after liability insurer's denial of coverage includes a false claim or collusion in which the plaintiffs agree to share the recovery with the insured. *Chomat*, 919 So.2d 535 (Fla.App. 3 Dist.,2006)

badge of fraud Factors from which an inference of fraud can be drawn.

bad law 1. A court opinion that fails to follow precedent or statutes. 2. A court opinion whose broader implications are unfortunate even though probably accurate for the narrow facts before the court.

bad title Title that is so defective as to be unmarketable.

bail 1. Money or other property deposited with the court as security to ensure that the defendant will reappear at designated times. Failure to appear forfeits the security. 2. Release of the defendant upon posting this security. 3. The one providing this security.

bailable offense An offense for which an accused is eligible for bail.

bail bond A surety contract under which the surety will pay the state the amount of the bond if the accused fails to appear in court.

bailee One to whom property is entrusted under a contract of bailment.

bailiff A court officer with duties in court, e.g., keep order.

bail jumping See jump bail.

bailment A delivery of personal property by one person to another under an express or implied contract whereby the property will be redelivered when the purpose of the contract is completed.

> Although the term "bailment" is difficult to define concisely, it is generally a contractual relationship among parties in which the subject matter of the relationship is delivered temporarily to and accepted by one other than the owner. *S & W Air Vac Systems*, 697 So.2d 1313 (Fla.App. 5 Dist.,1997)

bailment for hire A bailment under which the bailee is paid.

bailor One who delivers property to another under a contract of bailment.

bailout 1. Financial help to one in need of rescue. 2. Seeking alternative tax treatment of income.

bait and switch Using a low-priced item to lure a customer to a merchant who then pressures the customer to buy another item at a higher price.

> Bait and switch describes an offer which is made not in order to sell the advertised product at the advertised price, but rather to draw the customer to the store to sell him another similar product which is more profitable to the advertiser. *Fendrich*, 842 So.2d 1076 (Fla.App. 4 Dist.,2003)

balance 1. To calculate the difference between what has been paid and what is due. 2. To check to ensure that debits and credits are equal. 3. The equality of debits and credits. 4. See balancing test.

balance sheet A dated statement showing assets, liabilities, and owners' investment.

balancing test Weighing competing interests or values in order to resolve a legal issue.

balloon note A note on a loan calling for a large final payment and smaller intervening periodic payments.

ballot A paper or other media on which to vote; a list of candidates.

ban 1. To prohibit. 2. An announcement.

banc Bench. See also en banc.

banish See exile.

bank A financial institution that receives money on deposit, exchanges money, makes loans, and performs similar functions.

> Bank means any person having a subsisting charter or other lawful authorization, under the laws of this or any other jurisdiction, authorizing such person to conduct a general commercial banking business. The term "bank" does not include a credit union or an association. F.S.A. § 658.12(2)

bank bill See bank note.

bank credit Money a bank allows a customer to borrow.

bank draft A check that one bank writes on its account with another bank.

banker's lien The right of a bank to seize property of a depositor in the bank's possession to satisfy a customer's debt to the bank.

bank note A promissory note issued by a bank payable to bearer on demand and usable as cash. Also called bank bill.

bankrupt 1. Unable to pay debts as they are due. 2. A debtor undergoing a bankruptcy proceeding.

bankruptcy 1. The federal process by which a bankruptcy court gives a debtor relief by liquidating some or all of the unsecured debts or by otherwise rearranging debts and payment schedules. 2. Insolvency.

bankruptcy estate Assets of a debtor when bankruptcy is filed.

bankruptcy trustee See trustee in bankruptcy.

bar 1. The court or court system. 2. The courtroom partition behind which spectators sit. 3. All the attorneys licensed to practice in a jurisdiction. 4. The examination taken by attorneys to become licensed to practice law. 5. An impediment or barrier to bringing or doing something.

bar association An association of members of the legal profession.

bar examination See bar (4).

bare licensee One who enters the land for his or her own purposes, but with the express or implied consent of the occupier. Also called naked licensee.

> Plaintiff was a bare licensee to whom the defendants owed no duty except not to harm her willfully, wantonly or to set a trap for her or to expose her to danger recklessly or wantonly. *Schroeder*, 149 So.2d 564 (Fla.App.1963)

bareboat charter A document under which one who charters or leases a boat becomes for the period of the charter the owner for all practical purposes. Also called demise charter.

bargain 1. To negotiate the terms of a contract. 2. An agreement establishing the obligations of the parties.

bargain and sale deed A deed of conveyance without covenants.

bargaining agent A union bargaining on behalf of its members.

bargaining unit A group of employees allowed to conduct collective bargaining for other employees.

barratry 1. Persistently instigating or stirring up lawsuits. 2. Fraud or other misconduct by a captain or crew that harms the ship owner.

barrister An attorney in England and other Commonwealth countries who is allowed to try cases in specific courts.

barter To exchange goods or services without the use of money.

basis 1. The foundation; the underlying principle. 2. The cost or other amount assigned to an asset for income tax purposes.

bastard A child born before its parents were married or born from those who never married. An illegitimate child.

bastardy proceeding See paternity suit.

battered child syndrome A diagnosis that a child's injury or injuries are not accidental and are presumed to have been caused by someone of mature strength, such as an adult caregiver.

battered woman syndrome Psychological helplessness because of a woman's financial dependence, loneliness, guilt, shame, and fear of reprisal from her husband or boyfriend who has repeatedly battered her in the past.

> The battered woman's syndrome has been defined as a series of common characteristics that appear in women who are abused physically and psychologically over an extended period of time by the dominant male figure in their lives. *Rogers*, 616 So.2d 1098 (Fla.App. 1 Dist.,1993)

battery An intentional touching of the person of another that is harmful or offensive. Battery can be a tort and a crime.

bear 1. To produce or yield. 2. To carry.

bearer One who holds or possesses a negotiable instrument that is payable to bearer or to cash.

> Bearer means the person in possession of an instrument, document of title, or certificated security payable to bearer or indorsed in blank. F.S.A. § 671.201(5)

bearer paper Commercial paper payable to one who holds or possesses it.

belief The mind's acceptance that something is probably true or certain.

> "Belief" or "believes" denotes that the person involved actually supposed the fact in question to be true. Florida Rules of Professional Conduct, Preamble

belief-action There are no unconstitutional beliefs, but a person's actions can violate constitutional rights.

belligerent A country at war or in armed conflict.

below 1. Pertaining to a lower court in the judicial system. 2. Later in the document.

bench The court, the judge's seat, or the judiciary.

bench conference A meeting at the judge's bench between the judge and the attorneys out of the hearing of the jury. Also called a sidebar conference.

bench memo A memorandum of law by a party's attorney for a trial judge or by a law clerk for a judge.

bench trial A trial without a jury. Also called nonjury trial.

bench warrant A judge's direct order for the arrest of a person.

beneficial Tending to the benefit of a person.

beneficial interest A right to a benefit from property or an estate as opposed to the legal ownership of that property or estate.

> A resident has a "beneficial interest" in a trust if the resident has a vested interest, even if subject to divestment, which includes at least a current right to income and either a power to revoke the trust or a general power of appointment, . . . F.S.A. § 199.023(7)

beneficial owner See equitable owner.

beneficial use A right to the benefits of property when legal title to the property may be held by others.

beneficiary 1. A person whom a trust was created to benefit. 2. A person entitled to insurance benefits. 3. One who receives a benefit.

benefit Assistance, advantage, profit, or privilege; payment or gift.

benefit of clergy 1. A former right of clerics not to be tried in secular courts. 2. The approval or blessing given by a religious rite.

benefit of the bargain rule 1. In a fraud action, the damages should be the value as represented less the value actually received. 2. In a contract action, the damages should be what would place the victim in the position he or she would have been in if the contract had not been breached. Also called loss of bargain rule.

> The two standards for measuring damages in an action for fraud arising out of the sale of real property are the "benefit of the bargain rule," which awards as damages the difference between the actual value of the property and its value

had the alleged facts regarding it been true, and the "out-of-pocket rule," which awards as damages the difference between the purchase price and the real or actual value of the property; either measure of damages requires a plaintiff to prove the actual value of the property at the time of purchase. *Kind*, 889 So.2d 87 (Fla.App. 4 Dist.,2004)

bequeath To give property (sometimes only personal property) by will.

bequest Property (sometimes only personal property) given in a will.

best efforts Diligence more exacting than the duty of good faith.

best evidence rule To prove the content of a writing, recording, or phonograph, the original (or an acceptable duplicate) should be produced unless it is unavailable. Also called original document rule.

> The best evidence rule requires that if original evidence is available, then no evidence should be received which is merely substitutionary in nature. *State v. Eubanks*, 609 So.2d 107 (Fla.App. 4 Dist.,1992)

bestiality Sexual relations between a human and an animal.

bestow To give or convey.

best use See highest and best use.

betterment A property improvement beyond mere repairs.

beyond a reasonable doubt See reasonable doubt.

BFOQ See bona fide occupational qualification.

BFP See bona fide purchaser.

BIA Bureau of Indian Affairs (*www.doi.gov/bia*).

biannual 1. Twice a year. 2. Every two years.

bias A tendency or inclination to think and to act in a certain way. A danger of prejudgment. Prejudice.

bicameral Having two chambers or houses in the legislature.

bid 1. An offer to perform a contract for a designated price. 2. An offer to pay a designated price for property, e.g., auction bid.

bid and asked Price ranges quoted for securities in an over-the-counter market.

bid bond A bond to protect the government if a bidder fails to enter the contract according to its bid.

bid in A bid on property by its owner to set a floor auction price.

bid shopping A general contractor's use of a low subcontractor's bid as a tool to negotiate lower bids from other subcontractors.

biennial 1. Occurring every two years. 2. Lasting two years.

biennium A two-year period. This term is often used to describe the two-year term of the Florida Legislature that begins in November of an even-numbered year and ends in November of the next even-numbered year.

bifurcated trial A case in which certain issues are tried separately (e.g., guilt and punishment, liability and damages).

bigamy Marrying while still in a valid marriage with someone else.

bilateral contract A contract of mutual promises between the parties.

> A unilateral contract is one in which no promisor receives a promise as consideration for his promise. A bilateral contract is one in which there are mutual promises between two

parties to the contract; each party being both a promisor and a promisee. *Ballou*, 179 So.2d 228 (Fla.App.1965)

bilateral mistake See mutual mistake.

bill 1. A proposed statute. Legislation under consideration for enactment by a legislature. 2. The statute that has been enacted. 3. A statement of money owed. 4. Paper money. 5. A pleading that states a claim in equity. Also called bill in equity. 6. A list of specifics or particulars. 7. A draft. See bill of exchange.

billable Pertaining to tasks for which an attorney, paralegal, or other timekeeper can charge a client fees.

bill in equity See bill (5).

bill of attainder An act of the legislature that imposes punishment (e.g., death) on a specific person or group without a trial.

bill of exchange See draft (1).

bill of health A certificate on the health of a ship's cargo and crew.

bill of indictment A document asking the grand jury to determine whether enough evidence exists to bring a formal criminal charge against the accused.

bill of lading A document from a carrier that lists (and acknowledges receipt of) the goods to be transported and the terms of their delivery.

> Bill of lading means a document evidencing the receipt of goods for shipment issued by a person engaged in the business of transporting or forwarding goods, and includes an airbill. Airbill means a document serving for air transportation as a bill of lading does for marine or rail transportation, and includes an air consignment note or air waybill. F.S.A. § 671.201(6)

bill of pains and penalties An act of the legislature that imposes punishment (other than death) on a specific person or group without a trial.

bill of particulars A more detailed statement of the civil claims or criminal charges brought against another.

bill of review A request that a court of equity revise a decree.

bill of rights A list of fundamental rights, e.g., the first ten amendments to the U.S. Constitution.

bill of sale A document that conveys title to personal property from seller to buyer.

bind To place under a legal duty.

binder 1. A contract giving temporary protection to the insured until a formal policy is issued. 2. A statement (and often a deposit) to secure the right to purchase property.

> A binder is not policy of insurance but is generally taken to mean a contract either written or oral providing for interim insurance effective at the date of application and terminating at either completion or rejection of the principal policy. *Frank*, 310 So.2d 418 (Fla.App. 1975)

binding instruction See mandatory instruction.

bind over 1. To hold or transfer for further court proceedings. 2. To place under an obligation.

blackacre A fictitious name for a parcel of land. Also, whiteacre.

black code Laws of southern states regulating slavery.

black letter law A statement of a fundamental or basic principle of law. Also called hornbook law.

blackmail Unlawful demand of money or property under threat of bodily harm, property damage, accusation of crime, or exposure. Extortion.

black market Illegal avenues for buying and selling.

blanket bond 1. A bond protecting against loss from employee dishonesty. 2. A bond covering a group rather than named persons.

blank indorsement An indorsement without naming a person to whom the instrument is to be paid.

blasphemy Language or acts showing contempt for God or sacred matters.

blind trust A trust with a trustee who acts without control or influence by the owner or settlor to avoid a conflict of interest.

blockage rule A tax rule allowing a lower value for a large block of shares than the sum of their individual values.

blockbusting Persuading homeowners to sell by asserting that minority newcomers will lower property values.

blood alcohol concentration (BAC) The percentage of alcohol in a person's blood.

> The greater the blood alcohol concentration, the higher the breath alcohol concentration. The relationship between these two concentrations is derived by a formula. *Green*, 905 So.2d 922 (Fla.App. 1 Dist.,2005)

blotter A book recording daily events, e.g., arrests.

bluebook 1. Popular name of *A Uniform System of Citation*, a citation guidebook. 2. A directory of government offices and employees.

blue chip Pertaining to a high-quality investment stock.

blue flu Police officers call in sick as a labor protest.

blue laws Laws regulating Sunday commerce.

blue ribbon jury A jury with members having special skills.

blue sky laws State securities laws to prevent fraud.

BOA Based on arrest.

board 1. A group of persons with authority to manage or advise. 2. Regular meals.

boarder One to whom meals are supplied, often with a room.

board of aldermen A local legislative body, e.g., city council.

board of directors Individuals elected by shareholders to hire officers and set policy.

> Board of directors means the group of persons vested with the management of the affairs of the corporation irrespective of the name by which such group is designated, including, but not limited to, managers or trustees. F.S.A. § 617.01401(2)

board of education A government body that manages local public schools.

board of equalization A government agency with responsibility for ensuring that the tax burden is distributed fairly in a particular state or district.

board of pardons A government agency with the power to issue pardons.

board of parole See parole board.

board of supervisors The body that governs a county.

board of trade 1. An organization of businesses that promote common business interests. 2. The governing body of a commodities exchange.

bodily harm Physical damage to the body, including injury, illness, and pain.

bodily heir See heir of the body.

bodily injury Physical harm or damage to the body. Also called physical injury.

> Bodily injury means: 1. A cut, abrasion, bruise, burn, or disfigurement; 2. Physical pain; 3. Illness; 4. Impairment of the function of a bodily member, organ, or mental faculty; or 5. Any other injury to the body, no matter how temporary. F.S.A. § 501.001(4)(c)

body 1. A collection of laws. 2. The main section(s) of a document. 3. A person, group, or entity.

body corporate Another term for corporation.

body execution Taking a person into custody by order of the court.

body of the crime See corpus delicti.

body politic The people of a nation or state as a political group.

BOF Based on felony.

bogus Counterfeit, sham.

boilerplate Standard language commonly used in some documents.

boiler room sale A high-pressure phone sale of goods and services, e.g., securities.

bona fide In good faith; sincere.

bona fide occupational qualification (BFOQ) An employment qualification based on gender, religion, or other characteristic that is reasonably necessary for the operation of a particular business and hence is not an illegal requirement.

bona fide purchaser (BFP) One who has purchased property for value without notice of defects in the title of seller or of any claims in the property by others. Also called good faith purchaser, innocent purchaser.

> A purchaser for value, in good faith, before certification of such assessment of back taxes to the tax collector for collection. F.S.A. § 193.092(1)

bona immobilia Immovable property such as land.

bond 1. A certificate that is evidence of a debt in which the entity that issues the bond (a company or a governmental body) promises (a) to pay the bondholders a specified amount of interest for a specified amount of time and (b) to repay the loan on the expiration date. 2. An obligation to perform an act (e.g., payment of a sum of money) upon the occurrence or nonoccurrence of a designated condition. 3. A promise or binding agreement.

bond discount An amount that is lower than the face value of the bond.

bonded Placed under or secured by a bond.

bonded debt A debt that has the added backing or security of a bond.

bonded warehouse A private warehouse that stores imported goods subject to special taxes or custom duties.

bondholder One who holds a government, corporate, or commercial bond.

bond issue Bonds offered for sale at the same time.

bond premium An amount that is higher than the face value of the bond.

bondsman A surety; a person or business that guarantees a bond.

bonification A forgiveness of taxes, usually on exports.

bonus Extra; a consideration paid in addition to what is strictly due.

book 1. To enter charges against someone on a police register. The process is called booking. 2. To engage the services of someone. 3. Books: original financial or accounting records. Also called books of account. See also shop-book rule.

book entry 1. A note in a financial ledger or book. 2. A statement acknowledging ownership of securities.

> Book-entry form means that securities are not represented by a paper certificate but represented by an account entry on the records of a depository trust clearing system or, in the case of United States Government securities, a Federal Reserve Bank. F.S.A. § 280.02(5)

booking See book (1).

bookkeeper One who records financial accounts and transactions.

bookmaking Taking or placing or offering to take or place a bet for another.

bookie One engaged in bookmaking.

books; books of account See book (3).

book value 1. The value at which an asset is carried on a balance sheet. 2. Net worth.

Boolean search A computer search that allows words to be included or excluded by using operatives such as AND, OR, and NOT in the query.

boot 1. The taxable component in a transaction that is otherwise not taxable. 2. An additional payment or consideration.

bootlegger One who deals in (e.g., copies, sells) products illegally.

bootstrap sale Using the future earnings of a business to acquire that business.

border search A search upon entering the country, usually at the border.

borough A political subdivision of a state with self-governing powers.

borrowed servant rule See loaned servant doctrine.

bottomry A contract by which the owner of a ship borrows money for a voyage, giving the ship as security for the loan.

bought and sold notes Written confirmations of a sale from a broker to the buyer and seller.

bound 1. To identify the boundary. 2. Obligated. See also bind.

bound over See bind over.

bounty 1. A reward. 2. Generosity.

boycott A concerted refusal to work or do business with a particular person or business in order to obtain concessions or to express displeasure with certain practices of the person or business.

> For antitrust purposes, the term "group boycott" is also known as a collective refusal to deal. West's F.S.A. § 542.18. An essential element of an unlawful group boycott is that at least some of the boycotters are competitors of each other and the target. *St. Petersburg Yacht Charters*, 457 So.2d 1028 (Fla.App. 2 Dist.,1984)

Brady **material** Evidence known by the prosecution to be favorable to the defense must be disclosed to the defendant. *Brady v. Maryland*, 83 S. Ct. 1194 (1963)

brain death Irreversible cessation of circulatory and respiratory functions, or irreversible cessation of all functions of the entire brain, including the brain stem. Also called legal death.

> For legal and medical purposes, where respiratory and circulatory functions are maintained by artificial means of support so as to preclude a determination that these functions have ceased, the occurrence of death may be determined where there is the irreversible cessation of the functioning of the entire brain, including the brain stem, determined in accordance with this section. F.S.A. § 382.009(1)

branch A subdivision, member, or department.

Brandeis brief An appellate brief in which economic and social studies are included along with legal principles.

breach The breaking or violation of a legal duty or law.

breach of contract The failure to perform a contract obligation.

breach of promise to marry Breaking an engagement (promise) to marry.

breach of the peace A violation or disturbance of the public tranquility and order. Disorderly conduct.

> Breach of the peace is a generic term including all violations of the public peace, order, or decorum. *Edwards*, 462 So.2d 581 (Fla.App. 4 Dist.,1985)

breach of trust Violation of a fiduciary obligation by a trustee.

breach of warranty Breaking an express or implied warranty.

breaking a close Trespassing on land.

breaking and entering See burglary.

breaking bulk Unlawfully opening by a bailee of a container entrusted to his or her care and stealing the contents.

breathalyzer A device to measure blood alcohol concentration.

breve A writ.

bribe An offer, acceptance, or solicitation of an unlawful payment with the understanding that it will corruptly affect the official action of the recipient.

> Bribery means corruptly to give, offer, or promise to any public servant, or, if a public servant, corruptly to request, solicit, accept, or agree to accept for himself or herself or another, any pecuniary or other benefit not authorized by law with an intent or purpose to influence the performance of any act or omission which the person believes to be, or the public servant represents as being, within the official discretion of a public servant, in violation of a public duty, or in performance of a public duty. F.S.A. § 838.015(1)

bridge loan A short-term loan given until other funding is arranged.

brief 1. Shorthand for appellate brief, which is a document submitted by a party to an appellate court in which arguments are presented on why the appellate court should affirm (approve), reverse, or otherwise modify what a lower court has done. 2. A document submitted to a trial court in support of a particular position. 3. A summary of the main or essential parts of a court opinion. 4. Shorthand for a trial brief, which is an attorney's personal notes on how to conduct a trial.

bright-line rule A clear-cut (but sometimes overly simple) legal principle that resolves a dispute.

bring an action To sue someone.

broad interpretation See liberal construction.

broker An agent who arranges or negotiates contracts for others.

brokerage 1. The business or occupation of a broker. 2. The wages or commissions of a broker.

broker-dealer A firm that buys and sells securities as an agent for others and as a principal, buying or selling in its own name.

brutum fulmen 1. An empty threat. 2. An invalid judgment.

bubble An extravagant commercial project based on deception.

bucket shop A fraudulent business that pretends to be engaged in securities transactions.

buggery Sodomy or bestiality.

building code Laws that provide standards for constructing buildings.

building line Distances from the ends and sides of the lot beyond which construction may not extend.

bulk goods Goods not divided into parts or packaged in separate units.

bulk sale or transfer The sale of all or a large part of a seller's inventory, not in the ordinary course of the seller's business.

> Bulk transfer means the shipment of fuel by pipeline or marine vessel between terminals or from a refinery to a terminal. West's F.S.A. § 206.01(15)

bulletin An ongoing or periodic publication.

bull market A stock market climate of persistent rising prices.

bumping 1. Depriving someone of a reserved seat due to overbooking. 2. Replacing a worker with someone more senior.

burden 1. A duty or responsibility. 2. A limitation or hindrance.

burden of going forward The obligation to produce some evidence tending to prove (not necessarily conclusive evidence) its case. Also called burden of producing evidence, burden of production.

burden of persuasion The obligation to convince the trier of fact (judge or jury) that the party has introduced enough evidence on the truth of its version of the facts to meet the standard of proof, e.g., preponderance of the evidence. Also called risk of nonpersuasion.

burden of producing evidence See burden of going forward.

burden of production See burden of going forward.

burden of proof The obligation of proving the facts of one's claim. This obligation is met by meeting the burden of going forward and the burden of persuasion.

> Burden of establishing a fact means the burden of persuading the triers of fact that the existence of the fact is more probable than its nonexistence. West's F.S.A. § 671.201(8)

Burford **abstention** To avoid unnecessary federal-state friction, a federal court can refuse to review a state court's decision involving complex state regulations or sensitive state policies. *Burford v. Sun Oil Co.*, 63 S. Ct. 1098 (1943)

burglary 1. Entering a building of another with the intent to commit a felony therein. 2. Breaking and entering the dwelling house of another in the nighttime with the intent to commit a felony therein.

burgle To commit burglary; to burglarize.

bursar Someone in charge of funds, especially at a college.

business agent 1. One selected by union members to represent them. 2. A manager of another's business affairs.

> The term business agent means any person, without regard to title, who shall, for a pecuniary or financial consideration, act or attempt to act for any labor organization in: (a) The issuance of membership or authorization cards, work permits, or any other evidence of rights granted or claimed in, or by, a labor organization; or (b) Soliciting or receiving from any employer any right or privilege for employees. F.S.A. § 447.02(2)

business compulsion Exerting improper economic coercion on a business in a weak or vulnerable position. Also called economic duress.

business entry rule An exception to the hearsay rule allowing the introduction into evidence of entries (records) made in the ordinary course of business. Also called the business records exception.

business expense An amount paid for goods or services used in operating a taxpayer's business or trade.

business invitee Someone who has been expressly or impliedly invited to be present or to remain on the premises, primarily for a purpose directly or indirectly connected with business dealings between them. Also called business guest, business visitor.

> In actions involving premises liability, a business invitee is one who is invited to enter or remain on land for a purpose directly or indirectly connected with business dealings with the possessor of the land. *Moultrie*, 764 So.2d 637 (Fla.App. 1 Dist.,2000)

business judgment rule Courts will defer to good-faith decisions made by boards of directors in business dealings and presume the decisions were made in the best interests of the company.

business records exception See business entry rule.

business trust An unincorporated business in which a trustee manages its property for the benefit and use of the trust beneficiaries. Also called common law trust, Massachusetts trust.

business visitor See business invitee.

but-for test A test for causation: an event (e.g., injury) would not have happened without the act or omission of the defendant.

> The "but-for causation-in-fact-test" sets forth that to constitute proximate cause there must be such a natural, direct, and continuous sequence between the negligent act or omission and the plaintiff's injury that it can reasonably be said that but for the negligent act or omission the injury would not have occurred. *Deese*, 874 So.2d 1282 (Fla.App. 1 Dist.,2004)

buy and sell agreement An arrangement under which there is a right or duty of one or more owners of an entity to buy another owner's interest upon the occurrence of certain events, e.g., an owner dies or withdraws.

buyer in the ordinary course of business One who buys goods in good faith, without knowledge that the sale violates the rights of another person in the goods, and in the ordinary course from a person (other than a pawnbroker) in the business of selling goods of that kind. UCC 1-201(b)(9)

by-bidding Planting someone to make fictitious auction bids. Also called puffing.

bylaws Rules governing internal affairs of an organization.

by operation of law See operation of law.

bypass trust A trust designed to take full advantage of the unified credit against estate taxes by reducing the surviving spouse's estate.

by the entirety See tenancy by the entirety.

C

c Copyright, often printed as ©.

CA Court of Appeals.

cabinet An advisory board or council of a chief executive.

caduary Subject to forfeiture.

c.a.f. See cost and freight.

calendar A list of cases awaiting court action or bills awaiting legislative action.

calendar call A hearing to determine the status of, and establish court dates for, cases on the court calendar.

call 1. A demand for payment. 2. A demand to present bonds or other securities for redemption before maturity. 3. A property boundary landmark. 4. See call option.

callable Subject to be called and paid for before maturity.

callable bonds See redeemable bond.

call option The right to buy something at a fixed price.

call premium The added charge paid to redeem a bond prior to maturity.

calumny A false and malicious accusation.

camera See in camera.

cancellation 1. Striking or crossing out. 2. Invalidation, termination.

> Cancellation occurs when either party puts an end to the contract for breach by the other and its effect is the same as that of termination except that the canceling party also retains any remedy for breach of the whole contract or any unperformed balance. F.S.A. § 672.106(4)

c&f See cost and freight.

cannabis The plant from which marijuana is prepared.

canon A rule, law, or principle.

canonical disability An impediment justifying a church annulment.

canon law Ecclesiastical law; Roman church jurisprudence.

canons of construction Rules for interpreting statutes and contracts.

canvass 1. To examine carefully, e.g., the votes cast. 2. To solicit votes, contributions, opinions, etc.

capacity 1. Legal qualification or competency to do something. 2. The ability to understand the nature of one's acts. 3. Occupation, function, or role.

> Capacity to consent means that a vulnerable adult has sufficient understanding to make and communicate responsible decisions regarding the vulnerable adult's person or property, including whether or not to accept protective services offered by the department. F.S.A. § 415.102(3)

capias A writ requiring that someone be taken into custody.

capias ad respondendum A writ commanding the sheriff to bring the defendant to court to answer the claims of the plaintiff.

capias ad satisfaciendum A writ commanding the sheriff to hold a judgment debtor until the latter satisfies its judgment debt.

capias pro fine A writ commanding the sheriff to arrest someone who has not paid a fine.

capita Head, person. See also per capita.

capital 1. Assets available for generating more wealth. 2. Assets less liabilities; net worth. 3. Relating to the death penalty.

capital asset See fixed asset.

capital budget Projected spending to buy long-term or fixed assets.

capital gains tax A tax on the sale or exchange of a capital asset.

capital goods Assets (e.g., tools) used to produce goods and services.

capitalization 1. The total value of stocks and other securities used for long-term financing. 2. See capitalize.

capitalize 1. To treat an asset as capital; to classify an expenditure as a long-term investment. 2. To provide with investment funds. 3. To determine current value of cash flow.

capital loss Loss realized on the sale or exchange of a capital asset.

capital market The market for long-term securities.

capital punishment A death sentence.

capital stock 1. All of the stock a corporation is authorized to issue. Also called authorized stock. 2. The total par value of stock a corporation is authorized to issue.

> Capital stock means the aggregate of shares of nonwithdrawable capital issued. F.S.A. § 655.005(1)(d)

capital surplus Surplus other than retained earnings. Funds owners pay over par value.

capitation tax See poll tax.

capitulary A collection or code of laws.

capricious Impulsive; not based on evidence, law, or reason.

> Capricious action is one taken irrationally, without thought or reason. *Board of Clinical Laboratory Personnel*, 721 So.2d 317 (Fla.App. 1 Dist.,1998)

caption 1. The heading or introductory part of a pleading, court opinion, memo, or other document that identifies what it is, the names of the parties, the court involved, etc. 2. Arresting someone.

care 1. Caution in avoiding harm. 2. Heed. 3. Supervision or comfort.

career criminal See habitual criminal.

careless Absence of reasonable care; negligent.

carjacking Using violence or threats to take a vehicle from the driver.

> Carjacking means the taking of a motor vehicle which may be the subject of larceny from the person or custody of another, with intent to either permanently or temporarily deprive the person or the owner of the motor vehicle, when in the course of the taking there is the use of force, violence, assault, or putting in fear. F.S.A. § 812.133(1)

carnal knowledge Sexual intercourse.

carrier 1. A person or company engaged in transporting passengers or goods for hire. See also common carrier. 2. An insurance company.

> Carrier means every railroad company, pipeline company, water transportation company, private or common carrier, and any other person transporting motor or diesel fuel, casinghead gasoline, natural gasoline, naphtha, or distillate for others, either in interstate or intrastate commerce, to points within Florida, or from a point in Florida to a point outside of the state. F.S.A. § 206.01(6)

carrier's lien The legal right of a carrier to hold cargo until its owner pays the agreed shipping costs.

carry 1. To transport. 2. To bear the burden of. 3. To have in stock. 4. To list on one's accounts as a debt.

carryback Applying a loss or deduction from one year to a prior year.

carrying charge 1. Charges of a creditor, in addition to interest, for providing credit. 2. Costs involved in owning land, e.g., taxes.

carryover Applying a loss or deduction from one year to a later year.

carryover basis When property is transferred in a certain way (e.g., by gift), the basis of the property in the transferee is the same as (is carried over from) the transferor's basis.

cartel 1. An association of producers or sellers of any product joined together to control the production, sale, or price of the product. 2. An agreement between enemies while at war.

carve out To separate income from the property that generates it.

CASA Court appointed special advocate (*www.nationalcasa.org*).

case 1. A court's written explanation of how it applied the law to the facts to resolve a legal dispute. See also opinion. 2. A pending matter on a court calendar. 3. A client matter handled by a law office. 4. A statement of arguments and evidence. See also action on the case.

> In statute providing for reasonable attorney's fee to prevailing party in medical or hospital malpractice "action," word "action" is to be equated to "case," and thus filing of second amended complaint adding certain persons as parties defendant related back to original filing. *Theodorou*, 438 So.2d 400 (Fla.App. 4 Dist.,1983)

case agreed See agreed case.

casebook A law school textbook containing many edited court opinions.

caselaw (case law) The law found within court opinions. See also common law.

case method Learning law by studying court opinions.

case of first impression See first impression.

case-in-chief The presentation of evidence by one side, not including the evidence it introduces to counter the other side.

case or controversy For a federal court to hear a case, the plaintiff must have suffered a definite and concrete injury.

case reports See reporter (3).

case stated See agreed case.

cash basis Reporting or recognizing revenue only when actually received and expenses only when actually paid out.

cash dividend A dividend paid by a corporation in money.

cash flow 1. Cash from income-producing property. 2. Income less expenses over a designated period of time.

cashier's check A check drawn by a bank on its own funds, signed by a bank officer, and payable to a third party named by a customer.

cash out To receive cash for one's total ownership interest.

cash price A lower price if paid in cash rather than with credit.

> Cash price means the price at which a seller, in the ordinary course of business, offers to sell for cash the property or service that is the subject of the transaction. At the seller's option, the term "cash price" may include the price of accessories, services related to the sale, service contracts, and taxes and fees for license, title, and registration of the motor vehicle. The term "cash price" does not include any finance charge. F.S.A. § 520.02(2)

cash sale A sale in which the buyer and seller exchange goods and full payment in cash at the same time.

cash surrender value Cash available upon surrender of an insurance policy before it becomes payable in the normal course (e.g., at death). Also called surrender value.

cash value See fair market value.

castle doctrine See retreat rule.

casual 1. Unexpected. 2. Occasional. 3. Without formality.

casual ejector A fictitious defendant who casually enters the land to eject the person lawfully in possession of it.

casualty 1. A serious accident. 2. A person injured or killed.

casualty insurance Insurance against loss from accident. (Covers many different kinds of insurance.)

> Casualty insurance means automobile public liability and property damage insurance to be applied at the place of residence of the owner, or if the subject is a commercial vehicle, to be applied at the place of business of the owner; automobile collision insurance; fidelity bonds; burglary and theft insurance; and plate glass insurance. "Multiple peril" means a combination or package policy that includes both property coverage and casualty coverage for a single premium. F.S.A. § 185.02(2)

casualty loss Damage to property due to an event that is sudden, unexpected, and unusual in nature.

catching bargain An unconscionable purchase from one who has an estate in reversion or expectancy.

caucus A meeting of the members of a particular group, e.g., a political party.

causa A cause; what produces an effect.

causa causans The predominating effective cause.

causa mortis In contemplation of approaching death. Also phrased mortis causa.

causa proxima The immediate cause.

causa sine qua non "But-for" cause. Without (but-for) the act or omission, the event in question would not have occurred.

causation Bringing something about. Producing an effect.

> Causation is that act which, in natural and continuous sequence, unbroken by any intervening cause, produces injury, and without which injury would not have occurred. *Schatz*, 128 So.2d 901 (Fla.App.1961)

cause 1. Bringing something about. Producing an effect. 2. A reason, justification, or ground. 3. A lawsuit.

cause of action The facts that give a person a right to judicial relief. A legally acceptable reason for suing.

cautionary instruction A judge's caution or warning to the jury to avoid outside contact about the case, to ignore certain evidence, or to consider the evidence for a limited purpose.

caveat 1. A warning or admonition. 2. A party's notice filed in court asking that the case be stopped.

caveat actor Let the doer (the actor) beware.

caveatee The person being challenged by someone who files a caveat. The latter is the caveator.

caveat emptor Let the buyer beware. A buyer should examine and judge the product on his or her own.

> If the tenant has the same opportunities as the owner to discover a defect at the time of the leasing, then the rule of caveat emptor applies and the tenant takes the property as he finds it. *Butler*, 200 So. 226 (Fla.1941)

CC Circuit Court; County Court; Civil Code.

C corporation A corporation whose income is taxed at the corporate level; it has not chosen S corporation status. Also called subchapter C corporation.

CD Certificate of deposit.

cease and desist order A court or agency order prohibiting the continuation of a course of conduct.

cede 1. To surrender or yield. 2. To assign or transfer.

cedent A person who transfers something. One who cedes.

censor A person who examines material in order to identify and remove what is objectionable.

censure 1. An official reprimand. 2. To express formal disapproval.

census An official counting of a population.

center of gravity doctrine In conflict-of-law cases, courts apply the law of the place that has the most significant contacts or relationship with the matter in dispute.

> Significant relationship test applied to choice of law issues in tort actions is not a simple "center of gravity" or "contacts counting" test, but rather, court must determine which state or states have true interest in application of their law, by examining the various factual contacts in light of applicable principles; if only one state is interested, court should apply law of that state, while if two or more states are interested, court must determine which state has dominant interest and apply law of that state, and if no state has clearly dominant interest, court should apply law of place of injury. *Mezroub*, 702 So.2d 562 (Fla.App. 2 Dist.,1997)

ceremonial marriage A marriage entered in compliance with statutory requirements, e.g., obtaining a marriage license.

cert. See certiorari.

certificated Having met the qualifications for certification from a school or training program.

certificate A document that asserts the truth of something or that something has been done, e.g., that requirements have been met.

certificate of acknowledgement Confirmation that the signature on a document was made by a person who is who he or she claimed to be.

certificate of convenience and necessity An authorization from a regulatory agency that a company can operate a public utility.

certificate of deposit (CD) A document from a bank confirming that a named person has a designated amount of money in the bank, usually for a fixed term earning a fixed rate of interest. A time deposit.

certificate of incorporation A document issued by the state to a company that grants its status as a corporation.

certificate of occupancy A document confirming that the premises comply with building codes regulations.

> Request for certificate of occupancy or certificate of completion means a properly completed and executed application for: 1. A certificate of occupancy or certificate of completion. 2. A certificate of compliance from the private provider required pursuant to subsection (10). 3. Any applicable fees. F.S.A. § 553.791(1)(h)

certificate of title A document confirming who owns designated property, including who holds encumbrances such as liens.

certification 1. The act of affirming the truth or authenticity of something. 2. A request by a federal court that a state court resolve a state issue relevant to a case in the federal court. 3. The process by which a nongovernmental organization grants recognition to a person who has met the qualifications established by that organization.

certification mark Any word, name, symbol, or device used to certify some aspect of goods or services, e.g., their origin.

certified Having complied with the qualifications for certification.

certified check A check drawn on funds in a depositor's account whose payment is guaranteed by the bank on which it is drawn.

> The term "certified check" means a check accepted by the bank on which it is drawn. Acceptance may be made as stated in subsection (1) or by a writing on the check which indicates that the check is certified. The drawee of a check has no obligation to certify the check, and refusal to certify is not dishonor of the check. F.S.A. § 673.4091(4)

certified copy A duplicate of an original document, certified as an exact reproduction. Also called exemplified copy.

Certified Florida Legal Assistant (CFLA) A person who meets the certification qualifications of the Paralegal Association of Florida (which includes certification by the National Association of Legal Assistants). See section 1.1.

Certified Legal Assistant (CLA) The credential bestowed by the National Association of Legal Assistants (NALA) (*www.nala.org*) for meeting its criteria such as passing a national, entry-level certification exam.

Certified Public Accountant (CPA) An accountant who has met the requirements to be certified as a public accountant (*www.aicpa.org*).

certiorari (cert.) An order (or writ) by a higher court that a lower court send up the record of a case because the higher court has decided to use its discretion to review that case.

cession A surrender or yielding up.

cestui ("he who") One who benefits, a beneficiary.

cestui que trust Beneficiary of a trust. See also trust.

cf. Compare.

CFI Cost, freight, and insurance.

CFLA See Certified Florida Legal Assistant (and section 1.1).

CFR See Code of Federal Regulations (*www.gpoaccess.gov/cfr*).

Ch. Chancellor; chancery; chapter.

chain of causation The sequence of actions and omissions that led to or resulted in the harm or other event in question.

chain of custody A list of places an item of physical evidence has been in and the name of anyone who has possessed it over a period of time.

> "Chain of custody" refers to the methodology of tracking specified materials or substances for the purpose of maintaining control and accountability from initial collection to final disposition for all such materials or substances and providing for accountability at each stage in handling, testing, storing specimens, and reporting of test results. F.S.A. § 112.0455(e)

chain of title The history of ownership of land from the original title holder to the present holder.

challenge 1. A formal objection to the selection of a particular prospective juror. 2. A protest or calling into question.

challenge for cause An objection to selecting a prospective juror because of specified causes or reasons, e.g., bias.

challenge to the array A formal protest to the manner in which the entire pool or panel of prospective jurors has been selected.

chamber 1. A room, e.g., a judge's office. 2. A legislative body.

champerty Conduct by an individual (called the champertor) who promotes or supports someone else's litigation, often by helping to finance the litigation in exchange for a share in the recovery. (See F.S.A. §§ 877.01 and 877.02.)

> "Champerty" is a form of maintenance wherein one will carry on a suit in which he has no subject-matter interest at his own expense or will aid in doing so in consideration of receiving, if successful, some part of the benefits recovered. *Hardick*, 795 So.2d 1107 (Fla.App. 5 Dist.,2001)

chancellor 1. Judge in a court of equity. 2. An officer of high rank.

chancery 1. Equity jurisprudence. 2. A court of equity.

change of venue The transfer of a suit begun in one court to another court in the same judicial system.

chapter 1. A subdivision of a code. 2. A division of an organization.

Chapter 11 A category of bankruptcy (found in chapter 11 of the bankruptcy code) in which the debtor is allowed to postpone payment of debts in order to reorganize the capital structure of his or her business.

character evidence Evidence of a person's habits, personality traits, and moral qualities.

charge 1. To instruct a jury, particularly on the law pertaining to the verdict it must reach. 2. A jury instruction. 3. To accuse someone of a crime. 4. To impose a burden or obligation; to assign a duty. 5. To defer payment. 6. A person (e.g., a child) entrusted to the care of another. 7. Price.

chargé d'affaires A diplomatic officer of a lower rank.

charge off To treat or report as a loss.

charitable Having the character or purpose of the public good; philanthropic, eleemosynary.

> "Charitable purpose" means a function or service which is of such a community service that its discontinuance could legally result in the allocation of public funds for the

continuance of the function or service. It is not necessary that public funds be allocated for such function or service but only that any such allocation would be legal. F.S.A. § 196.012(7)

charitable contribution A gift of money or other property to a charitable organization.

charitable deduction An income tax deduction taken for gifts to a qualified tax-exempt charitable organization.

charitable remainder annuity trust A trust that pays designated amounts to beneficiaries for a period of time after which the trust property goes to a charity.

charitable trust A trust established to serve a purpose that is beneficial to a community. Also called public trust.

charter 1. The fundamental law governing a municipality or other local unit of government, authorizing it to perform designated functions. 2. A document creating an organization that states its fundamental purposes and powers. 3. The legal authorization to conduct business 4. To rent for temporary use.

chattel Personal property.

chattel mortgage A mortgage or lien on personal property as security for a debt.

chattel paper A document that is evidence of both a monetary obligation and a security interest in specific goods.

> "Chattel paper" means a record or records that evidence both a monetary obligation and a security interest in specific goods, a security interest in specific goods and software used in the goods, a security interest in specific goods and license of software used in the goods, a lease of specific goods, or a lease of specific goods and license of software used in the goods. F.S.A. § 679.1021(k)

check 1. A written order instructing a bank to pay on demand a certain amount of money from the check writer's account to the person named on the check (the payee). See also negotiable instrument. 2. To control; to hold within bounds. 3. To examine for accuracy; to investigate. 4. To deposit for safekeeping.

check kiting A form of bank fraud in which the kiter opens accounts at two or more banks, writes checks on insufficient funds on one account, and then, taking advantage of bank processing delays, covers the overdraft by depositing a check on insufficient funds from the other account. Also called kiting.

> Scheme by which depositor deposited checks drawn on various banks into his saving account at depositary bank and withdrew cash, obtained checks, wired funds out, or deposited funds into his checking accounts at depositary bank was "check-kiting" scheme even though it involved transfer of money within one bank between savings and checking accounts, and was thus covered by blanket bond insurance agreement as loss brought about by false pretenses; mere fact that depositary bank allowed depositor to draw immediately upon uncollected funds did not mean that it was not a check-kiting scheme. *NCNB Nat. Bank of Florida*, 477 So.2d 579 (Fla.App. 4 Dist.,1985)

checkoff An employer's deduction of union dues from employee wages and turning the dues over to the union.

checks and balances An allocation of powers among the three branches of government (legislative, executive, and judicial) whereby one branch can block, check, or review what another branch wants to do (or has done) in order to maintain a balance of power among the branches.

chief justice The presiding judge (called a justice) in a higher court. In a lower court, he or she is often called the chief judge.

child 1. A son or daughter. 2. A person under the age of majority.

child abuse Physically or emotionally harming a child, intentionally or by neglect.

child abuse report law A law that requires designated individuals (e.g., teachers) to report suspected child abuse to the state.

child molestation Subjecting a child to sexual advances, contact, or activity.

> For the purposes of this paragraph, the term "child molestation" means conduct proscribed by § 794.011 [sexual battery] or § 800.04 [lewd or lascivious offenses] when committed against a person 16 years of age or younger. F.S.A. § 90.404(2)

child neglect The failure to provide a child with support, medical care, education, moral example, discipline, and other necessaries.

child pornography Visual portrayal of a person under 18 engaged in sexual activity, actual or simulated.

child support The obligation of a parent to pay a child's basic living expenses.

chilling effect Being hindered or inhibited from exercising a constitutional right, e.g., free speech.

Chinese wall Steps taken in an office to prevent a tainted employee from having any contact with a particular case in order to avoid a disqualification of the office from the case. The employee is tainted because he or she has a conflict of interest in that case.

chit 1. A voucher for food and drinks. 2. A short letter or note.

choate Complete; perfected or ripened.

choate lien A perfected lien, enforceable without further steps.

choice of evils Acts otherwise criminal may be justifiable if performed under extraordinary circumstances out of some immediate necessity to prevent a greater harm from occurring. Also called necessity.

choice of law Deciding which jurisdiction's law should govern when an event involves the law of more than one jurisdiction.

chose Chattel; a thing.

chose in action 1. A right to recover something in a lawsuit, e.g., money. 2. The thing itself that embodies the right to sue. Also called thing in action.

> A chose in action is by definition a thing of which one has not the possession or actual enjoyment but only a right to demand by an action at law. 42 Fla.Jur.2d Property § 10 (1983). *Florida Citrus Nursery*, 570 So.2d 1355 (Fla.App. 2 Dist.,1990)

churning A broker's excess trading in a customer's account to benefit the broker (via commissions), not the client.

CIF See cost, insurance, and freight.

circuit 1. One of the 13 appellate subdivisions in the federal judicial system. 2. Pertaining to a court that has jurisdiction in several counties or areas. 3. A district traveled by a judge.

circular note See letter of credit.

circumstantial evidence Evidence of a fact that is not based on personal knowledge or observation from which another fact might be inferred. Also called indirect evidence.

> "Direct evidence" is that to which the witness testifies of his own knowledge as to the facts at issue, while "circumstantial evidence" is proof of facts and circumstances from which the trier of fact may infer that the ultimate facts in dispute existed or did not exist. *Davis*, 90 So.2d 629 (Fla.1956)

citation; cite 1. A reference to any legal authority printed on paper or stored in a computer database. 2. An order to appear in court to answer a charge. 3. An official notice of a violation.

citator A book, CD-ROM, or online service with lists of citations that can help assess the current validity of an opinion, statute, or other authority and give leads to additional relevant material.

cite checking Examining citations in a document to assess whether the format of the citation is correct, whether quoted material is accurate, and whether the law cited is still valid.

citizen A person born or naturalized in a country to which he or she owes allegiance and who is entitled to full civil rights.

citizen's arrest A private person making an arrest for a crime that is a breach of the peace committed in his or her presence or for reasonably believing the person arrested has committed a felony.

civil Pertaining to (a) private rights, (b) noncriminal cases, (c) the state or citizenship, (d) public order and peace, and (e) legal systems of Western Europe other than England.

civil action A lawsuit to enforce private rights.

> "Civil action" means all suits or claims of a civil nature in court, whether cognizable as cases at law or in equity or in admiralty. F.S.A. § 774.203(12)

civil arrest The arrest of the defendant until he or she satisfies the judgment.

civil assault The tort of assault.

civil code 1. A collection of statutes governing noncriminal matters. 2. The code containing the civil law of France, from which the civil code of Louisiana is derived.

civil commitment Noncriminal confinement of those who because of incompetence or addiction cannot care for themselves or who pose a danger to themselves or to society. Also called involuntary commitment.

civil conspiracy A combination of two or more persons acting in concert to commit an unlawful act and an overt act that results in damages.

civil contempt The refusal of the party to comply with a court order, resulting in punishment that can be avoided by compliance.

> As distinguished from "civil contempt," which is court coercion applied for benefit of a civil litigant, the only proper objective of "criminal contempt" is as punishment to vindicate authority of a court. *Pattinson*, 436 So.2d 975 (Fla.App. 5 Dist.,1983)

civil court A court that hears noncriminal cases.

civil damage law See Dram Shop Act.

civil death The status of a person who has lost civil rights (e.g., to vote) because of a conviction of certain crimes. Also called legal death.

civil disabilities Civil rights that are lost when a person is convicted of a serious crime (e.g., to drive a car).

civil disobedience Breaking the law (without using violence) to show the injustice or unfairness of the law.

civilian One who is not a police officer or in the military.

civil law 1. The law governing civil disputes. Any law other than criminal law. 2. The statutory or code law applicable in Louisiana and many Western European countries other than England.

civil liability Damages or other noncriminal responsibility.

civil liberties Basic individual rights that should not be unduly restricted by the state (e.g., freedom of speech).

civil penalty A fine or assessment for violating a statute or administrative regulation.

civil procedure Laws governing the mechanics of resolving a civil (noncriminal) dispute in a court or administrative agency.

civil rights Basic individual rights (e.g., to vote) guaranteed by the U.S. Constitution and by special statutes.

> Right to possess a firearm is a "civil right" under statute providing for suspension of a convicted felon's civil rights. F.S.A. § 944.292. *Thompson*, 438 So.2d 1005 (Fla.App. 2 Dist.,1983)

civil service Nonmilitary government employment, often obtained through merit and competitive exams.

> "Civil service" means any career, civil, or merit system used by any public employer. F.S.A. § 447.203(16)

civil union A same-sex relationship with the same *state* benefits and responsibilities the state grants spouses in a marriage.

CLA See Certified Legal Assistant (*www.nala.org*).

Claflin trust A trust that cannot be terminated by a beneficiary. Also called indestructible trust.

claim 1. A right to sue. 2. To demand as one's own or as one's right. 3. To assert something.

> "Claim" includes any request or demand, under a contract or otherwise, for money, property, or services, which is made to any employee, officer, or agent of an agency, or to any contractor, grantee, or other recipient if the agency provides any portion of the money or property requested or demanded, or if the agency will reimburse the contractor, grantee, or other recipient for any portion of the money or property requested or demanded. F.S.A. § 68.082(1)(b)

claim and delivery A suit to recover personal property that was wrongfully taken or kept.

claimant One who makes a demand or asserts a right or claim.

claim jumping Asserting a mining claim that infringes on the claim of another.

claim of right 1. A good-faith assertion that one was entitled to do something. 2. If a taxpayer receives income (without restrictions) that he or she claimed the right to have, it must be reported in the year received even if it may have to be returned in a later year.

claim preclusion See res judicata.

claims court A court in which a party seeks to resolve claims against the government, e.g., United States Court of Federal Claims.

claims-made policy Insurance that covers only claims actually filed (i.e., made) during the period in which the policy is in effect.

> "Claims-made policies," as opposed to occurrence policies, trigger coverage if the negligent or omitted act is discovered and brought to insurer's attention within the policy term. *U.S. Fire Ins. Co.*, 682 So.2d 620 (Fla.App. 3 Dist.,1996)

class A group with common characteristics, e.g., persons injured by the same product.

class action A lawsuit in which one or more members of a class sue (or are sued) as representative parties on behalf of everyone in the class, all of whom do not have to be joined in the lawsuit. Also called representative action.

class gift A gift to a group containing an unknown number of persons at the time the gift is made.

clause A subdivision of a sentence in a law or other document.

Clayton Act A federal antitrust statute prohibiting price discrimination and other monopolistic practices. 15 USC § 12.

CLE See continuing legal education.

clean bill A proposed statute (bill) that has been substantially revised and introduced to the legislature as a new bill.

clean bill of lading A bill of lading without qualifications.

clean hands doctrine A party may not be allowed to assert an equitable claim or defense if his or her conduct has been unfair or in bad faith. Also called unclean hands doctrine.

> Under the "clean hands" doctrine a decree for the payment of alimony or child support generally will not be vacated unless petitioner has paid up all alimony or support money due under such decree or by his petition shows his inability to do so. F.S.A. § 65.15. *Blanton*, 18 So.2d 902 (Fla.1944)

clear 1. Free from encumbrance. 2. To vindicate or acquit. 3. To pay a check according to the instructions of the maker. 4. To pass through a clearinghouse. 5. Obvious, unambiguous.

clearance card A letter from an employer given to a departing employee stating facts such as the duration of the latter's employment.

clear and convincing evidence Evidence demonstrating that the existence of a disputed fact is much more probable than its nonexistence. This standard is stronger than preponderance of the evidence but not as strong as beyond a reasonable doubt.

clear and present danger Imminent risk of severe harm, the test used to help determine whether the state can restrict First Amendment freedoms.

clearing 1. The process by which checks are exchanged and pass through the banking system. 2. A ship leaving port in compliance with laws.

clearinghouse A place where banks exchange checks and drafts drawn on each other and reconcile accounts.

clearly erroneous The definite and firm conviction of an appellate court that a mistake has been made by a lower court.

clear title 1. Title that is free of reasonable doubt as to its validity. Marketable title. 2. Title that is free of encumbrances.

clemency Leniency from the president or a governor to a criminal, e.g., a pardon or reduction in sentence. Also called executive clemency.

clergy-penitent privilege A privilege preventing spiritual advisors from disclosing confessions or religious confidences made to them. Also called priest-penitent privilege.

> (1)(b) A communication between a member of the clergy and a person is "confidential" if made privately for the purpose of seeking spiritual counsel and advice from the member of the clergy in the usual course of his or her practice or discipline and not intended for further disclosure except to other persons present in furtherance of the communication. (2) A person has a privilege to refuse to disclose, and to prevent another from disclosing, a confidential communication by the person to a member of the clergy in his or her capacity as spiritual adviser. F.S.A. § 90.505

clerical error A copying error or other minor mistake.

clerk 1. An official who manages records and files and performs other administrative duties, e.g., a court clerk. 2. A law student or recent law school graduate who works for a law office or judge, usually for a short period of time. 3. One who performs general office duties.

clerkship Employment as a clerk in a legal office. See clerk (2).

client One who hires or receives services from a professional, e.g., an attorney.

client security fund A fund (often run by the bar association) used to compensate victims of attorney misconduct.

> Clients' security fund. The board of governors may provide monetary relief to persons who suffer reimbursable losses as a result of misappropriation, embezzlement, or other wrongful taking or conversion by a member of The Florida Bar of money or other property that comes into the member's possession or control . . . . F.S.A. Bar Rule 1-8.4

client trust account An attorney's bank account that contains client funds that may not be used for office operating expenses. Also called trust account.

Clifford trust A fixed-term trust in which the principal is returned to the grantor after a period of time.

close 1. Land that is enclosed. 2. To bring to completion.

close corporation; closed corporation; closely held corporation A corporation whose shares are held by a small group, e.g., a family.

closed-end mortgage A mortgage loan whose principal cannot be increased during the life of the loan and cannot be prepaid.

closed shop A business whose employees must be members of a union as a condition of employment.

closing The meeting in which a transaction is finalized. Also called settlement.

> "Closing" means the delivery, exchange, and release of documents and funds for the completion of a transaction for the disposition of commercial real estate. West's F.S.A. § 475.701(3)

closing argument The final statements by opposing trial attorneys to the jury (or to the trial judge if there is no jury) summarizing the evidence and requesting a favorable decision. Also called final argument, summation, summing up.

closing costs Expenses incurred in the sale of real estate in addition to the purchase price.

cloture A legislative procedure to end debate and allow a vote.

cloud on title A claim or encumbrance on land, which, if valid, would affect or impair the title rights of the owner.

cluster zoning Modifications in zoning restrictions in exchange for other land being set aside for public needs, e.g., a park.

coaching Telling a witness how to give testimony on the stand.

COBRA See Consolidated Omnibus Budget Reconciliation Act.

coconspirator One who engages in a conspiracy with another. Under the conspirator exception to the hearsay rule, statements of one coconspirator can be admitted against another coconspirator if made in furtherance of the conspiracy.

> The "co-conspirator exception to hearsay rule" is that every act and declaration of each member of a conspiracy is the act and declaration of them all, and is therefore original evidence against each of them. *Farnell*, 214 So.2d 753 (Fla.App. 1968)

COD Collect on delivery.

code A systematic collection of laws, rules, or guidelines, usually organized by subject matter.

code civil The code containing the civil law of France. Also called the Code Napoléon.

codefendant One of two or more defendants sued in the same civil case or prosecuted in the same criminal case.

Code Napoléon See code civil.

code pleading See fact pleading.

codicil A supplement that adds to or changes a will.

codification Collecting and systematically arranging laws or rules by subject matter.

coercion Compelling something by force or threats. Overpowering another's free will by force or undue influence.

> "Coercion" means the exploitation of authority or the use of bribes, threats of force, or intimidation to gain cooperation or compliance. F.S.A. § 39.01(b)(1)

cognizable 1. Pertaining to what can be heard and resolved by a court. 2. Capable of being known.

cognizance 1. The power of a court to hear and resolve a particular dispute. 2. Judicial notice. 3. Awareness or recognition.

cognovit A written statement that acknowledges liability or the validity of a debt. The statement confesses judgment. A cognovit note (also called judgment note) is a promissory note containing a cognovit.

cohabitation Living together as a couple or in a sexual relationship.

coheir One of several persons to whom an inheritance passes or descends. A joint heir.

coif A ceremonial cap or other headpiece. See also Order of the Coif.

coinsurance A sharing of the risks between two or more insurers or between the insurer and the insured.

> "Umbrella or coinsurance policies" are designed to provide coverage only when amount of insured loss reaches predetermined level, such as in event of catastrophe. *Travelers Indem. Co.*, 550 So.2d 12 (Fla.App. 3 Dist.,1989)

COLA Cost of living adjustment.

cold blood Premeditated killing.

collapsible corporation A corporation set up to be sold or liquidated before it earns substantial income.

collateral 1. Property pledged as security for the satisfaction of a debt. 2. Not in the direct line of descent. 3. Not directly relevant. 4. Accompanying but of secondary importance.

collateral attack A challenge or attack against the validity of a judgment that is not raised in a direct appeal from the court that rendered the judgment.

collateral estoppel When parties have litigated and resolved an issue in one case, they cannot relitigate the issue in another case against each other even if the two cases raise different claims or causes of action. Also called direct estoppel, estoppel by judgment, estoppel by record, issue preclusion.

> The principle of "collateral estoppel" applies where the two causes of action are different, in which case the judgment in the first suit only estops the parties from litigating in the second suit issues common to both causes of action and which were actually adjudicated in the prior litigation. *Mass v. State*, 927 So.2d 157 (Fla.App. 3 Dist.,2006)

collateral fraud Deception by one party that does not pertain to the actual issues that were resolved in a trial but which prevented the other party from presenting its case fairly. Also called extrinsic fraud.

collateral heir One who is not of the direct line of the deceased, but comes from a collateral line, as a brother, aunt, or a cousin of the deceased. Also called heir collateral.

collateral order doctrine An appeal of a nonfinal order will be allowed if the order conclusively determines the disputed question, resolves an important issue that is completely separate from the merits of the dispute, and is effectively unreviewable on appeal from a final judgment.

collateral source rule The amount of damages caused by the tortfeasor shall not be reduced by any injury-related funds received by the plaintiff from sources independent of the tortfeasor such as a health insurance policy of the plaintiff.

> Evidence concerning personal injury plaintiffs' receipt of governmental benefits and resultant effect on plaintiffs' motivation to work was inadmissible in personal injury action; welfare benefits were inadmissible as "collateral source," and substantial likelihood of prejudice outweighed any marginal probative value. West's F.S.A. §§ 90.403, 768.76(2)(a). *Parker*, 695 So.2d 424 (Fla.App. 4 Dist.,1997)

collateral warranty A warranty of title given by someone other than the seller.

collation 1. A comparison of a copy with the original to determine the correctness of the copy. 2. Taking into account property already given to some heirs as an advancement.

collecting bank A bank handling a check for collection other than the payor bank.

collective bargaining Negotiations between an employer and representatives of its employees on working conditions.

> "Collective bargaining" means the performance of the mutual obligations of the public employer and the bargaining agent of the employee organization to meet at reasonable times, to negotiate in good faith, and to execute a written contract with respect to agreements reached concerning the terms and conditions of employment, except that neither party shall be compelled to agree to a proposal or be required to make a concession unless otherwise provided in this part. F.S.A. § 447.203(14)

collective mark A mark used by members of an organization (e.g., a union) to indicate membership or to identify what it offers.

colloquium Extrinsic facts showing that a defamatory statement was of and concerning the plaintiff. A complaint alleging such facts.

colloquy A formal discussion, e.g., between the judge and the defendant to determine if the defendant's plea is informed.

collusion 1. An agreement to commit fraud. 2. An agreement between a husband and wife that one or both will lie to the court to facilitate the obtaining of their divorce.

colorable 1. Plausible. Having at least some factual or legal support. 2. Deceptively appearing to be valid.

> The word "colorable" means "seemingly valid or genuine" and "intended to deceive." *Sult*, 906 So.2d 1013 (Fla.,2005)

color of law 1. Acting or pretending to act in an official, governmental capacity. 2. The pretense of law.

color of office Asserted official or governmental authority.

color of title A false appearance of having title to property.

comaker See cosigner.

combination The union or association of two or more persons or entities to achieve a common end. See also conspiracy, restraint of trade.

combination in restraint of trade An agreement among businesses to create a monopoly or otherwise stifle competition.

combination patent A combination of known elements which, when combined, accomplish a patentable function or result.

coming and going rule See going and coming rule.

comity Giving effect to the laws of another state, not as a requirement, but rather out of deference or respect.

> Rule of judicial "comity" has reference to principle in accordance with which courts of one state or jurisdiction will give effect to laws and judicial decisions of another state, not as matter of obligation, but out of deference and respect. *Kittel*, 194 So.2d 640 (Fla.App. 1967)

Comity Clause A provision in the U.S. Constitution which provides that "The Citizens of each State shall be entitled to all Privileges and Immunities of Citizens in the several States." U.S. Const. Art. IV, § 2, cl. 1.

commerce Buying, selling, or exchanging goods or services.

Commerce Clause The clause in the U.S. Constitution (Art. I, § 8, cl. 3) giving Congress the power to regulate commerce among the states, with foreign nations, and with Indian tribes.

commercial bank A bank with a variety of services such as providing loans, checking accounts, and safety deposit boxes.

commercial bribery The advantage secured over a competitor by corrupt dealings with agents of prospective purchasers.

commercial frustration An excuse not to perform a contract due to an unforeseen event not under the control of either party.

commercial impracticability See impracticability.

commercial law The law governing commercial transactions such as the sale and financing of goods and services.

commercial paper 1. A negotiable instrument (e.g., a draft, a promissory note) used in commerce. 2. A short-term, unsecured negotiable note, often sold to meet immediate cash needs.

commercial speech Expression related solely to the economic interests of the speaker and its audience.

> "Commercial speech" is expression related solely to economic interests of speaker and his audience, and in legal-professional context, its purpose is to engage lawyer for personal profit. *The Florida Bar*, 439 So.2d 835 (Fla.,1983)

commercial unit Goods considered a single whole for purposes of sale, the value of which would be materially impaired if divided into parts.

commingling Mixing what should be kept separate, e.g., depositing client funds in a single account with general law firm funds or an attorney's personal funds.

commission 1. The granting of powers to carry out a task. 2. A government body granted power to carry out a task. 3. Compensation, often a percentage of the value of the transaction. 4. The act of committing something, usually a crime.

commitment 1. An agreement or pledge to do something. 2. The act of institutionalizing someone as to a prison or mental hospital.

commitment fee A fee paid by a loan applicant for a lender's promise to lend money at a defined rate on a specified date.

committee 1. A group appointed to perform a function on behalf of a larger group. 2. A special guardian appointed to protect the interests of an incompetent person.

committee of the whole A special committee consisting of the entire membership of a deliberative body.

commodity Something useful; an article of commerce.

> "Commodity" means any goods, services, materials, merchandise, supplies, equipment, resources, or other article of commerce, and includes, without limitation, food, water, ice, chemicals, petroleum products, and lumber necessary for consumption or use as a direct result of the emergency. F.S.A. § 501.160(1)(a)

common 1. The legal right to use another's land or waters. 2. Land set apart for use by the general public. 3. Shared.

common carrier A company that holds itself out to the general public as engaged in transporting people or goods for a fee.

common disaster An event causing the death of two or more persons with shared interests, without clear evidence of who died first.

common enemy doctrine Landowners can fend off surface waters (e.g., rain) as needed, without liability to other landowners.

common law 1. Judge-made law in the absence of controlling statutory law or other higher law. Law derived from court opinions. 2. Law based on the legal system of England.

> Within meaning of statute providing that common laws of England which are of general and not local nature are in force in state if not inconsistent with Constitution and laws of United States and acts of state Legislature, the words "common laws of England" refer not only to the common law as declared by England, but also as declared by courts of American states. F.S.A. § 2.01. *DeGeorge*, 358 So.2d 217 (Fla.App.,1978)

common law action An action based on the common law. See also action at law.

common law copyright The author's proprietary interest in his or her creation before it has been made available to the pubic.

common law marriage A marriage entered without license or ceremony by persons who have agreed to marry, have lived together as husband and wife, and have held themselves out as such.

> No common law marriage entered into after January 1, 1968, shall be valid, . . . F.S.A. § 742.211. "Common law marriage" is a marriage that takes legal effect, without license or ceremony, when a couple live together as husband and wife, intend to be married, and hold themselves out to others as a married couple. *Lowe*, 766 So.2d 1199 (Fla.App. 4 Dist.,2000).

common law trust See business trust.

common nuisance See public nuisance.

Common Pleas The name of a trial court in some states (e.g., Ohio) and an intermediate appellate court in others.

common situs picketing Picketing an entire construction project even though the labor grievance is with only one subcontractor.

common stock Stock in a corporation with voting rights and the right to dividends after preferred stockholders have been paid.

commonwealth 1. A nation or state as a political entity. (In the United States, four states are officially designated commonwealths: KY, MA, PA, and VA.) 2. A political unit that is voluntarily united with the United States but is self-governing, e.g., Northern Mariana Islands.

community 1. A section or neighborhood in a city or town. 2. A group of people with common interests. 3. The marital entity that shares or owns community property.

community notification law See Megan's law.

community property Property in which each spouse has a one-half interest because it was acquired during the marriage (by a method other than gift or inheritance to one spouse only) regardless of who earned it.

community trust An entity that operates a charitable trust.

commutation 1. A change of punishment to one that is less severe. 2. An exchange or substitution.

commutative contract A contract in which what each party promises or exchanges is considered equal in value.

commutative justice A system of justice in which the goal is fundamental fairness in transactions among the parties.

commuted value The present value of a future interest or payment.

compact An agreement, often between states or nations.

company An association of persons who are engaged in a business.

company union An employer-controlled union of employees in a single company.

comparable worth Jobs requiring the same levels of skill should receive equal pay whether performed by men or women.

comparative negligence In a negligence action, the plaintiff's damages will be reduced in proportion to the plaintiff's negligence in causing his or her own injury.

> Under doctrine of "comparative negligence," if both plaintiff and defendant are at fault, plaintiff can still recover, but his or her recovery is limited to proportion of damages proximately caused by defendant's negligence; plaintiff's recovery is reduced by his or her percentage of fault. *Cody*, 682 So.2d 1147 (Fla.App. 4 Dist.,1996)

comparative rectitude When both spouses have grounds for a divorce, it will be granted to the spouse least at fault.

compelling state interest A substantial need for the state to act that justifies the resulting restriction on the constitutional right claimed by the person challenging the state's action.

compensating balance The minimum balance a bank requires one of its borrowers to have on deposit.

compensation 1. Payment of wages or benefits for services rendered. 2. Payment for a loss incurred. Indemnification.

compensatory damages Money to restore an injured party to his or her position prior to the injury or wrong. Actual damages.

competency proceeding A hearing to determine if someone has the mental capacity to do something, e.g., to stand trial.

competent 1. Having the knowledge and skill reasonably necessary to represent a particular client. 2. Having sufficient understanding to be allowed to give testimony as a witness. 3. Having the ability to understand the criminal proceedings, to consult with one's attorney, and to assist in one's own defense. 4. Having the capacity to manage one's own affairs.

> Competent representation requires the legal knowledge, skill, thoroughness, and preparation reasonably necessary for the representation. Florida Rules of Professional Conduct, Rule 4-1.1

competent evidence Evidence that is relevant and admissible.

> "Competent evidence" is evidence that is relevant and material to issue or issues presented for determination. *Gainesville Bonded Warehouse*, 123 So.2d 336 (Fla.1960)

compilation 1. A collection of laws, usually statutes. 2. An original work formed by the collection and assembling of preexisting works.

complainant One who files a complaint to initiate a civil lawsuit or who alleges that someone has committed a crime.

complaint 1. A plaintiff's first pleading, stating a claim against the defendant. Also called petition. 2. A formal criminal charge.

completion bond A bond given as insurance to guarantee that a contract will be completed within the agreed-upon time. Also called performance bond, surety bond.

complex trust See discretionary trust.

composition An agreement between a debtor and two or more creditors on what will be accepted as full payment.

compos mentis Of sound mind; competent.

compound 1. To adjust or settle a debt or other claim by paying a lesser amount. 2. To accept an illegal payment in exchange for not prosecuting a crime. 3. To calculate interest on both the principal and on interest already accrued. 4. A mixture of parts.

compound interest See compound (3).

compounding a crime Receiving something of value in exchange for an agreement to interfere with a prosecution or not to prosecute.

compromise To settle a dispute through mutual concessions.

compromise verdict A verdict that results when jurors resolve their inability to reach unanimity by conceding some issues to entice agreement on others.

comptroller A fiscal officer of an organization appointed to examine accounts, issue financial reports, and perform other accounting duties. Also spelled controller.

compulsion 1. Forcing someone to do or refrain from doing something. 2. An irresistible impulse.

compulsory arbitration Arbitration that parties are required to undergo to resolve their dispute.

compulsory counterclaim A claim that arises out of the same subject matter as the opposing party's claim.

> "Compulsory counterclaim" is defendant's cause of action arising out of transaction or occurrence that formed the subject matter of plaintiff's claim; claim will be barred unless raised by defendant in original suit. Fla.R.Civ.P. 1.170(a). *Yost*, 570 So.2d 350 (Fla.App. 1 Dist.,1990)

compulsory joinder Someone who must be joined as a party if his or her absence means that complete relief is not possible for the parties already in the lawsuit or that one or more of the parties may be subject to inconsistent or multiple liability.

compulsory process A summons or writ that compels a witness to appear in court, usually by subpoena or arrest.

compurgator Someone called to give testimony for the defendant.

computer crime The use of a computer to commit an illegal act, e.g., accessing or damaging computer data without authorization.

concealed weapon A weapon carried on a person in such a manner as to conceal it from the ordinary sight of another.

concerted Planned or accomplished together. Concerted activity is the conduct of employees who have joined together to achieve common goals on conditions of employment.

concert of action 1. A person cannot be prosecuted for both a substantive offense and a conspiracy to commit that offense where an agreement between two or more persons is a necessary element of the substantive offense. Also called Wharton's rule. 2. Concerted action (conduct planned by persons) results in liability for each other's acts.

conciliation 1. Conduct taken to restore trust in an effort to resolve a dispute. 2. Settlement of a conflict without undue pressure or coercion.

conclusion of fact An inference of fact drawn from evidence of another fact. See also finding of fact.

conclusion of law The result of applying the law to the facts. See also holding.

conclusive 1. Decisive. 2. Supported by substantial evidence.

conclusive presumption An inference of fact that the fact finder must find despite any evidence to the contrary. Also called irrebuttable presumption.

conclusory Pertaining to an argument that states a conclusion without providing the underlying facts to support the conclusion.

concur 1. To agree. 2. To accept a conclusion but for different reasons. See also concurring opinion.

concurrent 1. At the same time. 2. With the same authority.

concurrent cause A cause that acts together (simultaneously) with another cause to produce an injury or other result.

> Two separate and distinct causes that operate contemporaneously to produce a single injury. *Hadley*, 873 So.2d 378 (Fla.App. 5 Dist.,2004)

concurrent condition A condition that one party must fulfill at the same time that another party must fulfill a mutual condition.

concurrent covenants Two covenants that must be performed or ready to be performed simultaneously.

concurrent jurisdiction The power of two or more courts to resolve the same dispute. Also called coordinate jurisdiction.

concurrent negligence Negligence by two or more persons who, though not working in concert, combine to produce a single injury.

concurrent power A legislative power that can be exercised by the federal or state government, or by both.

concurrent resolution A measure that is adopted by both houses of the legislature but does not have the force of law.

concurrent sentence A sentence served simultaneously, in whole or in part, with another sentence.

concurring opinion A court opinion in which a judge agrees with the result of the majority opinion but for different reasons.

condemn 1. To set apart or expropriate (take) property for public use in exercise of the power of eminent domain. 2. To judge someone to be guilty. 3. To declare to be unfit.

condemnee A person whose property is taken for public use.

condition 1. An uncertain future event upon which a legal result (e.g., a duty to pay) is dependent. 2. A prerequisite.

conditional Depending on or containing a condition.

conditional bequest A gift in a will that will be effective only if a specific event (condition) occurs or fails to occur.

conditional contract An executory (i.e., unperformed) contract whose existence and performance depends on a contingency.

conditional fee 1. See contingent fee. 2. See fee simple conditional.

conditional privilege A right to do or say something that can be lost if done or said with malice. Also called a qualified privilege.

conditional sale A sale in which the buyer does not receive title until making full payment.

> The sale has been consummated under a conditional sales contract even though vendor holds legal title as security for payment of purchase price. *Kraemer*, 572 So.2d 1363 (Fla.,1990)

conditional use Permitted land use upon compliance with specified conditions. Also called special exception, special use.

condition of employment A job requirement.

condition precedent An act or event (other than a lapse of time) that must occur before performance becomes due.

condition subsequent An act or event that will, if it occurs, render an obligation invalid.

condominium A real estate interest that combines two forms of ownership: exclusive ownership of an individual unit of a multi-unit project and common ownership of the common project areas.

> "Condominium" means that form of ownership of real property created pursuant to this chapter, which is comprised entirely of units that may be owned by one or more persons, and in which there is, appurtenant to each unit, an undivided share in common elements. F.S.A. § 718.103(11)

condonation Overlooking or forgiving, e.g., one spouse's express or implied forgiveness of the marital fault of the other.

conference committee A committee consisting of members of both houses of the legislature that seeks to reach a compromise on two versions of the same bill the houses passed.

confession A statement acknowledging guilt.

> The term "confession" is restricted to an acknowledgment of guilt made by a person after an offense has been committed. *Brown*, 111 So.2d 296 (Fla.App.1959)

confession and avoidance A plea that admits some facts but avoids their legal effect by alleging new facts.

confession of judgment See cognovit.

confidence game Obtaining money or other property by gaining a victim's trust through deception.

confidential communication An exchange of information that is privileged—the exchange cannot be disclosed against the will of the parties involved.

confidential relationship 1. See fiduciary relationship. 2. A relationship that requires nondisclosure of certain facts.

confirmation 1. Giving formal approval. 2. Corroboration. 3. Rendering enforceable something that is voidable.

confiscation Seizing private property under a claim of authority.

conflict of interest Divided loyalty that actually or potentially harms someone who is owed undivided loyalty.

conflict of laws Differences in the laws of two coequal legal systems (e.g., two states) involved in a legal dispute. The choice of which law to apply in such disputes.

conformed copy An exact copy of a document with notations of what could not be copied.

conforming In compliance with the contract or the law.

> "Conforming" goods or performance under a lease contract means goods or performance that are in accordance with the obligations under the lease contract. F.S.A. § 680.1031(1)(d)

conforming use A use of land that complies with zoning laws.

confrontation Being present when others give evidence against you and having the opportunity to question them.

confusion of goods The mixing of like things belonging to different owners so that sorting out what each originally owned is no longer possible. Also called intermixture of goods.

conglomerate A corporation that has diversified its operations, usually by acquiring enterprises in widely different industries.

Congress 1. The national legislature of the United States. 2. A formal meeting of representatives of different groups (congress).

Congressional Record (Cong. Rec.) The official record of the day-to-day proceedings of Congress.

conjoint Joined together; having a joint interest.

conjugal Pertaining to marriage or spouses, e.g., the rights that one spouse has in the other's companionship, services, support, and sexual relations.

> "Conjugal" within meaning of dissolution judgment incorporating stipulation that alimony would terminate if former wife lived with another person in conjugal relationship meant of or belonging to marriage or marriage state; thus, condition required wife to live with another person in relationship at least similar to marriage relationship. *Herrero*, 528 So.2d 1286 (Fla.App. 2 Dist.,1988)

connecting-up Evidence demonstrating the relevance of prior evidence.

connivance A willingness or a consent by one spouse that a marital wrong be committed by the other spouse.

consanguinity Relationship by blood or a common ancestor.

conscience of the court The court's power to apply equitable principles.

conscientious objector A person who for religious or moral reasons is sincerely opposed to war in any form.

conscious parallelism A process, not in itself unlawful, by which firms in a concentrated market might share monopoly power.

consecutive sentences Sentences that are served one after the other—in sequence. Also called accumulative sentences, cumulative sentences.

consensus ad idem A meeting of the minds; agreement.

consent Voluntary agreement or permission, express or implied.

> "Consent" means an agreement, including all of the following: a. Understanding what is proposed based on age, maturity, developmental level, functioning, and experience. b. Knowledge of societal standards for what is being proposed. c. Awareness of potential consequences and alternatives. d. Assumption that agreement or disagreement will be accepted equally. e. Voluntary decision. F.S.A. § 39.01(3)

consent decree A court decree agreed upon by the parties.

consent judgment An agreement by the parties (embodied in a court order) settling their dispute.

consent search A search consented to by the person affected who has the authority to give the consent.

consequential damages Losses or injuries that do not flow directly from a party's action, but only from some of the consequences or results of such action.

conservator A person appointed by the court to manage the affairs of someone, usually an incompetent. A guardian.

consideration A bargained-for promise, act, or forbearance. Something of value exchanged between the parties.

> A promise, no matter how slight, can constitute sufficient "consideration" so long as a party agrees to do something that he or she is not bound to do. *Diaz*, 851 So.2d 843 (Fla.App. 2 Dist.,2003)

consignment Transferring goods to someone, usually for sale by the latter. The one transferring the goods is the consignor; the person receiving them is the consignee.

consignee, consignor See consignment.

consolidated appeal An appeal from two or more parties who file a joint notice of appeal and proceed as a single appellant.

Consolidated Omnibus Budget Reconciliation Act (COBRA) A federal statute that gives workers limited rights to keep their health insurance policy when they leave a job.

consolidation 1. A joining together or merger. 2. Combining two or more corporations that dissolve into a new corporate entity. 3. Uniting the trial of several actions into one court action.

consolidation loan A new loan that pays the balances owed on previous loans that are then extinguished.

consortium 1. The benefits that one spouse is entitled to receive from the other, e.g., companionship, cooperation, services, affection, and sexual relations. 2. The companionship and affection a parent is entitled to receive from a child and that a child is entitled to receive from a parent. 3. An association or coalition of businesses or other organizations.

> "Consortium" means much more than sexual relation between husband and wife and consists, also, of that affection, solace, comfort, companionship, conjugal life, fellowship, society, and assistance so necessary to successful marriage. *City of St. Petersburg*, 672 So.2d 42 (Fla.App. 2 Dist.,1996)

conspiracy An agreement between two or more persons to commit a criminal or other unlawful act or to perform a lawful act by unlawful means. Also called criminal conspiracy.

constable A peace officer whose duties (e.g., serving writs) are similar to (but not as extensive as) those of a sheriff.

constitution The fundamental law that creates the branches of government, allocates power among them, and defines basic some rights of individuals.

constitutional Pertaining to or consistent with the constitution.

constitutional court See Article III court.

constitutional fact A fact whose determination is decisive of constitutional rights.

constitutional law The body of law found in and interpreting the Constitution.

constitutional right A right guaranteed by a Constitution.

construction An interpretation of a law or other document. The verb is *construe*.

constructive True legally even if not factually.

constructive bailment An obligation imposed by law on a person holding chattels to deliver them to another.

constructive contempt See indirect contempt.

constructive contract See implied in law contract.

constructive delivery Acts that are the equivalent of the actual delivery of something.

constructive desertion The misconduct of the spouse who stayed home that justified the other spouse's departure from the home.

constructive discharge Acts by an employer that make working conditions so intolerable that an employee quits.

> The employer, by its illegal discriminatory acts, made working conditions so difficult that a reasonable person in his or her position would feel compelled to resign. *McCaw Cellular Communications*, 763 So.2d 1063 (Fla.App. 4 Dist.,1999)

constructive eviction A landlord's causing or allowing premises to become so uninhabitable that a tenant leaves.

constructive fraud A breach of a duty that violates a fiduciary relationship. Also called legal fraud.

constructive knowledge What one does not actually know, but should know or has reason to know and, therefore, is treated as knowing.

constructive notice Information the law assumes one has because he or she could have discovered it by proper diligence and had a duty to inquire into it.

constructive possession Control or dominion one rightfully has over property that he or she does not actually possess.

> Constructive possession exists where a person, without physically possessing a firearm, knows of its presence on the premises and has the ability to maintain control over it. F.S.A. § 790.23(1). *Hunter*, 914 So.2d 985 (Fla.App. 4 Dist.,2005)

constructive receipt of income Having control over income without substantial restriction even though not actually received.

constructive service See substituted service.

constructive trust A trust implied as an equitable remedy to prevent unjust enrichment by one who has obtained the legal right to property by wrongdoing. Also called implied trust, involuntary trust, trust de son tort, trust ex delicto, trust ex maleficio.

construe See construction.

consul An official in a foreign country who promotes the commercial and other interests of his or her own country.

consult; consultation Communication of information reasonably sufficient to permit the client to appreciate the significance of the matter in question. Florida Rules of Professional Conduct, Preamble

consumer A buyer of goods and services for personal use rather than for resale or manufacturing.

consumer credit Credit to buy goods or services for personal use.

consumer goods Products used or bought for personal, family, or household use.

> "Consumer goods or services" means any real property or any tangible or intangible personal property which is normally used for personal, family, or household purposes, including, without limitation, any such property intended to be attached to or installed in any real property without regard to whether it is so attached or installed, as well as cemetery lots and timeshare estates, and any services related to such property. F.S.A. § 501.059(b)

consumer lease A lease of personal property for personal, family, or household use.

consumer price index (CPI) A measurement by the Bureau of Labor Statistics of average monthly changes in prices of basic goods and services bought by consumers (*www.bls.gov/cpi*).

consummate 1. To complete or bring to fruition. 2. To engage in the first act of sexual intercourse after marriage.

contemner (contemnor) One who commits contempt.

contemplation of death The thought of death as a primary motive for making a transfer of property.

contemporaneous Existing or occurring in the same period of time.

contempt Disobedience of or disrespect for the authority of a court or legislature.

> "Contempt" is any act which is calculated to embarrass, hinder, or obstruct court in administration of justice, or which is calculated to lessen its authority or its dignity. *Milian*, 764 So.2d 860 (Fla.App. 4 Dist.,2000)

contest To challenge; to raise a defense against a claim.

contested Challenged; litigated.

contingency 1. A possible event. 2. Uncertainty. 3. A contingent fee.

contingent 1. Uncertain; pertaining to what may or may not happen. 2. Dependent; conditional.

contingent annuity An annuity whose commencement or exact terms of payment depend on an uncertain future event.

contingent beneficiary A person who receives a gift or insurance proceeds if a condition occurs.

contingent estate An estate that will become a present or vested estate if an event occurs or condition is met.

> An estate is a "contingent estate" if, in order for it to become a present estate, fulfillment of some condition precedent other than determination of preceding freehold estate is necessary. *Mahan*, 35 So.2d 725 (Fla.1948)

contingent fee A fee that is paid only if the case is successfully resolved by litigation or settlement. Also called conditional fee.

contingent interest An interest whose enjoyment is dependent on an uncertain event.

contingent liability Liability that depends on an uncertain event.

contingent remainder A remainder that is limited to take effect either to an uncertain person or upon an uncertain event. Also called executory remainder.

continuance An adjournment or postponement of a session.

continuing jurisdiction A court's power (by retaining jurisdiction) to modify its orders after entering judgment.

continuing legal education (CLE) Training in the law (often short term) received after completing one's formal legal training.

continuing offense An offense involving a prolonged course of conduct.

> Driving while intoxicated is a "continuing offense," being completed at every point along route of travel; as long as it continues unbroken, one prosecution may be had therefor at any point, regardless of whether an accident ultimately results. *State v. Stiefel*, 256 So.2d 581 (Fla.App. 1972)

continuing trespass Allowing a structure or other permanent invasion on another's land.

contra Against; in opposition to.

contraband Property that is unlawful to possess, import, export, or trade.

contract A legally enforceable agreement. A promise that, if breached, will entitle the aggrieved to a remedy.

contract carrier A private company that transports passengers or property under individual contracts, not for the general public.

Contract Clause A clause in the U.S. Constitution (art. I, § 10, cl. 1) providing that no state shall pass a law impairing the obligation of contracts.

contract for deed An agreement to sell property in which the seller retains title or possession until full payment has been made. Also called land sales contract.

> An "installment land sale contract," or so-called "contract for deed," evidences a sale of land and an obligation of vendor to convey and of purchaser to pay the purchase price in installments, usually extending over long period of time, and is essentially a security instrument taking the place of a purchase money mortgage. *H & L Land Co.*, 258 So.2d 293 (Fla.App. 1972)

contract implied in fact See implied in fact contract.

contract implied in law See implied in law contract.

contract of adhesion See adhesion contract.

contract under seal A signed contract that has the waxed seal of the signer attached. Consideration was not needed. Also called special contract, specialty.

contractor A person or company that enters contracts to supply materials or labor to perform a job.

contributing to the delinquency of a minor Conduct by an adult that is likely to lead to illegal or immoral behavior by a minor.

contribution 1. The right of one tortfeasor who has paid a judgment to be proportionately reimbursed by other tortfeasors who have not paid their share of the damages caused by all the tortfeasors. 2. The right of one debtor who has paid a common debt to be proportionately reimbursed by the other debtors.

> "Contribution" is partial payment made by each or any jointly or severally liable tortfeasors who share a common liability to an injured party. *Firestone Tire & Rubber Co.*, 353 So.2d 137 (Fla.App. 1977)

contributory 1. Helping to bring something about. 2 Pertaining to one who pays into a common fund or benefit plan.

contributory negligence Unreasonableness (negligence) by the plaintiff that helps cause his or her own injury or loss. Where recognized, it bars any recovery due to the defendant's negligence.

> Under Florida's "pure" comparative negligence scheme, liability is apportioned according to each party's percentage of negligence. See *Hoffman v. Jones*, 280 So.2d 431 (Fla.1973) (abolishing doctrine of contributory negligence). *Connell*, 944 So.2d 1174 (Fla.App. 1 Dist.,2006)

controlled substance A drug whose possession or use is prohibited or otherwise strictly regulated.

controller See comptroller.

controlling interest Ownership of enough of the stock of a company to be able to control it.

controversy A dispute that a court can resolve; a justiciable dispute. An actual rather than a hypothetical dispute.

contumacy Refusal to obey a court order. Contempt.

convenience and necessity See certificate of convenience and necessity.

convention 1. An agreement or treaty. 2. A special assembly.

conventional 1. Customary. 2. Based on agreement rather than law.

conventional mortgage A mortgage that is not government insured.

conversation See criminal conversation.

conversion 1. An intentional interference with personal property that is serious enough to force the wrongdoer to pay its full value. An action for conversion is called trover. 2. Changing the nature of property.

> "Conversion" occurs when a person asserts a right of dominion over chattel which is inconsistent with the right of the owner and deprives the owner of the right of possession. *Estate of Villanueva*, 927 So.2d 955 (Fla.App. 2 Dist.,2006)

convertible security One kind of security (e.g., bond) that can be exchanged for another kind (e.g., stock).

conveyance A transfer of an interest in land. A transfer of title.

conveyancer One skilled in transferring interests in land.

convict 1. To find a person guilty of a crime. 2. A prisoner.

conviction 1. A finding of guilty of a crime. 2. A firm belief.

cooling off period 1. A period of time during which neither side can take any further action. 2. The time given to a buyer to cancel the purchase.

cooperative 1. A business owned by customers that use its goods and services. 2. A multiunit building owned by a corporation that leases units to individual shareholders of the corporation.

> "Cooperative" means that form of ownership of real property wherein legal title is vested in a corporation or other entity and the beneficial use is evidenced by an ownership interest in the association and a lease or other muniment of title or possession granted by the association as the owner of all the cooperative property. F.S.A. § 719.103(12)

coordinate jurisdiction See concurrent jurisdiction.

coparcenary An estate that arises when several persons inherit property from the same ancestor to share equally as if they were one person or one heir. Also called estate in coparcenary, parcenary.

coparcener A concurrent or joint heir through coparcenary. Also called parcener.

copyhold Tenure as laid out in a copy of the court roll (an old form of land tenure).

copyright (©) The exclusive right for a fixed number of years to print, copy, sell, or perform original works. 17 U.S.C. § 101.

coram nobis ("before us") An old remedy allowing a trial court (via a writ of error) to vacate its own judgment because of factual errors. If the request to vacate is made to an appellate court, the remedy is called coram vobis ("before you").

> A petition for a writ of "error coram nobis" is filed to bring to the attention of a court facts that, if known at the time judgment was rendered, would have prevented rendition of the judgment. *State ex rel. Butterworth*, 714 So.2d 404 (Fla.,1998)

coram vobis See coram nobis.

core proceeding A proceeding that invokes a substantive bankruptcy right. 28 U.S.C.A. § 157(b).

corespondent 1. The person who allegedly had sexual intercourse with a defendant charged with adultery. 2. A joint respondent.

corner Dominance over the supply of a particular commodity.

coroner A public official who inquires into suspicious deaths.

corporal punishment Punishment inflicted on the physical body.

> "Corporal punishment" means the moderate use of physical force or physical contact by a teacher or principal as may be necessary to maintain discipline or to enforce school rule. However, the term "corporal punishment" does not include the use of such reasonable force by a teacher or principal as may be necessary for self-protection or to protect other students from disruptive students. F.S.A. § 1003.01(7)

corporate-opportunity doctrine Corporate directors and officers must not take personal advantage of business opportunities they learn about in their corporate role if the corporation itself could pursue those opportunities.

corporate veil Legitimate corporate actions are not treated as shareholder actions. See piercing the corporate veil.

corporation An organization that is an artificial person or legal entity that has limited liability and can have an indefinite existence separate from its shareholders.

corporation counsel An attorney who works for an incorporated municipality.

corporeal Tangible; pertaining to the body.

corporeal hereditament Anything tangible that can be inherited, e.g., land.

corpus 1. Assets in a trust. Also called res, trust estate, trust fund. 2. Principal as opposed to interest or income. 3. A collection of writings. 4. The main part of a body (anatomy).

corpus delicti ("body of the crime") The fact that a loss or injury has occurred as a result of the criminal conduct of someone.

> Corpus delicti means literally "the body of the crime" and is regularly used in appellate decisions to mean the legal elements necessary to show that a crime was committed. *State v. Colorado*, 890 So.2d 468 (Fla.App. 2 Dist.,2004)

corpus juris A collection or body of laws.

correction 1. The system of imposing punishment and treatment on offenders. 2. Removing an error. 3. A market adjustment.

correspondent An intermediary for an organization that needs access to a particular market.

corroborating evidence Supplemental or supporting evidence.

corruption of blood Punishment by taking away the right to inherit or transfer property to blood relatives.

corrupt practices act A statute regulating campaign contributions, spending, and disclosure.

cosigner One who signs a document along with another, often to help the latter secure a loan. The cosigner can have repayment obligations upon default of the other. Also called comaker.

cost and freight (c&f)(c.a.f.) The price includes the cost of the goods and of transporting them.

cost basis The acquisition costs of purchasing property.

cost, insurance, and freight (CIF) The price includes the cost of purchasing, insuring, and transporting the goods.

cost-of-living clause A clause providing an automatic wage or benefit increase tied to cost-of-living rises as measured by indicators such as the Consumer Price Index.

costs Court-imposed charges or fees directly related to litigation in that court, e.g., filing fees. (Usually does not include attorney fees.) Also called court costs.

> "Costs" are expenses incurred in prosecuting or defending an action. *Lee County*, 698 So.2d 1371 (Fla.App. 2 Dist.,1997)

costs to abide event Court costs that will be awarded to the prevailing party at the conclusion of the case.

cotenancy An interest in property whereby two or more owners have an undivided right to possession.

cotrustees Two or more persons who administer a trust together.

council An assembly or body that meets to advise or to legislate.

counsel 1. An attorney. A client's lawyer. Also called counselor, counselor at law. 2. Advice. 3. To give advice, to advise.

counselor See counsel (1).

count In pleading, a separate claim (cause of action) or charge.

counterclaim An independent claim by one side in a case (usually the defendant) filed in response to a claim asserted by an opponent (usually the plaintiff).

> Counterclaims and affirmative defenses are separate and distinct terms; "counterclaim" is [a defendant's] cause of action which seeks affirmative relief, while "affirmative defense" defeats the plaintiff's cause of action by denial or confession and avoidance. *Haven Federal Sav. & Loan Ass'n*, 579 So.2d 730 (Fla. 1991)

counterfeit To copy without authority in order to deceive by passing off the copy as genuine; fraudulent imitation, forgery.

countermand To change or revoke instructions previously given.

counteroffer A response by someone to whom an offer is made that constitutes a new offer, thereby rejecting the other's offer.

counterpart A corresponding part or a duplicate of a document.

countersign To sign in addition to the signature of another in order to verify the identity of the other signer.

county The largest territorial and governmental division within most states.

county commissioners Officers who manage county government.

coupon An interest or dividend certificate attached to a bond or other instrument that can be detached and presented for payment.

course of business What is usually and normally done in a business. Also called ordinary or regular course of business.

course of dealing A pattern of prior conduct between the parties.

course of employment Conduct of an employee that fulfills his or her employment duties.

> Under going and coming rule, "in the course of employment" refers to the time, place, and circumstances under which the accident occurs, and "arising out of" refers to origin or cause. West's F.S.A. § 440.092(2). *Swartz*, 726 So.2d 783 (Fla.App. 1 Dist.,1998)

course of performance Repeated occasions for performing a contract in the past by either party with knowledge of the nature of the performance and opportunities for objection to it.

court 1. A unit of the judicial branch of government that applies the law to disputes and administers justice. 2. A judge or group of judges on the same tribunal.

court costs See costs.

court en banc See en banc.

court-martial A military court for trying members of the armed services for offenses violating military law.

court of appeals The middle appeals court in most judicial systems and the highest appellate court in a few.

court of chancery See chancery (2), equity (1).

court of claims A court that hears claims against the government for which sovereign immunity has been waived.

court of common pleas (C.P.) 1. A trial court in several states, e.g., Ohio, Pennsylvania. 2. An appellate court in some states.

court of equity See court of law, equity (1).

court of law 1. A court that applied the common law as opposed to a court of equity that applied equitable principles. 2. Any court or judicial tribunal.

court reporter See reporter.

covenant A promise or contract, e.g., a promise made in a deed or other legal instrument.

covenantee One to whom a promise by covenant is made.

covenant for quiet enjoyment A grantor's promise that the grantee's possession will not be disturbed by any other claimant with a superior lawful title.

covenant marriage A form of marriage that requires proof of premarital counseling, a promise to seek marital counseling when needed during the marriage, and proof of marital fault to dissolve.

covenant not to compete A promise in an employment contract or contract for the sale of a business not to engage in competitive activities, usually within a specified geographic area and for limited time. Also called restrictive covenant.

covenant of seisin An assurance that the grantor has the very estate in quantity and quality that he or she purports to convey to the grantee. Also called right-to-convey covenant.

covenant of warranty An assurance that the grantee has been given good title and a promise to provide compensation if the title is attacked.

covenantor One who makes a promise by covenant to another.

covenant running with the land A covenant whose benefits or duties bind all later purchasers of the land.

> Covenants are divisible into two major classes: "real covenants" which run with land and bind heirs and assigns of covenantor, and "personal covenants" which bind only covenantor personally. Real covenant running with the land concerns enjoyment of property conveyed, while personal covenant is collateral to or is not immediately concerned with property granted. *Caulk*, 661 So.2d 932 (Fla.App. 5 Dist.,1995)

cover The right of a buyer, after breach by the seller, to purchase goods in substitution for those due from the seller.

coverage The amount and extent of risk included in insurance.

coverture The legal status of a married woman whereby her civil existence for many purposes merged with that of her husband.

craft union A labor union whose members do the same kind of work (e.g., plumbing) across different industries. Also called horizontal union.

credibility Believability; the extent to which something is worthy of belief.

credit 1. The ability to acquire goods or services before payment. 2. Funds loaned. 3. An accounting entry for a sum received. 4. A deduction from the amount owed.

credit bureau A business that collects financial information on the creditworthiness of potential customers of businesses.

credit insurance Insurance against the risk of a debtor's nonpayment due to insolvency or other cause.

credit line See line of credit.

creditor One to whom a debt is owed.

> "Creditor" means any person who offers or extends credit creating a debt or to whom a debt is owed, but does not include any person to the extent that they receive an assignment or transfer of a debt in default solely for the purpose of facilitating collection of such debt for another. F.S.A. § 559.55(3)

creditor beneficiary A third person who is to receive the benefit of the performance of a contract (of which he or she is not a direct party) in satisfaction of a legal duty owed to him or her by one of the parties of that contract.

creditor's bill An equitable proceeding brought by a judgment creditor to enforce the judgment out of the judgment debtor's property that cannot be reached by ordinary legal process.

credit rating An assessment of one's ability to repay debts.

crime Conduct defined as criminal by the government.

crime against humanity Conduct prohibited by international law that is knowingly committed as part of a widespread or systematic attack against any civilian population.

crime against nature See sodomy.

crimen falsi A crime involving false statements, e.g., perjury.

crime of passion A crime committed in the heat of an emotionally charged moment.

criminal 1. One who has committed or been convicted of a crime. 2. Pertaining to crimes.

criminal action A prosecution for a crime.

criminal assault See assault.

criminal attempt See attempt.

criminal conspiracy See conspiracy.

criminal contempt An act directed against the authority of the court that obstructs the administration of justice and tends to bring the court into disrepute.

> "Criminal contempt" proceedings are initiated to vindicate court's authority or to punish conduct in violation of court order. *Landingham*, 685 So.2d 946 (Fla.App. 1 Dist.,1996)

criminal conversation (crim. con.) A tort that is committed when the defendant has sexual relations with the plaintiff's spouse.

criminal forfeiture An action against a defendant convicted of a crime to seize his or her property as part of the punishment.

criminalize To declare that specific conduct will constitute a crime.

criminal law Laws defining crimes, punishments, and procedures for investigation and prosecution. Also called penal law.

criminal mischief See malicious mischief.

criminal negligence Conduct that is such a gross deviation from the standard of reasonable care that it is punishable as a crime.

criminal procedure The law governing the investigation and prosecution of crimes, including sentencing and appeal.

criminal syndicalism Advocacy of crime or other unlawful methods of achieving industrial or political change.

criminal trespass Knowingly entering or remaining on land with notice that this is forbidden.

criminology The study of the causes, punishment, and prevention of crime.

critical legal studies (CLS) The theory that law is not neutral but exists to perpetuate the interests of those who are rich and powerful. *Critical race theory* emphasizes the disadvantages imposed on racial minorities under this theory.

critical stage A step in a criminal investigation or proceeding that holds significant consequences for the accused, at which time the right to counsel applies.

cross action 1. A claim brought by the defendant against the plaintiff in the same action. Sometimes called a counterclaim. 2. A claim brought by one defendant against another defendant or by one plaintiff against another plaintiff in the same action. Also called a crossclaim.

cross appeal An appeal by the appellee in the case that the appellant has appealed.

cross bill An equitable claim brought by the defendant against the plaintiff or another defendant in the same suit.

crossclaim See cross action (2).

> A pleading may state as a crossclaim any claim by one party against a co-party arising out of the transaction or occurrence that is the subject matter of either the original action or a counterclaim therein, or relating to any property that is the subject matter of the original action. Florida Rules of Civil Procedure, Rule 1.170(g)

cross collateral 1. Pooling collateral among participants. 2. Collateral used to secure additional loans or accounts.

cross-complaint 1. A claim by the defendant against another party in the same case. 2. A claim by the defendant against someone not now a party in the case that is related to the claim already filed against the defendant.

cross-examination Questioning a witness by an opponent after the other side called and questioned that witness.

crown cases A criminal case brought in England.

cruel and unusual punishment Degrading or disproportionate punishment, shocking the conscience and offending human dignity.

cruelty The intentional or malicious infliction of serious mental or physical suffering on another.

> [The t]erm "cruel," as used in statute setting forth aggravating circumstance authorizing death penalty, means designed to inflict high degree of pain with utter indifference to, or even enjoyment of, suffering of others. F.S.A. § 921.141(5)(h). *Magill*, 428 So.2d 649 (Fla.,1983)

cta See cum testamento annexo.

culpable At fault; blameworthy.

cum Together with, along with.

cum testamento annexo (cta) Concerning administration of an estate where no executor is named in the will, or where one is named but is unable to serve. Administration with the will annexed.

cumulative That which repeats earlier material and consolidates it with new material. Added and combined into one unit.

> "Cumulative annual factor" means the product of all annual factors certified under this act prior to the fiscal year for which salaries are being calculated. F.S.A. § 145.19(2)(b)

cumulative dividend A dividend that, if not paid in one period, is added to dividends to be paid in the next period.

cumulative evidence Additional evidence tending to prove the same point as other evidence already given.

cumulative legacy An additional gift of personal property in the same will (or its codicil) to the same person.

cumulative sentences See consecutive sentences.

cumulative voting A type of voting in which a voter is given as many votes as there are positions to fill and can use the votes for one candidate or spread them among several candidates.

curative Tending to correct or cure a mistake or error.

curator 1. A guardian or custodian of another's affairs. 2. One appointed by the court to be in charge of a decedent's estate until letters are issued.

cure 1. To remove a legal defect or error. 2. The seller's right, after delivering defective goods, to redeliver conforming goods.

current asset Property that can readily be converted into cash.

current liabilities A debt that is likely to be paid within the current business cycle, usually a year.

curtesy A husband's right to lifetime use of land his deceased wife owned during the marriage if a child was born alive to them.

curtilage The land (often enclosed) immediately surrounding and associated with a dwelling house.

custodial interrogation Questioning by law enforcement officers after a person is taken into custody or otherwise deprived of his or her freedom in any significant way.

custodian One with responsibility for the care and custody of property, a person, papers, etc.

custody The protective care and control of a thing or person.

> There are four factors which determine whether a suspect is in "custody" for *Miranda* purposes: (1) the manner in which police summon the suspect for questioning; (2) the purpose, place, and manner of interrogation; (3) the extent to which the suspect is confronted with the evidence of his or her guilt; and (4) whether the suspect is informed that he or she is free to leave the place of questioning. *Lagasse*, 923 So.2d 1287 (Fla.App. 4 Dist.,2006)

custom 1. An established practice that has acquired the force of law. 2. A tax (duty) on the importation and exportation of goods.

cy-pres As near as possible. The intention of the author of an instrument (e.g., will, trust) will be carried out as closely as possible if carrying it out literally is impossible. To prevent the failure of the instrument, the court reforms the instrument using this guideline.

D

DA 1. District Attorney (called a state attorney in Florida). 2. Deposit account.

dactylography The study of identification through fingerprints.

damage An injury or loss to person, property, or rights.

damages Monetary compensation a court can award for wrongful injury or loss to person or property.

damnum absque injuria A loss that cannot be the basis of a lawsuit because it was not caused by a wrongful act.

dangerous instrumentality An object or condition that in its normal operation is an implement of destruction or involves grave danger.

> Under Florida's "dangerous instrumentality doctrine," an owner of a motor vehicle is strictly and vicariously liable when he voluntarily entrusts a motor vehicle to an individual whose negligent operation causes damage to another. *Davis*, 917 So.2d 350 (Fla.App. 1 Dist.,2005)

date of issue The date fixed or agreed upon as the beginning or effective date of a security or document in a series (e.g., bonds).

date rape Rape committed by the victim's social escort.

day in court The right to assert your claim or defense in court.

daybook A book on which daily business transactions are recorded.

dba (d/b/a) Doing business as. A trade name; an assumed name.

dbn See de bonus non.

DC District Court; District of Columbia.

DCA See district court of appeal.

dead freight The amount paid for the portion of a ship's cargo space that is contracted for but not used.

deadlock 1. A standstill due to a refusal of the parties to compromise. 2. The threatened destruction of a business that results when contending shareholders owning an equal number of shares cannot agree.

deadly force Force that is likely or intended to cause death or great bodily harm.

> The term "deadly force" means force that is likely to cause death or great bodily harm and includes, but is not limited to: (a) The firing of a firearm in the direction of the person to be arrested, even though no intent exists to kill or inflict great bodily harm; and (b) The firing of a firearm at a vehicle in which the person to be arrested is riding. F.S.A. § 776.06(1)

deadly weapon A weapon or other instrument intended to be used or likely to be used to cause death or great bodily harm. Also called lethal weapon.

dead man's statute A rule making some statements of a dead person inadmissible when offered to support claims against the estate of the dead person.

dealer 1. One who buys goods for resale to others. 2. One who buys and sells securities on his or her own account rather than as an agent.

death Permanent cessation of all vital functions and signs.

> Death means the absence of life as determined, in accordance with currently accepted medical standards, by the irreversible cessation of all respiration and circulatory function, or as determined, in accordance with § 382.009, by the irreversible cessation of the functions of the entire brain, including the brain stem. F.S.A. § 765.511(2)

deathbed declaration See dying declaration.

death certificate An official record of someone's death, often including vital information such as the date and cause of death.

death knell exception A nonfinal order is appealable if delaying the appeal will cause a party to lose substantial rights.

death penalty Capital punishment; a death sentence.

death qualified rule In a death penalty case, prospective jurors who oppose the death penalty should not be selected.

death tax See estate tax, inheritance tax.

death warrant A court order to carry out a death sentence.

debar To prohibit someone from possessing or doing something.

de bene esse Conditionally allowed for now.

debenture A bond or other debt backed by the general credit of a corporation and not secured by a lien on any specific property.

de bonis non (DBN) Of the goods not administered. An administrator de bonis non is an administrator appointed (in place of a former administrator or executor) to administer the remainder of an estate.

debit A sum owed; an entry made on the left side of an account.

debt An amount of money that is due; an enforceable obligation.

> Debt or consumer debt means any obligation or alleged obligation of a consumer to pay money arising out of a transaction in which the money, property, insurance, or services which are the subject of the transaction are primarily for personal, family, or household purposes, whether or not such obligation has been reduced to judgment. F.S.A. § 559.55(1)

debt capital Money raised by issuing bonds rather than stock.

debtor One who owes a debt, usually money.

debtor in possession A debtor in bankruptcy while still running its business.

debt service Payments to be made to a lender, including interest, principal, and fees.

deceased A dead person.

decedent A dead person.

decedent's estate Property (real and personal) in which a person has an interest at the time of his or her death.

deceit Willfully or recklessly misrepresenting or suppressing material facts with the intent to mislead someone.

decertify 1. To withdraw or revoke certification. 2. To declare that a union can no longer represent a group of employees.

decision A determination of a court or administrative agency applying the law to the facts to resolve a conflict.

decisional law Case law; the law found in court opinions.

declarant A person who makes a declaration or statement.

declaration 1. A formal or explicit statement. 2. An unsworn statement. 3. The first pleading of the plaintiff in an action at law.

declaration against interest A statement made by a nonparty that is against his or her own interest. The statement can be admitted as an exception to the hearsay rule if it was made by someone with personal knowledge who is now not available as a witness.

> Differences between well-recognized exceptions to hearsay rule of admissions of party-opponent or adverse party, and declarations against interest, are that an admission is made by party to litigation, while a declaration against interest is made by non-party; admission comes into evidence despite presence at trial of its author, while general hearsay rule concerning unavailability of declarant applies in case of declarations against interest. F.S.A. § 90.803. *Castaneda ex rel. Cardona*, 884 So.2d 1087 (Fla.App. 4 Dist.,2004)

declaration of trust The establishment of a trust by one who declares that he or she holds the legal title to property in trust for another.

declaratory judgment A binding judgment that declares rights, status, or other legal relationships without ordering anything to be done.

declaratory statute A statute passed to remove doubt about the meaning of an earlier statute. Also called expository statute.

decree 1. A court order. 2. The decision of a court of equity.

decree nisi A decree that will become absolute unless a party convinces the court that it should not be. Also called order nisi, rule nisi.

decretal Pertaining to a decree.

decriminalization A law making legal what was once criminal.

dedication A gift of private land (or an easement) for public use.

> Common law dedication is a setting apart of land for public use, to constitute which there must be an intention by owner clearly indicated by his words or acts to dedicate such land to public use and acceptance by public of the dedication. *Mingledorff*, 388 So.2d 632 (Fla.App., 1980)

deductible 1. What can be taken away or subtracted. 2. The amount of a loss the insured must bear before insurance payments begin.

deduction The part taken away, e.g., an amount that can be subtracted from gross income when calculating adjusted gross income.

deed 1. A document transferring (conveying) an interest in land. 2. An act; something that is done or carried out.

deed of trust A security instrument (similar to a mortgage) in which title to real property is given to a trustee as security until the debt is paid Also called trust deed, trust indenture.

deem To treat as if; to regard something as true or present even if this is not actually so.

deep pocket An individual, business, or other organization with resources to pay a potential judgment. The opposite of *shallow pocket.*

Deep Rock doctrine A controlling shareholder's loan to its own company that is undercapitalized may, in fairness, be subordinated in bankruptcy to other loan claims.

deface To mar or destroy the physical appearance of something.

de facto 1. In fact. 2. Functioning or existing even if not formally or officially encouraged or authorized.

> A de facto merger occurs where one corporation is absorbed by another without formal compliance with the statutory requirements for a merger. *Laboratory Corp. of America,* 813 So.2d 266 (Fla.App. 5 Dist.,2002)

de facto corporation An enterprise that attempts to exercise corporate powers even though it was not properly incorporated in a state where it could have incorporated and where it made a good faith effort to do so.

de facto government A government that has assumed the exercise of sovereignty over a nation, often by illegal or extralegal means.

de facto segregation Segregation caused by social, economic, or other factors rather than by state action or active government assistance.

defalcation 1. A fiduciary's failure to account for funds entrusted to it. Misappropriation; embezzlement. 2. The failure to comply with an obligation.

defamation The publication of a written (or gestured) defamatory statement (libel) or an oral one (slander) of and concerning the plaintiff that harms the plaintiff's reputation.

> Claims for common law defamation require unprivileged publication to a third party of some false and defamatory statement concerning another, with fault amounting to at least negligence on behalf of the publisher, with damage ensuing. Communication is defamatory if it tends to harm the reputation of another as to lower him or her in the estimation of the community or deter third persons from associating or dealing with the defamed party. *Mile Marker,* 811 So.2d 841 (Fla.App. 4 Dist.,2002)

default 1. The failure to carry out a duty. 2. The failure to appear.

default judgment A judgment against a party for failure to file a required pleading or otherwise respond to the opponent's claim.

defeasance 1. The act of rendering something null and void. 2. An instrument that defeats the force or operation of an estate or deed upon the fulfillment of a condition.

defeasible Subject to being revoked or avoided.

defeasible fee See fee simple defeasible.

defeat To prevent, frustrate, or circumvent; to render void.

defect A shortcoming; the lack of something required.

defective Lacking in some particular that is essential to completeness, safety, or legal sufficiency.

defend 1. To protect or represent someone. 2. To contest or oppose.

defendant One against whom a civil action or criminal prosecution is brought.

defender 1. One who raises defenses. 2. One who represents another.

defense 1. An allegation of fact or a legal theory offered to offset or defeat a claim or demand. 2. The defendant and his or her attorney.

deferred annuity An annuity that begins payment at a future date.

deferred compensation Work income set aside for payment in the future.

> Section 61.075(5)(a)4 defines marital assets to include all vested and nonvested benefits, rights, and funds accrued during the marriage in deferred compensation plans and programs. As the term implies, deferred compensation consists of funds already earned but for which payment is deferred. *Ruberg,* 858 So.2d 1147 (Fla.App. 2 Dist.,2003)

deferred income Income to be received in the future, after it was earned.

deficiency 1. A shortage or insufficiency. 2. The amount still owed.

deficiency judgment A judgment for an unpaid balance after the creditor has taken the secured property of the debtor.

deficit 1. An excess of outlays over revenues. 2. An insufficiency.

defined benefit plan A pension plan where the amount of the benefit is fixed but the amount of the contribution is not.

defined contribution plan A pension plan where the amount of the contribution is generally fixed but the amount of the benefit is not.

definite failure of issue See failure of issue.

definite sentence See determinate sentence.

definitive Complete; settling the matter.

defraud To use deception to obtain something or harm someone.

degree 1. The measure or scope of the seriousness of something; a grade or level of wrongdoing. 2. One of the steps in a process. 3. A step in the line of descent.

degree of care The standard of care that is required.

degree of proof The level of believability or persuasiveness that one's evidence must meet.

dehors Beyond the scope, outside of.

de jure Sanctioned by law; in compliance with the law.

> A de jure officer, who rests on right, has lawful title without possession, while a de facto officer, who rests on reputation, has possession and performs the duties under color of title without being technically qualified to act. *State ex rel. Hawthorne,* 28 So.2d 589 (Fla.1946)

de jure segregation Segregation allowed or mandated by the law.

del credere agent A business agent or factor who guarantees the solvency and performance of the purchaser.

delectus personae The right of a partner to exercise his or her preference on the admission of new partners.

delegable duty A responsibility that one can ask another to perform.

delegate 1. To appoint a representative. 2. A representative.

delegation 1. The granting of authority to act for another. 2. The persons authorized to act as representatives.

deliberate 1. To weigh or examine carefully. 2. Intentional.

deliberative process privilege The government can maintain secrecy when needed to ensure the free exchange of ideas in the making of policy.

delict, delictum A tort or offense; a violation of the law.

delinquency 1. A violation of duty. 2. The failure to pay a debt. 3. Misconduct, unruly, or immoral behavior by a minor.

delinquent 1. Pertaining to that which is still due; in arrears. 2. Failing to abide by the law or to conform to moral standards. 3. A minor who has committed an offense or other serious misconduct.

> [D]elinquent act means a violation of any law of this state, the United States, or any other state which is a misdemeanor or a felony or a violation of a county or municipal ordinance which would be punishable by incarceration if the violation were committed by an adult. F.S.A. § 985.03

delisting Removing a security from the list of what can be traded on an exchange.

delivery 1. The act by which something is placed in the possession or control of another. 2. That which is delivered.

demand 1. To claim as one's due or right. 2. The assertion of a right.

demand deposit Any bank deposit that the depositor may withdraw (demand) at any time without notice.

demand loan A loan without a set maturity date that the lender can demand payment of at any time. A call loan.

demand note A note that must be paid whenever the lender requests (demands) payment.

> If the note is payable on demand, the note is dishonored if presentment is duly made to the maker and the note is not paid on the day of presentment. F.S.A. § 673.5021(1)(a)

demeanor Outward or physical appearance or behavior; deportment.

demesne 1. Domain 2. Land a person holds in his or her own right.

de minimis Very small; not significant enough to change the result.

demise 1. A lease. A conveyance of land to another for a term. 2. The document that creates a lease. 3. To convey or create an estate or lease. 4. To transfer property by descent or by will. 5. Death.

demise charter See bareboat charter.

democracy A system of government controlled by the people directly or through elected representatives.

demonstrative bequest; demonstrative legacy A gift by will payable out of a specific fund.

> A "demonstrative legacy" is a bequest of a certain sum of money, stock, or other property payable out of a particular fund, property, or security, but it cannot constitute a gift of the corpus, nor can it show a purpose of releasing the general estate from liability in event the particular fund, property, or security should fail. *Park Lake Presbyterian Church*, 106 So.2d 215 (Fla.App.1958)

demonstrative evidence Evidence (other than testimony) addressed to the senses. Physical evidence offered for illumination and explanation, but otherwise unrelated to the case. Also called autoptic evidence.

demur 1. To state a demurrer. 2. To take exception.

demurrer A pleading that admits, for the sake of argument, the allegations of fact made by the other party in order to show that even if they are true, they are do not entitle this party to relief.

denial 1. A declaration that something the other side alleges is not true. 2. Rejection; refusing to do something.

de novo Anew; as if for the first time. See trial de novo.

depecage Under conflicts of law principles, a court can apply the laws of different jurisdictions to different disputes in the same case.

dependency 1. A geographically separate territory under the jurisdiction of another country or sovereign. 2. A relationship in which one person relies on another for society or a standard of living.

dependent 1. One who derives his or her main support from another. 2. A person who can be claimed as a personal exemption by a taxpayer.

dependent covenant A party's agreement or promise whose performance is conditioned on and subject to prior performance by the other party.

> A "dependent covenant" is a covenant which depends upon the prior performance of some act or condition, or as otherwise defined, an agreement to do or omit to do something with reference to the thing on which it depends and of which it relates, and the courts construe covenants as dependent where the act of each party is to be done or performed at the same time. *Nolan*, 196 So. 193 (Fla.1940)

dependent relative revocation The revocation of an earlier will was intended to give effect to a later will, so if the later will is inoperative, the earlier will shall take effect.

depletion An exhausting or reduction during the taxable year of oil, gas, or other mineral deposits and reserves.

deponent One who gives testimony at a deposition.

deport To banish or exile someone to a foreign country.

depose 1. To question a witness in a deposition. 2. To give testimony. 3. To remove from office or power.

deposit 1. To place for safekeeping. 2. An asset placed for safekeeping. 3. Money given as security or earnest money for the performance of a contract. Also called security deposit.

> A bank "deposit" merely constitutes a chose in action or right to money; it is a debt owing by depository collectible by owner. *In re Thourez' Estate*, 166 So.2d 476 (Fla.App.1964)

depositary A person or institution (e.g., bank) that receives an asset for safekeeping.

depositary bank The first bank to which checks or other deposits are taken for collection.

deposition A method of discovery by which parties or their prospective witnesses are questioned outside the courtroom before trial.

deposition de bene esse A deposition of a witness who will not be able to testify at trial, taken in order to preserve his or her testimony.

depository The place where an asset is placed and kept for safekeeping.

depreciable life The period over which an asset may reasonably be expected to be useful in a trade or business. Also called useful life.

depreciation A gradual decline in the value of property caused by use, deterioration, time, or obsolescence.

deputy One duly authorized to act on behalf of another.

deregulate To lessen government control over an industry or business.

derelict 1. Abandoned property. 2. Delinquent in a duty.

dereliction 1. A wrongful or shameful neglect or abandonment of one's duty. 2. The gaining of land from the water as a result of a shrinking back of the sea or river below the usual watermark.

derivative 1. Coming from another; secondary. 2. A financial instrument whose value is dependent on another asset or investment.

derivative action 1. A suit by a shareholder to enforce a corporate cause of action. Also called a derivative suit, representative action. 2. An action to recover for a loss that is dependent on an underlying tort or wrong committed against someone else.

> A "derivative action" is generally defined as a cause of action on behalf of a stockholder to enforce a right of action that exists on behalf of the corporation. *Fox*, 801 So.2d 175 (Fla.App. 5 Dist.,2001)

derivative evidence Evidence that is inadmissible because it is derived or spawned from other evidence that was illegally obtained.

derivative suit See derivative action (1).

derivative work A translation or other transformation of a preexisting work.

derogation 1. A partial repeal or abolishing of a law, as by a subsequent act that limits its scope or force. 2. Disparaging or belittling, or undermining something or someone.

descend To be transferred to persons entitled to receive a deceased's assets by intestate succession. To pass by inheritance.

descendant Offspring; person in the bloodline of an ancestor.

descent A transfer to persons entitled to receive a deceased's assets by intestate succession. Passing by inheritance.

descent and distribution 1. See intestate succession. 2. The passing of a decedent's assets by intestacy or will.

desecrate To violate something that is sacred; to defile.

desegregation The elimination of policies and laws that led to racial segregation.

desertion 1. The voluntary, unjustified leaving of one's spouse for an uninterrupted period of time with the intent not to return to resume marital cohabitation. 2. The willful failure to fulfill a support obligation. 3. Remaining absent (without authority) from one's military place of duty with the intent to remain away permanently.

> Abandonment of duty by quitting ship before termination of engagement, without justification and with intention of not returning. *Carson*, 123 So.2d 35 (Fla.App.1960)

design defect A flaw rendering a product unreasonably dangerous because of the way in which it was designed or conceived.

designer drug A synthetic substitute for an existing controlled substance or drug, often made to avoid anti-drug laws.

destination contract A contract in which the risk of loss passes to the buyer when the seller tenders the goods at the destination.

destructibility of contingent remainders A contingent remainder must vest before or at the end of the preceding estate, or it fails (is destroyed).

desuetude 1. Discontinuation of use. 2. The equivalent of a repeal of a law by reason of its long and continued nonuse.

detainer 1. Withholding possession of land or goods from another. Keeping someone or something in your custody. See also unlawful detainer. 2. A request or writ that an institution continue keeping someone in custody.

> A "detainer" is a request filed by a criminal justice agency with the institution in which a prisoner is incarcerated, asking the institution either to hold the prisoner for the agency or to notify the agency when release of the prisoner is imminent. *Chapman*, 910 So.2d 940 (Fla.App. 5 Dist.,2005)

detention Holding in custody; confinement.

determinable 1. Capable of coming to an end (terminable) upon the occurrence of a contingency. 2. Susceptible of being determined, ascertained, or settled.

determinable fee See fee simple determinable.

determinate sentence A sentence to confinement for a fixed period. Also called definite sentence.

determination 1. The final decision of a court or administrative agency. 2. The ending of an estate or property interest.

detinue An action for the recovery of personal property held (detained) wrongfully by another.

detraction Transferring property to another state upon a transfer of the title to it by will or inheritance.

detriment 1. Any loss or harm to person or property. 2. A legal right that a promisee gives up. Also called legal detriment.

> In context of child custody disputes, the term "detriment" means circumstances which produce or are likely to produce in child mental, physical, or emotional harm of lasting nature. *In Interest of B.B.*, 559 So.2d 1277 (Fla.App. 2 Dist.,1990)

detrimental reliance A loss, disadvantage, or change in one's position for the worse because of one's reliance on another's promise.

devaluation A reduction in the value of a currency in relation to other currencies.

devastavit An act of omission, negligence, or misconduct of an administrator or other legal representative of an estate.

devest See divest.

deviation Departure from established or usual conduct or ideology.

deviation doctrine A variation in the terms of a will or trust will be allowed to avoid defeating the purposes of the document.

device 1. A mechanical or electronic invention or gadget. 2. A scheme.

devise The gift of property (sometimes only real property) by a will.

> "Devise," when used as a noun, means a testamentary disposition of real or personal property and, when used as a verb, means to dispose of real or personal property by will or trust. The term includes "gift," "give," "bequeath," "bequest," and "legacy." A devise is subject to charges for debts, expenses, and taxes as provided in this code, the will, or the trust. F.S.A. § 731.201(8)

devisee The person to whom property is devised or given in a will.

devisor The person who devises or gives property in a will.

devolution The transfer or transition of a right, title, estate, or office to another or to a lower level. The verb is *devolve*.

devolve See devolution.

dicta See dictum, which is the singular form of dicta.

dictum 1. An observation made by a judge in an opinion that is not essential to resolve the issues before the court; comments that go beyond the facts before the court. Also called obiter dictum. 2. An authoritative, formal statement or announcement.

dies A day; days, e.g., dies non juridicus: A day on which courts are not open for business.

diet The name of the legislature in some countries.

digest An organized summary or abridgment. A set of volumes that contain brief summaries of court opinions, arranged by subject matter and by court or jurisdiction.

dilatory plea A plea raising a procedural matter, not on the merits.

diligence 1. Persistent activity. 2. Prudence, carefulness.

dilution Diminishing the strength or value of something, e.g., voting strength by increasing the number of shares issued, uniqueness of a trademark by using it on too many different products.

> "Dilution" as used in statute intended to prevent dilution of distinctiveness and value of trade name and mark even where there is absence of competition between parties or of confusion as to source of goods or services focuses on uniqueness or distinctiveness of name and mark and requires some proof that use of name and mark decreases its commercial value; if plaintiff holds distinctive mark, it is enough that defendant has made significant use of very similar mark. F.S.A. § 495.151. *Blanding Automotive Center*, 568 So.2d 490 (Fla.App. 1 Dist.,1990)

diminished capacity or **responsibility** A mental disorder not amounting to insanity that impairs or negates the defendant's ability to form the culpable mental state to commit the crime. Also called partial insanity.

diminution in value As a measure of damages, the difference between the fair market value of the property with and without the damage.

diplomatic immunity A diplomat's exemption from most laws of the host country.

direct 1. To command, regulate, or manage. 2. To aim or cause to move in a certain direction. 3. Without interruption; immediate. 4. In a straight line of descent, as opposed to a collateral line.

direct attack An attempt to have a judgment changed in the same case or proceeding that rendered the judgment, e.g., an appeal.

direct cause See proximate cause.

direct contempt A contempt committed in the presence of the court or so near the court as to interrupt its proceedings.

> Contemptuous conduct in immediate presence of court is "direct contempt"; contempt outside court's presence is "indirect contempt." *E.T. v. State*, 587 So.2d 615 (Fla.App. 1 Dist.,1991)

direct damages See general damages.

directed verdict A judge's decision not to allow the jury to deliberate because only one verdict is reasonable. In federal court, the verdict has been replaced by a *judgment as a matter of law* (see this phrase).

direct estoppel See collateral estoppel.

direct evidence Evidence that, if believed, proves a fact without using inferences or presumptions; evidence based on what one personally saw, heard, or touched. Also called positive evidence.

direct examination The first questioning of a witness by the party who has called the witness. Also called examination in chief.

direct line A line of descent traced through those persons who are related to each other directly as descendants or ascendants.

director 1. One who directs or guides a department, organization, or activity. 2. A member of the board that oversees and controls the managers or officers of an entity such as a corporation.

directory Nonmandatory. Pertaining to a clause or provision in a statute or contract that is advisory rather than involving the essence of the statute or contract.

directory trust A trust whose details will by filled out by later instructions.

direct tax A tax imposed directly on property rather than on the transfer of property or on some other right connected with property.

disability 1. Legal incapacity to perform an act. 2. A physical or mental condition that limits one's ability to participate in a major life activity such as employment. Also called incapacity.

> "Disability" is not simply employee's diminution of wage-earning capacity; rather, it is incapacity to carry on, in any field of endeavor, work which will equal or surpass income earned at time of injury. F.S.1989, § 440.02(10). *Delgado*, 606 So.2d 658 (Fla.App. 1 Dist.,1992)

disaffirm To repudiate; to cancel or revoke consent.

disallow To refuse to allow; to deny or reject.

disavow To repudiate; to disclaim knowledge of or responsibility for.

disbar To expel an attorney or revoke his or her license to practice law.

disbursement Paying out money; an out-of-pocket expenditure.

discharge 1. To relieve of an obligation. 2. To fulfill an obligation. 3. To release or let go. 4. To cancel a court order. 5. To shoot. 6. To release from employment or service.

> To "discharge" a destructive device, for purposes of statute imposing mandatory minimum 20-year sentence if defendant discharged destructive device, device must explode, that is, it must function as it was intended. F.S.A. § 775.087(2)(a). *Wallace*, 860 So.2d 494 (Fla.App. 4 Dist.,2003)

discharge in bankruptcy The release of a bankrupt from all nonexempted debts in a bankruptcy proceeding.

disciplinary rule (DR) A rule stating the minimum conduct below which no attorney should fall without being subject to discipline.

disclaimer The repudiation of one's own or another's claim, right, or obligation.

disclosure 1. The act of revealing that which is secret or not known. 2. Complying with a legal duty to provide specified information.

discontinuance 1. The plaintiff's withdrawal or termination of his or her suit. 2. In zoning, the abandonment of a use.

discount 1. An allowance or deduction from the original price or debt. 2. The amount by which interest is reduced from the face value of a note or other financial instrument at the outset of the loan. 3. The amount by which the price paid for a security is less than its face value.

discounting Converting future cash flows into a present value.

discount rate 1. A percentage of the face amount of commercial paper (e.g., note) that an issuer pays when transferring the paper to a financial institution. 2. The interest rate charged by the Federal Reserve to member banks.

discoverable Pertaining to information or other materials an opponent can obtain through a deposition or other discovery device.

discovered peril doctrine See last clear chance doctrine.

discovery Compulsory exchanges of information between parties in litigation. Pretrial devices (e.g., interrogatories) to obtain information about a suit from the other side.

discredit To cast doubt on the credibility of a person, an idea, or evidence.

discretion 1. The power or right to act by the dictates of one's own judgment and conscience. 2. The freedom to decide among options. 3. Good judgment; prudence.

> Discretion connotes no hard and fast rules but requires that such discretion be not exercised arbitrarily, but with regard to what is right and just under the circumstances and law, governed by reason and conscience of judge to a just end. *Bryan*, 156 So.2d 885 (Fla.App.1963)

discretionary review An appeal that an appellate court agrees to hear when it has the option of refusing to hear it.

discretionary trust A trust giving the trustee discretion to decide when a beneficiary will receive income or principal and how much. Also called complex trust.

discrimination 1. Differential imposition of burdens or granting of benefits. 2. Unreasonably granting or denying privileges on the basis of sex, age, race, nationality, religion, or handicap.

> "Discrimination" refers to differential treatment, such as where a state or local regulation places a greater economic burden on those outside state, with an attendant economic advantage to those within state. *Reinish*, 765 So.2d 197 (Fla.App. 1 Dist.,2000)

disenfranchise To deprive someone of a right or privilege, e.g., the right to vote. Also called disfranchise.

disfranchise See disenfranchise.

disgorge To surrender unwillingly.

dishonor To refuse to accept or pay a draft or other negotiable instrument when duly presented.

disinheritance Taking steps to prevent someone from inheriting property.

disinterested Objective; without bias; having nothing to gain or lose.

disintermediation The withdrawal by depositors of funds from low-yielding bank accounts for use in higher-yielding investments.

disjunctive allegations Assertions pleaded in the alternative, e.g., he stole the car or caused it to be stolen.

dismissal 1. An order that ends an action or motion without additional court proceedings. 2. A discharge; an order to go away.

dismissal without prejudice Termination of the action that is not on the merits, meaning that the party can return later with the same claim.

dismissal with prejudice Termination of the action that is the equivalent of an adjudication on the merits, meaning that the party is barred from returning later with the same claim.

disorderly conduct Behavior that tends to disturb the peace, endanger the health of the community, or shock the public sense of morality.

> Whoever commits such acts as are of a nature to corrupt the public morals, or outrage the sense of public decency, or affect the peace and quiet of persons who may witness them, or engages in brawling or fighting, or engages in such conduct as to constitute a breach of the peace or disorderly conduct, shall be guilty of a misdemeanor of the second degree.... F.S.A. § 877.03

disorderly house A dwelling where acts are performed that tend to corrupt morals, promote breaches of the peace, or create a nuisance.

disparagement The intentional and false discrediting of the plaintiff's product or business (sometimes called trade libel when written or slander of goods when spoken) or the plaintiff's title to property (sometimes called slander of title) resulting in specific monetary loss.

> Bothmann's primary cause of action is for slander of title, or more appropriately called disparagement of title or property. In a disparagement action the plaintiff must allege and prove the following elements: (1) A falsehood (2) has been published, or communicated to a third person (3) when the defendant-publisher knows or reasonably should know that it will likely result in inducing others not to deal with the plaintiff and (4) in fact, the falsehood does play a material and substantial part in inducing others not to deal with the plaintiff; and (5) special damages are proximately caused as a result of the published falsehood. *Bothmann*, 458 So.2d 1163 (Fla.App. 3 Dist.,1984)

disparate impact Conduct that appears neutral on its face but that disproportionately and negatively impacts members of one race, sex, age, disability, or other protected group.

disparate treatment Intentionally treating some people less favorably than others because of sex, age, race, nationality, religion, or disability.

dispensation An exemption from a duty, burden, penalty, or law.

disposition 1. The act of distributing or transferring assets. 2. The final ruling or decision of a tribunal. 3. An arrangement or settlement. 4. Temperament or characteristics.

dispossess To evict from land; to deprive of possession.

disputable presumption See rebuttable presumption.

dispute 1. A controversy. 2. The conflict leading to litigation.

disqualification That which renders something ineligible or unfit.

disseisin Wrongful dispossession of another from property.

dissent 1. A judge's vote against the result reached by the judges in the majority on a case. 2. A dissenting opinion.

dissipation 1. Wasting, squandering, or destroying. 2. The use of marital property by a spouse for a personal purpose.

> Where one spouse uses marital funds for his or her own benefit and for a purpose unrelated to the marriage at a time when the marriage is undergoing an irreconcilable breakdown. *Murray*, 636 So.2d 536 (Fla.App. 1 Dist.,1994)

dissolution 1. Cancellation. 2. The act or process of terminating a legal relationship or organization. 3. A divorce.

dissolution of marriage See divorce.

dist. ct. District court.

distinguish To point out an essential difference; to demonstrate that a particular court opinion is inapplicable to the current legal dispute.

distrain To take and hold the personal property of another until the latter performs an obligation.

distrainee A person who is distrained.

distrainer or **distrainor** One who seizes property under a distress.

distraint Property seized to enforce an obligation.

distress Seizing property to enforce an obligation, e.g., a landlord seizes a tenant's property to secure payment of delinquent rent.

> A distress writ shall be issued by a judge of the court which has jurisdiction of the amount claimed. The writ shall enjoin the defendant from damaging, disposing of, secreting, or removing any property liable to distress from the rented real property after the time of service of the writ until the sheriff levies on the property, the writ is vacated, or the court otherwise orders. F.S.A. § 83.12

distress sale 1. A foreclosure sale; a forced sale to pay a debt. 2. A sale at below market rates because of a pressure to sell.

distributee One who shares in the distribution of an estate. An heir.

distribution 1. The apportionment and division of something. 2. The transfer of property under the law of intestate succession after estate taxes and other debts are paid. 3. The transfer of proceeds from the sale of assets by a bankruptcy trustee to creditors of the estate.

distributive finding A jury's finding in part for the plaintiff and in part for the defendant.

distributive justice A system of justice where the goal is the fair allocation of available goods, services, and burdens.

district A geographic division for judicial, political, electoral, or administrative purposes.

district attorney A prosecutor representing the government in criminal cases in an area or district. Also called prosecuting attorney or state attorney.

district court A trial court in the federal and some state judicial systems.

district court of appeal (DCA) The intermediate appeals court in Florida (*www.flcourts.org*).

disturbance of the peace See breach of the peace.

divers Various, several.

diversion 1. Turning aside or altering the natural course or route of a thing. 2. An alternative to criminal prosecution leading to the dismissal of the charges if the accused completes a program of rehabilitation. Also called diversion program, pretrial diversion, or pretrial intervention.

diversity of citizenship The disputing parties are citizens of different states. This fact gives jurisdiction (called diversity jurisdiction) to a United States District Court when the amount in controversy exceeds $75,000.

divest To dispose of or be deprived of rights, duties, or possessions. Also spelled devest.

divestiture 1. The selling, spinning off, or surrender of business assets. 2. The requirement that specific property, securities, or other assets be disposed of, often to avoid a restraint of trade.

divided custody A custody arrangement in which the parents alternate having full custody (legal and physical) of a child.

dividend A share of corporate profits given pro rata to stockholders.

divisible Capable of being divided.

divisible contract A contract with parts that can be enforced separately so that the failure to perform one part does not bar recovery for performance of another.

divisible divorce A divorce decree that dissolves the marriage in one proceeding but that resolves other marital issues such as property division and child custody in a separate proceeding.

> Under "divisible divorce" concept, dissolution proceeding has two separable aspects, that which relates to marital res and that which relates to property rights and obligations of parties. *Birnbaum*, 615 So.2d 241 (Fla.App. 3 Dist.,1993)

division of fee See fee division.

divorce A declaration by a court that a validly entered marriage is dissolved. Also called dissolution of marriage.

divorce a mensa et thoro See legal separation.

divorce a vinculo matrimonii An absolute divorce that terminates the marital relationship.

DNA fingerprinting The process of identifying the genetic makeup of an individual based on the uniqueness of his or her DNA pattern. Deoxyribonucleic acid (DNA) is the carrier of genetic information in living organisms.

DNR Do not resuscitate (a notice concerning terminally ill persons).

dock 1. The space in a criminal court where prisoners stand when brought in for trial. 2. A landing place for boats.

docket 1. A list of pending court cases. 2. A record containing brief notations on the proceedings that have occurred in a court case.

docket number A consecutive number assigned to a case by the court and used on all documents filed with the court during the litigation of that case.

doctor of jurisprudence See Juris Doctor.

doctor-patient privilege. A patient and doctor can refuse to disclose communications between them concerning diagnosis or treatment. Also called physician-patient privilege.

> Communications between a patient and a psychiatrist, as defined in § 394.455, shall be held confidential and shall not be disclosed except upon the request of the patient or the patient's legal representative. F.S.A. § 456.059

doctrine A rule or legal principle.

document 1. Any physical or electronic embodiment of words or ideas (e.g., letter, X-ray plate). 2. To support with documentary evidence or with authorities. 3. To create a written record.

documentary evidence Evidence in the form of something written.

document of title A document giving its holder the right to receive and dispose of goods covered by the document (e.g., a bill of lading).

doing business Carrying on or conducting a business.

doli capax Capable of having the intent to commit a crime.

dolus Fraud; deceitfulness.

domain 1. Land that is owned; an estate in land. 2. Absolute ownership and control. 3. The territory governed by a ruler.

Dombrowski **doctrine** To protect First Amendment rights, a federal court can enjoin state criminal proceedings based on a vague statute. *Dombrowski v. Pfister*, 85 S. Ct. 1116 (1965)

domestic Concerning one's own country, state, jurisdiction, or family.

domestic corporation A corporation established in a particular state.

domestic partners Persons in a same-sex (or unmarried opposite-sex) relationship who are emotionally and financially interdependent and who register with the government to receive marriage-like benefits.

domestic relations Family law (e.g., the law on adoption and divorce).

domestic violence Actual or threatened physical injury or abuse by one member of a family or household on another member.

domicile 1. The place where someone has physically been present with the intention to make that place a permanent home; the place to which one would intend to return when away. 2. The place where a business has its headquarters or principal place of business. 3. The legal residence of a person or business. (*Residence* and *domicile* are sometimes used interchangeably.)

> "Domicile" means the place where a client legally resides, which place is his or her permanent home. Domicile may be established as provided in § 222.17. Domicile may not be established in Florida by a minor who has no parent domiciled in Florida, or by a minor who has no legal guardian domiciled in Florida, or by any alien not classified as a resident alien. F.S.A. § 393.063(12)

domiciliary Someone who has established a domicile in a place.

domiciliary administration The administration of an estate in the state where the decedent was domiciled at the time of death.

dominant estate The parcel of land that is benefited from an easement. Also called dominant tenement.

dominant tenement See dominant estate.

dominion Ownership or sovereignty; control over something.

> Supreme authority, a synonym to power. *Nichols*, 152 So.2d 486, *489 (Fla.App.1963)

donated surplus Assets contributed by shareholders to a corporation.

donatio A gift or donation.

donative intent The donor's intent that title and control of the subject matter of the gift be irrevocably and presently transferred.

donee One to whom a gift or power of appointment is given.

donee beneficiary A nonparty to a contract who receives the benefit of the contract as a gift.

donor One who makes a gift, confers a power, or creates a trust.

dormant In abeyance, suspended; temporarily inactive.

dormant judgment An unsatisfied judgment that has remained unexecuted for so long that it needs to be revived before it can be executed.

dormant partner A partner who receives financial benefits from a business, but does not run it and may be unknown to the public. Also called a silent partner, a sleeping partner.

double hearsay A hearsay statement contained within another hearsay statement.

double indemnity Twice the benefit for losses from specified causes.

double insurance Overlapping insurance whereby an insured has two or more policies on the same subject and against same the risks.

double jeopardy A second prosecution for the same offense after acquittal or conviction; multiple punishments for the same offense.

double taxation Taxing the same thing twice for the same purpose by the same taxing authority during identical taxing periods.

double will See mutual wills (1).

doubt Uncertainty of mind. See also reasonable doubt.

doubtful title Title that raises serious doubts as to its validity.

dower A wife's right to a life estate in one-third of the land her deceased husband owned in fee at any time during the marriage.

> Dower and curtesy are abolished. F.S.A. § 732.111

down payment An amount of money paid by the buyer to the seller at the time of sale, which represents only a part of the total cost.

dowry Property that a woman brings to her husband upon marriage.

DR See disciplinary rule.

draft 1. An unconditional written order (e.g., a check) by the first party (called the drawer) instructing a second party (called the drawee or payor, e.g., a bank) to pay a specified sum on demand or at a specified time to a third party (called the payee) or to bearer. Also called bill of exchange. 2. A preliminary version of a plan, drawing, memo, or other writing. 3. Compulsory selection; conscription.

> An instrument is a "note" if it is a promise and is a "draft" if it is an order. If an instrument falls within the definition of both "note" and "draft," a person entitled to enforce the instrument may treat it as either. F.S.A. § 673.1041(5)

Dram Shop Act A law imposing civil liability on a seller of liquor to one whose intoxication causes injury to a third person. Also called civil damage law.

draw 1. To prepare a legal document. 2. To withdraw money. 3. To make and sign (e.g., draw a check to pay the bill). 4. To pick a jury. 5. An advance against profits or amounts owed.

drawee The bank or other entity ordered to pay the amount on a draft.

drawer One who makes and signs a draft for the payment of money.

> "Drawer" means any person who writes a personal check and upon whose account the check is drawn. F.S.A. § 560.402(7)

Dred Scott case The U.S. Supreme Court case holding that slaves and former slaves were not citizens even if they lived in states where slavery was not legal. *Scott v. Sanford,* 60 U.S. 393 (1867)

driving under the influence (DUI); driving while intoxicated (DWI) The offense of operating a motor vehicle while impaired due to alcohol or drugs. States may treat DWI as more serious than or the same as DUI.

droit A legal right; a body of law.

drug-free zone Geographic areas (e.g., near schools) where conviction of a drug offense will lead to increased punishment.

dry 1. Without duties. 2. Prohibiting the sale or use of liquor.

dry trust See passive trust.

dual capacity doctrine An employer may be liable in tort to its employee if it occupies, in addition to its capacity as employer, a second capacity that confers on it obligations independent of those imposed on an employer.

dual citizenship The status of a person who is a citizen of the United States and of another country at the same time.

dual contract Two contracts by the same parties for the same matter or transaction, something entered to mislead others.

dual-purpose doctrine An employee injured on a trip serving both business and personal purposes is covered under workers' compensation if the trip would have been made for the employer even if there were no personal purpose.

> The "dual purpose doctrine" provides that an injury which occurs as the result of a trip, a concurrent cause of which was a business purpose, is within the course and scope of employment, even if the trip also served a personal purpose, such as going to and coming from work. F.S.A. § 440.092(2). *Swartz,* 788 So.2d 937 (Fla.,2001)

dubitante Having doubt.

duces tecum Bring with you. See also subpoena duces tecum.

due 1. Payable now or on demand; owing. 2. Proper, reasonable.

due-bill An acknowledgement of indebtedness; an IOU.

due care See reasonable care.

due course See holder in due course.

due diligence Reasonable prudence and effort in carrying out an obligation.

due notice Notice likely to reach its target; legally prescribed notice.

due process of law Fundamental fairness in having a dispute resolved according to established procedures and rules, e.g., notice, hearing.

DUI See driving under the influence.

duly In due and proper form or manner.

dummy 1. One who buys property and holds the legal title for someone else, usually to conceal the identity of the real owner. 2. Sham.

dummy corporation A corporation formed to avoid personal liability or conceal the owner's identity, not to conduct a legitimate business.

dumping 1. Selling in quantity at a very low price. 2. Selling goods abroad at less than their fair market price at home. 3. Shifting a nonpaying patient onto another health care provider.

dun To make a demand for payment.

duplicate A copy or replacement of the original.

duplicity 1. Deception. 2. Improperly uniting two or more causes of action in one count or two or more grounds of defense in one plea. 3. Improperly charging two or more offenses in a single count of an indictment.

duress 1. Coercion; the unlawful use of force or threat of force. 2. Wrongful confinement or imprisonment.

> "Duress" in making a payment is that degree of constraint or danger either actually inflicted or threatened and impending, sufficient to overcome the mind and will of a person of ordinary firmness. *Soneet R. Kapila, P.A.,* 817 So.2d 866 (Fla.App. 4 Dist.,2002)

duress of goods A tort of seizing or detaining another's personal property and wrongfully requiring some act before it is returned.

Durham **test** See insanity (3).

duty 1. A legal or moral obligation that another has a right to have performed. 2. The obligation to conform to a standard of conduct prescribed by law or by contract. Also called legal duty. 3. A function or task expected to be performed in one's calling. 4. A tax on imports or exports.

duty of tonnage See tonnage (2).

dwelling house The building that is one's residence or abode.

DWI See driving while intoxicated.

dying declaration A statement of fact by one conscious of imminent death about the cause or circumstances of his or her death. An exception to the hearsay rule. Also called deathbed declaration.

> "Dying declaration" to be admissible in evidence must be shown to have been made with knowledge that death was imminent and inevitable, and any expressions of one mortally wounded at time of making an alleged dying declaration, tending to show that deceased then believed his death was imminent, are admissible for purpose of determining whether declaration then made and offered in evidence was in fact a dying declaration. *Covington,* 200 So. 531 (Fla.1941)

dynamite instruction See *Allen* charge.

E

E&O See errors and omissions insurance.

earmarking To set aside or reserve for a designated purpose.

earned income Income (e.g., wages) derived from labor and services.

earned income credit A refundable tax credit on earned income for low income workers who have dependent children and who maintain a household.

earned premium The portion of an insurance premium that has been used thus far during the term of a policy.

earned surplus The surplus a corporation accumulates from profits after dividends are paid. Also called retained earnings.

earnest money Part of the purchase price paid by a buyer when entering a contract to show the intent and ability to carry out the contract.

earnings report A company report showing revenues, expenses, and losses over a given period and the net result. Also called an income statement, profit-and-loss statement.

easement A property interest in another's land that authorizes limited use of the land, e.g., a right-of-way across private property.

> Easement means any strip of land created by a subdivider for public or private utilities, drainage, sanitation, or other specified uses having limitations, the title to which shall remain in the name of the property owner, subject to the right of use designated in the reservation of the servitude. F.S.A. § 177.031(7)(a)

easement appurtenant An easement interest that attaches to the land and passes with it when conveyed.

easement by implication See implied easement.

easement by prescription See prescriptive easement.

easement in gross A personal right to use the land of another that usually ends with the death of the person possessing this right. An easement that does not benefit a particular piece of land.

> An easement unconnected with nor for the benefit of any dominant estate. *Platt*, 382 So.2d 414 (Fla.App., 1980)

easement of access The right to travel over the land of another to reach a road or other location.

easement of necessity A right-of-way that arises by implication or operation of law in favor of a grantee who has no reasonable access to its land or to a road except over other lands owned by the grantor or by a stranger.

eavesdrop To listen to another's private conversation without consent.

ecclesiastical Pertaining to the church. See also canon law.

ECF See electronic court filing.

economic duress See business compulsion.

economic realities test The totality of commercial circumstances that a court will examine to determine the nature of a relationship.

economic strike A strike over wages, hours, working conditions, or other conditions of employment, not over an unfair labor practice.

edict A formal decree, command, law, or proclamation.

EEOC Equal Employment Opportunity Commission (*www.eeoc.gov*).

effect 1. That which is produced. 2. To bring about or cause.

effective assistance of counsel Representation provided by an attorney using the skill, knowledge, time, and resources of a reasonably competent attorney in criminal cases.

effective date The date a law, treaty, or contract goes into effect and becomes binding or enforceable.

effective tax rate The percentage of total income actually paid for taxes.

effects Personal property; goods.

efficient cause See proximate cause.

efficient intervening cause See intervening cause.

efficient market A market in which material information on a company is widely available and accurately reflected in the value of the stock.

eggshell skull An unusually high vulnerability to injury.

egress The means or right to leave a place. The act of leaving.

Eighth Amendment The amendment to the U.S. Constitution that prohibits cruel and unusual punishment and excessive fines and bails.

ejectment An action for the recovery of the possession of land and for damages for the wrongful dispossession.

> Common-law ejectment abolished. In ejectment it is not necessary to have any fictitious parties. Plaintiff may bring action directly against the party in possession or claiming adversely. F.S.A. § 66.011

ejusdem generis Where general words follow a list of particular words, the general words will be interpreted as applying only to things of the same class or category as the particular words in the list.

election A selection among available persons, conduct, rights, etc.

election by spouse The right of a widow or widower to choose between what a deceased spouse gives the surviving spouse by will or the share of the decedent's estate designated by statute.

election of remedies A choice by a party between two inconsistent remedies for the same wrong.

> Doctrine of election of remedies is the act of choosing between two or more different and co-existing modes of procedure and relief allowed by law on the same state of facts. *Diamond R. Fertilizer Co.*, 743 So.2d 547 (Fla.App. 5 Dist.,1999)

elective share The statutory share a surviving spouse chooses over what the will of his or her deceased spouse provides.

elector 1. A voter. 2. A member of the electoral college.

electoral college A body of electors chosen to elect the president and vice president based on the popular vote in each individual state.

electronic court filing (ECF) A method of filing documents in court electronically.

electronic signature Any letters, characters, or symbols, manifested by electronic or similar means, executed or adopted by a party with an intent to authenticate a writing. A writing is electronically signed if an electronic signature is logically associated with such writing. F.S.A § 668.003(4).

eleemosynary Having to do with charity.

element 1. A constituent part of something. 2. A portion of a rule that is a precondition of the applicability of the entire rule.

elisor A person appointed by the court to perform duties of a disqualified sheriff or coroner.

eloign To remove something in order to conceal it from the court.

emancipation 1. Setting free. 2. The express or implied consent of a parent to relinquish his or her control and authority over a child.

embargo A government prohibition of ships into or out of its waters or of the exchange of goods and services to or from a particular country.

embezzlement Fraudulently taking personal property of another, which was initially acquired lawfully because of a position of trust.

> Embezzlement is broadly defined as the fraudulent appropriation of another's property by a person to whom it has been entrusted or into whose hands it has lawfully come. *Taccariello*, 664 So.2d 1118 (Fla.App. 4 Dist.,1995)

emblements The crops produced by the labor of a tenant.

embracery The crime of corruptly trying to influence a jury by promises, entertainments, etc. Also called jury tampering.

emend To correct or revise.

emergency doctrine 1. One will not be liable for ordinary negligence when confronted with an emergency situation he or she did not aid in creating. Also called imminent peril doctrine, sudden emergency doctrine. 2. A warrantless search is allowed if the police have an objectively reasonable belief that an emergency has occurred and that someone within the residence is in need of immediate assistance. 3. In an emergency, consent to medical treatment for a child or unconscious adult will be implied if no one is available to give express consent.

eminent domain The power of government to take private property for public use upon the payment of just compensation. The exercise of eminent domain is called *condemnation*.

> Eminent domain is the exercise of a government's power to take private property for public good. Eminent domain power is limited by State Constitution provision that any taking of private property for public purpose must be with full compensation to owner. West's F.S.A. Const. Art. 10, § 6. *State, Dept. of Health and Rehabilitative Services*, 418 So.2d 1032 (Fla.App. 2 Dist.,1982)

emolument Payment or other benefit for an occupation or office.

emotional distress Mental or emotional suffering or pain, e.g., depression, shame, worry. Also called mental anguish, mental distress, mental suffering.

empanel See impanel.

employee One hired by another who has the right to control the employee in the material details of how the work is performed.

Employee Retirement Income Security Act (ERISA) A federal statute creating the Pension Benefit Guaranty Corporation to regulate private pension plans (29 USC § 1001) (*www.pbgc.gov*).

employee stock ownership plan (ESOP) An employee benefits plan that primarily invests in the shares of stock of the employer creating the plan.

employers' liability See workers' compensation.

employment at will See at-will employee.

emptor A buyer or purchaser. See also caveat emptor.

enabling statute The statute that allows (enables) an administrative agency to carry out specified delegated powers.

enact To make into a law, particularly by a legislative body.

enacting clause A clause in a statute (often in the preamble) that states the authority by which it is made (e.g., "Be it enacted. . .").

enactment 1. The method or process by which a bill in a legislature becomes a law. 2. A statute.

en banc or **in banc** By the full membership of a court as opposed to one of its smaller groupings or panels. Also called by the full bench or full court.

encroach To trespass, interfere with, or infringe on another's property or rights. Also spelled incroach.

encumbrance Every right to, interest in, or claim on land that diminishes the value of land, e.g., a mortgage or easement. Also spelled incumbrance.

> Encumbrance means a right, other than an ownership interest, in real property. The term includes mortgages and other liens on real property. F.S.A. § 679.1021(1)(ff)

encumbrancer Someone who holds an encumbrance (e.g., a lien) against land.

endorsee See indorsee.

endorsement 1. See indorsement. 2. A modification to an insurance policy. An insurance policy rider.

endorser See indorser.

endowment 1. A special gift or fund for an institution. 2. An endowment insurance policy will pay the insured a stated sum at the end of a definite period, or, if the insured dies before such period, pay the amount to the person designated as beneficiary.

> Endowment fund means an institutional fund, or any part thereof, not wholly expendable by the institution on a current basis under the terms of the applicable gift instrument. F.S.A. § 1010.10(2)(a)

enfeoff To invest someone with a freehold estate. See also feoffment.

enforcement Forcing someone to comply with a law or other obligation.

enfranchisement 1. Giving a right or franchise, e.g., the right to vote. 2. Freeing someone from bondage.

engage 1. To hire or employ. 2. To participate.

English rule See American rule.

engrossment 1. Copying or drafting a document (e.g., a bill) for its final execution or passage. 2. Preparing a deed for execution. 3. Buying up or securing enough of a commodity in order to obtain a monopoly.

engrossed bill The version of a bill passed by one of the chambers of the legislature after incorporating amendments or other changes.

enjoin 1. To require a person to perform or to abstain from some act. 2. To issue an injunction.

enjoyment 1. The ability to exercise a right or privilege. 2. Deriving benefit from possession.

enlarge 1. To make or become bigger. 2. To allow more time.

Enoch Arden doctrine The presumption that a spouse is dead after being missing without explanation for a designated number of years.

enroll To register or record officially.

enrolled agent An attorney or nonattorney authorized to represent taxpayers at the Internal Revenue Service.

enrolled bill A bill that is ready to be sent to the chief executive after both chambers of the legislature have passed it.

entail To impose a limitation on who can inherit real property; it does not pass to all the heirs of the owner.

enter 1. To place anything before a court or on the court record. 2. To go into or onto. 3. To become part of or party to.

enterprise 1. A venture or undertaking, often involving a financial commitment. 2. Any individual, partnership, corporation, association, or other legal entity, and any union or group of individuals associated in fact although not a legal entity. 18 USC § 1961(4). See also RICO.

> Elements necessary to prove an enterprise, as utilized in state racketeering statute are: (1) an ongoing organization, formal or informal, with a common purpose of engaging in a course of conduct, which (2) functions as a continuing unit. F.S.A. § 895.02(3). *Helmadollar*, 811 So.2d 819 (Fla.App. 5 Dist.,2002)

enterprise liability theory Liability for harm caused by a product is spread over the entire industry or enterprise that made the product.

enticement 1. The tort of wrongfully (a) encouraging a wife to leave or stay away from her husband or (b) forcing or encouraging a child to leave or stay away from his or her parent. 2. The crime of luring a child to an area for sexual contact.

entire Whole, without division; indivisible.

entirety The undivided whole; the entire amount or extent. See also tenancy by the entirety.

entitlement 1. The right to benefits, income, or other property. 2. The right to receive a government benefit that cannot be abridged without due process.

entity An organization that has a legally independent existence that is separate from its members.

entrapment Conduct by a government official that instigates or induces the commission of a crime by someone not ready and willing to commit it in order to prosecute him or her for that crime.

> The defense of entrapment prevails when the defendant's criminal design has its origin in the minds of government officials, and where the government officials implant the disposition to commit a crime in the defendant's mind, thereby actively inducing the commission of the crime. *Rogers*, 277 So.2d 838 (Fla.App. 1973)

entry 1. The act of making a notation or record; the notation or record itself. 2. The act of presenting something before the court for or on the record. 3. The right or act of going into or onto real property. 4. Entering a building with one's whole body, a part of the body, or a physical object under one's control (for purposes of burglary).

enumerated Specifically or expressly listed or mentioned (e.g., the enumerated powers of Congress in the U.S. Constitution).

enure See inure.

en ventre sa mere In its mother's womb; an unborn child. Also spelled in ventre sa mere.

environmental impact statement (EIS) A detailed report on the potential positive and negative environmental effects of a proposed project or law.

Environmental Protection Act F.S.A. § 403.412.

envoy A diplomat of the rank of minister or ambassador.

EO See executive order.

eo die On that day.

eo instanti At that instant.

eo nomine By that name.

Equal Employment Opportunity Commission (EEOC) The federal regulatory agency that enforces antidiscrimination laws (*www.eeoc.gov*).

equality The status of being equal in rights, privileges, immunities, opportunities, and duties.

> Equality means two participants operating with the same level of power in a relationship, neither being controlled nor coerced by the other. F.S.A. § 985.03(32)(b)

equalization 1. The act or process of making equal; bringing about uniformity or conformity to a common standard. 2. Adjusting tax assessments to achieve fairness.

equal protection of the law A constitutional guarantee that the government will not deny a person or class of persons the same treatment it gives other persons or other classes under like circumstances. 14th Amendment, U.S. Constitution.

Equal Rights Amendment A proposed amendment to the U.S. Constitution that did not pass. ("Equality of rights under the law shall not be denied or abridged by the United States or by any State on account of sex.")

equipment Implements needed for designated purposes or activities, including goods that do not qualify as consumer goods, farm products, or inventory.

> [T]he term "industrial equipment" includes, but is not limited to, tractors, road rollers, cranes, forklifts, backhoes, and bulldozers. The term "industrial equipment" also includes other vehicles that are propelled by power other than muscular power and that are used in the manufacture of goods or used in the provision of services. F.S.A. § 493.6101(22)

equitable 1. Just; conformable to the principles of what is right. 2. Available or sustainable in equity or under the principles of equity.

equitable adoption A child will be considered the adopted child of a person who agreed to adopt the child but failed to go through the formal adoption procedures.

> To summarize, the child to be adopted pursuant to an agreement between his natural parent and the adoptive parent cannot specifically enforce his adoption by the deceased adoptive parent. But because of the agreement he can obtain specific enforcement of the benefits that would accrue from such adoption. This remedy is sometimes referred to as an equitable adoption. *In re Adoption of R.A.B.*, 426 So.2d 1203 (Fla.App. 4 Dist.,1983)

equitable abstention doctrine Where an order of a state agency predominantly affects local matters, a federal court should refuse to exercise its equity powers to restrain enforcement of the order if adequate state judicial relief is available to the aggrieved party.

equitable action An action seeking equitable remedy relief (e.g., an injunction) rather than damages.

equitable assignment An assignment that, though invalid at law, will be enforced in equity.

equitable defense A defense (e.g., unclean hands, laches) that was once recognized only by courts of equity but is now recognized by all courts.

equitable distribution The fair, but not necessarily equal, division of all marital property upon divorce in a common law property state.

equitable election An obligation to choose between two inconsistent or alternative rights or claims (e.g., a party cannot accept the benefits of a will and also refuse to recognize the validity of the will in other respects).

equitable estate An estate recognized by courts of equity.

equitable estoppel The voluntary conduct of a person will preclude him or her from asserting rights against another who justifiably relied on the conduct and who would suffer damage or injury if the person is now allowed to repudiate the conduct. Also called estoppel in pais.

> Equitable estoppel is the effect of the voluntary conduct of a party whereby he is absolutely precluded, both at law and in equity, from asserting rights which perhaps have otherwise existed, either of property or of contract, or of remedy, as against another person, who has in good faith relied upon such conduct and has been led thereby to change his position for the worse, and who on his part acquires some corresponding right, either of property, or of contract or of remedy. *Major League Baseball*, 790 So.2d 1071 (Fla.,2001)

equitable lien A restitution right enforceable in equity to have a fund or specific property, or its proceeds, applied in whole or part to the payment of a particular debt or class of debts.

equitable mortgage Any agreement to post certain property as security before the security agreement is formulized.

equitable owner The person who is recognized in equity as the owner of the property even though bare legal title to the property is in someone else. Also called beneficial owner.

equitable recoupment Using a claim barred by the statute of limitations as a defense to offset or diminish another party's related claim.

equitable relief An equitable remedy (e.g., injunction, specific performance) that is available when remedies at law (e.g., damages) are not adequate.

equitable restraint doctrine A federal court will not intervene to enjoin a pending state criminal prosecution without a strong showing of bad faith and irreparable injury. Also called Younger abstention. *Younger v. Harris*, 91 S. Ct. 746 (1971).

equitable servitude See restrictive covenant (1).

equitable title 1. The right (enforceable against the trustee) to the beneficial enjoyment of the trust property or corpus under the terms of the trust. 2. The right of the person holding equitable title to have legal title transferred to him or her upon the performance of specified conditions.

> Equitable title is a right, imperfect at law, but which may be perfected by the aid of a court of chancery by compelling parties to do that which in good faith they are bound to do, or removing obstacles interposed in bad faith to the prejudice of another. *Tyler*, 821 So.2d 1121 (Fla.App. 4 Dist.,2002)

equitable tolling A litigant may sue after the statute of limitations has expired if, despite due diligence, he or she was prevented from suing due to inequitable circumstances, e.g., wrongful concealment of vital information by the other party.

equity 1. Justice administered according to fairness in a particular case, as contrasted with strictly formalized rules once followed by common-law courts. 2. Fairness, justice, and impartiality. 3. The monetary value of property in excess of what is owed on it. Net worth. 4. Shares of stock in a corporation.

equity capital The investment of owners in exchange for stock.

equity court A court with the power to apply equitable principles.

equity financing Raising capital by issuing stock, as opposed to bonds.

equity loan A loan to a homeowner that is secured by the amount of equity in the home at the time of the loan. A home equity loan.

equity of redemption Before foreclosure is finalized, the defaulting debtor-mortgagor can recover (redeem) the property upon payment of the debt plus interest and costs. Also called right of redemption.

> Like the legal mortgagor, the land contract buyer has an "equity of redemption" which is a right recognized in equity to redeem his land from the consequences of default in payment of debt secured by the land, by fully paying the debt at any time before the judicial sale of the land becomes final. *White*, 566 So.2d 832 (Fla.App. 5 Dist.,1990)

equivalent 1. Equal in value or effect; essentially equal. 2. Under the doctrine of equivalents, an accused patent infringer cannot avoid liability for infringement by changing only minor or insubstantial details of the claimed invention while retaining the invention's essential identity.

ERA See Equal Rights Amendment.

erase 1. To wipe out or obliterate written words or marks. 2. To seal from public access.

ergo Therefore; consequently.

***Erie* doctrine** Federal courts in diversity cases will apply the substantive law of the state in which the federal court is situated, except as to matters governed by the U.S. Constitution and acts of Congress. *Erie v. Tompkins*, 58 S. Ct. 817 (1938).

ERISA See Employee Retirement Income Security Act.

erroneous Involving error, although not necessarily illegal.

error A mistaken judgment or incorrect belief as to the existence or the consequences of a fact; a false application of the law.

errors and omissions insurance (E&O) Insurance against liability for negligence, omissions, and errors in the practice of a particular profession or business. A form of malpractice insurance for nonintentional wrongdoing.

escalator clause A clause in a contract or lease providing that a payment obligation will increase or decrease depending on a measurable standard such as changing income or the cost-of-living index. Also called fluctuating clause.

escape clause A provision in a contract or other document allowing a party to avoid liability or performance under defined conditions.

escheat A reversion of property to the state upon the death of the owner when no one is available to claim it by will or inheritance.

***Escobedo* rule** Statements of a suspect in custody who is the focus of a police investigation are inadmissible if not told of his or her right to counsel and to remain silent. *Escobedo v. Illinois*, 84 S. Ct. 1758 (1964).

escrow Property (e.g., money, a deed) delivered to a neutral person (e.g., bank, escrow agent) to be held until a specified condition occurs, at which time it is to be delivered to a designated person.

> "Escrow" means the delivery to, or deposit with, an escrow agent of funds or property to be held and disbursed by such escrow agent consistent with the provisions of this act.

"Escrow agent" means: (a) A savings and loan association or bank located in Florida or any other financial institution located in Florida having a net worth in excess of $5 million; (b) An attorney who is a member in good standing of The Florida Bar; (c) A real estate broker . . . ; or (d) A title insurance agent. . . . F.S.A. § 498.005(6)&(7)

ESOP See employee stock ownership plan.

espionage Spying to obtain secret information about the activities or plans of a foreign government or rival company.

Esq. See esquire.

esquire (Esq.) A courtesy title given to an attorney.

essence 1. The gist or substance of something. 2. That which is indispensable. See also time is of the essence.

establish 1. To make or institute. 2. To prove. 3. To make secure.

establishment 1. A business or institution. 2. The act of creating, building, or establishing. 3. Providing governmental sponsorship, aid, or preference. 4. The people or institutions that dominate a society.

Establishment Clause Government cannot establish an official religion, become excessively entangled with religion, nor endorse one form of religion over another. First Amendment, U.S. Constitution.

estate 1. An interest in real or personal property. 2. The extent and nature of one's interest in real or personal property. 3. All of the assets and liabilities of a decedent after he or she dies. 4. All of the property of whatever kind owned by a person. 5. Land.

"Estate" means the property of a decedent that is the subject of administration. F.S.A. § 731.201(12)

estate at sufferance The interest that someone has in land he or she continues to possess after the permission or right to possess it has ended. Also called holdover tenancy, tenancy at sufferance.

estate at will See tenancy at will.

estate by the entirety See tenancy by the entirety.

estate for years An estate whose duration is known at the time it begins. A tenancy for a term.

estate from year to year See periodic tenancy.

estate in common See tenancy in common.

estate in expectancy See future interest.

estate of inheritance An estate that may be inherited.

estate planning Presenting proposals on how a person can have assets distributed at death in a way that will achieve his or her goals while taking maximum advantage of tax and other laws.

estate pur autre vie See life estate pur autre vie.

estate tail See fee tail.

estate tax A tax on the transfer property at death; the tax is based on the value of what passes by will or intestacy. Also called death tax.

estimated tax The current year's anticipated tax that is paid quarterly on income not subject to withholding.

estop To stop or prevent something by estoppel.

estoppel 1. Stopping a party from denying something he or she previously said or did, especially if the denial would harm someone who reasonably relied on it. 2. Stopping a party from relitigating an issue.

Word "estoppel" or "estop," as used in workmen's compensation cases, refers to state of affairs which arises when claimant, employer, or other person does some act or refrains from doing some act which will prevent him from averring anything to contrary at some later time. F.S.A. § 440.29. *Painter*, 223 So.2d 33 (Fla. 1969)

estoppel by deed A party to a deed will be stopped from denying the truth of a fact stated in a deed (e.g., that the party owns the land being transferred) as against someone induced to rely on the deed.

estoppel by judgment See collateral estoppel.

estoppel by laches Denial of relief to a litigant who unreasonably delayed enforcing his or her claim.

estoppel by record See collateral estoppel.

estoppel by silence Estoppel against a person who had a duty to speak, but refrained from doing so and thereby misled another.

estoppel certificate A signed statement certifying that certain facts are correct (e.g., that mortgage payments are current) as of the date of the statement and can be relied upon by third parties.

estoppel in pais See equitable estoppel.

estover 1. The right to use, during a lease, any timber on the leased premises to promote good resource management. 2. Support or alimony.

Estovers signify sustenance, or aliment, or nourishment. *In re Gilbert's Estate*, 36 So.2d 213 (Fla.1948)

et al. And others.

ethical 1. Conforming to minimum standards of professional conduct. 2. Pertaining to moral principles or obligations.

ethics 1. Rules that embody the minimum standards of behavior to which members of an organization are expected to conform. 2. Standards of professional conduct.

et seq. And following. When used after a page or section number, the reference is to several pages or sections after the one mentioned.

et ux. And wife.

et vir. And husband.

Euclidian zoning Comprehensive zoning in which every square foot of the community is within some fixed zone and is subject to the predetermined set of land use restrictions applicable to that zone. Zoning by district.

eurodollar A U.S. dollar on deposit in a bank outside the United States, especially in Europe.

euthanasia The act of painlessly putting to death those persons who are suffering from incurable diseases or conditions. Also called mercy killing.

The act or practice of painlessly putting to death persons suffering from incurable and distressing disease as an act of mercy. *Gilbert*, 487 So.2d 1185 (Fla.App. 4 Dist.,1986)

evasion 1. The act of avoiding something, usually by artifice. 2. The illegal reduction of tax liability, e.g., by underreporting income.

evasive answer An answer that neither admits nor denies a matter.

evergreen agreement A contract that automatically renews itself.

eviction 1. The use of legal process to dispossess a land occupier. 2. Depriving one of land or rental property he or she has held or leased.

evidence Anything that could be offered to prove or disprove an alleged fact. Examples: testimony, documents, fingerprints.

evidence aliunde See extrinsic evidence.

evidentiary fact 1. A subsidiary fact required to prove an ultimate fact. 2. A fact that is evidence of another fact.

evidentiary harpoon Deliberately introducing inadmissible evidence in order to prejudice the jury against the accused.

ex; Ex. without, from, example; Exchequer.

ex aequo et bono According to dictates of equity and what is good.

examination 1. Questioning someone under oath. 2. An inspection.

> "Examination" includes employment tests and other structured, systematic instruments used to assess the essential knowledge, skills, abilities, minimum qualifications, and other job-related requirements possessed by an applicant as a basis for any employment decision by an agency. F.S.A. § 110.215(2)(c)

examination in chief See direct examination.

examined copy A copy of a record or other document that has been compared with the original and often sworn to be a true copy.

examiner One authorized to conduct an examination; one appointed by the court to take testimony of witnesses.

except 1. To leave out. 2. Other than.

exception 1. An objection to an order or ruling of a hearing officer or judge. 2. The act of excluding or separating something out (e.g., a judge excludes something from an order; a grantor retains an interest in property transferred). 3. That which is excluded.

excess Pertaining to an act, amount, or degree that is beyond what is usual, proper, or necessary.

excess insurance Supplemental insurance coverage available once the policy limits of the other insurance policies are exhausted.

> [E]xcess policy means a policy that provides insurance protection for large commercial property risks and that provides a layer of coverage above a primary layer insured by another insurer. F.S.A. § 215.555(2)(c)

excessive Greater than what is usual, proper, or necessary.

excessive bail A sum that is disproportionate to the offense charged and beyond what is reasonably needed to deter evasion by flight.

excess of jurisdiction Action taken by a court or other tribunal that is not within its authority or powers.

excessive verdict A verdict that is clearly exorbitant and shocking.

exchange 1. A transaction (not using money) in which one piece of property is given in return for another piece of property. 2. Swapping things of value. 3. The conversion of the money of one country for that of another. The price of doing so is the rate of exchange. 4. Payment using a bill of exchange or credits. 5. An organization bringing together buyers and sellers of securities or commodities, e.g., New York Stock Exchange.

Exchequer The treasury department in England.

excise A tax that is not directly imposed on persons or property but rather on performing an act (e.g., manufacturing, selling, using), on engaging in an occupation, or on the enjoyment of a privilege.

excited utterance A statement relating to a startling event or condition, made while under the stress of excitement caused by the event or condition. An exception to the hearsay rule.

> Statement qualifies for admission as an "excited utterance" when: there is an event startling enough to cause nervous excitement; the statement was made before there was time for reflection; and the statement was made while the person was under the stress of the excitement from the startling event. West's F.S.A. § 90.803(2). *Charlot*, 679 So.2d 844 (Fla.App. 4 Dist.,1996)

exclusion 1. Denial of entry, admittance, or admission. 2. A person, event, condition, or loss not covered by an insurance policy. 3. Income that does not need to be included in gross income.

exclusionary rule Evidence obtained in violation of the constitution (e.g., an illegal search and seizure), will be inadmissible.

exclusive Not allowing others to participate; restricted; belonging to one person or group.

exclusive agency An agreement in which the owner grants a broker the right to sell property to the exclusion of other brokers, but allows the owner to sell the property through his or her own efforts.

> An "exclusive right to sell" on part of broker divests owner of his inherent right to dispose of his property, whereas an "exclusive agency to sell" merely prohibits placing of property for sale in hands of any other agent but does not prohibit sale of property by owner himself. *Wilkins*, 257 So.2d 573 (Fla.App. 1971)

exclusive jurisdiction The power of a court to hear a particular kind of case to the exclusion of all other courts.

exclusive listing An agreement giving only one broker the right sell the owner's property for a defined period. Also called exclusive agency listing.

ex contractu Arising from or out of a contract.

exculpate To free from guilt or blame.

exculpatory clause A clause in a lease or other contract relieving a party from liability for injury or damages he or she may wrongfully cause.

exculpatory evidence Any evidence tending to show excuse or innocence.

exculpatory-no doctrine An individual who merely supplies a negative and exculpatory response to an investigator's questions cannot be prosecuted for making a false statement to a government agency even if the response is false. The doctrine preserves the individual's self-incrimination protection.

ex curia Out of or away from court.

excusable neglect The failure to take the proper step (e.g., to file an answer) at the proper time that will be excused (forgiven) because the failure was not due to carelessness, inattention, or recklessness but rather was due to (a) an unexpected or unavoidable hindrance or accident, (b) reliance on the care and vigilance of one's attorney, or (c) reliance on promises made by an adverse party.

> To establish "excusable neglect," as required to set aside a default judgment, a party must file an affidavit or a sworn statement that sets forth the facts explaining or justifying

the mistake or inadvertence. *Coquina Beach Club Condominium Ass'n*, 813 So.2d 1061 (Fla.App. 2 Dist.,2002)

excuse A reason one should be relieved of a duty or not be convicted.

ex delicto Arising from a tort, fault, crime, or malfeasance.

ex dividend (x)(xd) Without dividend. Upon purchase of shares ex dividend, the seller, not the buyer, receives the next dividend.

execute 1. To complete, perform, or carry into effect. 2. To sign and do whatever else is needed to finalize a contract or other instrument to make it legal. 3. To enforce a judgment. 4. To put to death.

> Word "executed" means completion of service on a defendant, for purposes of the statute providing that a prosecution is commenced when either an indictment or information is filed, provided the capias, summons, or other process issued on such indictment or information is executed without unreasonable delay. F.S.A. § 775.15(5). *Sutton*, 784 So.2d 1239 (Fla.App. 2 Dist.,2001)

executed contract 1. A contract that has been carried out according to its terms. 2. See execute (2).

executed trust A trust in which nothing remains to be done for it to be carried out.

execution 1. Carrying out or performing some act to its completion. 2. Signing and doing whatever else is needed to finalize a document and make it legal. 3. The process of carrying into effect the decisions in a judgment. A command (via a writ) to a court officer (e.g., sheriff) to seize and sell the property of the losing litigant in order to satisfy the judgment debt. Also called general execution, writ of execution. 4. Implementing a death sentence.

execution sale See forced sale.

executive 1. Pertaining to that branch of government that is charged with carrying out or enforcing the laws. 2. A managing official.

executive agreement An agreement between the United States and another country that does not require the approval of the Senate.

executive clemency See clemency.

executive order (EO) An order issued by the chief executive pursuant to specific statutory authority or to the executive's inherent authority to direct the operation of government agencies and officials.

executive privilege The privilege, based on the separation of powers, that exempts the executive branch from disclosing information in order to protect national security and also to protect confidential advisory and deliberative communications among government officials.

executive session A meeting of a board or governmental unit that is closed to the general public.

executor A person appointed by someone writing a will (a testator) to carry out the provisions of the will.

executory Yet to be executed or performed; remaining to be carried into operation or effect; dependent on a future performance or event.

executory contract A contract that is wholly unperformed or in which substantial duties remain to be performed by both sides.

executory interest A future interest created in one other than the grantor, which is not a remainder and vests upon the happening of a condition or event and in derogation of a vested freehold interest.

executory trust A trust that cannot be carried out until a further conveyance is made. Also called imperfect trust.

executrix A woman appointed by a will to carry it out. A female executor.

exemplar 1. Nontestimonial identification evidence, e.g., fingerprints, blood sample. 2. A typical example; a model.

exemplary damages See punitive damages.

exemplification An official copy of a public record, ready for use as evidence.

exemplified copy See certified copy.

exempt Relieved of a duty others still owe.

exemption 1. Release or freedom from a duty, liability, service, or tax. 2. A right of a debtor to retain a portion of his or her property free from the claims of creditors. 3. A deduction from adjusted gross income.

> "Exemption" means the process by which a proposal that would otherwise require a certificate of need may proceed without a certificate of need. F.S.A. § 408.032(6)

exercise 1. To make use of. 2. To fulfill or perform; to execute.

ex facie On its face; apparently.

ex gratia As a matter of grace; as a favor rather than as required.

exhaustion of remedies Using available dispute-solving avenues (remedies) in an administrative agency before asking a court to review what the agency did.

> The doctrine of "exhaustion of administrative remedies" precludes judicial intervention in executive branch decision making where administrative procedures can afford the relief a litigant seeks. *Florida Fish and Wildlife Conservation Com'n*, 838 So.2d 648 (Fla.App. 1 Dist.,2003)

exhibit 1. A document, chart, or other object offered or introduced into evidence. 2. An attachment to a pleading, instrument, or other document.

exigency (exigence) An urgent need, requiring an immediate response.

exigent circumstances 1. An emergency justifying the bypassing of normal procedures. 2. An emergency requiring swift action to prevent imminent threat to life or property, escape, or destruction of evidence.

exile 1. Banishment from the country. 2. A person banished.

ex officio Because of or by virtue of one's position or office.

exonerate To free or release from (a) guilt, blame or (b) responsibility, duty.

> To exonerate means to free from blame; to exculpate; also, to relieve from the blame or burden of; to relieve or set free from blame, reproach. *Cira*, 903 So.2d 367 (Fla.App. 2 Dist.,2005)

exoneration 1. Releasing or freeing from (a) guilt, blame or (b) responsibility, duty. 2. The right to be reimbursed by reason of having paid what another should be compelled to pay. 3. A surety's right, after the principal's debt has matured, to compel the principal to honor its obligation to the creditor.

ex parte With only one side present; involving one party only.

ex parte order A court order requested by one party and issued without notice to the other party.

expatriation 1. The abandonment of one's country and becoming a citizen or subject of another. 2. Sending someone into exile.

expectancy 1. The bare hope (but more than wishful thinking) of receiving a property interest of another, such as may be entertained by an heir apparent. 2. A reversion or remainder.

expectation damages The cost of restoring the non-breaching party to the position in which it would have been if the contract not been breached. Also called expectancy damages.

expectation of privacy The belief that one's activities and property would be private and free from government intrusion.

> For purposes of the Fourth Amendment, a "reasonable expectation of privacy" exists if individual had exhibited an actual, subjective expectation of privacy which society is prepared to recognize as reasonable. *Randall*, 458 So.2d 822 (Fla.App. 2 Dist.,1984)

expenditure 1. The act of spending or paying out money. 2. An amount spent. An expense.

expense 1. What is spent for goods and services. 2. To treat (write off) as an expense for tax and accounting purposes.

experience rating A method of determining insurance rates by using the loss record (experience) of the insured over a period of time.

expert One who is knowledgeable, through experience or education, in a specialized field.

expert witness A person qualified by scientific, technical, or other specialized knowledge or experience to give an expert opinion relevant to a fact in dispute.

export 1. To carry or send abroad. 2. A commodity that is exported.

expository statute See declaratory statute.

ex post facto After the fact; operating retroactively.

ex post facto law A law that punishes as a crime an act that was innocent when done, that makes punishment more burdensome after its commission, or that deprives one of a defense that was available when the act was committed.

> "Ex post facto" law is one which applies to events occurring before it existed, and which disadvantages affected offender. *Blankenship*, 521 So.2d 1097 (Fla.,1988)

exposure The financial or legal risk one has assumed or could assume.

express Definite; unambiguous and not left to inference. Direct.

express agency The actual agency created when words of the principal specifically authorize the agent to take certain actions.

express authority Authority that the principal explicitly grants the agent to act in the principal's name.

express condition A condition agreed to by the parties themselves rather than imposed by law.

express contract An oral or written agreement whose terms were stated by the parties rather than implied or imposed by law.

> Where an agreement is arrived at by words, oral or written, the contract is said to be an "express contract." *Waite Development*, 866 So.2d 153 (Fla.App. 1 Dist.,2004)

expressio unius est exclusio alterius A canon of interpretation that when an author (e.g., the legislature) expressly mentions one thing, we can assume it intended to exclude what it does not mention.

express malice 1. Ill will, the intent to harm. Actual malice; malice in fact. 2. Harming someone with a deliberate mind or formed design.

express notice See actual notice.

express power A power that is specifically listed or mentioned.

express repeal An overt statement in a statute that it repeals an earlier statute.

express trust A trust created or declared in explicit terms for specific purposes, usually in writing.

express waiver Oral or written statements intentionally and voluntarily relinquishing a known right or privilege.

express warranty A seller's affirmation of fact, description, or specific promise concerning a product that becomes part of the basis of the transaction or bargain.

expropriation The government's taking of private property for public purposes. See also eminent domain.

expulsion A putting or driving out; a permanent cutting off from the privileges of an institution or society.

expunge To erase or eliminate.

expungement of record The process by which the record of a criminal conviction, an arrest, or an adjudication of delinquency is destroyed or sealed after the expiration of a designated period of time.

ex rel. (ex relatione) Upon relation or information. A suit ex rel. is brought by the government in the name of the real party in interest (called the realtor).

ex rights (x)(xr) Without certain rights, e.g., to buy additional securities.

extension 1. An increase in the length of time allowed. 2. An addition or enlargement to a structure.

extenuating circumstances See mitigating circumstances.

exterritoriality See extraterritoriality.

extinguishment The destruction or cancellation of a right, power, contract, or estate.

extort To compel or coerce; to obtain by force, threats, or other wrongful methods.

extortion 1. Obtaining property from another through the wrongful use of actual or threatened force, violence, or fear. 2. The use of an actual or apparent official right (i.e., color of office) to obtain a benefit to which one is not entitled. See also blackmail.

> "Bribery" is offense committed by one corruptly offering, giving, or receiving anything of value to influence his official action, while "extortion" consists in demanding illegal fee or gift to influence official conduct. *Richards*, 197 So. 772 (Fla.1940)

extra 1. Additional. 2. Beyond or outside of.

extradition The surrender by one state (or country) to another of an individual who has been accused or convicted of an offense in the state (or country) demanding the surrender.

extrajudicial Outside of court and litigation. Done or given outside the course of regular judicial proceedings.

A "judicial confession" is one made in court in the due course of legal proceedings, and an "extrajudicial confession" is one made out of court. *Louette v. State* 152 Fla. 495, 12 So.2d 168 (Fla.1943)

extralegal Not governed, regulated, or sanctioned by law.

extraneous evidence See extrinsic evidence.

extraordinary remedy A remedy (e.g., habeas corpus, writ of mandamus) allowed by a court when more traditional remedies are not adequate.

extraordinary session A session of the legislature called to address a matter that cannot wait till the next regular session. Also called special session.

extraordinary writ A special writ (e.g., habeas corpus) using a court's discretionary or unusual power. Also called prerogative writ.

extraterritoriality The exemption of diplomatic personnel from the jurisdiction of the local law of countries where they are posted. Also called exterritoriality.

extrinsic evidence External evidence; evidence that is not contained in the body of an agreement or other document; evidence outside of the writing. Also called extraneous evidence, evidence aliunde.

extrinsic fraud See collateral fraud.

ex warrants (x)(xw) Without warrants. See also warrant (3).

eyewitness A person who saw or experienced the act, fact, or transaction about which he or she is giving testimony.

F

fabricated evidence Evidence that is manufactured or made up with the intent to mislead.

face 1. That which is apparent to a spectator; outward appearance. 2. The front of a document.

face amount 1. The amount of coverage on an insurance policy. 2. See par value.

face value See par value.

facial Pertaining to what is apparent in a document—the words themselves—as opposed to their interpretation.

In a "facial takings claim," the landowner maintains that the mere enactment of the regulation constitutes a taking of all affected property without adequate procedures to provide prompt, just compensation, while in an "as-applied claim," the landowner challenges the regulation in the context of a concrete controversy specifically regarding the impact of the regulation on a particular parcel of property. F.S.A. Const. Art. 10, § 6. *Lost Tree Village Corp.*, 838 So.2d 561 (Fla.App. 4 Dist.,2002)

facilitation Aiding; making it easier for another to commit a crime.

facility of payment clause A provision in an insurance policy permitting the insurer to pay the death benefits to a third person on behalf of the beneficiary.

facsimile 1. An exact copy of the original. 2. Transmitting printed text or pictures by electronic means. Fax.

fact A real occurrence. An event, thing, or state of mind that actually exists or that is alleged to exist, as opposed to its legal consequences.

Issues of fact embrace disputes between the state and the defendant as to what actually existed or occurred at the particular time and place in question. *Simmons*, 36 So.2d 207 (Fla.1948)

fact-finder The person or body with the duty of determining the facts. If there is a jury, it is the fact-finder; if not, it is the judge or hearing officer. Also called trier of fact.

fact-finding The determination of the facts relevant to a dispute by examining evidence.

factor 1. One of the circumstances or considerations that will be weighed in making a decision, no one of which is usually conclusive. 2. A circumstance or influence that brings about or contributes to a result. 3. An agent who is given possession or control of property of the principal and who sells it for a commission. 4. A purchaser of accounts receivable at a discount.

factoring The purchase of accounts receivable at a discounted price.

factor's act A statute that protects good-faith buyers of goods from factors or agents who did not have authority to sell.

fact pleading Pleading those alleged facts that fit within the scope of a legally recognized cause of action. Also called code pleading.

fact question See issue of fact.

factual impossibility Facts unknown by or beyond the control of the actor that prevent the consummation of the crime he or she intends to commit.

factum 1. A fact, deed, or act, e.g., the execution of a will. 2. A statement of facts.

factum probandum The fact to be proved.

factum probans The evidence on the fact to be proved; an evidentiary fact.

failure 1. The lack of success. 2. An omission or neglect of something expected or required. Deficiency.

failure of consideration Failure of performance. The neglect, refusal, or failure of one of the contracting parties to perform or furnish the agreed upon consideration.

Failure of consideration is an affirmative defense and is the neglect, refusal, or failure of one of the parties to perform or furnish the consideration agreed upon. *Torbron*, 579 So.2d 165 (Fla.App. 5 Dist.,1991)

failure of issue Dying without children or other descendants who can inherit. Also called definite failure of issue.

failure to prosecute A litigant's lack of due diligence (e.g., failure to appear) in pursuing a case in court. Want of prosecution.

faint pleader Pleading in a misleading or collusive way.

fair Free from prejudice and favoritism, evenhanded; equitable.

fair comment The honest expression of opinion on a matter of legitimate public interest.

fair hearing A hearing that is conducted according to fundamental principles of procedural justice (due process), including the rights to an impartial decision maker, to present evidence, and to have the decision based on the evidence presented.

fair market value The amount at which property would change hands between a willing buyer and a willing seller, neither being under any compulsion to buy or sell and both having reasonable knowledge of the relevant facts. Also called cash value, market value, true value.

Fair market value, for deficiency judgment purposes, is defined as amount that would be paid for property to willing seller, not compelled to sell, by willing buyer, not compelled to buy, considering all reasonable uses to which property is adapted. *Savers Federal Sav. & Loan Ass'n*, 498 So.2d 519 (Fla.App. 1 Dist.,1986)

fairness doctrine A former rule of the Federal Communications Commission that a broadcaster must provide coverage of issues of public importance that is adequate and that fairly reflects differing viewpoints. Replaced by the equal-time doctrine.

fair preponderance of the evidence See preponderance of the evidence.

fair trade laws Statutes that permitted manufacturers or distributors of brand goods to fix minimum retail prices.

fair trial A trial in which the accused's legal rights are safeguarded, e.g., the procedures are impartial.

fair use The privilege of limited use of copyrighted material without permission of the copyright holder.

fair warning A due process requirement that a criminal statute be sufficiently definite to notify persons of reasonable intelligence that their planned conduct is criminal.

faith 1. Confidence. 2. Reliance or trust in a person, idea, or thing.

false 1. Knowingly, negligently, or innocently untrue. 2. Not genuine.

false advertising A misdescription or deceptive representation of the specific characteristics of products being advertised.

false arrest An arrest made without privilege or legal authority.

false impersonation See false personation.

false imprisonment The intentional confinement within fixed boundaries of someone who is conscious of the confinement or is harmed by it.

> (1) The tort of false imprisonment or false arrest is defined as the unlawful restraint of a person against his will, the gist of which action is the unlawful detention of the plaintiff and the deprivation of his liberty. *Escambia*, 680 So.2d 571 (Fla.App. 1 Dist.,1996). (2) The term false imprisonment means forcibly, by threat, or secretly confining, abducting, imprisoning, or restraining another person without lawful authority and against her or his will. F.S.A. § 787.02(1)(a)

false light An invasion-of-privacy tort committed by unreasonably offensive publicity that places another in a false light.

false personation The crime of falsely representing yourself as someone else for purposes of fraud or deception. Also called false impersonation.

false pretenses Obtaining money or other property by using knowingly false statements of fact with the intent to defraud.

> To constitute offense of obtaining property by false pretenses there must be representation of a past or existing fact or circumstance by defendant to another for purpose of obtaining property from the latter, representation must be false in fact, it must have been made with knowledge of its falsity, with intent to deceive the other party, it must have been believed by other party, who must have parted with his property to defendant because of representation. F.S.A. § 817.01. *Ex parte Stirrup*, 19 So.2d 712 (Fla.1944)

false representation See misrepresentation.

false return 1. A false statement filed by a process server, e.g., falsely stating that he or she served process. 2. An incorrect tax return. A tax return that is knowingly incorrect.

false statement 1. A falsehood. 2. Knowingly stating what is not true. Covering up or concealing a fact.

false swearing See perjury.

false verdict A verdict that is substantially unjust or incorrect.

falsi crimen See crimen falsi.

falsify To forge or alter something in order to deceive. To counterfeit.

family 1. A group of people related by blood, adoption, marriage, or domestic partnership. 2. A group of persons who live in one house and under one head or management.

> Family means the spouse, parent, grandparent, stepmother, stepfather, child, grandchild, brother, sister, half-brother, half-sister, adopted child of parent, or spouse's parent of an injured party. F.S.A. § 90.4026(1)(c)

family car See family purpose.

family court A special court with subject matter jurisdiction over family law matters such as adoption, paternity, and divorce.

family farmer A farmer whose farm has income and debts that qualify it for Chapter 12 bankruptcy relief. 11 USC § 101(18).

family law The body of law that defines relationships, rights, and duties in the formation, existence, and dissolution of marriage and other family units.

family purpose (automobile/car) doctrine The owner of a car who makes it available for family use will be liable for injuries that result from negligent operation of the car by a family member.

Fannie Mae Federal National Mortgage Association (FNMA) (*www.fanniemae.com*).

FAS See free alongside ship.

fascism A system of government characterized by nationalism, totalitarianism, central control, and often, racism.

fatal Pertaining to or causing death or invalidity.

fatal error See prejudicial error.

fatal variance A variance between the indictment and the evidence at trial that deprives the defendant of the due process guarantee of notice of the charges or exposes him or her to double jeopardy.

> Where there was a fatal variance between information and trial testimony as to victim and location of burglary, Green was convicted of uncharged offense, a fundamental error. *Green*, 714 So.2d 594, 595 (Fla. 2d DCA 1998)

***Fatico* hearing** A proceeding to hear arguments on a proposed sentence for the defendant. *Fatico v. U.S.*, 603 F.2d 1053 (2d Cir. 1979).

fault An error or defect in someone's judgment or conduct to which blame and culpability attaches. The wrongful breach of a duty.

favored beneficiary A beneficiary in a will who is suspected of exerting undue influence on the decedent in view of the relative size of what this beneficiary receives under the will.

FBI Federal Bureau of Investigation (*www.fbi.gov*).

FCC Federal Communications Commission (*www.fcc.gov*).

FDA Food and Drug Administration (*www.fda.gov*).

FDIC Federal Deposit Insurance Corporation (*www.fdic.gov*).

fealty Allegiance of a feudal tenant (vassal) to a lord.

feasance The performance of an act or duty.

featherbedding Requiring a company to hire more workers than needed.

Fed 1. Federal. 2. Federal Reserve System (*www.federalreserve.gov*).

federal United States; pertaining to the national government of the United States.

Federal Circuit Court of Appeals for the Federal Circuit (*www.cafc.uscourts.gov*), one of the 13 federal courts of appeal.

federal common law Judge-made law created by federal courts when resolving federal questions.

federal courts Courts with federal jurisdiction created by the U.S. Constitution under Article III or by Congress under Article I. The main federal courts are the U.S. district courts (trial courts), the U.S. circuit courts of appeals, and the U.S. Supreme Court.

federalism The division of powers between the United States (federal) government and the state governments.

federal magistrate See magistrate.

federal preemption See preemption.

federal question A legal issue based on the U.S. Constitution, a statute of Congress, a treaty, or a federal administrative law.

Federal Register (Fed. Reg.) The official daily publication for rules, proposed rules, and notices of federal agencies and organizations, as well as executive orders and other presidential documents (*www.gpoaccess.gov/fr*).

federal rules Rules of procedure that apply in federal courts (*www.uscourts.gov/rules/newrules4.html*).

Federal Tort Claims Act (FTCA) The federal statute that specifies the torts for which the federal government can be sued because it waives sovereign immunity for those torts (28 USC §§ 2671 et seq., 1346).

federation An association or joining together of states, nations, or organizations into a league.

fee 1. Payment for labor or a service. 2. An estate in land that can be passed on by inheritance.

fee division A single billing to a client covering the fee of two or more lawyers who are not in the same firm. Florida Rules of Professional Conduct, Rule 4-1.5

fee simple An estate over which the owner's power of disposition is without condition or limitation, until he or she dies without heirs. Also called fee simple absolute.

> Where any real estate has heretofore been conveyed or granted or shall hereafter be conveyed or granted without there being used in the said deed or conveyance or grant any words of limitation, such as heirs or successors, or similar words, such conveyance or grant, whether heretofore made or hereafter made, shall be construed to vest the fee simple title or other whole estate or interest which the grantor had power to dispose of at that time in the real estate conveyed or granted, unless a contrary intention shall appear in the deed, conveyance, or grant. F.S.A. § 689.10

fee simple absolute See fee simple.

fee simple conditional A fee that is limited or restrained to particular heirs, exclusive of others. Also called conditional fee.

fee simple defeasible A fee that is subject to termination upon the happening of an event or condition.

fee simple determinable A fee subject to the limitation that the property automatically reverts to the grantor upon the occurrence of a specified event.

fee splitting A single bill to a client covering the fee of two or more attorneys who are not in the same law firm.

> A division of legal fees between attorney who handles matters and attorney who referred such to him or her. A dividing of a professional fee for specialist's medical services with the recommending physician. Where a member of a profession divides the compensation he receives from a patient with another member of same profession or any person who has sent patient to him or has called him into consultation. *Practice Management Associates*, 614 So.2d 1135 (Fla.App. 2 Dist.,1993)

fee tail An estate that can be inherited by the lineal heirs, e.g., children (not the collateral heirs) of the first holder of the fee tail. Also called estate tail. If the estate is limited to female lineal heirs, it is a fee tail female; if it is limited to male lineal heirs, it is a fee tail male.

fee tail female; fee tail male See fee tail.

fellow servant rule An employer will not be liable for injuries to an employee caused by the negligence of another employee (a fellow servant). This rule has been changed by workers' compensation law.

felon Someone convicted of a felony.

felonious 1. Malicious. Done with the intent to commit a serious crime. 2. Concerning a felony.

felonious assault A criminal assault that amounts to a felony.

felonious homicide Killing another without justification or excuse.

felony Any crime punishable by death or imprisonment for a term exceeding a year; a crime more serious than a misdemeanor.

> Felony means a criminal offense that is punishable under the laws of this state, or that would be punishable if committed in this state, by death or imprisonment in the state penitentiary; a crime in any other state or a crime against the United States which is designated as a felony; or an offense in any other state, territory, or country punishable by imprisonment for a term exceeding one year. F.S.A. § 493.6101(23)

felony murder rule An unintended death resulting from the commission or attempted commission of certain felonies is murder.

feme covert A married woman.

feme sole An unmarried woman.

fence 1. A receiver of stolen property. 2. To sell stolen property to a fence. 3. An enclosure or boundary about a field or other space.

feoffee One to whom a feoffment is conveyed. A feoffor conveys it.

feoffment The grant of land as a fee simple (i.e., full ownership of an estate). The grant of a freehold estate.

ferae naturae Of a wild nature; untamed, undomesticated.

Feres **doctrine** The federal government is not liable under the Federal Tort Claims Act for injuries to members of the armed services where the injuries arise incident to military service. (*Feres v. U.S.*, 71 S. Ct. 153 (1950)

fertile octogenarian rule A person is conclusively presumed to be able to have children (and therefore heirs) at any age.

feudalism A social and political system in medieval Europe in which laborers (serfs) were bound to and granted the use of land in return for services provided to their lords.

FHA Federal Housing Administration (*www.hud.gov/offices/hsg/fhahistory.cfm*).

fiat 1. An authoritative order or decree. 2. An arbitrary command.

FICA Federal Insurance Contributions Act (a statute on social security payroll taxes).

fiction of law See legal fiction.

fictitious 1. Based on a legal fiction. 2. False; imaginary.

fictitious name 1. The name to be used by a business. A d/b/a (doing business as) name. 2. An alias.

> Name used by plaintiff partnership in action on deposit receipt contract was a "fictitious name" within contemplation of statutory definition because it did not reasonably reveal to defendant the names of the partners. F.S.A. §§ 865.09, 865.09(2)(b), (5). *Aronovitz*, 322 So.2d 74 (Fla.App. 1975)

fictitious payee A payee on a check named by the drawer or maker without intending this payee to have any right to its proceeds.

fictitious person See artificial person.

fidelity bond or **insurance** A contract whereby the insurer agrees to indemnify the insured against loss resulting from the dishonesty of an employee or other person holding a position of trust.

> Insurance guaranteeing the fidelity of persons holding positions of public or private trust, or indemnifying banks, thrifts, brokers, or other financial institutions against loss of money, securities, negotiable instruments, other specified valuable papers, or tangible items of personal property caused by larceny, misplacement, destruction, or other stated perils, including loss while being transported in an armored motor vehicle or by messenger and including insurance for loss caused by the forgery of signatures on, or alteration of, specified documents and valuable papers. F.S.A. § 624.6065(1)

fides Faith, honesty, veracity.

fiduciary One whose duty is to act in the interests of another with a high standard of care. Someone in whom another has a right to place great trust and to expect great loyalty.

fiduciary bond A bond that a court requires of fiduciaries (e.g., trustees, executors) to guarantee the performance of their duties.

fiduciary duty A duty to act with the highest standard of care and loyalty for another's benefit, always subordinating one's own personal interests.

fiduciary relationship A relationship in which one owes a fiduciary duty (see this phrase) to another, e.g., attorney-client relationship. Also called confidential relationship.

> Fiduciary relationship means a relationship based upon the trust and confidence of the vulnerable adult in the caregiver, relative, household member, or other person entrusted with the use or management of the property or assets of the vulnerable adult. F.S.A. § 415.102(10)

fiduciary shield doctrine A person's business in a state solely as a corporate officer does not create personal jurisdiction over that person.

field warehousing Financing by pledging inventory under the control of the lender or a warehouser working on behalf of the lender.

fieri facias (fi. fa.) A writ or order to a sheriff to seize and sell the debtor's property to enforce (satisfy) a judgment.

fi. fa. See fieri facias.

FIFO First in, first out. An inventory flow assumption by which the first goods purchased are assumed to be the first goods used or sold.

Fifth Amendment The amendment to the U.S. Constitution that provides rights pertaining to grand juries, double jeopardy, self-incrimination, due process of law, and just compensation for the taking of private property.

fighting words Words likely to provoke a violent reaction when heard by an ordinary citizen and consequently may not have free-speech protection.

> For purpose of the disorderly conduct statute which, in application to verbal conduct, is constitutionally limited to "fighting words" or false words reporting a physical hazard and likely to cause harm, "fighting words" are those which are likely to cause the average person to whom they are addressed to fight. West's F.S.A. Const. Art. 1, § 4; F.S.A. § 877.03; *Clanton*, 357 So.2d 455 (Fla.App. 1978)

file 1. To deliver a document to a court officer so that it can become part of the official collection of documents in a case. To deliver a document to a government agency. 2. To commence a lawsuit. 3. A law firm's collection of documents for a current or closed case.

file wrapper The entire record of the proceedings on an application in the U.S. Patent and Trademark Office. Also called prosecution history.

file wrapper estoppel One cannot recapture in an infringement action the breadth of a patent previously surrendered in the patent office.

filiation 1. The relationship between parent and child. 2. A court determination of paternity.

filiation proceeding A judicial proceeding to establish paternity.

filibuster A tactic to delay or obstruct proposed legislation, e.g., engaging in prolonged speeches on the floor of the legislature.

filing A document delivered to a court or government agency.

filius nullius ("son of nobody") An illegitimate child.

final 1. Not requiring further judicial or official action. 2. Conclusive. 3. Last.

final argument See closing argument.

final judgment; final decree A judgment or decree that resolves all issues in a case, leaving nothing for future determination other than the execution or enforcement of the judgment.

> Final judgment means a judgment, including any supporting opinion, that determines the rights of the parties and concerning which appellate remedies have been exhausted or the time for appeal has expired. F.S.A. § 501.203(1)

final submission Completing the presentation (including arguments) of everything a litigating party has to offer on the facts and law.

finance 1. To supply with funds; to provide with capital or loan money to. 2. The management of money, credit, investments, etc.

finance charge The extra cost (e.g., interest) imposed for the privilege of deferring payment of the purchase price.

> Finance charge means the cost of consumer credit as a dollar amount. The term "finance charge" includes any charge payable directly or indirectly by the buyer and imposed directly or indirectly by the seller as an incident to or a condition of the extension of credit. The term "finance charge" does not include any charge of a type payable in a comparable cash transaction. F.S.A. § 520.02(6)

finance company A company engaged in the business of making loans.

financial institution A bank, trust company, credit union, savings and loan association, or similar institution engaged in financial transactions with the public such as receiving, holding, investing, or lending money.

financial responsibility law A law requiring owners of motor vehicles to prove (through personal assets or insurance) that they can satisfy judgments against them involving the operation of the vehicles.

financial statement A report summarizing the financial condition of an organization or individual on or for a certain date or period.

financing statement A document filed as a public record to notify third parties, e.g., prospective buyers or lenders, that there may be an enforceable security interest in specific property.

find To make a determination of what the facts are.

finder Someone who finds or locates something for another. An intermediary who brings parties together (e.g., someone who secures mortgage financing for a borrower).

finder of fact See fact-finder.

finder's fee A fee paid to someone for finding something or for bringing parties together for a business transaction.

finding of fact The determination of a fact. A conclusion, after considering evidence, on the existence or nonexistence of a fact.

fine 1. To order someone to pay a sum of money to the state as a criminal or civil penalty. 2. The money so paid.

fine print The part of an agreement or other document containing exceptions, disclaimers, or other details, often difficult to read.

fingerprint The unique pattern of lines on a person's fingertip that can be made into an impression, often for purposes of identification.

firefighter's rule Negligence in causing a fire or other dangerous situation furnishes no basis for liability to a firefighter, police officer, or other professional who is injured while responding to the danger.

> *Potts v. Johnson*, 654 So.2d 596, 598 (Fla. 3d DCA 1995) § 112.182, Fla.Stat.(1990) abolished the common law rule, the "firefighter rule," that firefighters and police officers upon the land of another while carrying out their official duties occupied the status of a mere licensee. *Worth*, 697 So.2d 945 (Fla.App. 4 Dist.,1997)

firm 1. A business or professional entity. 2. Fixed, binding. See also law firm.

firm offer An offer that remains open and binding (irrevocable) for a period of time until accepted or rejected.

First Amendment The amendment to the U.S. Constitution that provides rights pertaining to the establishment and free exercise of religion, freedom of speech and press, peaceful assembly, and petitioning the government.

first degree The most serious level of an offense.

first-degree murder Killing another with premeditation, with extreme cruelty or atrocity, or while committing another designated felony.

first impression Concerning an issue being addressed for the first time.

first in, first out See FIFO.

first lien; first mortgage A lien or mortgage with priority that must be satisfied before other liens or mortgages on the same property.

first offender A person convicted of a crime for the first time and who, therefore, may be entitled to more lenient sentencing or treatment.

first refusal See right of first refusal.

fiscal Pertaining to financial matters, e.g., revenue, debt, expenses.

fiscal year Any 12 consecutive months chosen by a business as its accounting period (e.g., 7/01/08 to 6/30/09).

> "Fiscal year" means an accounting period of 12 months or less ending on the last day of any month other than December. . . . F.S.A. § 220.03(1)

fishing expedition Unfocused questioning or investigation. Improper discovery undertaken with the purpose of finding an issue.

fitness for a particular purpose See warranty of fitness for a particular purpose.

fix 1. To determine or establish something, e.g., price, rate. 2. To prearrange something dishonestly. 3. To fasten or repair. 4. An injection or dose of heroin or other illegal drug.

fixed asset An asset (e.g., machinery, land) held long-term and used to produce goods and services. Also called capital assets.

fixed capital Fixed assets. Money invested in fixed assets.

> Fixed capital outlay means the appropriation category used to fund real property (land, buildings, including appurtenances, fixtures and fixed equipment, structures, etc.), including additions, replacements, major repairs, and renovations to real property which materially extend its useful life or materially improve or change its functional use and including furniture and equipment necessary to furnish and operate a new or improved facility, when appropriated by the Legislature in the fixed capital outlay appropriation category. F.S.A. § 216.011(1)(p)

fixed charges Expenses or costs that must be paid regardless of the condition of the business (e.g., tax payments, overhead).

fixed income Income that does not fluctuate (e.g., interest on a bond).

fixed liability 1. A debt that is certain as to obligation and amount. 2. A debt that will not mature soon; a long-term debt.

fixed rate An interest rate that does not vary for the term of the loan.

fixture Something that is so attached to land as to be deemed a part of it. An item of personal property that is now so connected to the land that it cannot be removed without substantial injury to itself or the land.

> "Fixtures" means items that are an accessory to a building, other structure, or land and that do not lose their identity as accessories when installed but that do become permanently attached to realty. F.S.A. § 212.06(14)(b)

flagrante delicto See in flagrante delicto.

flat rate A fixed payment regardless of how much of a service is used.

flight Fleeing to avoid arrest or detention.

float 1. The time between the writing of a check and the withdrawal of the funds that will cover it. 2. The total amount representing checks in the process of collection. 3. To allow a given currency to freely establish its own value as against other currencies in response to supply and demand.

floater policy An insurance policy that is issued to cover items that have no fixed location (e.g., jewelry that is worn).

floating capital Funds available for current needs; capital in circulation.

floating debt Short-term debt for current needs.

floating interest rate A rate of interest that is not fixed; the rate may fluctuate by market conditions or be pegged to an index.

floating lien A lien on present and after-acquired assets of the debtor during the period of the loan.

floating zone A special detailed use district of undetermined location; it "floats" over the area where it may be established.

floor 1. The minimum or lowest limit. 2. Where legislators sit and cast their votes. 3. The right of someone to address the assembly.

floor plan financing A loan secured by the items for sale and paid off as the items are sold.

Florida Registered Paralegal (FRP) One who meets the definition of paralegal (see this term in the dictionary) and the requirements for registration with The Florida Bar as set forth in the Rules Regulating The Florida Bar, Rule 20-2.1(a) (see also section 1.1).

flotsam Goods that float on the sea when cast overboard or abandoned.

> Where a ship is derelict, or where goods have been thrown out of a vessel to lighten her (jetsam), or have been sunk but tied to some floating mark to show the place (lagan) or have been washed out of the ship and remain afloat (flotsam), in those cases, also, the property belongs to the Crown in its office of Admiralty, unless the owner establishes his claim to it. *State By and Through Ervin*, 95 So.2d 902 (Fla.1957)

FLSA Fair Labor Standards Act (29 USC § 201) (*www.dol.gov/esa/whd/flsa*).

FNC See forum non conveniens.

FOB See free on board.

FOIA See Freedom of Information Act.

follow 1. To accept as authority. 2. To go or come after.

forbearance Deciding not to take action, e.g., to collect a debt.

for cause For a reason relevant to one's ability and fitness to perform a duty as a juror, employee, fiduciary, etc.

force Strength or pressure directed to an end; physical coercion.

forced heir A person who by law must receive a portion of a testator's estate even if the latter tries to disinherit that person.

forced sale 1. A court-ordered sale of property to satisfy a judgment. Also called execution sale. 2. A sale one is pressured to make.

force majeure An unexpected event; an irresistible and superior force that could not have been foreseen or avoided.

forcible detainer 1. Unlawfully (and often by force) keeping possession of land to which one is no longer entitled. 2. See forcible entry and detainer.

forcible entry Taking possession of land with force or threats of violence. Using physical force to enter land or gain entry into a building.

forcible entry and detainer 1. A summary, speedy, and adequate remedy to obtain the return of possession of land to which one is entitled. Also called forcible detainer. 2. Using physical force or threats of violence to obtain and keep possession of land unlawfully.

foreclosure The procedure to terminate the rights of a defaulting mortgagor in property that secured the mortgagor's debt. The lender-mortgagee can then sell the property to satisfy the remaining debt.

> In foreclosure, the unpaid amount of the debt is determined and the owner is given one last opportunity to "redeem" his property by payment of all sums due, failing which the property is sold at public sale conducted under court authority and the proceeds of the sale are applied to pay or reduce the unpaid balance on the debt, with any surplus available to those having inferior rights in the mortgaged property. *Cain & Bultman, Inc.*, 409 So.2d 114 (Fla.App. 5 Dist., 1982)

foreign Pertaining to another country or to one of the 50 states of the United States other than the state you are in.

foreign administrator A person appointed in another state or jurisdiction to manage the estate of the deceased.

foreign commerce Trade involving more than one nation.

foreign corporation A corporation chartered or incorporated in one state or country but doing business in another state or country.

foreign exchange 1. The currency of another country. 2. Buying, selling, or converting one country's currency for that of another.

foreman 1. The presiding member and spokesperson of a jury. 2. A superintendent or supervisor of other workers. Also called foreperson.

forensic 1. Belonging to or suitable in courts of law. 2. Pertaining to the use of scientific techniques to discover and examine evidence. 3. Concerning argumentation. 4. Forensics: ballistics or firearms evidence.

forensic medicine The science of applying medical knowledge and techniques in court proceedings to discover and interpret evidence.

"Forensic client" or "client" means any defendant who is mentally ill, retarded, or autistic and who is committed to the department pursuant to this chapter and: (a) Who has been determined to need treatment for a mental illness or training for retardation or autism; (b) Who has been found incompetent to proceed on a felony offense or has been acquitted of a felony offense by reason of insanity; (c) Who has been determined by the department to: 1. Be dangerous to himself or herself or others; or 2. Present a clear and present potential to escape; and (d) Who is an adult or a juvenile prosecuted as an adult. F.S.A. § 916.106(7)

foreperson See foreman.

foreseeability The extent to which something can be known in advance; reasonable anticipation of something.

forestalling the market Buying products on their way to market in order to resell them at a higher price.

forfeiture The loss of property, rights, or privileges because of penalty, breach of duty, or the failure to make a timely claim of them.

> Generally, a forfeiture is a loss of some right or property as a penalty for some illegal act or because of breach of a legal obligation. *Brinkley*, 769 So.2d 468 (Fla.App. 5 Dist.,2000)

forgery 1. Making a false document or altering a real one with the intent to commit a fraud. 2. The document or thing that is forged.

form 1. Technical matters of style, structure, and format not involving the merits or substance of something. 2. A document, usually preprinted as a model, to be filled in and adapted to one's needs. 3. See forms of action.

formal 1. Following accepted procedures or customs. 2. Pertaining to matters of form as opposed to content or substance. 3. Ceremonial.

formal contract 1. A contract under seal or other contract that complies with prescribed formalities. 2. A contract in writing.

forma pauperis See in forma pauperis.

former adjudication See collateral estoppel and res judicata on when a former adjudication (prior judgment) on the merits will prevent relitigating issues and claims.

former jeopardy, defense of A person cannot be tried or prosecuted for the same offense more than once. See also double jeopardy.

> "Former jeopardy" is constitutional and statutory guarantee that an accused will not be put in jeopardy twice for the same offense. F.S.A. Const. Art. 1, § 9. *State v. Fisher*, 264 So.2d 857 (Fla.App. 1972)

forms of action The procedural devices or actions (e.g., trespass on the case) that are used to take advantage of common-law theories of liability.

fornication Sexual relations between unmarried persons or between married persons who are not married to each other.

> Fornication is sexual intercourse between an unmarried man or a married man and an unmarried woman. F.S.A. § 798.03. *Tatzel v. State*, 356 So.2d 787 (Fla. 1978)

forswear 1. To give up something completely. To renounce something under oath. 2. To swear falsely; to commit perjury.

forthwith Without delay; immediately.

fortiori See a fortiori.

fortuitous Happening by chance or accident rather than by design.

forum 1. The court; the court where the litigation is brought. 2. A setting or place for public discussion.

forum domicilii The court in the jurisdiction where a party is domiciled.

forum non conveniens (FNC) The discretionary power of a court to decline the exercise of the jurisdiction it has when the convenience of the parties and the ends of justice would be better served if the action were brought and tried in another forum that also has jurisdiction.

> "Forum non conveniens" is a common law doctrine addressing the problem that arises when a local court technically has jurisdiction over a suit but the cause of action may be fairly and more conveniently litigated elsewhere. F.S.A. RCP Rule 1.061. *Strauss*, 855 So.2d 167 (Fla.App. 4 Dist.,2003)

forum rei The court in the jurisdiction where the defendant is domiciled or the subject matter of the case is located.

forum selection clause A contract clause stating that any future litigation between the parties will be conducted in a specified forum (jurisdiction).

forum shopping Choosing a court or jurisdiction where you are most likely to win.

forward contract An agreement to buy or sell goods at a specified time in the future at a price established when the contract is entered. The agreement is not traded on an exchange.

foster home A home that provides shelter and substitute family care temporarily or for extended periods when a child's own family cannot properly care for him or her, often due to neglect or delinquency.

foundation 1. A fund for charitable, educational, religious, or other benevolent purpose. 2. The underlying basis or support for something. Evidence that shows the relevance of other evidence.

founder One who establishes something, e.g., an institution or trust fund.

founding father A leader in establishing a country or organization.

four corners The contents of a written document; what is written on the surface or face of a document.

four-corners rule 1. The intention of the parties to a contract or other instrument is to be ascertained from the document as a whole and not from isolated parts thereof. 2. If a contract is clear on its face, no evidence outside the contract may be considered to contradict its terms.

frame 1. To formulate or draft. 2. To produce false evidence that causes an innocent person to appear guilty.

franchise 1. The right to vote. 2. A contract that allows a business (the franchisee) the sole right to use the intellectual property and brand identity, marketing experience, and operational methods of another business (the franchisor) in a certain area. 3. A government authorization to engage in a specified commercial endeavor or to incorporate.

> A "franchise" is a special privilege conferred by the government on individuals or corporations that does not belong to the citizens of a country generally by common right. *Alachua County*, 737 So.2d 1065 (Fla.,1999)

franchisee The person or entity granted a franchise.

franchise tax A tax on the privilege of engaging in a business.

franchisor The person or entity that grants a franchise.

franking privilege The privilege of sending certain matter through the mail without paying postage. Also called frank.

fraternal benefit association or **society** A nonprofit association of persons of similar calling or background who aid and assist one another and promote worthy causes.

fratricide The killing of a brother or sister.

fraud A false statement of material fact made with the intent to mislead by having the victim rely on the statement. A tort is committed if the victim suffers actual damage due to justifiable reliance on the statement.

> "Fraud" is a knowing false statement of fact made with intent that it cause action in reliance and it does cause such action to detriment of victim of knowing false statement. *La Pesca Grande Charters*, 704 So.2d 710 (Fla.App. 5 Dist.,1998)
>
> "Fraud" or "fraudulent" denotes conduct having a purpose to deceive and not merely negligent misrepresentation or failure to apprise another of relevant information. Florida Rules of Professional Conduct, Preamble

fraud in fact See positive fraud.

fraud in law Constructive or presumed fraud.

fraud in the factum A misrepresentation about the essential nature or existence of the document itself.

fraud in the inducement Misrepresentation as to the terms other aspects of a contractual relation, venture, or other transaction that leads (induces) a person to agree to enter into the transaction with a false impression or understanding of the risks or obligations he or she has undertaken.

fraud on the market theory When false information artificially inflates the value of a stock, it is presumed that purchasers on the open market relied on that information to their detriment.

Frauds, statute of See statute of frauds.

fraudulent Involving fraud.

> For the purposes of this section, a person commits a "fraudulent insurance act" if the person knowingly and with intent to defraud presents . . . any written statement as part of . . . or in support of, an application for the issuance of . . . any insurance policy, or a claim for payment . . . which the person knows to contain materially false information concerning any fact material thereto or if the person conceals, for the purpose of misleading another, information concerning any fact material thereto. F.S.A. § 626.989(1)

fraudulent concealment 1. Taking affirmative steps to hide or suppress a material fact that one is legally or morally bound to disclose. 2. An equitable doctrine that estops a defendant who concealed his or her wrongful conduct from asserting the statute of limitations.

fraudulent conveyance Transferring property without fair consideration in order to place the property beyond the reach of creditors.

FRCP Federal Rules of Civil Procedure. See federal rules.

free 1. Not subject to the legal constraint of another. 2. Not subject to a burden. 3. Having political rights. 4. To liberate. 5. Without cost.

> For the purposes of this subsection, a "free" service warranty is: 1. A service warranty for which no identifiable and additional charge is made to the purchaser of such real property, personal property, or services. . . . F.S.A. § 634.436(b)

free alongside ship (FAS) The quoted price includes the cost of delivering the goods to a designated point alongside of the ship. The risk of loss is with the seller up to this point.

free and clear Not subject to liens or other encumbrances.

freedom of association The right protected in the First Amendment to join with others for lawful purposes.

freedom of contract The right of parties to enter a bargain of their choice subject to reasonable government regulation in the interest of public health, safety, and morals.

freedom of expression The rights protected in the First Amendment concerning freedom of speech, press, and religion.

Freedom of Information Act (FOIA) A federal statute making information held by federal agencies available to the public unless the information is exempt from public disclosure (5 USC § 552). Many states have equivalent statutes for state agencies.

freedom of religion The right protected in the First Amendment to believe and practice one's form of religion or to believe in no religion. In addition, the right to be free of governmental promotion of religion or interference with one's practice of religion.

freedom of speech The right protected in the First Amendment to express one's ideas without government restrictions subject to the right of the government to protect public safety and to provide a remedy for defamation.

freedom of the press The First Amendment prohibition against government restrictions that abridge the freedom of the press such as imposing prior restraint or censorship.

freedom of the seas The right of ships to travel without restriction in the sea beyond the territorial waters of any nation.

free exercise clause The clause in the First Amendment stating that "Congress shall make no law . . . prohibiting the free exercise" of religion.

freehold An estate in land for life, in fee simple, or in fee tail. An estate in real property of uncertain or unlimited duration, unlike a leasehold, which is for a definite period of time.

freelance paralegal See independent paralegal.

free on board (FOB) In a sales price quotation, the seller assumes all responsibilities and costs up to the point of delivery on board.

> Unless otherwise agreed the term "F.O.B." (which means "free on board") at a named place, even though used only in connection with the stated price, is a delivery term under which: (a) When the term is "F.O.B. the place of shipment," the seller must at that place ship the goods in the manner provided in this chapter § 672.504) and bear the expense and risk of putting them into the possession of the carrier; or (b) When the term is "F.O.B. the place of destination," the seller must at her or his own expense and risk transport the goods to that place and there tender delivery of them in the manner provided in this chapter (§ 672.503); . . . F.S.A. § 672.319(1)

freeze To hold something (e.g., wages, prices) at a fixed level; to immobilize or maintain the status quo.

freeze-out Action by major shareholders or a board of directors to eliminate minority shareholders or to marginalize their power.

fresh Prompt; without material interval.

fresh complaint rule A victim's complaint of sexual assault made to another person soon after the event is admissible.

fresh pursuit 1. A police officer, engaged in a continuous and uninterrupted pursuit, can cross geographic or jurisdictional lines to arrest a felon even if the officer does not have a warrant. 2. A victim of property theft can use reasonable force to obtain it back just after it is taken. Also called hot pursuit.

> "Fresh pursuit exception" allows officers, who attempt to detain or arrest within their territorial jurisdiction, to continue to pursue fleeing suspects even though suspect crosses jurisdictional lines. West's F.S.A. § 901.25. *State v. Phoenix*, 428 So.2d 262 (Fla.App. 4 Dist.,1982)

friendly Pertaining to someone who is favorably disposed; not hostile.

friendly suit A suit brought by agreement between the parties to obtain the opinion of the court on their dispute.

friend of the court See amicus curiae.

friendly takeover The acquisition of one company by another that is approved by the boards of directors of both companies.

fringe benefits Benefits provided by an employer that are in addition to the employee's regular compensation (e.g., vacation).

frisk To conduct a pat-down search of a suspect in order to find concealed weapons.

frivolous 1. Involving a legal position that cannot be supported by a good-faith argument based on existing law or on the need for a change in the law. 2. Clearly insufficient on its face.

> "Frivolous action," which requires award of attorney fee's to opposing party, is one that is so readily recognizable as devoid of merit on face of record that its character may be determined without argument or research. F.S.A. § 57.105. *Wood*, 546 So.2d 88 (Fla.App. 2 Dist.,1989)

frivolous appeal An appeal that is devoid of merit or one that has no reasonable chance of succeeding.

frolic Employee conduct outside the scope of employment because it is personal rather than primarily for the employer's business.

front A person or organization acting as a cover for illegal activities or to disguise the identity of the real owner or principal.

frontage The land between a building and the street; the front part of property.

front-end load A sales fee or commission (the load) levied at the time of making a stock or mutual fund purchase.

frozen assets Nonliquid assets. Assets that cannot be easily converted into cash.

FRP See Florida Registered Paralegal (and section 1.1).

fructus The fruit or produce of land.

fruit 1. The effect, consequence, or product of something. 2. Evidence resulting from an activity.

fruit and tree doctrine One cannot avoid taxation on income simply by assigning it to someone else.

fruit of the poisonous tree doctrine Evidence derived directly or indirectly from illegal governmental activity (e.g., an illegal search and seizure), is inadmissible as trial evidence.

> "Fruit of the poisonous tree doctrine" is a court-made exclusionary rule which forbids the use of evidence in court if it is the product or fruit of a search or seizure or interrogation carried out in violation of constitutional rights. *Hatcher*, 834 So.2d 314 (Fla.App. 5 Dist.,2003)

fruits of crime Stolen goods or other products of criminal conduct.

frustration Preventing something from occurring. Rendering something ineffectual.

frustration of contract or **purpose** See commercial frustration.

FTC Federal Trade Commission (*www.ftc.gov*).

fugitive One who flees in order to avoid arrest, prosecution, prison, service of process, or subpoena to testify (18 USC § 1073).

full age See age of majority.

full bench; full court See en banc.

full coverage Insurance with no exclusions or deductibles.

full faith and credit A state must recognize and enforce (give full faith and credit to) the legislative acts, public records, and judicial decisions of sister states. U.S. Constitution, Art. IV, § 1.

full settlement An adjustment of all pending matters and the mutual release of all prior obligations existing between the parties.

full warranty A warranty that covers labor and parts for all defects.

functus officio Without further official authority once the authorized task is complete.

fund 1. Money or other resources available for a specific purpose. 2. A group or organization that administers or manages money. 3. To convert into fixed-interest, long-term debt.

fundamental Serving as an essential component; basic.

fundamental error See plain error.

fundamental law Constitutional law; the law establishing basic rights and governing principles.

fundamental right A basic right that is either explicitly or implicitly guaranteed by the constitution.

funded debt 1. A debt that has resources earmarked for the payment of interest and principal as they become due. 2. Long-term debt that has replaced short-term debt.

fungible Commercially interchangeable; substitutable; able to be replaced by other assets of the same kind. Examples: grain, sugar, oil.

> "Fungible" with respect to goods or securities means goods or securities of which any unit is, by nature or usage of trade, the equivalent of any other like unit. Goods which are not fungible shall be deemed fungible for the purposes of this code to the extent that under a particular agreement or document unlike units are treated as equivalents. F.S.A. § 671.201(17)

future advances Funds advanced by a lender after creation of, but still secured by, the mortgage or other security agreement.

future damages Sums awarded for future pain and suffering, impairment of earning capacity, future medical expenses, and other future losses.

future earnings Income that a party is no longer able to earn because of injury or loss of employment.

future estate See future interest.

future interest An interest in real or personal property in which possession, use, or other enjoyment is future rather than present. Also called estate in expectancy, future estate.

> "Future interest" means an interest that takes effect in possession or enjoyment, if at all, later than the time of its creation. F.S.A. § 739.102(7)

futures Commodities or securities sold or bought for delivery in the future.

futures contract A contract for the sale or purchase of a commodity or security at a specified price and quantity for future delivery.

FY Fiscal year.

G

GAAP Generally Accepted Accounting Principles.

gag order 1. A court order to stop attorneys, witnesses, or media from discussing a current case. 2. An order by the court to bind and gag a disruptive defendant during his or her trial.

gain 1. Profit; excess of receipts over costs. 2. Increments of value.

gainful employment Available work for pay.

gambling Risking money or other property for the possibility—chance—of a reward. Also called gaming.

game laws Laws regulating the hunting of wild animals and birds.

gaming See gambling.

GAO General Accountability Office (*www.gao.gov*).

gaol A place of detention for temporary or short-term confinement; jail.

garnishee; garnishor (garnisher) A garnishee is the person or entity in possession of a debtor's property that is being reached or attached (via garnishment) by a creditor of the debtor. The creditor is the garnishor (garnisher).

garnishment A court proceeding by a creditor to force a third party in possession of the debtor's property (e.g., wages) to turn the property over to the creditor to satisfy the debt.

> Garnishment consists of notifying a third party to retain something he has belonging to defendant, to make disclosure to the court concerning it, and to dispose of it as court shall direct. *Schlosser*, 602 So.2d 628 (Fla.App. 2 Dist.,1992)

gavelkind A feudal system under which all sons shared land equally upon the death of their father.

gender discrimination Discrimination based on one's sex or gender.

GBMI Guilty but mentally ill. See also insanity.

general administrator A person given a grant of authority to administer the entire estate of a decedent who dies without a will.

general agent An agent authorized to conduct all of the principal's business affairs, usually involving a continuity of service.

general appearance Acts of a party from which it can reasonably be inferred that the party submits (consents) to the full jurisdiction of the court.

> When party appears in court to contest subject matter jurisdiction, that party has made "general appearance" which results in waiver of defense of lack of personal jurisdiction. *Coto-Ojeda*, 642 So.2d 587 (Fla.App. 3 Dist.,1994)

general assembly A legislative body in some states.

general assignment A transfer of a debtor's property for the benefit of all creditors. See also assignment for benefit of creditors.

general average contribution rule When one engaged in a maritime venture voluntarily incurs a loss (e.g., discards part of the cargo) to avert a larger loss of ship or cargo, the loss incurred is shared by all who participated in the venture.

general bequest A gift in a will payable out of the general assets of the estate. A gift in a will of a designated quantity or value of property.

general contractor One who contracts to construct an entire building or project rather than a portion of it; a prime contractor who hires subcontractors, coordinates the work, etc. Also called original contractor, prime contractor.

general counsel The chief attorney or law firm that represents a company or other organization in most of its legal matters.

General Court The name of the legislature in Massachusetts and in New Hampshire.

general creditor See unsecured creditor.

general court-martial A military trial court consisting of five members and one military judge, which can impose any punishment.

general damages Damages that naturally, directly, and frequently result from a wrong. The law implies general damages to exist; they do not have to be specifically alleged. Also called direct damages.

> In a breach of contract action, "general damages" are those damages which naturally and necessarily flow or result from injuries alleged. *Hardwick Properties*, 711 So.2d 35 (Fla.App. 1 Dist.,1998)

general demurrer A demurrer challenging whether an opponent has stated a cause of action or attacking a petition in its entirety. See also demurrer.

general denial A response by a party that controverts all of the allegations in the preceding pleading, usually the complaint.

general deposit Placing money in a bank to be repaid upon demand or to be drawn upon from time to time in the usual course of banking business.

general devise A gift in a will to be satisfied out of testator's estate generally; it is not charged upon any specific property or fund.

general election A regularly scheduled election.

general execution See execution (3).

general finding A finding in favor of one party and against the other.

general jurisdiction The power of a court to hear any kind of case, with limited exceptions.

> General jurisdiction, as distinguished from specific jurisdiction, does not require that the plaintiff's cause of action

arise out of the nonresident defendant's contacts with the forum state; rather defendant must be found to have maintained continuous and systematic general business contacts with the forum. *QSR, Inc.*, 766 So.2d 271 (Fla.App. 4 Dist.,2000)

general intent The state of mind in which a person is conscious of the act he or she is committing without necessarily understanding or desiring the consequences of that action.

general law A law that applies to everyone within the class regulated by the law.

general legacy A gift of personal property in a will that may be satisfied out of the general assets of the testator's estate.

general lien A lien that attaches to all the goods of the debtor, not just the goods that caused the debt.

general partner A business co-owner who can participate in the management of the business and is personally liable for its debts.

general partnership A partnership in which all the partners are general partners, have no restrictions on running the business, and have unlimited liability for the debts of the business. An association of two or more persons to carry on as co-owners of a business for profit.

general power of appointment A power of appointment exercisable in favor of any person that the donee (i.e., the person given the power) may select, including the donee him or herself.

> General power of appointment means a power of appointment under which the holder of the power, whether or not the holder has the capacity to exercise it, has the power to create a present or future interest in the holder, the holder's estate, or the creditors of either. F.S.A. § 732.2025(3)

general power of attorney A grant of broad powers by a principal to an agent.

general statute A statute that operates equally upon all persons and things within the scope of the statute. A statute that applies to persons or things as a class. A statute that affects the general public.

general strike Cessation of work by employees throughout an entire industry or country.

general verdict A verdict for one party or the other, as opposed to a verdict that answers specific questions.

general warrant A blanket warrant that does not specify the items to be searched for or the persons to be arrested.

general warranty deed See warranty deed.

General Welfare Clause The clause in the federal constitution giving Congress the power to impose taxes and spend for defense and the general welfare. U.S. Constitution, Art. I, § 8, cl. 1.

generation-skipping transfer A transfer of assets to a family member who is more than one generation below the transferor, e.g., from grandparent to grandchild.

generation-skipping trust Any trust having younger generation beneficiaries of more than one generation in the same trust. A trust that makes a generation-skipping transfer.

generic 1. Relating to or characteristic of an entire group or class. 2. Not having a brand name. Identified by its nonproprietary name.

> Generic terms by their nature cannot serve to identify source of goods or services because generic term is one that is commonly used as name of kind of goods; thus,

generic terms are not protectable. *Great Southern Bank*, 625 So.2d 463 (Fla.,1993)

generic drug A drug not protected by trademark that is the same as a brand name drug in safety, strength, quality, intended use, etc.

genetic markers Separate genes or complexes of genes identified as a result of genetic tests. In paternity cases, such tests may exclude a man as the biological father, or may show how probable it is that he is the father.

Geneva Conventions International agreements on the conduct of nations at war, e.g., protection of civilians, treatment of prisoners of war.

genocide Acts committed with intent to destroy, in whole or in part, a national, ethnic, racial, or religious group, e.g., killing members of the group, causing them serious mental harm, or imposing measures designed to prevent births within the group.

gentleman's agreement An agreement, usually unwritten, based on trust and honor. It is not an enforceable contract.

genuine Authentic; being what it purports to be; having what it says it has.

germane Relevant; on point.

gerrymander Dividing a geographic area into voting districts in order to provide an unfair advantage to one political party or group by diluting the voting strength of another party or group.

gestational surrogacy The sperm and egg of a couple are fertilized in vitro in a laboratory; the resulting embryo is then implanted in a surrogate mother who gives birth to a child with whom she has no genetic relationship.

gift A transfer of property to another without payment or consideration. To be irrevocable, (a) there must be a delivery of the property; (b) the transfer must be voluntary; (c) the donor must have legal capacity to make a gift; (d) the donor must intend to divest him or herself of title and control of what is given; (e) the donor must intend that the gift take effect immediately; (f) there must be no consideration (e.g., payment) from the donee; (g) the donee must accept the gift.

> The essential elements of a gift are donative intent, delivery, and acceptance. *Mercurio*, 552 So.2d 236 (Fla.App. 4 Dist.,1989)

gift causa mortis A gift made in contemplation of imminent death subject to the implied condition that if the donor recovers or the donee dies first, the gift shall be void.

gift in contemplation of death See gift causa mortis.

gift inter vivos See inter vivos gift.

gift over A gift of property that takes effect when a preceding estate in the property ends or fails.

gifts to minors act The Uniform Transfers to Minors Act covering adult management of gifts to minors, custodial accounts for minors, etc.

gift tax A tax on the transfer of property by gift, usually paid by the donor, although a few states tax the donee.

gilt-edged 1. Of the highest quality. 2. Pertaining to a very safe investment.

Ginnie Mae (GNMA) Government National Mortgage Association (*www.ginniemae.gov*).

gist The central idea or foundation of a legal action or matter.

give To make a gratuitous transfer of property. See also gift.

giveback A reduction in wages or other benefits agreed to by a union during labor bargaining.

gloss A brief explanatory note. An interpretation of a text.

GNP See gross national product.

go bare To engage in an occupation or profession without malpractice insurance.

go forward 1. To proceed with one's case. 2. To introduce evidence.

going and coming rule The scope of employment usually does not include the time when an employee is going to or coming from work. Respondeat superior during such times does not apply.

> The "going and coming rule" provides that injuries sustained while traveling to or from work do not arise out of and in the course of employment and, therefore, are not compensable. F.S.A. § 440.092(2). *Swartz*, 788 So.2d 937 (Fla.,2001)

going concern An existing solvent business operating in its ordinary and regular manner with no plans to go out of business.

going-concern value What a willing purchaser, in an arm's length transaction, would offer for a company as an operating business as opposed to one contemplating liquidation.

going private Delisting equity securities from a securities exchange. Going from publicly owned corporation to a close corporation.

going public Issuing stock for public purchase for the first time; becoming a public corporation.

golden parachute Very high payments and other economic benefits made to an employee upon his or her termination.

golden rule 1. A guideline of statutory interpretation in which we presume that the legislature did not intend an interpretation that would lead to absurd or ridiculous consequences. 2. Urging jurors to place themselves in the position of the injured party or victim.

good 1. Sufficient in law; enforceable. 2. Valid. 3. Reliable.

good behavior Law-abiding. Following the rules. A standard used to grant inmates early release.

good cause A cause that affords a legal excuse; a legally sufficient ground or reason. Also called just cause, sufficient cause.

> The physical inability to perform a job constitutes "good cause" for separation from employment which is attributable to the employer within meaning of statute providing that individuals seeking unemployment compensation benefits shall be disqualified when they leave employment voluntarily without good cause attributable to the employer. F.S.A. § 443.101(1)(a). *Belcher*, 882 So.2d 486 (Fla.App. 5 Dist.,2004)

good consideration Consideration based on blood relationship or natural love and affection. Also called moral consideration.

good faith A state of mind indicating honesty and lawfulness of purpose; the absence of an intent to seek an undue advantage; a belief that known circumstances do not require further investigation.

good faith bargaining Going to the bargaining table with an open mind and a sincere desire to reach agreement.

good faith exception Evidence is admissible (in an exception to the exclusionary rule) if the police reasonably rely on a warrant that is later invalidated because of the lack of probable cause.

good faith purchaser See bona fide purchaser.

goods 1. Movable things other than money or intangible rights. 2. Any personal property.

Good Samaritan Someone who comes to the assistance of another without a legal obligation to do so. Under Good Samaritan laws of most states, a person aiding another in an emergency will not be liable for ordinary negligence in providing this aid.

> Any person, including those licensed to practice medicine, who gratuitously and in good faith renders emergency care or treatment . . . at the scene of an emergency outside of a hospital, doctor's office, or other place having proper medical equipment, without objection of the injured victim or victims thereof, shall not be held liable for any civil damages as a result of such care or treatment or as a result of any act or failure to act in providing or arranging further medical treatment where the person acts as an ordinary reasonably prudent person would have acted under the same or similar circumstances. F.S.A. § 768.13(2)(a)

goods and chattels 1. Personal property. 2. Tangible personal property.

good time Credit for an inmate's good conduct that reduces prison time.

good title A valid title; a title that a reasonably prudent purchaser would accept. Marketable title.

goodwill The reputation of a business that causes it to generate additional customers. The advantages a business has over its competitors due to its name, location, and owner's reputation.

govern 1. To direct or control by authority; to rule. 2. To be a precedent or controlling law.

government 1. The process of governing. 2. The framework of political institutions by which the executive, legislative, and judicial functions of the state are carried on. 3. The sovereign power of a state.

governmental function 1. An activity of government authorized by law for the general public good. 2. A function that can be performed adequately only by the government. An essential function of government.

> A governmental function has to do with administration of some phase of government, that is to say, dispensing or exercising some element of sovereignty, while a proprietary function is one designed to promote comfort, convenience, safety, and happiness of citizens. *McPhee*, 362 So.2d 74 (Fla.App.,1978)

governmental immunity See sovereign immunity.

government contract A contract in which at least one of the parties is a government agency or branch.

government corporation A government-owned corporation that is a mixture of a corporation and a government agency created to serve a predominantly business function in the public interest.

government security A security (e.g., a treasury bill) issued by the government or a government entity.

governor A chief executive official of a state of the United States.

grace period Extra time past a due date given to avoid a penalty (e.g., cancellation) that would otherwise apply to the missed date.

graded offense A crime that can be committed in different categories or classes of severity, resulting in different punishments.

graduated lease A lease for which the rent will vary depending on factors such as the amount of gross income produced.

graduated payment mortgage (GPM) A mortgage that begins with lower payments and that increase over the term of the loan.

graduated tax See progressive tax.

graft Money or personal gain unlawfully received because of one's position of public trust.

grandfather clause A special exemption for those already doing what will now be prohibited or otherwise restricted for others.

> Ordinarily, as applied to regulation of a profession, a "grandfather clause" exempts from the examination prerequisite to obtaining a license those already bona fide engaged in practice of a profession being regulated for the first time. *Eslin*, 108 So.2d 889 (Fla.1959)

grand jury A jury of inquiry that receives accusations in criminal cases, hears the evidence of the prosecutor, and issues indictments when satisfied that a trial should be held.

grand larceny Unlawfully taking and carrying away another's personal property valued in excess of a statutorily set amount (e.g., $100).

grant 1. To give property or a right to another with or without compensation. 2. To transfer real property by deed or other instrument. 3. Something given or transferred.

grantee The person to whom a grant is made or property is conveyed.

grant-in-aid Funds given by the government to a person or institution for a specific purpose, e.g., education or research.

granting clause That portion of a deed or instrument of conveyance that contains the words of transfer of an interest.

grantor The person who makes the grant or conveys property.

grantor-grantee index A master index by grantor name to all recorded instruments (e.g., deeds, mortgages) allowing you to trace the names of sellers and buyers of land up to the present owner.

grantor trust A trust in which the grantor is taxed on its income because of his or her control over the income or corpus.

gratis Without reward or consideration. Free.

gratuitous 1. Given or granted free, without consideration. 2. Unwarranted; unjustified.

gratuitous bailment A bailment in which the care and custody of the bailor's property by the bailee is without charge or expectation of payment.

> A gratuitous bailment arose when the wife left her personalty in the husband's possession without contemplating any direct or indirect compensation in his favor and, thus, without contemplation of any mutual benefit. *Benz*, 557 So.2d 124 (Fla.App. 3 Dist.,1990)

gratuitous promise A promise made by one who has received no consideration for it.

gravamen The essence of a grievance; the gist of a charge.

gray market A market where goods are legally sold at lower prices than the manufacturer would want or that are imported bearing a valid United States trademark, but without consent of the trademark holder.

great bodily injury A significant or substantial injury or damage; a serious physical impairment. Also called serious bodily harm.

great care The amount of care used by reasonable persons when involved in very important matters. Also called utmost care.

Great Charter See Magna Carta.

Great Writ See habeas corpus.

green card The government-issued registration card indicating the permanent resident status of an alien.

greenmail Inflated payments to buy back the stock of a shareholder (a raider) who has threatened a corporate takeover.

Green River ordinance An ordinance that prohibits door-to-door commercial solicitations without prior consent.

grievance 1. An injury or wrong that can be the basis for an action or complaint. 2. A charge or complaint. 3. A complaint about working conditions or about a violation of a union agreement.

grievance procedure Formal steps established to resolve disputes arising under a collective bargaining agreement.

> Grievance procedure means an established set of rules that specify a process for appeal of an organizational decision. F.S.A. § 408.7056(c)

gross 1. Glaring, obvious. 2. Reprehensible. 3. Total; before or without diminution or deduction.

gross estate The total assets of a person at his or her death before deductions are taken.

gross income All income from whatever source before exemptions, deductions, credits, or other adjustments.

gross lease A lease in which the tenant pays only rent; the landlord pays everything else, e.g., taxes, utilities, insurance, etc.

gross national product (GNP) The total value of all goods and services produced in a given period.

gross negligence 1. The intentional failure to perform a manifest duty in reckless disregard of the consequences to the life or property of another. 2. The failure to use even slight care and diligence. Also called willful negligence.

> Gross negligence means that the defendant's conduct was so reckless or wanting in care that it constituted a conscious disregard or indifference to the life, safety, or rights of persons exposed to such conduct. F.S.A. § 400.0237(2)(b)

gross receipts The total amount of money (and any other consideration) received from selling goods or services.

ground 1. Foundation; points relied on. 2. A reason that is legally sufficient to obtain a remedy or other result.

ground rent 1. Rent paid to the owner for the use of undeveloped land, usually to construct a building on it. 2. A perpetual rent reserved to the grantor (and his or her heirs) from land conveyed in fee simple.

group annuity A policy that provides annuities to a group of people under a single master contract.

group boycott Agreements among competitors within the same market tier not to deal with other competitors or market participants.

group insurance A single insurance policy covering a group of individuals, e.g., employees of a particular company.

group legal services See prepaid legal services.

growth stock The stock in a company that is expected to have higher than average growth, particularly in the value of the stock.

GSA General Services Administration (*www.gsa.gov*).

guarantee 1. An assurance that a particular outcome will occur, e.g., a product will perform as stated or will be repaired at no cost. Also called guaranty. 2. A promise to fulfill the obligation of another if the latter fails to do so. 3. To give security. 4. Security given.

guaranteed stock The stock of one corporation whose dividends are guaranteed by another corporation, e.g., by a parent corporation.

guarantor One who makes a guaranty; one who becomes secondarily liable for another's debt or performance.

guaranty 1. A promise to fulfill the obligation of another if the latter fails to do so. 2. See guarantee (1).

> Warranty is distinguishable from a guaranty. Both are collateral contracts; but guaranty is an undertaking to answer for another's liability, while warranty is an undertaking that a certain fact regarding the subject of the contract is what it has been represented to be, and relates to some undertaking made ordinarily by the party who makes the warranty. *Vilord*, 226 So.2d 245 (Fla.App. 1969)

guardian A person who lawfully has the power and duty to care for the person, property, or rights of another who is incapable of managing his or her affairs (e.g., a minor, an insane person).

guardian ad litem (GAL) A special guardian appointed by the court to represent the interests of another (e.g., a minor) in court. See also ad litem.

> Guardian ad litem means a person who is appointed by the court having jurisdiction of the guardianship or a court in which a particular legal matter is pending to represent a ward in that proceeding. F.S.A. § 744.102(9)

guardianship 1. The office, duty, or authority of a guardian. 2. The fiduciary relationship that exists between guardian and ward.

guest 1. A passenger in a motor vehicle who is offered a ride by someone who receives no benefits from the passenger other than hospitality, goodwill, and the like. 2. One who pays for the services of a restaurant or place of lodging. 3. A recipient of one's hospitality, especially at home.

guest statute A statute providing that drivers of motor vehicles will not be liable for injuries caused by their ordinary negligence to nonpaying guest passengers.

guilty 1. A defendant's plea that accepts (or does not contest) the criminal charge against him or her. 2. A determination by a jury or court that the defendant has committed the crime charged. 3. Responsible for criminal or civil wrongdoing.

H

habeas corpus ("you have the body") A writ designed to bring a party before a court in order to test the legality of his or her detention or imprisonment. Also called the Great Writ.

> A writ that may be invoked by any person who seeks release from custody or confinement which is asserted to be unlawful. Upon application to any Justice or judge, the persons may test the legality of their detention, not as to guilt or innocence, but solely as to whether the commitment to custody was lawful and the retention in custody is in accordance with the requirements of due process. (*www.floridasupremecourt.org/pub_info/system2.shtml*) *State ex rel. Paine*, 166 So.2d 708 (Fla.App.1964)

habeas corpus ad faciendum et recipiendum A writ to move a civil case (and the body of the defendant) from a lower to a higher court.

habeas corpus ad prosequendum A writ issued for the purpose of indicting, prosecuting, and sentencing a defendant already confined within another jurisdiction.

habeas corpus ad testificandum A writ used to bring in a prisoner detained in a jail or prison to give evidence before the court.

habendum clause The portion of a deed (often using the words *to have and to hold*) that describes the ownership rights being transferred (i.e., the estate or interest being granted).

habitability The condition of a building that allows it to be enjoyed because it is free from substantial defects that endanger health or safety.

habitable Suitable or fit for living.

habitation 1. Place of abode; one's dwelling or residence. 2. Occupancy.

habitual Customary, usual, regular.

habitual criminal A repeat offender. Also called career criminal, recidivist.

half blood (half brother, half sister) The relationship between persons who have the same father or the same mother, but not both.

halfway house A house in the community that helps individuals make the adjustment from prison or other institutionalization to normal life.

hand down To announce or file an opinion by a court.

handicap A physical or mental impairment or disability that substantially limits one or more of a person's major life activities.

harassment Intrusive or unwanted acts, words, or gestures (often persistent and continuing) that have a substantial adverse effect on the safety, security, or privacy of another and that serve no legitimate purpose.

> Harassment means a course of conduct directed at a specific person that: 1. Causes substantial emotional distress in such person; and 2. Serves no legitimate purpose. F.S.A. § 914.24(3)(a)

harbor To shelter or protect, often clandestinely and illegally.

hard cases Cases in which a court sometimes overlooks fixed legal principles when they are opposed to persuasive equities.

hard labor Forced physical labor required of an inmate.

harm 1. Loss or detriment to a person. 2. To injure.

harmless Not causing any damage.

harmless error An error that did not prejudice the substantial rights of the party alleging it. Also called technical error.

Hatch Act A federal statute that prohibits federal employees from engaging in certain types of political activities (5 USC § 1501).

hate crime A crime motivated by hatred, bias, or prejudice, based on race, color, religion, national origin, ethnicity, gender, or sexual orientation of another individual or group of individuals.

> The penalty for any felony or misdemeanor shall be reclassified as provided in this subsection if the commission of such felony or misdemeanor evidences prejudice based on the race, color, ancestry, ethnicity, religion, sexual orientation, national origin, mental or physical disability, or advanced age of the victim: 1. A misdemeanor of the second degree is reclassified to a misdemeanor of the first degree. . . . F.S.A. § 775.085(1)(a)

have and hold See habendum clause.

hazard 1. A risk or danger of harm or loss. The chance of suffering a loss. 2. Danger, peril.

hazardous Exposed to or involving danger. Risky.

H.B. House Bill. A proposed statute considered by the House of Representatives.

headnote A short-paragraph summary of a portion of a court opinion printed before the opinion begins. Also called syllabus.

head of household 1. The primary income earner in a household. 2. An unmarried taxpayer (or married if living and filing separately) who maintains a home that for more than one-half of the taxable year is the principal place of abode of certain dependents, such as an unmarried child.

head tax See poll tax.

healthcare proxy See advance directive.

health maintenance organization (HMO) A prepaid health insurance plan consisting of a network of doctors and healthcare institutions that provide medical services to subscribers.

hearing 1. A proceeding designed to resolve issues of fact or law. Usually, an impartial officer presides, evidence is presented, etc. The hearing is *ex parte* if only one party is present; it is *adversarial* if both parties are present. 2. A meeting of a legislative committee to consider proposed legislation or other legislative matters. 3. A meeting in which one is allowed to argue a position.

hearing officer; hearing examiner See Administrative Law Judge.

hearsay 1. What one learns from another rather than from first-hand knowledge. 2. An out-of-court statement offered to prove the truth of the matter asserted in the statement. A "statement, other than one made by the declarant while testifying at the trial or hearing, offered in evidence to prove the truth of the matter asserted." Federal Rule of Evidence 801(c).

> Hearsay is a statement, other than one made by the declarant while testifying at the trial or hearing, offered in evidence to prove the truth of the matter asserted. F.S.A. § 90.801(c)

heart balm statute A law abolishing heart balm actions, which are actions based on a broken heart or loss of love (e.g., breach of promise to marry, alienation of affections, criminal conversation).

heat of passion Fear, rage, or resentment in which a person loses self-control due to provocation. Also called hot blood, sudden heat of passion.

hedge To safeguard oneself from loss on a bet, bargain, or speculation by making compensatory arrangements on the other side. To reduce risk by entering a transaction that will offset an existing position.

hedge fund A special investment fund that uses aggressive (higher risk) strategies such as short selling and buying derivatives.

hedonic damages Damages that cover the victim's loss of pleasure or enjoyment of life.

heinous Shockingly odious or evil.

heir 1. One designated by state law to receive all or part of the estate of a person who dies without leaving a valid will (intestate). Also called heir at law, legal heir. 2. One who inherits (or is in line to inherit) by intestacy or by will.

> "Heirs" or "heirs at law" means those persons, including the surviving spouse, who are entitled under the statutes of intestate succession to the property of a decedent. F.S.A. § 731.201(18)

heir apparent See apparent heir.

heir at law See heir (1).

heir collateral See collateral heir.

heir of the blood One who inherits because of a blood relationship with the decedent in the ascending or descending line.

heir of the body A blood relative in the direct line of descent, e.g., children, grandchildren (excluding adopted children).

heir presumptive See presumptive heir.

heirs and assigns Words used to convey a fee simple estate.

held Decided. See also hold.

henceforth From this (or that) time on.

hereafter 1. From now on. 2. At some time in the future.

hereditament 1. Property, rights, or anything that can be inherited. 2. Real property.

hereditary Capable of being inherited. Pertaining to inheritance.

hereditary succession See intestate succession.

herein In this section; in the document you are now reading.

hereto To this (document or matter).

heretofore Before now; up to now.

hereunder 1. By the terms of or in accordance with this document. 2. Later in the document.

herewith With this or in this document.

heritable Capable of being inherited.

hermeneutics The science or art of interpreting documents.

hidden asset Property of a company that is either not stated on its books or is stated at an undervalued price.

hidden defect A deficiency in property that could not be discovered by reasonable and customary observation or inspection and for which a lessor or seller is generally liable if such defect causes harm. Also called inherent defect, latent defect.

high crime A major offense that is a serious abuse of governmental power. Can be the basis of impeachment and removal from office.

highest and best use The use of property that will most likely produce the highest market value, greatest financial return, or the most profit.

high-low agreement A compromise agreement under which the parties set a minimum (floor) and maximum (ceiling) for damages. The defendant will pay at least the floor (if the jury awards less than this amount) but no more than the ceiling (if the jury awards over that amount).

high seas That portion of the ocean or seas that is beyond the territorial jurisdiction of any country.

high-water line or **mark** The line on the shore to which high tide rises under normal weather conditions.

hijack To seize possession of a vehicle from another; to seize a vehicle and force it to go in another direction.

HIPAA Health Insurance Portability and Accountability Act. A federal statute providing protections such as maintaining the privacy of personal health information (*www.hhs.gov/ocr/hipaa*).

hire 1. To purchase the temporary use of a thing. 2. To engage the services of another for a fee.

hiring hall An agency or office operated by a union (or by both union and management) to place applicants for work.

hit and run The crime of leaving the scene of an accident without being identified.

> Unidentified truck from which steel beam had fallen off, which beam caused insured's automobile accident when other driver hit beam lying on highway and caused beam to strike insured's vehicle, constituted a "hit-and-run vehicle" *Denoia,* 843 So.2d 285 (Fla.App. 3 Dist.,2003)

HMO See health maintenance organization.

hoard To accumulate assets beyond one's reasonable needs, often anticipating an increase in their market price.

Hobbs Act A federal anti-racketeering act that makes it illegal to obstruct, delay, or affect interstate commerce or attempt to conspire to do so by robbery, physical violence, or extortion (18 USC § 1951).

hobby losses A nondeductible loss suffered when engaged in an activity that is not pursued for profit.

hodgepodge See hotchpot.

hold 1. To possess something by virtue of lawful authority or title. 2. To reach a legal conclusion; to resolve a legal dispute. 3. To restrain or control; to keep in custody. 4. To preside at.

holder 1. One who has possession of something, e.g., a check, bond, document of title. 2. One who has legally acquired possession of a negotiable instrument (e.g., a check, a promissory note) and who is entitled to receive payment on the instrument.

holder for value Someone who has given something of value for a promissory note or other negotiable instrument.

holder in due course (HDC)(HIDC) One who gives value for a negotiable instrument in good faith, without any apparent defects, and without notice that it is overdue, has been dishonored, or is subject to any claim or defense.

> The holder of an instrument if: (a) The instrument when issued or negotiated to the holder does not bear such apparent evidence of forgery or alteration or is not otherwise so irregular or incomplete as to call into question its authenticity; and (b) The holder took the instrument: 1. For value; 2. In good faith; 3. Without notice that the instrument is overdue or has been dishonored or that there is an uncured default with respect to payment of another instrument issued as part of the same series; 4. Without notice that the instrument contains an unauthorized signature or has been altered; 5. Without notice of any claim to the instrument described in § 673.3061; and 6. Without notice that any party has a defense or claim in recoupment. . . . F.S.A. § 673.3021(1)

hold harmless To assume any liability in a transaction thereby relieving another from responsibility or loss. Also called save harmless.

holding 1. A court's answer to or resolution of a legal issue before it. 2. A court ruling. 3. Property owned by someone.

holding company A company that owns stock in and supervises the management of other companies.

holding period The length of time a taxpayer owns a capital asset, which determines whether a gain or loss will be short-term or long-term.

holdover tenancy See estate at sufferance.

holdover tenant A tenant who retains possession of the premises after the expiration of a lease or after a tenancy at will has been ended.

holograph A handwritten document.

holographic will A will written entirely by the testator in his or her own handwriting, often without witnesses.

home equity conversion mortgage A first mortgage that provides for future payments to a homeowner based on accumulated equity.

homeowner's policy A multiperil insurance policy covering damage to a residence and liability claims based on home ownership.

homeowner's warranty (HOW) A warranty and insurance protection program offered by many home builders, providing protection for 10 years against major structural defects. A construction warranty.

home port doctrine A vessel engaged in interstate and foreign commerce is taxable only at its home port (e.g., where it is registered).

home rule A designated amount of self-government granted to local cities and towns.

homestead The dwelling house and adjoining land where the owner or his or her family lives.

homestead exemption laws Laws that allow a householder or head of a family to designate a residence and adjoining land as his or her homestead that, in whole or part, is exempt from execution or attachment for designated general debts.

> The word "homestead" in the statute setting forth limitations on the devise of homestead property refers to the word "homestead" as used in the Constitution requiring that homestead property subject to exemptions be owned by the head of a family. West's F.S.A. § 732.4015. *Holden,* 420 So.2d 1082 (Fla.,1982)

homicide The killing of one human being by another. Whether the killing is a crime depends on factors such as intent.

homologate To approve; to confirm officially.

Hon. Honorable.

honor To accept or pay a check or other negotiable instrument when presented for acceptance or payment.

To "honor" is to pay or to accept and pay, or where a credit so engages to purchase or discount a draft complying with the terms of the credit. F.S.A. § 671.201(21)

honorable discharge A declaration by the government that a member of the military left the service in good standing.

honorarium A fee for services when no fee was required.

honorary trust A trust that may not be enforceable because it has no beneficiary to enforce it. Example: a trust for the care of a pet.

horizontal agreement An agreement between companies that directly compete at the same level of distribution, often in restraint of trade.

horizontal merger The acquisition of one company by another company producing the same or a similar product and selling it in the same geographic market. A merger of corporate competitors.

horizontal price fixing An agreement by competitors at the same market level to fix or control prices they will charge for their goods or services.

horizontal privity The relationship between a supplier and a nonpurchasing party who is affected by the product, such as a relative of the buyer or a bystander.

horizontal property acts A statute on condominiums or cooperatives.

horizontal restraint See horizontal agreement.

horizontal union See craft union.

hornbook A book summarizing the basics or fundamentals of a topic.

hornbook law See black letter law.

hostile environment sexual harassment A work setting in which severe and pervasive conduct of a sexual nature creates a hostile or offensive working environment.

hostile fire 1. A fire that breaks out or spreads to an unexpected area. 2. Gunfire from an enemy.

hostile possession Possession asserted to be superior to or incompatible with anyone else's claim to possession.

hostile witness A witness who manifests bias or prejudice, who appears aligned with the other side, or who refuses to answer questions. Also called adverse witness.

> A witness becomes "hostile" when he is called with the expectation that he will give testimony favorable to the calling party, but who thereafter proves to be unwilling or adverse, to the complete surprise of the calling party. *Poitier*, 303 So.2d 409 (Fla.App. 1974)

hot blood See heat of passion.

hot cargo 1. Goods produced or handled by an employer with whom a union has a dispute. 2. Stolen goods.

hotchpot Mixing or blending all property, however acquired, in order to divide it more equally. Also called hodgepodge.

> "Hotchpot" is bringing into the estate of an intestate an estimate of value of advancements made by the intestate to his or her children, in order that whole may be divided in accordance with statute of descents. F.S.A. § 734.07. *Livingston*, 141 So.2d 794 (Fla.App.1962)

hot pursuit See fresh pursuit.

house 1. Living quarters; a home. 2. One of the chambers of a legislature (e.g., U.S. House of Representatives, Md. House of Delegates).

house bill (H.B.)(H.) Proposed legislation considered by the House of Representatives.

housebreaking Breaking and entering a dwelling-house with the intent to commit any felony therein. Also called burglary.

house counsel An attorney who is an employee of a business or organization, usually on salary. Also called in-house counsel.

household 1. Belonging or pertaining to the house and family. 2. A group of persons living together.

> Family or household member means spouses, former spouses, persons related by blood or marriage, persons who are presently residing together as if a family or who have resided together in the past as if a family, and persons who are parents of a child in common regardless of whether they have been married. F.S.A. § 741.28(3)

House of Representatives (H.R.) See house (2).

H.R. See House of Representatives.

H. Res. House resolution. See also concurrent resolution.

H.R. 10 plan See Keogh plan.

humanitarian doctrine See last clear chance doctrine.

hung jury A jury so irreconcilably divided in opinion that a verdict cannot be agreed upon.

husband-wife immunity See interspousal immunity.

husband-wife privilege See marital communications privilege.

hybrid security A security that combines the features of a debt instrument and an equity instrument.

hypothecate To pledge property as security or collateral for a debt without transferring title or possession.

hypothesis An assumption or theory to be proven or disproven.

hypothetical 1. Based on conjecture; not actual or real, but presented for purposes of discussion and analysis. 2. A set of assumed facts presented for the sake of argument and illustration.

hypothetical question A question in which the person being interviewed (e.g., an expert witness) is asked to give an opinion on a set of facts that are assumed to be true for purposes of the question.

I

ibid. In the same place; in the work previously cited or mentioned.

ICE Immigration and Customs Enforcement (*www.ice.gov*).

ICJ See International Court of Justice (*www.icj-cij.org*).

id. The same. (Id. refers to the case or other authority cited immediately above or before in the text or footnotes.)

idem sonans Sounding the same. A misspelled signature can be effective if the misspelled name sounds the same as the correct spelling.

identify 1. To establish the identity of someone or something. 2. To associate or be associated with. 3. To specify the subject of a contract.

identity of interests Two persons being so closely related that suing one acts as notice to the other. Being only nominally separate.

> For purposes of determining whether the addition of a new party to an action relates back to the original complaint, on the ground that the new party is sufficiently

related to an original party such that the addition would not prejudice the new party, the "identity of interest" is manifested in such circumstances as when the companies (1) operate out of a single office; (2) share a single telephone line; (3) have overlapping officers and directors; (4) share consolidated financial statements and registration statements; (5) share the same attorney; and (6) receive service of process through the same individual at the same location. F.S.A. RCP Rule 1.190(c). *Roback*, 837 So.2d 1061 (Fla.App. 4 Dist.,2003)

identity of parties Two persons being so closely related that a judgment against one will bar (via res judicata) a later suit against the other.

identity theft Knowingly transferring or using a means of identification of another person with the intent to commit any unlawful activity.

i.e. That is; in other words.

IFP See in forma pauperis.

ignoramus We do not know. (A notation by a grand jury indicating a rejection of the indictment.)

ignorance The absence of knowledge.

ignorantia juris non excusat Ignorance of the law excuses no one.

illegal Against the law; prohibited by law.

illegal entry 1. Unauthorized entry with intent to commit a crime. 2. Entry into a country by an alien at the wrong time or place or by fraud; or eluding immigration officers when here.

illegality That which is contrary to law.

illegally obtained evidence Evidence collected in violation of a suspect's statutory or constitutional rights.

illegitimate 1. Born out of wedlock. 2. Contrary to law.

illicit Not permitted, illegal; improper.

illicit cohabitation Two unmarried persons living together as man and wife.

Illinois Land Trust See land trust.

illusory Deceptive, based on false appearances; not real.

An illusory trust is a trust arrangement which takes the form of a trust, but because of powers retained in the settlor has no real substance and in reality is not a completed trust. *In re Herron's Estate*, 237 So.2d 563 (Fla.App. 1970)

illusory contract An agreement in which one party's consideration is so insignificant that a contract obligation cannot be imposed.

illusory promise An apparent promise that leaves the promisor's performance entirely within the discretion of the promisor.

imbecility Severe mental retardation or cognitive dysfunction.

imitation Substantial duplication; resembling something enough to cause confusion with the genuine article.

immaterial Not material. Tending to prove something not in issue.

immaterial variance A discrepancy between the pleading and the proof that is so slight it misleads no one.

immediate annuity An annuity bought with a lump sum that starts making payments soon after its purchase.

immediate cause The last of a series or chain of events that produced the occurrence or result; a cause immediate in time to what occurred.

immemorial Beyond human memory. Exceptionally old.

immigrant A foreigner who comes into a country with the intention to live there permanently.

imminent Near at hand; about to occur.

imminent peril doctrine See emergency doctrine.

immoral Contrary to good morals; inimical to public welfare according to the standards of a given community.

immovables Land and those things so firmly attached to it as to be regarded as part of it; property that cannot be moved.

immunity 1. Exemption or freedom from a duty, penalty, or liability. 2. A complete defense to a tort claim whether or not the defendant committed the tort. 3. The right not to be subjected to civil or criminal prosecution.

immunize To grant immunity to; to render immune.

impact rule A party may recover emotional distress damages in a negligence action only if he or she suffered accompanying physical injury or contact.

The impact rule provides that, before a plaintiff can recover damages for emotional distress caused by the negligence of another, the emotional distress suffered must flow from the physical injuries the plaintiff sustained in an impact, and therefore, unless the emotional damages resulted from a physical injury, the impact rule precludes recovery. *School Bd. of Miami-Dade County*, 906 So.2d 1109 (Fla.App. 3 Dist.,2005)

impair To cause something to lose some or all of its quality or value.

impair the obligation of contracts To nullify or materially change existing contract obligations. See also Contract Clause.

impanel To enlist or enroll. To enroll or swear in (a list of jurors) for a particular case. Also spelled empanel.

imparl 1. To delay a case in an attempt to settle. 2. To seek a continuance for more time to answer and pursue settlement options.

impartial Favoring neither side; unbiased.

impasse A deadlock in negotiations. The absence of hope of agreement.

impeach To attack; to accuse of wrongdoing; to challenge the credibility of.

impeachment 1. An attack or challenge because of impropriety, bias, or lack of veracity. 2. A procedure against a public officer before a quasi-political court (e.g., a legislative body), instituted by written accusations called articles of impeachment that seek his or her removal from office.

The object of impeachment is to attack the credibility of a witness, and where this genuinely is the predominant purpose of the questioning, evidence so introduced is not being admitted to prove the truth of the matter asserted within hearsay definition but rather to show why witness is not trustworthy. West's F.S.A. § 90.801(1)(c). *Ellis*, 622 So.2d 991 (Fla.1993)

impediment A legal obstacle that prevents the formation of a valid marriage or other contract.

imperfect Missing an essential legal requirement. Unenforceable.

imperfect trust See executory trust.

impersonation Pretending or representing oneself to be another.

impertinent Irrelevant or not responsive to the issues in the case.

implead To bring a new party into the lawsuit on the ground that the new party may be liable for all or part of the current claim. The procedure is called impleader or third-party practice.

> A general partner against which an action is commenced under subsection (1) may: (a) Implead in the action any other person that is liable under subsection (1) and compel contribution from the person. F.S.A. § 620.1509(3)

implied Expressed by implication; suggested by the circumstances.

implied acquittal A guilty verdict on a lesser included offense is an implied acquittal of the greater offense about which the jury was silent.

implied agency An actual agency established through circumstantial evidence.

implied authority Authority that is necessary, usual, and proper to perform the express authority delegated to the agent by the principal.

implied consent Consent inferred from the surrounding circumstances.

implied consent law A law providing that a person who drives a motor vehicle in the state is deemed to have given consent to a test that determines the alcoholic or drug content of that person's blood.

implied contract An implied in fact contract or an implied in law contract (see these terms).

implied in fact Inferred from the facts and circumstances.

implied in fact contract An actual contract whose existence and the parties' intentions are inferred from facts rather than by express agreement.

> A "contract implied in fact" is an enforceable contract that is inferred in whole or in part from the parties' conduct, not solely from their words. A "contract implied in law" does not require an agreement, but a "contract implied in fact" does. *CDS and Associates*, 743 So.2d 1223 (Fla.App. 4 Dist.,1999)

implied in law Imposed by law; arising by operation of law.

implied in law contract An obligation created by the law to avoid unjust enrichment. Also called constructive contract, quasi contract.

implied easement An easement created by law when land is conveyed that does not contain an express easement, but one is implied as an intended part of the transaction. Also called easement by implication, way of necessity.

implied malice Malice that is inferred from conduct, e.g., reckless disregard for human life. Also called legal malice, malice in law.

implied notice Knowledge implied from surrounding facts so that the law will treat one as knowing what could have been discovered by ordinary care.

implied powers Powers presumed to have been granted because they are necessary to carry into effect expressly granted powers.

implied promise A fictional promise created by law to impose a contract liability, and thereby avoid fraud or unjust enrichment.

implied trust See constructive trust, resulting trust.

implied warranty A warranty imposed by operation of law regardless of the parties' intent. See also warranty of fitness for a particular purpose, warranty of habitability, warranty of merchantability.

imply 1. To suggest; to state something indirectly. 2. To impose or declare something by law.

import To bring goods into a country from a foreign country.

impossibility That which no person in the course of nature or the law can do or perform; that which cannot exist.

impossibility of performance doctrine A defense to a breach of contract when performance becomes objectively impossible, not due to anyone's fault.

> The two theories of "impossibility of performance" and "frustration of purpose" as grounds for rescission of contract are distinct; the first theory refers to those factual situations where purposes for which contract was made have, on one side, become impossible to perform; the second theory refers to that condition surrounding contracting parties where one of the parties finds that purposes for which he bargains, and which purposes were known to the other party, have been frustrated because of failure of consideration or impossibility of performance by the other party. *Crown Ice Mach. Leasing Co.*, 174 So.2d 614 (Fla.App.1965)

imposts A duty that is levied. An import tax.

impotence The inability to perform the act of sexual intercourse.

imposter One who deceives by pretending to be someone else.

impound To seize and take into custody of the law.

impoundment 1. Seizing and taking something into custody of the law. 2. Refusing to spend money appropriated by the legislature.

impracticability 1. A defense to breach of contract when performance can be undertaken only at an excessive and unreasonable cost. 2. Difficulty or inconvenience of joining all parties because of their large number.

impracticable Excessively burdensome to perform.

impress 1. To force someone into public service, e.g., military service. 2. To impose a constructive trust. The noun is *impressment.*

impression See first impression.

imprimatur ("let it be printed") Official approval to publish a book.

imprison To put in prison; to place in confinement.

improper 1. Not in accord with proper procedure or taste. 2. Wrongful.

improved land Land that has been developed, e.g., by adding roads.

improvement An addition to or betterment of land (usually permanent) that enhances its capital value. Something beyond mere repairs.

> The word "improvements" shall mean such repairs, replacements, additions, extensions and betterments of and to a project as are deemed necessary to place such project in proper condition for the safe, efficient and economic operation thereof, or necessary to preserve a project or to maintain adequate service to the public. F.S.A. § 159.02(11)

improvident Lacking in care and foresight. Ill-considered.

impulse A sudden urge or thrusting force within a person.

impunity Exemption or protection from penalty or punishment.

impute To credit or assign to; to ascribe. To attribute to another or to make another responsible because of a relationship that exists.

imputed disqualification If one attorney or employee in a firm has a conflict of interest with a client, the entire firm is ineligible to represent that client. Also called vicarious disqualification.

imputed income A monetary value assigned to certain property, transactions, or situations for tax purposes (e.g., the value of a home provided by an employer for an employee).

imputed knowledge Information that a person does not actually know, but should know or has reason to know and, therefore, is deemed to know.

imputed negligence Negligence of one person that is attributed to another solely because of a special relationship between them.

> When A is negligent but B is not, imputed negligence means that, by reason of some relationship existing between A and B, the negligence of A is to be charged against B, although B has played no part in it, has done nothing whatever to aid or encourage it, or indeed has done all that he possibly can to prevent it. *Guyton*, 525 So.2d 948 (Fla.App. 1 Dist.,1988)

in absentia In the absence of.

inadequate remedy at law An ineffective legal remedy, e.g., damages, justifying a request for an equitable remedy, e.g., injunction.

inadmissible Cannot be received and considered.

inadvertence An oversight; a consequence of carelessness, not planning.

inalienable Incapable of being bought, sold, transferred, or assigned. Also called unalienable.

in banc See en banc.

in being In existence; existing in life.

in blank Not identifying a particular indorsee. Not filled in.

Inc. Incorporated.

in camera In private with the judge; in chambers; without spectators.

incapacity 1. The existence of a legal impediment preventing action or completion. 2. Physical or mental inability. 3. See disability (2).

incarcerate To imprison or confine in jail.

incendiary 1. A bomb or other device designed to cause fire. 2. One who maliciously and willfully sets fire to property.

incest Sexual intercourse between a man and woman who are related to each other within prohibited degrees (e.g., brother and sister).

> Whoever knowingly marries or has sexual intercourse with a person to whom he or she is related by lineal consanguinity, or a brother, sister, uncle, aunt, nephew, or niece, commits incest, which constitutes a felony of the third degree . . . F.S.A. § 826.04

in chief 1. Main or principal. 2. See case-in-chief.

inchoate Begun but not completed; partial.

inchoate crime A crime in its early stage, constituting another crime. The inchoate crimes are attempt, conspiracy, and solicitation.

inchoate dower A wife's interest in the land of her husband during his life; a possibility of acquiring dower.

inchoate lien A lien in which the amount, exact identity of the lienor, and time of attachment must await future determination.

incident 1. Connected with, inherent in, or arising out of something else. 2. A dependent or subordinate part. 3. An occurrence.

incidental Depending upon and secondary to something else.

incidental beneficiary One who will be benefited by performance of a promise but who is neither a promisee nor an intended beneficiary.

incidental damages 1. The additional expenses reasonably incurred because of a breach of contract. 2. In class actions, those damages that flow directly from liability to the class as a whole on claims forming the basis of the injunctive or declaratory relief.

incident of ownership An ownership right retained in an insurance policy, e.g., the right to change beneficiaries.

incite To urge, persuade, stir up, or provoke another.

included offense See lesser included offense.

income Money or other financial gain derived from one's business, labor, investments, and other sources.

> "Income" means any form of payment to an individual, regardless of source, including, but not limited to: wages, salary, commissions and bonuses, compensation as an independent contractor, worker's compensation, disability benefits, annuity and retirement benefits, pensions, dividends, interest, royalties, trusts, and any other payments, made by any person, private entity, federal or state government, or any unit of local government. F.S.A. § 61.046(7)

income in respect of a decedent (IRD) The right to income earned by a decedent at death that was not included in his or her final income tax return.

income splitting Seeking a lower total tax by allocating income from persons in higher tax brackets to those in lower tax brackets.

income statement See earnings report.

income tax A tax on the net income of an individual or entity.

in common Shared together equally.

incompatibility Such discord between a husband and wife that it is impossible for them to live together in a normal marital relationship.

incompetent 1. Failing to meet legal requirements; unqualified. 2. Not having the skills needed. Physically or mentally impaired.

> "Incapacity" or "incompetent" means the patient is physically or mentally unable to communicate a willful and knowing health care decision. For the purposes of making an anatomical gift, the term also includes a patient who is deceased. F.S.A. § 765.101(8)

incompetent evidence Evidence that is not admissible.

inconsistent Not compatible. Mutually repugnant; the acceptance of one fact, position, or claim implies the abandonment of the other.

in contemplation of death With a view toward death. See contemplation of death.

incontestability clause An insurance policy clause providing that after a period of time (e.g., two years), the insurer cannot contest it on the basis of fraud, mistake, or statements made in the application.

inconvenient forum See forum non conveniens.

incorporate 1. To form a corporation. 2. To combine or include within.

incorporation by reference Making one document a part of another document by stating that the former shall be considered part of the latter.

incorporation doctrine See selective incorporation.

incorporator A person who is one of the original founders (formers) of a corporation.

incorporeal Not having a physical nature; intangible.

> The common-law right of property in literary or intellectual productions which entitles author to use of the production before publication is exclusive as against the world, and it is an "intangible incorporeal right" that exists apart from the property in the paper on which the production is written. *Schleman*, 15 So.2d 754 (Fla.1943)

incorporeal hereditament An intangible land right that is inheritable.

incorrigible Incapable of being corrected or reformed. Unmanageable.

increment An increase or addition in amount or quality.

incriminate 1. To charge with a crime; to accuse someone. 2. To show involvement in the possibility of crime or other wrongdoing.

incriminating Tending to demonstrate criminal conduct.

incriminating statement A statement that tends to establish a person's guilt.

> "Incriminating response" refers to any response, whether inculpatory or exculpatory, that the prosecution may seek to introduce at trial. *Lewis*, 754 So.2d 897 (Fla.App. 1 Dist.,2000)

incriminatory Charging or showing involvement with a crime.

incroach See encroach.

inculpatory Tending to show involvement with crime.

incumbent 1. One presently holding an office. 2. Obligatory.

incumbrance See encumbrance.

incur To become liable or subject to; to bring down upon oneself.

indebitatus assumpsit An action based on undertaking a debt.

indecent Sexually vulgar, but not necessarily obscene.

indecent assault Unconsented sexual contact with another.

indecent exposure Displaying one's self in public (especially one's genitals) in such manner as to be offensive to common decency.

indecent speech Vulgar or offensive (but not necessarily obscene) speech concerning sexual or excretory activities and organs.

indefeasible Not capable of being defeated, revoked, or made void.

indefinite Not definite or fixed; lacking fixed boundaries.

indefinite failure of issue A failure of issue (dying without descendants who can inherit) whenever it occurs.

indefinite sentence See indeterminate sentence.

indemnify To compensate or promise to compensate someone for a specified loss or liability that has resulted or that might result.

indemnitee A person who is indemnified by another.

indemnitor A person who indemnifies another.

indemnity 1. The duty of one person to pay for another's loss, damage, or liability. 2. A right to receive compensation to make one person whole from a loss that has already been sustained but which in justice ought to be sustained by the person from whom indemnity is sought.

> "Indemnity" is a right which inures to one who discharges duty owed by him but which, as between himself and another, should have been discharged by the other. *Rosati*, 848 So.2d 467 (Fla.App. 5 Dist.,2003)

indemnity insurance Insurance covering losses to the insured's person or to his or her own property. Also called first-party insurance.

indenture 1. A deed with the top of the parchment having an irregular (indented) edge. 2. A written agreement under which bonds and debentures are issued; the agreement sets forth terms such as the maturity date and the interest rate. 3. An apprenticeship agreement.

independent 1. Not subject to control or limitation from an outside source. 2. Not affiliated; autonomous.

independent agency A government board, commission, or other agency that is not subject to the policy supervision of the chief executive.

independent contractor One who operates his or her own business and contracts to do work for others who do not control the method or administrative details of how the work is performed.

> "Independent contractor" means a person, other than an agency, engaged in any business and who enters into a contract, including a provider agreement, with an agency. F.S.A. § 112.3187(3)(d)

independent counsel 1. An outside attorney hired to conduct an investigation or perform other special tasks. 2. Counsel chosen by an insured or with the approval of the insured, but paid by the insurer.

independent covenant An obligation that is not conditioned on performance by the other party.

independent paralegal An independent contractor who sells his or her paralegal services to, and works under the supervision of, one or more attorneys. In some states (*but not in Florida*) independent paralegals can sell their services directly to the public without attorney supervision. Also called freelance paralegal or legal technician.

independent source rule Illegally obtained evidence will be admitted if the government shows that it is also obtained through sources wholly independent of the illegal search or other constitutional violation.

indestructible trust See Claflin trust.

indeterminate Not designated with particularity; not definite.

> "Indeterminate value contracts" means annuity contracts, life insurance contracts, and contracts upon the lives of beneficiaries under life insurance contracts when such annuities or contracts provide variable or indeterminate benefits, values, or premiums. F.S.A. § 627.8015(1)

indeterminate sentence A prison sentence that is not fixed by the court but is left to the determination of penal authorities within minimum and maximum time limits set by the court. Also called indefinite sentence.

index fund A mutual fund that seeks to match the results of a stock market index, e.g., the S&P 500.

indexing 1. Adjusting wages or other payments to account for inflation. 2. Tracking investments to an index, e.g., the S&P 500.

Indian reservation Land set apart for tribal use of Native Americans (American Indians).

indicia Signs or indications of something; identifying marks.

indict To bring or issue an indictment.

indictable Subject or liable to being indicted.

indictable offense A crime that must be prosecuted by indictment.

indictment A formal accusation of crime made by a grand jury.

indigent 1. Impoverished. 2. Without funds to hire a private attorney.

indignity Humiliating, degrading treatment of another.

indirect contempt Behavior outside the presence of the judge that defies the authority or dignity of the court. Also called constructive contempt.

indirect evidence See circumstantial evidence.

indirect tax A tax upon some right, privilege, or franchise.

indispensable evidence Evidence essential to prove a particular fact.

indispensable party A party so essential to a suit that no final decision can be rendered without his or her joinder. The case cannot be decided on its merits without prejudicing the rights of such a party.

> "Indispensable parties" are necessary parties so essential to a suit that no final decision can be rendered without their joinder; an indispensable party is one whose interest will be substantially and directly affected by the outcome of the case and one whose interest in the subject matter is such that if he is not joined a complete and efficient determination of the equities and rights between the other parties is not possible. *Department of Revenue ex rel. Preston*, 871 So.2d 1055 (Fla.App. 2 Dist.,2004)

individual retirement account (IRA) A special account in which qualified persons can set aside a certain amount of tax-deferred income each year for savings or investment. The amount is subject to income tax upon withdrawal at the appropriate time.

indorse To place a signature on a check or other negotiable instrument to make it payable to someone other than the payee or to accept responsibility for paying it. Also spelled endorse.

indorsee The person to whom a check or other negotiable instrument is transferred by indorsement. Also spelled endorsee.

indorsement 1. Signing a check or other negotiable instrument to transfer or guarantee the instrument or to acknowledge payment. 2. The signature itself. Also spelled endorsement.

> The term "indorsement" means the act of a payee or holder in writing his or her name on the back of an instrument without further qualifying words other than "pay to the order of" or "pay to" whereby the property is assigned and transferred to another. F.S.A. § 199.185(1)(l)

indorser One who transfers a check or other negotiable instrument by indorsement.

inducement 1. The benefit or advantage that motivates a promisor to enter a contract. 2. An introductory statement in a pleading, e.g., alleging extrinsic facts that show a defamatory meaning in a libel or slander case. 3. Persuading or influencing someone to do something.

industrial relations The relationship between employer and employees on matters such as collective bargaining and job safety.

industrial union A labor union with members in the same industry (e.g., textiles) irrespective of their skills or craft. Also called vertical union.

industry An occupation or business that is a distinct branch of manufacture and trade, e.g., the steel industry.

inebriated Intoxicated; drunk.

ineffective assistance of counsel See effective assistance of counsel.

in equity Pertaining to (or in a court applying) equitable principles.

inescapable Being helpless to avoid a result by oneself; inevitable.

in esse In being, actually existing.

in evidence Before the court, having been declared admissible.

inevitable accident See unavoidable accident.

inevitable discovery doctrine Illegally obtained evidence is admissible if it inevitably would have been discovered by lawful means.

> To apply "inevitable discovery doctrine," allowing evidence obtained as result of unconstitutional police search to be admitted if evidence would ultimately have been discovered by legal means, there must be only a reasonable probability of discovery of evidence by lawful means, not an absolute certainty. *Minter-Smith*, 864 So.2d 1141 (Fla.App. 1 Dist.,2003)

infamous 1. Having a notorious reputation; shameful. 2. Denied certain civil rights due to conviction of a crime.

infamous crime A crime punishable by imprisonment or the loss of some civil rights.

infancy 1. See minority (1). 2. Childhood at its earliest stage.

infanticide The murder or killing of an infant soon after its birth.

inference 1. A process of reasoning by which a fact to be established is deduced from other facts. Reaching logical conclusions from evidence. 2. A deduction or conclusion reached by this process.

> An "inference" is a permissible deduction from the evidence which the jury may reject or accord such probative value as it desires, and it is descriptive of the factual conclusion that a jury may draw from sufficient circumstantial evidence. *Fenster*, 785 So.2d 737 (Fla.App. 4 Dist.,2001)

inferior court Any court that is subordinate to the highest court within its judicial system. Also called lower court.

infeudation Granting legal possession of land in feudal times.

infirm Lacking health; weak or feeble.

infirmative Tending to weaken a criminal charge.

infirmity Physical or mental weakness; frailty due to old age.

in flagrante delicto In the act of committing an offense.

infliction of emotional distress See intentional infliction of emotional distress.

in force In effect; legally operative.

informal Not following formal or normal procedures or forms.

informal contract 1. An oral contract. 2. A binding contract that is not under seal.

informal proceedings Proceedings that are less formal (particularly in applying the rules of evidence) than a court trial.

informant See informer.

in forma pauperis (IFP) With permission (as a poor person) to proceed without paying filing fees or other court costs.

information A formal accusation of a criminal offense from the prosecutor rather than from a grand jury indictment.

information and belief Good faith belief as to the truth of an allegation, not based on firsthand knowledge.

informed consent Agreement to let something happen based on having a reasonable understanding of the benefits and risks involved.

> "Informed consent" means consent voluntarily given by a person after a sufficient explanation and disclosure of the subject matter involved to enable that person to have a general understanding of the treatment or procedure and the medically acceptable alternatives, including the substantial risks and hazards inherent in the proposed treatment or procedures, and to make a knowing health care decision without coercion or undue influence. F.S.A. § 765.101(9)

informed intermediary A skilled and knowledgeable individual (e.g., a doctor) in the chain of distribution between the manufacturer of a product and the ultimate consumer. Also called learned intermediary.

informer A person who informs against another; one who brings an accusation against another on the basis of a suspicion that the latter has committed a crime. Also called informant.

> An undisclosed person who confidentially volunteers material information of violations of the law to officers charged with enforcement of that law. *State v. Bogard*, 388 So.2d 1296 (Fla.App., 1980)

informer's privilege The government's limited privilege to withhold the identity of persons who provide information of possible violations of law.

infra Below; later in the text.

infraction A violation (often minor) of a law, agreement, or duty.

infringement An invasion of a right; a violation of a law or duty.

infringement of copyright The unauthorized use of copyrighted material (17 USC § 106).

infringement of patent An unauthorized making, using, offering for sale, selling, or importing an invention protected by patent (35 USC § 271(a)).

infringement of trademark The unauthorized use or imitation of a registered trademark on goods of a similar class likely to confuse or deceive (15 USC § 1114).

in futuro At a future time.

ingress The act or right of entering.

in gross In a large sum or quantity; undivided.

in haec verba In these words; verbatim.

inherent Existing as a permanent or essential component.

"Inherent risk" means those dangers or conditions that are characteristic of, intrinsic to, or an integral part of skateboarding, inline skating, paintball, and freestyle bicycling. F.S.A. § 316.0085(b)

inherently dangerous Being susceptible to harm or injury in the nature of the product, service, or activity itself. Requiring great caution.

inherent defect See hidden defect.

inherent power A power that must necessarily exist in the nature of the organization or person, even if not explicitly granted.

inherent right A fundamental, nontransferable right that is basic to the existence of a person or organization. An inalienable right.

inherit 1. To take by inheritance. 2. To take by will.

inheritance 1. Property received by an heir when an ancestor dies without leaving a valid will (i.e., intestate). 2. Property received through the will of a decedent.

inheritance tax A tax on the right to receive property by descent (intestate succession) or by will. Also called death tax, succession tax.

in hoc In this regard.

in-house counsel See house counsel.

in invitum Against an unwilling party.

initial appearance The first criminal court appearance by the accused during which the court informs him or her of the charges, makes a decision on bail, and determines the date of the next proceeding.

initiative The electorate's power to propose and directly enact a statute or change in the constitution or to force the legislature to vote on the proposal.

injunction A court order requiring a person or organization to do or to refrain from doing something.

injuria absque damno A legal wrong, from which no loss or damage results, will not sustain a lawsuit for damages.

injuria non excusat injuriam One wrong does not justify or excuse another wrong.

injurious falsehood 1. The publication of a false statement that causes special damages. 2. The publication of a false statement that is derogatory to plaintiff's business of a kind calculated to prevent others from dealing with the business or otherwise to interfere with its relations with others, to its detriment. Sometimes called disparagement.

> An action for disparagement of title falls within the group of torts collectively titled "injurious falsehoods." An action for injurious falsehood protects economic interests of the injured party against pecuniary loss. *Callaway Land & Cattle Co.*, 831 So.2d 204 (Fla.App. 4 Dist.,2002)

injury 1. Any harm or damage to another or oneself. 2. An invasion of a legally protected interest of another.

in kind 1. Of the same species or category. 2. In goods or services rather than money.

in lieu of In place of.

in limine At the outset. Preliminarily. See also motion in limine.

in loco parentis In the place of a parent; assuming the duties of a parent without adoption.

inmate A person confined in a prison, hospital, or other institution.

"Inmate" means a male or female offender who is committed, under sentence to, or confined in, a penal or correctional institution. F.S.A. § 941.56(d)

innocence 1. The absence of guilt. 2. The lack of cunning or deceit.

innocent Free from guilt; untainted by wrongdoing.

innocent agent One who engages in illegal conduct on behalf of the principal wrongdoer without knowing of its illegality.

innocent construction rule If words can be interpreted as harmless or defamatory, the harmless interpretation will be adopted.

innocent party 1. One who has not knowingly or negligently participated in wrongdoing. 2. One without actual or constructive knowledge of any limitations or defects.

innocent purchaser See bona fide purchaser.

innocent spouse A spouse who did not know or have reason to know that the other spouse understated the taxes due on their joint tax return.

innocent trespasser One who enters the land of another under the mistaken belief that it is permissible to do so.

inn of court An association or society of the main trial attorneys (called barristers) in England that has a large role in their legal training and admission to practice.

innominate Belonging to no specific class.

innuendo 1. The portion of a complaint that explains a statement's defamatory meaning when this is not clear on its face. 2. An indirect derogatory comment or suggestion.

inoperative No longer in force or effective.

in pais Done informally or without legal proceedings.

in pari delicto In equal fault; equally culpable.

in pari materia Upon or involving the same matter or subject. Statutes in pari materia are to be interpreted together to try to resolve any ambiguity or inconsistency in them.

> Doctrine of "in pari materia" is a principle of statutory construction that requires that statutes relating to the same subject or object be construed together to harmonize the statutes and to give effect to the legislature's intent. *Florida Dept. of State*, 916 So.2d 763 (Fla.,2005)

in perpetuity Forever.

in personam Against the person. See also personal judgment.

in personam jurisdiction See personal jurisdiction.

in posse Capable of being; not yet in actual being or existence.

in praesenti At the present time; now.

in propria persona (in pro per) In one's own person. See pro se.

inquest An inquiry by a coroner or medical examiner to determine the cause of death of a person who appears to have died suddenly or by violence.

> As used in this chapter, the term "inquest" means a formal, nonadversary, nonjury presentation of evidence concerning a death, discovered by the medical examiner, state attorney, and law enforcement agency during their respective examinations and investigations into the death. F.S.A. § 936.002

inquiry 1. A careful examination or investigation. 2. A question.

inquiry notice Knowledge of facts that would lead a reasonably cautious person to inquire further.

inquisitorial system The fact-finding system in some civil law countries in which the judge has a more active role in questioning the witnesses and in conducting the trial than in an adversary system.

in re In the matter of. A way of designating a court case in which there are no adversary parties in the traditional sense.

in rem (against the res or thing) Pertaining to a proceeding or action binding the whole world in which the court resolves the status of a specific property or thing. The action is not against a person.

> Every cause of action the object of which requires the court to act directly on property or on title to property is an in rem action. *Publix Super Markets*, 502 So.2d 484 (Fla.App. 5 Dist.,1987)

in rem jurisdiction The court's power over a particular res, which is a thing within the territory over which the court has authority.

INS Immigration and Naturalization Service, now U.S. Citizenship and Immigration Services (*www.uscis.gov*).

insane delusion An irrational, persistent belief in nonexistent facts.

insanity 1. That degree of mental illness that negates an individual's legal responsibility or capacity to perform certain legal actions. Also called lunacy. 2. Model Penal Code test: As a result of a mental disease or defect, the accused lacks substantial capacity to appreciate the criminality of his or her conduct or to conform the conduct to the law. Also called substantial capacity test. 3. *Durham* test: The unlawful act was the product of mental disease or mental defect. 4. *M'Naghten* test: Laboring under such a defect of reason, from disease of the mind, as not to know the nature and quality of the act the accused was doing, or if the accused did know it, he or she did not know that it was wrong. Also spelled *McNaghten*. Also called right-and-wrong test. 5. Irresistible impulse test: An urge to commit an act induced by a mental disease so that the person is unable to resist the impulse to commit the act even if he or she knows that the act was wrong.

> Insanity is established when: (a) The defendant had a mental infirmity, disease, or defect; and (b) Because of this condition, the defendant: 1. Did not know what he or she was doing or its consequences; or 2. Although the defendant knew what he or she was doing and its consequences, the defendant did not know that what he or she was doing was wrong. Mental infirmity, disease, or defect does not constitute a defense of insanity except as provided in this subsection. F.S.A. § 775.027

inscription Entering, enrolling, or registering a fact or name on a list or record.

in se In and of itself. See malum in se.

insecurity clause A clause stating that a party may accelerate payment or performance or require collateral (or additional collateral) when he or she feels insecure because of a danger of default.

insider 1. One with knowledge of facts not available to the general public. 2. An officer or director of a corporation or anyone who owns more than 10 percent of its shares.

insider trading Conduct by corporate employees (or others who owe a fiduciary duty to the corporation) who trade in their company's stock based on material, nonpublic information, or who tip others about confidential corporate information. Trading in securities based on material, nonpublic information acquired in violation of a duty of confidence owed to the source of the information.

insolvency The condition of being unable to pay one's debts as they mature or fall due in the usual course of one's trade and business.

in specie In kind; in the same or like form.

inspection An examination of the quality or fitness of something.

installment A part of a debt payable in stages or successive periods.

installment contract A contract that requires or authorizes the delivery of goods in separate lots to be separately accepted or paid for. UCC 2-612.

> An "installment contract" is one which requires or authorizes the delivery of goods in separate lots to be separately accepted, even though the contract contains a clause "each delivery is a separate contract" or its equivalent. F.S.A. § 672.612(1)

installment credit A commercial arrangement in which the buyer pays for goods or services in more than one payment (often at regular intervals), for which a finance charge may be imposed.

installment loan A loan to be repaid in specified (often equal) amounts over a designated period.

installment note See serial note.

installment sale A commercial arrangement in which a buyer makes an initial down payment and agrees to pay the balance in installments over a period of time. The seller may keep title or take a security interest in the goods sold until full payment is made.

instance 1. Bringing of a law suit. 2. Occurrence. 3. Urgent insistence.

instant 1. Now under consideration. 2. The present.

instanter At once.

in statu quo In the same condition in which it was.

instigate To stimulate or goad someone to act; to incite.

in stirpes See per stirpes.

institute 1. To inaugurate or begin. 2. An organization that studies or promotes a particular area. 3. Legal treatise or textbooks.

institution 1. The commencement of something. 2. An enduring or established organization. 3. A place for the treatment of those with special needs. 4. A basic practice or custom, e.g., marriage.

instruction See charge (1).

instrument 1. A formal written document that gives expression to or embodies a legal act or agreement, e.g., contract, will. 2. See negotiable instrument. 3. A means by which something is achieved.

instrumentality A means or agency by which something is done.

insubordination Intentional disregard of instructions. Disobedience.

insufficient evidence Evidence that cannot support a finding of fact.

insurable Capable of being insured against loss.

insurable interest Any actual, legal, and substantial economic interest in the safety or preservation of the subject of the insurance.

insurance A contract to provide compensation for loss or liability that may occur by or to a specified subject by specified risks.

insurance adjuster A person who investigates, values, and tries to settle insurance claims.

insurance broker An intermediary or middleman between the public and an insurer on insurance matters such as the sale of an insurance policy. A broker is not tied to a particular insurance company.

> An "insurance broker" solicits insurance orders from the general public and is not bound by contract to work for or solicit insurance for any particular insurance company. *Amstar Ins. Co.*, 862 So.2d 736 (Fla.App. 5 Dist.,2003)

insurance policy An instrument in writing by which one party (insurer) engages for the consideration of a premium to indemnify another (insured) against a contingent loss by providing compensation if a designated event occurs, resulting in the loss.

insurance trust A trust containing insurance policies and proceeds for distribution under the terms of the trust.

insure 1. To obtain insurance. 2. To issue a policy of insurance.

insured The person covered or protected by insurance.

insurer The underwriter or insurance company that issues insurance.

insurgent One in revolt against government or political authority.

insurrection A rising of citizens or subjects in revolt against civil authority. Using violence to overthrow a government.

intangible 1. Without physical form. 2. Property or an asset that is a "right" (e.g., copyright, option) rather than a physical object even though the right may be evidenced by something physical such as a written contract.

> "Intangible property rights" are group of rights inhering in person's relation to physical thing, as right to possess or use, and may arise from contract. *Department of Transp.*, 705 So.2d 584 (Fla.App. 5 Dist.,1997)

intangible asset; intangible property See intangible (2).

integrated bar A bar association to which all lawyers must belong if they want to practice law. Also called unified bar. The Florida Bar is an integrated bar.

integrated contract A contract that represents the complete and final understanding of the parties' agreement.

integration 1. Bringing together different groups, e.g., different races. 2. Making something whole or entire. Combining into one.

integration clause A contract clause stating that the writing is meant to represent the parties' entire and final agreement. Also called merger clause.

intellectual property Intangible property rights that can have commercial value (e.g., patents, copyrights, trademarks, trade names, trade secrets) derived from creative or original activity of the mind or intellect.

intend 1. To have in mind as a goal; to plan. 2. To mean or signify. See also intent.

intended use doctrine Manufacturers must design their products so that they are reasonably safe for their intended users.

intendment The true meaning or intention of something.

intent 1. Design, plan, or purpose in performing an act. 2. The desire to cause the consequences of one's act (or failure to act) or the knowledge with substantial certainty that the consequences will follow from what one does (or fails to do).

intention 1. The purpose or design with which an act is done. Goal. See also intent. 2. Determination or willingness to do something.

intentional Deliberately done; desiring the consequences of an act or knowing with substantial certainty that they will result.

intentional infliction of emotional distress (IIED) The tort of intentionally or recklessly causing severe emotional distress by an act of extreme or outrageous conduct. Also called outrage.

> A cause of action for "intentional infliction of severe mental or emotional distress," more appropriately called "outrageous conduct causing severe emotional distress," essentially involves deliberate or reckless infliction of mental suffering on another, even if unconnected to any other actionable wrong. *Dominguez*, 438 So.2d 58 (Fla.App. 3 Dist.,1983)

inter alia Among other things.

intercept 1. To seize benefits owed to a parent to cover delinquent child support obligations. 2. To covertly acquire the contents of a communication via an electronic or other device. To wiretap.

interdict 1. To forbid, prevent, restrict. 2. To intercept and seize. 3. An injunction or prohibition. 4. One incapacitated by an infirmity.

interest 1. A right, claim, title, or legal share in something; a right to have the advantage accruing from something. 2. A charge that is paid to borrow money or for a delay in its return when due.

interested Involved, nonobjective; having a stake in the outcome.

Interest on Lawyers' Trust Accounts (IOLTA) A program in which designated client funds held by an attorney are deposited in a bank account, the interest from which can be used (often through a foundation) to help finance legal services for low-income persons.

interference 1. Hindering or obstructing something. 2. Meddling. 3. A patent proceeding to determine who has priority in an invention.

interference with prospective advantage The tort of intentionally interfering with a reasonable expectation of an economic advantage, usually a commercial or business advantage.

> Intentional interference with an expectancy is a relatively new and undeveloped tort. It apparently evolved from the commercial tort of interference with prospective advantage. The elements of this evolving tort include: (1) the existence of an expectancy; (2) intentional interference with the expectancy through tortious conduct; (3) causation; and (4) damages. *Whalen*, 719 So.2d 2 (Fla.App. 2 Dist.,1998)

interim 1. Intervening time; meantime. 2. Temporary.

interim order A temporary order that applies until another order is issued.

interlineation Writing between the lines of an existing document.

interlocking director A member of the board of directors of more than one corporation at the same time.

interlocutory Not final; interim.

interlocutory appeal An appeal that occurs before the trial court reaches its final judgment.

interlocutory decree An intermediate decree or judgment that resolves a preliminary matter or issue.

> A decree is "interlocutory," and therefore subject to reconsideration and modification, when it leaves any question in the cause open for future judicial determination. *State v. Milne*, 921 So.2d 792 (Fla.App. 5 Dist.,2006)

interlocutory injunction See preliminary injunction.

interlocutory order An order made before final judgment on an incidental or ancillary matter. Also called intermediate order.

interloper One who meddles in the affairs of others.

intermeddler See officious intermeddler.

intermediary A go-between or mediator who tries to resolve conflicts.

intermediary bank Any bank (other than a depositary or payor bank) to which an item is transferred in the course of collection.

intermediate In the middle position.

intermediate court An appellate court below the court of last resort.

intermediate order See interlocutory order.

intermittent easement An easement that is used only occasionally.

intermixture of goods See confusion of goods.

intern 1. To restrict or confine a person or group. 2. A student obtaining practical experience and training outside the classroom.

internal law The law within a state or country; local law.

internal revenue Tax revenue from internal (not foreign) sources.

Internal Revenue Code (IRC) The federal statute in title 26 of the U.S. Code that codifies federal tax laws.

Internal Revenue Service (IRS) The federal agency responsible for enforcing most federal tax laws (*www.irs.gov*).

internal security Laws and government activity to counter threats from subversive activities.

international agreements Contracts (e.g., treaties) among countries.

International Court of Justice (ICJ) The judicial arm of the United Nations that renders advisory opinions and resolves disputes submitted to it by nations (*www.icj-cij.org*).

international law The legal principles and laws governing relations between nations. Also called law of nations, public international law.

International Paralegal Management Association (IPMA) An association of paralegal managers at law firms and corporations (*www.paralegalmanagement.org*).

internment The confinement of persons suspected of disloyalty.

interplead 1. To file an interpleader. 2. To assert your claim or position on an issue in a case already before the court.

interpleader A remedy or suit to determine a right to property held by a disinterested third party (called the stakeholder) who is in doubt about ownership and who, therefore, deposits the property with the trial court to permit interested parties to litigate ownership.

If more than one person claims title or possession of the goods, the bailee is excused from delivery until he or she has had a reasonable time to ascertain the validity of the adverse claims or to bring an action to compel all claimants to interplead and may compel such interpleader, either in defending an action for nondelivery of the goods, or by original action, whichever is appropriate. F.S.A. § 677.603

Interpol International Criminal Police Organization; a coordinating group for international law enforcement (*www.interpol.int*).

interpolation Inserting words in a document to change or clarify it.

interpose To submit or introduce something, especially a defense.

interpret To explain the meaning of language or conduct. To construe.

interpretive rule The rule of an administrative agency that explains or clarifies the meaning of existing statutes and regulations.

interrogation A methodical questioning of someone, e.g., a suspect.

"Interrogation" takes place, for purposes of state constitutional self-incrimination clause restrictions on interrogation, when a person is subject to express questions, or other words or actions, by a state agent, that a reasonable person would conclude are designed to lead to an incriminating response. F.S.A. Const. Art. 1, § 9. *J.G.*, 883 So.2d 915 (Fla.App. 1 Dist.,2004)

interrogatories A discovery device consisting of written questions about a lawsuit submitted by one party to another.

in terrorem clause A clause with a threat, e.g., a clause in a will stating that a gift to a beneficiary will be forfeited if he or she contests the validity of the will. Also called a no-contest clause.

inter se; inter sese Among or between themselves.

interspousal Relating to or between husband and wife.

interspousal immunity Spouses cannot sue each other for personal torts, e.g., battery. Also called husband-wife immunity.

interstate Involving two or more states.

interstate commerce The exchange of goods or services (commerce) between two or more states of the United States (including a U.S. territory or the District of Columbia).

interstate compact An agreement between two or more states (and approved by Congress) that is designed to address common problems.

interval ownership See time-sharing.

intervening Coming or occurring between two times or events.

intervening cause A new and independent force that breaks the causal connection between the original wrong and the injury; a later cause that so interrupts the chain of events as to become the proximate cause of the injury. Also called efficient intervening cause.

Under the "intervening negligence doctrine," the original negligence is not regarded as the "proximate cause" of the injury, even though the injury might not have occurred but for the original negligence, if an independent efficient cause intervenes between the negligence and the injury and the original negligence does not directly contribute to the force or effectiveness of the intervening cause. *St. Fort ex rel. St. Fort*, 902 So.2d 244 (Fla.App. 4 Dist.,2005)

intervenor A person with an interest in real or personal property who applies to be made a party to an existing lawsuit involving that property.

intervention The procedure by which a third person, not originally a party but claiming an interest in the subject matter of the suit, is allowed to come into the case to protect his or her own interests.

inter vivos Between or pertaining to the living.

inter vivos gift A gift that takes effect when the donor is living.

Basic elements necessary to establish a "gift inter vivos," thereby giving rise to creation of a joint account of money with the right of survivorship, are: (1) clear intention of donor to transfer a present interest, (2) delivery by surrender of dominion and control to the donee, and (3) acceptance of gift by the donee. *Williams*, 255 So.2d 273 (Fla.App. 1971)

inter vivos trust A trust that takes effect when its creator (the settler) is living. Also called living trust.

intestacy Dying without a valid will.

intestate 1. Without making a valid will. 2. The person who dies without making a valid will.

intestate succession The transfer of property to the relatives of a decedent who dies without leaving a valid will. Also called descent and distribution, hereditary succession.

in testimonium In witness; in evidence whereof.

in the matter of See in re.

intimidate To coerce unlawfully.

in toto In total; completely.

intoxication A significantly lessened physical or mental ability to function normally, caused by alcohol or drugs.

intra Within.

intrastate commerce Commerce that occurs exclusively within one state.

intra vires Within the power; within the scope of lawful authority.

intrinsic Pertaining to the essential nature of a thing.

intrinsic evidence The evidence found within the writing or document itself.

intrinsic fraud Fraud that goes to the existence of a cause of action or an issue in the case, e.g., perjured testimony.

For purposes of an independent action to set aside a judgment due to fraud, "intrinsic fraud" is fraudulent conduct that arises within a proceeding and pertains to the issues in the case that have been tried or could have been tried. *Department of Revenue ex rel. Stephens*, 915 So.2d 717 (Fla.App. 5 Dist.,2005)

intrinsic value The true, inherent, and essential value of a thing, not depending on externals, but the same everywhere and to everyone.

intrusion 1. Wrongfully entering upon or taking something. 2. See invasion of privacy (1)(c).

inure 1. To take effect. 2. To habituate. Also spelled enure.

in utero In the uterus.

invalid 1. Having no legal effect. 2. A disabled person.

invasion 1. An encroachment on the rights of others. 2. Making payments from the principal of a trust rather than from its income.

invasion of privacy 1. Four separate torts. (a) Appropriation: The use of a person's name, likeness, or personality for commercial gain without authorization. (b) False light: Unreasonably offensive publicity that places another in a false light. (c) Intrusion: An unreasonably offensive encroachment or invasion into someone's private affairs or concerns. (d) Public disclosure of a private fact: Unreasonably offensive publicity concerning the private life of a person. 2. A constitutional prohibition of unreasonable governmental interferences with one's private affairs or effects.

invention The creation of a potentially patentable process or device through independent effort. The discovery of a new process or product.

inventory 1. A detailed list of property or assets. 2. Goods in stock held for sale or lease or under contracts of service, raw materials, works in process, or materials used or consumed in a business.

in ventre sa mere See en ventre sa mere.

inverse condemnation A cause of action for the taking of private property for public use without proper condemnation proceedings.

> "Inverse condemnation" is cause of action by property owner to recover value of property that has been de facto taken by agency having power of eminent domain where no formal exercise of that power has been undertaken. *Sarasota Welfare Home*, 666 So.2d 171 (Fla.App. 2 Dist.,1995)

inverse order of alienation doctrine One seeking to collect on a lien or mortgage on land sold off in successive parcels must collect first from any land still with the original owner; if this land is insufficient to satisfy the debt, he or she must resort to the parcel last sold, and then to the next to the last, and so on until the debt is satisfied.

invest 1. To use money to acquire assets in order to produce revenue. 2. To give power or authority to. 3. To devote to a task; to commit.

investiture See livery of seisin.

investment advisor One who, for compensation, engages in the business of advising others (directly or through publications) on the value of securities or the advisability of investing in, purchasing, or selling securities, or who, as a part of a regular business, publishes reports about securities.

investment bank A financial institution engaged in underwriting, selling securities, raising capital, and giving advice on mergers and acquisitions.

investment company A company in the business of investing, reinvesting, or trading in securities (15 USC § 80a-3). A company that sells shares and invests in securities of other companies. Also called an investment trust.

investment contract A contract in which money is invested in a common enterprise with profits to come solely from the efforts of others.

investment income Income from investment capital rather than income resulting from labor. Also called unearned income.

investment securities Instruments such as stocks, bonds, and options used for investment.

investment tax credit A credit against taxes, consisting of a percentage of the purchase price of capital goods and equipment.

investment trust See investment company.

invidious discrimination An arbitrary classification that is not reasonably related to a legitimate purpose. Offensively unequal treatment.

invited error rule On appeal, a party cannot complain about an error for which he or she is responsible, such as an erroneous ruling that he or she prompted or invited the trial court to make.

> Under the "invited error doctrine," a party may not make or invite error at trial and then take advantage of the error on appeal. *Bryan*, 930 So.2d 693 (Fla.App. 3 Dist.,2006)

invitee One who enters land upon the express or implied invitation of the occupier of the land to use the land for the purpose for which it is held open to the public or to pursue the business of the occupier.

invocation 1. Calling upon for assistance or authority. 2. The enforcement of something. The verb is *invoke*.

invoice A document giving the price and other details of a sale of goods or services.

involuntary 1. Not under the control of the will. 2. Compulsory.

involuntary bailment A bailment arising by an accidental, nonnegligent leaving of personal property in the possession of another.

involuntary bankruptcy Bankruptcy forced on a debtor by creditors.

involuntary commitment See civil commitment.

involuntary confession A confession obtained by threats, improper promises, or other unlawful pressure from someone in law enforcement.

involuntary conversion The loss or destruction of property through theft, casualty, or condemnation.

involuntary dismissal A dismissal of an action for failure to prosecute the action or to comply with a court rule or order.

involuntary dissolution The forced termination of the existence of a corporation or other legal entity.

involuntary intoxication Intoxication resulting when one does not knowingly and willingly ingest an intoxicating substance.

involuntary manslaughter The unintentional killing of another without malice while engaged in an unlawful activity that is not a felony and does not naturally tend to cause death or great bodily harm or while engaged in a lawful activity with a reckless disregard for the safety of others.

> The killing of a human being by the act, procurement, or culpable negligence of another in cases where such killing shall not be justifiable or excusable homicide or murder, or the death of a human being caused by the operation of a motor vehicle by any person while intoxicated. *Houser*, 474 So.2d 1193 (Fla.,1985)

involuntary nonsuit The dismissal of an action when the plaintiff fails to appear, gives no evidence on which a jury could find a verdict, or receives an adverse ruling that precludes recovery.

involuntary servitude The condition of being compelled to labor for another (with or without compensation) by force or imprisonment.

involuntary trust See constructive trust.

IOLTA See Interest on Lawyers' Trust Accounts.

IPMA See International Paralegal Management Association (*www.paralegalmanagement.org*).

ipse dixit An unproven or unsupported assertion made by a person.

ipso facto By that very fact; in and of itself.

ipso jure By the law itself; by the mere operation of law.

IRA See individual retirement account.

IRC See Internal Revenue Code.

irrational Illogical, not guided by a fair assessment of the facts.

irrebuttable presumption See conclusive presumption.

irreconcilable differences A no-fault ground of divorce that exists when persistent, unresolvable disagreements between the spouses lead to an irremediable breakdown of the marriage.

irrecusable Cannot be challenged or rejected.

irregular Not according to rule, proper procedure, or the norm.

irrelevant Not tending to prove or disprove any issue in the case.

irremediable breakdown See irretrievable breakdown.

irreparable Not capable of being repaired or restored.

irreparable injury Harm that cannot be adequately redressed by an award of monetary damages. An injunction, therefore, is possible.

> "Irreparable injury" for purposes of statute allowing injunction to enforce covenant not to compete when such injury is present, means in essence that injunction is only practical mode of enforcement. F.S.A. § 542.33. *Jewett Orthopaedic Clinic*, 629 So.2d 922 (Fla.App. 5 Dist.,1993)

irresistible impulse See insanity (5).

irretrievable breakdown A no-fault ground of divorce that exists when there is such discord and incompatibility between the spouses that the legitimate objects of matrimony have been destroyed and there is no reasonable possibility of resolution. Also called irremediable breakdown.

irrevocable Not capable of being revoked or recalled.

irrevocable trust A trust that cannot be terminated by its creator.

IRS See Internal Revenue Service (*www.irs.gov*).

issuable 1. Open to debate or litigation. 2. Allowed or authorized for issue or sale. 3. Possible.

issue 1. To send forth, announce, or promulgate. 2. A legal question. A point or matter in controversy or dispute. 3. Offspring; lineal descendants, e.g., child, grandchild. 4. A group or class of securities offered for sale in a block or at the same time. Also called stock issue. 5. The first delivery of a negotiable instrument.

issue of fact A dispute over the existence or nonexistence of an alleged fact. The controversy that exists when one party asserts a fact that is disputed by the other side. Also called question of fact or fact question.

issue of law A question of what the law is, what the law means, or how the law applies to a set of established, assumed, or agreed-upon facts. Also called legal question or question of law.

issue preclusion See collateral estoppel.

item 1. An instrument or a promise or order to pay money handled by a bank for collection or payment. 2. An entry on an account. 3. A part of something.

itemized deduction A payment that is allowed as a deduction from adjusted gross income on a tax return.

J

J Judge; justice.

jactitation False boasting; false claims causing harm.

JAG See Judge Advocate General.

jail A place of confinement, usually for persons awaiting trial or serving sentences for misdemeanors or minor crimes.

jailhouse lawyer An inmate who is allowed to give legal assistance and advice to other prisoners if the institution provides no alternatives.

Jane Doe; Jane Roe A fictitious name for a female party in legal proceedings if the real name is unknown or is being kept confidential.

***Jason* clause** A clause in a bill of lading requiring a general average contribution (see this phrase). *The Jason*, 32 S. Ct. 560 (1912).

jaywalking Failure to use crosswalks or to comply with other regulations for crossing the street.

J.D. See Juris Doctor.

***Jencks* rule** After a witness called by the federal prosecutor has testified on direct examination, the court shall, on motion of the defendant, order the prosecution to produce any statement of the witness in the possession of the prosecution that relates to the subject matter of the testimony to aid the defendant in the cross-examination of this witness. 18 USC § 3500(b); *Jencks v. U.S.*, 77 S. Ct. 1007 (1957).

> The items sought are examples of work product in its purest and narrowest sense, to which the accused is not ordinarily entitled, except perhaps as may be required under the *Jencks* rule, i.e., made available to the accused at trial for purposes of effective cross-examination within the scope of the right of confrontation. *State v. Gillespie*, 227 So.2d 550 (Fla.App. 1969)

jeopardy The risk of conviction and punishment once a criminal defendant has been placed on trial. Legal jeopardy.

jeopardy assessment If the collection of a tax appears to be in question, the IRS may assess and collect the tax immediately without going through the usual formalities.

jetsam Goods abandoned at sea that sink and remain underwater. Goods that the owner voluntarily throws overboard in an emergency in order to lighten the ship.

jettison To discard or throw overboard in order to lighten the load of a ship in danger. Goods thrown overboard for this purpose.

Jim Crow law A law that intentionally discriminates against blacks.

JJ Judges; justices.

JNOV See judgment notwithstanding the verdict.

jobber 1. One who buys goods from manufacturers and sells them to retailers. A wholesaler. 2. One who does odd jobs or piecework.

John Doe; Richard Roe A fictitious name for a male party in legal proceedings if the real name is unknown or is being kept confidential.

joinder Uniting two or more parties as plaintiffs, two or more parties as defendants, or two or more claims into a single lawsuit.

joinder of issue The assertion of a fact by a party in a pleading and its denial by the opposing party. The point in litigation when opponents take opposite positions on a matter of law or fact.

joint 1. Shared by or between two or more. 2. United or coupled together in interest or liability.

joint account An account of two or more persons containing assets that each can withdraw in full, and, upon the death of one of them, is payable to the others rather than to the heirs or beneficiaries of the decedent.

joint adventure See joint venture.

joint and mutual will A single will executed by two or more persons disposing of property owned individually or together that shows that the devises or dispositions were made in consideration of one another.

joint and several Together as well as individually or separately.

joint and several liability Legally responsible together and individually. Each wrongdoer is individually responsible for the *entire* judgment; the plaintiff can choose to collect from one wrongdoer or from all of them until the judgment is satisfied.

> Joint and several liability allows a claimant to recover all damages from one of multiple defendants even though that particular defendant may be the least responsible defendant in the cause. West's F.S.A. § 768.81(3). *Agency for Health Care Admin.*, 678 So.2d 1239 (Fla.,1996)

joint and survivor annuity An annuity with two beneficiaries (e.g., husband and wife) that continues to make payments until both beneficiaries die.

joint annuity An annuity with two beneficiaries that stops making payments when either dies.

joint bank account See joint account.

joint committee A legislative committee whose membership is from both houses of the legislature.

joint custody This phrase can mean (a) joint legal custody in which both parents share the right to make the major decisions on raising their child, who may reside primarily with one parent, (b) joint physical custody in which the child resides with each parent individually for alternating, although not necessarily equal, periods of time, or (c) both joint legal custody and joint physical custody.

> The mother and father jointly are natural guardians of their own children. . . . If the parents are given joint custody, then both shall continue as natural guardians. F.S.A. § 744.301(1)

joint enterprise See joint venture.

joint estate A form of joint ownership, e.g., joint tenancy, tenancy in common, tenancy by the entirety.

joint legal custody See joint custody.

joint liability Two or more parties together have an obligation or liability to a third party. Liability that is owed to a third party by two or more parties together.

joint lives The duration of an estate lasting until either one of two named persons dies.

joint obligation An obligation incurred by two or more debtors to a single performance to one creditor.

joint ownership Two or more persons who jointly hold title to, or have an interest in, property.

joint physical custody See joint custody.

joint resolution A resolution passed by both houses of a legislative body.

joint return A federal, state, or local tax return filed by a husband and wife together regardless of who earned the income.

joint stock company An unincorporated association of individuals who hold shares of the common capital they contribute. Also called stock association.

joint tenancy Property that is owned equally by two or more persons (called joint tenants) with the right of survivorship. Joint tenants have one and the same interest; accruing by one and the same conveyance, instrument, or act; commencing at one and the same time; with one and the same undivided possession.

> In joint tenancy, in addition to unity of possession, the interest must be the same, must have originated in the identical conveyance, and must therefore have commenced simultaneously, and there is the added characteristic of survivorship. *Andrews*, 21 So.2d 205 (Fla.1945)

joint tortfeasors Two or more persons who together commit a tort. One or more persons jointly or severally liable in tort for the same loss to person or property.

jointure A widow's freehold estate in lands (in lieu of dower) to take effect on the death of her husband and to continue during her life.

joint venture An association of persons who jointly undertake some commercial enterprise in which they share profits. An agreement among members of a group to carry out a common purpose, in which each has an equal voice in the control and direction of the enterprise. Also called joint adventure, joint enterprise.

> For purposes of this section, joint venture means any association of two or more business concerns to carry out a single business enterprise for profit, for which purpose they combine their property, capital, efforts, skills, and knowledge. F.S.A. § 287.09451(4)(n)

joint will A single testamentary instrument (will) executed by more than one person. It can dispose of property owned individually and jointly.

joint work A work prepared by two or more authors with the intention that their contributions be merged into inseparable or interdependent parts of a unitary whole (17 USC § 101).

Jones Act The federal statute that provides a remedy to seamen injured in the course of employment due to negligence (46 USC § 30104).

journal 1. A book in which entries are made, often on a regular basis. 2. A periodical or magazine.

journalist's privilege 1. The privilege of a journalist not to disclose information obtained while gathering news, including the identity of sources. Also called reporter's privilege. 2. The qualified privilege of the media (asserted in defamation actions) to make fair comment about public figures on matters of public concern.

> A professional journalist has a qualified privilege not to be a witness concerning, and not to disclose the information, including the identity of any source, that the professional journalist has obtained while actively gathering news. F.S.A. § 90.5015(2)

journeyman A person who has progressed through an apprenticeship in a craft or trade and is now qualified to work for another.

joyriding Driving an automobile without authorization but without the intent to steal it.

J.P. See justice of the peace.

J.S.D. Doctor of Juridical Science.

judge 1. A public officer appointed or elected to preside over and to administer the law in a court of justice or similar tribunal. 2. To resolve a dispute authoritatively.

judge advocate A legal officer or adviser in the military. A legal officer on the staff of the Judge Advocate General.

Judge Advocate General (JAG) The senior legal officer in the army, navy, or air force (see, e.g., *www.jag.navy.mil*).

judge-made law 1. Law created by judges in court opinions. Law derived from judicial precedents rather than from statutes. 2. A court decision that fails to apply the intent of the legislature. Also called judicial legislation.

judgment The final conclusion of a court that resolves a legal dispute or that specifies what further proceedings are needed to resolve it.

> Judgment is court's decision on merits as to whether plaintiff shall obtain relief sought in litigation. *Makar*, 553 So.2d 298 (Fla.App. 1 Dist.,1989). Until rendered, the decision of a trial judge is not a judgment. *Carr*, 578 So.2d 347 (Fla.App. 1 Dist.,1991).

judgment as a matter of law A judgment on an issue in a federal jury trial (and in some state jury trials) ordered by the judge against a party because there is no legally sufficient evidentiary basis for a reasonable jury to find for that party on that issue. The judgment may be rendered before or after the verdict. In some state courts, the judgment is called a *directed verdict* if it is rendered before the jury reaches a verdict and a *judgment notwithstanding the verdict* (JNOV or judgment n.o.v.) if it is rendered after the jury reaches a verdict.

judgment book The book or docket in which the clerk enters the judgments that are rendered.

judgment by default See default judgment.

judgment creditor A person in whose favor a money judgment (damages) is entered or who becomes entitled to enforce it.

judgment debtor A person ordered to pay a money judgment (damages) rendered against him or her.

judgment in personam See personal judgment.

judgment in rem A judgment concerning the status or condition of property. The judgment is against or on the property, not a person. See also in rem.

judgment lien A lien on property of a judgment debtor giving the judgment creditor the right to levy on it to satisfy the judgment.

judgment nisi ("a judgment unless") A judgment that will stand unless the party affected by it appears and shows cause against it.

judgment non obstante veredicto See judgment notwithstanding the verdict.

judgment note See cognovit.

judgment notwithstanding the verdict (JNOV) A court judgment that is opposite to the verdict reached by the jury. Also called judgment non obstante veredicto or judgment n.o.v. In federal court, it is called a *judgment as a matter of law* (see this phrase).

> A JNOV is appropriate only in situations where there is no evidence upon which a jury could rely in finding for the non-movant. *McQueen*, 909 So.2d 491 (Fla.App. 5 Dist.,2005)

judgment n.o.v. See judgment notwithstanding the verdict.

judgment on the merits A judgment, rendered after evidentiary inquiry and argument, determining which party is in the right, as opposed to a judgment based solely on a technical point or procedural error.

judgment on the pleadings A judgment based solely on the facts alleged in the complaint, answer, and other pleadings.

judgment proof A person without assets to satisfy a judgment.

judgment quasi in rem A judgment determining a particular person's interest in specific property within the court's jurisdiction. See also quasi in rem.

judicature 1. The judiciary. 2. The administration of justice. 3. The jurisdiction or authority of a judge.

judicial Pertaining to the courts, the office of a judge, or judgments.

judicial act A decision or other exercise of power by a court.

judicial activism Writing court decisions that invalidate arguably valid statutes, fail to follow precedent, or that inject the court's political or social philosophy. Sometimes called judicial legislation.

judicial admission A deliberate, clear statement of a party on a concrete fact within the party's peculiar knowledge that is conclusive upon the party making it, thereby relieving the opposing party from presenting any evidence on it.

judicial bonds Generic term for bonds required by a court for appeals, costs, attachment, injunction, etc.

judicial discretion The ability or power of a court (when it is not bound to decide an issue one way or another) to choose between two or more courses of action. Also called legal discretion.

> Judicial discretion means a discretion exercised within limits of applicable principles of law and equity, and the exercise of which, if clearly arbitrary, unreasonable, or unjust, when tested in light of such principles, amounting to an abuse of such discretion, may be set aside on appeal. *Ellard*, 77 So.2d 617 (Fla.1955)

judicial economy Efficiency in the use of the courts' resources.

judicial immunity The exemption of judges from civil liability arising out of the discharge of judicial functions.

judicial legislation 1. Statutes creating or involving the courts. 2. See judge-made law (2), judicial activism.

judicial lien A lien that arises by judgment, sequestration, or other legal or equitable process or proceeding (11 USC § 101).

judicial notice A court's acceptance of a well-known fact without requiring proof of that fact.

> Judicial notice is the cognizance of certain facts which judges and the jurors may properly take and act upon without proof because they already know them. *Mitchum*, 251 So.2d 298 (Fla.App. 1971)

judicial power The power of the court to decide and pronounce a judgment and carry it into effect between parties in the case.

judicial question A question that is proper for the courts to resolve.

judicial restraint Courts should resolve issues before them without reaching other issues that do not have to be resolved, follow precedent closely without injecting personal views and philosophies, and defer to the right of the legislature to make policy.

judicial review 1. The power of a court to interpret statutes and administrative laws to determine their constitutionality. 2. The power of a court to examine the legal and factual conclusions of a lower court or administrative agency to determine whether errors were made.

judicial sale A sale based on a court decree ordering the sale.

judicial separation See legal separation.

judiciary The branch of government vested with the judicial power; the system of courts in a country; the body of judges; the bench.

jump bail To fail to appear at the next scheduled court appearance after having been released on bail.

junior Subordinate; lower in rank or priority.

junior bond A bond that has a lower payment priority than other bonds.

junior lien A lien that has a lower priority than other liens on the same property.

junk science Unreliable, potentially misleading scientific evidence.

> When predictions are not based on proven methodology they lack the competence justifying consideration by the trier of fact because they provide no factual assistance, only prejudice, speculation, and/or what some may call junk science. *Westerheide*, 767 So.2d 637 (Fla.App. 5 Dist.,2000)

jura Rights; laws.

jural Pertaining to law, justice, rights, and legal obligations.

jurat A certificate of a person before whom a writing was sworn. A certification by a notary public that the person signing the writing (e.g., an affidavit) appeared before the notary and swore that the assertions in the writing were true.

jure By the law; by right.

juridical Relating to the law or the administration of justice.

juris Of law; of right.

jurisdiction 1. The power of a court to decide a matter in controversy. 2. The geographic area over which a particular court has authority. 3. The scope of power or authority that a person or entity can exercise. See also personal jurisdiction, in rem jurisdiction, quasi in rem jurisdiction, and subject-matter jurisdiction.

> Jurisdiction means a state, territory, or possession of the United States; the District of Columbia; the Commonwealth of Puerto Rico; or a Canadian province. F.S.A. § 322.50(1)
>
> Jurisdiction is generally defined as power of court lawfully to hear and determine cause. *Hall*, 677 So.2d 88 (Fla.App. 1 Dist.,1996)

jurisdictional amount See amount in controversy.

jurisdictional dispute Competing claims by different unions that their members are entitled to perform certain work.

jurisdictional facts Those facts that must exist before the court can properly take jurisdiction of the particular case.

jurisdiction in personam See personal jurisdiction.

jurisdiction in rem See in rem jurisdiction.

jurisdiction of the subject matter See subject-matter jurisdiction.

jurisdiction quasi in rem See quasi in rem jurisdiction.

Juris Doctor (J.D.) Doctor of law. The standard degree received upon completion of law school. Also called doctor of jurisprudence.

jurisprudence The philosophy of law; a science that ascertains the principles on which legal rules are based. The system of laws.

jurist A legal scholar; a judge.

juristic person See artificial person.

juror A member of a jury.

jury A group of persons selected to resolve disputes of fact and to return a verdict based on the evidence presented to them.

jury box The courtroom location where the jury observes the trial.

jury charge See charge (1).

jury commissioner An official in charge of prospective jurors.

jury instructions See charge (1).

jury list A list of citizens who could be called for jury duty.

jury nullification A jury's refusal to apply a law perceived to be unjust or unpopular by acquitting a defendant in spite of proof of guilt.

> Appellant's jury nullification argument would have encouraged the jurors to ignore the court's instruction and apply the law at their caprice. While we recognize that a jury may render a verdict at odds with the evidence or the law, neither the court nor counsel should encourage jurors to violate their oath. *Harding*, 736 So.2d 1230 (Fla.App. 2 Dist.,1999)

jury panel A list or group of prospective jurors. Also called venire.

jury tampering See embracery.

jury trial The trial of a matter before a judge and jury as opposed to a trial solely before a judge. The jury decides the factual issues.

jury wheel A system for the storage and random selection of the names or identifying numbers of prospective jurors.

jus (**jura** plural) Law; system of law; right; power; principle.

jus accrescendi The right of survivorship or accrual.

jus cogens A rule or legal principle that the parties cannot change.

jus gentium The law of nations; international law.

jus publicum 1. Public law. 2. State ownership of land.

just Conforming to what is legal or equitable.

just cause See good cause.

just compensation Compensation that is fair to both the owner and the public when the owner's property is taken for public use through eminent domain. Also called adequate compensation.

> Just compensation within the constitutional provision prohibiting the taking of private property without just compensation did not include damages for destruction of reasonable fair market value of lessees' business located on the land condemned but only included the value of the land, appurtenances, leasehold, and damage to remainder. *State Road Dept. v. Bramlett*, 189 So.2d 481 (Fla. 1966)

jus tertii The right of a third person or party.

justice 1. A judge, usually of a higher court. 2. The proper administration of the law; the fair resolution of legal disputes.

justice court A lower court (e.g., a justice of the peace court) that can hear minor civil or criminal matters.

justice of the peace (J.P.) A judicial magistrate of inferior rank with limited jurisdiction over minor civil or criminal cases.

justiciable Appropriate for court resolution.

justifiable Warranted or sanctioned by law. Defensible.

justifiable homicide Killing another when permitted by law (e.g., in self-defense).

justification A just or lawful reason to act or to fail to act.

juvenile One under 18 (or other age designated by law) and, therefore, not subject to be treated as an adult for purposes of the criminal law.

juvenile court A special court with jurisdiction over minors alleged to be neglected or juvenile delinquents.

juvenile delinquent A minor (e.g., someone under 18) who has committed an act that would be a crime if committed by an adult. Also called youthful offender.

K

k Contract.

kangaroo court A sham legal proceeding in which a person's rights are disregarded and the result is a foregone conclusion due to bias.

K.B. See King's Bench.

keeper A person or entity that has the custody or management of something or someone.

Keogh plan A retirement plan for self-employed taxpayers, the contributions to which are tax deductible. Also called H.R. 10 plan.

KeyCite The citator on Westlaw that allows online checking of the subsequent history of cases, statutes, and other laws.

key number A number assigned to a topic by West Group in its indexing or classification system of case law.

key man insurance Life insurance on employees who are crucial to a company. The company pays for the insurance and is the beneficiary.

kickback A payment made by a seller of a portion of the purchase price to the buyer or to a public official in order to induce the purchase or to influence future business transactions.

> As used in this section, the term kickback means a remuneration or payment back pursuant to an investment interest, compensation arrangement, or otherwise, by a provider of health care services or items, of a portion of the charges for services rendered to a referring health care provider as an incentive or inducement to refer patients for future services or items, when the payment is not tax deductible as an ordinary and necessary expense. F.S.A. § 456.054(1)

kiddie tax A popular term used for the tax paid by parents at their rate for the investment (unearned) income of their children.

kidnapping Taking and carrying away a human being by force, fraud, or threats against the victim's will and without lawful authority.

kin One's relatives; family, kindred.

kind Generic class; type. See also in kind.

kindred Family, relatives.

King's Bench (K.B.) One of the superior courts of common law in England. If the monarch is a queen, the court is called Queen's Bench.

kiting See check kiting.

knock-and-announce rule Police must announce their presence before forcibly entering premises to be searched. An exception (called the useless-gesture exception) exists if the occupants already know why the police are there.

knock down Final acceptance of a bid by an auctioneer.

knowingly With awareness or understanding; conscious or deliberate; intentionally.

> Knowingly means having actual knowledge of or acting with deliberate ignorance or reckless disregard for the prohibition involved. F.S.A. § 443.131(3)(g)(4)(a)

> "Knowingly," "known," or "knows" denotes actual knowledge of the fact in question. Florida Rules of Professional Conduct, Preamble

knowledge Acquaintance with fact or truth. Understanding obtained by experience or study. Awareness.

L

labor Mental or physical exertion or work, usually for a wage.

labor contract A collective bargaining agreement between a union and an employer covering wages, conditions of labor, and related matters.

laborer's lien A lien on property of someone responsible for paying for the work of a laborer on that property.

Labor-Management Relations Act The federal statute that covers procedures to settle strikes involving national emergencies, protects employees who do not want to join the union, and imposes other restrictions on unions (29 USC § 141). Also called Taft-Hartley Act.

labor organization A union.

labor union See union.

laches A party's unreasonable delay in asserting a legal or equitable right and another's detrimental good-faith change in position because of the delay.

> Laches is based on unreasonable delay in asserting known right which causes undue prejudice to party against whom claim is asserted. *Baker*, 920 So.2d 689 (Fla.App. 2 Dist., 2006)

lading See bill of lading.

LAMA See International Paralegal Management Association (*www.paralegalmanagement.org*).

lame duck 1. An elected official still in office who has not been or cannot be reelected. 2. A member of a stock exchange who has overbought and cannot meet his or her obligations.

lame duck session A legislative session conducted after the election of new members but before they are installed.

land 1. The surface of the earth, anything growing or permanently attached to it, the airspace above the earth, and what exists beneath the surface. 2. An interest in real property.

land bank A federally created bank under the Federal Farm Loan Act organized to make loans on farm land at low interest rates.

land grant A gift or donation of public land by the government to an individual, corporation, or other government.

landlord The owner who leases land, buildings, or apartments to another. Also called lessor.

Landlord means the owner or lessor of a dwelling unit . . . . Tenant means any person entitled to occupy a dwelling unit under a rental agreement. F.S.A. § 83.43(3)&(4)

landlord's lien The right of a landlord to levy upon goods of a tenant in satisfaction of unpaid rents or property damage.

landmark 1. A monument or other marker set up on the boundary line of two adjoining estates to fix such boundary. 2. Historically important. A landmark case establishes new and significant legal principles.

land sales contract See contract for deed.

land trust A trust that gives legal and equitable title of real property to a trustee but management and control of the property to the trust beneficiary. Also called Illinois Land Trust.

land use planning The use of zoning laws, environmental impact studies, and coordination efforts to develop the interrelated aspects of a community's physical environment and its social and economic activities.

lapping Theft of cash receipts from a customer that is covered up by crediting someone else's receipts to that customer.

lapse 1. To end because of a failure to use or a failure to fulfill a condition. 2. To fail to vest because of the death of the prospective beneficiary before the death of the donor. 3. A slip, mistake, or error. 4. A period of time.

lapsed Expired; no longer effective.

larcenous Having the character of or contemplating larceny.

larceny The wrongful taking and carrying away of another's personal property with the intention to deprive the possessor of it permanently.

> Larceny is the stealing, taking, and carrying away of personal property of another with intent to deprive the owner thereof of the property permanently, or to convert it to the taker's or someone else's use. *Canada*, 139 So.2d 753 (Fla. App.1962)

larceny by trick Larceny by using fraud or false pretenses to induce the victim to give up possession (but not title) to personal property.

lascivious Tending to incite lust; obscene.

last antecedent rule Qualifying words will be applied only to the word or phrase immediately preceding unless the qualifying words were clearly intended to apply to other language in the document as well.

last clear chance doctrine A plaintiff who has been contributorily negligent in placing himself or herself in peril can still recover if the negligent defendant had the last opportunity (clear chance) to avoid the accident and failed to exercise reasonable care to do so. Also called discovered peril doctrine, humanitarian doctrine, supervening negligence.

> Last clear chance doctrine is applicable if injured party has already come into position of peril, injuring party then or ᵗhereafter becomes, or in exercise of ordinary prudence should have become, aware of such fact and that party in peril either cannot reasonably escape from it, or apparently will not avail himself of opportunities to do so, and injuring party subsequently has opportunity by exercise of reasonable care to save the other from harm, but fails to exercise such care. *Williamson*, 208 So.2d 302 (Fla.App. 1968)

last in, first out (LIFO) An accounting assumption that the last goods purchased are the first ones sold or used.

last resort The end of the appeal process, referring to a court from which there is no further appeal.

last will The testator's most recent will before dying.

latent Concealed; dormant or not active.

latent ambiguity A lack of clarity in otherwise clear language that arises when some extrinsic evidence creates a necessity for interpretation.

> A latent ambiguity, as distinct from a patent ambiguity, arises where the language employed in a contract is clear and intelligible and suggests but a single meaning, but some extrinsic fact or extraneous evidence creates a necessity for interpretation or a choice among two or more possible meanings. *Mac-Gray Services*, 915 So.2d 657 (Fla.App. 2 Dist.,2005)

latent defect See hidden defect.

lateral support right The right to have land in its natural state supported by adjoining land.

laundering Concealing or disguising the source or origin of something (e.g., money) that was obtained illegally.

law 1. A rule of action or conduct prescribed by a controlling authority and having binding force. 2. The aggregate body of rules governing society. 3. The legal profession.

law clerk 1. An attorney's employee who is in law school studying to be an attorney or is waiting to pass the bar examination. 2. One who provides research and writing assistance to a judge.

law day 1. The date on which a mortgagor can avoid foreclosure by paying the debt on the mortgaged property. 2. May 1, the date each year set aside to honor our legal system.

law enforcement officer Someone empowered by law to investigate crime, make arrests for violations of the criminal law, and preserve the peace.

law firm A lawyer or lawyers in a law partnership, professional corporation, sole proprietorship, or other association authorized to practice law; or lawyers employed in the legal department of a corporation or other organization. Florida Rules of Professional Conduct, Preamble.

lawful Legal, authorized by law.

law journal A legal periodical of a law school or bar association. See also law review.

law list A list or directory of attorneys containing brief information relevant to their practice.

law merchant The practices and customs of those engaged in commerce that developed into what is known today as commercial law.

law of nations See international law.

law of nature See natural law.

law of the case doctrine An appellate court's determination of a legal issue binds both the trial court and the court on appeal in any subsequent appeal involving the same case and substantially the same facts.

> The "law of the case doctrine," a principle of judicial estoppel, requires that questions of law actually decided on appeal must govern the case in the same court and the trial court, through all subsequent stages of the proceedings. The trial court is bound to follow prior rulings of the appellate court on issues implicitly addressed or necessarily considered by the appellate court so long as the facts on which the appellate court based its decision continue to be the facts of the case. *Woolin*, 920 So.2d 1151 (Fla.App. 3 Dist.,2006)

law of the land 1. The law that applies in a country, state, or region. 2. Due process of law and related constitutional protections.

law of the road Traffic laws.

law reports, law reporters See reporter (3), report (2).

law review (L. Rev.) A legal periodical (usually student-edited) published by a law school. Also called law journal.

Law School Admission Test (LSAT) A standardized aptitude test used by many law schools in making decisions on admission.

lawsuit A court proceeding that asserts a legal claim or dispute. Also called a suit.

lawyer See attorney (1).

lay 1. Nonprofessional; not having expertise. 2. Nonecclesiastical; not belonging to the clergy. 3. To state or allege in a pleading.

layaway A seller's agreement with a consumer to hold goods for sale at a later date at a specified price.

layoff A temporary or permanent termination of employment at the will of the employer.

> Layoff means termination of employment due to a shortage of funds or work, or a material change in the duties or organization of an agency, including the outsourcing or privatization of an activity or function previously performed by career service employees. F.S.A. § 110.107(23)

lay witness A person giving only fact or lay (not expert) opinion testimony.

LBO See leveraged buyout.

lead counsel The attorney managing the case of a client with several attorneys. The primary attorney in a class action.

leading case An opinion that has had an important influence in the development of the law on a particular point.

leading question A question to someone being interviewed or examined that suggests the answer within the question.

learned intermediary See informed intermediary.

lease 1. A contract for the use or possession of real or personal property for a designated rent or other consideration. Ownership of the property is not transferred.
2. To let or rent.

> "Lease," "let," or "rental" means leasing or renting of living quarters or sleeping or housekeeping accommodations in hotels, apartment houses, roominghouses, tourist or trailer camps and real property, . . . F.S.A. § 212.02(10)

leaseback The sale of property to a buyer who gives the seller the right to lease the property from the buyer. Also called sale and leaseback.

leasehold An estate in real property held by a tenant/lessee under a lease; property held by a lease.

leave 1. To give in a will; to bequeath. 2. To withdraw or depart. 3. Permission to do something, e.g., to be absent from work or military service.

leave of court A court's permission to perform or refrain from a procedural step during litigation.

ledger A book used to record business transactions.

legacy 1. Any gift in a will. 2. A gift of personal property in a will. 3. Something handed down from an ancestor.

> A specific legacy is a gift by will of property which is particularly designated and which is to be satisfied only by the receipt of particular property described. A general legacy or devise is one which does not direct the delivery of any particular property, is not limited to any particular asset, and may be satisfied out of general assets belonging to estate of testator and not otherwise disposed of in will. *In re Parker's Estate*, 110 So.2d 498 (Fla.App. 1 Dist.1959)

legal 1. Authorized, required, permitted, or involving the law. 2. Pertaining to law rather than to equity.

legal age See age of consent, age of majority, age of reason.

legal aid A system (often government-funded) of providing legal services to people who cannot afford counsel.

legal assistant See paralegal.

legal cap Long ruled paper in tablet form.

legal capital The par or stated value of outstanding stock. Also called stated capital.

legal cause See proximate cause.

legal certainty test A court will find federal diversity jurisdiction on the basis of the plaintiff's complaint unless it appears to a legal certainty that the claim is for less than the jurisdictional amount.

legal conclusion A statement of legal consequences, often without including the facts from which the consequences arise. See also conclusion of law.

legal consideration See valuable consideration.

legal custody 1. The right and duty to make decisions about raising a child. 2. The detention of someone by the government.

> Legal custody means a legal status created by court order or letter of guardianship which vests in a custodian of the person or guardian, whether an agency or an individual, the right to have physical custody of the child and the right and duty to protect, train, and discipline the child and to provide him or her with food, shelter, education, and ordinary medical, dental, psychiatric, and psychological care. F.S.A. § 39.01(33)

legal death See brain death, civil death.

legal description A description of real property by various methods (e.g., by metes and bounds), including a description of portions subject to any easements or other restrictions.

legal detriment See detriment.

legal discretion See judicial discretion.

legal duty See duty (2).

legal entity An artificial person (e.g., a corporation) that functions in some ways as a natural person (e.g., it can sue and be sued).

legalese Technical language or jargon used by attorneys.

legal ethics Rules that embody the minimum standards of behavior to which members of the legal profession are expected to conform.

legal fiction An assumption of fact made by a court in order to dispose of a matter with justice even though the fact may not be true.

legal fraud See constructive fraud.

legal heir See heir (1).

legal holiday A day designated as a holiday by the legislature. A day on which court proceedings and service of process cannot occur.

legal impossibility A defense asserting that the defendant's intended acts, even if completed, would not amount to a crime.

> Impossibility of performance of agricultural contracts varies according to whether seller contracts to sell his own produce, in which case individual crop failure constitutes "legal impossibility," or whether an obligation is assumed to furnish produce regardless of source; but in the latter case there is still a concept of legal impossibility. *Holly Hill Fruit Products*, 275 So.2d 583 (Fla.App. 1973)

legal injury An invasion of a person's legally protected interest.

legal interest 1. A legally protected right or claim. A legal share of something. 2. A rate of interest authorized by law.

legal investments Those investments, sometimes called legal lists, in which banks and other financial institutions may invest.

legal issue A legal question. See also issue of law.

legality 1. Lawfulness; the state of being in accordance with law. 2. A technical legal requirement.

legalize To make or declare legal that which was once illegal.

legal list See legal investments.

legal malice 1. Pertaining to wrongful conduct committed or continued with a willful or reckless disregard for another's rights. 2. Malice that is inferred. Also called implied malice.

> Malice essential to cause of action for malicious prosecution may be of two kinds: (1) actual or subjective malice, sometimes called "malice in fact", which results in intentional wrong, and (2) "legal malice," which may be inferred from circumstances such as a want of probable cause, even though no actual malevolence or corrupt design is shown. *Wilson*, 118 So.2d 101 (Fla.App.1960)

legal malpractice The failure of an attorney to use such skill, prudence, and diligence as reasonable attorneys of ordinary skill and capacity commonly possess and exercise under the same circumstances. Professional misconduct or wrongdoing by attorneys.

legal name The designation of a person or entity recognized by the law.

legal notice Notification of something in a manner prescribed by law.

legal opinion An attorney's interpretation (often in writing) of how the law applies to facts in a client's case.

legal positivism The legal theory that the validity of laws is based, not on natural law or morality, but on being duly enacted or decreed by the three branches of government and accepted by society.

legal proceedings Formal actions in court or administrative tribunals to establish legal rights or resolve legal disputes.

legal question See issue of law.

legal realism The legal theory that the development of law in court opinions is based on public policy and social science considerations rather than on a pure or rigid legal analysis of rules.

legal representative One who represents the legal interests of another, e.g., one who is incapacitated.

> Legal representative means a guardian, conservator, survivor, or personal representative of a recipient or applicant, or of the property or estate of a recipient or applicant. F.S.A. § 409.901(11)

legal reserve Assets that a business (e.g., insurance company, bank) must set aside to be available to meet the demands of its customers.

legal residence The residence required by law for legal purposes, e.g., receipt of process. See also domicile (3).

legal separation A court order allowing spouses to live separately and establishing their rights and duties while separated, but still married. Also called divorce a mensa et thoro, judicial separation, limited divorce.

legal technician See independent paralegal.

legal tender Coins and currencies that can be used to pay debts.

legal title 1. A title that is recognizable and enforceable in a court of law. 2. A title that provides the right of ownership but no beneficial interest in the property. See also beneficial interest.

legatee The person to whom personal property (and sometimes real property) is given by will.

> A residuary legatee is one who is designated by testator in his will to receive the residue, being the personal estate of testator not effectually disposed of by his will and which remains after payment of debts and satisfaction of particular legacies. *In re Levy's Estate*, 196 So.2d 225 (Fla.App. 1967)

legation A diplomatic mission; the staff and premises of such a mission.

legislate To enact laws through legislation. To make or pass a law.

legislation 1. The enactment of laws by a legislative body. 2. Law or laws passed by a legislature. 3. A statute; a body of statutes.

legislative Pertaining to the enactment of laws by a legislative body.

legislative council A body that plans legislative strategy, primarily between sessions of the legislature.

legislative counsel The person or office that assists legislators by conducting research and drafting proposed legislation.

legislative court See Article I court.

legislative history Hearings, debates, reports, and all other events that occur in the legislature before a bill is enacted into a statute.

legislative immunity An immunity from civil suit enjoyed by a member of the legislature while engaged in legislative functions.

legislative intent The design, aim, end, or plan of the legislature in passing a particular statute.

legislative rule A rule of an administrative agency based on its quasi-legislative power. An administrative rule that creates rights or assigns duties rather than merely interprets a governing statute. Also called substantive rule.

legislative veto A legislative method of rejecting administrative action. The agency's action (e.g., a rule) would be valid unless nullified by resolutions of the legislature. On the unconstitutionality of such vetoes, see *INS v. Chadha*, 103 S. Ct. 2764 (1983).

legislator A member of a legislative body.

legislature The assembly or body of persons that makes statutory laws for a state or nation.

legitimacy 1. The condition of being born within a marriage or acquiring this condition through steps provided by law.

2. The condition of being in compliance with the law or with established standards.

legitimate 1. Lawful, valid, or genuine. 2. Born to married parents or to parents who have legitimated the child.

> Child born or conceived during lawful marriage is a legitimate child. *Matter of Adoption of Baby James Doe*, 572 So.2d 986 (Fla.App. 1 Dist.,1990)

legitimation 1. Making legitimate or lawful. 2. The procedure of legalizing (legitimating) the status of an illegitimate child.

legitime A portion of decedent's estate that must be reserved for a forced heir such as a child. See also forced heir.

lemon law A law giving a buyer of a new car with major defects the right to a refund or to have it replaced.

> The Legislature recognizes that a motor vehicle is a major consumer purchase and that a defective motor vehicle undoubtedly creates a hardship for the consumer. . . . It is . . . the intent of the Legislature to provide the statutory procedures whereby a consumer may receive a replacement motor vehicle, or a full refund, for a motor vehicle which cannot be brought into conformity with the warranty provided for in this chapter. F.S.A. § 681.101

lend 1. To provide money to another for a period of time, often for an interest charge. 2. To give something of value to another for a fixed or indefinite time, with or without compensation, with the expectation that it will be returned.

lese majesty A crime against the sovereign, e.g., treason. Also spelled leze majesty.

lessee A person who rents or leases property from another. A tenant.

> "Lessee" means a natural person who rents personal property pursuant to a rental-purchase agreement. "Lessor" means a person or corporation who, in the ordinary course of business, regularly offers to rent personal property, or arranges for personal property to be rented, pursuant to a rental-purchase agreement. F.S.A. § 559.9232(b)&(c)

lesser included offense A crime composed solely of some but not all of the elements of a greater crime so that it would be impossible to commit the greater offense without committing the lesser. Also called included offense.

lessor A person who rents or leases property to another. A landlord.

let 1. To allow. 2. To lease or rent. 3. To award a contract to one of the bidders.

lethal weapon See deadly weapon.

letter A writing that grants a power, authority, or right.

letter of attornment A letter to a tenant stating that the premises have been sold and that rent should be paid to the new owner.

letter of credit (LOC) An engagement by a bank or other issuer (made at the request of a customer) to honor demands for payment by a third party upon compliance with conditions stated in the letter. Also called circular note.

> Letter of credit means a definite undertaking that satisfies the requirements of § 675.104 by an issuer to a beneficiary at the request or for the account of an applicant or, in the case of a financial institution, to itself or for its own account, to honor a documentary presentation by payment or delivery of an item of value. F.S.A. § 675.103(j)

letter of intent (LOI) A nonbinding writing that states preliminary understandings of one or both parties to a possible future contract.

letter rogatory A court's request to a court in a foreign jurisdiction for assistance in a pending case, e.g., to take the testimony of a witness in the other jurisdiction.

letter ruling A written statement issued to a taxpayer by the IRS that interprets and applies the tax laws to a specific set of facts.

letters of administration The court document that authorizes a person to manage the estate of someone who has died without a valid will.

letters of marque A government authorization to a private citizen to seize assets of a foreign country.

letters patent A public document issued by the government that grants a right, e.g., a right to the sole use of an invention.

letters testamentary A formal document issued by a court that empowers a person to act as an executor of a will.

letter stock See restricted security.

levari facias A writ of execution to satisfy a party's judgment debt out of his or her profits and other assets.

leverage 1. The use of credit or debt to increase profits and purchasing power. The use of a smaller investment to generate a larger rate of return through borrowing. 2. Added power or influence.

leveraged buyout (LBO) Taking over a company by using borrowed funds for a substantial part of the purchase. The sale of a corporation in which at least part of the purchase price is obtained through debt assumed by the corporation.

levy 1. To assess or impose a tax, charge, or fine. 2. To seize assets in order to satisfy a claim. 3. To conscript into the military. 4. To wage or carry on. 5. A tax, charge, or fine.

> A levy is a limited legislative function which declares the subject and rate of taxation; it does not comprehend the entire process by which taxes are imposed. *Metropolitan Dade County*, 448 So.2d 515 (Fla.App. 3 Dist.,1984)

lewd Indecent, obscene; inciting to lustful desire.

lex Law or a collection of laws.

lex fori The law of the forum where the suit is brought.

LexisNexis A fee-based legal research computer service (*www.lexisnexis.com*).

lex loci contractus The law of the place where the contract was formed or will be performed.

lex loci delicti The law of the place where the wrong (e.g., the tort) took place.

leze majesty See lese majesty.

liability 1. The condition of being legally responsible for a loss, penalty, debt, or other obligation. 2. The obligation owed.

liability insurance Insurance in which an insurer pays covered damages the insured is obligated to pay a third person.

> Liability insurer means an insurer issuing a commercial general liability insurance policy in this state to a contractor that provides coverage for liability arising out of completed operations performed by the contractor or on the contractor's behalf. F.S.A. § 627.441(b)

liability without fault See strict liability.

liable Obligated in law; legally responsible.

libel 1. A defamatory statement expressed in writing or other graphic or visual form such as by pictures or signs. See also defamation. 2. A plaintiff's pleading in an admiralty or ecclesiastical court.

libelant The complainant in an admiralty or ecclesiastical court.

libelee The defendant in an admiralty or ecclesiastical court.

libelous Defamatory; constituting or involving libel.

libel per quod A writing that requires extrinsic facts to understand its defamatory meaning. Libel that requires proof of special damages.

libel per se A written defamatory statement that is actionable without proof that the plaintiff suffered special damages. Libel that is defamatory on its face.

liberal construction An expansive or broad interpretation of the meaning of a statute or other law to include facts or cases that are within the spirit and reason of the law.

liberty 1. Freedom from excessive or oppressive restrictions imposed by the state or other authority. 2. A basic right or privilege.

license 1. Permission to do what would otherwise be illegal or a tort. 2. The document that evidences this permission.

> License means a franchise, permit, certification, registration, charter, or similar form of authorization required by law, but it does not include a license required primarily for revenue purposes when issuance of the license is merely a ministerial act. F.S.A. § 120.52(9)

licensee 1. One who enters land for his or her own purposes or benefit, but with the express or implied consent of the owner or occupier of the land. 2. One who has a license.

licensor One who gives or grants a license.

licentious Without moral restraint. Disregarding sexual morality.

licit Permitted by law, legal.

lie 1. A deliberately or intentionally false statement. 2. To make a false statement intentionally. 3. To be sustainable in law.

lie detector See polygraph.

lien A charge, security, or encumbrance on property; a creditor's claim or charge on property for the payment of a debt.

> Lien means a charge against or interest in goods to secure payment of a debt or performance of an obligation, but the term does not include a security interest. F.S.A. § 680.1031(r)

lien creditor One whose claim is secured by a lien on particular property of the debtor.

lienee One whose property is subject to a lien.

lienholder; lienor One who has a lien on the property of another.

life annuity An annuity that guarantees payments for the life of the annuitant.

life-care contract A contract (often with a nursing care facility) to provide designated health services and living care for the remainder of a person's life in exchange for an up-front payment.

life estate An interest in property whose duration is limited to the life of an individual. Also called estate for life, life tenancy.

life estate pur autre vie A life estate whose duration is measured by the life of someone other than the possessor of the estate. Also called estate pur autre vie.

life expectancy The number of years a person of a given age and sex is expected to live according to statistics.

life in being The remaining length of time in the life of a person who is in existence at the time that a future interest is created.

life insurance A contract for the payment of a specified amount to a designated beneficiary upon the death of the person insured.

> "Life insurance" is insurance of human lives. . . . A "life insurer" or "life insurance company" is an insurer engaged in the business of issuing life insurance contracts, including contracts of combined life and health and accident insurance. F.S.A. § 624.602(1)&(2)

life interest An interest in property whose duration is limited to the life of the party holding the interest or of some other person.

life tenant One who possesses a life estate. A tenant for life.

LIFO See last in, first out.

lift To rescind or stop.

like-kind exchange The exchange of property held for productive use in a trade or business or for investment on which no gain or loss shall be recognized if such property is exchanged solely for property of like kind or character that is to be held either for productive use in a trade or business or for investment (26 USC § 1031).

limine See in limine, motion in limine.

limitation 1. Restriction. 2. The time allowed by statute for bringing an action at the risk of losing it. See also statute of limitations.

limited (Ltd.) 1. Restricted in duration or scope. 2. A designation indicating that a business is a company with limited liability.

limited admissibility Allowing evidence to be considered for isolated or restricted purposes.

limited divorce See legal separation.

limited jurisdiction The power of a court to hear only certain kinds of cases. Also called special jurisdiction.

limited liability Restricted liability; liability that can be satisfied out of business assets, not out of personal assets.

limited-liability company (L.L.C.) A hybrid business entity with features of a corporation and a partnership. The company has a legal existence separate from its members/owners who can participate in the management of the company and have limited liability.

> "Limited liability company" or "company" means a limited liability company organized and existing under this chapter. F.S.A. § 608.402(16)

limited-liability partnership (L.L.P.) A type of partnership in which a partner has unlimited liability for his or her wrongdoing but not for the wrongdoing of other partners.

limited partner A partner who takes no part in running the business and who incurs no liability for partnership obligations beyond the contribution he or she invested in the partnership.

limited partnership (L.P.) A type of partnership consisting of one or more general partners who manage the business and who are personally liable for partnership debts, and one or more limited partners who take no part in running the business and who incur no liability for partnership obligations beyond the contribution they invested in the partnership.

> "Limited partnership," except in the phrases "foreign limited partnership" and "foreign limited liability limited partnership," means an entity, having one or more general

partners and one or more limited partners, which is formed under this act by two or more persons or becomes subject to this act as the result of a conversion or merger under this act, or which was a limited partnership governed by the laws of this state when this act became a law and became subject to this act under § 620.2204(1) or (2). The term includes a limited liability limited partnership. F.S.A. § 620.1102(12)

limited power of appointment A power of appointment that restricts who can receive property under the power or under what conditions anyone can receive it. Also called special power of appointment.

limited publication The distribution of a work to a selected group for a limited purpose, and without the right of reproduction, distribution, or sale.

limited purpose public figure See public figure.

limited warranty A warranty that does not cover all defects or does not cover the full cost of repair.

lineage Line of descent from a common ancestor.

lineal Proceeding in a direct or unbroken line; from a common ancestor.

lineal heir One who inherits in a line either ascending or descending from a common source, as distinguished from a collateral heir.

line item veto The chief executive's rejection of part of a bill passed by the legislature, allowing the rest to become law with his or her signature.

line of credit The maximum amount of money that can be borrowed or goods that can be purchased on credit. Also called credit line.

> The term "line of credit," whenever used in this chapter, means an arrangement under which one or more loans or advances of money may be made available to a debtor in one transaction or a series of related transactions. F.S.A. § 687.0303(1)

lineup A group of people, including the suspect, shown at one time to a witness, who is asked if he or she can identify the person who committed the crime. The procedure is called a showup if the witness is shown only one person.

link-in-chain principle The privilege against self-incrimination covers questions that could indirectly connect (link) someone to a crime.

liquid Consisting of cash or what can easily be converted into cash.

liquidate 1. To pay and settle a debt. 2. To wind up the affairs of a business or estate by identifying assets, converting them into cash, and paying off liabilities.

liquidated claim A claim as to which the parties have already agreed what the damages will be or what method will be used to calculate the damages that will be paid.

liquidated damages An amount the parties agree will be the damages if a breach of contract occurs. Also called stipulated damages.

> Damages are "liquidated" when the proper amount to be awarded can be determined with exactness from the cause of action as pleaded, i.e., from a pleaded agreement between the parties, by an arithmetical calculation, or by application of definite rules of law. *Morales Sand & Soil*, 923 So.2d 1229 (Fla.App. 4 Dist.,2006)

liquidity The condition of being readily convertible into cash.

lis pendens 1. A pending lawsuit. 2. A recorded notice that an action has been filed affecting the title to or right to possession of the real property described in the notice. Also called notice of pendency. 3. Jurisdiction or control that courts acquire over property involved in a pending lawsuit.

list 1. A court's case docket. 2. A series or registry of names. 3. See listing.

listed security A security that is bought or sold on an exchange.

listing 1. A contract between an owner of real property and a real estate agent authorizing the latter to find a buyer or tenant in return for a fee or commission. 2. A contract between a firm and a stock exchange, covering the trading of that firm's securities on the stock exchange. 3. Making a schedule or inventory.

> "Listing period" means the period of time residential property is listed for sale with a licensed real estate broker, beginning on the date the residence is first listed for sale and ending on either the date the sale of the residence is closed, the date the residence is taken off the market, or the date the listing contract with the real estate broker expires. F.S.A. § 634.301(9)

list price The published or advertised retail price of goods.

literal construction See strict construction.

literary property 1. The corporal or physical embodiment (e.g., a book) of an intellectual production. 2. The exclusive right of an owner to possess, use, and dispose of his or her intellectual productions.

literary works Under copyright law, works, "expressed in words, numbers, or other verbal or numerical symbols or indicia, regardless of the nature of the material objects, such as books, periodicals, manuscripts, phonorecords, film, tapes, disks, or cards, in which they are embodied." Audiovisual works are not included. (17 USC § 101.)

litigant A party in litigation.

litigate To resolve a dispute or seek relief in a court of law.

litigation 1. The formal process of resolving a legal dispute through the courts. 2. A lawsuit.

litigious Prone to engage in disputes and litigation.

littoral Concerning or belonging to the shore or coast.

livery of seisin A ceremony to transfer legal title of land (e.g., deliver a twig, as a symbol of the whole land). Also called investiture.

living apart As a ground for divorce, the spouses live separately for a designated period of consecutive time with no present intention of resuming marital relations.

living trust See inter vivos trust.

living will A formal document that expresses a person's desire not to be kept alive through artificial or extraordinary means if in the future he or she suffers from a terminal condition.

> Any competent adult may, at any time, make a living will or written declaration and direct the providing, withholding, or withdrawal of life-prolonging procedures in the event that such person has a terminal condition, has an end-stage condition, or is in a persistent vegetative state. F.S.A. § 765.302(1). "Terri's law" which authorizes the Governor to issue a one-time stay to prevent the withholding of nutrition and hydration from a patient in a persistent vegetative state violated separation of powers. *Bush v. Schiavo*, 885 So.2d 321 (Fla.,2004)

LL.B.; LL.M.; LL.D. Law degrees: bachelor of laws (LL.B.), master of laws (LL.M.), doctor of laws (LL.D.). See also Juris Doctor.

LKA Last known address.

L.L.C. See limited liability company.

L.L.P. See limited liability partnership.

load The charge added to the cost of insurance or securities to cover commissions and administrative expenses. See also no-load.

loan 1. Anything furnished for temporary use. 2. The act of lending.

loan commitment An enforceable promise to make a loan for a specified amount on specified terms.

loaned servant doctrine When an employer lends its employee to another employer for some special service, the employee becomes (for purposes of respondeat superior liability) the employee of the party to whom he or she has been loaned with respect to that service.

loan for consumption A contract in which a lender delivers to a borrower goods that are consumed by use, with the understanding that the borrower will return to the lender goods of the same kind, quantity, and quality.

loan for use A loan of personal property for normal use and then returned.

loan ratio The ratio, expressed as a percentage, of the amount of a loan to the value of the real property that is security for the loan.

loansharking Lending money at excessive rates with the threat or actual use of force to obtain repayment.

> (g) "Loan sharking" or "shylocking" means the act of any person as defined herein lending money unlawfully under subsection (2) . . . (2) Unless otherwise specifically allowed by law, any person making an extension of credit to any person, who shall willfully and knowingly charge, take, or receive interest thereon at a rate exceeding 25 percent per annum but not in excess of 45 percent per annum, or the equivalent rate for a longer or shorter period of time, whether directly or indirectly, or conspires so to do, shall be guilty of a misdemeanor of the second degree. . . . F.S.A. § 687.071(g)(2)

loan value The maximum amount one is allowed to borrow on a life insurance policy or other property.

lobbying Attempts to influence the policy decisions of a public official, particularly a legislator.

lobbyist One in the business of lobbying.

local action An action that must be brought in a particular state or county, e.g., where the land in dispute is located.

> Under the "local action rule," a suit primarily seeking transfer of title to real property is considered to be quasi in rem and is required to be brought in the county where the land is situated. *Ocean Bank*, 902 So.2d 833 (Fla.App. 1 Dist.,2005)

local agent A person who takes care of a company's business in a particular area or district.

local assessment A tax upon property in a limited area for improvements (e.g., sidewalk repair) that will benefit property within that area.

local law 1. A law that is limited to a specific geographic region of the state. 2. The law of one jurisdiction, usually referring to a jurisdiction other than the one where a case is in litigation.

local option The right of a city or other local government to accept or reject a particular policy, e.g., Sunday liquor sales.

local union A unit or branch of a larger labor union.

lockdown The confinement of inmates to their cells or dorms, usually as a security measure.

lockout Withholding work from employees or temporarily closing a business due to a labor dispute.

lockup A place of detention in a police station, court, or other facility while awaiting further official action. A holding cell.

loco parentis See in loco parentis.

locus A locality. The place where a thing occurs or exists.

locus contractus The place where the last act is performed that makes an agreement a binding contract.

locus delicti The place of the wrong. The place where the last event occurred that was necessary to make the party liable.

locus in quo The place or scene of the occurrence or event.

locus poenitentiae The last opportunity to reconsider and withdraw before legal consequences (civil or criminal) occur.

> A critical factor in determining whether delivery has been accomplished is whether the grantor retained the "locus poenitentiae," or opportunity to change his or her mind. *Sargent*, 673 So.2d 979 (Fla.App. 4 Dist.,1996)

locus sigilli (L.S.) The place where a document's seal is placed.

lodestar A method of calculating an award of attorney fees authorized by statute. The number of reasonable hours spent on a case is multiplied by a reasonable hourly rate. Sometimes considered above the lodestar are the quality of representation and the risk that there would be no fee.

lodger One who uses a dwelling without acquiring exclusive possession or a property interest, e.g., one who lives in a spare room of a house.

logrolling Trading political votes or favors.

LOI See letter of intent.

loitering Remaining idle in essentially one place. Walking about aimlessly.

> Offense of "loitering and prowling" has two elements: defendant loitered or prowled in place, at time, or in manner not usual for law-abiding citizens; and such loitering and prowling were under circumstances that warranted justifiable and reasonable alarm or immediate concern for safety of persons or property in vicinity. F.S.A. § 856.021. *Freeman*, 617 So.2d 432 (Fla.App. 4 Dist.,1993)

long Holding securities or commodities in the hope that prices will rise.

long-arm statute A statutory method of obtaining personal jurisdiction by substituted service of process over a non-resident defendant who has sufficient purposeful contact with a state.

long-term capital gain The gain (profit) realized on the sale or exchange of a capital asset held for the required period of time.

lookout 1. Keeping careful watch. 2. One who keeps careful watch.

Lord Campbell's Act A statute giving certain relatives of a decedent a wrongful-death claim for a tort that caused the death of the decedent.

Lord Mansfield's rule Testimony of either spouse is inadmissible on whether the husband had access to the wife at the time of conception if such evidence would tend to declare the child to be illegitimate.

loser-pays See American rule.

loss 1. Damage, detriment, or disadvantage to person or property. 2. The amount by which expenses exceed revenues. 3. The amount by which the basis of property exceeds what is received for it.

loss leader An item sold by a merchant at a low price (e.g., below cost) in order to entice people to come into the store.

loss of bargain rule See benefit of the bargain rule.

loss of consortium Interference with the companionship, services, affection, and sexual relations one spouse receives from another.

loss payable clause An insurance clause designating someone other than the insured to receive insurance proceeds.

> "Open loss payable clause" in property insurance policy is one simply stating that loss, if any, is payable to specified person as his interest shall appear, or uses other equivalent words; it merely identifies person who may collect policy proceeds. *Secured Realty Inv. Fund*, 678 So.2d 852 (Fla.App. 3 Dist.,1996)

loss ratio The ratio between claims paid out and premiums received by an insurance company.

lost property Property that the owner has parted with through neglect or inadvertence and the whereabouts of which is unknown to the owner.

lost-volume seller A seller who, upon a buyer's breach, resells the goods to a second buyer who would have bought the same kind of goods from the seller even if the first buyer had not breached.

lost will A decedent's executed will that cannot be located.

lot 1. One of several parcels into which real property is divided. 2. A number of associated persons or things taken collectively. 3. A number of units of something offered for sale or traded as one item. 4. The shares purchased in one transaction.

lottery A scheme for the distribution of prizes by chance for which a participant pays something of value to enter.

lower court See inferior court.

L. Rev. See law review.

L.P. See limited partnership.

LSAT See Law School Admission Test.

Ltd. See limited.

lucid interval A temporary restoration to sanity, during which an insane person has sufficient intelligence to enter a contract.

> For purposes of determining testamentary capacity of individual who has been declared legally incompetent, a "lucid moment" is a period of time during which the individual returned to a state of comprehension and possessed actual testamentary capacity. *American Red Cross*, 708 So.2d 602 (Fla.App. 3 Dist.,1998)

lucrative title Title acquired without giving consideration.

lucri causa The intent to derive profit. For the sake of gain.

lump-sum alimony See alimony in gross.

lump-sum payment A single amount paid at one time.

lunacy See insanity (1).

luxury tax An excise tax on expensive, nonessential goods.

lying in wait Waiting and watching for an opportune time to inflict bodily harm on another by surprise.

lynch law Seizing persons suspected of crimes and summarily punishing them without legal trial or authority.

M

MACRS See Modified Accelerated Cost Recovery System.

magistrate 1. A judicial officer who has some of but not all the powers of a judge. Also called referee. In federal court, the duties of a U.S. magistrate were once performed by a U.S. commissioner. 2. A public civic officer with executive power.

magistrate court An inferior court with limited jurisdiction over minor civil or criminal matters. Also called police court.

Magna Carta The Great Charter of 1215, considered the foundation of constitutional liberty in England.

Magnuson-Moss Warranty Act A federal statute requiring warranties for consumer products to be written in plain and easily understood language (15 U.S.C. § 2301 et seq.).

mail box rule 1. The proper and timely mailing of a document raises a rebuttable presumption that the document has been received by the addressee in the usual time. 2. A prisoner's court papers are deemed filed when given to the proper prison authorities. 3. A contract is formed upon the act of mailing where the use of the mail is authorized by both parties.

> Under the "mailbox rule," a pro se inmate's postconviction pleading is deemed filed when the inmate entrusts the document to prison officials for further delivery or processing. *Pagan*, 899 So.2d 1203 (Fla.App. 2 Dist.,2005)

mail fraud The use of the U.S. Postal Service to obtain money by false pretenses or to commit other acts of fraud (18 USC § 1341).

mail-order divorce Obtaining a divorce from a state or country with no jurisdiction to award it, because, for example, neither spouse was domiciled there.

maim The infliction of a serious (and often disabling) bodily injury.

main purpose rule Under the statute of frauds, contracts to answer for the debt of another must be in writing *unless* the main purpose of the promisor's undertaking is his or her own benefit or protection.

maintain 1. To make repairs or perform upkeep tasks. 2. To bear the expenses for the support of. 3. To declare or affirm. 4. To continue or carry forward. 5. To involve oneself or meddle in another's lawsuit.

maintenance 1. Support or assistance. See also separate maintenance. 2. Keeping something in working order. 3. Becoming involved or meddling in someone else's lawsuit.

> Maintenance is defined as an officious intermeddling in a suit which in no way belongs to the intermeddler, by maintaining or assisting either party to the action, with money or otherwise to prosecute or defend it. *Hardick*, 795 So.2d 1107 (Fla.App. 5 Dist.,2001)

major dispute A dispute under the Railway Labor Act that relates to the formation or alteration of a collective bargaining agreement (45 USC § 155).

major federal action Projects that require an environmental impact statement because of their significant environmental effects.

majority 1. The age at which a person is entitled to the management of his or her own affairs and to the enjoyment of adult civil rights. 2. Greater than half of any total.

majority opinion The opinion in which more than half of the voting judges on the court joined.

make To formalize the creation of an instrument; to execute.

make law 1. To enact a law. To legislate. 2. To establish or expand upon a prior legal principle or rule in a court opinion.

maker One who signs a promissory note or other negotiable instrument.

make-whole rule An insurer cannot enforce subrogation rights against settlement funds until the insured is fully compensated (made whole). An insured who settles with a third-party tortfeasor is liable to the insurer-subrogee only for any excess received over the total amount of the insured's loss.

mala fides See bad faith (1).

mala in se See malum in se.

mala prohibita See malum prohibitum.

malefactor One who is guilty of a crime or offense. A wrongdoer.

malfeasance Wrongdoing, usually by a public official.

malice 1. The intentional doing of a wrongful act without just cause or excuse. 2. The intent to inflict injury; ill will. 3. Reckless or wanton disregard.

> Element of malice requires evidence that the defendant acted with ill will, hatred, spite, or an evil intent. *Slocum*, 757 So.2d 1246 (Fla.App. 4 Dist.,2000)

malice aforethought 1. A fixed purpose or design to do some physical harm to another. 2. In a murder charge, the intention to kill, actual or implied, under circumstances that do not constitute excuse (e.g., insanity) or justification (e.g., self-defense) or mitigate the degree of the offense to manslaughter.

malice in fact See actual malice (1).

malice in law See implied malice.

malicious 1. Doing a wrongful act intentionally and without just cause or excuse. 2. Pertaining to conduct that is certain or almost certain to cause harm.

malicious mischief Intentional, wanton, or reckless damage or destruction of another's property. Also called criminal mischief.

malicious prosecution A tort with the following elements: (a) To initiate or procure the initiation of civil or criminal legal proceedings; (b) without probable cause; (c) with malice or an improper purpose; (d) the proceedings terminate in favor of the person against whom the proceedings were brought.

> The elements of an action for malicious prosecution are: the instigation of a criminal proceeding by the defendant; its termination in favor of the plaintiff; the exercise of malice by the defendant; want of probable cause; and damage. *Maybin*, 606 So.2d 1240 (Fla.App. 2 Dist.,1992)

malpractice 1. The failure of a professional to exercise the degree of skill commonly applied under the circumstances by an ordinary, prudent, and reputable member of the profession in good standing. 2. Professional misconduct.

malum in se A wrong in itself; an act that is inherently and essentially evil and immoral in its nature (plural: mala in se).

malum prohibitum An act that is wrong because laws prohibit it; the act is not wrong in itself (plural: mala prohibita).

manager One who administers an organization or project.

managing agent A person given general powers to exercise judgment and discretion in dealing with matters entrusted to him or her.

mandamus A court order or writ to a public official to compel the performance of a ministerial act or a mandatory duty.

> A writ by which a court may compel an official to perform a duty the law requires but that the official has failed or refused to perform. (*www.floridasupremecourt.org/pub_info/system2.shtml*)

mandate 1. A court order, especially to a lower court. 2. To require. 3. An authorization to act.

> Mandamus is a remedy to compel performance of ministerial act which respondent has clear legal duty to perform. *Miller*, 825 So.2d 427 (Fla.App. 4 Dist.,2002)

mandatory Compulsory, obligatory.

mandatory injunction An injunction that requires an affirmative act or course of conduct.

mandatory instruction An instruction to the jury that if it finds that a certain set of facts (laid out by the judge) exists, then it must reach a verdict for one party and against the other. Also called binding instruction.

mandatory sentence A sentence of incarceration that, by statute, must be served; the judge has no discretion to order alternatives.

manifest 1. Evident to the senses, especially to sight. 2. A list of a vehicle's cargo or passengers.

manifest necessity Extraordinary circumstances requiring a mistrial; a retrial can occur without violating principles of double jeopardy.

manifesto A formal, public statement declaring policies or intentions.

manifest weight of the evidence, against the As a standard of review, an opposite finding is clearly called for; the verdict is unreasonable, arbitrary, or not based on the evidence.

manipulation Activity designed to deceive investors by controlling or artificially affecting the price of securities, e.g., creating a misleading appearance of active trading. Also called stock manipulation.

Mann Act A federal statute making it a crime to transport someone in interstate or foreign commerce for prostitution or other sexually immoral purpose (18 USC § 2421).

manslaughter The unlawful killing of another without malice.

> The killing of a human being by the act, procurement, or culpable negligence of another, without lawful justification according to the provisions of chapter 776 and in cases in which such killing shall not be excusable homicide or murder, according to the provisions of this chapter, is manslaughter, a felony of the second degree. . . . F.S.A. § 782.07(1)

manual 1. Made or performed with the hands. 2. A book with basic practical information or procedures.

manumission The act of liberating a slave from bondage.

Mapp **hearing** A hearing in a criminal case to determine whether seized evidence is admissible. *Mapp v. Ohio*, 81 S. Ct. 1684 (1961).

Marbury v. Madison The U.S. Supreme Court case that ruled that the courts can determine whether an act of Congress is constitutional. 5 U.S. 137 (1803).

margin 1. The edge or border. 2. An amount available beyond what is needed. 3. The difference between the cost and the selling price of a security. 4. An amount a buyer on credit must give to a securities broker to cover the broker's risk of loss. 5. The difference between the value of collateral securing a loan and the amount of the loan.

margin account An account allowing a client to borrow money from a securities broker in order to buy more stock, using the stock as collateral.

margin call A demand by a broker that a customer deposit additional collateral to cover broker-financed purchases of securities.

marijuana or **marihuana** A drug prepared from cannabis plant leaves.

marine insurance Insurance that covers hazards encountered in maritime transportation, including risks of river and inland navigation.

marital agreement 1. A contract between spouses. See also postnuptial agreement, separation agreement. 2. See premarital agreement.

marital communications privilege A spouse has a privilege to refuse to disclose and to prevent others from disclosing private or confidential communications between the spouses during the marriage. Also called husband-wife privilege, spousal privilege.

> (1) A spouse has a privilege during and after the marital relationship to refuse to disclose, and to prevent another from disclosing, communications which were intended to be made in confidence between the spouses while they were husband and wife. (2) The privilege may be claimed by either spouse or by the guardian or conservator of a spouse. The authority of a spouse, or guardian or conservator of a spouse, to claim the privilege is presumed in the absence of contrary evidence. F.S.A. § 90.504

marital deduction The amount of the federal estate and gift tax deduction allowed for transfers of property from one spouse to another (26 USC § 2056).

marital portion The part of a deceased spouse's estate that must be received by a surviving spouse.

marital property Property acquired by either spouse during the marriage that does not constitute separate property, plus any appreciation of separate property that occurs during the marriage. See also separate property.

> Marital assets and liabilities include: 1. Assets acquired and liabilities incurred during the marriage, individually by either spouse or jointly by them; 2. The enhancement in value and appreciation of nonmarital assets resulting either from the efforts of either party during the marriage or from the contribution to or expenditure thereon of marital funds or other forms of marital assets, or both; 3. Interspousal gifts during the marriage; 4. All vested and nonvested benefits, rights, and funds accrued during the marriage in retirement, pension, profit-sharing, annuity, deferred compensation, and insurance plans and programs; and 5. All real property held by the parties as tenants by the entireties, whether acquired prior to or during the marriage, shall be presumed to be a marital asset. If, in

any case, a party makes a claim to the contrary, the burden of proof shall be on the party asserting the claim for a special equity. F.S.A. § 61.075(5)(a)

maritime Pertaining to the sea, navigable waters, and commerce thereon.

maritime contract A contract on ships, commerce or navigation on navigable waters, transportation by sea, or maritime employment.

maritime law See admiralty.

mark 1. Language or symbols used to identify or distinguish one's product or service. Short for servicemark and trademark. 2. A substitute for the signature.

market 1. The place or geographic area where goods and services are bought and sold. 2. An exchange where securities or commodities are traded. 3. The geographical or economic extent of commercial demand.

marketable Capable of attracting buyers; fit to offer for sale.

marketable title A title that a reasonably prudent buyer, knowing all the facts, would be willing to accept.

> Agreement to convey good title or marketable title to realty can be discharged only by conveyance of a title unencumbered and free from reasonable doubt as to any question of law or fact necessary to sustain its validity. *Peters*, 163 So.2d 59 (Fla.App.1964)

market-maker Any "dealer who, with respect to a security, holds himself out (by entering quotations in an inter-dealer communications system or otherwise) as being willing to buy and sell such security for his own account on a regular or continuous basis." 15 USC § 78c(a)(38).

market order An order to buy or sell securities at the best price currently obtainable.

market price The prevailing price in a given market. The last reported price.

market share The percentage of total industry sales made by a particular company.

market value See fair market value.

mark up 1. The process by which a legislative committee puts a bill in its final form. 2. An increase in price, usually to derive profit.

marriage 1. The legal union of one man and one woman as husband and wife. 2. The status of being a married couple.

> For purposes of interpreting any state statute or rule, the term marriage means only a legal union between one man and one woman as husband and wife, and the term spouse applies only to a member of such a union. F.S.A. § 741.212(3)

marriage certificate The document filed by the person performing a marriage ceremony containing evidence that the ceremony took place.

marriage license The document (issued by the government) giving a couple authorization to be married.

marriage settlement See premarital agreement, separation agreement.

marshal 1. A federal judicial officer (U.S. Marshal) who executes court orders, helps maintain security, and performs other duties for the court. 2. A local police or fire department official.

marshaling 1. Arranging, ranking by priority, or disposing in order. 2. An equitable principle compelling a senior creditor to attempt to collect its claim first from another source that is unavailable to a junior creditor.

Marshaling is applied to avoid prejudice to the rights of a purchaser of mortgaged property and to prevent injustice to junior creditors. *Valparaiso Bank*, 512 So.2d 298 (Fla.App. 1 Dist.,1987)

martial law Rule (or rules) imposed by military authorities over civilian matters.

Martindale-Hubbell Law Directory A set of books that contain a state-by-state list of attorneys and a digest of state and foreign laws.

Mary Carter **agreement** A contract in which one or more defendants (a) agree to remain in the case, (b) guarantee the plaintiff a certain minimum monetary recovery regardless of the outcome of the lawsuit, and (c) have their liability reduced in direct proportion to the increase in the liability of the nonagreeing defendants. *Booth v. Mary Carter Paint Co.*, 202 So. 2d 8 (Fla.Dist.Ct.App., 1967).

mass picketing Picketing in large numbers, usually obstructing the ingress and egress of the target's employees, customers, or suppliers.

Massachusetts trust See business trust.

master 1. An employer. A principal who hires others and who controls or has the right to control their physical conduct in the performance of their service. 2. An officer appointed by the court to assist it in specific judicial duties (e.g., take testimony). Also called special master. 3. One who has reached the summit of his or her trade, and who has the right to hire apprentices and journeymen. 4. Main or central.

master agreement A labor agreement at one company that becomes the pattern for agreements in an entire industry.

master and servant An employer-employee relationship in which the employer reserves the right to control the manner or means of doing the work.

> A master is a species of principal, and a servant a species of agent; master and servant are not, however, wholly synonymous with the terms principal and agent. An agent is not only employed by the principal but represents him as well, and an agency contemplates contractual liability on the part of the principal arising from the acts of the agent, whereas, the servant merely acts for the principal usually according to his direction without discretion. *Lynch*, 31 So.2d 268 (Fla.1947)

master deed The major condominium document that will govern individual condominium units within a condominium complex.

master in chancery An officer in a court of equity who acts as an assistant to the judge in tasks such as taking testimony.

master limited partnership A limited partnership whose ownership interest is publicly traded.

master of laws (LL.M.) An advanced law degree earned after obtaining a Juris Doctor (J.D.) degree.

master plan A comprehensive land-use plan for the development of an area.

master policy An insurance policy that covers a group of persons, e.g., health or life insurance written as group insurance.

material 1. Essential, important, or relevant; having influence or effect. 2. Pertaining to concrete, physical matter.

> Statement is "material," for purposes of a claim that the state knowingly presented false testimony, if there is any

reasonable likelihood that it could have affected the judgment of the jury. *Davis*, 928 So.2d 1089 (Fla.,2005)

material allegation An allegation that is essential to a claim or defense.

material alteration A change in a document or instrument that alters its meaning or effect.

material breach A failure to perform a substantial part of a contract, justifying rescission or other remedy.

material evidence Relevant evidence a reasonable mind might accept.

material fact An influential fact; a fact that will affect the result.

material issue An important issue the parties need to resolve.

materialman One who furnishes materials (supplies) for construction or repair work.

material witness A witness who can give testimony on a fact affecting the merits of the case.

> A "material witness" is one who possesses information going to some fact affecting the merits of the cause and about which no other witness might testify. *Sardinas*, 805 So.2d 1024 (Fla.App. 3 Dist.,2001)

maternal Pertaining to, belonging to, or coming from the mother.

matricide The killing of one's mother.

matrimonial action A divorce proceeding or other action pertaining to the status of a marriage.

matter 1. A case or dispute; the subject for which representation is sought. 2. Something that a tribunal can examine or establish.

matter in controversy 1. The subject of litigation. 2. The amount of damages sought.

matter of See in re.

matter of fact A subject involving the truth or falsity of a fact.

matter of law A subject involving the interpretation or application of the law. See also judgment as a matter of law.

matter of record Pertaining to a subject that is part of or within an official record.

mature Due or ripe for payment, owing; developed, complete.

maxim A principle; a general statement of a rule or a truth.

mayhem The crime of depriving another of a limb or of disabling, disfiguring, or rendering it useless, especially for self-defense.

MBE Multistate bar examination.

McNabb-Mallory **rule** Confessions or incriminating statements can be excluded from evidence if obtained during a period of unnecessary delay in taking the accused before a magistrate. *McNabb*, 63 S. Ct. 608 (1943); *Mallory*, 77 S. Ct. 1356 (1957).

McNaghten **rule** See insanity (4).

M.D. 1. Middle District. 2. Doctor of medicine.

MDL See multidistrict litigation.

MDP See multidisciplinary practice.

mean high tide The average height of all the high waters (tides) over a complete or regular tidal cycle of 18.6 years.

means 1. That which is used to attain an end. A cause. 2. Assets or available resources.

means test The determination of eligibility for a public benefit based on one's financial resources.

mechanic's lien A right or interest in real or personal property (in the nature of an encumbrance) that secures payment for the performance of labor or the supply of materials to maintain or improve the property. Also called artisan's lien.

mediation A method of alternate dispute resolution (ADR) in which the parties submit a dispute to a neutral third person (the mediator) who helps the parties resolve their dispute without litigation; he or she does not render a decision resolving it for them.

> "Mediation" means a process whereby a neutral third person called a mediator acts to encourage and facilitate the resolution of a dispute between two or more parties. It is an informal and nonadversarial process with the objective of helping the disputing parties reach a mutually acceptable and voluntary agreement. The role of the mediator includes, but is not limited to, assisting the parties in identifying issues, fostering joint problem solving, and exploring settlement alternatives. F.S.A. § 39.01(42)

mediator See mediation.

Medicaid A federal-state public assistance program that furnishes health care to people who cannot afford it.

medical examiner A public officer who conducts autopsies and otherwise helps in the investigation and prosecution of death cases.

> [M]edical examiner means any district medical examiner, associate medical examiner, or substitute medical examiner acting pursuant to this chapter, as well as any employee, deputy, or agent of a medical examiner or any other person who may obtain possession of a photograph or audio or video recording of an autopsy in the course of assisting a medical examiner in the performance of his or her official duties. F.S.A. § 406.135(1)

Medicare A federal program of medical insurance for the elderly.

meeting of creditors A bankruptcy hearing or meeting in which creditors can examine the debtor.

meeting of the minds Mutual agreement and assent of the parties to the substance and terms of their contract.

Megan's law A state law (named in honor of a victim) requiring the registration of sex offenders and a method of notifying the community when they move into an area. Also called community notification law.

> The Florida statute, entitled the Florida Sexual Predators Act, is similar to many "Megan's Laws" enacted in virtually every state. State v. Robinson, 873 So.2d 1205 (Fla.,2004). The state has a compelling interest in protecting the public from sexual predators and in protecting children from predatory sexual activity, and there is sufficient justification for requiring sexual predators to register and for requiring community and public notification of the presence of sexual predators. § 775.21(3)(c) Fla. Stat. (Supp.1998).

memorandum 1. A written statement or note that is often brief and informal. 2. A brief record of a transaction or occurrence. 3. A written analysis of how the law applies to a given set of facts.

memorandum decision (mem.) The decision of a court with few or no supporting reasons, often because it follows established principles. Also called memorandum opinion.

memorandum of points and authorities A document submitted to a trial court that makes arguments with supporting

authorities for something a party wishes to do, e.g., have a motion granted.

memorial 1. A statement of facts in a petition or demand to the legislature or to the executive. 2. A summary or abstract of a record.

mensa et thoro Bed and board. See also legal separation.

mens rea A guilty mind that produces the act. The unlawful intent or recklessness that must be proved for crimes that are not strict liability offenses.

mental anguish See emotional distress.

mental cruelty Conduct causing distress that endangers the mental and physical health of a spouse (a fault ground for divorce).

> "Mental cruelty" as cause for divorce on ground of "extreme cruelty" means course of conduct by one spouse toward the other such as to impair mental and physical health of the other to the extent that maintaining and continuing marriage relationship is rendered unbearable. Steele, 177 So.2d 873 (Fla.App.1965)

mental defect or **disease** See insanity (2) and (3).

mental distress; mental suffering See emotional distress.

mercantile Commercial; involving the business of merchants.

merchant A person in the business of purchasing and selling goods.

merchantable Fit for the ordinary purposes for which the goods are used. The noun is merchantability.

mercy killing See euthanasia.

meretricious Involving vulgarity, unlawful sexual relations, or insincerity.

merger 1. The fusion or absorption of one duty, right, claim, offense, estate, or property into another. 2. The absorption of one company by another. The absorbed company ceases to exist as a separate entity.

> The doctrine of "merger" operates to extinguish a cause of action on which a judgment is based and bars a subsequent action for the same cause. Chrestensen, 906 So.2d 343 (Fla.App. 4 Dist.,2005)

merger clause See integration clause.

meritorious Legally plausible. Having merit; not frivolous.

merits See on the merits.

mesne Intermediate; occurring between two periods or ranks.

mesne process Any writ or process issued between commencement of the action and execution of the judgment.

mesne profits Profits accruing between two periods while held by one in wrongful possession.

> The measure of "mesne profits" recoverable by successful plaintiff in ejectment is value of use and occupation of land during period of defendant's wrongful possession, which value of use is measured by value of rents and profits. F.S.A. § 70.01 et seq. Kester, 15 So.2d 201 (Fla.1943)

messuage A dwelling house, its outbuildings, and surrounding land.

metes and bounds A system of describing the boundary lines of land with their terminal points and angles on the natural landscape.

metropolitan Pertaining to a city and its suburbs.

Mexican divorce A divorce granted by a court in Mexico by mail order or when neither spouse was domiciled there.

migratory divorce A divorce obtained in a state to which one or both spouses briefly traveled before returning to their original state.

military commission A military court for violations of martial law.

military government A government in which civil or political power is under the control of the military.

military jurisdiction Jurisdiction of the military in the areas of military law, military government, and martial law.

military law A system of laws governing the armed forces.

military will; military testament A will that may be valid even if it does not comply with required formalities when made by someone in military service. Also called sailor's will, seaman's will, soldier's will.

militia A citizen military force not part of the regular military.

mill One-tenth of one cent.

mineral A lifeless substance formed or deposited through natural processes and found either in or upon the soil or in the rocks beneath the soil.

> Whenever the word "minerals" is hereafter used in any deed, lease, or other contract in writing, said word or term shall not include any of the following: topsoil, muck, peat, humus, sand, and common clay, unless expressly provided in said deed, lease, or other contract in writing. F.S.A. § 689.20

mineral lease A contract or other form of authorization to explore, develop, or remove deposits of oil, gas, or other minerals. A mining lease allows such activity in a mine or mining claim.

mineral right The right to explore for and remove minerals, with or without ownership of the surface of the land.

miner's inch A unit for measuring water flow through a hole one-inch square in a miner's box (about nine gallons a minute).

minimal diversity A plaintiff is a citizen of one state and at least one of the defendants is a citizen of another state.

minimum contacts Purposely availing oneself of the privilege of conducting activities within a state, thus invoking the benefits and protections of its laws. (Basis of personal jurisdiction over a nonresident.)

minimum-fee schedule A bar association list of the lowest fees an attorney can charge for designated legal services. Such lists violate antitrust law.

minimum wage The lowest allowable wage certain employers may pay.

mining lease See mineral lease.

minister 1. An agent; one acting on behalf of another. 2. An administrator in charge of a government department. 3. A diplomatic representative or officer.

ministerial Involving a duty that is to be performed in a prescribed manner without the exercise of judgment or discretion.

> A duty or act is "ministerial," for purposes of mandamus, when there is no room for exercise of discretion, and the performance being required is directed by law. *RHS Corp.*, 736 So.2d 1211 (Fla.App. 4 Dist.,1999)

ministry The duties or functions of a religious minister.

minitrial An abbreviated presentation of each side's case that the parties agree to make to each other and to a private, neutral third party, followed by discussions that seek a negotiated settlement. An example of alternate dispute resolution.

minor A person under the legal age, often 18. One who has not reached the age of majority.

minority 1. The status of being below the minimum age to enter a desired relationship (e.g., marriage) or perform a particular task. Also called infancy, nonage. 2. The smaller number. 3. A group of persons of the same race, gender, or other trait that differs from the dominant or majority group in society and that is often the victim of discrimination.

minority opinion An opinion of one or more justices that disagrees with the majority opinion. It is often a dissenting opinion.

minority shareholder Any shareholder who does not own or control more than 50 percent of the voting shares of a corporation.

minute book The book maintained by the court clerk containing a record (the minutes) of court proceedings.

minutes A record of what occurred at a meeting.

***Miranda* warnings** Prior to any custodial interrogation, a person must be warned that: (a) he or she has a right to remain silent, (b) any statement made can be used as evidence against him or her, and (c) he or she has the right to his or her own attorney or one provided at government expense. *Miranda v. Arizona*, 86 S. Ct. 1602 (1966).

> Rule that statements made by individual while under custodial interrogation may not be introduced as evidence against him or her unless he or she first has been informed of certain rights, including right to have counsel present during custodial interrogation, are commonly known as "Miranda rights" and are designed to protect individual's Fifth Amendment right against compelled self-incrimination by offsetting inherently compelling pressures of custodial interrogation. *Sapp*, 690 So.2d 581 (Fla.,1997)

Mirandize To give a suspect the *Miranda* warnings.

misadventure An accident or misfortune (e.g., killing), often occurring while performing a lawful act.

misapplication The wrongful use of legally possessed assets.

misappropriate To take wrongfully; to use someone else's property to one's own advantage without permission. See also appropriation (2).

misbranding The use of a label that is false or misleading.

miscarriage of justice A fundamentally unfair result.

miscegenation Marriage between persons of different races.

mischarge An erroneous charge to a jury.

mischief 1. Conduct that causes discomfort, hardship, or harm. 2. The evil or danger that a statute is intended to cure or avoid.

misconduct Wrongdoing; a breach of one's duty.

> "Misconduct" which would disqualify a claimant from receiving unemployment benefits usually involves repeated violations of explicit policies after several warnings. West's F.S.A. § 443.036(29). *Leith*, 884 So.2d 1160 (Fla.App. 2 Dist.,2004)

misdelivery Delivery of mail or goods to someone other than the specified or authorized recipient.

misdemeanant A person convicted of a misdemeanor.

misdemeanor A crime, not as serious as a felony, punishable by fine or by detention in an institution other than a prison or penitentiary.

> The term "misdemeanor" shall mean any criminal offense that is punishable under the laws of this state, or that would be punishable if committed in this state, by a term of

imprisonment in a county correctional facility, except an extended term, not in excess of 1 year. F.S.A. § 775.08(2)

misdemeanor-manslaughter The unintentional killing of a human being while committing a misdemeanor.

misfeasance Improper performance of an otherwise lawful act.

misjoinder Improper joining of parties, causes of action, or offenses.

mislay To forget where you placed something you intended to retrieve.

misleading Leading one astray or into error, often intentionally.

misprision 1. Nonperformance of a duty by a public official. 2. A nonparticipant's concealment or failure to disclose a crime. Misprision of felony occurs when the crime involved is a felony.

misrepresentation 1. Any untrue statement of fact. 2. A false statement of fact made with the intent to deceive. Also called false representation. See also fraud.

> Any manifestation by words or other conduct by one person to another that, under the circumstances, amounts to an assertion not in accordance with the facts. *Travelodge Intern.*, 382 So.2d 789 (Fla.App., 1980)

mistake An unintentional act, omission, or error arising from ignorance, surprise, imposition, or misplaced confidence.

mistake of fact 1. An unconscious ignorance or forgetfulness of the existence or nonexistence of a material fact, past or present. 2. An honest and reasonable belief in the existence of circumstances, which, if true, would make the act for which the person is indicted an innocent act.

mistake of law A misunderstanding about legal requirements or consequences.

mistrial A trial terminated before its normal conclusion because of unusual circumstances, misconduct, procedural error, or jury deadlock.

mitigate To render less painful or severe.

mitigating circumstances Facts that can be considered as reducing the severity or degree of moral culpability of an act, but do not excuse or justify it. Also called extenuating circumstances.

> Evidence is "mitigating" if, in fairness or in the totality of the defendant's life or character, it may be considered as extenuating or reducing the degree of moral culpability for the crime committed. *Evans*, 808 So.2d 92 (Fla.,2001)

mitigation-of-damages rule An injured party has a duty to use reasonable diligence to try to minimize his or her damages after the wrong has been inflicted. Also called avoidable consequences.

mittimus 1. An order commanding that a person be detailed or conveyed to a prison. 2. An order for the transfer of records between courts.

mixed nuisance A nuisance that injures the public at large and also does some special damage to an individual or class of individuals.

mixed question of law and fact An issue involving the application of the law to the facts when the facts and the legal standards are not in dispute.

M'Naghten rule See insanity (4).

MO See modus operandi.

model act A statute proposed to all state legislatures for adoption.

Model Penal Code A proposed criminal law code of the American Law Institute. For its test for insanity, see insanity (2).

Model Rules of Professional Conduct The current ethical rules for attorneys recommended to the states by the American Bar Association.

modification An alteration or change; a new qualification.

> "Modification" means a child custody determination that changes, replaces, supersedes, or is otherwise made after a previous determination concerning the same child, regardless of whether it is made by the court that made the previous determination. F.S.A. § 61.503(11)

Modified Accelerated Cost Recovery System (MACRS) A method to calculate the depreciation tax deduction over a shorter period.

modus Manner or method.

modus operandi (MO) A method of doing things, e.g., a criminal's MO.

moiety 1. One-half. 2. A portion or part.

molest 1. To abuse sexually. 2. To disturb or harass.

money 1. Coins and paper currency or other legal medium of exchange. 2. Assets that are readily convertible into cash.

money demand A claim for a specific dollar amount.

money had and received An action to prevent unjust enrichment when one person obtains money that in good conscience belongs to another.

money judgment The part of a judgment that requires paying money (damages).

money laundering See laundering.

money market The financial market for dealing in short-term financial obligations such as commercial paper and treasury bills.

money order A type of negotiable draft purchased from an organization such as the Postal Service and used as a substitute for a check.

money supply The total amount of money circulating and on deposit in the economy.

monition 1. A summons to appear in an admiralty case. 2. A warning.

monopoly A market where there is a concentration of a product or service in the hands of a few, thereby controlling prices or limiting competition. A power to control prices or exclude competition.

> "Monopoly service" means a telecommunications service for which there is no effective competition, either in fact or by operation of law. F.S.A. § 364.02(9)

month to month tenancy A lease without a fixed duration that can be terminated on short notice, e.g., a month. See also periodic tenancy.

monument Natural or artificial boundary markers or objects on land.

moot 1. Pertaining to a nonexistent controversy where the issues have ceased to exist from a practical point of view. 2. Subject to debate.

moot case A case that seeks to resolve an abstract question that does not rest upon existing facts.

moot court A simulated court where law students argue a hypothetical case for purposes of learning and competition.

moral 1. Pertaining to conscience or to general principles of right conduct. 2. Pertaining to a duty binding in conscience but not in law. 3. Demonstrating correct character or behavior.

"Good moral character" means a personal history of honesty, fairness, and respect for the rights and property of others and for the laws of this state and nation. F.S.A. § 493.6101(7)

moral certainty A very high degree of probability although not demonstrable to an absolute certainty. Beyond a reasonable doubt.

moral consideration See good consideration.

moral evidence Evidence based on belief or the general observations of people rather than on what is absolutely demonstrable.

moral hazard The risk or probability that an insured will destroy the insured property or permit it to be destroyed to collect on the insurance.

moral right A right of integrity enjoyed by the creator of a work even if someone else now owns the copyright. Examples include the right to be acknowledged as the creator and to insist that the work not be distorted.

moral turpitude Conduct that is dishonest or contrary to moral rules.

moratorium Temporary suspension. A period of delay.

more or less An approximation; slightly larger or smaller.

morgue A place where dead persons are kept for identification or until burial arrangements are made.

mortality tables A guide used to predict life expectancy based on factors such as a person's age and sex.

mortgage An interest in property created by a written instrument providing security for the performance of a duty or the payment of a debt. A lien or claim against property given by the buyer to the lender as security for the money borrowed.

Whenever property belonging to one person is held by another as security for indebtedness of the other, transaction is in effect a "mortgage." F.S.A. § 697.01. *Kirkland*, 702 So.2d 620 (Fla.App. 4 Dist.,1997)

mortgage bond A bond for which real estate or personal property is pledged as security that the bond will be paid as stated in its terms.

mortgage certificate Document evidencing one's ownership share in a mortgage.

mortgage commitment A written notice from a lending institution that it will advance mortgage funds for the purchase of specified property.

mortgage company A company that makes mortgage loans, which it then sells to investors.

mortgagee A lender to whom property is mortgaged.

mortgage market The existing supply and demand for mortgages, including their resale. Rates and terms being offered by competing mortgagees.

mortgagor The debtor who mortgages his or her property; one who gives legal title or a lien to the mortgagee to secure the mortgage loan.

mortis causa See causa mortis.

mortmain statute A statute that restricts one's right to transfer property to institutions such as churches that would hold it forever.

"Mortmain statutes" allow voiding of deathbed charitable bequests, under certain circumstances, on ground that testators who know they are dying may be peculiarly susceptible to influence. *Martin*, 687 So.2d 903 (Fla.App. 4 Dist.,1997)

most favored nation clause (MFN) A treaty promise that each side will grant to the other the broadest rights that it gives any other nation.

motion An application for an order or ruling from a court or other decision-making body.

motion for a more definite statement A request that the court order the other side to make its pleading more definite, since it is so vague or ambiguous that one cannot frame a responsive pleading.

motion in limine A request for a ruling (often on the admissibility of evidence) prior to the trial or at a preliminary time during the trial.

motion to dismiss A request, usually made before the trial begins, that the judge dismiss the case because of lack of jurisdiction, insufficiency of the pleadings, or the reaching of a settlement.

motion to strike A request that the court remove specific statements, claims, or evidence from the pleadings or the record.

motion to suppress A request that the court eliminate from a criminal trial any illegally secured evidence.

motive A cause or reason that moves the will and induces action or inaction.

In criminal law motive may be defined as that which leads or tempts the mind to indulge in a criminal act, or as the moving power which impels to action for a definite result. It is distinguishable from intent, the purpose of which is to use a particular means to effect a certain result. *Dewey*, 186 So. 224 (Fla.1938)

movables Things that can be carried from one place to another. Personal property.

movant One who makes a motion or applies for a ruling or order.

move To make an application or request for an order or ruling.

moving papers Papers or documents submitted in support of a motion.

mug 1. To criminally assault someone, often with the intent to rob. 2. A human face. A mug shot is a photograph of a suspect's face.

mulct 1. A penalty or punishment such as a fine. 2. To defraud a person of something.

mulier 1. A woman; a wife. 2. A son who is legitimate.

multidisciplinary practice (MDP) A partnership of attorneys and nonattorney professionals that offers legal and nonlegal services.

multidistrict litigation (MDL) Civil actions with common questions of fact pending in different federal district courts that are transferred to one district solely for consolidated pretrial proceedings under a single judge before returning to their original district courts.

multifarious 1. Improperly joined claims, instructions, or parties. 2. Diverse.

multilateral agreement An agreement among three or more parties.

multiple access The defense in a paternity case that more than one lover had access to the mother during the time of conception.

multiple listing An arrangement among real estate agents whereby any member agent can sell property listed by another agent. The latter shares the fee or commission with the broker who made the sale.

multiplicity 1. A large number or variety of matters or particulars. 2. The improper charging of a single offense in several counts.

> "Multiplicity" occurs when the state charges a single offense in more than one count, an action which raises double jeopardy concerns. *State v. Rubio*, 917 So.2d 383 (Fla.App. 5 Dist.,2005)

multiplicity of actions Several attempts to litigate the same right or issue against the same defendant.

municipal 1. Pertaining to a city, town, or other local unit of government. 2. Pertaining to a state or nation.

municipal bond A bond or other debt instrument issued by a state or local unit of government to fund public projects. Also called municipal security.

municipal corporation A city, county, village, town, or other local governmental body established to run all or part of local government. Also called municipality.

> "Municipal corporation" is instrumentality of state established for more convenient administration of local government, and is possessed of certain governmental powers which it may exercise only in manner prescribed in law by which it is created. *Turk*, 47 So.2d 543 (Fla.1950)

municipal court An inferior court with jurisdiction over relatively small claims or offenses arising within the local area where it sits.

municipal ordinance See ordinance.

municipality 1. The body of officials elected or appointed to administer a local government. 2. See municipal corporation.

municipal securities See municipal bond.

muniments Documents used to defend one's title or other claim.

murder The unlawful, premeditated killing of a human being.

> "Second-degree murder" is the unlawful killing of another when perpetrated by act imminently dangerous to another, evincing depraved mind regardless of human life but without any premeditated design to effect death of any particular individual. F.S.A. § 782.04. *Luke*, 204 So.2d 359 (Fla.App. 1967)

mutatis mutandis With the necessary changes in any of the details.

mutilate 1. To maim, to dismember, to disfigure someone. 2. To alter or deface a document by cutting, tearing, burning, or erasing, without totally destroying it.

mutiny An insurrection or uprising of seamen or soldiers against the authority of their commanders.

mutual Reciprocal, common to both parties. In the same relationship to each other.

mutual company A company owned by its clients or customers.

mutual fund An investment company with a pool of assets, consisting primarily of portfolio securities, and belonging to the individual investors holding shares in the fund.

mutual insurance company An insurance company that has no capital stock and in which the policyholders are the owners.

mutuality An action by each of two parties; reciprocation; both sides being bound.

mutuality of contract; mutuality of obligation 1. Liability or obligation imposed on both parties under the terms of the agreement. 2. Unless both sides are bound, neither is bound.

mutual mistake A mistake common to both parties wherein each labors under a misconception respecting the terms of the agreement. Both contracting parties misunderstand the fundamental subject matter or term of the contract. Mistake of both parties on the same fact. Also called bilateral mistake.

> A mistake is a "mutual mistake" when the parties agree to one thing and then, due to either a scrivener's error or inadvertence, express something different in the written instrument. *BrandsMart U.S.A.*, 901 So.2d 1004 (Fla.App. 4 Dist.,2005)

mutual wills 1. Separate wills made by two persons, which are reciprocal in their provisions and by which each testator makes testamentary disposition in favor of the other. Also called double will, reciprocal will. 2. Wills executed pursuant to an agreement between testators to dispose of their property in a particular manner, each in consideration of the other.

N

naked licensee See bare licensee.

naked power A mere authority to act, not accompanied by any interest of the holder of the power in the subject-matter of the power.

naked trust See passive trust.

NALA See National Association of Legal Assistants (*www.nala.org*).

NALS See National Association of Legal Secretaries, now called NALS, the Association for Legal Professionals (*www.nals.org*).

named insured The person specifically mentioned in an insurance policy as the one protected by the insurance.

> Named insured means a person, usually the owner of a vehicle, identified in a policy by name as the insured under the policy. F.S.A. § 627.732(4)

Napoleonic Code See code civil.

narcotic Any addictive drug that dulls the senses or induces sleep.

National Association of Legal Assistants (NALA) A national association of paralegals (*www.nala.org*).

National Association of Legal Secretaries A national association of legal secretaries and paralegals, now called NALS, the Association for Legal Professionals (*www.nals.org*).

national bank A bank incorporated under federal law.

National Federation of Paralegal Associations (NFPA) A national association of paralegals (*www.paralegals.org*).

nationality The status that arises as a result of a person's belonging to a nation because of birth or naturalization.

nationalization The acquisition and control of privately owned businesses by the government.

Native American A member of the indigenous peoples of North, South, and Central America.

natural affection The affection that naturally exists between parent and child and among other close relatives.

natural death Death not caused by accidental or intentional injury.

natural heirs Next of kin by blood (consanguinity) as distinguished from collateral heirs or those related by adoption.

naturalization The process by which a person acquires citizenship after birth.

natural law A system of rules and principles (not created by human authority) discoverable by our rational intelligence as growing out of and conforming to human nature.

natural monument Boundary markers or objects on land that are not artificial.

natural object of bounty Descendants, surviving spouse, and other close relatives who are assumed to become recipients of the estate of a decedent.

natural person A human being. See also artificial person.

> For the purpose of this section, the term "natural person" means an individual. For the purpose of this section, the term "person" includes a natural person, corporation, association, trust, general partnership, limited partnership, joint venture, firm, proprietorship, or any other entity which may hold a license or certificate as a specialty insurer. F.S.A. § 628.4615(d)(e)

natural right A right based on natural law.

navigable water A body of water over which commerce can be carried on.

navigation The art, science, or business of traveling the sea or other navigable waters in ships or vessels.

N.B. (nota bene) Note well, take notice, attention.

necessaries 1. The basic items needed by family members to maintain a standard of living. 2. Food, medicine, clothing, shelter, or personal services usually considered reasonably essential for preservation and enjoyment of life. 3. Goods or services reasonably needed in a ship's business for a vessel's continued operation.

necessary 1. Essential. 2. Logically true.

Necessary and Proper Clause The clause in the U.S. Constitution (Art. I, § 8, cl. 18) giving Congress the power to enact laws that are needed to carry out its enumerated powers.

necessary party A party with a legal or beneficial interest in the subject matter of the lawsuit and who should be joined if feasible.

necessity 1. A privilege to make reasonable use of someone's property to prevent immediate harm or damage to person or property. 2. See choice of evils. 3. Something necessary or indispensable.

ne exeat A writ that forbids a person from leaving the country, state, or jurisdiction of the court.

negative act Not acting when a duty to act exists.

negative averment An allegation of a fact that must be proved by the alleging party even though the allegation is phrased in the negative.

negative covenant A promise not to do or perform some act.

> A negative covenant: where one party promises that he will not do certain things. *Corporate Management Advisors*, 756 So.2d 246 (Fla.App. 5 Dist.,2000)

negative easement An easement that precludes the owner of land subject to the easement (the servient estate) from doing an act which would otherwise be lawful.

negative evidence Testimony or other evidence about what did not happen or does not exist.

negative pregnant A negative statement that also implies an affirmative statement or admission (e.g., "I deny that I owe $500" may be an admission that at least some amount is owed).

neglect 1. The failure to perform an act one has a duty to perform. 2. Carelessness. See also child neglect.

negligence Harm or damage caused by not doing what a reasonably prudent person would have done under like circumstances. A tort with the following elements: (a) a duty of reasonable care, (b) a breach of this duty, (c) proximate cause, (d) actual damages.

> Negligence is the failure to use that degree of care, diligence, and skill that is one's legal duty to use in order to protect another person from injury. *Miriam Mascheck*, 264 So.2d 859 (Fla.App. 1972)

negligence per se Negligence as a matter of law when violating a statute that defines the standard of care.

negligent Unreasonably careless. See also neglect, negligence.

negligent entrustment Creating an unreasonable risk of harm by carelessly allowing someone to use a dangerous object, e.g., a car.

negligent homicide Death due to the failure to perceive a substantial and unjustifiable risk that one's conduct will cause the death of another person.

negligent infliction of emotional distress (NIED) Carelessly causing someone to suffer substantial emotional distress.

negotiability words Words that make an instrument negotiable, e.g., "to the order of."

negotiable 1. Legally capable of being transferred by indorsement or delivery. See also negotiation (1). 2. Open to compromise.

negotiable bill of lading A bill of lading that requires delivery of goods to the bearer of the bill or, if to the order of a named person, to that person.

negotiable instrument Any writing (a) signed by the maker or drawer; (b) containing an unconditional promise or order to pay a sum certain in money; (c) is payable on demand or at a definite time; and (d) is payable to order or to bearer. UCC § 3-104(a).

> The term negotiable instrument means a written document that is legally capable of being transferred by indorsement or delivery. The term "indorsement" means the act of a payee or holder in writing his or her name on the back of an instrument without further qualifying words other than "pay to the order of" or "pay to" whereby the property is assigned and transferred to another. F.S.A. § 199.185(l)

negotiate 1. To bargain with another concerning a sale, settlement, or matter in contention. 2. To transfer by delivery or indorsement. See also negotiation (1).

negotiated plea See plea bargaining.

negotiation 1. The transfer of an instrument through delivery (if the instrument is payable to bearer), or through indorsement and delivery (if it is payable to order) in such form that the transferee becomes a holder. 2. The process of submitting and considering offers.

nemo est supra leges No one is above the law.

nepotism Granting privileges or patronage to one's relatives.

net The amount that remains after all allowable deductions.

net assets See net worth.

net asset value (NAV) The per share value of a company or mutual fund measured by its assets less debts divided by the number of shares.

net estate The portion of a probate estate remaining after all allowable deductions and adjustments.

> Net estate means the net estate as determined under the provisions of the applicable federal revenue act. F.S.A. § 198.01(9)

net income Income subject to taxation after allowable deductions and exemptions have been subtracted from gross or total income.

net lease A lease in which the tenant pays not only rent, but also items such as taxes, insurance, and maintenance charges.

net listing A listing in which the amount of real estate commission is the difference between the selling price of the property and a minimum price set by the seller.

net operating loss (NOL) The excess of allowable deductions over gross income.

net premium 1. The amount of an insurance premium less expenses such as commission. 2. The amount required by an insurer to cover the expected cost of paying benefits.

net weight The weight of an article after deducting the weight of the box or other wrapping.

net worth The total assets of a person or business less the total liabilities. Also called net assets.

> Net worth means total assets minus total liabilities pursuant to generally accepted accounting principles. F.S.A. § 494.001(20)

net worth method To reconstruct the income of a taxpayer, the IRS compares his or her net worth at the beginning and end of the tax year and makes adjustments for personal expenses and allowable deductions.

neutral Not taking an active part with either of the contending sides; disinterested, unbiased.

neutrality laws Acts of Congress that forbid military assistance to either of two belligerent powers with which we are at peace.

ne varietur It must not be altered (a notary's inscription).

new and useful For an invention to be patented, it must be novel and provide some practical benefit.

newly discovered evidence Evidence discovered after the trial and not discoverable before the trial by the exercise of due diligence.

new matter In pleading, a fact not previously alleged by either party in the pleadings.

newsman's privilege See journalist's privilege.

new trial Another trial of all or some of the same issues that were resolved by judgment in a prior trial.

new value Newly given money or money's worth in goods, services, new credit, or release by a transferee of property previously transferred (11 USC § 547(a)(2)).

> New value means money; money's worth in property, services, or new credit; or release by a transferee of an interest in property previously transferred to the transferee. The

term does not include an obligation substituted for another obligation. F.S.A. § 679.1021(eee)

next friend Someone specially appointed by the court to look after the interests of a person who cannot act on his or her own (e.g., a minor). Also called prochein ami.

next of kin 1. The nearest blood relatives of the decedent. 2. Those who would inherit from the decedent if he or she died intestate.

nexus A causal or other connection or link.

NFPA See National Federation of Paralegal Associations (*www.paralegals.org*)

NGO Nongovernmental organization.

NGRI Not guilty by reason of insanity.

nighttime 1. The period between sunset and sunrise when there is not enough daylight to discern a person's face. 2. Thirty minutes after sunset to 30 minutes before sunrise.

nihil dicit ("he says nothing") The name of the judgment against a defendant who omits to plead or answer the plaintiff.

nihil est ("there is nothing") A form of return made by a sheriff when he or she has been unable to serve a writ.

nil (nihil) Nothing.

nisi Unless. Refers to the rule that something will remain or be valid unless an opponent comes forward to demonstrate otherwise.

nisi prius (n.p.) ("unless before") A civil trial court with a jury (in New York and Oklahoma).

NLRB National Labor Relations Board (*www.nlrb.gov*).

no action letter A letter from a government agency that no action will be taken against a person based on the facts before the agency.

no bill A grand jury statement that the evidence is insufficient to justify a formal charge or indictment. Also called not found.

no contest 1. See nolo contendere. 2. See in terrorem clause.

no evidence A challenge to the legal sufficiency of the evidence to support a particular fact finding.

no eyewitness rule If there is no direct evidence (e.g., eyewitness testimony) of what decedent did or failed to do immediately before an injury, the trier of facts may infer that decedent was using ordinary care for his or her own safety.

no fault Pertaining to legal consequences (e.g., granting a divorce, paying insurance benefits) that will occur regardless of who was at fault or to blame.

> New, unregistered, although otherwise registerable, station wagon which was taken out of automobile dealership for a test drive was a "motor vehicle" within Florida automobile reparations reform act, the so-called "no fault" act. F.S.A. §§ 319.23(5), 627.730, 627.731, 627.732(1). *Deel Motors*, 305 So.2d 811 (Fla.App. 1974)

no knock search warrant A warrant that authorizes the police to enter the premises without first announcing themselves.

nolle prosequi (nol-pros) A formal notice by the government that a criminal prosecution will not be pursued.

no-load Sold without a commission.

nolo contendere ("I will not contest it") A plea in a criminal case in which the defendant does not admit or deny the charges. The effect of the plea, however, is similar to a plea of guilty in that the defendant can be sentenced to prison, fined, etc. Also called no contest, non vult contendere.

nol-pros See nolle prosequi.

nominal 1. In name only; not real or substantial. 2. Trifling.

nominal consideration Consideration so small as to bear no relation to the real value of what is received.

nominal damages A trifling sum (e.g., $1) awarded to the plaintiff because there was no significant loss or injury suffered, although a technical invasion of rights did occur.

> The sum of $750 exceeded "nominal damages"; the award should not have exceeded $1. *State, Dept. of Corrections v. Niosi*, 583 So.2d 441 (Fla.App. 4 Dist.,1991)

nominal party A party who has no interest in the result of the suit or no actual interest or control over the subject matter of the litigation but is present to satisfy a technical rule of practice.

nominal trust See passive trust.

nominee 1. One who has been nominated or proposed for an office or appointment. 2. One designated to act for another. An agent.

nominee trust 1. A trust in which the trustee lacks power to deal with the trust property except as directed by the trust beneficiaries. 2. A trust in which property is held for undisclosed beneficiaries.

nonaccess A paternity defense in which the alleged father asserts the absence of opportunities for sexual intercourse with the mother.

nonage See minority (1).

non assumpsit A plea in an assumpsit action that the undertaking was not made as alleged.

non compos mentis Not of sound mind. Mentally incompetent.

nonconforming use A use of land that is permitted because the use was lawful prior to a change in the zoning law even though the new law would make the use illegal.

> Existing uses shall be considered lawful prior nonconforming uses, notwithstanding rezoning or continuous, rotated, or relocated uses within the annexed property. *County of Volusia v. City of Deltona*, 925 So.2d 340 (Fla.App. 5 Dist.,2006)

noncore proceeding A nonbankruptcy proceeding related to the debtor's estate that, in the absence of a petition in bankruptcy, could have been brought in a state court.

nondelegable duty An affirmative duty that cannot be escaped by entrusting it to a third party such as an independent contractor.

nonexclusive listing See open listing.

nonfeasance The failure to perform a legal duty.

nonintervention will A will providing that the executor shall not be required to account to any court or person.

nonjoinder The failure to join a necessary person to a suit.

nonjury trial See bench trial.

nonjusticiable Inappropriate or improper for judicial resolution.

nonmailable Pertaining to what cannot be transported by U.S. mail because of size, obscene content, etc.

nonnegotiable 1. Not capable of transfer by indorsement or delivery. 2. Fixed; pertaining to what will not be bargained.

non obstante veredicto Notwithstanding the verdict. See judgment notwithstanding the verdict.

nonperformance The failure or refusal to perform an obligation.

nonprofit corporation A corporation whose purpose is not to make a profit. Also called not-for-profit corporation.

non prosequitur ("he does not prosecute") A judgment against a plaintiff who fails to pursue his or her action.

nonrecourse creditor A creditor who can look only to its collateral for satisfaction of its debt, not to the debtor's other assets.

nonresident alien One who is neither a citizen nor a resident of the country he or she is presently in.

> Nonresident alien shall mean those individuals from other nations who can provide documentation from the Bureau of Citizenship and Immigration Services evidencing permanent residency status in the United States. For the purposes of this chapter, a "nonresident alien" shall be considered a "nonresident." F.S.A. § 370.01(17)

non sequitur A conclusion that does not logically follow from what precedes it.

nonstock corporation A corporation whose ownership is not determined by shares of stock.

nonsuit A termination or dismissal of an action by a plaintiff who is unable to prove his or her case, defaults, fails to prosecute, etc.

nonsupport The failure to provide food, clothing, and other support needed for living to someone to whom an obligation of support is owed.

nonuse The failure to exercise a right or claim.

non vult contendere A plea of no contest ("He will not contest"). See also nolo contendere.

no par stock Stock issued without a value stated on the stock certificate.

noscitur a sociis ("it is known by its associates") A word with multiple meanings is often best interpreted with regard to the words surrounding it.

> Under the "noscitur a sociis doctrine," a word is known by the company it keeps, and one must examine the other words used in a string of concepts to derive the drafters' intent. *Aerothrust Corp.*, 904 So.2d 470 (Fla.App. 3 Dist.,2005)

no-strike clause A commitment by a labor union not to strike during the period covered by the collective bargaining agreement.

nota bene See N.B.

notarial Performed or taken by a notary public.

notarize To certify or attest, e.g., the authenticity of a signature.

notary public One authorized to perform notarial acts such as administering oaths, taking proof of execution and acknowledgment of instruments, and attesting the authenticity of signatures.

> "Civil-law notary" means a person who is a member in good standing of The Florida Bar, who has practiced law for at least 5 years, and who is appointed by the Secretary of State as a civil-law notary. F.S.A. § 118.10(1)(b)

note See promissory note.

not-for-profit corporation See nonprofit corporation.

not found See no bill.

not guilty 1. A jury verdict acquitting the accused. 2. A plea entered by the accused that denies guilt for a criminal charge.

not guilty by reason of insanity (NGRI) A verdict of not guilty because of a finding of insanity. See also insanity.

notice 1. Information or knowledge about something. 2. Formal notification. 3. Knowledge of facts that would naturally lead an honest and prudent person to make inquiry.

> Actual notice means notice that is given directly, in person or by telephone, to a parent or legal guardian of a minor, by a physician, at least 48 hours before the inducement or performance of a termination of pregnancy, and documented in the minor's files. F.S.A. § 390.01114(a).

notice by publication Notice given through a broad medium such as a general circulation newspaper.

notice of appeal Notice given to a court (through filing) and to the opposing party (through service) of an intention to appeal.

notice of appearance A formal notification to a court by an attorney that he or she is representing a party in the litigation.

notice of pendency See lis pendens (2).

notice pleading Pleading by giving a short and plain statement of a claim that shows the pleader is entitled to relief.

notice to quit A landlord's written notice to a tenant that the landlord wishes to repossess the leased premises and end the tenancy.

notorious 1. Well-known for something undesirable. 2. Conspicuous.

notorious possession Occupation or possession of property that is conspicuous or generally known. Also called open possession.

NOV See judgment notwithstanding the verdict.

novation The substitution by mutual agreement of one debtor for another or of one creditor for another, whereby the old debt is extinguished, or the substitution of a new debt or obligation for an existing one.

novelty That which has not been known or used before. Innovation.

NOW account An interest-bearing savings account on which checks can be written. NOW means negotiable order of withdrawal.

NSF check (not sufficient funds) A check that is dishonored because the drawer of the check does not have sufficient funds to cover it.

nude Lacking something essential.

nudum pactum ("a bare agreement") A promise or undertaking made without any consideration.

nugatory Without force; invalid.

nuisance A substantial interference with the reasonable use and enjoyment of private land (private nuisance); an unreasonable interference with a right that is common to the general public (public nuisance).

> Nuisance means a condition in which pestiferous arthropods occur in such numbers as to be annoying, obnoxious, or inimical to human comfort. F.S.A. § 388.011(9)

nuisance per se An act, occurrence, or structure that is a nuisance at all times and under all circumstances.

null; null and void Having no legal effect; binding no one.

nulla bona "No goods" on which a writ of execution can be levied.

nullification 1. The state or condition of being void or without legal effect. 2. The process of rendering something void.

nullify To invalidate; to render void.

nullity Having absolutely no legal effect. Something that is void.

nullius filius ("the son of no one") An illegitimate child.

nul tiel record ("no such") A plea asserting that the record relied upon in the opponent's claim does not exist.

nunc pro tunc ("now for then") With retroactive effect. As if it were done as of the time that it should have been done.

nuncupative will An oral will declared or dictated in anticipation of imminent death.

NYSE New York Stock Exchange (*www.nyse.com*).

O

oath 1. A solemn declaration. 2. A formal pledge to be truthful.

> An "oath" is an unequivocal act, before an officer authorized to administer oaths, by which the person knowingly attests to the truth of a statement and assumes the obligations of an oath. *Crain*, 914 So.2d 1015 (Fla.App. 5 Dist.,2005)

obiter dictum See dictum (1).

object 1. To express disapproval; to consider something improper or illegal and ask the court to take action accordingly. 2. The end aimed at; the thing sought to be accomplished.

objection 1. A formal disagreement or statement of opposition. 2. The act of objecting.

objective 1. Real in the external world; existing outside one's subjective mind. 2. Unbiased. 3. Goal.

obligation 1. Any duty imposed by law, contract, or morals. 2. A binding agreement to do something, e.g., to pay a certain sum.

obligee The person to whom an obligation is owed; a promisee or creditor.

obligor The person under an obligation; a promisor or debtor.

obliterate To destroy; to erase or wipe out.

obloquy Abusive language; disgrace due to defamatory criticism.

obscene Material that enjoys no free-speech protection if: (a) the average person, applying contemporary community standards, finds that the work, taken as a whole, appeals to the prurient interest in sex; (b) the work depicts or describes, in a patently offensive way, sexual conduct specifically defined by the applicable state law; and (c) the work, taken as a whole, lacks serious literary, artistic, political, or scientific value.

> "Obscene" means that status of a communication which: 1. The average person applying contemporary community standards would find, taken as a whole, appeals to the prurient interests; 2. Describes, in a patently offensive way, deviate sexual intercourse, sadomasochistic abuse, sexual battery, bestiality, sexual conduct, or sexual excitement; and 3. Taken as a whole, lacks serious literary, artistic, political, or scientific value. F.S.A. § 365.161

obscenity 1. See obscene. 2. Conduct tending to corrupt the public morals by its indecency or lewdness.

obsolescence Diminution in value caused by changes in taste or new technology, rendering the property less desirable on the market; the condition or process of falling into disuse.

obstruction of justice Conduct that impedes or interferes with the administration of justice (e.g., hindering a witness from appearing).

obvious Easily discovered or readily apparent.

occupancy 1. Obtaining possession of real property for dwelling or lodging purposes. 2. The period during which one is in actual possession of land.

> Occupancy, within meaning of the fire policy, is largely a matter of intent; it does not of necessity involve a continuous bodily presence on the insured premises. *Independent Fire Ins. Co.*, 362 So.2d 980 (Fla.App.,1978)

occupation 1. Conduct in which one is engaged. 2. One's regular employment or source of livelihood. 3. Conquest or seizure of land.

occupational disease A disease resulting from exposure during employment to conditions or substances detrimental to health.

Occupational Safety and Health Administration (OSHA) A federal agency that develops workplace health and safety standards, and conducts investigations to enforce compliance (*www.osha.gov*).

occupation tax A tax imposed for the privilege of carrying on a business or occupation.

occupying the field A form of preemption (see this word) where a federal rule is so pervasive that no room is left for states to supplement it.

occurrence policy Insurance that covers all losses from events that occur during the period the policy is in effect, even if the claim is not actually filed until after the policy expires.

> Occurrence policies trigger carrier's liability if the error or omission occurs during period of policy coverage, regardless of date of discovery or date the claim is made or asserted. *U.S. Fire Ins. Co.*, 682 So.2d 620 (Fla.App. 3 Dist.,1996)

odd lot An irregular or nonstandard amount for a trade, e.g., less than 100.

odd lot doctrine For workers' compensation, permanent total disability may be found in the case of workers who, while not altogether incapacitated for work, are so handicapped that they will not be employed regularly in any well-known branch of the labor market.

odious Arousing strong dislike; base, vile, detestable, disgraceful, scandalous.

odium Contempt or intense dislike. Held in disgrace.

of age See adult, majority (1).

of counsel 1. An attorney who is semiretired or has some other special status in the law firm other than regular member or employee. 2. An attorney who assists the principal attorney in a case.

offender One who has committed a crime or offense.

offense A crime or violation of law for which a penalty can be imposed.

offensive 1. Disagreeable, objectionable, displeasing. 2. Offending the personal dignity of an ordinary person who is not unduly sensitive. 3. Taking the offensive; on the attack; aggressive.

offer 1. A proposal presented for acceptance or rejection. 2. To request that the court admit an exhibit into evidence.

> Offer means any solicitation, advertisement, inducement, or other method or attempt to encourage any person to become a purchaser. F.S.A. § 509.502(9)

offeree The person to whom an offer is made.

offering The sale or offer for sale of an issue of securities.

offer of compromise An offer to settle a case.

offer of proof Telling the court what evidence a party proposes to present after the judge has ruled it inadmissible so that a record will be made for a later appeal of this ruling.

offeror The party who makes an offer.

office 1. A position of trust and authority. 2. A place where everyday administrative business is conducted. 3. A unit or subdivision of government.

officer A person holding a position of trust, command, or authority in organizations.

officer of the court A person who has a responsibility in carrying out or assisting in the administration of justice in the courts, such as judges, bailiffs, court clerks, and attorneys.

official 1. An elected or appointed holder of a public office. An officer. 2. Concerning that which is authorized. 3. Proceeding from, sanctioned by, or pertaining to an officer.

Official Gazette Publication of the U.S. Patent and Trademark Office.

official immunity The immunity of government employees from personal liability for torts they commit while performing discretionary acts within the scope of their employment.

official notice The equivalent of judicial notice when taken by an administrative law judge or examiner.

official report or **official reporter** A collection of court opinions whose printing is authorized by the government.

officious intermeddler One who interferes in the affairs of another without justification (or invitation) and is generally not entitled to restitution for any benefit he or she confers. Also called intermeddler.

> Officious intermeddling, as a necessary element of champerty, is offering unnecessary and unwanted advice or services or being meddlesome in high-handed or overbearing way. *Kraft*, 668 So.2d 679 (Fla.App. 4 Dist.,1996)

offset A deduction; that which compensates for or counters something else. See also setoff.

Old Age, Survivors, and Disability Insurance A federal program providing financial benefits for retirement and disability. Also called Social Security.

oligarchy Government power in the hands of a few persons.

oligopoly A market structure in which a few sellers dominate sales of a product, resulting in high prices.

ombudsman One who investigates and helps resolve grievances that people have within or against an organization, often employed by the organization.

omission 1. The intentional or unintentional failure to act. 2. Something left out or neglected.

> An omission sufficient to apply the doctrine of equitable estoppel means negligent or culpable omission where the party failing to act was under a duty to do so. *Pasco*, 364 So.2d 850 (Fla.App.,1978)

omnibus bill 1. A legislative bill that includes different subjects in one measure. 2. A legislative bill covering many aspects of one subject.

omnibus clause 1. A clause in an instrument (e.g., a will) that covers all property not specifically mentioned or known at the time. 2. A clause extending liability insurance coverage to persons using the car with the permission of the named insured.

on all fours Pertaining to facts that are exactly the same, or almost so; being a very close precedent.

on demand Upon request; when demanded.

onerous Unreasonably burdensome or one-sided.

on information and belief See information and belief.

on its face Whatever is readily observable, e.g., the language of a document. See also face.

on or about Approximately.

one man (person), one vote The equal protection requirement that each qualified voter be given an equal opportunity to participate in an election.

on point 1. Germane, relevant. 2. Covering or raising the same issue (in a case, law review article, etc.) as the one before you.

on the brief Helped to research or write the appellate brief.

on the merits Pertaining to a court decision that is based on the facts and on the substance of the claim, rather than on a procedural ground.

on the pleadings Pertaining to a ruling based on the allegations in the pleadings rather than on evidence presented in a hearing.

on the record Noted or recorded in the official record of the proceeding.

open 1. Visible, apparent, exposed. 2. Still available or active. 3. Not restricted. 4. Not resolved or settled.

open account 1. A type of credit from a seller that permits a buyer to make purchases on an ongoing basis without security. 2. An unpaid account.

In commercial transactions, an "open account" should refer to an unsettled debt, arising from items of work or labor, goods sold, and other open transactions not reduced to writing, sole record of which is usually the account books of owner of demand, and it should not include express contracts or obligations that have been reduced to writing. *H & H Design Builders*, 639 So.2d 697 (Fla.App. 5 Dist.,1994)

open and notorious Conspicuous, generally recognized, or commonly known.

open court A court in session to which the general public may or may not be invited.

open end 1. Without a defined time or monetary limit. 2. Allowing further additions or other changes.

open-end mortgage A mortgage that allows the debtor to borrow additional funds without providing additional collateral.

open field doctrine No violation of one's constitutional right to privacy occurs when the police search an open field without a warrant.

The "open fields doctrine," which stands for the proposition that the Fourth Amendment's protection of one's person, house, papers, and effects does not extend to the open fields, does not extend to warrantless search of

closed structure on fenced property. *Norman*, 379 So.2d 643 (Fla., 1980)

opening statement An attorney's statement to the jury made before presenting evidence that summarizes the case he or she intends to try to establish during the trial.

open listing A listing available to more than one agent in which the owner agrees to pay a commission to any agent who produces a ready, willing, and able purchaser. Also called nonexclusive listing.

open market An unrestricted competitive market in which any buyer and purchaser is free to participate.

open order An order placed with a broker that remains viable (open) until filled or the client cancels the order.

open policy See unvalued policy.

open possession See notorious possession.

open price The amount to be paid has yet to be determined or settled.

open shop A business in which union membership is not a condition of employment.

operating lease A short-term lease that expires before the end of the useful life of the leased property.

operating loss See net operating loss.

operation of law The means by which legal consequences are imposed by law, regardless of the intent of the parties involved.

opinion 1. A court's written explanation of how it applied the law to the facts to resolve a legal dispute. 2. A belief or conclusion expressing a value judgment that is not objectively verifiable.

Opinion testimony of lay witnesses. If a witness is not testifying as an expert, the witness's testimony about what he or she perceived may be in the form of inference and opinion when: (1) The witness cannot readily, and with equal accuracy and adequacy, communicate what he or she has perceived to the trier of fact without testifying in terms of inferences or opinions . . . and (2) The opinions and inferences do not require a special knowledge, skill, experience, or training. F.S.A. § 90.701

opinion evidence Beliefs or inferences concerning facts in issue.

opinion of the attorney general Formal legal advice from the chief law officer of the government to another government official or agency.

opportunity cost Benefits a business foregoes by choosing one course of action (e.g., an investment) over another.

opportunity to be heard A due process requirement of being allowed to present objections to proposed government action that would deprive one of a right.

oppression 1. An act of cruelty; conduct intended to frighten or harm. 2. Excessive and unjust use of authority. 3. Substantial inequality of bargaining power of the parties to the contract and an absence of real negotiation or a meaningful choice on the part of the weaker party.

option 1. An agreement that gives the person to whom the option is granted (the optionee) the right within a limited time to accept an offer. The right to buy or sell a stated quantity of securities or other goods at a set price within a defined time. 2. An opportunity to choose.

option contract A unilateral agreement to hold an offer open. See option (1).

An option contract, in contrast to executory right of first refusal, is a contract in which the seller makes an irrevocable offer to sell on specified terms and which creates in the buyer a power of acceptance; it is therefore an executed contract. *Steinberg*, 837 So.2d 503 (Fla.App. 3 Dist.,2003)

optionee The person to whom an option is granted.

OR Own recognizance. See also personal recognizance.

oral Spoken, not written.

oral argument A spoken presentation to the court on a legal issue, e.g., telling an appellate court why the rulings of a lower tribunal were valid or were in error.

oral contract See parol contract.

oral trust A trust established by its creator (the settler) by spoken words rather than in writing.

oral will See nuncupative will.

ordeal An ancient form of trial in which the innocence of an accused person was determined by his or her ability to come away from an endurance test (e.g., hold a red-hot iron in the hand) unharmed.

order 1. A command or instruction from a judge or other official. 2. An instruction to buy or sell something. 3. The language on a check (or other draft) directing or ordering the payment or delivery of money or other property to a designated person.

Order means a written instruction to pay money signed by the person giving the instruction. The instruction may be addressed to any person, including the person giving the instruction, or to one or more persons jointly or in the alternative but not in succession. An authorization to pay is not an order unless the person authorized to pay is also instructed to pay. F.S.A. § 673.1031(1)(f)

order bill of lading A negotiable instrument, issued by a carrier to a shipper at the time goods are loaded aboard ship, that serves as a receipt that the carrier has received the goods for shipment, as a contract of carriage for those goods, and as documentary evidence of title to those goods.

ordered liberty The constitutional balance between respect for the liberty of the individual and the demands of organized society.

order nisi See decree nisi.

Order of the Coif An honorary organization of law students whose membership is based on excellence.

order paper A negotiable instrument payable to a specific person or to his or her designee (it is payable to order, not to bearer).

order to show cause See show cause order.

ordinance 1. A law passed by the local legislative branch of government (e.g., city council) that declares, commands, or prohibits something. Also called municipal ordinance. 2. A law or decree.

ordinary Usual; regularly occurring.

ordinary care Reasonable care under the circumstances.

Ordinary care, in the case of a person engaged in business, means observance of reasonable commercial standards, prevailing in the area in which the person is located, with respect to the business in which the person is engaged. F.S.A. § 673.1031(g)

ordinary course of business See course of business.

ordinary income Wages, dividends, commissions, interest earned on savings, and similar kinds of income; income other than capital gains.

ordinary life insurance See whole life insurance.

ordinary negligence The failure to use reasonable care (often involving inadvertence) that does not constitute gross negligence or recklessness. Sometimes called simple negligence.

ordinary prudent person See reasonable man (person).

organic Inherent, integral, or basic.

organic law The fundamental law or constitution of a state or nation; laws that establish and define the organization of government.

organization A society or group of persons joined in a common purpose.

organize To induce persons to join an organization, e.g., a union.

organized crime A continuing conspiracy among highly organized and disciplined groups to engage in supplying illegal goods and services.

The Legislature found that organized crime involves various patterns of unlawful conduct, including the illegal use of force, fraud, and corruption, that its operatives use Florida's own laws governing business enterprises for unlawful purposes, and that its corruption of legitimate business provides an outlet for illegally obtained capital, harms innocent investors, entrepreneurs, merchants, and consumers, interferes with free competition, and thereby constitutes a substantial danger to the economic and general welfare of the State of Florida. *State v. Otte*, 887 So.2d 1186 (Fla.,2004)

organized labor Employees in labor unions.

original 1. The first form, from which copies are made. 2. New and unusual.

original contractor See general contractor.

original document rule See best evidence rule.

original intent The meaning understood by the framers or drafters of the U.S. Constitution, a statute, a contract, or other document.

original jurisdiction The power of a court to be the first to hear and resolve a case before it is reviewed by another court.

original-package doctrine Goods imported into a state cannot be taxed by that state if they are in their original packaging when shipped.

original promise A promise, made for the benefit of the promisor, to pay or guarantee the debt of another.

original writ The first process or initial step in bringing or prosecuting a suit.

origination fee A fee charged by the lender for preparing the loan documents and processing the loan.

orphan's court See probate court.

OSHA See Occupational Safety and Health Administration (*www.osha.gov*).

ostensible Apparent; appearing to be accurate or true.

ostensible agency An agency that arises when the principal's conduct allows others to believe that the agent possesses authority, which in fact does not exist.

ostensible authority The authority a principal intentionally or by lack of ordinary care allows a third person to believe the agent possesses. See also apparent authority.

Apparent or ostensible authority arises where a principal allows or causes others to believe the agent possesses such authority, as where the principal knowingly permits the agent to assume such authority or where the principal by his actions or words holds the agent out as possessing it. *Singer*, 510 So.2d 637 (Fla.App. 4 Dist.,1987)

OTC See over-the-counter.

our federalism Federal courts must refrain from hearing constitutional challenges to state action when federal action is regarded as an improper intrusion on the right of a state to enforce its own laws in its own courts.

oust To remove; to deprive of possession or of a right.

ouster Turning out (or keeping excluded) someone entitled to possession of property. Wrongful dispossession.

outlaw 1. To prohibit or make illegal. 2. A person excluded from the benefits and protection of the law. 3. A fugitive.

out-of-court Not part of a court proceeding.

out-of-court settlement The resolution or settlement of a legal dispute without the participation of the court.

out-of-pocket expenses Expenditures made out of one's own funds.

out-of-pocket rule The damages awarded will be the difference between the purchase price and the real or actual value of the property received.

> The two standards for measuring damages in an action for fraud arising out of the sale of real property are the "benefit of the bargain rule," which awards as damages the difference between the actual value of the property and its value had the alleged facts regarding it been true, and the "out-of-pocket rule," which awards as damages the difference between the purchase price and the real or actual value of the property; either measure of damages requires a plaintiff to prove the actual value of the property at the time of purchase. *Kind*, 889 So.2d 87 (Fla.App. 4 Dist.,2004)

output contract A contract in which one party agrees to sell its entire output, which the other party agrees to buy during a designated period.

outrage See intentional infliction of emotional distress.

outrageous Shocking; beyond the bounds of human decency.

outside director A member of a board of directors who is not an officer or employee of the corporation.

outstanding 1. Uncollected, unpaid. 2. Publicly issued and sold.

over Passing or taking effect after a prior estate or interest ends or is terminated.

overbreadth doctrine A law is invalid, though designed to prohibit legitimately regulated conduct, if it is so broad that it includes within its prohibitions constitutionally protected freedoms.

overdraft 1. A check written on an account for an amount that exceeds the funds available in the account. 2. The act of overdrawing a bank account.

overhead The operating expenses of a business (e.g., rent, utilities) for which customers or clients are not charged a separate fee.

overissue To issue shares in an excessive or unauthorized quantity.

overreaching Taking unfair advantage of another's naiveté or other vulnerability, especially by deceptive means.

> Overreaching has been defined as that which results from an inequality of bargaining power or other circumstances in which there is an absence of meaningful choice on the

part of one of the parties. *Schreiber*, 795 So.2d 1054 (Fla.App. 4 Dist.,2001)

override 1. To set aside, supersede, or nullify. 2. A commission paid to managers on sales made by subordinates. 3. A commission paid to a real estate agent when a landowner makes a sale on his or her own (after the listing agreement expires) to a purchaser who was found by the agent.

overrule 1. To decide against or deny. 2. To reject or cancel an earlier opinion as precedent by rendering an opposite decision on the same question of law.

overt act 1. An act that reasonably appears to be about to inflict great bodily harm, justifying the use of self-defense. 2. An outward act from which criminality may be implied. 3. An outward objective action performed by one of the members of a conspiracy.

over-the-counter (OTC) 1. Sold or transferred independent of a securities exchange. 2. Sold without the need of a prescription.

owelty Money paid to equalize a disproportionate division of property.

ownership The right to possess, control, and use property, and to convey it to others. Having rightful title to property.

oyer Reading a document aloud in court or a petition to have such a reading.

oyer and terminer A special court with jurisdiction to hear treason and other criminal cases. A judge's commission to hear such cases.

oyez Hear ye; a call announcing the beginning of a court proceeding or a proclamation.

P

P.A. See professional association.

PAC See political action committee.

PACE See Paralegal Advanced Competency Exam (*www.paralegals.org*).

PACER See Public Access to Court Electronic Records (*pacer.psc.uscourts.gov*).

pack 1. To assemble with an improper purpose. 2. To fill or arrange.

pact 1. A bargain. 2. An agreement between two or more nations or states.

pactum An agreement. See also nudum pactum.

paid-in capital Money or property paid to a corporation by its owners for its capital stock.

paid-in surplus That portion of the surplus of a corporation not generated by profits but contributed by the stockholders. Surplus accumulated by the sale of stock at more than par value.

pain Physical discomfort and distress.

pain and suffering Physical discomfort or emotional distress; a disagreeable mental or emotional experience.

pains and penalties See bill of pains and penalties.

pais See in pais.

palimony Support payments ordered after the end of a nonmarital relationship if the party seeking support was induced to sustain or initiate the relationship by a promise of support or if support is otherwise equitable.

The counterclaim asserted a claim was one for "palimony," which is not a recognized cause of action in this state. Without attempting to define what may or may not be "palimony," this case simply involves whether these parties entered into a contract for support, which is something that they are legally capable of doing. *Crossen*, 673 So.2d 903 (Fla.App. 2 Dist.,1996)

palming off Misrepresenting one's own goods or services as those of another. Also called passing off.

***Palsgraf* rule** Negligence liability is limited to reasonably foreseeable harm. *Palsgraf v. Long Island R. Co.*, 162 N.E. 99 (NY 1928).

pander To engage in pandering. A panderer is one who panders.

pandering The recruitment of prostitutes. Acting as a go-between to cater to the lust or base desires of another.

panel 1. A group of judges, usually three, who decide a case in a court with a larger number of judges. 2. A list of persons summoned to be examined for jury duty or to serve on a particular jury. 3. A group of attorneys available in a group legal services plan.

paper A written or printed document that is evidence of a debt. Commercial paper; a negotiable instrument.

paper loss; paper profit An unrealized loss or gain on a security or other investment that is still held. Loss or profit that will not become actual until the asset is sold or closed out.

papers Pleadings, motions, and other litigation documents filed in court.

paper title The title listed or described on public records after the deed is recorded. Also called record title.

par 1. An acceptable average or standard. 2. See par value.

paralegal A person with legal skills who works under the supervision of an attorney or who is otherwise authorized by law to use his or her skills; this person performs substantive tasks that do not require all the skills of an attorney and that most secretaries are not trained to perform. Also called legal assistant.

A person with education, training, or work experience, who works under the direction and supervision of a member of The Florida Bar and who performs specifically delegated substantive legal work for which a member of The Florida Bar is responsible. Rules Regulating The Florida Bar, Rule 20-2.1(a) (see also section 1.1)

Paralegal Advanced Competency Exam (PACE) The certification exam of the National Federation of Paralegal Associations for experienced paralegals (*www.paralegals.org*).

parallel citation A citation to an additional reporter where you can read the same court opinion.

paramount title Superior title as among competing claims to title.

paraphernalia 1. Property kept by a married woman on her husband's death in addition to her dower. 2. Equipment used for an activity.

parcel 1. To divide into portions and distribute. 2. A small package or wrapped bundle. 3. A part or portion of land.

parcenary See coparcenary.

parcener See coparcener.

pardon An act of government exempting an individual from punishment for crime and from any resulting civil disabilities.

parens patriae The state's power to protect and act as guardian of persons who suffer disabilities (e.g., minors, insane persons).

Parens patriae, which is Latin for "parent of his or her country," describes the state in its capacity as provider of protection to those unable to care for themselves. The doctrine derives from the common-law concept of royal prerogative, recognized by American courts in the form of legislative prerogative. *Global Travel Marketing*, 908 So.2d 392 (Fla.,2005)

parent A biological or adoptive mother or father of another.

parental kidnapping A parent's taking and removing his or her child from the custody of a person with legal custody without the latter's consent with the intent of defeating the custody jurisdiction of the court that currently has such jurisdiction.

parental liability law A law that makes parents liable (up to a limited dollar amount) for torts committed by their minor children.

parental rights The rights of a parent to raise his or her children, receive their services, and control their income and property.

parent corporation A corporation that controls another corporation (called the subsidiary corporation) through stock ownership.

To hold a parent corporation liable for the acts of its subsidiary, the parent's control must be high and very significant, such that the subsidiary functions for the sole purpose of achieving the parent's interests. *Banco Continental*, 922 So.2d 395 (Fla.App. 3 Dist.,2006)

pari delicto See in pari delicto.

pari materia See in pari materia.

parish 1. A territorial government division in Louisiana. 2. An ecclesiastical division of a city or town administered by a pastor.

parity Equality in amount, status, or value.

parliament A legislative body of a country, e.g., England.

parliamentarian An expert who provides advice on parliamentary law.

parliamentary Pertaining to the parliament or to its rules.

parliamentary law Rules of procedure to be followed by legislatures and other formal organizations.

parol 1. Spoken rather than in writing. 2. An oral statement.

parol contract A contract that is not in writing. Also called oral contract.

parole Allowing a prisoner to leave confinement before the end of his or her sentence.

Parole is not an act of amnesty and does not terminate a sentence legally imposed but is that procedure by which a prisoner who must in any event be returned to society at some future time is allowed to serve last portion of sentence outside prison under strict supervision as preparation for eventual return to society. F.S.A. § 947.16. *Sellers*, 15 So.2d 293 (Fla.1943)

parole board A government agency that decides if and under what conditions inmates can be released before completing their sentences.

parolee An ex-prisoner who has been placed on parole.

parol-evidence rule Prior or contemporaneous oral statements cannot be used to vary or contradict a written contract the parties intended to be final.

The parol-evidence rule is a substantive rule of law and reduced to its essence provides that a written document intended by the parties to be the final embodiment of their agreement may not be contradicted, modified, or varied by parol evidence. *King*, 867 So.2d 1224 (Fla.App. 5 Dist.,2004)

parole officer A government official who supervises persons on parole.

partial average See particular average.

partial breach A nonmaterial breach of contract that entitles a party to a remedy but not the right to consider the contract terminated.

partial disability A worker's inability to perform jobs he or she could perform before a work injury, even though still able to perform other gainful jobs subject to the disability.

partial insanity See diminished capacity.

partial verdict A verdict that is not the same on all the counts charged or on all the defendants in the trial. A verdict that consists of a finding of guilt on some counts and innocence on others.

particeps criminis A participant in a crime; an accomplice or accessory.

participation loan A loan issued or owned by more than one lender.

particular average An accidental partial loss of goods at sea by one who must bear the loss alone. Also called partial average.

particular estate An estate less than a fee simple, e.g., life estate.

particular lien A right to hold property as security for labor or funds expended on that specific property. Also called special lien.

particulars The details. See also bill of particulars.

partition The dividing of land held by co-owners into distinct portions, resulting in individual ownership.

partner 1. One who has united with others to form a partnership. 2. Two or more persons engaged in a jointly owned business.

partnership A voluntary association of two or more persons to place their resources in a jointly owned business or enterprise, with a proportional sharing of profits and losses.

> [T]wo or more persons [who] carry on as coowners of a business with the understanding that there will be a proportional sharing of the profits and losses between them. For the purposes of this chapter, a partner is a person who participates fully in the management of the partnership and who is personally liable for its debts. F.S.A. § 440.02(21)

partnership association A hybrid type of business with characteristics of a close corporation and a limited partnership.

part performance rule When an oral agreement fails to meet the requirements of the statute of frauds, the agreement may sometimes still be enforced when a relying party has partly performed the agreement.

party 1. One who brings a lawsuit or against whom a lawsuit is brought. 2. One who is concerned with, has an interest in, or takes part in the performance of an act. 3. A formal political association.

party aggrieved See aggrieved party.

party in interest See real party in interest.

party to be charged One against whom another seeks to enforce a contract.

par value An amount stated in a security, policy, or other instrument as its value. Also called face amount, face value, par, stated value.

pass 1. To utter or pronounce. 2. To transfer. 3. To enact into law by a legislative body. 4. To approve. 5. To forego.

passage Enactment into law by a legislative body.

passbook A bank document that records a customer's account activities.

passenger Any occupant of a motor vehicle other than the operator.

> A person rightfully taking passage in, without exercising control over management of, a motor vehicle, as distinguished from the operator or person responsible at time for its operation. *Peery*, 5 So.2d 694 (Fla.1942)

passim Here and there; in various places throughout.

passing off See palming off.

passion Any strong emotion that often interferes with cool reflection of the mind. See also heat of passion.

passive 1. Submitting without active involvement. 2. Inactive.

passive negligence The unreasonable failure to do something; carelessly permitting defects to exist.

passive trust A trust whose trustee has no active duties. Also called dry trust, naked trust, nominal trust, simple trust.

passport A document that identifies a citizen, constitutes permission to travel to foreign countries, and acts as a request to foreign powers that the citizen be allowed to pass freely and safely.

past consideration An earlier benefit or detriment that was not exchanged for a new promise.

past recollection recorded A written record of a matter about which a witness now has insufficient memory. The record may be read into evidence if it was made or adopted by the witness when the matter was fresh in his or her memory. Fed. R. Evid. 803(5). An exception to the hearsay rule. Also called recorded recollection.

> The . . . following are not inadmissible as evidence, even though the declarant is available as a witness: (5) Recorded recollection.—A memorandum or record concerning a matter about which a witness once had knowledge, but now has insufficient recollection to enable the witness to testify fully and accurately, shown to have been made by the witness when the matter was fresh in the witness's memory and to reflect that knowledge correctly. A party may read into evidence a memorandum or record when it is admitted, but no such memorandum or record is admissible as an exhibit unless offered by an adverse party. F.S.A. § 90.803

patent 1. A grant of a privilege or authority by the government. 2. A grant made by the government to an inventor for the exclusive right to make, use, and sell an invention for a term of years.

patentable Suitable to be patented because the device or process is novel, useful, and nonobvious.

patent defect See apparent defects.

patentee A person to whom a patent is granted; the holder of a patent.

patent infringement See infringement of patent.

patent medicine Packaged medicines or drugs sold over the counter under a trademark or other trade symbol.

paternity The state or condition of being a father.

paternity suit A court action to determine whether a person is the father of a child for whom support is owed. Also called bastardy proceeding.

> Paternity proceeding means an administrative action commenced by the Department of Revenue to order genetic testing and establish paternity pursuant to this section. F.S.A. § 409.256(1)(f)

patient-physician privilege See doctor-patient privilege.

pat. pend. Patent (application is) pending.

patricide 1. Killing one's father. 2. One who has killed his or her father.

patrimony 1. Heritage from one's ancestors. 2. That which is inherited from a father. 3. The total value of a person's rights and obligations.

patronage 1. The power to offer political jobs or other privileges. 2. Assistance received from a patron. 3. The customers of a business.

pattern 1. A reliable sample of observable features. 2. A model.

pauper A person so poor that he or she needs public assistance.

pawn To deliver personal property to another as security for a loan.

pawnbroker A person in the business of lending money upon the deposit of personal property as security.

> Pawnbroker means any person, corporation, or other business organization or entity which is regularly engaged in the business of making pawns. . . . Pawn means either of the following transactions: 1. Loan of money.—A written or oral bailment of personal property as security for an engagement or debt, redeemable on certain terms and with the implied power of sale on default. 2. Buy-sell agreement.—An agreement whereby a purchaser agrees to hold property for a specified period of time to allow the seller the exclusive right to repurchase the property. A buy-sell agreement is not a loan of money. F.S.A. § 538.03(c)&(d)

payable 1. Able to be paid. 2. Money or a balance owed.

payable to bearer Payable to whoever possesses the instrument.

payable to order Payable to a named person, the payee.

payee One to whom or to whose order a check or other negotiable instrument is made payable. One who receives money.

payer or **payor** One who makes or should make payment, particularly on a check or other negotiable instrument.

payment 1. The partial or full performance of an obligation by tendering money or other consideration. 2. An amount paid.

payment bond A guarantee from a surety that laborers and material suppliers will be paid if the general contractor defaults.

> The payment bond required to exempt an owner under this part shall be furnished by the contractor in at least the amount of the original contract price before commencing the construction of the improvement under the direct contract, and a copy of the bond shall be attached to the notice of commencement when the notice of commencement is recorded. The bond shall be executed as surety by a surety insurer authorized to do business in this state and shall be conditioned that the contractor shall promptly make payments for labor, services, and material to all lienors under the contractor's direct contract. F.S.A. § 713.23(1)(a)

payment in due course Payment made in good faith at or after maturity to the holder without notice that his or her title is defective.

payment into court Property deposited into court for eventual distribution by court order.

payor See payer.

payroll tax 1. A tax on employees based on their wages. 2. A tax on employers as a percentage of wages paid to employees.

P.C. See professional corporation.

PCR See postconviction relief.

P.D. 1. See public defender. 2. Police department.

peace Orderly behavior in the community. Public tranquility.

peaceable 1. Without force or violence. 2. Gentle, calm.

peaceable possession 1. Possession that is continuous and not interrupted by adverse claims or attempts to dispossess. 2. Peaceful enjoyment.

peace bond A bond required of one who threatens to breach the peace.

peace officers A person designated by public authority to keep the peace and to arrest persons suspected of crime.

peculation Misappropriation of money or goods. Embezzlement.

pecuniary Relating to money.

> Anything of value in the form of money, a negotiable instrument, or a commercial interest or anything else the primary significance of which is economic advantage. . . . F.S.A. § 895.04(4)(a)

pecuniary interest A financial interest, e.g., the opportunity, directly or indirectly, to share in the profit (or loss) derived from a transaction.

pederasty Sexual relations (oral or anal) between a man and boy.

penal Concerning or containing a penalty.

penal action 1. A civil action based on a statute that subjects a wrongdoer to liability in favor of the person wronged as a punishment for the wrongful act. 2. A criminal prosecution.

penal bond A bond obligating the payment of a specified penalty (called the penal sum) upon nonperformance of a condition.

penal code A compilation of statutes on criminal law.

penal institution See penitentiary.

penal law See criminal law.

penal statute A statute that defines a crime and its punishment.

> Statute is "penal" if it imposes punishment for offense committed against state; term includes all statutes which command or prohibit acts and establish penalties for their violations to be recovered for purpose of enforcing obedience to law and punishing its violation. *Dotty,* 197 So.2d 315 (Fla.App. 1967)

penal sum See penal bond.

penalty 1. Punishment for a criminal or civil wrong. 2. An extra charge imposed if a stated condition (e.g., late payment) occurs.

penalty clause A contract clause imposing a stated penalty (rather than actual damages) for nonperformance.

pendency While waiting; while still undecided.

pendent Undecided; pending.

pendente lite During the progress of the suit; pending the litigation.

pendent jurisdiction The power of a court to hear a claim over which it has no independent subject-matter jurisdiction if the facts of the claim are closely enough related on the facts of a main claim over which it does have such jurisdiction.

> A federal court may hear and decide state law claims over which it ordinarily has no subject matter jurisdiction if the state claims arise from a common nucleus of operative fact with a federal claim over which that court does have jurisdiction. *Andujar*, 659 So.2d 1214 (Fla.App. 4 Dist.,1995)

pending Under consideration; begun but not yet completed.

penetration An intrusion, however slight, of any object or any part of the defendant's body into the genital or anal openings of the victim's body.

penitentiary A place of confinement for persons convicted of crime, usually serious crimes. Also called penal institution, prison.

Pennoyer **rule** A personal judgment requires personal jurisdiction. *Pennoyer v. Neff*, 95 U.S. 714 (1877).

penny stocks High-risk equity securities, often selling at less than $1 a share and usually not traded on an approved securities exchange.

penology The study of prisons and the rehabilitation of criminals.

pen register A device that records the numbers dialed on a telephone but not the conversations themselves.

> "Pen register" means a device or process that records or decodes dialing, routing, addressing, or signaling information transmitted by an instrument or facility from which a wire or electronic communication is transmitted, but such information does not include the contents of any communication. F.S.A. § 934.02(20)

pension Regularly paid funds as a retirement or other benefit.

pension plan A plan of an employer, primarily to pay determinable retirement benefits to its employees or their beneficiaries.

penumbra doctrine Implied constitutional rights, e.g., the right of privacy, exist on the periphery of explicit constitutional rights.

peonage Illegally compelling one to perform labor to pay off a debt.

people The prosecution in a criminal case representing the citizenry.

peppercorn A small amount; nominal consideration.

per By; for each.

per annum Annually.

per autre vie See pur autre vie.

per capita 1. For each person. 2. Divided equally among each person.

percentage depletion A method of taking a depletion deduction based on a percentage of gross income from an oil or gas well.

percentage lease A lease in which the rent is a percentage of gross or net sales, often with a minimum required payment.

per curiam opinion (an opinion "by the court" as a whole) A court opinion, usually a short one, that does not name the judge who wrote it.

per diem By the day; an allowance or amount of so much per day.

peremptory 1. Conclusive; final. 2. Without need for explanation.

peremptory challenge The right to challenge and remove a prospective juror without giving any reasons. Such challenges, however, cannot be used to discriminate against a protected minority.

> "Peremptory challenge" is a challenge that need not be supported by any reason, although a party may not use such a challenge in a way that discriminates against a protected minority. *Shannon*, 770 So.2d 714 (Fla.App. 4 Dist.,2000)

peremptory instruction An instruction by the judge to the jury that it must obey. (The equivalent of a directed verdict.)

perfect 1. Complete, executed. 2. To follow all procedures needed to complete or put in final form so that it is legally enforceable.

perfected Completed, executed; legally enforceable.

perfect tender rule Exact (perfect) performance by the seller of its obligations can be a condition of the enforceability of the contract.

performance The fulfillment of an obligation according to its terms.

performance bond See completion bond.

peril That which may cause damage or injury; exposure to danger.

peril of the sea A peril peculiar to the sea that cannot be guarded against by ordinary human skill and prudence.

periodic Happening at fixed intervals; recurring now and then.

periodic alimony Alimony paid indefinitely at scheduled intervals. Also called permanent alimony.

periodic tenancy A tenancy that continues indefinitely for successive periods (e.g., month to month, year to year) unless terminated by the parties.

perjury Making a false statement under oath concerning a material matter with the intent to provide false testimony. Also called false swearing.

> In decisional law, "perjury" is defined as the willful giving of false testimony under lawful oath on a material matter in a judicial proceeding. (Per Boyd, J., with two Judges concurring and one Judge concurring specially.) F.S.A. § 837.02. *Adams*, 394 So.2d 411 (Fla., 1981)

perks See perquisites.

permanent Continuing indefinitely.

permanent alimony See periodic alimony.

permanent injunction An injunction issued after a court hearing on the merits of the underling issues. Also called perpetual injunction.

permissive 1. Allowable; optional. 2. Lenient.

permissive counterclaim A counterclaim that does not arise out of the same transaction or occurrence that is the basis of the plaintiff's claim.

permissive joinder The joinder of a party that is allowed (but not required) if the claims involved arise out of the same occurrence and there are questions of law or fact that will be common to all the parties.

permissive presumption A presumption that allows (but does not require) the fact finder to infer the presumed fact.

A "permissive inference" allows, but does not require, the trier of fact to infer an elemental fact from proof of a basic fact and does not place any burden on the defendant; in this situation, the basic fact may constitute prima facie evidence of the elemental fact. *State v. Rygwelski,* 899 So.2d 498 (Fla.App. 2 Dist.,2005)

permissive use A use expressly or impliedly within the scope of permission.

permissive waste A tenant's failure to use ordinary care to preserve and protect the property, such as allowing deterioration for lack of repair.

permit 1. To expressly agree to the doing of an act. 2. A formal document granting the right to do something. A license.

perp (slang) Perpetrator of a crime.

perpetrate To commit or carry out an act, often criminal in nature.

perpetrator A person who commits a crime or other serious wrong.

perpetual injunction See permanent injunction.

perpetual lease A lease of land with no termination date.

perpetual succession The uninterrupted (perpetual) existence of a corporation even though its owners (shareholders) change.

perpetuation of testimony Procedures to ensure that the testimony of a deposition witness will be available for trial.

perpetuity 1. Continuing forever. 2. A future interest that will not vest within the period prescribed by law.

perquisites (perks) Incidental benefits in addition to salary.

per quod Needing additional facts or proof of special damages.

per se In itself; inherently. Without needing additional facts.
  "Per se antitrust violations" may be established with relatively little proof; in general, only proof of particular conduct which is considered inherently pernicious is necessary, and an unlawful effect of that conduct upon competition is presumed. F.S.A. §§ 542.01 et seq. *St. Petersburg Yacht Charters,* 457 So.2d 1028 (Fla.App. 2 Dist.,1984)

persecution The offensive infliction of suffering or harm upon those who differ in race, religion, sexual orientation, or beliefs.

person A natural person, plus legal entities such as corporations that the law endows with some of the rights and duties of natural persons.

personal Pertaining to a person or to personal property.

personal bond A bail bond with no sureties.

personal chattel Tangible or intangible personal property.

personal effects Articles intimately or closely associated with the person (e.g., clothing, jewelry, wallet).

personal exemption A deduction from adjusted gross income for an individual and qualified dependents.

personal injury (PI) Injury, damage, or invasion of one's body or personal rights. Harm to personal (as opposed to property) interests.

personality The legal status of being a person.

personal judgment A judgment against the person (over whom the court had personal jurisdiction) that may be satisfied out of any property of that person. Also called judgment in personam.

personal jurisdiction A court's power over a person to adjudicate his or her personal rights. Also called *in personam*

jurisdiction. More limited kinds of jurisdiction include the court's power over a person's interest in specific property (*quasi in rem jurisdiction*) or over the property itself (*in rem jurisdiction*).

personal knowledge Firsthand knowledge rather than what others say.

personal liability An obligation that one can be forced to pay or satisfy out of personal (not just business) assets.
  "Personal liability" means personal liability for a debt, liability, or other obligation of an organization which is imposed on a person that coowns, has an interest in, or is a member of the organization. F.S.A. § 620.2101(10)

personal notice Information communicated directly to a person.

personal property Everything, other than real property, that can be owned, e.g., a car, a stock option.

personal recognizance Pretrial release of a defendant in a criminal case without posting a bond, based solely on a promise to appear. Release on own recognizance (ROR).

personal representative A person appointed to administer the estate and legal affairs of someone who has died or who is incapacitated.
  "Personal representative" means the executor, administrator, or curator of the decedent, or, if there is no executor, administrator, or curator appointed, qualified, and acting, then any person who is in the actual or constructive possession of any property included in the gross estate of the decedent or any other person who is required to file a return or pay the taxes due under any provision of this chapter. F.S.A. § 198.01(2)

personal right A right that inheres in the status of an individual as opposed to his or her estate or property rights.

personal service Handing a copy of a notice or summons to the defendant.

personalty Personal property.

personam See in personam, personal judgment.

per stirpes Taking the share a deceased ancestor would have been entitled to (had he or she lived) rather than taking as individuals in their own right. Taking by right of representation. Also called in stirpes.

persuasive authority Any source a court relies on in reaching its decision that it is not required to rely on.

pertinent Relevant to an issue.

petit Lesser, minor.

petition 1. A formal written request. 2. A complaint.
  "Petition" means a written request to the court for an order. F.S.A. § 731.201(26)

petitioner One who presents a petition or complaint to a tribunal.

petit jury An ordinary jury called and sworn in (impaneled) to try a particular civil or criminal case. Also called petty jury, trial jury. See also grand jury.

petition in bankruptcy A formal application from a debtor to a bankruptcy court to file for bankruptcy.

pettifogger 1. One who quibbles over trivia. 2. An incompetent, ill-prepared attorney who sometimes engages in questionable practices.

petty Of less importance or merit.

petty jury See petit jury.

petty larceny The larceny or stealing of personal property with a value below a statutorily set amount (e.g., $200).

petty offense A minor violation of the law, e.g., a traffic violation.

p.h.v. See pro hac vice.

physical Pertaining to the body or other material (non-mental) things.

physical evidence See real evidence (1).

physical fact A thing or action that can be perceived by the senses.

physical-fact rule The testimony of a witness that is positively contradicted by physical facts can be disregarded.

physical injury See bodily injury.

physician-patient privilege See doctor-patient privilege.

PI See personal injury.

picket To patrol or demonstrate outside a business or other organization in order to protest something it is doing or proposing and thereby pressure it to change.

pickpocket One who secretly steals something from another's person.

> "Where no force is exerted upon the victim's person, as in the case of a pickpocket, only a larceny is committed." The act of stealthily picking a person's pocket, without any accompanying resistance or struggle, does not constitute robbery. In the "pickpocket" offense the victim suffers no emotional response simply because the victim is unaware of the theft. *Robinson v. State,* 680 So.2d 481 (Fla.App. 1 Dist.,1996)

piecework Work for which one is paid by the number of units produced.

piercing the corporate veil A process by which a court disregards the limited liability normally afforded corporations and instead imposes personal liability on officers, directors, and shareholders.

pilferage Stealing; petty larceny.

pillage Using force or violence to rob someone, often in times of war.

pimp One who solicits customers for prostitutes.

pioneer patent A patent concerning a function or advance never before performed or one of major novelty and importance.

piracy 1. Robbery or seizure of a ship at sea or airplane in motion. See also hijack. 2. Copying in violation of intellectual property laws.

P.J. Presiding judge.

P.L. See public law.

place of abode One's residence or domicile.

placer claim A mining claim to loose minerals in sand or gravel.

plagiarism Using another's original ideas or expressions as one's own.

plain error An obvious, prejudicial error an appellate court will hear even if it was not raised at trial. Also called fundamental error.

plain meaning The usual and ordinary meaning given to words by reasonable persons at the time and place of their use.

plaintiff The person who initiates a civil action in court.

plaintiff in error The appellant; the party bringing the appeal.

plain view doctrine An officer can seize objects without a warrant if they can be plainly be seen, there is probable cause they are connected to a crime, and the officer is lawfully present.

> The "plain view doctrine" allows police to seize contraband in plain view when the seizing officer is in a location he has a legal right to be, the incriminating character of the evidence is immediately apparent, and the seizing officer has a lawful right of access to the object. *Minter-Smith,* 864 So.2d 1141 (Fla.App. 1 Dist.,2003)

planned unit development (PUD) Development of land areas where standard zoning rules are suspended to achieve mixed-use flexibility.

plant patent A patent granted to someone who invents or discovers and asexually reproduces any distinct and new variety of plant.

plat 1. A map showing streets, easements, etc. 2. A small land area.

> "Plat or replat" means a map or delineated representation of the subdivision of lands, being a complete exact representation of the subdivision and other information in compliance with the requirement of all applicable sections of this part and of any local ordinances. F.S.A. § 177.031(14)

plea 1. The first pleading of the defendant in a civil case. 2. The defendant's formal response to a criminal charge, e.g., not guilty.

plea bargaining Negotiations whereby an accused pleads guilty to a lesser included offense or to one of multiple charges in exchange for the prosecution's agreement to support a dismissal of some charges or a lighter sentence. Also called plea agreement, negotiated plea.

plead To file a pleading, enter a plea, or argue a case in court.

pleadings Formal litigation documents (e.g., a complaint, an answer) filed by parties that state or respond to claims or defenses of other parties.

> The formal allegations by the parties of their respective claims and defenses. *Buzzi,* 921 So.2d 14 (Fla.App. 3 Dist.,2006)

plea in abatement A plea objecting to the timing or other defect in the plaintiff's claim without challenging its merits.

plea in bar A plea that seeks a total rejection of a claim or charge.

plebiscite A vote of the people on a proposed law or policy.

pledge 1. Delivering personal property as security for the payment of a debt or other obligation. A bailment for this purpose. 2. A solemn promise or agreement to do or forbear something.

> A deposit of corporeal personal property as security, with an express or implied power of sale upon default. A bailment of personal property as a security for some debt or engagement. *Aetna Ins. Co.,* 211 So.2d 44 (Fla.App. 1968)

pledgee The person to whom something is delivered in pledge.

pledgor The person who pledges; the one who delivers goods in pledge.

plenary 1. Complete, unlimited. 2. Involving all members.

plenary jurisdiction A court's unlimited judicial power over the parties and subject matter of a legal dispute.

plenipotentiary Someone (e.g., a diplomat) with full powers to act.

PLI Practising Law Institute (*www.pli.edu*).

plottage The additional value of adjacent, undeveloped lots when combined into a single tract.

PLS See professional legal secretary (*www.nals.org*).

plurality The largest number of votes received even though this number is not more than half of all votes cast or that could have been cast.

plurality opinion The controlling opinion that is joined by the largest number of judges on the bench short of a majority.

pluries Process (e.g., a writ) that issues in the third (or later) instance, after earlier ones have been ineffectual.

PMI See private mortgage insurance.

pocket part A pamphlet inserted into a small pocket built into the inside back (and occasionally front) cover of a book. The pamphlet contains text that supplements or updates the material in the book.

pocket veto The president's "silent" or indirect rejection of a bill by not acting on it within 10 weekdays of receiving it if the legislature adjourns during this period.

POD account Pay-on-death account. An account payable to the owner during his or her life, and upon death, to a designated beneficiary.

point 1. A distinct legal position or issue. 2. A fee or service charge equal to one percent of the principal amount of the loan. 3. A unit for measuring the price or value of stocks or other securities.

> "Total offense score" results from adding the sentence points for primary offense, additional offense, and victim injury. Fla. R. Crim. P. Rule 3.702(d)(7)

point of error A lower court error asserted as a ground for appeal.

point reserved An issue on which the trial judge will rule later in the trial, allowing the case to proceed. Also called reserved point.

points and authorities See memorandum of points and authorities.

poisonous tree doctrine See fruit of the poisonous tree doctrine.

poison pill Steps by a corporation to discourage a hostile takeover, e.g., issuing new shares that would increase the takeover costs.

police A unit of the government charged with maintaining public order primarily through the prevention and investigation of crime.

police court See magistrate court.

police power The power of the state to enact laws, within constitutional limits, to promote public safety, health, morals, and convenience.

> Term "police power," in context of substantive due process, is valid governmental power that promotes public health, safety, welfare, or morals. The concept of police power is used more narrowly to describe a government action which regulates property without constituting a taking. *Conner*, 567 So.2d 515 (Fla.App. 2 Dist.,1990)

policy 1. The principles by which an organization is managed. 2. An insurance contract. 3. A lottery-type numbers game.

policyholder An owner of an insurance policy, usually the insured.

political action committee (PAC) An organization (other than a political party or candidate committee) that uses fundraising or contributions to advocate the election or defeat of a clearly identified candidate for office or the victory or defeat of a public question.

political asylum See asylum (2).

political offense Crimes against a state or political order, e.g., treason.

political question A question that a court should not resolve because it concerns policy choices that are constitutionally committed for resolution to the legislative or executive branches or because of the absence of judicially discoverable and manageable standards for resolving it.

poll the jury To ask each juror how he or she voted on the verdict.

poll tax A tax imposed on each individual regardless of income. Also called capitation tax, head tax.

polyandry Having more than one husband at the same time.

polygamy Having more than one spouse at the same time.

polygraph An instrument to record physiological processes, e.g., blood pressure, to detect lying. Also called lie detector.

polygyny Having more than one wife at the same time.

Ponzi scheme A fraudulent investment scheme whereby returns to investors are financed, not through the success of an underlying business venture, but from the funds of newly attracted investors.

> A fraudulent investment scheme in which money contributed by later investors generates artificially high dividends for the original investors, whose example attracts even larger investments. *Weldon*, 863 So.2d 395 (Fla.App. 3 Dist.,2003)

pool 1. To combine for a common purpose. 2. A combination or agreement by persons or companies to carry out a joint purpose. 3. A sum of money made up of stakes contributed by bettors in a game of chance.

popular Pertaining to the general public.

pornography The portrayal of erotic behavior designed to cause sexual excitement. The portrayal is protected unless it is obscene.

port authority A government agency that plans and regulates traffic through a port by sea vessels, airplanes, public transportation, etc.

portfolio All the investments held by one person or institution.

port of entry The port where goods and travelers from abroad may enter the country. The port containing a station for customs officials.

positive evidence See direct evidence.

positive fraud Fraud that is actual or intentional rather than implied or constructive. Also called actual fraud, fraud in fact.

positive law Law actually and specifically enacted by a proper authority, usually a legislative body.

positivism See legal positivism.

posse See in posse.

posse comitatus ("the power or force of the county") Citizens called by the sheriff for special purposes, e.g., to help keep the peace.

possession 1. The actual custody or control of something. 2. That which one holds, occupies, or controls. 3. That which one owns.

> "Possession" is defined as having personal charge or exercising right of ownership, management, or control over article in question. *State v. Brider*, 386 So.2d 818 (Fla.App., 1980)

possession is nine-tenths of the law A false adage that nevertheless reflects the truth that the law does not always make it easy for a rightful property owner to oust someone in wrongful possession.

possessor One who has possession or custody of property.

possessory Relating to, founded on, or claiming possession.

possessory action An action to assert the right to keep or maintain possession of property.

possessory interest The right to exert control over specific property to the exclusion of others whether or not the right is based on title.

possibility of reverter The interest remaining in a grantor who conveys a fee simple determinable or a fee simple conditional. Any reversionary interest that is subject to a condition precedent. Also called reverter.

post To send by mail. See also posting.

postconviction relief (PCR) A remedy sought by a prisoner to challenge the legality of his or her conviction or sentence. A prisoner's collateral attack of his or her final judgment.

postdate To insert a date that is later than the actual date.

posterity 1. All descendants of a person. 2. Future generations.

posthumous Referring to events occurring after the death of a person.

posting 1. A form of substituted service of process by placing process in a prominent place (e.g., the front door of the defendant's residence). 2. The transfer of an original entry of debits or credits to a ledger. 3. The steps followed by a bank in paying a check. 4. Making something available on the Internet. 5. Making payment.

> "Post" or "posting" means placing the document referred to on the site of the improvement in a conspicuous place at the front of the site and in a manner that protects the document from the weather. F.S.A. § 713.01(24)

postmortem 1. Pertaining to what occurs after death. 2. See autopsy.

postnuptial agreement An agreement between spouses on the division of their property in the event of death or divorce.

postpone 1. To put off. 2. To subordinate or give a lower priority.

post-trial discovery Discovery procedures (e.g., deposition) conducted after judgment to help enforce (e.g., collect) a judgment.

pourover trust A trust that receives property from a will.

pourover will A will that transfers property to a trust.

poverty affidavit A written declaration of one's finances for purposes of qualifying for free legal services or other public benefit.

power 1. The right, ability, or authority to do something. 2. The right of a person to produce a change in a given legal relation by doing or not doing a given act. 3. Control over another.

power coupled with an interest A right or power to do some act, together with an interest in the subject matter on which the power is to be executed.

power of acceptance The right of an offeree to create a contract by accepting the terms of the offer.

power of appointment A power created when one person (the donor) grants another (the donee) authority to designate beneficiaries of the donor's property.

> "General power of appointment" means a power of appointment under which the holder of the power, whether or not the holder has the capacity to exercise it, has the power to create a present or future interest in the holder, the holder's estate, or the creditors of either. F.S.A. § 732.2025(3)

power of attorney A document that authorizes another to act as one's agent or attorney-in-fact.

power of sale The right to sell property, e.g., the right of a trustee or mortgagee to sell the real property mortgaged in the event of a default.

pp. Pages.

PPO Preferred provider organization, a group of health care providers.

practice 1. A repeated or customary action; habitual performance. 2. The rules, forms, and methods used in a court or administrative tribunal. 3. The exercise of a profession or occupation.

practice of law Using legal skills to assist a specific person resolve his or her specific legal problem. The work of a lawyer in counseling and representing clients on legal matters.

> Paralegal engaged in "unlicensed practice of law" by participating in settlement negotiations as if he were legal counsel for one of the parties; paralegal's acts included discussing case law and legal strategy with clients, speaking on behalf of clients, and arguing the legal merits of cases. *The Florida Bar*, 816 So.2d 587 (Fla.,2002)

praecipe 1. A formal request that a court take some action. 2. A writ ordering an action or a statement of why it should not be taken.

praedial See predial.

praesenti See in praesenti.

prayer for relief The portion of a complaint or other pleading that sets forth the requested relief (e.g., damages) sought from the court.

preamble A clause at the beginning of a law (e.g., statute) or instrument (e.g., contract) setting out its objectives.

precarious Uncertain; at the whim or discretion of someone.

precatory Embodying a recommendation, hope, or advice rather than a positive command or direction; pertaining to a wish.

precedent A prior decision that can be used as a standard or guide in a later similar case.

precept 1. A rule imposing a standard of conduct or action. 2. A warrant, writ, or order.

precinct A subdivision or other geographical unit of local government.

preclusion order An order preventing a party from introducing specific evidence, usually because of a violation of discovery rules.

precognition A pretrial questioning of a potential witness.

precontract A contract designed to prevent a person from entering another contract of the same nature with someone else.

predatory pricing A company's artificially low prices designed to drive out competition so that it can reap monopoly profits at a later time.

predecessor One who goes or who has gone before. A prior holder.

predial Pertaining or attached to land. Also spelled praedial.

predisposition A defendant's tendency or inclination to engage in certain conduct, e.g., illegal activity.

preemption 1. Under the Supremacy Clause, federal laws take precedence over (preempt) state laws when Congress (a) expressly mandates the preemption, (b) regulates an area so pervasively that an intent to preempt the entire field may be inferred, or (c) enacts a law that directly conflicts with state law. 2. The right of first purchase.

> "Preemption doctrine" insures that legislatively intended allocation of jurisdiction between administrative agencies and judiciary is maintained without disruption which would flow from judicial incursion into province of agency. *Hill Top Developers*, 478 So.2d 368 (Fla.App. 2 Dist.,1985)

preemptive right The right of a stockholder to maintain a proportionate share of ownership by purchasing a proportionate share of any new stock issues. Also called subscription right.

pre-existing duty rule When a contracting party does or promises something that it is already legally obligated to do, there is no adequate consideration because the party has not incurred a detriment.

prefer 1. To submit for consideration; to file or prosecute. 2. To give advantage, priority, or privilege.

preference 1. Making a payment or a transfer by an insolvent debtor to one of the creditors, to the detriment of the other creditors. 2. The choice of one over another; the choice made.

preferential shop A job site in which union members are given priority or advantage over non-union members in hiring, promotion, etc.

preferred dividend A dividend payable to preferred shareholders, which has priority over dividends payable to common shareholders.

preferred risk An insurance classification of people who statistically have fewer accidents or have better health records and who, therefore, are often eligible for a reduced rate.

preferred stock Stock in a corporation that has a claim to income (dividends) or liquidation assets ahead of holders of common stock.

prejudice 1. Bias. A leaning toward or against one side of a cause for a reason other than merit. 2. Detriment or harm to one's legal rights.

> Before a court can dismiss an information for a prosecutor's violation of a discovery rule or order, the trial court must find that the prosecutor's violation resulted in prejudice to defendant; "prejudice" means something which affects the ability of defendant to properly prepare for trial. F.S.A. RCrP Rule 3.220(n). *State v. Carpenter*, 899 So.2d 1176 (Fla.App. 3 Dist.,2005)

prejudicial error An error justifying a reversal because it probably affected the outcome and was harmful to the substantial rights of the party objecting to the error. Also called fatal error, reversible error.

preliminary Introductory; prior to the main body or theme.

preliminary examination See preliminary hearing.

preliminary hearing A pretrial hearing on whether probable cause exists that the defendant committed a crime. Also called preliminary examination, probable cause hearing.

> An adversarial preliminary hearing is defined as a hearing in which the seizing agency is required to establish probable cause that the property subject to forfeiture was used in violation of the Act. See § 932.701(2)(f), Fla. Stat. (2000). *City of Coral Springs*, 803 So.2d 847 (Fla.App. 4 Dist.,2002)

preliminary injunction A temporary order to preserve the status quo and prevent irreparable loss of rights prior to a trial on the merits. Also called interlocutory injunction, temporary injunction.

premarital agreement A contract made by two persons about to be married that covers spousal support, property division, and related matters in the event of the separation of the parties, the death of one of them, or the dissolution of the marriage by divorce or annulment. Also called antenuptial agreement, marriage settlement, prenuptial agreement.

premeditated Considered, deliberated, or planned beforehand.

premise A statement that is a basis of an inference or conclusion.

premises 1. Land, its buildings, and surrounding grounds. 2. The part of a deed describing the interest transferred and related information, e.g., why the deed is being made. 3. The foregoing statements.

premium 1. An extra payment or bonus. 2. The payment to an insurance company to keep the policy. 3. The amount by which the market value of a bond or other security exceeds its par or face value.

prenuptial agreement See premarital agreement.

prepackaged bankruptcy (prepack) A plan negotiated between debtor and creditors prior to filing for bankruptcy.

prepaid legal services A plan by which a person pays premiums to cover future legal services. Also called legal plan, group legal services.

prepayment penalty An extra payment imposed when a promissory note or other loan is paid in full before it is due.

preponderance of evidence The standard of proof that is met when the evidence establishes that it is more likely than not that the facts are as alleged. Also called fair preponderance of the evidence.

prerogative An exclusive right or privilege of a person or office.

prerogative writ See extraordinary writ.

prescription 1. A method of acquiring ownership or title to property or rights by reason of continuous usage over a designated period of time. 2. An order for drugs issued by a licensed health professional. 3. A direction; a practice or course or action that is ordered. 4. The laying down or establishing of rules or directions.

> There is a distinction between acquiring of title by adverse possession and the acquiring of a prescriptive right. In the former, title must be through possession. In the latter, a prescriptive right is through the use of the privilege without actual possession. In acquisition of the title by adverse possession, the possession must be exclusive, while in acquisition of a prescriptive right, the use may be in common with the owner or the public. *Hunt*, 121 So.2d 697 (Fla.App.1960)

prescriptive easement An easement created by an open, adverse, continuous use of another's land under claim of right over a designated period of time.

presence 1. Being physically present. 2. Being in physical proximity to or with something, including a sensory awareness of it.

present 1. Currently happening. 2. In attendance. 3. Under examination.

present danger See clear and present danger.

presentence report A probation report on the background of a convicted offender to assist the judge in imposing a sentence.

present estate An interest in property that can be possessed and enjoyed now, not just in the future. Also called present interest.

presenting bank Any bank presenting an item except a payor bank.

present interest See present estate.

present memory refreshed See present recollection refreshed.

presentment 1. A grand jury's accusation of crime that is not based on a prosecutor's request for an indictment. 2. Producing a check or other negotiable instrument for acceptance or payment.

> The term "presentment" means a demand made by or on behalf of a person entitled to enforce an instrument: (a) To pay the instrument made to the drawee or a party obliged to pay the instrument or, in the case of a note or accepted draft payable at a bank, to the bank; or (b) To accept a draft made to the drawee. F.S.A. § 673.5011(1)

present recollection refreshed A use by witnesses of writings or other objects to refresh their memory so that testimony can be given about past events from present recollection. Also called present memory refreshed, present recollection revived, refreshing memory or recollection.

presents This document being considered; the present instrument.

present sense impression A statement describing or explaining an event or condition made while perceiving it or immediately thereafter.

present value The amount of money you would have to be given now in order to produce or generate, with compound interest, a certain amount of money in a designated period of time. Also called present worth.

> "Present value" means the amount as of a date certain of one or more sums payable in the future, discounted to the date certain. The discount is determined by the interest rate specified by the parties if the rate is not manifestly unreasonable at the time the transaction is entered into. . . . F.S.A. § 671.201(C)(3)

preside To be the person in authority; to direct the proceedings.

president The chief executive officer of an organization or country.

presidential elector See electoral college.

president judge The presiding or chief judge on some courts.

presume To take for granted as true before establishing it as such.

presumption An assumption or inference that a certain fact is true once another fact is established.

presumption of death A presumption that a person is no longer alive after being missing without explanation for a set period of time.

presumption of fact An inference; a logical inference or conclusion that the trier of the facts is at liberty to draw or refuse to draw.

presumption of innocence An accused cannot be convicted of a crime unless the government proves guilt beyond a reasonable doubt. The accused does not have the burden of proving his or her innocence.

presumption of law A particular conclusion the court must reach in absence of evidence to the contrary.

> A "presumption of law" is a preliminary "rule of law" which may be made to disappear in the face of rebuttal evidence but which, in the absence thereof, compels a decision in favor of the one who relies on it. *Locke*, 113 So.2d 402 (Fla.App.1959)

presumption of paternity; presumption of legitimacy A man is presumed to be the natural father of a child if he and the child's natural mother are married to each other and the child is conceived or born during the marriage. The presumption also applies if he receives the child into his home and holds the child out as his natural child.

presumption of survivorship In a common disaster involving multiple victims, a younger, healthier victim is presumed to have died after the others in the absence of evidence to the contrary.

presumptive 1. Providing a logical basis to believe; probable. 2. Created by or arising out of a presumption.

> "Presumptive death" means a determination by a court of competent jurisdiction that: (a) A death of a resident of this state has occurred or is presumed to have occurred, but the body of the person involved has not been located or recovered; . . . F.S.A. § 382.012(1)

presumptive evidence Evidence sufficient to establish a given fact and which, if not rebutted or contradicted, will remain sufficient.

presumptive heir A person who can inherit if a closer relative is not born before the ancestor dies. Also called heir presumptive.

presumptive trust See resulting trust.

pretermit To pass by, omit, or disregard.

pretermitted heir A child or spouse omitted in a will by a testator.

pretext arrest A valid arrest for an improper reason, e.g., to investigate a different offense for which an arrest is not valid.

pretrial conference A meeting of the attorneys and the judge (or magistrate) before the trial to attempt to narrow the issues, to secure stipulations, and to make a final effort to settle the case without a trial.

pretrial detention Keeping someone in custody before trial.

pretrial discovery Devices parties can use to uncover facts that will help them prepare for trial (e.g., depositions, interrogatories).

pretrial diversion; pretrial intervention See diversion (2).

pretrial order A judge's order before a trial stating the issues to be tried and any stipulations of the parties.

prevail 1. To be in general use or practice. 2. To succeed.

prevailing party The party winning the judgment.

preventive detention Detaining someone before trial to prevent fleeing, future antisocial behavior, or self-inflicted harm.

preventive justice Restraining orders, peace bonds, and other remedies designed to keep the peace and prevent future wrongdoing.

price discrimination A difference in price a seller charges different customers for the same product or one of like quality.

price fixing An agreement on prices that otherwise would be set by market forces. Any means calculated to eliminate competition and manipulate price.

> Literal meaning of term "price fixing" connotes that in horizontal arrangements two or more competitors have literally fixed a price and in vertical arrangements that a supplier and a dealer have fixed a resale price. F.S.A. § 542.18. *St. Petersburg Yacht Charters*, 457 So.2d 1028 (Fla.App. 2 Dist.,1984)

price supports Devices (e.g., government subsidies) to keep prices from falling below a set level.

priest-penitent privilege See clergy-penitent privilege.

prima facie 1. On the face of it, at first sight. 2. Sufficient.

prima facie case A case as presented that will prevail until contradicted and overcome by contrary evidence.

prima facie evidence Sufficient evidence of a fact unless rebutted.

> "Prima facie evidence" is such as in judgment of law is sufficient to establish the fact and, if unrebutted, remains sufficient for that purpose. *Merit Clothing Co.*, 218 So.2d 779 (Fla.App. 1969)

prima facie tort The intentional infliction of harm without justification, resulting in special damages.

primary activity A strike, picketing, or other action directed against an employer with whom a union has a labor dispute.

primary authority Any law (e.g., case, statute) that a court could rely on in reaching a decision.

primary boycott Action by a union to urge its members and the public not to patronize a firm with which the union has a labor dispute.

primary election An election by a party's voters to select (nominate) candidates to run in a general election.

primary evidence The best or highest quality evidence available.

primary jurisdiction doctrine Although a case is properly before a court, if there are issues requiring administrative expertise, the court can refrain from acting until the administrative agency acts.

primary liability Liability for which one is directly responsible, rather than secondarily after someone else fails to pay or perform.

primary market 1. The market where new issues of securities are first sold. 2. The main target of an initial offering of goods and services.

prime contractor See general contractor.

prime rate The lowest rate of interest charged by a bank to its best (most creditworthy) customers for short-term loans.

primogeniture 1. The status of being the first-born of siblings. 2. The right of the oldest son to inherit the entire estate.

principal 1. The amount of debt not including interest. 2. The initial sum invested. 3. A perpetrator of a crime. 4. One who permits an agent to act on his or her behalf. 5. One with prime responsibility for an obligation. 6. See corpus (2).

"Principal" means the face value of the debt or obligation. F.S.A. § 216.0442(h)

prior 1. Before in time or preference. 2. An earlier conviction.

prior art Any relevant knowledge, acts, and descriptions that pertain to, but predate, the invention in question.

prior consistent statement An earlier statement made by a witness that supports what he or she is now saying at the trial.

prior inconsistent statement An earlier statement made by a witness that conflicts what he or she is now saying at the trial.

priority A legal preference or precedence, e.g., the right to be paid first.

prior lien A lien with rights superior to other liens.

prior restraint A judicial or other government restriction on a publication before it is published.

prison See penitentiary.

prisoner A person in police custody serving a prison sentence.

privacy The absence of unwanted attention into one's private concerns or affairs. Being left alone. See also invasion of privacy.

> Place and time when a person has a reasonable expectation of privacy means a place and time when a reasonable person would believe that he or she could fully disrobe in privacy, without being concerned that the person's undressing was being viewed, ... F.S.A. § 810.145(c)

privacy law A law that restricts the public's access to personal information maintained by the government. See also invasion of privacy.

private 1. Pertaining to individual or personal matters as opposed to public or official ones. 2. Restricted in use to designated persons or groups. 3. Confidential. 4. Not sold or offered to the general public.

private act See private law (2).

private bill A proposal for a private law. See private law (2).

private corporation A corporation established by private individuals for a nongovernmental or nonpublic purpose.

private foundation A charitable organization whose main source of funds is not the general public.

privateer A privately owned ship authorized by the government to attack enemy ships.

private international law Conflict of laws involving different states or countries. See also international law.

private investigator Someone other than a police officer who is licensed to do detective work or to conduct investigations.

private law 1. The law governing private persons and their interelationships. 2. A law that applies to specifically named persons or groups and has little or no permanence or general interest. A special law.

private mortgage insurance (PMI) Insurance to protect the lender if the debtor dies or defaults.

private necessity A privilege to make reasonable use of another's property to prevent an immediate threat of harm or damage to one's private property.

private nuisance A substantial interference with the reasonable use and enjoyment of private land.

> A "private nuisance" exists where there is a substantial interference with comfort, repose, and enjoyment of the home. *Overby*, 163 So.2d 532 (Fla.App.1964)

private offering A sale of an issue of securities to a limited number of persons. Also called private placement.

private person One who is not a public official, public figure, or member of the military.

private placement 1. The placement of a child for adoption by the parents or their intermediaries rather than by a state agency. 2. See private offering.

private sale A sale that was not open to the public through advertising, auction, or real estate agents.

> A casual or private sale means any sale other than that by a licensed dealer. F.S.A. § 320.131(1)(b)

private statute See private law (2).

privatize Convert from government control or ownership to the private sector.

privies See privy.

privilege 1. A special legal benefit, right, immunity, or protection. 2. A defense that authorizes conduct that would otherwise be wrongful.

privilege against self-incrimination 1. A criminal defendant cannot be compelled to testify. 2. The right not to answer incriminating questions by the government that could directly or indirectly connect oneself to the commission of a crime.

privileged Protected by a privilege, e.g., does not have to be disclosed.

privileged communication A communication that does not have to be disclosed. A statement protected by privilege.

Privileges and Immunities Clause The clause in the U.S. Constitution (Art. IV, § 2) that "citizens of each state shall be entitled to all Privileges and Immunities of citizens" in every other state. A state cannot discriminate within its borders against citizens of other states.

privity A relationship that persons share in property, a transaction, or a right. Mutuality of interest.

> To be in "privity" with one who is a party to a lawsuit, one must have an interest in the action such that she will be bound by the final judgment as if she were a party. *Gentile*, 718 So.2d 781 (Fla.,1998)

privity of contract The relationship that exists between persons who enter a contract with each other.

privity of estate A mutual or successive relationship to the same rights in property.

privy A person who is in privity with another; someone so connected with another as to be identified with him or her in interest (plural: privies).

prize 1. A reward given to a winner. 2. A vessel seized during war.

pro For.

probable cause 1. A reasonable belief that a specific crime has been committed and that the defendant committed the crime. Also called sufficient cause. 2. A reasonable belief that evidence of a crime will be found in a particular place. 3. A reasonable ground for a belief in the existence of supporting facts.

> A reasonable ground of suspicion supported by circumstances strong enough in themselves to warrant a cautious person in belief that the named suspect is guilty of the offense charged. *State, Dept. of Highway Safety*, 866 So.2d 737 (Fla.App. 3 Dist.,2004)

probable cause hearing See preliminary hearing.

probate 1. A court procedure to establish the validly of a will and to oversee the administration of the estate. 2. To establish the validity (of a will); to administer (an estate) under court supervision.

probate court A court for probating wills, supervising the administration of estates, and handling related family law issues. Also called orphan's court, surrogate's court.

probate estate Assets owned by the decedent at death plus assets later acquired by the decedent's estate.

probation 1. The conditional release of a person convicted of a crime in lieu of a prison sentence. Conditions can include attending drug counseling and remedial training. 2. A trial or test period for a new employee to determine competence and suitability for the job.

probationer A convicted offender on probation.

probation officer A government employee who supervises probationers.

probative Furnishing proof; tending to prove or disprove.

probative evidence Evidence that contributes toward proof.

probative fact A fact from which an ultimate or decisive fact may be inferred or proven.

probative value The extent to which evidence tends to establish whatever it is offered to prove.

> Evidence having probative value is evidence "tending to prove" something. *Rahyns*, 752 So.2d 617 (Fla.App. 4 Dist., 1999)

pro bono Concerning or involving legal services that are provided for the public good (pro bono publico) without fee or compensation. Sometimes also applied to services given at a reduced rate. Shortened to pro bono.

procedendo A writ ordering a lower court to proceed to judgment.

procedural due process Minimum requirements of procedure (e.g., notice and the opportunity to be heard) that are constitutionally mandated before the government deprives a person of life, liberty, or property.

> "Procedural due process" under State Constitution guarantees to every citizen the right to have that course of legal procedure which has been established in judicial system for protection and enforcement of private rights; it contemplates that defendant shall be given fair notice and afforded a real opportunity to be heard and defend in an orderly procedure, before judgment is rendered against him. F.S.A. Const. Art. 1, § 9. *J.B. v. Florida Dept. of Children and Family Services*, 768 So.2d 1060 (Fla.,2000)

procedural law A law that governs the steps or mechanics of resolving a dispute in a court or administrative agency.

procedure A method or process by which something is done, e.g., to resolve a legal dispute in court or in an administrative agency.

proceeding 1. A part or step in a lawsuit, e.g., a hearing. 2. A sequence of events. 3. Going forward or conducting something.

proceeds Money derived from some possession, sale, or other transaction. The yield.

process 1. A summons, writ, or court order, e.g., to appear in court. 2. Procedures or proceedings in an action or prosecution.

process server Someone with the authority to serve or deliver process.

prochein ami See next friend.

proclamation An official and public declaration.

pro confesso As having accepted responsibility or confessed.

proctor One who manages the affairs of another. A supervisor.

procuration The appointment of an agent. A power of attorney.

procurement 1. Obtaining or acquiring something. 2. The persuasion of another to engage in improper sexual conduct.

procurement contract A government contract to acquire goods or services.

procuring cause 1. See proximate cause. 2. The chief means by which a sale of property was effected, entitling the broker to a commission.

prodition Treason.

produce 1. To bring forth or yield. 2. Products of agriculture.

producing cause See proximate cause.

product Something produced by physical labor, intellectual effort, or natural processes. A commercial item that is used or consumed.

production of documents See request for production.

products liability A general term that covers different causes of action (e.g., negligence, strict liability in tort, and breach of warranty) based on defective products that cause harm.

> "Product liability" means liability for damages because of any personal injury, death, emotional harm, consequential economic damage, or property damage, including damages resulting from the loss of use of property, arising out of the manufacture, design, importation, distribution, packaging, labeling, lease, or sale of a product, but does not include the liability of any person for those damages if the product involved was in the possession of such a person when the incident giving rise to the claim occurred. F.S.A. § 627.942(7)

profert The document relied on in the pleading is produced in court.

professional association (P.A.) 1. Two or more professionals (e.g., doctors) who practice together. 2. A group of professionals organized for a common purpose, e.g., continuing education, lobbying.

professional conduct See Model Rules of Professional Conduct.

professional corporation (P.C.) A corporation of persons performing services that require a professional license, e.g., attorneys.

> The term "professional corporation" means a corporation which is organized under this act for the sole and specific purpose of rendering professional service and which has as its shareholders only other professional corporations, professional limited liability companies, or individuals who themselves are duly licensed or otherwise legally authorized to render the same professional service as the corporation. F.S.A. § 621.03(2)

professional legal secretary (PLS) A certification credential of NALS, the Association for Legal Professionals (*www.nals.org*).

professional responsibility Ethical conduct of professionals.

proffer To tender or offer.

profiling Targeting, suspecting, or selecting out individuals based on group characteristics, e.g., race.

profit The gross proceeds of a business transaction less the costs of the transaction; excess of revenue over expenses. Gain.

profit-and-loss (P&L) statement See earnings statement.

profit à prendre The right to enter another's land and remove something of value from the soil or the products of the soil. Also called right of common.

profiteering Making excessive profits through unfair advantage.

profit sharing A company plan in which employees can share profits.

pro forma 1. Perfunctorily; as a formality. 2. Provided in advance for purposes of description or projection.

progressive tax A type of graduated tax that applies higher tax rates as one's income range increases. Also called graduated tax.

pro hac vice (p.h.v.) ("for this particular occasion") Pertaining to permission given to an out-of-state attorney to practice law in the jurisdiction for this case only.

prohibited degree A relationship too close to be allowed to marry.

prohibition 1. Suppression or interdiction; an order forbidding something. 2. A law preventing the manufacture, sale, or transportation of intoxicating liquors. 3. See writ of prohibition.

prohibitory injunction A court order that a person refrain from doing a specific act. An injunction that maintains the status quo.

prolixity Superfluous statements of fact in a pleading or as evidence.

promise 1. A manifestation of an intention to act or to refrain from acting in a specified way so as to justify the promisee in understanding that a commitment has been made. 2. To make a commitment.

> "Promise" means a written undertaking to pay money signed by the person undertaking to pay. An acknowledgment of an obligation by the obligor is not a promise unless the obligor also undertakes to pay the obligation. F.S.A. § 673.1031(i)

promisee The person to whom a promise has been made.

promisor The person who makes a promise.

promissory estoppel The rule that a promise (not supported by consideration) will be binding if (a) the promisor makes a promise he or she should reasonably expect will induce action or forbearance by the promisee, (b) the promise does induce such action or forbearance, and (c) injustice can be avoided only by enforcement of the promise.

> Doctrine of "promissory estoppel" broadly stated is that a promise, which promisor should reasonably expect to induce action or forbearance of substantial character on part of promisee and which does produce such action or forbearance, is binding if an injustice can be avoided only by enforcement of promise. *Southeastern Sales & Service Co.,* 172 So.2d 239 (Fla.App.1965)

promissory note A written promise to pay. An unconditional promise in writing made by one person to another, signed by the maker, engaging to pay on demand, or at a fixed or determinable future time, a certain sum of money, to order or to bearer. Also called note.

promissory warranty A commitment by the insured that certain facts will continue or remain true after the insurance policy takes effect.

promoter 1. One who promotes or furthers some venture. 2. One who takes preliminary steps in the organization of a corporation or business.

promulgate 1. To announce officially. 2. To put into effect.

pronounce To declare formally.

proof 1. The effect of being persuaded by evidence that a fact has been established or refuted. 2. Evidence that establishes something.

proof beyond a reasonable doubt See reasonable doubt.

proof of claim A written statement a creditor files with the bankruptcy court showing the amount and character of the debt owed to the creditor.

> Proof of claim shall consist of a written statement under oath signed by the claimant or his or her attorney in fact and shall be in such form as the office requires. F.S.A. § 663.178 (1)

proof of loss Providing an insurer with the information and evidence needed to determine its liability under an insurance policy.

proof of service Evidence that a summons or other process has been served on a party in an action. Also called certificate of service, return of service.

proof to a moral certainty See moral certainty.

pro per See in propria persona, pro se.

proper lookout The duty of a driver to see what is clearly visible or what in the exercise of due care would be visible.

proper party A person whose interest may be affected by the action and, therefore, may be joined, but whose presence is not essential for the court to adjudicate the rights of others.

property 1. That which one can possess, enjoy, or own. 2. The right of ownership. 3. The quality or characteristic of a thing.

property settlement An agreement dividing marital property between spouses upon separation or divorce. A court judgment on this division.

property tax A tax on real or personal property that one owns, the amount often dependent on the value of the property.

prophylactic Acting to prevent something.

proponent An advocate; one who presents or offers an argument, proposal, or instrument.

proposal An offer or plan.

propound To offer or propose for analysis or acceptance.

proprietary 1. Owned by a private person or company. 2. Pertaining to ownership.

> "Proprietary software" means data processing software that is protected by copyright or trade secret laws. F.S.A. § 119.011(10)

proprietary drug A drug that has the protection of a patent.

proprietary function A function of a municipality that (a) traditionally or principally has been performed by private enterprise, or (b) is conducted primarily to produce a profit or benefit for the government rather than for the public at large.

proprietary interest One's right or share based on property ownership.

proprietary lease A lease in a cooperative apartment between the owner-cooperative and a tenant-stockholder.

proprietor The owner of property, e.g., a business. See also sole proprietorship.

pro rata Proportionately; according to a certain rate or factor.

pro rata clause A clause in an insurance policy that the insurer will be liable only for the proportion of the loss represented by the ratio between its policy limits and the total limits of all available insurance.

> The carrier had included in its policy a "pro rata" clause, limiting its liability to its fractional share of all insurance on the building. *Mierzwa*, 877 So.2d 774 (Fla.App. 4 Dist.,2004)

prorate To divide, calculate, or distribute proportionally.

proscription A prohibition or restriction.

pro se (on one's own behalf) Appearing for or representing oneself. Also called in propria persona, pro per.

prosecute To initiate and pursue a civil case or a criminal case.

prosecuting attorney See district attorney, prosecutor (1), state attorney.

prosecuting witness The person (often the victim) who instigates a criminal charge and gives evidence.

prosecution 1. Court proceedings to determine the guilt or innocence of a person accused of a crime. 2. The prosecuting attorney or the government in a criminal case. 3. Pursuing a lawsuit.

prosecution history See file wrapper.

prosecutor 1. The representative of the government in a criminal case. The state attorney. 2. One who instigates a prosecution or files a complaint.

prosecutorial discretion The right of prosecutors to decide whether to charge someone for a crime, whether to plea bargain, and whether to ask for a particular sentence.

prosecutory Involving or relating to a prosecution.

prospective Pertaining to or applicable in the future; expected.

prospective law A law applicable to cases or events arising after its enactment.

prospectus A document containing facts on a company designed to help a prospective investor decide whether to invest in the company.

prostitution Engaging in sexual activities for hire.

> "Prostitution" means the giving or receiving of the body for sexual activity for hire but excludes sexual activity between spouses. F.S.A. § 796.07(a)

pro tanto For so much; to the extent of.

protected class A group of people (e.g., members of a minority race) given special statutory protection against discrimination.

protection Defending or shielding from harm; coverage.

protection order See restraining order.

protective custody Being held under force of law for one's own protection or that of the public.

protective order 1. A court order designed to protect a person from harassment or undue burden or expense during litigation. 2. See restraining order.

protective trust A trust designed to protect trust assets from the spendthrift tendencies of the beneficiary.

pro tem (pro tempore) For the time being; temporarily.

protest 1. A formal declaration of dissent or disapproval. 2. A written declaration (often by a notary public) that a check or other negotiable instrument was presented but not paid or accepted. 3. A disagreement that a debt is owed but paying it while disputing it.

prothonotary A chief clerk of court.

protocol 1. The etiquette of diplomacy. 2. A brief summary of a document, e.g., a treaty. 3. The first copy or draft of a treaty; an amendment of a treaty. 4. The formal record or minutes of a meeting.

prove To establish a fact or position by sufficient evidence.

province 1. A division of the state or country. 2. A sphere of expertise or authority.

provision 1. A section or part of a legal document. 2. A stipulation.

provisional remedy A temporary remedy, pending final court action.

proviso A condition, exception, or stipulation in a law or document.

provocation Inciting another to do a particular deed.

proximate Nearest or closest; close in causal connection.

proximate cause The legally sufficient cause of an event when (a) the defendant is the cause in fact of the event, (b) the event was the foreseeable consequence of the original risk created by the defendant, and (c) there is no policy reason why the defendant should not be liable for what he or she caused in fact. Also called direct cause, efficient cause, legal cause, procuring cause, producing cause.

> "Proximate cause," or "legal cause," in language of standard jury instructions, consists of two essential elements: causation in fact and foreseeability, with the former often characterized in terms of a "but for" test. *Anglin*, 472 So.2d 784 (Fla.App. 1 Dist.,1985)

proxy 1. An agent; one authorized to act for another. 2. The authorization to act for another.

proxy marriage The performance of a valid marriage ceremony through agents because one or both of the prospective spouses are absent.

proxy statement A document mailed to shareholders giving information on matters for which the company is seeking proxy votes.

prudent Cautious; careful in adapting means to ends.

> Practically wise, judicious, careful, discreet, circumspect, sensible. *A.O. v. Department of Health and Rehabilitative Services*, 696 So.2d 1358 (Fla.App. 5 Dist.,1997)

prudent investor rule A trustee must use such diligence and prudence in managing and investing a trust fund as a reasonable person would use.

prurient Pertaining to a shameful or morbid interest in sex.

P.S.; p.s. 1. Public Statute (P.S.). See public law (1). 2. Postscript (p.s.).

psychotherapist-patient privilege A patient can refuse to disclose, and can prevent others from disclosing, confidential communications between patient and psychotherapist involving the patient's diagnosis or treatment.

public 1. The community at large. 2. Open for use by everyone. 3. Traded on the open market.

Public Access to Court Electronic Records (PACER) An electronic public access service that allows subscribers to obtain case and docket information from federal courts via the Internet (*pacer.psc.uscourts.gov*).

public accommodation A business or place that is open to, accepts, or solicits the patronage of the general public.

> "Public accommodation" means a common carrier, airplane, motor vehicle, railroad train, motor bus, streetcar, boat, or other public conveyance or mode of transportation; hotel; lodging place; place of public accommodation, amusement, or resort; and other places to which the general public is invited, subject only to the conditions and limitations established by law and applicable alike to all persons. F.S.A. § 413.08(c)

public act See public law (1).

public administrator Someone appointed by the court to administer an intestate estate when relatives or associates of the decedent are not available to do so.

publication 1. Making something known to people. 2. Communication of a statement to someone other than the plaintiff.

public bill A legislative proposal for a public law.

public contract A contract (often with a private person or business) in which a government buys goods or services for a public need.

public convenience and necessity Reasonably meeting the needs of the public, justifying the grant of public funds or a license for a project or service.

public corporation 1. A company whose shares are traded on the open market. Also called publicly held corporation. 2. A corporation owned by the government and managed under special laws in the public interest.

public defender (P.D.) An attorney appointed by a court and paid by the government to represent indigent defendants in criminal cases.

public domain 1. Work product or other property that is not protected by copyright or patent. A status that allows access to anyone without fee. 2. Government-owned land.

public duty doctrine The government is not liable for a public official's negligent conduct unless it is shown that the official breached a duty owed to the injured person as an individual as opposed the breach of an obligation owed to the public in general.

public easement An easement for the benefit of the general public.

public figure A person who has assumed special prominence in the affairs of society. A public figure for a limited purpose is a person who has voluntarily become involved in a controversy of interest to the general public.

public forum Settings or places traditionally available for public expression and debate, such as public streets and the radio.

public hearing A hearing open to the general public.

publici juris ("of public right") Being owned by the public and subject to use by anyone.

public interest 1. A matter of health or welfare that concerns the general public. 2. The well-being of the public.

public interest law Law involving broad societal issues.

public international law See international law.

public land Government-owned land.

public law (P.L.)(Pub. L.) 1. A statute that applies to the general public or to a segment of the public and has permanence or general interest. Also called public act, public statute. 2. Laws governing the operation of government or relationships between government and private persons. The major examples are constitutional law, administrative law, and criminal law.

publicly held corporation See public corporation (1).

public necessity The privilege to make a reasonable use of someone's property to prevent an immediate threat of harm or damage to the public.

public nuisance Unreasonably interfering with a right of the general public. An act that adversely affects the safety, health, morals, or convenience of the public. Also called common nuisance.

> A "public nuisance" violates public rights, subverts public order, decency, or morals, or causes inconvenience or damage to the public generally. *Orlando Sports Stadium*, 262 So.2d 881 (Fla. 1972)

public offering A sale of stock to the public on the open market.

public office A position created by law by which an individual is given power to perform a public function for a given period.

> "Public office" means any federal, state, county, municipal, school, or other district office or position which is filled by vote of the electors. F.S.A. § 97.021(30)

public official An elected or appointed holder of a public office.

public policy Principles inherent in customs and societal values that are embodied in a law.

public property Government-owned property.

public purpose Benefit to or welfare of the public as a goal of government action.

public record A record the government must keep that may or may not be open to the public.

public records exception Some written statements that would normally be excluded as hearsay may be admitted into evidence if they qualify as public records and reports (Federal Rules of Evidence Rule 803(8)).

public sale A sale in which members of the public are invited to become buyers.

public security Bonds, notes, certificates of indebtedness, and other instruments evidencing government debt.

public service commission A government commission that supervises or regulates public utilities.

public statute (P.S.) See public law (1).

public trial A trial that the general public can observe.

public trust See charitable trust.

public use 1. A use that confers some benefit or advantage to the public. A use affecting the public generally, or any number thereof, as distinguished from particular individuals. 2. A use of an invention by one under no restriction or obligation of secrecy to the inventor.

> Public use is one which is fixed and definite, in which public has an interest, and the terms and manner of its enjoyment must be within the control of the state and must be available to all people equally, although it is not essential that the benefits of the public use be received by the whole public or even a large part of it. *Devon-Aire Villas*, 490 So.2d 60 (Fla.App. 3 Dist.,1985)

public utility A company or business that regularly supplies the public with some commodity or service that is of public consequence and need (e.g., electricity).

public works Construction, demolition, installation, or repair work on roads, dams, and similar structures done under contract with public funds.

public wrong An offense against the state or the general community, e.g., a crime, public nuisance, or breach of a public contract.

publish To make known, to make public; to distribute or disseminate.

puffing 1. A seller's opinion consisting of an exaggeration of quality or overstatement of value. 2. See by-bidding.

> Salesmen's talk comprised of affirmation of value of goods or opinion or commendation of goods is "puffing" and does not create warranty. F.S.A. § 672.313(2). *Lou Bachrodt Chevrolet*, 570 So.2d 306 (Fla.App. 4 Dist.,1990)

puisne Subordinate in rank.

***Pullman* abstention** Federal courts can refrain or postpone the exercise of federal jurisdiction when a federal constitutional issue might be mooted or presented in a different posture by a state court determination of pertinent state law. *Railroad Comm'n v. Pullman*, 61 S. Ct. 643 (1941).

punishment Any fine, penalty, confinement, or other sanction imposed by law for a crime, offense, or breach of a duty.

punitive damages Damages that are added to actual or compensatory damages in order to punish outrageous or egregious conduct and to deter similar conduct in the future. Also called exemplary damages, smart money, vindictive damages.

pur autre vie For or during the life of another. Also spelled per autre vie.

purchase Acquisition by buying; receiving title to property by a means other than descent, inheritance, or gift.

purchase money mortgage A mortgage taken back when purchasing property to secure payment of the balance of the purchase price.

purchase money resulting trust A trust imposed when title to property is transferred to one person, but the entire purchase price is paid by another.

purchase money security interest (PMSI) A security interest taken or retained by a seller to secure all or part of the price of the collateral, or a security interest taken by one who gives value that is used by the debtor to acquire the collateral.

> "Purchase-money obligation" means an obligation of an obligor incurred as all or part of the price of the collateral or for value given to enable the debtor to acquire rights in or the use of the collateral if the value is in fact so used. F.S.A. § 679.1031(b)

purchaser One who acquires property by buying it for a consideration.

pure accident See unavoidable accident.

pure plea A plea stating matters not in the bill to defeat the claim.

pure race statute See race statute.

purge To clear or exonerate from a charge or of guilt.

purloin To steal.

purport 1. To appear to be; to claim or seem to be. 2. Meaning.

purpose Goal or objective.

purposely Intentionally; with a specific purpose.

purpresture An encroachment on public rights or the appropriation to private use of that which belongs to the public.

pursuant to In accordance with; under.

pursuit of happiness The phrase in the Declaration of Independence interpreted to mean the right to be free in the enjoyment of our faculties, subject to restraints that are necessary for the common welfare.

purview The body, scope, or extent of a something, e.g., a statute or other law.

putative Generally regarded or reputed, believed.

putative father A man reputed or alleged to be the biological father of a child born out of wedlock.

> Putative father means an individual who is or may be the biological father of a child whose paternity has not been established and whose mother was unmarried when the child was conceived and born. F.S.A. § 409.256(1)(g)

putative marriage A marriage that has been solemnized in proper form and celebrated in good faith by one or both parties, but which, by reason of some legal infirmity, is either void or voidable.

put option The right to sell a specified security or commodity at a specified price. See also call option.

pyramid scheme A sales device or plan (illegal in many states) in which participants are recruited to pay the person who recruited them, hoping to receive payments from the persons they recruit. A pyramid scheme rewards participants for inducing other people to join the program, whereas a Ponzi scheme operates strictly by paying earlier investors with money tendered by later investors.

pyramiding Speculating on stocks or commodities by using unrealized (paper) profits as margin for more purchases.

Q

Q.B. Queen's Bench. See King's Bench.

QDRO See qualified domestic relations order.

QTIP Qualified terminable interest property.

qua As; in the character or capacity of.

quaere Ask, question; a query.

qualification 1. A quality or circumstance that is legally or inherently necessary to perform a function. 2. A restriction or modification in a document or transaction.

qualified 1. Eligible; possessing legal power or capacity. 2. Restricted or imperfect.

qualified acceptance A counteroffer; an acceptance that modifies the offer.

qualified disclaimer An irrevocable and unqualified refusal by a person to accept an interest in property (26 USC § 2518).

qualified domestic relations order (QDRO) A court order that allows a nonemployee to reach retirement benefits of an employee or former employee in order to satisfy a support or other marital obligation to the nonemployee.

> A QDRO creates or recognizes the existence of an alternate payee's right to, or assigns to an alternate payee the right to, receive all or a portion of the benefits payable with respect to a participant under a plan. *DeSantis*, 714 So.2d 637 (Fla.App. 4 Dist.,1998)

qualified immunity A government official's immunity from liability for civil damages when performing discretionary functions if his or her conduct does not violate clearly established statutory or constitutional rights of which a reasonable person would have known.

qualified indorsement An indorsement that limits the liability of the indorser of a negotiable instrument.

qualified privilege See conditional privilege.

qualify 1. To make oneself fit or prepared. 2. To limit or restrict.

quantum meruit ("as much as he deserves") 1. An equitable theory of recovery based upon an implied agreement to pay for benefits or goods received. 2. The measure of damages imposed when a party prevails on the equitable claim of unjust enrichment.

quantum valebant An action seeking payment for goods sold and delivered based on an implied promise to pay as much as the goods are reasonably worth.

quarantine Isolation of persons, animals, goods, or vehicles suspected of carrying a contagious disease.

quare clausum fregit See trespass quare clausum fregit.

quash To vacate or annul; to suppress completely.

quasi Somewhat the same, but different; resembling.

quasi contract See implied in law contract.

quasi corporation A body or entity (often part of the government) that has some of the characteristics of a corporation but is not a corporation in the full sense.

quasi estoppel A party should be precluded from asserting, to another's disadvantage, a right or claim that is inconsistent with a position previously taken by the party.

> A plea of quasi-estoppel applies to a litigant who attempts to occupy inconsistent positions during the course of litigation. *Savino*, 92 So.2d 817 (Fla.1957)

quasi in rem jurisdiction A court's power over a person, but restricted to his or her specific interest in property within the territory over which the court has authority.

quasi judicial Pertaining to the power of an administrative agency (or official in the executive branch) to hear and determine controversies between the public and individuals in a manner that resembles a judicial trial.

quasi legislative Pertaining to the power of an administrative agency (or official in the executive branch) to write rules and regulations in a manner that resembles the legislature.

quasi-suspect classification A classification such as one based on gender or illegitimacy that will receive intermediate scrutiny by the court to determine its constitutionality.

Queen's Bench (Q.B.) See King's Bench.

question 1. An issue to be resolved. 2. Something asked; a query.

question of fact; question of law See issue of fact; issue of law.

quia emptores A 1290 English statute that had the effect of facilitating the alienation of fee-simple tenants.

> After the statute quia emptores enabled tenants in fee simple to alienate their lands at pleasure, under the common law, the beneficiary of a trust holding real estate in fee, in which no one else was interested, could, on becoming of age, ignore and terminate any restraint on his right to alienate it. *In re Jones' Will*, 289 So.2d 42 (Fla.App. 1973)

quia timet An equitable remedy to be protected from anticipated future injury where it cannot be avoided by a present action at law.

quick assets Cash and assets readily convertible into cash (other than inventory).

quid pro quo Something for something; giving one thing for another. Quid pro quo sexual harassment exists when an employer conditions an employment benefit upon sexual favors from an employee.

quiet 1. Free from interference or adverse claims. 2. To make secure.

quiet enjoyment Possession of land that is not disturbed by superior ownership rights asserted by a third person.

quiet title action An action to resolve conflicting claims to land. An action asserting an interest in land and calling on others to set forth their claims.

quit 1. To surrender possession. 2. To cease.

qui tam action An action in which a private plaintiff is allowed to sue under a statute that awards part of any penalty recovered to the plaintiff and the remainder to the government.

quitclaim 1. To transfer the extent of one's interest. 2. To surrender a claim.

quitclaim deed A deed that transfers any interest or claim the grantor may have, without warranting that the title is valid.

quittance A release from debt.

quod vide (q.v.) A reference directing the reader elsewhere in the text for more information.

quorum The minimum number of members who must be present in a deliberative body before business may be transacted.

quota 1. An assigned goal; the minimum sought. 2. A proportional part or allotment.

quotation 1. A word-for-word reproduction of text from another source. 2. A statement of current price.

quotient verdict A verdict on damages reached when the jurors agree to average the figures each juror states as his or her individual verdict.

> Jurors' accepting as the verdict a figure arrived at by dividing by the number of jurors the sum of the jurors' opinions as to the value of damage was improper as a quotient verdict and constituted ground for new trial, but a new trial on such ground would be limited to damages. *Niebla*, 533 So.2d 816 (Fla.App. 3 Dist.,1988)

quo warranto A court inquiry (by writ) to determine whether someone exercising government power is legally entitled to do so.

> The writ of quo warranto, although rarely sought, is available to challenge the right of public officials to hold the offices to which they claim entitlement. (*www.floridasupremecourt.org/ pub_info/system2.shtml*)

q.v. See quod vide.

R

® The symbol indicating registration of a trademark or service mark with the U.S. Patent and Trademark Office.

race The historical division of humanity by physical characteristics. A grouping based on ancestry or ethnic characteristics.

race notice statute A recording law giving priority to the first party to record a claim, unless this person had notice of an unrecorded prior claim.

race statute A recording law giving priority to the first party to record a claim, even if this person had notice of another's unrecorded prior claim. Also called pure race statute.

racial discrimination Discrimination based on one's race.

racketeer One who commits racketeering.

Racketeer Influenced and Corrupt Organizations Act (RICO) A federal statute imposing civil and criminal penalties for racketeering offenses such as engaging in a pattern of fraud, bribery, extortion, and other acts enumerated in the statute (18 USC § 1961). Some states have enacted similar statutes.

racketeering Crime engaged in as a business or organized enterprise, often involving illegal activity such as extortion, bribery, gambling, prostitution, and drug sales.

> "Pattern of racketeering" activity means engaging in at least two incidents of racketeering conduct that have the same or similar intents, results, accomplices, victims, or methods of commission or that otherwise are interrelated by distinguishing characteristics and are not isolated incidents, provided at least one of such incidents occurred after the effective date of this act and that the last of such incidents occurred within 5 years after a prior incident of racketeering conduct. F.S.A. § 895.02(4)

raid 1. An effort to entice personnel or customers away from a competitor. 2. A hostile attempt to take over a corporation by share purchases. 3. A sudden attack or forcible entry by law enforcement.

railroad To rush someone through without due care or due process.

rainmaker An attorney who brings fee-generating cases into the office due to his or her contacts or reputation.

raise 1. To increase. 2. To invoke or put forward. 3. To gather or collect. 4. To create or establish.

raise a check To increase the face amount of a check fraudulently.

rake-off A share of profits, often taken as a payoff or bribe.

RAM See reverse annuity mortgage.

ransom Money or other payment sought for the return of illegally detained persons or property.

rape Nonconsensual sexual intercourse.

> Sexual battery means oral, anal, or vaginal penetration by, or union with, the sexual organ of another or the anal or vaginal penetration of another by any other object; however, sexual battery does not include an act done for a bona fide medical purpose. F.S.A. § 794.011(1)(h)

rape shield law A law imposing limits on defendant's use of evidence of the prior sexual experiences of an alleged rape victim.

rap sheet The arrest and conviction record of someone.

rasure Erasing part of a document by scraping.

ratable 1. Able to be evaluated or apportioned. 2. Taxable. 3. Proportionate.

rate 1. Relative value. A measure or degree in relationship to another measure. 2. Cost or price.

rate base The fair value of the property of a utility (or other entity) upon which a reasonable return is allowed.

rate of exchange See exchange (3).

rate of return Earnings or profit as a percentage of an investment.

ratification 1. An adoption or confirmation of a prior act or transaction, making one bound by it. 2. Formal approval.

> Ratification is the express or implied adoption by a person of an act or contract entered into on his behalf by another without authority. *Port Largo Club*, 476 So.2d 1330 (Fla.App. 3 Dist.,1985)

ratio decidendi The ground, reason, principle, or rule of law that is the basis of a court's decision.

rational basis test A law will be upheld as constitutional if it rationally furthers a legitimate government objective.

ravish 1. To rape. 2. To seize and carry away by force.

re In the matter of; concerning or regarding.

reacquired stock See treasury securities (1).

ready, willing, and able Having sufficient funds, capacity, and desire to complete the transaction.

reaffirmation 1. A confirmation or approval of something already agreed to. 2. An agreement by a debtor to pay an otherwise dischargeable debt.

real 1. Pertaining to stationary or fixed property such as land. 2. True or genuine.

real chattel A real property interest that is less than a freehold or fee interest. An example is a lease of land.

real defense A defense such as duress and fraud in the factum that is good against everyone, including a holder in due course.

real estate See real property.

real estate broker An agent or intermediary who negotiates or arranges agreements pertaining to the sale and lease of real property.

> Broker means a person who, for another, and for a compensation or valuable consideration directly or indirectly paid or promised, expressly or impliedly, or with an intent to collect or receive a compensation or valuable consideration therefor, appraises, auctions, sells, exchanges, buys, rents, or offers, attempts or agrees to appraise, auction, or negotiate the sale, exchange, purchase, or rental of business enterprises or business opportunities or any real property or any interest in or concerning the same, . . . F.S.A. § 475.01(1)(a)

real estate investment trust (REIT) A business that invests in real estate on behalf of its shareholders.

Real Estate Settlement Procedures Act (RESPA) A federal law on disclosure of settlement costs in the sale of residential property financed by a federally insured lender (12 USC § 2601).

real evidence 1. Evidence that was actually involved in the incident being considered by the court. Also called physical evidence. 2. Evidence produced for inspection at trial.

realization 1. Conversion of an asset into cash. 2. The receipt by a taxpayer of actual economic gain or loss from the disposition of property.

realized gain or loss The difference between the amount realized on the disposition of property and the adjusted basis of the property.

real party in interest The person who benefits from or is harmed by the outcome of the case and who by substantive law has the legal right to enforce the claim in question. Also called party in interest.

real property Land and anything permanently attached or affixed to the land such as buildings, fences, and trees. Also called real estate, realty.

> "Real property" means all lands, including improvements and fixtures thereon, and property of any nature appurtenant thereto or used in connection therewith and every estate, interest, right, and use, legal or equitable, therein, including but not limited to terms for years and liens by way of judgment, mortgage, or otherwise. F.S.A. § 163.340(13)

realtor A real estate broker or agent, often a member of the National Association of Realtors (*www.realtor.org*).

realty See real property.

reapportionment Redrawing boundaries of a political subdivision to reflect population changes, leading to a reallocation of legislative seats. Also called redistricting. Compare gerrymander.

reargument Another presentation of arguments before the same court.

reason 1. An inducement, motive, or ground for action. 2. The faculty of the mind to form judgments based on logic.

reasonable Sensible and proper under the circumstances. Fair.

> "Reasonable" or "reasonably" when used in relation to conduct by a lawyer denotes the conduct of a reasonably prudent and competent lawyer. Florida Rules of Professional Conduct, Preamble

reasonable care The degree of care a person of ordinary prudence and intelligence would use under the same or similar circumstances to avoid injury or damage. Also called due care, ordinary care.

reasonable diligence The care and persistence of an ordinarily prudent person under the same or similar circumstances.

reasonable doubt Doubt that would cause prudent people to hesitate before acting in matters of importance to themselves. The standard of proof needed to convict someone of a crime is proof beyond a reasonable doubt.

> A reasonable doubt is not a mere possible doubt, a speculative, imaginary or forced doubt. Such a doubt must not influence you to return a verdict of not guilty if you have an abiding conviction of guilt. On the other hand, if, after carefully considering, comparing and weighing all the evidence, there is not an abiding conviction of guilt, or, if, having a conviction, it is one which is not stable but one which wavers and vacillates, then the charge is not proved beyond every reasonable doubt and you must find the defendant not guilty because the doubt is reasonable. Std.Crim.Jury Instr., 3.7 (*www.floridasupremecourt.org/jury_instructions/instructions.shtml#*)

reasonable force Force that an average person of ordinary intelligence in like circumstances would deem necessary.

reasonable man (person) A person who uses ordinary prudence under the circumstances to avoid injury or damage. (A legal guide or standard.) Also called ordinary prudent person.

reasonable suspicion A particularized and objective reason based on specific and articulable facts for suspecting someone of criminal activity.

reasonable time As much time as is needed, under the particular circumstances involved, to do what a contract or duty requires to be done.

> By failing to seek rescission of contract for purchase of television satellite system until buyer had been in possession

of system for one and one-half years, buyer did not act "within a reasonable time" within meaning of statute authorizing revocation of acceptance. F.S.A. § 672.608. *Central Florida Antenna Service*, 503 So.2d 1351 (Fla.App. 5 Dist.,1987)

reasonable use A use of one's property that is consistent with zoning rules and does not interfere with the lawful use of surrounding property.

reasonable woman test A female plaintiff states a prima facie case of hostile environment sexual harassment when she alleges conduct that a reasonable woman would consider sufficiently severe or pervasive to alter the conditions of employment and create an abusive working environment.

rebate A reduction or return of part to the price.

rebellion Organized, open, and armed resistance to a constituted government or ruler by a subject.

rebut To refute, oppose, or repel.

rebuttable presumption An inference of fact that can be overcome by sufficient contrary evidence. Also called disputable presumption.

> A rebuttable presumption gives particular effect to a certain group of facts in the absence of further evidence, and the presumption provides a prima facie case which shifts to defendant the burden to go forward with evidence to contradict or rebut fact presumed. *Gulle*, 174 So.2d 26 (Fla.1965)

rebuttal Arguments or evidence given in reply to explain or counter an opponent.

recall 1. Removing a public official from office before the end of his or her term by a vote of the people. 2. A request by the manufacturer to return a defective product. 3. Revocation of a judgment.

recant To repudiate or retract something formally.

recapitalization A change or adjustment in the capital structure (stock, bonds, or other securities) of a corporation.

recaption Retaking chattels once in your possession or custody.

recapture 1. To retake or recover. 2. The recalculation of tax liability in order to remove improperly taken deductions or credits.

receipt 1. Written acknowledgment of receiving something. 2. Taking physical possession of something. 3. Receipts: income, money received.

receivable 1. Awaiting collection. 2. The amount still owed.

receiver A person appointed by the court to manage property in litigation or in the process of bankruptcy.

receivership The condition of a company or individual over whom a receiver has been appointed. See receiver.

receiving stolen property Receiving or controlling stolen movable property of another, knowing that it has been stolen.

> Offense of "dealing in stolen property" is committed not merely by possession stolen property knowing same to be stolen, which was essentially former offense of "receiving stolen property," but, rather, offense of "dealing" in stolen property is committed by one who "traffics" in such property, meaning "to sell, transfer, distribute, dispense, or otherwise dispose of property," or "to buy, receive, possess, obtain control of, or use property with intent to sell, transfer, distribute, dispense, or otherwise dispose of such property." F.S.A. §§ 812.012(7)(a, b), 812.019. *Coley*, 391 So.2d 725 (Fla.App., 1980)

recess An interval when business is suspended without adjourning. A temporary cessation of judicial proceedings.

recidivism The tendency to return to a life of crime.

recidivist Repeat offender; habitual criminal.

reciprocal 1. Given or owed to each other. 2. Done in return.

reciprocal negative easement When an owner sells a portion of land with a restrictive covenant that benefits the land retained by the owner, the restriction becomes mutual.

reciprocal wills See mutual wills (1).

reciprocity A mutual exchange of the same benefits or treatment.

recision See rescission.

recital The formal setting forth of facts or reasons.

reckless Consciously failing to exercise due care but without intending the consequences; wantonly disregarding risks.

> One is guilty of reckless driving if he or she drives automobile in willful or wanton disregard for safety of persons or property. F.S.A. § 316.192(1). *LaValley*, 633 So.2d 1126 (Fla.App. 5 Dist.,1994)

reckless disregard Conscious indifference to consequences.

reckless endangerment Creating a substantial risk of major injury or death.

recklessness Knowing but disregarding a substantial risk that an injury or wrongful act may occur.

reclamation 1. Converting unusable land into land that is usable. 2. A seller's right to recover possession of goods from an insolvent buyer.

recognition 1. A formal acknowledgment or confirmation. 2. The point at which a tax on gain or loss is accounted for.

recognizance An obligation recorded in court to do some act required by law, e.g., to appear at all court proceedings.

> "Personal recognizance" means an agreement by a motorist made at the time of the issuance of a traffic citation that he or she will comply with the terms of that traffic citation. F.S.A. § 322.50(6)

recollection The act of recalling or remembering.

reconciliation 1. The voluntary resumption of full marital relations. 2. The bringing of financial accounts into consistency or agreement.

reconduction 1. Renewing a lease. 2. The forcible return of illegal aliens.

reconsideration A review or reevaluation of a matter.

reconstruction 1. Rebuilding. 2. Re-creating an event.

reconveyance A transfer back. The return of something, e.g., title.

record 1. To make an official note of; to enter in a document. 2. A formal account of some act or event, e.g., a trial. 3. The facts that have been inscribed or stored.

recordation The formal recording of an instrument (e.g., a deed) with a county clerk or other public registry.

record date A date by which a shareholder must officially own shares in order to be entitled to a dividend or to vote.

recorded recollection See past recollection recorded.

recorder 1. An officer appointed to maintain public records, e.g., recorder of deeds. 2. A magistrate or judge with limited jurisdiction in some states.

recorder's court A court with limited criminal jurisdiction.

recording act; recording statute A law on recording deeds and other property instruments in order to establish priority among claims.

record owner Anyone recorded in a public registry as the owner.

record title See paper title.

recoupment 1. The defendant's right to a deduction from the plaintiff's damages due to plaintiff's breach of duty arising from the same contract. 2. An equitable remedy that permits the offset of mutual debts based on the same transaction or occurrence. 3. A reimbursement or recovery.

> "Recoupment" is purely defensive matter springing from same transaction as plaintiffs' cause of action, which is available only to reduce or satisfy plaintiffs' claim. *Kellogg*, 807 So.2d 669 (Fla.App. 4 Dist.,2001)

recourse 1. Turning or appealing for help; a way to enforce a right. 2. The right of a holder of a negotiable instrument to recover against an indorser or other party who is secondarily liable. 3. The right to reach other assets of the debtor if the collateral is insufficient.

recover 1. To obtain by court judgment or legal process. 2. To have restored; to regain possession.

recovery 1. That which is awarded by court judgment or legal process. 2. Restoration.

recrimination 1. A charge by the accused against the accuser. 2. An accusation that the party seeking the divorce has committed a serious marital wrong that in itself is a ground for divorce.

recross-examination Another cross-examination of a witness after redirect examination.

recusal A judge's (or other decision maker's) removal of him or herself from a matter because of a conflict of interest. Also called recusation. The verb is *recuse*.

redaction Revising or editing a text. Removing confidential or inappropriate parts of a text.

reddendum A provision in a deed in which the grantor reserves something out of what had been granted (e.g., rent).

redeemable bond A bond that the issuer may call back for payment before its maturity date. Also called callable bond.

redemption 1. Buying back; reclaiming or regaining possession by paying a specific price. Recovering what was mortgaged. 2. The repurchase of a security by the issuing corporation. 3. Converting shares into cash.

> Phrase "right of redemption" takes on different meanings depending upon whether it is being used in a relation to mortgagor or mortgagee; when used with respect to mortgagor, it refers to his right to satisfy mortgage indebtedness which encumbers his property, but when used with reference to junior mortgagee, it refers to his right to satisfy prior mortgage by payment of the debt it secures and thereby become equitably subrogated to all rights of prior mortgagee. *Islamorada Bank*, 452 So.2d 61 (Fla.App. 3 Dist.,1984)

red herring 1. A diversion from the main issue; an irrelevant issue. 2. A preliminary prospectus.

redhibition Avoiding a sale due to a major defect in the thing sold.

redirect examination Another direct examination of a witness after he or she was cross-examined.

rediscount rate The rate the Federal Reserve System charges a member bank on a loan secured by paper the bank has already resold.

redistricting See reapportionment.

redlining 1. The discriminatory practice of denying credit or insurance to geographic areas due to the income, race, or ethnicity of its residents. 2. Showing the portions of an earlier draft of a text that have been stricken out.

redraft A second note or bill drafted by the original drawer after the first draft has been dishonored.

redress Damages, equitable relief, or other remedy.

reductio ad absurdum Disproving an argument by showing that it leads to an absurd consequence or conclusion.

reduction to practice The point in time at which an invention is sufficiently tested to demonstrate it will work for its intended purpose.

redundancy Needless repetition; superfluous matter in a pleading.

reentry Retaking possession of land.

reexchange The expenses incurred due to a dishonor of a bill of exchange in a foreign country.

refer To send for further consideration or action.

referee A person to whom a judge refers a case for specific tasks, e.g., to take testimony and to file a report with the court.

referee in bankruptcy A court-appointed officer who performs administrative and judicial functions in bankruptcy cases. Now called a bankruptcy judge.

reference 1. The act of referring or sending a case for further consideration or action. 2. A source of information. 3. A citation in a document.

referendum The electorate's power to give final approval to an existing provision of the constitution or statute of the legislature.

refinance To replace one loan for another on different terms.

reformation An equitable remedy to correct a writing so that it embodies the actual intent of the parties.

> "Reformation" is an equitable remedy which acts to correct an error not in the parties' agreement but in the writing which constitutes the embodiment of that agreement. *Kolski*, 731 So.2d 169 (Fla.App. 3 Dist.,1999)

reformatory A correctional institution for youthful offenders.

refreshing memory or **recollection** See present recollection refreshed.

refugee One seeking refuge in one country after being unwilling or unable to return to another.

refund 1. The return of an overpayment. 2. The return of the price paid for the returned product. 3. To finance again; to refinance.

refunding Refinancing a debt. Replacing a bond with a new bond issue.

reg. See regulation.

regent 1. A member of the governing board of a school. 2. A governor or ruler.

regime 1. A system of rules. 2. The current government.

register 1. To record formally. 2. To enroll. 3. A book containing official facts. 4. One who keeps official records. 5. A probate judge.

registered bond See registered security.

registered check A check guaranteed by a bank for a customer who provides funds for its payment.

registered mail Mail that is numbered and tracked by the U.S. Postal Service to monitor a safe delivery.

registered paralegal One who meets the definition of paralegal (see this term in the dictionary) and the requirements for registration with The Florida Bar as set forth in the Rules Regulating The Florida Bar, Rule 20-2.1(a) (see also section 1.1).

registered representative A representative who meets the requirements of the Securities and Exchange Commission to sell securities to the public.

registered security 1. A stock, bond, or other security whose owner is recorded (registered) by the issuer. 2. A security for sale for which a registration statement has been filed.

register of ships A customs list containing data on vessels, e.g., their owner and country of registration.

registrar The official in charge of keeping records.

registration Inserting something in an official record; formally applying or enrolling. The process by which persons or institutions list their names on an official roster.

> "Registration" means a state operating license on a vessel which is issued with an identifying number, an annual certificate of registration, and a decal designating the year for which a registration fee is paid. F.S.A. § 327.02(33)

registration statement A statement disclosing relevant financial and management data to potential investors in the securities of a company.

registry 1. A book or list kept for recording or registering documents or facts, e.g., a deed, the nationality of a ship. 2. A probate judge.

regressive tax A tax whose rate decreases as the tax base increases.

regs. See regulation.

regular course of business See course of business.

regular session One of the meetings scheduled at fixed times.

regulate To adjust or control by rule, method, or principle.

regulation (reg.) 1. A rule governing conduct; the management of conduct by rules. 2. An administrative agency's rule or order that carries out statutes or executive orders that govern the agency.

Regulation D A regulation of the Securities and Exchange Commission governing the limited offer and sale of unregistered securities.

regulatory agency A government agency that regulates an area of public concern and that can implement statutes by issuing regulations.

regulatory offense 1. A crime created by statute. 2. A minor offense. Also called a public-welfare offense.

regulatory taking Government regulation that deprives a private owner of all or substantially all practical uses of his or her property.

rehabilitation 1. Restoration of credibility to an impeached witness. 2. Improving the character of an offender to prevent recidivism. 3. A reorganizing of debts in bankruptcy.

rehearing An additional hearing to correct an error or oversight.

reimburse 1. To pay back. 2. To indemnify.

reinstate To restore; to place again in a former condition or office.

reinsurance A contract by which one insurer (called the reinsurer) insures all or part of the risks of another insurer; insurance for insurers.

> "Reinsurance" is a contract that one insurer makes with another to protect the first insurer from a risk he has already assumed; it is not a contract against loss by fire, accident, or other hazard as provided in original policy but is one against loss on account of an outstanding contract of insurance or a bond and thus is one to indemnify original insurer for any loss it may sustain, and only if contract contains a clear written assumption of liability to original insured can policyholder bring suit against the reinsurer. *McDonough Const. Corp.*, 190 So.2d 617 (Fla.App. 1966)

REIT See real estate investment trust.

rejection A refusal to accept something, e.g., an offer, performance.

rejoinder Defendant's response to a plaintiff's reply or replication.

relation back The rule that an act done at one time is considered by a fiction of the law to have been done at a prior time.

relative A person related by blood or marriage.

relator 1. See ex rel. 2. An informer. 3. One who applies for a writ.

release 1. To set free from custody. 2. To discharge or relinquish a claim against another. 3. To allow something to be communicated or published. 4. The giving up of a right, claim, interest, or privilege.

> A "release" is an outright cancellation or discharge of the entire obligation as to one or all of the alleged joint wrongdoers; however, a "covenant not to sue" recognizes that the obligation or liability continues, but the injured party agrees not to assert any rights grounded thereon against a particular covenantee. *Rosen*, 802 So.2d 291 (Fla.,2001)

release on own recognizance (ROR) See personal recognizance.

relevance Logically connected to the matter at hand. Being relevant.

relevant Logically tending to establish or disprove a fact. Pertinent. Relevant evidence is evidence having any tendency to make the existence of a fact more probable or less probable than it would be without the evidence.

reliance Faith or trust felt by someone; dependence on someone.

relict A widow or widower.

reliction The gradual alteration of land by withdrawing water.

> Accretion is the extension of land area due to a gradual, natural, and imperceptible build up of additional land by the accumulation of alluvium material. Reliction is a similar increase of land area due to the lowering of the water level by natural causes. *State, Dept. of Natural Resources v. Contemporary Land Sales*, 400 So.2d 488 (Fla.App.,1981)

relief 1. Redress sought from a court. 2. Assistance to the poor.

religion A belief system of faith and worship, often involving a supernatural being or power and moral or ethical rules.

rem See in rem.

remainder 1. A future estate or interest arising in someone other than the grantor or transferor (or the heirs of either) that will take effect upon the natural termination of the prior estate. 2. That which is left over; the remaining portions not otherwise disposed of.

    "Remainder beneficiary" means a person entitled to receive principal when an income interest ends. F.S.A. § 738.102(11)

remainderman One who holds or is entitled to a remainder.

remand 1. To send back for further action. 2. To return to custody.

remediable Capable of being remedied.

remedial 1. Intended to correct wrongs and abuses. 2. Providing an avenue of redress.

remedial action 1. Action to solve long-term environmental damage. 2. Action to redress an individual wrong.

remedial statute 1. A statute that provides a remedy or means to enforce a right. 2. A statute designed to correct an existing law.

remedy 1. The means by which a right is enforced or the violation of a right is prevented or redressed. 2. To correct.

remise To give up or release.

remission 1. Canceling or relinquishing a debt or claim. 2. Pardon or forgiveness.

remit 1. To send or forward. 2. To transmit (money). 3. To refer for further action. 4. To cancel or excuse; to pardon. 5. To mitigate.

remittance Money sent (or the sending of money) as payment.

remitter 1. A person who purchases an instrument from its issuer if the instrument is payable to an identified person other than the purchaser. 2. The relation back of a later defective title to an earlier valid one. 3. Sending a case back to a lower court. 4. One who sends payment to another.

remittitur The power of the court to order a new trial unless a party agrees to reduce the jury verdict in its favor by a stated amount.

    If the court finds that the amount awarded [by verdict] is clearly excessive or inadequate, it shall order a remittitur or additur, as the case may be. If the party adversely affected by such remittitur or additur does not agree, the court shall order a new trial in the cause on the issue of damages only. F.S.A. § 768.043

remonstrance A statement of grievances or reasons against something.

remote 1. Removed in relation, space, or time. 2. Minor or slight.

remote cause 1. A cause too removed in time from the event. 2. A cause that some independent force took advantage of to produce what was not the probable or natural effect of the original act.

removal The transfer of a person or thing from one place to another, e.g., transfer of a case from one court to another.

render To pronounce or deliver. To report formally.

rendition 1. Returning a fugitive to a state where he or she is wanted. 2. Making or delivering a formal decision.

renewal A reestablishment of a legal duty or relationship.

renounce To repudiate or abandon.

rent Cash or other consideration (often paid at intervals) for the use of property.

    "Rent" means the periodic payments due the landlord from the tenant for occupancy under a rental agreement and any other payments due the landlord from the tenant as may be designated as rent in a written rental agreement. F.S.A. § 83.43(6)

rent-a-judging A method of alternate dispute resolution in which the parties hire a private person (e.g., a retired judge) to resolve their dispute.

rental 1. Something rented. 2. Rent to be paid.

rent strike An organized effort by tenants to withhold rent until grievances are resolved, e.g., repair of defective conditions.

renunciation The abandonment or waiver of a right or venture.

renvoi The doctrine under which the court of the forum, in resorting to a foreign law, adopts the rules of the foreign law as to conflict of laws, which rules may in turn refer the court back to the law of the forum.

    The "renvoi" principle is applicable where the forum's conflict of laws rule requires that the law of a foreign jurisdiction be applied, but the conflict of law rule of the foreign jurisdiction requires that the law of the forum be applied. *Nahar*, 656 So.2d 225 (Fla.App. 3 Dist.,1995)

reopen To allow new evidence to be introduced in a trial that was completed. To review a closed case.

reorganization A financial restructuring of a corporation for purposes of achieving bankruptcy protection, tax benefits, or efficiency.

reorganization plan A corporation's proposal to a bankruptcy court for restructuring under Chapter 11.

rep. See report, reporter, representative, republic.

reparable injury An injury for which money compensation is adequate.

reparation Compensation for an injury or wrong. Expiation.

repeal The express or implied abrogation of a law by a legislative body. Rescind.

repeat offender Someone convicted of a crime more than once.

replacement cost The current cost of creating a substantially equivalent structure or other asset.

replevin An action to recover possession of personal property wrongfully held or detained and damages incidental to the detention.

    "Replevin" is a possessory statutory action at law in which main issue is right of possession, and in essence partakes of action in rem rather than in personam. *Delacruz*, 221 So.2d 772 (Fla.App. 1969)

replevin bond A bond posted by the plaintiff when seeking replevin.

replevy To regain possession of personal property through replevin.

replication A plaintiff's response to the defendant's plea or answer.

reply A plaintiff's response to the defendant's counterclaim, plea, or answer.

reply brief The appellate brief filed by the appellant in response to the appellee's brief. A brief responding to an opponent's brief.

repo 1. An agreement to buy back a security. 2. See repossession.

report (rep.) 1. A written account of a court decision. 2. A volume (or set of volumes) of court opinions. Also called reports. 3. A volume (or set of volumes) of administrative decisions. 4. A formal account or descriptive statement.

reporter (rep.) 1. The person in charge of reporting the decisions of a court. 2. The person who takes down and transcribes proceedings. 3. A volume (or set of volumes) of court opinions. Also called case reports.

reporter's privilege See journalist's privilege (1).

reports See report (2).

repose See statute of repose.

repossession (repo) The taking back of property, e.g., a creditor's seizure of property bought on credit by a debtor in default.

representation 1. The act of representing or acting on behalf of another. 2. A statement of fact expressed by words or conduct, often made to induce another's conduct. 3. See also per stirpes.

> "Represent" or "representation" means actual physical attendance on behalf of a client in an agency proceeding, the writing of letters or filing of documents on behalf of a client, and personal communications made with the officers or employees of any agency on behalf of a client. F.S.A. § 112.312(22)

representative (rep.) 1. One who acts on behalf of another. 2. A legislator. 3. Serving as an example.

representative action See derivative action; class action.

reprieve A stay or postponement in carrying out a sentence.

reprimand An official declaration that an attorney's conduct was unethical. The declaration does not affect the attorney's right to practice law. A *private reprimand* is not disclosed to the public; a *public reprimand* is.

reprisal Action taken in retaliation.

reproductive rights Rights pertaining to one's reproductive and sexual life, e.g., using contraceptives, access to abortion.

republic (rep.) Government in which supreme authority lies with the voters who act through elected representatives. A republican form of government.

republication 1. Repetition of a statement already published or communicated once. 2. Steps that reestablish a revoked will, e.g., adding a codicil to it.

repudiation 1. Denial or rejection. 2. Declaring a refusal to perform.

repugnant Incompatible; irreconcilably inconsistent.

reputation The views or esteem others have of a person.

request for admission A method of pretrial discovery in which one party asks another to admit the truth of any matter that pertains to a statement or opinion of fact or the application of law to fact.

> A party may serve upon any other party a written request for the admission of the truth of any matters within the scope of rule 1.280(b) set forth in the request that relate to statements or opinions of fact or of the application of law to fact, including the genuineness of any documents described in the request. Fla.R.Civ.P. Rule 1.370(a)

request for instructions A party's request that the trial judge provide the jury with the instructions stated in the request.

request for production A method of pretrial discovery consisting of a demand that the other side make available documents and other tangible things for inspection, copying, and testing.

requirements contract A contract in which the buyer agrees to buy all of its goods and services from a seller, which agrees to fill these needs during the period of the contract.

requisition 1. A formal request or demand. 2. The seizure of property by the state.

res 1. The subject matter of a trust or will. 2. A thing or object, a status.

res adjudicata See res judicata.

resale A sale of goods after another buyer of those goods breaches its contract to buy them.

resale price maintenance A form of vertical price-fixing by which a manufacturer sets the price at which its buyers resell to others.

rescind 1. To annul or repeal. 2. To cancel a contract.

rescission A party's cancellation of a contract because of a material breach by the other party or by mutual agreement. Also spelled recision.

> To "rescind" a contract is not merely to terminate it, but to abrogate and undo it from the beginning. *Richard Bertram & Co.*, 155 So.2d 409 (Fla.App.1963)

rescript 1. A direction from a court to a clerk on how to dispose of a case. 2. The decision of the appellate court sent to the trial court.

rescue doctrine An injured rescuer can recover from the original tortfeasor who negligently caused the event that precipitated the rescue.

reservation 1. A right or interest created for the grantor in land granted to the grantee. 2. A tract of land to which a Native American tribe retains the original title or which is set aside for its use. 3. A condition through a limitation, qualification, or exception.

reserve 1. To keep back or retain. 2. A fund set aside to cover future expenses, losses, or claims.

> "Contingency reserve" means a special premium reserve which is in addition to other premium reserves required by law and which is established for the protection of policyholders against the effect of adverse economic cycles. F.S.A. § 635.011(2)

reserve banks Member banks of the Federal Reserve System.

reserve clause A contract clause giving club owners a continuing and exclusive right to the services of a professional athlete.

reserved point See point reserved.

reserved powers Powers not delegated to the federal government by the U.S. Constitution nor prohibited by it to the states are and hence reserved to the states or to the people. (U.S. Const. amend. X.)

reserve price The minimum auction price a seller will accept.

res gestae declarations Spontaneous or unfiltered statements made in the surrounding circumstances of an event (e.g., excited utterances) are sometimes admissible as exceptions to the hearsay rule.

> "Res gestae" consist of circumstances, facts, and declarations which grow out of the main fact and serve to illustrate its character, and which are so spontaneous and contemporaneous with the main fact as to exclude the idea of deliberation or fabrication. *State v. Adams*, 683 So.2d 517 (Fla.App. 2 Dist.,1996)

residence 1. Living or remaining in a particular locality for more than a transitory period but without the intent to stay there indefinitely. If this intent existed, the place would be a domicile. Sometimes, however, *residence* and *domicile* are treated as synonyms. 2. A fixed abode or house.

residency The place where one has a residence.

resident One who occupies a dwelling and has an ongoing physical presence therein. This person may or may not be a domiciliary.

> "Resident" means a person who has his or her principal place of domicile in this state for a period of more than 6 consecutive months, who has registered to vote in this state, who has made a statement of domicile pursuant to § 222.17, or who has filed for homestead tax exemption on property in this state. F.S.A. § 320.01(35)

resident agent One authorized to accept service of process for another.

resident alien A noncitizen who legally establishes a long-term residence or domicile in this country.

residual 1. Pertaining to that which is left over or what lingers. 2. Payment for reuse of a protected work.

residuary What is left over. See also residuary estate.

residuary bequest A bequest of the residuary estate.

residuary clause A clause in a will disposing of the residuary estate.

residuary devise A devise of the residuary estate.

residuary estate The remainder of an estate after all debts and claims are paid and after all specific bequests (gifts) are satisfied. Also called residuary, residue, residuum.

residuary legacy A legacy of the residuary estate.

residuary legatee The person who receives the residuary estate.

residue What is left over. See also residuary estate.

residuum What is left over. See also residuary estate.

res inter alios acta ("a thing done among others") A person cannot be affected by the words or acts of others with whom he or she is in no way connected, and for whose words or acts he or she is not legally responsible.

res ipsa loquitur ("the thing speaks for itself") An inference of the defendant's negligence arises when the event producing the harm (a) was of a kind that ordinarily does not occur in the absence of someone's negligence, (b) was caused by an agency or instrumentality within the defendant's exclusive control, and (c) was not due to any voluntary action or contribution on the part of the plaintiff.

resisting arrest Intentionally preventing a peace officer from effecting a lawful arrest.

res judicata ("a thing adjudicated") A final judgment on the merits will preclude the same parties from later relitigating the same claim and any other claim based on the same facts or transaction that could have been raised in the first suit but was not. Also called claim preclusion.

> The doctrine of "res judicata" applies to a cause of action when there is a judgment on the merits, rendered in a former suit between the parties, on the same cause of action, by a court of competent jurisdiction; such a judgment is conclusive as to every matter offered to support or defeat the claims, and also to every matter that might have been litigated and determined in that action. *Burns,* 914 So.2d 451 (Fla.App. 4 Dist.,2005)

res nova A question the courts have not yet addressed.

resolution 1. An expression of the opinion or will of an assembly or group. 2. A decision or authorization. The verb is *resolve.*

resort A place or destination to obtain redress or assistance.

RESPA See Real Estate Settlement Procedures Act.

respite A delay, e.g., a temporary suspension of the execution of a sentence, additional time to pay a debt.

respondeat superior ("let the master answer") An employer or principal is responsible (liable) for the wrongs committed by an employee or agent within the scope of employment or agency.

> Most jurisdictions, including Florida, recognize that independent of the doctrine of respondeat superior, an employer is liable for the willful tort of his employee committed against a third person if he knew or should have known that the employee was a threat to others. *Anderson Trucking Service,* 884 So.2d 1046 (Fla.App. 5 Dist.,2004)

respondent 1. The party against whom a claim, petition, or bill is filed. 2. The party against whom an appeal is brought; the appellee.

responsibility 1. Being accountable, liable, or at fault. 2. A duty.

responsible bidder An experienced, solvent, available contract bidder.

responsive Constituting an answer or response; nonevasive.

responsive pleading A pleading that replies to a prior pleading of an opponent.

rest To indicate to the court that a party has presented all of the evidence he or she intends to submit at this time.

Restatements Treatises of the American Law Institute (e.g., *Restatement (Second) of Torts*) that state the law and indicate changes in the law that the Institute would like to see implemented (*www.ali.org*).

restitution 1. Making good or giving an equivalent value for any loss, damage, or injury. 2. An equitable remedy to prevent unjust enrichment.

restraining order A court order not to do a threatened act, e.g., to harass someone, to transfer assets. Also called protection order, protective order.

restraint Restriction, prohibition; confinement.

restraint of marriage An inducement or obligation not to marry that results from a condition attached to a gift.

restraint of trade Contracts or combinations that tend to or are designed to eliminate competition, artificially set prices, or otherwise hamper a free market in commerce.

restraint on alienation A provision in an instrument (e.g., a deed) that prohibits or restricts transfers of the property by the grantee.

restricted security Stock whose sale to the public is restricted. The stock is not registered with the Securities and Exchange Commission. Also called letter stock.

restrictive covenant 1. A restriction created by covenant or agreement (e.g., in a deed) on the use of land. Also called equitable servitude. 2. See covenant not to compete.

> "Restrictive covenants" are private promises or agreements creating negative easements or equitable servitudes which are enforceable as rights arising out of contract. *Kilgore,* 676 So.2d 4 (Fla.App. 1 Dist.,1996)

restrictive indorsement An indorsement that limits or conditions the further negotiability of the instrument.

resulting trust A remedy used when a person makes a disposition of property under circumstances that raise the inference that he or she did not intend to transfer a beneficial interest to the person taking or holding the property. Also called implied trust, presumptive trust.

> Traditionally, a "resulting trust" arises where the purchase money of land is paid by one person, and the title is taken in the name of another, the party taking the title is presumed to hold it in trust for him who pays the purchase price. *International Alliance*, 902 So.2d 959 (Fla.App. 4 Dist.,2005)

resulting use An implied use remaining with the grantor in a conveyance without consideration.

retailer A business that sells goods to the ultimate consumer.

retain 1. To engage the services of or employ. 2. To hold.

retainage A portion of the contract price withheld to assure that the contractor will satisfy its obligations and complete the project.

retained earnings See earned surplus.

retainer 1. The act of hiring or engaging the services of someone, usually a professional. 2. An amount of money (or other property) a client pays a professional as a deposit or advance against future fees, costs, and expenses of providing services.

> Retainers are funds paid to guarantee the future availability of the lawyer's legal services and are earned by the lawyer upon receipt. Retainers are not funds against which future services are billed. Florida Rules of Professional Conduct, Rule 5-1.1 (Official Comment)

retaliatory eviction An eviction because the tenant has complained about the leased premises.

retirement 1. Voluntarily withdrawing from one's occupation or career. 2. Taking out of circulation.

retirement plans Pension or other benefit plans for retirement.

retraction Withdrawing a declaration, accusation, or promise. Recanting.

retraxit Voluntary withdrawal of a lawsuit that cannot be rebrought.

retreat rule Before using deadly force in self-defense against a deadly attack, there is a duty to withdraw or retreat if this is a safe alternative, unless (under the castle doctrine) the attack occurs in one's home or business.

> "Duty to retreat" rule has an exception, known as the "castle doctrine," which espouses that one is not required to retreat from one's residence, or one's "castle," before using deadly force in self-defense, so long as the deadly force is necessary to prevent death or great bodily harm. *State v. James*, 867 So.2d 414 (Fla.App. 3 Dist.,2003)

retrial A new trial of a previously tried case.

retribution Punishment that is deserved.

retroactive Applying or extending to a time prior to enactment or issuance. Also called retrospective.

retrocession Ceding back something, e.g., title, jurisdiction.

retrospective See retroactive.

return 1. A report of a court officer on what he or she did with a writ or other court instrument. 2. Profit. 3. See tax return.

return day The day on which a litigation event must occur, e.g., file an answer, appear in court.

return of service See proof of service.

rev'd See reversed.

revenue Gross income; total receipts.

revenue bond A government bond payable by public funds.

> "Revenue bonds" shall mean bonds or other obligations secured by and payable from the revenues derived from rates, fees and charges collected by a district from the users of the facilities of any water system or sewer system, or both . . . . F.S.A. § 153.52(9)

Revenue Procedure The position of the Internal Revenue Service on procedural requirements for matters before it.

Revenue Ruling (Rev. Rul.) The opinion of the Internal Revenue Service of how the tax law applies to a specific transaction.

revenue stamp A stamp used to certify that a tax has been paid.

reversal An appellate court's setting aside of a lower court decision.

reverse annuity mortgage (RAM) A mortgage on a residence in which the borrower receives periodic income and the loan is repaid when the property is sold or the borrower dies. Also called reverse mortgage.

reversed (rev'd) Overturned on appeal.

reverse discrimination Discrimination against members of a majority group, usually because of affirmative action for a minority group.

reverse mortgage See reverse annuity mortgage.

reverse stock split Calling in all outstanding shares and reissuing fewer shares with greater value.

reversible error See prejudicial error.

reversion The undisposed portion of an estate remaining in a grantor when he or she conveys less than his or her whole estate and, therefore, retains a portion of the title. The residue of the estate left with the grantor.

> A reversion is defined as the residue of an estate left in the grantor, to commence in possession after the determination of some particular estate granted out by him. It is also described as the returning of land to the grantor, or his heirs, after the grant is over. *Sorrels*, 105 So. 106 (Fla.1925)

reversionary interest The interest that a person has in the reversion of property. See reversion. Any future interest left in a transferor.

reversioner A person who is entitled to an estate in reversion.

revert To turn back; to return to.

reverter See possibility of reverter.

revest To vest again with a power or interest.

rev'g Reversing.

review 1. To examine or go over a matter again. 2. The power of a court to examine the correctness of what a lower tribunal has done. Short for judicial review (see this phrase).

Revised Statutes (R.S.)(Rev. Stat.) A collection of statutes that have been revised, rearranged, or reenacted as a whole.

revival Renewing the legal force or effectiveness of something.

revocable Susceptible of being withdrawn, canceled, or invalidated.

revocable trust A trust that the maker (settlor) can cancel or revoke.

The central characteristic of a "revocable trust" is that the settlor has the right to recall or end the trust at any time, and thereby regain absolute ownership of the trust property; in this way, a revocable trust is similar to a "Totten trust" under New York law, which is a bank account which the depositor holds "in trust for" or "as trustee for" the beneficiary. *Siegel*, 920 So.2d 89 (Fla.App. 4 Dist.,2006)

revocation Canceling, voiding, recalling, or destroying something.

revolving credit An extension of credit to customers who may use it as desired up to a specified dollar limit.

Rev. Rul. See Revenue Ruling.

Rev. Stat. See Revised Statutes.

RFP Request for production; request for proposals.

Richard Roe See John Doe.

RICO See Racketeer Influenced and Corrupt Organizations Act.

rider An amendment or addition attached to a legislative bill, insurance policy, or other document.

right 1. Morally, ethically, or legally proper. 2. A legal power, privilege, immunity, or protected interest one can claim.

right-and-wrong test See insanity (4).

right of action The right to bring a suit. A right that can be enforced.

right of common See profit á prendre.

right of election See election by spouse.

right of first refusal A right to equal the terms of another offer.

> "Right of first refusal" is right to elect to take specified property at same price and on same terms and conditions as those continued in good faith offer by third person if owner manifests willingness to accept offer; right is clearly executory right. *Steinberg*, 837 So.2d 503 (Fla.App. 3 Dist., 2003)

right of privacy See invasion of privacy.

right of redemption 1. A mortgagor's right to redeem property after it has been foreclosed. 2. See equity of redemption.

right of re-entry The estate that the grantor may acquire again upon breach of a condition under which it was granted.

right of survivorship A joint tenant's right to receive the entire estate upon the death of the other joint tenant.

right of way 1. The right to pass over the land of another. 2. The right in traffic to pass or proceed first.

> "Right-of-way" means land dedicated, deeded, used, or to be used for a street, alley, walkway, boulevard, drainage facility, access for ingress and egress, or other purpose by the public, certain designated individuals, or governing bodies. F.S.A. § 177.031(16)

right to bear arms The Second Amendment right "to keep and bear arms."

right-to-convey covenant See covenant of seisin.

right to counsel A constitutional right to an appointed attorney in some criminal and juvenile delinquency cases when the accused cannot afford private counsel.

right to die A right of a competent, terminally ill adult to refuse medical treatment.

right to travel A constitutional right to travel freely between states.

right-to-work law A state law declaring that employees are not required to join a union as a condition of receiving or retaining a job.

rigor mortis Muscular rigidity or stiffening shortly after death.

riot Three or more persons assembled together for a common purpose and disturbing the peace by acting in a violent or tumultuous manner.

riparian right The right of owners of land adjoining a waterway to make reasonable use of the water, e.g., for ingress, egress, and fishing.

ripeness doctrine A court will decline to address a claim unless the case presents definite and concrete issues, a real and substantial controversy exists, and there is a present need for adjudication. See also justiciable.

risk The danger or hazard of a loss or injury occurring.

risk capital An investment of money or property in a business, often a new venture involving high risk. See also venture capital.

risk of loss Responsibility for loss, particularly during transfer of goods. The danger of bearing this responsibility.

risk of nonpersuasion See burden of persuasion.

robbery Unlawfully taking property from the person of another (or in his or her presence) by the use of violence or threats.

> "Robbery" means the taking of money or other property which may be the subject of larceny from the person or custody of another, with intent to either permanently or temporarily deprive the person or the owner of the money or other property, when in the course of the taking there is the use of force, violence, assault, or putting in fear. F.S.A. § 812.13(1)

Robert's Rules of Order Rules for conducting meetings. A parliamentary manual.

rogatory letters See letter rogatory.

roll 1. The record of official proceedings. 2. An official list.

rollover 1. Refinancing or renewing a short-term loan. 2. Reinvesting funds in a plan that qualifies for the same tax treatment.

Roman Law The legal system and laws of ancient Rome that is the foundation of civil law in some European countries.

root of title The recorded conveyance that begins a chain-of-title search on specific real property.

ROR Release on own recognizance. See personal recognizance.

Roth IRA An individual retirement account with nondeductible contributions but tax-free distributions after age $59\frac{1}{2}$.

round lot The unit of trading securities, e.g., 100 shares.

royalty 1. Payment for each use of a work protected by copyright or patent. 2. Payment for the right to extract natural resources.

R.S. See Revised Statutes.

rubric 1. The title of a statute. 2. A rule. 3. A category. 4. A preface.

rule 1. An established standard, guide, or regulation. 2. A court procedure. 3. The controlling authority. 4. To decide a point of law.

rule against accumulations Limits on a trust's accumulation of income.

rule against perpetuities No interest is valid unless it must vest, if at all, within 21 years (plus a period of gestation) after the death of some life or lives in being (i.e., alive) at the time the interest was created.

> "Rule against perpetuities" requires that a contingent future interest vest on or before expiration of a life or lives in being plus 21 years plus period of gestation. *In re McCune's Estate*, 214 So.2d 56 (Fla.App. 1968). See Florida Uniform Statutory Rule Against Perpetuities, F.S.A. § 689.225.

rule in Shelley's case When in the deed or other instrument an estate of freehold is given to a person and a remainder to his or her heirs in fee or in tail, that person takes the entire estate—a fee simple absolute.

rule in Wild's case If X devises land to Y and Y's children, the devise is a fee tail (if Y has no children at the time of the devise) but a joint tenancy (if Y has children at that time).

rulemaking The process and power of an administrative agency to make rules and regulations.

rule nisi See decree nisi.

rule of completeness A party may introduce the whole of a statement if any part is introduced by the opposing party.

rule of four The U.S. Supreme Court will accept a case on certiorari if at least four justices vote to do so.

rule of law 1. A legal principle or ruling. 2. Supremacy of law.

rule of lenity When there is ambiguity in a criminal statute, particularly as to punishment, doubts are resolved in favor of the defendant.

> The "rule of lenity" provides that when the language of a criminal sentencing statute is ambiguous, the statute must be construed favorably to the accused. West's F.S.A. § 775.021. *Walker*, 880 So.2d 1262 (Fla.App. 2 Dist.,2004)

rule of reason 1. In antitrust cases, the issue is whether the restraint's anticompetitive effects substantially outweigh the procompetitive effects for which the restraint is reasonably necessary. 2. A requirement to consider pertinent evidence and reasonable alternatives in decision making.

rules committee A legislative committee establishing agendas and procedures for considering proposed legislation.

rules of professional conduct See Model Rules of Professional Conduct.

ruling A judicial or administrative decision.

run 1. To apply or be effective. 2. To expire because of elapsed time. 3. To accompany or go with a conveyance.

runaway shop An employer who relocates or transfers work for antiunion reasons.

runner 1. One who solicits business, especially accident cases. 2. An employee who delivers and files papers.

running account A continuous record kept to show all the transactions (charges and payments) between a debtor and creditor.

running with the land See covenant running with the land.

S

sabotage Willful destruction of property or interference with normal operations of a government or employer.

safe harbor Protection from liability if acting in good faith.

said Before mentioned; aforementioned.

sailor's will See military will.

salable Fit to be offered for sale. Merchantable.

salary Compensation for services paid at regular intervals.

sale The transfer of title to property for a consideration or price. A contract for this transfer.

> Sale means any transfer, exchange or barter in any manner, or by any means whatever. Retail sale or sale at retail means a sale to a consumer or to any person for any purpose other than resale. F.S.A. § 210.01(3)&(4)

sale and leaseback See leaseback.

sale by sample A sale of goods in quantity or bulk with the understanding that they will conform in quality with a sample.

sale in gross A sale of land in which the boundaries are identified but the quantity of land is unspecified or deemed to be immaterial.

sale on approval A conditional sale that is absolute only if the buyer is satisfied with the goods, whether or not they are defective.

sale or return A sale to a merchant buyer who can return any unsold goods (even if not defective) if they were received for resale.

sales tax A tax on the sale of goods and services, computed as a percentage of the purchase price.

salvage 1. Property saved or remaining after a casualty. 2. Rescue of assets from loss. 3. Payment for saving a ship or its cargo.

salvage value An asset's value after its useful life for the owner has ended.

same evidence test When the same acts violate two distinct statutory provisions, the double-jeopardy test of whether there are two offenses or one is whether each provision requires proof of a fact the other does not.

sanction 1. A penalty for a violation. 2. Approval or authorization.

S&L See savings and loan association.

sane Of sound mind; able to distinguish right from wrong.

> All persons are presumed to be sane. . . . Insanity is established when: (a) The defendant had a mental infirmity, disease, or defect; and (b) Because of this condition, the defendant: 1. Did not know what he or she was doing or its consequences; or 2. Although the defendant knew what he or she was doing and its consequences, the defendant did not know that what he or she was doing was wrong. Mental infirmity, disease, or defect does not constitute a defense of insanity except as provided in this subsection. F.S.A. § 775.027

sanitary Pertaining to health and hygiene.

sanity The condition of having a sound mind.

sanity hearing A hearing to determine fitness to stand trial or whether institutionalization is needed.

satisfaction The discharge or performance of a legal obligation.

> Satisfaction of lien means full payment of a debt or release of a debtor from a lien by the lienholder. F.S.A. § 319.001(10)

satisfaction contract A contract in which the stated standard of performance is the satisfaction of one of the parties (e.g., a contract giving an employer sole discretion to decide if an employee should be terminated for unacceptable work).

satisfaction of judgment 1. Full payment or compliance with a judgment. 2. A document so stating.

satisfaction piece A statement by the parties that the obligation between them has been paid or satisfied.

save harmless See hold harmless.

saving clause 1. A clause in a statute that preserves certain rights, remedies, privileges, or claims. 2. See severability clause. 3. See saving-to-suitors clause.

savings and loan association (S&L) A financial institution that specializes in making mortgage loans for private homes.

saving-to-suitors clause A statutory clause allowing certain admiralty claims to be brought in nonadmiralty courts. (28 USC § 1333) Also called saving clause.

savings bank trust See Totten trust.

savings bond A U.S. government bond that cannot be traded.

S.B. See senate bill.

scab A worker who crosses a picket line to work or otherwise acts in disregard of positions or demands of a union. Also called strikebreaker.

scalper One who resells something at an inflated price for a quick profit.

scandalous matter Irrelevant matter in a pleading that casts a derogatory light on someone's moral character or uses repulsive language.

scènes à faire General themes that cannot be copyrighted.

schedule A written list or plan. An inventory.

scheduled property A list of properties with their values.

scheme A plan of action, often involving deception.

scienter 1. Intent to deceive or mislead. 2. Knowingly done.
> Scienter is defined as knowingly, to signify guilty knowledge, and is an integral element of making false promises or committing a breach of trust. *Brod*, 188 So.2d 575 (Fla.App. 1966)

sci. fa. See scire facias.

scilicet That is to say. See ss.

scintilla A minute amount; a trace.

scire facias (sci. fa.) 1. A writ ordering one to appear on a matter of record and show cause why another should not be able to take advantage of that record. 2. The procedure by which a lienholder prosecutes a lien to judgment.
> Scire facias is not a new action, but only a step in the original cause of a remedial nature to effectuate the lien already in existence. *B. A. Lott, Inc.*, 14 So.2d 667 (Fla.1943)

scope of authority An agent's express or implied authorization to act for the principal.

scope of employment That which is foreseeably done by an employee for an employer under the latter's specific or general control.

S corporation A corporation whose shareholders are taxed on the income of the corporation. Also called subchapter S corporation.

screened The isolation of a lawyer, paralegal, or other employee from any participation in a matter through the timely imposition of procedures within a firm that are reasonably adequate under the circumstances to protect information that the isolated person is obligated to protect under law. Florida Rules of Professional Conduct, Preamble.

scrip 1. A substitute for money. 2. A document entitling one to a benefit. 3. A document representing a fraction of a share.

scrip dividend A dividend in the form of the right to receive future issues of stock.

script 1. Handwriting. 2. The original document.

scrivener One who prepares documents. A professional copyist or drafter.

seal An impression or sign to attest the execution of an instrument or to authenticate the document.

sealed bid A bid that is not revealed until all bids are submitted.

sealed records Publicly filed documents that are kept confidential.

sealed verdict A jury verdict not yet officially given to the court.

seaman's will See military will.

search An examination by police of private areas (e.g., one's person, premises, or vehicle) in an attempt to discover evidence of a crime.
> In order to be classified as a search, law enforcement conduct must violate a constitutionally protected reasonable expectation of privacy. *State v. Rabb*, 920 So.2d 1175 (Fla.App. 4 Dist.,2006)

search and seizure See unreasonable search.

search warrant A court order allowing a law enforcement officer to search designated areas and to seize evidence of crime found there.

seasonable Within the agreed-upon time; timely; at a reasonable time.

seaworthy Properly constructed and equipped for a sea voyage.

SEC See Securities and Exchange Commission.

secession The act of withdrawing.

secondary Subordinate; inferior.

secondary authority Any nonlaw a court can rely on in its decision. Writings that describe or explain, but do not constitute, the law.

secondary boycott A boycott of customers or suppliers with whom the union has no labor dispute to induce them to stop dealing with a business with whom the union does have a labor dispute. The boycott can include picketing.
> When the coercion extends to customers of the person or persons boycotted and attempts to coerce them on pain of being boycotted themselves unless they refrain from dealing with the person boycotted, it is called a secondary boycott. *Paramount Enterprises*, 140 So. 328 (Fla.1932)

secondary easement An incident to an easement that allows those things necessary to the full enjoyment of the easement.

secondary evidence Evidence that is not the stronger or best evidence.

secondary liability Liability that applies only if the wronged party cannot obtain satisfaction from the person with primary liability.

secondary market A market for previously available goods or services.

secondary meaning Public awareness that a common or descriptive name or symbol identifies the source of a particular product or service.

secondary picketing See secondary boycott.

second-degree murder The unlawful taking of human life without premeditation or other facts that make the crime first-degree murder.

second-look See wait and see.

second mortgage A mortgage with a ranking in priority that is immediately below a first mortgage on the same property.

secretary The corporate officer in charge of keeping official records.

secret partner A partner whose identity is not known by the public.

secta 1. Followers. 2. A lawsuit.

section 1. A subdivision of a law or document. 2. A square mile area.

secundum 1. Second. 2. According to.

secured Backed by collateral, a mortgage, or other security.

secured creditor; secured party A creditor who can reach collateral of the debtor if the latter fails to pay the debt.

> "Secured party" means: 1. A person in whose favor a security interest is created or provided for under a security agreement, whether or not any obligation to be secured is outstanding; . . . 4. A person to whom accounts, chattel paper, payment intangibles, or promissory notes have been sold; . . . F.S.A. § 679.1021(1)(sss)

secured transaction A contract in which the seller or lender is a secured creditor.

securities See security (2).

Securities and Exchange Commission (SEC) The federal agency that regulates the issuance and trading of securities in order to protect investors and maintain fair and orderly markets (*www.sec.gov*).

securities broker One in the business of buying and selling securities for others.

securitize To convert an asset into a security offered for sale.

security 1. Collateral that guarantees a debt or other obligation. 2. A financial instrument that is evidence of a debt interest (e.g., a bond), an ownership/equity interest, (e.g., a stock) or other specially defined rights (e.g., a futures contract). 3. Surety. 4. The state of being secure.

security agreement An agreement that creates or provides for a security interest.

security deposit See deposit (3).

security interest A property interest that secures a payment or the performance of an obligation.

> "Security interest" means an interest in personal property or fixtures which secures payment or performance of an obligation. The term also includes any interest of a consignor and a buyer of accounts, chattel paper, a payment intangible, or a promissory note in a transaction which is subject to chapter 679. . . . F.S.A. § 671.201(37)

sedition Communicating, agreeing to, or advocating lawlessness, treason, commotions, or revolt against legitimate authority.

seditious libel Libelous statements designed to incite sedition.

seduction Wrongfully inducing another, without the use of force, to engage in sexual relations.

segregation The unconstitutional separation of people based on categories such as race, religion, or nationality.

seise To hold in fee simple.

seisin or **seizin** Possession of land under a claim of freehold estate.

seize To take possession forcibly.

seizure Taking possession of person or property.

select committee A committee set up for a limited or special task.

selective enforcement Enforcing the law primarily against a member of certain groups or classes of people, often arbitrarily.

selective incorporation The process of making only some of the Bill of Rights applicable to the states through the Fourteenth Amendment. Total incorporation makes all of them applicable.

Selective Service System A federal agency in charge of military registration and, if needed, a draft (*www.sss.gov*).

selectman An elected municipal officer in some towns.

self-authenticating Not needing extrinsic proof of authenticity.

self-dealing Acting to benefit oneself when one should be acting in the interest of another to whom a fiduciary duty is owed.

self-defense The use of force to repel threatened danger to one's person or property.

> A person is justified in the use of force, except deadly force, against another when and to the extent that he reasonably believes that such conduct is necessary to defend himself or another against such other's imminent use of unlawful force. However, he is justified in the use of deadly force only if he reasonably believes that such force is necessary to prevent imminent death or great bodily harm to himself or another or to prevent the imminent commission of a forcible felony. F.S.A. § 776.012. *Adams*, 727 So.2d 997 (Fla.App. 2 Dist.,1999)

self-employment tax Social security tax on the self-employed.

self-executing Immediately or automatically having legal effect.

self-help Acting to redress a wrong without using the courts.

self-incrimination Acts or declarations by which one implicates oneself in a crime; exposing oneself to criminal prosecution.

self-insurance Funds set aside by a business to cover any loss.

> For the purposes of §§ 627.551 and 627.651, self-insurance includes any plan, fund, or program . . . for the purpose of providing for employees or their beneficiaries through such individual, partnership, association, corporation, trustee, governmental unit, employer, or employee organization, or any other group, benefits in the event of sickness, accident, disability, or death. F.S.A. § 624.031

self-proving Not requiring proof outside of the documents themselves.

self-serving declaration An out-of-court statement benefiting the person making it.

sell To transfer an asset by sale.

seller One who sells enters a contract to sell.

semble It would appear.

senate The upper chamber of a two-house (bicameral) legislature.

senate bill (S.B.)(S.) A bill pending or before passage in the Senate.

senior Higher in age, rank, preference, or priority.

senior interest An interest that is higher in precedence or priority.

seniority Greater rights than others based on length of service.

senior judge A judge with the longest tenure or who is semi-retired.

senior lien A lien on property that has priority over other liens.

senior mortgage A mortgage that has priority over other mortgages.

sentence Punishment imposed by the court on one convicted of a crime.

Under the sentencing guidelines, the term "sentence" refers to the term of incarceration and not any term of probation. *Sullivan*, 801 So.2d 185 (Fla.App. 5 Dist.,2001)

SEP See simplified employee pension plan.

separability clause See severability clause.

separable Capable of being separated.

separable controversy A dispute that is part of the entire controversy, yet by its nature is independent and can be severed from the whole.

separate Distinct, not joined.

separate but equal Segregated with equal opportunities and facilities.

separate maintenance Support by one spouse to another while separated.

separate property Property acquired by one spouse alone (a) before marriage, (b) during marriage by gift, will, or intestate succession, or (c) during marriage but after separating from the other spouse.

separate trial An individual (separate) trial of one of the defendants jointly accused of a crime or of one of the issues in any case.

separation Living separately while still married.

separation agreement A contract between spouses who have separated or who are about to separate in which the terms of their separation (e.g., child custody, property division) are spelled out.

separation of powers The division of government into judicial, legislative, and executive branches with the requirement that each branch refrain from encroaching on the authority of the other two.

sequester 1. To separate or isolate a jury or witness. 2. To seize or take and hold funds or other property. Sometimes called sequestrate.

sequestrate See sequester.

sequestrator One who carries out an order or writ of sequestration.

sergeant at arms An officer who keeps order in a court or legislature.

serial bonds A number of bonds issued at the same time but with different maturity dates.

serial note A promissory note payable in regular installments. Also called installment note.

seriatim One by one in a series; one following after another.

series bonds Groups of bonds usually issued at different times and with different maturity dates but under the same indenture.

serious bodily harm See great bodily injury.

servant One employed to perform service, whose performance is controlled by or subject to the control of the master or employer.

[A] servant [is] a species of agent . . . the servant merely acts for the principal usually according to his direction without discretion. *Lynch*, 31 So.2d 268 (Fla 1947).

serve To deliver a legal notice or process.

service 1. Delivery of a legal notice or process. 2. Tasks performed for others. 3. To pay interest on.

service by publication Publishing a notice in a newspaper or other media as service of process upon an absent or nonresident defendant.

service charge An added cost or fee for administration or handling.

servicemark (SM) See mark (1).

service of process A formal delivery of notice to a defendant that a suit has been initiated to which he or she must respond.

servient estate The track of land on which an easement is imposed or burdened. Also called servient tenement.

For purposes of easements, a "dominant estate" is the land benefitted by the easement, while the "servient estate" is the land burdened by the easement. *Tyler*, 821 So.2d 1121 (Fla.App. 4 Dist.,2002)

servitude 1. An easement or similar right to use another's land. 2. The condition of forced labor or slavery.

session 1. A continuous sitting of a court, legislature, council, etc. 2. Any time in the day during which such a body sits.

session laws (S.L.; sess.) Uncodified statutes enacted by a legislature during a session, printed chronologically.

set aside 1. To vacate a judgment, order, etc. 2. Set-aside: Something reserved for a special reason.

setback The distance that buildings are set back from property lines.

setoff 1. A defendant's claim against the plaintiff that is independent of the plaintiff's claim. 2. A debtor's right to reduce a debt by what the creditor owes the debtor.

settlement 1. An agreement resolving a dispute without full litigation. 2. Payment or satisfactory adjustment of an account. 3. Distributing the assets and paying the debts of an estate. 4. See closing.

As used in this section, the term "settlement" means an agreement entered into between a manufacturer and consumer that occurs after a dispute is submitted to a procedure or program or is approved for arbitration before the board. F.S.A. § 681.114(3)

settlement option Choices available to pay life insurance benefits.

settlor One who makes a settlement of property (e.g., one who creates a trust). Also called trustor.

severability clause A clause in a statute or contract providing that if parts of it are declared invalid, the remaining parts shall continue to be effective. Also called saving clause, separability clause.

several 1. A few. 2. Distinct or separate, e.g., a person's several liability is distinct from (and can be enforced independently of) someone else's liability.

severally Apart from others, separately.

severalty The condition of being separate or distinct.

severance 1. Separating claims or parties. 2. Removing; cutting off.

severance tax A tax on natural resources removed from the land.

sewer service Falsely claiming to have served process.

sex discrimination Discrimination that is gender-based.

sexual abuse; sexual assault Rape or other unlawful sexual contact with another.

sexual harassment Unwelcome conduct of a sexual nature on the job.

sexual predator A person with a propensity to commit sexual assault.

shadow jurors Persons hired by one side to observe a trial as members of the general audience and, as the trial progresses, to give feedback to a jury consultant hired by the attorney of one of the parties, who will use the feedback to assess strategy for the remainder of the trial.

shall 1. Is required to, must. 2. Should. 3. May.

sham Counterfeit, a hoax; frivolous, without substance.

> "Sham pleading" is one that while in good form is false in fact, or one good in form but false in fact and not pleaded in good faith. F.S.A. RCP Rule 1.150. *St. John Medical Plans*, 711 So.2d 1329 (Fla.App. 3 Dist.,1998)

sham transaction Conduct with no business purpose other than tax avoidance.

share 1. The part or portion that you contribute or own. 2. An ownership interest in a corporation. A unit of stock.

share and share alike To divide equally.

shareholder One who owns a share in a corporation. Also called stockholder.

shareholder's derivative action See derivative action (1).

shelf registration Registration with the Securities and Exchange Commission involving a delayed stock sale.

shell corporation A corporation with no assets or active business.

Shelley's Case See rule in Shelley's case.

shelter An investment or other device to reduce or defer taxes.

shepardize To use *Shepard's Citations* to find data on the history and currentness of cases, statutes, and other legal materials. See also citator.

sheriff's deed A deed given a buyer at a sheriff's sale.

sheriff's sale A forced sale based on a court order.

shield law 1. A law to protect journalists from being required to divulge confidential sources. 2. See rape shield law.

shifting income Transferring income to someone in a lower tax bracket.

shifting the burden Transferring the burden of proof (or the burden to produce evidence) from one party to another during a trial.

shipment contract A sale in which the risk of loss passes to the buyer when the seller duly delivers the goods to the carrier.

> Contract for sale of goods which stipulates place where goods sold are to be sent by carrier but contains no explicit provisions allocating risk of loss while the goods are in possession of carrier and no delivery terms such as "F.O.B." place of destination, without more, constitutes a "shipment contract" wherein risk of loss passes to buyer when seller duly delivers the goods to the carrier under a reasonable contract of carriage for shipment to the buyer. F.S.1977, §§ 672.319(1)(b), 672.503 comment, 672.504, 672.509(1). *Pestana*, 367 So.2d 1096 (Fla.App., 1979)

shop A place of business.

shop-book rule A rule allowing regularly kept original business records into evidence by as an exception to the hearsay rule.

shoplifting The theft of goods displayed for sale.

shop steward A union official who helps enforce the union contract.

short sale A sale of a security the seller does not own that is made by the delivery of a security borrowed by, or for the account of, the seller.

short summons A summons with a shorter-than-usual response time.

short-swing profit Profit earned on stock by a corporate insider within six months of purchase or sale.

short-term capital gain Gain from the sale or exchange of a capital asset held for less than a year or other designated short term.

show To establish or prove.

show cause order A court order to appear and explain why the court should not take a proposed action to provide relief.

shower One who takes the jury to a scene involved in the case.

showup See lineup.

shut-in royalty A payment by a lessee to continue holding a functioning well that is not being currently utilized due to a weak oil or gas market.

shyster Slang for an unscrupulous attorney.

sic A signal alerting the reader that you are quoting exactly, including the error in the quote.

sidebar conference See bench conference.

sight draft A draft payable on demand when shown.

sign 1. To affix one's signature (or mark substitute). 2. To indicate agreement.

signatory The person or nation signing a document.

signature One's name written by oneself. A word, mark, or symbol indicating identity or intended to authenticate a document.

> "Signature" means the name or mark of a person as written by that person. When an "X" is used as a signature on a document, the document must include the printed names, signatures, and addresses of two persons who witnessed the signing, or the document must be notarized. F.S.A. § 121.021(61)

signing statement An announcement by the president upon signing a bill into law that states the president's objections, interpretation, or intention in implementing the law.

silent partner See dormant partner.

silent witness theory Evidence such as photographs may be admitted without testimony of a witness if there is sufficient proof of the reliability of the process that produced the evidence.

silver platter doctrine The former rule that evidence obtained illegally by state police is admissible in federal court if no federal officer participated in the violation of the defendant's rights.

> Prior to the decision in *Elkins v. United States*, 364 U.S. 206 (1960), law enforcement officers could receive under the 'silver platter' doctrine evidence illegally seized by state police without the knowledge or cooperation of the federal authorities. *Bernovich*, 272 So.2d 505 (Fla. 1973)

simple 1. Not aggravated. 2. Uncomplicated. 3. Not under seal.

simple assault; simple battery An assault or battery not accompanied by aggravating circumstances.

> Simple battery is defined in section 784.03(1)(a), Florida Statutes (1999), as having occurred when a person: "1. [a]ctually and intentionally touches or strikes another person against the will of the other; or 2.[i]ntentionally causes

bodily harm to another person." *Beard*, 842 So.2d 174 (Fla.App. 2 Dist.,2003)

simple interest Interest on the principal only, not on any interest earned on the principal.

simple negligence See ordinary negligence.

simple trust 1. A trust requiring the distribution of all trust income to the beneficiaries. 2. See passive trust.

simpliciter Simply; unconditionally.

simplified employee pension plan (SEP) An employee benefit plan consisting of an annuity or an individual retirement account.

simulated sale A sham sale in which no consideration was exchanged.

Simultaneous Death Act A statute providing that when two people die together but without evidence of who died first, the property of each may be disposed of as if each survived the other.

> Unless a contrary intention appears in the governing instrument: (1) When title to property or its devolution depends on priority of death and there is insufficient evidence that the persons have died otherwise than simultaneously, the property of each person shall be disposed of as if that person survived. . . . F.S.A. § 732.601

sine die ("without day") With no day being designated.

sine prole (s.p.) Without issue.

sine qua non An essential condition.

single-juror charge A jury instruction stating that if a single juror is not reasonably satisfied with the plaintiff's evidence, the jury cannot find for the plaintiff.

single-publication rule Only one defamation cause of action exists for the same communication, even if it was heard or read by many.

sinking fund Regular deposits and interest accrued thereon set aside to pay long-term debts.

SIPC Securities Investor Protection Corporation (*www.sipc.org*).

sister corporations Corporations controlled by the same shareholders.

sistren Sisters. Female colleagues.

sit 1. To hold a session. 2. To occupy an office.

sit-down strike Employees' refusal to work while at the work site.

sitting In session.

situs Position. The place where a thing happened or is located.

S.J.D. Doctor of Juridical Science.

skip person A recipient of assets in a generation-skipping transfer.

skiptracing Efforts to locate persons (e.g., debtors) or assets.

S.L. See session laws.

slander Defamation that is oral or gestured.

> "Slander" is a spoken or oral defamation of another which is published to others and which tends to damage that person's reputation, ability to conduct that person's business or profession, and which holds that person up to disgrace and humiliation. *Scott*, 907 So.2d 662 (Fla.App. 5 Dist.,2005)

slander of goods; slander of title See disparagement.

slander per se Slander that accuses a person of unchastity or sexual misconduct, of committing a crime of moral

turpitude, of engaging in business or professional misconduct, or of having a loathsome disease.

SLAPP See Strategic Lawsuit Against Public Participation.

slavery A status or system of enforced labor and bondage.

sleeping partner See dormant partner.

slight care More than the absence of care but less than ordinary care.

> "Slight care" is the equivalent of "gross negligence." F.S.A. § 320.59. *Cadore*, 91 So.2d 806 (Fla.1957)

slight negligence The failure to exercise great care.

slip law One act of the legislature printed in a single pamphlet.

slip opinion The first printing of a single court opinion.

slowdown Causing production to decrease as a union or labor protest.

SM Servicemark. See mark (1).

small-claims court A court that uses more informal procedures to resolve smaller claims—those under a designated amount.

small loan acts Laws on interest-rate limits for small consumer loans.

smart money 1. See punitive damages. 2. Funds of a shrewd investor.

smuggle To import or export goods illegally without paying duties.

social guest One invited to enter or remain on another's property to enjoy private hospitality, not for a business purpose.

society 1. An association of persons united for a common purpose. 2. Companionship and love among family members.

sodomy Oral sex or anal intercourse between humans, or between humans and animals. Also called unnatural offense.

soil bank A federal program paying farmers not to grow certain crops.

soldier's will See military will.

sole actor doctrine The knowledge of an agent is treated as the knowledge of his or her principal.

sole custody Only one parent makes all child-rearing decisions.

sole proprietorship A form of business that does not have a separate legal identity apart from the one person who owns all assets and assumes all debts and liabilities.

solicitation 1. A request for something. 2. Enticing or urging someone to commit a crime. 3. An appeal or request for clients or business.

> Soliciting patients, either personally or through an agent, through the use of fraud, intimidation, undue influence, or a form of overreaching or vexatious conduct. A "solicitation" is any communication which directly or implicitly requests an immediate oral response from the recipient. F.S.A. § 462.14(1)(m)

solicitor 1. One who solicits. 2. A lawyer for a city or government agency. 3. A British lawyer who prepares documents and gives clients legal advice but (unlike a barrister) does not do extensive trial work.

solicitor general A high-ranking government litigator.

solvent Able to meet one's financial obligations.

Son of Sam law A law against criminals earning income by selling the story of their crime to the media.

sound 1. Healthy; able. 2. Marketable. 3. Well-founded. 4. To be actionable.

source of law The authority for court opinions or statutes, e.g., constitutions, other court opinions and statutes, and custom.

sovereign 1. Having supreme power. 2. The ruler or head of state.

sovereign immunity The sovereign (i.e., the state) cannot be sued in its courts without its consent. Also called governmental immunity.

> Section 768.28(9), Florida Statutes (1985), defines sovereign immunity as follows: No officer, employee, or agent of the state or of any of its subdivisions shall be held personally liable in tort or named as a party defendant in any action for any injury or damage suffered as a result of any act, event, or omission of action in the scope of her or his employment or function, unless such officer, employee, or agent acted in bad faith or with malicious purpose or in a manner exhibiting wanton and willful disregard of human rights, safety, or property. . . . *Williams*, 619 So.2d 983 (Fla.App. 5 Dist.,1993)

sovereignty Supreme political authority.

s.p. 1. Same principle. 2. See sine prole.

speaker The chairperson or presiding officer of an assembly.

speaking demurrer A demurrer that alleges facts that are not in the pleadings. See also demurrer.

speaking motion Saying more than called for by the motion or pleading.

special act See private law (2).

special administrator An estate administrator with limited duties.

special agent An agent delegated to do a specific act.

special appearance Appearing solely to challenge the court's jurisdiction.

special assessment An additional tax on land that benefits from a public improvement.

special contract 1. An express contract with explicit terms. 2. See contract under seal.

special counsel An attorney hired by the government for a particular matter.

special court-martial An intermediate level of court-martial.

special damages Actual and provable economic losses, e.g., lost wages.

> "Special damages" are not likely to occur in usual course of events, but may reasonably be supposed to have been in contemplation of parties at time they made contract. Special damages consist of items of loss which are peculiar to party against whom breach was committed and would not be expected to occur regularly to others in similar circumstances. *Hardwick Properties*, 711 So.2d 35 (Fla.App. 1 Dist.,1998)

special demurrer A challenge to the form of a pleading.

special deposit A deposit in a bank made for safekeeping or for some special application or purpose.

special exception 1. A challenge to the form of a claim. 2. See conditional use.

special-facts rule A duty of disclosure exists when special circumstances make it inequitable for a corporate director or officer to withhold information from a stockholder.

special finding A finding of essential facts to support a judgment.

special grand jury A grand jury called for a limited or special task.

special guaranty A guarantee enforceable only by designated persons.

> "General guaranty" is one addressed to all persons generally and may generally be enforced by anyone to whom it is presented who acts upon it, while "special guaranty" is one addressed to a particular entity, and under it ordinarily only named or specifically described promisee acquires rights. *New Holland*, 579 So.2d 215 (Fla.App. 5 Dist.,1991)

special indorsement An indorsement that specifies the person to whom the instrument is payable or to whom the goods are to be delivered.

special interrogatory A separate question a jury is asked to answer.

specialist One possessing special expertise, often certified as such.

special jurisdiction See limited jurisdiction.

special jury A jury chosen for its special expertise or for a case of special importance. Also called struck jury.

special law See private law (2).

special lien See particular lien.

special master See master (2).

special meeting A nonregular meeting called for a special purpose.

special power of appointment See limited power of appointment.

special power of attorney A power of attorney with limited authority.

special prosecutor An attorney appointed to conduct a criminal investigation of a matter.

special session See extraordinary session.

special trust A trust whose trustee has management duties other than merely giving trust assets to beneficiaries. Also called active trust.

specialty See contract under seal.

special use See conditional use.

special use valuation Real property valued on its actual current use rather than on its best possible use.

special verdict A jury's fact findings on fact questions given to it by the judge, who then states the legal consequences of the findings.

> "Special verdict," in contrast to "general verdict," is one in which civil jury makes separate findings on basis of evidence presented, referring the decision on the facts found as a matter of law to the court. *Turner*, 673 So.2d 532 (Fla.App. 1 Dist.,1996)

special warranty deed 1. A deed in which the grantor warrants title only against those claiming by or under the grantor. 2. A quitclaim deed.

specie 1. See in specie. 2. Coined money.

specification 1. A list of contract requirements or details. 2. A statement of charges. 3. Invention details in a patent application.

specific bequest A gift of specific or unique property in a will.

specific denial A denial of particular allegations in a claim.

specific devise A devise of a specific property.

specific intent Desiring (intending) the precise criminal consequences that follow one's act.

specific legacy A gift of specific or unique property in a will.

specific performance An equitable remedy directing the performance of a contract according to the precise terms agreed upon by the parties.

spectograph A machine used for voiceprint analysis.

speculation 1. Seeking profits through investments that can be risky. 2. Theorizing in the absence of sufficient evidence and knowledge.

speculative damages Damages that are not reasonably certain; damages that are too conjectural to be awarded.

speech Spoken communication.

Speech or Debate Clause The clause in the U.S Constitution (Art. I, § 6, cl. 1) giving members of Congress immunity for what they say during their legislative work.

speedy trial A trial that begins promptly after reasonable preparation by the prosecution and is conducted with reasonable dispatch. "In all criminal prosecutions, the accused shall enjoy the right to a speedy and public trial. . . ." U.S. Const. amend. VI.

spendthrift One who spends money irresponsibly.

spendthrift trust A trust whose assets are protected against the beneficiary's improvidence and are beyond the reach of his or her creditors.

> A "spendthrift trust" is one created to provide a fund for maintenance of another, and at the same time securing it against the other's improvidence or incapacity for self-protection. *Waterbury*, 32 So.2d 603 (Fla.1947)

spin-off A new and independent corporation that was once part of another corporation whose shareholders will own the new corporation.

spirit of the law The underlying meaning or purpose of the law.

split See stock split.

split gift A gift from a spouse to a nonspouse that is treated as having been given one-half by each spouse.

split-off A new corporation formed by an existing corporation, giving shares of the new corporation to the existing corporation's stockholders in exchange for some of their shares in the existing corporation.

split sentence A sentence served in part in an institution and suspended in part or served on probation for the remainder.

> A "true split sentence" consists of a total period of confinement with a portion of the confinement period suspended and the defendant placed on probation for that suspended portion. *Johnson*, 927 So.2d 251 (Fla.App. 2 Dist.,2006)

splitting a cause of action Suing on only part of a cause of action now and on another part later.

split-up Dividing a corporation into two or more new corporations.

spoliation Intentionally destroying, altering, or concealing evidence.

sponsor 1. One who makes a promise or gives security for another. 2. A legislator who proposes a bill.

spontaneous declaration An out-of-court statement or utterance (made with little time to reflect or fabricate) about a perceived event. An exception to the hearsay rule.

> A spontaneous declaration or excited utterance has been held to be a "firmly rooted" hearsay exception. *State v. Frazier*, 753 So.2d 644 (Fla.App. 5 Dist.,2000)

spot zoning Singling out a lot or small area for different zoning treatment than similar surrounding land.

spousal abuse Physical, sexual, or emotional abuse of one's spouse.

spousal privilege See marital communications privilege.

spousal support See alimony.

spread The difference between two amounts, e.g., the buyer's bid price and the seller's asked price for a security.

springing use A use that is dependent or contingent on a future event.

sprinkling trust A trust that spreads income among different beneficiaries at the discretion of the trustee.

spurious Counterfeit or synthetic; false.

squatter One who settles on land without legal title or authority.

squeeze-out An attempt to eliminate or weaken the interest of an owner, e.g., a minority shareholder.

ss. 1. Sections. 2. Sometimes used to abbreviate scilicet, meaning to wit.

SSI See Supplemental Security Income.

stake 1. A deposit to be held until its ownership is resolved. 2. A land boundary marker. 3. A bet. 4. An interest in a business.

stakeholder See interpleader.

stale No longer effective due to the passage of time.

stalking Repeatedly following or harassing someone, who is thereby placed in reasonable fear of harm.

> Cyberstalk means to engage in a course of conduct to communicate, or to cause to be communicated, words, images, or language by or through the use of electronic mail or electronic communication, directed at a specific person, causing substantial emotional distress to that person and serving no legitimate purpose. F.S.A. § 784.048(d)

stamp tax The cost of stamps affixed to legal documents such as deeds.

stand See witness stand.

standard 1. A yardstick or criterion. 2. Customary.

standard deduction A fixed deduction from adjusted gross income, used by taxpayers who do not itemize their deductions.

standard mortgage clause A mortgage clause stating that the interest of the mortgagee will not be invalidated by specified acts of the mortgagor.

standard of care The degree of care the law requires in a particular case, e.g., reasonable care in a negligence case.

standard of need A level of need qualifying one for public benefits.

standard of proof The degree to which the evidence of something must be convincing before a fact finder can accept it as true.

standing A person's right to seek relief from a court.

standing committee An ongoing committee.

standing mute A defendant refusing to answer or plead to the charge.

standing orders Rules adopted by a court governing practice before it.

Star Chamber 1. An early English court known for arbitrariness. 2. A term used to describe an arbitrary or secret tribunal or proceeding.

stare decisis ("stand by things decided") Courts should decide similar cases in the same way. Precedent should be followed.

> Precedent must be followed except when departure is necessary to vindicate other principles of law or to remedy continued injustice. *Haag*, 591 So.2d 614 (Fla.,1992)

stat. Statute.

state 1. A sovereign government. 2. A body of people in a defined territory organized under one government.

state action 1. Conduct of a government. 2. Court proceedings made available to protect or enforce conduct of a private person or entity.

state attorney The chief prosecuting officer of all criminal trial courts in his or her circuit. Also called state's attorney, prosecutor, district attorney.

state bank A bank chartered by a state.

stated account See account stated.

stated capital See legal capital.

stated value See par value.

statement 1. An assertion of fact or opinion. 2. An organized recitation of facts.

statement of affairs A list of assets and debts.

state of mind 1. One's reasons and motives for acting or failing to act. 2. See mens rea. 3. The condition or capacity of a mind.

state-of-mind exception An out-of-court declaration of an existing motive or reason is admissible as an exception to the hearsay rule.

> [T]he following are not inadmissible as evidence . . . (a) A statement of the declarant's then-existing state of mind, emotion, or physical sensation, including a statement of intent, plan, motive, design, mental feeling, pain, or bodily health, when such evidence is offered to: 1. Prove the declarant's state of mind, emotion, or physical sensation at that time or at any other time when such state is an issue in the action. . . . F.S.A. § 90.803

state's attorney See state attorney.

state secrets Government information that would threaten national security or compromise diplomacy if disclosed to the public.

state's evidence Testimony of one criminal defendant against another.

states' rights 1. The political philosophy that favors increased powers for state governments as opposed to expanding the powers of the federal government. 2. Powers not granted to the federal government and not forbidden to the states "are reserved to the states" and the people. U.S. Const. amend. X.

status crime; status offense 1. A crime that consists of having a certain personal status, condition, or character. Example: vagrancy. 2. Conduct by a minor that, if engaged in by an adult, would not be legally prohibited.

status quo The existing state of things.

statute 1. A law passed by the state or federal legislature that declares, commands, or prohibits something. 2. A law passed by any legislative body.

statute of frauds A law requiring some contracts (e.g., one that cannot be performed within a year of its making) to be in writing and signed by the party to be charged by the contract.

statute of limitations A law stating that civil or criminal actions are barred if not brought within a specified period of time.

statute of repose A law barring actions unless brought within a designated time after an act of the defendant. The law extinguishes the cause of action after a fixed period of time, regardless of when the cause of action accrued.

> A "statute of repose," in contrast to a statute of limitations, is a substantive statute which not only bars enforcement of an accrued cause of action but may also prevent the accrual of a cause of action where the final element necessary for its creation occurs beyond the time period established by the statute; it provides a substantive right to be free from liability after the established time period. *American Bankers Life Assur. Co.*, 905 So.2d 189 (Fla.App. 3 Dist.,2005)

statute of uses An old English statute that converted certain equitable titles into legal ones.

Statutes at Large The United States Statutes at Large is the official chronological collection of the acts and resolutions of a session of Congress.

statutory Pertaining to or required by a statute.

statutory construction The interpretation of statutes.

statutory employer An employer of a worker covered by workers' compensation.

statutory foreclosure A nonjudicial foreclosure of a mortgage.

statutory lien A lien created by statute.

statutory rape Sexual intercourse with a person under a designated age (e.g., 16) even if the latter consents.

stay The suspension of a judgment or proceeding.

> A "stay of proceedings" essentially postpones the action until a contingency occurs, and is not an appealable non-final order. F.S.A. R.App.P.Rule 9.130(a). *Department of Children and Families*, 840 So.2d 432 (Fla.App. 5 Dist.,2003)

stealing Unlawfully taking and keeping the property of another.

stenographic record The transcript of a trial or deposition.

step-up basis The tax basis of inherited property, which is its value on the date the donor died or on the alternate valuation date.

step transaction doctrine For tax purposes, a series of formally separate steps are treated as a single transaction.

stet ("let it stand") 1. Leave the text unchanged (usually meaning undo the last correction). 2. A stay.

steward See shop steward.

sting An undercover operation to catch criminals.

stipulated damages See liquidated damages.

stipulation 1. An agreement between parties on a matter, often so that it need not be argued or proven at trial. 2. A requirement or condition.

> A "stipulation" is an agreement, admission, or concession made in a judicial proceeding. *McGoey*, 736 So.2d 31 (Fla.App. 3 Dist.,1999)

stirpes See per stirpes.

stock 1. An ownership interest or share in a corporation. 2. The capital raised by a corporation, e.g., through the sale of shares. 3. Goods to be sold by a merchant.

stock association See joint stock company.

stockbroker One who buys or sells stock on behalf of others.

stock certificate Documentary evidence of title to shares of stock.

stock corporation A corporation whose capital is divided into shares.

stock dividend A dividend paid in additional shares of stock.

> In a "stock dividend" there is capitalization of earnings or profit and distribution of shares which represent assets transferred to capital, whereas in a "stock split" there is a mere increase in the number of shares without altering the amount of capital or surplus. The distinguishing feature is the permanent retention of earnings in the business through formal transfer of earned surplus, legally available for dividends, to a capital account. *Keller Industries*, 203 So.2d 644 (Fla.App. 1967)

stock exchange The place at which shares of stock are bought and sold.

stockholder See shareholder.

stockholder's derivative action See derivative action (1).

stock in trade 1. Inventory for sale. 2. Equipment used in business.

stock issue See issue (4).

stock manipulation See manipulation.

stock market See market (2).

stock option A right to buy or sell stock at a set price within a specified period of time.

stock right A shareholder's right to purchase new stock issues before the public can make such purchases.

stock split Each individual share is split into a larger number of shares without changing the total number of shareholders.

stock warrant See warrant (3).

stolen property Property taken by theft or embezzlement.

stop and frisk Temporary detention, questioning, and "patting down" of a person whom the police reasonably believe has committed or is about to commit a crime and may have a weapon. Also called *Terry* stop. *Terry v. Ohio*, 88 S. Ct. 1868 (1968).

> "Terry stop," or temporary investigative "stop and frisk," is permissible if the detention is temporary and reasonable under the circumstances and only if the police officer has a well-founded suspicion that the individual detained has committed, is committing, or is about to commit a crime. *Saturnino-Boudet*, 682 So.2d 188 (Fla.App. 3 Dist.,1996)

stop-loss order An order to buy or sell securities when they reach a particular price. Also called stop order.

stop order 1. An instruction of a customer who has written a check that his or her bank should not honor it. A stop-payment order. 2. See stop-loss order.

stoppage in transit (in transitu) A seller's right to repossess goods from a carrier before they reach the buyer when payment by the latter is in doubt.

stop-payment order See stop order (1).

straddle The option to purchase or sell the same asset.

straight bill of lading A bill of lading that names a specific person to whom the goods are to be delivered.

straight life insurance See whole life insurance.

straight-line depreciation Depreciation computed by dividing the purchase price of an asset (less its salvage value) by its estimated useful life.

stranger Someone not a participant or party to a transaction.

Strategic Lawsuit Against Public Participation (SLAPP) A meritless suit brought primarily to chill the free speech of the defendant.

> A SLAPP suit is one filed by developers, unhappy with public protest over a proposed development, filed against leading critics in order to silence criticism of the proposed development. *Florida Fern Growers Ass'n*, 616 So.2d 562 (Fla.App. 5 Dist.,1993)

straw man 1. A cover or front. 2. A fictitious person or argument.

street name A broker's name on a security, not that of its owner.

strict construction A narrow construction; nothing is taken as intended that is not clearly expressed in the literal language of the law or document. Also called literal construction.

strict foreclosure A transfer of title (of the mortgaged property) to the mortgagee without a foreclosure sale upon the mortgagor's default.

stricti juris According to a strict or narrow construction of the law.

strict liability Legal responsibility even if one used reasonable care and did not intend harm. Also called absolute liability, liability without fault.

strict scrutiny The standard requiring a government to show its law is the least restrictive way to further a compelling state interest.

> Under "strict scrutiny," which applies to certain classifications and fundamental rights, a court must review the legislation to ensure that it furthers a compelling state interest through the least intrusive means; the legislation is presumptively unconstitutional, and the state must prove that the legislation furthers a compelling state interest through the least intrusive means. *North Florida Women's Health and Counseling Services*, 866 So.2d 612 (Fla.,2003)

strike 1. An organized work stoppage or slowdown by workers in order to press demands. 2. To remove something.

strikebreaker See scab.

strike suit A shareholder derivative action that is baseless.

striking a jury Selecting a jury for a particular or special case.

struck jury 1. A jury chosen by a process that allows the parties to take turns striking names from a large panel of prospective jurors until a sufficient number exists for a jury. 2. See special jury.

structuring Altering a currency transaction in such as way as to avoid a currency reporting requirement. 31 U.S.C. §§ 5316, 5324(c)(3)

style The title or name of a case.

suable Capable of being sued.

sua sponte On one's own motion; voluntarily.

sub Under; secondary.

subagent Someone used by an agent to perform a duty for the principal.

subchapter C corporation See C corporation.

subchapter S corporation See S corporation.

subcontract A contract that performs all or part of another contract.

subcontractor One who performs under a subcontract.

subdivision 1. The division of something into smaller parts. 2. A portion of land within a development.

subinfeudation A feudal system of vassals creating vassals of their own.

subjacent support The support of land by land that lies beneath it.

subject 1. A citizen or resident under another; one governed by the laws of a sovereign. 2. A theme or topic acted upon.

subject-matter jurisdiction The power of the court to resolve a particular category of dispute.

sub judice Under judicial consideration; before a court.

sublease A lease of leased premises. A lease (called a sublease, subtenancy, or underlease) granted by an existing lessee (called a sublessor) to another (called a sublessee, subtenant, or undertenant) of all or part of the leased premises for a portion of the sublessor's original term.

> "Sublease" means a lease of goods the right to possession and use of which was acquired by the lessor as a lessee under an existing lease. F.S.A. § 680.1031(1)(w)

sublessee; sublessor See sublease.

subletting The granting of a sublease.

submission 1. Yielding to authority. 2. An argument to be considered.

sub modo Within limits; subject to qualifications.

sub nominee (sub nom.) Under the name or title.

subordinate 1. One who works under another's authority. 2. To place in a lower priority or rank.

subordination agreement An agreement to accept a lower priority than would otherwise be due.

suborn To induce another to commit an illegal act, e.g., perjury.

subornation of perjury Instigating another to commit perjury.

subpoena A command to appear in a court, agency, or other tribunal.

subpoena ad testificandum A command to appear to give testimony.

subpoena duces tecum A command to appear and bring specified things, e.g., records.

subrogation The substitution of one party (called the subrogee) in place of another party (called the subrogor), along with any claim, demand, or right the latter party had.

> Generally speaking, "subrogation" is the substitution of one person to position of another with reference to legal claim or right. *Wolf*, 706 So.2d 881 (Fla.App. 3 Dist.,1998)

subrogee; subrogor See subrogation.

subscription 1. A signature; the act of writing one's name on a document. 2. An agreement to purchase new securities of a corporation.

subscription right See preemptive right.

subsequent Occurring or coming later.

subsidiary 1. Under another's control. 2. A branch or affiliate.

subsidiary corporation A corporation owned or controlled by another corporation.

sub silentio Under silence; without specific reference or notice.

substance 1. The material or essential part of a thing. 2. A drug.

substantial 1. Not imaginary. 2. Considerable in amount or degree.

> "Substantial" when used in reference to degree or extent denotes a material matter of clear and weighty importance. Florida Rules of Professional Conduct, Preamble

substantial capacity test See insanity (2).

substantial compliance Compliance with the essential requirements.

> "Substantial compliance" means that the circumstances which caused the creation of the case plan have been significantly remedied to the extent that the well-being and safety of the child will not be endangered upon the child's remaining with or being returned to the child's parent. F.S.A. § 39.01(71)

substantial evidence Relevant evidence a reasonable mind might accept as adequate to support a conclusion.

substantial justice A fair proceeding or trial even if minor procedural errors are made.

substantial performance Performance of the essential terms of a contract or agreement.

substantiate To establish by supporting evidence. To support with proof.

substantive due process The constitutional requirement (based on the Fifth and Fourteenth Amendments) that legislation be rationally related to a legitimate government purpose.

> "Substantive due process" protects the full panoply of individual rights from unwarranted encroachment by the government and implicates the vagueness doctrine, as applied to legislative action. F.S.A. Const. Art. 1, § 9. *Westerheide*, 767 So.2d 637 (Fla.App. 5 Dist.,2000)

substantive evidence Evidence offered to support a fact in issue.

substantive law Nonprocedural laws that define or govern rights and duties.

substantive rule See legislative rule.

substituted basis The basis of property in the hands of the transferor becomes the transferee's basis of that property.

substituted service Service by an authorized method (e.g., by mail) other than personal service. Also called constructive service.

substitution Taking the place of another.

subtenancy; subtenant See sublease.

subversive Pertaining to the overthrow or undermining of a government.

succession 1. Obtaining property or interests by inheritance rather than by deed or contract. The acquisition of rights upon the death of another. 2. Taking over or continuing the rights of another entity.

succession tax See inheritance tax.

successor A person or entity that takes the place of or follows another.

> [T]he term "successor entity" includes any trust, receivership, or other legal entity governed by the laws of this state to which the remaining assets and liabilities of a dissolved corporation are transferred and which exists solely for the purposes of prosecuting and defending suits by or against the dissolved corporation. . . . F.S.A. § 607.1406(15)

successor in interest One who follows another in ownership or control of property.

sudden emergency doctrine See emergency doctrine (1).

sudden heat of passion See heat of passion.

sue To commence a lawsuit.

sue out To ask a court for an order.

suffer 1. To feel physical or emotional pain. 2. To allow or admit.

sufferance The absence of rejection; passive consent.

sufficient Adequate for the legal purpose involved.

> The sufficiency of the evidence standard is a test of whether the evidence presented is legally adequate to permit a verdict, whereas weight of the evidence tests whether a greater amount of credible evidence supports one side of an issue or the other. *State v. Brockman,* 827 So.2d 299 (Fla.App. 1 Dist.,2002)

sufficient cause See good cause, probable cause (1).

sufficient consideration Consideration that creates a binding contract.

suffrage The right to vote.

suicide The voluntary termination of one's life.

sui generis ("of its own kind") Unique.

sui juris ("of one's own right") Possessing full civil rights.

suit See lawsuit.

suitor A plaintiff, one who sues.

sum certain An exact amount.

summary 1. Not following usual procedures. 2. Done quickly. 3. Short or concise.

summary court-martial The lowest-level court-martial.

summary judgment A judgment on a claim or defense rendered without a full trial because of the absence of genuine conflict on any of the material facts involved.

summary jury trial A nonbinding trial argued before a mock jury as a case evaluation technique and an incentive to settle.

summary proceeding A nonjury proceeding that seeks to achieve a relatively prompt resolution.

summary process A special procedure that provides an expeditious remedy.

summation; summing up See closing argument.

summons 1. A notice directing the defendant to appear in court and answer the plaintiff's complaint or face a default judgment. 2. A notice directing a witness or juror to appear in court.

> "Summons" means any subpoena, subpoena duces tecum, order, or other legal process which requires the production of documents. F.S.A. § 92.153(1)(d)

sumptuary Regulating personal expenditures; restricting immorality.

Sunday closing laws See blue laws.

sunset law A law that automatically terminates a program unless it is affirmatively renewed.

sunshine law A law requiring increased public access to government meetings and records.

suo nomine In one's own name.

Superfund A government fund for hazardous-waste cleanup.

superior Having a higher rank, authority, or interest.

superior court A trial court in most states.

supermajority Two-thirds, 60 percent, or any other voting requirement of greater than half plus one.

supersede To supplant; to annul by replacing.

supersedeas A writ or bond to stay the enforcement of a judgment.

superseding cause An intervening cause that is beyond the foreseeable risk originally created by the defendant's unreasonable acts or omissions and thereby cuts off the defendant's liability.

> Therefore, an intervening cause is material in determining legal cause only insofar as it supersedes a prior wrong as the proximate cause of any injury, by breaking the sequence between the prior wrong and the injury. Accordingly, a superseding cause is one that operates, in succession to a prior wrong, as the proximate cause of an injury. 38 Fla. Jur. 2d, Negligence § 70

supervening cause A superseding cause.

supervening negligence See last clear chance doctrine.

supplemental jurisdiction Jurisdiction over a claim that is part of the same controversy over which the court already has jurisdiction.

supplemental pleading A pleading that adds facts to or corrects an earlier pleading.

Supplemental Security Income (SSI) A government income benefit program (part of social security) for the aged, blind, or disabled.

supplementary proceeding A new proceeding that supplements another, e.g., to help collect a judgment.

support 1. Provide a standard of living. 2. Maintenance with necessities. 3. Foundation.

suppress To stop or prevent.

suppression hearing A pretrial criminal hearing to decide if evidence was seized illegally and should be inadmissible (i.e., suppressed).

suppression of evidence 1. A prosecutor's failure to disclose exculpatory evidence to the defense. 2. Evidence held inadmissible at a suppression hearing.

supra Above; mentioned earlier in the document.

supremacy Being in a higher or the highest position of power.

Supremacy Clause The clause in the U.S. Constitution (Art. VI, cl. 2) that has been interpreted to mean that when valid federal law and state law conflict, federal law controls.

supreme court 1. The highest court in the federal and in most state judicial systems. 2. In New York, it is a trial court with some appellate jurisdiction. 3. The Supreme Court of Appeals is the highest state court in West Virginia. 4. The Supreme Judicial Court is the highest state court in Maine and Massachusetts.

surcharge 1. An added charge or tax. 2. A charge imposed on a fiduciary for misconduct.

surety One who becomes liable for the payment of another's debt or the performance of another's contractual obligation. The surety generally becomes primarily and jointly liable with the other, the principal.

> "Surety" is an insurer of the debt or obligation, while a "guarantor" is an insurer of ability or solvency of the principal where there is a conditional guaranty or guaranty

of collection. *A & T Motors*, 158 So.2d 567 (Fla.App. 3 Dist.1963)

surety bond See completion bond.

suretyship The contractual relation whereby one person (the surety) agrees to answer for the debt, default, or miscarriage of another (the principal), with the surety generally being primarily and jointly liable with the principal.

surplus What is left over. The amount remaining after the purpose of a fund or venture has been accomplished.

surplusage Extraneous matter or words in a statute, pleading, or instrument that do not add meaning.

surprise Something unexpected, often unfairly so.

surrebuttal A rebuttal to a rebuttal.

surrejoinder An answer of the defendant to a rejoinder.

surrender 1. To return a power, claim, or estate. 2. To release.

surrender value See cash surrender value.

surrogacy The status or act of being a substitute for another.

surrogate 1. A substitute for another. 2. A probate judge.

surrogate mother A woman who gestates an embryo and bears a child for another person. The surrogate relinquishes her parental rights.

> "Gestational surrogate" means a woman who contracts to become pregnant by means of assisted reproductive technology without the use of an egg from her body. F.S.A. § 742.13(5)

surrogate's court See probate court.

surtax 1. An additional tax added to something already taxed. 2. A tax levied on a tax.

surveillance Close and continual observation of a person or place.

survey 1. A map that measures boundaries, elevations, and structures on land. 2. A study or poll.

survival action An action brought on behalf of a decedent to recover damages the decedent suffered up to the time of his or her death. The action seeks what the decedent would have sought if he or she had not died.

> No cause of action dies with the person. All causes of action survive and may be commenced, prosecuted, and defended in the name of the person prescribed by law. F.S.A. § 46.021

survivorship See right of survivorship.

survivorship annuity An annuity that continues paying benefits to the survivor of the annuitant after the latter's death.

suspect classification A classification in a statute whose constitutional validity (under the Equal Protection Clause) will be measured by the standard of strict scrutiny. An example would be a preference in a statute on the basis of race, alienage, or national origin.

suspended sentence A sentence that is imposed but postponed, allowing the defendant to avoid prison if he or she meets specified conditions.

suspension A temporary delay or interruption, e.g., the removal of the right to practice law for a specified period.

suspicion A belief that someone has or may have committed wrongdoing but without proof.

sustain 1. To uphold or agree with. 2. To support or encourage. 3. To endure, withstand, or suffer.

swear 1. To take or administer an oath. 2. To talk obscenely.

sweating Questioning an accused through harassment or threats.

sweetheart deal An arrangement providing beneficial treatment that is illegal or ethically questionable.

syllabus 1. A brief summary or outline. 2. See headnote.

symbolic delivery The constructive delivery of property by delivering something that represents the property, e.g., a key to a building.

symbolic speech Nonverbal activity or conduct that expresses a message or thought, e.g., the hood worn by the KKK; expressive conduct.

sympathy strike A strike against an employer with whom the workers do not have a labor dispute in order to show support for other workers on strike.

synallagmatic Reciprocal, bilateral.

syndicalism A movement advocating control of industry by labor unions. Criminal syndicalism is an act or plan intended to accomplish change in industrial ownership or government by means of unlawful force, violence, or terrorism.

syndicate A group formed to promote a common interest.

synopsis A brief summary.

T

tacit Understood without being openly stated; implied by silence.

tacking 1. One claiming adverse possession adds its period of possession to that of a previous possessor to meet the statutory period. 2. Gaining priority for a lien by joining it to a superior lien.

tail Limitation in the right of inheritance. See fee tail.

tail female Limitation to female heirs. See fee tail.

tail male Limitation to male heirs. See fee tail.

taint 1. A defect or contamination. 2. A felony conviction.

tainted evidence Illegally obtained evidence.

take 1. To seize or obtain possession. 2. To acquire by eminent domain.

takeover Obtaining control, management, or ownership.

taking See take.

talesman A prospective juror. A bystander called to serve on a jury.

tamper To meddle or change something without authorization.

TANF See Temporary Assistance to Needy Families.

tangible Having physical form. Capable of being touched or seen.

> "Tangible personal property" means all goods, chattels, and other articles of value (but does not include the vehicular items enumerated in § 1(b), Art. VII of the State Constitution and elsewhere defined) capable of manual possession and whose chief value is intrinsic to the article itself. F.S.A. § 192.001(11)(d)

target corporation A corporation that someone wants to take over.

tariff 1. A tax paid on categories of imported or exported goods. 2. A list of rates or fees charged for services.

tax Compulsory monetary payments to support the government.

taxable Subject to taxation.

taxable estate A decedent's gross estate less allowable deductions.

taxable gift See gift tax.

taxable income Gross income less deductions and exemptions.

taxable year; tax year A calendar year or a taxpayer's fiscal year.

tax avoidance Using lawful tax-reducing steps and strategies.

tax benefit rule When already deducted losses and expenses are recovered in a later year, the recovery is listed as income in the later year.

tax bracket The range of income to which the same tax rate is applied.

tax certificate An instrument issued to the buyer of property at a tax sale entitling him or her to the property after the redemption period.

> "Tax certificate" means a legal document, representing unpaid delinquent real property taxes, non-ad valorem assessments, including special assessments, interest, and related costs and charges, issued in accordance with this chapter against a specific parcel of real property and becoming a first lien thereon, superior to all other liens, except as provided by § 197.573(2). F.S.A. § 197.102(3)

tax court A court that hears appeals involving tax disputes.

tax credit A subtraction from the tax owed rather than from income.

tax deduction A subtraction from income to arrive at taxable income.

tax deed A deed given to the purchaser by the government to property purchased at a tax sale.

tax deferred Not taxable until later.

tax evasion; tax fraud See evasion (2).

tax exempt; tax free Not subject to taxation.

tax home One's principal place of employment or business.

taxing power A government's power to impose taxes.

tax lien A government's lien on property for nonpayment of taxes.

tax preference items Regular deductions that must be factored back in when calculating the alternative minimum tax.

tax rate The percentage used to calculate one's tax.

tax refund An overpayment of taxes that can be returned or credited.

tax return The form used to report income and other tax information.

tax roll A government list of taxable assets and taxpayers.

> Tax rolls and assessment rolls are synonymous and mean the rolls prepared by the property appraiser pursuant to chapter 193 and certified pursuant to § 193.122. . . . "Ad valorem tax roll" means the roll prepared by the property appraiser and certified to the tax collector for collection. F.S.A. § 197.102(6)&(7)

tax sale The forced sale of property for nonpayment of taxes.

tax shelter An investment or other device to reduce or defer taxes.

tax title The title obtained by a buyer of property at a tax sale.

technical error See harmless error.

teller 1. A bank employee who receives and pays out money. 2. A vote counter at an election.

temporary Lasting for a limited time; transitory.

temporary alimony An interim order of spousal support pending the final outcome of the action for divorce or legal separation. Also called alimony pendente lite.

Temporary Assistance to Needy Families (TANF) The welfare program that replaced Aid to Families with Dependent Children (AFDC) (42 U.S.C. § 601)

temporary injunction See preliminary injunction.

temporary restraining order (TRO) An order maintaining the status quo pending a hearing on the application for a permanent injunction.

tenancy 1. The possession or holding of real or personal property by right or title. 2. Possession or occupancy of land under a lease.

tenancy at sufferance See estate at sufferance.

tenancy at will A lease with no fixed term or duration. Also called estate at will.

tenancy by the entirety A form of joint tenancy for a married couple. Co-ownership of property by spouses with a right of survivorship. Also called estate by the entirety.

> In a tenancy by the entirety, in addition to all of the unities of joint tenancy, there is the additional unity of persons resulting from relationship of husband and wife, and neither holder may alone sever the estate. *Andrews*, 21 So.2d 205 (Fla.1945)

tenancy for years A tenancy for any predetermined time period, not just for years. Also called tenancy for a term.

tenancy from year to year See periodic tenancy.

tenancy in common Ownership of property by two or more persons in shares that may or may not be equal, each person having an equal right to possess the whole property but without the right of survivorship. Also called estate in common.

tenant 1. One who pays rent to possess another's land or apartment for a temporary period. 2. One who holds a tenancy.

tenantable Habitable, fit for occupancy.

tenant for life One who holds a life estate.

tender 1. To offer payment or other performance. 2. An offer.

tender of delivery An offer of conforming goods by the seller.

tender offer An offer to purchase shares at a fixed price in an attempt to obtain a controlling interest in a company.

tender years doctrine In custody disputes, very young children should go to the mother unless she is unfit.

> The tender years doctrine gives a preference to the mother of a child of tender years in matters of custody determination, and, under the doctrine, with other essential factors being equal, the mother of the infant of tender years should receive prime consideration for custody. *Johnson*, 884 So.2d 1169 (Fla.App. 2 Dist.,2004)

tenement 1. An apartment or other residence. 2. An estate of land.

ten-K (10-K) A company's annual financial report filed with the SEC.

tentative trust See Totten trust.

tenure 1. The right to permanent employment subject to termination for cause in compliance with procedural safeguards. 2. The right to hold land subordinate to a superior.

term 1. A fixed period. 2. A word or phrase. 3. A contract provision.

terminable interest An interest that ends upon a given time or condition.

termination 1. The end of something. 2. Discontinuation.

term life insurance Life insurance for a specified or limited time.

term loan A loan that must be paid within a specified date.

term of art A word or phrase with a special or technical meaning. Also called word of art.

territorial Pertaining to a particular area or land.

territorial court A court in a U.S. territory, e.g., Guam.

territorial waters Inland and surrounding bodies of water controlled by a nation, including water extending three miles offshore.

territory 1. A geographical area. **2.** A part of the United States with its own branches of government but not part of or within any state.

terrorem clause A condition in a will that voids gifts to any beneficiary who contests the will. Also called no-contest clause.

> Florida courts will not enforce a penalty which is disproportionate to the damages and is agreed upon in order to enforce performance of a contract and held in terrorem over the promisor to deter him from breaking his promise. *Coleman*, 766 So.2d 427 (Fla.App. 5 Dist.,2000)

terrorism Politically motivated violence against noncombatants. Using or threatening violence to intimidate for political or ideological goals.

Terry **stop** See stop and frisk.

testament A will.

testamentary Pertaining to a will.

testamentary capacity Sufficient mental ability to make a will. Knowing the nature of a will, the extent of one's property, and the natural objects of one's bounty.

> Testamentary capacity is the ability of testator to mentally understand in general way the nature and extent of property to be disposed of, and testator's relation to those who would naturally claim a substantial benefit from the will, as well as a general understanding of the practical effect of the will as executed. *American Red Cross*, 708 So.2d 602 (Fla.App. 3 Dist.,1998)

testamentary class A group of beneficiaries under a will whose number is not known when the will is made.

testamentary disposition A transfer of assets to another by will.

testamentary gift A gift made in a will.

testamentary intent The intent to make a revocable disposition of property that takes effect after the testator's death.

testamentary trust A trust created in a will and effective on the death of the creator.

testate 1. Having died leaving a valid will. 2. See testator.

testate succession Acquiring assets by will.

testator One who has died leaving a valid will. Also called testate.

testatrix A female testator.

test case Litigation brought to create a new legal principle or right.

teste The clause in a document that names the witness.

testify To give evidence as a witness. To submit testimony under oath.

testimonium clause A clause in the instrument giving the date on which the instrument was executed and by whom.

testimony Evidence given by a witness under oath.

test oath An oath of allegiance and fidelity to the government.

theft Taking personal property with the intent to deprive the owner of it permanently. Larceny.

> "Retail theft" means the taking possession of or carrying away of merchandise, property, money, or negotiable documents; altering or removing a label, universal product code, or price tag; transferring merchandise from one container to another; or removing a shopping cart, with intent to deprive the merchant of possession, use, benefit, or full retail value. F.S.A. § 812.015(1)(d)

theory of the case The application of the law to the facts to support the judgment you are seeking.

Thibodaux **abstention** A federal court can abstain from exercising its federal jurisdiction when facing difficult and unresolved state law issues involving policy. *Louisiana Power v. Thibodaux*, 79 S. Ct. 1070 (1959).

thief One who commits larceny or theft.

thing in action See chose in action.

third degree Overly aggressive or abusive interrogation techniques.

third party A nonparty or nonparticipant who is involved in a transaction in some way.

third-party beneficiary One for whose benefit a contract is made but who is not a party to the contract.

> Third-party beneficiaries to a contract are those persons whom the parties to the contract intended to primarily and directly benefit. *Tartell*, 668 So.2d 1105 (Fla.App. 4 Dist.,1996)

third-party complaint A defendant's complaint against someone who is not now a party on the basis that the latter may be liable for all or part of what the plaintiff might recover from the defendant.

third-party neutral A person, such as a mediator, arbitrator, conciliator, or evaluator, who assists the parties, represented or unrepresented, in the resolution of a dispute or in the arrangement of a transaction. Florida Rules of Professional Conduct, Rule 4-2.4

third-party plaintiff A defendant who files a third-party complaint.

third-party practice See implead.

threat An expression of an intent to inflict pain or damage.

three-judge court A panel of three judges hearing a case.

three-strikes law A statute imposing harsher sentences for persons convicted of their third felony.

through bill of lading A contract covering the transport of cargo from origin to destination, including the use of additional carriers.

ticket 1. A paper giving the holder a right. 2. A traffic citation.

tideland Land covered and uncovered each day by the action of tides.

tie-in See tying arrangement.

time-barred Pertaining to a claim barred by a statute of limitations.

time bill See time draft.

time deposit A bank deposit that remains in the account for a specified time and is not payable on demand before that time without penalty.

time draft A draft payable on a specified date. Also called time bill.

time immemorial Time beyond the reach of memory or records.

time is of the essence The failure to do what is required by the time specified will be considered a breach of the contract.

timely Within the time set by contract or law.

time note A note payable only at a definite time.

time, place, or manner restriction The government can restrict the time, place, or manner of speech and assembly, but not their content.

time-sharing Joint ownership of property that is used or occupied for limited alternating time periods. Also called interval ownership.

> Section of Real Estate Time-Sharing Act, by defining time-share period as that period of time when purchaser is entitled to possession and use clearly indicates that "time-share period" refers to single period of time less than a year, within a year, when purchaser thereof is entitled to use rights he has purchased. West's F.S.A. §§ 721.01 et seq., 721.03(1), 721.05(28). *All Seasons Resorts*, 455 So.2d 544 (Fla.App. 1 Dist.,1984)

tippee One who receives material inside information about a company. See also insider trading.

title The legal right to control, possess, and dispose of property. All ownership rights in property.

title company A company that issues title insurance.

title insurance Insurance for losses incurred due to defects in the title to real property.

title search A determination of whether defects in the title to real property exist by examining relevant public records.

title state See title theory.

title theory The theory that a mortgagee has title to land until the mortgage debt is paid. States that so provide are called title states.

TM See trademark.

to-have-and-to-hold clause See habendum clause.

toll 1. Payment for the use of something. 2. To stop the running of.

tombstone ad An advertisement (sometimes printed in a black-border box) for a public securities offering.

tonnage 1. The weight carrying capacity of ships. 2. A duty on ships.

tontine A financial arrangement among a group in which the last survivor receives the entire fund.

Torrens title system A system for land registration under which a court issues a binding certificate of title.

tort A civil wrong (other than a breach of contract) for which the courts will provide a remedy such as damages.

> Torts have defined elements, whether intentional or negligent. Ultimate facts must be pled to allege that the conduct in question consists of those elements which make the conduct actionable in tort. Example, an assault. *Doe v. Evans*, 814 So.2d 370 (Fla.,2002)

tortfeasor A person who has committed a tort.

tortious Pertaining to conduct that can lead to tort liability.

tortious interference with prospective advantage See interference with prospective advantage.

total breach A breach that so substantially impairs the value of the contract to the injured party at the time of the breach that it is just in the circumstances to allow recovery of damages based on all the injured party's remaining rights to performance.

total disability Inability to engage in any gainful occupation.

> Trial court did not err in limiting recovery by insured for "total disability" to one week, where insured worked about five hours daily at her usual and regular employment during all of period in question, and she was able to perform a large portion of her regular duties. *Scott*, 158 So.2d 532 (Fla.App.1963)

total incorporation See selective incorporation.

total loss Damage beyond physical repair; complete destruction.

Totten trust A trust created by a deposit of funds in a bank account in trust for a beneficiary. The trustee is the depositor, who retains the power to revoke the trust. Also called savings bank trust, tentative trust.

to wit That is to say, namely.

township 1. A political subdivision, usually part of a county. 2. A square tract that is six miles on each side.

tract index A publicly kept index of parcels (tracts) of land.

trade Commerce. Buying, selling, or bartering goods or services.

trade acceptance A bill of exchange drawn by a seller on the buyer of goods for the amount of the purchase, and accepted for payment by the buyer at a set time.

trade association An organization of businesses in an industry that promotes the interests of the industry.

trade dress The total image or overall appearance of a product.

trade fixture Personal property affixed to the realty by a tenant who uses it in its business and has the right to remove it.

trade libel See disparagement.

trademark (TM) A distinctive word, mark, or emblem that serves to identify a product with a specific producer and to distinguish it from others. See also infringement.

trade name A name or symbol that identifies and distinguishes a business.

trade secret A business formula, pattern, device, or compilation of information known only by certain individuals in the business and used for competitive advantage.

> "Trade secret" means information, including a formula, pattern, compilation, program, device, method, technique, or process that: (a) Derives independent economic value, actual or potential, from not being generally known to, and not being readily ascertainable by proper means by, other persons who can obtain economic value from its disclosure or use; and (b) Is the subject of efforts that are reasonable under the circumstances to maintain its secrecy. F.S.A. § 688.002(4)

trade union A union or workers in the same trade or craft.

trade usage A practice or method of dealing having such regularity of observance in a place, vocation, or trade as to justify an expectation that it will be observed in the transaction in question.

traffic 1. Commerce or trade. 2. Transportation of people or things.

tranche A slice or portion of a bond offering or other investment.

transact To have dealings; to carry on.

transaction 1. The act of conducting something. 2. A business deal.

transactional immunity Immunity from prosecution for any matter about which a witness testifies.

transcript A word-for-word account. A written copy of oral testimony.

transfer To deliver or convey an interest. To place with another.

transfer agent An agent appointed by a corporation to keep records on registered shareholders, handle transfers of shares, etc.

transferee One to whom an interest is conveyed.

transfer payments Payments made by the government to individuals for which no services or goods are rendered in return.

transferred-intent doctrine The defendant may be held responsible for a wrong committed against the plaintiff even if the defendant intended a different wrong against a different person.

> The doctrine of transferred intent operates to transfer defendant's intent with respect to intended victim to unintended victim. *Miller*, 636 So.2d 144 (Fla.App. 1 Dist.,1994)

transfer tax A tax imposed on the transfer of property by will, inheritance, or gift.

transitory action An action that can be tried wherever the defendant can be personally served.

transmit To send or transfer something (e.g., an interest, a message) to another person or place.

transmutation The voluntary change of separate property into marital property or vice versa.

traveler's check A cashier's check that requires the purchaser's signature when purchased and countersigned when cashed.

traverse A formal denial of material facts stated in an opponent's pleading.

treason An attempt by overt acts to overthrow the government of the state to which one owes allegiance or to give aid and comfort to its foreign enemies. Under Article III, section 3 of the U.S. Constitution, "Treason against the United States, shall consist only in levying war against them, or in adhering to their enemies, giving them aid and comfort. No person shall be convicted of treason unless on the testimony of two witnesses to the same overt act, or on confession in open court."

treasurer An officer with responsibility over the receipt, custody, and disbursement of moneys or funds. The chief financial officer.

treasure trove Valuable property found hidden in a private place and whose owner is unknown.

treasury 1. The funds of an organization. 2. The place where such funds are stored.

Treasury bill (T-bill) A short-term debt security of the U.S. government that matures in a year or less.

Treasury bond (T-bond) A long-term debt security of the U.S. government that matures in more than ten years.

treasury certificate An obligation of the U.S. government with a one-year maturity and interest paid by coupon.

Treasury note (T-note) An intermediate-term debt security of the U.S. government that matures in more than one year but not more than ten years.

treasury securities 1. A corporation's stock that it reacquires. Also called treasury stock. 2. Debt instruments of the U.S. government.

> Treasury shares means shares of a corporation that belong to the issuing corporation, which shares are authorized and issued shares that are not outstanding, are not canceled, and have not been restored to the status of authorized but unissued shares. F.S.A. § 607.01401(29)

treatise A book that gives an overview of a topic, often in-depth and scholarly.

treaty A formal agreement between two or more nations.

Treaty Clause The provision in the U.S. Constitution giving the president the power to make treaties with the advice and consent of the U.S. Senate. U.S. Const., Art. II, § 2.

treble damages Three times the amount of damages found to be owed.

trespass A wrongful interference with another's person or property.

> Whoever, without being authorized, licensed, or invited, willfully enters or remains in any structure or conveyance, or, having been authorized, licensed, or invited, is warned by the owner or lessee of the premises, or by a person authorized by the owner or lessee, to depart and refuses to do so, commits the offense of trespass in a structure or conveyance. F.S.A. § 810.08(1)

trespass de bonis asportatis Wrongfully taking and carrying away the goods of another.

trespasser A wrongdoer who commits a trespass.

trespass on the case See action on the case.

trespass quare clausum fregit Wrongfully entering the enclosed land of another.

trespass to chattels An intentional interference with another's personal property, resulting in dispossession or intermeddling.

trespass to land A wrongful entry on another's land.

trespass vi et armis A wrongful interference with another's person or property through force.

trial A judicial proceeding that applies the law to evidence in order to resolve conflicting legal claims.

trial brief 1. An attorney's presentation to a trial court of the legal issues and positions of his or her client. 2. An attorney's strategy notes for trial. Also called trial book, trial manual.

trial by ordeal See ordeal.

trial court The first court that provides a complete forum to hear evidence and arguments on a legal claim. A court of original jurisdiction. Also called court of first instance.

trial de novo A new trial as if a prior one had not taken place.

trial jury See petit jury.

tribal land Reservation land held by a tribe for its community.

tribunal A court or other body that adjudicates disputes.

trier of fact See fact-finder.

TRO See temporary restraining order.

trover See conversion (1).

true bill A grand jury's notation on a bill of indictment that there is enough evidence for a criminal trial. A grand jury indictment.

true value See fair market value.

trust A device or arrangement by which its creator (the settlor or trustor) transfers property (the corpus) to a person (the trustee) who holds legal title for the benefit of another (the beneficiary or cestui que trust).

> If the intention is that the money shall be kept or used as a separate fund for the benefit of the depositor or third person, a "trust" is created. However, if the intention is that the person receiving the money shall have unrestricted use thereof, being liable to pay a similar amount with or without interest to the depositor or a third person, a "debt" is created. *Bankers Life & Cas.*, 199 So.2d 482 (Fla.App. 1967)

trust account See client trust account.

trust company A company or bank that serves as a trustee for trusts. A trust officer is the employee in charge of a trust.

trust deed 1. The document setting up a trust. 2. See deed of trust.

trust de son tort See constructive trust.

trustee The person or company holding legal title to property for the benefit of another.

trustee in bankruptcy A person appointed or elected to administer the estate of a debtor in bankruptcy.

trust estate See corpus (1).

trust ex delicto See constructive trust.

trust ex maleficio See constructive trust.

trust fund See corpus (1).

trust fund doctrine An insolvent corporation's assets are held in trust for its creditors.

> The trust fund doctrine which imposes individual liability to creditors upon the corporation's directors who, when the corporation is insolvent, accept conveyance of corporate property upon any other consideration than the full value of the property paid in cash. *Garnett*, 145 So.2d 295 (Fla.App.1962)

trust indenture 1. The document specifying the terms of a trust. 2. See deed of trust.

trust instrument The document setting up a trust.

trust officer See trust company.

trustor See settlor.

trust receipt A document stating that a dealer/borrower is holding goods in trust for the benefit of the lender.

trust territory A territory placed under the administration of a country by the United Nations.

trusty A trusted prisoner given special privileges and duties.

truth-in-lending Required disclosure of credit terms.

try 1. To litigate. 2. To decide a legal dispute in court.

turnkey contract A contract in which the builder agrees to complete the work of building and installation to the point of readiness for occupancy.

turnover order A court order that the losing litigant transfer property to the winning litigant.

turntable doctrine See attractive nuisance doctrine.

turpitude Depravity.

twisting Deception to induce an insured to switch insurance policies.

two-dismissal rule A voluntary dismissal of a second action operates as a dismissal on the merits if the plaintiff has previously dismissed an action involving the same claim.

two-issue rule A jury verdict involving two or more issues will not be set aside if the verdict is supported as to at least one of the issues.

> The two-issue rule holds that in the absence of a proper objection to the use of a general verdict, no error can be found as to one of multiple theories of liability submitted to the jury. *LRX, Inc.*, 922 So.2d 984 (Fla.App. 4 Dist.,2005)

two-witness rule In a perjury or treason case, proof of falsity of the testimony cannot be established by the uncorroborated testimony of a single witness.

tying arrangement A seller conditions the sale of one product or service on the buyer's purchase of a separate product or service.

U

uberrima fides Highest degree of good faith.

ubi Where.

UCC See Uniform Commercial Code.

UCCC Uniform Consumer Credit Code.

UCMJ Uniform Code of Military Justice.

UFTA Uniform Fraudulent Transfer Act.

ukase An official decree or proclamation.

ultimate facts Facts essential to a cause of action or a defense.

> Ultimate facts are those found in that vaguely defined area lying between evidentiary facts on the one side and conclusions of law on the other and are the final resulting effects which are reached by the process of logical reasoning from the evidentiary facts. *Feldman*, 389 So.2d 692 (Fla.App.,1980)

ultrahazardous See abnormally dangerous.

ultra vires Beyond the scope of corporate powers; unauthorized.

umbrella policy An insurance policy that covers risks not covered by homeowners, automobile, or other standard liability policies.

umpire A neutral person asked to resolve or help resolve a dispute.

unalienable See inalienable.

unanimous opinion An opinion in which all judges or justices are in full agreement.

unauthorized practice of law (UPL) Engaging in acts that require either a license to practice law or other special authorization by a person who does not have the license or special authorization.

unavoidable accident An accident that could not have been prevented by ordinary care. Also called inevitable accident, pure accident.

> An unavoidable accident is a casualty occurring as result of matters beyond knowledge, actual or implied, of the person charged, and over which he has no control, and he is relieved of liability for reason that he is not guilty of actionable negligence. *Tropical Exterminators*, 171 So.2d 432 (Fla.App.,1965)

uncertificated security A security not represented by an instrument, the transfer of which is registered on the issuer's books.

unclean hands doctrine See clean hands doctrine.

unconditional Without contingencies or conditions.

unconscionable So one-sided as to be oppressive and grossly unfair.

unconstitutional Contrary to or inconsistent with the constitution.

uncontested Unopposed; without opposition.

uncontrollable impulse An impulse or urge that cannot be resisted.

undercapitalized Insufficient capital to run a profitable business.

under color of law See color of law.

underlease See sublease.

under protest Waiving no rights; to be challenged later, but paid now.

undersigned The person signing at the end of the document or page.

understanding 1. A meeting of the minds; agreement. 2. Interpretation.

undertaking 1. A promise or guaranty. 2. A bail bond. 3. A task.

undertenant See sublease.

under the influence See driving under the influence.

underwriting 1. Assuming a risk by insuring it. The process of deciding whether to insure a risk. 2. An agreement to buy the shares of a new issue of securities not purchased by the public.

undisclosed principal A principal whose existence and identity are not revealed by the agent to a third party.

undivided interest; undivided right; undivided title The interest of each individual in the entire or whole property rather than in a particular part of it.

undivided profits Accrued profit a corporation has not distributed.

undue influence Improper persuasion, coercion, force, or deception that substitutes the will of one person for the free will of another.

> Undue influence, required for invalidation of a will, is conduct which must amount to overpersuasion, duress, force, coercion, or artful or fraudulent contrivances to such a degree that there is destruction of the free agency of will power of the one making the will. *In re Carpenter's Estate*, 239 So.2d 506 (Fla.App. 1970)

unearned income 1. Income that has been received but not yet earned, e.g., prepaid rent. 2. See investment income.

unemployment compensation Temporary income from the government to persons who have lost their jobs (for reasons other than misconduct) and are looking for work.

unethical In violation of standards of practice or an ethical code.

unfair competition Passing off one's goods or services as those of another. Trade practices that unfairly undermine competition.

unfair labor practice Acts by workers, employers, or unions that are illegal under laws on labor-management relations.

unified bar See integrated bar.

unified transfer tax A single or unified federal tax on property transfers during one's life and at death.

uniform Without change or variation; the same in all cases.

Uniform Commercial Code (UCC) A law adopted in all states (with some variations) on commercial transactions (e.g., sale of goods, negotiable instruments).

Uniform Code of Military Justice (UCMJ) The rules governing discipline in the armed forces.

uniform laws Laws proposed by the National Conference of Commissioners on Uniform State Laws to state legislatures, which may adopt, modify, or reject them (*www. nccusl.org*).

unicameral Having one house or chamber in the legislature.

unilateral Affecting only one side; obligating only one side.

unilateral contract A contract in which only one party makes a promise and the other party completes the contract by rendering performance.

> A unilateral contract is one in which no promisor receives a promise as consideration for his promise. A bilateral contract is one in which there are mutual promises between two parties to the contract; each party being both a promisor and a promisee. *Ballou*, 179 So.2d 228 (Fla.App.1965)

unilateral mistake A mistake by only one of the parties to a contract.

unincorporated association A group of persons formed (but not incorporated) to promote a common enterprise or objective.

uninsured motorist coverage Insurance protection when injured by motorists without liability insurance.

union An association that negotiates with employers on labor issues.

union certification A government declaration that a particular union is the bargaining representative of a group of workers.

union shop A business where all workers must join the union.

United States (U.S.) The federal government.

United States Attorney An attorney who represents the federal government.

United States Code (USC) An official codification of permanent and public federal statutes organized by subject matter.

United States Commissioner See magistrate (1).

United States courts The federal courts (*www.uscourts.gov*).

United States Marshal See marshal (1).

United States Magistrate See magistrate (1).

United States Reports (U.S.) The official collection of opinions of the U.S. Supreme Court.

United States Statutes at Large See Statutes at Large.

United States Trustee A federal official appointed by the U.S. Attorney General with statutory oversight responsibility over bankruptcy court cases (28 U.S.C. § 581).

unit investment trust A trust investing in a portfolio of securities.

unit rule Valuing shares by multiplying the sale price of one share on a stock exchange by the total number of shares.

unity The four elements of a joint tenancy: 1) *unity of interest* (the interests of all the joint tenants have the same nature, extent, and duration); 2) *unity of title* (all the joint tenants had their estate created by the same instrument); 3) *unity of time* (the interests of all the joint tenants vested at the same time); and 4) *unity of possession* (all the joint tenants have the right to possess the whole property).

In order to entitle an owner of a dominant estate to a way of necessity over a servient estate both properties must have at one time been owned by the same party; this requirement is called a "unity of title." F.S.A. § 704.01(1). *Dixon*, 448 So.2d 554 (Fla.App. 5 Dist.,1984)

universal agent An agent with full powers to act for the principal.

unjust enrichment Receiving a benefit that in justice and in equity belongs to another.

An action for money had and received, or the more modern action for unjust enrichment is an equitable remedy requiring proof that money had been paid due to fraud, misrepresentation, imposition, duress, undue influence, mistake, or as a result of some other grounds appropriate for intervention by a court of equity. *Hall*, 686 So.2d 653 (Fla.App. 5 Dist.,1996)

unlawful Contrary to the law; illegal.

unlawful arrest An arrest without a warrant or probable cause.

unlawful assembly Three or more persons who meet to do an unlawful act or a lawful act in a violent, boisterous, or tumultuous manner.

unlawful detainer Remaining in possession of real property unlawfully by one whose original possession was lawful.

unlawful entry 1. A trespass on real property. 2. Entering a country illegally.

unlawful force The wrongful use of force against another.

unliquidated Not determined or specified; not ascertained in amount.

unlisted security A security not registered with a stock exchange.

unmarketable title A title an ordinary prudent buyer would not accept.

unnatural offense See sodomy.

unnecessary hardship Ground for a variance from a zoning regulation based on the unreasonableness of its application.

unprofessional conduct Conduct that violates the ethical code.

unrealized Pertaining to a gain or loss on paper. See realization (2).

unreasonable Irrational; arbitrary or capricious.

Unreasonable adverse effects on the environment means any unreasonable risk to humans or the environment, taking into account the economic, social, and environmental costs and benefits of the use of any pesticide. F.S.A. § 487.021(65)

unreasonable restraint of trade A restraint of trade whose anticompetitive effects outweigh its procompetitive effects.

unreasonable search A search conducted without probable cause or consent, or that is otherwise illegal.

unrelated business income Income of a non-profit organization that is taxable because it is not substantially related to the organization's main purpose.

unrelated offenses Crimes that are separate and independent.

unresponsive Not answering the question or charge; irrelevant.

unreviewable Not ripe or suitable for review by a court or other body.

unsecured creditor A creditor unprotected by a lien or other security in any property of the debtor. Also called general creditor.

unsound 1. Unhealthy 2. Not based on sufficient evidence or analysis.

unsworn Not given under oath.

untenantable Unfit for the purpose leased.

untimely Too soon or too late.

unvalued policy An insurance policy in which the value of the thing insured is not agreed upon and stated in the policy. Also called open policy.

unwritten law Law derived from custom. Law not formally promulgated but collected from court opinions and learned treatises.

UPA Uniform Partnership Act.

UPC Uniform Probate Code.

UPL See unauthorized practice of law.

upset price The lowest action price a seller will accept.

U.S. See United States.

usage A custom or practice that is widely known or established.

A usage of trade is any practice or method of dealing having such regularity of observance in a place, vocation or trade as to justify an expectation that it will be observed with respect to the transaction in question. F.S.A. § 671.205(2)

USC See United States Code.

USCA United States Code Annotated.

U.S.D.C. United States District Court.

use 1. Taking, employing, or applying something. 2. The value of something. 3. The profit or benefit of land. 4. A purpose.

useful Having practical utility.

useful life See depreciable life.

use immunity Compelled statements cannot be used in a later criminal trial.

useless-gesture exception See knock-and-announce rule.

use tax A tax on goods bought outside the state.

usufruct A right to use another's property without damaging it.

usurious Pertaining to usury.

usury Lending money at an interest rate above what is authorized by law.

The four elements of "usury" are: (1) a loan, express or implied; (2) an understanding between parties that money loaned is to be returned; (3) payment or agreement to pay a greater rate of interest than is allowed by law; and (4) a corrupt intent to take more than the legal rate. *Lord*, 209 So.2d 692 (Fla.App.,1968)

utility 1. Usefulness, providing a benefit. 2. See public utility.

UTMA Uniform Transfers to Minors Act.

utmost care See great care.

utter 1. To place or send into circulation. 2. To say or publish. See also excited utterance.

uttering forged instruments Knowingly presenting false instruments with the intent to harm. F.S.A. § 831.02.

ux. (uxor) Wife. See also et ux.

V

v. Versus; volume.

VA Veterans Administration, now the Department of Veterans Affairs (*www.va.gov*).

vacant succession Succession when no one claims it, when all the heirs are unknown, or when all the known heirs to it have renounced it.

vacate 1. To cancel or set aside. 2. To surrender possession.

vacation 1. Cancellation or setting aside. 2. A period of time between sessions or terms.

vacatur ("it is annulled") Setting aside.

vagrancy Wandering without a home or lawful means of support.

> It is unlawful for any person to loiter or prowl in a place, at a time or in a manner not usual for law-abiding individuals, under circumstances that warrant a justifiable and reasonable alarm or immediate concern for the safety of persons or property in the vicinity. F.S.A. § 856.021(1)

vague Unclear or imprecise.

vagueness Not giving fair warning of what is commanded or prohibited.

> The void-for-vagueness doctrine requires that a penal statute define the criminal offense with sufficient definiteness that ordinary people can understand what conduct is prohibited and in a manner that does not encourage arbitrary and discriminatory enforcement. *State v. Rubio*, 917 So.2d 383 (Fla.App. 5 Dist.,2005)

valid Having the force of law; legally sufficient. Meritorious.

valuable consideration A benefit to the promisor or detriment to the promisee. Any valid consideration. Also called legal consideration.

valuation 1. Determining the value of something. 2. The appraised price.

value 1. Monetary worth. 2. Usefulness; desirability. 3. Consideration.

value-added tax (VAT) A tax on whatever additional value is added at the various stages of production.

valued policy An insurance policy in which the value of the thing insured is agreed upon and stated in the policy as the amount to be paid in the event of a loss.

vandalism Willful or malicious destruction of property.

variable annuity An annuity in which benefit payments fluctuate with the performance of the fund's earnings.

variable-rate mortgage (VRM) See adjustable-rate mortgage.

variance 1. Permission not to follow a zoning requirement. 2. An inconsistency between two allegations, positions, or provisions.

> Variance means a decision by an agency to grant a modification to all or part of the literal requirements of an agency rule to a person who is subject to the rule. F.S.A. § 120.52(18)

VAT See value-added tax.

vehicular homicide Killing while operating a motor vehicle illegally, particularly with gross negligence.

vel non Or not; or without it.

venal Corruptible; available for bribes.

vendee A buyer.

vendor A seller.

vendor's lien A seller's lien securing the unpaid purchase price.

venire See jury panel.

venire facias A writ requiring the sheriff to summon a jury.

venireman, veniremember, venireperson A prospective member of a jury.

venture A business enterprise or other undertaking that often has an element of risk and speculation.

venture capital An investment in a business, often involving potentially high risks and gains. Also called risk capital.

venue The proper county or geographical area in which a court with jurisdiction may hear a case. The place of the trial.

> Venue concerns the privilege of being accountable to a court in a particular location. *Walters*, 332 So.2d 684 (Fla.App. 1976)

veracity Accuracy, truthfulness.

verbal Concerned with words; expressed orally.

verbal act An utterance to which the law attaches duties and liabilities.

verdict The jury's decision on the fact questions it was asked to resolve.

verification 1. Confirmation of correctness. 2. A declaration (often sworn) of the authenticity or truth of something.

versus (vs.)(v.) Against (e.g., Smith vs. Jones).

vertical integration The performance within one business of two or more steps in the chain of production and distribution.

vertical merger A merger between two businesses with a buyer-seller relationship with each other.

vertical price fixing An attempt by someone in the chain of distribution to set prices that someone lower on that chain will charge. An attempt by a supplier to fix the prices charged by those who resell its products.

vertical union See industrial union.

vest To give an immediate, fixed right of present or future enjoyment. To confer ownership or title.

vested Fixed; absolute, not subject to be defeated by a condition.

> Vested or vesting means the guarantee that a member is eligible to receive a future retirement benefit upon completion of the required years of creditable service for the employee's class of membership, even though the member may have terminated covered employment before reaching normal or early retirement date. F.S.A. § 121.021(45)(a)

vested estate; vested interest An estate or interest in which there is a present fixed right either of present or of future enjoyment.

vested remainder An estate in land that presently exists unconditionally in a definite or ascertained person, but the actual enjoyment of it is deferred until the termination of a previous estate.

vested right A right that cannot be infringed upon or taken away.

veto A chief executive's rejection of a bill passed by the legislature.

vexatious Without reasonable or just cause; annoying.

viable 1. Able to live outside the womb. 2. Practicable.

viatical settlement A contract of a terminally ill person to sell his or her life insurance policy, allowing the buyer to collect the death benefits.

vicarious Experienced, endured, or substituting for another.

vicarious disqualification See imputed disqualification.

vicarious liability Liability imposed on one party for the conduct of another, based solely upon the status of the relationship between the two.

Under the concept of vicarious liability, a person whose liability is imputed based on the tortious acts of another is liable for the entire share of comparative responsibility assigned to the other. *American Home Assur. Co.*, 908 So.2d 459 (Fla.,2005)

vice 1. In substitution for; in place of. 2. Immoral; illegal; defect.

vicinage Vicinity; the area or locale where the crime was committed from which prospective jurors will be drawn.

victim impact statement Comments made during sentencing by a victim on the impact of the crime on his or her life.

victimless crime A crime with a consenting victim or without a direct victim, e.g., drug use or possession.

victualer One who serves food prepared for eating on the premises.

videlicet See viz.

vi et armis With force and arms.

vinculo matrimonii Marriage bond. See divorce a vinculo matrimonii.

vindictive damages See punitive damages.

violation 1. Breaching a law or rule. 2. Rape or sexual assault.

violent Involving great or extreme physical or emotional force.

vir 1. A man. 2. A husband.

virtual representation doctrine A person may be bound by a judgment even though not a party if one of the actual parties in the suit is so closely aligned with that person's interests as to be his or her virtual representative.

vis (power) Force; disturbance.

visa An authorization on a passport giving the holder permission to enter or leave a country.

visitation Time allowed someone without custody to spend with a child.

vis major An irresistible force or natural disaster; a loss caused by nature that was not preventable by reasonable care.

vital statistics Public records on births, deaths, marriages, diseases, etc.

vitiate To impair or destroy the legal efficacy of something.

viva voce By word of mouth, orally.

viz (abbreviation for videlicet) Namely, in other words.

void 1. Having no legal force or binding effect. 2. To invalidate.

void ab initio Invalid from its inception or beginning.

voidable Valid but subject to being annulled or declared void.

A voidable assessment is one made in good faith but is irregular or unfair. *Dade County v. Transportes Aereos*, 298 So.2d 570 (Fla.App. 1974)

voidable preference A debtor's transfer of assets to a creditor (before filing for bankruptcy) that constitutes an advantage over other bankruptcy creditors.

void for vagueness A law that is so obscure that a reasonable person could not determine what the law purports to command or prohibit.

voir dire ("to speak the truth") A preliminary examination of (a) prospective jurors for the purpose of selecting persons qualified to sit on a jury or (b) prospective witnesses to determine their competence to testify.

volenti non fit injuria ("to a willing person it is not wrong") There is no cause of action for injury or harm endured by consent.

voluntary 1. By choice; proceeding from a free and unconstrained will. 2. Intentional. 3. Without consideration; gratuitous.

voluntary bankruptcy A petition for bankruptcy filed by the debtor.

voluntary bar A bar association that attorneys are not required to join.

voluntary commitment Civil commitment or institutionalization with the consent of the person committed or institutionalized.

voluntary dismissal A dismissal of a suit at the plaintiff's request.

voluntary manslaughter The intentional, unlawful killing of someone without malice or premeditation. Murder reduced to manslaughter.

To prove the crime of Attempted Voluntary Manslaughter, the State must prove the following element beyond a reasonable doubt: (Defendant) committed an act [or procured the commission of an act], which was intended to cause the death of (victim) and would have resulted in the death of (victim) except that someone prevented (defendant) from killing (victim) or [he] [she] failed to do so. F.S.A. Std.Crim.Jury Instr., 6.6

voluntary trust 1. A trust created by express agreement. 2. A trust created as a gift.

voluntary waste Harm to real property committed by a tenant intentionally or negligently.

volunteer 1. One who voluntarily performs an act (e.g., pays someone's debt) without a duty to do so. 2. One who acts without coercion.

vote A formal expression of one's choice for a candidate or position.

voter One who votes or who has the qualifications to vote.

voting stock Stock entitling a holder to vote, e.g., for directors.

voting trust An agreement between stockholders and a trustee whereby the rights to vote the stock are transferred to the trustee.

vouch To give a personal assurance or to serve as a guarantee.

voucher 1. A receipt for payment. 2. An authorization to pay.

vouching-in A mechanism whereby a defendant in a proceeding may notify a non-party, the vouchee, that a suit is pending against the defendant and that, if liability is found, the defendant will look to the vouchee for indemnity and hold it to the findings in that suit.

The general rule of indemnification, the vouching-in rule, is that an indemnitor who has notice of the suit filed against the indemnitee by the injured party and who is afforded an opportunity to appear and defend it is bound by a judgment rendered against the indemnitee as to all material questions determined by the judgment, if the judgment is rendered without fraud or collusion. *Camp, Dresser & McKee*, 853 So.2d 1072 (Fla.App. 5 Dist.,2003)

VRM See adjustable-rate mortgage.

vs. See versus.

W

***Wade* hearing** A pretrial hearing on the admissibility of lineup or other identification evidence. *United States v. Wade*, 87 S. Ct. 1926 (1967).

wage Payments made to a hired person for his or her labor or services.

> Wages means and includes all compensation paid by an employer or his or her agent for the performance of service by an employee, including the cash value of all compensation paid in any medium other than cash. F.S.A. § 448.07(1)(c)

wage and hour laws Statutes on minimum wages and maximum work hours.

wage assignment 1. A court order to withhold someone's wages in order to satisfy a debt. An attachment by a creditor of a debtor's wages. 2. A contract transferring the right to receive wages.

wage earner's plan A new payment schedule or plan for the payment of all or a portion of a debtor's debts in a Chapter 13 bankruptcy when the debtor still has regular income.

wager policy An insurance policy to one with no insurable interest in the risks covered by the policy.

wait and see Basing the rule against perpetuities on vesting that actually occurs rather than what might occur. Also called second look.

waiting period The time that must elapse before the next legal step can occur or a right can be exercised.

waiver The express or implied voluntary relinquishment of a right, claim, or benefit.

> Waiver is the voluntary and intentional relinquishment of a known right. *Clear Channel Metroplex*, 922 So.2d 229 (Fla.App. 3 Dist.,2005)

walkout A labor strike or departure in protest.

want of consideration A total lack of consideration for a contract.

wanton A conscious disregard of consequences. Malicious.

war Armed conflict between nations, states, or groups.

war crimes Conduct in violation of international laws governing wars.

ward 1. A person (e.g., minor) placed by the court under the care or protection of a guardian. 2. A division of a city or town.

warden A superintendent or person in charge.

warehouseman; warehouser Someone in the business of offering storage facilities.

warehouseman's lien A lien of a warehouseman in goods it is storing that provides security for unpaid storage charges.

warehouse receipt A receipt issued by a person engaged in the business of storing goods for hire. The receipt is a document of title.

warrant 1. A court order commanding or authorizing a specific act, e.g., to arrest someone, to search an area. 2. A document providing authorization, e.g., to receive goods or make payment. 3. A long-term option to purchase stock at a given price. Also called stock warrant. 4. To guarantee or provide a warranty.

> Warrant means an order issued by a court authorizing law enforcement officers to take physical custody of a child. F.S.A. § 61.503(17)

warrantless arrest An arrest made without a warrant. The arrest is proper if a misdemeanor is committed in the officer's presence or if the officer has probable cause to believe that a felony has been committed.

warranty 1. A commitment imposed by contract or law that a product or service will meet a specified standard. 2. A guarantee in a deed that assures the conveyance of a good and clear title.

> Warranty is distinguishable from a guaranty. Both are collateral contracts; but guaranty is an undertaking to answer for another's liability, while warranty is an undertaking that a certain fact regarding the subject of the contract is what it has been represented to be, and relates to some undertaking made ordinarily by the party who makes the warranty. *Vilord*, 226 So.2d 245, *247 (Fla.App. 1969)

warranty deed A deed in which the grantor promises to convey a specified title to property that is free and clear of all encumbrances. Also called general warranty deed.

warranty of fitness for a particular purpose An implied warranty that goods will meet a buyer's special need when the seller knows the buyer is relying on the seller's expertise for such need.

warranty of habitability An implied promise by a landlord that the premises are free of serious defects that endanger health or safety.

warranty of merchantability An implied promise that the goods are fit for the ordinary purposes for which they are used.

warranty of title A seller's warranty that he or she owns what is being sold and that there are no undisclosed encumbrances on it.

wash sale A deceptive transaction involving the sale and purchase of securities that does not change beneficial ownership.

waste 1. Serious harm done to real property that affects the rights of holders of future interests in the property. 2. Refuse.

wasting asset An asset with a limited life or subject to depletion.

wasting trust A trust, the res of which consists of property that is gradually being depleted by payments to the beneficiaries.

watered stock 1. Stock issued at less than par value. 2. Stock issued at an inflated price.

water rights Rights to use water in its natural state, e.g., a lake.

waybill The non-negotiable document containing details of a carrier's contract for the transport of goods and acknowledging their receipt.

way of necessity See implied easement.

ways and means Methods and sources for raising government revenue.

weapon An instrument used for combat or to inflict great bodily harm.

weight of the evidence The inclination of the evidence to support one side over another; the persuasiveness of the evidence presented.

> There is a distinction between the "sufficiency of the evidence" standard, used in determining whether a judgment of acquittal is appropriate, and the "weight of the evidence" standard used in evaluating a motion for new trial: "sufficiency of the evidence" is a test of whether the evidence presented is legally adequate to permit a verdict, whereas "weight of the evidence" tests whether a greater amount of credible evidence supports one side of an issue or the other. *State v. Brockman*, 827 So.2d 299 (Fla.App. 1 Dist.,2002)

welfare 1. The well-being and the common blessings of life. 2. Public assistance; government aid to those in need.

well-pleaded complaint rule Federal-question jurisdiction exists only when a federal issue is presented on the face of the plaintiff's complaint.

Westlaw (WL) West Group's system of computer-assisted legal research (*www.westlaw.com*).

Wharton rule See concert-of-action rule.

whereas 1. That being the case; since. 2. Although.

whereby By means of which; through which.

whiplash Injury to the cervical spine (neck) due to a sudden jerking of the head.

whistleblower One who discloses wrongdoing. A worker who reports employer wrongdoing to a public body.

whiteacre See blackacre.

white-collar crime A nonviolent crime, often involving a business.

white knight One who helps prevent a hostile takeover of a target corporation.

white slavery Forced prostitution.

whole law All the law in a jurisdiction, including choice of law rules.

whole life insurance Insurance covering the insured's entire life, not just for a term. Also called ordinary life insurance, straight life insurance.

wholesale Selling goods to one who is in the business of reselling them.

widow's (or widower's) allowance Part of a decedent's estate set aside by law for the surviving spouse, which most creditors cannot reach.

widow's (or widower's) election See election by spouse.

wildcat strike A strike called without authorization from the union.

Wild's case See rule in Wild's case.

will 1. An instrument that a person makes to dispose of his or her property upon his or her death. 2. Desire or choice.

> Will means an instrument, including a codicil, executed by a person in the manner prescribed by this code, which disposes of the person's property on or after his or her death and includes an instrument which merely appoints a personal representative or revokes or revises another will. F.S.A. § 731.201(36)

will contest A challenge to the validity of a will.

willful Voluntary, intentional, deliberate.

> A conscious motion of the will; voluntary; knowingly; deliberate. Intending the result which actually comes to pass; designed; intentional; purposeful; not accidental or involuntary. *Jones*, 912 So.2d 686 (Fla.App. 1 Dist.,2005)

willful negligence See gross negligence.

will substitute An alternative method or device (e.g., life insurance) that is used to achieve all or part of what a decedent's will is designed to accomplish.

wind up To settle the accounts and liquidate the assets of a business about to be dissolved.

wire fraud A scheme to defraud using interstate electronic communication.

wiretapping Connecting a listening device to a telephone line to overhear conversations. Electronic eavesdropping.

with all faults As is; no warranty given.

withdraw 1. To remove, take back, or retract. 2. To take (funds) out of.

withholding tax Income taxes taken from one's salary or other income.

without prejudice With no loss or waiver of rights or privileges.

> Use of the words "without recourse" in an endorsement on the back of a note made it a "qualified endorsement" under negotiable instruments law, but did not destroy the negotiable character of instrument or prevent endorsees from taking as holders in due course. *Davis*, 114 So.2d 703 (Fla.App.1959)

without recourse Disclaiming liability to subsequent holders in the event of non-payment.

with prejudice Ending all further rights; ending the controversy.

witness 1. To see, hear, or experience something. 2. A person who gives testimony, often under oath.

witness protection A government program that relocates witnesses and gives them a new identity to protect them from retaliation because of their testimony.

witness stand The place in court where a witness gives testimony.

wobbler An offense that could be charged as a felony or a misdemeanor.

words actionable in themselves Words that constitute libel per se or slander per se.

words of art See terms of art.

words of limitation In a conveyance or will, words that describe the duration or quality of an estate being transferred.

words of negotiability See negotiability words.

words of purchase Words designating the recipients of a grant.

work The physical or mental exertion of oneself for a purpose. Labor.

workers' compensation A no-fault system of benefits for workers injured on the job. Also called employers' liability.

> Workers' compensation law means a law respecting a program administered by this state or the United States to provide benefits, funded by a responsible employer or its insurance carrier, for occupational diseases or injuries or for disability or death caused by occupational diseases or injuries. F.S.A. § 774.203(32)

work for hire An employee-authored work whose copyright is owned by the employer.

workhouse A jail for persons convicted of lesser offenses.

working capital Current assets of a business less its current liabilities.

working papers A permit certifying one's right to work.

workout A restructuring of the payment and other terms of a debt.

work product rule Material prepared by or for an attorney in anticipation of litigation is not discoverable, absent a showing of substantial need.

> In ordering discovery of the materials when the required showing has been made, the court shall protect against disclosure of the mental impressions, conclusions, opinions, or legal theories of an attorney or other representative of a party concerning the litigation. Fla.R.Civ.P. Rule 1.280(b)(3)

work release program A program allowing inmates to leave the institution for employment during part of the day.

work stoppage A cessation of work, often due to a labor dispute.

work-to-rule A slowdown due to excessive compliance with work rules.

World Court The International Court of Justice (*www.icj-cij.org*).

worth 1. The monetary or emotional value of something. 2. Wealth.

worthier title doctrine A person who receives by will what he or she would have inherited as an heir by intestacy, takes as an heir.

wraparound mortgage A second mortgage in which the lender of additional funds assumes the payments on the first mortgage.

wreck The cast-aside wreckage of a ship or its cargo.

writ A written court order to do or refrain from doing an act.

write-down; write-up A reduction (write-down) or an increase (write-up) in the value of an asset as noted in an accounting record.

write-off Removing a worthless asset from the books of account.

writing A tangible or electronic record of a communication or representation, including handwriting, typewriting, printing, photostating, photography, audio or video recording, and e-mail. Florida Rules of Professional Conduct, Preamble.

writ of assistance A writ to transfer possession of land after a court has determined the validity of its title.

> A writ of assistance is a form of process issuing out of chancery to transfer possession of land the title to and right to possession of which have been previously adjudicated. *Sarasota-Fruitville Drainage Dist*, 25 So.2d 498 (Fla.1946)

writ of capias See capias.

writ of certiorari See certiorari.

writ of coram nobis See coram nobis.

writ of error An appellate court's writ that the record of a lower court proceeding be delivered for review.

writ of error coram nobis See coram nobis.

writ of execution See execution (3).

writ of habeas corpus See habeas corpus.

writ of mandamus See mandamus.

writ of ne exeat See ne exeat.

writ of possession A writ to repossess real property.

writ of prohibition A writ to correct or prevent judicial proceedings that lack jurisdiction.

> A writ by which a court may prevent a lower tribunal from acting upon matters that are not within its jurisdiction or from exceeding its lawful powers. (*www.floridasupremecourt.org/pub_info/system2.shtml*)

writ of quo warranto See quo warranto.

writ of right A writ issued as a matter of course or right.

writ of supersedeas See supersedeas.

wrong A violation of the right of another. A breach of duty.

wrongdoer One who does what is illegal.

wrongful birth action An action by parents of an unwanted impaired child for negligence in failing to warn them of the risks that the child would be born with birth defects. The parents seek their own damages.

> The primary object of a wrongful birth claim is to recover damages for the extraordinary expense of carrying for an impaired or deformed child, over and above routine rearing expenses. *Kush*, 616 So.2d 415 (Fla.,1992)

wrongful conception See wrongful pregnancy action.

wrongful death action An action by a decedent's next of kin for their damages resulting from a wrongful injury that killed the decedent.

wrongful discharge Terminating employment for a reason that violates a contract, the law, or public policy.

wrongful life An action by or on behalf of an unwanted impaired child for negligence that precluded an informed parental decision to avoid the child's conception or birth. The child seeks its own damages.

wrongful pregnancy action An action by parents of an unwanted healthy child for negligence in performing a sterilization procedure. Also called wrongful conception.

X

x 1. The mark used as the signature of someone who is illiterate. 2. See ex dividend. 3. See ex rights. 4. See ex warrants.

Y

year-and-a-day rule Death occurring more than one year and a day after the alleged criminal act cannot be a homicide, e.g., murder, manslaughter.

> The "year and a day" rule should be abolished. At common law, if more than a year and a day elapsed between the infliction of an injury and the death of the party injured, that injury was conclusively presumed not to be the cause of death. *Jones*, 518 So.2d 295 (Fla.App. 2 Dist.,1987)

yellow-dog contract A contract forbidding union membership.

yield 1. To relinquish or surrender. 2. Profit stated as an annual rate of return on an investment.

Younger **abstention** See equitable restraint doctrine.

youthful offender See juvenile delinquent.

Z

z-bond A bond payable upon satisfaction of all prior bond classes.

zealous witness A witness overly eager or anxious to help one side.

zero coupon bond A bond that does not pay interest.

zipper clause A contract clause that closes out bargaining during the contract term, making the written contract the exclusive statement of the parties' rights and obligations.

zone An area set aside or that has distinctive characteristics.

zone of danger test To recover for negligent infliction of emotional distress, the plaintiff must have been frightened due to actual personal physical danger caused by defendant's negligence.

zone of employment The place of employment and the area thereabout, including the means of ingress and egress under control of the employer.

zone of privacy Activities and areas of a person given constitutional protection against unreasonable intrusion or interference.

> Florida's constitutional right to privacy provision states that the right to privacy "shall not be construed to limit the public's right of access to public records." Art. I, § 23, Fla. Const. *Alterra Healthcare Corp.*, 827 So.2d 936 (Fla.,2002)

zoning Geographic divisions within which regulations impose land use requirements covering permissible uses for buildings, lot size limitations, etc.

Index